ARCHAEOLOGICAL SERVICE
EXCAVATION & SURVEY REPORT NO 14

EXCAVATIONS AT CHESTER

25 BRIDGE STREET 2001

TWO THOUSAND YEARS OF URBAN LIFE IN MICROCOSM

Dan Garner

with contributions by
Diane Backhouse, John Carrott, H E M Cool, Julie Edwards, Peter Guest, Allan Hall, David Higgins, Deborah Jaques, Alison Jones, Harry Kenward, Quita Mould, Peter Owen, Thom Richardson, Ian Smith, David Starley, Penelope Walton Rogers, Margaret Ward, and Hugh Willmott

Drawings by
David Higgins, Tim Morgan, Cheryl Quinn, Gill Reaney and Susie White

Finds photography
Simon Warburton

Conservation
**Yannick Minvielle-Debat,
York Archaeological Trust**

Volume editor
Peter Carrington

*Chester
City Council*

Published by Chester City Council

ISBN 978-1-872587-21-9

Archaeological Service
27 Grosvenor Street
Chester CH1 2DD
Tel: +44 (0)1244 402009
Fax: +44 (0)1244 347522
Email: archaeology@chester.gov.uk
www: http://www.chester.gov.uk/archaeology

Printed by W H Evans
Knutsford Way
Sealand Road Industrial Estate
Chester CH1 4NS

Foreword

DEBENHAMS became involved with archaeology in Chester following a decision to extend the Browns of Chester store. The proposed extension, to the rear of the store, lay in the backlands of the city's famous Rows, and trial archaeological excavation on the site had shown that it contained buried evidence from the Roman period to the present day. As part of the planning consent for the store extension Debenhams agreed to the provision of a range of archaeological works, the results of which are presented in this book.

To fully analyse the results of the excavation a variety of specialists were involved, who examined the soils for evidence of the past environmental conditions, looked at the animal bones for evidence of diet, butchery and the keeping of animals, including pets, and studied the artefacts for clues on how people lived. Indeed, the information in this book is drawn not just from the archaeological excavation itself, but also from accompaning studies undertaken as part of the project, including research into wills, title deeds and other documents relating to the owners of the properties along the Rows, and maps and plans showing changes and development along the Rows since the sixteenth century.

Together the various strands of information have built up a picture of life in the Rows, in particular giving rich and fascinating detail on the lives of early city traders who lived along the Rows from the medieval period onwards. Some unexpected discoveries were also made – such as the fourteenth-century elephant bone found in a sixteenth-century cess pit in the back garden of a Row property and fragments of a type of sixteenth-century armour known as a 'jack of plate'.

This book presents a unique insight into the lives of people who lived and worked in this part of the Chester Rows, and Debenhams are proud to continue the trading connection of this site. We are delighted to have funded and been involved with the most extensive backland exploration in the city, especially having seen the wealth of knowledge, covering 2000 years, that has been produced. We trust that this book will therefore be of interest not only to researchers but to the people of Chester now and in the future.

Stephen Hallam
Debenhams plc

I AM delighted to introduce this important work of scholarship. With the forthcoming demise of Chester City Council, this report on archaeological excavations in Bridge Street will be the last and largest of a series of fourteen published under its aegis, the first having been in 1978. They represent an enduring contribution to our knowledge of the city's heritage. The series constitutes a fine legacy that the City Council can be proud to bequeath to its successor, the unitary authority of Cheshire West and Chester.

The excavation was carried out in 2001 and gives a fascinating insight into the lives of some of the people who lived and traded in Chester, especially between the sixteenth and eighteenth centuries. These buildings in Bridge Street were occupied or owned by prominent and wealthy citizens: as established traders in the city, they would have been Freemen. This impressive undertaking has brought together the collective expertise of our archaeological specialists. They have examined fragments of pottery, glass, and animal remains, they have looked at the contents of domestic rubbish pits and have succeeded in building up an accurate picture of how the post-medieval occupants of Bridge Street lived their lives. From the City records the experts have traced the names of some of the occupiers and their businesses. Those Cestrians cannot have imagined that their lives would generate such microscopic attention in the twenty-first century. Within this final volume of the series you will find, almost as asides, those little discoveries and observations that bring these people to life. The book will be a powerful source for the popular interpretation of life in Chester at that time: it will be consulted by students of Chester's history, by enthusiasts, academics and the more enquiring visitor to the city. Anyone who delves into it will be rewarded by the exceptional detail of its content.

I thank everyone who has been concerned with this publication, in particular Debenham plc for their generous funding, Gifford and Partners for their work as lead contractor of the excavation, the City's archaeology team for applying their accumulated expertise, and Chester City Council for its unswerving support for this project and its predecessors.

Councillor Hilarie McNae
Historic Environment Champion for Chester and Freeman of the City of Chester

Contents

Contents

Illustrations

Illustrations

Tables

Tables

Contributors

Omission from List of Contributors

Lead cloth seals	Geoff Egan MA, PhD, FSA, FMA (*Museum of London Specialist Services*)
Stratigraphic report and discussion	Dan Garner BA (*formerly Gifford and Partners, latterly Chester City Council*)
Standing building report	Peter Owen BA, MIFA (*Gifford and Partners*)
Documentary research	Diane Backhouse (*formerly Gifford and Partners*)
Roman building materials and pottery	Alison Jones BA, AIFA (*Chester City Council*)
Roman samian pottery	Margaret Ward MA, MIFA (*Freelance samian consultant*)
Post-Roman building materials and pottery	Julie Edwards BA (*Chester City Council*)
Clay tobacco pipes and other pipeclay objects	David Higgins BA, PhD, MIFA (*Liverpool University*)
Roman glass, beads, copper alloy, stone objects and organic artefacts	H E M Cool BA, PhD, FSA. MIFA (*Barbican Research Associates*)
Post-Roman glass	Hugh Willmott BA, MA, PhD, FSA, MIFA (*Sheffield University*)
Coins and tokens	Peter Guest BA, PhD, FSA (*Cardiff University/Barbican Research Associates*)
Iron	Quita Mould BA, MA, FSA (*Barbican Research Associates*)
Jack of plate analysis and report	Thom Richardson BA, PhD, FSA (*Keeper of Armour and Oriental Collections, Royal Armouries Museum, Leeds*) and David Starley PhD (*formerly Science Officer, Royal Armouries Museum, Leeds*)
Textiles	Penelope Walton Rogers Dip Acc, FSA (*The Anglo-Saxon Laboratory*)
Mammal, bird and amphibian bone	Ian Smith BA, MSc (*Chester City Council*)
Drawings	David Higgins BA, PhD, MIFA; Tim Morgan MAAIS (*Freelance illustrator*); Cheryl Quinn BA, AAHI (*Chester City Council*); Gill Reaney (*Gifford and Partners*); Susie White PhD
Finds photography	Simon Warburton (*formerly Chester City Council*)
Conservation	Yannick Minvielle-Debat BSc (*University of Bradford*); York Archaeological Trust (elephant bone)
Plant, invertebrate and fish remains	John Carrott and Deborah Jaques (*Palaeoecology Research Services*), Allan Hall MA, PhD, Harry Kenward BSc (*University of York*)
Carbon 14 dating	Beta Analytic

Acknowledgements

Site staff
Ian Grant, George Luke, Ken Owen (*Supervisors*); David Tonks (*Database supervisor*); Geoff Couling (*Palaeoenvironmental supervisor*); Clare Ahmad, Elizabeth Callendar (*Finds supervisors*)

Titania Berks, Ian Davies, John Foulkes, Amanda Garrett, Lisa Gooch-Butler, Anthony Hanna, Mark Hart, Laurence Hayes, Chris Healey, Chris Jones, Greg Jones, Peter Jones, George Lacey, Andy McBrien, Clare Maxfield, Heike Neumann, David Pepper, John Roberts, Eryl Williams (*Site assistants*)

Volunteers - initial finds processing and recording
Liz Bailey, John Bailey, David Cartwright, Susan Chambers, the late Brian Curzon, Averil Downs, Heather Hidden, Debbie Morton, Cathy Roberts, the late Geoff Rhodes, Simon Skelling, Monica Webster

Industrial residue assessment
Dr Gerry McDonnell (*Bradford University*)

English Heritage
Sue Stallibrass (*Regional Archaeological Science Adviser*)

Client team
Stephen Hallam (*Debenhams, Project Co-ordinator*), Philip Topham (*Browns store manager*), Kari Galloway (*Browns store liaison*)

Design Team
Howard Richardson (*MPM Capita*), Barry Watts (*Thomason Partnership*), S Russell (*Roberts and Partners*), Dennis Faller (*Simons Design*), Keith Gilchrist (*Fitzsimon & Co*)

Main Contractors - Simpsons Shopfitting
Ian Hildreth (*Contracts director*), Stuart Sey (*Project manager*), Gary Francis (*Site manager*)

In-store display
Jonathan Duval (*idmedia*)

The volume editor would like to express his thanks to Anne Thompson (*Gifford and Partners*) and Mike Morris (*City Archaeologist, Chester City Council*) for their support in bringing this project to fruition.

Summary

THE early periods of the site's history were only investigated in comparatively small areas. These were limited to the locations of two escalator pits (in Plot 6) and in the area of the ramp which cut across the back of Plots 1–3. The earliest phase of activity reached in these areas was associated with the timber phases of the Roman legionary fortress. It was clear that Roman construction had entirely removed any pre-Roman layers. A small number of worked prehistoric lithics were found to be scattered throughout the stratigraphy, but none of this material could be ascribed to a particular period and it can only be regarded as an indicator or 'background noise', which when added to the existing body of evidence from elsewhere in the centre of Chester lends weight to the suggestion that it was an important site throughout prehistory.

In many respects the late medieval and post-medieval archaeology from the site produced groundbreaking results, not in terms of the nature but of the sheer quantities of various classes of material present in many well dated groups. In this respect there are not yet any comparable sites elsewhere in Chester or at other urban sites in the North-West: this clearly demonstrates the importance of the site both regionally and nationally.

It was possible to identify six distinct plots, five of which appeared to belong to properties fronting onto Bridge Street and one of which appeared to belong to a property fronting on to Newgate Street. It was also possible to identify the property boundary running from north to south across the site which effectively marked the midway point between Bridge Street and Newgate Street, providing clear evidence for a planned layout of the properties in this part of Chester. Although the property boundaries appeared to be late medieval in date it is tempting to see them as part of an earlier burgage plot system with their origins in the Norman town plan.

Phase I: Roman
The earliest activity on the site was represented by an east–west road of rammed gravel, running along the north side of the fortress baths. On the north side of the road was a drainage ditch, beyond which were a series of enigmatic deposits containing small quantities of domestic waste. These features were probably associated with the earliest phase of the fortress.

This phase was followed by the construction of a stone-founded building in the first half of the second century. Only the western and northern walls were exposed during the excavation and little of its interior was available for investigation. However, it was finished with *opus signinum* flooring and painted wall plaster. Associated with this building was an external stone paved area which represented either a north–south road to the west of the building or a courtyard. A drain had been constructed in the north-east corner of this surface using folded sheets of lead capped with roof tiles. This drain emptied into a large pit. The surface was covered in layers which were probably associated with the Antonine dereliction of the fortress. Subsequently, the area was given a new surface of sandstone brash. The second-century building was apparently refurbished at this time, being given a new coating of wall plaster and a new *opus signinum* floor surface. These developments were probably part of the early third-century reconstruction work seen in other parts of the fortress.

After the road surface had been in use for a while, a north–south stone sewer was inserted in the centre of the excavation area and a rammed pebble surface was laid on either side. A tributary drain was later added to the sewer and ran from the north-west corner of the building, suggesting that the latter was still in use during the later third century.

Phases II and III: Late Roman–Late Saxon
The silts of the sewer produced fourth-century artefacts suggesting that it was in use for the remaining part of the fortresses occupation and possibly beyond. The stone-founded building was apparently in a ruinous state by the fourth century, and although its precise fate is uncertain, it appears to have been deliberately demolished. A new timber post hole structure was erected along the line of the western wall of the old building sometime in the fourth century or later: whether this was an entirely new building or a repair is unclear. The high level of residuality present in the artefact record complicated the dating of this activity and a suite of radiocarbon dates did little to help clarify the situation. It is possible that this activity related to a sub-Roman phase, possibly during the fifth or sixth centuries, during which Chester could have continued to function as an administrative centre along similar lines to Wroxeter, long after the 'official' end of Roman Britain in 410.

The next activity on the site appeared to have no regard for the earlier Roman street plan or building layout. It was characterised by the cutting of large pits, probably for stone-robbing, into the now silted-up Roman sewer and associated road surfaces. One such pit produced evidence for the burning of peat, an unusual fuel type for Chester. Further pitting and a possible clay oven base superseded this activity. In all likelihood this sequence of pits and occupation layers represented continued use of the site between the fifth/sixth century and the Norman conquest. This time a suite of radiocarbon dates helped to clarify the site chronology.

Phase IV: Early medieval (Norman–14 century)
Prior to the formalisation of the plots in the late medieval period the entire area appeared to have been given over to cultivation, with evidence for intermittent midden-spreading and little else. Samples from the cultivation soils produced large quantities of elder seeds, which may indicate that the area was left unused for relatively long intervals.

Phase V: Late medieval (14–late 15 century)
By the late medieval period clear plots had been established and their boundaries marked by substantial, well built stone walls. The area of the excavation was confined to the backs of these plots, so none of the main buildings could be investigated. However, in their earli-

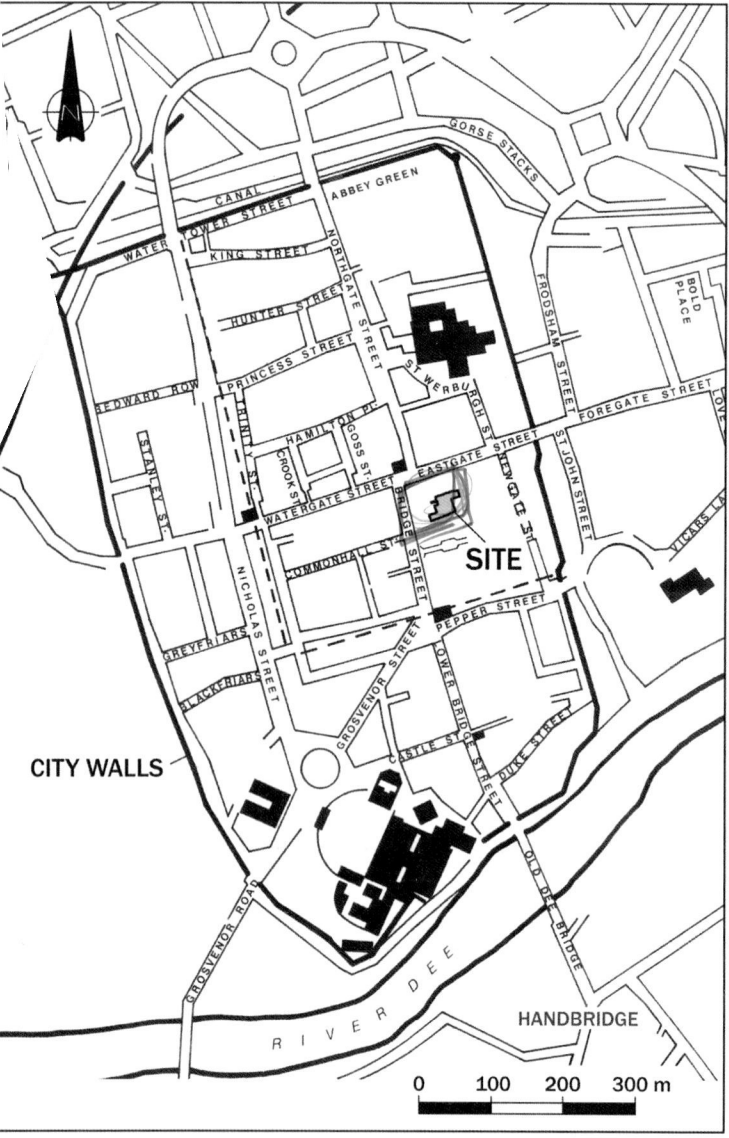

III 1.1.1 Chester: map of city centre showing excavation site. (Scale 1/10,000)

often possible to link archaeological and documentary evidence, giving insights into the status of the occupants and trends in Chester's general economic fortunes.

Phase VI: Late 15–mid-17 century

By the sixteenth century the ovens and stone-lined cess pit had fallen into disuse. The latter began to fill with rubbish, including a discarded curio in the form of an elephant's ulna. However, the boundary walls were still maintained and a stone culvert was inserted between Plots 1 and 2. In some instances smaller stone-lined cess pits were constructed at the back of the plots. The whole of Plot 6 was turned into a formal garden.

This phase also produced the remains of a set of armour, which may relate to the siege of the city during the English Civil War. From this period onwards the site produced large assemblages of all classes of material which provided many indicators of the status, wealth and activities of the inhabitants.

Phase VII: Mid- to late 17–early 18 century

Activity in this phase mirrored that of the earlier phases, with a continuation of the late medieval property boundaries and further pitting and rubbish disposal. In many cases the activity was initiated with the construction of a cess pit (usually with a structure of timber or stone, but in one instance made from cow horn cores). After a period of use this was either backfilled with the upcast of a new pit or became a convenient hole for rubbish disposal. In Plot 2 a brick oven was built in the partially backfilled Phase V stone-lined cess pit. This was conceivably associated with sugar refining. The Phase VI culvert between Plots 1 and 2 was completely rebuilt in the early eighteenth century, indicating a continued requirement for good drainage.

Phases VIII and IX: Early 18–end of 19 century
(c 1720–1900)

From the mid- to late eighteenth century the individual plots appear to have broken down to some degree. This was mainly apparent in the southern half of the site where low-status brick and sandstone buildings were constructed. The function of these buildings appears to have varied between warehouses (eg the 'Ursula Keyes' building behind 19 Bridge Street) and dual-purpose domestic/commercial accommodation (eg Fletcher's Buildings). The organisation of these buildings seems to have been based on a series of interlinked passageways and courtyards. Nineteenth-century census returns hint at a large population of people occupying this area of the city, with some sixty occupants attributed to Fletcher's Buildings alone. Plot 4 was the possible exception to this downward trend as, prior to the construction of the 'Ursula Keyes' building, it was occupied by an eighteenth-century sandstone structure which was served by a stone-lined cess pit fed by a stone culvert and which had a brick-lined well: no other property within the excavation area had such luxuries.

Phase X: 20 century

This phase largely comprises the foundations and services of buildings demolished in 2001 and discussed under Building Recording.

est form each plot contained a stone-built oven at the very back, possibly for baking and/or brewing. There were no obvious signs of manufacture associated with these ovens and samples taken from them did not suggest a specific function. The property in Plot 2 was also furnished with a substantial well built stone cess pit, which was apparently cleaned out on a regular basis.

This character of this phase suggested a certain degree of affluence and a concerted effort to formalise boundaries. Given that the area was so far removed from the street frontage, this argues for an expanding and increasingly prosperous population.

Once the property boundaries had been established they apparently remained fossilised within the townscape, continuing to be respected until the end of the eighteenth century, when accelerating urbanisation led to a demand for increased domestic housing and commercial premises. This period of some three hundred years was mainly characterised by repeated rubbish disposal, either during the deliberate backfilling of cess pits or the accumulation of midden-type deposits. As this rubbish-disposal could be related to specific street-front properties and could be accurately dated using the ceramics, it was

The Site

Dan Garner

THE site lay on high ground near the centre of Chester (Ill 1.1.1). To the north and west it was bounded by buildings fronting onto Eastgate Street and Bridge Street respectively; to the east by the rear of properties fronting onto Newgate Street. In terms of the Roman legionary fortress it was situated on the east side of the *praetentura*, just to the north of the baths. It would also have lain within the late Saxon *burh*. In medieval times the site straddled several properties fronting onto both Bridge Street and Newgate Street. Ultimately, during the late eighteenth and nineteenth centuries these backlands became the focus for housing catering for the urban poor, until clearances freed up the site for redevelopment as the offices and printworks for the *Chester Chronicle*. These occupied most of the site for much of the twentieth century, and the general fabric of the standing buildings was of late eighteenth–early nineteenth-century date, with mid- to late nineteenth- and early twentieth-century additions and later extensions and alterations attributable to the 1960s. These buildings had little architectural merit and were in a dilapidated condition by the start of excavation and recording in 2001.

The Project

This report presents the results of a scheme of archaeological work required by a westward extension to 'Brown's of Chester' (Debenhams), which at that time stretched between Eastgate Street and the Grosvenor shopping centre. The fieldwork was carried out during the winter of 2001/2 by Gifford and Partners. Seven trial holes had already been excavated in 1996 in advance of an abortive redevelopment scheme, while two surveys of the rear range of 19 Bridge Street had been carried out in 1998 and 2000; further recording of the standing buildings was undertaken as part of the present project. A detailed study was also made of the documentary evidence relating to the site. Post-excavation work was managed by the City Council's archaeological service.

In general terms the site was well preserved, with 3.5–4 m of archaeological deposits surviving. However, some periods were better represented than others, and a finished excavation height of 25.1 m OD meant that over much of the site the earlier phases remained unexcavated, as they were to be preserved *in situ*. The northern part of the site had apparently been graded prior to the construction of the twentieth-century buildings associated with the *Chronicle* print works; only in the yard area to

1

INTRODUCTION

the rear of 19 Bridge Street had the earlier ground level been preserved. This indicated that up to one metre of archaeological deposits had been removed, largely representing the eighteenth- and nineteenth-century phases of this part of the site. Only the deepest features such as wells, cellars and rubbish pits had survived this grading exercise. Because of the natural fall of the site from north to south and the survival of pre-existing buildings, the southern half of the site had avoided this truncation. Four areas of the site had been voided by nineteenth- and twentieth-century cellarage, but this amounted to less than five percent of the total area investigated. Apart from the areas mentioned above, modern ground disturbance had largely been limited to concrete wall footings/stanchions and drain runs/manholes/grids, which had generally only disturbed the top one metre of the site.

No waterlogging was encountered, and this led to a generally low yield of palaeoenvironmental data, despite an extensive sampling strategy. The generally sandy nature of the soils encountered also led to poor preservation of pollen grains, further limiting the scope for palaeoenvironmental study, although there were exceptions to this in two of the sixteenth-century cess pits. However, a few exceptions, where anaerobic conditions had prevailed, did provide good preservation of plant and insect remains. Other classes of find such as bone, glass and ceramics were well preserved, whilst most metal objects had suffered from active corrosion.

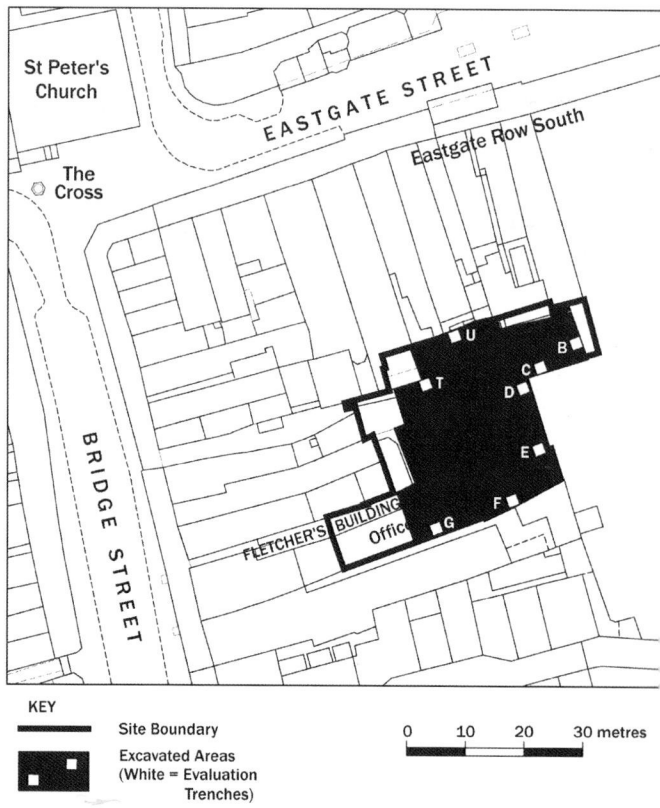

Ill 1.1.2 Trench location plan. (Scale 1/1250)

Archaeological and Historical Background

Bridge Street corresponds to the main north–south street of the Roman fortress (*via praetoria*). During the Roman period the eastern side of Bridge Street, principally to the south of the present site, was occupied by the main fortress bath house. In 1963 sections of the north wall of the colonnaded hall (*basilica*) of this bath house were revealed during work in a cellar behind no 29; it was found to have been laid in a rock-cut trench *c* 1.82 m deep and *c* 1.18 m thick, and survived in places to a height of eleven courses (Mason *et al* 2005, 13). This wall was again uncovered during evaluation work in 1996 (Emery 1996).

However, little is known about the fortress plan to the north of the baths, in the area occupied by the present site. By analogy with other fortresses one would expect the south side of the *via principalis* (medieval and modern Eastgate Street and Watergate Street) to have been occupied by the tribunes' houses. Excavation undertaken in the cellar of Brown's in 1960 revealed an *opus signinum* floor, several walls and evidence for a hypocaust. The quality of the finds from this excavation suggested that this might have been the site of one of these houses (Thompson 1967; Mason *et al* 2005, xii). However, the southern limit of these buildings is uncertain and it is possible that they extended further south

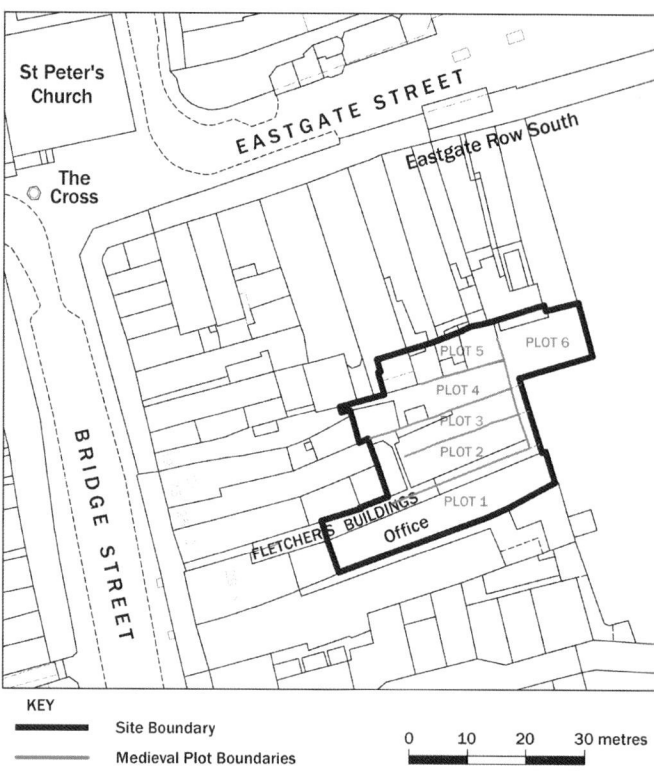

Ill 1.2.1 Medieval plot location plan. (Scale 1/1250)

Ill 1.2.2 Extract from Braun map (1580). The area investigated is circled. (Not to scale)

than has been assumed. Floors of mosaic and *opus signinum* were found during work in 1901 on the present site, along the north side of the passage to Fletcher's Buildings (Newstead 1902, 104). The information recovered from the 1996 evaluation trenches and the geotechnical test pits excavated in 2000 produced further evidence for stone-founded buildings with mosaic and *opus signinum* floors and walls decorated with painted plaster. Three broad phases of Roman activity were identified: phase 1 (*c* 70–90), comprising the earliest Roman activity, culminating in the construction of large stone-founded buildings and associated *opus signinum* floors; phase 2 (*c* 90–120), comprising occupation layers and a pit with an associated lead water pipe; phase 3 (*c* 120–300), comprising thick deposits of sand and clay containing large quantities of building material. Amongst the finds recovered were several military items, including a scale from a suit of *lorica squamata*.

The late and post-Roman sequence on the site remained unclear, although, from the exploratory work undertaken in 1996 and 2000, it would appear that there was a period characterised by the continued deposition of building material-rich layers, possibly serving as house platforms or floors. Subsequently, there was a phase of pitting. These pits may have been associated with buildings fronting onto Bridge Street and, although dating material was lacking, they could have spanned a fairly long period of time between the fifth and ninth centuries.

Soon after the Norman Conquest the area may have been divided into burgage plots fronting onto Bridge Street and Newgate Street (Ill 1.2.1). The width for each plot may have been *c* 66 feet or 4 perches (*c* 20 m); these often seem to have been further subdivided into fractions of 11 feet (most commonly 22 x 33 feet divisions are apparent). The length of these plots varied but a length of *c* 264 feet or 16 perches (*c* 80 m) was common. The average distance between the street-frontages on Bridge Street and Newgate Street is 140 m, suggesting that the burgage plots were *c* 70 m long. Furthermore, it is possible that a service lane divided the backs of these plots. These property boundaries could be plotted onto the development site to predict which properties the land was attached to during this period.

By the thirteenth century the area would have had well established property divisions, with houses presenting an almost continuous frontage along Bridge Street and being served by gardens and orchards to the rear. The 1996 and 2000 investigations identified deposits of this date behind the street frontages thought to be associated with cultivation.

Three factors are thought to have contributed to the origins of the Row buildings during the thirteenth century: the fire of 1278, which reputedly destroyed a significant part of the town; the use of Chester as a military base by Edward I for his campaigns against the Welsh; and the grant of the city's first charter in 1300. By the 1250s domestic and commercial structures were closely intertwined, with references to buildings on Northgate Street containing dwellings, shops and undercrofts. Recording work in 1985 at 12 Watergate Street suggested that some Row-type buildings may already have been in existence in parts of the city prior to 1237 (Ward 1988, 45–9).

During the fourteenth and fifteenth centuries a continuous Row system developed along the main street frontages. However, certain high-status buildings also began to appear behind the street-front properties. This is attested on Northgate Street in the early fourteenth century by a reference to a stone *solarium* owned by Richard of Wheatley, Sheriff of Chester, and located 15 royal ells (13.72 m) behind the frontage on the western side of the street. Other buildings which might be expected to rear of properties fronting on to the main streets are indicated by documentary references and include stables, granges, chapels and dovecotes. During extension work to Brown's in 1926 large quantities of medieval pottery were recovered, along with fourteenth–fifteenth-century floor tiles. The 1996 and 2000 investigations only identified further cultivation deposits attributable to this period, suggesting that the development area continued to be used as gardens. However, they produced good evidence for pits in evaluation trenches B and G, and masonry structures associated with internal and external surfaces in evaluation trenches E and F, all datable to the sixteenth century. By contrast, Braun's map of *c* 1580, followed by Speed's map of 1610, continued to show orchards and gardens to the rear of narrow street-front buildings (Ill 1.2.2).

The earliest recorded permission to enclose a Row was granted to Sir Richard Grosvenor in 1643, for a property in Lower Bridge Street, and an etching dated 1700 shows the site of 23–9 Bridge Street at different stages of Row development. The results of the 1996 and 2000 investigations again produced good evidence for seventeenth-century activity, including pits, deposits and surfaces, possibly indicating that the sixteenth-century structure in the area of Trenches E and F was still in use. Excavations in 1926 near the entrance to St Michael's Row exposed numerous cess- and rubbish pits dating from the sixteenth to the eighteenth centuries, some of which were dug to a depth of 3.96 m beneath Row level (Newstead 1928).

Much of the backland area on the eastern side of Bridge Street appears to have been developed before 1795, as is shown on James Hunter's map of that year (Ill 1.2.3). The building to the rear of 19 Bridge Street can be identified, as can the long strip building to the south of Fletcher's

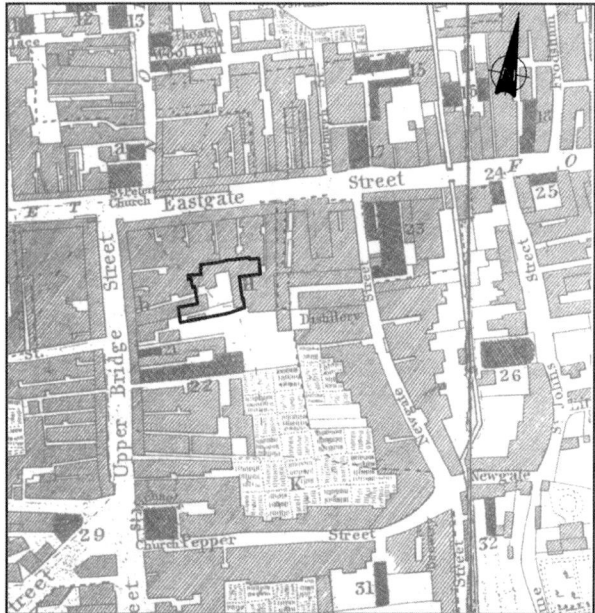

Ill 1.2.3 Extract from James Hunter map (1795). (Not to scale)

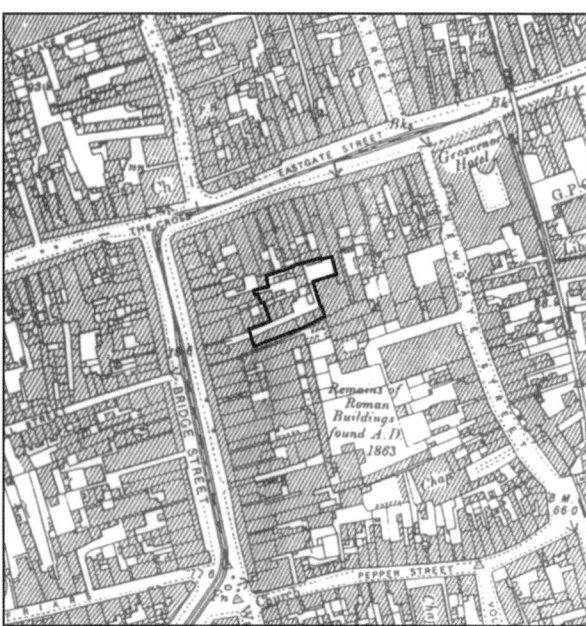

Ill 1.2.4 Extract from OS 1/500 map (second edition, 1899). (Not to scale)

some activity in these buildings, possibly associated with the master chemist thought to be occupying 27 Bridge Street Row in 1851. This late phase of development demonstrates the site's last use as residential and workshop space prior to its shift to modern retail.

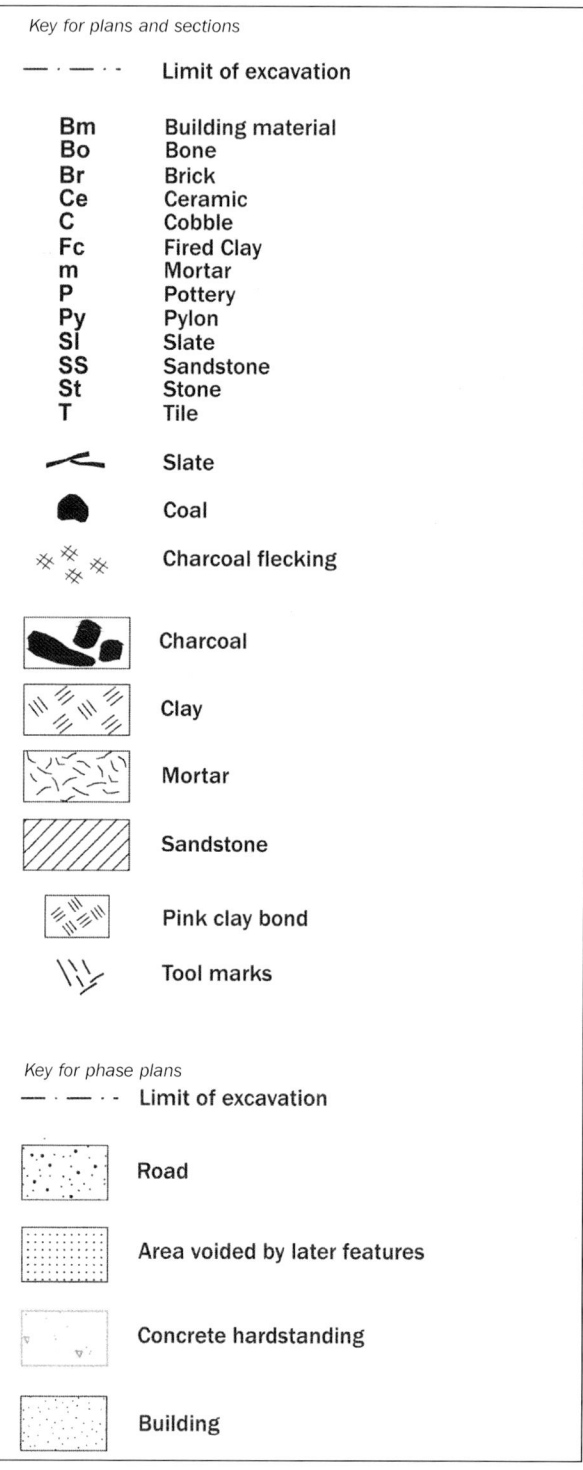

Ill 2.1.1 Key to excavation drawing conventions

Buildings alley, to the rear of 29–31 Bridge Street Row. These buildings are also shown on Wood's map of 1833 and the first edition OS map of 1875. The second edition OS map of 1899 demonstrates that the Fletcher's Buildings alley was shortened and given a dogleg to the north sometime between 1872 and 1898 (Ill 1.2.4). Nevertheless, a large central part of the quadrangle formed by Bridge Street, Eastgate Street, Newgate Street and Pepper Street remained as cultivated land up to 1795. Much of the development on the north side of the Fletcher's Buildings alley to the south of 19 Bridge Street dates from around 1898–1911, though prior to this – certainly by 1872 – the area appears to have been occupied by courtyards and buildings accessed *via* the 19 Bridge Street building. During the archaeological work undertaken in 2000, Trench G produced evidence for the back of a circular brick oven of nineteenth-century date. This hints at

The Excavation   Dan Garner

Phase I: Roman

Phase Ia (Ill 2.1.5)

THE earliest activity on the site comprised deposits predating the stone-founded building described below under Phase Ic. They probably relate to the timber phase of the fortress.

At the eastern end of the site within the area of Evaluation Trench B and Escalator Pit B a slot was excavated on either side of the east–west wall (134)/(978)/(1027) of the Phase Ic building. This revealed the earlier stratigraphic sequence (Ill 2.1.2).

To the north of the wall the earliest deposit identified was a dark grey clay silt, (155), flecked with charcoal and decomposed bone fragments. This lay directly above the natural subsoil and produced pottery which was exclusively grey ware, including a jar and an indented ?beaker of late first-century date. This deposit was subsequently covered by a layer of clean buff sand, (154). This in turn was covered by a mixed deposit, (153), comprising equal quantities of buff sand and reddish brown clay with occasional fragments of red sandstone.

A similar deposit to (155) was encountered to the south of the wall. This deposit, (1065), was a dark greyish brown silty clay flecked with charcoal. Although only the top 100 mm of this context was excavated it appeared to be filling a feature cut into the top of the natural subsoil.

A sterile deposit of light orange-brown silty sand, (1063), covered deposit (1065). The differential build up of deposits on either side of the wall would have created a stepped ground surface c 300 mm higher to the south than to the north. This was peculiar as the natural ground surface in the excavated area sloped from north to south on a similar gradient to modern Bridge Street. Thus the evidence suggested a building platform on the footprint of the Phase Ic building, even though evidence for the structure itself was presumably removed by the construction of wall (134).

Within the area of Evaluation Trench C (Ill 2.1.3) the earliest deposit recorded was a clean mid-brown sand, (160), which apparently overlay a sandstone brash deposit that was not investigated. Above this was a deposit of dark grey sandy silt, (159), which contained fragments of tile, mussel shell and charcoal; it seems probable that this deposit (159) was the equivalent of (155) and (1065) in Evaluation Trench B.

Above (159) was a clean mid-grey silty clay, (158), which produced a sherd of Verulamium area mortarium dated 70–140. This was in turn covered by a deposit of mid-yellow-brown sandy clay, (157), containing fragments of abraded tile and late first-century grey ware. Sample <5112> taken from deposit (157) produced fragments of charcoal and ironworking waste, possibly indicating low-level ironsmithing in the vicinity.

2

FIELDWORK

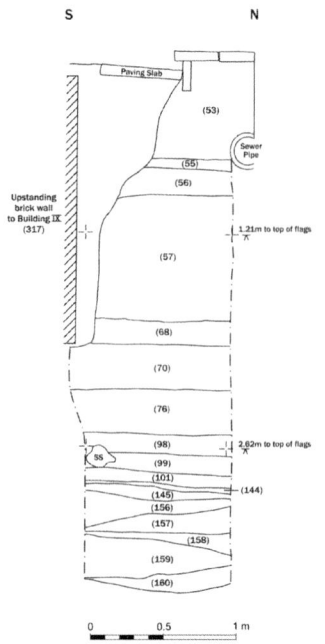

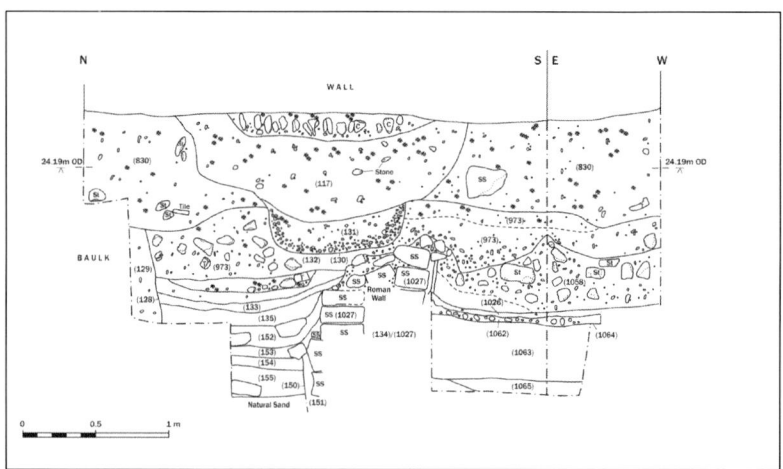

III 2.1.2 Evaluation Trench B: W-facing section. (Scale 1/50)

III 2.1.3 Evaluation Trench C: E-facing section.
(Scale 1/50)

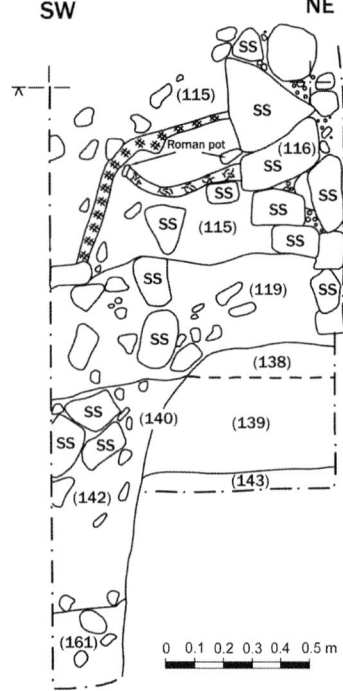

III 2.1.4 Evaluation Trench D: E-facing section. (Scale 1/25)

The sequence of deposits examined in Evaluation Trench C seemed to follow a pattern alternating between a deposit with a level upper horizon and one with an upper horizon falling from north to south, following the natural gradient of the site. From this it may follow that deposits (160) and (157) accumulated on level floor surfaces in two phases of a building, and that deposits (159) and (158) were deliberately laid as part of a levelling exercise between the two phases. This hypothesis would make the sandstone brash seen below deposit (160) the primary floor level and (158) a later clay floor laid on top of a thick accumulation of domestic waste (159).

Within the area of Evaluation Trench D (Ill 2.1.4) examination of fragmentary deposits revealed a green silty sand, (143), lying directly above the natural subsoil. This deposit produced a sherd of grey ware pottery of the late first century; sample <5111> produced fragments of charcoal and fish bone. (143) was sealed by a deposit of light brown silty sand, (139), which in turn was covered by a deposit of reddish brown sand, (138).

Within the area of the ramp excavation and the access pit the main feature consisted of an east–west cambered road surface, (1259). Its construction involved the cutting of a terrace, (1260), into the natural sand along the northern side to create a level base. Within the access pit the earliest Roman road surface, (283), was a mid-reddish brown sandstone brash 60 mm thick, which was laid directly on top of layer (284). Evaluation Trench K, excavated in 1996, located this road surface further east; here the road was set on a base of sandy clay which produced late first-century grey ware (Ill 2.1.6).

Phase Ib (Ill 2.1.7)

The main event of Phase Ib was the resurfacing of the east–west road described above. The resurfacing layer, (1252), comprised densely set and well compacted fragments of sandstone, from which were recovered a sherd of Holt pottery dated 90/100–130 and fragments of south Gaulish amphora dated *c* 70–mid-third century (Ill 2.1.6).

This new road surface was bounded to the north by a ditch, (1244), 0.2 m deep. This ditch presumably served as a roadside drain. The fill, (1243), was a dark reddish brown, sand silt loam containing pottery dated to the late first–early/middle second century and a Dressel 20 am-

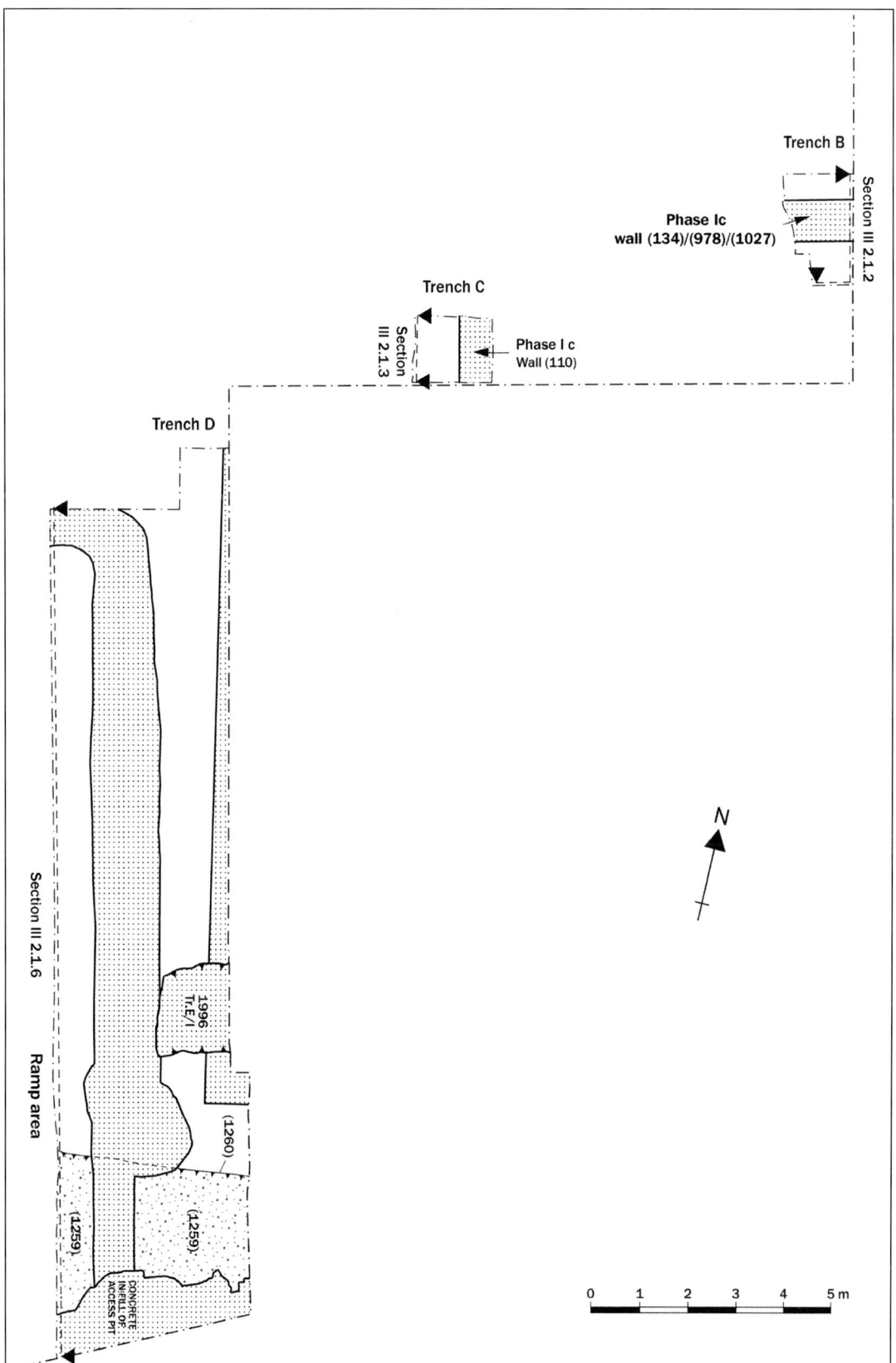

Trench B

Section III 2.1.2

Phase Ic
wall (134)/(978)/(1027)

Trench C

Section III 2.1.3

Phase I c
Wall (110)

Trench D

Section III 2.1.6

N

1996
Tr.E/I

(1260)

(1259)

(1259)

CONCRETE
INFILL OF
ACCESS PIT

Ramp area

| 0 | 1 | 2 | 3 | 4 | 5 m |

III 2.1.5 Phase Ia: plan. (Scale 1/125)

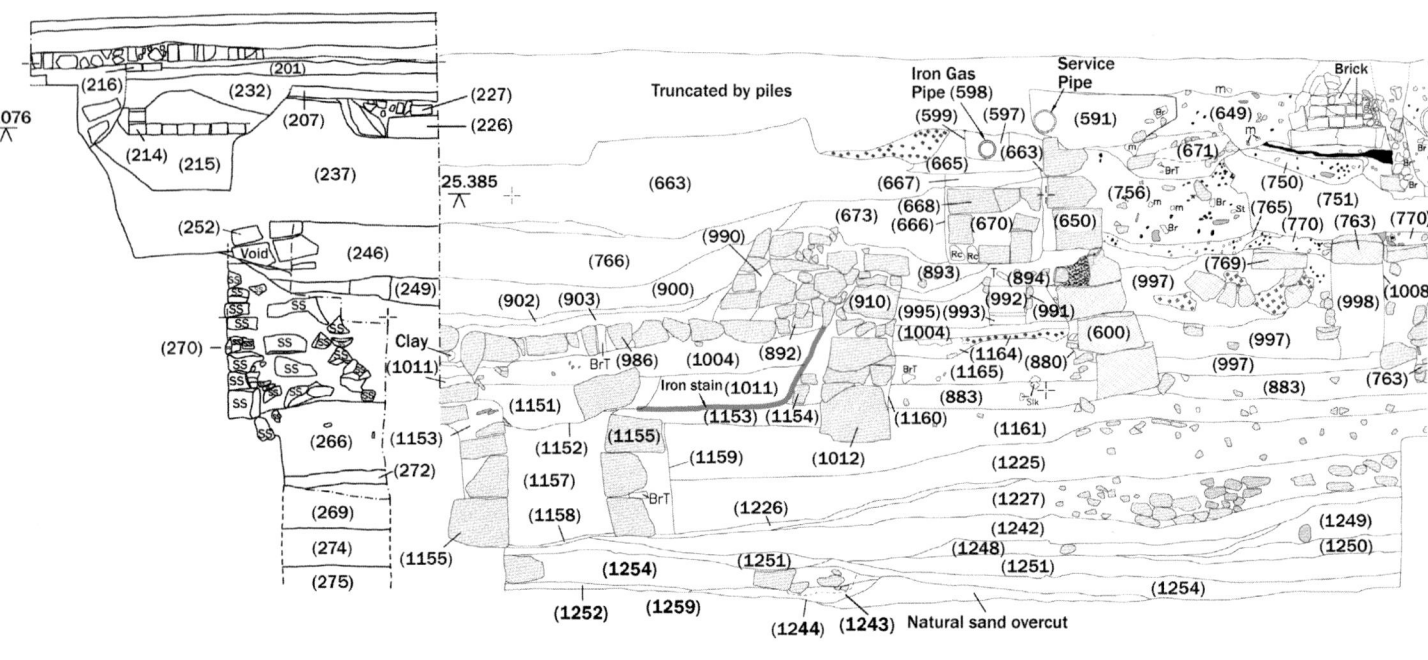

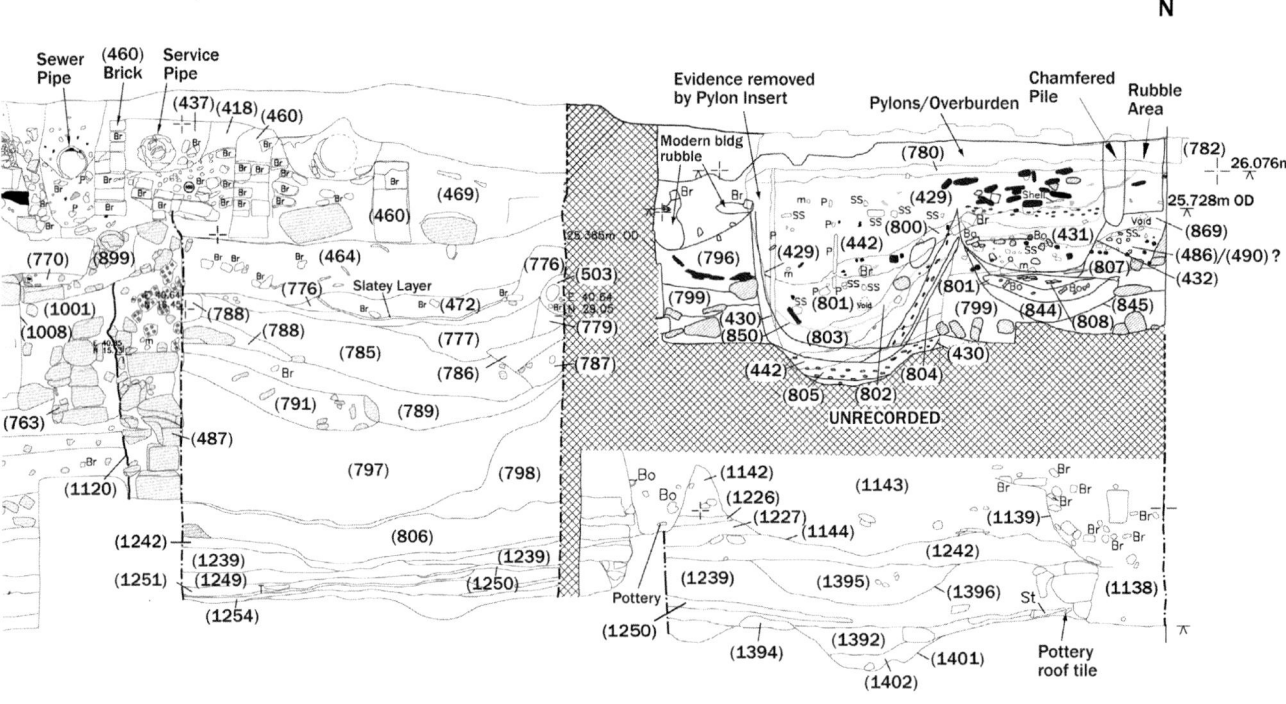

III 2.1.6 Ramp area: E-facing section. (Scale 1/50)

phora (late first–mid third century). This context was also recorded as (1255) and (1256). A sample of the fill, < 5133>, produced charred cereal grains as well as fish bone, including eel and possibly cod.

The ditch must have silted up fairly quickly and was subsequently partially covered by an extensive layer, (1254), which formed over the entire area of the ramp excavation to the north of the road. This layer was a dark reddish grey silty sand containing mineralised charcoal flecks concentrated at the interface with the overlying Phase Ic layer, (1251). It was observed during excavation that there were river-worn pebbles concentrated towards the base of layer (1254), and a single sherd of Holt orange ware dated 90/100–130 was recovered.

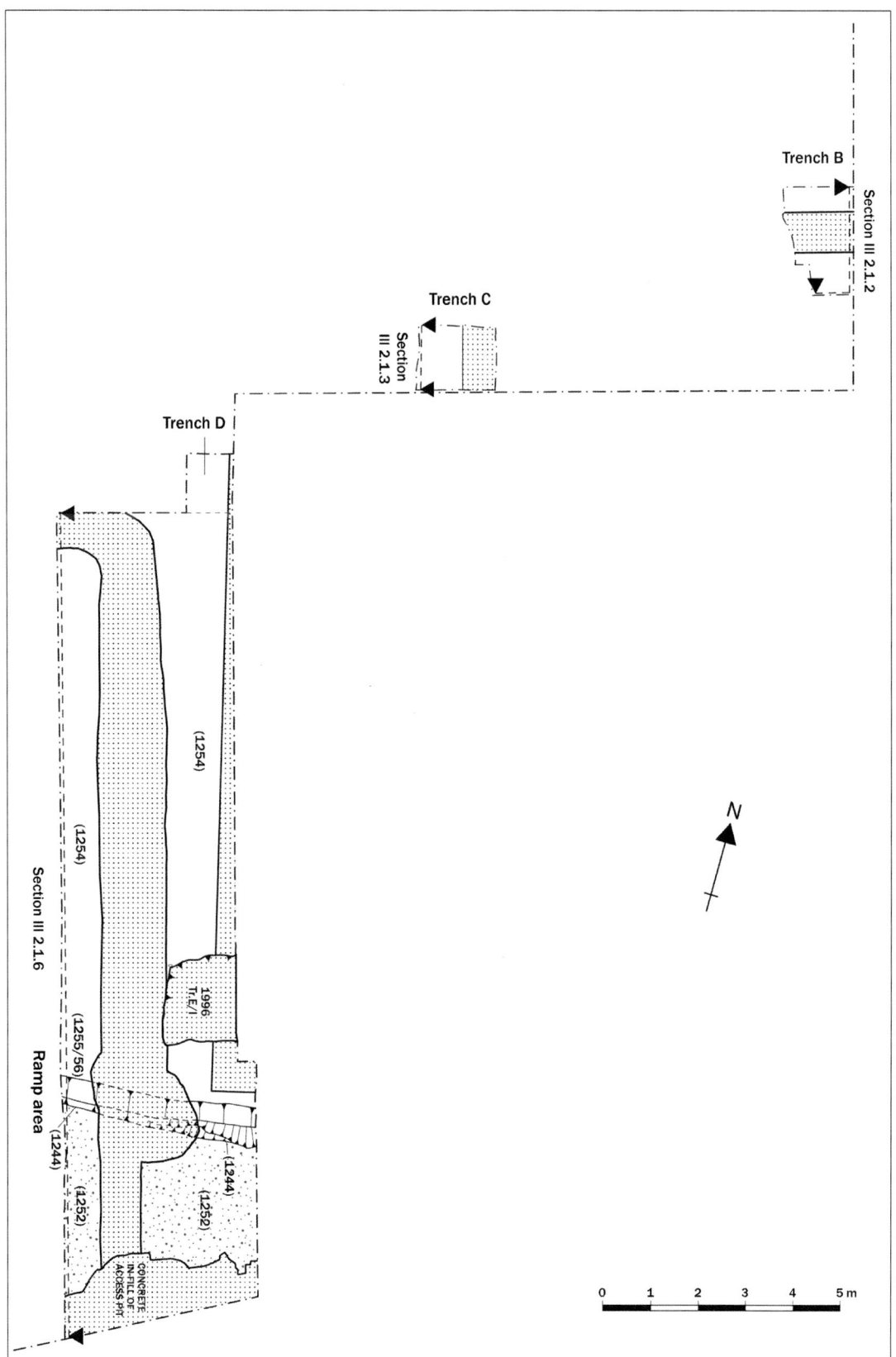

III 2.1.7 Phase Ib: plan. (Scale 1/125)

Phase Ic (Ills 2.1.8–.10)

This sub-phase could broadly correspond to either the partial rebuilding of the fortress in stone in the early second century or the renovation evidenced in the 160s. It was characterised by the construction of stone-founded Building I(i), largely occupying the area to the east of the 2001 excavations beneath the existing Debenhams store. To the west of this building was evidence for a paved yard or side road and a lead-lined drain which emptied into a large pit. The end of the sub-phase was marked by deposit (144), (1250) and (1388), which could represent a phase of abandonment.

Building I(i)

At the eastern end of the site, within the area of Evaluation Trench B and Escalator Pit B, an east–west trench 0.7 m deep x 1 m wide, (150), was excavated into Phase Ia layer (153) for the construction of the sandstone wall footing (134)/(1027). The footing had an average width of 0.8 m and comprised coursed sandstone blocks bonded in a reddish brown clay; at least seven courses survived. The backfill (151) of the construction trench contained Holt pottery of *c* 90/100–130. The southern (internal) face of this wall had at least two coats of plaster applied to it: the outer render was a pale brown sand mortar covered with a white lime wash; the inner render was earthen (possibly daub) with a thin lime wash. Both of these renders had been applied before the laying of the floor (1026) and thus may have been contemporary with mortar floor surface (1064). This floor was only exposed over an area of 1.5 x 1.5 m and had apparently been laid on top of Phase Ia deposit (1063) (Ill 2.1.2).

It is assumed that Evaluation Trench C lay within the footprint of Building I(i). The primary deposit thought to be associated with the structure was a layer of red sandstone brash, (156), possibly forming the sub-base to a floor. This layer produced Holt pottery dated *c* 90/100–130. Directly above the brash was a well made floor, (145). It was of similar construction to floor (1064) in Evaluation Trench B, comprising sandstone, cobbles and pebbles rammed into a compact surface and bonded in lime mortar. The upper surface of this floor showed signs of scorching, with some of the pebbles appearing to be fire-cracked and fused together (Ill 2.1.3).

A footing for a north–south wall, (111), was detected on the eastern side of Evaluation Trench C. Its western side was exposed for a length of 1.2 m and was at least 0.4 m wide. The wall foundation itself, (110), comprised sandstone fragments bonded in clay. Its western face had been given a coat of lime plaster, (108), as seen on wall (134)/(1027). However, unlike wall (134) there was no evidence for upstanding masonry. Although this could be explained by stone-robbing episodes, it is possible that the superstructure was constructed from *pisé* (compacted earth rendered in mortar) (Tim Strickland *pers comm*). This wall probably represented an internal partition within Building I(i).

A small circular post hole, (149), 0.2 m diameter and 0.15 m deep, was cut into surface (145). The fill, (148), was a mid-brown silty sand containing small amounts of charcoal, tile and mortar flecks. This post hole could have a multitude of explanations, but its small size suggested that it represented a temporary structure such as a scaf-

Ill 2.1.8 Phase Ic: wall (1245) of Building I(i), looking E.

fold used during decoration or refurbishment of the building. A mortar patch, (109), was applied to the top of the post hole after the post had been removed, achieving a neat repair to the floor.

Subsequently, a thin layer of black sandy silt, (144), formed over floor (145) and mortar patch the (109). This layer produced Holt pottery. This layer had certain affinities with layer (1250)/(1388) in the ramp excavation (Ill 2.1.6) and it is possible that these layers all formed as part of the hiatus episode recorded elsewhere within the fortress at Chester during the Antonine period.

At the beginning of this phase a substantial north–south footing of angular, coarsely split sandstone blocks was inserted along the eastern edge of the ramp excavation. The southern end of the foundation trench, (1246), had been cut into the silt of the Phase Ib roadside ditch, (1244), as well as being excavated through layer (1254) to a depth of *c* 0.6 m. This wall is interpreted as the western side of Building I(i). The superstructure of the wall, (1245), was *c* 0.8 m thick and was composed of dressed red sandstone facing blocks with a sandstone rubble core, bonded with stiff mid-red-brown clay. The wall was not excavated along its full length or width as it continued underneath the west-facing section of the trench. The southern end of the wall formed a corner with an east–west wall of similar construction, being *c* 0.8 m wide and having foundations 0.8 m deep. Pottery recovered from the foundation trench included South Gaulish samian ware (*c* 90–110), and Holt pottery.

Road/yard surface (1394)

To the west of wall (1245) the northern half of the ramp excavation area produced patchy but consistent evidence for a well made surface, (1394). This comprised flat sandstone fragments set within brash laid against the external face of wall (1245). This surface may have formed an external yard area or road surface to the west of Building I(i).

At the southern end of the ramp area a layer of mid-yellowish brown silty clay, (1251), formed above Phase Ib layer (1254) and contained Holt pottery dated *c* 90/100–30, also late first century grey and black-on-brown wares and a south Gaulish Dr 37 bowl (70–110).

In the north-western corner of the ramp excavation an east–west gully, (1401), was recorded cutting into surface (1394). This was 1.2 m wide and 0.3 m deep, with concave sides and an irregular concave base. The lower fill, (1402), was greyish brown silt containing a small

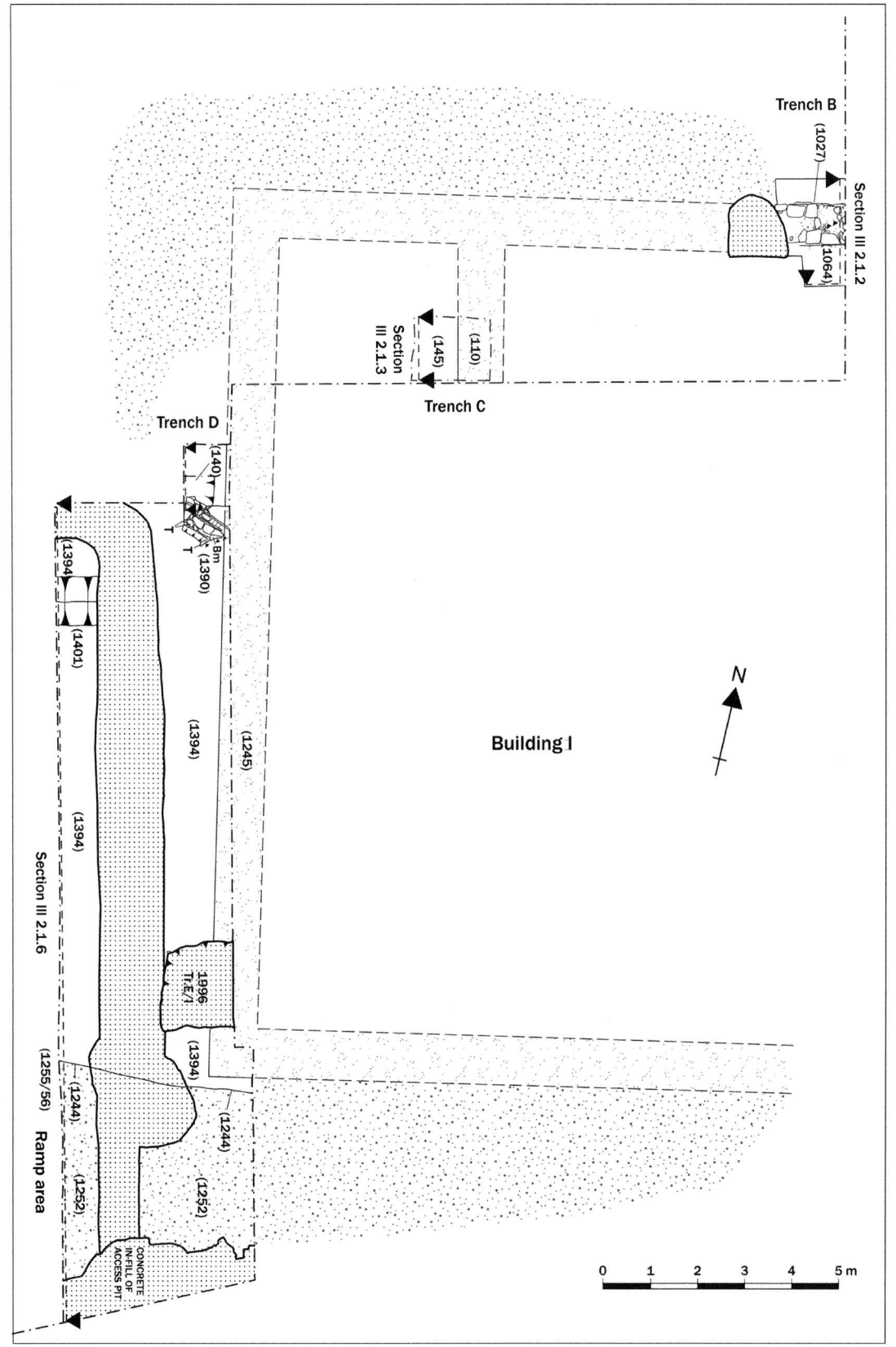

III 2.1.9 Phase Ic: plan. (Scale 1/125)

percentage of charcoal, while the upper fill, (1392), was a dark brown-grey, charcoal-rich silt which produced Holt pottery and South Gaulish samian of *c* 80–110 and Severn Valley ware, probably dating from 120. A sample from the upper fill, <5139>, produced fish bone including flat fish. This feature may have been a drain: the western end of the gully had been removed by the cut for the Phase Ie drain (1241) and could have connected into a predecessor of this feature.

Subsequently surface (1394) and layer (1251) were covered by a black-brown sandy silt, (1388)/(1250), containing small amounts of fragmented roof tile (including a Warry group D *tegula*, dated *c* 240–380). This layer covered the whole of the ramp excavation and produced South Gaulish samian ware (*c* 70–110) and a late third-century black-burnished 1 cooking pot. Samples from the layer, <5136> and <5134>, produced charred cereal grain and fish bone including flat fish.

Drain (1390) and pit (140)

In the north-eastern corner of the ramp excavation a square pit, (140), had been cut through layer (1388); it had been partly exposed in Evaluation Trench D. The upper fill, (142), was a light reddish brown clayey sand containing probable Holt orange wares, samian pottery, and a fragment of a portable oven (*clibanus*). The lower fill, (161), was a grey clay sand which also produced Holt pottery. The original function of the pit was not determined but a lead-lined drain, (1390), fed into it and suggested that it had functioned as a drain or latrine (Ill 2.1.4 and .10).

The lead-lined drain was originally identified in Trench D as a lead pipe, (137), split along its upper face and subsequently filled with a dark grey-brown silt. The ramp excavation established that the drain was cut into layer (1388) and ran south-east–north-west from the edge of wall (1245) to the lip of pit (140), with a fall towards the pit. The lining of the cut, (1389), was constructed from overlapping rectangular sheets of lead bent to form a U shape. The final sheet overhung the edge of pit (140), allowing foul water to discharge freely into the pit. One side of the lining was supported by a line of sandstone fragments averaging *c* 0.3 m in diameter. The channel was capped by a line of complete roof tiles (*tegulae*).

Underlying the lead lining in the base of the cut was a green-grey silt, (1393). This could either have been formed by seepage during the use of the drain or during the construction prior to the insertion of the lead lining. The fill of the lead lining itself had a greeny grey hue, (1391), possibly cess contaminated with lead.

Ill 2.1.10 Phase Ic: lead-lined drain (1390), looking S.

Phase Id (Ills 2.1.11–.12)

This sub-phase represents renovation and refurbishment of existing features, mainly Building I(i) and the east–west road, in the third century.

At the eastern end of the site, within the area of Evaluation Trench B and Escalator Pit B, a deposit of light reddish brown sandstone brash, (152), had been laid against the northern face of wall (134)/(1027 to a depth of *c* 150 mm. This layer was thought to be an external surface to the north of Building I(i) and could be evidence for an east–west road. A layer of reddish brown sandy clay, (135), accumulated above surface (152) and produced pottery which included an imitation black-burnished 1 jar dated *c* 120–200 (Ill 2.1.2).

Building I(i)

The Phase Ic floor surface (1064) in Evaluation Trench B was covered in a layer of crushed and broken sandstone fragments (1062) *c* 60 mm thick. Immediately above this was laid a mortar floor surface (*opus signinum*) (979/1026), which lay up against, and was therefore later than, the second layer of wall plaster noted on the southern face of wall (134)/(1027).

Within the area of Evaluation Trench C a further area of mortar floor, (101), was found, covering most of the trench except where wall (111) was situated. It consisted of an aggregate of crushed tile and fragments of painted wall plaster and had been subjected to random patching suggesting a prolonged period of use (Ill 2.1.3).

Ill 2.1.11 Phase Id: *opus signinum* (1026) surface of Building I(i), looking N.

Road/yard surface (1239)

Towards the centre of the ramp area was a layer of yellow clay mottled with patches of reddish brown silty sand, (1249). This layer appeared to have been dumped on the Phase Ic occupation layer (1250)/(1388) and appeared to have no practical function. Pottery recovered included South Gaulish Samian ware of the period 70–110 and a Wilderspool mortarium dated to the second century. Subsequently, a compacted sandstone brash in a sandy matrix, (1239), was laid over the northern edge of layer (1249) and extended over the northern half of the ramp area, probably to function as an external surface. Layer (1239) produced three limestone *tesserae* and second-century pottery. A similar sandstone brash deposit, (1248), was laid over the south part of layer (1249) and was almost certainly contemporary with layer (1239). Layer (1248) stopped 0.5 m short of the edge of the east–west road

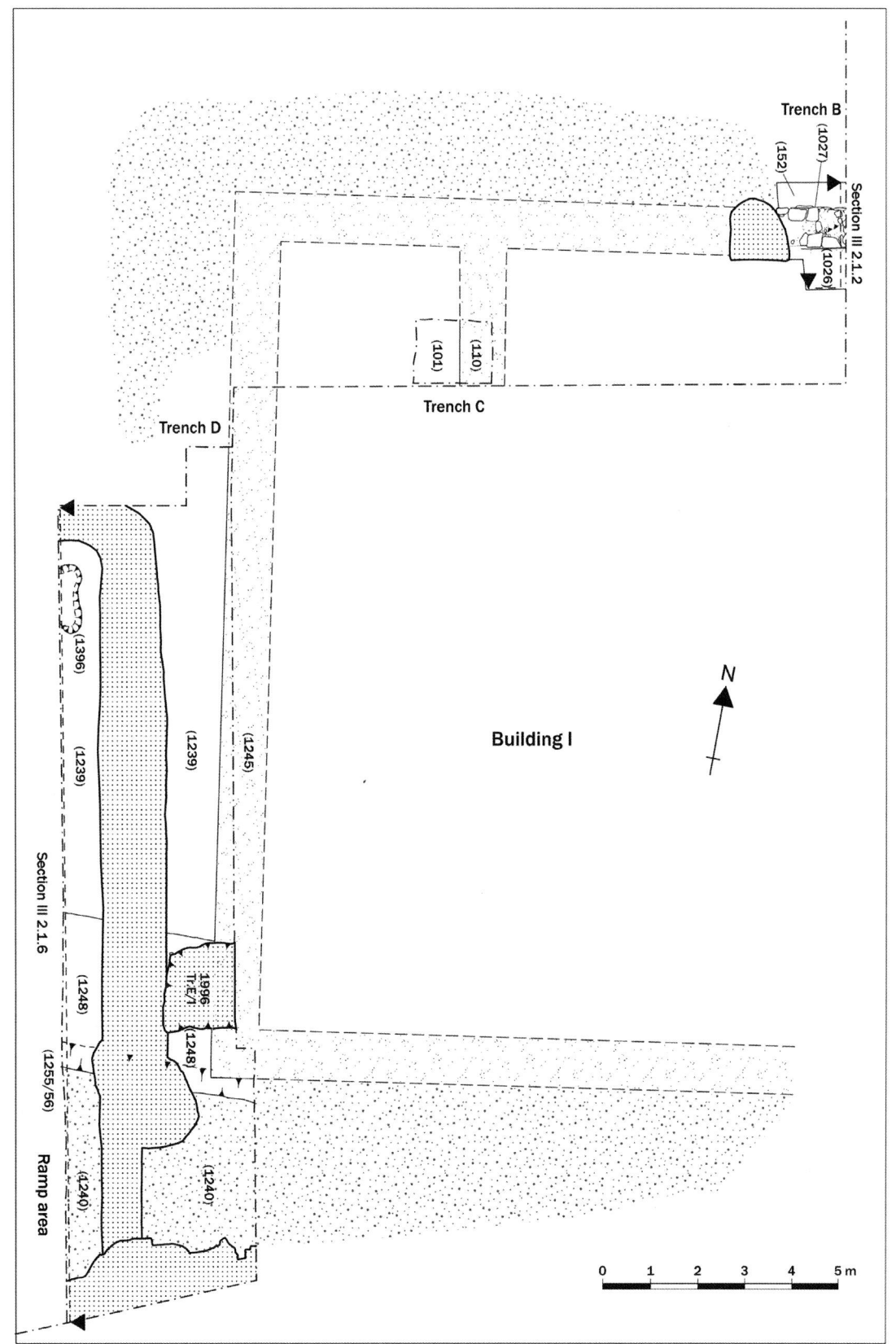

III 2.1.12 Phase Id: plan. (Scale 1/125)

surface (1240), and it is possible that the marginal area between the two surfaces was left to act as a drain (Ill 2.1.6). Pit (1396), which was apparently used as a rubbish pit, was cut into layer (1239). The fill, (1395), was a reddish brown silty sand containing demolition material and Holt pottery, plus south Gaulish samian (probably 80–100).

East–west road (1240)

A new surface, (1240), was added to the east–west road at about the same time that the sandstone brash surfaces (1239) and (1248) were laid. Layer (1240) was a grey to reddish brown gritty sand, containing sandstone fragments and water-worn pebbles, probably derived from river bed deposits, rammed to form a level surface. Only one sherd of grey ware was found within this surface, of late first-century date.

Layer (1240) probably represented the same road surface as (274), seen in the access pit excavation (Ill 2.1.6). Layer (274) comprised rounded sandstone fragments laid to form a rough surface, with the gaps between the larger fragments being filled with small rounded pebbles rammed into a dark greyish brown sandy silt. This was interpreted as the highest surviving surface of the road that formed an east–west thoroughfare along the northern side of the fortress baths. It produced Holt pottery dated 90/100–130; however, it was found to be lie on a layer of mid-grey clayey silt, (275), which in turn sealed a layer of yellowish brown silty clay, (276), that produced a probable Mancetter-Hartshill sherd dated *c* mid-second to early fourth century. Sample <5015> from layer (276) contained small amounts of charred cereal and unidentifiable fish bone.

A layer of dirty mid-yellowish brown silty clay, (1242), subsequently formed across most of the ramp area to a depth of *c* 0.3 m. This layer sealed surfaces (1239) and (1248) as well as encroaching on to the northern edge of road surface (1240). Layer (1242) produced Holt pottery and South Gaulish Samian of 70–100. Sample <5135> from (1242) produced charred cereal and fish bone, possibly mackerel, as well as hammerscale.

Phase Ie (Ills 2.1.13–15)

This marked the final episode in Phase I and was dominated by the construction of a substantial sandstone sewer down the centre of the ramp excavation no earlier than the mid-third century.

Building I(i)

No direct evidence was found for occupation during this phase within Evaluation Trench B, but a series of sand and silt lenses had built up against the southern face of wall (1027) after the insertion of floor (1026).

Within the area of Evaluation Trench C, after a period of prolonged use and wear, floor (101) was resurfaced in mortar, (107) The extent of the resurfacing suggested that there may have been timber partition walls along its northern and western edges when the deposit was laid. This surface was subsequently cut by a small post hole, (147), *c* 0.2 m in diameter with a homogeneous fill, (146). This post hole may again indicate the erection of scaffolding for refurbishment of the building.

Road/yard surface (1227)

A compact reddish brown sandstone brash layer, (1227), was laid down at the beginning of Phase Ie. It occupied all of the ramp area from the edge of road surface (1240) to the northern limit of the ramp excavation and may have formed an external surface. Very few finds were present, but some pottery was recovered, including black-burnished 1 pottery of mid-third-century date.

Sewer (1182)

Shortly after the laying of surface (1227) a substantial north–south sewer was inserted down the centre of the ramp excavation, running parallel to the wall foundation (1245). The sewer itself comprised a pair of parallel sandstone walls with a course of capping blocks set in a construction trench, (1241), cut through layer (1227). The walls, (1182), were constructed of blocks measuring on average 0.5 x 0.5 x 0.15 m and generally stood to four courses in height, although one section had survived to five courses; on average the height was 0.6–0.7 m (Ills 2.1.13 and .15). The bonding was generally a mixture of clay and dry stone construction. However, the upper part of the build incorporated a mixture of friable pinky brown mortar containing charcoal and small pebbles and sandstone brash. The mortar had been used to set the sandstone into the construction cut, and this characteristic helped to define the edges of the structure. The capping stones typically measured 0.95 x 0.74 x 0.15 m and some bore tooling marks of no particular pattern. There was no structural base to the feature as it was set on the top of the firm natural buff sand subsoil.

At its northern end the sewer branched to the northwest, but it was not possible to ascertain whether it had once continued northwards because of severe truncation by a later robber pit, (1139).

The primary silt in the sewer, (1148), was a light grey-green sandy silt which was only present in the northern half of the run. This produced a wide variety of ceramics, glass, animal bone, building material and metalwork, including a copper alloy spoon and black-burnished 1 pottery dated early to mid-second century. A sample of the silt, <5132>, produced abundant very rotted shell fragments of mussel and oyster, as well as a good assemblage of fish bone.

Within the area of Evaluation Trench F, the lowest level reached was a rammed pebble surface bonded with a light skim of lime mortar, (125). This surface was laid onto a compact layer of sandstone and was almost certainly the uppermost level of the east–west road encountered in the ramp and access pit excavations.

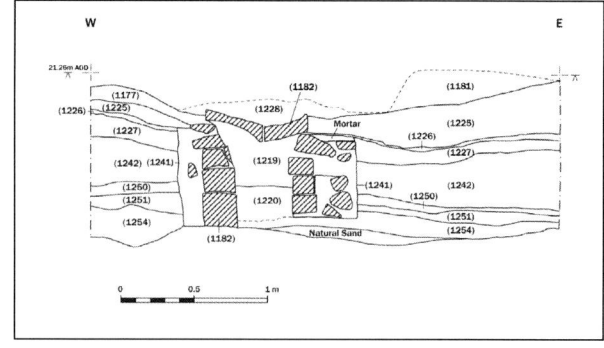

Ill 2.1.13 Phase Ie sewer (1182): S-facing section. (Scale 1/50)

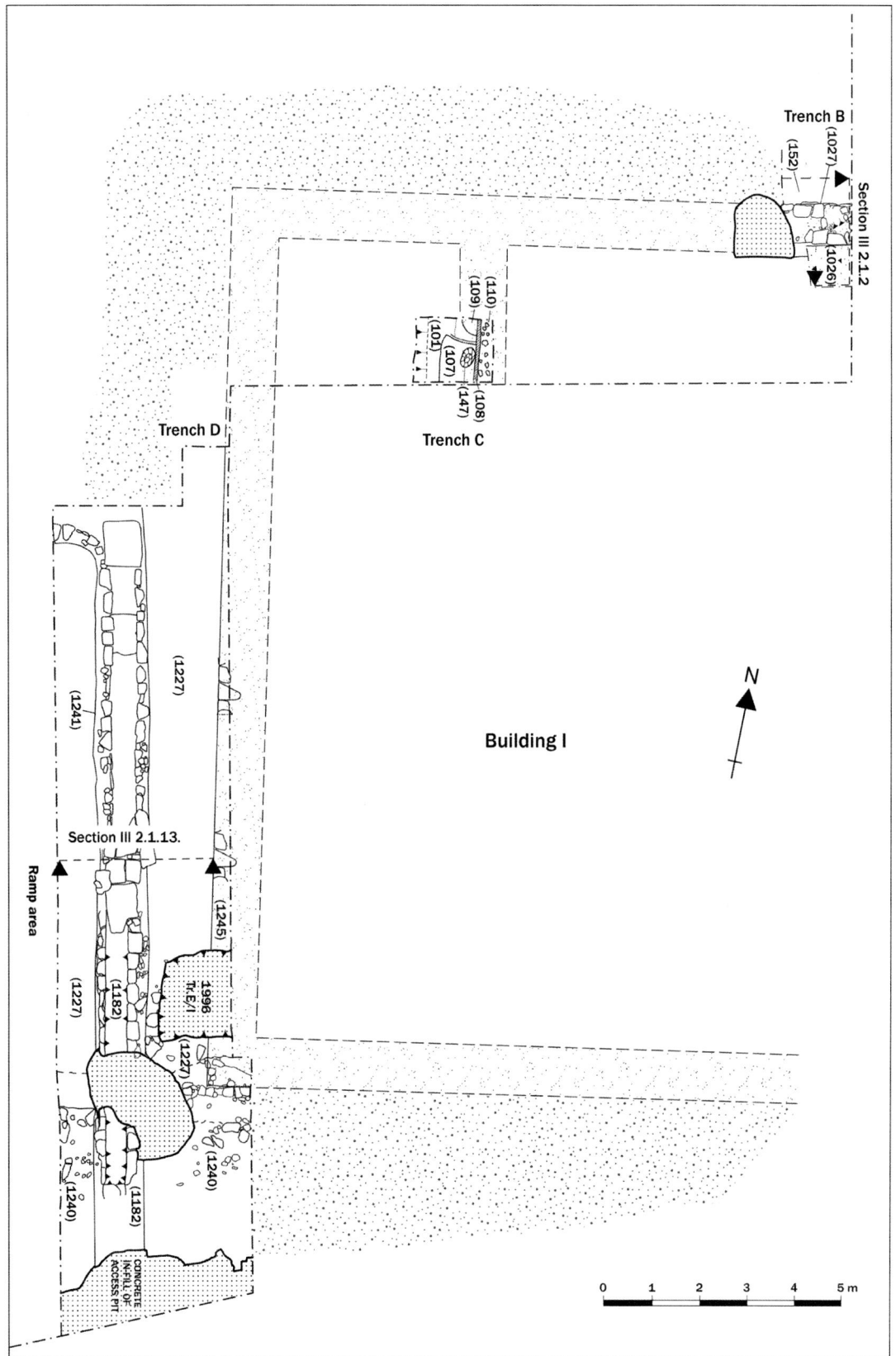

Trench B

(1027)

(152)

Section III 2.1.2

(1026)

(110)

(109)

(101)

(107)

(147)

(108)

Trench C

Trench D

(1227)

(1241)

Section III 2.1.13.

Ramp area

(1245)

1996
Tr.E/I

(1227)

(1182)

(1227)

(1240)

(1240)

(1182)

CONCRETE
IN-FILL OF
ACCESS PIT

Building I

N

0   1   2   3   4   5 m

III 2.1.14   Phase Ie: plan. (Scale 1/125)

A line of sandstone blocks bonded in clay, (120), was found running on an east–west alignment along the southern side of Evaluation Trench F. The surface (125) was laid up against these blocks, suggesting that they predated it. The most likely interpretation is that structure (120) represented the northern side of a sewer (of similar construction to that of (1182) found in the ramp area), serving the east–west road.

To the west, in Evaluation Trench G, two sandstone structures were cut into a layer of light brown silt sand, (95). The first, (94), comprised a line of sandstone blocks aligned east–west on the same line as (120) in Evaluation Trench F. A similar sandstone structure, (92), was bonded to the northern side of structure (94) and was aligned north–south. The fill, (93), of the construction trench of structure (92) produced three joining sherds of a Dragendorff form 29 samian bowl dated 70–85. As in Evaluation Trench F these structures are likely to represent elements of the sewer network associated with the east–west road situated to the north of the fortress baths.

III 2.1.15 Phase Ie: sewer (1182), looking N.

Phase II: Late Roman–'Dark Age'

This phase includes all of the stratigraphy that is likely to have accumulated between the fourth century and *c* AD 900. It was difficult to tie down exact dates for this phase; however, some of the archaeology must broadly correspond to the currently defined first two major phases of post-Roman activity in Chester (as defined in Ward *et al* 1994, 116), namely the sub-Roman and British phase

(fifth to seventh centuries), when Chester was part of the kingdom of Powys; and the first period of Mercian rule (late seventh to late ninth century).

Phase IIa (III 2.1.16)

This sub-phase probably represented the final period of Roman occupation within the fortress. The final archaeological event may have been the formation of layer (1237)/ (1225)/(1142), representing abandonment *c* 370.

Demolition of Building I(i)

In the area of Evaluation Trench B and Escalator Pit B, layer (133) comprised a series of interspersed lenses, alternating between light brown sand and light brown clay, containing sandstone and tile fragments. This layer appeared to run up to and over the northern edge of wall (134)/(1027) of Building I(i), suggesting that the building had been levelled by this time.

As described under Phase Ie the area immediately to the south of wall (1027) had accumulated a significant depth of sediment suggestive of abandonment. During Phase II these sediments were covered by a thick deposit of building debris (1058). This debris only existed to the south of the wall, and the section shows that the wall had toppled or had been pulled down in this direction. The debris lay over the *opus signinum* floor (1026) and as such was at the same stratigraphic height as layers (99) and (98) in Evaluation Trench C, implying that the Phase IIb post hole building II(i) identified in the ramp area did not extend this far east (Ills 2.1.2–.3).

In the area of Evaluation Trench D, layer (119) was a dark reddish brown sandy silt containing fragments of Roman building material, sandstone fragments and pottery dating from the late first to mid-second century onwards. This was the equivalent of layer (1142)/(1225) in the ramp excavation (Ill 2.1.6).

Road surface (1226)

The first event of Phase IIa in the ramp excavation was the laying of a rammed pebble surface (1226) across most of the area. The surface was laid over the edges of the sandstone sewer (1182) in a way that suggested the sewer was still functioning. At the northern end of the ramp this surface was capped by a lime mortar skim which still existed in patches and probably served to consolidate the road construction. The same thing was also observed above the Roman road surface in Evaluation Trench F (*see* above, Phase Ie context (125)). A possible patch of resurfacing to road (1226) may be represented by isolated clay deposit (1224).

Sewer (1182)

The secondary silting of the main north–south sewer was represented by fill (1220), which was a brown sandy clay *c* 250 mm thick (Ill 2.1.13). The thickness of this silt demonstrated a prolonged period of use, during which little maintenance was being undertaken. Finds included Oxfordshire white ware dated 240–400+ and a number of *tesserae*.

The upper fill, (1219), was a brown silt clay loam. Finds included a fragment of fourth-century copper alloy bracelet and a possible Oxfordshire red colour-slipped sherd dated 240–400+. A radiocarbon date was sought from a

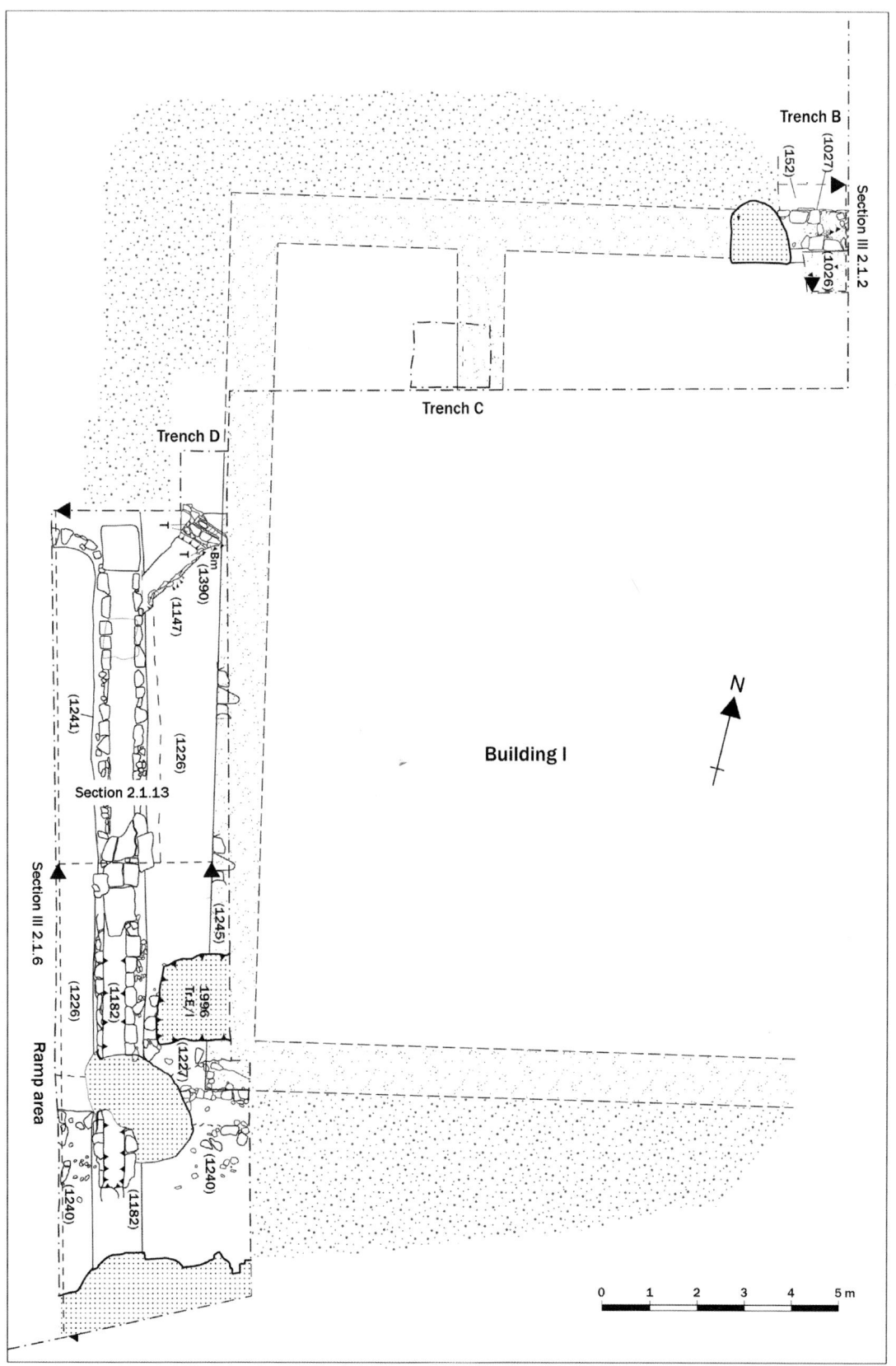

Ill 2.1.16   Phase IIa: plan. (Scale 1/125)

carefully selected animal bone sample: this produced a 2 sigma result of cal AD 115 to 330 (Beta - 170990), demonstrating that the material working its way into the drain silts had a high element of residuality.

Sewer tributary (1147)

Cut (1147) was a north-east–south-west trench which cut through surface (1226) and formed a branch connecting with the north–south sewer constructed in Phase Ie. It was clearly an addition to the Phase Ie sewer because the bottom courses of the latter were left *in situ* at the junction. The sewer itself, (1145), was stone built and was set within the trench. The side walls were constructed from sandstone blocks bonded in reddish brown clay and supported capping stones made from flat abraded sandstone blocks (no decoration or tool marks were visible). The sewer flowed from the north-east (the direction of Building I(i)) to the junction with sewer (1182).

This branch had subsequently become choked along its entire length by a homogeneous sandy silt, (1146). The silt had inclusions of charcoal flecking and building material including abraded sandstone and lumps of mortar, but was much sandier toward the base of the sewer, with small concentrations of yellow cess-like material. Finds included black-burnished 1 pottery dated 120+.

Abandonment layer (1237)/(1225)/(1142)

Layer (1237) was a spread of sandstone rubble north of Phase Id road surface (1240) which overlay the corner of wall (1245) and could be associated with the collapse of the wall. Layer (1225) was a mid-reddish brown silt sand loam 0.2 m thick, containing some large fragments of *opus signinum* and pale grey gritty mortar as well as herringbone floor tiles which were probably derived from the adjacent bath building. This deposit physically sealed road surface (1226). Residual material in it included a coin of Trajan (98–117), black-burnished 1 pottery dated to the late third century, and an unusual bone handle (SF 8787). At the northern end of the ramp area (1225) was overlain by (1142), which produced a ?late second to early third-century black-burnished 1 plain-rimmed dish and Dressel 20 amphorae dated *c* 150–225.

Phase IIb (Ills 2.1.17–.18)

This sub-phase broadly corresponded to Ward's phase 1. Although, at one end of the spectrum Building II(i) described below could have been mid-fourth-century, this does not fit with the established sequence of fortress development and maintenance during the final phase of Roman occupation: a fifth-century context may be more likely. The final acts of this sub-phase appeared to be characterised by pit-digging, although whether this activity took place after the end of Building II(i) was unclear.

The area of Escalator Pit A was characterised by two phases of clay floor interleaved by a lens of black silt thought to be an occupation deposit. Only one post hole was identified, and if a structure was present in this area it was fairly ephemeral, quite unlike the post hole Building II(i) recorded in the ramp area. The first floor, (1042), ran into the northern and eastern baulks of the pit. It had been laid to a thickness 0.10 m and was composed of a light yellowish brown sandy clay mixed with about 20%

sand rammed to form a flat surface. Post hole (1043) was 0.52 m in diameter and 0.11 m deep and was located within 0.1 m of the southern limit of floor (1042). Its fill, (1040), was a reddish brown sandy clay and contained black-burnished 1 pottery dated 120+, iron *lorica* links and an amber-orange glass bead of late Roman type. The second floor, (1038), was composed of pink clay which occupied an area 1.4 x 0.95 m on the eastern side of the pit. Layer (1039) was a very thin black clay lens rich in charcoal fragments, which appeared to define three sides of a rectangle (Ill 2.1.19).

In the area of Evaluation Trench C, layer (99) was a compact mid-red-brown sand, containing fragments of sandstone, mortar and tile. The deposit was thought to have been compacted by its use as a surface and as such it may well represent an internal floor surface to Building II(i), the western wall of which was identified in the ramp area (*see* below). The layer contained a fragment of a fourth-century copper alloy bracelet.

Above surface (99) was a layer of dark red-brown silt sand, (98), which may have been an occupation deposit over surface (99) within Building II(i). This layer produced crucible fragments and copper alloy waste, suggesting that metalworking was taking place in the building. *Tesserae*, iron waste and daub/fired clay were also present. This occupation layer was covered by a layer of mid-yellow-brown sand silt, (76), containing another fragment of a fourth-century copper alloy bracelet (Ill 2.1.3).

Sewer maintenance trench (1229)

A north–south gully, (1229), was excavated through layer (1225) in order to expose the capping stones of sewer (1182) along the entire length of the ramp excavation, probably to aid site drainage and maintain the flow of the sewer. The upcast from this excavation may well be represented by deposit (1181), which ran in a line parallel with the eastern edge of cut (1229). This gully was subsequently filled with a dark greyish brown sandy silt, (1228), very reminiscent of upper sewer fill (1219) (Ill 2.1.13). This produced residual Central Gaulish samian ware dating to *c* 120–200.

Building II(i)

This building was defined by a north–south line of unevenly spaced post holes, (1141), (1137) and (1218), cut into deposit (1181). They were roughly 2 m apart and followed the line of the Roman stone wall (1245). The holes were circular in plan, although only half of each was exposed because they ran into the section. The most exposed example, (1218), had a concave base, was 1.20 m in diameter and 0.60 deep. The respective fills, (1140), (1136) and (1183), were characterised as dark brown sandy silts, containing large sandstone packing stones (set in clay in at least one instance) and soft rounded, burned limestone fragments. The size of these post holes indicated a substantial building, quite capable of being more than one storey in height (Ill 2.1.18).

The main piece of dating evidence for this structure came from a coin dated 330–5 found within the packing material (1136) of post hole (1137), as well as a fourth-century Lower Nene Valley black colour-coated vessel, which demonstrated that the structure had to be built after this date, despite the fact that the accepted sequence

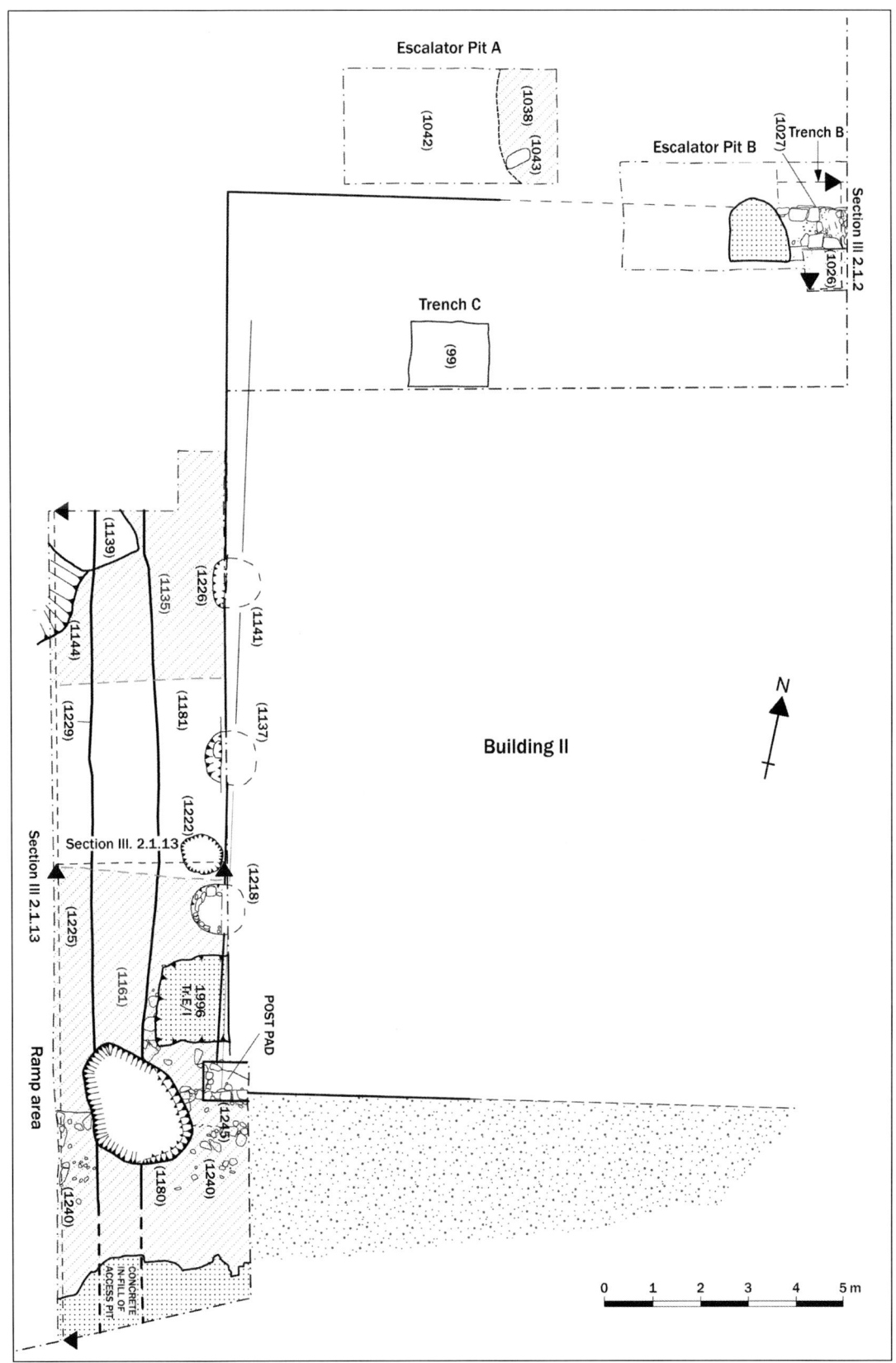

Ill 2.1.17 Phases IIb and c: plan. (Scale 1/125)

Ill 2.1.18 Phase IIb: post hole (1137) of Building IIb, looking E.

for the fortress places the final major phase of rebuilding *c* 300. It is also clear that this building replaced Building I(i), the end of which was signified by layer (1237) in the ramp area and layer (1058) in Escalator Pit B.

Pit (1222)

Pit (1222) was circular in plan, 0.70 in diameter and 0.30 deep. It was out of alignment with and shallower than the three post holes attributed to Building II(i), but would still have been on the line of the wall and probably represented a structural feature. It may have been a repair replacing (1218); If so, this would argue for a reasonably long life for the building. The fill, (1221), was a mid-yellowish brown silty sand and produced Nene Valley ware dated mid-second to fourth century.

Pit group (1144) and (1139)

Pit (1144) was sub-circular in plan, 2.2 m in diameter and 0.40 m deep, with a steep profile and a flat, regular base (Ill 2.1.6). The fill, (1143), was a pale orange brown sandy silt which contained pottery including Oxfordshire red colour-coated ware dated 240–400+. The pit may have been dug in order to remove stone from the Phase Ie sewer (1182), suggesting that the latter had gone out of use by this time, although its presence was still detectable.

Pit (1139) was 1.2 m in diameter and 0.60 m deep. It had extensively removed the northern end of the earlier pit fill, (1143), and may have been dug as a second phase of stone-robbing from the Roman sewer. The fill, (1138), was a yellowish brown sandy silt, thought to be derived from the disposal of midden-type waste: this was apparently supported by the evidence from the environmental sampling which indicated organic waste of faecal origin. The pit's apparent function as a cess pit implies that there was a need for another means of disposing of sewage, now that the Roman sewer had gone out of use. Radiocarbon dates were sought from two carefully selected animal bone samples. These produced two 2 sigma results of cal AD 60 to 240 (Beta - 170989) and cal BC 45 to cal AD 120 (Beta - 170988). This implied a strong residual element to the assemblage from this pit, which was further supported by analysis of the fish bone recovered from sample <5129>.

Layer (1135) was an orange brown silty clay which occupied the northern end of the ramp excavation and was sealed above by Phase IIc layer (1132). This contained rubble and demolition debris, although it stopped short of containing enough rubble to be called a demolition layer. It contained much residual Roman material

including *tesserae*, a fragment of fourth-century copper alloy bracelet and a Oxfordshire red colour-coated wall-sided mortarium dated 240–400+.

Stone-robbing pit (1180)

Pit (1180) was oval in plan with dimensions 2.4 x 1.85 x 0.90 m. It was interpreted as a robber pit cut to extract stone from sewer (1182). The fill, (1179), was a mid- to dark brown silty loam containing degraded animal bones, sandstone rubble, mortar fragments, Roman roof tile and burnt limestone. This was stratigraphically the earliest point that East Gaulish samian ware and late Roman shell-tempered ware (dated 360+) occurred on the site.

In Evaluation Trench F a shallow pit, (127), was cut into road surface (125). The fill, (126), was a mid-brown silty sand containing sandstone fragments.

Phase IIc (Ill 2.1.17)

This period of cultivation and soil generation corresponds to Ward's phase 2: first period of Mercian rule (late seventh to late ninth century). It is thought to represent a 'dark earth' horizon, which has been noted elsewhere within the fortress.

Within the area of the ramp excavation and the access pit, layer (269) was recorded lying directly above Phase Id road surface (274). The layer was a light brown sandy silt, containing a *denarius* of Caracalla and Mancetter-Hartshill mortaria dated to the late second century or later (Ill 2.1.6).

Layer (1132) was identified at the northern end of the ramp excavation as a greyish brown sandy silt. The coarse components and finds were evenly distributed throughout and it was interpreted as a shallow cultivation soil. An intrusive sherd of late Saxon Chester ware was recovered from it as well as residual late Roman material, including bone pins, many *tesserae*, a fourth-century copper alloy bracelet and shell-tempered ware dated 360+. The presence of Chester ware suggests that the area was still being cultivated by Phase III and would tie this horizon in with the Phase III pit (277) and layer (272) in the access pit excavation. Layer (1161) was a brown sandy silt, containing burned white limestone fragments and was interpreted as a shallow cultivation soil. It produced residual late Roman material including a coin (House of Constantine, 335–40) and Nene Valley black colour-coated ware dated to the fourth century. Layer (1177) was a mid-grey sandy loam which covered most of the ramp area. Coarse components all increased in size and frequency towards the interface with demolition deposit (1225), and deposit (1181). It was again interpreted as a shallow cultivation soil which had been truncated by Phase III feature (1175). It produced residual late Roman material including a fourth-century copper alloy bracelet and shell tempered ware.

In Evaluation Trench F layer (121) sealed pit (127) and the road surface (125). It was a mid-brown silty sand containing fragments of tile, *tesserae* and mortar. The residual late Roman material included a black-burnished 1 jar of early to mid-fourth-century date and Nene Valley black colour-coated ware dated mid-second to late fourth century.

In Evaluation Trench G two layers were recorded with a combined thickness of 0.5 m. Layer (75) was a greyish brown silty sand containing lenses of charcoal flecks and a black-burnished 1 beaker dating to the ?early to mid-second century. Layer (77) was a reddish brown sand containing similar coarse components to Phase III layer (74). Pottery included black-burnished 1 and a grey ware bowl dated 220+. Layer (75) was thought to be the equivalent of layer (121) in Evaluation Trench F.

Phase III: Late Saxon (AD 907–1066)

(Ills 2.1.19–.20)

This phase broadly corresponds to Ward's phases 3 and 4 (1994, 116): from the foundation of the Saxon *burh* in AD 907 to the Viking raid of 980; and the decline between 980 and the Norman Conquest of 1066. Owing to the scant evidence no sub-phases have been attempted.

Layer (132) in Evaluation Trench B was a compact mid-red-brown sandy clay up to 0.35 m thick containing an even mix of sandstone, mortar and tile and sealing earlier Roman structural remains. The top of this deposit formed a fairly hard level surface and is thought to be the equivalent of layer (973) in the main excavation of the escalator pit. The latter was an undulating reddish brown sandy clay beneath (972) at the eastern edge of the area above Roman wall (1027). Layer (1018), a mid-red-brown sandy silt at the western edge of the escalator pit may also have been the same layer. These layers may have been deposited to form a level base on which to lay a clay surface (Ill 2.1.2).

Layer (1022) in Escalator Pit A was an orange sandy silt up to 0.70 m thick beneath (974) and sealing (1038) (Ill 2.1.19). Only Roman finds were recovered. A sample of animal bone produced a 2 sigma AMS date of cal AD 215–400 (Beta - 170987). A dog coprolite was also identified from the bulk sample (Ill 2.1.19).

In Evaluation Trench C, pit (96) was cut into Phase II layer (76) and was only partially exposed within the trench. It was roughly circular with a diameter of 1 m and a depth of 0.5 m. The fill, (97), was a dark brown sandy silt, which produced a fragment of an iron horseshoe of tenth–eleventh-century type and some metalworking waste. Layer (70) was a mid-yellow-brown sand silt 0.30 m thick, containing Roman tile, sandstone and mortar fragments which covered all of the trench and sealed pit fill (97); it also produced a copper alloy bead of ninth-to tenth-century Norse type. This deposit was probably contemporary with deposit (1022) in Escalator Pit A.

In Evaluation Trench D, layer (115) was a reddish brown sandy clay containing fragments of sandstone, tile and mortar. As with Evaluation Trenches B and C this deposit was thought to be post-Roman in character and may be the equivalent of layer (1134) in the ramp excavation.

Layer (106) in Evaluation Trench F was a dark red-brown sandy silt, containing fragments of Roman building material including tile, mortar, and sandstone. It may have been the same as layer (272) in the access pit excavation. A fragment of crucible was recovered from this layer, and although there is a high risk that it was a residual Roman artefact it could indicate metalworking in the vicinity.

Layer (74) in Evaluation Trench G was a light red brown sand clay containing high percentages of Roman building material.

The access pit produced the most abundant C14 evidence for late Saxon occupation from the entire excavation programme. It is therefore interesting to note that Chester ware was significant by its absence from both the fills of pit (277) and layer (272).

Pit (277) was a circular pit 1.1 m in diameter and 0.25 m deep cut into Phase II layer (269). The pit had four very distinctive fills which in plan had the appearance of a series of concentric circles (the outer most circle being the earliest fill, (281)). As three of the four fills produced evidence for charred plant remains it seems likely that this pit represented a hearth. All four fills, (278) to (281), were sampled in their entirety, samples <5016> to <5019> respectively, and so we can be confident that the lack of artefactual evidence is real and not a result of excavation technique. Charred oat seeds from the uppermost fill, (278), produced a 2 sigma AMS date of cal AD 795–1000 (Beta - 170532). The sample taken from fill (278) produced charred nutlets of sedge, which could be interpreted as evidence for the burning of peat as a fuel; other fuel was probably represented by wood charcoal (hazel roundwood). All of the other plant remains recovered from the samples indicated charred food debris, from the cooking of food consisting in large part of pulses and whole or milled grain.

Layer (272) was a mid-grey-green cess-like clayey silt up to 0.15 m thick containing Roman tile fragments. It was thickest in the south-west corner of the access pit and thinned to the north and east. The layer sealed pit (277) on the southern edge of the trench. The layer was sampled, <5014>, and bread/club wheat seeds produced a 2

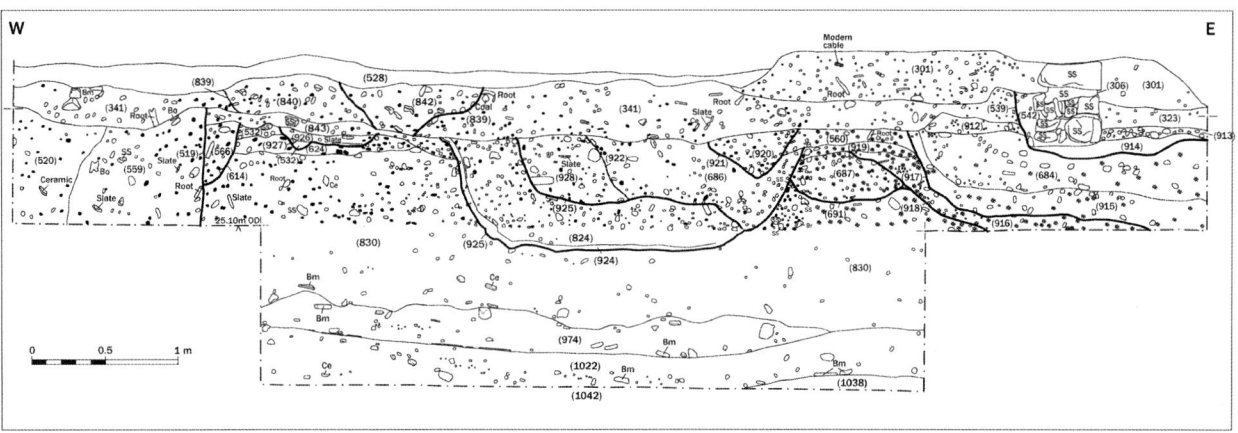

Ill 2.1.19 Escalator Pit A: S-facing section. (Scale 1/50)

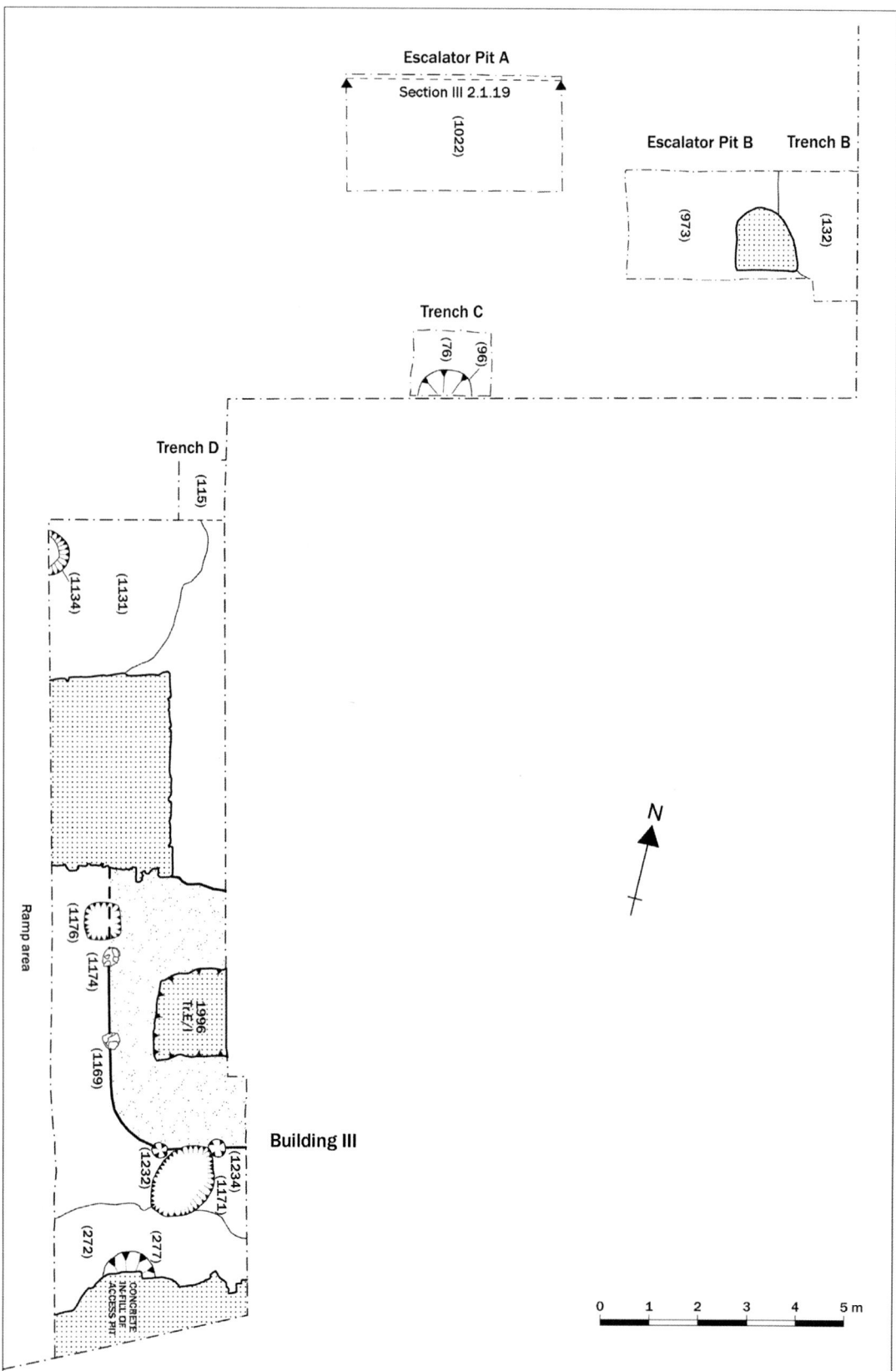

III 2.1.20 Phase III: plan. (Scale 1/125)

sigma AMS date of cal AD 785–1040 (Beta - 170531). Some of the fish bone preservation from this layer was described as 'battered', possibly as the result of having passed through the human digestive system – thus suggesting that it had resulted from the spreading of cess.

A basin-shaped pit, (1134), was cut into layer (1132) at the north end of the ramp excavation, being 0.94 m in diameter, 0.245 m deep (only part-excavated as the feature extended into the edge of the area of excavation). The fill, (1133), was a black silt. Layer (1131) was a grey brown silt *c* 0.10 m thick, and was thought to be a cultivation soil.

Building III(i)

This building was defined by a group of four post holes forming a right-angle in the southern half of the ramp excavation. The area enclosed measured at least 4 m north–south by 2.6 m east–west, but the limits of excavation and truncation by later features rendered the building plan incomplete. There were no internal surfaces or features associated with the structure.

Post hole (1174) was sub-circular in plan, 0.35 m in diameter and 0.25 m deep. The fill, (1173), was a light brown clayey silt, sub-angular sandstone being used for packing stones for the post. Post hole (1169) was circular in plan, 0.34 m in diameter and 0.35 m deep. The fill, (1168), was a light brown clayey silt. Sub-angular sandstone again acted as packing stones for the post. However, the stones were not arranged to form a post pipe, so the post had probably been removed for reuse. Post holes (1232) and (1234) were both circular in plan, 0.30 m in diameter and 0.03 m deep. The fills, (1231) and (1233) respectively, were a mid-brown silty sand.

Pits

Pit (1171) was oval in plan and was cut into Phase II layer (1161) and the edge of post hole (1234). The fill, (1170), was a dark olive green silty clay loam. It was sealed by cultivation soil (883) (dated 1250+).

Cut (1176) was roughly square in plan with rounded corners, convex sides and a flat base. The lower fill, (1175), was a green silty clay 0.15 m thick which was entirely sampled, <5124>, and produced charred cereal, hazelnut and *ficus*, as well as fragments of shell, coprolite and fish bone. Upper fill (1178) was a mid-green-brown sand silt 0.10 m thick. The fills were indicative of the pit's use as a cess pit.

Phase IV: Early medieval

(Norman–14 century)

Very little in this phase of activity can be dated to pre-1250. As on other excavation sites in Chester there seems to have been a 'Norman hiatus', with archaeologically observed activity between *c* 1066 and 1250 being limited to the generation of cultivation soils, probably because other activity, eg building, was concentrated on the street frontages, which are usually inaccessible to investigation. The next significant event in the ramp area was the excavation of a ditch, (1127), which would appear to have delimited the eastern ends of the future Plots 2, 3 and 4. Several other ephemeral pits and post holes appeared at this time but very little sense could be made of

these dispersed features. The final episode seemed to consist of an increase in backland activity and the subdivision of earlier properties, with the boundaries to Plot 2 being delimited by an imposing sandstone wall. Ovens were evidenced in Plots 3 and 6, and a possible metalworking hearth was recorded in Evaluation Trench C.

Plot 1 (III 2.1.21)

Cultivation soil (883)

Cultivation soil (883) covered the entire area of the ramp excavation, with the exception of areas voided by later archaeological features such as ditch cut (1127) and the Phase V cut (1120) for the stone-lined cess pit (487). The layer was a dark grey brown, sand silt loam 0.18 m thick, containing pottery dated 1250+, and an iron object which might be either a leather worker's punch, a blacksmith's cold drill or an armour-piercing arrowhead.

Layer (266)/(268) recorded in the access pit (Ill 2.1.6) was a dark greyish brown silty sand and probably represents a continuation of the cultivation soil (883) described above; it contained pottery of thirteenth–fourteenth-century date. The sample from this context, <5013>, produced uncharred elder seeds, charred cereal (bread/club wheat, barley and rye – possibly residual from Phase III?) and fish bone, including herring and eel.

Evaluation Trench G

Layer (34) covered the whole of Evaluation Trench G and was a dark brown silty clay containing pottery of mid-thirteenth- and fourteenth-century date. Layer (47) was a dark brown sandy silt containing pottery of thirteenth–early fourteenth-century date and was interpreted as a medieval cultivation soil. Trench (52) was excavated during the construction of an east–west sandstone wall, (51). This was constructed from angular sandstone blocks bonded in a yellow brown clay, and was possibly associated with Phase V wall (45) in Evaluation Trench F.

Plot 2 (Ills 2.1.22 and .24–5)

Layer (883), described in Plot 1 above, continued into Plot 2.

Pit (1002)

Pit (1002) was represented by one quadrant of a circular cut, the other three quadrants lying beyond the limits of excavation, 2 m in diameter and 0.80 m deep. It was cut into the cultivation soil (883) and contained a single fill (1001), which was a pink-grey brown silty clay containing pottery dated 1250+. Whatever the original function of the pit the single fill of clay and sandstone rubble suggests a strong desire to fill it in and create a level surface.

Boundary ditch (1127)

Ditch (1127) was a cut 1.5 m wide, running north–south along the eastern side of the ramp excavation. The fills, (1126) and (1125), consisted of grey brown silty clays, with horizon distinction being made on coarse components. The upper fill, (1125), produced pottery dated 1250+.

Boundary wall (600)

Trenches (880) and (1150) defined a rectilinear cut forming three sides of a rectangular property boundary at the back of Plot 2 (Ills 2.1.22 and .25). The trench was filled by sandstone wall, (600), which survived to a height of up to five courses. Most of the blocks had tooling marks on the facing stones (both point and flat tooling; some in cross-hatching, some overlaid with opposing cross-hatching). The top three courses were bonded with a sandy lime mortar of pale brown colour and were composed of well dressed facing stones to the north, south and east; the internal face was very roughly hewn and unfinished, which suggests that the blocks were made for the job rather than being reused. The lower two courses were bonded with a mid-yellowish brown clay and were likewise rough-hewn. A short cross halfpenny dated 1180–1247 was recovered from the clay bonding of the wall. The fact that the top three courses were dressed suggests they were above ground level at the time the wall was built.

The backfill to construction trench (880)/(1150) was a dark grey silty clay, (882)/(1006).

Plot 3 (Ills 2.1.21, .23 and .24)

Cultivation soil (1119)

Cultivation soil (1119) covered all of Plot 3 in the ramp excavation area and was a very dark grey-black silty clay which produced pottery dated 1250+. This was thought to be the same as layer (883) in Plots 1 and 2.

Post hole (1122)

Post hole (1122) was a circular feature cut into cultivation soil (1119). The fill, (1121), was found to contain clay and medieval ceramic of thirteenth–fourteenth-century date. It was sealed by (873), a dark grey brown silty clay which produced ceramics dated 1250+.

Oven (871)

A subrectangular construction pit, (872), had been cut into layer (873) and contained oven structure (871), which ran under the western edge of the ramp excavation, where the remainder was lost through modern mini-piling. The oven was constructed of sandstone blocks bonded with a sandy lime mortar, forming an oval shape that narrowed dramatically to the west (Ill 2.1.23). The original base of the oven comprised a well laid stone floor bonded with clay; this had subsequently been covered by a thin surface of clay, heated to a biscuit hardness. Pottery dating 1250+ was recovered from within the fabric of the structure. The lowest fill, (875), comprised yellow and black sand and charcoal resulting from the use of the oven. The upper fill, (874), was a brown silt which probably accumulated after a period of disuse. This was covered by layer (799), a brownish grey silty sand containing pottery dated 1250+.

Hearth (849)

Hearth (849) was an area of bright orange sand and orange friable clay sitting in a shallow scoop in the top of layer (799). Small amounts of well oxidised animal bone, which had been subject to high levels of heat, were found within it, as well as pottery of thirteenth–fourteenth-century date.

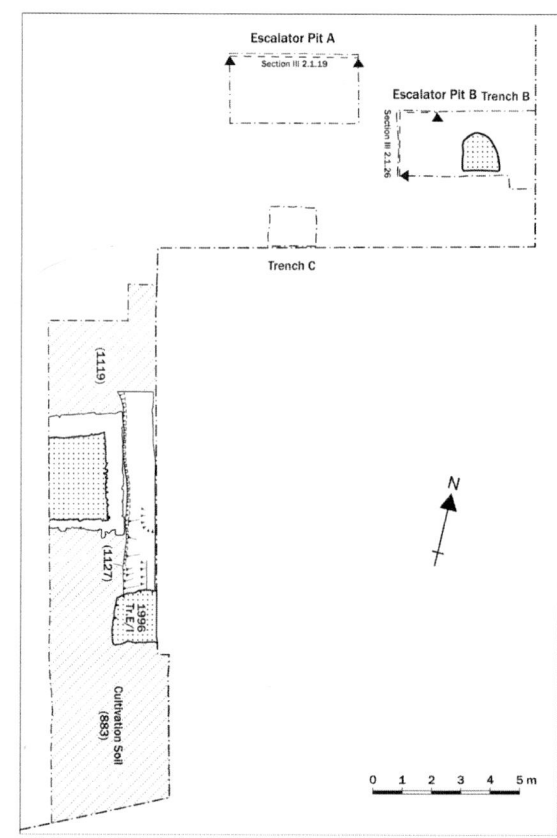

Ill 2.1.21 Phase IV: plan of earlier features. (Scale 1/250)

Ill 2.1.22 Phase IV Plot 2 boundary wall (600): E-facing section.

Ill 2.1.23 Phase IV Plot 3: oven (871), looking E.

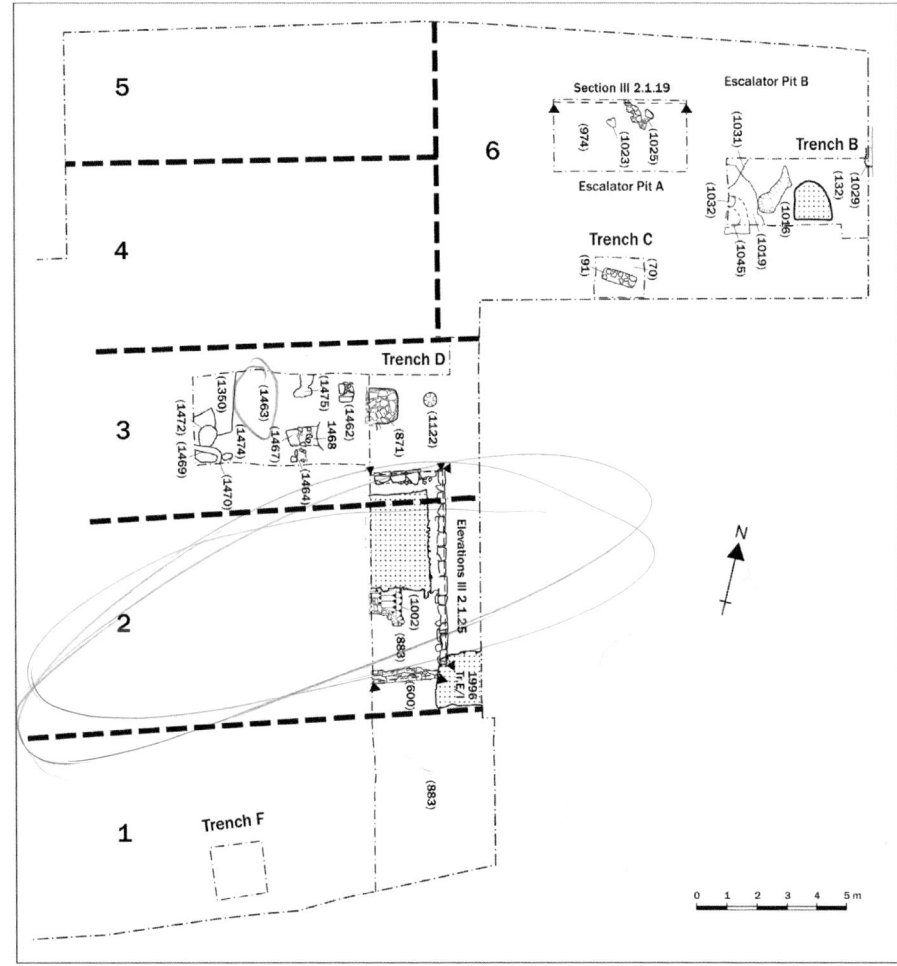

III 2.1.24 Phase IV:
general arrangement of plots.
(Scale 1/250)

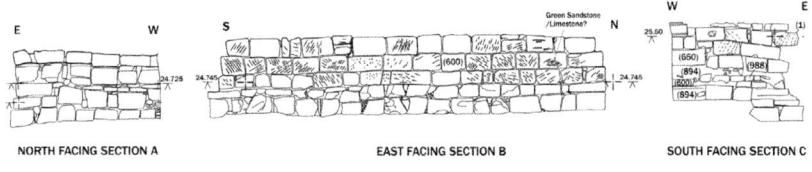

III 2.1.25 Phase IV Plot 2 boundary wall (600):
elevation. (Scale 1/125)

Layer (1479)

Layer (1479) was an arbitrary spit which included clay surface (1463). This was excavated quickly to reach a required depth of 25 m OD in this area for construction purposes.

Clay floor (1463)

Context (1463) was an orange clay layer which emerged on removal of layer (1350); it may have been the internal surface of a building. Substantial walls protruded through this layer, one to the east, aligned north–south, and one to the south-east, aligned east–west (1467). The relationship between the two walls had been destroyed by pit cut (850).

Layer (1475)

Layer (1475) was a lime mortar spread that was identified for planning purposes but remained unexcavated as it was below 25 m OD.

Post hole (1464)

Post hole (1464) was circular in plan and was cut into (1479). Its fill, (1465), was a mid-brown clay. The post pipe was defined by the sandstone post-packing, which suggested that the post had decayed *in situ*.

Sandstone wall (1467)

Sandstone wall (1467) was aligned east–west and was truncated to the east by cut (850). The wall comprised reused blocks bonded in clay, with two courses surviving. Both the north and south faces were well dressed. The construction trench (1466) was cut into layer (1479) and was backfilled with (1468).

Ditch (1469)

Ditch (1469) was aligned east–west. The fill (1470) was not excavated.

Hearth (1472)

Hearth (1472) comprised a shallow pit filled with a pink clay which was removed to reveal a mid-brown, charcoal-rich silty clay, (1471), which was not excavated.

Pit (1474)

Pit (1474) was a small oval feature oriented east–west, filled by (1473). This was not excavated.

Oven (1462)

Oven (1462) was a sandstone structure below layer (1350). The stones were set into the underlying deposit, and sand had been placed in and around the inner sides but not along the outer edge. A spread of mortar appeared to be set against the stones spreading to north and west. It seems likely that this was the western part of the hearth/oven earlier discovered in the ramp area (*see* (871) above).

Plot 6 (Ills 2.1.21, .24 and .26)

Pit (128)/(1029)

Pit (128)/(1029) was a rectangular steep-sided pit with a flat base that was cut into deposit (132)/(973) in Evaluation Trench B (Ill 2.1.2). The upper fill, (129)/(1030), was a dark reddish brown sandy clay containing a relatively high percentage of animal bone; the sample <5114> produced charred cereal and fish bone including herring, eel and flat fish. The lower fill, (141)/(1041), was a dark grey charcoal-rich sandy silt which was also sampled, <5115> and produced fish bone including conger eel. This pit was revisited during the excavation of Plot 6 and was recorded as cut (1029). The upper fill was recorded as (1030) and the lower as (1041).

Post hole (1032)

Post hole (1032) in Escalator Pit B was circular in plan and was well defined against sandy layer (1018) through which it cut. The fill, (1034), was a greyish brown sandy loam, sealed by clay hearth (1045). The fill was sampled, <5116>, and produced charred cereal and fish bone including herring and flat fish, and a 2 sigma AMS date of cal AD 1150–1270 (Beta - 170530) was obtained from a sample of the charred grain.

Pit (1031)

A curved pit (1031) ran into the baulk in the north-west corner of Escalator Pit B. The fill, (1033), was a dark brown sandy loam, containing early medieval pottery. A sample, <5099>, produced charred cereal and fish bone including herring and flat fish. This pit was presumably broadly contemporary with post hole (1032) as they were both cut through the same layer (1018) and sealed by clay floor (1019).

Oven (1045)

Oven (1045) comprised a layer of orange red clay that had been fired to a biscuit hardness towards its centre. It was located in the south-west corner of Escalator Pit B and showed some signs of discoloration due to exposure to intense heat (Ill 2.1.26). The extent of the oven was uncertain as it ran into two baulks and had been truncated to the south by pit (681). The oven had no apparent construction cut and was laid directly on top of post hole (1032). It was overlain by layer (1048), a mid-grey-brown clay loam that probably represents the sooting of the oven prior to disuse.

Clay floor (1019)

Floor (1019) was a deposit of orange clay in the south-west corner of Escalator Pit B (Ill 2.1.26). There was some broken building material at the base of the layer. This floor is almost certainly associated with oven base (1045) and the two in combination may attest a workshop or even a dwelling. Layer (1017)/(1035) was a greyish brown silty clay loam running north–south through the middle of the escalator pit. It was thought to be levelling material for floor (1019).

Pit (1016)

Pit (1016) was an irregularly shaped cut in the centre of the escalator pit. It was roughly linear and aligned north-east to south-west with post hole depressions in the base at either end and therefore could have been a beam slot. The fill, (1015), was a dark greyish brown silty clay, which had few inclusions, but a sample, <5096>, produced charred cereal and fish bone including flat fish.

Hearth (91)

Hearth (91) in Evaluation Trench C was a shallow feature filled with large fragments of Roman tile apparently laid to form a base. No cut was identified, but the feature lay above layer (70). Layer (69) overlay the tile and consisted of a black silt sand containing a high percentage of industrial waste associated with ironworking.

Layer (68) covered the entire trench and sealed hearth (91). It was a yellowish brown sandy silt containing sandstone and Roman tile fragments (Ill 2.1.3).

Building IV(i)

Deposit (1025) in Escalator Pit B was a linear scatter of sandstones of various sizes up to 400 mm. The stones formed what could have been a rudimentary wall, although the lack of bonding materials, faces, courses and infill make it a difficult feature to assess properly. All the stones peeled straight off onto layer (1022) beneath.

Post hole (1023) was sub-triangular in plan and so slight as to not really have sides or a break of slope. The feature was oriented north-west-south-east lengthways and cut layer (1022). Its fill, (1024), was a dark brown silty clay. Post hole (1046) was located in the north-west corner of the escalator pit and filled by (1047). Post hole (1057) had a post pipe defined by the associated packing stones.

Layer (974) was an orange brown silty sand, covering all of the escalator pit excavation.

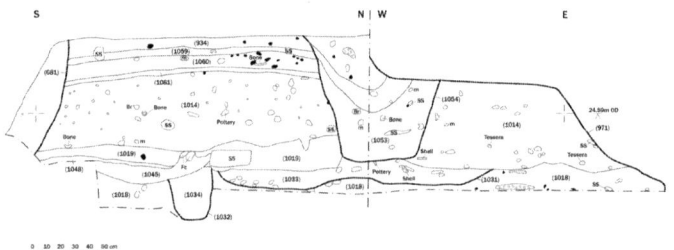

Ill 2.1.26 Escalator Pit B: E- and S-facing sections. (Scale 1/50)

Phase V: Late medieval (14–late 15 century)

The precise chronology of the later medieval developments on the site remains uncertain but at some point in
the fourteenth–fifteenth century the area was formally
divided by substantial stone walls. The main north–south
boundary, marking the mid-point between Bridge Street
and Newgate Street, had already been set out in Phase IV.
Ovens were constructed at the backs of these individual
properties, some quite elaborate in design. Their precise
use remains obscure, but baking and brewing are possibilities. In one case the fabric of the oven contained a
large quantity of reused medieval floor tile. This phase
also saw the digging of pits for the disposal of cess and
domestic waste. Among these was a large stone-built structure in Plot 2: this remained in use until the sixteenth
century and is discussed in more detail in Phase VI.

Plot 1 (Ills 2.1.28–9)

Plot 1 was the most southerly property within the excavation. It was separated from Plot 2 by an east–west strip
that had been used to construct a culvert. None of the
other plots were delimited by such a feature and it is
possible that this was due to the fact that Plot 1 occupied
the northern side of an earlier, larger, plot, while Plots 2–

4 lay within what had been a separate plot. The Phase V
plan has been subdivided into (a–b), (c) and (d) in order
to illustrate the developments in each plot more clearly.

Pit (1163)

The earliest Phase V feature identified in the plot was a
sub-circular pit, (1163), 0.50 m deep with nearly vertical
sides and a flat base. It was cut into the Phase IV cultivation soil (883). The fill, (1162), was a mid-grey-brown
silty clay which was sealed by cultivation layer (1164).

Cultivation soils

Contexts (264), (261), 1165), (1164), (1004), (67), (66),
(64), (1838), (1849), (1900) represent a collection of
brown clayey loam deposits which were spread throughout Plot 1. All had the general characteristics of
cultivation soils and were rich in residual Roman building material. They lay directly above Phase IV cultivation
soil (883) and produced ceramics of fourteenth–fifteenth-
century date. Layer (995) was a dark grey brown sandy
silt loam which overlay deposit (1004) and only survived
in a fragmentary state owing to truncation by later wall
foundation cuts (994) and (1005). Its general character
suggested that it was another cultivation soil, while occasional dark olive green cess lenses within the matrix
suggested manuring during cultivation.

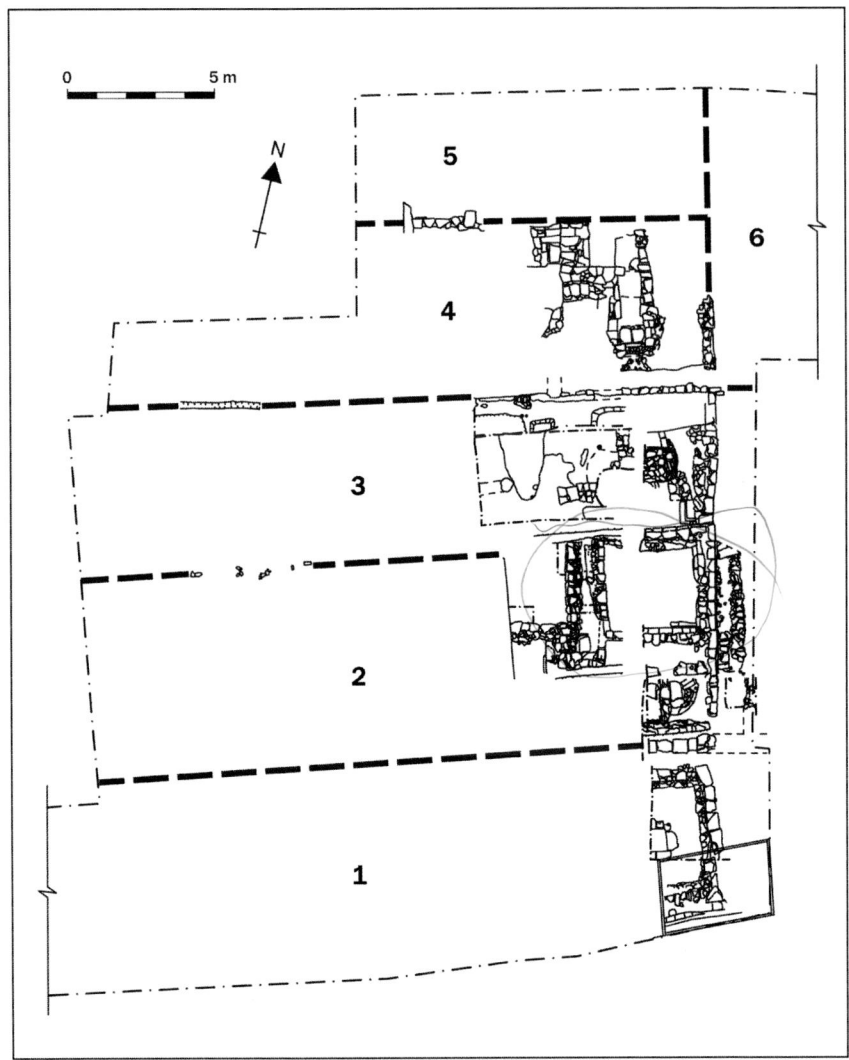

Ill 2.1.27 Phase V: general arrangement of plots. (Scale 1/250)

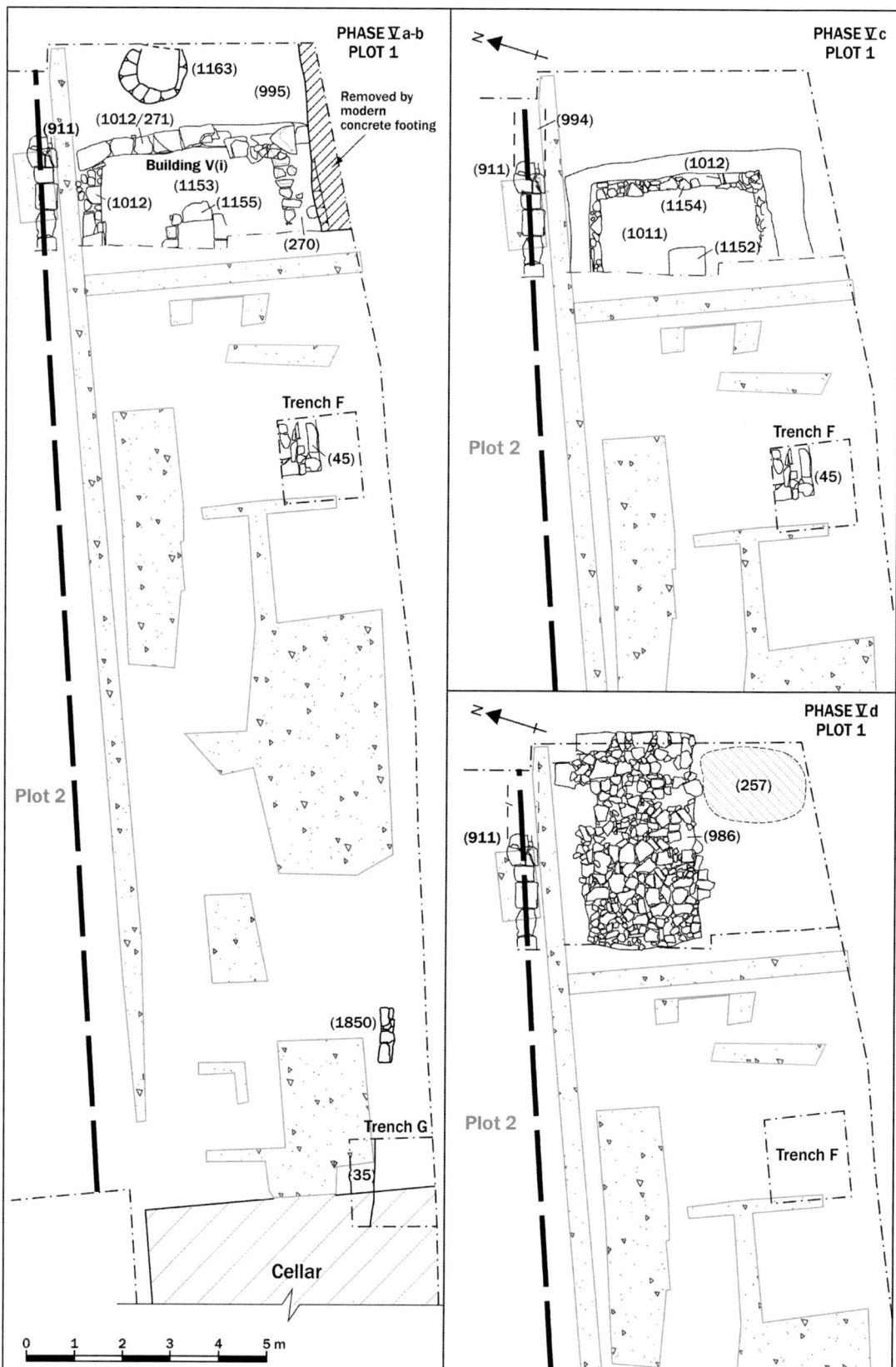

III 2.1.28 Phase V Plot 1: plan. (Scale 1/125)

28

Building V(i)

The walls of Building V(i) defined the north, south and east limits of Plot 1 and may have served simply as property boundary walls. However, the identification of what have been interpreted as internal floor surfaces suggests that the walls were also part of a roofed structure.

Walls (1012)/(270)/(271)

Sandstone wall (1012)/(270)/(271) was built on a terraced foundation cut, (1160) and consisted of very roughly hewn blocks, some with broad flat tooling marks, bonded with a stiff reddish yellow clay. It generally only survived to a height of two courses, except on the southern side where it rose to a height of six courses, possibly owing to a terrace on the adjacent property to the south. Fourteenth–fifteenth-century pottery was recovered from the bonding material. Wall (45) in Evaluation Trench F may represent the south-western corner of the building. The western continuation of the southern boundary of the plot may be formed by walls (1850) and (35), the latter located in Evaluation Trench G.

Floor (1153)/(267)/(262)

Floor (1153)/(267)/(262) was formed by a reddish yellow clay deposit laid evenly within the bounds of wall (1012) and compacted to form a firm surface. It partially overlay oven structure (1155), suggesting that the oven had already been built by the time the surface was laid. Thirteenth–fourteenth-century pottery was recovered from the floor make-up.

Oven (1155)

The oven or hearth (1155) was built in a construction trench, (1159), 0.43 m wide x 0.67 m deep with vertical sides and a flat base. The oven itself comprised heat reddened and heavily sooted red sandstone blocks with both wide, flat cross-hatched tooling, and narrow skew tooling, suggesting reuse of earlier masonry. It was rectangular in plan, with a short north–south cross wall bonded with a white, soft sandy lime mortar to two east–west oriented side walls. All three walls survived to a height of three courses and the internal face was partially rendered with the same mortar as was used to bond the structure. A thin lens of blue-black soot, (1158), lay within the base of the oven. This was covered by a dump of mid-yellow-brown soil, (1157), which was rich in building debris and appeared to represent the deliberate backfilling of the oven after it had fallen into disuse.

Reflooring (260)/(1011)

After clay floor (1153) had been laid, a single course of poor quality red sandstone rubble bonded with a reddish yellow clay, (1154), was added around the base of the internal faces of wall (1012). This addition is puzzling as it did not appear to improve the appearance or structural integrity of the original wall. Both (1153) and (1154) were covered with a distinct ironpan-like staining which may indicate the remains of decomposed organic matter such as wood. (1154) may therefore have been a dwarf wall which supported the joists for a raised timber floor inserted after oven (1155) had gone out of use. Fourteenth–fifteenth-century pottery was recovered from the bonding material of (1154). Subsequently, a third floor was laid within the bounds of wall (1012), consisting of a layer of mid-yellow-brown clay, (260)/(1011). This layer again produced fourteenth–fifteenth-century pottery.

Hearth (1152)

After the laying of clay floor (1011), a square cut, (1152), was dug through the floor surface in the position of the earlier oven (1155). The cut was filled with a dark brown silty clay, (1151), which was flecked with tiny flecks of charcoal and produced pottery of fourteenth–fifteenth-century date. The cut also contained tooled sandstone blocks, indicating that the feature may have functioned as a domestic hearth.

Culvert (991)/(993)

To the north of Building V(i) was an east–west cut, (994), which marked the boundary between Plots 1 and 2 and had been cut into cultivation soil (995). The cut served as the construction trench for a stone drain, which comprised a basal course of sandstone slabs set in a reddish brown clay, (993). On these was constructed a pair of parallel walls formed from sandstone slabs set on edge and again bonded in clay, (991). A course of sandstone slabs, (911), formed a cap. The culvert eventually became choked with a dark greenish grey, gritty sandy silt, (992). A probable coprolite was noted during the excavation of this silt, along with frequent streaks of light yellow fibrous material, and sample <5097> produced fig pips suggestive of the presence of faecal matter.

The culvert was overlain by a dark reddish brown deposit containing blocks of angular sandstone rubble, (908). This deposit lay just south of Phase IV boundary wall (600) delimiting the southern edge of Plot 2 and could represent a local collapse, leading to the episode of rebuilding represented by (650), discussed below.

Ill 2.1.29 Phase V Plot 1: culvert (991)/(993), looking E.

Yard/road surface (986)/(259)

The final development in Plot 1 during Phase V was the establishment of an external surface, (986)/(259). No eastern limit was found where one might have been expected along the main north–south property division and the surface continued into the eastern edge of excavation, suggesting that it functioned as a road between Bridge Street and Newgate Street. The surface was made up of angular fragments of sandstone that had been laid with a flat upper surface. The interstices were filled by reddish brown silty sand which contained fourteenth–fifteenth-century pottery. The layer of sandstone brash, (257) found on the south-eastern side of Plot 1 probably represented a localised resurfacing.

Plot 2 (Ills 2.1.30–5)

Cultivation soils (996), (651), (1656)

Layer (996) was a greyish brown silty clay in the south-eastern area of Plot 2 which partly overlay the internal face of Phase IV wall (600). It only survived in a fragmentary state, but may indicate a period of cultivation at the back of Plot 2 prior to the construction of cess pit (1008). Layer (651) was a similar deposit to the south of wall (600). Layer (1656) occupied an extensive area in the western part of Plot 2 and produced pottery of fourteenth–fifteenth century date.

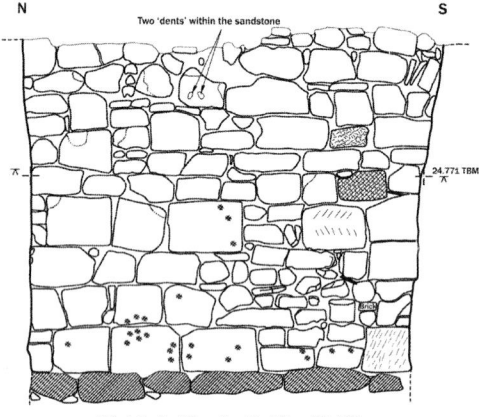

West Facing Elevation B of Cess Pit 487

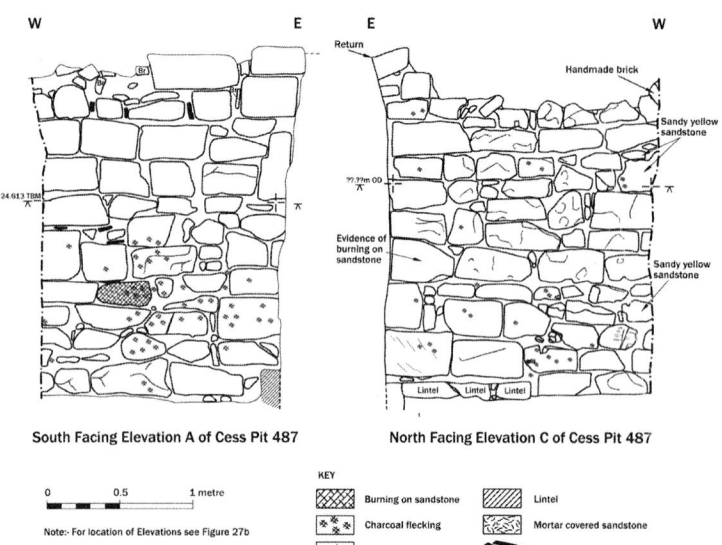

South Facing Elevation A of Cess Pit 487   North Facing Elevation C of Cess Pit 487

KEY

▨ Burning on sandstone	⧄ Lintel	
✳ Charcoal flecking	▨ Mortar covered sandstone	
⁄⁄⁄ Chisel marks	➤ Slate	

Ill 2.1.30 Phase V Plot 2 cess pit (487): elevations. (Scale 1/50)

Stone-lined cess pits (998), (487)

A steep-sided pit, (1008), was cut 0.70 m into cultivation soil (1004) in the south-eastern corner of Plot 2. This was lined with sandstone blocks bonded in pink-brown clay, (998). The structure had the appearance of two walls joined at right-angles on the northern and eastern sides of the pit; the southern side of the structure was formed by boundary wall (600) and the western side was not located within the excavation. The void created between cut (1008) and the stone lining was filled with sandstone rubble and dark greyish brown silty clay, (1007). After a period of use as a cess pit this feature was deliberately backfilled with reddish brown silty clay (997) and angular sandstone blocks, possibly derived from the collapse of the lining. The creation of this cess pit may have been indirectly responsible for the structural problems later evidenced in the adjoining section of wall (600), which are described below.

To the north of the cess pit a foundation trench, (981), was cut for wall (763), which survived as a single course of sandstone blocks bonded in clay with good quality facings. The eastern end of the wall was bonded to boundary wall (600) with a white lime mortar. The construction trench was backfilled with a brown sandstone-rich clay, (980). The function of the wall is unclear, but it served to divide the eastern end of Plot 2 into two separate areas, which were subsequently used for very different purposes. The angle between walls (763) and (600) was filled by a dump of gritty white lime mortar mixed with sand. It produced late medieval pottery and probably represented a building episode after the construction of wall (763), but before the building of oven (767).

To the north of wall (763) a large rectangular cut, (1120), 2.17 m deep was excavated to facilitate the construction of another stone-lined cess pit, (487). This cut removed virtually all traces of cultivation soil (996) from the eastern end of Plot 2. The lining itself was also rectangular and comprised reused sandstone masonry bonded in pink clay, and included at least one architectural fragment, a corbel. On the bottom of the west-facing elevation and halfway along the base of the north-facing elevation was a stepped footing. The pit appears to have been well maintained and routinely emptied during Phase V; hence its subsequent filling is discussed in Phases VI and VII. To the west of the cess pit a series of layers formed, (1311) and (1333). The lower layer, (1311), produced fourteenth–fifteenth-century pottery (Ills 2.1.30–1).

Ill 2.1.31 Phase V Plot 2: cess pit (487), looking E.

30

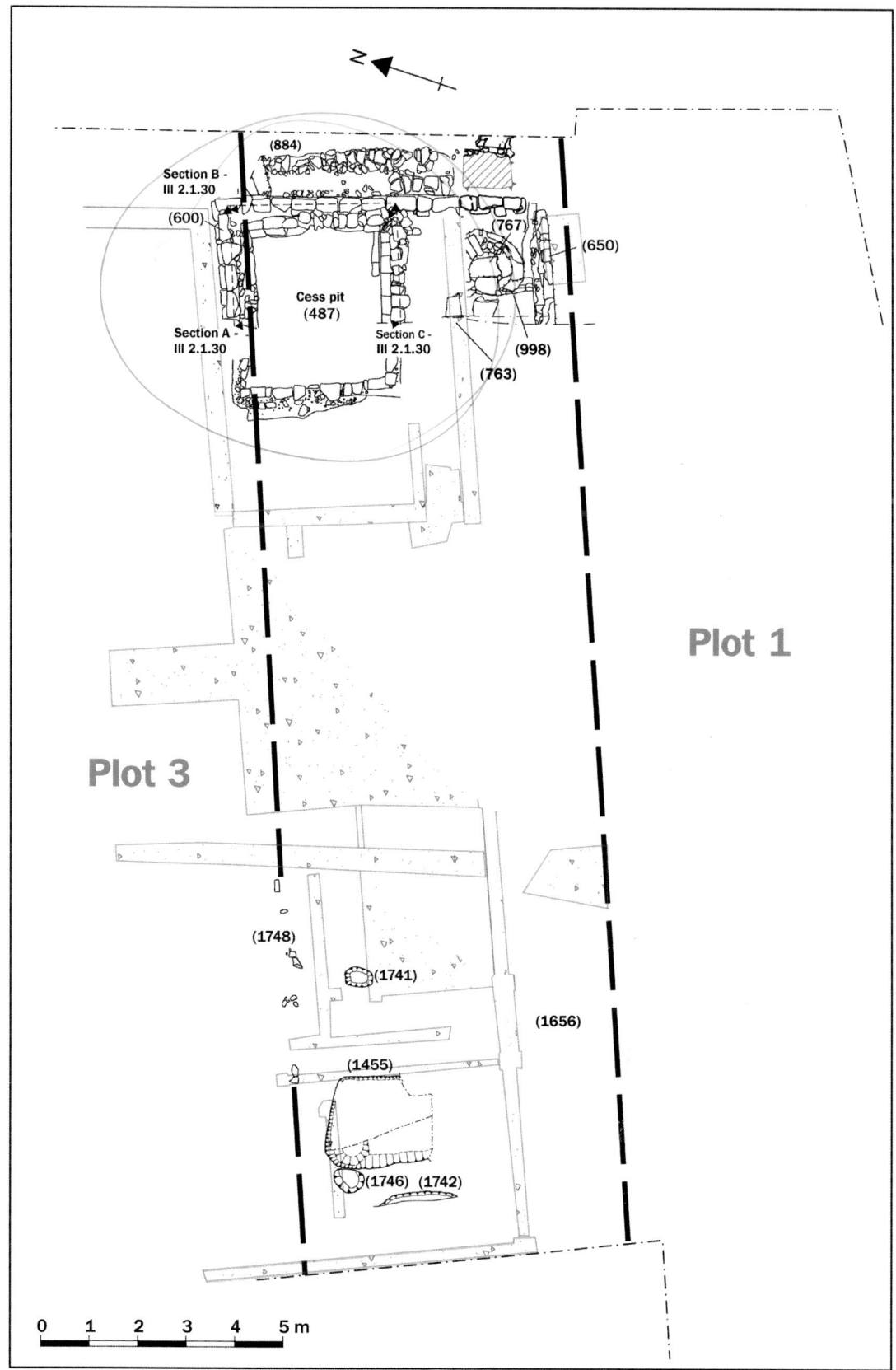

III 2.1.32 Phase V Plot 2: plan. (Scale 1/125)

Oven (767)

After the disuse and backfilling of cess pit (1008)/(998) a shallow construction trench, (1000), was cut for the foundation for a sandstone oven, (767) (Ill 2.1.33), bonded in reddish brown clay. The floor of the oven was made of sandstone slabs, whilst the two remaining courses walls comprised sandstone blocks with their internal faces cut to a curve, suggesting a circular, domed superstructure. There was an opening to the oven on the western side, with the base of an east–west flue defined by a course of sandstone blocks (769)/(1347)/(1346), again bonded with reddish brown clay. A pink clay, (999), was packed into the void between the cut (1000) and the oven structure (767) during construction.

The black, charcoal-rich fill of the oven, (888), and the adjoining flue, (769), was probably related to the oven's primary use. However, none of the sandstone blocks was reddened or discoloured by heat, suggesting that it may have been used for relatively low temperature firing, such as baking. Overlying (888) was a grey-brown silty clay deposit, (768)/(1352), containing many sandstone block fragments, thought to derive from the collapse of the oven superstructure and possibly from adjacent wall (763). Subsequently a dump of mid-pink-brown clay rich in building debris, (770)/(1351)/(1329), was used to backfill the flue. This in turn was levelled off with a deposit of greyish brown silty clay, (1334), which contained late medieval pottery. A series of brown clay deposits rich in sandstone rubble was recorded overlying oven (767) and wall (763), probably from the demolition or collapse of the wall. The uppermost of these deposits, (760), produced pottery dated to the fourteenth–fifteenth century.

Ill 2.1.33 Phase V Plot 2: oven (767), looking E.

Ditch (1129)

After the construction of boundary wall (600), the Phase IV ditch to its east, (1127), was recut, (1129). It probably served as an open drain at the rear of Plot 2. It was at least 10 m long and was seen to run north into Plot 3 but was not detected in Plot 1, where terracing may have removed all trace of it. The primary fills, (1124) and (1123), were lenses of brown clay which appeared to act as a lining to the base of the cut and may have been deliberately deposited to improve water retention. No evidence of silting was noted before the feature was deliberately backfilled with dumps of clay and building debris, (881).

Culvert (884)

After the backfilling of ditch (1129) another cut, (1066), was excavated along the back of the Plot 2 boundary wall to accommodate culvert (884). A deposit of greyish brown clay, (879), along the eastern edge of the cut possibly represented the upcast from its excavation and produced late fifteenth–sixteenth-century pottery. The culvert itself was constructed of large flat sandstone flags bonded by pink clay. It was probably contemporary with culvert (991) in Plot 1 and they were almost certainly linked; however, any proof of this relationship had been removed by Evaluation Trench E. The culvert eventually became choked with a build-up of greyish brown silty clay (1130), a sample from which, <5123>, produced wood charcoal and charred cereal. A series of layers, (877)/(790), formed over the top of the culvert: these were characterised by small amounts of building debris and may indicate activity to the east of the excavation. Pottery dated to the fifteenth–sixteenth century was recovered from (877).

Boundary wall repair (988) and (650)

The south-eastern corner of the boundary wall of Plot 2, (600), established in Phase IV, seems to have been prone to structural weakness, and during Phase V several attempts were made to rebuild sections of it. The first attempt appears to have involved the removal of a section of the wall to within two courses of its foundation; this event was identified as cut (989)/(1322) which cut cultivation soil (996). Once the section of wall had been taken down new courses of sandstone blocks were laid, bonded with grey and light yellowish brown clay, (988); these blocks appear to have been deliberately wedge-

Ill 2.1.34 Phase V Plots 2 and 3: boundary walls, looking S.

shaped to level the courses on the uneven foundation of the original wall. Subsequently (988) itself appears to have failed and a deposit of sandstone rubble and dark grey-brown silt loam, (894)/(1323), containing fourteenth–fifteenth-century pottery formed over the lower courses of the wall, possibly representing debris from a collapse. The second rebuilding, (650), was founded on this layer of debris and comprised reused sandstone blocks bonded with a grey sticky clay that survived to four courses in height. Layer (894) also overlay culvert (991) in Plot 1, and thus demonstrated that the culvert was inserted, and may even have gone out of use, prior to the collapse and repair of wall (600).

Pits (1455) and (1740)
A large subrectangular pit, (1455), 0.80 m deep with a north–south orientation was excavated roughly 10 m to the west of stone-lined cess pit (1008) (Ill 2.1.35). The base of this pit was beyond the limit of archaeological excavation (25 m OD). The lowest fill excavated, (1633), was a mid greenish grey silty clay containing lenses of brown grey and dark grey-black material which produced fourteenth–fifteenth-century pottery. This was sealed by a lens of lime over which had been deposited a light yellow-brown silty clay upper fill, (1632). This upper fill also produced fourteenth–fifteenth-century pottery. A sample from this deposit, <5161>, produced seeds of fig, blackberry and grape as well as decayed faecal concretions. Insect analysis suggested that there might have been waste material from brining, but generally the fauna indicated the presence of foul decaying matter. The nature of the fills to this feature strongly suggests its use as a cess pit.

Another pit, sub-circular and steep-sided with a depth of at least 0.5 m, (1742), was partially exposed on the western limit of excavation in the plot. The lowest fill excavated was a greenish grey clayey silt, (1745), again suggesting use as a cess pit. This was covered by a dump of greyish brown clayey silt and building debris, (1744), containing late medieval/transitional pottery. The pit was finally backfilled with a reddish brown clayey silt, (1743).

Post holes (1741) and (1746)
A pair of stone-packed post holes, (1741) and (1746), was located on the northern side of the plot close to the boundary with Plot 3. The respective brown clayey silt fills, (1740) and (1747), contained several large sandstone fragments, probably used for post-packing, and fill (1747) also produced a sherd of late medieval pottery.

These features appeared to be placed parallel to the northern boundary of the plot and could be the vestiges of a timber building for which no further evidence was found.

Fence line (1748)
Further groups of sandstone fragments set into cultivation soil (1656) at intervals of 0.5 to 1.0 m were given a group context of (1748); they were not excavated as they were below 25 m OD, but they appeared to form an east–west alignment along the northern boundary of the plot and may indicate part of a timber fence line.

Possible oven (1749)
Structure (1749) consisted of a single course of sandstone fragments in a semicircular plan, set into cultivation soil (1656). It was not excavated as it lay below 25 m OD. The structure was orientated north–south and had no bonding material between the stones or any evidence for a construction cut. The interior of the semicircle contained a charcoal-rich deposit, and this together with the shape of the structure suggested that it was another oven.

Plot 3 (Ill 2.1.36)

Pit (1118)
A sub-circular pit, (1118), was cut into Phase IV cultivation layer (1161); it had steep sides and a U-shaped profile (dimensions: 1.36 x 0.99 x 0.22 m). The fill, (1117), was a mid-brown clay silt with a high percentage of sandstone rubble, which produced pottery dated to the fourteenth–fifteenth century. This pit was actually located to the east of the Plot 3 boundary wall (496) and may have been at the back of an adjacent property that would have fronted on to Newgate Street.

Pit (845)
A shallow sub-circular pit, (845), was cut into (799)/(849) (dimensions 0.80 x 0.40 x 0.115 m). The primary fill, (844), was a lens of brownish grey silt which was the result of natural weathering and indicated that the feature had remained open for a period of time before its backfilling. A small deposit of coal and ash, (809), lay directly above this silting and produced pottery of fourteenth–fifteenth-century date; this deposit was thought to be the result of hearth sweepings, but the animal bone recovered suggested evidence for leatherworking. A quantity of oyster shell, (808), was dumped on top of this coal and ash prior to the pit being backfilled with a brown grey silt, (807), that contained late medieval pottery.

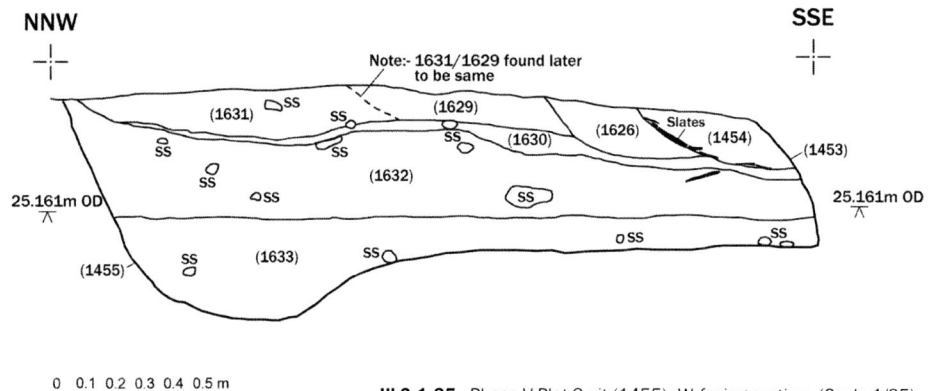

NNW — **SSE**

Note:- 1631/1629 found later to be same

25.161m OD — 25.161m OD

0 0.1 0.2 0.3 0.4 0.5 m

Ill 2.1.35 Phase V Plot 2 pit (1455): W-facing section. (Scale 1/25)

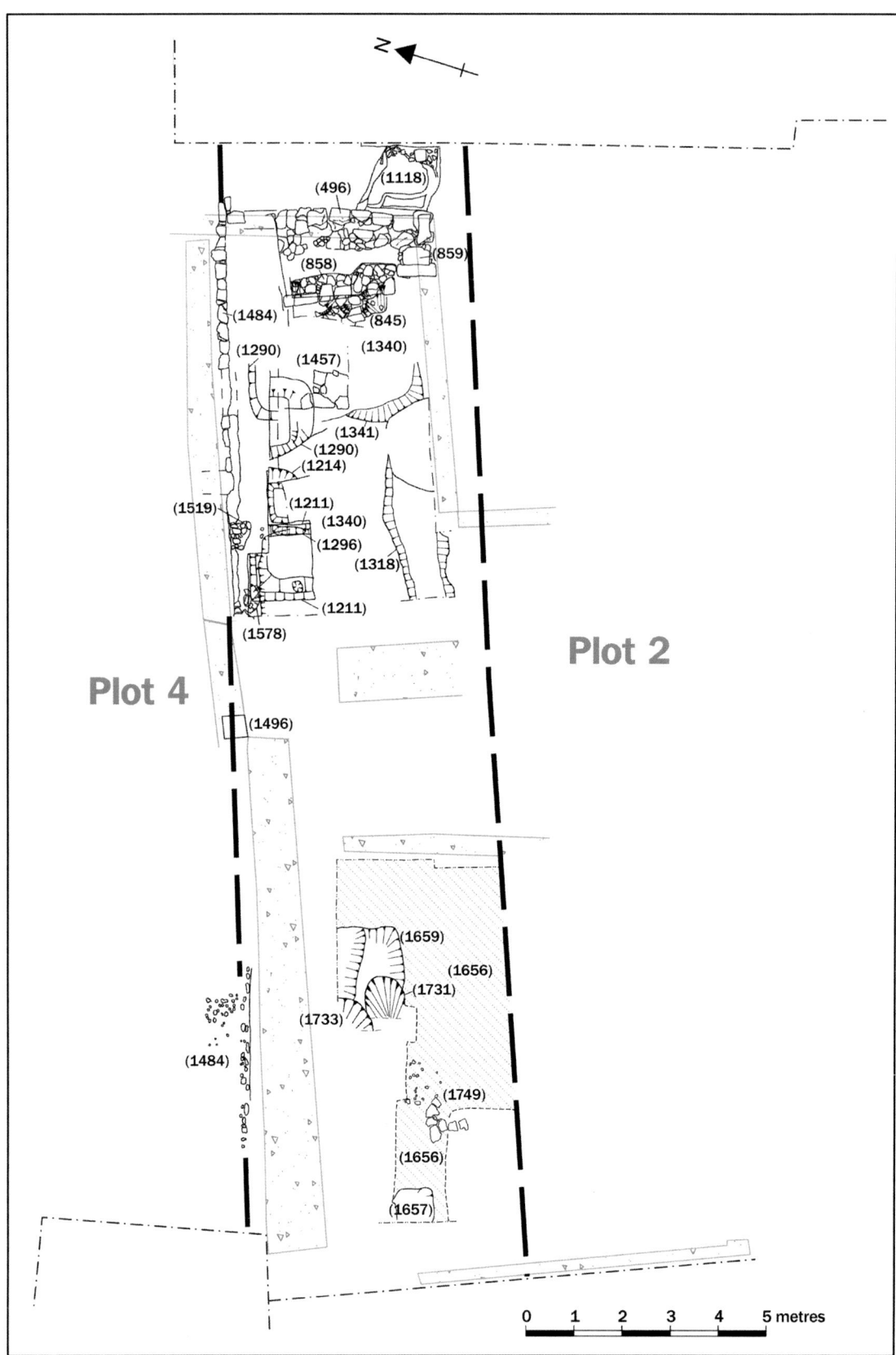

III 2.1.36 Phase V Plot 3: plan. (Scale 1/125)

Deposits (796), (792), (870) and (854)

A sequence of localised silty clay deposits had formed at the eastern end of Plot 3 against the northern face of boundary wall (600) to a combined thickness of 0.8 m. The full extent of these deposits had been obscured by the construction of several later walls; however, most of these deposits produced pottery of fourteenth–fifteenth-century date.

Boundary wall (496)/(858)

A cut, (866), was excavated along the back of Plot 3 on a north–south alignment in order to construct the foundation for boundary wall (496). The wall was constructed of reused red sandstone blocks bonded with clay, and survived to a height of three courses, with the stones on the eastern face of the wall being well dressed (as was true with the masonry of wall (600) to the south in Plot 2). The western side of this boundary wall appears to have subsequently been given a new face of dressed sandstone blocks, (858), which sat in their own construction trench, (865). This new component of the wall survived to a height of two courses bonded in clay. The space between this insertion and the original wall, (496), was filled with a mix of sandstone and clay rubble. A deposit of clay rich in sandstone rubble and fragments of slate overlay (858).

Structure (859)

A series of three sandstone steps, (859), had been built against the western side of boundary wall (496)/(858), creating a flight rising from west to east (ie towards the eastern boundary of the plot). These steps sat in a construction trench (867) that had been stepped in line with the overlying structure. The steps themselves comprised reused sandstone blocks bonded in clay and set in a bed of clay and sandstone rubble; this bonding material produced pottery dated 1250+.

Wall (1457)

A short length of sandstone wall, (1457), lay to the west of boundary wall (496)/(858) and only survived to a height of one course. It appeared to represent the western end of an east–west wall, although its function remains uncertain. Construction trench (1458) contained a backfill, (1459), of pink clay and sandstone fragments.

Subsequent to the disuse of the wall, a layer of dark reddish brown sandy clay, (1340), formed across the whole of the central portion of Plot 3 and contained pottery of fourteenth–fifteenth-century date

Pit (1341)

A heavily truncated pit, (1341), had been cut into layer (1340); this was thought to have originally been oval in plan. The fill, (1342), was a mid-brown to yellowish brown sandy loam, with a lens of charcoal at the base, and contained pottery dated to the fourteenth–fifteenth century.

Cultivation soil (1319)

A relatively thin layer of mid-brown loam, (1319), covered much of the eastern part of Plot 3 and was interpreted as a cultivation soil. It produced pottery and a copper alloy buckle folding clasp of late thirteenth–early fifteenth-century date.

Cultivation soil (490) and (790)

Layer (490) was a spread of greenish grey silty clay at the western end of Plot 3 which overlay clay and rubble deposit (495) and contained pottery of fourteenth–fifteenth-century date. An extensive layer of mid-brown sandy clay, (790), also covered the top of wall (858) and was thought to be contemporary with (490). Layer (790) had the characteristics of a cultivation soil and produced late medieval pottery.

Ditch (1318)

An east–west ditch, (1318), with steep sides and a flat base (2.50 x 1.05 x 0.46 m), was cut through cultivation soil (1319) and ran parallel with the southern boundary of Plot 3. The primary fill, (1344), was a mid-reddish grey sandy clay, probably indicating a period of weathering or natural silting whilst the feature remained open, during which residual pottery of thirteenth–fourteenth-century date was deposited. The upper fill, (1317), was a mid-reddish brown sandy clay, rich in carbonised material, fragments of roofing slate and metalworking waste (some degraded mussel shell was noted by the excavator but it was too fragile to recover). This upper fill appeared to be a deliberate dump of domestic waste containing pottery of fourteenth–fifteenth-century date, probably intended to backfill the feature once it had become obsolete.

Cultivation soil (1292)/(1293)/(1294)/(1304)/(1656)

Another cultivation soil, (1292)/(1293)/(1304), was represented by a dark reddish brown silty clay loam, distinguished by the presence of a high amount of carbonised fragments and 'purple' lime; it had formed over ditch fill (1317). This was an extensive horizon covering the whole of Plot 3, and produced pottery of fourteenth–fifteenth-century date.

Pit (1290)

Pit (1290) was a heavily truncated sub-circular feature towards the north-eastern corner of the plot. It had steep sides and a flat base. The single fill, (1217), appeared to be alternating lenses of dark orange brown clay and charcoal-rich loam containing pottery of fourteenth–fifteenth-century date and a long cross penny (1279–1489). The fill contained frequent sandstone fragments and seemed to represent an episode of deliberate backfilling, implying that the pit had not remained open for long.

Post hole (1296)

A sub-circular post hole (1296) (0.70 x 0.24 x 0.20 m) was dug at about the same time as pit (1290) was dug. The fill, (1295), was a mid-reddish brown sandy silty loam, containing fourteenth–fifteenth-century pottery.

Clay oven base? (1211)/(1214)

A shallow rectangular cut, (1211), with a flat base was cut into cultivation soil (1292) and the backfill of post hole (1296). The fill, (1205)/(1213), was a compact light brownish red sandy clay, which contained fourteenth–fifteenth-century pottery. It was felt during the excavation that this feature represented a clay floor, but its dimensions do not support this and the base of an oven maybe a better interpretation.

Boundary wall (1484)

A long feature, (1521)/(1797), oriented east–west along the northern edge of Plot 3 was cut through cultivation soil (1293) and formed the foundation trench for sandstone boundary wall (1484). The wall survived to a height of three courses and was composed of roughly dressed blocks bonded in clay. The lower fill of the foundation trench, (1520), was a dark reddish brown sandy clay that contained fourteenth–fifteenth-century pottery and was sealed by an upper fill of pink clay, (1517). This wall was connected to the eastern boundary wall (496) at the northeast corner of the plot and presumably served to re-establish an earlier property division. A cultivation soil (1485) lay to the south of wall (1484) and was associated with it.

Post hole (1519)

A substantial post hole, (1519) (0.30 x 0.44 x 0.60 m), was cut into foundation trench fill (1517). It was circular in plan and tapered to a point at the base. The fill, (1518), was a dark reddish brown sandy clay. Given that it lay on the boundary between properties it was very likely a fence post setting, but it was very large and deep for such a purpose and other interpretations are possible.

Deposit (1092)/(869)

This deposit was a reddish brown sandstone-rich sandy loam which survived patchily along the southern edge and in the north-west corner of Plot 3 and contained pottery of thirteenth–fourteenth-century date. Later pitting had removed much of this deposit, but it is possible that it represented an external surface.

Pit group (1659), (1731) and (1733)

A group of three intercutting pits was situated towards the western end of Plot 3. Pit (1659) was the earliest in the sequence and was cut into cultivation soil (1656). It was square in plan, with steep sides that stepped in towards the base, forming a shelf before the sides dropped off again to a flat base. The primary fill, (1738), was a light brown silt that was entirely sealed with a secondary fill of yellow clay, (1728); both of these fills produced pottery of fourteenth–fifteenth-century date. The pit was subsequently backfilled with mid-brown silty clay, (1729). A shallow sub-circular pit (1731) was later cut into the upper fill of pit (1659). This later pit was filled with a single dump of mid-brown silty clay, (1732), although some larger slates were thought to have been deliberately placed to line the base of the cut. Pit (1733) was the latest in the sequence as it was seen to be cutting pit fill (1732). The pit was again fairly shallow and circular in shape, with steep sides and a flat base. As with pit (1731) it was systematically backfilled with a charcoal-rich brown silty clay, (1734), containing some domestic rubbish.

Layer (1654)

Layer (1654) was a thin layer of charcoal-rich dark greyish brown silty clay, which produced pottery of fourteenth–fifteenth-century date and a long cross penny (1279–1377).

Pit (1657)

A shallow rectangular pit, (1657), was partially exposed on the western limit of excavation in Plot 3. It cut cultivation soil (1656). The fill, (1658), was a pink-brown silt clay containing building debris; suggesting that the pit had been deliberately backfilled.

Demolition layers (1655), (1649), (1641) and (1640)

After the backfilling of pit (1657) much of the western end of Plot 3 was covered by a series of large dumps of brown clay silts rich in building debris, mainly comprising fragments of grey roofing slate and red sandstone. The lower layers, (1655) and (1649), were particularly rich in slate fragments, whilst layer (1641) had a high content of small sandstone chippings and produced pottery of fourteenth–fifteenth-century date. The uppermost layer, (1640), contained an even mix of slate and sandstone as well as fragments of lime mortar/plaster and pottery, again of fourteenth–fifteenth-century date. These layers must represent a major building episode further west towards the street frontage, indicating that the back of the property was temporarily used as a tipping ground for both masons' and slaters' waste.

Plot 4 (Ills 2.1.37–9)

As with Plots 1–3, activity in Plot 4 seems to have involved periods of cultivation, the establishment and confirmation of property limits with substantial stone boundary walls, and the construction of a stone oven. The oven in particular was a substantial structure and would presumably have been built to last. Unfortunately very little evidence was recovered to suggest its precise function, but it could have been associated with a brewhouse at the back of the property.

Cultivation soils

The eastern part of Plot 4 appears to have been completely covered by a layer of cultivation soil, (1588)/(1661)/(1663), characterised as a greyish brown silty loam. A deep layer, (1586)/(1660)/(1590)/(1662)/(1571)/(1603)/(1615), also encountered in several areas at the eastern end of the plot, again consisted of a greyish brown silt loam but was characterised by a large number of yellow flecks, possibly representing decomposed straw or animal bone. The upper horizon was thought to have become compacted through its use as a ground surface for a prolonged period of time. Both groups of soil produced fourteenth–fifteenth-century pottery.

Boundary wall (1570)

A north–south foundation trench, (1072), was cut into these cultivation soils at the eastern edge of the plot for the construction of wall (1570), which formed the boundary between Plot 4 to the west and Plot 6 to the east. The wall consisted of angular sandstone blocks bonded in reddish brown clay and survived to a height of 0.6 m. There was some evidence for a dressed face to the west. This wall was probably bonded with southern boundary wall (1484), described above under Plot 3. Pottery of fourteenth–fifteenth-century date was recovered from the construction trench.

Oven (1568)

A substantial pit (1071) had also been cut into the cultivation soils at the back of the plot in order to facilitate the construction of a large sandstone oven, (1568) (Ills

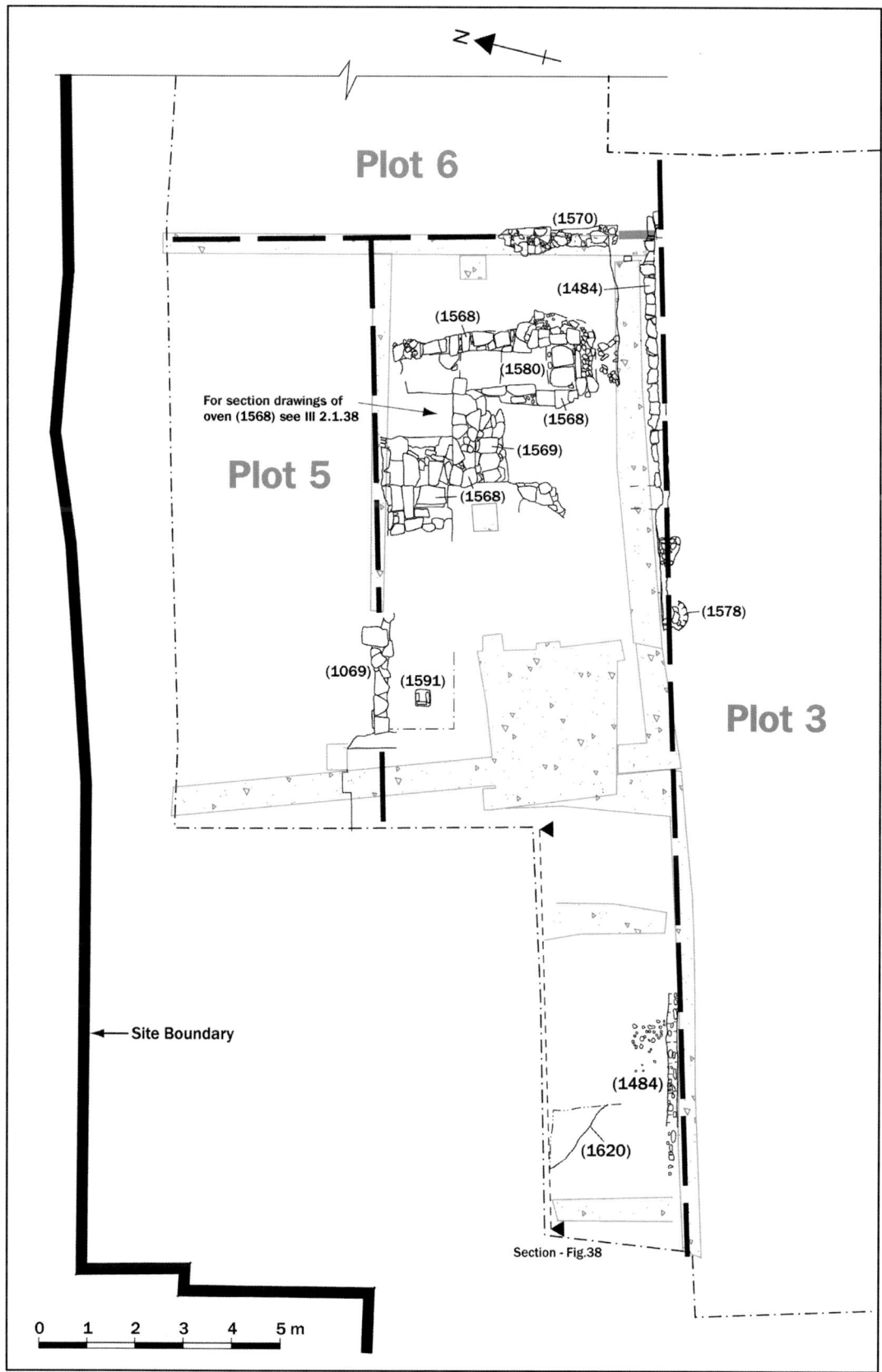

Ill 2.1.37 Phase V Plot 4: plan. (Scale 1/125)

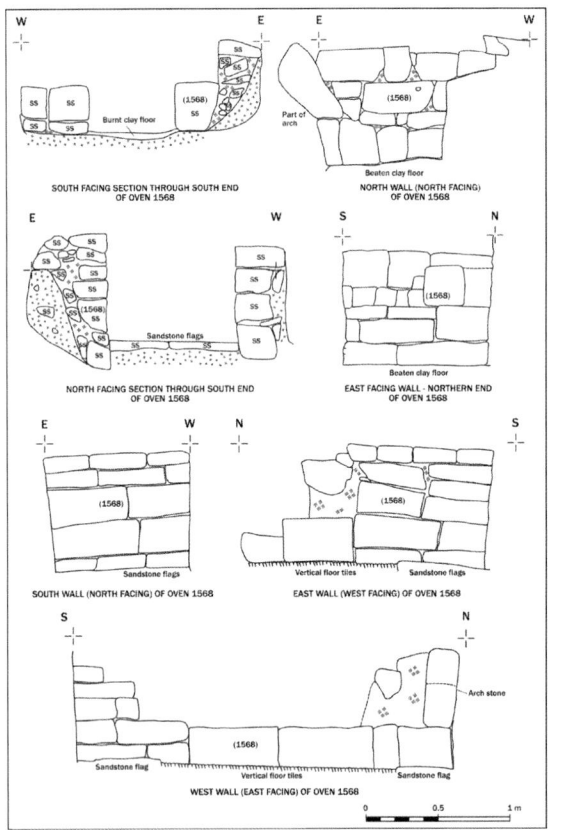

Ill 2.1.38 Phase V Plot 4 oven (1568): elevations and sections. (Scale 1/50)

Ill 2.1.39 Phase V Plot 4: oven (1568), looking S.

2.1.38–9). The oven was square and was aligned north–south with the stokehole and firing area at the northern end, connected *via* a flue to the oven. The structure had been damaged and partially destroyed by later pitting, but the southern area survived well enough to be able to demonstrate that it had been constructed of large dressed sandstone blocks bonded in red clay. The northern end of the flue had two stones from a spanning arch still in place, and beyond this the sunken stoking area was accessed from ground level by a set of stone steps rising from east to west. The floor, (1580), was of mixed construction with an area of sandstone flags at the southern end within the oven and at the northern end at the stokehole. The floor of the flue had the appearance of a cobbled surface comprising reused fragments of decorated medieval floor tile and Roman ceramic roof tile set on edge: this could represent a repair. There was evidence of oxi-

dation and burning in the area of the floor around the stokehole and in some areas of the flue this had subsequently been covered with a light skim of lime mortar.

The stoking/rake-out area to the north of the opening for the flue was first covered with a deposit of dark yellowy brown clay silt, (1585), which was sampled, < 5153>. This end of the feature was subsequently filled with successive dumps of reddish brown clay, (1584), and dark grey sandy silt, (1582), the latter of which produced late medieval pottery. The floor of the oven and flue was covered with a deposit of coarse black charcoal-rich sand, (1579), which again produced pottery of late medieval date. This deposit was sampled, < 5152>, and charred oat awns were recovered. Finally, a succession of greyish brown clayey silt deposits, (1581) and (1583), then filled all of the oven, flue and stoking/rake-out area: the latter again produced late medieval pottery. A layer of brown silty clay, (1589)/(1563), containing building debris and late medieval pottery formed over the oven backfill and may imply that the superstructure was systematically dismantled and removed for reuse.

A very chopped about fragment of sandstone wall (1569), bonded in mid-yellow-brown sandy clay, (1587), survived on an east–west alignment towards the eastern end of the plot, and possibly represents part of another oven.

Gully (1620)

The south-western side of a trench, (1620), was identified at the western end of the plot, aligned north-west to south-east. It ran from the northern limit of the excavation and was exposed for a length of 1.8 m before being removed by later pitting. The function of this gully is uncertain, but it clearly was not associated with any property divisions: it may have served as a drain.

Post holes (1578) and (1591)

A pair of post holes was cut into layer (1589)/(1563), one on the southern side of the plot and the other on the northern side. The first, (1578), had been deliberately backfilled with water-worn cobbles after the post had been removed, (1577), whilst the second, (1591), contained sandstone packing stones, implying that the post had rotted *in situ*. No dating evidence was recovered from either of these features.

Plot 5 (Ills 2.1.40–1)

The northern limit of Plot 5 lay beyond the limits of the excavation and roughly three-quarters of the area available for investigation had been removed by a nineteenth-century cellar. Two further areas within the plot had been removed by twentieth-century building foundations. This meant that only a relatively small block of medieval stratigraphy was preserved. As with Plots 1 to 4, the activity within Plot 5 seems to have involved periods of cultivation, the establishment and confirmation of property limits with substantial stone boundary walls and the cutting of cess pits.

Cultivation soils and surface (1669), (1668), (1667)

All of the undisturbed area within Plot 5 was covered with a layer of dark brown clayey loam, (1669), which was interpreted as a cultivation soil and produced pot-

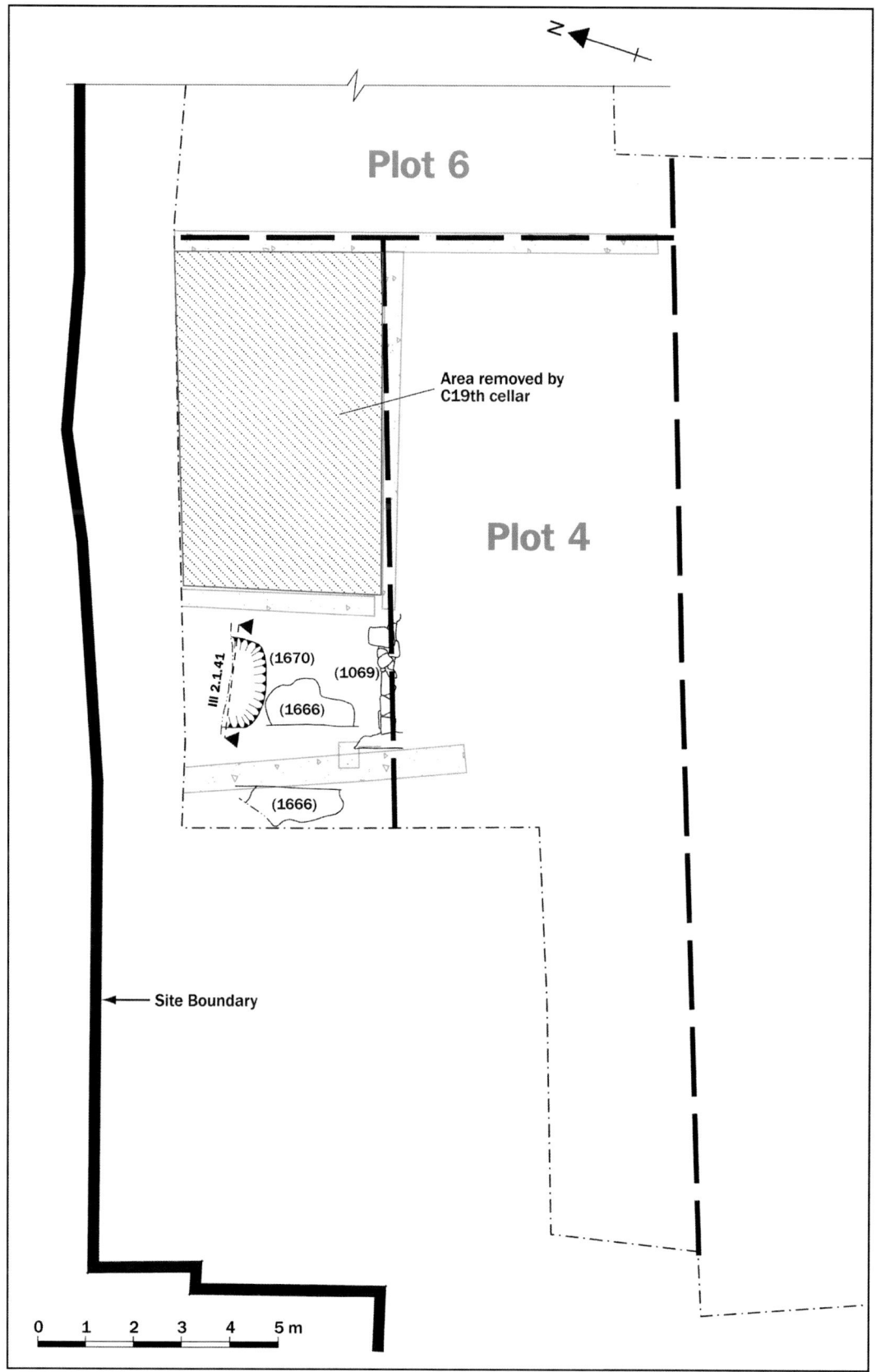

Plot 6

Area removed by
C19th cellar

Plot 4

III 2.1.41

(1670)

(1069)

(1666)

(1666)

Site Boundary

0 1 2 3 4 5 m

III 2.1.40 Phase V Plot 5: plan. (Scale 1/125)

tery dated to the second half of the thirteenth century. The thickness of this layer was not established as it extended below the depth of archaeological excavation. This cultivation soil had been covered by a layer of red-brown sandy clay mixed with crushed sandstone and gravel, (1668), which was thought to represent a surface. This surface was subsequently covered by another dark brown clayey loam cultivation soil, (1667), which produced late medieval pottery.

Boundary wall (1069)

A shallow east–west foundation trench, (1070), for boundary wall (1069) was identified cutting cultivation soil (1667) on the southern edge of the plot. Only the base course of the wall survived. It consisted of roughly dressed red sandstone blocks with a dressed north face, bonded in red-brown clay.

Adjacent to the boundary wall and overlying cultivation soil (1667) was a patchy deposit of grey-black silt and bright orange, biscuit-fired clay, (1666). This was undoubtedly the result of *in-situ* burning and produced pottery of fourteenth–fifteenth-century date.

Pit (1670)

The southern half of a sub-circular pit 0.31 m deep, (1670), was identified on the northern limit of excavation. The pit was cut into cultivation soil (1667) and had steep sides tapering towards the base. The lowest fill excavated, (1673)/(1674), was a pale yellow sandy clay, which was sealed by a thin deposit of broken and crushed coal fragments, (1672), which contained late medieval pottery. The upper part of the pit was filled with a mid-brown sand clay silt, (1671), containing building debris and pottery dated to the thirteenth–fourteenth century. This was almost certainly a cess pit, but the lower fills were not explored in the excavation and only its secondary function of a convenient place for rubbish disposal could be confirmed.

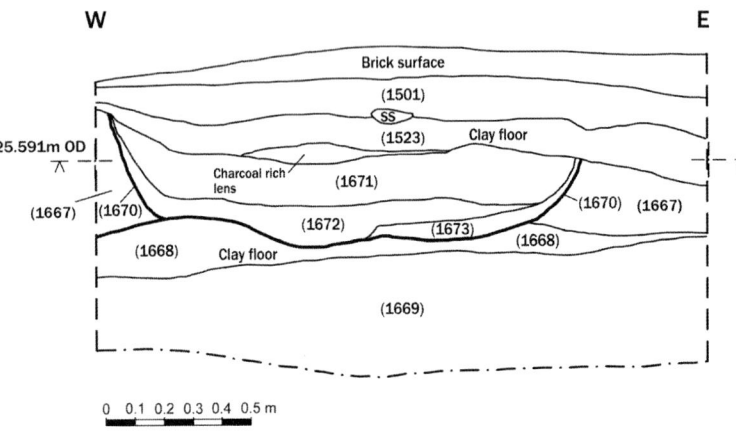

Ill 2.1.41 Phase V Plot 5 pit (1670): S-facing section. (Scale 1/25)

Plot 6 (Ill 2.1.42)

Plot 6 was assumed to lie within a single property as no boundaries were identified within the excavation other than the western one with Plots 4 and 5. It was larger than Plots 1 to 4, which may imply that the same level of burgage plot subdivision did not take place on the Newgate street frontage. The evidence from Plot 6 otherwise

mirrors that from the other plots in Phase V, exhibiting evidence for periods of cultivation followed by the digging of cess pits and some possible indications for the planting of a garden.

Cultivation soil

The plot was covered in a thick layer of homogeneous dark greyish brown loam, (57)/(117)/(1014)/(700)/(972)/(830)/(938)/(705)/(723)/(959)/(934)/(685). It was encountered in many disparate areas, owing in the main to the density of later post-medieval pitting. This layer has been interpreted as a cultivation soil and consistently produced fourteenth–fifteenth-century pottery. A certain amount of later intrusive material also was recovered from these layers, but this is not surprising considering the amount of later pitting that had taken place.

Pits (975)/(1054)/(1020), (971), (1055), (701), (707)

A circular pit, (975)/(1054)/(1020), 1.30 m deep with a U-shaped profile, was cut into the cultivation soils between escalator pits A and B. The primary fill, (976)/(1021), was a dark greyish brown silty clay with a cess-like appearance, which contained pottery dated 1250+ and large fragments of sandstone. A sample from this fill, <5095>, produced charred cereal. A dump of dark greyish brown silty clay, (1050,) covered this primary silting, and in turn was covered with a deposit of broken slate fragments mixed with a yellow silty clay, (1051)/(1049). The upper part of the pit was filled with a dark greyish brown silty clay, (1052)/(1053), containing coarse blocks of sandstone, suggesting that the pit had been deliberately backfilled. The primary fill of the pit would suggest that it had functioned as a cess pit before it was deliberately backfilled

A rectilinear pit, (971), oriented north–south 0.53 m deep with steep sides and a flat base was cut into the cultivation soils. It was apparently filled in a single operation with a mid-red-brown sandy loam, (968), containing thirteenth–fourteenth-century pottery.

In Escalator Pit B at the eastern end of the plot a thin lens of orange sand, (1061), lay directly above the cultivation soils. This was covered by a deposit of brown sandy loam, (1060), which in turn was covered by an orange-brown sandy clay deposit, (1059). These deposits may have been formed from the upcast for the excavation of a pit such as (975)/(1054)/(1020) (Ill 2.1.26).

Pit (1055) was only partially uncovered within the excavation area, but it appeared to be sub-circular in plan, oriented north–south with steep sides and a flat base. It was backfilled with a single deposit of reddish brown silty clay, (1056), very similar in appearance to the cultivation soils through which it was cut.

A shallow oval pit (701), 0.27 deep, was identified cutting into the cultivation soils. It had the characteristics of having been created by the removal of a large shrub or small tree. The fill was a dark brown clayey loam, (702), containing fourteenth–fifteenth-century pottery

Well (967)

Also cut into the cultivation soils at the eastern end of the plot to the north of Escalator Pit B was a large sub-rounded pit, (967), 0.45 m deep with vertical sides which continued to plunge below the limit of excavation, leading to the suggestion that it may have been the top of a

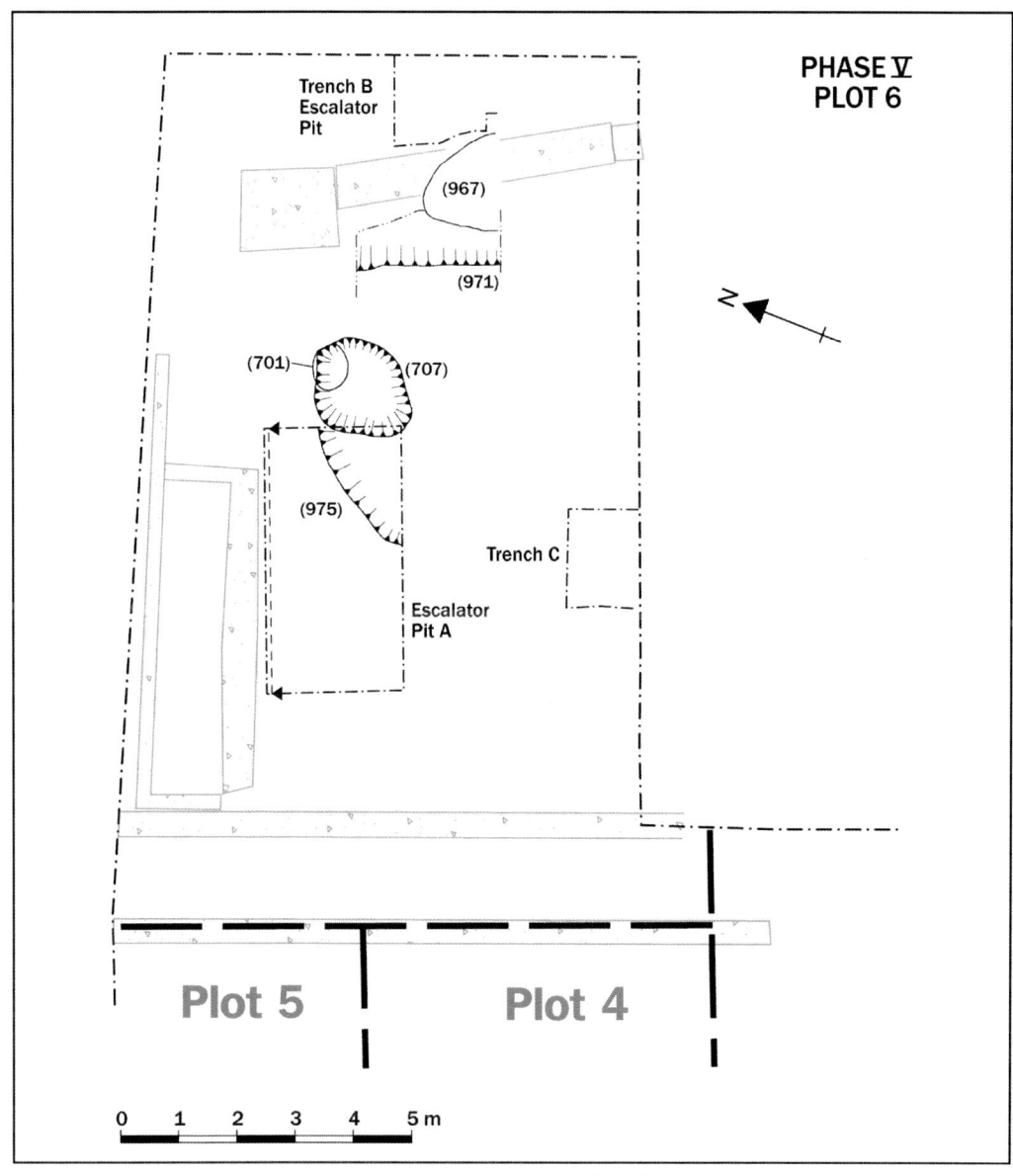

III 2.1.42 Phase V Plot 6: plan. (Scale 1/125)

well. The pit had been systematically backfilled with sandstone rubble and large rounded cobbles mixed in a dark greyish brown clay loam, (966), containing fourteenth–fifteenth-century pottery.

Garden soil (624)

The western half of the plot was covered by a brown silty clay layer, (624), containing late medieval pottery. This had all the characteristics of a cultivation soil and could represent a garden or allotment soil. The layer was sampled for pollen, <5049> and <5072>, with negative results.

Phase VI: Late 15–mid-17 century

Plot 1 (IIIs 2.1.44–7)

It was apparent that until the later seventeenth century Plot 1 had occupied an artificial terrace with a significantly lower ground surface than Plot 2 to the north. This terrace appears to have developed gradually rather than being the result of a deliberate construction episode, as a

result of the natural downward slope towards the River Dee. Consequently most of the archaeology recorded in this phase was only uncovered at the eastern end of the plot, where excavations for the access pit and ramp went deeper than elsewhere. Elsewhere, the Phase VI archaeology remained largely unexcavated as it lay beneath the formation level for the new building, except where it was revealed in evaluation trenches and piling locations along the southern edge of the plot. The phase plans for Plot 1 have been divided into a, b and c in order to illustrate more clearly the structural sequence.

Boundary wall (910)

At the eastern end of the plot the surviving four courses of an east–west wall, (910), were exposed for a length of 2.7 m along the northern boundary of the plot. The wall was constructed from sandstone blocks bonded with red clay. The blocks were well dressed on the northern face but had an unfinished appearance on south face. The upper surfaces of all of the blocks were marked with flat chisel marks in a cross-hatched pattern. The wall was built within a construction trench, (1005).

41

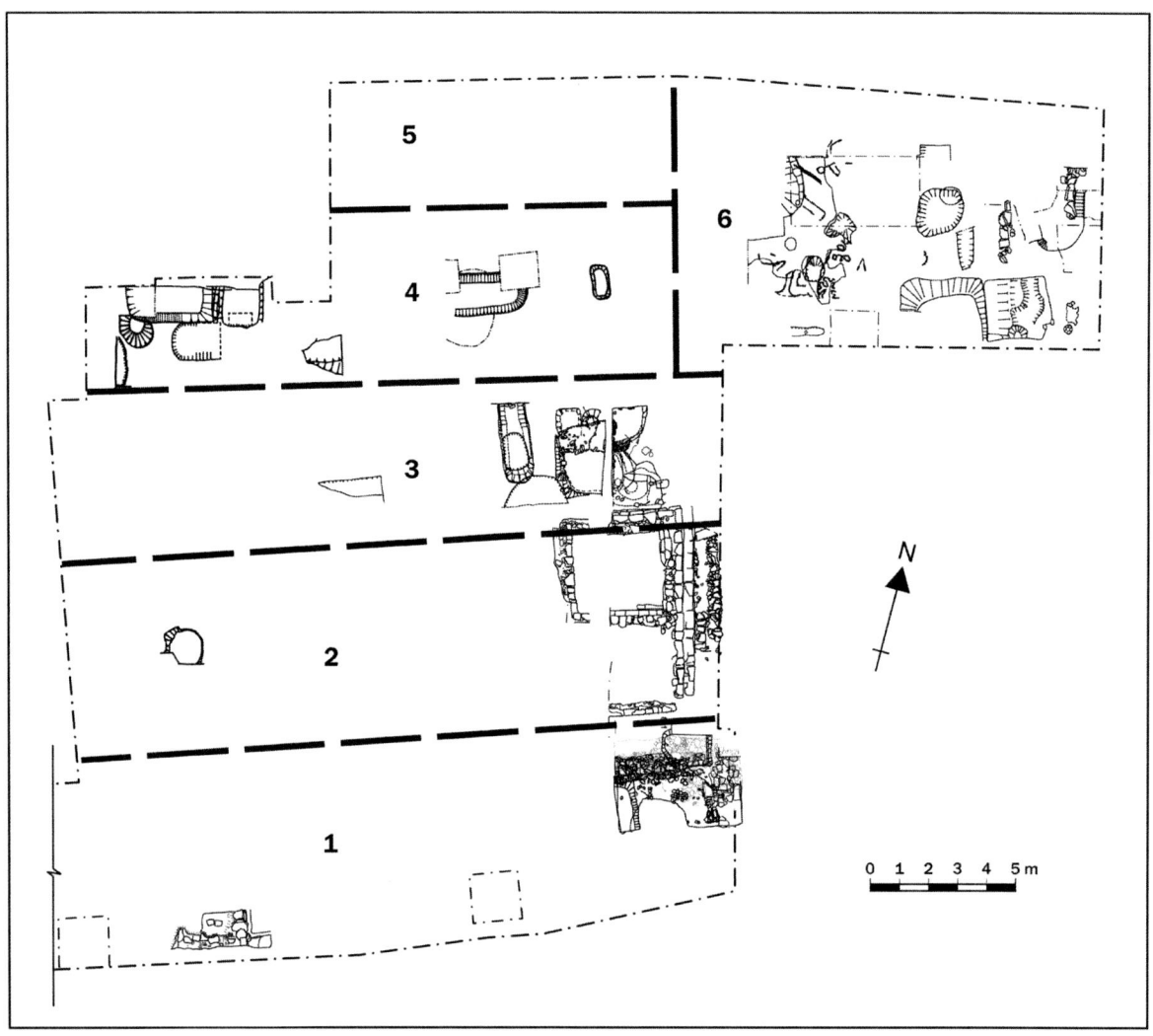

III 2.1.43 Phase VI: general arrangement of plots. (Scale 1/250)

Structure (892), (252), (896), (897) and (990)

Slightly to the south of and parallel to boundary wall (910) was a sandstone wall, (892), which was exposed for a length of 3.2 m. Wall (892) was set at right-angles to structure (896)/(897) and comprised roughly shaped sandstone blocks five courses high bonded in stiff yellowish brown clay and roughly dressed along the southern face. A post hole, (886), was identified cut into the top of wall (892) at its western end, suggesting that (892) was only intended to be a dwarf wall, with the post hole representing the traces of a timber superstructure.

On the southern edge of Plot 1 another east–west wall, (252), had been built parallel to wall (892). It was of similar construction and character to (892) and had been built within construction trench (253). The backfill of the construction trench backfill, (258), was recorded but did not produce any dating evidence.

Along the eastern edge of Plot 1 two large worked sandstone blocks, (897), were found to have been laid on the Phase V yard or road surface, (986). The blocks had been deliberately placed in a north–south alignment, but had not been bonded in anyway. Behind these blocks was a deposit of smaller more roughly shaped sandstone blocks bonded with a yellowish brown clay, (896), which clearly had a structural function.

A shallow post setting, (255), was identified to the south of (252); the fill, (254), comprised a single flat piece of sandstone laid on the base of the cut as a pad stone and a series of packing stones

Within the area defined by these walls a sequence of layers were recorded overlying the Phase V stone surface (986). The lowest layer in the sequence was a spread of sandstone brash and fragments with occasional pockets of reddish brown loamy sand, (983), which covered the whole of the excavated area at the back of Plot 1. This was covered by a patchy lens of reddish brown clayey silt, (987)/(249). A band of reddish brown clay, (982), overlay (987) with a small break approximately half way along its length. This band of clay ran parallel to wall (892) and the ends were defined by a series of broken roofing slates which may have formed the seating for a superstructure, such as the base for a vat or oven. A lens of dark grey silt, (984), containing flecks of lime mortar had formed above (982). This was covered by an extensive layer of reddish brown clayey silt, (909), which in turn was covered by a spread of light brown silt, (905)/(256), which was rich in fragments of lime mortar and produced pottery dated broadly to the sixteenth century.

A single post hole, (906), was cut into layer (905) and was filled with a sterile grey-brown clayey silt, (907).

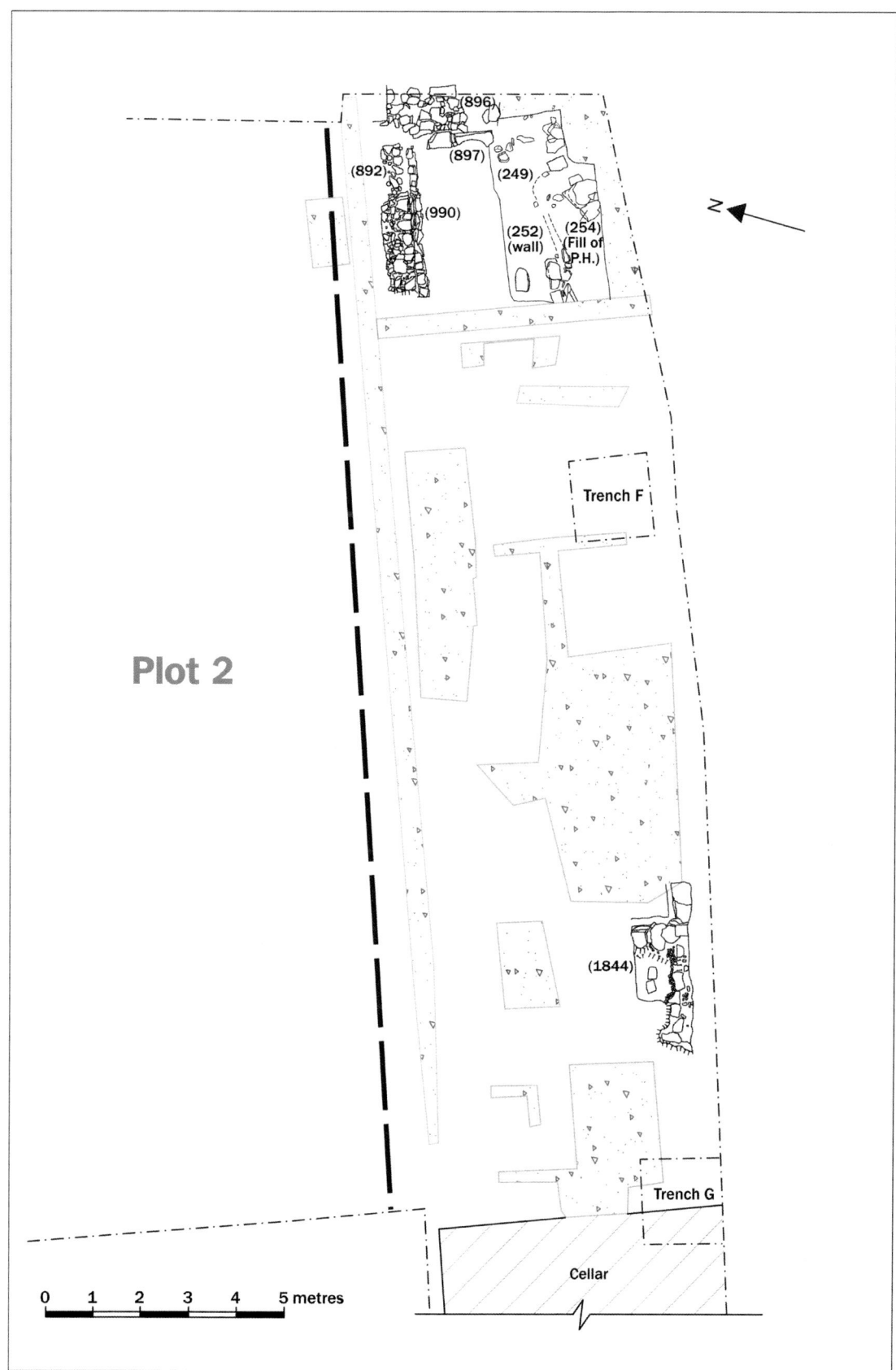

III 2.1.44 Phase VIa Plot 1: plan. (Scale 1/125)

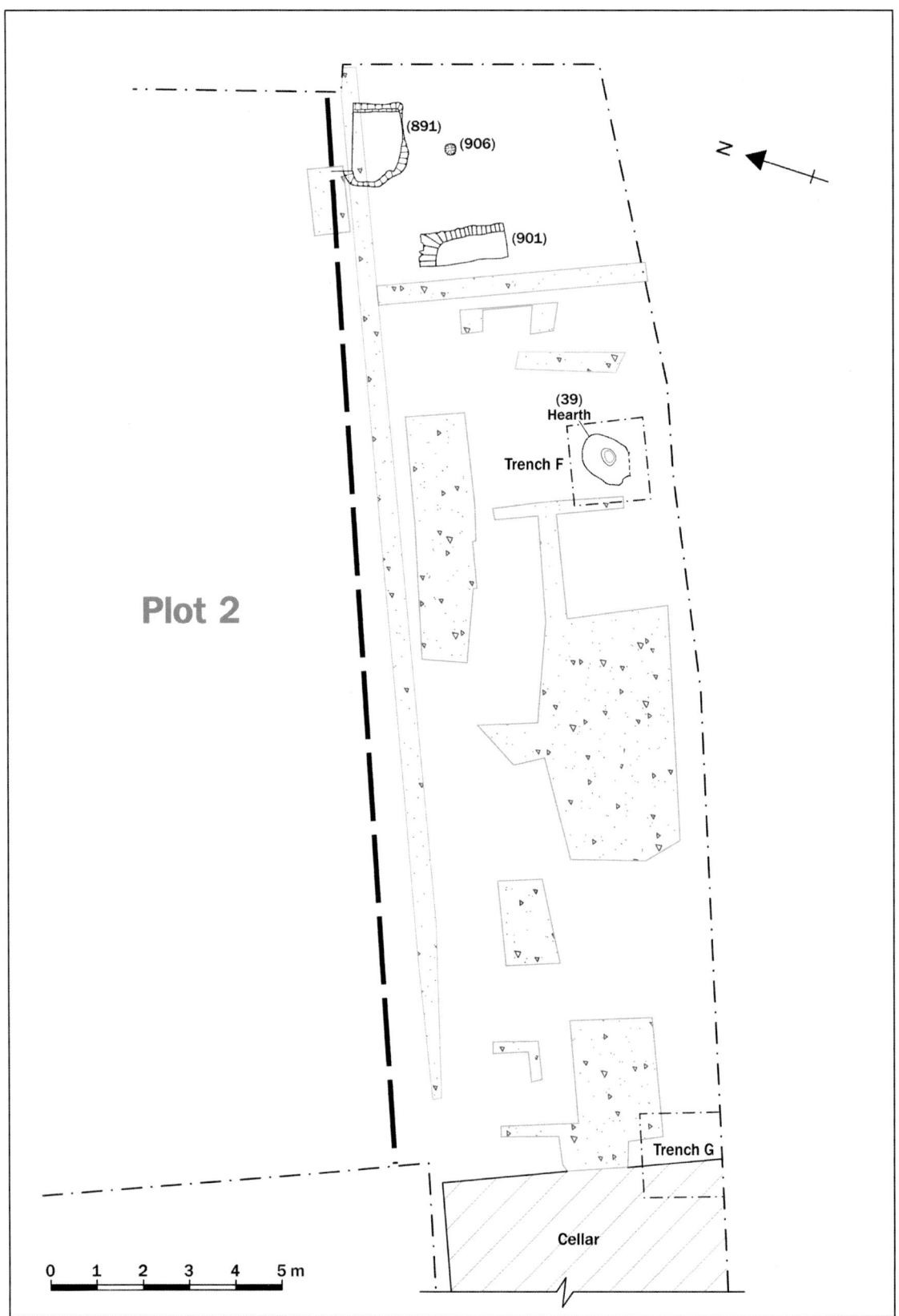

III 2.1.45 Phase VIb Plot 1: plan. (Scale 1/125)

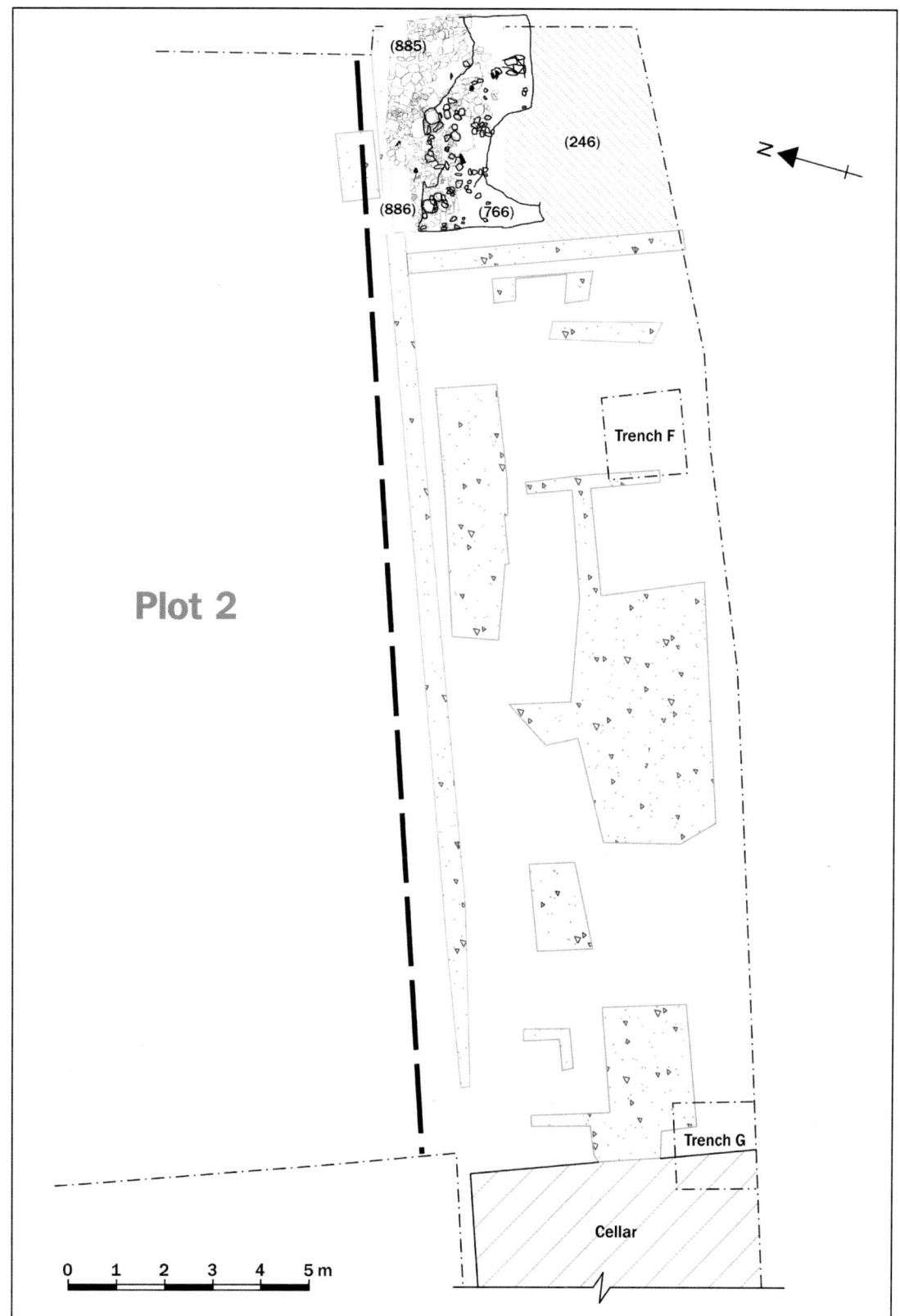

(885)

(246)

Z

(886)   (766)

Plot 2

Trench F

0 1 2 3 4 5 m

Trench G

Cellar

Ill 2.1.46 Phase VIc Plot 1: plan. (Scale 1/125)

Once the post hole had filled with silt a patchy clay layer, (904), formed over an area 1.85 x 1.3 m and this may have represented an internal floor surface. A substantial deposit of reddish brown sand, (895,) containing a high percentage of sandstone fragments formed over the entire area to a thickness of 0.55 m; this had the character of quarry waste and possibly represents the byproduct of stone masonry somewhere in the vicinity.

A layer of clay and sandstone rubble, (893), later formed on the top of walls (892) and (910), possibly representing a rubble spread formed after the partial collapse of one or both of these structures. Subsequently, a lining of sandstone slabs and blocks, (990), was laid against the southern face of wall (892) at an angle of fifteen degrees from vertical. The stones were set in reddish brown clay and there was no clear pattern to the coursing, although the larger slabs were two or three courses high. This structure apparently sat within a cut in layer (893).

Hearth (39)
To the west of this structure, and towards the southern boundary of the plot, a sequence of layers was excavated within Evaluation Trench F. The lowest layers, (43) and (44), were thought to be associated with the destruction of Phase V wall (45) and produced pottery ranging in date from late medieval to seventeenth century.

A sub-circular bowl-shaped pit, (39), had been cut into the top of layer (44) and had a diameter of 0.9 m and a depth of 0.16 m. The primary fill, (37), was grey sandy silt containing heat-cracked stone and round charcoal twigs, suggesting that it had functioned as a small domestic hearth. The fill produced pottery dated to the fourteenth–fifteenth century. The upper fill, (38), was almost entirely made up of lime mortar fragments and represented the deliberate backfilling of the pit. A layer of dark olive green silty sand, (28)/(41), containing flecks of white mortar and fourteenth–fifteenth-century pottery covered the hearth. This in turn was covered by a layer of brown silty sand, (65), which contained pottery of mid-seventeenth-century date.

Structure (1844)
Towards the south-western corner of the plot part of an east–west wall, (1844), was exposed during the insertion of concrete pile foundations. This consisted of large irregular sandstone blocks bonded in brown clay with a dressed southern face and survived to a height of two courses in places. The wall was only exposed for a length of 1.5 m and continued beyond the edges of excavation in both directions. A second wall on a north–south alignment was clearly part of the same building; this extended north beyond the limits of excavation and may have formed an internal partition.

To the north and west of these walls there was a floor surface constructed from sandstone blocks, (1883), but like the walls this surface continued beyond the limits of the excavation. The surface was covered by a sequence of layers rich in building debris, possibly from structure (1844) itself. The lowest layer in the sequence was a thick layer of brown silty clay, (1843), which was rich in roofing slate fragments and was interpreted as a deliberate dump of material. This in turn was covered by an equally thick layer of clay and sandstone rubble, (1848), which was also thought to be the result of deliberate tipping.

Above this were two layers of mortar-rich reddish brown clay, (1847) and (1842). Unfortunately, no dating evidence was recovered from this sequence and it is ascribed to Phase VI on the basis of the stratigraphic evidence.

Pits (891), (901), (250) and post hole (886)
In the north-eastern corner of the plot there was a subrectangular pit with a stepped profile, 0.69 m deep, (891). This pit was filled in a single operation with a dump of sandstone fragments and large water-worn cobbles, (890); a small amount of silt had formed between the coarse components and this produced seventeenth-century pottery. The nature of the fill suggests that the pit was deliberately backfilled shortly after it was excavated. It may have been intended to function as a soakaway to assist with drainage at the back of the plot.

Further west a north–south linear pit 0.60 m deep, (901) was cut into the reddish brown sand (895), with the northern end terminating at sandstone wall (892); the western and southern edges of the pit continued beyond the limits of excavation. The primary fill, (903), was a dark olive green silt, suggesting that it had been formed from cess; this was sampled, <5092>. Upper fills (902) and (900) consisted of dark brown silty sands containing building debris including broken roofing slate, indicative of deliberate backfilling. It seems likely that the primary function of this feature was to serve as a cess pit and that after a period of use it was deliberately filled in with fairly neutral material.

A third pit, (250), was identified to the south of pit (891). Little detail was recorded about it but the fill, (251), produced pottery dated to between the late fifteenth century and 1600.

Both pits (891) and (901) were sealed by a layer of sandstone rubble and water-worn cobbles, (885), which covered an area 4.5 x 2.5 m. This layer also contained a large architectural fragment, possibly a door or window lintel, suggesting that the material was derived from the collapse or demolition of a structure nearby. Pottery of seventeenth-century date was recovered from this layer. This layer was cut by a square post hole, (886). The fill, (887), consisted of a reddish brown sandy clay and sandstone fragments that were arranged randomly and probably represented disturbed post packing. The post hole may represent part of a fence line marking the boundary between Plots 1 and 2.

Post hole (886) was covered by a thick layer of brown sandy loam, (766), which covered an area 4.3 x 2.6 m;

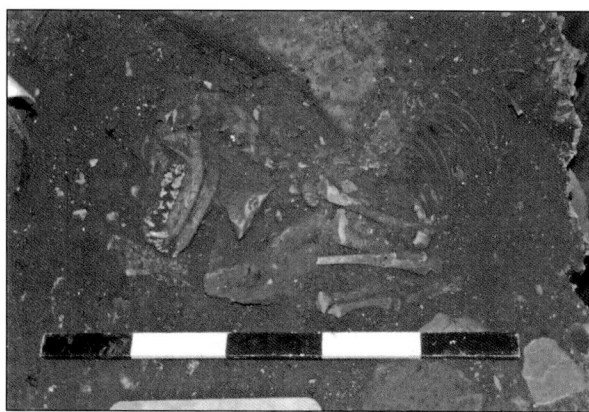

Ill 2.1.47 Phase VI Plot 1: articulated dog burial from (766).

this was rich in building debris and produced seventeenth-century pottery. An articulated dog burial was recorded within the layer: this must have occupied a grave cut which was not identified during excavation (Ill 2.1.47). A second layer of building debris, (673), subsequently covered the same area and produced pottery of late sixteenth–early seventeenth-century date. This layer had been encountered further to the south during the excavation of the access pit (Ill 2.1.6), where it was recorded as layer (246); this layer produced pottery of early to mid-seventeenth-century date and a set of sixteenth-century armour known as a 'jack of plate'.

In the extreme south-west corner of the plot a layer of light yellowish brown clay, (33), was exposed in Evaluation Trench G. This layer was rich in lumps of white mortar and produced pottery dated to the late sixteenth–seventeenth century.

Plot 2 (Ills 2.1.48–.50)

Cess pit (487)

The construction of the stone-lined cess pit (487) was discussed under Phase V. The pit ceased to be emptied during Phase VI, and after an initial build up of cess-rich sediments at the base of the pit a deliberate and consistent attempt seems to have been made to backfill it. The primary sediment, (806), consisted of interleaved lenses of clay and silt containing fragments of glazed floor tile and large fragments from black-glazed sixteenth-century drinking cups. In the north-western corner of the structure and partially buried in the sediment (806) was a broken femur from an adult elephant (radiocarbon dated to cal AD 1290–1410).

A sample of this sediment, < 5081 >, showed and abundance of fruit seeds that had clearly been eaten – very largely grape, fig, and apple. Insect remains were also fairly numerous and the species which dominated (*Omalium ?allardi*) is a likely invader of foul matter in the pit. Many of the other species were also components of house fauna and may have been attracted to the odour of faeces or may alternatively have been introduced in floor sweepings, together with a human flea. Parasite eggs were also noted and analysis suggested they were either *Trichuris trichiura* or *T. suis*, the whipworms of humans and pigs respectively, or perhaps both. The presence of the parasite eggs clearly indicates that faecal material formed a component of these deposits. The results of the sample analysis would seem to strongly support an argument for (806) being formed while the cess pit was still in use.

The pit was subsequently filled with a series of rubbish dumps represented by (798), (797), (791), (789), (788), (787), (786) and (785). These fills were characterised by the presence of a range of building materials, including hand-made brick, grey roofing slate and a distinctive type of late medieval glazed floor tile: this might argue for the fills having accumulated over a short period of time. However, the dating evidence suggests a more complex picture, with lower fill (798) producing a nearly complete German stoneware cup dated *c* 1500–50, whilst upper fills (791), (789) and (785) produced pottery of late sixteenth- or early seventeenth-century date.

The nature and origins of these dumps of rubbish are complex and they are likely to derive from a variety of sources and processes. Some produced several herring

and flatfish vertebrae (recorded from fills (791) and (798)) which were crushed – damage characteristic of ingestion and passage through the human gut – indicating that these remains were likely to originate from faecal material. Meanwhile, remains of gorse were abundant in fill (785), and were recorded from two of the other fills of this feature; these probably represent domestic waste. Although not always charred, such remains from combustible raw material seem likely to have arrived, with the abundant coal and cinders recovered from many of the fills, from hearths and fireplaces, if not ovens. Fill (785) also produced grains of sprouted barley and abundant remains of hops which might suggest that some of the waste was generated by brewing.

Oven (778)

After the formation of fill (785) the filling of the cess pit seems to have halted and the area was brought back into use as the site of an oven. This was sub-circular with the remains of a flue on the western side, (778) (Ills 2.1.48–9). The sides were built of hand-made brick bonded with clay and survived to a height of two courses, while the base was formed from roughly shaped sandstone flags. The whole oven sat within a shallow construction cut, (784), which had been backfilled with a clay-rich deposit (779); the latter produced pottery of sixteenth–seventeenth-century date. It is tempting to suggest that the hops and sprouted barley recovered from the underlying fill (785) were actually associated with this oven, implying that it might have been associated with a brewing house at the back of the plot. Once the oven had gone out of use it was deliberately dismantled down to its lower courses and the interior was backfilled with deposit (777).

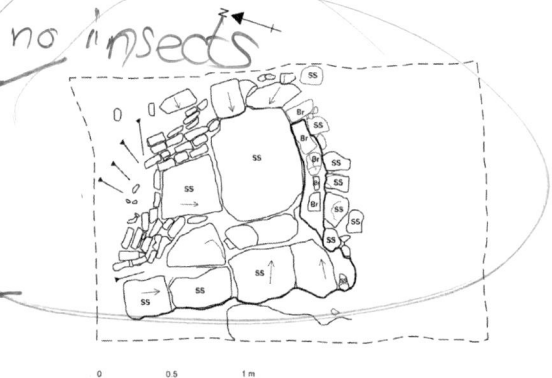

no insects

Ill 2.1.48 Phase VI Plot 2 oven (778): plan. (Scale 1/50)

Ill 2.1.49 Phase VI Plot 2: oven (778), looking E.

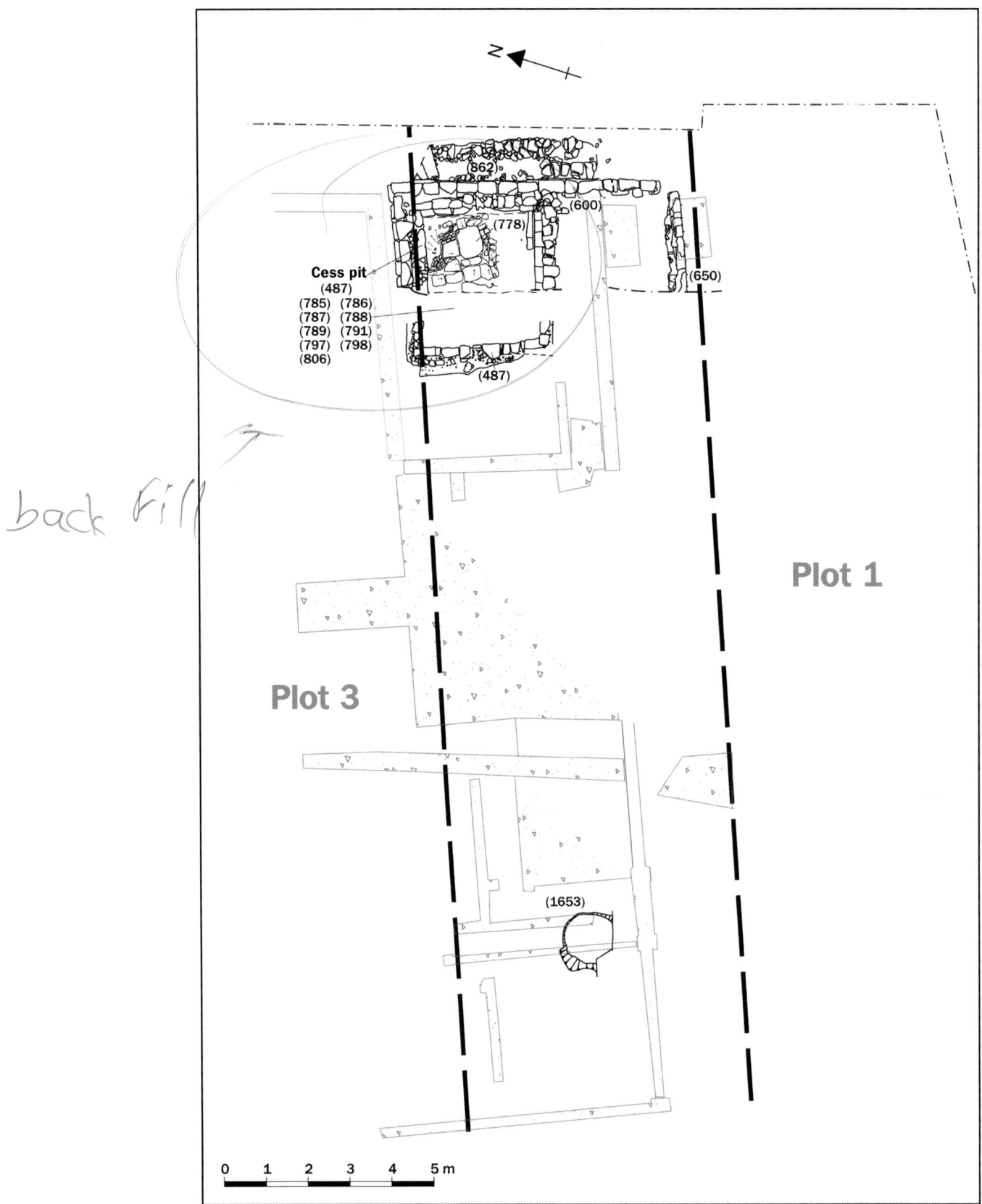

Ill 2.1.50 Phase VI Plot 2: plan. (Scale 1/125)

Subsequently, the systematic backfilling of the cess pit began again with successive dumps of material, represented by (776) and (503). Deposit (776) contained quite a high component of hand-made brick, probably derived from the dismantling of the oven. Late medieval glazed floor tile was also recovered from this deposit, as well as pottery of sixteenth–early seventeenth-century date and an iron textile-processing spike. The upper deposit, (503), produced fragments of clay tobacco pipe of seventeenth-century date; this was the first instance of this artefact type within the of deposits associated with the cess pit.

Alleyway (862)

Beyond the eastern boundary of the plot a layer of coal and clinker, (876), was spread down the entire length of wall (600). This only produced late medieval pottery. This coal and clinker was subsequently covered by a layer of reddish brown sandstone brash, (868). Both layers may have been laid as the hardcore base for the construction of surface (862). This surface comprised small sandstone blocks, occasional water-worn cobbles and pottery of sixteenth–seventeenth-century date which had been rammed to form an area of paving which sloped away from the boundary wall. It is possible that it formed an alleyway at the rear of Plot 2, the slope possibly aiding drainage from the back of the plot towards the culvert (884) constructed in Phase V. This interpretation may be supported by a shallow cut at the southern end of the surface, which appeared to have been made in order to re-expose the top of the culvert and thus improve drainage. This cut was subsequently filled with fairly sterile sandy silt, (878).

Surface (862) was either well maintained or was not in use for very long, as before any depth of silting could form over it the southern half of the surface was covered by a succession of deposits rich in building materials. These deposits, (775), (774), (772) and (773), contained quantities of sandstone (including one large dressed sandstone block), mortar and grey roofing slate. These may have been dumped during maintenance work associated with boundary wall (600).

Deposits (746), (771), (765), (756) and (751)

In the south-eastern corner of Plot 2, a series of deposits formed over the disused oven (767) described in Phase V. The lower of these deposits, (746) and (771), contained bricks and sandstone blocks which could represent tumble from the partial collapse of either wall (600) or the superstructure of cess pit (487); they also contained pottery of late sixteenth–early seventeenth-century date and fragments of clay tobacco pipe. Subsequent deposits, (765), (756) and (751), appear to represent a sequence of rubbish dumps, all of which contained fragments of glazed medieval floor tile and pottery of late medieval or transitional date which clearly must be residual. The occurrence of coal and clinker in all of these later deposits suggests that at least some of the material originated as hearth sweepings from domestic fireplaces. Further rubbish deposits, (671) and (750), were later dumped in this area and contained pottery of sixteenth–early seventeenth-century date; again this material appears to have mixed origins, with evidence for some cess-like material as well as further evidence of coal and clinker from hearth sweepings. The final deposit in this sequence was a dump of white sandy lime mortar, (743), which was probably discarded after the completion of a building episode somewhere within Plot 2.

Cess pit (1653)

At the western end of Plot 2 a sub-circular pit, (1653), 0.6 m deep had been excavated. The fill, (1635), contained post-medieval pottery. A sample from the fill, <5166>, produced similar results to that from the cess pit fill (806), confirming the primary use of the feature.

Plot 3 (Ills 2.1.51–3)

Nearly all of the activity identified in Plot 3 during Phase VI was confined to the eastern end of the plot. With the exception of two enigmatic post holes the only structural evidence was the continued maintenance and use of the boundary walls described in Phase V. The overwhelming majority of the features appear to have been cess pits, which were often used for the disposal of domestic refuse once they had become defunct. On two occasions the cess pit zone appears to have been divorced from the rest of the plot by the excavation of a ditch, with access on the southern side presumably having been regulated by a gate. This arrangement implies some order and planning to the disposal of sewage in the plot, although this was clearly not on the same scale as the large cess pit in Plot 2. A barrier in the form of a ditch may have been needed to prevent livestock from straying into the area and falling into one of the open pits.

Post hole (494) and pit (479)

A single post setting, (494), was identified at the eastern end of the plot, with a fill of fairly sterile greenish grey silt, (493). Its function must remain a matter of conjecture, but it may indicate the presence of a light timber structure such as a shed or animal pen at the back of the plot. This part of Plot 3 was subsequently covered by two successive deposits of silty clay, (486) and (485), which produced pottery dated *c* 1400–1600.

The upper deposit, (485), was later cut by a small, shallow rectangular pit, (479), which had been partially removed to the west by later pit (430). The pit could not have remained open for very long, as before any silting could occur it was backfilled in a single event represented by coal-rich deposit (478). Unlike many of the pits in this phase no evidence was recovered to suggest that this had served as a cess pit, but some domestic waste was present in the form of animal bone, indicating that this pit was ultimately used to dispose of domestic rubbish. Once pit (479) had been filled in this part of the plot was covered by another layer of silty clay, (476), containing fragments of brick and interpreted as a cultivation soil.

Pit group (475), (477), (468) and (432)

After cultivation soil (476) had formed at the eastern end of the plot a series of small, shallow pits was excavated in the area, but none of these survived in their entirety owing to the later cutting of pit (430)/(850). The earliest pit in the sequence, (475), was cut directly into layer (476) and had surviving dimensions of 1.1 x 0.93 x 0.20 m. The pit was backfilled in a single episode represented by (473), which contained domestic refuse including pottery dated to the fourteenth–fifteenth century. A second pit, (477), was then cut in fill (473) and had surviving dimensions of 0.56 x 0.57 x 0.25 m. This pit was thought to be a recut of pit (475), and the green silty character of its fill, (474), would argue for its having served as a cess pit.

Pit fill (474) was later cut by a third pit, (468), which was a steep-sided sub-circular feature with surviving dimensions of 1.6 x 0.8 x 0.61 m. The eastern side of pit (468) appeared to have been partially lined with cut sandstone fragments that possibly indicated an attempt to invest the pit with some form of structure. The pit again appears to have been backfilled in a single episode, and the green-brown colouration of fill (467) would suggest that the disposal of cess was a primary function. The fill, (467), also contained domestic refuse including animal bone and pottery dated to the late sixteenth or seventeenth century. After fill (467) had been covered by a localised deposit of silty clay, (466), a fourth pit, (432), was excavated in the same area; it was again sub-circular, with steep sides, a flat base and surviving dimensions measuring 1.20 x 0.50 m. Pit (432) was also backfilled in a single episode, (431), with material that was derived from domestic refuse. The green colouration of fill (431) would again indicate that the primary function had been to serve as a cess pit.

Features (860), (864) and (856)
To the west of the pit group a second group of features had been heavily disturbed by the later cutting of pit (430)/(850). The earliest was a shallow rectangular pit, (860), which had surviving dimensions of 1.1 m north–south x 0.90 east–west and a depth of 0.30 m. Its fill, (857), was rich in building debris including roofing slate and fragments of lime mortar, together with pottery dated between the late fifteenth century and 1600, and seems to have been deposited in one episode.

After the backfilling of pit (860) a circular pit, (864), was excavated immediately to the east and had surviving dimensions of 0.76 x 0.35 m. The size of pit (864) might suggest that it was in fact a timber post setting. The later insertion of a sharpened wooden stake, (856), into the top of its fill, (863), may support this argument, but (863) did not contain any obvious packing stones. The base of the stake appeared to have been left to rot *in situ*.

Ditch (1289)
To the west of pit (860) was a ditch, (1289), aligned roughly north–south with almost vertical sides with a flat base. It ended about two metres short of the southern boundary to the plot. The primary clay-rich fill of the ditch, (1288), contained pottery of fourteenth–fifteenth-century date and may have acted as a lining, suggesting that the feature was designed to retain water. Secondary fills (1204) and (1215) contained a mixture of domestic waste and building debris, apparently dumped into the ditch as part of a systematic backfilling process; the lower fill, (1204), produced pottery of late sixteenth-century date.

Pit group (1207), (1321), (1303) and (1298)
An oval pit, (1207), 0.35 m deep, was later cut into the backfill of ditch (1289). The lower fills of the pit, (1209) and (1208), had the appearance of yellowish green silty lenses interleaved with charcoal-rich silt, suggesting that its primary function had been as a cess pit. The upper fill, (1210), was a fairly sterile brown loam.

To the south of (1207) a second sub-circular pit, (1321), had also been cut into the southern end of the backfilled ditch (1289), but the southern half of this pit had been removed by later disturbance; its surviving depth was 0.60 m. It had a single fill, (1320), which was greyish green in colour, suggesting that it had formed during use of the feature as a cess pit. The eastern edge of this pit was subsequently cut by another circular pit, (1303), which had been almost entirely removed by later pit (430)/(850), and survived as a crescent-shaped feature. Pit (1303) also appears to have functioned as a cess pit as it was filled by a series of lenses, (1302), which alternated between greyish green cess and purple-brown coal and ash tips and produced pottery of seventeenth-century date.

Pit (1298) lay immediately to the north of (1303) and had again been almost entirely removed by pit (430)/(850); it survived as a rectangular feature. It had been backfilled in a single event and no indication of its original function could be discerned. The fill, (1297), consisted of a mix of clay and sandstone fragments, together with small amounts of domestic waste probably derived from hearth sweepings: this included seventeenth-century pottery.

Pit (430)/(50)
During Phase VI the eastern end of Plot 3 was dominated by the excavation of pit (430)/(850) (Ills 2.1.52–.3). The pit was actually excavated archaeologically at two separate times as the centre of the pit had been removed by a north–south alignment of concrete mini-piles which had been inserted prior to the beginning of the excavation. The eastern quarter of the pit was recorded as cut (430) and had two distinct fills, (442) and (429), whilst the western three-quarters were recorded as cut (850) and had a far more complex sequence of eight fills, represented by (852), (805), (851), (804), (803), (802), (801) and (800). It was thought by the excavators that fill (429) was broadly contemporary with fills (851), (804), (803), (802), (801) and (800). Fill (442) only appeared in the eastern quarter of the pit, and fills (852) and (805) only occurred in the western three-quarters.

The overall cut appeared to be sub-circular in plan and measured 2.5 x 2.5 x 1.24 m. The northern side was stepped, possibly to allow access for maintenance, whilst the other three sides were nearly vertical, tapering in slightly towards a flat base. Lower fill (442) had a dark green colour, strongly suggesting that the primary function had been as a cess pit; domestic waste was also recovered from this fill, including seventeenth-century pottery and a heavily weathered glass beaker of early sixteenth-century date. The remaining fills appear to have comprised a systematic backfilling with dumps of domestic rubbish. This included some fine and rare glass vessels, most notably from (429) and (800); the majority of these could be dated to the first half of the seventeenth century. This dating is corroborated by a stamped clay tobacco pipe stem from fill (429), dated *c* 1610–40.

Recut ditch (1106)/(1197)
To the west of pit (430)/(850) was a possibly contemporary recut of ditch (1289), designated (1106)/(1197). This had removed the central portion of pit (1207). Unlike the earlier ditch it showed no evidence for a clay lining. Before any silting could occur it was completely backfilled

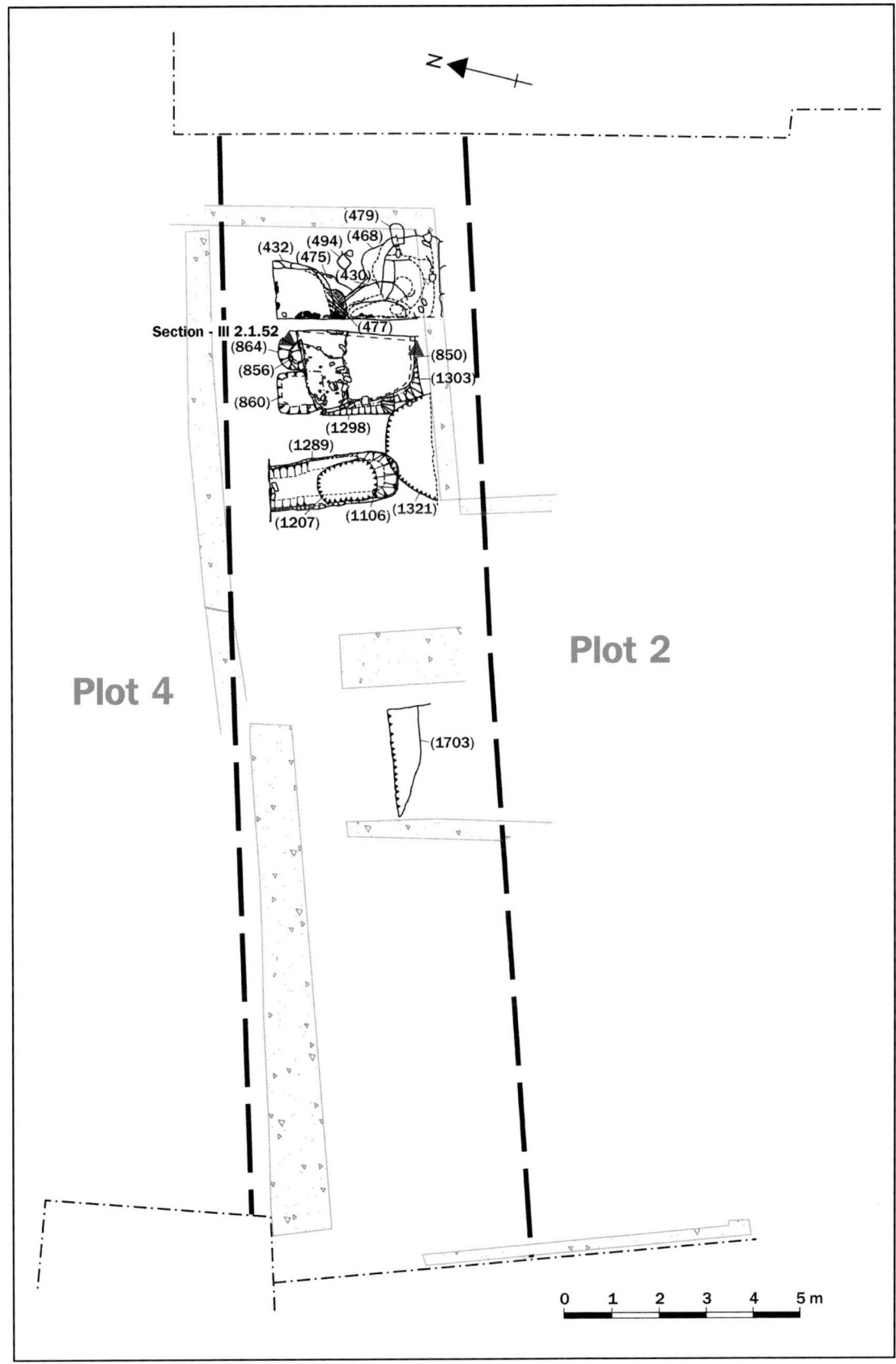

III 2.1.51 Phase VI Plot 3: plan. (Scale 1/125)

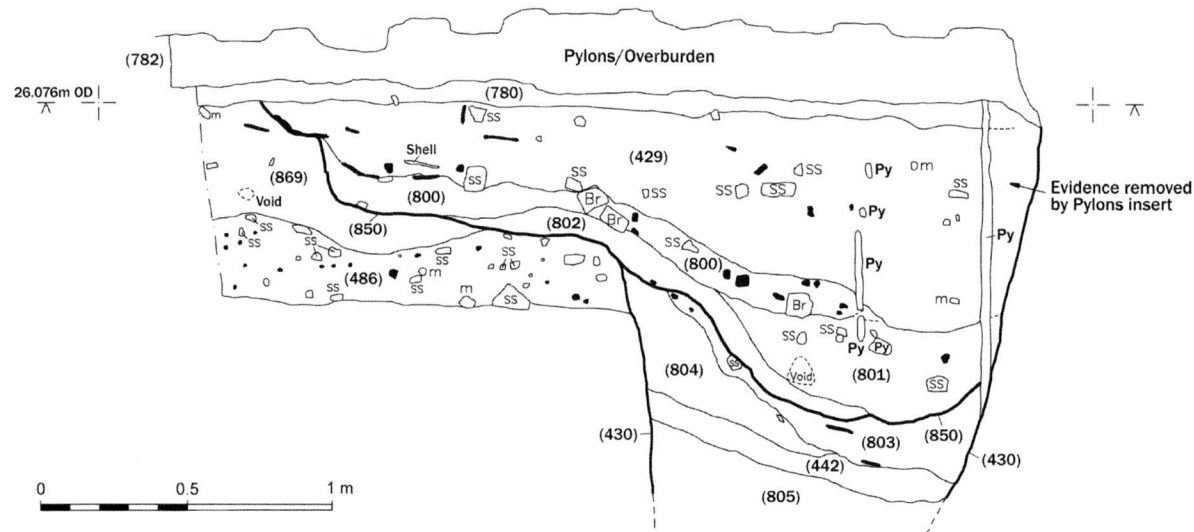

Ill 2.1.52 Phase VI Plot 3 pit (430)/(850): S-facing section. (Scale 1/25)

with loamy soils, (1196)/(1101), which were rich in charcoal, coal and clinker probably derived from domestic hearth sweepings.

Approximately four metres to the west of the recut ditch was a shallow east–west gully, (1703). This was filled with a cessy greenish brown silt, (1702), which contained pottery dated to the late fifteenth–early seventeenth century. Later pitting had entirely divorced the gully (1703) from its original context, but the cessy nature of the fill would suggest that its function was connected to the numerous cess pits excavated in the area.

Layer (1200)

The final event of Phase VI in Plot 3 was the formation of deposit (1200) over the top of ditch fill (1196)/(1101) on the northern side of the plot. Deposit (1200) contained late medieval material and appeared to be a redeposited dump of soil possibly representing the upcast from the excavation of one of the many pits in the area.

Plot 4 (Ills 2.1.54–5)

Pits (1619), (1624), (1606) and (1544)

The earliest activity in Plot 4 was concentrated at the western end of the excavation and began with the cutting of an oval pit, (1619). This had been partly removed at its eastern end by later disturbance. The pit had steep sides and a flat base with surviving dimensions measuring 2.40 x 1.30 x 0.65 m. Pit (1619) appeared to have been backfilled in a single event with a mixture of clay and domestic refuse that contained pottery dated late fifteenth century+.

The north-eastern corner of pit (1619) was later removed by the cutting of a second rectangular shaped pit, (1624), that appeared to have been dug on a north–south alignment. The northern edge of this pit was beyond the limits of excavation, but the excavated portion had nearly vertical sides, a flat base and exposed dimensions measuring 0.80 x 0.47 x 0.40 m. The primary fill, (1697), comprised a fairly thick deposit of interleaved lenses of green and brown silt that produced pottery dated to the mid-sixteenth century. The samples taken from fill (1697),

Ill 2.1.53 Phase VI Plot 3: pit (430)/(850), looking W.

<5171> and <5172>, clearly indicated that it contained human faecal matter, and this would suggest that the feature had functioned as a cess pit. Later fills (1698) and (1600) comprised dumps of loamy material containing charcoal and domestic waste that were probably intended to backfill the pit once it had gone out of use.

About two metres to the west of pit (1619) the edge of another sub-circular pit, (1606), was only partially exposed as it extended west beyond the limit of excavation; the surviving dimensions were 1.45 x 0.60 x 1.05 m. The pit had vertical sides and the fill, (1605), was a mass of clay and blocks of angular sandstone, which suggest a deliberate backfilling event. The backfill was subsequently covered by a sterile layer of light brown sand, (1542), that spread east over an area 2 x 2.3 m and contained pottery of fourteenth–fifteenth century date. This sand was subsequently cut by sub-circular pit (1544), which was 1.08 m in diameter and 0.65 m deep. The northern edge of pit (1544) was had been removed by the cutting of pit (1541), but it had steep sides tapering to a concave base. The primary fill, (1548), comprised alternating lenses of silt and sand rich in fragments of coal that were probably derived from hearth sweepings. The pit was subsequently filled with a dump of mixed building debris, (1543), and domestic waste including pottery dated to the late fifteenth century.

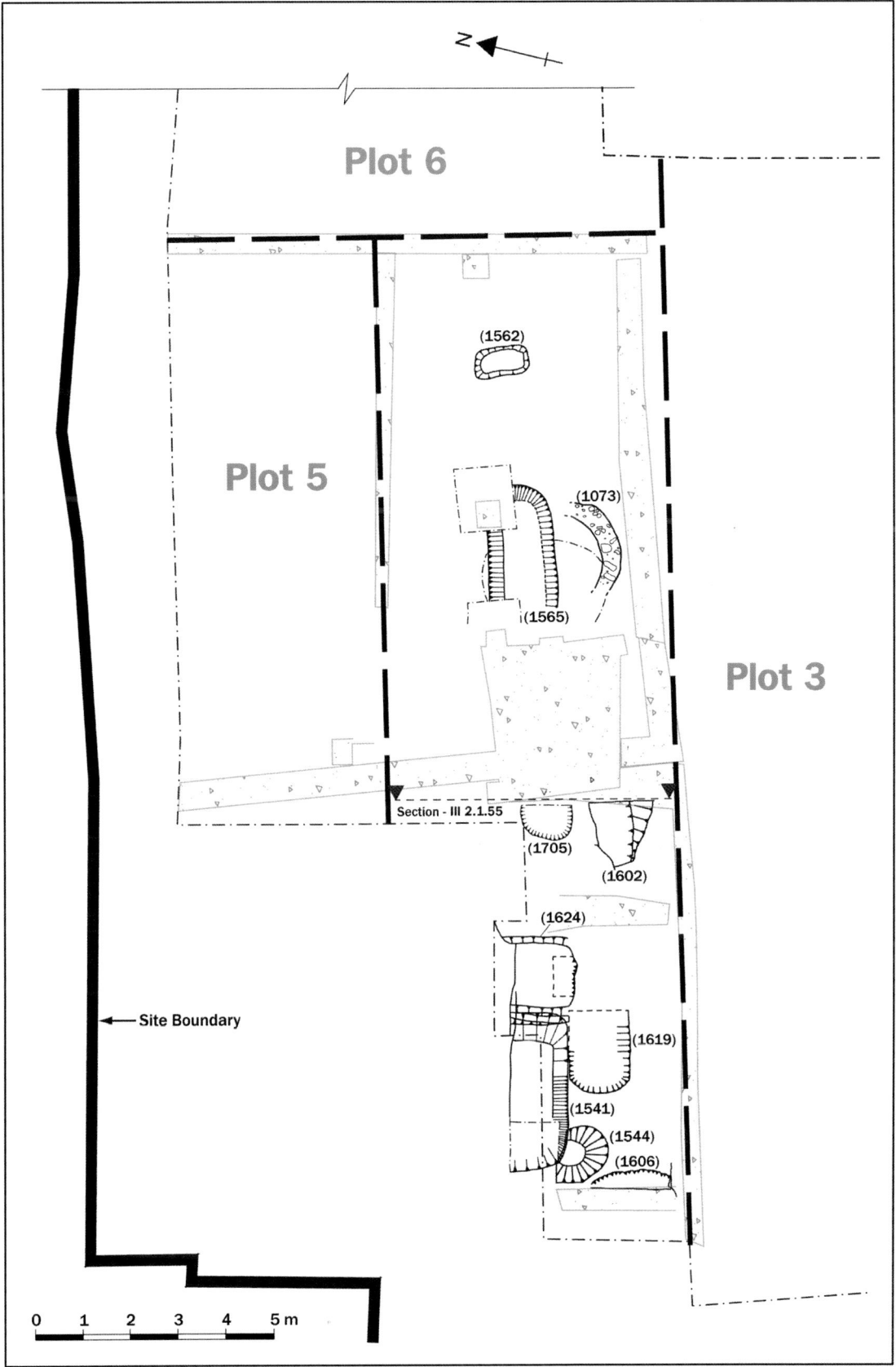

Plot 6

Plot 5

Plot 3

(1562)

(1073)

(1565)

Section - III 2.1.55

(1705)

(1602)

(1624)

(1619)

◄— Site Boundary

(1541)

(1544)

(1606)

0   1   2   3   4   5 m

III 2.1.54 Phase VI Plot 4: plan. (Scale 1/125)

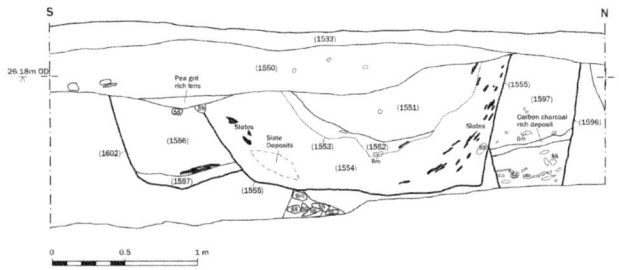

Ill 2.1.55 Phase VI Plot 4: S-facing section. (Scale 1/50)

Pits (1562) and (1073)

At the eastern end of Plot 4 two pits were identified. The first, (1562), was kidney-shaped and measured 1.20 x 0.46 x 0.60 m; it was oriented north–south with a steep slope at the northern end and a more gradual slope at the southern side. The character and profile of the pit would suggest that it resulted from the removal of a tree bole. The fill, (1561), consisted almost entirely of charcoal which might suggest that the tree bole was burnt *in situ*; fourteenth–fifteenth-century pottery was also present. The second pit, (1073), had been heavily disturbed by later features, but it appeared to be a sub-circular pit 2 m in diameter. The fill, (1567), produced pottery dating to between the late fifteenth century and *c* 1600 and a piece of worked sandstone that had the appearance of being a socketed base to an ornamental object.

Pits (1705), (1602) and (1623)

Towards the centre of Plot 4 was a group of three pits that had been heavily truncated by later pitting. Pit (1705) was sub-circular in plan and measured 1.05 m in diameter and was 0.40 m deep. The fill, (1704), consisted of lenses of olive green cessy material on top of which was dumped a mixed brown clay containing building debris and pottery dated to the sixteenth–seventeenth century. To the south of this pit was a second sub-circular pit, (1602), that had been cut by three later pits and had surviving dimensions of 1.17 x 1.01 x 0.88 m (Ill 2.1.55). The primary fill, (1557), was black owing to the high content of coal/charcoal/carbonised material present in the matrix, and could represent an episode of rubbish-dumping in the base of the pit immediately after its original function had ceased. Upper fill (1556) was greenish brown in colour implying that it was derived from the deposition of cess and faecal matter and this would imply that in the case of (1602) use as a cess pit was a secondary function. The third pit, (1623), only survived in a fragmentary state and was recorded as having a single fill (1622).

Pit (1541)

At the western end of Plot 4 a large subrectangular pit, (1541), was partly exposed by the excavation and had excavated dimensions of 1.80 x 1.20 x 0.85 m. The pit was aligned roughly east–west and had nearly vertical sides and a flat base. The primary fill, (1549), was a mid-brown silty clay, distinguished from upper fill (1540) by the concentration of coal fragments within the matrix. Upper fill (1540) was also a mid-brown silty clay that contained small quantities of building material, suggesting that it was part of the systematic backfilling of the

pit. Fills (1549) and (1540) did not present any evidence to suggest that pit (1541) had functioned as a cess pit, but they did produce pottery of a consistently early seventeenth-century date.

To the north of pit (1541) a deposit of black coal/charcoal-rich material, (1827), was identified covering an area roughly 0.70 m in diameter. This deposit was similar in character to lower pit fill (1549), and this might imply that the two contexts derived from the same event.

Pit (1565)

Pit (1565) was located in the western half of Plot 4 on a parallel alignment to pit (1541). It was subrectangular in plan with surviving dimensions 2.65 x 1.40 x 0.90 m. The base of the pit was not fully excavated because it continued beneath the limit of excavation in this area. The fill, (1566), was a dark grey-brown sand silt which produced pottery of a seventeenth-century date and a Hanns Krauwinckel jetton dated 1586–1635.

Plot 5 (Ill 2.1.54)

Most of the earlier archaeology in Plot 5 had been removed by the insertion of a full-height cellar during the nineteenth century (*see* Phase IX), and as a consequence Phase VI remains were confined to the western end of the plot beyond the limit of the cellar. The evidence was limited to the presence of two clay floor horizons separated from one another by a series of occupation layers. The floors are assumed to be internal, although no wall remains were identified in the plot during this phase.

The sequence began with the deposition of a layer of red-brown clay, (1523), which survived over an area 2.36 x 4.5 m and was interpreted as a floor surface. The central portion of the surface was covered by a lens of greenish grey material, (1501), which was interpreted as an occupation deposit. Both lens (1501) and the clay surface were subsequently covered by layer (1806), which contained late medieval pottery.

A second layer of red-brown clay, (1500), was subsequently laid over the same area as the earlier one. The horizon between the base of layer (1500) and the top of layer (1806) had a high concentration of degraded shell fragments and pottery dated to the fourteenth–fifteenth century. Layer (1500) was again interpreted as a floor surface and was covered by a possible occupation layer, (1805), which again produced pottery dated to the fourteenth–fifteenth century. Layer (1805) was in turn covered by layer (1804).

Plot 6 (Ills 2.1.56–9)

The sequence of development in Plot 6 appeared to demonstrate three broad changes in land use. The earliest activity in this phase appeared to be the establishment of a formal knot garden over the western half of the plot. This was in stark contrast to the large cess pit identified on the eastern edge of the excavation. The evidence for a division between the two areas may just represent a functional division within a single plot or may indicate a property boundary, implying that by the sixteenth century Plot 6 was in fact part of the backyards of two properties fronting on to Eastgate Street to the north. A subsequent change in use appears to have been repre-

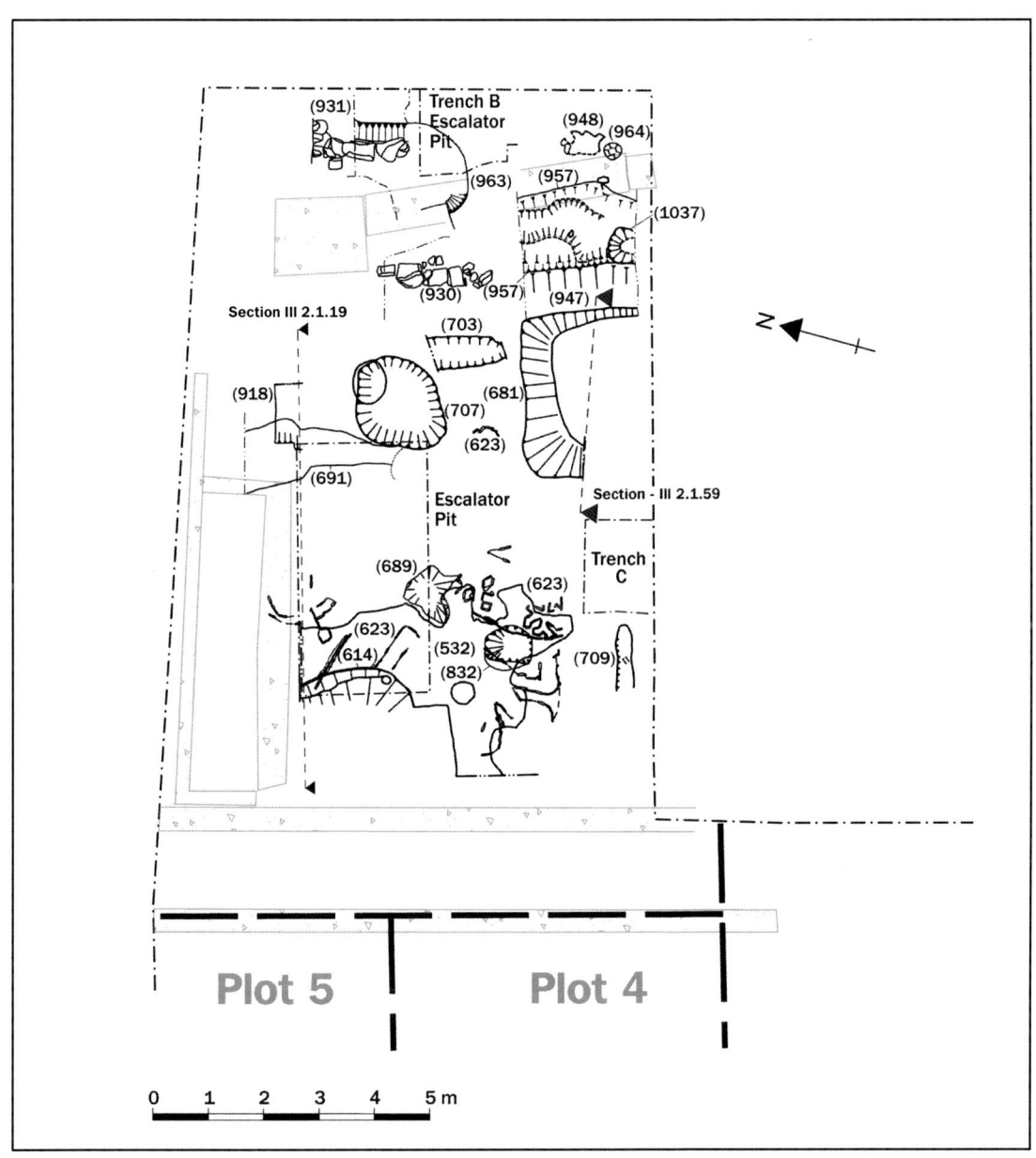

III 2.1.56 Phase VI Plot 6: plan. (Scale 1/125)

sented by the replacement of the formal garden with a light timber building. The earlier cess pit seems to have been deliberately backfilled and replaced by a mixed timber and stone building containing a cobbled surface and a hearth or oven base. These buildings were presumably ancillary buildings to the rear of their respective properties; no specific functions can be assigned to either of them. The final change of land use consisted of the removal of the buildings and the commencement of an intense cycle of pit-digging and systematic backfilling probably associated with sewage management.

'Knot garden' (623)

The western half of the plot appears to have been covered by elements of what has been interpreted as a formal knot garden, (623), covering an area approximately 4.60 x 5.80 m (Ills 2.1.57–8). The evidence consisted of broken and reused roofing slates which had been set on edge in a series of geometric patterns including parallel lines, curving lines, diamond shaped boxes, lines which converged

in points at about thirty degrees, and a flower which could be either a clover, a *fleur de lis* or a four-petalled rose. These slate configurations were interpreted as borders for flower beds, possibly designed for an intricate planting scheme of different flora. At the centre of this intricate scheme of slate borders there was a heart-shaped pit, (689). This pit had been deliberately backfilled with clay and sandstone rubble, (690), and produced pottery dating to between the late sixteenth and eighteenth centuries. The central location of the pit could suggest that it was made by the root bole of an ornamental shrub such as a bay tree, which would have formed a focal point of the design. Thus the dated material in the pit indicates when the formal garden was disposed of. Many of the borders were sampled for pollen in the hope that it would be possible to reconstruct elements of this planting scheme. Unfortunately, the sandy soil was not conducive to the preservation of pollen grains and the results proved entirely negative. Braun's map of 1586 (Ill 1.2.2) clearly shows formal knot gardens covering much of the areas behind the buildings fronting on to Bridge Street and Eastgate Street including the area occupied by Plot 6. On the south side of the garden there was an accumulation of garden soils represented by layers (712) and (711).

Some of the elements of the formal garden were cut by pit (832). It had a single fill, (833), which was a mixture of building debris and domestic rubbish suggestive of deliberate backfilling. The pit may have been left by the removal of a tree or large shrub which had established itself within the formal garden during a period of neglect; it may have been removed at the same time as the tree represented by pit (689).

Pit (701) was a similar sized oval shaped feature with dimensions of 0.76 x 0.60 x 0.27 m, which was adjacent to the line of boundary ditch (691). The fill, (702), had the appearance of redeposited medieval cultivation soil with some larger fragments of sandstone mixed in and producing fourteenth–fifteenth-century pottery; it probably represented a single deliberate backfilling event, after the removal of a tree or shrub, and thus may be contemporary with pit (832).

Boundary ditch (691)

On the northern side of the plot, to the east of the garden, a fragment of a shallow north–south ditch, (691), was identified. It is likely that its southern end had been removed by a later group of pits, including pit (681). The ditch had been filled with building debris and household refuse, (687), which included pottery of early seventeenth-century date. A fragment of the southern end of a parallel ditch may be represented by gully (703); the fill, (704), contained pottery dated between the late fifteenth and early seventeenth centuries. The line of ditches (691)/(703) may have originally delimited the eastern extent of the formal garden or alternatively represented a property division.

Cess pit (89)/(112)/(963)

To the east of the ditch (691) in the north-eastern corner of the plot a thick layer of dark brown silty clay, (977), formed over an area of 1.0 x 0.66 m. This was subsequently truncated by the excavation of a large pit, (89)/(112)/(963), which was more than 0.48 m deep (the base was not reached as it lay beneath the limit of excavation). The lowest fill encountered in this pit was a greyish brown silty clay, (113)/(962), which had a relatively high charcoal content as well as containing building debris and domestic refuse. The secondary fill, (124)/(960), was a reddish brown sandy silt containing a high percentage of large water-worn cobbles and sandstone fragments, suggestive of deliberate backfilling. The upper fill, (90)/(949), was a very mixed deposit truncated on two sides by modern services and produced late medieval to sixteenth-century pottery. The pit was clearly very deep and probably represents a large cess pit, although this could not be confirmed by excavation.

Surface (680)/(532)/(717)

A series of brown silty clay layers, (831), (697), (719) and (826), subsequently formed over the formal garden and contained pottery dating from the fifteenth to the seventeenth centuries. These layers were then covered by a surface represented by contexts (680), (532) and (717), which covered an area 4 x 2.2 m. The surface was com-

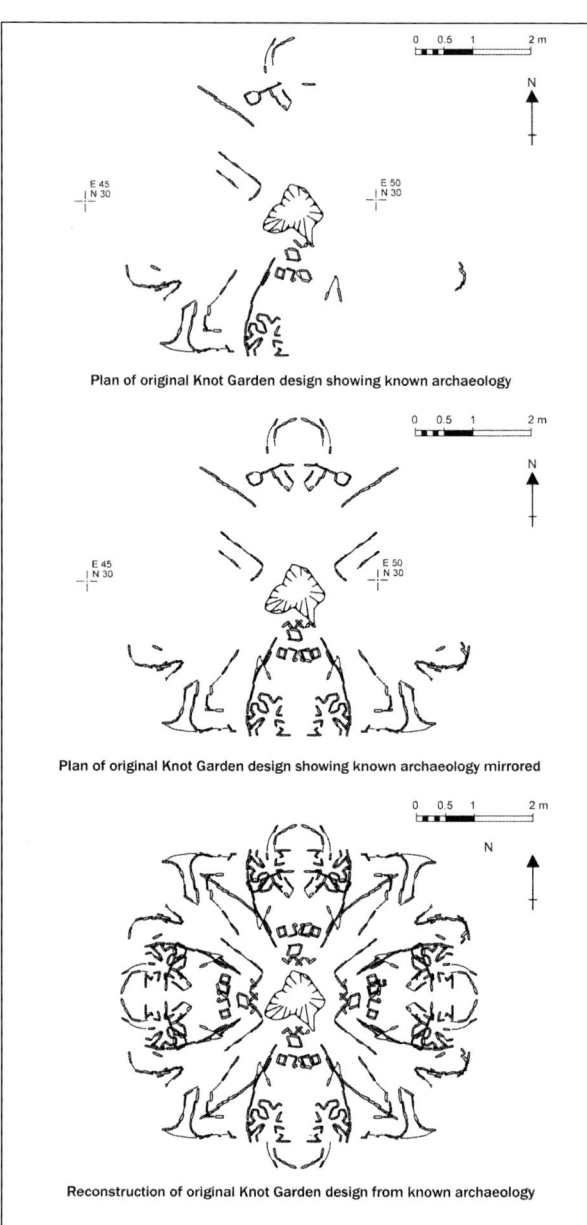

Plan of original Knot Garden design showing known archaeology

Plan of original Knot Garden design showing known archaeology mirrored

Reconstruction of original Knot Garden design from known archaeology

Ill 2.1.57 Phase VI Plot 6 'knot garden': plan of excavated remains and reconstruction. (Scale 1/50)

Ill 2.1.58 Phase VI Plot 6: element of knot garden, looking W.

pact and largely comprised fragments of red sandstone, although some fragments of hand-made brick and grey roofing slate were also present. It has been interpreted as a floor surface, probably belonging to a lightly constructed timber outbuilding. Another element of this building may be represented by slot (709), which ran along the southern edge of the floor surface on an east–west alignment. The western end of slot (709) was removed by later pitting. The fill, (710), was a greenish brown silty clay containing pottery of fourteenth–fifteenth-century date.

Stone building

This building lay at the east end of the plot and was represented by two parallel walls, (930), (931), aligned north–south and set into the upper fill of cess pit (963). Both were constructed from roughly shaped sandstone blocks bonded with red clay. Beyond the southern surviving limit of the two walls an area of sandstone fragments, (88), bonded in a greyish brown silty clay, (84), was identified as a possible surface. This surface had clearly subsided into the underlying pit and was subsequently covered by an olive green cess-rich deposit, (87), which produced late medieval–sixteenth-century pottery.

Beyond surface (88), in the south-eastern corner of the plot, lay a post hole, (964). Its fill, (965), was a sterile mid-brown sandy silt. A second sub-rounded post hole, (1037), lay to the west of (964). The dark brown silty clay fill, (1036), contained some large sandstone fragments which may have originally served as packing stones; if so these stones had clearly been disturbed during the removal of the timber. These post holes may be associated with the building represented by walls (930) and (931) as (964) appeared to align with the eastern wall (931) while (1037) aligned with wall (930).

Hearth (958)

A shallow subrectangular pit, (948,) later removed the upper portion of post hole (964). Its fill was entirely composed of biscuit-fired orange-red clay, (958), interpreted as the base of a hearth or oven. As with post hole (964), this hearth may have been associated with use of the building represented by walls (930) and (931). The hearth was subsequently covered by a layer of dark brown silty clay, (835), which was spread over an area 2.2 x 1 m and contained pottery of seventeenth-century date.

Pit (681)

A layer of cultivation soil, (947), formed to the west of hearth (948) and covered an area 2.1 x 2.15 m; this may have been contemporary with layers (835) and (1028). The layer produced a copper alloy buckle, possibly of mid-sixteenth century date.

Pit (681) was cut into layer (947) and was only partly uncovered on the southern side of the plot, where it had probably removed the southern end of boundary ditch (691) (Ill 2.1.59). The base of the pit was not excavated as it was beneath the limit of excavation; however, it was square in plan with almost vertical sides. The fills of the pit suggested that it had been systematically backfilled over a short period of time using material derived from a variety of different activities. The lowest fill encountered, (728), was entirely composed of a tip of small coal fragments. This was overlaid by a deposit of red sandy clay, (729), rich in small lumps of lime mortar and hand-made brick fragments. Above this was a greyish brown silty clay deposit, (730), dominated by many broken fragments of grey roofing slate. This waste is characteristic of the trimming of roofing slates and probably attests the re-roofing of an adjacent building. The slateworking waste was covered by a deposit of greyish brown clay, (724), which produced pottery of sixteenth–seventeenth-century date. This in turn was covered by a deposit of sandy loam, (692)/(699), up to 0.8 m thick, which resembled the medieval cultivation soils described in Phase V and produced late medieval and sixteenth-century pottery. A thin lens of brown sand rich in lime mortar, (829), sealed these lower fills and contained late medieval pottery. The uppermost fill, (828), comprised a dump of sandstone fragments and large water-worn cobbles and contained late medieval and sixteenth-century pottery.

Gully (957)

To the east of pit (681) lay a gully aligned roughly north–south and cut into layer (835)/(1028). Its profile indicated steep sides and a concave base. Both of the fills, (956) and (955), comprised charcoal-rich loams containing fragments of sandstone and hand-made brick, suggestive of deliberate backfill. It was interpreted as a boundary ditch, but was not detected further to the north and it may have been a more localised feature, possibly part of a drain leading to one of the myriad of pits identified in this area.

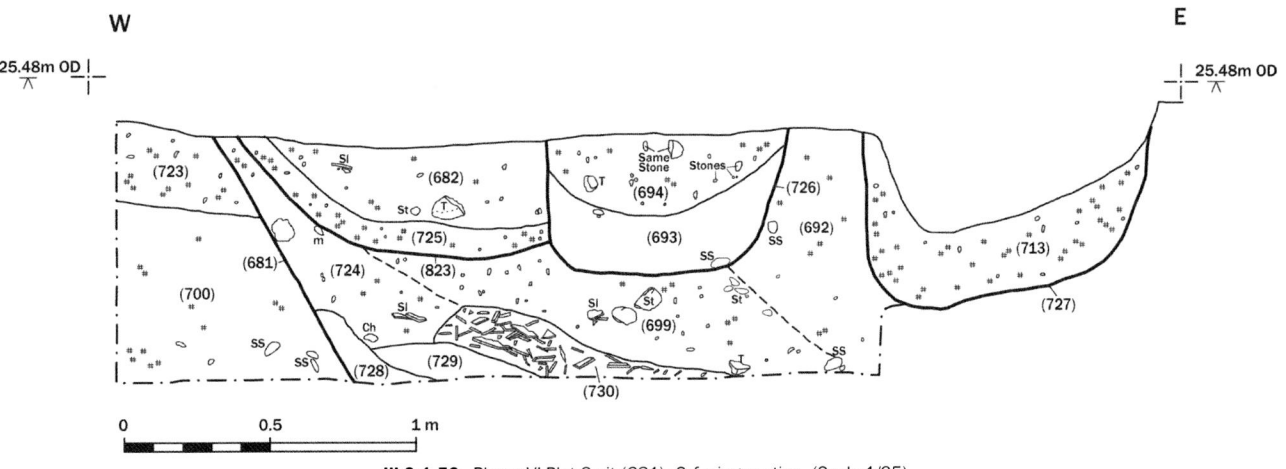

Ill 2.1.59 Phase VI Plot 6 pit (681): S-facing section. (Scale 1/25)

Pits (614), (927) and (707)

Pits (614) and (927) were both cut into the surface (680)/ (532) of the postulated timber building. Pit (614) had an irregular shape which was caused by a tremendous amount of root disturbance along its edges. The primary fill, (608), was almost entirely composed of small coal fragments which may have been derived from a domestic hearth. The secondary fill, (565), was a pale orange silty clay which contained sandstone rubble and building material suggestive of deliberate backfilling and pottery of sixteenth–seventeenth-century date. The upper fill, (566), was an orange-brown sandy silt reminiscent of the medieval cultivation soils described in Phase V, suggesting that it was in fact redeposited cultivation soil. The few coarse components probably derived from deliberate backfilling rather than natural silting. It also produced pottery of fourteenth–fifteenth-century date.

Pit (927) was only identified in the northern section of the excavation trench. The fill, (926), was a dark brown silty clay containing a mixture of building debris and hearth sweepings, probably indicating that it was backfilled over a short period of time. The fragment of pit (918) was likewise partially exposed towards the northern edge of the plot. It was not fully excavated as the base lay below the limit of excavation. The fill, (916), had regular lumps of red clay in its make up and relatively small amounts of domestic waste, suggesting that it was backfilled in a single event. A layer of dark brown silty clay, (919)/(843), subsequently formed over (916) and more generally over the northern side of Plot 6 and is thought to be derived from horticultural activity in the vicinity. Pit (707) was cut along the line of boundary ditches (691)/(703) and entirely removed sections of these features. Again, the base was not reached as it lay below the limit of the excavation. The fill, (706), contained building debris including hand-made brick and sandstone fragments, suggesting that it had been backfilled in a single event. Domestic debris was also recovered, including pottery dated to between the late fifteenth and early seventeenth centuries.

Adjacent to pit (707) towards the centre of the plot was a layer of mid-brown sandy loam, (683), unevenly mixed with concentrations of stones and building material and covering an area 2.2 x 2.4 m. The layer produced pottery dating to the seventeenth century and a residual iron horseshoe of Norman type.

Phase VII: Mid- to late 17–early 18 century

Plot 1 (Ills 2.1.61–2)

A large central area of the Phase VII archaeology in Plot 1 was heavily truncated or entirely removed by a late twentieth-century reinforced concrete base and servicing pit constructed for an industrial-sized printing press when the site was occupied by the *Chester Chronicle* newspaper. A similar level of destruction was also identified in a linear zone along the northern boundary of the plot, this time caused by nineteenth-century wall foundations associated with Fletcher's Buildings, and the laying of sewer pipes and other services during the early twentieth century.

Pits (242), (244) and (247)

The south-eastern corner of Plot 1 was covered by a layer of light reddish brown silty clay, (240), which contained moderate amounts of building debris and pottery dating from the mid-seventeenth to the early eighteenth century. This layer was cut by three pits. The largest, (242), was subrectangular in plan and orientated east–west. It had fairly vertical sides and was filled with a dark brown coal-rich deposit, (243), which contained pottery of mid- to late seventeenth-century date. The second pit, (244), was also subrectangular in plan, only this time it was orientated north–south and was quite shallow; the fill, (245), contained pottery of seventeenth–early eighteenth-century date. The third pit, (247), lay just to the west of pit (242) and was interpreted as the rounded end to a linear shaped feature aligned east–west (the western extent of the feature was not ascertained during the excavation). The fill, (248), produced seventeenth-century pottery.

Layer (237)/(663)/(1884)/(1887)/(1891)

The entire excavated area of Plot 1 was subsequently covered by a layer of dark greyish brown sandy silt up to 0.48 m thick, (237), which contained frequent small abraded fragments of building debris. The coarse components in this layer were well mixed and it was also characterised by frequent lumps of dark grey silt which were thought to be derived from midden-spreading; this led to its interpretation as a cultivation deposit. The deposition of this layer effectively negated the terracing effect noted in earlier phases at the boundary between Plots 1 and 2. A large assemblage of material was recovered from this layer. The pottery was consistently dated from the mid- to late seventeenth to the early eighteenth century, with the majority of the clay tobacco pipes giving a date bracket of *c* 1610–80, with some early eighteenth-century pieces also present; a small assemblage of early to mid-seventeenth-century glass vessels and a musket ball were also recovered from this layer. This material is clearly quite mixed and either represents wholesale tipping of soil imported to the site as part of a massive backfilling exercise or a gradual build-up of cultivation soil during the second half of the seventeenth century and the early part of the eighteenth century.

Culvert (666)/(1916)

Along the northern boundary of Plot 1 a stone-built culvert was traced for a length of at least 15 m on an east–west alignment. The drain was initially recorded in the ramp excavation area as sitting in a construction cut (666), which was dug through layer (663). The structure of the drain consisted of a flat base, (672), formed from sandstone blocks and large water-worn cobbles. On this base were built two parallel walls, (669), 0.3 m in height; the walls consisted of sandstone blocks bonded in puddled red clay and were up to two courses high in places. The tops of the walls were used to seat a course of roughly shaped blocks, (668), which served as a capping to the drain (Ill 2.1.61). The upper part of the construction trench was subsequently backfilled, first with a reddish grey sandy silt, (667), which produced seventeenth–eighteenth-century pottery, and then with an upper fill of brown sandy silt, (664)/(665), which was very similar in appearance to layer (663) and may well have been the redeposited upcast from the excavation of the construction trench.

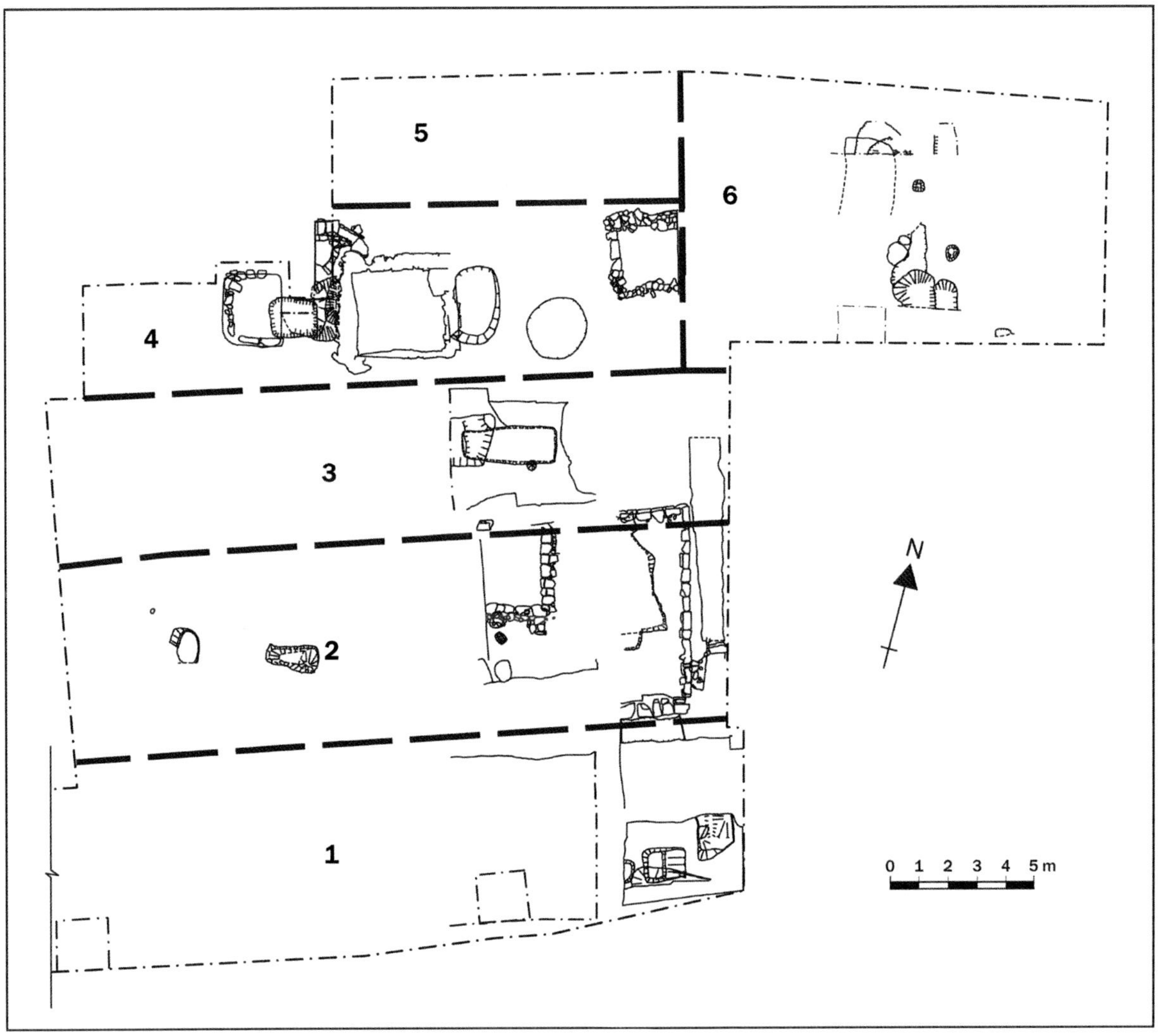

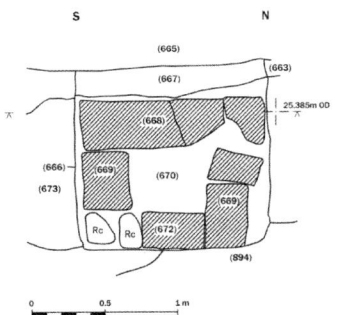

Ill 2.1.60 Phase VII: general arrangement of plots. (Scale 1/250)

Ill 2.1.61 Phase VII Plot 1 culvert (666): E-facing section. (Scale 1/50)

This upper fill contained pottery of late seventeenth-century date.

The culvert was recorded further to the west during the subsequent grading exercise (although it did not survive in as good a condition), and at least two tributary drains were detected within Plot 1. It appeared to have become choked with silt, (670), after a period of use; the silt was sampled, < 5056>, and found to contain small fragments of pottery dating to the eighteenth–nineteenth century.

Hearth (1910) and pit (1905)
A large sandstone block, (1910), measuring 1.45 x 0.60 x 0.35 m was found lying horizontally near the southern

boundary of Plot 1. There was evidence for *in situ* burning on the upper surface of the block and it was interpreted as the base to a hearth or fireplace. Part of this hearth/fireplace had later been removed by the cutting of a large rectangular pit, (1905), orientated east–west and measuring 0.65 x 1.73 x 0.76 m. The base of the pit contained a thin lens of green cess-like material, subsequently covered by a dump of charcoal-rich building debris, (1897), which contained pottery of late seventeenth–mid-eighteenth-century date. The nature of the fill suggests that pit (1897) was a cess pit which was deliberately backfilled after a period of use. Fill (1897) was later covered by a compact layer of reddish brown sandy clay, (1898), which produced pottery of seventeenth–eighteenth-century date.

Pits (73), (63) and (27)
Layer (237)/(663)/(1884)/(1887)/(1891) was not identified in Evaluation Trench F, probably because of the sequence of intercutting pits encountered, and as a result it is hard to reconcile the stratigraphy with the archaeology in the rest of Plot 1. However, the following sequence was recorded.

At the bottom of the sequence was a small subrectangular cess pit, (73), which had steep sides, a flat base and excavated dimensions of 0.8 x 0.5 x 0.5 m. The fill was an

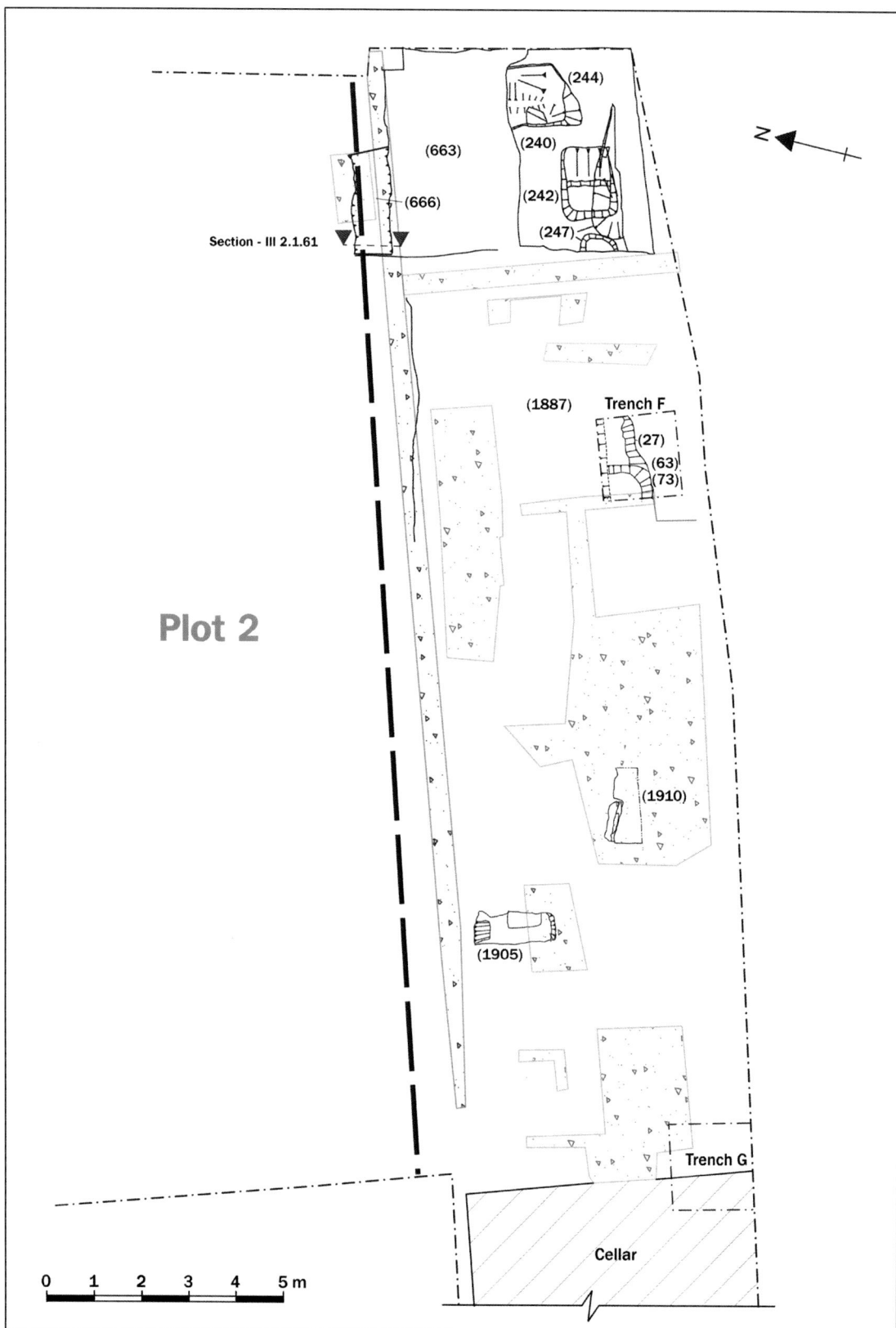

III 2.1.62 Phase VII Plot 1: plan. (Scale 1/125)

olive green silty clay, (72), which contained fragments of mineralised wood/bark and eighteenth-century pottery. Pit (73) was partly removed by the later digging of pit (63), which had excavated dimensions of 0.50 x 0.66 x 0.32 m. The primary fill of pit (63) was a thin layer of brown clay, (62), which might have acted as a lining to the pit; above this was a secondary fill of olive green silty sand, (61), which contained pottery of late seventeenth–early eighteenth-century date.

Pit fill (61) was a covered by a layer of dark olive green silty sand, (49), which would appear to be derived from an accumulation of cessy material. Layer (49) was cut by an east–west aligned pit, (27), with excavated dimensions of 1.66 x 0.80 x 0.64 m, which had a stepped profile and a flat base. The fill, (26), was an olive green silty loam with some fibrous material noted during excavation; it produced seventeenth–eighteenth-century pottery.

Pits (73), (63) and (27) may represent a single cess pit recut on two separate occasions. In each case the green organic-rich fills strongly indicate the purpose of the pit or pits.

Pit (32)

Layer (237)/(663)/(1884)/(1887)/(1891) was not identified in Evaluation Trench G either, although it is possible that layers (12) and (4) were broadly equivalent, and as a result it is hard to reconcile the stratigraphy with the archaeology in the rest of Plot 1. The following sequence was recorded.

A rectilinear pit, (32), aligned roughly north–south was identified with excavated dimensions of 1.04 x 0.5 x 0.5 m. The fill, (31), comprised a dark brown silty clay, although it was noted that the sides and base appeared to be lined with broken fragments of grey roofing slate. The fill also produced pottery of seventeenth–eighteenth-century date. It was sealed by a layer of brick and sandstone rubble, (12), which in turn was covered by a layer of charcoal-rich silt, (4).

Plot 2 (III 2.1.63)

At the eastern end of Plot 2 the medieval boundary wall (600) continued to dictate the sequence of layer deposition. As mentioned previously, it seems likely that features and layers recorded to the east of wall (600) were probably not within the property defined as Plot 2 but rather belonged to a different property fronting on to Newgate Street.

In this narrow strip of land a sequence of deposits were recorded which in hindsight probably represented the successive fills of a single large cess pit unrecognised during the excavation, as they all sloped sharply from west to east. The lowest deposit in the sequence was a brown sandy silt, (499), which covered an area 6 m long and 0.6 m wide. This was covered by a deposit of greyish brown clayey silt, (481), which was rich in clinker, coal and charcoal and produced a collection of copper alloy pins. Upper deposit (480)/(492) comprised a dump of light orange-brown clay and building debris indicative of deliberate backfilling. The whole sequence of deposits produced pottery of sixteenth–seventeenth-century date.

Walls (646) and (655)

On the southern edge of deposit (480)/(492) a small rem-

nant of a sandstone wall, (646), with surviving dimensions of 1.60 x 0.55 x 0.20 m was identified butting up to the back of boundary wall (600). The wall was aligned north–south and consisted of a mixture of sandstone blocks and small stone fragments bonded by both a pinkish sandy lime mortar and clay. The blocks were uneven and bonded in a fairly haphazard manner with uncoursed rough faces, suggesting that the wall was built in haste with no particular concern as to its outer appearance. The base of the wall was partly covered by a discrete deposit, (652), comprising sandstone rubble flecked with lime mortar which was thought to represent debris from the collapse of the wall. This deposit was covered by a similar deposit, (659), which was distinguished by having fewer sandstone fragments within its matrix; this upper deposit produced pottery of seventeenth–eighteenth-century date and clay tobacco pipes dated 1640–70. After the formation of deposit (659) an additional fragment of sandstone wall, (655), was added to the remnant of wall (646) on an east–west alignment. Wall (655) consisted of roughly hewn sandstone blocks bonded in pink mortar which survived to a height of two courses.

Layer (459)

An extensive layer of mid-brown clayey silt, (459), subsequently covered the strip of land to the east of the boundary wall. This layer extended beyond the northern boundary of Plot 2, along the back of Plot 3 to the southern boundary of Plot 4 and was interpreted as a cultivation soil. It produced pottery of late seventeenth–early eighteenth-century date and clay tobacco pipes dated 1660–80.

Cess pit (465)

To the west of boundary wall (600) a hollow, (465), had persisted in the location of the Phase V cess pit (487). Only the eastern side of the hollow was uncovered during the excavation, but the north–south dimension suggested that it had a diameter of about 3.4 m. The primary fill, (472), was an orange-red clay rich in building debris, including window glass and more of the late medieval decorated floor tile that had been deposited in this area during Phase VI. It also produced pottery dated *c* 1670–early 1700s, clay tobacco pipes dated 1660–80 and glass bottle fragments of late seventeenth–early eighteenth-century date. This was covered by a thick deposit of dark brown organic-rich silt, (464), which contained late seventeenth-century pottery, glass vessels and clay tobacco pipes dated 1630–1700. Above this was a thick dump of building debris represented by fills (463) and (491) that were rich in artefacts including late seventeenth-century pottery, late seventeenth–early eighteenth-century glass vessels and clay tobacco pipes dated 1680–1720. The upper fill of the hollow, (489), was a green cess-like deposit which produced no datable finds. The hollow has been interpreted primarily as a cess pit, but it seems to have served as a means for disposal of domestic rubbish in a secondary capacity. This led to the accumulation of a large assemblage of material which would appear to be broadly contemporary, with a date of deposition shortly after 1702, indicated by a Queen Anne ale measure mark on one of the pottery tankards. This assemblage also included a small group of sugar cone mould fragments.

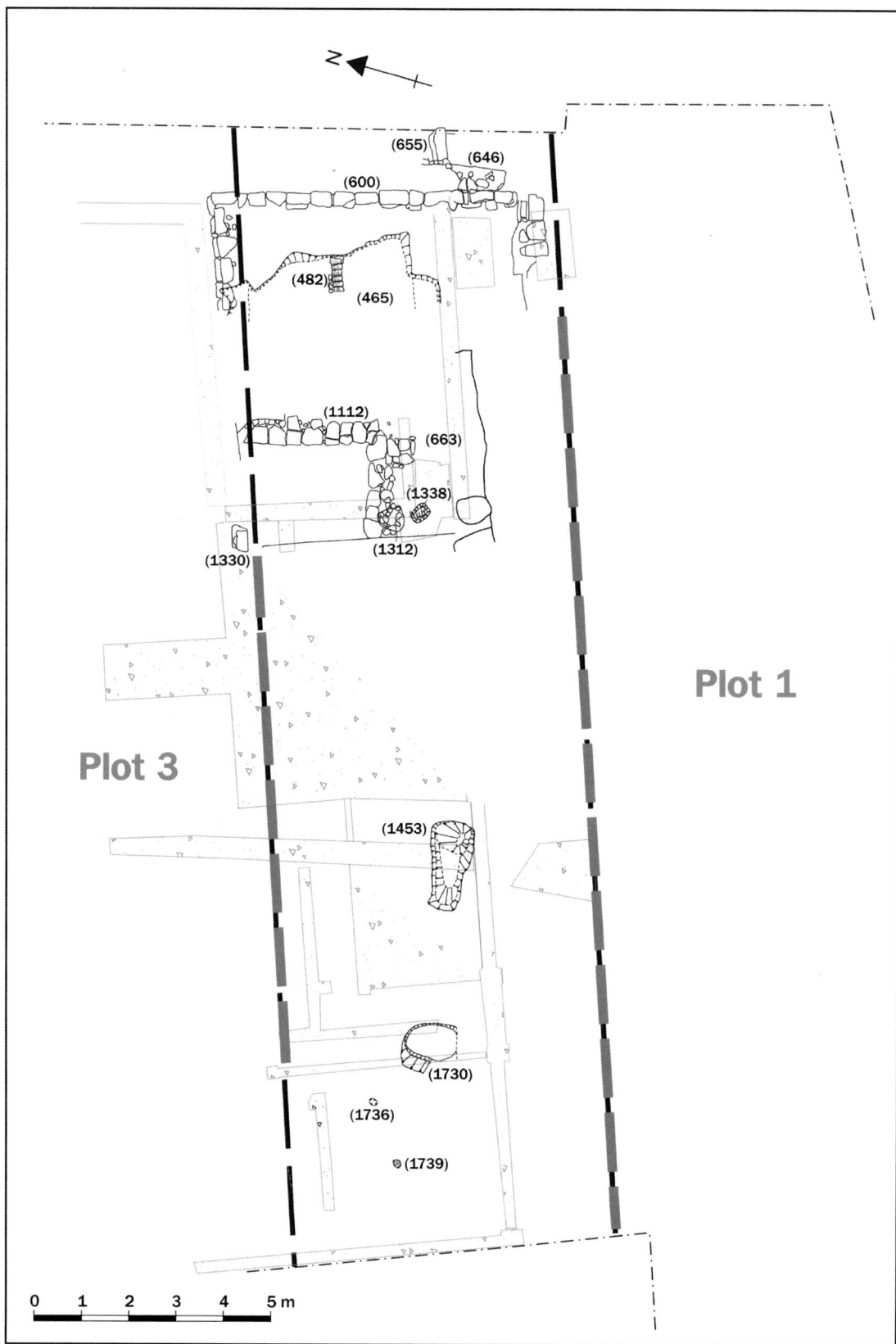

III 2.1.63 Phase VII Plot 2: plan. (Scale 1/125)

A short section of brick wall bonded with a pink-white sandy mortar, (482), was subsequently built over the top of pit (465) on an east–west alignment. This wall probably belonged to a small outbuilding of which no other trace was found. It was covered by a layer of building debris, (440), which produced clay tobacco pipes dated 1660–1720, suggesting that the layer did not long post-date the underlying pit (465).

Layer (1327)/(1328)/(1343)/(1345)
To the west of cess pit (465) there was an extensive layer of dark greyish brown silty clay, (1327)/(1328)/(1343)/(1345), which was rich in building debris. No dating evidence was recovered from this layer but it was overlain by a discrete deposit of greenish grey silty clay, (1310), which produced pottery of seventeenth–eighteenth-century date.

Cess pit (1112)/(1330)
The western side of layer (1327)/(1328)/(1343)/(1345) had been completely removed by the cutting of a substantial pit, (1316)/(1335). This pit had been partially removed on its western side by the construction of a brick cellar during Phase IX, but the surviving dimensions suggested that it was square in plan (approximately 3 x 3 m) and at least 0.95 m deep. The north, south and east sides of the pit had been lined with sandstone walls, (1112) and (1330), consisting of well dressed blocks bonded in red clay; pottery of late seventeenth-century date was recovered from the bonding material. The walls survived to a height of at least five courses (0.95 m), although their base lay beneath the limit of excavation. This structure was very similar in size and construction to the earlier cess pit located immediately to the east and described in Phases V and VI. The lowest fill of the pit was a reddish grey silty clay, (1336). This was covered by a dump of light brown silt which had an ash-like quality and produced pottery of sixteenth–seventeenth-century date. Above this was a dump of building debris and clay, (1308). This was covered by a deposit of yellowish green silt, (1307), which was very rich in coal fragments and contained pottery of late seventeenth–early eighteenth-century date and clay tobacco pipes dated 1680–1720.

Pit (1312) and post hole (1338)
On the southern edge of the stone pit lining (1112), two features, (1312) and (1338), had been cut into layer (1327)/(1328)/(1343)/(1345). Pit (1312) was a shallow circular cut with vertical sides. The fill, (1309), was a coal-rich purple silty clay containing late seventeenth–early eighteenth-century pottery and clay tobacco pipes dated 1680–1720. Just to the south of the pit was the cut for a circular post hole, (1338). This was filled with a pinkish brown silty clay, (1339), which was rich in brick and stone rubble, suggesting that the hole had been deliberately backfilled after removal of the post. It is possible that this pair of features was associated with a light timber superstructure covering the top of cess pit (1316)/(1335). Both pit (1312) and post hole (1338) were covered by a layer of brown sand silt, (1304), which produced clay tobacco pipes dated to the seventeenth–eighteenth century.

Pit (1730)
Towards the western end of Plot 2 an oval pit 0.55 m deep, (1730), was identified cutting into the fills of an underlying Phase V cess pit (1455). The primary fill, (1634), produced seventeenth–eighteenth-century pottery and a collection of copper alloy pins. Above this was a mottled deposit, (1630), which in turn was covered by a reddish brown sandy clay, (1629)/(1631), which also contained pottery of seventeenth–eighteenth-century date. This was sealed by a dump of dark reddish brown sandy silt, (1627), and a deposit of light grey ash and lime mortar, (1626), which was rich in broken fragments of grey roofing slate; both (1627) and (1626) produced pottery of mid-seventeenth–eighteenth-century date. The upper part of the pit was filled by a succession of deposits of building debris, (1628) and (1454), which also contained material of seventeenth–eighteenth-century date.

A pair of stake holes, (1736) and (1739), was identified to the west of pit (1730) at a spacing of about 1 m; each was approximately 0.15 m in diameter and 0.2 m deep with profiles that tapered to a point. Stake hole (1739) was thought to be at an angle but this was thought to be a result of the stake having been forcibly removed rather than the stake having been deliberately set off-vertical. Stake hole (1736) was backfilled with a slate-rich silty clay, (1735). The stake holes were thought to be contemporary and probably formed part of a fence or light timber superstructure associated with cess pit (1730).

Pit (1453)
A couple of metres to the east of cess pit (1730) there was a subrectangular pit 0.60 m deep, (1453), aligned roughly east–west. The pit sloped down from west to east and had been backfilled with a dump of sandstone rubble, (1452), containing seventeenth-century pottery. There was no indication as to the pit had originally served as a cess pit, but it appears to have been deliberately infilled before any silting could take place, suggesting that it did not remain open for very long. The pit and the surrounding area were later covered by a layer of brown silt, (1451), which contained seventeenth-century pottery.

Plot 3 (III 2.1.64)

Layer (459)
As was mentioned under Plot 2, the easternmost edge of Plot 3 was covered by a layer of mid-brown clayey silt, (459), which produced pottery of late seventeenth–early eighteenth-century date and clay tobacco pipes dated 1660–80. This layer extended north from Plot 2 and is thought to occupy the back of a separate property fronting on to Newgate Street.

Pits (1192) and (1189)/(1691)
Towards the eastern end of Plot 3 was a large subrectangular pit 0.32 m deep (1192), aligned east–west. The fill, (1193), was a greenish yellow sandy clay which was rich in domestic hearth scrapings and contained pottery of mid- to late seventeenth-century date and clay tobacco pipes dated 1640–70. The nature of this fill would imply that the pit had served as a cess pit prior to its deliberate backfilling.

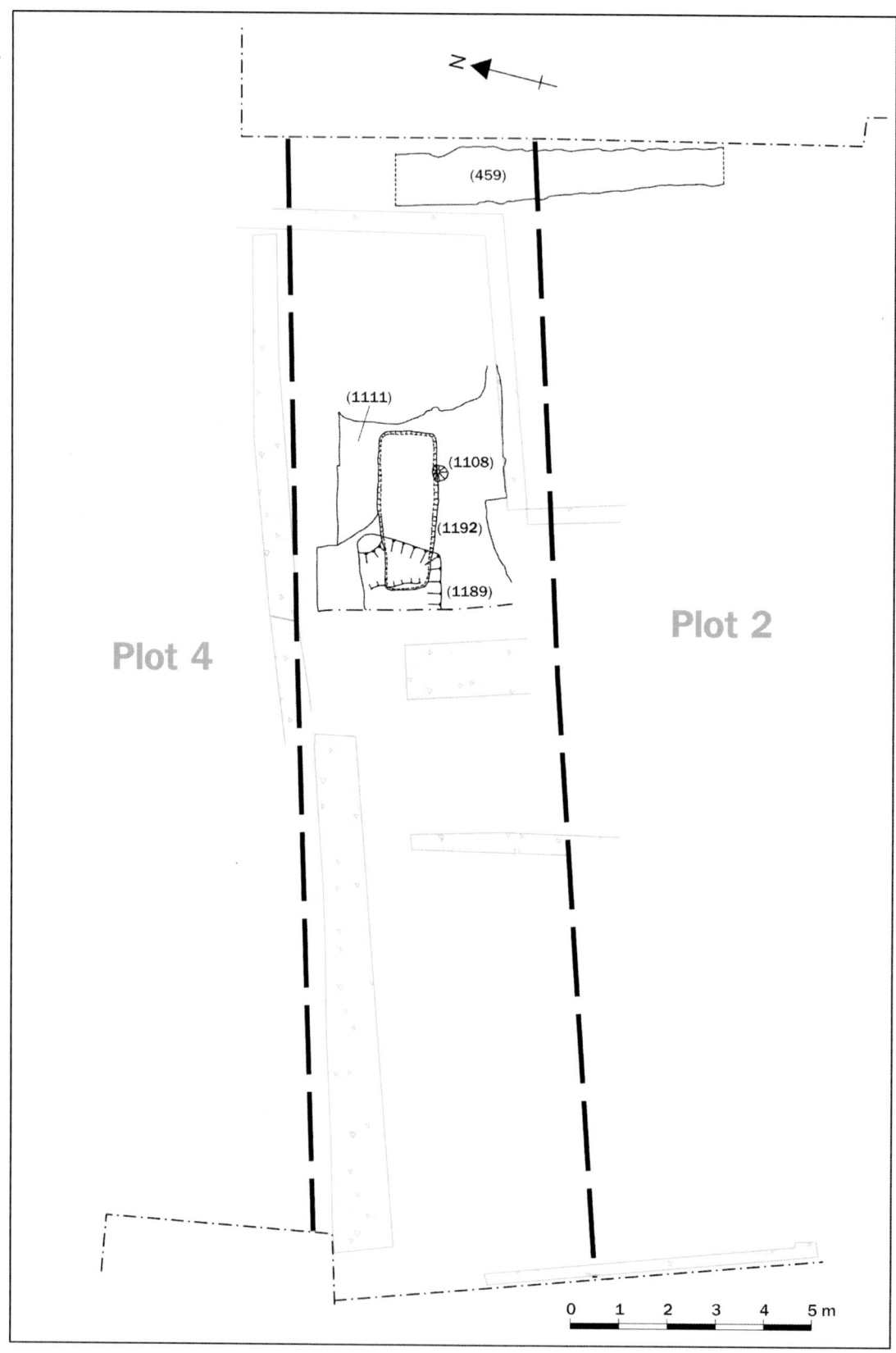

III 2.1.64   Phase VII Plot 3: plan. (Scale 1/125)

The western end of pit (1192) had been partly removed by the cutting of a second subrectangular pit 0. 27 m deep, (1189)/(1691); this second pit had itself been partly removed at its western end by the construction of a brick cellar during Phase IX. The primary fill, (1190), was composed almost entirely of orange-yellow sand containing late seventeenth-century pottery. Above this was a lens of greyish green clay, (1191), which was itself covered by a thick upper fill of dark brown silt, (1098), suggestive of deliberate backfilling. Fill (1098) contained seventeenth-century pottery and a pipeclay figurine of a lady in 'Tudor style' clothing.

Both pits were subsequently covered by an extensive layer of dark reddish brown sandy clay, (1111), which contained pottery of late seventeenth–early eighteenth-century date and clay tobacco pipes dated 1680–1720.

Stake hole (1108)

An isolated stake hole, (1108), was identified cutting into layer (1111). It had steep sides tapering to a blunt point. The fill, (1107), was a reddish grey silty clay which contained seventeenth–eighteenth-century pottery.

Plot 4 (Ills 2.1.65–8)

Plot 4 was completely dominated during Phase VII by a complicated series of intercutting cess pits. An attempt has been made here to describe them in chronological order, although this has proved difficult as the date-ranges on some of the pits are quite broad and stratigraphic relationships could not always be established. It was generally thought that pits (1807)/(1621), (1506) and (1508)/(1560) were the earliest in the phase and that they were followed by pits (1522) and (1696), and finally pit group (1593), (1553), (1596), (1555) and (1612).

Ill 2.1.66 Phase VII Plot 4: pit (1807)/(1621), looking W.

Horn-core pit (1807)/(1621)

At the western end of Plot 4 a rectangular pit 1.1 m deep, (1807)/(1621), was excavated on a north–south alignment (Ills 2.1.65–6). It had vertical sides and a flat base. All four sides had a lining, (1609)/(1796), constructed entirely from cattle horn cores some twenty courses in height. The cores had been laid with distal (pointed) ends pointing both into and out of the pit and some had skull fragments still attached. In places, fragments of pottery and tile had been used to level the coursing of the horn cores or to fill gaps. There was no deliberate clay or other bonding. The sides of the pit were stable and it appears likely that they were porous. It therefore seems probable that it had been used as a cess pit. Around the top of the lining a sandstone wall, (1598), had been built, comprising roughly shaped blocks bonded in red clay and surviving to two courses in height. It is possible that this wall represented the base of a building such as a latrine, standing over the pit. The primary fill of the pit, (1881), was a dark brown sandy clay, which was covered by a black silty sand, (1699), containing burnt bone, wood charcoal and seventeenth-century pottery. The upper fill, (1608), was a black silt which contained clay tobacco pipes of seventeenth–eighteenth-century date; sample <5162> from fill (1608) produced hop fruits suggesting that brewing may have been going on in the vicinity.

Pit (1506)

Towards the centre of the plot was an oval pit 1.2 m deep, (1506). The primary fill, (1515), was an orange-brown silt which produced pottery of seventeenth–eighteenth-century date; sample <5150> from the fill contained fragments of leaves from the box plant, which may indicate a formal garden in the vicinity. Above this was a deposit of black silt, (1514), which contained clay tobacco pipes dated 1610–50. The upper fill, (1507), was a greenish brown silt which contained clay tobacco pipes dated 1640–70.

Pit (1508)/(1560) and cess pit (1522)

To the east of pit (1506) there was a shallow subrectangular pit, (1508)/(1560), 0.20 m deep. The primary fill, (1516), was a dark brownish green charcoal-rich silt containing early to mid-seventeenth-century pottery. The upper fill, (1509), was a light brown charcoal-rich sandy silt containing clay tobacco pipes dated 1650–1720.

Once pit (1508)/(1560) had been completely filled in, a layer of grey silty clay, (1495), formed over the top of it. This layer was subsequently cut through during the ex-

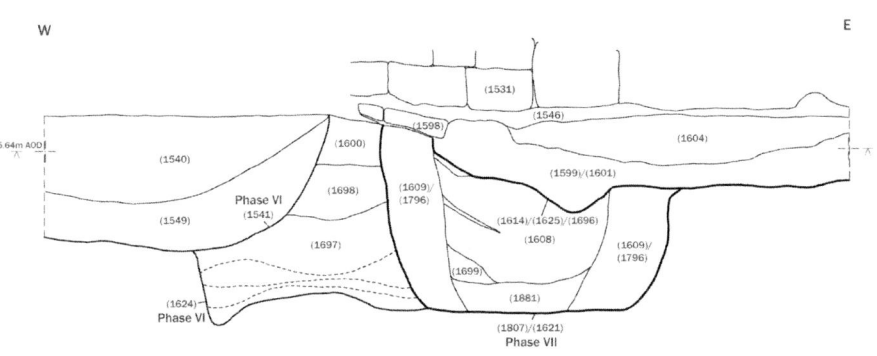

Ill 2.1.65 Phase VII Plot 4 pit (1807)/(1621) and (1696): S-facing section. (Scale 1/50)

Ill 2.1.67 Phase VII Plot 4: pit (1522), looking W.

cavation of pit (1522), which was roughly square and at least 1.2 m deep (Ill 2.1.67). All four sides of the pit had been lined with roughly shaped sandstone blocks bonded in red clay, (1494); the northern side of the lining had been heavily disturbed during the construction of the Phase IX cellar in Plot 5. The lowest fill encountered was a reddish brown loamy clay, (1559), containing quite high quantities of building debris, pottery of late seventeenth–early eighteenth-century date and clay tobacco pipes dated 1660–80. This was covered by a lens of greenish grey silty clay, (1558), the very fine texture of which suggested a slow natural accumulation of silt within the pit, possibly while it was still open but unused. A deposit of light grey sand, (1513), lay above lens (1558) and mainly comprised a large quantity of oyster shell which could have been derived from a single barrel of oysters which had perhaps gone off. A deposit of dark grey silty clay, (1505), had been dumped on top of (1558). This was covered by the uppermost fill, (1504), which consisted of orange-brown silty clay rich in fragments of clay tobacco pipes which were dated 1680–1710.

Pit (1696)/(1614)/(1625)

Pit (1696)/(1614)/(1625) was cut into the upper fills of the horn core pit (1807)/(1621); it was subrectangular in plan and was 0.42 m deep. The primary fill, (1695), was a dark grey silty clay which contained cattle horn cores which were probably redeposited from the underlying pit. Above this was a dark reddish grey silt clay, (1694), which was in turn covered by a deposit of green silt, (1607), that contained early eighteenth-century pottery. The next fill in the sequence was a dark greyish green organic-rich silt, (1599), which was overlain by a dark greenish grey sandy loam (1601). The uppermost fill, (1604), was a dark reddish grey silty clay. These fills produced a huge assemblage of domestic waste and it has been suggested that it may be derived from a household clearance. The pottery consistently dated to the late seventeenth and early eighteenth century, and mugs from fill (1599) had ale measure marks with the initials, 'AR', (Queen Anne); this places the deposition no earlier than 1702, while clay tobacco pipe bowls from the higher fills, (1601) and (1604), were dated 1710–30.

Pit group (1593), (1553), (1596), (1555) and (1612)

Pit (1696)/(1614)/(1625) was followed by a complex sequence of five intercutting pits, which appear to have been dug and then systematically filled in.

A subrectangular pit (1593) with concave sides and a flat base was cut into the upper fill, (1604), of pit (1696)/(1614)/(1625); it had excavated dimensions of 1.80 x 1.22 x 0.40 m and was aligned north–south. The fill, (1592), was a dark greyish brown silty clay and contained early eighteenth-century pottery.

Fill (1592) was partly removed during the cutting of pit (1553), which was a subrectangular pit aligned north–south with excavated dimensions of 2.23 x 0.88 x 0.4 m. The primary fill, (1552) was a dark greyish brown silty clay which was quite rich in fragments of grey roofing slate and contained pottery of seventeenth–eighteenth-century date. This was covered by upper fill (1551), which was a mid-brown silty clay and again contained seventeenth–eighteenth-century pottery.

Pit (1596) was located to the north of pit (1553); only about twenty-five percent of it had survived truncation by later features; it was probably originally sub-circular and 1.20 m deep. The fill, (1597), was a mid-grey-brown sandy silt rich in building debris, including late medieval floor tile and pottery dated to the seventeenth–eighteenth century.

Pit (1555) was cut into both the upper fill, (1551), of pit (1553) and fill (1597) of pit (1596). It was a subrectangular pit of which more than half had been removed by later pit (1545); it appeared to have been aligned north–south and was 0.44 m deep. The fill, (1554), was a mid-grey-brown silty clay containing humic material thought by the excavator to represent degraded coprolites. Pottery of late seventeenth–early eighteenth-century date was also present.

Pit (1612) was located to the north of pit (1555) and was cut into fill (1597) of pit (1596). It was 0.34 m deep. It appeared quite irregular in plan and again only survived as a fragment owing to truncation by later features. The fill, (1613), was a mottled yellowish brown silty loam which produced no datable artefacts.

Layers (1550), (1546) and (1533)

After the pit-digging had ceased in the central part of Plot 4 a series of thick layers were deposited over an area measuring 4.7 x 1.6 m. These layers were probably originally more extensive but they had been truncated to the west by terracing undertaken in Phase VIII and to the east by the cutting of pit (1545). The earliest of these layers, (1550), was 0.4 m thick and comprised a mid-grey-brown silty clay containing eighteenth-century pottery. This was covered by a layer of dark reddish grey sandy loam, (1546), which contained lenses of green silt and pottery of early eighteenth-century date. Above this was a mid-yellow-brown sandy silt 0.2 m thick which contained pottery dated to the late seventeenth–early eighteenth century. These three layers had a combined depth of nearly 1 m and were similar in character to the fills of pit (1696)/(1614)/(1625), which suggests that they may have been part of a large midden deposited in the centre of Plot 4.

Plot 5

No archaeological deposits in this plot were assigned to this phase.

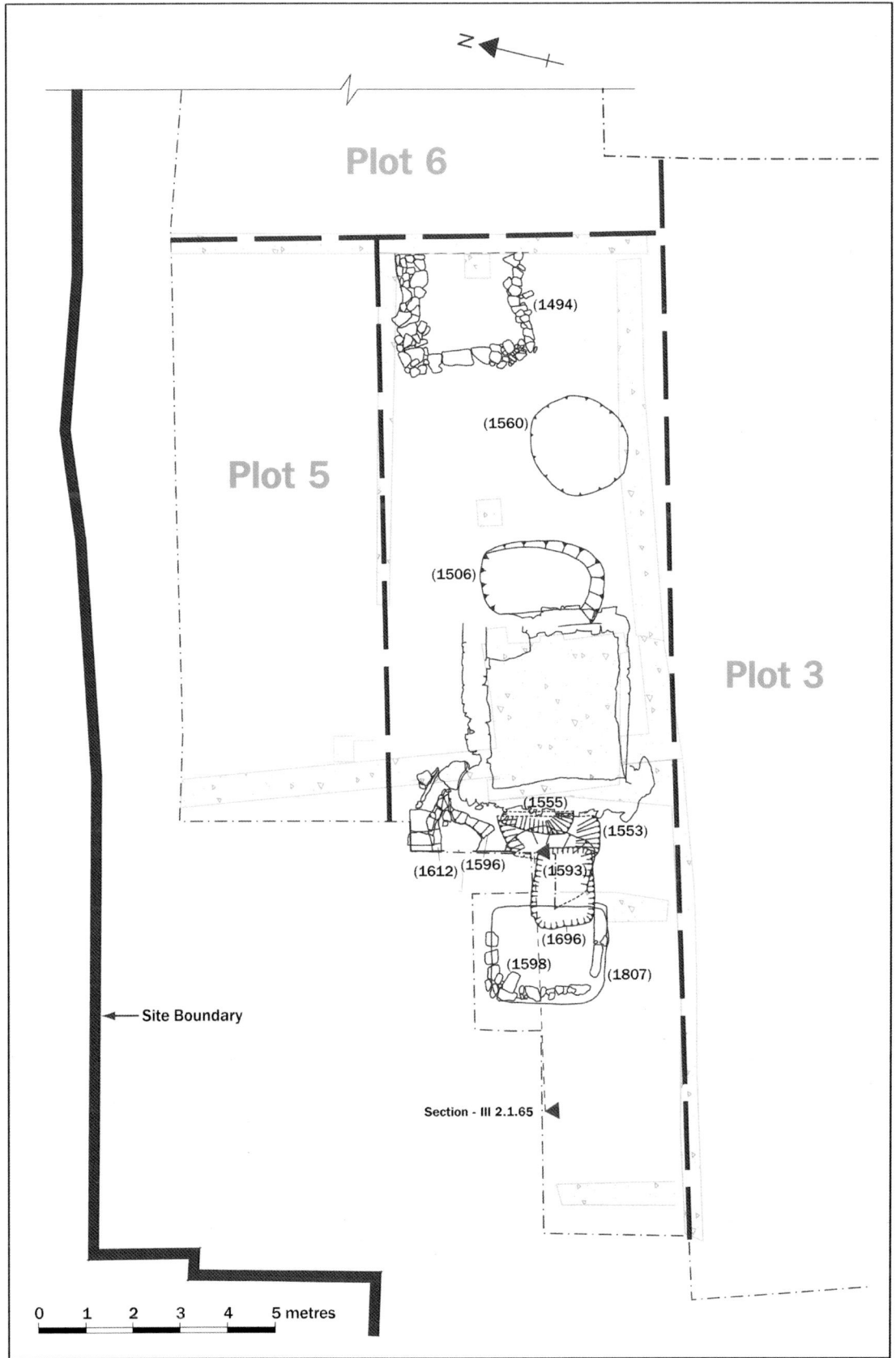

N

Plot 6

(1494)

(1560)

Plot 5

(1506)

Plot 3

(1555)

(1553)

(1612) (1596)

(1593)

(1696)

(1598)

(1807)

← Site Boundary

Section - III 2.1.65 ◄

0 1 2 3 4 5 metres

III 2.1.68 Phase VII Plot 4: plan. (Scale 1/125)

67

Plot 6 (Ills 2.1.69–.70)

Pit group (925), (923) and (922)

Only the northern end of pit (925) was found, as the remainder had been removed by a twentieth-century service trench. It was 0.58 m deep. The base was only reached in Escalator Pit A as it lay beyond the general limit of excavation. The pit was cut along the same line as the Phase VI boundary ditch. The primary fill, (924), was a yellowish brown silty clay which seemed to line the edges of the pit. This was covered by a dump of brown silty clay, (824), which appeared to represent deliberate backfilling and contained pottery dated to the late seventeenth–early eighteenth century.

After the backfilling, the northern end of the pit was partly removed by the cutting of a shallow pit, (923). The southern part of this pit had been removed by a twentieth-century boundary wall foundation, but it may have originally been circular with a diameter of 0.74 m and a depth of 0.36 m. The pit had a single fill, (928), which was a medium brown silty clay very similar in appearance to (824) and could only be distinguished by an accumulation of slate fragments which had collected towards the base of the fill. Fill (928) was again interpreted as deliberate backfilling.

An oval pit, (922), was later cut into pit fill (928) and was 0.61 m deep. This pit was filled by a deposit of mid-greyish brown clayey loam containing building debris, (686), which not only filled pit (922) but also covered the adjoining area to a depth of 0.3 m.

Building VII(i)

A collection of three post holes was identified to the south of pit group (925), (923) and (922). They appeared to be evenly spaced and of similar dimensions, suggesting that they were contemporary. The northernmost post hole, (819), was cut into Phase VI deposit (683); the fill, (818), was a dark brown clayey silt rich in brick fragments which may have served as packing material. Approximately 2 m to the south was a second post hole, (837), which had been truncated by later pitting in the vicinity. The fill, (838), was a charcoal-rich mid-grey-brown sandy clay. The third post hole, (933), lay about 2 m to the east of (837); it was filled with a mid-brown sandy silt, (932), rich in building debris. It seems likely that these post holes represent the south-western corner of an outbuilding to which a function cannot be ascribed.

Pits (929) and (679)

To the south of Building VII(i) was an irregularly shaped pit, (929), which had been partially removed at its southern end by pit (823). It had a single fill, (688), which consisted of a charcoal-rich dark brown-black silty clay, which produced late seventeenth-century pottery.

The western edge of pit (929) had been cut by pit (679); this was slightly oval in plan. The fill, (678), was a charcoal-rich dark brown sandy loam which probably formed as the result of sweepings from a domestic hearth.

Layer (560)/(388)/(389)/(817)

After pit (679) had been deliberately backfilled a layer of mid-brown loam, (560)/(388)/(389)/(817), formed over almost all of Plot 6 to a depth of 0.16 m. This layer contained an even mixture of building and domestic debris that included pottery of early eighteenth-century date. It has been interpreted as a garden/cultivation soil.

Pits (823) and (726)

After the formation of layer (560)/(388)/(389)/(817) a large oval pit, (823), was dug into the southern side of earlier pit (929); its southern extent had later been removed by the construction trench to the upstanding brick wall of Brown's department store. It was 0.4 m deep. The primary fill, (725), was a charcoal-rich dark purple-brown sandy loam which contained seventeenth-century pottery and was probably derived from domestic hearth sweepings. Upper fill (682) was a dark greyish brown clayey loam which probably represented deliberate backfill and produced pottery of eighteenth-century date.

The eastern side of pit (823) was cut by a second oval-shaped pit, (726), which had again been truncated on its southern side by the construction trench to the standing brick wall of Brown's department store; it was 0.45 m deep. The primary fill, (693), was a light brown sand containing a high proportion of small sandstone pebbles. This was covered by an upper fill of mid-brown sandy loam, (694,) containing seventeenth–eighteenth-century pottery.

Pit (940)

To the east of pit (726) was a layer of coal-rich dark brown-black sandy loam, (939), which covered an area 2 x 2.3 m in the south-eastern corner of the plot and was up to 0.18 m thick. It contained lenses of sand which demonstrated tip lines indicative of rapidly deposited material. Layer (939) was cut by an oval pit, (940), 0.47 m deep, which had been truncated on its southern side by the construction trench to the standing brick wall of Brown's department store. The fill, (941), was a mid-brown sandy loam which produced no dating evidence. Subsequently, an area of cobbled surface, (954), was laid to the north-east of pit (940) and covered an area 3.35 x 0.50 m along the eastern end of Plot 6. This surface may have been more extensive further to the east or alternatively represents a garden path.

Pits (917) and (921)

Towards the north-eastern corner of Plot 6 part of a large pit, (917), 0.65 m deep was identified; the full extent of the pit could not be ascertained owing to the limits of excavation and truncation by twentieth-century service trenches. The lower fill, (915), was a medium brown silty clay which contained a fairly even distribution of wood charcoal. Upper fill (684) was a dark brown clayey loam rich in building debris and appeared to represent deliberate backfilling. The upper fill was later covered by a layer of red sand, (912), which was rich in sandstone chippings and was interpreted as a levelling layer above the pit; the chippings may indicate stoneworking in the vicinity.

To the west of pit (917) there was a small oval-shaped pit, (921), 0.33 m deep. The fill, (920), was a slightly charcoal-rich medium brown silty clay. This feature was quite enigmatic, but may have represented the root bole from a small tree or shrub.

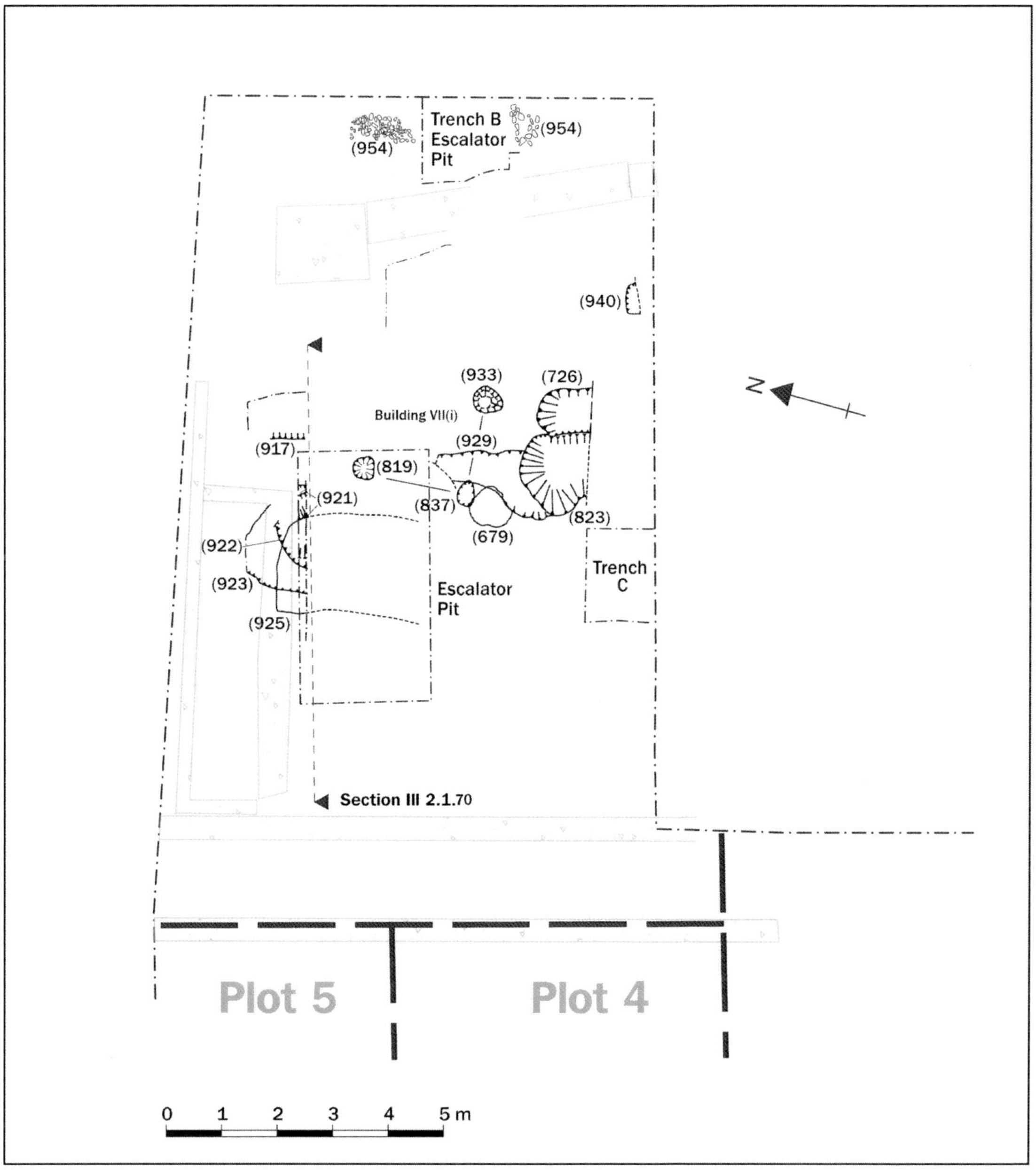

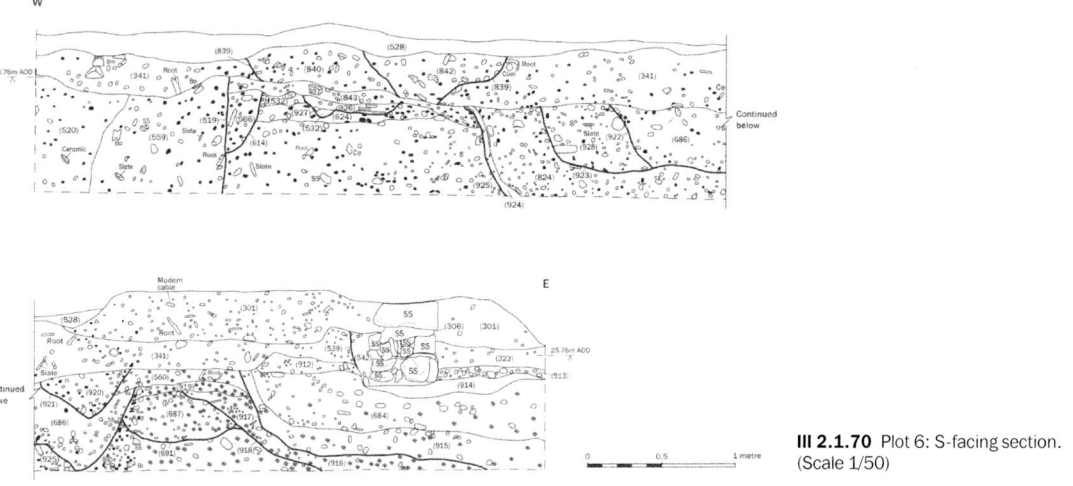

III 2.1.69 Phase VII Plot 6: plan. (Scale 1/125)

III 2.1.70 Plot 6: S-facing section. (Scale 1/50)

Phase VIII: Early 18–early 19 century

(c 1720–c 1810)

Plot 1 (Ills 2.1.72–3)

The remains of at least two separate buildings were identified in Plot 1 during Phase VIII. These tallied closely with the buildings shown on the plan of 1879 (Ill 3.1.1) suggesting that once they had been built they stayed in use for over one hundred years. The documentary research suggests that they did not exist in 1770 and that they were probably built between 1803 and 1808; they certainly appear to have been in existence by 1813, when they were purchased by John Fletcher. The plan for Plot 1 has been subdivided into Phases VIII a and b in order to illustrate developments more clearly.

Building VIII(i)

Structure VIII(i) comprised a square building at the eastern end of Plot 1 which would have originally had external dimensions of 6 x 6 m and internal dimensions of 5 x 5 m. Evidence for the lines of the north, east and west walls was still present, but the southern wall had been replaced by a massive concrete retaining wall during the construction of the Grosvenor shopping centre in the 1960s. The north wall, (575), east wall, (231), and west wall, (1888), were all constructed in the same manner, suggesting that they were part of an entirely new building on an otherwise vacant plot. In each case the walls had been set in a shallow foundation trench, (662), roughly 0.8 m wide and 0.2 m deep. The foundation itself varied slightly, as in the case of walls (231) and (1888) it consisted of a single course of red sandstone slabs, while wall (575) had an additional two courses of red sandstone blocks, (661), which had been bonded in a pale brown lime mortar and had a well dressed northern face covered in fine cross-hatched flat chisel marks. The reason for this is likely to have been that walls (231) and (1888) were in fact partition walls between adjoining terrace properties to the east and west (Structure VIII(ii)), while wall (575) was an external wall facing north and received some additional embellishment as a result. In the case of all three surviving walls, the upstanding structure was composed of hand-made bricks bonded in a soft pale brown mortar (identical to that observed in (661)), which produced a single sherd of pottery dated to the eighteenth–nineteenth century. The brickwork was two courses deep and laid in an English cross-bond pattern; it was noted that several layers of white lime wash were still adhering to the internal faces of the walls. During demolition work on the standing buildings it was noted that part of a timber roof gable had been preserved in the rebuilt upper storeys of wall (231), indicating a building at least two storeys high.

Oven/vat base (236)/(224)

There was evidence that an oven or vat base, (236)/(224), had been inserted into the south-eastern corner of Building VIII(i) after it was built. This was clearly shown by the fact that the eastern wall, (231), of the building had been given a lime mortar render prior to the construction of the oven/vat base. The base had the appearance of being semicircular in plan with an upper structure of hand-made brick, (224), which was founded on two courses of reused sandstone blocks, (236). The internal face of the brickwork had been rendered with a thin skim of lime mortar, whilst behind this the remaining space in the corner of the building had been filled with a mass of rubble sandstone and brick bonded in lime mortar.

An isolated deposit of red-brown silt, (239), covered an area 0.45 x 0.20 m immediately west of the base. The deposit was rich in charcoal/coal/ash as well as red sandstone chippings and produced pottery of seventeenth–eighteenth-century date. This material was covered by a slightly more extensive deposit of brown silty clay, (238), which contained many fragments of sandstone and lime mortar flecks.

Floor (225)/(643)

The entire internal area of Building VIII(i) had been covered with a floor surface of lime mortar, (225)/(643), which only survived as a patchy layer and contained pottery of mid-seventeenth- to mid-eighteenth-century date.

Associated features (226), (605), (603) and (234)

On the western side of Building VIII(i) there was a collection of features which appeared to run north–south, parallel with wall (1888). All three of the features had been cut into floor (225)/(643) and sub-sequently backfilled with very similar material, implying that they were broadly contemporary. It was thought that all three features were possibly associated with timber structures, and it seems possible that they might represent either the remains of a timber staircase leading up to first-floor level or alternatively a timber partition wall associated with a lobby. If either of these interpretations is valid then it would argue for the entrance to Building VIII(i) having been situated in the north-western corner.

The southernmost feature was a large sub-circular pit, (226), 0.32 m deep. The base of the pit contained one centrally placed sandstone block which seemed deliberately positioned and might have served as a pad stone for a timber post. This was covered by a dump of material made up almost entirely of red sandstone brash, (233); above this was an upper fill of sandstone rubble, (227). Both fills (233) and (227) were suggestive of deliberate backfilling and produced pottery of seventeenth–eighteenth-century date.

To the north of pit (226) was a short slot, (605), 0.40 m deep. It had a flat base, which suggested that it was intended to accommodate a structural element such as a short length of timber sill beam. To the north of this slot was an oval pit, (603), 0.20 m deep, possibly a post hole. Both slot (605) and pit (603) were filled with a reddish brown sandstone brash, ((604) and (602) respectively), which was identical to the lower fill, (233), of pit (226); (604) produced pottery of eighteenth-century date.

A fourth pit, (234), was also filled with a red-brown sandstone brash, (235), which produced pottery dated 1720+; however, it had no direct relationship with features (226), (605) or (603) and it remains enigmatic.

Pits (228), (654), (657) and (219)

There is some evidence to suggest that Building VIII(i) went through a period of disuse or abandonment as a series of pits was identified cutting into floor surface (225)/(643).

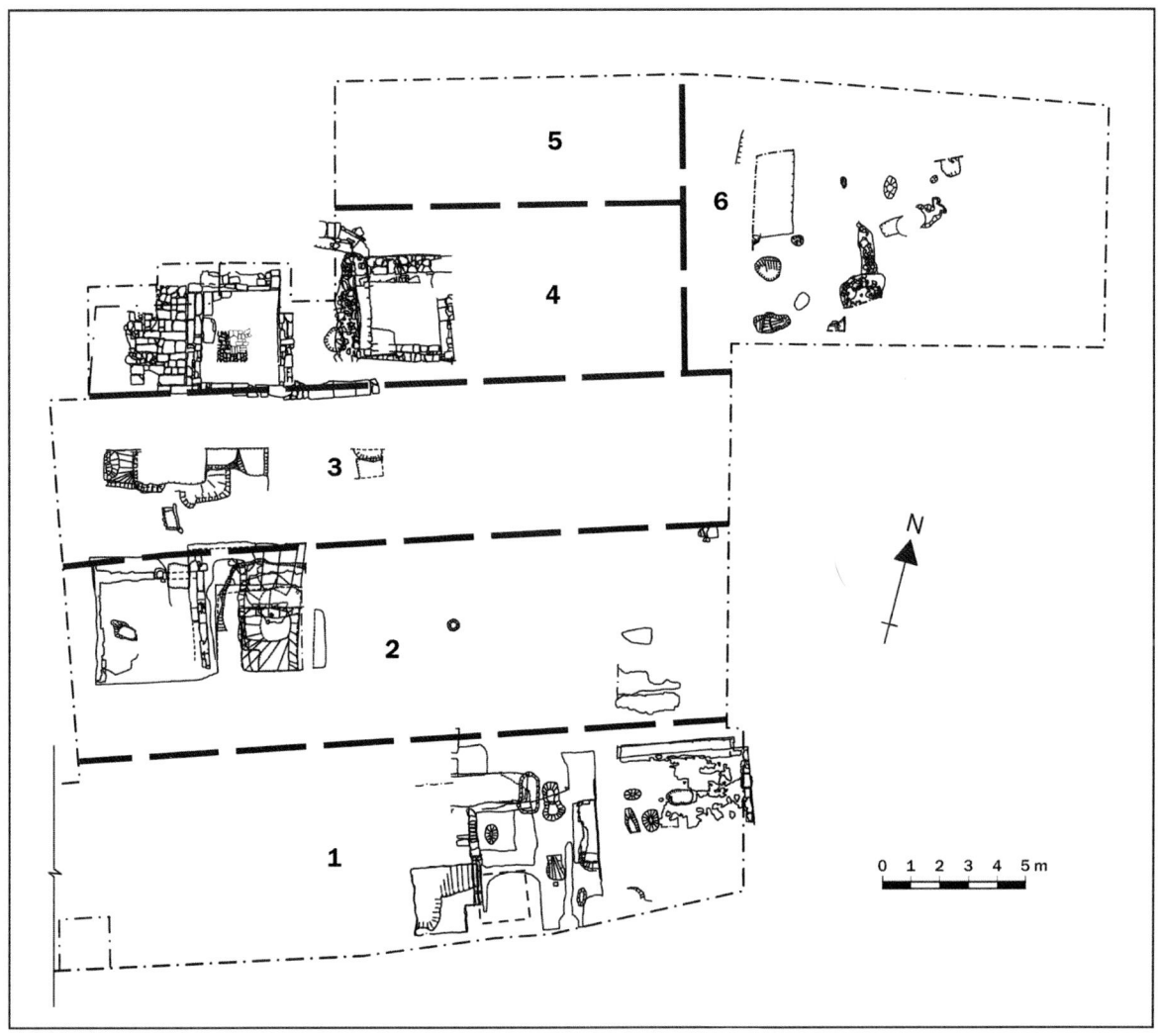

III 2.1.71 Phase VIII: general arrangement of plots. (Scale 1/250)

A sub-circular pit, (228), 0.37 m deep, was identified in the south-western corner of Building VIII(i). The fill, (229), was a mid-greyish brown silty sand which was rich in fragments of coal and clinker likely to be sweepings from a domestic hearth. Approximately 2 m to the north of pit (228) was a sub-circular pit, (654), 0.35 m deep. The fill, (653), was a mid-brown clayey silt which contained pottery dated to the mid-eighteenth century or later. Less than 1 m to the north-east of pit (654) there was another subrectangular pit, (657), 0.60 m deep. The fill, (656), was a greyish brown silty loam which again contained pottery dated to the mid-eighteenth century or later.

The largest of these pits was a subrectangular pit, (219), which was situated in the southern half of the building and was 1 m deep. The lower three fills of this pit, (223), (221) and (222), consisted of brown loams which were very similar to the soils the pit was dug into, suggesting that they represented redeposited upcast. Above these fills was a dump of mortar and sand, (220), containing building debris and pottery of late seventeenth–eighteenth-century date. This was covered by upper fill (218), which comprised a greyish brown sandy silt very similar in character to the overlying layer, (207); fill (218) produced eighteenth-century pottery and a gaming counter fashioned from a broken sherd of pottery.

Layer (207)
The fills of pit group (228), (654), (657) and (219) were subsequently covered with a layer of dark greyish brown sandy silt, (207), which covered the entire interior of Building VIII(i). Layer (207) produced pottery dated to the eighteenth century and a copper alloy button of eighteenth–nineteenth-century date; it also contained a selection of gaming counters fashioned from broken sherds of pottery and a die made from a piece of animal bone. This layer was thought to have accumulated during reoccupation of Building VIII(i) and was sampled, <5004>.

Building VIII(ii)
Building VIII(ii) comprised a square building immediately to the west of Building VIII(i) and would have originally had external dimensions of 6 x 5 m and internal dimensions of 5 x 4 m. Evidence for the lines of the east wall (1888) and west wall (1810) was still present in the archaeological record, but the southern wall had been replaced by a massive concrete retaining wall during the construction of the Grosvenor shopping centre in the 1960s. The northern wall had been removed and all that remained was the robber trench, (1909), which had been backfilled with a mix of building debris rich in fragments of lime mortar, (1908); this was done prior to the digging

71

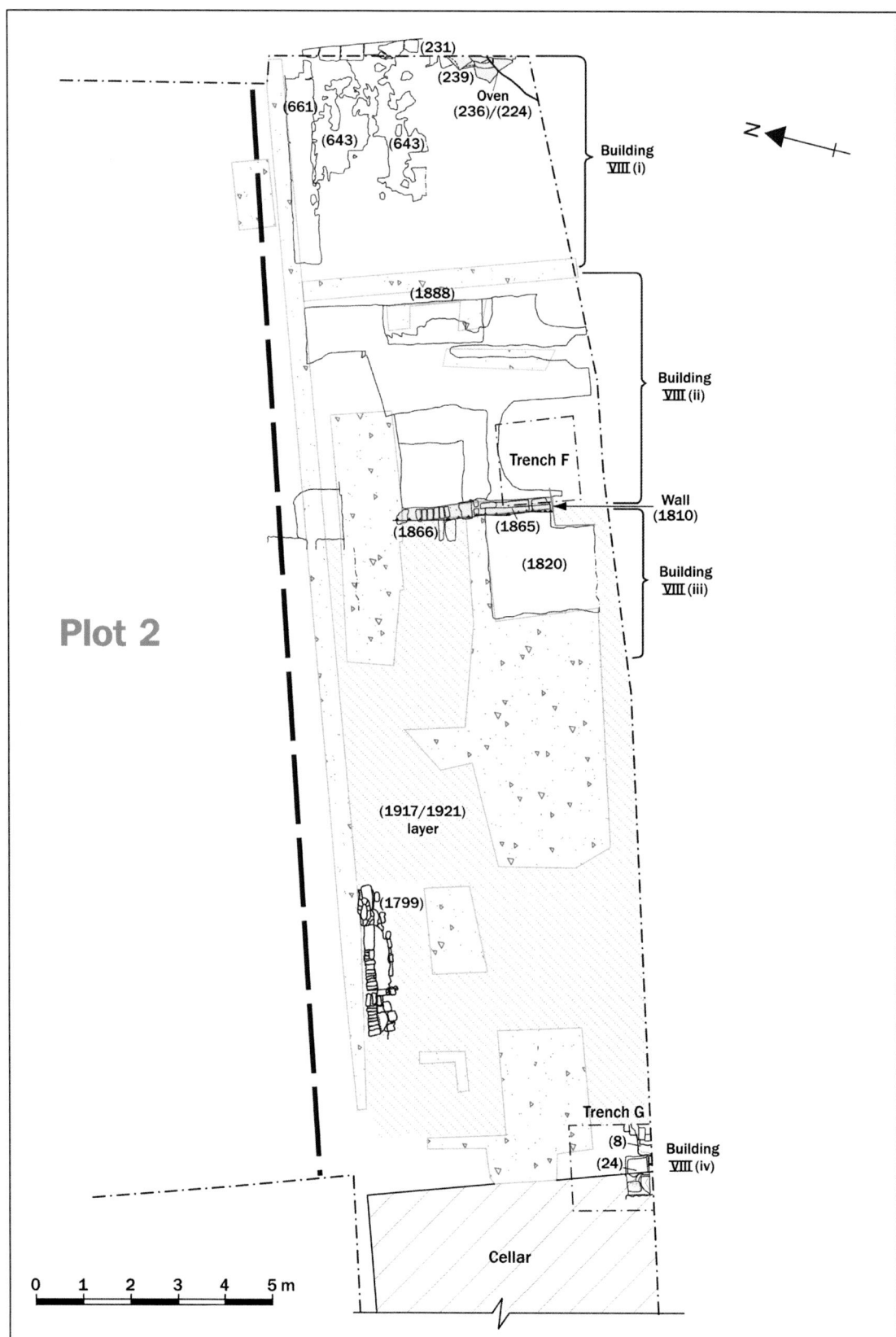

III 2.1.72 Phase VIIIa Plot 1: plan. (Scale 1/125)

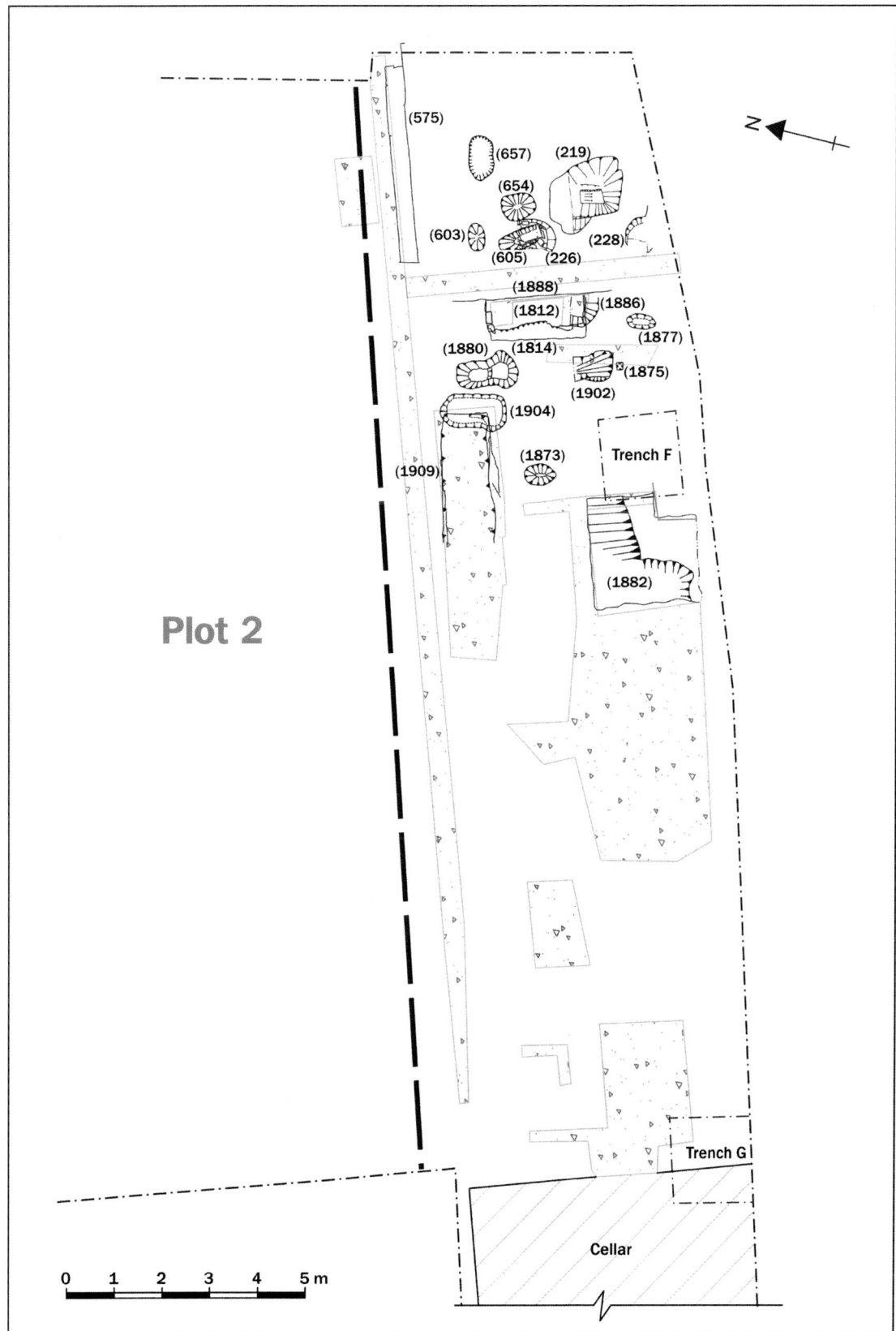

Plot 2

(575)

(657)

(219)

(654)

(603)

(605) (226) (228)

(1888)

(1812) (1886)

(1877)

(1880) (1814)

(1875)

(1902)

(1904)

Trench F

(1909)

(1873)

(1882)

(1882)

Trench G

Cellar

0   1   2   3   4   5 m

III 2.1.73   Phase VIIIb Plot 1: plan. (Scale 1/125)

73

of another construction trench thought to be associated with alterations to Fletcher's Buildings during Phase IX. The details of the construction methods used for wall (1888) are described above under the description for Building VIII(i). Wall (1810) was set in a shallow foundation trench, (1866), which was 0.52 m wide and 0.24 m deep; the wall foundation itself was comprised entirely of hand-made brick bonded in lime mortar and survived to a height of two courses. A backfill deposit of brown silty sand, (1867), within the foundation trench produced pottery dated 1720+. Walls (1888) and (1810) were thought to form partitions between adjoining terrace properties to the east and west (Buildings VIII(i) and (iii)).

Pits (1886), (1902), (1880) and (1904)

Unlike in Building VIII(i) no floor surfaces were identified within Building VIII(ii) and it was therefore impossible to be certain whether this group of pits predated the building or were dug into the floor in the same manner as some of the pits in Building VIII(i). However, it is clear that pit (1886) had been backfilled prior to the construction of brick chimney breast (1812), but it is not clear whether or not the pit also predated wall (1888). The pits appeared to be arranged in two pairs, (1886) being parallel with (1902) and (1880) being parallel with (1904). As pits (1886) and (1902) appear to have functioned as cess pits it is tempting to draw on the documentary research which has several references associated with the Fletchers to 'two houses of convenience' or 'two privies'.

Pit (1886) was located along the eastern edge of Building VIII(ii) and was cut on its northern side by the construction trench (1814) of brick chimney breast (1812). It was sub-circular with a depth of 0.52 m. The fill, (1885), was a greyish green silt that was cess-like in appearance and contained pottery and clay tobacco pipes of seventeenth–nineteenth-century date.

Less than 1 m to the west of pit was a subrectangular pit, (1902), 0.25 m deep. The fill, (1901), was a coal-flecked dark yellowish brown sand silt containing pottery of seventeenth–eighteenth-century date.

On the northern side of the building was a small 'hour-glass'-shaped pit, (1880), 0.4 m deep. The fill, (1879), was a greyish brown silty clay containing large amounts of building debris including grey roofing slate and sandstone fragments suggestive of deliberate backfilling. The fill, (1879), again produced pottery of seventeenth–eighteenth-century date.

Adjacent to the western side of pit (1880) was an oval pit, (1904), 0.15 m deep. The fill, (1903), was a mid-brown silty clay containing a high percentage of grey roofing slate fragments and pottery of seventeenth–eighteenth-century date.

Chimney breast (1812)

Approximately midway along the length of wall (1888) was a rectangular foundation trench, (1814), measuring 2.3 x 0.9 x 0.4 m. It contained a hollow three-sided brick and stone structure, (1812), 2.3 x 0.63 x 0.42 m, with the fourth side being formed by wall (1888). It was constructed from reused sandstone blocks and hand-made bricks bonded in lime mortar. It had clearly been added after wall (1888) was built and had the appearance of the base

to a brick chimney breast. Within (1812) was a deposit of black-brown silty clay, (1871), containing large lumps of unburnt coal; the deposit also produced pottery of eighteenth–nineteenth-century date and a number of copper alloy pins. The upper part of the interior of structure (1812) contained a deposit of light greyish brown sand, (1813), which contained a large percentage of brick rubble and flecks of lime mortar; it also produced pottery dated to the mid-eighteenth century or later.

Layer (19)/(1819)

After the construction of the chimney breast the whole of the interior of the building was covered with a layer of dark yellowish brown loam, (1819), which contained pottery of early eighteenth-century date. It is not clear whether this layer represents an occupation deposit associated with people living in Building VIII(ii) or abandonment/disuse of the property.

Associated features (18), (1875), (1877) and (1873)

After the formation of layer (1819) a series of features were dug within the building. The general nature of these features suggests that the building was not being used as a dwelling at the time.

Towards the southern side of the building there was evidence for a single timber stake hole of square section, (1875). The fill, (1874), was a mid-brownish grey sand containing flecks of mortar and mid-eighteenth- to nineteenth-century pottery.

To the east of stake hole (1875) was a shallow oval-shaped pit, (1877), 0.12 m deep. The base of the pit was occupied by the skeleton a single adult cat, with the remainder of the fill, (1876), comprising a mid-reddish brown silty clay. Quite clearly this pit was dug in order to bury the cat.

On the western edge of the building, adjacent to wall (1810), there was an oval pit, (1873), 0.21 m deep. The fill, (1872), was a dark brown silt containing building debris and pottery of eighteenth-century date.

In the south-western corner of the building there was another oval pit, (18), 0.35 m deep. The fill, (17), was a dark greyish black loam containing a lot of building debris indicative of deliberate backfilling.

Building VIII(iii)

Building VIII(iii) lay immediately west of VIII(ii). The evidence for the building had largely been removed by twentieth-century disturbance mainly associated with the construction of a large concrete base for a printing press. The only structural element remaining was the partition wall, (1810), described under Building VIII(ii) above. However, Building VIII(iii) can be inferred from the plan of 1879 and by the presence of a lime mortar floor, (1820), which was identical to floor (225)/(643) found in Building VIII(i). This floor was found in the south-eastern quadrant of the building and was about 10 mm thick. The mortar contained lenses of soft building sand within it.

Layer (1917)/(1921)

To the north and west of Buildings VIII(ii) and VIII(iii) there was an extensive layer of dark brown clay silt, (1917)/(1921), which was rich in building debris and was interpreted as a demolition or levelling layer.

Layer (1837)

The western end of Plot 1 was covered by a layer of reddish brown silty clay, (1837), that was 0.20 m thick and contained pottery of late seventeenth–eighteenth-century date. Layer (1837) was rich in building debris and was interpreted as a demolition or levelling layer; as such it may be broadly contemporary with layer (1917)/(1921).

Building VIII(iv)

Structural evidence for Building VIII(iv) was observed within Evaluation Trench G at the western end of Plot 1 and was also represented by brick wall (799). The evidence consisted of a small section of north–south wall, (8), built in a shallow foundation trench, (25). It comprised a foundation course of red sandstone blocks on which was set a course of hand-made bricks bonded in a light brown lime mortar. At its southern end the wall was bonded to an east–west wall, (24), which only survived as a foundation course of sandstone blocks lying beneath the upstanding northern wall of the Grosvenor shopping centre. Wall (24) was built within a shallow foundation trench, (29), which also contained a backfill deposit, (30), containing seventeenth–eighteenth-century pottery.

Floor (3)

In the corner of Building VIII(iv) as defined by walls (8) and (24) there was a small area covered by a patchy layer of lime mortar, (3). This was interpreted as the remnants of a mortar floor which was probably contemporary with the floor (643)/(225) found in Building VIII(i) and floor (1820) found in Building VIII(iii).

Plot 2 (Ills 2.1.74–6)

As with Plot 1 the plan for Plot 2 has been subdivided into Phases VIIIa and b in order to show the development of the plot more clearly.

Layer (649)

In the south-eastern corner of Plot 2 a layer of dark yellowish brown silty clay, (649), covered an area approximately 2 x 1 m and was rich in building debris including fragments of decorated medieval floor tile. It also produced seventeenth–eighteenth-century pottery.

Sandstone wall (648)/(647)

To the south of layer (649) was the remnant of a brick and sandstone wall, (647), built in a shallow foundation trench (498). It consisted of blocks and roughly shaped fragments, with a brick rubble core, (648); the whole structure was bonded in a mixture of pale brown mortar and red clay. The location of this structure tallies with a boundary wall shown on the plan of 1879 adjacent to the 'ashpit' and 'closets' and this may well have been its original function; wall (647) closely follows the line of earlier southern boundary walls between Plots 1 and 2.

Sandstone wall (645)

Another fragment of wall, (645), survived in the north-eastern corner of Plot 2 and consisted of sandstone blocks of varying size bonded in lime mortar. No obvious function can be attached to this fragment. Late eighteenth–early nineteenth-century pottery was recovered from the foundation trench.

Cess pit (848)

Along the eastern edge of Plot 2, and at the limit of excavation, the very edge of a large sub-circular cess pit, (848), was encountered. This pit had been almost totally removed by the cutting of a Phase IX foundation trench, (582). The fill of the pit, (847), consisted of a green silt which contained pottery dated 1760+. The top of the pit had been capped with a deposit of sand and clay, (488), which contained clay tobacco pipes dated 1680–1720.

Post hole (1306)

Towards the centre of Plot 2 a single circular post hole, (1306), was identified. The fill, (1305), was a dark brown clayey silt rich in building debris which produced pottery of seventeenth–eighteenth-century date.

Pit (1642)

Towards the western end of Plot 2 there was a large subrectangular pit, (1642), 0.5 m deep. The fill, (1636), was a mid-brown silt rich in fragments of grey roofing slate, which appeared to be the result of deliberate backfilling. The fill contained pottery dating from 1720 to the middle of the eighteenth century. Although the base of the pit was not reached within the limits of the excavation, it is likely that it represented a backfilled cess pit. The southern end of the pit had subsequently been partly covered by a deposit of red-brown sandstone brash, (1652).

Layers (1439) and (1737)

The western half of Plot 2 was covered by an extensive layer of light brown clayey silt, (1439), which produced clay tobacco pipes dated 1610–1730. This was interpreted as a deliberately deposited levelling layer, as it contained an almost complete jar, which was unlikely to have survived intact in, for example, a cultivation soil. Along the northern side of Plot 2 a layer of orange-brown clayey silt, (1737), had been deposited on top of layer (1439) in an east–west band covering an area of 3.22 x 0.6 m.

Pits (1441), (1647) and (1444)

Layer (1439) was cut by a series of pits. Pit (1441) was a steep-sided, sub-circular shaped cut 0.28 m deep. It had a single fill, (1440), of purple-brown sandy silt which contained building debris and domestic waste.

Pit (1647) was square in plan with vertical sides and a flat base, 0.37 m deep. The primary fill, (1646), was a thin deposit of dark greyish brown silty clay lining the base of the pit and was rich in fragments of coal and charcoal. The remainder of the pit was filled with a dump of dark greyish brown silty clay, (1645), which was rich in domestic waste including pottery dated 1720–50.

Pit (1444) was located in the same place as earlier pit (1642) and might represent a hollow caused by the settlement of the earlier pit fills rather than a new pit cut. It had a subrectangular shape and was 0.65 m deep. The lower fill, (1443), was composed entirely of pieces of broken purple-grey roofing slate (some perforated with nail holes), which almost certainly came from the reroofing of a building in the vicinity. The upper fill, (1447), was a dark brown sandy clay containing lenses of ash and clinker which were probably derived from domestic hearth sweepings.

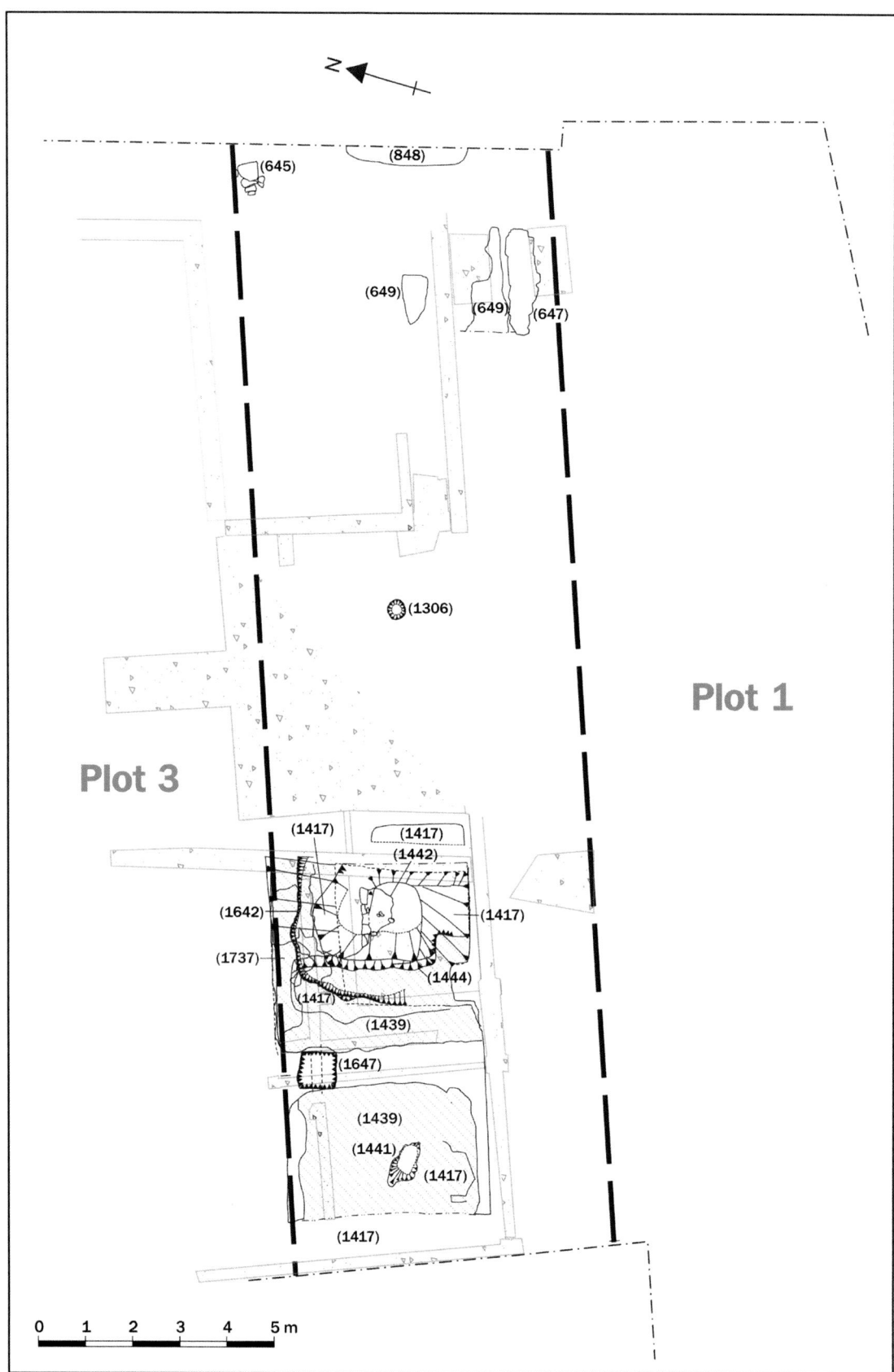

III 2.1.74 Phase VIIIa Plot 2: plan. (Scale 1/125)

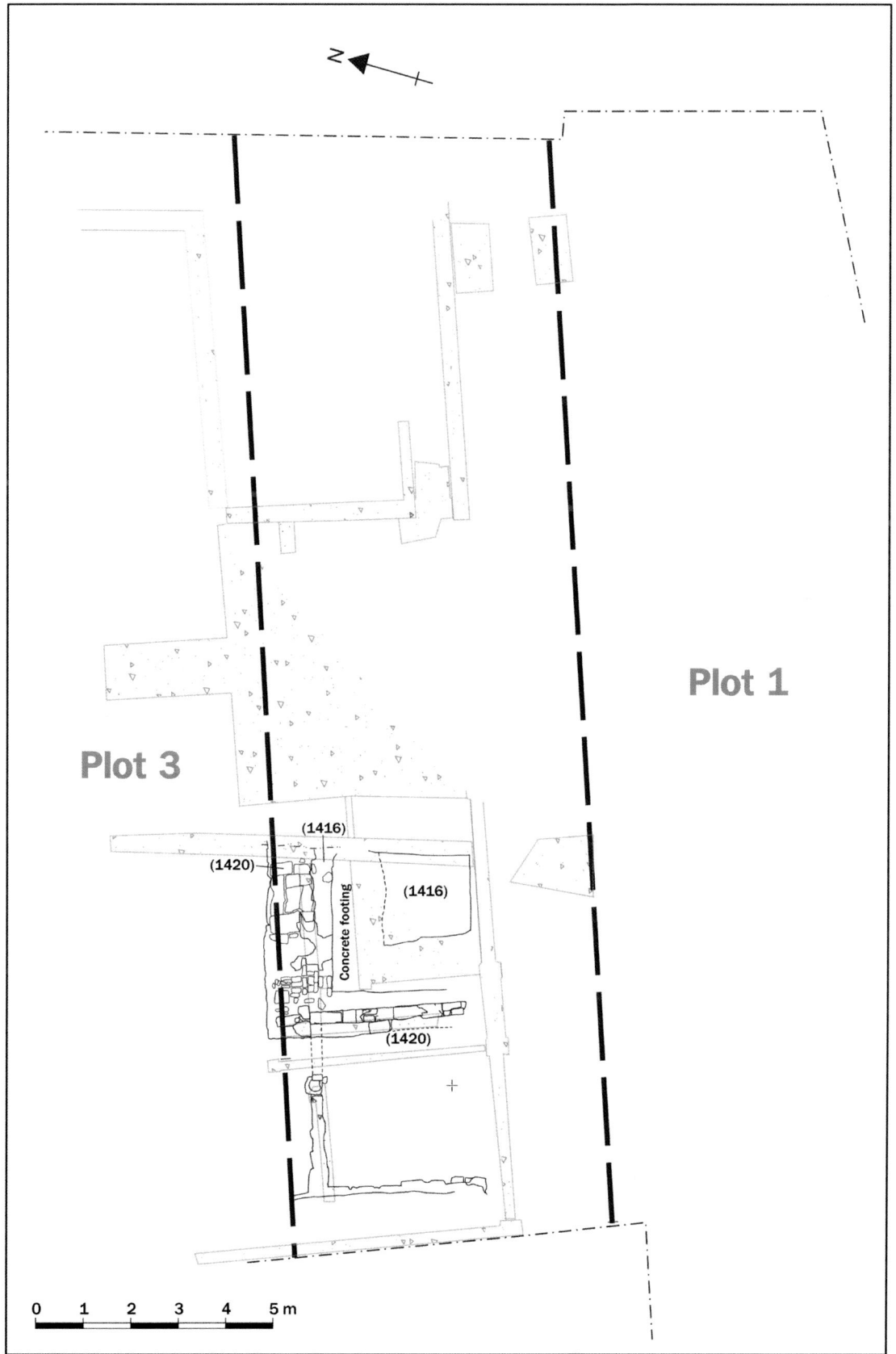

Plot 1

Plot 3

(1416)

(1420)

(1416)

Concrete footing

(1420)

0 1 2 3 4 5 m

Ill 2.1.75 Phase VIIIb Plot 2: plan. (Scale 1/125)

Hearth (1442)

Hearth (1442) sat above backfilled pit (1444) and consisted of a single course of sandstone blocks bonded with red clay. To the south of these sandstone blocks there was a roughly semicircular area of fire-reddened clay and the entire structure had excavated dimensions of 1.25 x 1.00 x 0.10 m

Layer (1432)

Pits (1441), (1647) and hearth (1442) were subsequently covered by a layer of dark brown sandy clay, (1432), which covered an area approximately 5 x 4 m. Layer (1432) contained some domestic waste including pottery dated to the late seventeenth–eighteenth century and was interpreted as a levelling layer associated with the construction of Building VIII(v).

Building VIII(v)

Building VIII(v) was situated at the western end of Plot 2 and, as with Buildings VIII(i) to (iv) in Plot 1, it was thought to be generally in the right place for one of the houses shown on the northern side of the Fletcher's Buildings passage. The north, east and west wall foundations to Building VIII(v) survived and indicated a square building plan with external dimensions of approximately 4 x 4 m. Within the building fragments of two surviving floor surfaces were identified, implying that an internal partition had originally existed on a north–south alignment.

Floor (1420)

Prior to the laying of floor (1420) a series of make-up layers were deposited within the general footprint of Building VIII(v). The earliest of these layers was a mortar-rich brown silt, (1421), which contained pottery dated to the mid-eighteenth century or later. This was covered

by a layer of fairly clean yellow sand, (1417), which produced a halfpenny of George II dated 1727–60. Floor surface (1420) only survived in a patchy state owing to truncation by later phases of building; it comprised a mixture of sandstone flags and hand-made bricks bonded in a grey-white lime mortar which covered an area 3 x 3 m. The north, east and west edges of this floor were delimited by sandstone wall foundations on which there had been a brick superstructure which survived to a height of three courses in places and was bonded in grey-white lime mortar (Ill 2.1.76).

Floor (1416)

There had clearly been an internal partition within Building VIII(v), as the western part of the building's footprint was covered by a layer of white lime mortar, (1416), which covered an area 2.1 x 1.85 m and contained eighteenth-century pottery. This had again been laid above levelling sand (1417) and was thus thought to be contemporary with (1420). Layer (1416) was interpreted as an internal floor surface identical in character to floor surface (225)/ (643) in Building VIII(i) in Plot 1.

Plot 3 (Ills 2.1.77–9)

Pits (1681) and (1686)

A layer of brick and sandstone rubble, (1689), had been deposited towards the centre of Plot 3. This was cut by a subrectangular pit, (1681), which had been heavily truncated by the construction of a brick cellar during the late nineteenth or early twentieth century. Its fill, (1684), produced pottery of late seventeenth-early eighteenth–century date. The northern edge of the pit had been removed by pit (1686), which was sub-circular and 0.42 m deep. The northern half of pit (1686) had been truncated by twentieth-century concrete foundations. Its fill, (1687), produced eighteenth-century pottery.

To the east of pits (1681) and (1686) a couple of deposits were identified which were thought to be the fills of a cess pit. Unfortunately all of the edges of this pit had been removed by nineteenth- and twentieth-century construction trenches and none of the dimensions could be ascertained. The earlier deposit was a purple silt, (1701), which contained ash and clinker probably derived from domestic hearth sweepings; this was sealed by (1700). Both deposits (1701) and (1700) had a diameter in excess of 2.2 m and produced pottery dating to the early to mid-eighteenth century (Ill 2.1.77).

Ill 2.1.76 Phase VIII Plot 2: floor (1420), looking W.

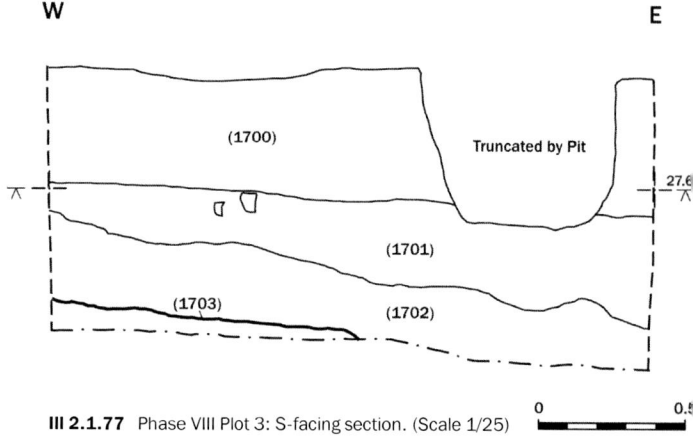

Ill 2.1.77 Phase VIII Plot 3: S-facing section. (Scale 1/25)

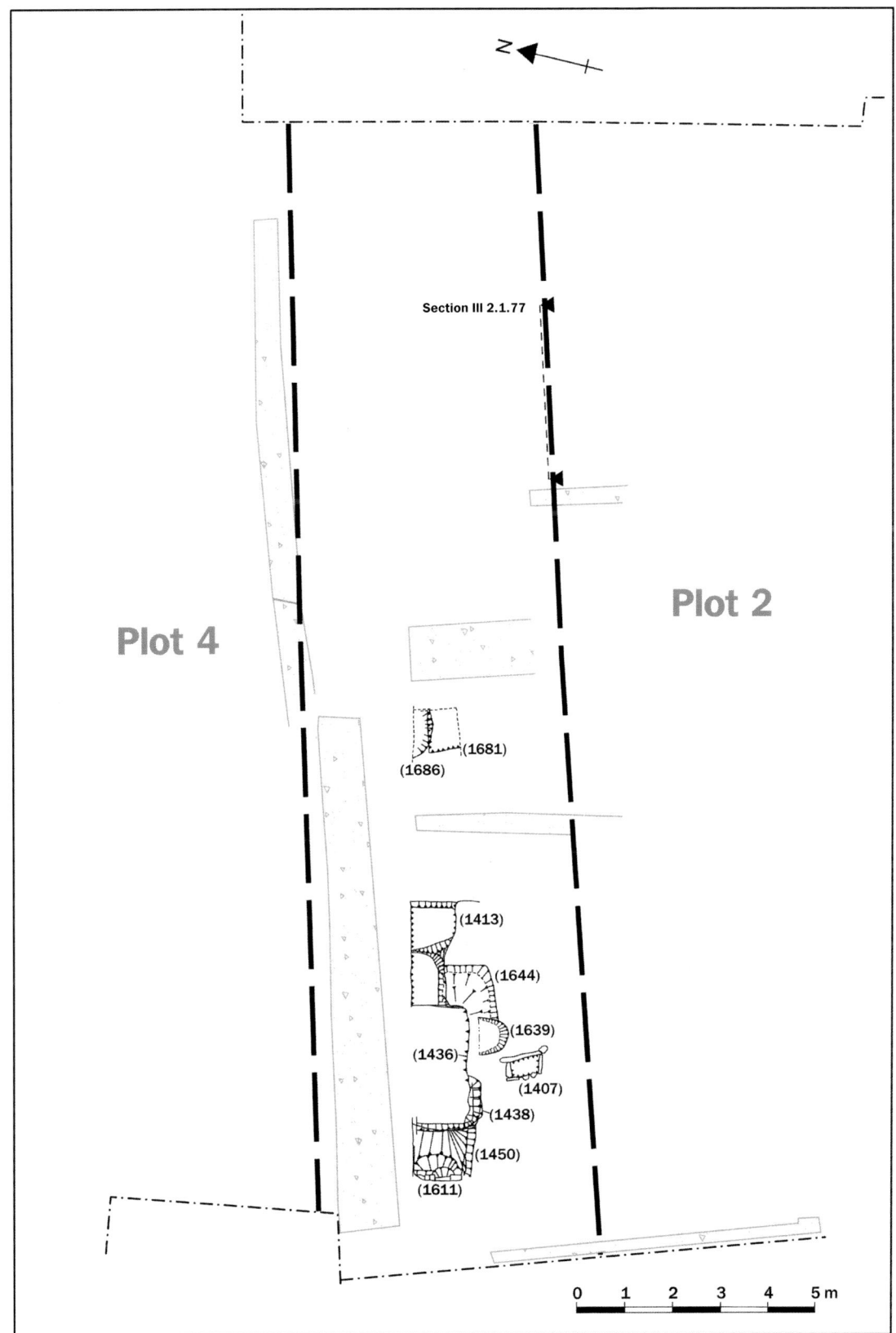

Section III 2.1.77

Plot 4

Plot 2

(1681)
(1686)

(1413)

(1644)

(1639)

(1436)

(1407)

(1438)

(1450)

(1611)

0   1   2   3   4   5 m

III 2.1.78   Phase VIII Plot 3: plan. (Scale 1/125)

Layer (1637)

At the western end of Plot 3 a layer of charcoal-rich dark brown silty sand, (1637, had been deposited over an area 2.47 x 2.05 m. This layer contained a lot of building debris, including a high percentage of grey roofing slate fragments; it also produced pottery of eighteenth-century date and fragments of sugar mould.

Pits (1413), (1644) and (1639)

Layer (1637) had been cut by three successive pits, (1413), (1644) and (1639); all of these pits had been partly removed on their northern sides by later pit (1436). The southern part of pit (1413) had also been removed by a twentieth-century concrete pier base. The base of the pit was defined by a thin lens of green silt which implied that its primary function had been as a cess pit. The bulk of the fill, (1406), was a dark brown sandy silt rich in building debris and domestic waste, suggestive of deliberate backfilling. It produced pottery dated 1720+ and clay tobacco pipes dated 1610–1750.

The second of these pits was (1644), which was 0.53 m deep. The primary fill, (1648), was a thin band of yellowish green silty clay, again suggesting that the primary function had been as a cess pit. The upper fill, (1643), was a charcoal-rich brown sandy silt containing a high percentage of sandstone fragments, which was thought to represent deliberate backfilling.

The latest pit, (1639), was sub-circular and 0.36 m deep. It had been backfilled in a single event with a dark brown sandy silt, (1638), which contained a lot of building debris and a late medieval copper alloy hooked tag.

Layer (1405)

After the backfilling of pit (1639) an extensive layer of dark brown loam, (1405), was deposited over the western end of Plot 3 and covered an area 4.65 x 3.1 m. This layer was rich in building debris and contained lenses of charcoal which may indicate tipping lines for a succession of imported materials; it also contained pottery of late seventeenth–eighteenth-century date.

Pits (1450), (1438), (1436) and (1611)

At the western end of Plot 3 a succession of pits was dug into layer (1405).

Pit (1450) was only partially exposed within the excavation; its eastern and western edges had been removed by later pits (1438) and (1611) respectively; it was 0.77 m deep. This pit appeared to have been lined with a thin layer of clay, above which was a cess-like lens of green silt. The lowest fill encountered was a mid-reddish brown silt, (1449), which contained rare lenses of white lime. The upper fill, (1448), was a mid-brownish black silty loam that was rich in building debris and produced pottery of late seventeenth–early eighteenth-century date.

Pit (1438) had partly removed pit (1450) and had itself had been heavily truncated by the cutting of later pit (1436); its was 0.69 m deep. The primary fill, (1437), was a charcoal-rich mid-yellowish green silty clay likely to be derived from the use of the feature as a cess pit. The upper fill, (1445), was a dump of reddish brown silty clay rich in building debris and containing pottery of seventeenth–eighteenth-century date.

Pit (1436) had partly removed the eastern side of pit (1438). Its northern half had in turn been removed by

later cut (1415); it was 0.40 m deep. The fill, (1435), was a dark purple ash-rich silt which contained abundant fragments of coal and was probably derived from domestic hearth sweepings.

Pit (1611) had partly removed the western side of pit (1450) and had itself been truncated on its western side by twentieth-century concrete wall footing (1400); it was 0.28 m deep. The fill, (1610), was a mid-grey-green silty clay which contained moderate amounts of charcoal and late seventeenth-century pottery.

Hearth (1407)

To the south of pit group (1450), (1438), (1436) and (1611) was a subrectangular sandstone structure, (1407), which consisted of slabs of sandstone set on edge to line all four sides of a construction cut, (1446). The base of the cut was covered by a single horizontally laid sandstone slab. The structure had the overall appearance of a hollow chamber measuring 1.0 x 0.61 x 0.37 m which was interpreted as the base of a domestic hearth (Ill 2.1.79). The interior had initially been filled with a thin deposit of black silt, (1409), which had the appearance of soot and contained carbonised material. This was covered by a dump of light grey ash-like silt, (1408), which was rich in fragments of mortar and produced pottery of seventeenth–eighteenth-century date.

Ill 2.1.79 Phase VIII Plot 3: hearth (1407), looking E.

Plot 4 (Ills 2.1.80–3)

Stone-lined cess pit (1371)

Stone-lined cess pit (1371) was located towards the centre of Plot 4 and sat within a square construction cut, (1545), 4.16 m deep. Only the upper 1.4 m of this pit was excavated as the lower portion lay beyond the limits of excavation. The lining, (1371), was exposed to a height of 1.94 m on the western side, suggesting that much of the upper 0.5 m of the pit had been removed during twentieth-century construction work associated with the *Chester Chronicle* print works. The lining itself consisted of roughly shaped sandstone rubble bonded in puddled red clay (Ill 2.1.81).

The remains of a culvert, (1379), fed into the northwestern corner of the cess pit. This was constructed in a shallow curvilinear trench, (1384), 0.5 m deep. It was built entirely of red sandstone and consisted of a base of slabs onto which had been built a pair of walls one course high; these supported a capping of further slabs (Ill

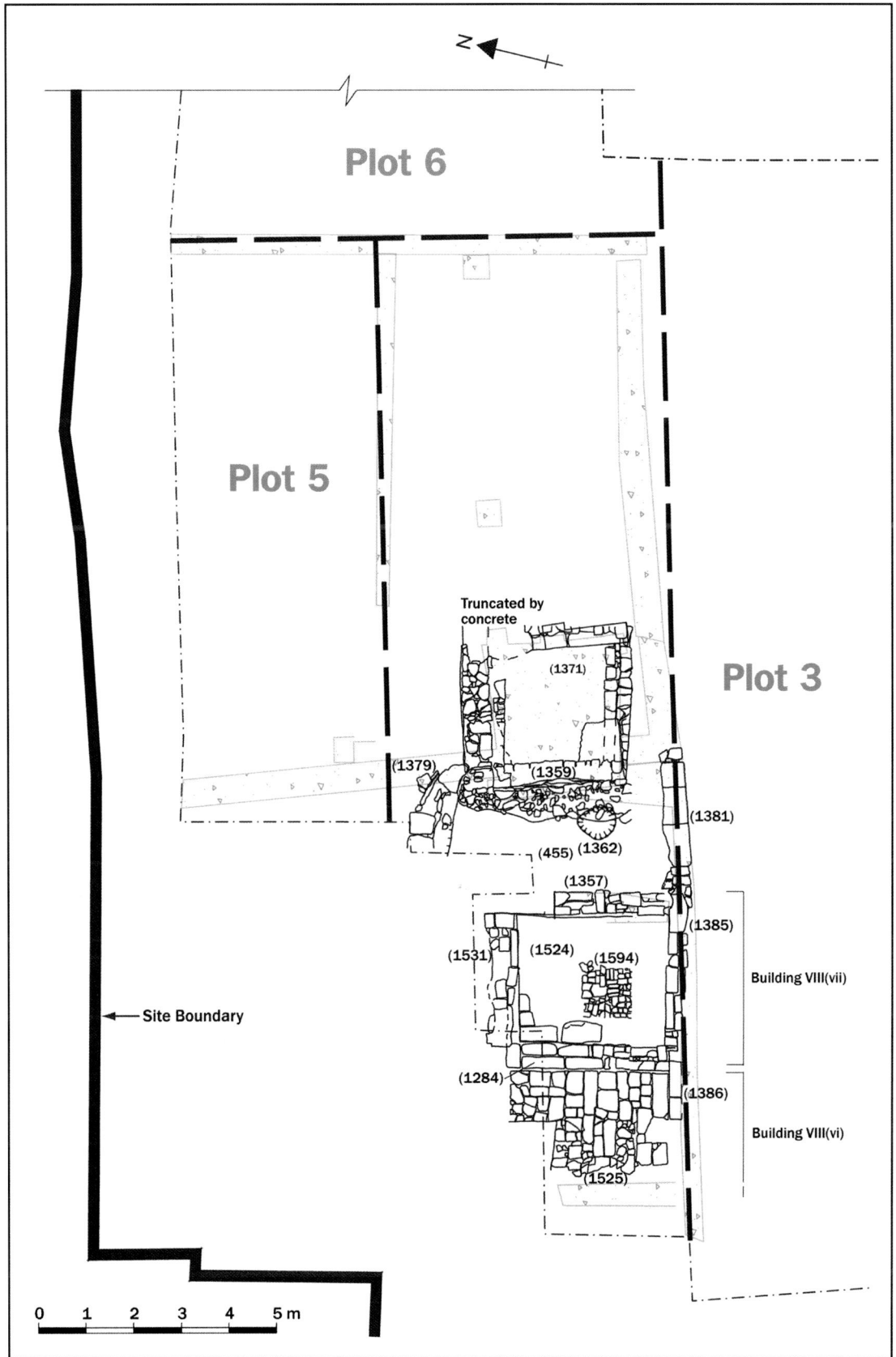

Plot 6

Plot 5

Plot 3

Truncated by concrete

(1371)

(1379)

(1359)

(1381)

(455) (1362)

(1357)

(1385)

(1531)

(1524)

(1594)

Building VIII(vii)

(1284)

(1386)

Building VIII(vi)

(1525)

← Site Boundary

0 1 2 3 4 5 m

III 2.1.80 Phase VIII Plot 4: plan. (Scale 1/125)

III 2.1.81 Phase VIII Plot 4: cess pit (1371), looking W.

III 2.1.82 Phase VIII Plot 4: culvert (1379), looking NW.

2.1.82). The culvert had eventually become choked with a greyish black sandy silt, (1380), which was heavily disturbed by modern animal burrowing.

Layer (455)/(1538)

Either after or during the construction of the cess pit a thick deposit of dark greyish brown sandy loam, (455)/(1538), was evenly spread over an area 2.4 x 5.15 m immediately to the west. This deposit contained lenses of green cess-like silt, cattle horn cores and residual pottery of late seventeenth–early eighteenth-century date and was thought to be associated with the upcast from the excavation of pit (1371).

Post hole (1362)

On the eastern side of layer (455)/(1538) a large sub-circular post hole (1362) had subsequently been excavated. The sides of the cut were lined with large sandstone fragments, (1361), which would have served as

packing material around the post. The post pipe itself was filled with a dark brown silty clay, (1360), containing late seventeenth–early eighteenth-century pottery. This post hole is hard to interpret but it possibly represents a repair to the superstructure which would have originally stood above cess pit (1371).

Southern boundary wall (1386), (1385) and (1381)

The southern boundary of Plot 4 appears to have been rebuilt during Phase VIII in the form of a sandstone wall which survived for a length of approximately 10 m; its eastern end had been removed during twentieth-century construction work associated with the *Chester Chronicle* print works. This wall was clearly not of one build but rather appeared to have evolved over a period of time as structures were erected within the plot. The most westerly section of the wall was represented by (1386), which was composed of small roughly shaped sandstone blocks bonded in a sandy lime mortar; it was 4 m long, 0.45 m thick and survived to a height of 1.2 m.

To the east of wall (1386) a later wall, (1385), had been constructed in a shallow construction trench, (1536). Wall (1385) was butted to the eastern end of wall (1386) and consisted of much larger sandstone blocks which had been more carefully dressed and were bonded in pale brown lime mortar. The wall was 2.75 m long 0.48 m wide and survived to height of 0.9 m. After construction the foundation trench had been backfilled with a dark brown silty clay, (1537), which produced pottery dated 1720+.

The easternmost section of the boundary wall was represented by (1381), which was built within a much deeper construction trench, (1382), which had cut into the southern edge of layer (455)/(1538). Wall (1381) was bonded with a pink-brown lime mortar and consisted of neatly shaped medium-sized sandstone blocks interspersed with sections of hand-made bricks laid in English Garden Wall bond; it was 3.7 m long, 0.6 m thick and survived to a height of 0.65 m. The foundation trench had been backfilled with a brown silty clay, (1383), which produced pottery of seventeenth–eighteenth-century date.

Building VIII(vi)

Building VIII(vi) was a rectangular structure aligned north–south with external dimensions of 4 x 2.15 m. It was defined by walls (1386), (1531) and (1284) and its interior was covered by a sandstone floor, (1525). There were no other internal features to indicate whether or not Building VIII(vi) had served as a domestic dwelling.

The southern wall was represented by property boundary wall (1386), described above. The northern wall, (1531), was only partly exposed at the northern limit of excavation; it consisted of large sandstone blocks bonded in a sandy lime mortar. Although originally part of Building VIII(vi), it extended eastwards beyond wall (1284), to which it was bonded, and later demarcated the northern side of Building VIII(vii).

The eastern wall, (1284), later formed a partition wall between Building VIII(vi) and Building VIII(vii). It comprised three courses of roughly shaped sandstone blocks bonded in a pale brown lime mortar and was 3.44 m long, 0.5 m wide and survived to a height of 0.61 m. Both the east and west faces of the wall had been well dressed; however, the east face was quite weathered, suggesting that it may have once served as an external wall, whilst the west face appeared scorched, possibly as the result of a conflagration within the building.

The whole interior of the building was covered by a thin layer of greyish brown silty clay, (1539), which produced pottery dated 1720+. This was in turn covered by a deposit of yellowish brown sand, (1535), which was interpreted as bedding material for the laying of sandstone floor (1525) and produced pottery dated from the middle of the seventeenth to the middle of the eighteenth century. The floor itself, (1525), consisted of neatly laid sandstone slabs with surviving dimensions of 3.35 x 2.15 m; silt between the slabs produced pottery dated to the middle of the eighteenth century or later. The western part of the floor had been removed by the foundations of the Phase IX rear range of 19 Bridge Street.

Building VIII(vii)

Building VIII(vii) was a rectangular structure aligned north–south with external dimensions of 4 x 3.8 m. It was defined by walls (1386), (1357), (1531) and (1284) and the interior of the building was covered by a brick floor, (1285) (Ill 2.1.83). There were no other internal features to indicate whether or not Building VIII(vii) had served as a domestic dwelling.

The southern wall was represented by boundary wall (1386), described above. The eastern wall, (1357), was built within a deep construction trench, (1532), which was cut into the western side of layer (455)/(1538). The wall consisted of three courses of large sandstone blocks bonded in lime mortar and was 3.44 m long, 0.65 m thick and survived to a height of 0.36 m. The northern wall, (1531), comprised large sandstone blocks bonded in a sandy lime mortar. It appears to have originally been part of the earlier Building VIII(vi), as it extended west beyond wall (1284) The western wall, (1284), formed a partition between Buildings VIII(vi) and (vii).

Within the footprint of Building VIII(vii) there was a thin layer of dark greenish grey sandy silt, (1524), which was interpreted as bedding material for the laying of the floor; it produced pottery dated to the mid-eighteenth century or later. Above this was laid floor surface (1285), which was predominantly made from reused hand-made bricks but also included some water-worn cobbles and patches of pale brown mortar. The floor surface covered the whole interior of Building VIII(vii). A small sub-rounded hole, (1595), had been made in the centre of the

Ill 2.1.83 Phase VIII Plot 4: brick surface (1285) of Building VIII(vii), looking S.

floor, possibly as the result of settlement by underlying cess pits; this was subsequently filled with a brick and sandstone repair (1594).

Plot 6 (Ill 2.1.84)

Documentary research suggests that Plot 6 may have come into the Fletcher estate between 1796 and 1811, when it was probably part of 'an acre of land in the Parish of St Peter'. A deed recording the purchase of the estate by John Fletcher in 1813 describes the area as a 'larger garden' on the north side of Fletcher's Buildings, and in a deed of 1879 it is described as 'a drying ground'. Although the earlier eighteenth-century use of Plot 6 seems typical of that seen in Plots 1–4, it would appear that by the later part of the eighteenth-century it had become used as a garden, and in fact remained open ground until the start of the recent extension to the Debenhams department store in 2001.

Pits (519), (621), (714), (532), (632), (674) and (609)

The earliest activity during Phase VIII appears to have been the cutting and later backfilling of seven dispersed pits which probably functioned as cess pits. In most instances these pits were stratigraphically contemporary.

The largest of these pits was located on the western edge of Plot 6 and consisted of a subrectangular cut, (519), which measured roughly 4 x 2 x 0.72 m. The earliest fill, (613), was a yellowish brown sandy silt which contained a high percentage of domestic waste, including part of a tankard dated 1720+. The upper fills, (559), (520) and (531), comprised a succession of brown silty clay deposits rich in building debris, early eighteenth-century pottery and clay tobacco pipes dated 1610–1800; these upper fills appeared to have been deposited in quick succession and probably represented the systematic backfilling of the pit. A single post hole, (611), was identified on the southern edge of the pit (519); it measured 0.3 x 0.38 x 0.15 m and was filled with a pale brown sandy silt, (612). This post hole may indicate that a timber superstructure had once been positioned above the pit while it was in use as a cess pit.

Pit (621) was oval in plan and 0.24 m deep. It had been truncated to the south by the cutting of a late nineteenth-century service trench. The fill, (622), was a greenish brown silty clay suggestive of use as a cess pit.

Pit (714) was subrectangular, 0.30 m deep, and had been truncated on the north-east side by the cutting of telegraph pole (373). The fill, (715), was a mid-brown silty clay containing domestic waste, which suggested that the pit had been deliberately backfilled.

Pit (532) was subrectangular in plan, 0.15 m deep and orientated roughly north–south; the southern end of the pit had been removed by the cutting of pit (632). It appeared to have been lined with broken pieces of grey roofing slate, which were covered by a dark brown silty clay fill, (540). The upper fill, (533), consisted of a dump of sandstone fragments which had clearly been used in an attempt to deliberately backfill the pit.

Pit (632) lay approximately 1.2 m to the south of pit (714) and was 0.42 m deep. The lower fills, (637) and (677), consisted of dark brown silty clay containing building debris and domestic waste including pottery of seventeenth–eighteenth-century date. The pit was unu-

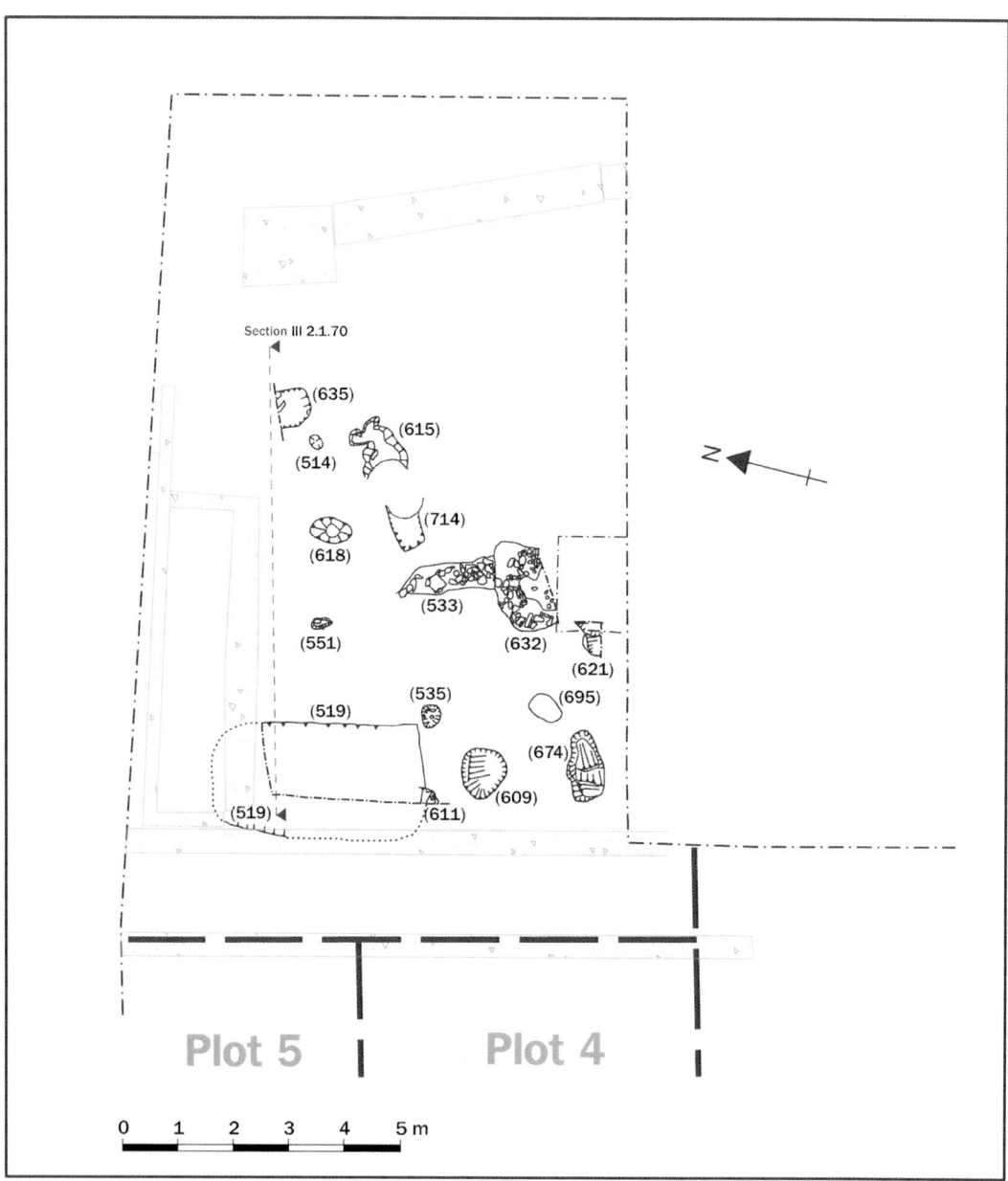

Section III 2.1.70

(635)

(615)

(514)

(714)

(618)

(533)

(551)

(632)

(621)

(695)

(535)

(519)

(674)

(519) (611) (609)

Plot 5   Plot 4

0 1 2 3 4 5 m

III 2.1.84 Phase VIII Plot 6: plan. (Scale 1/125)

sual in that a drystone wall of sandstone blocks, (631), appeared to have been built down the centre of the long axis of the pit after the initial infilling with (637) and (677); this wall effectively divided the pit in two. After the construction of wall (631), an orange-brown sandy clay, (676), was deposited in the southern half of the pit, whilst a deposit of sandstone brash, (639), was laid in the northern half. The top of the pit was then filled with a deposit of charcoal and coal mixed in a dark brownish black silty clay, (633), which contained eighteenth-century pottery.

Pit (674) was located in the south-western corner of Plot 6 and was 0.32 m deep. The base of the pit was cut in a series of three descending steps running from west to east. The fill, (675), was a brownish grey clayey silt containing building debris and domestic waste including pottery of seventeenth–early eighteenth century date.

Pit (609) lay approximately 1 m to the north of pit (674) and comprised a circular cut 0.23 m deep. The pri-

mary fill, (610), was a reddish brown clayey sand, which was covered by an upper fill of dark greyish brown silty clay, (617).

Tree bole pits (635), (615), (618), (551), (535) and (695)

A total of six rather irregularly shaped pits was also identified in Plot 6. They were all cut from the same stratigraphic horizon and appeared to be arrayed in a rough arc, running from pit (635) in the north-east to pit (695) in the south-west. The evidence of root disturbance in all of these pits led to their being interpreted as resulting from the removal of root boles of large shrubs or small trees and as such probably belonged to the later eighteenth-century use of Plot 6 as a garden.

The northern half of pit (635) was not exposed during the excavation; it was 0.07 m deep. Pit (615) had a very irregular shape and had been partly removed on its western side by telegraph pole cut (373); it was 0.12 m deep.

Pit (618) was circular in plan with a depth of 0.11 m. Pit (551) was oval in plan with a V-shaped profile and was 0.08 m deep. Pit (535) was a slightly irregular oval cut 0.16 m deep. Pit (695) was 0.20 m deep.

The brown sandy backfills of these pits, (636), 616), (619), (538), (536) and (696), were all reminiscent of cultivation soils. (696), the fill of (695), produced pottery of late eighteenth–nineteenth-century date.

Cat burial (514)

Just to the west of pit (635) was a small sub-rounded shallow pit, (514), which had been dug for the purpose of burying the remains of a domestic cat. The fill, (515), was a mid-brown silty loam which probably represented the redeposited material from the excavation of the pit and produced eighteenth-century pottery.

Layers (638), (698) and (534)

Towards the south-east corner of Plot 6 was a hollow which had formed as the result of ground settlement into underlying cess pit (680), described in Phase VI. This hollow was systematically filled in with a sequence of layers: the lowest of these was a greyish brown clayey silt, (638); above this was a reddish brown sandy clay, (698) followed by (534), which produced clay tobacco pipes dated to the eighteenth–nineteenth century.

Layer (56)/(341)/(349)/(324)/(1573)

The whole of Plot 6 was eventually covered by an extensive layer of dark yellowish brown clayey loam, (56)/(341)/(349)/(324)/(1573), which was interpreted as a cultivation soil and probably represented the use of the plot in the later eighteenth century as a garden. The layer produced pottery dated from 1720 to 1800.

Evaluation Trench B

A shallow pit, (103), was identified during the excavation of Evaluation Trench B, and although it was not interpreted at the time it seems possible that it represented another tree bole pit. The primary fill, (104), was a buff/yellow sand and this was covered by an upper fill of dark brown loam (102).

Phase IX: Early 19 century–c 1900

The distinction between the end of Phase VIII and the beginning of Phase IX was slightly arbitrary. Many of the buildings described in Phase VIII were clearly mapped on the plan accompanying a deed of 1879 and were largely unchanged from the time of their purchase by John Fletcher in 1813. The documentary research suggested that these buildings did not exist in 1770 and in fact were most likely to have been built between 1803 and 1808. However, the dating evidence from the archaeological excavation suggested that many of the buildings were in fact older than 1803–8, with a construction date sometime after *c* 1760. It is clear that several of them stayed in use during Phase IX as dwellings, and this has served to complicate our understanding and interpretation of the stratigraphy. A crucial turning point in the development of the site is indicated by the deed of sale of 1879: shortly after this, in 1882, the area marked as the 'drying ground' (Plot 6) was exchanged by the Browns for a similar-sized plot further east owned by the Duke of Westminster. This was possibly done to facilitate the construction of an extension to the Brown's store (currently owned by Debenhams plc); the extension was clearly marked on the second edition 1:2,500 OS map of 1899. This extension would have removed the eastern end of Fletcher's Buildings and the event seems to be an appropriate point to end this phase of the narrative.

Plot 1 (Ills 2.1.85 and .87)

Building VIII(i)
Layer (217)

A layer of silt (217) had been deposited in the south-east corner of Building VIII(i) at the beginning of Phase IX. This layer produced pottery of eighteenth–nineteenth-century date and a sample, <5003>, indicated the presence of charred cereal grains and fig pips, probably derived from faecal material.

Hearth (209)

Layer (217) was subsequently cut by a subrectangular construction trench, (210), that measured 1.12 x 0.8 x 0.6 m. This cut had been stepped in at a depth of 0.4 m to create a shelf on all four sides. This shelf provided the base for the construction of brick structure (209), which consisted of a four-sided 'box' made of hand-made bricks, one course wide and 6 courses high, bonded in lime mortar (Ill 2.1.85). The outer limits of cut (210) were backfilled after the construction of structure (209) with a dark grey sand silt, (211), that contained pottery of nineteenth-century date. There was evidence to suggest that the internal face of brick structure (209) had been whitewashed. It was interpreted as the ashpit for a domestic hearth. The interior of the structure was subsequently filled in with a deposit of clinker and grey, ash-like silt, (208), that contained a coin of George III dated 1800 and fragments of ironwork from a suspended vessel (possibly a cauldron). A sample, <5002>, taken from (208) produced evidence for box leaf fragments, heather and rye rachis that may indicate the remnants of a straw floor covering or fuel.

On the south-eastern side of hearth (209) there were the fragmentary remains of another brick structure (212), which consisted of a hand-made brick wall bonded in lime mortar, aligned south-east to north-west and surviving to a height of two courses. Wall (212) sat in a shallow construction trench, (213), and was thought to be part of the base to a domestic fireplace associated with ashpit (209).

Ill 2.1.85 Phase IX Plot 1: hearth (209) of Building VIII(i), looking N.

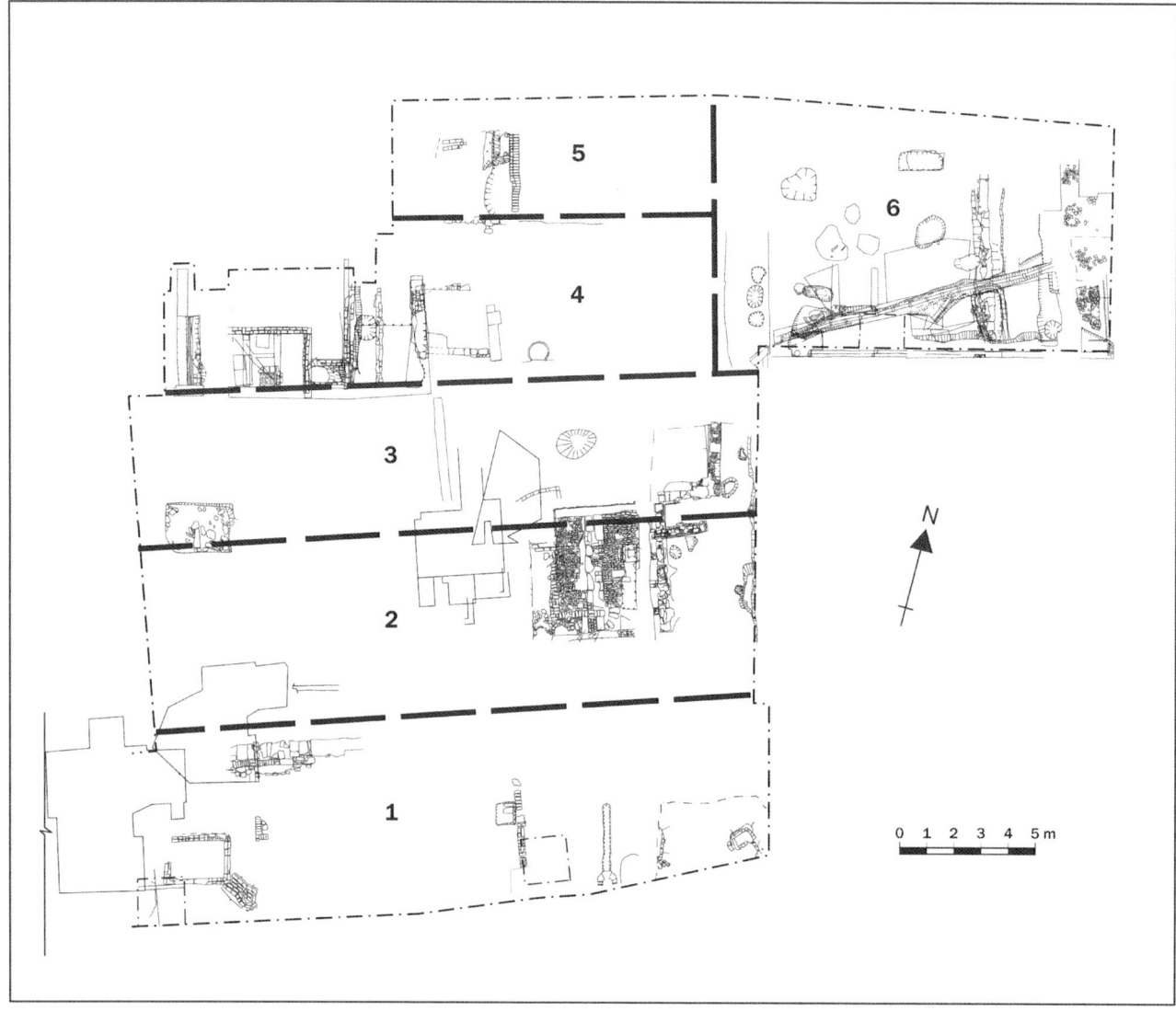

Ill 2.1.86 Phase IX: general arrangement of plots. (Scale 1/250)

Hearth (214)

Just inside and parallel to the west wall of Building VIII(i) there was a second subrectangular construction trench, (215). This contained another brick 'box' structure, (214), that was very similar in character and dimensions to structure (209) and was likewise interpreted as the ashpit for a domestic hearth. The primary fill within the structure was a pale grey silt, (230), which produced a copper alloy button bearing the military insignia of the Royal Artillery. The upper fill, (232), was composed entirely of coal and clinker and contained pottery of eighteenth–nineteenth-century date.

Floor (216)/(577)

A layer of dark grey silt sand, (201)/(601), had formed over the entire interior of Building VIII(i) to a depth of 0.2 m. This contained building debris and pottery of nineteenth-century date. It was interpreted as a levelling layer prior to the laying of floor (216). A layer of clean yellow sand, (585), had been laid on top of layer (201)/(601) and was used as bedding material for the laying of a quarry tile floor, (216)/(577), comprising 9" x 9" tiles. The evidence for floor (216)/(577) only survived in the corners of Building VIII(i) as most of it had been removed during the laying of a twentieth-century concrete floor, (200).

Pit (205)

In the north-eastern side of Building VIII(i) a shallow rectangular pit, (205), had been dug into layer (201). The base of the pit was occupied by two horizontally laid quarry tiles (each measuring 9" x 9"), implying that the pit was contemporary with floor (216) and had been dug to accommodate something. This sort of feature has been noted elsewhere, often in country cottages where the low ceiling has prevented the accommodation of a tall object such as a grandfather clock. The pit was subsequently backfilled with a grey-brown silt sand, (206), which contained nineteenth–twentieth-century pottery. Fill (206) was sampled, <5001>, and found to contain insect remains including specimens of the oriental cockroach.

Deposit (640)

A deposit of dark brown silt sand, (640), formed over an area 0.80 x 0.82 x 0.10 m; it probably indicated the location of a shallow cut in floor (216)/(577) which had been largely removed when concrete floor (200) was inserted into Building VIII(i) during the twentieth century. It produced pottery dated to the mid-eighteenth–nineteenth century.

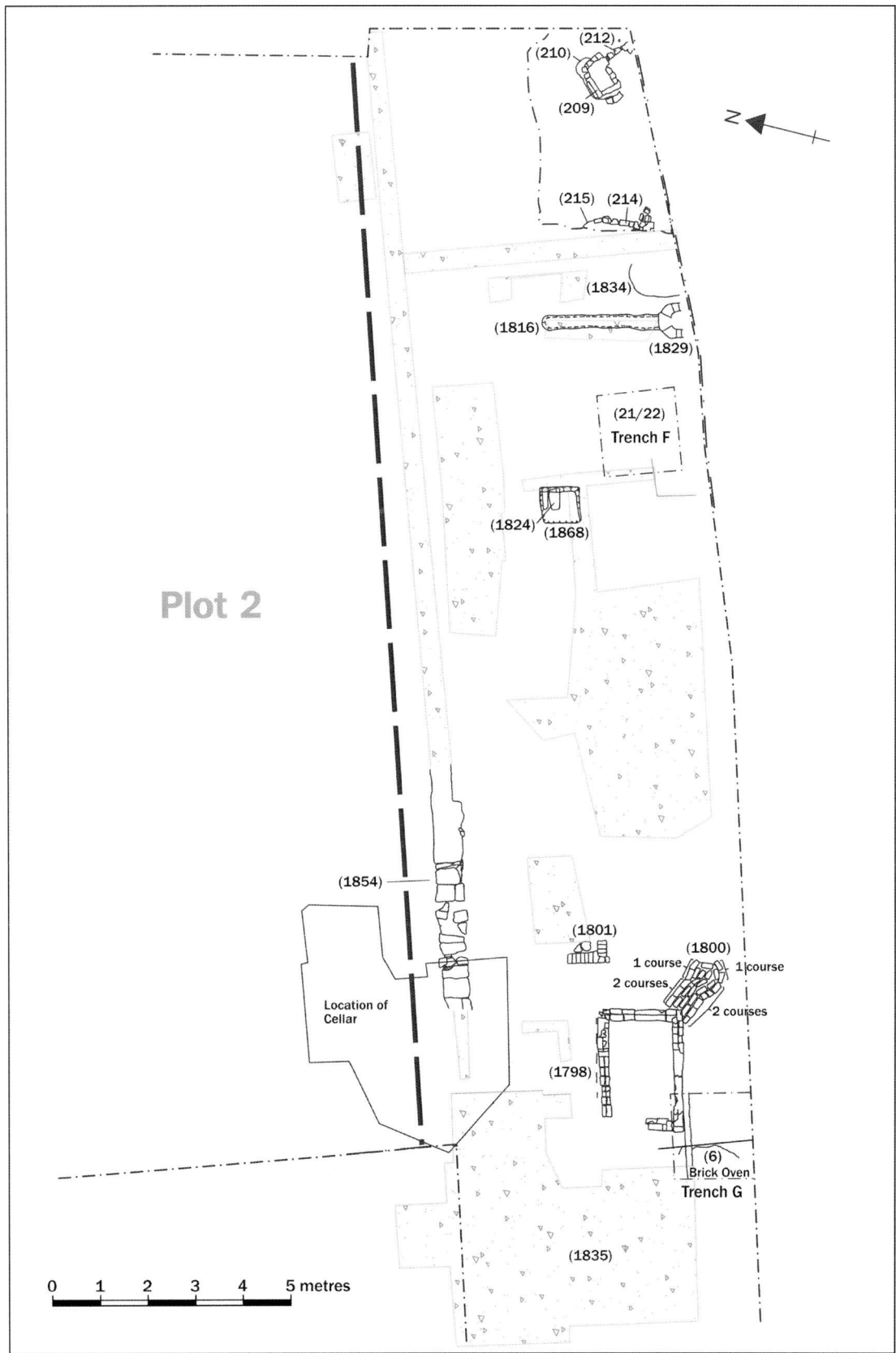

Plot 2

(212)
(210)
(209)

(215) (214)

(1834)
(1816)
(1829)

(21/22)
Trench F

(1824)
(1868)

(1854)

(1801)
(1800)
1 course
2 courses
1 course
2 courses

Location of
Cellar

(1798)

(6)
Brick Oven
Trench G

(1835)

0 1 2 3 4 5 metres

Ill 2.1.87 Phase IX Plot 1: plan. (Scale 1/125)

87

Layer (644)

Just to the north of Building VIII(i) a layer of mortar-rich pale brown sand silt, (644), had been deposited over an area 0.65 x 0.34 m. Pottery of nineteenth–twentieth-century date was recovered from the layer.

Building VIII(ii)
Floor (16)/(1839)

The interior of Building VIII(ii) was largely covered by a compact layer of mottled brown clay, (16)/(1839), which contained small fragments of building debris and pottery dated to the late eighteenth–nineteenth century. The upper surface of the layer was so even and compact that it was felt likely that it had served as an internal floor surface for the building.

Slot (1816)

A north–south slot, (1816), measuring 2.55 x 0.32 x 0.13 m had been excavated in floor surface (1839) in the southeastern quarter of Building VIII(ii). The slot had a flat base and is likely to have accommodated a timber sill beam, perhaps to create an internal partition wall or to support a timber staircase allowing access to an upper floor within the building. It had been filled with dark brown silty clay, (1815), that contained eighteenth–nineteenth-century pottery; this is likely to have been introduced after the removal of any timber structure and therefore relates to its disuse rather than construction.

Pit (1829)

The southern end of slot (1816) was later removed by the cutting of a circular pit, (1829), which had surviving dimensions of 0.80 x 0.50 x 0.27 m. The pit was filled with a dump of material (1828) that contained nineteenth-century pottery and was rich in carbonised wood and clinker, thought to be derived from domestic hearth sweepings; this might imply that the pit was associated with a hearth within Building VIII(ii).

Pit (1834)

To the east of pit (1829) another circular pit, (1834), was cut into floor (1839) with excavated dimensions of 1.0 x 0.60 x 0.50 m. The function of the pit could not be verified, but it had apparently been deliberately backfilled with a dump of building debris, (1818), which contained nineteenth-century pottery.

Building VIII(iii)
Base (1824)

On the eastern side of the footprint of the Phase VIII Building VIII(iii) and adjacent to the partition wall (1810) within Building VIII(ii), a square base, (1824), had been constructed within a shallow construction trench, (1868). The base comprised two courses of roughly shaped sandstone blocks bonded in a pale pink-brown lime mortar with dimensions of 0.44 x 0.40 x 0.27 m The construction trench had been backfilled with dark grey-brown silty clay, (1869), which contained pottery dating to between the late eighteenth and the early twentieth century. The structure was interpreted as the foundation for a buttress to wall (1810), implying that the row of buildings had begun to become unstable and required structural maintenance in order to keep them standing.

Ill 2.1.88 Phase IX Plot 1: oven (1800) of Building VIII(iv), looking NW.

Building VIII(iv)
Oven/flue (1800)

Towards the south-west corner of Building VIII(iv) a shallow subrectangular trench, (1851), measuring 1.52 x 0.77 x 0.16 m had been excavated at floor level in order to construct brick structure (1800). This comprised a solid brick base and upstanding brick walls that formed a circular chamber, with a shaft feeding into it on a northwest–south-east alignment (Ill 2.1.88). A deposit of black sand silt, (1803), had formed within structure (1800) and was noteworthy for a high concentration of burnt coal and carbonised material. It was thought likely that this structure was, in fact, the base of a small oven or vat associated with a domestic function such as baking or the boiling of water and as such probably predated the conversion of the area to the *Chester Chronicle* offices.

Layers (1808), (1836), (1831) and (1830)

A large area on the interior of building VIII(iv) including the area occupied by oven structure (1800) was covered with a series of layers that were rich in building debris. These layers consisted of a series of grey-brown clay silts deposited in the following sequence: (1808), (1836), (1831) and (1830). All of these layers contained a high percentage of grey roofing slate and lime mortar fragments indicating the demolition of a building in the vicinity. The uppermost layer (1830) produced pottery dating to the late eighteenth–early nineteenth century and it is thought that the demolition event suggested would have been immediately prior to the construction of the *Chester Chronicle* offices between 1820 and 1840.

Wall (7)

In the position of Evaluation Trench G a north–south brick wall (7) survived to a height of five courses. The wall was set within a foundation trench, (23), and comprised hand-made bricks bonded in white lime mortar. Pottery recovered from the construction trench indicated a date of 1830+, which suggested that this wall was a later partition added to Building VIII(iv) but predating the construction of the *Chester Chronicle* offices.

Oven (6)

A brick oven was partially exposed within Evaluation Trench G; its construction trench, (10), clearly postdated brick wall (7). The superstructure, (6), consisted of four courses of brick laid in a semicircular shape and bonded in pink lime mortar, with dimensions of 0.73 x 0.32 x

0.32 m, founded a square brick and mortar plinth measuring 0.6 x 0.7 x 0.6 m. The latter contained a brick stamped 'Buckley Brick & Tile Co Limited'. The oven had been backfilled with light grey silt sand, (11), which produced pottery of nineteenth–twentieth-century date.

Building IX(i)
Wall (1854)/(1864)
The northern side of the area occupied by Building VIII(iv) had been heavily disturbed by the construction of a substantial wall foundation, (1854). The sandstone foundation was aligned east–west and consisted of roughly shaped sandstone blocks bonded in lime mortar with a width of 0.6 m. This new wall line corresponded precisely with the location of the northern wall of the 'Fletcher's Building' structure recorded in 2001 prior to demolition work and is likely to represent the building referred to as 'the Chronicle Offices' on the 1879 plan. In some places the remains of the brick superstructure, (1864), were still bonded to the foundation by a hard white mortar. The wall would have originally continued east along the northern side of the footprint of Building VIII(iii), but it had been entirely removed in this area during the 2001 demolition work. The standing building survey had noted that the architectural style of this structure would suggest a construction date between the 1820s and the 1840s, which would tally with the proposed date for the relocation of the *Chronicle* offices to Bridge Street suggested by the documentary research.

Cellar (1835)
At the very western end of Plot 1 a full-height cellar was recorded as structure (1835). This cellar was housed within the Fletcher's Buildings block and had been recorded during the standing building recording exercise prior to demolition in 2001. In the final phase of the building's use as the *Chronicle* offices, the cellar was accessed *via* a trapdoor and ladder and had been used as a 'tank room' (housing a large iron water tank used in the printing process). The cellar was largely built of bricks bonded in a hard lime mortar, similar to the mortar used in the construction of wall (1864), although dressed sandstone blocks were noted in the lower courses of the south and west walls. The north wall of the cellar still had a cellar light or coal chute accessed *via* the Fletcher's Buildings alleyway; whilst the south-east corner contained a partially surviving feature that might either have served as a narrow flight of stairs into the cellar or as a vent for air circulation. The cellar is likely to have been contemporary with the redevelopment at this end of Plot 1 associated with the conversion/construction of the *Chronicle* offices between 1820 and 1840.

Fletcher's Buildings alley
This area was heavily truncated by the lines of several modern services, including a 4" ceramic sewer pipe, and iron gas pipe and lead water pipe – all of which ran along the alleyway on an east–west alignment. The area was further disturbed by the insertion of concrete stanchion bases associated with the buildings demolished in 2001.

Layer (1912)
To the north of Buildings VIII(i)/(ii) was a layer of mid-reddish brown sandy clay, (1912), which covered the area

defined as the alleyway serving Fletcher's Buildings on the 1879 plan. This layer was rich in building debris and was interpreted as a demolition deposit that may have been associated with a rebuilding phase during the nineteenth century.

Slot (1914)
The southern side of layer (1912) had been removed by an east–west slot, (1914), which ran parallel to the northern side of brick wall (1854). The slot was 0.8 m wide, 0.34 m deep and could be traced westwards for a length of 2.7 m. It was filled with a dark reddish brown sandy clay, (1913), that was rich in building debris and contained nineteenth-century pottery. It was thought likely that the slot was associated with the construction of brick wall (1854).

Plot 2 (Ills 2.1.89–.90)

Tree bole pits (471), (450) and (458)
The eastern end of Plot 2 seems to have remained open ground for a while at the beginning of Phase IX. An irregularly shaped pit, (471), 0.3 m deep lay at the very back of the plot and had been partly removed by the brick foundations of the extension to Brown's department store during the 1880s/1890s. The pit had the irregular sides and base usually associated with animal burrowing or the root bole of a tree or shrub. It had been deliberately backfilled with a dump of ash and clinker, (470), which was probably derived from domestic hearth sweepings; an unusual engraved ivory handle was recovered from this fill.

To the north-west of pit (471) was a second smaller pit, (450), which was sub-circular in plan and 0.18 m deep. Its fill was a very dark brown sand silt rich in charcoal, (451). A sample from this fill, <5040>, produced tomato seeds, which might suggest that a tomato plant had been planted in this spot while it was still open ground.

Pit (458) lay to the north-east of (450) and was subrectangular in plan and 0.09 m deep. The fill, (457), was a very dark brown clay loam rich in domestic rubbish which was probably derived from hearth sweepings. Again, it seems likely that this pit represents another root bole of a small tree or shrub.

Layer (418)/(441)
The whole of the eastern end of Plot 2 was subsequently covered by a layer of dark brown silt, (418)/(441), to a depth of 0.2 m. This layer was very rich in building debris and appeared to represent a clearance episode prior to a new phase of construction. During the 2001 demolition work this layer was disturbed by the passage of heavy plant and some modern contamination occurred, but the majority of the pottery from the layer would seem to date after *c* 1830.

Post hole (1300)
Approximately 10 m to the west of layer (418)/(441) there was a layer of light yellow-brown sandy silt, (1301), which had largely been removed by the later construction of cellar (1089). This layer had been cut by a small post hole, (1300), 0.40 m deep, which had vertical sides leading to a rounded base. The post hole had a single fill of dark grey brown sandy silt, (1299), which contained pot-

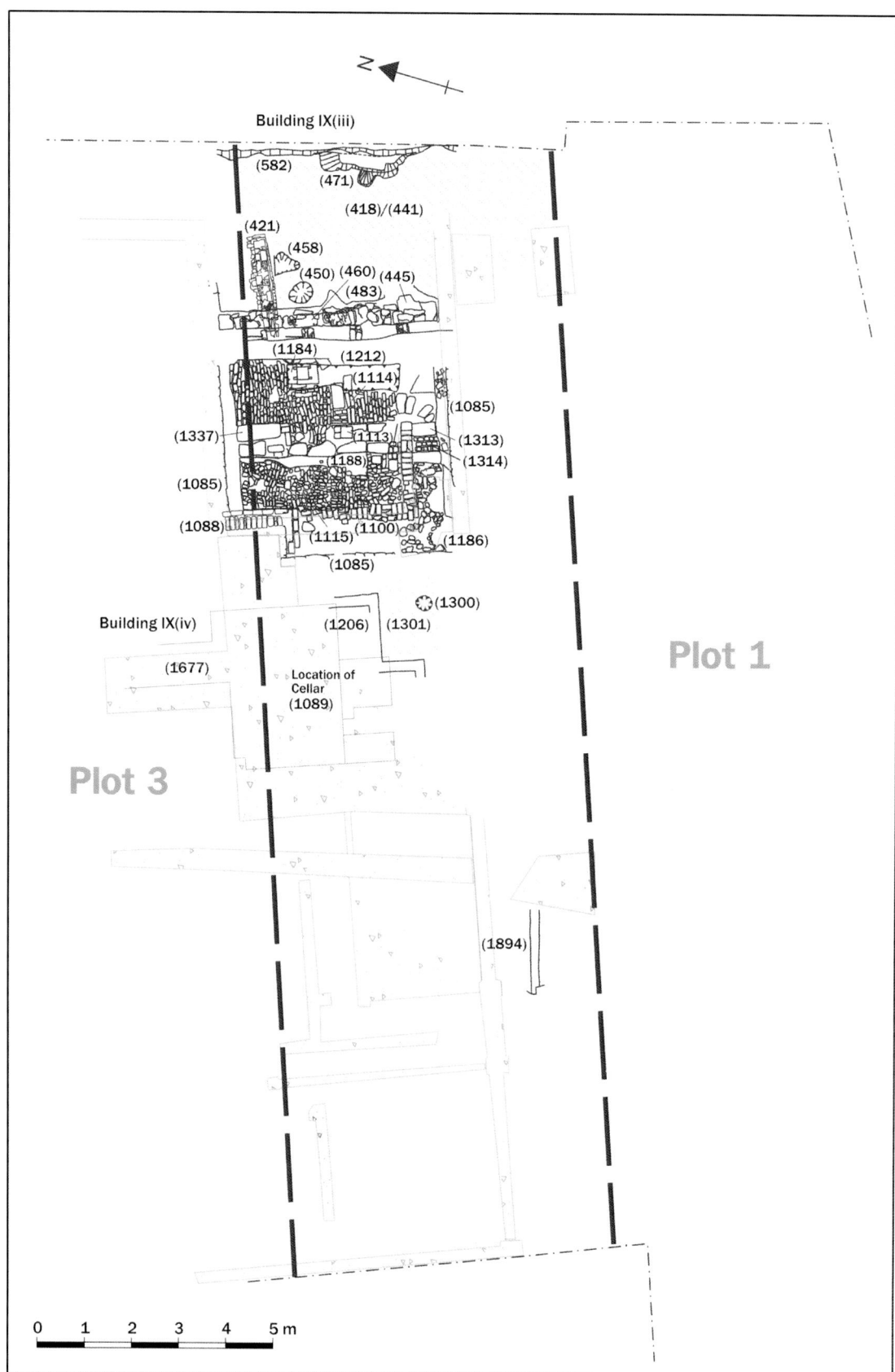

Building IX(iii)

(582)

(471)

(418)/(441)

(421)

(458)

(450) (460) (445)

(483)

(1184)

(1212)

(1114)

(1085)

(1337)

(1113)

(1313)

(1188)

(1314)

(1085)

(1088)

(1115) (1100)

(1186)

(1085)

(1300)

Building IX(iv)

(1206) (1301)

(1677)

Location of
Cellar
(1089)

Plot 1

Plot 3

(1894)

0 1 2 3 4 5 m

III 2.1.89 Phase IX Plot 2: plan. (Scale 1/125)

Ill 2.1.90 Phase IX Plot 2: closets and ash pit, looking S.

tery of eighteenth-century date. This post hole is hard to interpret but it may have been part on an earlier fence line within Plot 2.

Building IX(ii): The 'Closets & Ash Pit'

The plan of conveyance dated to 1879 shows an area towards the eastern end of Plot 2 which is labelled 'closets & ash pit'. This structure was located during the 2001 excavation, and the presence of green silt between the pointing on the brickwork of the walls and floor made it clear that it had functioned as a fairly poorly maintained latrine. The structure was square in plan, with dimensions of 4.5 x 4.5 m and was given a group context (1206) for planning purposes. The eastern side was delimited by brick walls (445) and (460); the western and southern sides by brick wall (1100); and the northern side by the existing sandstone boundary wall (1085) (Ill 2.1.90). The floor level of the structure, (1114)/(1115), would appear to have been deliberately set approximately 0.5 m beneath the surrounding ground level, giving the building a subterranean aspect, with access *via* a small flight of steps, (1313), on the southern side. Internal partitions suggested that the eastern side was occupied by five 'closets', while the western side contained the ash pit. The individual closets did not appear to have had any drainage and probably housed removable containers such as buckets. These buckets were probably emptied into the ash pit area where ash from domestic hearth sweepings would have been used to keep the stench at bay. The 'ash pit would in effect have been a temporary holding pen and was probably intermittently emptied by the night soil man and carted away to be spread on outlying fields.

Walls (445) and (460)

The eastern wall of Building XI(ii) survived to a height of three courses with dimensions of 4.60 x 1.00 x 0.60 m. It was constructed from a mixture of reused sandstone blocks and hand-made brick bonded in a pink-white lime mortar and set in a shallow construction trench, (483). The construction trench had been backfilled with a grey-brown sand silt, (484), which was rich in building debris (including fragments of chimney pot) and pottery dating to the nineteenth century.

Along the western face of wall (445) were four short returning walls, (460), aligned east–west, each bonded to

wall (445) and of similar construction. These walls were evenly spaced to leave five compartments approximately 0.6 m wide and originally 0.8 m long; the western end of all four walls had been removed by a line of mini-piles inserted into the ground prior to the start of excavation in 2001. It seems extremely likely that these five small compartments represented the 'closets' referred to on the 1879 plan.

Wall (1100)

The western and southern walls of the building were represented by wall (1100) which formed an L-shaped structure composed entirely of hand-made bricks bonded with lime mortar. The western wall had surviving dimensions of 2.5 x 0.6 x 0.35 m, while those of the southern wall were 1.8 x 0.6 x 0.35 m.

Partition wall (1337) and (1113)

The western half of Building IX(ii) appeared to have been separated from the closets, as indicated by the remains of a north–south cross wall, (1337), at the northern end of the building. Wall (1337) was constructed from a mixture of reused sandstone blocks and hand-made bricks bonded in clay and had surviving dimensions of 1.50 x 0.36 x 0.45 m. The remaining length of the partition had two openings, each approximately 1 m wide, separated by a brick column, (1113). To the west of the partition the floor consisted of a brick surface, (1115), bonded in lime mortar; this surface had suffered from major settlement at its southern end where it overlay a Phase VIII cess pit. An area of the brick surface at the northern end of the partition was removed during excavation and an underlying layer of dark brown sand silt, (1287), was revealed which produced pottery of nineteenth-century date. This western part of the building is thought to represent the 'ash pit' referred to on the 1879 plan.

Brick yard surface (1114), steps (1313)/(1314) and path (1186)/(1201)

The area between the closets and the ash pit appears to have functioned as an open yard with a surface constructed from a mixture of sandstone blocks and bricks bonded in lime mortar, (1114). This surface had been laid on successive dumps of ash and coal, (1291), and brown clay, (1216), which had served to level the area prior to the construction of the yard and produced nineteenth-century pottery. On the eastern side of the yard was an arrangement of four sandstone blocks held together with two iron bands that formed the top to a possible drain, (1184). Beneath the blocks was a square brick chamber measuring 0.62 x 0.415 x 0.10 m which was connected to a length of ceramic salt-glazed 4" sewer pipe, running south towards the Fletcher's Buildings alleyway. The ceramic pipe sat within a shallow cut, (1212), which had been backfilled with dark grey-brown silt clay, (1104). This appears to have been a later addition and constituted the only *in-situ* sewerage within Building IX(ii).

At the southern edge of surface (1114), four sandstone slabs had been laid around the eastern end of wall, (1100), and led to a pair of sandstone steps, (1313), which ascended to the west. In between the steps there was a small area covered by a brick surface, (1314), that would have served to lessen the gradient of ascent/descent to the closets and ash pit. At the top of the upper step of (1313) there was a cobbled sandstone surface, (1186), which formed a path that continued west to the south-west corner of Building IX(ii), before turning north and running parallel with the external face of wall (1100). The northern arm of path (1186) gradually petered out and appeared to have been affected by later disturbance, represented by a layer of dark brown sand silt, (1286), which produced pottery dated after 1865. This disturbance was later covered by a layer of ash and clinker which was recorded as layer (1201).

Wall (421)

To the east of wall (460) there was a short length of brick wall, (421), measuring 2.10 x 0.50 x 0.22 m. The wall was aligned east–west and consisted of hand-made bricks bonded with a pink-brown lime mortar and survived to a height of four courses. It was set in a shallow foundation trench, (452), which had been backfilled with grey-brown clay, (453), rich in building debris. This wall appeared to be a later addition, forming part of a lean-to structure on the eastern side of the closets and ash pit; the specific function of this new building could not be ascertained.

Layers (1187), (1109) and (1096)/(742)/(469)

The area of the closets and ash pit appears to have gone out of use during the later nineteenth century. This is likely to have been after the land conveyance deal between the Grosvenors and the Browns in 1879. The first layer to accumulate in the yard area was a dump of lime mortar fragments, (1187), mixed with a pale yellow-green silt about 0.19 m thick which presumably represented a build up of cess in the yard area. This was subsequently covered with a layer of dark greyish brown silt clay, (1109), which contained domestic refuse, including pottery of nineteenth-twentieth-century date. This was then covered by another layer of grey silt clay, (1096)/(742)/(469), which was 0.4 m thick and contained a high percentage of building debris and clay tobacco pipes dated 1850–1900. Layer (1096)/(742)/(469) also produced a small assemblage of bone tooth brushes, as well as a large assemblage of glass and stoneware bottles, many of which were marked with the name 'Davies & Shepheard'. This material may have derived from a clearance of the chemist's shop on Bridge Street Row which is likely to have occurred shortly before the construction of Davies and Shepheard's new warehouse in 1901.

Building IX(iii)
Wall (582)

The eastern ends of Plots 2 and 3 were delimited by a substantial brick wall, (582), which still formed the western edge of the Brown's store building in 2001. The wall appeared to be of a single phase of construction which the cartographic evidence suggests was undertaken sometime between 1882 and 1899. The wall was recorded as part of the standing building survey in 2001.

Building IX(iv)

Building IX(iv) was sited to the west of IX(ii), towards the centre of Plot 2; it also extended north into Plot 3. The building was recorded as group context (1085) for planning purposes and consisted of wall foundation (1088), drain/chute (1086), cellar (1089) and cellar stair well (1677), which was located in Plot 3. Some of this building was still standing prior to demolition in 2001 and has been included in the standing building recording section of this report. It would appear likely that the cellar of this building was excavated in 1901 during which a section of mosaic floor was recorded by Robert Newstead. The report indicated that the cellar was part of a new building erected as a warehouse for Davies and Shepheard's chemists shop on this part of Bridge Street Row; as such the construction of the cellar and associated building marks the end of Phase IX in Plot 2.

Cellar (1089), (1677) and chute (1086)

Cellar (1089) was roughly square in plan, measuring 3.5 x 3.5 m, and was aligned to the cardinal points. The walls stood to their full height and were constructed from brick bonded with a hard white lime mortar. On the southern side of the cellar there was a square recess rising to modern ground level that would have served as cellar light. Access was gained to the cellar on the northern side by a flight of seven steps, (1677), constructed in the same way as the walls. The floor was covered with a surface of 9" x 9" quarry tiles laid on to a bedding layer of yellow sand.

The north-eastern corner of the cellar was connected to a brick chute, (1086), which was orientated east–west and fell towards the cellar on a slight curve. The walls of the chute were constructed from bricks bonded in lime mortar and survived to a height of three courses. The base of the chute was also made of brick, except where it entered the cellar, and had been formed from grey roofing slate. The chute had been backfilled with brownish grey silt clay, (1093), which was rich in building debris and contained a high percentage of corks and wooden bottle tops possibly derived from the chemist's shop. It is uncertain what this chute was used for, but it appears to have served to channel something into the cellar; this was probably water and presumably had something to do with the chemist's warehouse arrangements.

Wall (1088)

Brick wall (1088) was an L-shaped structure bonded to the eastern side of the cellar and to the southern side of chute (1086), measuring 1.60 x 1.00 x 0.48 m. The wall appeared to be a later addition and probably represented an internal partition within the superstructure of the chemist's warehouse.

Wall (1894)

Towards the western end of the Fletcher's Buildings alleyway there was an east–west brick wall, (1894), that was exposed for a length of 1.6 m. The brickwork sat in construction cut (1896) and survived to a height of two courses and was bonded with a sandy yellow lime mortar. The wall had been heavily disturbed by later services and its function was hard to discern, but it was felt possible that it was associated with the inspection hatch to an earlier phase of services.

Plot 3 (III 2.1.91)

Pits (462) and (795)

At the eastern end of Plot 3 there was again some evidence to suggest that the area remained open ground for a while at the beginning of Phase IX. As with Plot 2 there were several irregularly shaped features which may have been left by the removal of the root boles of small trees or shrubs. The first of these was a kidney-shaped pit, (462), 0.45 m deep and with irregular sides and base. The pit had a single fill of light yellowish brown sand, (461), which appeared to have been deposited as a deliberate backfilling exercise.

To the south-west of pit (462) was a second larger sub-circular pit, (795), 0.22 m deep. The pit had two fills, the lower of which was a light yellow-brown silt clay, (794), that was rich in fragments of burnt coal and clinker. The upper fill, (793), was a dump of yellow clay also rich in coal and clinker. Pit (795) also seemed likely to have been left by the removal of the root bole of a small tree or shrub.

Pit (1097)

The central portion of Plot 3 was covered with a thin layer of reddish brown loam, (1090), which was thought to represent a relict garden soil and produced pottery of late eighteenth–nineteenth-century date. The pit was cut into layer (1090) and lay to the north of Building IX(iv). It was oval in plan and was 0.25 m deep with steep sides sloping to a rounded base. The pit had a single fill of dark brown loam, (1091), containing lenses of lime mortar. These lenses might imply that the pit had served as a latrine: if so, it is likely that it predated Building IX(iv) to the south. To the north of pit (1097) was a deposit of sterile pink clay, (1099), which may have been the remains of the upcast from the excavation of the pit.

Pit (1434)

At the western end of Plot 3 was a large rectangular pit, (1434), aligned east–west and 1.00 m deep. Only the upper fill, (1433), was excavated, as the base of the pit lay beneath the 25 m OD limit of excavation. (1433) consisted of a dump of sandstone blocks sitting in a mid-brown silt clay and produced nineteenth-century pottery. It had the appearance of deliberate backfill and it is likely that the pit functioned as a latrine, possibly before the construction of the 'closets & ash pit' building IX(ii).

Plot 4 (III 2.1.92)

Building IX(v): Rear range of 19 Bridge Street

This comprised a three-storey rectangular strip building that was still standing prior to demolition in 2001 and has been included in the standing building recording section of this report where it is interpreted as a warehouse. Only the eastern gable wall, (1370), was within the excavation area and much of the excavated area within Plot 4 comprised the backyard and outbuildings associated with the building's use.

East gable wall (1370)

This substantial wall foundation, (1370), had excavated dimensions of 3.92 x 0.55 x 1.49 m and consisted of bricks laid in English Garden wall bond using a hard pink-grey lime mortar. The foundation sat in trench (1529), which had been backfilled with brownish grey silt clay (1528) which produced pottery of eighteenth–nineteenth-century date.

Layer (1387)

To the immediate east of wall foundation (1370) there was a layer of dark grey-brown sand silt, (1387), which covered an area measuring 3.60 x 2.64 x 0.20 m and was seen to be sealing the backfill (1528) of wall foundation cut (1529). The layer contained some building debris and may have been associated with the construction of Building IX(v).

Pit (1365)

To the east of layer (1387) was a steep-sided, oval pit, (1365), 0.60 m deep. The pit had been backfilled with a grey silt sand, (1364), containing domestic waste; there were no indications that it had served as a cess pit. The top of the pit was covered by substantial sandstone blocks, (456), forming a north–south structure 1.3 m in length. The function of this masonry could not be established.

Pit (1365) and structure (456) were subsequently covered by a layer of dark brown sandy loam (1280) which measured 2.7 x 2.3 m and was interpreted as a garden soil.

Cess pit (1526)/(1359)

During Phase VIII a large stone-lined cess pit, (1371), had been identified towards the centre of Plot 4 but was not fully investigated because it was deeper than the limit of excavation. However, it was possible to establish that the north, west and south sides of this structure had been refaced with a new wall, (1359), possibly in an attempt to strengthen the structure and prolong its use. The new wall comprised a mixture of bricks and sandstone blocks bonded in a pink-brown lime mortar. The eastern side of the cess pit had also been refaced, but this time with a wall, (1526), composed only of brick laid in an English Garden Wall bond. The insertion of these new walls reduced the internal dimensions of the cess pit to 3.8 x 3.8 m. The renovation work could not be accurately dated but the cess pit was subsequently backfilled with a dump of domestic rubbish, (1527), which included pottery of late nineteenth-century date.

Garden terrace walls

Immediately to the west of cess pit (1526/1359) was a north–south brick wall, (1279), which survived to a height of nine courses. It was built in English Garden Wall bond and bonded in pink-grey mortar. The wall sat within a construction trench, (1366). Along with wall (1263), this formed a raised terrace which occupied the entire width of Plot 4 and covered an area three metres east–west. The

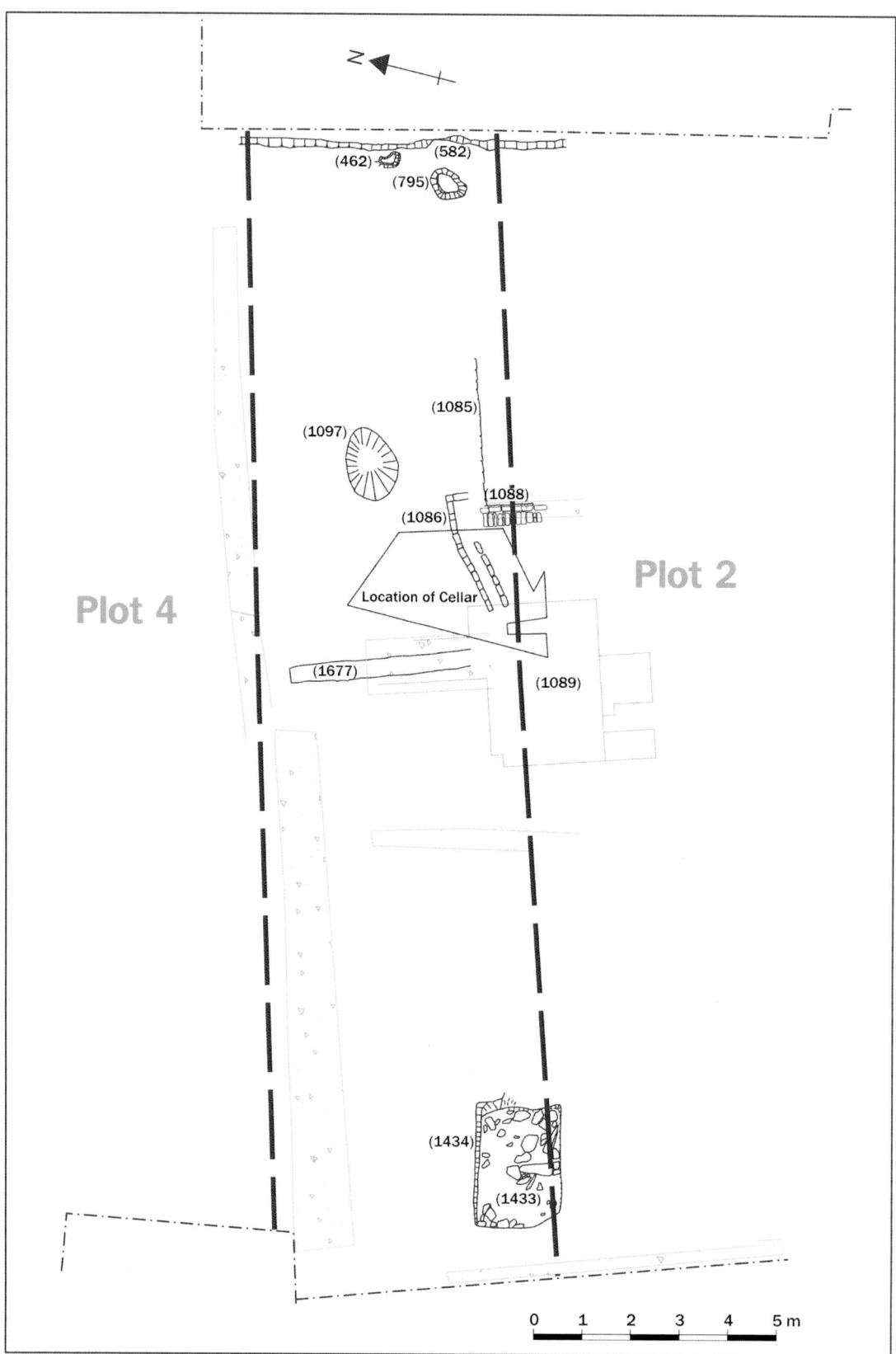

III 2.1.91 Phase IX Plot 3: plan. (Scale 1/125)

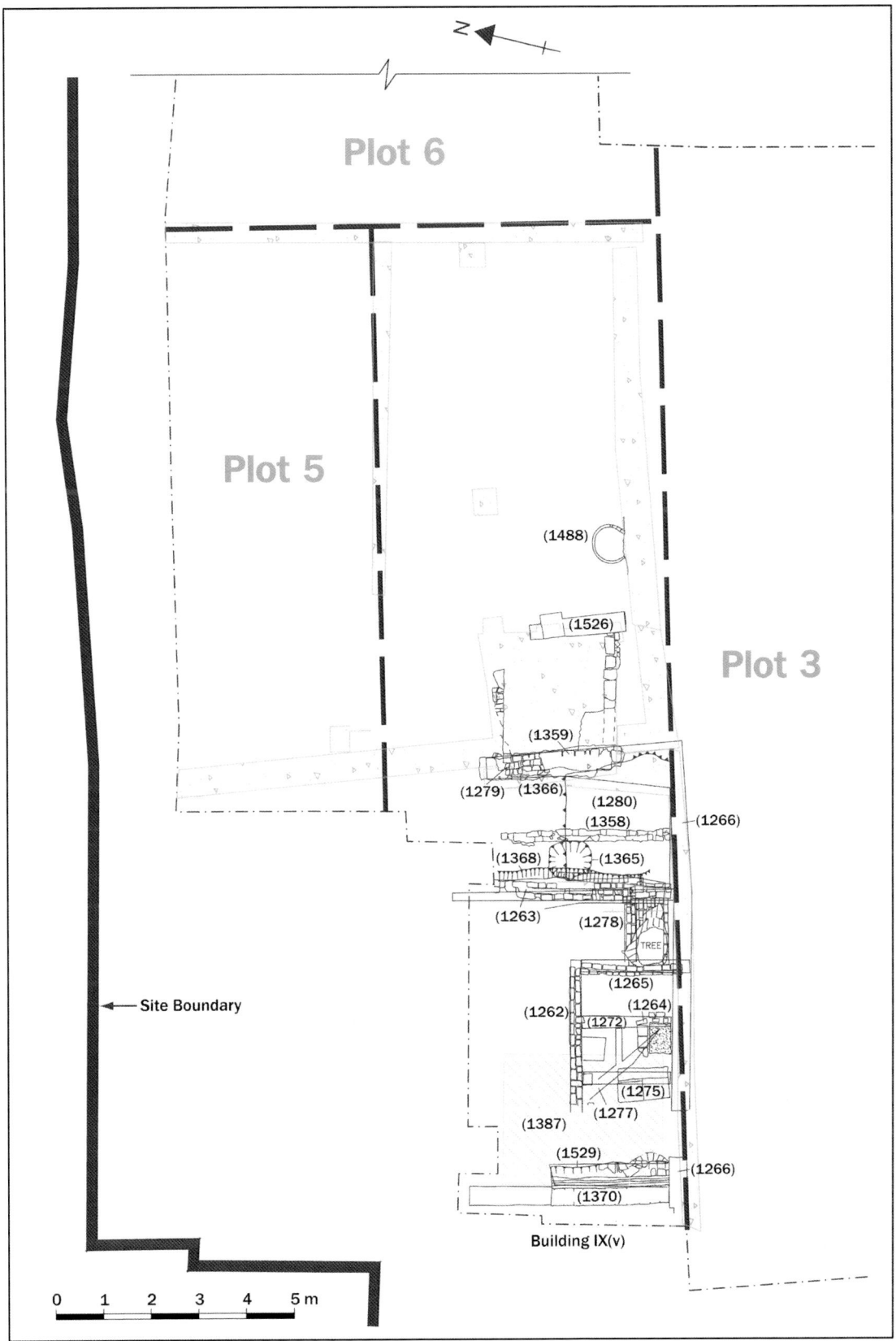

Ill 2.1.92 Phase IX Plot 4: plan. (Scale 1/125)

95

terrace created a zone between cess pit (1526)/(1359) and the yard area at the back of Building IX(v).

Approximately 5 m to the east of wall Building IX(v) there was a north–south brick wall, (1358), which appeared to form the western side of a terrace within Plot 4. The foundation cut, (1368), had vertical sides and a flat base and was seen to be cutting sandstone structure (456). The wall itself appeared to have at least two phases to its construction. The earlier phase was slightly offset to the east and consisted of a brick foundation 0.3 m wide, onto which had been built a poorly faced superstructure, (1358), which survived to a height of six courses with dimensions of 3.72 x 0.27 x 0.80 m. The brickwork was bonded in a hard pink-brown mortar but was not pointed, suggesting that the wall was not intended to be seen. Wall (1263) may have served as a refacing of the original wall as it lay directly to the west and was constructed in English Garden Wall bond, which would have complemented the eastern gable wall of the 19 Bridge Street building. Wall (1263) was bonded in a well pointed pink-grey lime mortar.

Boundary wall (1266)

During Phase VIII the southern edge of Plot 4 had been defined by a substantial sandstone boundary wall, (1386)/(1385)/(1381), some of which survived until demolition work in 2001. However, during Phase IX this boundary wall was repaired and heightened with a length of brick wall, (1266), which had surviving dimensions of 7.70 x 0.34 x 0.89 m. The wall had nine courses of brick surviving in English Garden Wall bond, similar to terrace wall (1263). It sat within a construction trench, (1367), where it ran across the southern end of the garden terrace defined by walls (1263) and (1279) and it clearly postdated both of these walls.

Building IX(vi)

In the corner formed between garden terrace wall (1263) and southern boundary wall (1266) a small brick structure, (1278), was subsequently constructed. It measured 1.23 x 1.13 m and survived to a height of 0.7 m. The interior had a brick surface which would have raised the internal height of the floor above that of the exterior yard. The structure probably served as a toilet, although there was no evidence for drainage: it probably housed a night-soil bucket.

Building IX(vii)

Building IX(vii) lay immediately to the west of IX(vi) and appears to have superseded it. It comprised a rectangular structure built against the northern face of boundary wall (1266) and was given a group context, (1267), which included brick walls (1272), (1275), (1265) and (1262). All four walls were apparently built in English Garden Wall bond and were bonded in a pale brown lime mortar. Wall (1272) formed a central north–south partition, creating two small rooms of similar dimensions. The easternmost of these rooms had been given a floor surface of 9 x 9" quarry tiles. The building was accessed from the north and, like Building IX(vi), probably served as toilets. Again, there was no evidence for drainage during Phase IX and so probably housed night-soil buckets.

Well (1488)

To the east of cess pit (1526)/(1359) a circular brick structure, (1488), was identified with an internal diameter of 1.73 m. It was made of hand-made bricks bonded in red clay and was interpreted as a well; only the top 0.95 m of this structure was excavated owing to the limits imposed on the depth of excavation. It sat within a construction cut, (1490), with a diameter of 2.05 m, which had been backfilled with mid-yellow-brown silt clay, (1489), which was devoid of artefacts. The interior of the well had been backfilled with a mid-grey silt sand, (1491), which was rich in ash, clinker and domestic rubbish, including pottery dated to the nineteenth century.

Plot 5 (III 2.1.93)

Cess pit (1487)

The earliest Phase IX feature within Plot 5 was a rectangular shaped pit, (1487), at the western end of the plot. The pit had steep sides and a flat base and was 0.26 m deep. It had been backfilled with a greyish green silt loam, (1486), which contained pottery of nineteenth-century date. A sample from the fill, <5143>, was found to contain plant remains (*ficus* and *vitis*) which would imply it had served as a cess pit.

Building IX(viii)
Cellar (1477)/(1476)

The easternmost three-quarters of Plot 5 were entirely taken up by a substantial cellar measuring at least thee metres north–south and seven metres east–west. The western end of the cellar was defined by brick wall (1477), 0.35 m thick and bonded with light grey lime mortar. This wall was built within a construction trench, (1067)/(1665), which had vertical sides and a flat base; it had been backfilled with a grey-brown loam, (1502), which was rich in building debris. The southern side of the cellar was defined by wall (1476), which was composed of well dressed sandstone blocks bonded in an off-white lime mortar. Whilst the cellar was still in use the internal face of wall (1476) had been covered in a hard cement render. Ultimately it had been carefully backfilled with tightly packed rows of complete bricks, (1478), in order to avoid later ground settlement; it is believed that this was done immediately prior to the construction of the new *Chester Chronicle* newspaper buildings during the early 1960s. Only the top one metre of the cellar was investigated as the lower part lay beneath the limit of excavation.

Wall (1498)

To the west of the cellar a short length of brick wall, (1498), was identified running east–west and measuring 0.90 x 0.36 x 0.11 m. The wall was built in a shallow construction trench, (1068), with a square terminus at its eastern end. The purpose of the wall is unknown but is likely to have been associated with Building IX(viii).

Layer (1499)

To the south of wall (1498) there was a thin layer of greyish black silt clay, (1499), that covered an area measuring 1.50 x 0.60 x 0.04 m. The layer was rich in charcoal but produced no datable artefacts.

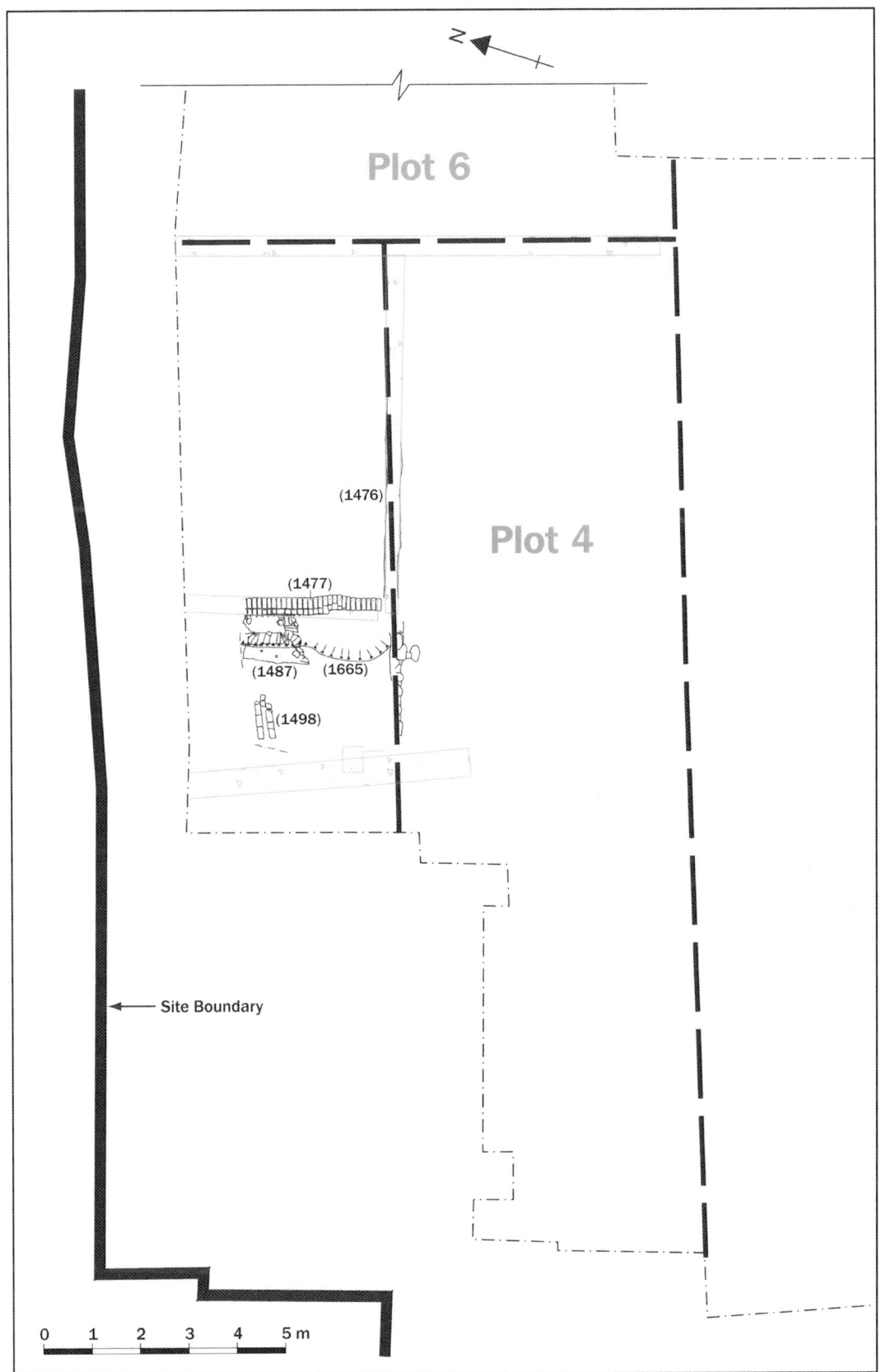

Plot 6

Plot 4

(1476)

(1477)

(1487)   (1665)

(1498)

Site Boundary

0 1 2 3 4 5 m

Ill 2.1.93 Phase IX Plot 5: plan. (Scale 1/125)

Plot 6 (Ills 2.1.94–6)

Phase IXa

Throughout most of the nineteenth century the cartographic evidence suggests that a large proportion of Plot 6 was open ground. The plan of 1879 labels this area as 'The Drying Grounds', the eastern boundary of which was represented by sandstone wall (306). To the east of this boundary wall the 1875 OS map shows an area that looks like alleyway, which was probably represented by cobbled surface (313). A lead water pipe, (564), had been installed by excavating a trench through this cobbled surface and then reinstating the cobbles, suggesting that the surface stayed in use after the installation. Piped water was introduced to the city between 1826 and 1831.

Although the label 'The Drying Grounds' seems to be self-explanatory, the evidence suggests that it was an area liable to become overgrown, as suggested by the numerous tree-bole pits attributable to this phase. The area also seems to have been a convenient place to bury family pets, as evidenced by the dog and cat burials identified. A square timber structure (Building IX(ix)) in the southwestern corner of the plot may have been a privy.

Pit group (727), (606) and (628)

Towards the centre of the southern side of Plot 6 a complicated sequence of intercutting pits and deposits was identified and seen to predate boundary ditch (539)/(555), thus representing some of the earliest activity in Phase IX. The pits are likely to represent the remains of a series of cess pits in this part of the plot.

The earliest event was the cutting of a large oval pit, (727), which was aligned roughly north–south and was 0.70 m deep. It had been truncated at the south end by a later wall foundation, (395), but had a U-shaped profile on the surviving short axis. The pit had been deliberately backfilled with a dump of purple-brown ash, (713), which was probably derived from hearth sweepings.

To the west of pit (727) the northern edge of a second large pit, (606), was identified; most of the pit had been removed by later wall foundation (395) and it had surviving dimensions of 2.10 x 0.50 x 0.50 m. Pit (606) had been backfilled with a dump of dark brown silt clay, (607), which was rich in building debris and contained pottery dated to the nineteenth–twentieth century. Roughly 1 m to the north of pit (606) was a discrete deposit of dark brown silt clay, (630), which was rich in building debris and contained nineteenth-century pottery. It is possible that (630) was the upcast from the excavation of pit (606) or, in view of its similarity with (607), it could have been the remnants of the material used in the backfill.

Almost directly above pit (727) a second large, north–south oval pit, (628), was subsequently dug. The southern extent of the pit had again been removed by wall foundation (395), leaving excavated dimensions of 2.08 x 0.90 x 0.27 m. The pit had been backfilled with a deposit of dark brown silt, (629), which was rich in coal and charcoal fragments. A deposit of dark brown silt clay rich in building debris, (548)/(558), had been dumped to the west of the pit and covered an area 2.30 x 0.75 x 0.30 m. Deposit (548)/(558) produced pottery dated to the nineteenth–twentieth century and was thought to represent the upcast from the excavation of pit (628).

Boundary ditch (390)/(539)/(555)

A linear feature was recorded in three sections as cuts (390), (539) and (555); these were later seen to be part of a single shallow ditch 1 m wide and 0.28 m deep, which cut across the eastern third of Plot 6 on a north–south alignment. The southern end of the ditch became indistinct as it reached later wall foundation (395); however, it was demonstrated to have cut backfilled pit (628) and thus postdated it. The ditch was traced for a length of roughly 8 m before it ran beyond the northern edge of the excavation. The primary fill was a yellow-brown sand silt, (391)/(542)/(554), up to 0.18 m thick and rich in building debris and charcoal. The upper fill, (553), was a grey-brown silt clay 0.1 m thick and rich in fragments of lime mortar/plaster and charcoal. Only residual finds were recovered from this ditch but it is likely to be earlier than *c* 1875 as it was later cut by the foundation trench of boundary wall (306), described below. Ditch (390)/(539)/(555) is thought to mark the creation of a new boundary which effectively divided Plot 6 into two properties; subsequent parallel developments either side of the boundary seem to bear this out.

Wall (306)

The upper boundary ditch fill, (553), was later cut by wall construction trench (397), which was directly above and parallel with ditch (390)/(539)/(555) along its entire length. The construction trench had vertical sides and a flat base, being 0.55 m wide and 0.4 m deep. The primary fill, (914), was a charcoal-rich dark brown silt clay which possibly represented a layer of trample in the trench prior to the construction of the wall. The wall, (306), had been constructed directly on top of fill (914) and consisted of roughly shaped sandstone blocks bonded in lime mortar which formed a surviving structure 6.04 x 0.4 x 0.45 m. After the wall foundation had been constructed the remaining construction trench was backfilled with a mid-grey-brown sand loam, (401)/(913), rich in building debris. This wall appears to reinforce the property boundary marked by ditch (390)/(539)/(555) and is shown on the 1st edition OS map of 1875.

Layers (396), (511), (827) and (513)

To the east of the property boundary first defined by ditch (390)/(539)/(555) and then later by wall (306), the area of the excavation had been heavily disturbed by the line of late nineteenth-century sewer pipe trenches, (360) and (339), and a twentieth-century concrete and brick inspection hatch, (335). In spite of this later disturbance a stratigraphic sequence was still discernable in the archaeological record.

The earliest horizon in the area east of boundary wall (306) consisted of the remnants of several discrete layers, the main significance of which was the dating material which they contained. The earliest was a layer of dark grey-brown clay loam, (396), which covered an area measuring 2.1 x 0.4 m. The western side of layer (396) was subsequently covered by a layer of mid-brown sand silt, (511), which produced pottery dated to the nineteenth–twentieth century and covered an area measuring 1.90 x 0.94 m. To the south of layer (511) there was another discrete layer of dark brown sand silt, (827), which covered an area measuring 2.45 x 0.90 m. Layer (827) was rich in small fragments of coal and also produced pottery

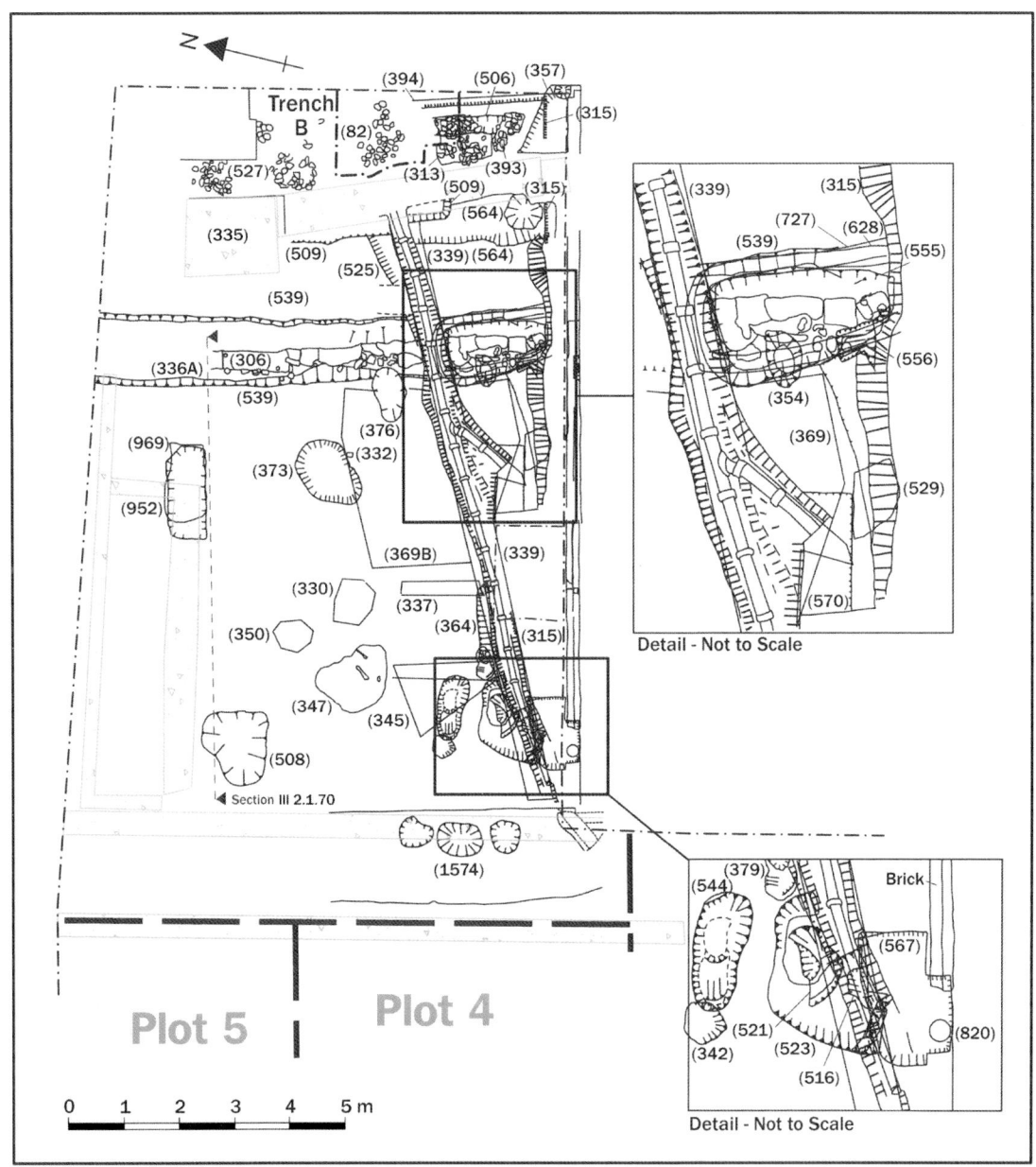

III 2.1.94 Phase IX Plot 6: plan. (Scale 1/125)

dating to the nineteenth–twentieth century. Finally, to the west of layer (511) there was a patchy layer of light yellow-brown sand loam, (513), which survived over an area measuring 1 x 0.22 m and produced pottery dating to the eighteenth–twentieth century.

Cobbled surface (527)/(82)/(313)

A fairly extensive cobbled surface was subsequently laid in the area to the east of boundary wall (306), but it had been badly disturbed by later twentieth-century activity and it only survived in dispersed patches. The northern limit was marked by three isolated areas of cobbling, (527), made from water-worn cobbles up to 70 mm in diameter. To the south, another intact patch of cobbling, (82,) was encountered within Evaluation Trench B, where an area measuring 1.5 x 0.5 m was recorded. Further south again a third area of cobbling, (313), was recorded covering an area measuring 1.1 x 0.85 m; in this case the cobbles were set in pale yellow sand which contained nineteenth-century pottery.

Wheel ruts (506), (377) and (366)

A short length of a gully, (506), could be seen cutting through layer (511) on a north–south alignment. It had surviving dimensions of 0.60 x 0.35 x 0.07 m and a U-shaped profile. The fill, (505), was a dark brown silt loam containing water-worn cobbles that were probably derived from surface (313), suggesting that the cutting of gully (506) had disturbed the surface. Fill (505) produced pottery dating to the nineteenth–twentieth century.

Approximately 2 m to the west of gully (506) was a pair of parallel slots. The first, (377), had surviving dimensions of 1.66 x 0.12 m and was aligned north–south; the slot was filled with yellow-brown silt clay (378). Adjacent to and cutting slot (377) was parallel slot, (366), which had surviving dimensions of 1.58 x 0.46 x 0.20 m, although it was noted that the width and depth were variable along the length. Slot (366) was filled with a dark brown silt, (367), which produced nineteenth–twentieth century pottery and a residual copper alloy token.

It seems likely that all three slots were probably wheel

ruts caused by cart wheels rolling along cobbled surface (527)/(82)/(313).

Water pipe trench (564)

A shallow trench, (564), had been excavated into cobbled surface (313) on a north–south alignment and had surviving dimensions of 2.40 x 0.90 x 0.18 m. The base of the cut was still occupied by a length of lead water pipe 2 m long with a diameter of 20 mm. Above the pipe had been deposited a backfill of mid-brown silt loam, (512), which contained nineteenth-century pottery. The upper part of fill (512) was rich in cobbles and fragments of sandstone which implied some attempt to reinstate the surface, suggesting that it was still functional at the time the water pipe was installed. Piped water was first introduced to Chester between 1826 and 1831.

Repair to surface (313)

A small pit, (392), measuring 0.85 x 0.35 x 0.20 m had appeared within cobbled surface (313) after the laying of water pipe (564). It may represent a pothole in the cobbled surface created by wear and tear; the subsequent fill, (393), was nearly entirely composed of water-worn cobbles, implying a deliberate attempt to repair the surface.

Building IX(ix)

The existence of a square timber structure measuring approximately 1.5 x 1.5 m was suggested by a series of three slots, (337), (364) and (345) (group context (398)), situated in the south-west corner of the plot. The absence of a slot on the northern side may indicate the position of a doorway. The presence of *ficus/vitis* plant remains and dog/pig coprolite may suggest that this structure was a privy.

The eastern and southern sides of the building were defined by a continuous L-shaped slot 0.28 m wide and 0.28 m deep, with vertical sides and a flat base. The eastern side was recorded as cut (337) and extended for 1.47 m, whilst the southern side was recorded as cut (364) and was recorded for a length of 1.22 m. The lower fill of slots, (337) and (364) ,was a mid-grey-brown silt clay (365) rich in coal and slate fragments. The upper fill, (338), was a light red-grey silt clay rich in charcoal and ash which was probably derived from domestic hearth sweepings.

The western side of the building was defined by slot (345), which ran parallel to slot (337); it had vertical sides, a flat base and excavated dimensions of 1.89 x 0.38 x 0.40 m. Slot (345) had a series of four successive fills: the lowest was a charcoal-rich black silt clay, (384); above this was a grey-red ash deposit, (383), which was rich in domestic waste. The southern half of the slot was then filled with grey-orange silt clay, (346), which contained nineteenth–twentieth-century pottery; the upper fill of the slot was a mid-grey-brown silt clay, (381).

Adjoining the western side of slot (345) was a short east–west gully, (544), measuring 1.20 x 0.57 x 0.48 m. This gully had a primary fill of red-brown silt clay, (547), which could have acted as a lining. A lower fill of dark grey-brown silt clay, (546), was subsequently deposited in the gully and an environmental sample, <5033>, produced evidence of charred pulses and *ficus/vitis*. The upper fill, (545), was a mid-grey-brown silt clay which produced fragments of coprolite, probably derived from dog or pig;

this fill was also sampled, <5032>, producing evidence of charred cereal and *ficus/vitis*. Gully (544) was rather enigmatic but the environmental evidence suggested the possibility that it had contained faecal material and as such may have acted as a drain associated with Building IX(ix).

Pit (523)

To the south-west of Building IX(ix) there was a pit which at the time of excavation was interpreted as a series of three intercutting features allocated cut numbers (523), (521), and (516). However, it became apparent that this was a single sub-circular pit 0.4 m deep. The three fills of this pit were, in fact, each ascribed an individual cut number and from this information it is possible to suggest the following depositional sequence. The lowest fill was a green-brown silt clay, (524), that contained nineteenth-century pottery. This was covered by a deposit of grey-brown silt clay, (522), and an upper fill of mid-grey-brown silt clay, (517), which contained domestic waste. The nature of the lower fill suggests that this pit had functioned as a latrine.

Pits (969), (952), (839) and (841)

To the west of wall (306) and on the northern edge of the excavation there were two pairs of intercutting rectangular pits. These pits were all relatively shallow and subrectangular in shape, but excavation revealed nothing about their function or purpose.

The first pair comprised pits (969) and (952). (969) had steep sides, a flat base and was 0.32 m deep. The pit was backfilled with grey-brown clay, (970), which was rich in building debris and domestic waste. The later pit, (952), was situated in almost the same spot and on the same alignment as pit (969) and had a similar profile and depth. It was backfilled with dark brown silt clay (953) that was rich in building debris and domestic waste.

The second pair consisted of pits (839) and (841). (839) was 0.35 m deep and had been backfilled with a mid-brown silt clay, (840), which contained some domestic waste. Pit (841) had been excavated into this fill (840); it was smaller in plan and was 0.27 m deep Pit (841) had been backfilled with mid-brown silt clay (842).

Dog burial (376) and cat burials (354)

Immediately to the west of boundary wall (306) there was a group of animal burials which presumably represent a small pet cemetery. These burials were situated along the line of wall (306) and clearly respected the boundary. Along with the evidence for shrubs and trees described below, it seems probable that these burials were deposited at a time when the area was functioning as open ground.

The most northerly burial consisted of an oval pit aligned east–west, (376), measuring 1 x 0.55 m. The base of the pit was filled with the articulated remains of a single adult dog. The pit had been deliberately backfilled with pale brown silt clay, (375) (Ill 2.1.95).

To the south of pit (376) was a subrectangular shaped pit, (354), again aligned east–west and measuring 0.58 x 0.30 x 0.12 m. The base of the pit was filled with the articulated remains of two adult cats which appeared to have been buried at the same time; the lower cat had been placed with its head to the west while the second cat had been placed on top of the first with its head to the east (Ill

III 2.1.95 Phase IX Plot 6: dog burial (376), looking E.

III 2.1.96 Phase IX Plot 6: cat burials (354), looking N.

2.1.96). The pit had been deliberately backfilled with dark grey sand loam, (353).

Tree bole pits (556), (529), (336), (350), (330), (328)/ (347), (326), (342), (508), (379) and (1574)

Aside from the animal burials the remaining features to the west of boundary wall (306) were all shallow and often irregularly shaped pits which have been interpreted as the sites of root boles. These pits did not appear to follow any sort of arrangement and are unlikely to have been part of a formal planting scheme, so it seems more likely that they indicate a period of disuse and the natural growth of vegetation.

Pit (556) had an irregular shape and profile and was 0.40 m deep. It had been backfilled with a deposit of dark brown clay silt, (557).

Pit (529) was subrectangular in shape and was 0.08 m deep. It was backfilled with a deposit of mortar-rich brown silt clay, (530).

Pit (336) was only partially exposed within the area of excavation but was irregular in shape and 0.33 m deep. It was backfilled with dark grey-brown sand loam, (352), rich in charcoal, ash and coal probably derived from hearth sweepings; a sample, < 5021>, produced charred cereal, pulses and *ulex*. To the west of pit (336) there was a small rectangular stake hole, (332), filled with a dark brown silt, (331), which suggested that the base of the stake had rotted *in situ*.

Pit (350) was an irregular semicircle in plan and was 0.30 m deep. It was backfilled with mid-grey-brown silt loam, (351), which was rich in fragments of brick and produced pottery dated to the late eighteenth–nineteenth century.

Pit (330) was an irregular D-shaped cut 0.30 m deep. The backfill was a mid-brown clay silt, (329), which was rich in building debris.

Pit (328)/(347) was an irregular, kidney-shaped cut 0.35 m deep, with irregular sides and an uneven base. The backfill was mid-grey-brown silt loam, (327)/(348), containing some building debris.

Pit (326) was an irregular rectangular cut 0.30 m deep. The backfill was a mid-grey-brown sand loam, (325), containing some building debris.

Pit (342) was oval in plan and was 0.30 m deep. The backfill was a dark brown silt clay, (343), rich in building debris, charcoal and ash.

Pit (508) was slightly heart-shaped in plan with irregular sides and was 0.30 m deep. The lower fill, (518), produced a penny of Edward III. The upper fill was mid-brown sand silt, (507), which had concentrations of charcoal within it; sample <5028> produced charred cereal and *ficus/vitis*.

Pit (379) was an irregular oval 0.16 m deep. The backfill was a mid-orange-grey silt clay, (380), which contained building debris and a cat's skull; the presence of the latter might suggest that this was a disturbed pet burial.

Pit group (1574) was a north–south alignment of three sub-circular pits along the western edge of Plot 6. The pits were each approximately 0.3 m deep and running from north to south were 0.54 m, 0.8 m and 0.5 m in diameter. The fills produced pottery of nineteenth-century date.

Phase IXb

Prior to the installation of ceramic drain (355), a large square pit, (369), was excavated to the west of wall (306). This pit was apparently immediately filled with brick demolition rubble which was not well compacted. Presumably the intention was to create a well drained area of ground. It is tempting to suggest that the rubble was derived from the demolition of wall (306) or the row of terraced buildings to the south, in preparation for the building of the Brown's store extension. The exact function of the pit is not certain, but it may have been designed as a soakaway prior to the installation of more effective drainage.

The brick building bordering the southern edge of Plot 6 (now part of Brown's department store) postdates the plan of 1879 but is shown on the second edition OS map of 1898. This new building appears to have encroached on the southern part of 'Drying Ground' and would have necessitated the demolition of boundary wall (306). Associated with the construction of the Brown's building, ceramic drains (355) and (359) appear to have been laid to service the rainwater goods from the roof. Generally ceramic sewer pipes were being installed in the city from 1892, and all built-up areas of the city had been furnished with ceramic foul drain pipes by 1902 (Matthews 1995). Ceramic drain (355) was certainly cut through the remains of wall (306).

An odd addition to this area was the installation of a telegraph pole, which appears to have respected the Brown's building of 1879–98 but predated the construction of the twentieth-century brick outbuildings later occupying the northern part of the plot and the western garden boundary wall (528). It is uncertain whether the telegraph pole and its accompanying stanchion bases predated the ceramic drains (355) and (359), but they do appear to be stratigraphically contemporary with the Brown's shop wall (317). It is tempting to see this feature as part of the evolution in communication technology being exploited by the *Chester Chronicle*. Certainly the presence of this structure would have rendered the area useless for any other purpose.

Soakaway (369)

The earliest feature to appear within Plot 6 during Phase IXb was a large square pit, (369)/(372), to the west of wall (306). Pit (369)/(372) measured 2.98 x 2.91 x 0.26 m and had steep sides and a flat base; the cutting of its eastern edge had slightly disturbed dog burial (376). The pit had been backfilled with brick rubble and pale yellow-brown sand, (368), within which was a lump of brick masonry still bonded together in lime mortar, (370). The loose backfill had been covered by a deposit of dark brown silt clay, (344), which would have served to reinstate the pit to the height of the surrounding ground surface. The pit was thought to have functioned as a soakaway, although it probably was not in use for long before the insertion of more permanent sewerage.

Building IX(x)

The eastern end of Plot 6 was defined by the existing wall of Brown's department store (Debenhams), which was probably constructed after 1879 and before *c* 1898. The building was largely outside of the scope of the excavation and was retained within the new development; only the western wall was examined as part of the archaeological work. The foundations were first exposed within Evaluation Trench B, where they were recorded as a north–south brick foundation, (79), within a foundation trench, (81), which had been backfilled with loose rubble and mortar, (80). The wall was re-examined during the main excavation phase and the foundation trench, (394), was recorded as 0.85 m deep. The trench backfill, (395), was recorded as a mid-brown sandy loam which produced pottery of nineteenth–twentieth-century date.

Building IX(iii)
Brick wall (317)

The southern side of Plot 6 was delimited by a substantial brick wall, (317), which still formed the northern edge

of Brown's department store building at the beginning of the excavation in 2001. The wall was aligned east–west and appeared to be of a single phase of construction, which the cartographic evidence suggests was undertaken sometime between 1882 and 1899. The wall was recorded as part of the standing building survey in 2001. The brick foundation, (317,) was 1 m deep and sat in a foundation trench (315)/(816), which had been backfilled with dark brown silt loam (316)/(815) which contained nineteenth–twentieth-century pottery.

Sewer/drain pipe (355) and (359)

A complex network of sewer pipes was introduced to Plot 6 during Phase IXb. As the pipes were seen to be connected to the drainage for the guttering of Building IX(iii) it seems likely that they were contemporary with its construction and therefore dated to the period 1882–99.

The principal branch of the sewer pipe was aligned roughly east–west with a slight fall from west to east. It comprised twenty segments of salt-glazed ceramic pipe, (355). Each segment was 650 mm long and had a diameter of 130 mm; the joints had each been sealed with mortar. The pipe had been laid in a trench, (339), which had vertical sides and measured 10.5 x 0.5 x 0.5 m. This had been entirely backfilled with dark brown clay silt, (340), containing building debris. The western end of the pipe was supported by a brick and mortar structure, (569), measuring 0.80 x 0.24 x 0.40 m. This structure sat within a separate construction trench, (567), suggesting that it may have been a later addition, perhaps to prevent the subsidence and collapse of the sewer. The backfill, (568), was dark grey silt clay rich in building debris.

The eastern end of pipe (355) formed a T junction with a second ceramic sewer pipe laid on a north–south alignment. This second pipe was laid in trench (509)/(525), measuring 2.62 x 0.30 x 0.32 m and with a fall from south to north terminating at a twentieth-century brick and concrete inspection chamber, (335). Trench (509)/(525) had been backfilled with very dark brown sand silt, (510)/(526), that contained pottery of nineteenth–twentieth-century date.

A short tributary branch of sewer pipe was recorded in the south-east corner of Plot 6, serving to carry rain water from roof furniture into the main sewer system. The sewer, (359), again consisted of sections of salt-glazed ceramic pipe identical to (355), forming an alignment falling from south-east to north-west. The ceramic pipe sat within a trench (357) which measured 1.40 x 0.70 x 0.20 m and had been backfilled with grey-brown silt loam, (358).

A second short tributary branch of sewer pipe was recorded at the south-western corner of Plot 6 serving to carry rain water from roof furniture into the main sewer system. This again consisted of sections of salt-glazed ceramic pipe identical to (355) and formed an alignment falling from south-west to north-east. The pipe sat within a trench, (820), measuring 1.30 x 0.82 x 1.02 m backfilled with dark grey silt clay (821) contained nineteenth–twentieth-century pottery.

Telegraph pole pit (373) and stanchion bases (58), (570) and (945)

A late addition to Plot 6 was the installation of a telegraph pole, (373), which appeared to respect the Browns building of 1879–98 but predated the construction of the twentieth-century brick outbuildings later occupying the northern part of the plot and the western garden boundary wall (528). It is uncertain whether the telegraph pole and its accompanying stanchion bases, (58), (570) and (945), predated the ceramic drains (355) and (359) but they did appear to be stratigraphically contemporary with the Brown's shop wall (317). It is tempting to see this feature as part of the evolution in communication technology being exploited by the *Chester Chronicle*.

The surviving base of the timber telegraph pole itself sat in a circular pit, (373), with a diameter of 1.06 m and a depth of 1 m. The pit had been backfilled with greyish brown sand silt, (374), which contained nineteenth-century pottery.

Three stanchion base pits, (58), (570) and (945), were also identified. Each pit was rectangular in plan measuring 1.17 x 0.52 x 0.90 m with vertical sides and a flat base. At the base of each pit was a length of timber, into the top of which was an iron fitting which probably originally held one end of a length of steel cable, the other end being attached to the top of the telegraph pole. Pit (58) was located in the area of Evaluation Trench C and was backfilled by (59) and (60). Pit (570) was located near twentieth-century manhole structure (335) and was backfilled with a succession of brown clay loam deposits, (620) and (571). Pit (945) was located on the northern side of Plot 6 and was backfilled with deposit (946).

Phase X: 20 century

This phase largely comprises the foundations and services of buildings demolished in 2001 and discussed under Building Recording.

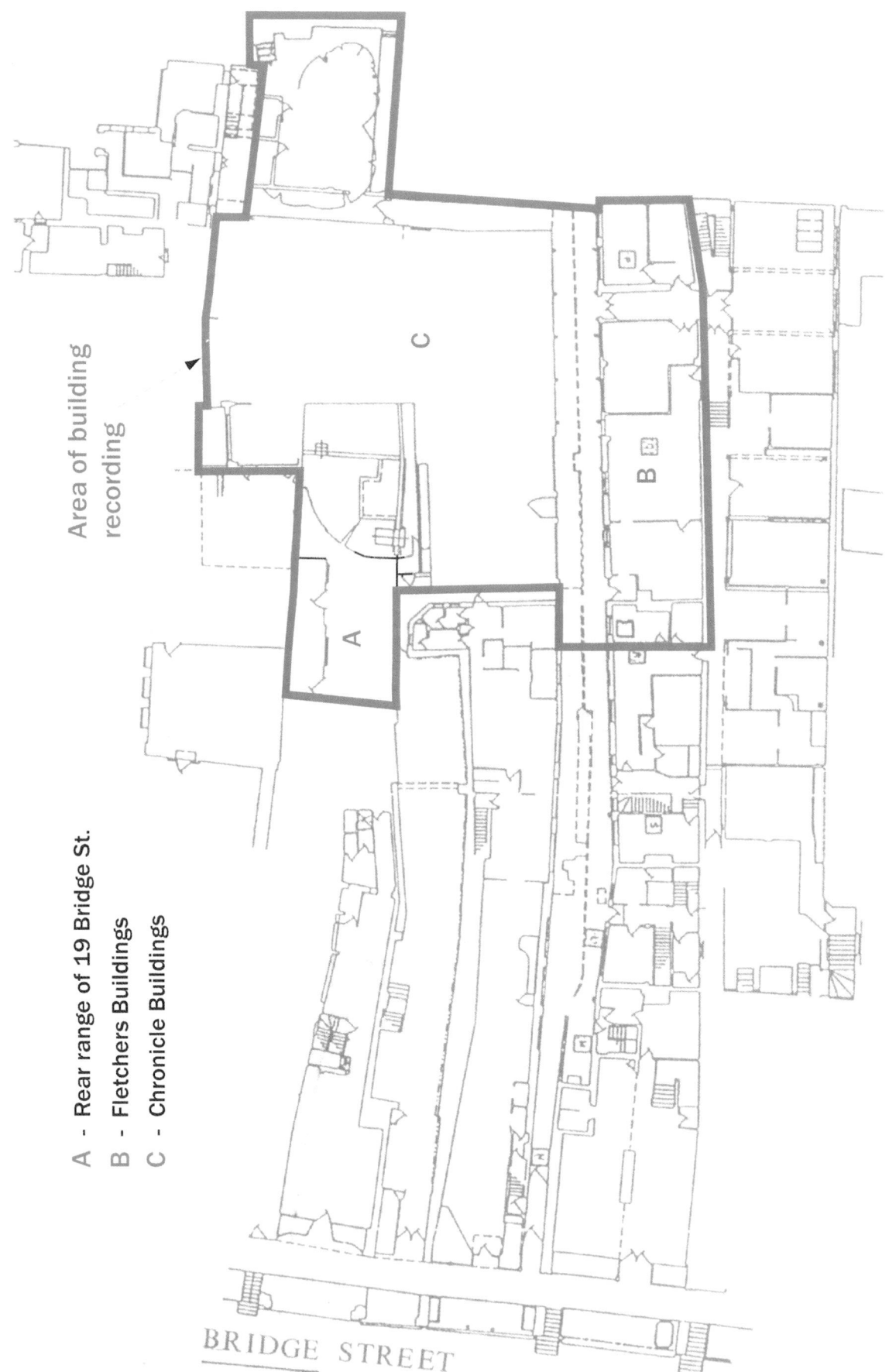

Area of building recording

A - Rear range of 19 Bridge St.
B - Fletchers Buildings
C - Chronicle Buildings

BRIDGE STREET

III **2.2.1** 19–29 Bridge Street before demolition: plan. (Not to scale)

Building Recording   Peter Owen

Introduction

This chapter gives an account of the buildings on the site that were demolished prior to the construction works for the Debenhams extension (Ill 2.2.1). One of these, the 'Ursula Keyes' building, which formed the rear range of 19 Bridge Street, had already been the subject of two building recording exercises (by Nigel Neil in 1998 and Archaeological Investigations in 2000). That work has been incorporated into this report and their contribution is duly acknowledged. The other buildings recorded during this project comprised two main elements: the early nineteenth-century buildings known as Fletcher's Buildings, which lay on the south side of the passageway to Bridge Street and formed part of the *Chester Chronicle* offices, and the 1960s buildings which formed the *Chester Chronicle* print works and further offices, to the north of the passageway. A measured survey was undertaken of all the buildings within the site and the data used to produce a set of scale drawings, some of which are reproduced in this report. A photographic record on 35 mm colour and monochrome film was made of the general views of the exterior of the buildings, including their setting, and also of the principal rooms, circulation areas and any surviving features of historic interest.

Rear range of 19 Bridge Street

To the west of the 1960s *Chester Chronicle* buildings lay the rear range of 19 Bridge Street, an eighteenth-century structure with possible earlier elements (Ill 2.2.2). This account of the building is based on the survey undertaken by Neil and the enhancement survey subsequently undertaken by Archaeological Investigations Ltd. The documentary research undertaken by Backhouse (*this volume*) has demonstrated that in the early nineteenth century the building was used as a warehouse by Robert Brittain, who operated a woollen drapery on Bridge Street Row.

The rear range of 19 Bridge Street consisted of a three-storey building constructed of brick in English garden wall bond. The gable roof was covered with asbestos concrete sheet with ceramic ridge tiles. A sandstone plinth, *c* 3.8 m long and *c* 0.35 m high, comprised of blocks up to 0.82 m long and 0.25 m deep, was visible at the base of the south elevation (Ill 2.2.3). That this represented the footings of an earlier building was confirmed during the excavation, which identified that a sandstone structure served by a stone-lined cess pit and a brick-lined well had previously occupied the site. The east elevation (Ill 2.2.4) contained a small rectangular window on the ground floor (Row level) and segmental arch-headed window openings with brick sills on the first and second floors. The north elevation (Ill 2.2.5) contained two segmental arch-headed doorways, and evidence for a third doorway was observed between these. There were also

Ill 2.2.2 Rear range of 19 Bridge Street: general view from NE.

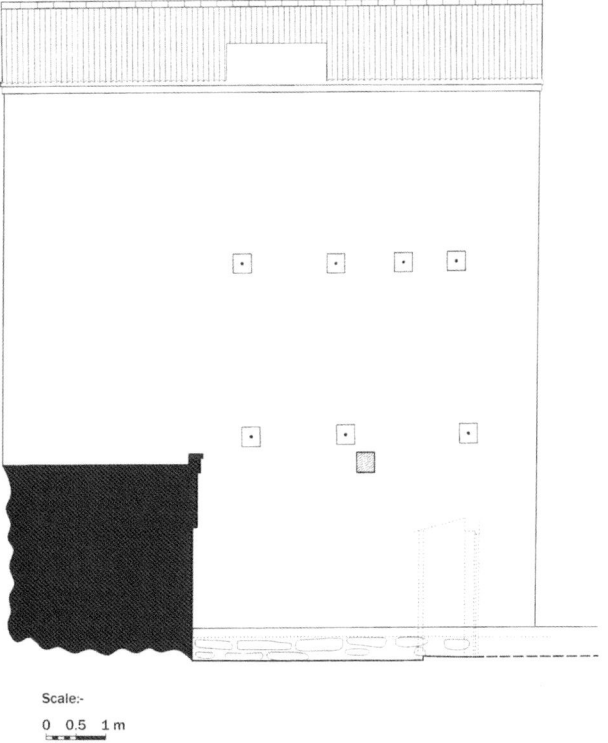

Scale:-

0   0.5   1 m

Ill 2.2.3 Rear range of 19 Bridge Street: S elevation. (Scale 1/125)

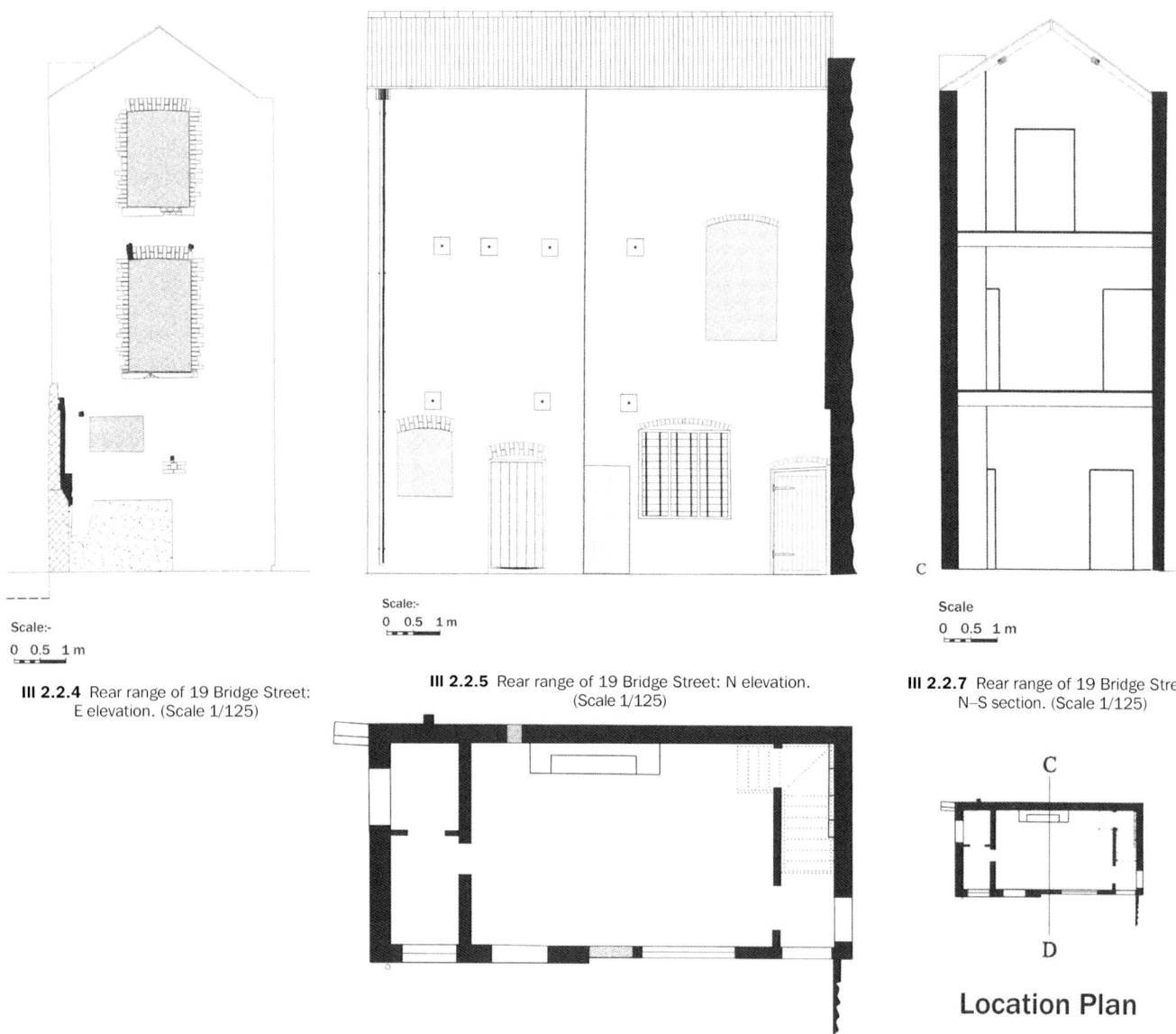

Scale:-

0 0.5 1 m

III 2.2.4 Rear range of 19 Bridge Street:
E elevation. (Scale 1/125)

Scale:-

0 0.5 1 m

III 2.2.5 Rear range of 19 Bridge Street: N elevation.
(Scale 1/125)

Scale

0 0.5 1 m

III 2.2.7 Rear range of 19 Bridge Street:
N–S section. (Scale 1/125)

C

D

Location Plan

Scale:-

0 0.5 1 m

III 2.2.6 Rear range of 19 Bridge Street: ground-floor plan. (Scale 1/125)

three segmental arch-headed windows, two on the ground floor (Row level) and one on the first floor. As can be seen in Ill 2.2.5, all three windows were of different dimensions.

Internally the ground floor was entered *via* the western doorway of the north elevation. This led into a small hallway which gave access to an enclosed stairway leading to the upper floors and a large ground-floor (Row-level) room with a centrally placed chimney breast set against the north wall. Two smaller rooms lay at the east end of the ground floor, one of which contained a stone sink and drainer. The first and second floors contained one main room each.

Immediately to the east of the rear of 19 Bridge Street lay a small brick-floored courtyard. This courtyard contained the brick foundations of two smaller demolished buildings. Another courtyard lay to the east of the *Chester Chronicle* buildings, associated with the rear of 32 Eastgate Street.

Fletcher's Buildings

These buildings consisted of part of a row of two-storey buildings, formerly houses, dating to the early nineteenth century and used as the *Chester Chronicle* newspaper's offices since the later part of that century. Ill 2.2.9 shows a general view, looking east along the passageway from Bridge Street Row: Fletcher's Buildings can be seen on the right-hand side. The north elevation of the building is shown in Ill 2.2.10

Fletcher's Buildings were built of hand-made brick in English garden wall bond. As can be seen from the change in roofline on the north elevation shown in Ill 2.2.11, they were made up of two distinct elements, the join running vertically down the centre of the figure. The roofline of the western portion had been altered to accommodate a later asphalt roof with pitched and flat sections. Interestingly, the new roof was installed over the original pitched slate roof, and at the time of this recording exer-

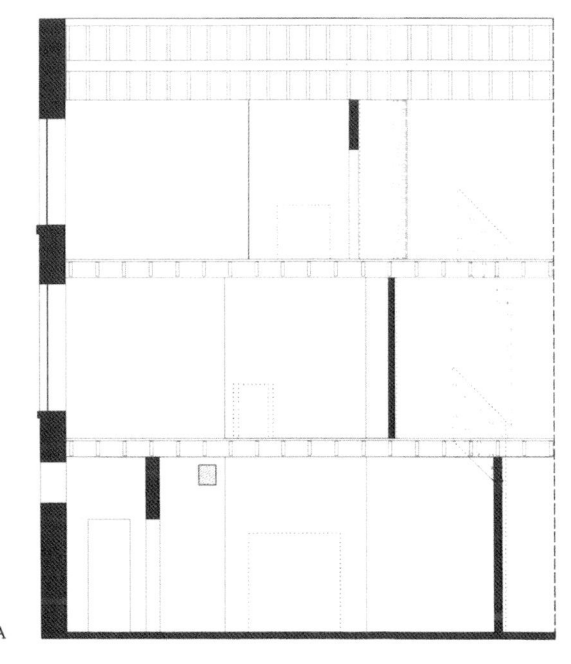

Scale

0 0.5 1 m

Ill 2.2.8 Rear range of 19 Bridge Street: E–W section. (Scale 1/125)

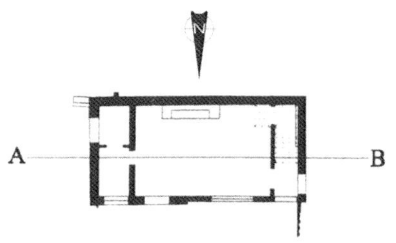

Location Plan

Ill 2.2.9 Fletcher's Buildings (*right*), seen from passageway
from Bridge Street Row.

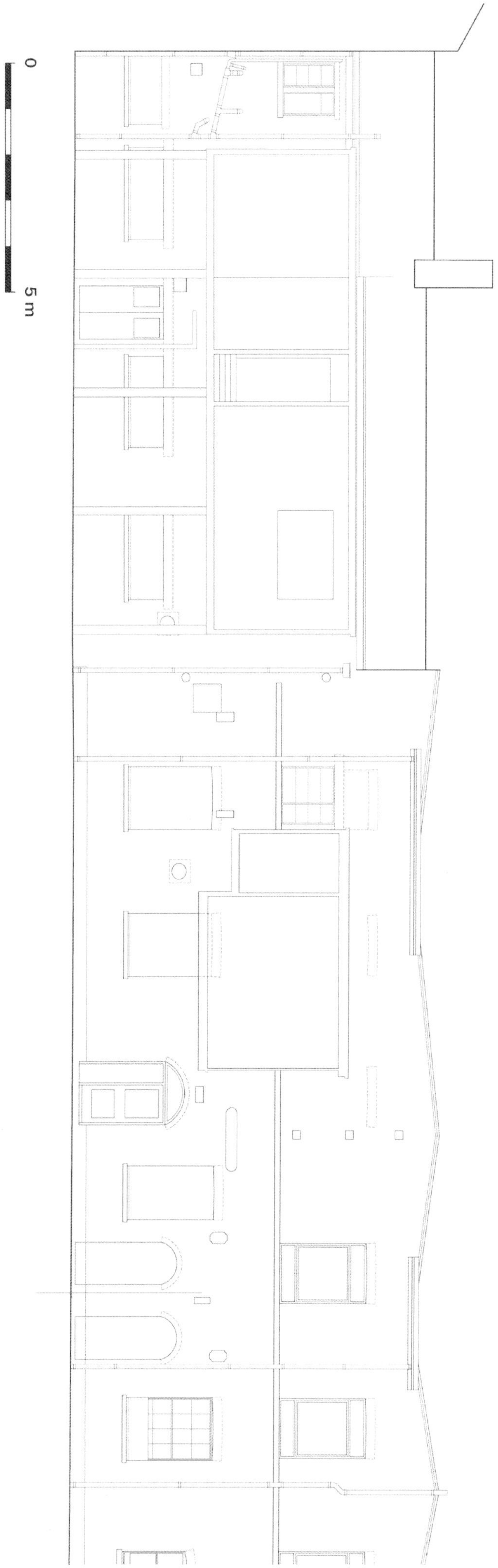

0

5 m

Ill 2.2.10 Fletcher's Buildings: N elevation. (Scale 1/125)

Ill 2.2.11 Fletcher's Buildings: detail of N elevation, showing change in roof line.

Ill 2.2.12 Fletcher's Buildings: first-floor chimney breast.

cise, portions of that earlier roof were visible through holes in the ceiling. The eastern portion had a slate pitched roof with the ridge running lengthwise.

Apart form the addition of first-floor walkways which led across the passage to the 1960s buildings on the north side of the passageway, the most obvious changes to the north elevation of the western portion of Fletcher's Buildings had been made to the windows. Some of the original windows had been fitted with late twentieth-century timber frames, whilst two retained timber eight-over-twelve sash frames. Two of the first-floor windows had been bricked up, whilst a third had been reduced in height to carry a metal window frame with a concrete lintel. The north elevation also had three arch-headed doorways, two of which had been bricked up. All of the windows in the eastern portion of the buildings had been altered to take metal frames or were completely new additions; all used concrete lintels. Most of the first-floor face of the eastern section was taken up by one of the two walkways that led across to the 1960s buildings on the north side of the passageway.

Within Fletcher's Buildings there had been considerable changes to the structure, all apparently part of adaptation of the building by the *Chester Chronicle* newspaper. One of the only original internal features that could be identified was the first-floor chimney breast on the south wall of the eastern portion of the building. The chimney breast only continued approximately halfway down the ground floor (Row-level) wall, where it was carried by iron supports (Ill 2.2.12). The decking of the first floor had been replaced and strengthened by the addition of steel joists between surviving wooden joists. These steel joists were supported by steel stanchions set into a concrete ring beam set within the floor of the ground floor (Row level). A hole that had been hacked through the concrete floor in front of one of the stanchions exposed what may have been a rubble-filled cellar. There is no other evidence for cellars beneath Fletcher's Buildings, apart from the small plant room in the western end, and it may be that most of the original 'cellars' (at street level) were filled in during the insertion of this steel framing.

The other changes within Fletcher's buildings had been the division of the ground-floor (Row-level) interior into smaller rooms by the use of stud walls faced with plasterboard, the insertion of which removed any traces of earlier interior layouts.

1960s *Chester Chronicle* buildings

The range of 1960s *Chronicle* buildings comprised a core element, consisting of remnants of a warehouse constructed in 1901 for Messrs Davies and Shepheard, surrounded on three sides by 1960s additions. The earlier element comprised a two-storey structure constructed in English garden wall bond brickwork with a hipped slate roof. Each floor originally consisted of a single room, although a breeze block partition wall had been inserted into the ground floor (Row level) to form a plant room. Externally, the east elevation of this element, and the west elevation of the building on the opposite side of the passageway to the garden courtyard, were faced in white glazed brick. However, the glazed bricks on the early element of the *Chronicle* buildings had a mortar gap of only 3–4 mm between courses, whilst the glazed bricks of the wall to the south had a mortar gap of 8 mm between courses, indicating that they probably formed two separate phases of construction.

The early element of the *Chronicle* building contained a trap door entrance to a cellar, which actually lay beneath part of the 1960s building to the south. The western end wall of this early element (and the continuation of the wall that formed the eastern elevation of the 1960s *Chronicle* buildings) were on a slightly different orientation to the rest of the building and followed the alignment of the passage leading to the garden courtyard. This difference in alignment was also mirrored in the alignment of the yards described above in the section on the rear of 19 Bridge Street and was presumably a reflection of the property boundaries to the back of the Rows. Another interesting feature was the 0.8 m-thick sloping brick wall which formed the north wall of the early element. There were no indications as to the origin of this wall and why it was so thick in relation to the other walls.

The remainder of the *Chronicle* building consisted of a two-storey structure built in stretcher bond brickwork and breeze block, with a flat asphalt roof dating to the 1960s. Many of the rooms had stud and plaster board partition walls and suspended false ceilings. The 1960s *Chronicle* building was connected to Fletcher's Buildings by two first-floor suspended corridors, the eastern corridor being twice the width of the western corridor, incorporating two small workrooms.

Discussion
Diane Backhouse

Introduction

THE documentary research for a site of this nature presents many problems. Even where plentiful material exists, the separate ownership of Row- and street-level buildings in Bridge Street, as in all the Chester Rows, and the subdivision and multiple occupation of premises and plots throughout their history, frequently make it impossible to tie references to specific properties. Medieval title deeds and City records may give the name of the street, but they rarely specify whereabouts or on which side, and prior to the late eighteenth century it is unusual for any distinction to be made between Upper and Lower Bridge Street. Street numbers first appear in Chester trade directories in 1846 (Williams) but these were altered around 1878 (Post Office Directory: Kelly ed 1878), and the numbering at Row and street level has always been different. In many cases identification of properties in documents is tentatively based on association between the names of close neighbours and references to adjacent premises, correlated with a conjectural street plan based on the 1:500 OS Town Plan of 1875 (Sheets 38.11.17–.18 and 38.11.22–3).

Obviously one of the main objectives of this study was to discover something of the activities carried out on the site, as witnessed in the documentary sources, and to relate them to the results of the excavation. One difficulty was that the documentation frequently referred only to the owner, who may or may not have been the occupier, and this was not only frustrating but could also be misleading. This was true not only of medieval title deeds, but also of rate books, probate records and the records of the City Assembly. Another major limitation of the documentary evidence in this case was that it generally related primarily to the properties fronting the Rows, and its relevance to the backland areas, with which this study is concerned, was frequently a matter of conjecture.

For the reasons outlined above the following account is patchy and lacking in continuity, and inevitably it contains almost as much speculation as fact, but even where firm evidence was lacking, enough material was found to give some impression of the professional lives, living conditions and social relationships of the occupants of the area, especially in the late seventeenth and eighteenth centuries for which wills and probate inventories are a particularly rich resource.

The site

With the exception of Plot 6, the early plot boundaries identified by the excavation followed quite closely the boundaries of what were originally five or six large properties, later subdivided, extending south from what is now known as 13–15 Bridge Street Row East to 31 Bridge Street Row East, as delineated on the 1/500 OS Town Plan of 1875. This plan was the earliest to show with any

3

DOCUMENTARY EVIDENCE

precision the layout and size of plots fronting the main streets of Chester, which, as is suggested elsewhere in this report, may contain elements of an earlier layout of large burgage plots. No street or Row numbers were identified in records earlier than Williams directory of 1846, in which the Row properties were numbered 8–13. By the time of the 1871 census the numbering was closer to the modern configuration, although there are inconsistencies resulting from the later subdivision of shops and premises and the different numbering of the properties at street level, which can be confusing. Where Plot 6 fits into this picture is not clear, although in the nineteenth century it formed part of the Fletcher's Buildings complex, which lay behind nos 27 and 29 Bridge Street Row (*see* below and Table 3.1). These properties lie within St Peter's parish, the southern and eastern boundaries of which are almost exactly coterminous with the southern and eastern boundaries of the excavation site, and St Michael's ward, which overlaps St Peter's parish on the north-eastern side of Bridge Street.

On the assumption that there was a connection between the owners and occupiers of these properties and the associated excavation plots to the rear, the data accumulated was, where possible, organised by phase, plot and owners and/or occupiers in an attempt to provide a framework for the history of the site, the emphasis being on the properties at Row level as being most likely to have had an impact on the land at the rear. Data which could not be linked to a particular plot was summarised separately. This information is set out in Tables 3.1 and 3.2. A more general chronological account, focussing on key documents, is given below.

Sources

A wide range of primary sources was consulted for the purpose of this study. The most rewarding were: maps (1580–1911); census returns (1841–91); trade directories (1781–1896); deeds and estate papers of the Barnston, Vernon, Grosvenor, Cholmondeley, Bavand and Anderton families; papers in the collections of Jolliffe, Wickham & Wood and Birch Cullimore, solicitors; parish (St Peter's), and ward (St Michael's) rate books; Chester Corporation deeds, lease books, Assembly books, Treasurers' accounts and Freemen's rolls; probate records; and the archive of the Chester Rows Research Project. These are all held by Chester & Cheshire Archives & Local Studies (referred to below as CCALS) with the exception of the Eaton charters, which are in the custody of the Duke of Westminster at Eaton Hall. Printed editions of the medieval title deeds of the Aston, Talbot, Egerton-Warburton, and Moore families, who also held property in Chester, and of the cartularies of St Werburgh's and Vale Royal abbeys, were also consulted. The scope of the project did not permit the random searching of unindexed records: consequently the Chester Portmote rolls, which may well contain relevant information, were not consulted, nor were the Exchequer and Chester Palatinate records in the National Archives at Kew. For the same reason, although relevant references were identified in the Mayors' and Sheriffs' books, these were not systematically searched, nor were several collections of family and estate papers that include material relating to Chester but are not indexed to street level.

In addition to the original records, a wide range of secondary sources was consulted. Of these the most useful were *The Rows of Chester* (Brown ed 1999) and the *Victoria Country History* vol 5 (1) (Lewis & Thacker eds 2003).

Phases IV and V: Early to late medieval

Although it is now generally accepted that by the late thirteenth century a continuous Row system, comprising dwellings, shops and undercrofts connected by raised walkways, with established property divisions, was in existence in the central area of the city and that Bridge Street Row East would have been a prime commercial site (Brown ed 1999, 18), identifiable references to the section of the Row which now includes nos 13–31 were conspicuously absent from the records searched. Deeds surviving from the middle of the fourteenth century indicated that the Corporation of Chester owned a substantial amount of property in Bridge Street, but where identifiable these appear to have been situated mainly on the corner near to the Cross (probably the premises later known as 1 Bridge Street and 1 Bridge Street Row, rebuilt for the City Council by Lockwood in 1888), the north-west corner of Bridge Street Row West, sometime known as Corvisers' (Shoemakers') Row', and property to the south of St Michael's church, probably in what is now Lower Bridge Street (eg CCALS ZCHD 2/1 (1356); ZCHB 6; ZTAR 1/8 (1554)).

The areas in between were presumably in private hands and so escaped official record until the sixteenth and seventeenth centuries, when their owners became liable for various fines and rents in respect of encroachments onto the street and Row walkways as a result of rebuilding and expansion (*see* below). Searches of medieval title deeds in private collections were, however, unproductive. Although all the more prominent Chester and Cheshire families, (eg Cholmondeley, Barnston, Vernon, Talbot, Aston, Warburton and Leche) seem to have owned property in Bridge Street, in the rare instances where the location was identifiable, it was once again usually on the western side, or in Lower Bridge Street (CCALS DCH/ DD/3, 5, 11, 12; DBA/ 35–7; DVE I/CI, DLE 67; Barker ed 1953; Beamont 1866). Similarly, references in the cartularies of St Werburgh's and Vale Royal abbeys indicate substantial landholdings in Bridge Street, but in the case of the latter, a reference of *c* 1299 to the 'eleven shops called the cobblers' shops' (Corvisers' Row again) locates it on the north-west corner (Brownbill ed 1914, 131).

In spite of the lack of evidence directly relevant to the study area during this period, enough references to Bridge Street existed to suggest the nature and size of the plots and buildings that may have occupied the site. As mentioned above, the topography of the site suggested that landholdings may originally have been considerably larger than they were later to become, and there was possible confirmation of this in some early documents. Exact measurements were rarely given in early title deeds, the extent of landholdings usually being defined by abuttals onto the land of neighbours, but David the Miller, who held office as sheriff in the 1290s, was granted a block of land with buildings in Bridge Street belonging to St Werburgh's abbey, for which he paid an annual rent of £2, suggesting that it was of some considerable size. Although its exact location is unknown, it is not impossible that it included the area of this study and already comprised a number of small shops within its bounds (Tait ed 1920–3, 341). Searches of the later estate records of the Dean and Chapter of Chester cathedral in the hope of identifying a possible location for this property and other lands in Bridge Street known to have been held by St Werburgh's abbey were unsuccessful (CCALS EDD 10/1/13, 7/29; Lewis & Thacker eds 2003, 31). Other individuals known to have occupied property in Bridge Street at this time were Peter the Clerk, chancellor to the Earl of Chester, who is thought to have owned a house on the corner of Castle Street and Lower Bridge Street on the site of the Old King's Head (Brown ed 1999,168), and Richard the Engineer, master mason to Edward I, mayor 1305–6, whose house stood adjacent to St Olave's church (Brown ed 1999, 15; Lewis & Thacker eds 2003, 53).

These comparatively grand, high-status houses were built of stone, an expensive material and not in common usage, so it may be of some significance that the undercroft of 15 Bridge Street/17–19 Bridge Street Row, basically a seventeenth-century house with an eighteenth-century façade, is spanned by two stone arches dated to the mid-fourteenth century. This type of structure has been described as possibly related to stone-built halls built parallel to the street, which would have required a wider frontage than the more usual right-angled halls common along the main streets of Chester (Brown ed 1999, 23, 38, 157). The accommodation in these town houses broadly conformed to a model common to medieval urban properties, modified in Chester by the existence of the Row walkway connecting adjoining houses at first-floor level. Basically, the commercial and retail areas were located at the front, facing the Row, while the domestic accommodation was located either at the rear, at Row level or above. Access to these domestic areas was through side passages, many of which still exist. The undercrofts and cellars, often in separate ownership, were generally used as storage areas, retail outlets or as ale-cellars, completely independent of the properties above, although it was not unusual for taverns to be situated under the houses of prominent citizens, which would commonly have had a brewhouse to the rear to provide for the needs of the household (Brown ed 1999, 75).

Although the plot boundaries and street frontages shown on the 1875 Town Plan may have changed little since the medieval period, the areas behind the main buildings only seem to have been intensively developed from the late eighteenth century. Before this time, apart from a few outbuildings such as brewhouses, bakehouses, and kilns, which were often built as separate structures because of the risk of fire, the backlands in Bridge Street would have consisted mainly of gardens and orchards, as illustrated in the first extant map of Chester by Braun & Hogenberg, dated 1580 (CCALS PM 14/1). A conveyance of 1393 among the deeds of the Warburton family described a house in Bridge Street with a chapel, dovecote and a garden granted by Ralph de Holland and Rosa his wife to Roger de Potter, citizen of Chester, but unfortunately there was no clue as to its exact location (Beamont 1866, 43). There was, of course, a less savoury aspect to these areas, which also, of necessity, included large numbers of rubbish- and cess-pits, now a prime source of archaeological evidence for lifestyle within the buildings on the Rows and for the trades and professions exercised there, as has been shown by this excavation (*see* also Ward 1981).

The clustering of specific trades and crafts in 'Rows' was common to all medieval urban centres, although in Chester the appellation has an additional meaning. As regards Bridge Street, such evidence as exists suggested a predominance of leatherworkers in the area, eg skinners, tanners, saddlers and glovers and there was fairly conclusive evidence that this was still the case in the mid-seventeenth century, even though by that date it had been popularly known as 'Mercers' Row' for at least a hundred and fifty years (Lewis & Thacker eds 2003, 51; *see* also below). A deed of 1438 among the estate records of the Talbot family referred to a piece of land in Bridge Street, occupied by a Richard Shotton, skinner, in 1438, and although the location of his property is uncertain, the appearance of numerous mercers and drapers as witnesses to this and associated documents in the series, suggested a possible connection with Bridge Street Row East (Barker ed 1953, nos 171, 205).

Phase VI: Late 15 to mid-17 century

The earliest known reference to Bridge Street Row East as 'Mercers' Row' dates from 1493 (Dodgson 1981, 21), and the best known is the presentment of Joan Steyner and Margery Bower before the Sheriff's Court in 1503 for making a fire in their cellars, the smoke from which rose into 'le Mercerrowe', causing a nuisance to their neighbours and passers-by (CCALS ZSB 5 fo 7v). Mercers' Row is also marked on Braun and Hogenberg's map of Chester of 1580, which shows it as running from the Cross about halfway to Pepper Street (CCALS PM 14/1). This supports the tradition that the bridge over Feathers' Lane, shown on the 1875 OS Town Plan, was the dividing line between Mercers' Row to the north and St Michael's Row to the south, and indicates that it included the whole of the frontage associated with the excavation site (CCALS DBE 49/29). Disappointingly, no further references to Mercers' Row as such were found in documents searched in the course of this study, which once again made identification of specific properties extremely difficult. There is no doubt, however, that this area was indeed a prime site, in keeping with the importance of the Mercers' Company in the economy and government of the city, and one would expect the archaeological evidence to reflect this (Lewis & Thacker eds 2003, 75).

References to the wills and inventories of twenty-four mercers were found in the Chester diocesan probate indexes for the period 1500–1700, and these were all examined not only for possible links with Mercers' Row but also for information regarding household possessions, lifestyle and stock in trade. Places of residence were rarely specifically mentioned, although there were references to shops, rows and stallboards, which suggested Row properties. Nothing was found to specifically link any of the documents searched with the excavation site, but a considerable amount of information was gleaned regarding the type of stock in trade that might be expected to impact upon it. For example, the inventory of William Dodd of the parish of St Bridget, dated 1598, lists fustian, velvet, taffeta, damask, serge, grosgrain, laces 'Taffeta hattes', 'french garters And girdells' 'Spanish & Naples Silk', silk and gold laces, lawn, cambric etc (CCALS WS 1598 William Dodd), and that of Owen Jones, dated 1611, also refers to a 'boultinge house', which presumably lay behind his Row property (CCALS WS 1611 Owen Jones). The inventory of John Bennett, of the parish of St Peter, dated 1667, lists plush, silk, tabby, sarcenet, drugget, stockings, hose, lace, ribbon etc, all 'In the Shop' (CCALS WS 1667 John Bennett). Interestingly, some of these inventories suggested that the mercers did not confine themselves to dealing in luxurious and expensive fabrics, but also diversified into other areas. The inventory of Kendrick Eyton, dated 1624, listed predominantly exotic dyestuffs and spices, the type of stock in trade that one would normally associate with a grocer, viz: 'Madder rootes', 'Gentian Roote' 'Tormerick', cardamon, heliboris niger, fenugreek, caraway, ambergris, nutmeg, comfits etc (CCALS WS 1624 Kendrick Eyton).

From the late sixteenth until the nineteenth century, parish and ward rate assessments for St Peter's parish and St Michael's ward provided lists of names for ratepayers in Bridge Street, but it is important to bear in mind that many of the properties in the Rows were not owner-occupied, and that the ratepayer could therefore have been the landlord rather than the tenant. A Poor Rate assessment of 1567 for the parish of St Peter, which included both sides of Bridge Street as far as Commonhall Street on the west and the southern boundary of 29–31 Bridge Street on the east, gave the names of numerous well-to-do citizens and merchants, and although it was impossible to establish from this source alone exactly where the properties of these individuals were located, collating it with other contemporary sources produced some interesting results (Morris 1895, 360).

One name on this list which may be relevant was that of William Wall, ironmonger, who was listed in the Chester Treasurers' accounts between 1568 and 1589 as the occupant of a shop in 'Bridge Street upone the est syde' formerly occupied by Thomas Dutton, and as owing 6d for 'iij posts set upon the City's ground' there, a reference to the trend in the late sixteenth century for extending the upper storeys of Row buildings out over the street on posts, which had to be licensed by the City Assembly, as did any form of encroachment on to the public highway (CCALS ZTAR 1/13 and 17). Wall, who held office as mayor 1586/7, was clearly a wealthy man, and his fragmentary will of 1599 included references to several houses in Bridge Street, although their exact location was not specified and there was no indication as to which was his normal place of residence (CCALS WS 1599 William Wall). However, in 1573 the City Assembly book listed him as owing 'iijs iiid' rent for a piece of 'voide grond' in Bridge Street upon which he had built what must have been a substantial house 91' long x 27' wide, and if this was indeed his home, and it was located on the east side of Bridge Street within the parish of St Peter, it must by deduction have been situated in Mercers' Row and very close to, if not within, the excavation site (CCALS ZAB 1 fo 152). William Wall's activities reflected the large-scale rebuilding which took place in the Chester Rows during this period, following what has been interpreted as a period of stagnation and decay the late fourteenth and fifteenth centuries, with many houses falling into disrepair, during (Brown ed 1999, 63–4).

From the sixteenth century onwards the available sources became more varied and interesting, although the evidence for identifying individual properties was still often inconclusive. Wills and probate inventories were of particular value, not only for the information they contained regarding possessions and status, but also for leads supplied by references to other family members, tenants, friends and neighbours. Of particular interest in this respect were the numerous wills and inventories of the Fletcher family, who were all involved in one way or another with the leather industry. The will of Robert Fletcher, skinner (d 1688), was probably the most useful document to have been discovered in the course of the research for this study (CCALS WS 1688 Robert Fletcher). It was most relevant to the late seventeenth and eighteenth centuries (Phase VII) and is therefore discussed in more detail below, but some of the references in it may throw light on the history of the site at an earlier period.

Although the exact location of Fletcher's property is uncertain, that it was situated on the eastern side of Bridge Street was specifically stated in his will, and correlation of the rate books of St Peter's parish and St Michael's ward, in both of which he was listed, together with references to a 'long garden' divided into three parts, indicated that it was situated south of the properties on the northeastern corner whose gardens abutted those of Eastgate Street, and therefore almost certainly formed some part of the excavation site (CCALS P63/7/2). The property was very substantial, comprising four dwelling houses, four shops, a cellar, a warehouse, a brewhouse, two coalhouses and two 'houses of convenience', but of particular interest for the earlier period was the cellar, which was described in the will as being in the occupation of a Thomas Minshull, ironmonger. A series of deeds and papers relating to the later history of the site, again discussed in more detail below, referred to this cellar as being formerly the 'Moon tavern', and further research in the indexes to the Chester City records revealed that this property first came into the hands of the Fletcher family on its purchase, along with other premises in Bridge Street, by a Robert Fletcher 'jr' feltmaker, in 1612 (CCALS ZL/Ch/4). The records of the Chester Assembly included numerous references to a Robert Fletcher 'the elder' and a Robert Fletcher 'the younger', usually described as 'hatmaker', at about the same date. Robert Fletcher 'the elder' was elected alderman in 1608/9 and held office as treasurer in 1611, during which year Robert Fletcher 'the younger' (presumably his son) held office as sheriff. Clearly Fletcher jr did not confine himself to hat-making, as in 1613 he was accused, with others, of infringing the rights of the Cardmakers' Company by buying and selling cards in the city while not being free of the company, and it may be that the felt-making side of his activities was also a diversification, although hat-making and felt-making were clearly related occupations (Groombridge 1956, 41, 49, 51, 69).

The very extensive inventory of a Robert Fletcher, dated 1617, listed a stock in trade which certainly suggested someone who exercised both of these crafts, including 'beavers', 'woll[en] felts', 'mens felts lined w[i]th velvett', 'collared hatts', 'Cappes', 'silver and goulde bandes', as well as a large quantity of fine fabrics, such as velvet, taffeta and silk, and the likelihood that it relates to the premises of the Robert Fletcher jr who purchased the 'Moon tavern' in 1612 is strong. Of particular interest was the unusually large quantity of arms and armour listed. The appearance of 'halberds ' and 'head-pieces' 'jackes' (steel-plated jackets) and 'corselets' in wills and inventories of this date is not unusual, as following various directives from the government and city authorities all citizens were required to equip themselves with at the very least a 'halberte & headpeece' in case of a national emergency (Morris 1895, 76–8), but the number of items listed here, including '1 head peece one backe & brest plate', 'iii halberds and a picke', 'ij Calevvers flaxe and tuch box' and a 'Jacke' was exceptional, and may be of significance in relation to the discovery of a jack of plates on the site. Fletcher's possessions were listed room by room, as was the custom, suggesting a substantial house and shop, including the 'Great Chamber', 'parlor', 'Chamber over the parlour', 'hall', 'the gallerye over the hall' (where most of his weaponry was stored), 'Chamber at the steare head', 'litell Chamber next adioyninge to the greate chamber', 'Nurses Chamber', 'butterye', 'smale butterye' 'Storehowse' etc.

His personal possessions were typical of those of a wealthy citizen, including large quantities of linen, hangings, carpets and embroidered cushions, wainscot, glass, pewter, and pictures (including, interestingly, 'one picture of armes'). They did not suggest any association with a tavern, but the 'Moon' tavern, if it was part of the premises, would have been situated in the undercroft, and probably in separate occupation (CCALS WS 1617 Robert Fletcher). Other members of the Fletcher family who appeared in the City records at this date were: James, George and Charles Fletcher (glovers), Thomas and John Fletcher (shoemakers), John Fletcher (skinner), and William Fletcher (draper) (Groombridge 1956, *passim*). That they were all related to each other seems indisputable, although exactly how remains difficult to establish, as is their place of residence, but it was clear from such of their wills and inventories as survive that they all enjoyed a considerable degree of wealth and status (eg CCALS WS 1609 Thomas Fletcher, alderman; WS 1625 James Fletcher, glover; WS 1627 Thomas Fletcher, glover).

The history of the site incorporating the 'Moon' tavern between 1614 and 1675, when it is known to have been in the ownership of the Robert Fletcher, skinner, who died in 1688 (*see* above and below), is unclear, but a St Peter's parish rate assessment for Bridge Street dated 1641 listed a 'mrs fffletcher' widow who is probably identifiable with the 'Isabell Fletcher' listed in the same source for 1651 (CCALS P63/7/1). No other clues were provided as to the exact locations of the premises referred to in this source, but that these entries were relevant would seem to be confirmed by a lease dated 18 July 1664 in the records of the Bavand family that referred to a chief rent of 20/- on a house in Bridge Street occupied by Isabell Fletcher, widow. No other details were given, but this must have been the same chief rent of 20/- mentioned in Robert Fletcher's will as due to 'Mr Edward Bavand' on his own residence in Bridge Street East in 1688 (CCALS ZCR 465/92).

It was unfortunate that in spite of the considerable amount of information that was uncovered regarding the Fletcher property, which must have taken up a substantial part of the excavation site, it was so difficult to locate it, even during the later phases of its history (*see* below).

One property for which this was not such a problem was that now known as 13 Bridge Street/13–15 Bridge Street Row, largely rebuilt in 1861 by the architect Edward Hodkinson for the Marquis of Westminster (Plot 5). An abstract of title among the Grosvenor mss gave an account of the descent of this property from 1605 to 1815, which established that the owner during the period 1609–39 was a John Sparke, who had inherited it through his marriage to Ann, heiress to Alexander Cotes (Eaton Hall, Grosvenor Mss, Box F 22). There was no physical description of this property, nor any reliable information to distinguish owners from occupiers until 1738 (*see* Table 3.1), but it may be significant that a William Sparke, merchant and ironmonger, who held office as mayor in 1632/3, was listed as a resident in Bridge Street in the St Peter's rate assessment of 1627/8 and in an assessment for St Michael's ward in 1629, which definitely located him on the north-eastern side of the street (CCALS P63/7/1; ZMB 32 fo 138).

William Sparke appeared frequently in the records of the City Assembly for this period, not only in his capacity as an active member of the Corporation, but more interestingly as the next-door neighbour of William Edwards, also an ironmonger and formerly Sparke's apprentice. In 1617 Edwards applied to the Corporation to extend his shop streetwards, claiming that it would 'beautifie and adorne' the city by making 'a uniformitie of building with all the rest of the shops from thence Northwards' to the Cross. He described his shop as being situated underneath the dwelling house of Sir Sackville Trevor, which illustrates the rather complicated arrangement in Chester at this period, whereby the houses of the gentry and nobility were often located above the shops at Row and street level, all of which were in completely different ownership and occupation (Groombridge 1956, 83–5). William Edwards, a Puritan, became a common councillor in 1623, alderman in 1631 and mayor in 1636/7 and was particularly well known for his feud with the Gamull family, which is thought to have been an element in the political alignments within the city at the outbreak of the Civil War. After openly declaring his support for Parliament, Edwards left the city to join his friend Sir William Brereton, the parliamentary commander, in 1642, returning as mayor and MP after the end of the siege in 1646. William Sparke, although less outspoken in his support, was also a sympathizer, and was one of only seven aldermen who retained their seat on the bench after the surrender (Johnson 1972, 206–9, 215–16, 218–20). Edwards was listed under Bridge Street in the St Peter's parish rate books between 1627/8 and 1641, but not thereafter, suggesting that on his return to Chester after the Civil War he lived elsewhere in the city (CCALS P63/7/1).

If William Sparke, ironmonger, was indeed the occupant of the house now known as 13–15 Bridge Street Row, then it is possible that the house occupied by William Edwards was the adjacent property, now known as 15 Bridge Street/17–19 Bridge Street Row (Plot 4). The external appearance of this building, with its flat Georgian front, is deceptive, as the room above the Row on the street front retains what is thought to be a seventeenth-century panelled plaster ceiling, as does the room above in the attic storey. The position of the very fine mouldings at the intersections of the ceiling panels in these rooms indicate that they were originally jettied and that the overhanging portion must have been removed when the house was modified during the Georgian period (CCALS ZCR 587/11 Part 8/14, nos 47–54; Brown ed 1999, 157; Hewitt 1887, 40–1). An engraving of 'St Peter's church and Bridge Street in 1700' shows this building as it looked before alteration, and its distinctive gable can also be identified in Moses Griffith's engraving of 'Bridge Street and Mercers' Row' in 1777 (Morris 1895, 288–9, 292–3). That this house was a gentleman's residence of some distinction in the late seventeenth century is clear (*see* below), but it is unfortunate that the only references to its earlier history that have been identified are apocryphal, with no basis in fact.

A story which apparently first appeared in 1681, and was subsequently accepted without question by Hanshall (1817), Hemingway (1831) and Morris (1895), and reproduced in almost every Chester guide and directory published in the nineteenth century, related that in the mid-sixteenth century this house was 'the most capital Inn..... known by the sign of the Blue Posts', and that in 1558 a Dr Henry Cole, Dean of St Paul's, stayed there while *en route* to Ireland with a commission from Mary Tudor for the suppression of heresy. The story went that during his stay he was visited by the Mayor of Chester, and that while explaining his errand he was overheard by the landlady, named as Mrs Elizabeth Mottershead, who, fearing for the safety of her brother, one John Edmunds who lived in Dublin, subsequently removed the commission from its box, replacing it with a pack of cards, the knave of clubs uppermost. By the time Dr Cole had arrived in Ireland, discovered what had happened, returned to England and obtained a new commission, Queen Mary was dead, and Mrs Mottershead was rewarded by the new queen with a pension of £40 a year.

This story was discredited in the late nineteenth century as a piece of anti-Catholic propaganda related to the Popish Plot, no evidence having been found in the State Papers either of Dr Cole's mission or of such a pension being granted, and research for this study found no proof of the existence of a hostelry called the 'Blue Posts' in Bridge Street at any time. However, the myth persisted, and an impressive nineteenth-century narrative painting of Mrs Mottershead in the act of positioning the playing card hangs in the lecture room of the Grosvenor Museum in Chester. Despite their lack of authenticity, successive accounts of this incident have proved useful in supplying clues to the occupation and use of this building at a later date (Broster 1821, 70; Catherall 1849, 30; Roberts 1851; Audsley 1891, 70; Gresty & Burghall nd, 70; Lockwood & Hewitt 1886, v–vii; Morris 1895, 72–3; *Cheshire Sheaf* ser 3, **1**, 1896, 3–5).

Phase VII: Mid- to late 17 to early 18 century

Documentary evidence for the house now known as 15 Bridge Street/17–19 Bridge Street Row during the late seventeenth century was firmer and more extensive. A collection of merchants' papers found in the attic of this house during recent restoration, including correspondence and bills addressed to a Matthew Anderton and dating *c* 1662–1716, provided a vital clue (CCALS ZCR 656).

Research in Chester City records and will indexes revealed the existence of two prominent citizens by that name: Matthew Anderton 'the elder', 'gentleman' (d 1693), and Matthew Anderton 'the younger' (d 1709). Both were members of the Innholders' Company (Bennett ed 1906–8) but operated as merchants and were actively involved in trade with Dublin. Because their careers overlapped it was not always clear to which Matthew Anderton the documents referred, but one of them held office as sheriff in 1686, while Matthew Anderton the younger was elected alderman in 1700, commissioner for the Dee 1701, and mayor 1703/4 (CCALS ZAB 3 ff 2, 20, 64, 80v, 114v–126v). During the 1660s Matthew Anderton the elder held office as deputy controller of customs at the port of Chester, and a number of the items in the collection of papers mentioned above were addressed to him at the Custom House (Bennett & Dewhurst 1940, 179–80).

That he definitely lived in Bridge Street Row East was confirmed by his regular appearance in St Peter's parish and St Michael's ward rate books from at least 1665 onwards, and in the hearth tax returns for 1664 he was listed as having seven hearths, the highest number in the ward (CCALS P63/7/2; microfilm 13/2). Additional confirmation was provided by his will, in which he devised to his wife Elizabeth 'all that Messuage Tenement and dwelling House wherein I now live, scituate in the Bridg street of the sd City of Chester', along with his shop in the holding of Mr Thomas Fernihough, draper, and the cellar in the holding of Jane Reece, widow. The will was accompanied by a detailed inventory, which suggested an establishment of some considerable size comprising a 'Brewhouse', 'Little parlour', 'Kitchen', 'Buttery', 'Backside', 'Dining Room', 'upper Street chamber', 'Hall Chamber', 'roome att the Stair head', 'Middle Chamber', 'passage chamber', 'roome over the Brewhouse', 'roome over the Kitchen', 'Closett at the Staire head'. The quantity of furniture, hangings, linen, crockery and glass listed in this inventory suggested a high-status dwelling, and references to 'one gross of Bottles' 'whiteware and glasses' are of significance in relation to finds discovered on this plot. However, there was no indication that this property was an inn (CCALS WS 1693 Matthew Anderton). Later entries in St Peter's parish rate books confirmed that Anderton's widow, Elizabeth, continued to live in the house, and Thomas Fearnihaugh to run his drapery business from the shop, until *c* 1710, but there was no reference specifically to Jane Reece. In 1720 the main house was occupied by Sarah Anderton, widow of Matthew Anderton the younger, and her son William (CCALS P63/7/2–3 and *see* below).

The presence of Thomas Fernihaugh in Bridge Street Row East was of interest in reflecting what may have been a gradual change in the nature of the businesses in Mercers' Row from dealers in luxury fabrics to traders in more practical, everyday textiles. Earlier evidence suggested that occupations in this area had always been fairly mixed, despite the name of the Row, and had included a significant number of ironmongers. However, by the mid- to late eighteenth century there was a definite preponderance of linen- and woollen drapers there, as was quite clear from entries in the Chester trade directories which began to appear at that time (*see* below Phase VIII). 17–19 Bridge Street/21–3 Bridge Street Row (Plot

3) was the location of one such business, that of Randle Vause, an exact contemporary and neighbour of Matthew Anderton, whose building activities on the site, recorded in a series of agreements found in the collection of Birch Cullimore solicitors, made it possible to identify not only his own property, but also that to the south (Plot 2: 21–3 Bridge Street and 25–7 Bridge Street Row) (CCALS DBC Acc 1720/4). These documents recorded that Vause bought the house from Robert Caddick, alderman, prior to the latter's death in 1681 and in the same year acquired the cellar, which was in separate ownership, from Humphrey Jones, another draper. He immediately started to demolish the house with the intention of rebuilding it and creating 'a New fabrick towards the street', and entered into agreements with Matthew Anderton the younger, his immediate neighbour to the north, and Elizabeth, Hannah and Abigail Aspinwall, daughters and co-heirs of the late Thomas Aspinwall, ironmonger, to the south, concerning the specifications for the reconstruction of the party walls, their subsequent main- tenance, the reuse of timbers, the replacement and maintenance of guttering, preservation of light etc.

An almost identical set of agreements was made in 1711 between Vause's widow Sarah (now Sparke) and her son John Vause, also a draper; Anderton's daughter-in-law Sarah and his grandson William; and John and Abigail Swan (née Aspinwall), suggesting that completion of this project had been considerably delayed. Of particular interest in these documents were references to the use of brick in relation to earlier timber structures, including a possible allusion to the timber overhanging gable of Anderton's house and its implications for the reconstruction of the south wall, but they were also extremely valuable in providing the names of the occupiers of these properties at this period. The cellars of both 21–3 and 25–7 Bridge Street Row were occupied by butchers, an increasingly common feature in this area, and the Row-level shop of the latter by a bookseller (*see* Tables 3.1 and 3.2). In his will of 1689 Randle Vause, bequeathing his property to his wife Sarah, referred additionally to a tailor and a periwig maker (CCALS WS 1689 Randle Vause and see Table 3.1).

Rate assessments for St Peter's parish indicated that Robert Caddick, from whom Vause bought his house, was resident there *c* 1641–50, and Thomas Aspinwall, his neighbour to the south (Plot 2), between *c* 1641 and 1675 (CCALS P63/7/1). Thomas Aspinwall is listed in the 1664 hearth tax returns as possessing four hearths, suggesting a fairly substantial establishment, although not as large as Anderton's (CCALS microfilm 13/2). In his will he requested burial in St Peter's church, which is confirmation of his place of residence, but he made only general references to his property in connection with the settlement of his debts and the maintenance of his daughters. His inventory was modest in comparison with those already described, but his house had some interesting features. In addition to the 'hall' (containing the mandatory 'halbert and head peece'), 'parlo[u]r', 'Chamber over the parlour', 'Chamber at ye stayre head', 'the other little chamber', 'buttery', 'brewhouse', 'kill' (kiln - containing thirty-six measures of malt), and shop, the inventory referred to a 'hatchelling house' containing 'one hatchel and a little table' suggesting that Aspinwall may have had a sideline as a ropemaker. It also lists '135li undrest

flax at 3d p[er] li' and '88li drest flax at 6d p[er] li' implying that the premises were also being used for flaxdressing, a possible link with later practices on the site (CCALS WS 1675 Thomas Aspinwall and *see* below).

The will of Robert Fletcher, skinner, dated 1688, to which reference has already been made, is of crucial importance to the history of the excavation site, even though it was not possible to locate his property with any precision. Although he was not a party to the building agreements between Ralph and Sarah Vause and their neighbours in 1681, his name appeared as a witness, which suggests that he lived nearby (CCALS DBC Acc 1720/4/ 1 and 3). It may also be significant that on Fletcher's death in 1688 it was Matthew Anderton who succeeded him as common councillor (CCALS ZAB 3 fo 20v). His exact relationship to the Robert Fletcher jr who purchased the 'Moon' Tavern in 1612 is obscure, but that there was a link would seem to be proven by references to him as lessor of the same property in 1675 and 1684 (CCALS ZL/Ch/10 and 12), and entries in rate books suggest that he was living in the area from 1665 at the latest (CCALS ZCAS 1 nos 56 and 88; P63/7/2). He was clearly a man of means, or at least had been until he embarked on a scheme of 'Newbuilding & repayringe' his house, which had cost him 'very neare ffoure Hundred Pounds' and put him considerably into debt.

Fletcher's own residence comprised a house, a shop in the Row, a brewhouse, coalhouse and 'house of Conveniency' and 'one third part (in three parts devided) of my long Garden lying next unto my warehouse', but he also owned three other houses, two of which also had a coalhouse, 'house of conveniency' and a third each of the remainder of the 'long Garden'. The brewhouse seems to have doubled as a 'washhouse' and was shared in common. In addition to the houses, Fletcher owned four shops, and the cellar, which is identified in later documents as the former 'Moon' tavern (*see* below). The occupiers of these properties were all named, and comprised an ironmonger, a tailor, a linendraper, a mercer, an apothecary and an aged aunt (*see* Tables 3.1 and 3.2). The reference to a warehouse, described as 'new built' is of interest as indicating that Fletcher stored his stock in trade on the premises, although, as there was no inventory attached to this will, we have no information as to its contents, nor any clues as to whether he actually engaged in any skinning activities on the site. A reference to him in a list of quit rents owed to the City in respect of one of his shops in 1686 describes him as 'Robte ffletcher of Corke', which suggests that he was a merchant involved in the Irish trade in animal skins rather than in the preparation of them (CCALS ZTAP 1 p 45). However, there is no doubt that such activity did take place along the main city streets. A coroner's inquest of 1718 refers to the death of John Pendlebury, apprentice to William Jennings, wetglover, who was suffocated by smoke from fires for the drying of skins in the storehouse of William Jennings in Bridge Street. It is not clear to which part of Bridge Street this refers, but it belies the common assumption that all such processes took place outside the city boundaries, whatever the rules and regulations may have been (CCALS ZQCI/19/16).

Wills were identified for most of Fletcher's tenants, but the only surviving inventory was that of Thomas Minshull, ironmonger, occupant of the cellar, which was clearly being used as a warehouse. Minshull's stock in trade, including flax, hemp, soap, brimstone, pitch, turmeric, fenugreek, pepper, ginger, 'whalebone', sugar, coriander, paper, 'horn combs' etc, is more suggestive of a grocer than an ironmonger and illustrates once again the very diverse interests of Chester's mercantile community (CCALS WS 1690 Thomas Minshull). Robert Fletcher's wife Ann, whom he appointed as executor, carried on his business after his death, and described in her own will (1696) how she managed to settle his debts 'by the moneys by me gott, in the way of Trade'. The inventory attached to this will was particularly useful in that it lists not only the contents of the rooms in the house (kitchen, dining room, three garrets, 'the darke Roome', brewhouse, 'Garden Room') but also those of the shop, which included a large number of muffs, '8 gray Catt skinns', '1 Wilde Catt's skinn', '9 black Catt skinns', '7 ffitchet skins' and '16 Lamb skinns' (CCALS WS 1696 Ann Fletcher).

The rebuilding activities of Randle Vause and Robert Fletcher illustrate a dramatic surge in such activity in Chester at this period, partly the consequence of a general rise in prosperity, and also possibly of damage and neglect suffered during the Civil War period. Surprisingly, these activities were completely unrecorded in the records of the City Assembly, which closely regulated all developments in the Rows and are particularly rich for the late seventeenth and early eighteenth centuries (Brown ed 1999, 77, 151): a search of the indexes to these records failed to reveal a single reference which could be identified with the area of Mercers' Row. The reason for this may be that the projects did not actually impinge on the Row, but it is also possible that many developments in the city which should have been licensed slipped through the net. However, as already mentioned, one of the problems in identifying properties in these records was that there was no differentiation between Upper and Lower Bridge Street until the late eighteenth century, and this has led to errors in previous research (Emery 1996). The apparent absence of any references to development could be explained by the simple fact that the vast majority of petitions and licences were for Row enclosures, which became very common in the predominantly residential area of Lower Bridge Street, while in Bridge Street Row East, possibly because of commercial pressures and the need to maintain easy access, there have never been any such enclosures.

Phase VIII: Early to late 18 century

The later history of the property formerly owned by Robert Fletcher, skinner, is documented in a collection of deeds among the records of Jolliffe, Wickham & Wood, solicitors (CCALS ZD/JWW/12–42) On the death of Fletcher's widow, Ann, in 1696, his estate was divided between his nephew and niece John and Hannah Ellis and sister Mary Yonge, and passed down through their descendants the Frith, Anderson, Entwistle and Smith families until its purchase in 1811 by John Fletcher, printer, proprietor of the *Chester Chronicle* (see below, Phase IX). This block of land did not include the area subsequently known as Fletcher's Buildings, which was acquired by John Fletcher in a separate conveyance in 1813 (see below), but we can infer that it was almost

certainly adjacent to it. Although it was still impossible to differentiate or locate the properties involved, the information concerning tenants and their occupations in these documents made it possible to build up a picture of the community living and working in the area during the whole of the eighteenth century and to follow the subtle changes in the nature of the structures on the site.

In his will of 1688 Robert Fletcher referred to four houses, four shops, a long garden divided into three parts, a cellar, a warehouse, a brewhouse, two coalhouses and two houses of convenience (see above). From 1702 to 1811 the same estate was fairly consistently described as consisting of five houses, three shops in the Row, two shops/cellars in the street, and two gardens, the only changes being that at some point between 1796 and 1811 the three shops in the Row were reduced to two, and in 1811 there was an additional reference to an acre of land in the parish of St Peter. Whether this referred to the extent of the property previously described or to a separate plot is not clear (CCALS ZD/JWW/16 and 40). In 1729 the names of nine occupants were given, comprising an upholsterer, tailor, cordwainer, joiner, grocer, clothier, watchmaker, butcher and spinster (see Table 3.1).

A search of the indexes to the Chester probate records revealed the existence of an extensive inventory and funeral accounts for the upholsterer Abner Scholes (d 1736), which were not only of interest for the details they provided of his very large establishment, personal possessions and stock in trade, but also for his personal and professional relationships with his neighbours, suggesting a close-knit and interdependent community. His premises (which may have comprised two houses) were listed in his inventory as a 'Gate-House' with a room above, a gallery, two staircases, pantry, kitchen, 'little parlour', 'large parlour', shop, 'House in the street Garrat', 'the small street Garrat', 'the Maid's Garrat', 'the Best Bed Chamber', 'the parlour', 'the Green Room', 'the little Bed Chamber', another kitchen, lumber room, brewhouse and coalhouse (CCALS WS 1736 Abner Scholes). His funeral accounts drawn up by his sister, Margery Dudley, referred to his coffin having been provided by 'Mr Wrench' (the joiner), and to a debt owed him by Robert Cawley (the watchmaker) (CCALS WS 1742 Abner Scholes).

In 1759 the premises were purchased by Alderman Gabriel Smith, another watchmaker, who along with a stationer, flaxdresser, tailor, tinman, and a butcher was resident on the site (see Table 3.1) (CCALS ZD/JWW/30). In 1811 only six occupants are listed, possibly related to the amalgamation of two of the shops. These included the same tinman or brazier who was living there in 1759, Messrs Hassall & Foulkes, liquor merchants, and four others whose occupations are unspecified (CCALS ZD/JWW/40).

Phase IX: Early 19 century–c 1900

The evidence for the early history of the structures which later became known as Fletcher's Buildings (Plots 1, 2 and 6) was found in a separate deed in the same collection as those referred to above, recording their purchase in 1813 by John Fletcher from Mrs Ratcliffe, widow of Joseph Ratcliffe, flaxdresser. In that year they comprised three messuages or dwelling houses, with a yard, two privies and a garden on the south side, fronted by the house on the Row (described as formerly the premises of a bookseller), and five messuages, yards, a lumber room, a washhouse, two privies, and a 'larger garden' on the north side, behind the shop and warehouse of Benjamin Whittell chemist. The names of thirteen occupants are given for these eight houses (*see* Table 3.1), including a linen-draper, a shoemaker, two plasterers, a mantua maker, a cooper, a brazier, a silversmith, a labourer and two widows, and presumably their families. An oblique reference to an earlier deed of 1770 indicated that these houses did not exist at that date, and a search of St Peter's rate books suggested that they were probably built between 1803 and 1808, which is consistent with the date of 1804 which appears on the rainwater head of no 23 Bridge Street/27 Bridge St Row (Plot 2 (part)), the building probably occupied by Benjamin Whittell, chemist (CCALS ZDJ/WW/42; P63/7/7–9).

For the late eighteenth and nineteenth centuries, as wills became more formulaic and inventories less common, trade directories replace them as the best tool for identifying individual occupants with houses, especially when they can be collated with other evidence such as rate books and (from 1841) census returns. They made it possible to trace the occupants of most of the properties on the excavation site through from 1781 to 1896 (*see* Table 3.1). They do have limitations, in that listing in them was by subscription only, so that they were not comprehensive, and street numbers did not appear until 1846. However, they give both name and occupation, and were of considerable assistance in fitting individual properties and their occupants into the street plan, which facilitated their identification in earlier and later sources.

The Joseph Ratcliffe from whose widow John Fletcher purchased the property later known as Fletcher's Buildings in 1813, is listed in the earliest extant directory of 1781 (Broster), and with his brother, William, also described as flaxdresser, in a directory of 1789 (Cowdroy). In 1783 he is also listed in St Peter's parish rate book with the highest-rated property on the eastern side of Bridge Street (CCALS P63/7/4). The administration of a Joseph Ratcliffe, flaxdresser (d 1747), of St Mary's parish was identified among the Chester diocesan probate records, but it seems likely that the first members of the family to operate on the Bridge Street site were his two sons William (admitted to the freedom 1752), and Joseph (admitted 1755), whose wills or administrations have not been identified (CCALS WS 1747 Joseph Ratcliffe; Bennett ed 1906–8, 347, 351). It follows that they were probably responsible for the development of the site for residential purposes, although whether this was new building or a reuse of older buildings was not clear (*see* below).

Although John Fletcher, printer, who took over the *Chester Chronicle* in 1783, purchased the Fletcher's Buildings site in 1813, the printing office remained on its original site in Hop Pole Yard, Northgate Street until at least 1829 (Pigot). An entrepreneur as well as a publisher, Fletcher was a friend of Thomas Telford and was involved in numerous engineering projects, including the construction of the Chester canal. He was also actively involved in city politics, holding office as mayor in 1825 and 1832. On his death on 7 January 1835 the business was taken over by his nephew Thomas Fletcher, and it was in the first edition of the newspaper to be pub-

lished after this event (16 January 1835) that the earliest reference to the printing office as being located in 'Fletcher's Buildings', and indeed the earliest reference to 'Fletcher's Buildings' at all, occurred. It was not clear whether the move to Fletcher's Buildings had been planned before John Fletcher's death, nor whether they were named after himself or his nephew, but that some expansion was in the pipeline was implied by Thomas Fletcher's announcement in the edition of 13 February 1835 that he had purchased new types and materials, and was expanding his range to bills, posters, circulars etc. The address of the *Chronicle* office, as distinct from the printing works, was given as 13 Bridge Street Row, which was the original numbering of the building now known as 29–31 Bridge Street Row (Plot 1), and it remained there until its removal to Commonhall Street. This was probably the Row shop occupied by George Bulkeley, bookseller, at the time of the purchase of the site in 1813 (CCALS Pigot 1828; Nuttall 1967, 63–75 and *see* Table 3.1).

Benjamin Whittell, chemist, who occupied the shop on the Row on the northern side of the passage to Fletcher's Buildings in 1813 (Plot 2 (part) - no 27 Bridge Street Row) was of particular interest in connection with the discovery of a collection of chemist's and apothecary's jars in the area formerly occupied by the two privies at the rear of this plot (*see* above). He first appeared in St Peter's parish rate assessments in 1800, and seems to have been the owner of two properties, a 'shop' occupied by himself, and an adjacent house occupied by a John Walker (CCALS P63/7/7). Whittell's shop is almost certainly identifiable with what is now 27 Bridge Street Row (Plot 2 (part)). He was listed as a 'druggist' in trade directories between 1818 and his death in 1826, when his business was taken over by Samuel Davies, who had joined him as partner in 1825. Surprisingly Benjamin Whittell was not listed in the Chester Freemen's registers, although a Charles Whittell, druggist, son of Robert Whittell, ropier, was admitted in 1802 (Bennett ed 1906–8, 420). When Benjamin Whittell died intestate in 1826, the administration of his goods was granted to a Robert Whittell of the City of Chester, gent, and a Thomas Whittell, also of Chester, ropier (CCALS WS 1826 Benjamin Whittell). A glance at the index to the Chester probate records confirmed that until the nineteenth century the Whittells were primarily a family of rope-makers, but there was nothing to suggest that they had any connection with Bridge Street Row prior to Benjamin's appearance in 1800.

Samuel Davies was one of the founder members of the Pharmaceutical Society and Chairman of the Mechanics' Institute at Chester, which later became the Chester Free Library. In 1855 he entered into partnership with Thomas Shepheard, a pioneer in microscopy and friend of Charles Kingsley, with whom he founded the Chester Society of Natural Science. After the death of Samuel Davies in 1857 the chemist's shop devolved to Shepheard, who was joined in 1893 by his son W F J Shepheard, an even more distinguished scientist than his father, who became an FCS in 1895 and an examiner to the Pharmaceutical Society in 1907. According to an interesting article published in the *Chemist & Druggist* in 1914, from which the above information has been obtained, W F J Shepheard 'added to his business some years ago a factory for making and bottling soda-water and other bev-

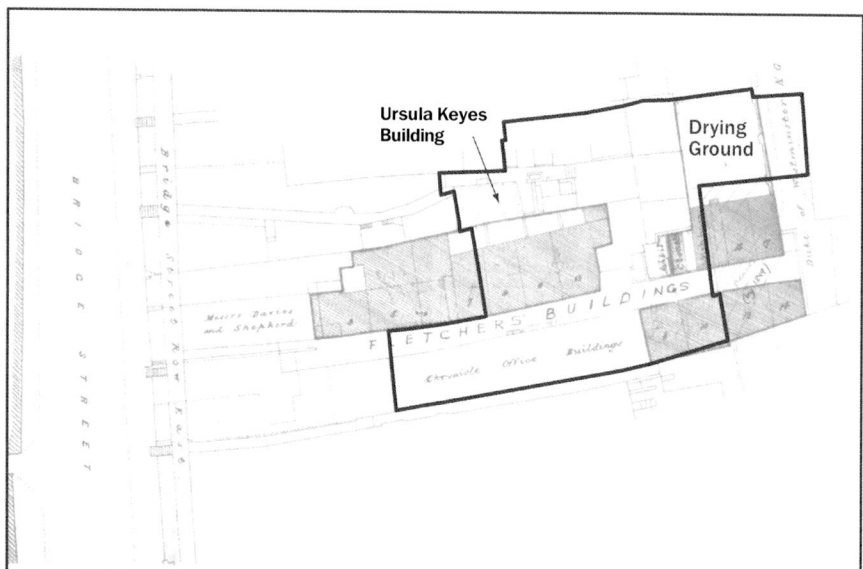

Ill 3.1.1 Plan from deed of sale of 1879. (Not to scale)

erages'. Where this factory was located is not stated, but it was probably not on the Bridge Street site (Anon 1914, 153–7). The business of Davies & Shepheard was listed in Chester trade directories until 1923. It was described in 1914 (*op cit*) as 'the oldest-established drug business in Chester'.

The later history of the Fletcher's Buildings site is documented in a deed in the collection of the Brown family, founders of Brown's of Chester, who acquired it in 1879 from a William Topham of Tarvin (CCALS ZCR 38/1). Recitals of earlier transactions in this document record that on the death of Thomas Fletcher in 1858 his estate passed to his son-in-law William Smith, but in respect of a outstanding mortgage taken out in 1839 the houses in the passage were conveyed to William Topham in 1860. The latter's will of 1888 describes him as a gentleman, but other entries in the Chester will indexes show that he was a member of a Chester family formerly closely associated with the skinning and tanning trades, with a tanyard and glue manufactory in Handbridge (eg CCALS WS 1835 Thomas Topham). There was, however, no indication that any such activities were carried out on the Fletcher's Buildings site, which was probably no more than an investment opportunity and continued to be used as domestic accommodation, dominated to the south by the *Chronicle* office buildings.

The deed of sale of 1879 was particularly valuable in that not only did it describe the property in great detail, giving the names of tenants, which could be collated with the 1881 census returns, but it was also accompanied by a plan showing all the dwellings in Fletcher's Buildings marked with their numbers. In total the property comprised fourteen dwellings (as distinct from eight in 1813), consisting of four to the south side of the passage and ten to the north, two of which were adjoined to the north by a piece of land described as a 'drying ground', probably the 'larger garden' referred to in 1813 (*see* above) (Plot 6). There was also a building adjoining no 15 described in the deed as a 'wash house with a room over', and privies in common. These are marked on the plan as 'Ashpit' and 'Closets', and are of particular interest as occupying the site of the sixteenth-century cess pit discovered during the excavation.

In 1882 the 'drying ground', described as an 'Open Yard with the strip of land now forming passage into Fletcher's Buildings' was exchanged by William and Charles Brown for another 'Open Yard' lying just to east of it, owned by the Duke of Westminster (Eaton Hall, Grosvenor Mss Box E 2.4). The reason for this is not specified, but it may have been related to a planned extension to Brown's department store which obliterated the eastern end of Fletcher's Buildings. This extension is clearly shown on the second edition of the 1:2500 OS map of 1899 (Sheet 38.11) and the piece of land involved in the transaction would have connected Fletcher's Buildings to the rear of Brown's department store in Eastgate Street.

A comparison of maps of Chester produced during the eighteenth and early nineteenth centuries (eg Hunter 1789; Poole 1791; Wood 1833) and the OS 1:500 Town Plan of 1875, showed the gradual shrinkage of the open area in the centre of the square bounded by Bridge Street East, Pepper Street, Newgate Street and Eastgate Street. This was at least partly the result of residential development following a surge in the city population after 1800, and the Fletcher's Buildings complex was one of many 'court' developments behind the street frontages which sprang up during this time. These were not always entirely new buildings; in some cases they constituted a reuse or redevelopment of existing outbuildings formerly associated with the houses on the street frontage, and it is possible that at least part of Fletcher's Buildings represented such a reuse (Brown ed 1999, 129–30; Lewis & Thacker eds 2003, 229). That it was a slum court and the scene of the kind of 'squalor, poverty, dirt and despair' described in a report in the *Chester Chronicle* in 1879 and characteristic of the courts which existed behind Watergate Street, Northgate Street and Lower Bridge Street is doubtful, but evidence derived from the census returns shows that at its peak in 1871, when it was actually described as 'Fletcher's Court', the population of Fletcher's Buildings was sixty-eight within sixteen households, a large number of people to be living in a confined area, if not exactly overcrowding.

At no time do the places of origin and occupations of the inhabitants of these houses recorded in the censuses suggest a migrant population including large numbers of lodgers, nor are they indicative of acute poverty. Rather, the impression is one of a lower working-class population of journeymen working in the leather trades (especially shoemakers), workers in the hotel and retail trade (eg hotel waiters and salesmen), domestic servants, railway workers, dressmakers and clerks, with a few labourers, laundresses and charwomen, and in 1861 a 'Professor of Music' and a 'Chelsea Pensioner'. The majority were Cheshire-, although not necessarily Chester-, born, with a number originating in the neighbouring counties of Shropshire, Staffordshire and North Wales; none were of Irish origin. The 1841 census returns suggest that the structures on the site had changed little since 1813, as, at eight, the number of houses remained the same and accommodated thirty-nine inhabitants. In 1851 the number of households was given as sixteen, indicating that during the intervening decade there had been either some new development or subdivision of the existing premises, and fifty-nine inhabitants were listed. Between 1851 and 1871 the number of households stabilised at sixteen, with the population of the court rising to sixty-eight in 1871, but by 1881 two of the houses at the south-eastern end (nos 12 and 14) were either uninhabited or had already been demolished to make way for the extension to Brown's to which reference has already been made (*see* above). In 1891 and 1901 only five houses were listed, reflecting the loss of the whole of the eastern end of the alleyway. In both years the population of Fletcher's Buildings was reduced to twenty-two, but its social composition was consistent with the earlier period (CCALS census microfilms: St Peter's, Chester 1841–1901).

A comparison of the census returns for the houses and shops on the Row frontage with entries in contemporary trade directories produced interesting results. The value of the census returns is that they show exactly who was living in the buildings on the night that the census was taken, while the directories list the names of the businesses located there. During the latter part of the nineteenth century there are discrepancies between the two, which, while confusing, reflect the trend for the owners of shops and businesses to move their families out of the city centre to leafier areas such as Boughton and Hough Green. Consequently, where there were no residents in the buildings overnight there was no need for them to be recorded at all and they were completely omitted. The other scenario was for the domestic part of the house to be turned over to use as staff accommodation or subdivided and rented out to smaller businesses, which makes it very difficult to identify individual properties in the returns, even when street or Row numbers are given (these appear first in the 1881 census returns, but are erratic and often inaccurate, reflecting a degree of confusion on the part of the enumerator). The results of a search of these returns, collated with the entries in the directories, have been entered into Tables 3.1 and 3.2, but it should be emphasized that some of the identifications are tentative only.

One business which was of particular interest in relation to the excavation area was that of the Brittain family, which occupied the building now known as 15 Bridge Street/17–19 Bridge Street Row (formerly the house of Matthew Anderton) between *c* 1781 and *c* 1857 (Plot 4).

A Robert Brittain, 'Woollen Draper', was listed in directories between 1781 and 1828 as operating from Bridge Street Row, although entries in the Chester probate indexes suggest that the business may have been established some time before this, presumably in different premises, as there is no entry under the name of Brittain in the St Peter's rate books before 1787 (P63/7/6) The administration of a Samuel Brittain, described as 'late of the City of Chester, Woollen Draper', dated 1814, refers to two individuals by the name of Robert Brittain, one of Hoole Bank, described as 'Esq,' and the other 'of the City of Chester, Woollen Draper', although their relationship is not specified (Broster 1781; Cowdroy 1789; Pigot 1818, 1828; WS 1814 Samuel Brittain). However, the will of a Robert Brittain of Hoole Bank, dated 1828, makes it clear that the two Roberts were father and son, and that by 1828 Robert senior had retired to his estates at Hoole Bank and handed over the management of the business to his son Robert junior. The will of 1828 is particularly useful in that it lists in great detail all Brittain's extensive property, including 'All that Dwellinghouse Shop and Warehouse situate on the East side of Upper Bridge Street..... now in the occupation of my..... son Robert Brittain and the Vaults beneath the same now in the occupation of Messieurs Hassall and Foulkes Wine Merchants' which he conveyed to trustees for the use of his son (CCALS WS 1828 Robert Brittain). The warehouse to which Brittain refers is almost certainly identifiable with the building formerly belonging to the Ursula Keyes Trust, which was demolished prior to the excavation, and which was the subject of a Standing Building Evaluation in 1998 (Neil 1998). It was presumably used for the storage of Brittain's stock in trade, although the description and photographs of some of the internal fittings prior to its demolition suggest that it may have subsequently been used at least partially as domestic accommodation (Neil 1998, 14)

On Robert Brittain's death in 1828 the business devolved to his son William Walker Brittain, who is listed in directories as 'Draper, Tailor & Hatter' (1846–50) and 'Clothier, Hatter & Undertaker' (1857–60). Census returns confirm that the family was still resident there in during this period, with one daughter, three shop assistants and two female servants in 1841, and two children together with three female and one male servant in 1851. The 1851 returns provide the additional information that Brittain employed seventeen men, who were presumably accommodated elsewhere (CCALS microfilm 2/35). There is no reference to the Brittain family in the 1861 returns, which include a note to the effect that two houses were being rebuilt (CCALS microfilm 234/20), and although it is known that no 13 Bridge Street/13–15 Bridge Street Row was rebuilt by the Duke of Westminster in that year, which may have affected the structure of the adjoining building (Brown ed 1999, 157), the complete absence of any references to the firm in directories after 1860 suggests that the business may have closed down at about that time.

During the nineteenth century Bridge Street Row maintained its reputation as the centre of the drapery trade in the city, as, in addition to the business of Brittain & Co, at least four other similar businesses were situated there, including that of Isaac Ewen, described in 1864 as 'hosier, glover, and baby linen and ladies outfitter' at 8 (later

13–15) Bridge Row (Plot 5) between 1851 and 1896, and John Higgins, 'Master Woolen Draper' listed between 1841 and 1871 at what may have been 13–14 (later 29–31 Bridge Street Row (Plot 1)), which was also the location of the *Chester Chronicle* office. Another business of note was that of Richard Taylor, 'Music Seller & Painter', who set up at 10 (later 21–3) Bridge Street Row *c* 1818, and after being joined by his sister Hannah, diversified into 'Toys & Fishing Tackle', trading until *c* 1861. There were at least two other toy shops on the Row, that of Elizabeth Duboc, the predecessor of Isaac Ewen at 8 (later 13–15) Bridge Street Row who was in business between *c* 1841 and 1850, and William Fitch who is listed at 11 (later 25) Bridge Street Row between 1857 and 1881. Interestingly, both were also described as hairdressers and perfumers. Between at least 1781 and 1860 a public house known as the 'Rising Sun' was located to the rear of 13–15 Bridge Street Row on land owned by the Duke of Westminster, presumably accessed through the passage to the south of Lowe's silversmith (11 Bridge Street Row). This disappeared from the record after the rebuilding of the house on the street front in 1861 (Eaton Hall, Grosvenor Mss Box A 2, Bundle 4; CCALS Chester directories 1781–1860; census returns 1841 and 1851 and *see* above).

A comparison of the 1871 and 1881 census returns and contemporary trade directories revealed the beginning of a new trend in the use and occupation of the buildings in Bridge Street Row, which was reflected elsewhere in the city. Particularly noticeable was the tendency for the actual residents to be housekeepers, servants, assistants and apprentices, while the owners of the businesses and their families were conspicuously absent, having moved out of town (CCALS census microfilms 24/35, 146/21, 265/24, fiche 34/93). Evidence from directories also indicates that some of the properties had been subdivided into many small offices, such as that of Norden & Mason, solicitors (1878), Harold Hignett, architect (1878) and the 'Ladies County Club' (1896), all located at 23 Bridge Street Row (CCALS Chester directories). Clearly, although many improvements were made to the public face of the Rows in the nineteenth century, the area was no longer the bustling thriving community that it had once been, as the prosperous merchants and craftsmen who had populated the area during earlier centuries were replaced by a transient population of shop assistants, office workers and domestic servants.

Summary of documents

Table 3.2.1 Summary of documentary evidence for the owners/occupiers of the plots

Plot 1 Nos 25–7 Bridge St/29–31 (formerly 13–14) Bridge St Row (including southern range of Fletcher's Buildings)

The site occupied by Fletcher's Buildings falls partly within Plot 1 (southern range) and partly within Plot 2 (northern range), divided by a central passageway. However, because of problems of differentiation in earlier records, information relating to both sides has been entered here

Phase	Date	Owners/Occupiers	Sources
VIII	c 1770–c 1789	Site occupied by William and Joseph Ratcliffe, flaxdressers (owners), and tenants (unnamed).	CCALS ZD/JWW/42, P63/7/5; Cowdroy 1789
	1789–pre 1813	George Bulkeley, bookseller and stationer, occupier of shop on Row (probably 29 Bridge St. Row).	Cowdroy 1789
IX	1808	Mrs Ratcliffe (owner), with 8 named tenants in 6–7 'houses' and two 'rooms', (? Fletcher's Buildings) viz: Robert Blythin, Ann Davies, ? Simpson, Step Crowfoot, David Bunn, Mr Gunney, Mrs Culm, Daniel Humphreys.	CCALS P 63/7/9
	1813	John Fletcher, printer, acquires whole of Fletcher's Buildings site from Mrs Ratcliffe, including the two shops either side of the passage on the Row occupied by George Bulkeley and Benjamin Whittle, chemist, 5 houses to the north and 3 to the south. 9 named occupants, viz: Benjamin Whittle, Stephen Crowfoot, shoemaker, David Bevin, labourer, Anne Davies, plaisterer, ? Gunnery, plaisterer, ? Culm, mantua maker, David Humphreys, cooper, ? Owen, brazier and John Walker, silversmith.	CCALS ZD/JWW/42
	1835	Premises inherited by Thomas Fletcher, nephew of John, on latter's death. Printing presses for *Chester Chronicle* moved to 13 (now 29) Bridge St Row at approx same time.	CCALS WS 1835 John Fletcher; *Chester Chronicle* 16 Jan 1835
	1841–61	John Higgins, woollen draper (at 14 (now 31) Bridge St Row).	CCALS 1841 Census Fiche HO107/130/10 fo 4v; 1851 Census Mf 2/35 HO107/2172 fo 250v; 1861 Census Mf 234/20 RG9/2630 fo 32
	1849	Site inherited by William Smith, son-in-law of Thomas Fletcher.	CCALS ZCR 38/1

Plot 1 Nos 25–7 Bridge St/29–31 (formerly 13–14) Bridge St Row (including southern range of Fletcher's Buildings) *(continued)*

Phase	Date	Owners/Occupiers	Sources
IX	1860	William Topham of Tarvin acquires Fletcher's Buildings from William Smith.	CCALS ZCR 38/1
	1878	Appleton and Bracegirdle, silk mercers, drapers, milliners and hosiers (at 31 Bridge St Row).	Post Office Directory 1878
	1879	William and Charles Brown, silk mercers acquire Fletcher's Buildings from William Topham.	CCALS ZCR 38/1
	1882	William and Charles Brown exchange the 'drying ground' (see Plot 6) for the strip of land belonging to the Duke of Westminster adjoining their Eastgate St premises.	Eaton Hall, Grosvenor Mss. Box E 2.4
	1846–96	Chester Chronicle Offices – Thomas Fletcher 1846–57 / William Smith, H Smith and co, 1860 / Ann Smith 1864–1874 / Richard Fletcher Smith 1878 / J Ward Jones 1896	CCALS Chester Directories 1846–96
		Fletcher's Buildings (N and S):	
	1841	8 households accommodating 39 inhabitants, including shoemaker, servants, butcher grocer etc.	CCALS 1841 Census Fiche HO107/130/10 fo 3v–4v
	1851	16 households accommodating 59 inhabitants, including shoemaker, blacksmith, stationer, milliner, laundress, housekeeper, clerk, waiter, dressmaker, domestic servant.	CCALS 1851 Census Mf 2/35 HO107/2172 ff 249r–250v
	1861	16 households accommodating 67 inhabitants, including servants, brazier, painter, dressmakers, shoemaker, hotel waiter, butcher, upholsterer and 'Professor of Music' etc.	CCALS 1861 Census Mf 234/20 RG9/2630 ff 32r–33v
	1871	16 households accommodating 68 inhabitants, including unemployed brazier, servants hotel waiter, stoker at railway, groom at livery stable, dressmaker, labourer, clerk, teacher of dancing, warehouseman, painter etc.	CCALS 1871 Census Mf 24/35 RG10/3731 ff 41v–43r
	1881	10 households accommodating 56 inhabitants, including traveller, salesman, domestic servant, cab driver, printers, gas fitter, retired gardener, waiter, charwomen (3), labourers (6), tobacconist etc.	CCALS 1881 Census Mf 146/21 RG11/3559 ff 41r–42r
	1891	6 households accommodating 22 inhabitants, including joiner, housemaid, butcher turner and fitter, striker, mantle maker, tobacconist, labourer, tailor etc	CCALS 1891 Census Mf 265/24 RG12/2864 ff.11r–11v
	1901	5 households accommodating 22 inhabitants, including quarryman, charwoman, dressmaker, mantlemaker, laundress, boilermaker, carter etc.	CCALS 1901 Census Mf 34/93 RG13/3372 ff 10v–11r

See also notes on Plots 2 and 6

Plot 2 (Part 1) No 23 Bridge St/27 (formerly 12) Bridge St Row (including northern range of Fletcher's Buildings).
For Fletcher's Buildings see notes on Plot 1

Phase	Date	Owners/Occupiers	Sources
VIII	c 1770–c 1789	Site owned and occupied by William and Joseph Ratcliffe flaxdressers.	See notes on Plot 1
IX	c 1800–26	Benjamin Whittell, chemist, owns shop on Row. Also rents adjoining property from Mrs Ratcliffe.	CCALS P63/7/7; WS 1826 Benjamin Whittell; Chester Directories 1818–28
	1808	Mrs Ratcliffe (owner) with 8 named tenants in 6–7 houses and 2 'rooms' (? Fletcher's Buildings).	See notes on Plot 1
	1813	John Fletcher acquires site from Mrs Ratcliffe (including house occupied by Benjamin Whittell).	See notes on Plot 1
	1826	Death of Benjamin Whittell.	CCALS WS 1826 Benjamin Whittell
	1826–57	Samuel Davies, Chemist and Druggist, succeeds to business of Benjamin Whittell.	CCALS Chester Directories; 1841 Census Fiche HO107/130/10 fo 4v; 1851 Census Mf 2/35 HO107/2172 fo 248v–249
	1857	Death of Samuel Davies.	CCALS WS 1857 Samuel Davies
	1857–1923	Thomas Shepheard takes over business of Samuel Davies, trading as Davies and Shepheard; joined in 1893 by his son William Shepheard.	*Chemist and Druggist* 1914; CCALS 1861 Census Mf 234/20 RG9/2630 fo 33v; 1871 Census Mf 24/35 RG10/3731 fo 43; 1881 Census Mf 146/21 RG11/3559 fo 41; 1891 Census RG12/2864 fo11; 1901 Census Fiche 34/93 fo 11

See also notes on Plot 1

Plot 2 (Part 2)   No 21 Bridge St/25 (formerly 11) Bridge St Row

Phase	Date	Owners/Occupiers	Sources
VII	c 1641–75	Thomas Aspinwall, ironmonger. Owner and occupier of house with 4 hearths 1664.	CCALSP63/7/1; WS 1675 Thomas Aspinwall
	1682	Property described as inheritance of Elizabeth, Hannah and Abigail Aspinwall, daughters and co-heirs of Thomas Aspinwall in agreement *re* rebuilding of house to N owned by Randle Vause (no 23 Bridge St Row).	CCALS DBC Acc 1720/4/2. *See also notes on Plot 3*
	1711	Described as in ownership of John and Abigail Swan (née Aspinwall) and Obadiah Rock in further agreement *re* rebuilding of house to N. Tenants named as Rachel Page, bookseller (Row shop), Ralph Pickmore, butcher (street), Robert Hayward, gent (unspec).	CCALS Acc 1720/4/8. *See also notes on Plot 3*
VIII	1742	Mrs Page (Rachel Page, bookseller) listed in rate books as tenant of house and shop belonging to 'Mrs Swan'.	CCALS P63/74
IX	c 1841–pre 1851	George Prichard, bookseller and family occupies shop in Row.	CCALS 1841 Census Fiche HO107/130/10 fo 5
	c 1846–50	Henry Bailey, perfumer, hairdresser and Berlin wool repository (shop only, home in Foregate St).	CCALS Chester Directories
	1857–81	William Fitch, hairdresser and perfumer.	CCALS Chester Directories; 1861 Census Mf 234/20 RG9/2630 fo 33v; 1871 Census Mf 24/35 RG10/3731 fo 43; 1881 Census Mf 146/21 RG11/3539 fo 40v
	1891	Andrew John Wright, perfumer.	CCALS Chester Directories; 1891 Census Mf 265/24 fo 10v

Plot 3 Nos 17–19 Bridge St/21–3 (formerly 10) Bridge St Row

Phase	Date	Owners/Occupiers	Sources
VII	c 1641–50	Robert Caddick, alderman (d 1681) listed in rate books.	CCALS P63/7/1; WS Robert Caddick
	1681	House referred to as recently purchased from Caddick by Randle Vause, linen draper, in agreement between Vause and Matthew Anderton (neighbour to N) *re* rebuilding of party wall in course of reconstruction of house.	CCALS DBC Acc 1720/4/3. *See also notes on Plot 2 (part 2) and Plot 4*
	1681	Cellar in same house in separate ownership of Humphrey Jones, draper, sold by him to Randle Vause, linen draper. Occupant Mary Appleton.	CCALS DBC Acc 1720/4/1
	1689	Property described in will of Randle Vause as messuage shops and cellar occupied by himself, Mary Appleton, widow, Thomas Hollwell, tailor, John Day, periwig maker.	CCALS WS 1689 Randle Vause
	1698	Sale of cellar confirmed to Sarah Vause (widow of Randle Vause) by Samuel, Hannah, Mary and Martha Jones (children of Humphrey Jones. Cellar still occupied by Mary Appleton.	CCALS DBC Acc 1720/4/5–6
	1711	House rebuilt by Sarah Sparke (formerly Vause) and her son John Vause further to agreements *re* party walls with Sarah and William Anderton (to N) and John and Abigail Swan (to S). Street level premises occupied by Joseph Dutton, butcher.	CCALS DBC Acc 1720/4/7–8. *See also notes on Plot 2 (part 2) and Plot 4*
	1720	House conveyed by William Vause to Sarah Sparke. Occupant Elizabeth Buckley.	CCALS DBC Acc 1720/4/9–12
IX	1818–29	Richard Taylor, music seller and painter.	CCALS Chester Directories
	1846–c 1861	Richard and Hannah Taylor, music sellers and dealers in toys and fishing tackle.	CCALS Chester Directories; 1851 Census Mf 2/35 HO107/2172 fo 248v; 1861 Census Mf 234/20 RG9/2630 fo 34
	c 1871	? Robert Thomas, bootmaker.	CCALS 1871 Census Mf 24/35 RG10/3731 fo 43
	1878	? Norden and Mason, solicitors. ? Harold Hignett, architect.	CCALS Chester Directories
	1881	William Parsons, gent and son (draper).	CCALS 1881 Census Mf 146/21 RG11/3559 fo 40v
	1891	Mary Edwards, 'Fancy Business'.	CCALS 1891 Census Mf 265/24 RG12/2864 fo 10v
	1891–1901	Mary Nixon, hairdresser and perfumer.	CCALS 1891 Census Mf 265/24 RG12/2864 fo 11; 1901 Census Fiche 34/93 fo 10v
	1896	?Ladies County Club. ?Miss Anne Pye, art teacher. ?Arthur Blayney, stationer.	CCALS Chester Directories

Plot 4 No 15 Bridge St/17–19 (formerly 9) Bridge St Row (including Ursula Keyes Building)

Phase	Date	Owners/Occupiers	Sources
VI	1558	Purported to be site of 'Blue Posts' Inn and incident (see main text).	Morris 1895, 72–3; Roberts 1851
	1617	? Shop of William Edwards, ironmonger, who applies to Assembly to extend streetwards. Described as beneath house of Sir Sackville Trevor.	Groombridge 1956, 83–5
VII	c 1660–93	House and shop (with 7 hearths in 1664) owned and occupied by Matthew Anderton Sr, merchant, innholder, alderman, sheriff and deputy controller of customs (d 1693). Other occupants named in his will (1693): Thomas Fernihaugh, draper (shop) and Jane Reece, widow (cellar).	CCALS ZCR 656; P63/7/2; WS 1693 Matthew Anderton
	1681	Agreement for rebuilding party wall to S between Matthew Anderton Sr and Ralph Vause, linen draper.	CCALS DBC Acc 1720/4/3. See also notes on Plot 2 (part 2) and Plot 3
	c 1693–1709	House inherited by Matthew Anderton Jr, mayor 1703–4 (d 1709).	CCALS WS 1709 Matthew Anderton
	c 1710–20	Mrs Anderton (widow of Matthew Jr) listed in rate books.	CCALS P63/7/2–3
	1711	Further agreement for rebuilding party wall to S between William and Sarah Anderton and Sarah Sparke.	CCALS DBC Acc 1720/4/7–8. See also notes on Plot 2 (part 2) and Plot 3
IX	1781–9	Robert Brittain and John Larden, woollen drapers (? shared premises).	CCALS Chester Directories
	1818–29	Robert Brittain and Son, Woollen Drapers and Tailors owners and occupiers of house and shop.	CCALS Chester Directories
		Robert Brittain Sr of Hoole Bank (d 1828). Will describes premises and refers to warehouse (probably Ursula Keyes Building) and vaults occupied by Hassall and Foulkes, wine merchants.	WS 1828 Robert Brittain
	c 1829–41	?Robert Brittain Jr succeeds to business, possibly retired by 1841 (d 1848).	CCALS Chester Directories; 1841 Census Fiche HO107/130/10 fo 5; WS 1848 Robert Brittain
	c 1841–60	William Walker Brittain, draper, hatter and undertaker, succeeds to business.	CCALS Chester Directories; 1851 Census Mf 2/35 HO107/2172 fo 248v
	1861	Census returns refer to 2 unoccupied houses in process of rebuilding. Possibly no 8 (13–15 Bridge St Row) and no 9 (17–19) Bridge St Row affected due to party walls.	CCALS 1861 Census Mf 234/20 RG9/2630 fo 34
	c 1871	?William Shenton, bootmaker.	CCALS 1871 Census Mf 265/24 RG10/3731 fo 43v
	1878	?George Watmough Webster, photographer.	CCALS Chester Directories
	c 1881–91	John Higginson, police constable and family.	CCALS 1881 Census Mf 146/21 RG11/3559 fo 40v; 1891 Census Mf 265/24 RG12/2864 fo 10v
	1886	?James Jones, bootmaker.	Lockwood & Hewitt 1886, v

Plot 5 No 13 Bridge St/13–14 (formerly 8) Bridge St Row (including the 'Rising Sun' public house at rear)

Phase	Date	Owners/Occupiers	Sources
VI	1605	House in ownership of Alexander Cotes of the City of Chester, gent.	Eaton Hall, Grosvenor Mss Box F 22
	1609	Property inherited by Sparke family.	Eaton Hall, Grosvenor Mss Box F 22
	1617	? House occupied by William Sparke, merchant and ironmonger.	Groombridge 1956, 83–5
VIII	1739	Property inherited by Thomas Adams on d of Mary Wood (née Sparke) Occupants named in will of Mary Wood (1738): Thomas Davies, woollen draper; Benjamin Boulton, flax dresser; John Wright, tailor.	Eaton Hall, Grosvenor Mss Box F22
IX	1781	Earliest reference to 'Rising Sun' public house.	CCALS Chester Directories
	1810	Occupants named as: Jane and Sarah Green, tea dealers; Joseph Ralph, butcher (cellar); Peter Hewitt (licensee of 'Rising Sun').	Eaton Hall, Grosvenor Mss Box F22
	1814	Dorothy Adams devises property to nephews Samuel and William Thomas for disposal by sale.	Eaton Hall, Grosvenor Mss Box F22
	1815	Property (including 'Rising Sun') sold to Robert, Earl Grosvenor Occupants named as: – Reece, milliner; Joseph Ralph, butcher; Peter Hewitt, publican.	Eaton Hall. Grosvenor Mss Box A2 Bdle 4
	1818–20	John Randle named as licensee of 'Rising Sun'.	CCALS Chester Directories

Plot 5 No 13 Bridge St/13–15 (formerly 8) Bridge St Row (including the 'Rising Sun' public house at rear) (continued)

Phase	Date	Owners/Occupiers	Sources
	1828–9	John Williams named as licensee of 'Rising Sun'.	CCALS Chester Directories
	1828–9	Theodore Duboc 'hairdresser from Paris' occupant of shop on Row.	CCALS Chester Directories
	c 1841–50	Elizabeth Duboc, Toy Warehouse and perfumer occupant of shop on Row.	CCALS Chester Directories; 1841 Census Fiche HO107/130 /10 fo 5
	c 1841–1851	Ann Roberts named as licensee of 'Rising Sun'.	CCALS Chester Directories; 1841 Census Fiche HO107/130 /10 fo 5; 1851 Census Mf 2/35 HO107/2172 fo 248
	c 1851–1896	Isaac England Ewen, hosier and haberdasher and occupant of house and shop on Row.	CCALS Chester Directories; 1851 Census Mf 2/35 HO107/ 2172 fo 248v; 1871 Census Mf 24/35 RG10/3731 fo 43v; 1881 Census Mf 146/21 RG11/ 3559 fo 40v
	1857–60	Thomas Orme named as licensee of 'Rising Sun'.	CCALS Chester Directories
	1861	House rebuilt by Edward Hodkinson for Marquis of Westminster. No further references to 'Rising Sun' public house.	Brown ed 1999, 157

Plot 6 Parcel of land to E of Plots 4 and 5, eventually forming the 'Drying Ground' to Fletcher's Buildings

Phase	Date	Owners/Occupiers	Sources
IX	1813	Referred to as the 'larger garden' in deed of conveyance of site later known as 'Fletcher's Buildings' from Mrs Ratcliffe to John Fletcher, printer.	CCALS ZD/JWW/42
	1879	Referred to as the 'drying ground' in deed of conveyance of Fletcher's Buildings from William Topham of Tarvin to William and Charles Brown (with plan).	CCALS ZCR 38/1
	1882	Open Yard with the strip of land now forming passage into Fletcher's Buildings' owned by Wiliam and Charles Brown, mercers, exchanged for 'Open Yard' to E of Fletcher's Buildings owned by Duke of Westminster.	Eaton Hall, Grosvenor Mss Box E 2.4
		See also notes on Plots 1 and 2	

Plot unspecified

Phase	Date	Owners/Occupiers	Sources
V	c 1356–1483	Numerous references to 'void' pieces of land in Bridge St.	CCALS ZCHB 6
VI	1503	Presentment of Joan Steyner and Margery Bower, widows, for making a fire in their cellars, the smoke from which was rising into 'le Mercerrowe' to the great nuisance of neighbours and passers-by.	CCALS ZSB 5 fo 7
	c 1554	Thomas Elton 'ij littell shoppes and plots thereunto adyonynge' on E side of Bridge St.	CCALS ZTAR 1/8
	1568–9	Thomas Dutton 'a shope now in occupacon of Will[ia]m Wall Iarnmonger' (possibly same property as formerly held by Elton).	CCALS ZTAR 1/13
	1573–87	Reference to house recently built on piece of void ground in Bridge St. by William Wall. Measurements given as 91' L x 27' W. Pays 6d pa for 3 posts holding it up. Referred to in 1587 as 'under the house where Mrs Dutton of Dutton did lately inhabit'.	CCALS ZAB 1 fo 152; ZTAR 1/17
	1599	Will of William Wall, ironmonger, alderman, treasurer 1576, mayor 1586–7. Refers to several properties, but not specific.	CCALS WS 1599 William Wall
	1603–4	Reference to house formerly of William Wall on E side of Bridge St as in tenure of Thomas Fletcher, alderman.	CCALS ZTAR 2/23
	1612	Robert Fletcher 'jr' feltmaker purchases property in Bridge St, including the 'Moon' tavern	CCALS ZL/Ch/4
	1613	Robert Fletcher furnishes Henry Darwall, glover, with musket in muster of trained soldiers.	Groombridge 1956, 66
	1617	Inventory of Robert Fletcher (feltmaker), including references to items of armour, including 'Jacke'.	CCALS WS 1617 Robert Fletcher
VII	c 1641–64	Mrs [Isabell] Fletcher, widow, listed in St. Peter's parish rate books, and as owing a chief rent of 20/- to Edward Bavand in respect of a house in Bridge St. (This chief rent is also referred to in the will of Robert Fletcher, skinner (d 1688) as due on his house).	CCALS P 63/7/1; ZCR 465/92
	1643–4	Robert Fletcher 'hatmaker' (possibly related to above) pays fine for 'enclosure' (probably an encroachment) in unspecified location.	CCALS ZTAR 3/51
	1664–88	Robert Fletcher listed in rate books for both St. Peter's parish and St. Michael's ward, which locates his property in the overlapping area on the NE section of Bridge St. Assessed for 2 hearths in Hearth Tax 1664.	CCALS P 63/7/2; ZCAS 1 nos 56 and 88; Hearth Tax 1664, Mf 13/2
	1675 and 1684	Robert Fletcher 'jr' skinner, lessor of tenement, incl 'Moon' tavern.	CCALS ZL/Ch/10 and 12

Plot unspecified (*continued*)

Phase	Date	Owners/Occupiers	Sources
VII	1686	Robert Fletcher 'of Corke' pays fines to City in respect of shop adjacent to that of Robert Radford and shop in holding of Francis Touchett (his tenants).	CCALS ZTAP 1
	1688	Death of Robert Fletcher, skinner, whose will describes property on E side of Bridge St comprising 4 houses, 4 shops, a 'long garden' divided into 3 parts, a cellar, a warehouse a brewhouse, 2 coalhouses, and 3 houses of convenience. Bequeathed to wife Ann for life. Occupants:	CCALS WS 1688 Robert Fletcher

	Robert Fletcher	: house and shop in Row, brewhouse in court, coalhouse, house of convenience, 1/3 of 'long garden'	
	John Jones, tailor	: house	CCALS WS 1693
	Aunt Wood'	: house, coalhouse, house of convenience, use of brewhouse, 1/3 of 'long garden'	
	Robert Radford, linen draper	: shop	CCALS WS 1696
	Charles Leech, mercer	: house, house of convenience, 1/3 of 'long garden'	CCALS WS 1698
	Francis Touchett, apothecary	: 2 shops, use of brewhouse	CCALS WS 1700
	Thomas Minshull, ironmonger	: cellar	CCALS WS 1690

Phase	Date	Owners/Occupiers	Sources
	1696	Death of Ann Fletcher, widow of Robert, who had continued to run business. Her inventory lists stock-in-trade including muffs and cat skins.	CCALS WS 1696 Ann Fletcher
VII–IX	1696–1811	Property of Robert Fletcher split between niece and nephew Hannah and John Ellis and sister Mary Yonge, passing down through their descendants the Frith, Anderson, Entwistle and Smith families. In 1811 property comprised 5 shops/cellars, 2 gardens and 1 acre of land.	CCALS ZD/JWW/12–42; WS 1690 John Ellis
VII	1699–1702	Cellar formerly 'Moon' tavern in occupation of Margaret Minshull, widow of Thomas.	CCALS ZD/JWW/12
VIII	1729	Occupants of site named in deed of Frith family as: Abner Scholes, upholsterer; Thomas Wright, tailor; John Cotgreave, cordwainer; Robert Wrench, joiner; Alice Cooke, spinster; Samuel Smith, grocer; Peter Frodsham, clothier; Robert Cawley, watchmaker; John Dutton, butcher (probably cellar).	CCALS ZD/JWW/17
	1759	Occupants of site named in conveyance of property from Thomas Entwistle to Gabriel Smith, watchmaker, as: Elizabeth Smith, widow; John Maddocks, yeoman; Thomas Ledsham, stationer; Benjamin Boulton, flaxdresser; John Wright, tailor; George Hastings, tinman; Gabriel Smith, watchmaker; Thomas Man, butcher (probably in cellar).	CCALS ZD/JWW/31
	1764	Occupants of site named in deed of Smith family as: Elizabeth Bavand, spinster; John Maddock, yeoman; Thomas Ledsham, bookseller; Mary Bolton, widow; John Wright, tailor George Hastings, tinman; Gabriel Smith, watchmaker; Thomas Williams, dealer in earthenware.	CCALS ZD/JWW/33
IX	1811	Occupants of site named in conveyance of site from Rev John Smith to John Fletcher, printer, as: George Hastings, brazier; Messrs Hassall and Foulkes (wine merchants); George Youd; Thomas Hogg; Sarah Heywood, widow; Joseph Davies, grocer	CCALS ZD/JWW/39

See also notes on Fletcher's Buildings (Plots 1, 2 and 6)

Table 3.2.2 Occupations of owners/occupiers of the plots

Phase	Plot 1	Plot 2 (part 1)	Plot 2 (part 2)	Plot 3	Plot 4	Plot 5	Plot 6	No plot
V								Mercer
VI					?Inn ?Ironmonger	?Ironmonger ?Merchant		Mercers Ironmonger Feltmaker Tavern
VII			Ironmonger Bookseller Butcher Gentleman	Linen draper Tailor Periwig maker Butcher	Merchant Innholder Gentleman			Hatmaker Skinner Tailor Linen draper Mercer Apothecary Ironmonger Tavern
VIII	Flaxdresser Bookseller	Flaxdresser	Bookseller			Woollen draper Flaxdresser Tailor		Upholsterer Tailor Cordwainer Joiner Grocer Clothier Watchmaker Butcher
VIII								Stationer Flaxdresser Bookseller Brazier Earthenware
IX	Printer Chemist Shoemaker Labourer Plasterer Mantua maker Cooper Brazier Silversmith Woollen draper Silk mercers Butcher Grocer Blacksmith Stationer Milliner Laundress Dressmaker Painter Upholsterer Tobacconist Joiner Tailor Waiter Stoker Groom Clerk Dancing teacher Warehouseman	Chemist Printer	Bookseller Perfumer Hairdresser Wool repository	Music seller Painter Toy dealer Fishing tackle Bootmaker Hairdresser Perfumer Stationer Solicitor Architect Art teacher	Woollen draper Wine merchant Bootmaker Photographer Police constable	Public house Tea dealer Butcher Milliner Hairdresser Toy warehouse Perfumer Hosier	Garden	Printer Brazier Wine merchant Grocer

Roman Building Materials

Alison Jones with a report on the
window glass by H E M Cool

Stone

Introduction

THIRTY-SEVEN items were recovered, comprising ten
(possibly eleven) column fragments, a fragment of a
moulded wall lining/panel, an inscribed panel and twenty-five indeterminate fragments, several of which were
worked.

Phases I and IIa

A single fragment of carved grey slate came from Phase
Ie. Phase IIa produced a piece of grey ?sandstone, partly
burnt on one side, and two fragments of pale grey biosparitic limestone coated in a chalky white ?cement.

Post-Roman phases and unstratified

Of the remaining thirty-four items, thirty came from the
post-Roman phases and four were unstratified. It is not
certain that all the indeterminate pieces are Roman in
date. Diagnostic fragments comprise a side edge fragment of an inscribed slate panel from Phase IV. Two letters
are visible: the base of a vertical stroke is just apparent at
the top, below is the main letter, 'M' or 'N'. It is part of a
new inscription rather than a further fragment of a previously discovered example (Dan Robinson *pers comm*). It
presumably originated from an inscription on a public
building.

There were also ten small column fragments of white
Purbeck marble, with a possible additional fragmentary
example from Phase VI (910), all presumably Roman in
date. The column fragments vary slightly in diameter,
ranging from 90 mm to 110 mm. The largest formed the
lower part of a base fragment, which probably explains
why it has a slightly increased diameter in comparison to
the other pieces; the base itself has a diameter of 150 mm.
There is also a large moulded fragment of Purbeck marble from Phase IV, which was possibly part of a panel or
wall lining.

Table 4.1.1 Purbeck marble column fragments quantified by phase and
context

Phase	Context	SF no	Dim (mm)
V	1589		Diam 91; surviving H 190
	1641		Surviving diam: 90; Surviving H 110
	1656	10125	Base diam 150; base th: 30; column diam 110
VI	949	10126	Diam 93; surviving H 195
	1501		Surviving diam 90; surviving H 80
IX	1502	10127	Diam 95; surviving H 220
	u/s		Diam 100; surviving H 170
	u/s		Diam 93; surviving H 115
	u/s		Diam 100; surviving H 225
	u/s		Diam 95; surviving H 110

Table 4.1.2 Indeterminate fragments of ?Roman stone building materials quantified by phase and context

Phase	Context	SF no	Material	Source	Condition	No	Comments
Ie	93		Grey slate	Probably N Wales		1	Carved
IIa	1146		Grey ?sandstone		Partly burnt on one side	1	Attached chalky lime deposits
	1225		Pale grey biosparitic limestone			2	Coated with white, chalky ?cement
IIb	1138		Grey slate	Probably N Wales		1	Thick frag of slab
III	74		White ?limestone			4	
	106		Grey slate	Probably N Wales		3	Worked
	106		White limestone			2	
IV	871	10124	White Upper Purbeck marble	S Dorset		1	Carved/moulded
	883		Red Triassic sandstone	Probably local		1	Worked
	1034		White limestone			1	Indet lump (?b mats)
	1125		White limestone			1	
V	57		Grey slate	Probably N Wales		1	
	67		White ?limestone			2	
	1661		White limestone			1	
	1669		Red Triassic sandstone	Probably local	Burnt	1	Worked; rounded section; traces of attached white lime mortar
VI	910		White Upper Purbeck marble	SE Dorset		1	Worked
X	80		White marble	?Pennines ?Italy		1	Worked
	780		White ?Tertiary limestone			1	Moulded

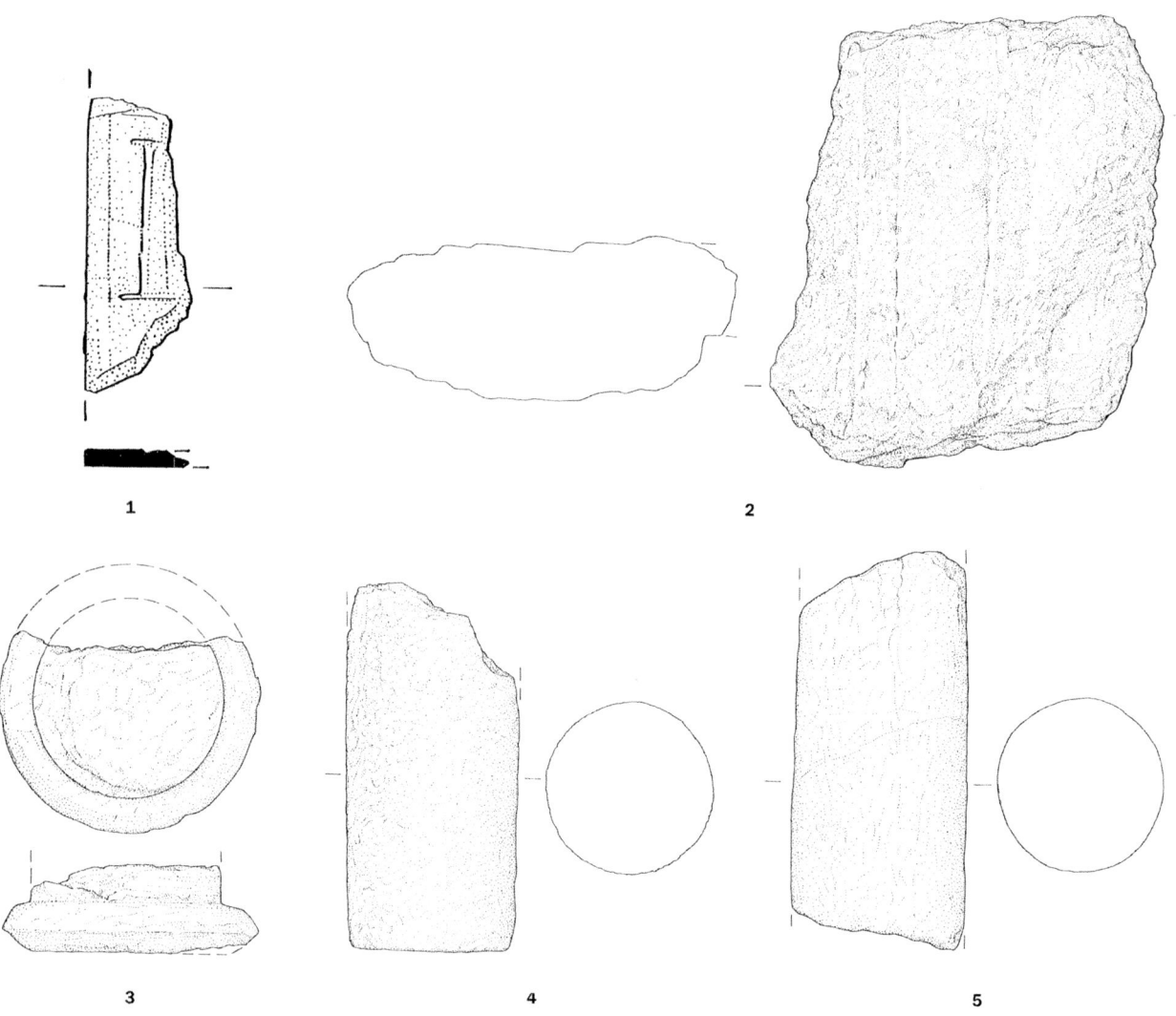

Ill 4.1.1 Roman stone building materials. (Scale: no 1: 1/2; nos 2–5: 1/4)

Catalogue

1   Fragment of an inscription in grey North Wales slate; side edge fragment with two letters; fire-scorched, causing it to split along a fault plane and resulting in an unusually thin base. Main letter is 'M' or 'N'; base of vertical stroke just visible at top; marking-out line visible for left margin. Surviving L 79 mm; surviving th 6 mm. (849): Phase IV; SF 9209. Ill 4.1.1.1.

2   Large moulded fragment of white Upper Purbeck marble. Surviving L *c* 230 mm; surviving W *c* 200 mm; surviving th *c* 75 mm. (871): Phase IV; SF 10124. Ill 4.1.1.2.

3   Column base of white Upper Purbeck marble with column stump. Base diam 150 mm; base th 30 mm; column diam 110 mm; complete surviving H 45 mm. (1656): Phase V; SF 10125. Ill 4.1.1.3.

4   Column fragment of white Upper Purbeck marble. Diam 93 mm; surviving H 195 mm. (949): Phase VI; SF 10126. Ill 4.1.1.4.

5   Column fragment of white Upper Purbeck marble. Diam 95 mm; surviving H 220 mm. (1502): Phase IX; SF 10127. Ill 4.1.1.5.

Discussion

The major period of quarrying for Purbeck marble in the Roman period was from *c* 43 to 200. However, it is also present in large quantities in fourth-century contexts in Britain, suggesting that the quarries remained active during this period (Williams 2002, 129). It was exploited for both ornamental and building purposes. Fragments of Purbeck marble were recovered from excavations at 25–9 Bridge Street in 1996, just to the south of the 2001 site, where they were perhaps most likely to have originated in the fortress bath house (Emery 1996, 35). A dedicatory inscription to Vespasian in Purbeck marble is known from the bath house itself, where it was recovered during excavations in 1963/4 (Robinson 2005, 103–5). Purbeck marble is not recorded from any other sites in the vicinity. Purbeck marble was used for moulded wall-linings and panels in the fortress bath house at Caerleon (Zienkiewicz 1986, 303–6). It was also much used for wall veneers, moulded panel edgings, *labra* (edgings), etc in the legionary baths at Exeter (Zienkiewicz 1986, 303).

Acknowledgements

With thanks to Kate Riddington (Assistant Keeper of Natural History at The Grosvenor Museum) for checking the identification of the stone, and to Dan Robinson (formerly Keeper of Archaeology at The Grosvenor Museum) for his comments on the slate inscription.

Tesserae

A group of 966 *tesserae* was recovered from the site. The Roman Phases I and IIa produced just 3 % of the site total; 95 % came from Phases IIb to X and 2% were unstratified.

Table 4.1.3 *Tesserae* from Roman phases quantified by phase and material

Phase	Colour	Material	No
Id	White	White limestone	7
	Black	Grey carboniferous limestone	2
Total			9
Ie	?Black	Pale grey quartzite	1
Total			1
IIa	White	White limestone	9
	Black	Grey carboniferous limestone	12
Total			21
Total			31

Table 4.1.4 *Tesserae* from post-Roman phases and unstratified quantified by phase and material

Phase	Colour	Material	No
IIb	White	White limestone	16
	White	White quartz	1
	?White	Pale grey limestone	1
	Black	Grey carboniferous limestone	28
Total			46
IIc	White	White limestone	20
	Black	Grey carboniferous limestone	85
	?Black	Pale grey carboniferous limestone	1
	Red	CBM	1
Total			107
III	White	White limestone	72
	Black	Grey carboniferous limestone	60
	?Black	Very pale grey carboniferous limestone	1
Total			133
IV	White	White limestone	52
	Black	Grey carboniferous limestone	134
	Red	Pale red sandstone	1
Total			187
V	White	White limestone	66
	Black	Grey carboniferous limestone	112
	?Black	Pale grey siltstone	1
	Red	Red sandstone	1
	Red	CBM	1
Total			181
VI	White	White limestone	29
	Black	Grey carboniferous limestone	52
	Black	Grey ?sandstone	1
	?Black	Pale grey biosparitic limestone	1
	Red	CBM	2
Total			85
VII	White	White limestone	18
	Black	Grey carboniferous limestone	36
	?Black	Pale grey siltstone	1
	Red	CBM	3
Total			58
VIII	White	White limestone	25
	Black	Grey carboniferous limestone	31
	?Black	Pale grey sandstone	1
	Red	CBM	4
Total			61
IX	White	White limestone	15
	Black	Grey carboniferous limestone	28
	Red	CBM	1
	Red	Sandstone	2
Total			46
X	White	White limestone	2
	Black	Grey carboniferous limestone	8
Total			10
U/S	White	White limestone	8
	Black	Grey carboniferous limestone	12
	?Black	Pale grey sandstone	1
Total			21
Total			935

Three colours were identified: black, white and red. Black *tesserae*, made from grey carboniferous limestone, comprise 62% of the assemblage; white *tesserae*, of white limestone, 35 %; and red *tesserae*, made from cut-down ceramic building material (12) or red sandstone (3) 2 %; the remaining 1 % comprise one ?white and five ?black *tesserae* composed of other stone, together with a fragment of intact mosaic embedded in concrete, SF 8696. The latter is composed of an indistinct pattern of three black and five white *tesserae*, formed of grey carboniferous limestone and white limestone respectively. There are also five examples of pairs of *tesserae* cemented together. All the other *tesserae* were found loose, although many retained traces of their original bedding cement.

Where measured, the *tesserae* range from 8 x 17 mm to 18 x 23 mm in cross-section and most are roughly cuboid. However, just over 12 % (119) are elongated and ranged in length from 26 to 41 mm. The majority of these (82%) are of grey carboniferous limestone; the remaining 18% are of white limestone. Six of the long *tesserae* came from the Roman phases; the remaining 95% (113) came from the post-Roman phases (111) or were found unstratified (2).

Phases I and IIa

The Roman phases produced only black and white *tesserae*. All are of limestone except for the black *tessera* from Ie, which is of pale grey quartzite. The absence of any other colours perhaps suggests that they came from a monochrome mosaic, presumably in a public building or a relatively high-status private dwelling on, or close to, the site.

Phase Id produced two long *tesserae*, one of white limestone from (275), SF 8301 (L 32 mm), and one of grey carboniferous limestone, from (1242), SF 9068 (L 28 mm).

Phase IIa produced two white limestone *tesserae* cemented together. Four elongated *tesserae* came from this phase, comprising one of white limestone from (1220), SF 9022 (L 29 mm) and three of grey carboniferous limestone: one from (1220), SF 9022, Sa 5131 (L 26.5 mm) and two from (1225), SF 9023 (L 30 and 33 mm).

Post-Roman phases and unstratified

The post-Roman phases produced red as well as black and white *tesserae*. Black and white *tesserae* made of stone other than grey carboniferous limestone or white limestone respectively comprise a ?*tessera* (or natural stone) of white quartz and ?black *tesserae* of soft pale grey siltstone, pale grey biosparitic limestone and pale grey sandstone. As already mentioned, the red *tesserae* are made of sandstone or reused ceramic building material.

Three pairs of complete black *tesserae* and one pair of white *tesserae* (one a fragment only) were found cemented together, plus the intact fragment referred to above. 113 of the elongated *tesserae* came from the post-Roman and unstratified assemblage: 83 % (94) are of grey carboniferous limestone and 17 % (19) of white limestone. They range in length from 26 to 41 mm, with 37 % between 26 and 29 mm and 63 % between 30 and 41 mm in length. 48 % were between 28 and 30 mm. Two of the eight *tesserae* in the intact fragment (one black and one white) are long and rectangular (with lengths of >26 and >30 mm); the remainder are cuboid.

Catalogue

1   A fragment of intact mosaic, comprising eight *tesserae* in two colours, embedded in concrete (*opus signinum*); three *tesserae* of grey carboniferous limestone and five of white limestone; surviving L *c* 55 mm; surviving W *c* 50 mm; surviving th *c* 45 mm. (1014): Phase V; SF 8696. Ill 4.1.2.

Discussion

The similarity of the *tesserae* in terms of source material and their consistent size suggest a common origin both geologically and in the mosaics from which they came. Geologically, the carboniferous limestone used to produce the majority of the black *tesserae* could have been obtained locally, probably from Halkyn Mountain in North Wales (Kate Riddington *pers comm*). The *tesserae* may have come from the same mosaic or from different mosaics laid at approximately the same time and /or they may have been produced at the same workshop. The predominance of dark grey and white limestone *tesserae*, together with the evidence provided by the surviving fragment, suggests that the mosaic from which they came was probably largely monochrome in design, while the high proportion of black to white *tesserae* suggests predominantly white patterns or figures set against a black background. It is natural to draw comparisons with the fragmentary mosaic floor from the fortress bath house, discovered in 1909 and described by Newstead as being set in 'a bed of concrete, 6–10 in thick', which was composed of 'pale to dark grey or blackish, and white' limestone *tesserae* (Newstead 1928, 117–18). Monochrome mosaic floors were also discovered on the same site between 1863 and 1865. These were described by Brushfield as being composed of *tesserae* of grey limestone and white chalk, which had an average cube size of 'three-fifths of an inch square' (1885, 39). Brushfield also referred to the discovery of *tesserae* of red 'baked clay' at the site (1885, 35) (*see* now Mason 2005, 17–18, 78–81, 106–7). *Tesserae* from the 1963/4 excavations of the baths varied in cross-section from *c* 10 x 17 mm to 20 x 25 mm, with some as much as 25 mm long (Dunn 2005, 89, no 10). This compares closely with those from 25 Bridge Street 2001. Loose *tesserae* of grey carboniferous and white limestone were found at 25–9 Bridge Street in 1996 and, as with the fragments of Purbeck marble also found there, are likely to come from the fortress baths (Emery 1996, *passim*). However, a fragment of mosaic floor 'composed of large black and white *tesserae* like many other examples found in Chester; the white *tesserae* being of chalk and the black of lias rock' was also found on the north side passage to Fletcher's Buildings during excavations in Bridge Street in 1901 (Newstead 1902, 104). Mason has suggested that it could have been from a senior officer's house or from a building occupied by the commander of an auxiliary regiment which fronted onto the *via praetoria* (2000, 15).

All of the elongated *tesserae* are made from either dark grey carboniferous limestone (the majority) or of white limestone; none occur in any other colour or material.

III 4.1.2 Fragment of intact mosaic (no 1). (Photo © A Jones)

These are most likely to have come from the fortress bath house, as they provided greater protection against possible damage from steam and water to the mortar floor in which they were embedded and thus to the hypocaust below (David Neal *pers comm*, 12 May 2006). The fact that the intact fragment of mosaic, SF 8696, is composed of a mixture of both elongated and cuboid *tesserae* may well indicate that most of the *tesserae* of dark grey carboniferous and white limestone, whether elongated or cuboid in shape, originated from the monochrome mosaics which adorned the fortress bath house.

Acknowledgements

With thanks to Kate Riddington (Assistant Keeper of Natural History at The Grosvenor Museum) for checking the identification of the stone and to David Heke for the use of his photographic studio.

Ceramic building material

Methodology

The ceramic building material (CBM) was assessed in terms of quantity, range, condition, source and date range and recorded to the level set out in the Archaeological Ceramic Building Materials Group (ACBMG) minimum standards draft document for the recovery, curation, analysis and publication of CBM (Hunter-Mann 2001), with the addition of part as a sub-term of form. Given the residual nature of the assemblage and the time and financial constraints on the post-excavation process, the report is in summary form only, with a brief description of the nature and character of the assemblage, organised by phase, followed by an overall discussion. A fuller version of the report and the archive are available for consultation in hard copy and as an MS Word file and Access database respectively.

Since an unusually large assemblage was expected from the site, a discard strategy was devised in advance of the excavation and detailed guidelines were drawn up for the selection and recording of material to be retained or discarded on site. Unfortunately, the strategy was not fully adhered to, and although all discarded CBM was recorded, this was only done in a summary fashion to the basic level of form, weight and fragment count per context. Only a very small proportion of discarded CBM was recorded by part, condition, measurement of complete dimensions and signs of use/reuse. The condition of the discarded CBM was also routinely recorded as 'abraded' on the proformas. The retained material exhibited a much greater variety in its condition. Despite this, however, it was still possible to gain useful statistical information regarding the quantity and range of the material recovered from the site.

For box tile types referred to in the text, *see* Appendices 4.1.1 and .2. For Twentieth Legion stamps from Holt, *see* Grimes 1930, 139–43; 211, fig 59 and 212, fig 60.3. For Twentieth Legion stamps from Holt, Chester and elsewhere, *see* Frere & Tomlin eds 1992, 175–94).

Introduction

The site produced a large assemblage of CBM, comprising 12,517 fragments with a weight of 1315.44 kg. Hand-collection produced 11,680 frags/1296.29 kg (93% by fragment count and 99% by weight of the total site assemblage). The remaining 837 fragments/19.151 kg (7% by fragment count and 1% by weight of the site assemblage) were retrieved from wet sieving. Almost 90% by fragment count and weight of the entire assemblage, comprising 11,244 fragments/1148.458 kg, was discarded: only 1273 fragments/166.98 kg were retained.

Table 4.1.5 lists the retained/discarded assemblages by phase and also the fragmentation index (average weight per fragment) by phase. The discarded material generally exhibited a greater degree of fragmentation than the retained material, although this was not so for Phases I, II and VII. In these phases the retained assemblages had a lower average weight per fragment than the discarded material.

Forms recovered comprise roof tiles (*tegulae* and *imbrices*/ridge tiles), antefixes, vaulting tube fragments, bricks, a ?chimney fragment, *opus spicatum* bricks, box tiles and ?half-box tiles, ?facing (or wall) tiles, and several unusual forms (described as 'oddities'), which probably had a specialised purpose or function (*see* Table 4.1.6), as well as indeterminate fragments. Combed and scored fragments were retained, as well as stamps, signatures, tally marks, graffiti, human, animal or other imprints, rare or unusual forms, complete forms and samples of the more common CBM types.

The discarded assemblage comprised roof tile (*tegulae* and *imbrices*/ridge tiles), brick and indeterminate fragments. *Tegulae* and indeterminate fragments were the major component, each comprising approximately 40% by weight of the total. *Imbrices*/ridge tiles comprised approximately 16% by weight of the discarded total. Bricks (62 fragments weighing 22,143 g) formed the smallest component, comprising a mere 2% by weight of the discarded total.

Tegulae form the largest component, by weight (42%), of the entire site assemblage, closely followed by indeterminate forms (36% by weight). *Imbrices*/ridge tiles comprise 15%, bricks and box tiles 3%. The remaining forms together comprise less than 1%. Apart from a single piece of chimney, fragments of facing (or wall) tile (*parietalis*), ?half box tile and vaulting tube form the rarest component by weight of the assemblage.

4 Building materials/Roman building materials

Table 4.1.5 Roman discarded and retained ceramic building material: total amount quantified by phase, no of fragments and weight

Phase	Discarded			Retained			Total		
	No	Wt (g)	Frag index (g)	No	Wt (g)	Frag index (g)	No	Wt (g)	Frag index (g)
I	169	30457	180.2	130	16530	127.2	299	46987	157.1
II	1543	193186	125.2	229	25859	112.9	1772	219045	123.6
III	1106	127978	115.7	62	15742	253.9	1168	143720	123
III/IV	1	8	8	0	0	0	1	8	8
IV	1416	160093	113.1	77	15062	195.6	1493	175155	117.3
V	2045	170138	83.2	236	23193	98.2	2281	193331	84.8
V/VI	13	3495	268.8	0	0	0	13	3495	268.8
VI	1225	98482	80.4	111	15230	137.2	1336	113712	85.1
VII	1133	107036	94.5	245	13328	54.4	1379	120378	87.3
VIII	838	87867	104.9	71	21843	307.6	909	109710	120.7
IX	783	60098	76.8	35	3241	92.6	817	63325	77.5
X	316	26305	83.2	28	6010	214.6	344	32315	93.9
Group Nos	66	989	15	1	74	74	67	1063	15.9
u/s	590	82326	139.5	48	10870	226.5	638	93196	146.1
Total	11244	1148458	102.1	1273	166982	131.2	12517	1315440	105.1

Table 4.1.6 Roman ceramic building material: forms quantified by phase, no of fragments and weight

132

Phase I

Only a tiny percentage of the site assemblage came from Phase I, comprising 299 fragments weighing 46,987 g (2% by fragment count and 4% by weight of the site assemblage. Although it was stipulated that all CBM from Roman contexts should be retained, unfortunately a large proportion of the Phase I material – 169 fragments – was discarded after summary recording on site.

Phase Ia

The five fragments retrieved from Phase Ia all came from Evaluation Trench C. They comprise indeterminate forms, including one burnt piece reused in the Roman period (the broken edges are coated in mortar) from ?levelling deposit (158). The remaining fragments came from ?levelling deposit (159). The fragmentation index of 12.4 g gives some indication of the small size and relative brokenness of the material from this sub-phase.

Phase Ib

A slightly larger group was recovered from Phase Ib, but again comprises indeterminate fragments, all from the area of the ramp excavation: eight from (1243), the fill of ?roadside drain (1244), and one from layer (1254). The fragmentation index of 49.7 g indicates a slightly lesser degree of brokenness than the previous sub-phase, but the fragments are still very small in size.

Phase Ic

Phase Ic produced the largest group by weight of the Phase I assemblage, (24488 g)). The fragmentation index of 255 g is the highest in Phase I, suggesting that the material was subjected to less disturbance than that from the other sub-phases.

The forms recovered from Ic are listed in Table 4.1.6. All came from the area of the ramp excavation. The *tegulae* fragments are of mixed condition and include an almost complete example of a Warry group A tile (dated up to AD 120) with a signature mark at one end, SF 9845, from (1389) (Warry 2006a, 2006b, 2007). Since (1389) represented the lead lining of sewer (1390), the smashed *tegula* may have originally formed a capping for the drain. Layer (1388) produced a *tegula* fragment with a signature, SF 9456, and another fragment with a ?nail hole and hobnail imprints in the upper surface, SF 9455. Holes are normally found in the lowest course of *tegulae* along a roof edge, which were sometimes nailed in to prevent them sliding off under the weight of the roof (Brodribb 1987, 11). A corner fragment with a partial Warry group ?D cutaway provides a *tpq* of 240–380 for Phase Ic). Five *imbrices*/ridge tile fragments were also retrieved from (1388) but all were discarded; one piece was described as being partially vitrified. A single brick was retrieved, comprising an edge fragment in good condition, also a single fragment of box tile of Chester type 4 (*see* Appendix 4.1.2 for a description of Chester box tile types). The latter is abraded, has a sanded exterior and a knife-cut air vent (the edge of which only is visible). The remainder of the group comprised 60 fragments/2389g of indeterminate form in mixed condition. One piece from layer (1250) is burnt and twenty-four pieces from (1388) are probably *opus signinum* fragments, as all are coated in mortar.

Phase Id

This phase produced the second largest group after Ic, with a fragmentation index of 159.9 g, the second highest in Phase I.

Only one fragment of *tegula* was retained, from layer (135) in Evaluation Trench B. It comprises a flange fragment in fresh condition, although burnt. All the discarded *tegulae* fragments were recorded as abraded on the proformas. Of the twenty-one fragments of *imbrices*/ridge tiles recovered, sixteen were discarded: from road surface (274) in the access pit area, road surface (1239) and layer (1242). They were of mixed condition and two fragments, both from (1239), were slightly burnt. One end fragment from (274) is unusual in that the upper surface is coated with a creamy wash. A similar coating occurs on an *imbrex*/ridge tile fragment from Phase IV (1125). Other forms comprise two bricks, one of which, from (1242) in the ramp excavation area, was discarded. Both examples were abraded. Sixty-four fragments of indeterminate form were recovered but only twenty-seven were retained. Ten pieces from (1242) were probably *opus signinum* fragments, as they are coated in mortar. The fragments are of mixed condition and two, both from (1239), are burnt.

Phase Ie

All the roof tiles recovered (both *tegulae* and *imbrices*/ridge tiles) were discarded and described as abraded. Of the 64 fragments of indeterminate form, only 7, all from primary fill (1148) of sewer (1182), in the ramp excavation area, were kept. The latter were of mixed condition; one is very burnt and two are slightly burnt. The fragmentation index of 59.5 is similar to that for Phase Ic.

Discussion

Only 2% by fragment count and 4% by weight of the site assemblage came from Phase I. Diagnostic fragments indicate a limited range of forms, comprising roof tile (both *tegulae* and *imbrices*/ridge tiles), bricks, box tile and indeterminate fragments. *Tegulae* and *imbrices*/ridge tiles together form the largest component by weight (62% and 14% respectively), followed by indeterminate fragments (17%), bricks (7%) and box tile (0.06%).

It is difficult to pinpoint the origin of the assemblage, but most of it is likely to have come from a stone building or buildings, possibly from Building I(i) in Phase Ic. However, a small group of indeterminate CBM was present in Phases Ia and Ib. Whether these came from an earlier timber building is dubious, as these may have been thatched or shingled rather than tiled.

The three brick fragments are represented by an edge fragment from the Phase Ic backfill of construction trench, (151), for wall (150) in Evaluation Trench B, which is 60 mm thick; by a corner fragment from I d (1239), which is 55 mm thick and a discarded fragment from Phase Id (1242) of unknown thickness. The first two are probably too thick to be the square form, *bessalis* (used to build hypocaust *pilae*), but they could have come from any of the other four large brick forms: square *pedalis*, rectangular *lydion*, square *sesquipedalis* or large square *tegula bipedalis*. The *pedalis* was used as a capping or base brick for *pilae* (Brodribb 1987, 36); the *lydion* was generally used for bonding or lacing courses in the walls of large public buildings or defences, although it was also used for flooring or for capping *pilae* (Brodribb 1987, 37 and 40). The *sesquipedalis* was used for flooring (Brodribb 1987, 41). The *tegula bipedalis* was the largest and thickest and probably the most versatile of these bricks. It was used, for example, to bridge the gaps between the *pilae* of a hypocaust, for bonding courses and occasionally in the construction of arches (Brodribb 1987, 41). Not many examples of the *bipedalis* used as a bridging brick between *pilae* have been found *in situ* in Britain. At Holt, they were used to face the walls below ground level on one side of a hypocaust (Brodribb 1987, 42).

The single box tile from Phase Ic again suggests the presence of a centrally heated building that was demolished or rebuilt before the close of this sub-phase. However, it could also have been left behind as a result of building activity or indeed it may have been intrusive in the phase. If it is in the correct phase, this could mean that Chester ?type 4 represents an early box tile form, although the different types could also have been contemporary, with the different keying marks and manu- facturing methods meaning that different types were used for slightly different purposes. In London and the south-east of England, lattice-scored keying seems to have been an early Roman feature, which was superseded by combing and roller-stamping in the early second century (Betts 2000, 3). Grimes (1930, 135–6) recognised six different box tile types at Holt, differentiated by size alone rather than by methods of manufacture or type of keying.

Fourteen fragments are burnt, coming from every sub-phase. One indeterminate fragment (from Phase Ia) shows evidence of reuse in the Roman period as it has Roman mortar attached to the broken edges; this piece is also burnt. Thirty-four of the indeterminate fragments (twenty-four from Ic (1388) and ten from Id (1242)) are probably *opus signinum* fragments, as all are small and coated in mortar. They probably represent coarse components which had fallen out of the softer mortar matrix. They presumably originated from the *opus signinum* floors Ic (1064) and I d (1026) of Building I(i). The burning which is evident on some of the pieces could have been the result of waste disposal, ie the use of fire to cleanse a rubbish dump. The burnt fragments from Ic (1250) and (1388) may have been associated with the burnt and fire-cracked floor surface (145) of Building I(i) in Ic, particularly the partially vitrified piece from (1388).

Apart from the box tile fragment, the Phase I group is not particularly informative as to the function and status of the building(-s) from which it originated. Central heating was used in public buildings, such as bath houses, and in high-status private accommodation.

Phase II

Phase II produced 1772 fragments/219,045 g, the largest group by weight from any phase.

Phase IIa

This sub-phase produced 25% by fragment count and 26% by weight of the Phase II assemblage, with a fragmentation index of 132.4 g.

103 fragments/31,612 g of *tegulae* were retrieved; only 14 fragments/8022 g were kept. The retained assemblage included SF 9449 from occupation layer (1142), comprising an end fragment, slightly abraded, with an unusual

double*, S-shaped signature. (*'Double signature' refers to the use of two fingers, rather than one, to make the mark in the wet clay). A complete *tegula*, fresh in appearance and smashed into six pieces, was recovered from Trench D, (119). SF 9476 from (1219) comprises a fairly fresh middle piece with a curved signature and SF 9761 from (1225) an abraded and burnt corner fragment with a partial lower cutaway and a curved signature. All the discarded fragments were described as abraded.

The *imbrex*/ridge tile fragments were in mixed condition; only three fragments were retained. One edge piece, fairly fresh in appearance, SF 9844 from road surface (1226), bears a signature mark parallel to the long edge. One discarded middle piece from fill (1146) of drain (1147) was described as 'overfired/misfired' and another discarded piece from layer (1237) was burnt; the remaining discarded fragments were all described as abraded.

Two *opus spicatum* bricks came from (1225), each comprising the end third of a playing-card shape. This rectangular shape was typical of Holt.

An edge fragment of a ?facing (or wall) tile with knife-scored, sanded underside (ie, the side which would have faced into the interior of a room; the scoring (keying) aided the adhesion of mortar or plaster (Betts 2000, 3)) and a smooth, upper face came from secondary fill (1220) of the main north–south sewer (1182). It is fairly fresh in appearance. Two edge fragments of brick were recovered, both bearing signature marks. Such marks are relatively unusual on bricks (Brodribb 1987, 102). SF 9562, from the upper fill (1219) of sewer (1182), comprises a curved signature and SF 9908 from (1220) <5131> bears an abraded ?signature.

An unusual tile ('oddity') was recovered from (1225). It has a smooth, bevelled edge, a finger groove parallel to the edge and an unsanded face with a knife-scoring. Similar oddities were recovered from IIc (1161), IV (1125) and VI (503), although the first two examples are also pierced by large oval vents. Their purpose and function are unclear, although they may be box tiles.

295 fragments/19,017 g of indeterminate form were recovered, of which only 116 fragments/1224g were retained (including 104 tiny fragments/443 g from (1220) <5131>). The retained assemblage is in mixed condition and includes three probable fragments of *opus signinum* (two from (1220) and one from (1219), all coated in mortar. It also includes a fresh edge piece from (1146) with Roman mortar (?*opus signinum*) attached to the edge and sanded underside. An abraded middle piece from occupation layer (1225) is also coated in ?Roman concrete. All the discarded material was described as abraded.

Catalogue

1   An 'oddity' (?box tile) with a smooth bevelled edge, a finger groove parallel to the edge and an unsanded exterior face which bears lattice knife-scoring; abraded; th 22 mm. (1225); SF 10128. Similar oddities were recovered from Phases IIc (1161), IV (1125) and VI (503). Ill 4.1.3.

Discussion

Phase IIa is thought to represent the final period of Roman occupation within the fortress. The CBM assemblage may therefore represent building debris from the late Roman or sub-Roman demolition of Building I(i).

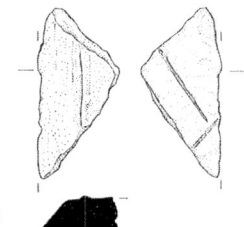

Ill 4.1.3 Phase IIa: brick/tile with bevelled edge.

A wide range of forms was present. These comprise roof tile (*tegulae* and *imbrices*/ridge tiles), brick, *opus spicatum* brick, ?facing (or wall) tile (*parietalis*), an unusual form ('oddity') and indeterminate forms. It is perhaps notable that no box tile was recovered, suggesting that the single fragment from Ic may have been intrusive. *Tegulae* and *imbrices*/ridge tiles together form the largest component by weight of the assemblage (55% and 7% respectively). Indeterminate forms make up 33% by weight of the assemblage, bricks 4% and the remaining forms together comprise just over 1%.

The group is small in quantity and in mixed condition. Only two fragments were burnt. Two indeterminate fragments show evidence of reuse in antiquity as both have Roman mortar attached to broken edges. The three probable *opus signinum* fragments probably originated from the concrete floors (1064) or (1026) of Building I(i) in Phases Ic or Id respectively

The two brick fragments comprise an edge piece from (1219), which has a thickness of 53–66 mm, and a ?brick edge from (1220), only 29 mm thick. The latter piece is perhaps more likely to be the end of a thicker-than-average *tegula*. It is probable that the example from (1219) came from any of the large brick forms discussed above (Phase I).

The abraded *opus spicatum* bricks came from the '*opus signinum* rich' deposit (1225). *Opus spicatum* bricks made at Holt had an average size of 113 x 75 (or 88) x 32 mm (Grimes 1930, 135). They were generally laid with the narrow edge down in a thick bed of concrete and arranged in a herringbone pattern. The resulting floor surface was both hard-wearing and long-lasting (Brodribb 1987, 50–3). Herringbone floors are not particularly common in Britain: plain brick floors paved with large square or rectangular bricks are more usual. At Chester, herringbone floors are known from the fortress bath house (Mason 2005, *passim*) and also from the extramural bathhouse in Watergate Street (Mason *forthcoming*). Herringbone flooring is known to have been used in bath houses at other British sites, as well as in a ?kitchen, a ?stable or cartshed and in other rooms of unknown function (Brodribb 1987, 52). It is possible that these bricks could have come from Building I(i) but the fortress bath house is perhaps a more likely source.

Phase IIb

Phase IIb and all subsequent phases and sub-phases represented major post-Roman activity at the Bridge Street site. A massive 95% by fragment count and 92% by weight of the total Roman CBM assemblage occurred residually or was found unstratified. This sub-phase produced the smallest group from Phase II, comprising 21% by fragment count and 19% by weight of the Phase II assemblage, with a fragmentation index of 109.9 g. This indicated a slightly higher degree of brokenness than IIa.

Only 4 fragments/1362 g of *tegulae* were retained. These include a battered ?flange fragment with a red slip from (1040). Other examples comprise SF 9466 from (1135), a slightly abraded middle fragment with ?deer hoof prints, and SF 9477 from fill (1228) of north–south gully (1229), a fairly fresh middle fragment with hobnail imprints. All the discarded *tegulae* were described as abraded. All 51 fragments/8980 g of *imbrices*/ridge tiles were discarded. Apart from one fragment from (1138), which was described as fresh, all the rest were recorded as abraded.

A probable chimney fragment, SF 9561, came from layer (1135); this wheel-thrown piece is abraded. A single box tile fragment, with a combed, unsanded exterior and sanded interior (Chester type 1), came from (1136), the packing material of post hole (1137). The piece is fairly fresh in appearance and the edge of an air vent survives where the tile is broken away. The edge fragment of a ?brick with a double, curved signature, SF 9448, was retrieved from fill (1138) of pit (1139).

243 fragments/10,741 g of indeterminate form were recovered, although only 31 fragments/87 g were retained. The retained assemblage includes three probable *opus signinum* fragments (with attached mortar) from Evaluation Trench F, fill (126) of pit (127), fill (1040) of post hole (1043) in Evaluation Trench B/Escalator Pit A and fill (1221) of post hole (1222). SF 8869 from (1135) comprises a small chip with a very faint ?stamp. The retained assemblage is in mixed condition; the discarded assemblage was mainly described as abraded, apart from eight fresh and two burnt fragments, all from (1138).

Catalogue
2   Wall fragment of ?chimney; wheel-thrown; abraded. (1135); SF 9561.

Phase IIc

301 fragments/54,647 g of *tegulae* were recovered, of which only 6 fragments/2214g were kept. The fragmentation index was 125 g. The discarded assemblage included an apparently complete Twentieth Legion stamp (recorded as LEG XX VV in the site archive) from (269). Unfortunately no rubbing was taken, nor was any record made of which Holt stamp type it was. SF 9467 from (1161) comprises a middle fragment with ?finger prints. SF 9451, also from (1161), is an end fragment with a looped signature, and SF 9782, also from (1161), comprises a middle piece with a double, curved signature. SF 9454 from (1177) comprises a corner fragment with an abraded partial stamp -]VV and a double, looped signature at the end edge. SF 9459, also from (1177), is a middle fragment with a faint, abraded signature.

121 fragments/18,734 g of *imbrices*/ridge tiles were retrieved, of which only 7 fragments/1274 g were retained. SF 9843 from (1161) comprises an edge piece with a scored ?signature parallel to the long edge; SF 9450, also from (1161), comprises a corner fragment with a signature across the gable.

The assemblage includes an almost complete example of the rare and unusual Jupiter Ammon antefix type – one of three examples of this form recovered from the site. It has a broken-off rear projection for insertion into an *imbrex* or ridge tile, is abraded and has traces of white lime wash over the moulded design.

Three brick fragments were recovered. A retained example from (269) has a lump of concrete (*opus signinum*) attached to the broken edges, indicating that it had been reused in antiquity. The piece from (1177) is pierced by a nail hole 9 mm in diameter.

A single *opus spicatum* brick, approximately two-thirds complete, came from (1161).

All the box tiles were retained. Three types were identified: the first, and most common, comprising twenty-five fragments, has a sanded interior and a combed, unsanded exterior (Chester type 1); the second, represented by a single example, has an unsanded interior and a sanded, knife-scored, exterior (Chester type 2); the third type, represented by two fragments, has a combed exterior and an unsanded interior (Chester type 3). It is possible that these different forms represent different periods of production or production at different workshops or possibly even slightly different functions. The single example of Chester type 2 from dark earth layer (1161) also bears the edge of a circular air vent 65 mm in diameter. It is unclear whether this type always had circular air vents. Three fragments bear traces of sooting from use on their interior surfaces and two have traces of mortar/plaster attached to their exterior surfaces.

Two unusual forms were recovered, from (1132) and (1161). The piece from (1132) comprises a square or rectangular form with an indented, knife-trimmed corner. It is closely comparable to the 'lugged bricks' from the fortress baths at Caerleon, which may have been used in vault construction (Zienkiewicz 1986, 325 and 326, fig 107, no 3). The piece from (1161) has a bevelled edge, a finger groove parallel to the edge, a lightly sanded underside and the edge of a curving (?oval) vent.

505 fragments/39,509 g of indeterminate form were recovered, of which only 5 fragments/573 g were retained. Among these, SF 9821 from (269) comprises a middle fragment with overlapping signatures. Roman mortar is attached to the upper and lower surfaces of this piece. SF 9719 from (1161) comprises a middle fragment with a signature mark.

Catalogue
3 An almost complete example of a Jupiter Ammon antefix with an integral *imbrex*-shaped back projection. The back projection forms a pointed gable at the top. The top scalloped section is broken off as is the bottom left corner, below the mouth. The piece is very abraded and bears traces of white limewash on all surfaces, including broken edges, which suggests that it results from reuse rather than from an original decorative coating. There are traces of burning on the left edge of the antefix. The fabric is hard, bright orange and sandy with abundant quartz inclusions and a harsh feel. It is closely comparable to Chester (Holt) pottery fabric 152 (NRFRC fabric code HOL OX (Tomber & Dore 1998, 207). H 155 mm; W (max complete) 130 mm; th (max complete) 25 mm; back projection: H 15 mm; W 120 mm; th 22 mm. (1177); SF 8932. Ill 4.1.4.
4 Square or rectangular brick with an indented, knife-trimmed corner (?a possible lugged brick). Max th *c* 50 mm; rectangular indent 70 x 30 mm. The lower surface is sanded and there are patches of Roman mortar on the smooth, upper surface; the edges are

Ill 4.1.4 Phase IIc: Jupiter Ammon antefix.

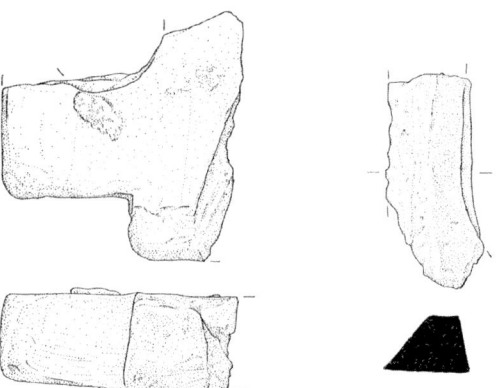

Ill 4.1.5 Phase IIc: brick with knife-trimmed corner. (Scale 1/4)

Ill 4.1.6 Phase IIc: brick/tile with bevelled edge and ?oval vent. (Scale 1/4)

sanded. (1132); SF 10129. A similar piece was recovered from Phase IV (974). Ill 4.1.5.
5 An 'oddity' (?box tile) with a bevelled edge, a finger groove parallel to the edge, a lightly sanded exterior face and the curving edge of an ?oval vent (the piece is broken at this point); abraded. Th 28 mm. (1161); SF 10130. The form is comparable to the oddity from Phase IIa (1225), as well as examples from Phases IV (1125) and VI (503). Ill 4.1.6.

Phase III

281 fragments of *tegulae*/79,743 g were recovered, although only 13 fragments/10,370 g were retained. The retained assemblage includes SF 9453 from (1179), an unusually thick end fragment with overlapping signature marks and the edge of a ?stamp. SF 9452, also from

(1179), is a middle fragment with a looped signature overlain by a worn indeterminate stamp. SF 9446 from (1022) is a middle piece with a sweeping, curved, double signature. SF 9447 from (1131) comprises a middle fragment of *?tegula* with a retrograde stamp, probably Holt type 27 (RIB **2** (4), 2463.28), and signature marks. SF 9444 from (1022) comprises a middle *?tegula* fragment with a double, curved signature; SF 9443, also from (1022), is a middle *?tegula* fragment with a looped signature, and SF 9458, also from (1022), is a middle *?tegula* fragment with an overlapping (?looped) signature.

133 fragments/19,899 g of *imbrex*/ridge tile were recovered; only 6 fragments/ 734 g of which were retained.

A middle fragment of ?vaulting tube came from cultivation layer (1131). It has a wall thickness of 6 mm and an external diameter of 80 mm. The latter falls just within the size range given by Mason for the vaulting tubes recovered from the fortress bath house in 1963/4 (Mason 1990, 218).

A middle fragment of brick came from (1170). The presence of Roman concrete attached to the broken edges indicates that it had been reused in antiquity.

There were twenty-three fragments of box tile, all of which were retained. Examples of types 1–3 are present (*see* above) as well as an additional type, (Chester type 4 (a single example), which has a sanded exterior and unsanded interior. Chester type 1 was the most common form, with eighteen fragments present, and one example each of Chester types 2 and 3. The remaining two pieces are of indeterminate type: although both have a combed exterior surface, the interior surfaces are missing. The interior surfaces of five fragments are sooted through use. Four fragments from (74) and layer (106) were reused in antiquity: Roman mortar adheres to their broken surfaces. The reused fragments are all of Chester type 1.

729 indeterminate fragments /40,306 g were recovered, of which only 18 fragments/866g were retained. Among these are SF 9812 from (74), a middle *?tegula* fragment with an incomplete ?graffito 'X'. SF 9814 from (106) is a middle *?tegula* fragment with a curved signature. SF 9815, also from (106), is a middle piece with a double, curved signature. SF 9445 from (1022) comprises a middle fragment of *?tegula* with quite deep hobnail impressions made while the clay was still wet. Warry has recently suggested that hobnail imprints on *tegulae* probably resulted from the officer in charge of the tile works testing the hardness of the drying tile with his foot (2006a, 16).

Catalogue

6   Middle fragment of *?tegula* with an incomplete ?graffito X; slightly abraded; th 27 mm. (74); SF 9812.

Phase IV

304 fragments of *tegulae*/74,472 g were recovered, of which only 13 fragments/5106 g were retained. These include SF 8863 from (34), a middle fragment with a partial Holt ?type 8 stamp [LEG X]X VV. SF 9811, also from (34), is a corner piece with the edge of a stamp of indeterminate type, L[EG XX VV], and a triple curved signature. Another triple curved signature, SF 9817, occurs on a middle fragment from (265). An end piece from (268) bears a hole with the remains of an iron nail still *in situ*.

The bottom row of *tegulae* on a roof are believed to have been held in place with nails (Brodribb 1987, 11). The holes were almost always placed in the top centre of the *tegula* (Warry 2006, 102). SF 9442 from (974) is a middle *?tegula* fragment with an abraded ?signature mark. SF 9760 from (883) is a middle fragment with an indeterminate ?paw print. SF 9819 from (268) was an end edge of *?tegula* with a looped signature and SF 9727 from (1125) is a middle fragment with fingerprints and a burnt upper surface.

143 fragments/30,832 g of *imbrices*/ridge tiles were retrieved, of which only 5 fragments/1392 g were retained. A small chip from (1125) bears a creamy slip wash on the upper surface; it is comparable to an end fragment of *imbrex*/ridge tile from Id (274).

The upper part of a rare lion's head antefix, SF 8773, came from layer (974) in Escalator Pit A.

Two ?vaulting tube fragments came from Phase IV. They comprise a middle fragment from (265) in the access pit excavation area and a shoulder fragment from layer (799).

Two complete *opus spicatum* bricks were recovered. The example from (266) has mortar attached to all faces except the long, upper surface, which is clearly worn through use. The second example came from (883).

Of the 35 brick fragments/13,930 g recovered only one piece was retained, an edge fragment, SF 853 from (34), with a double, curved signature mark and traces of lime wash, particularly on the upper surface.

Examples of Chester box tile types 1–4 were recovered. As with the preceding phases, type 1 is the most common form with thirty-eight fragments; types 2 and 3 produced two fragments each; there is only one example of type 4. Five fragments have mortar attached to their combed exterior surfaces.

A single fragment of ?facing (or wall) tile from (883) has a sanded underside with a knife-scored lattice pattern and a smooth upper surface.

Two unusual forms were recovered, from (974) and (1125). The piece from (974) is the corner fragment of a square or rectangular ?brick with a large knife-trimmed, square or rectangular indent. It is comparable to a fragment from Phase IIc (1132). The example from (1125) has a chamfered edge and two large, oval vents; it may be an unusual type of box tile.

960 indeterminate fragments/48,890 g were recovered, of which only 7 fragments/703 g were retained. The retained assemblage includes SF 9842 from (1119), a chip with a possible ?graffito. SF 9820 from (268) comprises a middle fragment with sanded and knife-scored underside and a double signature on the opposing face. A second, middle fragment from this context also bears a sanded and knife-scored underside, the scoring having been done in a lattice pattern. A similar middle piece from fill (1001) of pit (1002) has a sanded surface with a diamond-lattice pattern of knife scoring. It is possible that all these pieces are examples of Chester box tile type 2. SF 9818 from (268) bears a partial Holt type 1 (RIB **2** (4), 2463.29) legionary stamp, [LEG XX V]V; it is probably a middle *tegula* fragment. SF 9799 from (1033) is a chip only with a double, curved signature. SF 9470 from (974) is an edge fragment (end fragment if *tegula*) bearing an indeterminate paw print.

Catalogue

7   A fragment from the upper part only of a lion's head antefix, with knife-trimmed scallop edging and part of the pointed gable of an integral back projection (broken); chipped and abraded. The fabric is hard, bright orange and sandy with abundant quartz inclusions and a harsh feel. A slightly darker, self-coloured slip coats the upper moulded surface. H 71 mm; W 97 mm; th (max complete) 37 mm. (974); SF 8773. Ill 4.1.7.

8   Corner fragment of a tapering square or rectangular ?brick with a large knife-trimmed, square or rectangular indent, *c* 25 mm deep and extending to the broken edge, which is c 60 mm from the corner. The surviving edge and ?upper surface are sanded; a patch of mortar adheres to this sanded surface; abraded. Th 30–37 mm. (974); SF 10132. Comparable to the ?lugged brick from Phase IIc (1132), but thinner.

9   'Oddity' (?box tile) with a chamfered edge, finger grooves running parallel to the edge and a sanded exterior surface; pierced by two large oval vents; th 27 mm; vent diam *c* 54 mm. (1125); SF 10131. Ill 4.1.8.

Ill 4.1.7 Phase IV: upper part of lion's head antefix.

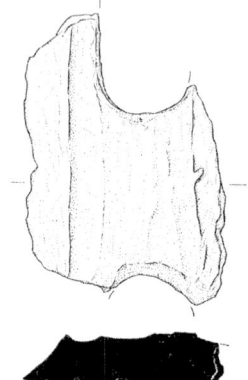

Ill 4.1.8 Phase IV: brick/tile with two oval vents. (Scale 1/4)

Phase V

Phase V produced 18% by fragment count and 15% by weight of the total assemblage, the second largest group after Phase II, with a fragmentation index of 84.9 g. The relatively low average weight indicated a fairly high degree of brokenness which was not unexpected in a large residual group and is similar to Phases VI, VII, IX and X.

A large group of 379 fragments of *tegulae*/70,898 g was recovered, of which only 34 fragments/7595 g were retained. The retained material includes SF 9834 from layer (490), a middle-end piece with a double, curved signature mark. A dog's paw print, SF 8767, appears on a burnt middle piece from structure (270). A middle fragment with the ?edge of a stamp (border only), SF 9816, came from (261). SF 9474 from (830) comprises a middle fragment with overlapping curved signatures. A signature, SF 9550, appears on a corner fragment of ?*tegula* from layer (1668). (490) produced a middle ?*tegula* fragment, SF 9835, with overlapping straight and curved signatures. A curved signature, SF 9480, occurs on a very abraded middle fragment of ?*tegula* from layer (1661). A curved signature, SF 9594, also appears on an edge/end fragment of ?*tegula* from fill (1740) of post-hole (1741). A middle-end piece of ?*tegula*, SF 9759, with a ?tally mark in the shape of a V cut into the end edge, as well as a curved signature on the upper surface, came from (1568). A looped signature, SF 9478, also occurs on a middle ?*tegula* fragment from (1293).

219 fragments of *imbrices*/ridge tiles/29,576 g were recovered, of which only 18 fragments/2175 g were retained. A middle piece from (117) has a pale orange/red slip wash coating the upper surface. SF 9840 from (966) is a corner piece with a scored signature mark running parallel to the long edge. The corners of two *imbrices*, from (830) and layer (1589), are distinctly tapered.

Five ?vaulting tube fragments comprise two edge pieces from (830) and (1014) and three middle pieces from (1004), (1641) and (1660).

Two *opus spicatum* brick fragments were retrieved. These comprise a two-thirds complete fragment from (790) and a half-length piece from (1568).

9 fragments of brick/4580 g were recovered, of which only 5/2985 g were retained. The retained material includes an edge piece from (1568) with a tapered nail hole (maximum diam 8 mm), which pierces the brick 67 mm in from the edge. A second edge piece from (1344) is also pierced by a similarly tapered nail hole (8–12 mm diam).

All of the box tiles recovered were retained. Seven have interior surfaces sooted through use. One fragment from (830) has white lime wash coating the combed exterior surface. Chester type 1 is the most common form, with nineteen fragments; there are five fragments of Chester type 3 and two of Chester type 4; a single example of an additional type (Chester type 5) – with sanded interior and unsanded exterior – came from (770). This example also has a partial circular air vent, as do two examples of Chester type 4, both from (1568). There are no certain examples of Chester type 2.

A single unusual form, comprising a flange fragment, came from (261).

1629 indeterminate fragments/82980 g, were recovered, of which only 134 fragments/5141 g were retained. The retained assemblage includes SF 9728 from (1660), a middle fragment with a partial triple, curved signature mark. SF 9722 from (1671) is a middle fragment with the edge of a ?stamp; SF 9801, also from (1671), comprises a middle piece with a ?signature mark. A middle fragment with looped signature, SF 9932, came from (1344). SF 9551, also from (1344), comprises a chip with a partial retrograded stamp]VV ?X[- probably Holt type 10 (RIB **2** (4), 2463.49). The fragment of a stamp, SF 9225, came from (1317) and SF 9457 from (1632) was a chip with a curved signature mark. A wide, curved signature, SF 9757, occurs on a middle piece from (1568) and a ?signature mark, SF 9563, on a chip from (1656). SF 9471 from fill (968) of (971) comprises a middle fragment with a double, curved signature and a ?signature mark, SF 9573, also occurs on a curving edge fragment from (992). An unusual piece came from (64) and comprises a curved upper surface decorated with combed lines. The curve suggests an *imbrex*/ridge tile but the combing suggests a box tile. A fragment from fill (1162) <5122>) is probably a piece of *opus signinum*, as mortar adheres to the broken edges/surfaces.

Phase VI

222 fragments of *tegulae*/48,915 g were recovered, of which only 15 fragments/3743 g were retained. SF 9837 from (797) comprises an end fragment with a double, curved signature mark. SF 9475, from (895), is an end fragment with a triple, curved signature and SF 9473 from layer (774) comprises a middle piece with a curved signature mark.

107 fragments of *imbrices*/ridge tiles/14,634 g were recovered, of which only 14 fragments/2932 g were retained. These include SF 9607 from (431), a battered and abraded middle fragment with a ?signature mark. A tapered edge fragment of *imbrex* was recovered from (485).

A complete *opus spicatum* floor brick came from (503).

5 fragments of brick/4029 g were recovered and all were retained. An edge piece, SF 8670 from (798), has a triple, curved signature mark overlaid by hobnail imprints. A very abraded and battered ?edge fragment from (1618) is pierced by a circular nail hole, 9 mm in diameter.

17 fragments of box tile/1797 g were recovered, all of which were kept. The group comprises fifteen examples of Chester type 1 and a single example of Chester type 3; there is also one indeterminate example, with a combed exterior, but no surviving interior surface.

An unusual form came from (503). It comprises a curved, smoothed edge with a finger groove along the base of the edge; the exterior surface is sanded and sooted with knife-scoring.

A large group of indeterminate CBM, comprising 982 fragments/43,045 g was recovered. Only 57 fragments/1437 g were retained. The retained assemblage includes SF 9846 from (1540), a soft and weathered middle fragment with an ?illegible ?graffito. A fragment from (797), *c* 35 mm thick, has one smooth face and one sanded face with knife-scoring. It is unclear whether it is a facing tile fragment or possibly a Chester type 2 box tile fragment, although it is probably too thick for the latter.

Catalogue

10 An 'oddity' (?box tile) comprising a curved, smoothed edge with a finger groove along the base of the edge; the exterior surface is sanded and sooted and bears knife-scoring; very abraded; th (max complete) 30 mm. (503); SF 10133. There are similar examples from Phases IIa (1225), IIc (1161) and IV (1125). Ill 4.1.9.

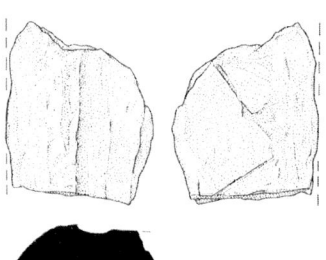

Ill 4.1.9 Phase VI: brick/tile with finger groove and lattice pattern. (Scale 1/4)

Phase VII

A large group of 227 *tegulae*/38,476 g was recovered, but only 12 fragments/3203 g were retained. The retained assemblage includes SF 9833 from (481), an end fragment with a double, curved signature. SF 9839 from (824) is a middle ?*tegula* fragment with a looping signature. SF 9441 from (663) comprises a middle ?*tegula* fragment with a triple, curved signature. SF 9502 from (1304) is a middle ?*tegula* fragment with a partial Webster type 40* (*Chester tile stamp series number) stamp LEG [XX VV] within an ansate frame. It is comparable to RIB **2** (4), 2463.56 (v), which is identified as a possible *Victoriniana* stamp, dated 265–7. Peter Warry has recently questioned the interpretation of the third V of RIB **2** (4), 2463.56 (Webster type 40) and RIB **2**, (4), 2463.57 (Webster type 43) as *V*(*ictoriniana*) ['Victorinus' own'] and has instead suggested that the third V stands for Viducius, a contractor who was apparently making CBM for the Twentieth Legion at Tarbock, Merseyside during the consulship of Verus (which Warry dates to AD 126 rather than 167) (Warry 2006, 60–5 and 156). SF 9487, also from (1304), comprises a middle ?*tegula* fragment with a double, curved signature.

102 fragments of *imbrices*/ridge tiles/14,951 g were recovered, but only 11 fragments/3404 g were retained. Layer (240) produced 12 fragments/2260 g of *tegulae* and *imbrices*/ridge tiles, all discarded. Unfortunately they were not recorded separately on the proformas.

A ?nozzle fragment of ?vaulting tube came from layer (817).

6 brick fragments/3004 g were recovered but only 2 fragments/794 g were retained. The retained assemblage includes SF 9838 from (824), which comprises an edge fragment with a double signature and the knife-trimmed edge of an ?air vent. The latter is an unusual form.

All the box tile fragments retrieved were retained, except for a corner fragment of ?box tile from (560). The group comprises eleven fragments of Chester type 1, two fragments of Chester type 2 and five fragments of indeterminate type, all with combed exterior surfaces. One fragment has a sooted interior through use. The middle fragment from (459) has quite clearly been combed with an eight-toothed comb.

Two fragments of ?half-box tile (*tegula hamata*) were recovered and retained. A battered edge fragment from layer (1304) has a thin flange and a sanded exterior. An abraded corner fragment from (1629) has sanded surfaces and edges. Half-boxes were a short-lived type which were in use in Roman Britain during the first century. They were largely superseded by ordinary box tiles in the Flavian period (Betts 2000, 4).

Two fragments of ?facing (or wall) tile were recovered, both from (824). Each has one smooth face; the opposing face is sanded and knife-scored in a lattice pattern.

A large group of indeterminate forms comprising 1008 fragments/59,055 g were recovered but only 198 fragments/3404 g were retained. The retained assemblage included SF 9831 from (459), which comprises a burnt/overfired middle fragment with a double, curved signature mark. A Holt type 28 stamp (RIB **2** (4), 2463.48), SF 9832, came from (463). A middle fragment of ?*tegula*, also from (463), SF 8232, bears hobnail imprints in the upper surface. An edge fragment from (682) has one smooth face and an opposing face sanded and knife-scored in a lattice pattern. It may have been a fragment of ?facing tile or Chester type 2 ?box tile. A possible *opus spicatum* fragment came from (1599) <5158>.

Catalogue

11 An edge fragment of brick with a double signature and the knife-trimmed edge of an ?air vent; an unusual form; th 44 mm. (824); SF 9838.

Phase VIII

142 fragments of *tegulae*/29,821g were recovered, of which only 15 fragments/4253 g were retained. These include SF 9598 from (1879), which comprises an end fragment with a curved signature mark. SF 9469 from (637) comprises a middle ?*tegula* fragment with a triple, curved signature; SF 9823, also from (341), is an edge/end ?*tegula* fragment with a triple, curved signature mark and SF 8419, also from (341), is a middle ?*tegula* fragment with an indeterminate partial stamp. A noteworthy datable form is a Warry group D tile (240–38) from (533) (Warry 2006a, 2006b, 2007).

98 fragments of *imbrices*/ridge tile/14,978 g were recovered, of which only 6 fragments/1888 g were retained. These include SF 9479 from (1636), an edge fragment with a signature mark running parallel to the edge.

The upper portion of a Jupiter Ammon antefix, SF 8418, came from (341). For similar examples from the site, compare SF 8932 from Phase IIc (1177) and SF 8417 from Phase IX (367). The fragment is fresh in appearance.

Three fragments of ?vaulting tube were retrieved. An end piece and a middle fragment came from (341) and a middle fragment from (56). The end fragment has a wall thickness of 9 mm and an external diameter of 80 mm, and thus falls just within the size range given by Mason for the vaulting tubes recovered from the fortress bath house in 1963/4 (Mason 1990, 218). The two middle fragments have a thickness of 8 mm, an external diameter of 50 mm (from (341) and a thickness of 7 mm and an external diameter of 60 mm (from (56). This indicates both the range in size and the degree of taper of these vaulting tubes.

7 fragments/3300 g of brick were recovered, all from (649), and all were discarded.

Of the fifteen fragments of box tile recovered, only one piece was discarded. The assemblage comprises seven fragments of Chester type 1, one each of Chester types 3 and 5 and six of indeterminate form, two of which have combed exterior surfaces.

A large group of indeterminate forms comprising 643 fragments/46,564 g, was retrieved. Only 32 fragments/

860 g were retained; 28 of these are very small pieces recovered during wet-sieving. The retained assemblage includes SF 9472 from (341), which comprises a middle piece with a double, curved signature. SF 9721, from (1637), also comprises a middle fragment with a double, curved signature. Two possible *opus signinum* fragments came from (1437) <5151>.

Catalogue

12 Upper fragment (top scalloped section) only of a Jupiter Ammon antefix; complete from just above the top of the right-hand spirally fluted, vertical column to half way up the incurving side of the first scallop edging on the right; H *c* 90 mm; W *c* 105 mm; th 48 mm. (341); SF 8418. Ill 4.1.10.

Ill 4.1.10 Phase VIII: upper part of Jupiter Ammon antefix.

Phase IX

117 fragments of *tegulae*/21,327 g were recovered, of which only 2 fragments/412 g were retained.

85 fragments of *imbrices*/ridge tiles/11,119 g were recovered, but only 8 fragments/1489g were retained. One very abraded middle piece from (620) appears to have been pierced by a nail hole. SF 9826 from (368), a ?middle fragment with a signature mark, had also been reused as there is mortar attached to the broken edges.

A middle fragment of a Jupiter Ammon antefix, SF 8417, comprising part of the god's face, came from (367).

A single fragment of ?vaulting tube came from (83) and comprises a fairly fresh middle fragment with a wall thickness of 7 mm and an external diameter of 60 mm.

16 fragments of brick/5068 g were recovered but all were discarded.

Two complete *opus spicatum* bricks were recovered, one from (395), the other from (512). The latter was reused in antiquity as Roman concrete is attached to all the surfaces.

Four fragments of box tile were recovered; all were retained. All the fragments are of Chester type 1 and one piece has an interior surface sooted through use.

A group of indeterminate forms, comprising 592 fragments/25,048 g was recovered, of which only 17 fragments/563 g were retained. These include SF 9171 from (1528), which comprises a middle fragment with a partial Holt type 27 (RIB **2** (4), 2463.28) retrograde stamp]EL, which was deeply impressed. SF 9909 from (1387) comprises a middle fragment with a ?signature mark. SF 9575 from (1433) is a chip only with a curved signature.

Catalogue

13 Face fragment of a Jupiter Ammon antefix, broken diagonally. The left side of the face is intact from immediately below the left eye, across the bridge of the nose to the right corner of the bearded chin. The very bottom edge of the left ram's horn is also present. A short section of horizontal spiral fluting survives along the bottom edge, as well as the stalk and base of a leaf in the bottom right corner, just above the horizontal fluting. The piece is chipped and fairly abraded. The fabric is hard, bright orange and sandy with abundant quartz inclusions and a harsh feel. It is closely comparable to Chester (Holt) pottery fabric 152 (NRFRC fabric code HOL OX (Tomber & Dore 1998, 207)). H 63 mm; W 61 mm; th (max complete) 25 mm. (367); SF 8417. Ill 4.1.11.

Ill 4.1.11 Phase IX: face of Jupiter Ammon antefix.

Phase X

65 fragments of *tegulae*/13,200 g were found, but only 8 fragments/3416 g were kept. These include SF 8724 from (407), a middle fragment with a partial Holt type 6 (RIB **2** (4), 2463.47) stamp LEG [XX VV]; SF 8095 from (320), a middle fragment with an almost complete Holt type 11 (RIB **2** (4), 2463.44) stamp [L]EG XX VV and a faint signature mark; and SF 9830, also from (320), a middle fragment with a looped signature.

47 fragments of *imbrices*/ridge tiles/6233 g were recovered, but only 5 fragments/1300 g were retained. These include SF 9827, a corner fragment from (407) with a double signature across the gable end; SF 9822, an edge fragment from (334) with a triple curved signature; and SF 9829, an edge fragment from (413) with a signature along the edge.

10 fragments of brick/1543g were recovered and all were discarded.

Eight fragments of box tile were recovered; all were retained. There are six fragments of Chester type 1 and one each of Chester types 2 and 5. A middle fragment of Chester type 1 from (407) is in an unusual fabric with streaks of white clay. There are also mortar traces on the interior and exterior surfaces, suggesting that the tile was reused. One piece has an interior sooted through use.

214 indeterminate fragments/10,338 g were recovered but only 7 fragments/295 g were retained. The retained group include SF 9905 (413), a fragment with a looped signature mark, and SF 9828, also from (413), a middle piece with a double, curved signature. SF 9841 from (1082) is a middle fragment with a ?signature mark on the smooth face. This ?signature mark could be a keying mark made with the fingers rather than with a comb or knife. The other face of this piece is sanded and knife-scored in a diamond lattice pattern. It may, therefore, have been a ?facing tile or a Chester ?type 2 box tile fragment. Another middle fragment from (407) also has a knife-scored lattice pattern on a sanded face, the other face being unsanded. It is also possible that this piece is a fragment of ?facing tile or ?box tile.

Unstratified

165 fragments of *tegulae*/37,231 g were recovered. The retained assemblage comprises 17 fragments/4986 g. These include SF 9847, a middle fragment with a double, curved signature mark which had clearly been reused in the Roman period as all the surfaces are coated in *opus signinum*; SF 9758, a middle fragment with a double, curved signature mark; SF 9756, a middle fragment with a curved signature mark; SF 9755, an edge fragment with an S-shaped signature; SF 9595, a middle fragment with a curved signature; SF 9512, a flange fragment with a ?cat's paw print; SF 9754, a middle fragment of ?*tegula* with a partial Holt ?type 2 (RIB **2** (4), 2463.4) stamp [LEG X]X VV; SF 9481, an end piece with a double, curved signature; SF 9751, a middle ?*tegula* fragment with the edge of a stamp, possibly a Holt type 1 (RIB 2 (4), 2463.29); SF 9749, an end fragment of ?*tegula* with a signature mark; and SF 9748, a middle ?*tegula* fragment with a double, curved signature mark.

107 fragments of *imbrices*/ridge tile/18,462 g were unstratified. Only 6 fragments/1677 g were retained. These include SF 9804, a corner fragment with a signature mark running parallel to the edge; SF 9803, an edge fragment with a signature running roughly parallel to the edge; SF 9752, a corner fragment with a signature running parallel to the edge; and SF 9750, a corner fragment with a signature mark halfway up the edge.

4 fragments of brick/1372 g were recovered; all were retained. SF 9753 was a middle fragment with the edge of a ?stamp. The group also includes an unusual tapering brick, SF 10134, pierced by a nail hole 9 mm in diameter and coated in white limewash.

There were 3 fragments of *opus spicatum* brick/673 g; again, all were retained. One fragment measures 105 mm, even though incomplete, and had clearly been longer than the standard 113 mm found at Holt (Grimes 1930, 135).

12 fragments of box tile/1440 g were recovered and all were kept. The group includes one example of an additional type, Chester type 6, which has a combed and sanded exterior surface and a sanded interior. There are nine fragments of Chester type 1 and two fragments of indeterminate type, both with combed exterior surfaces.

There is a single ?end fragment of ?facing (or wall) tile; both surfaces are unsanded but one bears a knife-scored lattice pattern, suggesting that it may have been a box tile fragment.

An unusual form has a smooth, rounded edge, a sanded lower surface and a smooth upper surface, knife-scored in a lattice pattern.

There were 345 fragments of indeterminate form/33,774 g, of which only 4 fragments/478 g were retained. These include SF 9582, a chip with a badly abraded partial stamp, LEG [XX VV], within an ansate frame. The stamp is too worn to identify with any certainty. Another small chip bears an unusual, closely packed, knife-scored lattice pattern on the surviving surface; it may be a box tile or facing tile fragment.

Catalogue

14 Middle fragment of an unusual tapering brick pierced by a nail hole and coated in white lime wash; abraded; th 34–45 mm; diam of nail hole 9 mm. U/S; SF 10134. Ill 4.1.12.

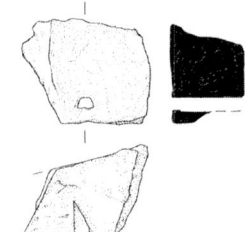

Ill 4.1.12 Phase X: tapering brick with nail hole. (Scale 1/4)

Discussion of Phases IIb–X and unstratified

The post-Roman and unstratified assemblage comprises 11,783 fragments/1210,878 g, 94% by fragment count and 92% by weight of the total site assemblage. The largest group, 18% by fragment count and 15% by weight of the site assemblage, came from Phase V.

A wide range of forms was recovered, comprising *tegulae*, *imbrices*, *imbrices*/ridge tiles, antefixes, ?vaulting tube fragments, a ?chimney fragment, bricks, *opus spicatum* bricks, box tiles, ?half-box tiles, ?facing (or wall) tiles, 'oddities' and indeterminate forms. *Tegulae* form the largest component by weight of the assemblage from post-Roman phases, 2287 fragments/490,952 g (19% by count and 40.5% by weight of the assemblage). Indeterminate forms account for 7922 fragments/443,478 g (67% by count and 37% by weight). *Imbrices* and *imbrices*/ridge tiles account for 10% by count and 16% by weight; bricks 1% by count and 3% by weight; and box tiles 1% by count and 3% by weight. The remaining forms each comprise less than 1% by count and weight

The assemblage is of mixed condition. 114 fragments were burnt, examples coming from every phase except VI/VII. Twelve fragments show evidence of reuse in the Roman period, all being coated in Roman mortar or concrete. There are twenty-two other fragments with evidence of reuse but the period at which this occurred is uncertain: two are definitely coated in post-Roman mortar. There are nine probable *opus signinum* fragments, all coated in Roman mortar/concrete. Thirty-three fragments of box tile are sooted through use. The 'oddity' from Phase VI was also slightly sooted and this may give some indication of its function.

Conclusion

Probably most of the ceramic building material was made at Holt, the works depot of the Twentieth Legion, which was founded in the late first century AD to supply the fortress at Chester with tile and pottery. There is some disagreement over the source of the Jupiter Ammon and lion's head antefixes and vaulting tubes. As no examples

of these forms were published in Grimes 1930, it is generally assumed that they were not made there. However, microscopic examination of the fabrics suggests that the clays used in their production were probably of local origin. Dating the end of ceramic building material production at Holt is problematic. Recent work by Peter Warry has cast doubt on the interpretation of the *Victoriniana* (268–70) and *Deciana* (249–51) stamps, which were thought to extend the known period of CBM production at Holt to the end of the third century. He also suggested that the ANTO (*Antoniniana*) stamped tiles (213–22) were not produced at Holt, as no examples have been found there, but were probably contracted out (2006a, 59–60, 85 and 138). Possibly the most significant items from the assemblage are the fragments of vaulting tube (*tubi fittili*), as these must have originated in the fortress bath house, where their presence suggests that they date to the reconstruction of the fortress and its buildings in the 220s and 230s (Mason 2002, 111).

Examples of all four of Warry's *tegula* lower cutaway groups are present. Group A comprises 61%, group B 12%, group C 3% and group D 5%; 19% were indeterminate. It is clear that the majority of the assemblage represents a period of construction between 90 and 140 (groups A and B), with a smaller group representing the period 160–380 (groups C and D). The rest of the CBM assemblage may have the same chronological distribution.

97% of the box tile fragments were combed; only 3% were knife-scored. In the south-east, knife-scored box tile were replaced by combed tiles about the early second century (Betts 2000, 3). The two types found on the current excavation could represent different buildings or phases of construction, or the knife-scored tiles may simply represent the using up of old stock.

Appendix 4.1.1: Box tile types from Holt

Defined on the basis of size only (Grimes 1930, 13–16). Measurements have been converted into millimetres.
1   Single box: 152 x 152 x 152 mm
2   Single box: 304 x 152 x 152 mm (ie as type 1 but twice the length)
3   Single box: 317 x 317 x 317 mm (ie as type 1 but twice the size)
4   Single box: 444 x 152 x 152 mm (ie as type 1 but three times the length)
5   Double box: 304 x 177 x 292 mm
6   Single box: 228 x 228 x 177 mm long

Appendix 4.1.2: Box tile types from Chester

Defined by Alison Jones on the basis of method of manufacture (eg location of moulding sand) and type of keying (ie knife-scored or combed). No complete examples have yet been found so no dimensions are available for comparison with the Holt types. For this reason, it cannot be stated with certainty that the following types are single or double box tiles. It is statistically more likely, however, that all, or most, are single box tiles.

25 Bridge Street 2001 types
1   Box with combed, unsanded exterior and sanded interior

2 Box with sanded, knife-scored exterior and unsanded interior
3 Box with combed, unsanded exterior and unsanded interior
4* Box with sanded exterior and unsanded interior (*Type 4 could be the unscored side of Type 2)
5* Box with smooth, unsanded exterior and sanded interior
   (*Type 5 could be the uncombed side of type 1 or the unscored side of Type 9]
6 Box with combed and sanded exterior and sanded interior

Nun's Field 1964 type

7 Box with combed exterior and unsanded interior impressed with ?vegetation (?grass/straw) (or is it just the rough impression of the wooden mould?)

Grey Friars Court 1976–8 and 1981 types

8 Box with sanded, knife-scored exterior and sanded interior
9 Box with unsanded, knife-scored exterior and sanded interior
10 Box with unsanded, knife-scored exterior and unsanded interior
11* Box with unsanded exterior and unsanded interior (*Type 11 could be the unscored side of type 10 or the uncombed side of type 3)

Acknowledgements

I should like to express my thanks to volunteers, Michael Bonsall, Liz and John Bailey, Susan Chambers and Simon Skelling for their invaluable help in the preparation of the archive.

Concrete

197 fragments of concrete were retrieved. Roman Phases I and IIa produced 135 fragments*; sixty-one came from post-Roman contexts; one was unstratified. (*This figure excludes (1026) sample <5126> from Id, which produced innumerable loose pieces of the original concrete matrix (pieces of red sandstone, broken CBM fragments and pebbles, all coated in lime mortar), as well as crumbling fragments of *opus signinum*).

Phases I and IIa

Most of the concrete from Phase I is in the form of small loose fragments of CBM coated in cement which has become detached from the concrete matrix. None was retrieved from Ia; Ib produced a single fragment; twenty fragments came from Ic; the remaining 104 fragments came from Id. They presumably derived from the concrete floors of Building I(i). Phase IIa produced just ten fragments, including a large fragment with surviving upper surface from the *opus signinum*-rich deposit (1225).

Post-Roman phases and unstratified

Sixty-two fragments were recovered, including eleven with surviving upper surfaces. The material is fragmentary and adds little to the interpretation of structures on the site, except to illustrate the use of concrete in the construction of floors and buildings.

Table 4.1.7 Roman concrete quantified by phase and no of fragments

Phase	Ib	Ic	Id	IIa	IIb	IIc	III	IV	V
No	1	20	104	10	5	5	9	9	14

Phase	VI	VII	VIII	IX	X	Groups	U/S
No	6	6	3	1	1	2	1

Catalogue

1 Large fragment with a smoothed upper surface and a chamfered edge; clear imprints of now-missing CBM in the lower surface. (77): Phase IIc.
2 Fragment with surviving upper surface. (1138): Phase IIc.
3 Large moulded, corner fragment. (1138): Phase IIc.
4 Three large adjoining pieces with surviving upper surface. (1022): Phase III.
5 Three large fragments, two adjoining, with surviving upper and lower surfaces. (871): Phase IV.
6 Large fragment with the imprint of CBM, a piece of which has adhered to the concrete. (706): Phase VI.
7 Thick fragment with a piece of red sandstone adhering to it. (800): Phase VI.
8 Fragment with surviving ?upper surface. (1193): Phase VII.
9 Fragment with a surviving edge/surface. (441): Phase IX.
10 Large fragment with a surviving surface. u/s.

Baked clay and daub

Six fragments of daub were recovered, all from post-Roman phases. It is not clear whether any or all are Roman in date. All were featureless except for a piece from (687) in Phase VI, which has a is of little significance and adds little to the interpretation of structures on the site, except to illustrate its use in the construction of nearby buildings.

Table 4.1.8 Baked clay and daub quantified by phase, context and no of fragments

Phase	Context	Sa no	No	Part	Comments
IV	129	0	1	Frag	
IV	1015	5096	1	Frag	
V	261	0	1	Frag	
V	768	5084	2	Frags	
VI	687	0	1	Corner	Smooth upper surface
Total			6		

Cement and plaster

Over eighty fragments of cement/plaster were recovered: Roman Phases I and IIa produced twelve fragments; sixty-six came from post-Roman phases and two were unstratified (*see* Table 4.1.9). Many of the fragments are in a poor condition and so are not easy to identify. It is possible that some may be post-Roman in date. In addition, many very crumbly indeterminate fragments came from (1182) in Phase Ie.

Thirty-three fragments could be positively identified as wall plaster, including some with traces of red paint, from Roman Phases Ic, Id and IIa and post-Roman Phases VI and VII. None are large enough to distinguish any clear pattern but one fragment from (1219) in Phase IIa appears to bear a linear design in red paint over the red painted background. The material is fragmentary and largely residual and adds little to the interpretation of structures on the site, except to illustrate its use in the nearby buildings.

Table 4.1.9 Roman cement/plaster quantified by (sub-)phase, context and no of fragments

Phase	Context	Condition	No	Description
Ic	142		1	Red-painted wall plaster
	1388		4	Tiny frags wall plaster; red painted surfaces
Id	101		3	Red-painted wall plaster
Ie	1148		1	Wall plaster
	1182	Many very crumbly frags	*0	*Incl many frags indet cement/plaster and lumps of red sandstone; ?sample (but no ample no on finds label)
Id	1242		*0	Several tiny frags wall plaster; red painted surfaces
Total Phase I			>9	
IIa	1219		3	Wall plaster: 1 x frag with red-painted surface (incl linear design in red paint)
Total Phase IIa			3	
IIb	1135		1	Red-painted wall plaster
	1138		1	Wall plaster; imprint of indet CBM frag on inner surface
Total Phase IIb			2	
IIc	75		1	Indet cement/plaster
IIc	77		1	Indet cement/plaster
IIc	1161	Crumbly	0*	*frags coarse pinky/orange indet ?cement
Total Phase IIc			>2	
III	74	Incl several crumbly frags	1	1 x frag indet cement/coarse plaster + several crumbly frags
	74		3	Wall plaster
	106		1	Indet cement/plaster
	1022		11	Indet cement/plaster
	1131		1	Small frag indet cement/plaster
Total Phase III			17	
IV			3	Indet cement or ?concrete
	883		2	Indet cement/plaster; 1 x frag with traces of lime ?plaster
	974		1	Indet cement /plaster (or ?opus signinum) with attached lime ?plaster
	1033		6	Indet cement/plaster
	1034		1	Indet cement/plaster
	1125		1	Indet cement/plaster
Total Phase IV			14	
V	870	Crumbly	10	?Wall plaster
	1155	Very crumbly	2	Several frags (incl 2 x adjoining pieces) indet cement/plaster
	1656		1	Indet ?cement/plaster or ?*opus signinum*
Total Phase V			13	
VI	717		1	Red-painted wall plaster
	785		1	Tiny frag ?wall plaster
	1704		1	Indet pinkish ?cement/?*opus signinum*
Total Phase VI			3	
VII	388		1	Red-painted wall plaster
	817		3	Indet cement/plaster
	936		1	Indet cement /plaster (or ?opus signinum) with attached lime ?plaster
	1193		1	Indet ?cement/plaster or ?opus signinum
Total Phase VII			6	
VIII	341		1	Wall plaster
	1819	Crumbly	1	Indet cement/plaster
Total Phase VIII			2	
IX	208		1	?wall plaster; grey painted surface
	1096		1	Indet cement/plaster
	1526		1	Indet ?cement of loosely-bonded crushed frags of Roman CBM
Total Phase IX			3	
	407		1	Indet cement
	1503		1	Wall plaster
Total Phase X			2	
	0		1	Indet grey ?cement/plaster
	0		3	Indet pinkish ?cement/plaster
Total u/s			4	

Window glass

H E M Cool

Introduction

All of the fragments of Roman window glass were of the cast variety which was used from the first to the third centuries. All were blue/green with the exception of a colourless fragment from a Phase V context (no 6). Apart from one fragment, it was all found residually. This was not surprising as cast window glass is thick and able to withstand redeposition, although it could also hint that glazed buildings were still standing on the site in the post-Roman period.

Phase I

1   Cast matt/glossy with rounded edge; area 4.5 cm². (1242).

Phase III

2   Cast matt/glossy; two fragments; area 7 cm². (1022).
3   Cast matt/glossy; area 10 cm². (973).
4   Cast matt/glossy; area 3.5 cm². (70).

Phase IV

5   Cast matt/glossy; two fragments; area 9 cm². (1030); SF 5114.

Phase V

6   Cast matt/glossy; colourless with rounded edge; area 16 cm². (879).
7   Cast matt/glossy with one grozed edge; area 7.5 cm². (996).
8   Cast matt/glossy; area 1.5 cm². (1632).
9   Cast matt/glossy; area 6 cm². (830).

Phase VI

10   Cast matt/glossy; two joining fragments; area 7 cm². (532).

Phase VII

11   Cast matt/glossy; area 11 cm². (560).
12   Cast matt/glossy; area 7.5 cm². (939).

Phase VIII

13   Cast matt/glossy with rounded edge; area 3 cm². (649).
14   Cast matt/glossy; area 0.5 cm2. (341); SF 5026.

Discussion of Roman building materials

The excavations at 25 Bridge Street produced a wide range of Roman building materials, which appears likely to have come from a variety of buildings. The purpose of this note is to examine what these might have been.

The *tubi fittili* (vaulting tubes) represent the only item that can be stated with certainty to have come from the fortress bath house. They are thought to date to the reconstruction of the vaulting over the bathing halls during a major refurbishment in the 220s and 230s (Mason 2002, 111). However, it is probable that many more items in the 25 Bridge Street assemblage also originated in the baths. Herringbone flooring composed of *opus spicatum* bricks, for example, was used in the original Flavian swimming baths, pools and *labrum* alcove. Although no concrete was recovered from the 1963/4 excavations, it was used as the main flooring and lining material for the pools and swimming baths of the Severan period refurbishment, when it replaced the original *opus spicatum* floors. Box tiles (*tubuli*) were used for the wall jacketing (*tubulatio*) of the heated rooms and also for the original Flavian vaulting of the bathing halls. Possible parallels for some of the specialised bricks from 25 Bridge Street are the 'lugged bricks' from the fortress baths at Caerleon, which are thought to have been used in vault construction in a similar way to armchair voussoirs (Zienkiewicz 1986, 325). The Flavian period brick-stack hypocaust pillars (*pilae*) were composed of *pedales* bricks; these were largely replaced by *bessales* bricks during the Severan reconstruction and finally by sandstone *pilae* in the fourth-century alterations. Roofing tiles comprising *tegulae* and *imbrices* were common finds at the fortress baths at both Exeter and Caerleon, and antefixes are also known, occurring with particular abundance at Exeter. On the other hand, *tegulae* and *imbrices*, at least, can be expected on all buildings in the fortress.

The inscription attributed to Vespasian attests the use of Purbeck marble in the early baths at Chester. Purbeck marble slabs, veneers, mouldings and *labra* are known from the fortress baths at Exeter (Bidwell 1979). At Caerleon, Purbeck marble was used as a decorative veneer from the earliest phase of the baths (*c* AD 75) and panels of this stone continued to adorn the interior until the final closure of the baths (Zienkiewicz 1986, 303).

Monochrome mosaic floors decorated all the chambers in the *sudatoria* and *frigidarium* of the baths in the Flavian period. In the fourth century, new monochrome mosaic floors were laid in the *sudatoria*. A large number of loose *tesserae* were recovered from 25 Bridge Street, as well as a single intact fragment of dark grey and white *tesserae* and five examples of pairs of *tesserae* cemented together. David Neal has suggested that the elongated *tesserae*, at least, must have come from the fortress bath house and that the group as a whole probably dates to the first century AD (D Neal *pers comm* 12 May 2006).

The walls and ceilings of the baths would have been decorated with painted plaster, and blocks of solid colour were commonly used for the lower sections of walls. Fragments of plaster with traces of a dark red wash were recovered from earlier excavations at the bath house and a small number of plaster fragments were recovered from 25 Bridge Street, including some with traces of red paint.

However, like the roof tiles, red-painted plaster has been found on a wide variety of buildings.

It is equally possible that a large part of the building material assemblage from 25 Bridge Street originated in the *scamnum tribunorum* to the north of the site. Unfortunately, although we have a fairly good understanding of the general layout and plan of tribunes' houses in both Britain and Europe, very little evidence has been recovered for their internal decoration. All the known tribunes' houses appear to have incorporated a central courtyard surrounded by living quarters and offices, although the general layout and the number of rooms varied greatly, seemingly making allowance for individual needs and tastes (Pitts & St Joseph 1985, 139). The senior tribune (*tribunus laticlavius*) probably occupied a larger and more elaborate house then the other tribunes (*tribuni augusticlavii*). However, a large courtyard house in the *scamnum tribunorum* at Caerleon, which contained a heated baths for the occupant's private use, is thought to have belonged to the *praefectus castrorum* rather than the senior tribune, as it also contained workshops (Zienkiewicz 1993, 75). This particular building produced evidence for good quality concrete floors and plastered walls, as well as box tiles, probably from the *tubulatio* of the small hypocausted room (Zienkiewicz 1993, 127).

Evidence for tribunes' houses in Chester has come firstly from investigations carried out in 1894 to the west of the *via praetoria* (Mason 2000, 15 and ill 13). Here, excavations in the vaults of Quellyn Roberts, Watergate Street South, revealed part of an apsidal building and three east–west walls. Part of a hypocaust floor with brick-stack *pilae* survived (one of the tiles bore a stamp of the Twentieth Legion), as well as a sandstone *pila*, probably of fourth-century date, voussoir tiles (?ie box tiles) and fragments of a monochrome mosaic floor set between *pilae* (Lawson 1928, 171). A range of rooms, at least one of which contained a hypocaust, was found during excavations in Brown's basement in 1960. Finds included two examples of Jupiter Ammon antefixes (Jones 2003). It is uncertain whether these remains formed part of a tribune's house or lay in the *scamnum* to the south (Thompson 1967, 22; Mason 2000, xii, ill 2). More recently, building work at 17–19 Watergate Street in 1985 revealed walls, floors and part of a small courtyard, which may have belonged to a tribune's house (Frere ed 1986, 387).

Thus, much of the Roman building material from 25 Bridge Street could have come from the baths: the vaulting tube fragments and the box tiles, as well as the unusual vented tiles and lugged or indented bricks, the slate inscription, the Purbeck marble column fragments and worked pieces, the *tesserae* and the lion's head and Jupiter Ammon antefixes. However, the assemblage could equally represent a mix of material from the bath house, the tribunes' houses and other buildings within the *scamnum* in which the site lay. For example, some of the *tesserae* could have come from the monochrome mosaic fragment discovered at Fletcher's Buildings in 1901 (Newstead 1902, 104). It is unlikely that we shall ever be likely to be specific about the origin of some of the more common materials, such as the roof tiles and plaster. It was unfortunate that such a small proportion of the 2001 assemblage came from closely dated contexts and that so much of the material recovered from Roman contexts appeared to be residual.

Post-Roman Ceramic Building Materials: Introduction

Julie E C Edwards

The medieval and post-medieval phases of the site produced a large quantity and wide range of ceramic building materials. These consisted of items that can generally be expected from excavations in Chester: medieval and post-medieval roof and floor tiles, medieval roof furniture, bricks (some of potential late medieval/early post-medieval date) and chimney fragments, as well as later post-medieval ornamental ceramic fittings.

Condition

As might be expected the assemblage is varied in condition. The medieval material, although mainly fragmentary, is generally in quite good condition: there is a low level of abrasion and there are many complete examples of late medieval–early post-medieval brick and floor tile. The floor tile varies in condition: as is common, many tiles are worn from use rather than as a result of post-depositional disturbance, although there are abraded pieces in the later post-medieval contexts. The roof tile is fragmentary but nevertheless in good condition, with very few abraded fragments: many pieces appear freshly broken. As a result of the collection policy all the retained post-medieval building material is in good condition and there was a high number of complete objects.

Given the large quantity of material and the limitations of the project it was only possible to examine in any detail the large stratified assemblages of floor tile and brick which it was felt might produce new information about their use in the city. A summary description is given of the roof tiles. All the retrieved building material was recorded according to form, general fabric type, broad date, condition, dimensions, number of fragments, with comments on features and surface treatment. All the data is stored in an Access database and in the paper archive.

Collection policy

The evaluation excavations carried out by Gifford & Partners produced a very large quantity of ceramic building material for all periods. It was felt that the quantities which would be retrieved from a full excavation would be unmanageable and it was requested that a discard policy be drawn up and employed.

This was done and in brief the later post-medieval brick and floor tile was recorded and disposed of on site when possible. A sample of each type was retained for record purposes. Samples were taken of the bricks from any *in situ* walls which could provide independent dating evidence. Medieval building material, glazed roof tiles, decorated tiles or brick and any object in an uncommon fabric or displaying unusual or outstanding features regardless of period should have been retained, and it was further required that large stratified assemblages should be examined by the post-Roman finds specialist before disposal. However, for various reasons the policy was difficult to implement and some medieval building material appears in the discard records and some assemblages were discarded before close examination.

Medieval Ceramic Building Material

Introduction

The total quantity of retained and discarded ceramic medieval and possibly medieval building material is set out in Table 4.3.1 and is described below.

Table 4.3.1 Retained medieval ceramic building material quantified by phase, no of fragments and weight

Phase	No	Wt (g)
I	6	290
II	5	191
IV	4	493
V	272	42810
VI	690	236104
VII	1250	90244
VIII	200	31915
IX	139	40059
X	113	19114

The quantity of and general type of discarded ceramic medieval building material is shown in Tables 4.3.2–.3.

Table 4.3.2 Discarded medieval ceramic building material quantified by phase, no of fragments and weight

Phase	No	Wt (g)
V	1	130
VI	49	22475
VII	33	10935
VIII	2	150
IX	8	1805
X	3	1100

Table 4.3.3 Range of discarded medieval ceramic building material quantified by form, no of fragments and weight

Form	No	Wt (g)
Brick	53	26295
Brick/Tile	39	9750
Tile	2	375
Tile/Indet	2	175

Floor tile

Introduction

The floor tiles were recorded within context groups. The assemblage from each context was laid out in order to identify any joining fragments. All the fragments from the same tile in each context were recorded together. Each tile was recorded by number of fragments, weight, dimensions, design, number of corners present, condition, surface treatment and shape of sides. The design on the tile was identified using the design series for Chester held by Chester Archaeology and where possible the Cheshire tile census (Rutter 1990c; Brotherton-Ratcliffe & Axworthy *in prep*). The designs therefore have two numbers in the text and records: the first number is that for the Chester series and the second for the county cen-

sus; where the designs do not appear in the census, only the Chester number appears. Because of the limited time available an extensive search through the sources to identify parallels and possible dating for new designs was not possible. For similar reasons limited work was done on tile fabrics, although at the time of recording fabric differences were noted for the two key groups and some provisional fabric groupings were made: these were recorded in the archive. Dating is dependent on that suggested by Eames (1980).

The tiles range in date from possible thirteenth or fourteenth-century decorated examples to late fifteenth- and/or sixteenth-century decorated and plain tiles. Three broad types of tiles are represented: decorated and undecorated mosaic and pseudo-mosaic tiles; square tiles (*c* 120 mm x 120 mm), chiefly with line-impressed decoration; and large thick square tiles (*c* 225 mm x 225 mm). The last are either line-impressed (in the style of Chester design 119), plain with a slipped and glazed surface, or plain and unglazed. The plain slipped tiles either have a clear glaze over a white slip, giving a yellow finish, or a copper green stained glaze over a white slip, giving a green or mottled green finish. Used in conjunction these tiles could form a chequered floor such as can be seen in late medieval and early post-medieval paintings and manuscript illustrations (Eames 1992, 7, fig 4). In northern Europe such floors appear to have replaced the highly decorated medieval tiled floors. Locally such large thick tiles, either plain or decorated, are not precisely dated but evidence from Chester cathedral, where similar tiles were associated with the Tudor reconstruction of the west entrance (unpublished), suggests that they are late medieval to early post-medieval in date, the large plain variety perhaps being used as late as the late sixteenth century.

Whilst a number of the tile designs are new to Chester, the majority are types which can be expected to occur on excavations in Chester, but such a large quantity had only previously been found associated with ecclesiastical establishments.

Table 4.3.4 Medieval floor tile: total amount quantified by phase, no of fragments and weight (149 contexts)

Phase	No	Wt (g)
II	1	114
IV	1	219
V	120	28888
VI	397	136191
VII	982	31760
VIII	40	10529
IX	52	9009
X	18	3633
Total	1611	220343

Floor tiles were concentrated in Phases V, VI and VII, where a large fragmentary assemblage was found, with smaller quantities appearing as residual components of later phases. Tiles of probable fifteenth-century date were found in Phases II and IV. Whilst the majority of tiles appeared to be a part of accumulated debris, three groups were deliberately deposited:

- A group from Phase V, reused to construct oven (1568);
- A large group used to backfill the stone-lined cess pit (487) in Phase VI;

- Others, probably derived from the same source as those in pit (487), used to construct the Phase VI oven (778) overlying the pit and to fill cess pit (465).

The last two groups form the largest assemblage of large square slipped or decorated tiles to have been found in Chester; generally they have only been previously found as fragments and in small quantities. It is these groups which are reported on below.

Phase V

Plot 4

Oven (1568)

A group of floor tiles comprising sixty-eight fragments (19035 g) was found forming the floor of the flue of the oven (1568). The assemblage is generally in a poor condition: some tiles display heavy wear on their decorated/glazed surface; mortar and a red clay bonding material appears in varying quantities on the surfaces and sides of some of the fragments and complete tiles; and mortar is also occasionally present on broken edges. Over half the pieces had been damaged by heat to such an extent that some are distorted across their depth, while others have damaged and discoloured glazes and some have fabrics which are reduced and almost vitrified. A number, however, are in remarkably good condition considering the nature of the context and one tile in particular, although clearly damaged during firing, is in such good condition that it appears never to have been used (no 2).

Table 4.3.5 Phase V Plot 4 oven (1568): medieval floor tile designs quantified by no of fragments and weight

Design no	No	Wt (g)
?144/357	3	702
120/113	2	503
124/137	4	740
136/357	2	506
196/1	1	210
196/1, 197/6, 198/46	1	377
196/1, 197/6?	1	224
196/1, 199/51	1	209
198/46	2	542
198/46, 199/51	1	769
198/46, 204/40	1	353
200/130?	1	160
201/142	1	208
202/28	1	98
203/33	1	75
205/50	3	568
206/76	1	325
208/-	1	199
209/8	1	260
210/-, 211/-	1	139
212/43	1	307
213/-, 219/349	2	598
214/-, 198/46	1	348
215/-, 196/1	1	545
216/-	1	259
217/-, 198/46	1	316
218/-	6	2161
221/56, 196/1	1	318
35/232	1	501
53/138	1	153
60/143	4	1033
Plain	12	4669
Unidentifiable	6	660

Note The design numbers represent the Chester series and the Cheshire census separated by a /; more than one set of numbers represents several stamp designs used on a single tile.

Clearly the tiles were not made to construct the oven and their use in this context was a secondary one. Their origin is unclear but there are at least two possibilities: they had been removed from the floor they were made for either because they needed to be replaced or because the building was being demolished; alternatively, they were kiln seconds or perhaps surplus stock. One identifying factor for a kiln second is evidence of overfiring but the heat of the oven no doubt would have caused similar damage to those tiles with which it was in direct contact. It was therefore difficult to use heat damage to decide between the two possibilities but wear and variety in date proved to be more useful.

The amount of wear on a number of the tiles clearly suggests use, as does the presence of mortar on the lower surface and side. Some of the burnt tiles do not show signs of wear, but they may still have seen use in an area of low footfall. Dated parallels could not be found for many of the tiles but the dates of those for which it was possible to suggest parallels varied from the earlier part of the fourteenth to the fifteenth century. The tiles therefore seem likely to have been reused from one or more buildings rather than being the products of a single kiln. The date of this reuse was unclear but was no earlier than sometime in the fifteenth century as late medieval pottery was found associated with the fill.

The forms comprise mosaic, pseudo-mosaic, rectangular and square tiles. As is common in Chester, the majority of the decorated pieces have line-impressed designs: there is only one two-colour tile. When a surface colour is discernible it is yellow or dark brown/black. It was difficult to determine whether the dark colour was a result of reduction or from a colouring of the glaze, although some pieces do appear to have a glaze which had been deliberately reduced rather than burnt from association with heat from the oven. The assemblage is noteworthy in Chester for its variety of stamp designs and mosaic shapes, many of which are unusual and have not been recorded before from the city or county. Some, whilst new to the city, have parallels in the Cheshire county census, whilst others are variants of previously recorded designs. The group therefore extends the range of designs from the city and county. The additions to the Chester stamp designs and mosaic shapes have been added to the stamp series for Chester. Within the variety of patterns and forms there was repeated use of small floral-type stamps, sometimes in groups of the same stamp or combined with one or two other stamps.

Mosaic tiles

Eleven pieces are from mosaic pieces. These largely consist of small squares or rectangles. Broken L-shaped fragments are perhaps from square shapes with cut-out centres; others with curved and straight edges could have been from a variety of abstract shapes, eg Rutter 1990c, fig 162, nos 46/20, 49/21, 50/14. Whilst there is some general similarity between the types found in this assemblage and those published in 1990, there are no exact parallels. Numbers 1–5 are unusual finds in Chester; 4 and 5 straddle the mosaic and pseudo-mosaic categories.

Catalogue

1 Half of a square tile with a centre from which a quatrefoil shape had been cut. The tile had been partly cut and broken along the diagonal to form a right-angled triangle. It has a white slip under a colourless glaze and two different line-impressed floral designs made by small stamps (196/1 and 197/6). A mass of fired red clay adheres to the central void and is presumably from the secondary usage in the oven. The slip- and glaze-covered surface at one end of the tile is crazed and apparently burnt. Chester mosaic shape 38. SF 10373. Ill 4.3.1.1.

2 A square with semicircular cut-outs in each side to form a cruciform shape. It, too, has a white slip under a colourless glaze and a design made by different small stamps. The tile is in very good condition with no signs of wear as though freshly made, although the decorated surface is marred by a kiln scar where another object had stuck to the surface. The piece does not have any discoloration from heat or burning. No parallels for either the stamps or shape appear to have been recorded from Cheshire, nor are any parallels shown by Eames (1980). The design is 208 in the Chester design series and 32 in the Chester mosaic shape series. SF 10371. Ill 4.3.1.2.

3 A tile with one straight and one curving edge from a Y-shaped mosaic. The tile has a simple line border, and a single floral stamp has been impressed at the crossing point of the three arms of the Y. Neither the stamp design nor the mosaic shape has been recorded previously in Chester, but the overall design appears to complement numbers 16–19 in the county census where the stamp is similar to that occurring on tile design 8. An almost black glossy glaze probably covered the surface but only remains intact along one edge; the remainder is crazed and badly heat damaged. The stamp design is 209 and the mosaic shape 33 in the Chester series. SF 10370. Ill 4.3.1.3.

4 Two joining pieces which appear to form a square tile with a central square cut-out. The two pieces are decorated with cinquefoil stamps similar to county census design 46. The decorated surface has a green speckled colourless glaze. The glaze and red sandy fabric is similar to 9. Chester stamp design 198 and mosaic shape 34. SF 10360. Ill 4.3.1.4.

A virtually identical tile design has been found at Wenlock priory in Shropshire (Eames 1980, 62 and vol 2, design 34): a large square tile has a small square cut from the centre and replaced by a small square glazed in a different colour. The same number of similar cinquefoil stamps as no 4 are arranged around the sides of the large square and the small square has a single stamp. The Wenlock examples are dated to the earlier fourteenth century (*op cit*, 356). No small squares were found in this group, but one stamped with a flower was found during the 1996 excavations of the nave of Chester cathedral nave (unpublished).

5 A fragment which, although broken, appears to be from a similarly shaped tile as no 4. However, it is slightly smaller and has a different design. As on pseudo-mosaic tiles the tile appears to be divided into grid squares with a small stamp in each. The two stamps which survive are similar to county census tile designs 1 and 5, 11 and 51. The yellow-coloured tile has a white slip under a colourless glaze. Chester stamp designs 196, 199 and mosaic shape 35. SF 10372. Ill 4.3.1.5.

6 A yellow-coloured mosaic tile with a line-impressed design under a white slip and colourless glaze, comparable to Chester census design 33. One example from the city has been published previously from the site of the Franciscan friary (Bennett 1921, no 10, facing page 17). Chester stamp design 203 and mosaic shape 36. SF 10352. Ill 4.3.1.6.

7 A small rectangular tile with a very dark glaze appearing black over line-impressed decoration consisting of two bands of decoration separated by vertical lines. The remains of two smaller tiles, SF 10351 and SF 10350, were also present, made by partly scoring and breaking a tile of similar design along the line between the bands of decoration. One of the smaller examples has a white slip with a colourless glaze appearing bright yellow and the other has a glaze which appears dark brown/black. Each tile represents one half of the design of the complete example, although they do not appear to be two halves of the same tile. There is a slight difference in thickness between SF 10351 and the other two pieces. SF 10349. Ill 4.3.1.7.

This decoration was not previously listed in the Chester design series but has been found at the site of the Franciscan friary (Bennett 1921, facing 17, fig 12) and the same design is present as Cheshire census no 50. An example of this design is present in the British Museum collection, no 144, found in Lichfield cathedral and suggested to be perhaps fifteenth century in date (Eames 1980, 326). The unbroken design is Chester stamp design 205 and mosaic 37.

8 A narrow rectangular border tile with the letters E and T in Lombardic lettering stamped through a white slip covering under a colourless glaze. The lettering is set between two border lines. A variety of lettered tiles has been found in the city but these letters in this style have not been recorded before. Chester design 221 and mosaic 41. SF 10363. Ill 4.3.1.8.

9 One corner of a square or rectangular tile. Two small stamps have been used in the surviving area of design. Cinquefoil 198/46 is repeated around the edge of the tile and in the centre there is a lion face design similar to Cheshire census 40. The surface of the tile is heavily worn but the remains of a clear glaze with green speckling are visible. The glaze, fabric and the cinquefoil are similar to that of no 4 and are possibly from the same production. SF 10362. Ill 4.3.1.9.

This lion face stamp, Chester stamp design 204, has not previously been recorded in the Chester design series, although it is one of two similar lion face stamps in the Cheshire census, the other being no 24. The stamp is similar to that found in design 115 in the British Museum collection from Wenlock Priory, Shropshire suggested to be earlier fourteenth century (Eames 1980, 356). A similar stamp is also known from Wales at Castell y Bere and Valle Crucis abbey (Lewis 1999, 89 and 194, no 726), where it was part of a group attributed to the first half of the fourteenth century.

10 A narrow rectangular tile, possibly a border tile, the surface of which is quite heavily worn although remains survive of a colourless glaze over a white slip. Three complete stamps can be seen, together with the remains of a fourth. Two small quatrefoil stamps similar to 196/1 separate two larger circular stamps. The complete larger stamp is the same design as that which appears on county census 17 and 56 and consists of a circle divided into interlocking mouchettes with trefoil heads. The design is comparable to that found on tiles from Llanfaes friary, Anglesey and dates to somewhere in the fourteenth–fifteenth century (Lewis 1999, 188 and 82, no 666). Chester design 221 and mosaic 41. SF 10363. Ill 4.3.1.10.

Pseudo-mosaic tiles

Three pseudo-mosaic tiles are present (nos 11, SF 10368; 12, SF 10374; 13, SF 10369: Ill 4.3.2.11–.13). Two are divided by scored lines into a squared grid and small stamps have been used to decorate some of the grid squares. Three different stamps are visible on no 11. Each stamp design has been recorded in the county census but not previously in the Chester series, 196/1,197/6 and 198/46. Two stamp designs, 198/46 and 199/51, appear on no 12. The third piece, no 13, is incomplete but appears to have been divided into squares and rectangles and decorated with a single stamped design, 196/1. Remains of glaze are present on all the pieces but two have heat- or fire-damaged surfaces and the third is very worn. Where intact glaze is visible it appears dark brown–black and no slip is visible. Given the context in which the tiles were found it can be suggested that this was a result of reduction through contact with great heat during the secondary use. However a pseudo-mosaic tile from the Benedictine nunnery in the city also has a reduced dark glaze over a red oxidised fabric. Other tiles in the 25 Bridge Street assemblage were similarly treated and it seems likely that the glaze colour was intentional.

All the tiles are incomplete but represent squares or rectangles *c* 30 mm thick. Only one piece has another complete dimension, the intact side being 129 mm long. The tiles are so similar as to suggest that they were produced together.

Rectangular tiles

A number of rectangular tiles (Chester mosaic shape 39) appear to have been intended to be viewed with the short sides to top and bottom (portrait style). They are distinctive because, with the exception of one (no 14), they do not appear in the Cheshire tile census nor in the British Museum catalogue (Eames 1980). The decoration incorporates small stamps within larger line-impressed designs covering the whole tile. Some of the small stamps are, however, similar to types which occur in the county census and on other tiles in this assemblage; it is the combination of the line-impressed designs with the small stamps that is significant. All are worn and some obviously burnt. The majority have a glaze which is dark and probably reduced, but it is difficult to determine whether this was deliberate or a result of secondary use in the oven; none are slipped. A number of plain tiles of similar shape and dimensions may also have been part of this group but other than an impressed line forming a border to the edges they all appear to be plain.

The group may have formed a border to a mosaic or other panel of tiles.

Catalogue

14 This is similar to county census no 43; the surface is very worn and glaze only remains in the line impression and on the side, where it varies in colour from black to a dark reduced green. The stylised leaf and stem perhaps belong with the lily design found on nos 15 and 16. Chester design 212. SF 10365. Ill 4.3.3.14.

15 A complete tile with an outline of a lily-shaped flower above a leaved stem. A small circular stamp similar to Cheshire census 349 has been impressed in the central area of the flower. Both the large flower design (Chester stamp design 213) and the small stamp (Chester stamp design 219) are unusual and have not been previously recorded from Chester. SF 10361. Ill 4.3.3.15.

16 A fragment with a similar but not identical flower design (Chester stamp design 214) as no 15. In the centre of the flower is a cinquefoil stamp similar to Cheshire census 46 (Chester stamp design 198). SF 10348. Ill 4.3.3.16.

17 An almost complete tile with a line-impressed architectural style design, Chester stamp design 215, which resembles a pinnacle with a trefoil-shaped arch below, the open area of which is infilled with small quatrefoil stamps (stamp design 196/1). SF 10367. Ill 4.3.3.17.

18 A fragment from a tile with a similar but not identical line-impressed design to no 17 but the area under the arch has been left blank. Chester stamp design 216. SF 10354. Ill 4.3.3.18.

19 This tile is included here because, although it is square, stylistically it is similar to the rectangular tiles and has similar dimensions in regard to width and thickness (82 mm square and 27 mm thick). The surface is worn, partly burnt and also obscured by various unidentified deposits, but unlike the other tiles it has a colourless glaze over an oxidised surface which when visible appears a pale yellowish brown. A cinquefoil stamp is at the centre, bordered by a four-sided design with simple *fleur de lis* at the corners. The cinquefoil stamp is similar to county census 46. Chester stamp designs 217 and 198, mosaic shape 40. SF 10364. Ill 4.3.3.19.

Line-impressed square tiles

20 Six fragments have a line-impressed design which has not been recorded previously at Chester. The design is similar to an incomplete design (no 209, cat nos 2814, 2816 and 13,662) in the British Museum catalogue (Eames 1980), which is found on examples from Lilleshall abbey, Shropshire, suggested to be ?fifteenth century. The surfaces are worn but all had a dark brown or black glaze. Two of the fragments join to make a complete tile. The pieces vary in thickness from 28 to 32 mm and the sides are *c* 130 mm. A similar but not the same design has been noted at Bangor cathedral (Lewis 1999, 84 and 190, no 695) but dates to the first quarter of the fourteenth century. Chester stamp design 218. SF 10359. Ill 4.3.4.20.

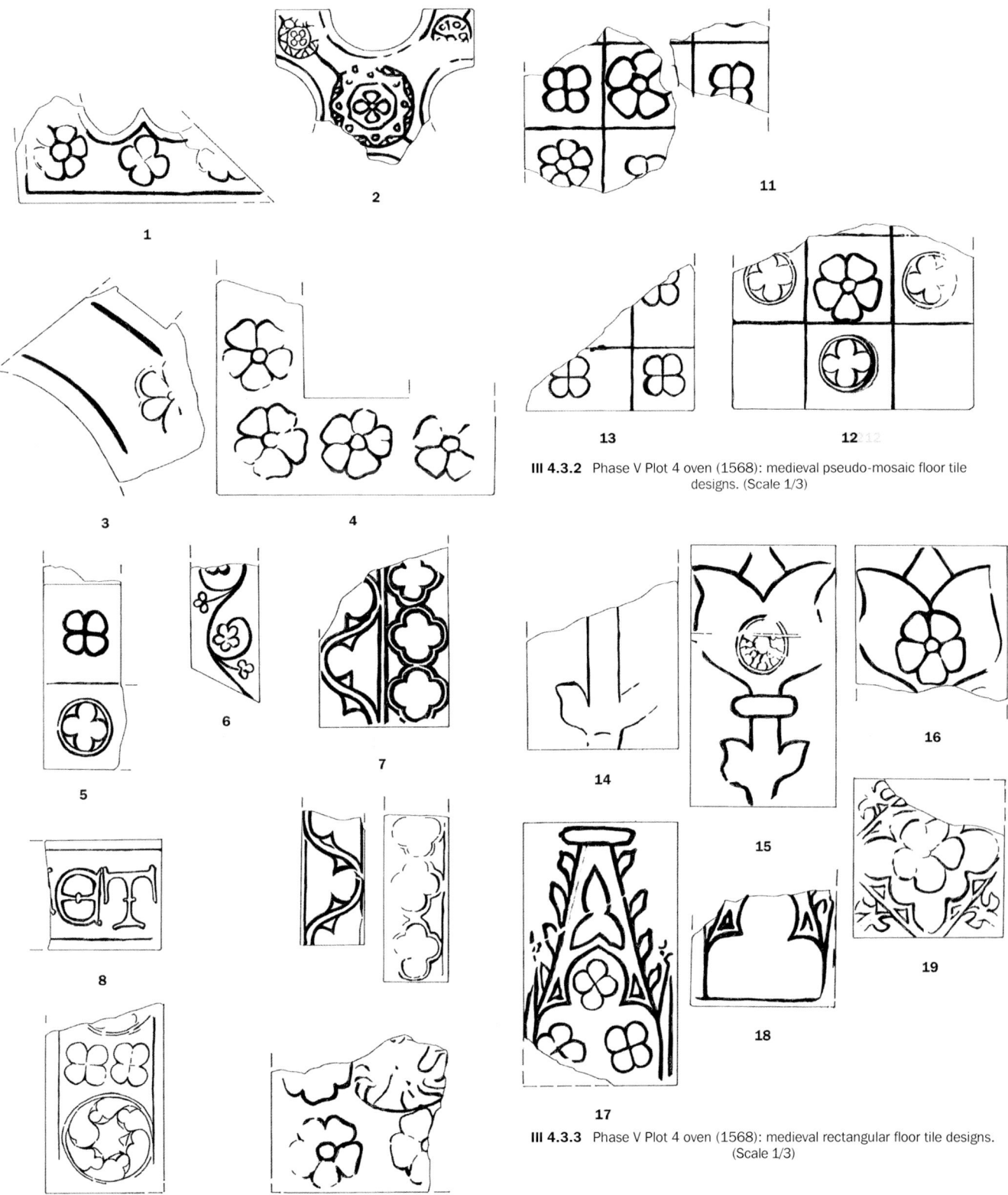

Ill 4.3.2 Phase V Plot 4 oven (1568): medieval pseudo-mosaic floor tile designs. (Scale 1/3)

Ill 4.3.3 Phase V Plot 4 oven (1568): medieval rectangular floor tile designs. (Scale 1/3)

Ill 4.3.1 Phase V Plot 4 oven (1568): medieval pseudo-mosaic floor tile designs. (Scale 1/3)

21 This fragment adds further detail to 120/113 found previously in Chester at the Dominican friary (Rutter 1990c, 246) and Chester cathedral and suggested to be fourteenth- or fifteenth-century in date, with known parallels only in Ireland. SF 10353. Ill 4.3.4.21.

22 A fragment which is probably part of the complete Cheshire census design no 142 which appears not to have been recorded from Chester previously. The glazed surface is damaged but a white slip appears to be present. Mrs Brotherton-Ratcliffe suggested that this design may have been used in conjunction with 60/143 to create a large panel. Chester stamp design 201. SF 10346. Ill 4.3.4.22.

23 Four fragments from design, 60/143, showing three hairs or rabbits which appear to be chasing each other in a circle. Each shares an ear with its neighbour, so that whilst each animal has two ears only three are shown. (Ill 4.3.4.23). A complete example of this line-impressed stamp design and several fragments were found at Chester cathedral during excavations of the nave in 1996 (Whitfield ed 2004, 290, no 246); previous to that the only other known occurrences were a complete example recorded from the Franciscan friary, Chester (Bennett 1921, fig 19, facing 26) and a fragment in Bangor Museum thought to be from Llanfaes friary, Anglesey (Lewis 1999, 81 and 187, no 662). The design has not been closely dated, although it appears on tiles which in size and finish appear similar to those of fourteenth–fifteenth century date; the Llanfaes example is suggested to be fourteenth century (Lewis 1999, 81).

The three hares/rabbits motif in this design is intriguing: the precise origin of the motif is unclear but it is found painted in late sixth–early seventh-century Buddhist cave temples at Dunhuang, China, from where it seems to have travelled along the Silk Road to northern Europe (Whitfield ed 2004, 290). It appears in a number of European churches; the most notable examples found in England are on ceiling bosses in several Devon churches (Greeves 2001). The only other currently known appearance of the motif on an English tile is from the church of St Mary the Virgin, Long Crendon, Buckinghamshire, where it is used in a two-colour tile (Haberly 1937, 168).

24 (and 24a) These pieces add additional information to designs 136/357 and 144/357. 136 and 144 are given the same number in the county census but the information from the larger fragments found at 25 Bridge Street suggests that they are two different designs. They were first identified from the excavations of the nave of Chester cathedral in 1996 and do not appear to be paralleled in the British Museum catalogue (Eames 1980). SF 10347 and SF 10358. Ill 4.3.4.24.

25 Similar to the incomplete county census no 76 and also number 688 in the Welsh series, found at Llanfaes friary, Anglesey (Lewis 1999, 189). The design appears to be a stylised *fleur de lis* with what is possibly a bird perched on one side (Lewis 1999, 83). The glaze appears pale brown with an area of green in the centre of the *fleur de lis*. The fragment is part of a triangular tile. It was common for triangular tiles to be made by drawing a line diagonally across a square tile and partially cutting through the tile before firing. After firing the tile would be snapped in half, leaving a characteristic break mark along the diagonal edge. However, this tile appears to have been cut right through the thickness before firing. Chester stamp design 206. SF 10356. Ill 4.3.4.25.

Two-colour tiles

26 This fragment almost completes design 35/232, found previously in Chester at the site of the Dominican friary (Rutter 1990c, 236) but undated. SF 10355. Ill 4.3.5.

20 21

22 23

24a

24

25

Ill 4.3.4 Phase V Plot 4 oven (1568): medieval line-impressed floor tile designs. (Scale 1/3)

Ill 4.3.5 Phase V Plot 4 oven (1568): medieval two-colour floor tile design 35/232. (Scale 1/3)

Phase VI

Plot 2

Fills of cess pit (487)

The pit contained 185 fragments (66948 g), including a quantity of large square tiles, some of which have line-impressed decoration whilst others are plain. The tiles had been coloured green or yellow by combining the use of a coating of slip with a colourless or coloured lead glaze. The similarity in condition of the tiles suggests that they came from a single floor which was taken up and discarded. However, a number of smaller tiles with designs of fourteenth–fifteenth-century date were also present and do not fit this hypothesis, although it was possible that they came from different parts of the same building as the larger tiles.

Two other groups in Plot 2 appear to be associated with this dump of tiles. The first was used in the construction of the Phase VI oven (778) which overlay cess pit (487); the second was included in the late seventeenth- to early eighteenth-century fill of cess pit (465) in Phase VII which overlay oven (778).

The majority of the tiles are worn on the upper decorated surface, with the more prominent areas of the design having completely lost their covering of glaze, although this often survives in good condition in the more deeply impressed areas. In contrast, the undersides and sides of the tiles display few signs of wear or abrasion and broken surfaces appear freshly broken. This suggests that the tiles became worn during use and that there was little or no time between the floor being dismantled and the tiles being deposited in the pit. Like the pottery in the pit there are joins between fragments in contexts throughout the fill, as well as between the topmost fill (785) and fragments in the overlying oven, (778).

As Tables 4.3.6–.8 and 4.3.10 show, a variety of different designs was found but two designs, numbers 119/188 and 13/108, dominated the cess pit (487), whilst 119/188 was most numerous in the assemblages from oven (778) and cess pit (465): these designs are discussed below. Descriptions and illustrations of the other tile designs can be found in Rutter 1990c.

Catalogue

27 Design 119/188 was the most numerous type in the (487) assemblage by sherd count and weight (also by number of corners present), with 90 fragments (36354 g). (Ill 4.3.6). Locally this design is only found on large square and relatively thick tiles, measuring *c* 225 mm x 225 mm x 35 mm, and this was the size of tile on which they were found in the pit. Previously only fragments of this design had been retrieved from excavations in Chester and its surrounding district, but two complete examples of the design were retrieved from the pit. Both tiles display an additional line which cuts across the design and suggests that the stamp was cracked. As the design consists of a repeated motif on each side of the square it is difficult to determine whether any of the fragments from the site are from tiles which had been stamped with a perfect uncracked stamp. The tiles from the pit and the overlying layers and oven were laid out but it was not possible to assemble an un-

Table 4.3.6 Phase VI Plot 2 cess pit (487) fills: medieval floor tile quantified by context, design no, no of fragments and weight

Context	Design no	No	Wt (g)
785	Unidentifiable	8	1685
785	106/126	1	611
785	119/188	23	6261
785	119/188 cracked	1	256
785	13/108	8	1026
785	195/197	1	589
785	52/189	6	786
Context total		48	11214
786	1/121	1	409
786	119/188	7	2368
786	119/188 cracked	1	757
Context total		9	3534
787	Unidentifiable	2	320
787	119/188	15	5070
787	13/108	5	1574
787	4/78	1	362
787	Plain	5	2001
Context total		28	9327
788	Unidentifiable	9	1607
788	109/337	2	823
788	119/188	11	4188
788	13/108	5	1598
788	13/108?	1	720
788	222/96	2	569
788	3/73	1	266
Context total		31	9771
789	119/188	2	811
789	13/108	1	80
789	02/81	1	355
789	222/96	2	711
789	Plain	1	3771
Context total		7	5728
791	Unidentifiable	3	151
791	13/108?	1	16
791	223/110	1	157
Context total		5	324
797	1/121	1	533
797	119/188	5	1356
797	119/188 cracked	3	1178
797	13/108	10	2913
797	2/81	3	1522
797	3/73	1	583
797	5/83	1	160
797	Plain	4	1607
Context total		28	9852
798	Unidentifiable	4	1876
798	119/188	10	4442
798	119/188 cracked	2	3362
Context total		16	9680
806	Unidentifiable	1	496
806	119/188	4	613
806	119/188 cracked	6	5692
806	Plain	2	717
Context total		13	7518

Table 4.3.7 Phase VI Plot 2 cess pit (487) fills: medieval floor tile designs quantified by no of fragments and weight, in weight order

Design no	No	Wt (g)
119/188	77	25109
119/188 cracked	13	11245
Plain	12	8096
13/108	29	7191
Unidentifiable	27	6135
2/81	4	1877
222/96	4	1280
1/121	2	942
3/73	2	849
109/337	2	823
52/189	6	786
13/108?	2	736
106/126	1	611
195/197	1	589
4/78	1	362
5/83	1	160
223/110	1	157

cracked example of the design. Further work attempting to assemble complete tiles from the entire site assemblage may have provided an answer but was beyond the boundaries of this project. As already discussed, this type is suggested to be late medieval/early post-medieval in date; a similar design has been found at Basingwerk abbey where it has been attributed a fifteenth century date (Lewis 1999, 93 no 752).

The surface of the tiles had been treated to give a variety of colours. Tiles appearing generally yellow in colour have a patchy white slip under a colourless glaze. In most cases the slip appears to have been roughly wiped or brushed over the surface, leaving striations and patches where the underlying red clay can be seen; some fragments appear to have just small patches or narrow bands of slip. Some examples have a glaze with bright green flecks, presumably from the addition of copper oxide to the glaze. None of the slipped examples have a solid green glaze, although some of the unslipped examples do. There are also fragments with a colourless glaze and no slip, thus giving them a brown appearance; it was not possible to determine whether these were from tiles which had areas of green in the glaze or had an overall colourless glaze.

28 Joining fragments of a variant on the above design were found in (785) and (778). The pieces are quite fragmentary and worn but they possibly match and expand design 52/189, which is very uncommon in Chester. A fragment which has a similar if not the same design was found in Gresford parish church, north-east Wales and dated to the fifteenth century (Lewis 1999, 93 no 756). Ill 4.3.6.

Fragments of large square tiles without line-impressed decoration were also found in the assemblage. Many of these were slipped in a similar way to the decorated types.

29 Design 13/108 appears on smaller tiles than numbers 27 and 28 and which are *c* 120 mm square and *c* 28 mm thick. There are 29 fragments of definite examples, weighing 7191 g and two possible examples weighing 736 g. They were generally found without a slip and the glaze colour varies from colourless to green. No date has yet been ascribed to this design in Chester (Rutter 1990c, 232–3) but Lewis places a similar tile from Valle Crucis in the same fifteenth century group as the designs on 27 and 28 (Lewis 1999, 93 no 754). Ill 4.3.6.

Oven (778) overlying cess pit (487)

Sixty fragments (29243 g) came from this feature: 19 from context (778), weighing 9444 g and 41 from (779) weighing 19799 g. Joins were noted between fragments in (778) and pit (487).

Table 4.3.8 Phase VI Plot 2 oven (778): medieval floor tile designs quantified by no of fragments and weight

Design no	No	Wt (g)
Unidentifiable	22	10408
52/189?	2	168
109/337	1	288
109/337?	1	113
119/188	21	9941
13/108	4	1391
189/378	3	1311
4/78	1	192

Phase VII

Plot 2

Fills of cess pit (465)

A total of 53 fragments of floor tile weighing 19386 g came from the fills of this potentially early eighteenth-century pit: 17 (6449 g) from context (463); 18 (6700 g) from (464); 12 (3377 g) from (472) and 6 (2860 g) from (491). As in (778) and (487), fragments carrying design 119/188 predominate. These tiles may have been derived from the underlying deposits in oven (778) and cess pit (487).

Table 4.3.9 Phase VII Plot 2 cess pit (465): medieval floor tile quantified by context, no of fragments and weight

Context	No	Wt (g)
463	17	6449
464	18	6700
472	12	3371
491	6	2860
Total	53	19386

Table 4.3.10 Phase VII Plot 2 cess pit (465): medieval floor tile designs quantified by no of fragments and weight

Design no	No	Wt (g)
Unidentifiable	18	5444
71/97	1	172
106/126	2	543
119/188	14	5908
13/108	1	250
189/378	1	689
2/81	4	532
48/84	1	38
Plain	11	5810

Discussion

It is difficult to suggest the origin of the tiles from (487), (778) and (465). Large groups of medieval floor tiles have not been found on secular sites in the city (except for the Feathers Lane group: *see* below). Their presence in sixteenth-century and later contexts may suggest that they were brought to the site as rubble after the dismantling of floors in a church or other ecclesiastical building at the Dissolution. There was already evidence from Phase V that tiles were reused as a construction material, and those in Phase VI may have also been deliberately acquired to backfill cess pit (487) and construct oven (778). The variety in the dates of the tiles could be used to support this theory but it could equally point to more than one source for the tiles on the site. If the tiles could be associated with the Dissolution a closer date could be applied to the backfilling of pit (487). However, the suggested late medieval date for the larger tiles was also a period when secular domestic households were acquiring tiled floors and thus these may be evidence of secular use. Another alternative is offered by a possible relaid medieval tile floor which was found during the nineteenth century in nearby Feathers Lane (Harrison 1850). The tiles therefore may have been initially reused to floor a building at the site. The discovery of this group clearly adds to the debate on the use of floor tiles in the city beyond ecclesiastical establishments.

27

28

III 4.3.6 Phase VI Plot 2 cess pit (487) fills: medieval floor tile designs.
(Scale 1/3)

29

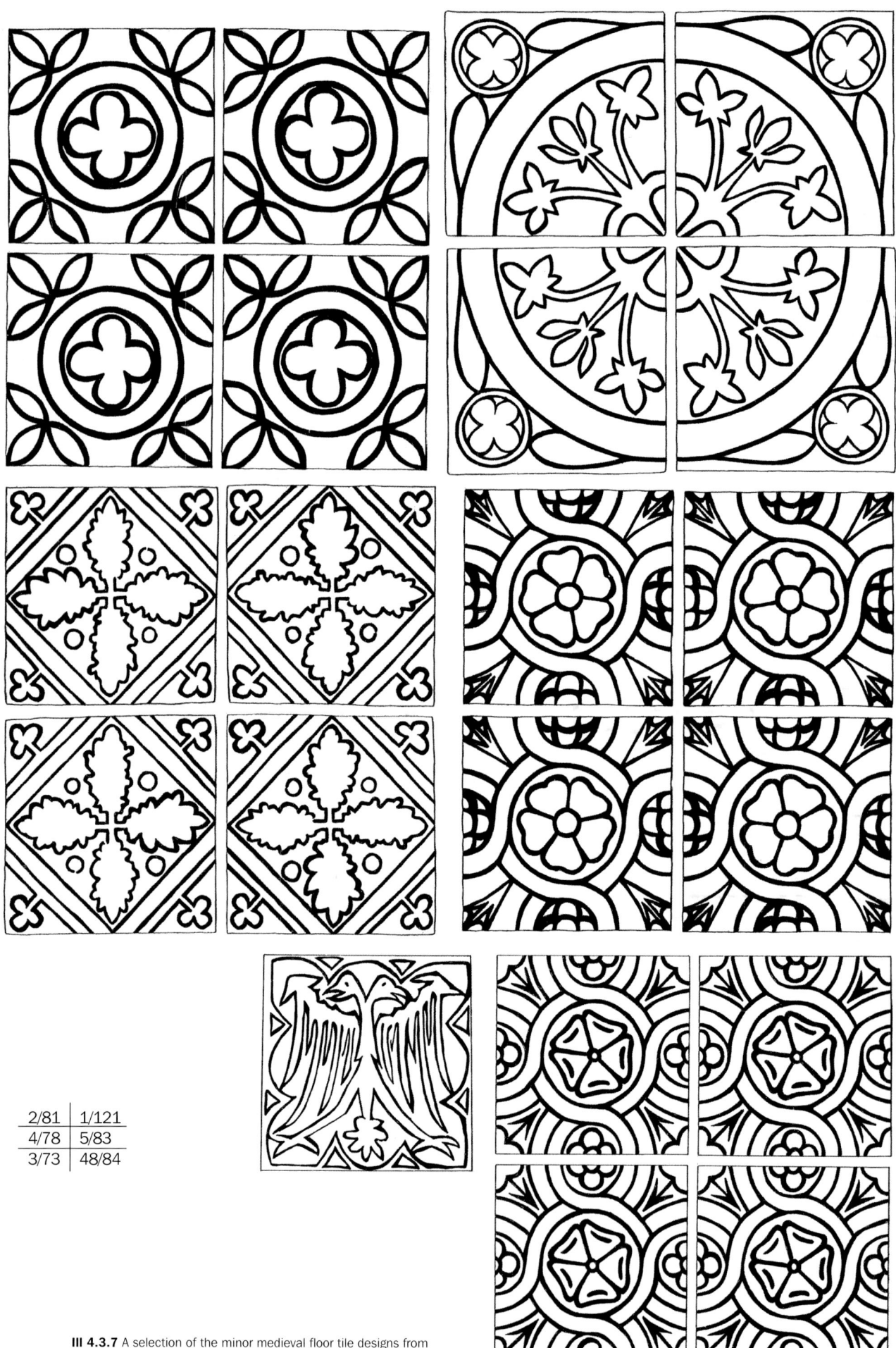

2/81	1/121
4/78	5/83
3/73	48/84

Ill 4.3.7 A selection of the minor medieval floor tile designs from cess pit (487), oven (778) and cess pit (465). (Scale 1/3)

156

48/84 | 109/337
106/126

III 4.3.8 A selection of the minor medieval floor tile designs from cess pit (487), oven (778) and cess pit (465). (Scale 1/3)

Roof tile

Roof tiles from the site were numerous and were represented predominantly by glazed ridge tiles, often decorated with crests, made from pink/white-firing Coal Measure clays. There was some variety in the size and shape of the crests and some unusual forms were present, eg in Phase VIII, context (1449). Red/grey-firing ridge tiles were also present. They were generally part-glazed and some had crests. There was also a smaller quantity of glazed and unglazed flat tiles.

In addition to roof tiles there was a small number of fragments which may have come from various pieces of roof furniture, eg finials from (1495), (1516), (1531), (1567), (1586), (1597) and also fragments of louvre, eg from (1495), although the majority of these came from post-medieval phases and only (1586) was from Phase V.

In general, large, well stratified assemblages of medieval roof tile and roof furniture have rarely been recovered in Chester and, whilst this assemblage was large and broadly stratified, there were no large closely datable assemblages. The principal contribution of the material from this site, in addition to illustrating the range that can be found, was the indication it gave of when ceramic roof tiles started to be deposited in the city: in this regard the sparsity of material before Phase V was striking.

There are two possible comparable groups from the city. The first was found during excavations at the site of the Chester Royal Infirmary in 1998 and contains a large dump of pink/white ridge tiles in the same fabric, size and overall appearance as the assemblage from 25 Bridge Street. It is to be hoped that when this assemblage is studied reference can be made to the present material. A possible waste dump of roof tiles was found during an evaluation by Liverpool Museum Field Archaeology Unit in George Street in 2001. Unusually most of these tiles, including ridge tiles, were in red-firing fabrics and the kiln they represented was obviously not the source of the tiles from the present site. The assemblage published from the Dominican friary was very fragmentary (Rutter 1990a) and it was not possible to examine and compare the material during the course of this project.

Table 4.3.11 Medieval roof tile: total amount quantified by phase, type, no of fragments and weight

Phase	Period	Object	No	Wt (g)
I	Medieval	Roof tile - ridge	2	277
II	Medieval	Roof tile	1	14
	Medieval	Roof tile - ridge?	1	21
	Medieval	Roof tile?	1	40
IV	Medieval	Roof tile - ridge	1	256
V	Medieval	Roof tile	72	4211
	Medieval?	Roof tile	1	82
	Medieval	Roof tile - flat	37	3302
	Medieval	Roof tile - flat?	1	82
	Medieval	Roof tile - ridge	13	1277
	Medieval?	Roof tile - ridge	1	241
	Medieval	Roof tile - ridge?	8	735
	Medieval	Roof tile?	2	78
VI	Medieval	Roof tile	51	3373
	Medieval?	Roof tile	1	93
	Medieval	Roof tile - flat	5	628
	Medieval	Roof tile - flat?	8	960
	Medieval?	Roof tile - flat?	1	188
	Medieval	Roof tile - ridge	61	6719
	Medieval	Roof tile - ridge?	10	732
	Medieval	Roof tile ?ridge	1	10
	Medieval	Roof tile?	1	98
	Medieval?	Roof tile?	2	48
	Medieval	Roof tile? - flat?	1	88
VII	Medieval	Roof tile	42	1653
	Medieval?	Roof tile	4	498
	Medieval	Roof tile - flat	8	776
	Medieval/ Post-medieval	Roof tile - flat	1	243
	Medieval?	Roof tile - flat	1	83
	Medieval	Roof tile - flat?	5	352
	Medieval?	Roof tile - flat?	4	735
	Medieval/ Post-medieval?	Roof tile - flat?	1	188
	Medieval	Roof tile - ridge	67	7311
	Medieval/ Post-medieval	Roof tile - ridge	5	605
	Medieval?	Roof tile - ridge	11	2057
	Medieval	Roof tile - ridge?	10	792
	Medieval?	Roof tile - ridge?	1	82
	Medieval	Roof tile/furniture	2	99
	Medieval	Roof tile/furniture?	1	20
	Medieval	Roof tile?	4	348
	Medieval/ Post-medieval	Roof tile?	2	4
	Medieval?	Roof tile? - ridge?	1	210
VIII	Medieval	Roof tile	43	2606
	Medieval	Roof tile - flat	1	267
	Medieval	Roof tile - flat?	2	35
	Medieval?	Roof tile - flat?	1	56
	Medieval	Roof tile - ridge	54	6101
	Medieval?	Roof tile - ridge	6	572
	Medieval	Roof tile - ridge?	8	644
	Medieval	Roof tile?	1	2
	Medieval	Roof tile? - ridge?	1	9
IX	Medieval	Roof tile	1	26
Total			571	49927

Post-Medieval Ceramic Building Material Julie E C Edwards

Brick

Methodology

No type series of bricks had previously been created for bricks from Chester and it was initially hoped that the assemblage could be used to form the basis of a series for the entire post-medieval period in the city. However, although bricks were sampled throughout the stratigraphic sequence, time limits meant that they could not all be analysed. However, it is hoped that the data from Phase VI can form the basis for future detailed work on the supply and use of brick in Chester.

All the building material, including bricks that were retained, was recorded according to object type by weight and fragment count; complete dimensions were recorded and a general fabric type noted along with comments on general appearance and condition.

There has been little archaeological study of the use of brick in Chester. This is partly because when bricks were found in the past they received little attention and were often not retrieved and also because well stratified assemblages have not been excavated. Exceptions are the discovery of a seventeenth-century brick kiln in Cuppin St in 1986 and a brick fireplace from a post-Dissolution building on the site of the Dominican friary at Nicholas Street Mews in 1988, neither of which has been published. Much of the evidence related to brick use in Chester has been derived from standing buildings and thus is limited to the later seventeenth and eighteenth centuries. Documentary references, however, do indicate earlier use of brick. Although brick is not thought to have been widely used in the city before 1600 (Brown ed 1999, 88), the Bricklayers Company was in existence in the sixteenth century (Simpson 1918, 55). Bricks were also noted in the St Mary-on-the-Hill churchwardens' accounts for the year Easter 1550–Easter 1551 (Earwaker 1898, 234): there was no indication of their use, although it appears that repairs were being carried out to the wall and floor of the church. There is an early reference to a brick wall in Upton, now a suburb of the city, in the Mayor's Books for 1603/4 (CCALS ZMB 28b). In the early seventeenth century the use of brick appears to have been restricted to chimneys and ovens (Brown ed 1999, 88), but a description of the city written in 1620s suggests that some brick houses had been built, and in 1625 Randle Holme is recorded as having built a brick house in Castle Lane (Brown ed 1999, 88). In Chester's rural district, Tattenhall hall, built in 1622, is of brick construction and exceptionally early examples of a brick building in the wider local region are Bach y Graig near Tremeirchion and Plas Clough, Denbigh, built under Flemish influence in 1567–9 (Brunskill 1997, 130–1). In the first half of the seventeenth century there are records of people being fined or restricted in their digging for clay for brick-making: the resulting pits were being left open and causing a nuisance (eg Groombridge 1956, 161, 194, 208). As the century progressed, the city's assembly appeared to be imposing financial controls over clay-digging and brick-making in Cow Lane and Hough Green (CCALS ZAB 2/166).

In the light of this documentary evidence it is perhaps not surprising that Phase VI produced an assemblage of brick consisting of 439 fragments and weighing 240368 g; of these 106 fragments/82893 g were retained for recording and analysis. These were concentrated in the suggested sixteenth-century pit (1073) in Plot 4, and in Plot 2 in the cess pit (487), the succeeding oven (778) and the overlying layer (776); the cess pit was backfilled in the sixteenth or very early seventeenth century and the final two contexts in the fill are dated to the early seventeenth century. As these deposits potentially contained the earliest material evidence yet found for brick in the city, it was decided, given the limited resources, to only publish the information from these groups. The discarded material from all phases was recorded by weight and fragment count; ideally fabric types should have been recorded as well but this was not possible. The totals are published below so that if excavations take place in a similar Row backland in the future the potential size of the assemblage can be anticipated and an appropriate strategy drawn up to record the material. When totalled the discarded and retained figures do show some differences in distribution across the site.

Table 4.4.1 Discarded post-medieval ceramic building material quantified by phase, no of fragments and weight

Phase	No	Wt (g)
III	1	105
V	30	13945
VI	305	136985
VII	471	236761
VIII	197	67162
IX	1094	819105
X	825	712231

Table 4.4.2 Range of discarded post-medieval ceramic building material quantified by form, no of fragments and weight

Form	No	Wt (g)
Brick	2544	1886558
Brick/Tile	42	10465
Brick?	2	1520
Chimney	2	1305
Drainpipe	238	40624
Floor tile	2	0
Floor/roof tile	46	0
Roof tile	4	1120
Roof tile - ridge	11	0
Tile	124	80837
Tile/Indet	2	175
Tile?	1	280
Indet	1	5

Table 4.4.3 Retained post-medieval brick quantified by phase, no of fragments and weight

Phase	No	Wt (g)
I	2	20
V	8	11425
VI	106	82893
VII	81	40956
VIII	57	68949
IX	66	149699
X	43	119410

Table 4.4.4 Discarded post-medieval brick quantified by phase, no of fragments and weight

Phase	No	Wt (g)
V	8	4355
VI	333	157475
VII	419	239126
VIII	186	65054
IX	954	775955
IX	644	644593

Table 4.4.5 Retained post-medieval brick quantified by plot, no of fragments and weight

Plot	No	Wt (g)
1	71	122935
2	109	159239
3	28	29596
4	128	121284
5	2	6693
6	25	33605

Table 4.4.6 Discarded brick quantified by plot, no of fragments and weight

Plot	No	Wt (g)
1	703	92395
2	592	508705
3	109	108173
4	59	34682
5	1	125
6	1080	1142478

When the discarded and retained totals for each phase were examined (*see* Tables 4.4.3–.4) there was a huge increase between Phases V and VI. When it was taken into account that over 50% of the Phase V retained brick was intrusive post-medieval material and the remainder was from insecurely stratified contexts, Phase VI could be said to see the introduction of brick into the archaeological record. Without accurate records for all the bricks found, the only further observation that can be made is that there was a further increase in Phase VII but a decreased number of bricks in Phase VIII before another increase in Phase IX. These figures reflect activity on the site regarding demolition and dumping rather than actual use, but they do display the increasing occurrence of brick which might have been expected in the city centre during the post-medieval period.

Plots 1, 2 and 6 produced the greatest numbers of bricks overall (Tables 4.4.5–.6) but amongst the bricks which were retained Plots 2 and 4 dominated, suggesting there was a clear bias in retention with bricks being kept from good deposits rather than perhaps make-up layers.

Fabrics

The bricks from Phase VI were laid out and grouped according to colour, hardness of fabric and range/quantity/size of inclusions. Six broad groups were observed and were recorded as BF 1–BF 6. The bricks from Phases VII and VIII were identified using these six groupings and two additional groupings were identified in Phase VII, but any bricks which differed from these eight were left unclassified, as were those from Phase IX.

The basic inclusions are all very similar, which was perhaps to be expected given that the documentary sources suggest that clay-digging for bricks was taking place within and just outside the walls of the city. An unusual feature is the presence of white Coal Measures clay in some examples. White clay is not known to outcrop in the city nor in the immediate vicinity: the nearest areas where these clays are known to have been exploited are in Flintshire, although there is a small area to the south of the city at Aldersey Green and Edgerley. It is possible that the white clay was brought into the city for other purposes and found its way accidentally into the brick clay whilst being used at the same sites as the brick-making; alternatively some of the red clays for bricks were perhaps being brought into the city from Coal Measure areas. The presence of very sparse fragments of granite in BF 1 is presumably attributable to erratics in the boulder clay. Further analysis of the brick fabrics is required in order to determine the source of the clays.

Further work is needed on defining these fabric groups. Some divisions are based on colour and hardness of fabric, both of which may be the result of kiln conditions and positioning within the kiln, and it is possible that some of the groups could be amalgamated. Early brick-making in the city appears to have been carried out when and where there was a need, so perhaps little uniformity need be expected. It was not until the second half of the seventeenth century that production was concentrated in the two areas of Hough Green and Cow Lane, but how uniform that production was is currently unclear. It is difficult to determine whether the differences between bricks are due to different makers or whether the bricks were used in different types of structure or whether there was a chronological factor at work. The answers require further and larger assemblages to be examined, but the number of similar bricks in the assemblages chosen here suggests that the assemblages represent different structures.

A brief examination of the brick samples from the Cuppin Street 1986 and Nicholas Street Mews 1988 excavations was made and there is a clear difference between these two assemblages. The Cuppin Street samples are quite uniform in finish and size and are larger in length and width than the examples from Phase VI on the 25 Bridge Street site. It is not until Phases VIII and IX that bricks of a similar length (*c* 240 mm) were recorded, although the Phase VII assemblage is very fragmentary and no complete bricks survive. The Nicholas Street Mews

group, however, contains a comparable range of sizes and fabric variations to the Phase VI assemblage, in particular bricks at the thinner end of the size range (*c* 40 mm).

The bricks all carry a variety of surface marks resulting from the manufacturing process. All have obvious 'upper' and 'lower' surfaces, with the upper being smoothed in some fashion and the lower often being uneven with straw or grass impressions; sometimes sand and small fragments of clay are embedded in the surface. The most common marks are parallel lines or scratches which appear to be the result of a wire being used to remove excess clay from the upper surface of the brick lengthwise (*see* Brunskill 1997, 24). On some examples the scratches curve at one end, as though finished with a flourish or sweep to one side. Similar parallel but vertical scratches are often present on the stretcher and header faces. Sometimes the smoothing on the sides stops short of the base, leaving an irregular upstanding ridge of clay running around the lower edges, as though the clay has bulged out under pressure. Distinct lines of smoothing in the same position on some examples suggest that this excess clay had sometimes been removed with a blade. A similar feature has been noted on frame-made bricks (Smith 1985, 42–3, fig 11).

On some examples one header face appears to have been smoothed but there are no scratch marks. Other faces appear roughly smoothed as though an implement had been swept along the side leaving bands of smoothing amidst uneven patches where bulges in the clay stood proud of the surface. Occasionally the upper surface is treated in the same manner, leaving upswept patches of clay. Both Brunskill (1997, 24) and Smith (1985, 42) describe the use of a stick to remove excess clay in addition to or instead of a wire.

A mark that occurs more in later phases but is nevertheless present in Phase VI is a long shallow gouge in the base which fans out at one end and is filled with parallel scratches across its width; the clay along one side of this mark appears to have been pushed over it, suggesting that something had been pushed under the brick to move it when the clay was still soft. Other marks include longitudinal pressure marks where bricks had been stacked on their sides whilst drying; these tend to be at an angle across the side. Such stacking marks are not common amongst this assemblage.

The variety of surface features suggests that different manufacturing methods were present, with some bricks shaped using a frame pushed over a lump of clay, as described by Smith, while others may have been moulded, with possibly different moulding methods being involved. Some of the examples which had smoothed surfaces without any trace of wire marks may have been slop-moulded, whilst others have been stock-moulded (Brunskill 1997, 24). Clearly further examination and comparative work is required in order to identify and confirm the methods of manufacture and to explore the introduction of brick building to Chester.

BF 1 A dull reddish brown in colour. The fabric is soft with a rough, slightly powdery feel and an irregular to hackly texture; abundant inclusions of ill-sorted quartz which vary from fine to coarse and are subangular and rounded, opaque white, colourless or clear; sparse mica mainly white but brown–gold is also present; moderate to sparse ill-sorted iron-rich black sub-angular fragments fine to coarse in size; sparse very coarse sandstone fragments and very sparse coarse angular granite fragments.

BF 2 A bright orange/red fabric which is hard with a rough feel and an irregular texture; fine to medium abundant and ill-sorted sub-angular opaque white, clear, colourless or pink stained quartz; moderate fine to medium irregular shaped black iron-rich fragments; sparse very coarse sub-rounded sandstone fragments; sparse sub-rounded coarse opaque white quartz fragments.

BF 3 A dark reddish brown colour with a hard fabric with a rough feel and a hackly texture. Inclusions consist of abundant ill-sorted fine to medium and moderate coarse quartz which is opaque white, clear or colourless; moderate fine to medium irregular and sub-rounded black or red iron-rich fragments; sparse very coarse irregularly shaped white clay pieces; sparse, coarse, sub-rounded sandstone fragments.

BF 5 A dark red fabric which is hard with a harsh feel and an irregular to hackly texture; abundant inclusions of ill-sorted quartz which vary from fine to medium and are sub-angular and angular, opaque white, colourless or clear; moderate angular and rounded opaque white medium to very coarse quartz fragments; angular and rounded white quartz fragments up to 2 mm; moderate fine to coarse angular and sub-angular iron-rich red or black fragments; sparse coarse to very coarse sub-angular sandstone fragments; sparse irregular coarse to very coarse pieces of white clay.

BF 6 A dull reddish brown in colour with streaks of pale red to buff. The fabric is hard with a rough feel and an irregular texture. Inclusions consist of abundant fine to coarse rounded and sub-angular opaque white, clear, colourless quartz; moderate fine to coarse irregular and sub-rounded black iron-rich fragments; sparse coarse lenses of fine red clay and irregular shaped fine to coarse pieces of white clay; sparse very coarse sub-rounded opaque white quartz.

Phase VI

Plot 2

Fills of cess pit (487)

The assemblage from the backfill of cess pit (487) is potentially the most interesting on the site. The date of the pottery from this feature and the absence of clay tobacco pipes suggest that it was backfilled sometime in the sixteenth century or in the very early years of the seventeenth century at the latest. The date at which the bricks were made is harder to determine, and it is possible that they came from a late medieval building, if not a sixteenth-century one. In general the edges of the bricks appear relatively sharp and the retained pieces whilst broken are not abraded, suggesting that they were part of a primary deposit rather than redeposited rubble. The brick assemblage is thus potentially the earliest to be retrieved from the city, and it was regrettable that a large proportion of it, including the bricks from the lowest fill, (806), was discarded before it could be examined in detail.

Two types of fabric are present amongst the retained assemblage. There is one example of BF 1, but the rest are in BF 5. Sizes are recorded in Table 4.4.7 below.

Table 4.4.7 Phase VI Plot 2 cess pit (487) fills: retained post-medieval brick quantified by context, fabric, no of fragments and weight, with dimensions

Context	Fabric	No	Wt (g)	L (mm)	W (mm)	Th (mm)
785	BF5	1	657	0	105	50
797	BF5	1	189	0	0	55
797	BF5	1	431	0	110	55
797	BF5	1	854	0	0	58
797	BF5	1	970	0	108	50
798	BF5	1	577	0	110	54
791	BF1	1	2260	215	105	55
Total		7	5938			

Table 4.4.8 Phase VI Plot 2 cess pit (487) fills: discarded post-medieval brick quantified by context, no of fragments and weight

Context	No	Wt (g)
785	6	1540
786	1	125
787	11	9850
788	0	4660
791	9	5140
797	11	5945
798	3	6240
806	5	1600
Total	46	35100

Oven (778) overlying pit (487)

As discussed above, the oven (778) was partly constructed from reused floor tiles of a similar type to those found in cess pit (487); indeed, there are joining fragments from (785) in the pit and oven (778). It is therefore possible that some or all of the bricks in the oven were also reused and may have come from the same source as those in the cess pit. However, although two pieces of brick are similar to an example from the pit, in general the retained bricks from the oven differ from the retained bricks from the pit. One type, BF 2, which appeared in greater quantity in layer (776) overlying the oven, is noticeably thinner than those in the cess pit and the upper surface is more concave. Single bricks often vary in thickness by as much as 10 mm across their width so that some are trapezoidal in section. Whilst some bricks have traces of blackening and discoloration of one end or side, none are badly burnt or vitrified and few appear to have been in direct contact with the heat source.

Table 4.4.9 Phase VI Plot 2 oven (778): retained post-medieval brick quantified by context, fabric, no of fragments and weight, with dimensions

Context	Fabric	No	Wt (g)	L (mm)	W (mm)	Th (mm)
778	BF 1	1	2341	0	110	60
778	BF 1	1	1745	0	110	58
778	BF 2	1	1604	0	107	47
778	BF 3	2	1518	230	110	60
779	BF 3	1	1274	0	115	55
779	BF 1	1	190	0	0	45
Total		7	8672			

Table 4.4.10 Phase VI Plot 2 oven (778): discarded post-medieval brick quantified by context, no of fragments and weight

Context	No	Wt (g)
778	1	1530
779	8	6260
Total	9	7790

Layer (776)

A total of 36 bricks, weighing over 31,000 g, were found in layer (776). They may have come from the oven, although only one fragment shows any sign of contact with a fire. The deposit has an increased number of BF 2 and BF 5 type bricks, similar to those from cess pit (487). One additional type is also present, BF 6, which is distinctive for having a marbled appearance caused by red and pinkish buff to white clay. Only four examples of this type were noted among the retained bricks recorded from Phases V–VI; three of them were in Phase VI, the other one in Phase VIII. The layer was dated on the pottery present to the sixteenth or early seventeenth century; fragments of blackware in the underlying oven suggested the later date. There were no clay pipes or vessel glass.

Table 4.4.11 Phase VI Plot 2 layer (776): retained post-medieval brick quantified by context, fabric, no of fragments and weight, with dimensions

Context	Fabric	No	Wt (g)	L (mm)	W (mm)	Th (mm)
776	BF 1	1	1400	0	107	47
776	BF 2	1	2590	224	106	55
776	BF 2	1	1236	0	94	44
776	BF 2	1	1131	0	108	47
776	BF 2	1	1239	0	112	50
776	BF 2	1	466	0	109	42
776	BF 2	1	2382	220	105	60
776	BF 5	1	911	0	105	50
776	BF 5	1	984	0	93	50
776	BF 5	1	1257	0	108	46
776	BF 5	1	508	0	110	45
776	BF 6	1	615	0	108	41
Total		12	14719			

Table 4.4.12 Phase VI Plot 2 layer (776): discarded post-medieval brick quantified by context, no of fragments and weight

Context	No	Wt g
776	23	16990

Plot 4

Fill of pit (1073)

The fill of this pit, (1567), produced one of the largest assemblages of bricks from Phase VI, and all those found appear to have been retained. The assemblage largely consists of fabrics BF 1 and BF 3 and, whilst fragmentary, they are generally thicker than those from cess pit (487), with a range between 55 and 80 mm; none with complete lengths survived. The assemblage is in a much poorer condition than the other brick groups and was possibly redeposited rubble rather than a primary deposit of demolition debris. The pit also contained a small group of pottery ranging in date from the late fifteenth century to *c* 1600; there were no clay pipes or glass vessels. This suggests that the bricks came from a structure demolished before the early seventeenth century.

Table 4.4.13 Phase VI Plot 4 pit (1073): post-medieval brick quantified by fabric, no of fragments and weight

Fabric	No	Wt (g)	L (mm)	W (mm)	Th (mm)
BF 1	1	1200	0	112	75
BF 1	1	1006	0	110	65
BF 1	1	627	0	0	65
BF 1	1	717	0	0	70
BF 1	1	571	0	112	60
BF 1	1	449	0	0	0
BF 1	1	908	0	112	60
BF 1	1	695	0	114	55
BF 1	1	501	0	0	0
BF 1	1	453	0	0	80
BF 1	1	173	0	0	0
BF 1	1	453	0	0	0
BF 1	1	388	0	0	66
BF 1	1	257	0	0	0
BF 1	1	240	0	0	0
BF 1	1	335	0	0	65
BF 1	1	301	0	0	73
BF 1	1	218	0	0	0
BF 1	1	42	0	0	0
BF 1	1	238	0	0	0
BF 1	1	515	0	110	0
BF 1	1	442	0	0	0
BF 1	1	522	0	0	70
BF 1	1	382	0	0	68
BF 1	1	123	0	0	0
BF 1	1	278	0	0	77
BF 1	13	1145	0	0	0
BF 1?	1	397	0	0	67
BF 1?	1	367	0	0	60
BF 1?	1	232	0	0	65
BF 1?	1	53	0	0	0
BF 1?	2	74	0	0	0
BF 3	1	342	0	0	68
BF 3	1	596	0	0	0
BF 3	1	397	0	0	0
BF 3	1	456	0	0	68
BF 3	1	535	0	0	68
BF 3	1	327	0	0	77
BF 3	1	286	0	0	70
BF 3	1	258	0	0	68
BF 3	1	55	0	0	0
BF 6?	1	186	0	0	0
Total	55	17740			

Roof tile

The dating and extent of use of ceramic roof tiles in the post-medieval period is unclear. In 1671 regulations were introduced to ban the use of thatch as a roofing material in Foregate Street, Eastgate Street, Northgate Street, Watergate Street and Bridge Street 'for ornament and for securing the City from fire' (CCALS ZAB 2/170v; ZA/B/ 2/170v–171): roofs were to be slated or tiled. This order suggests that thatch was still in use in the city and that roofing had perhaps changed little from the medieval period. It is perhaps significant that appearance was the first reason given and the named streets were the principal ones in the city: whilst fire was a real threat the sight of thatched buildings in the centre of the city was clearly a concern. That slate was in use in the medieval period is evident from archaeological finds and from documentary references to slates being brought by sea from Ogwen (eg Hewitt 1929, 140). The extent of use, however, is unclear. It is possible that it was restricted to prestigious buildings or buildings belonging to the wealthier inhabitants of the city (Hewitt refers to its use at Chester castle) but in the later medieval and early post-medieval period its use was possibly more common (Brown ed 1999, 74 and 88).

The reference to tiles as well as slate suggests there was a difference between the two and the assumption is that ceramic tiles were being stipulated. The identification of the types of ceramic roof tile in use in the broad medieval period is comparatively straightforward, although their production span is unclear, but the types of tile being produced in the periods covered by Phase VI and the early part of Phase VII are poorly understood. Ideally a detailed analysis and comparison of material from different phases and deposits would have been carried out in an attempt to elucidate chronological changes in fabric, form and surface treatment and to examine questions of residuality. However, this was not possible within the timeframe of the project. What is clear is the appearance in Phase VI of ridge tiles in a fine sandy red-firing fabric. These tiles are thicker than the medieval red- or grey-firing ridge tiles, and unlike the medieval types they are usually totally oxidised. A colourless glaze covers all or part of the upper surface; the glaze is rarely reduced and gives a glossy orange appearance. When these tiles first came into use is uncertain and they may be late medieval in date: they have therefore been catalogued as medieval/post-medieval. It is also unclear how far flat tiles continued in use into the post-medieval period and whether a post-medieval type can be recognised.

One clearly post-medieval tile was easily recognisable: the black-glazed ridge tiles made from hard, dark red Coal Measure clays that were often streaked with white clay. These tiles first appeared in Phase VII deposits; further work is required to establish where these tiles were made but Buckley is the most likely source.

Roof slates and ceramic ridge tiles are thus the principal roofing materials found on post-medieval excavations in Chester. It can be suggested that it was preferable to use North Wales slates or other materials for the sides of roofs and that the use of ceramic tiles was, as in the medieval period, largely restricted to ridge tiles. However the archaeological evidence requires further examination to establish the validity of this idea.

Table 4.4.14 Retained post-medieval roof tile quantified by phase, type, no of fragments and weight

Phase	Period	Object	No	Wt (g)
VII	Post-medieval	Roof tile	2	282
	Post-medieval?	Roof tile	1	147
	Post-medieval	Roof tile - ridge	2	60
	Post-medieval?	Roof tile - ridge	2	1013
	Post-medieval?	Roof tile - ridge?	1	511
VIII	Post-medieval	Roof tile	1	13
	Post-medieval?	Roof tile - flat?	1	47
	Post-medieval?	Roof tile - flat?	3	422
	Post-medieval	Roof tile - ridge	7	1412
	Post-medieval?	Roof tile - ridge	14	5509
	Post-medieval	Roof tile - ridge?	6	613
	Post-medieval?	Roof tile - ridge?	2	195
IX	Post-medieval	Roof tile - ridge	22	10160
	Post-medieval	Roof tile - ridge?	1	123
X	Post-medieval	Roof tile - ridge	15	3374
	Post-medieval?	Roof tile - ridge	1	32
	Post-medieval	Roof tile - ridge?	4	310
	Post-medieval	Roof tile?	1	24
Total			86	24247

Acknowledgements

I am grateful to Sue Andrew, Janet Axworthy and the late Elizabeth Brotherton-Ratcliffe for advice and help on various tile designs. Liz Bailey, John Bailey, David Cartwright, Susan Chambers, the late Geoff Rhodes and Simon Skelling all carried out tasks essential to the recording of the ceramic building material, and I am very grateful to them for giving up their time.

Roman Pottery

Samian   Margaret Ward

Introduction

RESOURCES did not allow for detailed work on the stamped and decorated ware to be undertaken, but a brief resumé is given here of those items considered to warrant publication.

The abbreviations SG, CG and EG are used in the tables and diagrams to indicate vessels which were produced in South Gaulish, Central Gaulish and East Gaulish workshops respectively. 'Ind' denotes a vessel of indeterminate form. For other terminology, *see* Bulmer 1979 and Webster 1996.

Where date ranges, rather than epochs such as 'Hadrianic–Antonine,' have been given, these should not be thought of as more precise. They were employed to facilitate detailed analysis of the material from each phase. A table and histogram are presented to summarise the forms, fabrics and date-ranges of the collection. Maximum numbers of vessels are given, since the estimation of minimum numbers is difficult and probably misleading, particularly in the case of collections containing a large proportion of fragments in poor condition.

Summary

The total of 452 sherds represented a maximum of 425 vessels. 118 vessels (28%) were from South Gaul, 301 vessels (71%) were from Central Gaul and only six vessels (1%) were East Gaulish. Table 5.1.1 gives details of the forms of vessel represented, and Ill 5.1.1 represents their date ranges.

In all, eleven vessels could have been produced before the Flavian period, but it is likely that most, if not all, of these were of Flavian origin. There were around ninety moulded bowls from South and Central Gaul. Seven or eight of the South Gaulish bowls were of form Dr 29 which was produced largely before *c* AD 85/90.

Among the material from second-century Central Gaul, fifteen vessels were likely to have been produced at Les Martres-de-Veyre, where activity was at its height in the Trajanic period. There were seven or more vessels which are likely to have been of Hadrianic origin in Central Gaul and one from South Gaul (Montans).

Of all the vessels represented, 25% was produced later than *c* 150 and 14% after *c* 160. Amongst these were seven mortaria of forms 45 and 43 which were made only after *c* 170: two were from East Gaul. Of the total of six East Gaulish vessels, two or three were produced at Rheinzabern and one or two at Trier in the period *c* 160/180–220/260. Another was a dish apparently made at La Madeleine in the Hadrianic–early Antonine period, and one was of uncertain form and origin in the second century. The La Madeleine piece was recovered from Phase IIb (1179); the remainder were found in later phases.

5

PORTABLE ARTEFACTS

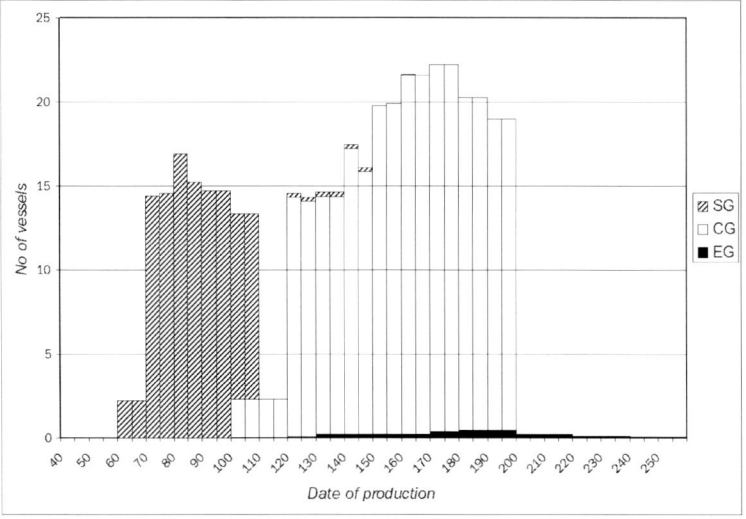

Table 5.1.1 Samian vessel forms quantified by fabric and max no of vessels

Form	SG	CG	EG	Total
C 11	1			1
C15		2		2
C 21		1		1
C 23		1		1
15/17 or 18	1			1
15/17R	1			1
15/17R or 18R	1			1
18 or 18R	3			3
18 or 18/31	1			1
18/31	2	2		4
18/31 or 31		1	1	2
18/31R		20		20
18/31R or 31R		10		10
18R	4			4
18R or 18/31R	2			2
31		15		15
31 or 31R		7		7
31R		22		22
31R group			1	1
22	1			1
27	12	6		18
33	6	51	1	58
35		1		1
36	4	5		9
38		4		4
40		1		1
43		1		1
45		4	2	6
46 or C 15		1		1
79		4		4
81		1		1
O&P pl 55.13		1		1
Bowl		2		2
Cup		1		1
Dish	2	9		11
Enclosed	1	3		4
Ind	40	68	1	109
29	6			6
29 or 37	1			1
30	3	4		7
30 or 37		3		3
37	26	50		76

There were eight or nine potters' stamps, four of them certainly Antonine. One was a rosette stamp and at least six had letters surviving which may prove attributable to specific potters. One or two were moulded bowls: see nos 13 and 20 in the styles of Butrio (?) and Advocisus.

The decorated bowls listed below have been selected largely for their significance in regard to our understanding of the site. The range of Central Gaulish potters represented was remarkably limited. Those recorded were attributed possibly to Butrio, who worked primarily under Hadrian; to the earlier- to mid-Antonine potters Albucius or Cinnamus (two bowls); and to those potters working exclusively after *c* 160, Casurius (two bowls) and Advocisus.

Other decorated fragments found in post-Roman contexts and not listed were attributable to the primarily Hadrianic potters Butrio and Potter X-5; the early-Antonine association of Cerialis-Cinnamus (two bowls including ovolo B144) and the standard style of Cinnamus (ovolo B143 and two examples of B231); and those potters working after *c* 160, Casurius and Iullinus or (more probably) Do(v)eccus.

The scrappy nature of the collection is reflected in the fact that as much as 25% comprised fragments of indeterminate form. Twenty-three vessels (in Phase II and later contexts) showed signs of wear from use, including one East Gaulish mortarium found in Phase V (1615). There were no graffiti, but one piece showed 'ownership marks' (no 3). Two vessels had seen repair work of the round, drilled variety (no 16) and, with traces of lead riveting, no 11). There were no definitely reworked pieces such as spindle whorls or counters, although there may be a badly battered example of the latter in Phase V (no 14). Two pieces in Phase VII appear to have been rubbed down or filed, and one of these may itself have been used as a rubber (*see* nos 17–18). Of the whole assemblage, 7% was burnt; all of it was found in Phase II or later contexts.

Phases I and IIa

Phase Ic

1 South Gaulish Dr 37; fragment of goose (probably Oswald 2289 rather than 2293) in a scroll with part of a leaf; apparently from the same bowl as two fragments in Phase III/IV (115) and Phase IV (119); (142). SF 10169. Flavian or Flavian–Trajanic. Ill 5.1.2.1.

2 South Gaulish Dr 30; adjoining rim and wall sherd with an ovolo whose long tongue has a trifid tip bent left, as used by Albanus iii, Amandus, Bassus, etc (*cf* Mees 1995, Taf 1.8; 6.2;10.8); below, divided panelling with two gladiators (Oswald 1007 and 1008) above a compartment filled with arrowheads and diagonal wavy lines. (1245); SF 10170. *c* 85–10. Ill 5.1.2.2.

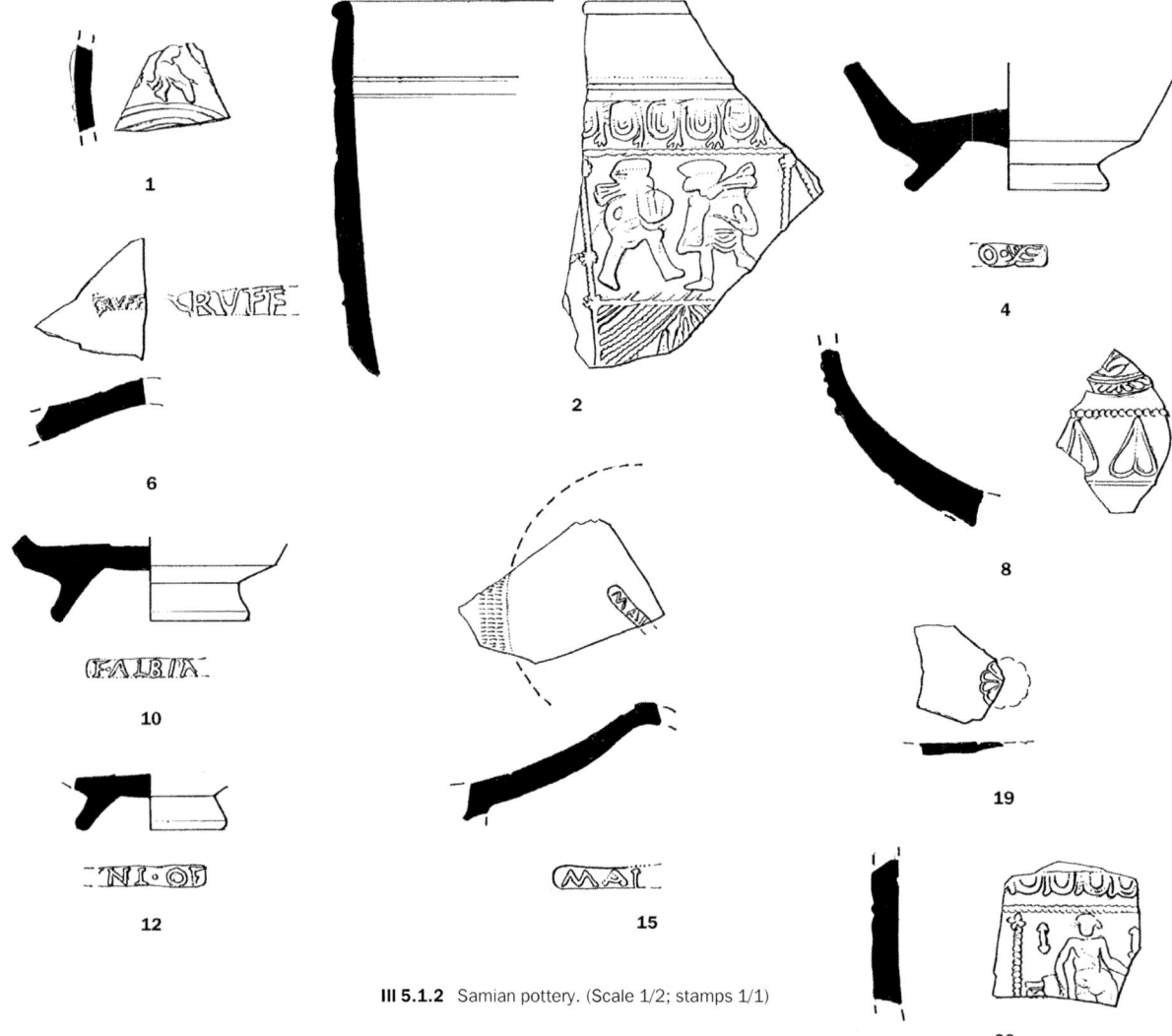

Ill 5.1.2 Samian pottery. (Scale 1/2; stamps 1/1)

Phase Ie

3   Central Gaulish Dr 31. The very worn footring has broken at one of at least two nicks which had been incised on the standing surface, probably as a mark of ownership. (1227). *c* 150–200.

4   Central Gaulish cup (probably form 33) with a fragment only of the potter's stamp reading]O with a decorative leaf. (1227); SF 8916. Trajanic–Hadrianic. Ill 5.1.2.4.

Phase IIa

5   Central Gaulish Dr 37; badly battered fragment of decoration: a vertical astragaloid border (Rogers A9) lies next to an indistinct group of figures. (1219). Probably the style of Cinnamus or Albucius, but at any rate in the range *c* 140–80.

Post-Roman phases

6   Central Gaulish Dr 18/31R; fragment only of the basal stamp reads RVFF[. (1135): Phase IIb; SF 8840. Probably a stamp of Ruffus ii and from Lezoux in the period *c* 130–60. Ill 5.1.2.6.

7   Central Gaulish Dr 37; the ovolo Rogers B223 lacking the core, along with a border which was probably A9. (1138): Phase IIb. Probably the style of Cinnamus rather than Casurius, in the period *c* 155–80.

8   Central Gaulish Dr 37; panelling with beadrow, festoon and leaf (Rogers J56) as used by Casurius. (1179): Phase IIb; SF 10171. *c* 160–90. Ill 5.1.2.8.

9   Central Gaulish Dr 37; badly blurred ovolo, probably Rogers B176, above beadrow A3. (1179): Phase IIb. Style of Casurius, *c* 160–190, but not from the same bowl as no 8.

10   Central Gaulish Dr 33; basal stamp F.ALBIN[. (1018): Phase III; SF 8748. Presumably a product of the Albinus who worked at Lezoux in the Hadrianic–Antonine period. Ill 5.1.2.10.

11   Central Gaulish Dr 18/31R; rimsherd broken at a round rivet- hole which retains traces of lead from the rivet. (974): Phase IV. *c* AD 120–60.

12   Central Gaulish Dr 33; stamped]ANI.OF. (1119): Phase IV; SF 9132. The product of a potter working at Lezoux in the Hadrianic–Antonine period. Ill 5.1.2.12.

13   Central Gaulish Dr 37; part of an ovolo and a corded border below, together with only a fragment which could perhaps represent an intra-decorative stamp of Butrio (*cf* S&S pl 60.679). (57): Phase V. *c* 125–45.

14   Central Gaulish Dr 37; fragment only of an ovolo above a wavy-line border and a double festoon. Possibly reworked as a counter, but the piece has been badly battered. (700): Phase V. *c* 120–60.

15 Central Gaulish Dr 31R; basal sherd stamped MAI[. (1660): Phase V; SF 9460. Probably the work of Maior i at Lezoux, *c* 160–200. Ill 5.1.2.15.

16 South Gaulish Dr 29; fragment only of a scroll, broken at a rivet-hole of the round, drilled variety. (697): Phase VI. Produced in the range *c* 60–85.

17 Central Gaulish Dr 37; thick basal sherd; parts of the edges appear to have been rubbed down. (1629): Phase VII. *c* 120–200.

18 Central Gaulish Dr 37. The edges and surfaces appear to have been rubbed down and the piece may itself have been used as a rubber. (1887): Phase VII. *c* 120–200.

19 Central Gaulish Dr 46 or Curle 15; base stamped with a rosette as used in the Hadrianic–Antonine period at Lezoux. (1112): Phase VIII; SF 10172. Ill 5.1.2.19.

20 Central Gaulish Dr 30; ovolo Rogers B102 and panelling; beaded borders (A2) with blurred ornaments at the junctions (C114) and filling motifs (Rogers U104). The indistinct figure is classified as Venus by Oswald (type 293A) and as a young satyr by Déchelette (type 325). For all these motifs on form 30, see S&S pl 113.26 from London; an intra-decorative advertisement stamp reads [ADVOCI]SI. (337): Phase IX; SF 9930. Advocisus worked at Lezoux in the period *c* 160–90. Ill 5.1.2.20.

Fine and coarse wares   Alison Jones

Methodology

The pottery was assessed in terms of quantity, range, condition, source and date range. Where macroscopic identification was insufficient, fabrics were examined using a binocular microscope at x20 magnification and were compared with samples from the Chester Roman pottery fabric reference collection. Where applicable, fabrics were also identified by National Roman Fabric Reference Collection (NRFRC) fabric code (Tomber & Dore 1998). Pottery was quantified and recorded by sherd count and weight on an MS Access database. The report comprises a brief description of the character of the assemblage, organised by phase, followed by discussion. The catalogues comprise only those sherds chosen for illustration.

Introduction

The site produced 4784 sherds with a weight of 107,939 g (*see* Table 5.1.2). Hand-collection produced 4060 sherds/104734 g (85% by sherd count and 97% by weight of the assemblage); the remaining 714 sherds/3051 g came from wet-sieving.

Table 5.1.2 Roman pottery: total amount quantified by (sub-) phase, no of sherds and weight

Phase	Sub-phase	Incl amphorae			Excl amphorae		
		No	Wt (g)	Average sherd wt (g)	No	Wt (g)	Average sherd wt (g)
I	Ia	13	93	7.15	13	93	7.15
	Ib	11	377	34.27	9	322	35.78
	Ic	113	2514	22.25	107	1498	14
	Id	207	2184	10.55	202	1948	9.64
	Ie	131	2291	17.49	122	1585	12.99
I total		475	7459	15.7	453	5446	12.02
II	IIa	401	12169	30.35	364	6510	17.88
	II	464	13219	28.49	418	6958	16.65
	IIc	216	8618	39.9	185	4767	25.77
II total		1081	34006	31.45	967	18235	18.85
III		391	12121	31	338	5821	17.22
III/IV		27	515	19.07	24	419	17.46
IV		444	8400	18.92	398	5439	13.67
V		633	13634	21.54	564	8788	15.58
V/VI		3	262	87.33	2	19	9.5
VI		406	6747	16.62	373	4942	13.25
VII		390	5847	14.99	362	4539	12.54
VIII		313	5220	16.68	282	3568	12.65
IX		189	2673	14.14	175	1886	10.78
IX/X		5	37	7.4	3	17	5.67
X		196	4455	22.73	174	2852	16.39
u/s		231	6563	28.41	205	3733	18.21
Total		4784	107939	22.56	4320	65704	15.21

The Roman phases, I and IIa, together produced 876 sherds/19,628 g (18% by sherd count and weight of the total assemblage). The post-Roman phases (IIb to X) produced 3677 sherds/81,748 g; 231 sherds/6563 g were unstratified. The post-Roman and unstratified assemblage comprised 82% by sherd count and weight of the site total. This was comparable to the Roman ceramic building material assemblage, where 90% by fragment count and weight came from post-Roman contexts or was unstratified.

Phase I

Only 10% by sherd count and 7% by weight of the entire pottery assemblage came from Phase. It comprises 475 sherds/7459 g with an average sherd weight (including amphorae) of 15.7 g, or of 12.02 g excluding amphorae, the bulk of which came from sub-phases Ic, Id and Ie. In comparison, the CBM assemblage from Phase I produced only 2% by fragment count and 4% by weight of the site total. A considerable proportion of the Phase I assemblage was retrieved from wet-sieving, comprising 219 sherds/1114 g.

Phase Ia
Description
All of the pottery from this sub-phase came from Evaluation Trenches B, C and D. Samples produced 2 sherds/3 g (15% by sherd count and 3% by weight of the sub-phase Ia total).

The stratigraphically earliest context in Trench B, deposit (155), which lay directly above the natural subsoil, produced 3 sherds/37 g of grey ware, including the body sherd of an indented ?beaker with vertical burnishing on the exterior and a girth groove on the shoulder. The form is presumably derived from that of colour-coated vessels. Its date is uncertain. The remaining two sherds comprises a jar rim and body sherd, probably from the same vessel, of late first-century date.

Trench C produced a total of 9 sherds/54 g. The silt deposit (159) produced six sherds of late first-century grey ware and one sherd of Holt orange ware, all indeterminate closed forms. The secondary clay floor, (158), produced the rim of a Verulamium region white ware mortarium. The main distribution of Verulamium region white wares, including mortaria, spanned the years *c* 70–140, although production at the kiln site lasted from *c* 50 to 165 (Tyers 1996, 199–201). The only pottery recovered from the latest context in Trench C, (157), is a single sherd of late first-century grey ware from an indeterminate closed form, from sample <5112>.

The stratigraphically earliest context in Evaluation Trench D, deposit (143), produced a single grey ware sherd from sample <5111>, probably from a jar, of late first-century date. The vessel is sooted externally and was probably used for cooking.

Catalogue
1   Rim of coarse grey ware jar; local product. B (155); SF 10135. Late first century. Ill. 5.1.3.1.
2   Rim of Verulamium region white mortarium with hooked rim; VER WH. C (158); SF 10136. Probably *c* 70–140. Ill 5.1.3.2.

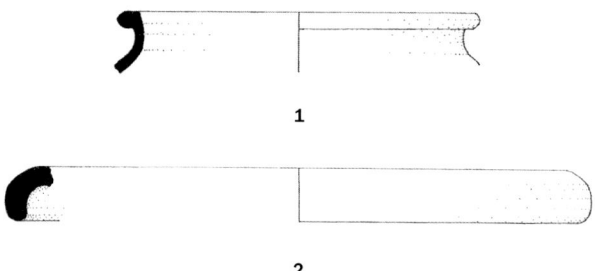

Ill 5.1.3 Phase Ia: Roman pottery. (Scale 1/4)

Discussion
Only coarse wares were recovered. Diagnostic forms comprise vessels relating to the preparation and serving of food and drink. The group is typical of pottery found in Chester dating to the late first–early second century.

Phase Ib
Description
All of the pottery from this sub-phase came from a group of contexts in the ramp area. 6 sherds/11 g came from samples (55% by sherd count and 3% by weight of the sub-phase Ib total).

The stratigraphically earliest context, (1252), which represented a resurfacing of the main east–west road, produced an indeterminate closed form in Holt oxidised ware – burnt and abraded – and the burnt body sherd of a south Gaulish wine amphora. The latter is most probably from form Gauloise 4 (G4), which was widely distributed in Britain, Gaul and the Rhineland. In Britain, Gauloise amphorae are found from the Flavian period through to the third century (Tyers 1996, 95).

(1243), the fill of the roadside drain, produced an indeterminate closed form in a slightly abraded black-on-brown fabric and oxidised wares, probably all Holt products. The only diagnostic form among the latter is a burnt and battered flat-rim bowl; the remainder comprise indeterminate closed forms. There is also a Holt white-slipped orange ware sherd from an indeterminate closed form with an abraded slip coating. The same context produced the burnt and abraded rim of an oxidised mortarium. The rim is strongly hooked and is reminiscent of Verulamium region forms. The fabric is definitely not Holt and the unusual rim form makes the source and date-range uncertain. The body sherd of a south Spanish olive oil amphora also came from (1243). The sherd is probably from form Dressel 20 produced in Baetican amphora fabric 1, which was used to produce the early variants of

Table 5.1.3 Phase Ia: Roman pottery quantified by common ware name, no of sherds and weight

Fabric	Source	NRFRC code	Date range	No	Wt (g)	Average sherd wt (g)
Grey	Cheshire Plain		Late 1 cent	11	68	6.2
Orange	Holt	HOL OX	*c* 90/100—130	1	2	2
White	Verulamium region	VER WH	Probably 70—140	1	23	23
Total				13	93	7.2

Table 5.1.4 Phase Ib: Roman pottery quantified by common ware name, no of sherds and weight

Fabric	Source	NRFRC code	Date range	No	Wt (g)	Average sherd wt (g)
Black-on-brown	Cheshire Plain		Late 1 cent	1	1	1
Orange	Holt	HOL OX	c 90/100—130	6	30	5
Orange	?	?		1	289	289
White-slipped orange	Holt	HOL WS	c 90/100—130	1	2	2
Amphora	Baetica, S Spain	BAT AM 1	Late 1—mid-3 cent	1	9	9
Amphora	S Gaul	GAL AM 1	c 70—3 cent	1	46	46
Total				11	377	34.3

this form (Tomber & Dore 1998, 84). The uppermost deposit in sub-phase Ib, (1254), which sealed the roadside drain, produced a single sherd from an indeterminate closed form in a probable Holt oxidised fabric.

Catalogue

3   Rim of coarse orange ware flat-rimmed bowl; burnt and battered; probably Holt; HOL OX. (1243); sample <5133>; SF 10137. c 90/100–130. Ill 5.1.4.3.

4   Rim of coarse orange ware mortarium with strongly hooked rim; burnt and abraded; probably a local product. (1243); SF 10138. Ill 5.1.4.4.

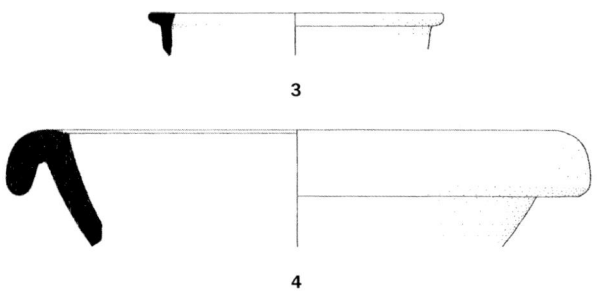

3

4

Ill 5.1.4 Phase Ib: Roman pottery. (Scale 1/4)

Discussion

Only coarse wares were recovered from Ib. Diagnostic forms comprise vessels relating to the transport, preparation, storage and serving of food and drink.

Phase Ic

Description

The pottery from this sub-phase came from Evaluation Trenches B, C and D and from a small group of contexts in the ramp area. Samples produced 49 sherds/257 g (43% by sherd count and 6% by weight of the Phase Ic total).

The only pottery from Trench B came from (151), the backfill of the construction trench (150) for Building I(i) and comprises a dish/bowl base in a ?Holt oxidised fabric.

Pottery came from just two contexts in Trench C – (156), the make up for the floor of Building I(i) and (144), a layer of black silt, which had formed over the floor – and comprises just three sherds of Holt oxidised ware weighing 13 g. That from (144) has a deposit of white limescale on the interior surface, suggesting that the vessel had been used for heating/cooking liquid or a liquid food such as soup or stew.

Only two contexts in Trench D produced pottery – pit fills (142) and (161). The lower fill, (161), produced a ?jar or ?flagon body sherd in a Holt oxidised fabric. The upper fill, (142), produced a small group of 17 sherds/784 g. Samian ware is represented by a south Gaulish Dr 37 bowl (with a date range of 70–110). Coarse pottery includes grey wares, which are presumably residual to this sub-phase, including a jar (slightly abraded) and an indeterminate closed form with traces of ?sooting on the exterior surface, suggesting that it had been used for cooking. Oxidised wares include a plain-rim dish and indeterminate closed forms, which are probably all Holt products. Two sherds are burnt (possibly as a result of rubbish disposal – ie burning the rubbish to cleanse it) and another contains a deposit of white limescale on its interior surface, suggesting its use as a cooking vessel. However, the weight total is largely composed of a single sherd (644 g), comprising the rim of a possible 'portable oven' or *clibanus* (SF 9600). This unusual find is closely comparable to the incomplete example from Holt illustrated in Grimes 1930, 184 and 212, fig 60, no 9. The thickened rim is decorated with thumb impressions, as is the Holt example, which is described as ''?an oven of red ware, height 21½ inches, diameter at base c 2 feet. Open type with thickened rim decorated with thumb impres-

Table 5.1.5 Phase Ic: Roman pottery quantified by common ware name, no of sherds and weight

Fabric	Source	NRFRC code	Date range	No	Wt (g)	Average sherd wt (g)
Samian	SG		tpq 90—110	15	118	7.9
Lead-glazed	Holt		c 90/100—130	1	1	1
Black-on-brown	Cheshire Plain		Late 1 cent	8	74	9.3
Grey	Cheshire Plain		Late 1 cent	28	184	6.6
Orange	Holt	HOL OX	c 90/100-130	44	1015	23.1
Orange	Cheshire Plain		Late 1—late 2 cent	1	35	35
Orange	Severn Valley	SVW OX 2	At least late 1 cent (to 4 cent)	1	4	4
BB 1	Poole, Dorset	DOR BB1	tpq late 3 cent	3	8	2.7
White-slipped orange	Holt	HOL WS	c 90/100-130	5	51	10.2
?White/ ?Amphora	?	?	?	1	8	8
Amphora	Baetica, S Spain	BAT AM 1	Late 1—mid-3 cent	2	427	213
Amphora	Probably Cadiz, S Spain	Probably CAD AM 1	Depends on form	2	549	274.5
Amphora	Probably S Gaul	Probably GAL AM 1	Probably c 70—3 cent	1	27	27
?Amphora	?	?	?	1	13	13
Total				113	2514	22.2

sions, semicircular opening near bottom, with moulded edge and thumb impressions round.' (Grimes 1930, 184). An almost identical rim in a coarse orange fabric was recovered during excavations at the amphitheatre between 1965 and 1969. In the report the rim was identified as medieval and from a 'large ?storage jar in coarse pink ware with deeply thumbed decoration' (Thompson 1976, 216, no 58 and fig 41). These ovens are thought to have been used to keep food hot for serving at table. Only four other published examples of *clibani* are known from Roman Britain, comprising two from Caerleon, one from Catterick and one from Prestatyn (Evans 2000, 303). The latter is of the same form as the Holt and Chester examples and was most probably also a product of the Holt kilns (Blockley 1989, 164, fig 67 and 165, no 75). A burnt or misfired white-slipped orange ?flagon sherd is probably also a Holt product.

In the ramp area, pottery recovered from the foundation trench for wall (1245) comprises a south Gaulish samian ware Dr 30 bowl (90–110) and a burnt Holt white-slipped orange sherd of indeterminate closed form. Most of the remaining contexts to produce pottery came from the road or yard area to the west of wall (1245). They comprise (1251), a silt-clay layer north of the east–west road, and (1250)(1388), a silt layer marking the end of the sub-phase. (1251) produced 18 sherds/242 g. Local coarse wares comprise a late first-century black-on-brown ?jar (slightly abraded), a late first-century grey ware ?jar base (slightly worn and with a sooted exterior), a white-

ular oxidised fabric with a grey core. Although Severn Valley ware first began to appear in small numbers in Chester from the late first century, it did not become common here until *c* 120–200 (Tyers 1996, 197). According to Manning, the marketing of Severn Valley ware at Chester and further north dates from the early second century (Manning 1993, 286). The presence of this sherd alongside the first appearance of black-burnished 1 suggests a *terminus post quem* for sub-phase Ic of *c* 120+ and also perhaps suggests that the preceding sub-phases predated *c* AD 120. There was quite a high proportion of residual late first-century grey and black-on-brown wares from this part of the site. The drain lining, (1389), produced just 4 sherds/603 g. They comprise Holt orange wares, including a flat, reeded-rim, carinated bowl (*cf* Grimes 1930, 217 fig 65) and a ?jar with a sooted exterior; as well as probable Cadiz fish sauce amphorae sherds. The Cadiz fabric was used for forms P & W 17 (Cam 186A), dated late first century BC–early second century AD; P & W 18 (Cam 186C), dated *c* 70–early second century AD; and P & W 19 (Beltran IIB), dated early/mid-first century–mid-second century (Peacock & Williams 1986, 120–5).

Catalogue

5   Rim of portable oven (*clibanus*) in coarse orange ware; Holt; HOL OX. D (142); SF 9600. *cf* Grimes 1930, 212 fig 60 no 9. Ill 5.1.5.5.

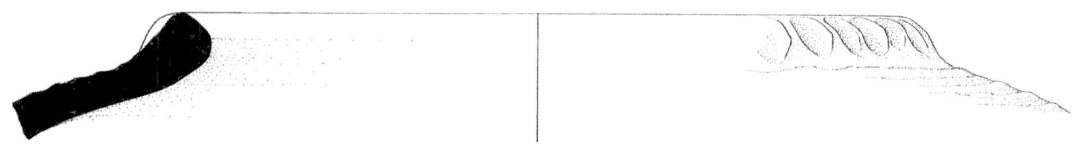

5

Ill 5.1.5 Phase Ic: Roman pottery. (Scale 1/4)

slipped orange flagon (slightly misfired and with a worn circular patch on the exterior), as well as probable Holt orange ware ?jars/?beakers and a ?lid. The latter comprises the ?knob handle of a lid from a large storage vessel (comparable to Grimes 1930, 155 and 218, fig 66, nos 101–2). The only fine ware from this context is a south Gaulish samian Dr 37 bowl (70–110). (1250) produced 24 sherds/146 g. Fine wares comprise south Gaulish samian ware – a Dr 27 cup (probably *c* 80–100) and a Dr 37 bowl (probably *c* 70/75–85/90). Local coarse wares comprise a black-on-brown ?jar and ?beaker and grey ware jars and a flat-rim bowl; indeterminate grey ware sherds are probably from jars (two sherds have sooted exterior surfaces). There are also probable Holt orange and white-slipped orange wares of indeterminate forms. A burnt sherd from an indeterminate buff amphora fabric was also retrieved. (1388) produced three sherds of black-burnished 1 – all from sample <5136> – which makes its first appearance in this sub-phase. They comprised two small sherds from indeterminate closed forms, one with a sooted exterior and probably from a cooking pot, and the abraded rim of a late third-century cooking pot (*cf* Gillam 1976, 65 fig 2 type 10).

(1392), the upper fill of the east–west gully (1401) produced an oxidised Severn Valley ware sherd dating from at least the later first century. This is in a hard vesic-

Discussion

A wide range of forms and fabrics was recovered from sub-phase Ic. Diagnostic forms comprise vessels relating to the transport, preparation, storage and serving of food and drink. Fine tableware, in the form of south Gaulish samian ware cups, bowls and a plate or plate/bowl and a fragment from a rare Holt lead-glazed vessel, make their first appearance in this sub-phase, as do a handful of coarse wares from non-local British sources, namely black-burnished 1 from Poole in Dorset and oxidised wares from the Severn Valley. The latter suggest imports from the early second century onwards – perhaps following the demise of the local industries at Holt and elsewhere on the Cheshire Plain (ie the producers of the late first-century grey and black-on-brown wares) – towards at least the close of this sub-phase. Imports of wine, olive oil and fish sauce from southern Gaul and southern Spain respectively are represented by amphorae fragments.

Phase Id

Description

All the pottery from this sub-phase came from Trench B, the access pit and ramp areas. Wet-sieving produced 95 sherds/234 g (46% by sherd count and 11% by weight of the sub-phase Id total). Intrusive material in Id comprised a single sherd of medieval pottery from (1242).

Table 5.1.6 Phase Id: Roman pottery quantified by common ware name, no of sherds and weight

Fabric	Source	NRFRC code	Date range	No	Wt (g)	Average sherd wt (g)
Samian	S Gaul		Probably 80—100	8	10	1.3
Samian	C Gaul		c 120—200	1	42	42
Orange mica-dusted	Holt		c 90/100—130	2	3	1.5
Black-on-brown	Cheshire Plain		Late 1 cent	47	174	3.7
Grey	Cheshire Plain		Late 1 cent	34	549	16.1
Grey (BB1 copy)	?	?	?c 120—200	1	20	20
Grey or orange	Cheshire Plain		Late 1—late 2 cent	1	15	15
Orange	Holt	HOL OX	c 90/100-130	60	524	8.7
Orange	?Wilderspool	?WIL OX	?Early—mid- to late 2 cent	3	122	40.7
Orange	Cheshire Plain		Late 1—late 2 cent	3	62	20.7
Orange	?Severn Valley	?SVW OX 2	?At least Late 1 cent+ (to 4 cent)	1	30	30
White-slipped orange	Holt	HOL WS	c 90/100—130	33	375	11.4
Orange/ CBM	Holt	HOL OX		5	10	2
White	probably Mancetter-Hartshill	?MAH WH	Probably mid-2—early 4 cent	1	2	2
White	probably Verulamium region	?VER WH	Probably 70—140	2	9	4.5
Amphora	Baetica, S Spain	BAT AM 1	Late 1—mid-3 cent	5	237	47.4
Total				207	2184	10.6

Layer (135), which immediately overlay the external surface in Trench B, produced 7 sherds/84 g. These comprise the polished/burnished rim of a grey ware jar or beaker and an imitation grey ware copy of a black-burnished 1 cooking pot with a deposit of white limescale on the interior. The burnished decoration is in the form of acute-angled lattice, placing it between *c* 120 and 200 (Tyers 1996, 185). Oxidised wares from (135) comprise a Holt indeterminate closed form and a roughcast beaker base, probably a Wilderspool vessel (early–mid- to late second century).

Pottery comprising 22 sherds/253 g was recovered from two contexts in the access pit: layer (276) and east–west road surface (274). The stratigraphically earliest deposit, (276), produced 17 sherds/33 g, the majority from sample <5015>. The two hand-collected sherds comprise an indeterminate Holt orange vessel and an indeterminate coarse white ware sherd. The latter is probably a Mancetter-Hartshill fabric (*c* mid-second–early fourth century). The sherds from sample <5015> comprise an indeterminate closed grey ware sherd and fourteen orange ware sherds. A jar or bowl in a Holt fabric is represented by two rim sherds, which probably came from the same vessel, although they do not join. The remaining sherds are from indeterminate closed forms and include eight sherds with external sooting, which probably came from a single vessel. All are probably Holt products. Road surface (274) produced a Holt oxidised flat-rim bowl with slight sooting on the exterior of the rim and a south Spanish Dressel 20 olive oil amphora.

178 sherds/1847 g came from a small group of six contexts in the area of the ramp excavation. The yellow clay layer, (1249), produced a south Gaulish samian Dr 18 plate, with a date range of 70–110, and a slightly abraded hooked rim mortarium in a probable Wilderspool fabric (early–mid-/late second century). Sandstone brash surface (1239) produced a residual battered sherd of black-on-brown ware in an indeterminate closed form, an incomplete smashed Holt white-slipped orange ?flagon as well as Cheshire Plain and Holt oxidised wares. These comprise a dish/bowl with battered exterior, an indeterminate closed form with a sooted exterior and a Holt

plain-rim dish. The oxidised wares also include the rim of a ?Severn Valley ware wide-mouthed jar with internal lid-seating and lines of burnishing on the exterior (comparable to Carrington 1977, fig 10.2 no 32 – for which there is no precise parallel in Webster 1976). The form is also comparable to wide-mouthed jar forms from Wilderspool (Hinchliffe *et al* 1992, 132, fig 72, no 446 and 149, fig 81, no 687). Webster suggests that the latter were probably the products of a different kiln, which was of a slightly later date than the products of the known kiln site at Wilderspool – perhaps mid- to late second rather than early to mid-/late second century (Hinchliffe *et al* 1992, 124). Sandstone brash deposit (846), the equivalent of (1239), produced the first central Gaulish samian vessel in Phase I, an indeterminate deep dish or shallow bowl with a date range of 120–200.

All the pottery from the remaining contexts in the ramp area (road surface (1240), equivalent to (274); layer (1242) over the road/yard area; and pit fill (1395)) was clearly residual. (1240) produced only one worn/abraded grey ware sherd of indeterminate form. Notable sherds from (1242) include a south Gaulish samian cup, Dr 27 cup, a Dr 18 or 18R plate and a Dr 37 bowl. The only other fine wares from (1242) comprise Holt orange mica-coated vessels (one with a sooted exterior). Diagnostic grey ware forms include jars, a lid and a beaker. A large sherd from a grey ware ?jar with zones of unusual combed and burnished lattice decoration separated by girth grooves has no obvious parallel. There are several other residual grey, orange and white-slipped orange wares – mainly Holt products. They are in mixed condition and some are burnt, probably resulting from the clearing/cleansing of old rubbish. Diagnostic orange ware forms comprise two flat, reeded-rim carinated bowls (*cf* Grimes 1930, 217, fig 65). A white-slipped orange tazza with frilled shoulder is comparable to Grimes 1930, 169 and 22, fig 73, 213 – only traces of the white slip coating survived. There are also Verulamium region white wares (probably flagons, as principal exports in this fabric were flagons and bowls (Tyers 1996, 199–201)), to be dated *c* 70–140. (1395) produced a south Gaulish samian Dr 27 cup (probably 80–100), late first-century grey wares and Holt orange and white-slipped orange wares. The only diagnostic orange wares comprise a plain-rim dish (comparable to Grimes 1930, 159 and 221, fig 69, nos 134–6) and a plain-rim dish with in-curving rim.

Catalogue

6   Base of coarse orange ware roughcast beaker; possibly a Wilderspool product; WIL OX. B (135); SF 10139. Possibly early–mid- to late second century. Ill 5.1.6.6.

7   Rim of a coarse orange ware wide-mouthed jar with internal lid seating; ?Severn Valley ware or ?Wilderspool. (1239); SF 10141. *cf* Carrington 1977, fig 10.2, no 32; Hinchliffe *et al* 1992, 132, fig 72, no 446 and 149, fig 81, no 687. No precise parallel for the form in Webster 1976. Ill 5.1.6.7.

8   Body sherd of a coarse grey ware ?jar with zones of combed and burnished lattice decoration, separated by girth grooves; source uncertain. (1242); SF 10142. Ill 5.1.6.8.

9   Rim of a coarse orange ware mortarium with hooked rim; probably Wilderspool; WIL OX. (1249); SF 10140. Possibly early–mid- to late second century. Ill 5.1.6.9.

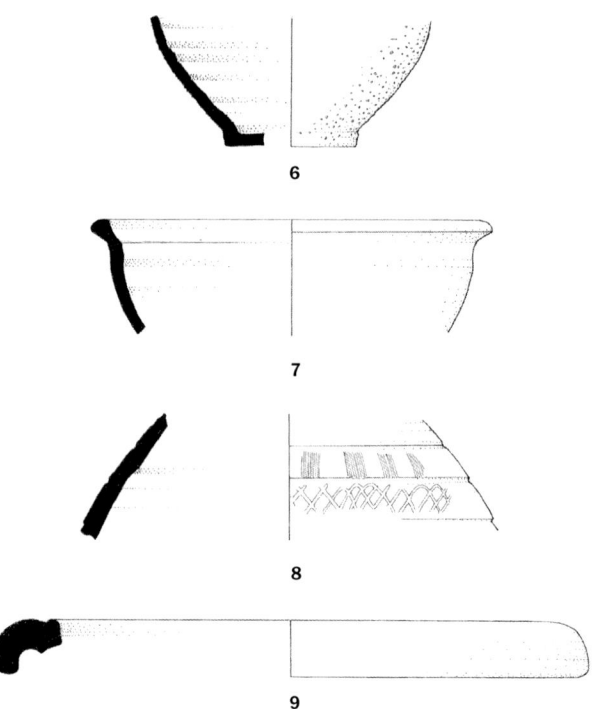

Ill 5.1.6 Phase Id: Roman pottery. (Scale 1/4)

Discussion

A wide range of forms and fabrics was recovered from sub-phase Id. Diagnostic forms comprise vessels relating to the transport, preparation, storage and serving of food and drink. Fine tableware comprises samian ware cups, plates and a bowl and Holt orange mica-coated wares. Samian ware from central Gaul makes its first appearance. Surprisingly, black-burnished 1 wares, which made their first appearance in the preceding sub-phase, are now absent, but there were grey ware copies of black-burnished forms. There was a high proportion of residual local coarse pottery, comprising late first century black-on-brown, and

grey wares as well as late first–early second-century orange and white-slipped orange wares. Residual Verulamium region white wares are also present. Probable Severn Valley ware continues to be represented (although only by a single sherd). Olive oil imports from southern Spain are represented by amphorae fragments.

Phase Ie
Description

The pottery from this sub-phase came from Evaluation Trenches C and G and the ramp area. Wet-sieving produced 67 sherds/709 g (51% by sherd count and 31% by weight of the Ie total). Intrusive material in Ie comprised a sherd of post-medieval pottery from (1148) and a post-medieval clay tobacco pipe stem from (1182).

Only 2 sherds/5 g were recovered from (107), the mortar floor of Building I(i) in Trench C. They comprise an indeterminate black-burnished 1 open form with sooted exterior surface and lattice or chevron burnished decoration on the exterior (*c* 120+) and an indeterminate ?Severn Valley ware form. The latter is a burnished and high-fired closed form, possibly a base with a vestigial footring. The form is uncertain.

Context (93) in Trench G, the fill of the construction trench of structure (92), produced 4 sherds/53 g of pottery. It comprises a south Gaulish samian Dr 29 bowl (70–85) and a ?Wilderspool white-slipped orange flagon handle.

A total of 125 sherds/2233 g came from just two contexts – (1227) (26 sherds/637 g) and (1148) (99 sherds/1596 g). A mid-third-century black-burnished 1 cooking pot, well burnished and with a sooted rim, came from (1227), the road/yard surface laid at the beginning of the sub-phase. No other black-burnished ware was recovered from (1227). The remaining pottery from (1227) comprise south Gaulish and central Gaulish samian ware bowls, a dish, a ?cup and indeterminate forms – the latest dated vessel being a central Gaulish Dr 31 bowl with a very worn footring, which had a date range of 150–200. Residual coarse pottery comprises local Holt orange and white-slipped orange wares. They are in mixed condition: some are burnt, others sooted and some slightly worn. Apart from the black-burnished ware, the only other British import from (1227) is a Verulamium region white ware sherd (probably *c* 70–140). Other imports from other provinces comprise sherds of south Spanish olive oil and south Gaulish wine amphorae (late first–mid-third century and *c* 70–third century respectively).

The pottery assemblage from (1148), the primary fill of sewer (1182), was also largely residual. Fine wares comprise south Gaulish samian ware bowls and indeterminate forms as well as black colour-coated roughcast beaker sherds (one from an indented vessel) in Anne Anderson's 'North Gaul 2' fabric, dated *c* 80–135. Recent work suggests that the source of 'Gallic roughcast fabric' was in the Argonne. A number of examples of indented roughcast beakers in 'North Gaul 2' fabric are known from Usk. Anne Anderson dates these vessels as distributed to Britain between *c* 80–135 (Webster in Manning 1993, 295). Local fine wares comprise Holt orange mica-coated wares (diagnostic forms include a burnt beaker, a slightly abraded bowl, and a burnt jar or beaker) as well as the rim of a white eggshell ware straight-sided cup (comparable to Grimes 1930, 165 and 223, fig 71, no 174). Webster has

Table 5.1.7 Phase Ie: Roman pottery quantified by common ware name, no of sherds and weight

Fabric	Source	NRFRC code	Date range	No	Wt (g)	Average sherd wt (g)
Samian	S Gaul		80–110	14	78	5.6
Samian	C Gaul		150–200	2	114	57
?Red cc	Holt		c 90/100–130	1	74	74
Black cc	?Argonne, N Gaul		?c 80–135	2	4	2
Orange mica-dusted	Holt		c 90/100–130	5	18	3.6
White eggshell	Holt		c 90/100–130	1	1	1
Grey or black-on-brown	Cheshire Plain		Late 1 cent	6	46	7.7
Grey	Cheshire Plain		Late 1 cent	20	149	7.5
Orange	Holt	HOL OX	c 90/100–130	30	350	11.7
Orange	Cheshire Plain		Late 1–late 2 cent	6	338	56.3
Orange or grey	Cheshire Plain		Late 1–late 2 cent	1	32	32
Orange/CBM	Holt	HOL OX		2	14	7
Orange	?Severn Valley	?SVW OX 2	?At least late 1 cent+ (to 4 cent)	1	1	1
BB1	Poole, Dorset	DOR BB1	c mid-3 cent	9	179	19.9
White-slipped orange	Holt	HOL WS	c 90/100–130	5	92	18.4
White-slipped orange	Probably Wilderspool	probably WIL WS	Probably early– mid- to late 2 cent	1	17	17
White-slipped orange	Cheshire Plain		Late 1–late 2 cent	9	12	1.3
White	Verulamium region	VER WH	Probably 70–140	2	33	16.5
White	Indet			1	10	10
Amphorae	Baetica, S Spain	BAT AM 1	Late 1–mid-3 cent	6	460	76.7
Amphorae	SG	GAL AM 1	Probably c 70–3 cent	1	22	22
Other amphorae	?	?	?	6	247	41.2
Total				131	2291	17.5

questioned whether the production of white eggshell wares was within the capabilities of the Holt potters and postulated that the close similarity between the Holt and Caerleon/Usk fabrics suggested that they were all the product of a single source 'at some remove from the sites themselves' (Webster in Manning 1993, 315–16). However, Grimes pointed out that 'the large quantity of fragments of this fine white pottery [at Holt] indicates that eggshell ware was ... made at Holt'. He also reported that white clays are associated with the carboniferous limestone of Flintshire and Denbighshire and that these could have been used for eggshell ware production (1930, 163).

Local coarse wares from (1148) comprise a late first-century grey ware lid and indeterminate closed forms, as well as Holt and other Cheshire Plain orange and white-slipped orange wares. Orange ware forms include flat-rim bowls (including one Holt vessel with flat, reeded rim comparable to Grimes 1930, 217, fig 65), a beaker, a jar or beaker, jars or flagons and indeterminate closed forms. A Holt plain-rimmed dish has traces of a red or self-coloured slip coating, darkened by burning. British imports from (1148) comprise a ?mortarium sherd in Verulamium region white ware (c 70–140) and black-burnished ware vessels. The latter include cooking pots (some of which are burnt/sooted; one of which has a deposit of white limescale on the interior) – one of which is dated to the early to mid-second century – and a slightly abraded ?dish with scribble decoration on the underside and inner surface of the sherd. The latter is a feature of plain-rimmed and bead-rimmed dishes rather than bowls. Amphorae from (1148) comprise sherds of south Spanish globular olive oil forms and three lids/stoppers of indeterminate forms.

A fairly high proportion of the residual pottery from (1148) is burnt, suggesting the cleansing of old rubbish through burning.

Discussion

A wide range of forms and fabrics was recovered from sub-phase Ie. Diagnostic forms comprise vessels relating to the transport, preparation, storage and serving of food and drink. There is a high proportion of residual wares, including many burnt sherds, probably the result of rubbish disposal through burning. Black-burnished ware is again present after disappearing in the preceding sub-phase. There is an increased proportion of fine wares (including black colour-coated wares from north Gaul as well as samian ware and Holt mica-coated and white eggshell wares). This may be a reflection of the larger assemblage size as these wares were all residual in this sub-phase.

Discussion of Phase I

Despite the small size of the Phase I assemblage, a wide range of fabrics and forms was recovered, comprising vessels used for the transport, storage, preparation and serving of food and drink. Notable forms comprise a *clibanus* (portable oven) rim fragment from Ie and a tazza (?incense burner) from Id. The pottery assemblage is in mixed condition. The date range is late first to late third century, but there is a large residual component to the assemblage. Most vessels fall within a date range from the late first to the early second century and comprised locally made grey wares and Holt oxidised wares. There is a small group of second-century vessels (including black-burnished wares, Wilderspool orange wares and some samian wares). A possible Mancetter-Hartshill white ware from Id dated from the middle of the second century onwards. The latest dated wares from Phase I comprise a mid-third-century black-burnished vessel from sub-phase Ie and a late third-century black-burnished 1 cooking pot from Ic. There is no east Gaulish samian and products of the Roman pottery industries of the later third and fourth centuries are notable by their absence.

Table 5.1.8 Phase IIa: Roman pottery quantified by common ware name, no of sherds and weight

Fabric	Source	NRFRC code	Date range	No	Wt (g)	Average sherd wt (g)
Samian	S Gaul		*tpq* probably 80—100	22	120	5.5
Samian	C Gaul		*tpq* 160—200	22	265	12
Red cc	Holt		c 90/100-130	3	26	8.7
Red cc	Lower Nene Valley	LNV CC	Mid-2—late 4 cent	1	1	1
Red cc	?Oxfordshire	?OXF RS	?240—400+	1	1	1
Red cc	?	?	?	2	27	13.5
Black cc	Lower Nene Valley	LNV CC	Mid-2—late 4 cent	1	1	1
Black cc	?Lezoux, C Gaul	?CNG BS	?c 150—early 3 cent	2	1	0.5
Orange mica-dusted	Holt		c 90/100—130	12	193	16.1
White eggshell	Holt		c 90/100—130	1	4	4
Black-on-brown	Cheshire Plain		Late 1 cent	1	15	15
Grey	Cheshire Plain		Late 1 cent	25	241	9.6
Orange	Holt	HOL OX	c 90/100—130	147	3554	24.2
Orange	Cheshire Plain		Late 1—late 2 cent	4	229	57.3
Orange	?Wilderspool	?WIL OX	?Mid- to late 2 cent	1	10	10
Orange	Severn Valley	SVW OX 2	2—3 cent	1	20	20
Orange/CBM	Holt	HOL OX		6	11	1.8
BB1	Poole, Dorset	DOR BB 1	*tpq* late 3 cent	57	773	13.6
Grey (BB1 copies)	?		?c 120+	12	269	22.4
White-slipped orange	Holt	HOL WS	c 90/100—130	29	387	13.3
White-slipped orange	?Wilderspool	?WIL WS	?Early— mid- to late 2 cent	1	169	169
White-slipped orange	Cheshire Plain		Late 1—late 2 cent	4	65	16.3
White	Mancetter-Hartshill	MAH WH	Mid 2—early 4 cent	1	1	1
White	Oxfordshire	OXF WH	240—400+	1	2	2
White	Oxfordshire	OXF ?PA	240—400+	1	37	37
White	Verulamium region	VER WH	c 70-140	1	70	70
White	?	?	?	5	18	3.6
Amphorae	Baetica, S Spain	BAT AM 1	Late 1—mid-3 cent	30	5353	178.4
Amphorae	S Gaul	GAL AM 1	Probably c 70—3 cent	5	75	15
Other amphorae	?	?	?	2	231	115.5
Total				401	12169	30.3

Phase II

Phase II produced the largest group of Roman pottery from any of the phases, comprising 1081 sherds/34,006g or 23% by sherd count and 31.5% by weight of the total site assemblage (see Table 5.1.2).

Phase IIa

Description

This sub-phase is thought to represent the final period of Roman occupation within the fortress, the final archaeological event being the formation of occupation layer (1237), (1225), (1142). Intrusive material in IIa comprise six sherds of medieval pottery from (1220) and a single sherd of post-medieval pottery from (1225).

Pottery from this sub-phase came from Evaluation Trench D and also from the area of the ramp excavation. The assemblage comprises 401 sherds/12,169g or 8% by sherd count and 11% by weight of the site total, almost all of it residual (*see* Table 5.1.8). 53 sherds/115g were retrieved from wet-sieving (ie 42% by sherd count but only 1% by weight of the IIa total).

Evaluation Trench D produced 56 sherds/1101g, all from layer (119) and all residual. Fine wares comprise samian ware vessels from south and central Gaul and orange mica-coated wares from Holt. Identifiable samian ware forms were a south Gaulish Dr 37 bowl (70–90); a central Gaulish Dr 37 bowl (100–140) and ?Dr 36 dish (70–110). The orange mica-dusted wares comprise a plain-rimmed bowl, slightly burnt (comparable to Grimes 1930, 161 fig 70 no 155) and the overfired rim of a ?beaker or ?jar (comparable to Grimes 1930, 151 and fig 63 no 50). Locally produced coarse wares comprise a late first-

century grey ware jar and Holt orange wares. Diagnostic Holt forms comprise three jars, all with sooted rims and/or exterior surfaces and a flat-rim bowl. Indeterminate sherds are probably mainly jars (six sherds were sooted externally), although three thin-walled sherds (two of which joined) are probably from a beaker. White-slipped orange wares from (119) were probably all Holt products. The only diagnostic form comprises the rim/neck of a ring-necked flagon. Indeterminate body sherds are probably also from flagons. One sherd is burnt. British imports comprise black-burnished 1 and white wares. The only diagnostic black-burnished vessel is the rim of a beaker or 'mini cooking pot' (probable early to mid-second century), from (119), for which there is no obvious parallel in Gillam 1976. White wares from (119) comprise a Verulamium region mortarium (c 70-140) with no grits surviving and an indeterminate closed form from ?Mancetter-Hartshill (?mid-second–early fourth century). This is the latest vessel in this trench. A buff-coloured body sherd may be an indeterminate amphora fabric. Otherwise, the only amphorae from Trench D comprise two adjoining sherds of a south Spanish olive oil vessel (late first–mid-third century), one of which is abraded.

A total of 345 sherds/11,068 g came from six contexts in the ramp excavation area. Road surface (1226) produced 19 sherds/633 g, all of them residual. No pottery was recovered from (1224), a possible resurfacing of this road. The only fine ware recovered comprised a south Gaulish samian Dr 37 bowl (probably *c* 80–100) and an indeterminate south Gaulish vessel (70–110). Local coarse wares comprise late first-century grey wares and Holt orange and white-slipped orange wares. No truly diagnostic sherds were recovered but orange ware forms probably

174

included a jar (burnt) and a ?platter or ?dish with burnished surfaces. Two indeterminate orange ware sherds are burnt. White-slipped orange wares probably include flagons (one sherd is slightly burnt). The only British import comprises an indeterminate black-burnished 1 open form (120+), the exterior of which is decorated with close-packed lattice. Amphorae sherds comprise south Spanish olive oil vessels; one from a Dressel 20 (late first–mid-third century); the other is fairly thin-walled and may be the earlier form Dressel 25 (Augustan–first century AD) or the later form Dressel 23 (third–fourth century).

Pottery from (1146), the fill of sewer tributary (1147), comprises a small group of 19 sherds/1482 g, again all residual. The only fine ware comprises a south Gaulish samian Dr 37 bowl (70–100). Local coarse wares comprise Holt orange and white-slipped orange wares and an indeterminate grey ware vessel (the latter burnt). The orange wares include the rim of an outsize jar, which joins another rim fragment from IIb (1228). The top of the rim is abraded and the interior surface has been smoothed. There is also the body sherd of a large ?flagon with a wide girth groove on the shoulder of the vessel (cf flagons in Grimes 1930, 220 fig 68, especially nos 123–6). The white-slipped orange wares include a Holt mortarium with abraded slip and mixed, mainly white quartz, grits. Apart from a grey ware copy of a black-burnished 1 cooking pot (c 120+) of uncertain provenance, the only British import is an indeterminate black-burnished 1 open form (also 120+). Amphorae from (1146) comprise Gallic wine jars (probably c 70 to the third century), the handle of a south Spanish olive oil vessel (possibly Dressel 25), and the spike of form ?Dressel 2–4 (Peacock & Williams Class 10) of uncertain provenance. The latter form is the most important western Mediterranean wine amphora of the early Empire (Peacock & Williams 1986, 106) and dates from the late first century BC to the mid-second century AD.

The lower fill, (1220), of the main north–south sewer produced a group of 104 sherds/2421 g, again all residual. Fine wares comprise samian wares from south and central Gaul, Holt orange mica-coated and red colour-coated wares. South Gaulish samian ware vessels comprise Dr 37 bowls (70–110) (one vessel was burnt black); a Dr 29 bowl (60–85) and a Dr 18 or 18R plate (60–90). The only central Gaulish vessels comprise a Dr 33 cup (140–200) and an indeterminate form (100–140). Diagnostic Holt forms comprise an orange mica-coated ?beaker with a narrow pedestal base (for which there was no parallel in Grimes 1930), and a flanged bowl (cf Grimes 1930, 222-fig 70, nos 157–9 for red-slipped versions of the same form). There is also a beaker with traces of a micaceous slip coating. The red colour-coated vessel is of indeterminate open form. No other fine wares were recovered. Local coarse pottery comprise late first-century grey wares (including a ?beaker), orange and white-slipped orange wares. The orange wares are all from Holt, apart from two burnt sherds of uncertain local source, which are probably flagons, and a large, flat-rim bowl with a single reed in the centre top of the rim. The latter vessel is in a pale orange, sandy fabric with a darker orange core. Identifiable Holt forms comprise a carinated bowl with flat rim (not reeded), which is burnt (cf Grimes 1930, 217, fig 65); a two-handled flagon, the handles of which, represented

by scars only, rises high up on the neck, with a single ring below the rim (cf Grimes 1930, 220, fig 68, nos 125 and 126 for the closest parallels. Swan has identified Holt type 125 as a 'North African type' (Swan 1999, 539 and 545 fig 3 no 25)); a burnt dish (cf Grimes 1930, 221 fig 69 no 31); a tazza with notched rim (cf Grimes 1930, 225, fig 73, no 214) and an abraded bowl with a rounded rim. There is no exact parallel for the latter in Grimes 1930. White-slipped orange wares from (1220) include a ?Wilderspool mortarium, the interior of which is worn through use (cf Hartley & Webster 1973, 102, fig 12, no 10). All other sherds are indeterminate forms, although most are probably flagons, from Holt or other Cheshire Plain sources. Two sherds are burnt and one is overfired/slightly burnt. British imports comprise black-burnished 1 wares from Poole, Dorset and white wares from Oxfordshire. Diagnostic black-burnished forms comprise cooking pots and a beaker. One cooking pot, dated to the mid-second century, has a wavy line decoration on the neck (cf Gillam 1976, 62, fig 1, no 2). Evidence for their use as cooking vessels comes from two sherds with a deposit of white limescale on the interior surfaces and one sherd with a sooted rim. One sherd was burnt and another has a partly oxidised exterior (?through burning). One indeterminate open vessel has been pierced while the clay was still wet – the hole appears to have been made by pushing a tool through from the exterior to the interior of the vessel. There is a rough area on the inside where excess clay had been pushed out from the hole. The white wares comprise the base of a bowl in Oxfordshire ?parchment ware and an indeterminate closed form in Oxfordshire white ware. These vessels represent the first appearance of Oxfordshire wares from the Roman phases. Production dated from c 240 to 400+ with extensive distribution from the Severn Valley to the Thames Estuary by the late third century. Distribution expanded and intensified during the fourth century (Tyers 1996, 178). Amphorae from (1220) comprise south Spanish olive oil vessels, mostly of form Dressel 20, two of which are slightly burnt; and one indeterminate form (probably either Dressel 23 or Dressel 25). The latter is slightly burnt.

The upper fill of the drain, (1219), produced 75 sherds/1232 g, again all residual. Fine wares comprise local forms as well as British and continental imports. Continental fine wares comprise samian vessels and black- slipped ?beaker fragments from Lezoux, central Gaul (c 50–early third century). The samian wares from south and central Gaul include a south Gaulish Dr 36 dish (70–110); central Gaulish wares include a badly battered Dr 37 bowl (possibly 150–180), a south Gaulish 18/31R or 31R plate/bowl or bowl (150–200a), a Dr 31R bowl with worn footring (160–200) and Dr 37 bowls (120–160 and possibly 150–180). Local fine wares comprise an indeterminate open form in Holt orange mica-coated ware and Holt red colour-coated wares, including a flanged bowl with a micaceous red slip on all surfaces (cf Grimes 1930, 222, fig 70, no 159, although the bead rim is grooved in the Bridge Street example); the fabric is comparable to Chester Holt fabric 436. A white eggshell beaker, also from Holt, is comparable to Grimes 1930, 223, fig 71, no 174. British imports include a black colour-coated beaker from the Lower Nene Valley with rouletted decoration, as well as an indeterminate form (both vessels c mid-second to late fourth century). These vessels represent the first appearance of Lower Nene Valley colour-coated wares in the Roman phases. The industry broadly dated from the mid-second to late fourth centuries but was probably most extensive during the third century, before the rise of the Oxfordshire potteries (Tyers 1996, 175). There is also a possible Oxfordshire red-slipped vessel of indeterminate form (*c* 240–400+).

Coarse wares from local and other British sources comprise a late first century black-on-brown ware jar – the only example of the ware recovered from sub-phase IIa. The only grey ware from (1219) comprises an imitation black-burnished 1 cooking pot with a sooted exterior; the angle of lattice suggests a date of *c* 200. Orange wares from Holt include a flagon (similar to Grimes 1930 220, fig 68, nos 119 and 126, although there is no exact parallel); a beaker with burnished exterior (*cf* Grimes 1930, 223 fig 71 nos 195–6); a bowl (*cf* Hinchliffe *et al* 1992, 67, fig 35, no 309 for form, although the published example was in a reduced fabric: there is no exact parallel in Grimes); and a dish with a wiped/smoothed exterior (*cf* Grimes 1930, 221, fig 68, no 130). Indeterminate Holt orange wares include a red-slipped ?mortarium rim or ?flange from a bowl. Two sherds are slightly burnt. The only non-Holt orange ware comprises a ?Wilderspool wide-mouthed, lid-seated jar with burnished rim (*cf* Hinchliffe *et al* 1992, 132, fig 72, no 446 and 149, fig 81, no 687). There are similar vessels in sub-phase IIb (1179) and II *c* (1161) and (1177). White-slipped orange wares from (1219) comprise indeterminate sherds, one of which is slightly burnt, probably all from Holt. British imports comprise black-burnished wares from Poole. Diagnostic forms comprise a cooking pot with sooted exterior and limescale on the interior (*c* 120–200) and a flat rim dish/bowl (mid- to late second century) (*cf* Gillam 1976, 69, fig 3, nos 38–40). Amphorae from (1219) comprise south Spanish olive oil vessels (late first to mid-third century) and ?Gallic wine vessels (probably *c* 70 to third century), one sherd of which is battered.

Layer (1237)/(1225)/(1142) produced 128 sherds/5300 g. If this layer represents the abandonment of the Roman site, it is noteworthy that no late Roman pottery was recovered from it. A late third-century black-burnished 1 cooking pot is the latest vessel from (1225), whereas one would have expected small but significant quantities of the latest black-burnished 1 forms, shell-tempered wares and late Oxfordshire red-slipped forms. However, most of the pottery comprises local wares of late first to early/mid-second-century date, second-century samian wares (with a few late first–early second-century vessels), second-century black-burnished 1 vessels and grey ware copies of black-burnished forms. The only exceptions are a black-burnished 1 dish (?late second–early third century), Baetican olive oil amphorae (broadly dated late first to mid-third century) and a Severn Valley ware jar (broadly dated from the second to third centuries).

(1225) produced 84 sherds/3540 g. Diagnostic samian forms comprised a south Gaulish Dr 37 bowl (70–110); a central Gaulish Dr 18/31R or 31R plate/bowls or bowls (120-160) and (130–170), the latter with worn footring; a central Gaulish Dr 33 cup (120–200, although probably before *c* 160); a central Gaulish Dr ?35 cup (140–200); a central Gaulish Dr 37 bowl (*c* 125–145?); and a central Gaulish Dr 40? 'cup' (160–200). Local fine wares comprise Holt orange mica-dusted vessels. Diagnostic forms

comprised a lid-seated ?flagon (*cf* Grimes 1930, 219, fig 67, no 115, although the published form is not lid-seated) and a flat-rim bowl (*cf* Grimes 1930, 221, fig 69, no 139, which occurs in both oxidised and reduced versions (page159)). An orange ware dish/platter of unknown provenance with a red slip coating is comparable to McPeake *et al* 1980, 27–9 and fig 7, no 2 for fabric and form. Also of unknown provenance is a vessel in a fine buff fabric with abundant white inclusions and traces of a red slip on the interior surface.

Local coarse wares comprise late first-century grey wares (one sherd with a sooted exterior) and Holt orange wares. The latter include a large flagon; a large bowl with traces of red slip on the inner surface (not in Grimes 1930); a flagon; a tazza with a sooted interior (*cf* Grimes 1930, 221, fig 69, no 130); a dish (*cf* Grimes 1930, 221 fig 69, no 132 for rim form, but the published example is smaller); a beaker with burnished exterior (not in Grimes 1930); a beaker(s) with clay roughcast decoration (one sherd burnt); and a mortarium (*cf* Grimes 1930, 213, fig 61, no 2). British imported coarse wares comprise black-burnished 1 wares from Poole. Diagnostic forms comprise a second-century bead rim ?bowl with slightly inward-turning rim (for closest parallel *cf* Holbrook & Bidwell 1991, 107 fig 30, no 30.1); a late third-century cooking pot (*cf* Gillam 1976, 65, fig 2 no 10); and a mid-second-century flat-rim dish/bowl. Four of the indeterminate vessels have sooted exteriors. There is also a grey ware copy of a black-burnished cooking pot (?*c* 120–200) and white (buff) wares of indeterminate provenance. The latter may be amphora sherds. Amphorae from (1225) comprise south Spanish olive oil sherds, both from form Dressel 20 (late first to mid-third century) and one sherd possibly from either form Dressel 25 or Dressel 23 (*see* above).

(1142) produced 44 sherds/1760 g, all residual. Diagnostic samian forms comprise two south Gaulish Dr 27 cups (70–110) – burnt – and (80–110); a south Gaulish Dr 18R plate (70–110); a central Gaulish Dr 81 heavy bowl with a slightly worn footring (120–160); a battered central Gaulish Dr 37 bowl (120–200); and a central Gaulish ?inkwell (120–200). Local fine wares comprise a Holt orange mica-coated ?bowl. Local coarse wares comprise late first-century grey wares and Holt orange wares. The grey wares include the spout of a 'feeding cup' or 'lamp filler' (*cf* Manning 1993, 110, fig 55, no 251 for a grey ware 'feeding cup' from Usk). Diagnostic orange wares from (1142) comprise a flanged bowl (*cf* Grimes 1930, 217, fig 65, nos 81 and 82); a two-handled flagon with cylindrical cornice-rimmed neck (*cf* Grimes 1930, 220, fig 68, no 127), also known from Holt in a reduced fabric; a beaker (*cf* Grimes 1930, 223 fig 71 nos 194–6); a flagon (probably from Holt); a clay roughcast beaker; and a burnt and battered lid with knob handle (?Holt). British coarse ware imports comprise Severn Valley ware, black-burnished 1 wares and grey ware copies of black-burnished forms. Recognisable black-burnished 1 forms comprised a cooking pot (120+); a flat rim dish/bowl (*cf* Gillam 1976, 69, fig 3, no 41); and a plain-rimmed dish with slight bead in the rim (?late second–early third century), with a chamfered or sagging base (*cf* Gillam 1976, 75, fig 5, no 78). Grey ware copies of black-burnished forms include a jar with sooted rim, dated on parallel for rim form in Gillam 1976 to the early to mid-second century, and a jar with sooted exterior (*c* 120-200). An oxidised Severn

Valley ware jar, second to third century in date, was also recovered (*cf* Carrington 1977, 157, fig 10.2, no 5).

Catalogue

10 Large coarse orange ware bowl with traces of red slip on the interior; probably Holt; HOL OX. (1225); SF 10146. No parallel in Grimes 1930; *c* 90/100–130. Ill 5.1.7.10.

11 Pedestal base of orange mica-coated ?beaker; Holt. (1220); SF 10144. No parallel in Grimes 1930; *c* 90/100–130. Ill 5.1.7.11.

12 Spout of coarse grey ware 'feeding cup' or 'lamp filler' with polished/burnished exterior; ?local product. (1142); SF 10147. Ill 5.1.7.12.

13 Adjoining rim sherds of an outsize coarse orange ware jar; probably Holt; HOL OX. (1146) and Phase IIb (1228); SF 10143. *c* 90/100–130. Ill 5.1.7.13.

14 Rim of large coarse orange ware flat-rimmed bowl with a single reed in the centre top of the rim; indeterminate local source. (1220); SF 10145. Ill 5.1.7.14.

15 Rim of a BB1 mini cooking pot/beaker; Poole Harbour, Dorset; DOR BB1. (119); SF 10189. Probably early–mid- to late 2 century. Ill 5.1.7.15.

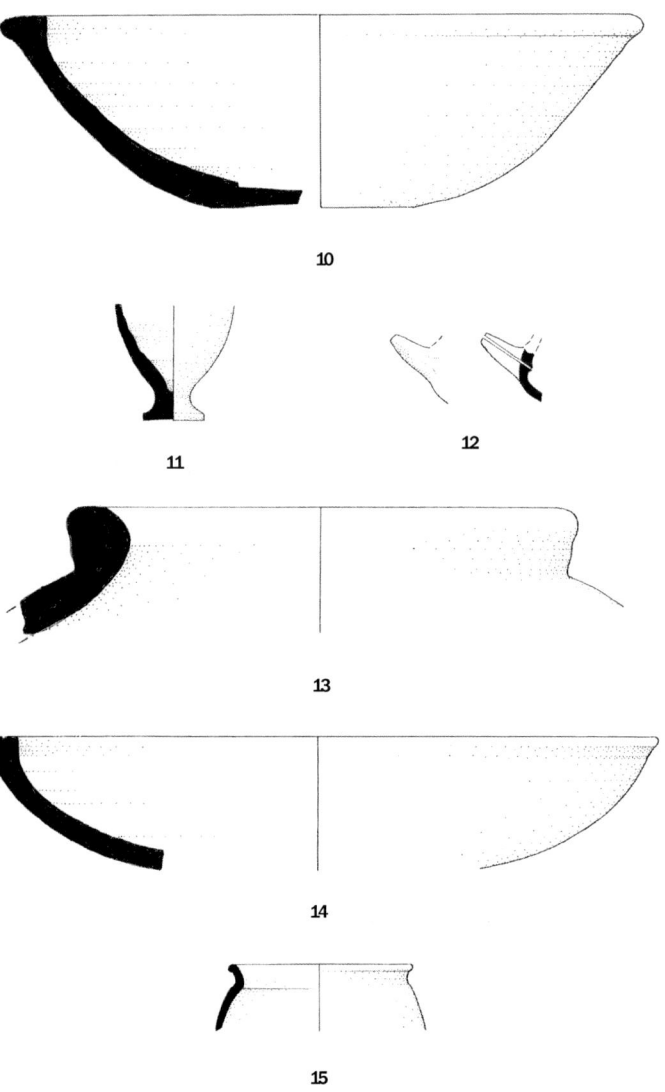

10

11

12

13

14

15

Ill 5.1.7 Phase IIa: Roman pottery. (Scale 1/4)

Discussion

A wide range of fabrics and forms was recovered from this sub-phase but almost all are residual. There were very few late Roman wares. The latest dated vessel is a late-third-century black-burnished 1 cooking pot from layer (1225). There are no fourth-century shell-tempered or calcite-gritted wares, although Lower Nene Valley colour-coated wares do make their first appearance in this sub-phase, alongside products of the Oxfordshire industry. However, the Lower Nene Valley wares do not include sherds diagnostic of fourth-century forms and the Oxfordshire sherds could only be broadly dated to *c* 240–400+. As well as samian wares from southern and central Gaul (notably none from east Gaul) and the Lower Nene Valley wares already mentioned, there is a small group of fine wares from Holt and black-slipped wares from Lezoux in central Gaul. Coarse wares comprise a large group of predominantly Holt oxidised wares but there are some second-century ?Wilderspool wares and one late second to third-century Severn Valley ware vessel. Black-burnished 1 wares comprise the second largest coarse ware group from IIa, followed by grey and white-slipped orange wares. The grey wares include a small but notable group of black-burnished 1 copies, dating from *c* 120+. One might have expected to see a decline in the proportion of black-burnished 1 vessels in a late fourth-century group (Tyers 1996, 79). Notable forms comprise tazze sherds, a 'feeding cup' or 'lamp filler' in coarse grey ware, a samian ware ?inkwell, and an outsize jar of unusual form (which cross-joins with a rim sherd from IIb). Considering the size of the assemblage from IIa, it is a little surprising that there was such a small group of mortaria, comprising just four vessels from Holt, ?Wilderspool and the Verulamium region. Wine and olive oil imports are represented by amphorae fragments from southern Gaul and southern Spain. The pottery assemblage is generally in good condition, with a only few abraded or burnt sherds.

Post-Roman Phases IIb–X and unstratified

The post-Roman and unstratified assemblage comprised 3,898 sherds/88,157 g, of which 442 sherds/1822 g were recovered from samples (11% by sherd count and 2% by weight of the post-Roman and unstratified total). Vessels of particular note are discussed briefly by phase below.

Phase IIb

Description

All the Roman pottery from Phase IIb came from the area of the ramp excavation. This sub-phase was notable for the first appearance of fourth-century pottery. Fill (1136) of post hole (1137) of Building II(i) produced a fourth-century Lower Nene Valley black colour-coated flagon or jug, alongside a coin dated 330–35. Fill (1179) of stone-robbing pit (1180) also produced three sherds of late Roman shell-tempered ware, comprising a jar base and two body sherds (probably from jars), dated *c* 360+. The source of these wares is uncertain, although a southern bias in their distribution suggests that it lay somewhere in southern England (Tomber & Dore 1998, 212). Tyers describes the fabric as South Midlands shell-tempered ware, which is abundant in late fourth-century assemblages in the east and south midlands, and suggests Harrold, Bedfordshire as a possible source (1996, 193). This, however, is discounted by Tomber & Dore, although it is acknowledged that similar rilled vessels were made there (1998, 212). For a description of the Harrold shelly ware fabric (HAR SH), *see* Tomber & Dore 1998, 115. The presence of these fourth-century sherds is notable, as they may support the suggestion that IIb began in the mid-fourth rather than the fifth century. However, only a handful of sherds can be assigned with confidence to this period; most of the assemblage is residual. Context (1179) also produced a sherd of east Gaulish samian, a Dr 18/31 or 31 plate/bowl or bowl with a date range of 130–160. This vessel represents the first appearance of east Gaulish samian on the site, although it is not a late form. Only one Oxfordshire red-slipped vessel was recovered, the rim of a wall-sided mortarium (*cf* Young 1977, 173, fig 67 no C97) from layer (1135), with a general date range of *c* 240–400+. A red slip-coated dish with overhung base was also recovered from (1135). It is comparable to Grimes 1930, 221 fig 69, no 137, which is recognised as a 'North African type' (Swan 1999, 539). A relatively large group of black-burnished 1 ware was recovered, but no vessels which date beyond the early to mid-third century. The grey wares include a high proportion of copies of black-burnished 1 cooking pots, including one jar from fill (1143) of pit (1144) which is comparable to Gillam 1976, 62, fig 1, no 7 (early to mid-third century). A Wilderspool white-slipped orange ware jar with a 'pulley-wheel' rim was recovered from (1143). The closest parallel for the form is Hartley & Webster 1973, 84 fig 5, no 39, which is described as a 'honey pot'. The latter example, however, lacks the 'pulley-wheel' rim of the Bridge Street vessel. Sherds of Baetican olive oil amphorae from (1135), (1138) and (1179) may have come from the later form, Dressel 23 (which dates from the third to fourth centuries), as they are too thin-walled for Dressel 20. However, they could equally have come from the earlier form, Dressel 25. IIb also saw an increase in the proportion of Gallic wine amphorae compared with IIa. Fill (1228) of gully (1229) produced the rim fragment of an outsize jar, which joins a rim sherd from IIa (1146) (*see* IIa above).

Phase IIc

Description

A single sherd of east Gaulish samian was recovered, a Dr 45 mortarium probably made at Trier in the third century. The base of an 'African-style' dish with an external recess at the wall/base junction was recovered from (1161) (*cf* Grimes 1930, 221, fig 69, no 137; Swan 1999b, 539). Fourth-century pottery was again recovered from sub-phase IIc. Lower Nene Valley vessels of this date comprise a black colour-coated flanged bowl (*cf* Howe *et al* 1980, 23 fig 6 no 70) from cultivation layer (1161) and a black colour-coated ?narrow-mouthed jar from (1177) (*cf* Howe *et al* 1980, 24 and fig 7, no 79 – although the upright neck on the Bridge Street vessel is more comparable to 25, fig 7, no 74, 'three-handled jar', which is dated to the late fourth–fifth century). A coin dated 335–340 was also recovered from (1161). The latest black-burnished 1 vessel is an early to ?mid-fourth-century cooking pot from (121) (*cf* Gillam 1976, 65, fig 2, no 13). As with sub-phase IIb, roughly 50% of the grey ware assemblage comprises copies of black-burnished 1 vessels. Two shell-tempered ware jars came from cultivation layers (1132) and (1177). An unusual white ware ?flagon with a wide splayed rim was recovered from shallow cultivation layer (1132). It is comparable to the Lower Nene Valley self-coloured ware narrow-mouthed jars illustrated in Howe *et al* 1980, 27, fig 8, nos 94–5, although the Bridge Street example has a much flatter, wider rim. The fabric is hard and fine, pale brown in colour with a grey core at the thickest part of the rim; the source was uncertain. Sherds of Baetican olive oil amphorae from (1132) and (1177) may have come from the third- to fourth-century form Dressel 23. A possible counter was recovered from (1177), comprising a fragment of a roughly formed disc of Baetican amphora fabric (NRFRC fabric code BAT AM 1). Rather surprisingly, it comprises the only pottery counter recovered from the site.

Catalogue

16 Rim of black colour-coated narrow-mouthed jar; burnt; Lower Nene Valley; LNV CC. (1177); SF 10149. Fourth century. Ill 5.1.8.16.
17 Rim of a shell-tempered ware jar; two adjoining sherds; ROB SH; source uncertain. (1177); SF 10148. *c* 360+. Ill 5.1.8.17.
18 Rim of a coarse white ware ?flagon with widely splayed rim; source uncertain. (1132); SF 10150. Ill 5.1.8.18.

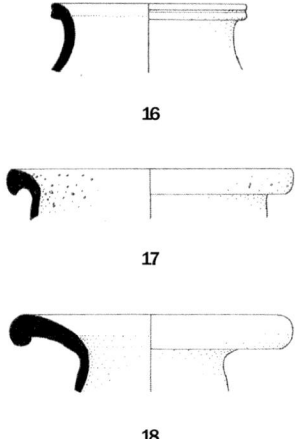

Ill 5.1.8 Phase IIc: Roman pottery. (Scale 1/4)

Phase III

Description

Phase III produced 8% by sherd count and 11% by weight of the site total, comprising an assemblage of 391 sherds/12,121 g. The Oxfordshire wares include an indeterminate parchment ware vessel with red-painted curvilinear and dot motifs from Evaluation Trench B levelling layer (132). According to Young, curvilinear decoration was sometimes used on the outer walls of jars or beakers (1977, 82). None of the Lower Nene Valley ware colour-coated sherds cane be dated more closely than mid-second to late fourth century. The latest black-burnished vessel is a ?late third to early fourth-century cooking pot from Evaluation Trench C layer (70) (*cf* Gillam 1976, 65 fig 2 no 11).

This phase saw the first appearance of fourth-century calcite-gritted ware, represented by two adjoining rim sherds of a Huntcliff type jar or cooking pot with characteristic internal lid-seating groove (*cf* Gillam 1968, 59, fig 19, no 163) from (1018) in Escalator Pit B. Such vessels are rare in Chester. There was also a shell-tempered ware ?jar sherd from (1175), the fill of cess pit (1176). The burnt base of a Holt coarse orange ware mortarium with a ?graffito inscription on the underside of the base came from layer (1022).

Catalogue

19 Two adjoining rim sherds of a calcite-gritted jar/cooking pot; Huntcliff, East Yorkshire; HUN CG. (1018) and Phase VI (566); SF 10151. *cf* Gillam 1968, 59 fig 19 no 163. *c* 360+. Ill 5.1.9.19.

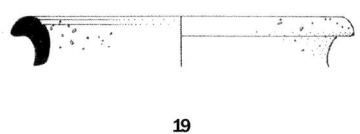

19

Ill 5.1.9 Phase III: Roman pottery. (Scale 1/4)

Phase IV

Description

This phase produced 9% by sherd count and 8% by weight of the total assemblage, comprising 444 sherds/8400 g. A central Gaulish Dr 18/31R plate/bowl (120–160) has a round rivet hole with traces of the lead rivet still in position, indicating that the vessel had been mended in antiquity. A single east Gaulish samian vessel, a Dr 31R bowl (dated 160–240) came from (974). None of the Oxfordshire wares can be dated more closely than *c* 240–400+. The latest dated black-burnished 1 vessels comprise a ?late third-century cooking pot rim from cultivation soil (1119), which also contained a coin dated 364–378, and a ?late third-century cooking pot (sooted) from (974). Fourth-century shell-tempered wares comprise a jar from ?post-Roman demolition layer (974) and an indeterminate body sherd from fill (1015) of pit (1016). A south Spanish Dressel 20 amphora rim in later Baetican fabric, BAT AM 2 (Tomber & Dore 1998, 85), also from (974), can be dated to *c* 250–300 (*cf* Peacock & Williams 1986, 138 fig 66 no 45). The assemblage includes a large group of Holt orange wares, a small but significant group of grey ware copies of black-burnished 1 forms and a small but notable group of Mancetter-Hartshill mortaria, including both hooked and hammerhead rim forms.

Phase V

Description

Phase V produced the second largest group of Roman pottery from the site after Phase II, comprising 633 sherds/13,634 g, or 13% by sherd count and weight of the total assemblage. The only east Gaulish samian vessels from Phase V are a Dr 33 cup (160–220) from layer (1654) and a Dr 45 mortarium (170–200) from layer (1615). Oxfordshire red-slipped vessels include a shallow bowl with out-turned rim, dated *c* 325–400+ from layer (1350) (*cf* Young 1977, 161, fig 59, type C50). There are two fourth-

century Lower Nene Valley ware black colour-coated forms: a ?flagon/jug from wall (496) and a flanged bowl from fill (1520) of pit (1521). The orange wares include a notable group of ?Wilderspool or ?Severn Valley ware wide-mouthed, lid-seated jars from (830), (996) and (1117). Similar groups of vessels were recovered from Phases Id (1239); IIa (1219); IIb (1179); IIc (1161) and (1177) and IV (268), (974) and (1119). Three such vessels were also found unstratified. Wilderspool versions of these vessels were recovered from the 1976 excavations at the site and were dated by Webster to the mid- to late second century (Hinchliffe *et al* 1992, 124; *cf* 132, fig 72, no 446 and 149, fig 81, no 687 for comparable forms). A Severn Valley ware version of the form from Chester is known from the YMCA 1976 excavations (Carrington 1977, 157 fig 10.2, no 32; the latter is undated and there are no parallels for the form in Webster 1976). Webster suggested that these jars were used for mixing and other kitchen use (Webster in Hinchliffe *et al* 1992, 127). A 'North African type' orange ware dish/platter with overhanging base and a well burnished interior was recovered from primary fill (1673) of pit (1670). The latest dated black-burnished vessels comprise an ?early to mid-fourth-century cooking pot from the upper fill, (1632), of pit (1455), and a ?late third-century cooking pot from cultivation soil (830). There is a small but significant group of grey ware copies of black-burnished 1 forms, including flanged bowls comparable to mid- to late third-century forms, from (830). Fourth-century shell-tempered wares comprise three jar rims and a probable jar sherd from cultivation soil (830), layers (1004) and (1615) and fill (1738) of pit (1659). The three jar rims are all burnt. The white wares include a Mancetter-Hartshill mortarium with red painted vertical stripes on the hammerhead rim (?third century) from fill (1162) of pit (1163). A battered amphora sherd in an indeterminate white on orange fabric from medieval cultivation layer (1656) shows the edge of a rivet hole, indicating that the vessel had been mended in antiquity.

Phase VI

Description

Phase VI produced 406 sherds/6747g, comprising 8.5% by sherd count and 6% by weight of the total assemblage. A South Gaulish samian Dr 29 bowl (60–85) from layer (697) has a broken rivet hole, indicating that the vessel was mended in antiquity. Oxfordshire red colour-coated wares include an abraded bowl with rouletted decoration from layer (977) (*cf* Young 1977, 166, fig 64, type C81). A Lower Nene Valley ware black colour-coated flanged-rim bowl (burnt) came from fill (87) of pit (89)/(112)/(963). Notable orange ware forms comprise a tazza with frilled edging around the carination from fill (692) of pit (681) (*cf* Grimes 1930, 225, fig 73, no 213) and a strainer fragment from fill (706) of pit (707) (*cf* Grimes 1930, 224, fig 72, no 209). A Wilderspool orange ware dish/bowl with red painted vertical stripes was recovered from ?oven (896). Wilderspool red-painted wares are fairly rare in Chester and this is the only example noted from the assemblage (Hartley 1981, 171–9). The latest dated black-burnished 1 vessel is an ?early to mid-fourth-century cooking pot from layer (771). A small group of grey wares includes just two copies of black-burnished

I forms, including a plain-rimmed dish from fill (702) of pit (701) and a jar (burnt) from upper fill (1540) of pit (1541) dated on rim form to early to mid-third century. A calcite-gritted Huntcliff-type jar rim, dated *c* 360+, was recovered from upper fill (566) of pit (614) (*cf* Gillam 1968, 59, fig 19, no 163 for form). It joins a rim sherd from Phase III (1018). A shell-tempered ware jar rim (slightly burnt) was recovered from fill (797) of cess pit (487). The amphorae include an indeterminate ribbed vessel in a micaceous orange fabric from layer (771). It is thin-walled with shallow broad ribs and may have been Peacock & Williams 1986 Class 45 (form British Biv), although the Bridge Street sherd is orange rather than deep reddish-brown in colour (Peacock & Williams 1986, 188–90; Tyers 1996, 103). There is also the hooked rim of a ?Dressel 38 with a handle scar just below the rim from fill (779) of oven (778) (Peacock & Williams Class 18; Cam 186C). These vessels are thought to have carried fish-based products.

Catalogue

20   Rim of a red-painted, coarse orange ware dish/bowl; Wilderspool. (896); SF 10153. Early to mid-/late second century. Ill 5.1.10.20.

21   Rim of a shell-tempered ware jar; ROB SH; source uncertain. (797); sample <5077>; SF 10152. *c* 360+. Ill 5.1.10.21.

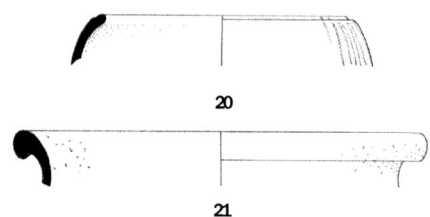

Ill 5.1.10 Phase VI: Roman pottery. (Scale 1/4)

Phase VII

Description

Phase VII produced 8% by sherd count and 5% by weight of the total assemblage, comprising a group of 390 sherds/ 5847 g. Oxfordshire red-slipped wares include a very battered plain rim ?bowl from fill (824) of pit (925) (*cf* Young 1977, 160 type C51). A Lower Nene Valley black colour-coated flanged bowl also came from (824) and the basal sherd (burnt), probably from a similar flanged bowl, from fill (245) of pit (244). The orange wares, which are dominated by Holt forms, include a possible face pot fragment from (824). A frilled tazza (burnt) in a probable Holt white-slipped orange fabric, was also recovered from (824). The latest dated black-burnished 1 vessels comprise a ?late third–early fourth-century flanged-rim bowl from (824); a ?late third or ?early fourth-century cooking pot (battered and sooted), also from (824); a ?late third– early fourth-century flanged bowl (battered, abraded and burnt) from fill (1592) of pit (1593); and a late third-century+ cooking pot from eighteenth-century cultivation soil (1891). The small group of grey wares include two copies of black-burnished 1 forms, both jars, one of which, from upper fill (1507) of pit (1506), is dated by rim form to the ?late third century. Shell-tempered vessels comprise a flanged bowl (burnt) and a rilled ?jar sherd (burnt), both from (824).

Catalogue

22   Body sherd of a coarse orange ware ?face pot; indeterminate local source. (824); SF 10154. Ill 5.1.11.22.

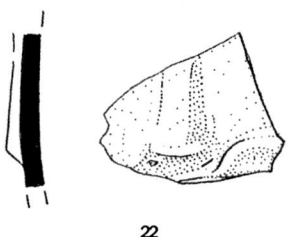

Ill 5.1.11 Phase VII: Roman pottery. (Scale 1/2)

Phase VIII

Description

Phase VIII produced 313 sherds/5220 g (6.5% by sherd count and 5% by weight of the total assemblage. The Oxfordshire red-slipped wares include a wall-sided mortarium (badly burnt) from layer (1637) (*cf* Young 1977, 175 fig 67, type C97). A large group of Holt orange wares was also recovered from this phase, including a dish of North African type, with rilling on the underside of the base, from layer (1439). A Holt orange ware bowl rim from layer (455) shows the broken edge of a ?rivet hole. The latest dated black-burnished 1 vessel is a late third-century flanged-rim dish/bowl from (341). Copies of black-burnished 1 forms comprise approximately one-quarter of the grey ware group. They include a ?mid-third-century jar with burnished rim (date based on comparable BB1 rim forms) from fill (638) of depression (680). The only fourth-century wares comprise two shell-tempered jars and an indeterminate body sherd, all from ?cultivation soil (341). Two of the sherds are burnt and one of the jars has a lid-seated rim.

Catalogue

23   Rim of a shell-tempered ware jar with internal lid seating; ROB SH; source uncertain. (341); SF 10155. *c* 360+. Ill 5.1.12.23.

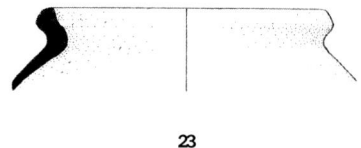

Ill 5.1.12 Phase VIII: Roman pottery. (Scale 1/4)

Phase IX

Description

Phase IX produced 4% by sherd count and 2.5% by weight of the site assemblage, comprising a group of 189 sherds/ 2673 g. Notable vessels include an Oxfordshire red-slipped ?bowl from fill (713) of cut (727) (*cf* Young 1977, 161 type C51 – especially type C51.6 'the most common Oxford colour-coat type') and a ?flagon/bottle sherd decorated with rouletted bands (abraded) from fill (352) of cut (336) (*cf* Young 1977, 149 fig 53 type C8 for probable form). An ?Oxfordshire red-slipped open vessel with abraded slip and edge of ?rivet hole was recovered from fill (316) of (315). The latest dated black-burnished 1 vessel is a late third-century cooking pot (sooted) from fill (629) of cut (628). Grey ware copies of black-burnished forms include a ?third-century flanged bowl from (629) (cf Gillam 1976, 69, fig 3, nos 43 and 44) and a ?mid-third-century jar from fill (571) of cut (570). A fourth-century shell-tempered rilled ?jar sherd was recovered from fill (348) of cut (347) – comprising the only clearly late Roman sherd from this phase. The white wares include a ?third-century Mancetter-Hartshill hammerhead rim mortarium, with red painted decoration on the rim, from fill (325) of cut (326).

Phase X

Description

Phase X produced a residual group of 196 sherds/4455 g, comprising 4% by sherd count and weight of the total assemblage. An Oxfordshire red-slipped wall-sided mortarium (c 240–400+) was recovered from layer (300), a very common, long-lived type (cf Young 1977, 173 and fig 67, type C97). Fourth-century Lower Nene Valley black colour-coated wares comprise a flanged bowl from fill (302) of cut (303) and a jar with grooved rim and neck from fill (407) of cut (406). For the latter form, which is rare in Chester, cf Howe et al 1980, fig 6, nos 69 and 70 and fig 7, no 74. The latest dated black-burnished 1 vessels comprise ?late third–early fourth-century cooking pots from cut (413), fill (563) of cut (360), and fill (334) of cut (333).

Catalogue

24 Rim of a black colour-coated jar with a grooved rim and neck; Lower Nene Valley; LNV CC. (407); SF 10156. cf Howe et al 1980, fig 6, nos 69 and 70 and fig 7 no 74: fourth century. Ill 5.1.13.24.

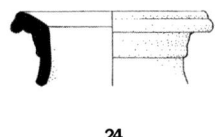

Ill 5.1.13 Phase X: Roman pottery. (Scale 1/4)

Unstratified

Description

A group of 231 sherds/6563 g was unstratified, comprising 5% by sherd count and 6% by weight of the total assemblage. Notable vessels comprise three more wide-mouthed, lid-seated Wilderspool or Severn Valley ware jars (*see* also Phases I, II, IV and V). A Holt coarse orange ware North African type dish with overhanging base was also recovered. Fourth-century wares comprise a calcite-gritted Huntcliff-type jar with typical down-turned, hooked rim with internal lid-seating groove and shell-tempered jars, one with lid-seated rim. A Mancetter-Hartshill mortarium has a rivet hole at the junction of the base and wall, indicating that the vessel had been mended in antiquity. A battered Dressel 20 amphora body sherd has a ?graffito 'X' close to the handle stub, SF 9806.

Catalogue

25 Rim of a calcite-gritted jar/cooking pot; Huntcliff, East Yorkshire; HUN CG. Unstratified; SF 10187. cf Gillam 1968, 59, fig 19, no 163. c 360+. Ill 5.1.14.25.

26 Body sherd of south Spanish Baetican olive oil amphora with graffito 'X' inscribed below the handle stub: BAT AM 1. Unstratified; SF 9806. Late first–mid-third century. Ill 5.1.4.26.

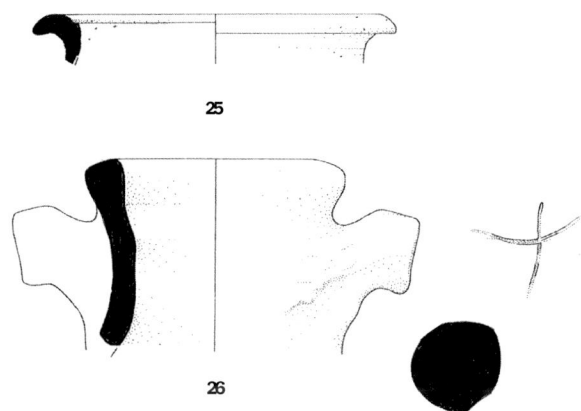

Ill 5.1.14 Unstratified Roman pottery. (Scale 1/4)

Discussion of Phases IIb–X

Phases IIb to X produced 3,677 sherds/81,748 g; 231 sherds/6563 g were unstratified. A wide range of fabrics and forms was recovered and the pottery is in mixed condition. The largest group came from sub-phases IIb and IIc, comprising 680 sherds/21,837 g). Phase V produced the second largest group with 633 sherds/13,634 g. The assemblage generally reflects the picture from the Roman phases, I and IIa, in that there is a large group of late first- to early second-century material – mainly locally produced grey, orange and white-slipped orange wares. Orange wares from the post-Roman phases form a major component of the site total, comprising a massive 38% by sherd count and 30% by weight. (In comparison, orange wares from the Roman phases comprise 35.5% by sherd count and 33.7% by weight of the I and IIa total). They are mainly Holt wares but also include some Wilderspool vessels and a small number of Severn Valley wares. Some of the grey wares are probably Holt products as there are both reduced and oxidised examples of the same forms (also published in Grimes 1930). There is a significant proportion of grey ware copies of black-burnished 1 forms, particularly cooking pots, with both acute and obtuse-angled lattice (which date the forms to pre-200 and post-200 respectively). Second-century wares include black-burnished 1 vessels, grey ware copies of black-burnished 1 wares, Mancetter-Hartshill white wares (dating from about the middle of the second century to the early fourth century), Lower Nene Valley wares (dating from about the middle of the second century to the late fourth century), Wilderspool wares (early to mid- to late second century), Severn Valley wares and samian wares (mainly central Gaulish vessels; some (very few) east Gaulish forms). Other second-century fine wares include occasional black colour coats from central Gaul (c 150 to early third century) and north Gaul (c 135/40–160+). Third-century material include a few black colour-coated sherds from Trier (c 180–250) and black-burnished 1 vessels (mainly cooking pots). However, the assemblage also comprises a small but significant group of late Roman wares which are absent or largely absent from the Roman phases. These comprise fourth-century shell-tempered wares (23 sherds/413 g), Huntcliff calcite-gritted jars (3 sherds/52 g), also 360+; fourth-century Nene Valley wares (mainly flanged bowls) and later third- and fourth-century black-burnished 1 wares (including flanged bowls and cooking pots), as well as Oxfordshire white and red-slipped wares (240–400+). Of the diagnostic vessels, aside from amphorae, the most common forms comprise beakers, jars, cooking pots, bowls, and dish/bowls, closely followed by flagons, cups and dishes. Rare but notable vessel forms comprise a single strainer and two tazze sherds. A wider range of amphorae is present, although wine amphorae from southern Gaul and olive oil vessels from southern Spain continue to form the largest component of the group. Unusually, only one counter is present - from IIc - made from a sherd of south Spanish olive oil amphora.

A small group of 'North-African type' vessels (four in number) was recovered from post-Roman phases IIb, IIc, V and VIII; a single vessel was also found unstratified. All five vessels are of similar form, comprising dishes with an overhanging base. Four are in a coarse oxidised Holt fabric; the source of the vessel from IIc, which has a red slip coating, is uncertain, although the form is comparable to Grimes 1930, 221 fig 69 no 137. The dish from Phase V has a well burnished interior and that from Phase VIII has distinctive rilling on the underside of the base. In addition, the Roman sub-phase IIa produced a single vessel of possible North African type, a two-handled flagon, comparable to Grimes 1930, 220 fig 68 no 125. Swan has suggested that the presence of these vessels at Holt and Chester, together with similar, locally made, vessels of North African type on the Antonine Wall, may indicate the presence of small numbers of North African soldiers in the vexillations which returned to Britain from the Mauretanian war in 149/150 (Swan 1999b, 423). Recent studies of the samian and the coins indicate that production at Holt probably began in the late Flavian period (possibly *c* 87) and continued until soon after the middle of the second century, possibly ending about 165/170 (Swan 1999b, 425; 2004, 262). The appearance of small numbers of Holt mortaria on the Antonine Wall also indicates that these continued to be produced at the kiln site until the mid-second century (Swan 1999b, 426).

Discussion of the assemblage

Source and date range

Local sources dominate the pottery assemblage, supplying approximately 62% of the site total. 80.6% of the Phase I total came from local sources, particularly Holt (*c* 90–130) and other indeterminate Cheshire Plain sources. Wilderspool (early/mid- to late second century) supplied just four sherds in Phase I. 55.6% of the Phase II assemblage came from local sources, with Holt again the main supplier. Ignoring the small groups from cross-over phases III/IV, V/VI and IX/X, approximately 62% of the pottery assemblages from Phases III to X came from local sources, again with Holt as the major supplier. 68% of the unstratified assemblage was also from local sources.

Overall, 17% of the assemblage is composed of British traded wares (ie pottery imported from non-local British sources). Phase I received just over 4% of its pottery supply from non-local British sources; Phase II 22.1% and Phases III–X, an average of 18%. Black-burnished 1 ware from Poole in Dorset was the major source, accounting for 10% of all traded wares reaching the site, with 1.6% of the assemblage being supplied by the white ware industries of Hartshill-Mancetter in Warwickshire. The major industries of Oxfordshire and the Lower Nene Valley again each provided just over 1% of the pottery assemblage. Verulamium-region white wares of the late first century appears in just three phases: I (five sherds), II (four sherds) and V (one sherd). Black-burnished 1 ware is the least common in Phase I and the most common in Phase II.

Continental imports comprised almost 20% of the site total, with 14.3% from Phase I, 21.5% from Phase II, and an average of 19% from Phases III to X. Central Gaulish samian supplied almost 7% of the site total. South Gaulish samian wares are dominant in Phase I (thirty-seven sherds as opposed to three central Gaulish sherds) but this pattern alters in Phase II, with twenty-seven sherds of south Gaulish samian but 83 sherds of central Gaulish samian. Baetican olive oil amphorae made up 5.3% of the pottery assemblage, Gallic wine amphorae 2.3%. Other sources, including south Spanish fish-sauce and Italian wine amphorae, made up approximately 2% of the site total.

There is a strong bias towards early pottery in the assemblage, which was another aspect of its domination by local wares, which mainly date to the late first to early second century. Second- and third-century material is rarer and there is only a small, although noteworthy, collection of fourth-century pottery. This consists of shell-tempered ware forms (23 sherds/413 g), especially jars; Lower Nene Valley ware black colour-coated forms (9 sherds/249 g), especially flanged bowls; black-burnished 1 cooking pots (3 sherds/43 g) and 'Huntcliff type' calcite-gritted jars (3 sherds/52 g). There was also an Oxfordshire red colour-coated bowl dated *c* 325–400+.

There was also a high level of residuality on the site from sub-phase Ie onwards. Second-century and later pottery only appears in quantity from Phase II, ie in late Roman and post-Roman deposits, and fourth-century pottery first occurs in sub-phase IIb. Even so, over half the Roman pottery in post-Roman layers continued to be made up of local, early wares.

The assemblage from the post-Roman phases appears to exhibit a fairly consistent pattern in both source and condition. The probable factors influencing its make-up are the truncation of later Roman deposits and a continuing cycle of disturbance and redeposition of material during later phases of activity (eg extensive pit-digging) on the site. The assemblage may represent redeposited material which originated on the site or in buildings nearby (eg the bath house to the south or the tribunes' houses to the north), or a mixture. When comparing the pottery assemblage with those from Browns 1960 (Thompson 1967; Rutland & Whitwell 1960), 25–9 Bridge Street 1996 (Emery 1996 and Newgate/Pepper Street 1963/4 (Mason *et al* 2005), the latter option seems more likely as there are close similarities in the range and date of the material. The same is true of the finds assemblages as a whole from these sites.

Forms

Indeterminate forms (including vessels described as 'flagon/bowl' or 'flagon/amphora' etc) account for 56.3% of the total assemblage. Of the diagnostic forms present, vessels for the transport of goods (amphorae and amphora lids) comprise 10% of the assemblage; Vessels used in food preparation and storage of food 11.5% (jars/cooking pots 8%, mortaria 3%; lids, strainer and *clibanus* less than 1%); vessels used for serving food and drink about 20% (beakers 2.5%, cups 2%, flagons 3%, bowls 9%, dishes 2%, platters and plates under 1% each); 'other' vessels (feeding cup, inkwell, tazze) 0.15% and gaming counters 0.02%. However, some coarse ware bowls have traces of sooting, sometimes around the rim, suggesting that they were used for cooking food, perhaps as lids or covers. The relatively high proportion of tableware to kitchen wares suggests a relatively high-status assemblage.

Condition

Condition was recorded for just 27.8% of the assemblage. This indicates that approximately 62% of sherds are in good condition. Approximately 12% of the total is burnt or slightly burnt, probably as a result of the use of bonfires to cleanse old rubbish. Only c 9.5% of the assemblage was recorded as abraded, slightly abraded or very abraded. 4% of sherds are sooted, indicating their use as cooking pots. Six vessels had rivet holes, indicating that they were mended in antiquity. This may have happened for a range of reasons: temporary shortage in supply, a lack of money to replenish stocks, or the desire to mend a favourite vessel. Although this evidence comes from such a small group, clearly a wide range of forms was deemed worthy of mending. They comprise two samian ware vessels, an ?Oxfordshire red-slipped vessel, a Mancetter-Hartshill mortarium, a Holt coarse orange ware bowl and an indeterminate amphora. Graffiti occurs on two, possibly three, vessels: a Holt orange ware mortarium, a Baetican olive oil amphora and possibly a central Gaulish samian vessel, although the incisions on the base of the latter may be accidental.

Appendix

Pottery from Brown's basement 1960

An examination of the excavators' notes in the Grosvenor Museum archive indicates the presence of a 'large quantity' of decorated samian, consisting of bowl forms Dr 29 and Dr 37 of late first- to mid-second-century types (Rutland & Whitwell 1960). Plain wares comprise forms Dr 27 and 33, plate Dr 18, plate/bowl Dr 18/31, bowl Dr 31, cup Dr 35, dish Dr 36 and bowl Ritterling 12. Coarse wares are dominated by locally produced wares. These include late first- to early second-century Holt forms in orange mica-coated, orange, and white-slipped orange fabrics, as well as late first-century grey and black-on-brown wares and indeterminate Cheshire Plain wares in orange and white-slipped fabrics. The latter may include some Wilderspool products of second-century date. British traded and continental wares comprise black-burnished 1 cooking pots, flat-rimmed dishes and a bead-rim dish, all of second-century date apart from two

cooking pots (one mid-second–early third-century, the other late second–mid-third century). There are also white wares of uncertain provenance, a Mancetter-Hartshill hammerhead mortarium dated 300–70 and amphora handle stamped DFITA and black colour coated vessels of indeterminate source. The latter comprise a beaker base and a lamp fragment. The high proportion of tablewares suggests a fairly high-status assemblage.

25–9 Bridge Street 1996

This evaluation produced pottery ranging from the late first to fourth centuries. The assemblage comprises a wide range of fabrics and forms from a range of sources but is dominated by locally produced orange wares (43.8% by sherd count). The relatively high proportion of tablewares to kitchen wares again indicates a fairly high-status assemblage. The finds assemblage as a whole bears a close similarity to that from 25 Bridge Street 2001 both in the range and quality of material recovered (Emery 1996, *passim*).

Newgate/Pepper Street 1963

Excavations on the site of the fortress bath house produced a poorly stratified pottery assemblage of just 656 sherds/29,237 g. 54% of the samian was from south Gaul and 44% from central Gaul; only one vessel was from east Gaul. Almost all the south Gaulish vessels are thought to have been produced in the Flavian period. The central Gaulish wares date mainly to the Hadrianic or Hadrianic–early Antonine periods, with few vessels produced after c 160. 55% of the fine and coarse wares (593 sherds) were unphased. The majority of the coarse ware assemblage comprises locally produced orange, white-slipped orange, grey and black-on-brown wares of ate first to early second-century date, with smaller groups of second, third and fourth-century wares. The latter include shell-tempered ware jars and a grey ware flanged bowl from Crambeck in east Yorkshire. Other British and continental imports comprise oxidised Wilderspool and Severn Valley wares, black-burnished 1 cooking pots and flanged bowls, Lower Nene Valley colour-coated wares, Mancetter-Hartshill mortaria (dated 240–370), Oxfordshire red colour-coated wares, black-slipped Rhenish wares and amphorae from southern Gaul and southern Spain. Forms are largely restricted to jars, beakers, bowls, flagons and mortaria (Mason *et al* 2005, 93–9).

Acknowledgements

I should like to express my thanks to volunteers, Liz and John Bailey and Simon Skelling for their invaluable help in the preparation of the archive.

Table 5.1.9 Roman pottery: total amount quantified by common ware name, phase, no of sherds and weight

	Phase															
	I		II		II		III/IV		IV		V		V/VI		VI	
Fabric	No	Wt (g)	No	Wt (g)	No	Wt (g)	No	Wt (g)	No	Wt (g)	No	Wt (g)	No	Wt (g)	No	Wt (g)
Samian	40	362	112	1169	43	468	2	10	31	230	59	511	1	8	35	220
Red cc	1	74	13	232	7	34	0	0	8	41	11	100	0	0	6	75
Black cc	2	4	12	101	11	31	0	0	3	9	16	87	0	0	10	127
Lead-glazed	1	1	0	0	0	0	0	0	0	0	0	0	0	0	0	0
Orange mica-dusted	7	21	23	357	3	25	0	0	2	10	3	52	0	0	2	11
White eggshell	1	1	2	5	0	0	0	0	0	0	0	0	0	0	0	0
Black-on-brown	56	249	3	60	5	41	0	0	1	1	0	0	0	0	0	0
Grey or black-on-brown	6	46	0	0	0	0	0	0	0	0	0	0	0	0	0	0
Grey	94	970	83	1269	30	386	0	0	36	254	39	684	0	0	24	337
Orange	158	2802	419	10192	145	3451	15	218	191	3335	319	5665	1	11	219	3119
Orange or grey	2	47	0	0	0	0	0	0	0	0	3	39	0	0	2	10
Orange or CBM	7	24	14	15	1	1	0	0	9	33	6	19	0	0	10	37
Red-slipped orange	0	0	0	0	0	0	0	0	1	34	1	35	0	0	2	22
BB1	12	187	166	2189	65	789	0	0	88	656	38	453	0	0	23	250
BB1 or grey	0	0	0	0	0	0	0	0	0	0	1	4	0	0	0	0
Shell-tempered	0	0	6	75	1	2	0	0	2	41	4	44	0	0	1	27
Calcite-gritted	0	0	0	0	1	12	0	0	0	0	0	0	0	0	1	17
White-slipped orange	54	549	89	1865	17	427	4	107	9	100	32	469	0	0	26	344
White	7	77	22	627	8	153	1	72	16	686	32	637	0	0	13	353
White or amphora	1	8	1	2	0	0	1	8	0	0	0	0	0	0	0	0
Amphora	26	2037	115	15778	54	6301	4	100	47	2970	69	4835	1	243	32	1798
Indet mortarium fabric	0	0	1	70	0	0	0	0	0	0	0	0	0	0	0	0
Total	475	7459	1081	34006	391	12121	27	515	444	8400	633	13634	3	262	406	6747

Table 5.1.10 Roman pottery: total amount quantified by form, phase, no of sherds and weight

	Phase															
	I		II		III		III/IV		IV		V		V/VI		VI	
Form	No	Wt (g)	No	Wt (g)	No	Wt (g)	No	Wt (g)	No	Wt (g)	No	Wt (g)	No	Wt (g)	No	Wt (g)
Flagon	17	246	58	2045	11	365	7	181	2	16	8	214	0	0	6	110
Flagon/amphora	0	0	0	0	0	0	1	8	0	0	0	0	0	0	0	0
Flagon/bottle	0	0	0	0	0	0	0	0	0	0	0	0	0	0	0	0
Flagon/bowl	0	0	0	0	0	0	0	0	0	0	0	0	0	0	0	0
Flagon/jar/beaker	0	0	1	11	0	0	0	0	0	0	0	0	0	0	0	0
Flagon/jar	0	0	0	0	0	0	0	0	2	25	0	0	0	0	0	0
Flagon/jug	0	0	2	61	0	0	0	0	0	0	3	168	0	0	0	0
Beaker	15	148	37	415	14	87	0	0	8	46	13	65	0	0	7	27
Beaker/jar	0	0	1	8	0	0	0	0	0	0	0	0	0	0	0	0
Inkwell	0	0	1	7	0	0	0	0	0	0	0	0	0	0	0	0
Jar	66	464	67	1530	8	217	1	12	13	269	26	501	0	0	16	335
Outsize jar	0	0	2	619	0	0	0	0	0	0	0	0	0	0	0	0
Jar/beaker	8	29	0	0	0	0	0	0	1	8	0	0	0	0	0	0
Jar/bowl	3	147	0	0	0	0	0	0	1	12	0	0	0	0	2	139
Jar/flagon	5	429	5	301	0	0	0	0	1	5	3	485	0	0	2	110
Cooking pot	7	128	54	851	17	173	0	0	25	143	5	60	0	0	8	74
Mini cooking pot/beaker	0	0	1	8	0	0	0	0	0	0	0	0	0	0	0	0
Bowl	31	533	99	2850	49	1137	3	25	38	812	61	1266	0	0	36	724
Bowl/mortarium	0	0	1	4	0	0	0	0	0	0	1	9	0	0	0	0
Bowl/jar	0	0	0	0	0	0	0	0	1	5	0	0	0	0	2	147
Cup	9	62	28	153	3	56	0	0	5	20	10	41	0	0	5	25
Cup/dish	0	0	0	0	0	0	0	0	0	0	0	0	0	0	0	0
Feeding cup	0	0	1	13	0	0	0	0	0	0	0	0	0	0	0	0
Mortarium	6	417	26	1601	11	1046	0	0	14	810	26	830	0	0	10	430
Dish/bowl	3	114	21	409	4	80	0	0	18	322	31	494	0	0	15	258
Dish/platter	0	0	1	17	0	0	0	0	0	0	0	0	0	0	0	0
Dish	8	136	20	528	15	385	0	0	6	147	6	89	0	0	9	126
Plate	4	3	2	11	2	6	0	0	0	0	1	1	0	0	1	3
Plate/bowl	0	0	9	111	3	9	0	0	1	11	1	4	1	8	1	2
Plate/bowl or bowl	0	0	6	97	2	59	0	0	0	0	0	0	0	0	0	0
Plate or plate/bowl	1	3	1	3	0	0	0	0	0	0	0	0	0	0	1	5
Platter	0	0	0	0	0	0	0	0	0	0	0	0	0	0	0	0
Lid	5	129	5	115	0	0	0	0	3	46	2	15	0	0	4	83
Strainer	0	0	0	0	0	0	0	0	0	0	0	0	0	0	1	11
Tazza	1	18	2	27	0	0	0	0	0	0	0	0	0	0	1	17
Counter	0	0	1	7	0	0	0	0	0	0	0	0	0	0	0	0
Clibanus	1	644	0	0	0	0	0	0	0	0	0	0	0	0	0	0
Amphora	22	2014	114	15771	53	6300	3	96	46	2961	69	4846	1	243	32	1798
Amphora lid	4	23	0	0	1	1	1	4	1	9	2	7	0	0	0	0
Indet closed	221	1533	378	5157	146	1858	11	189	183	2052	240	3310	1	11	158	1623
Indet open	21	189	77	1012	15	240	0	0	27	317	40	513	0	0	28	348
Indet	10	26	46	249	36	101	0	0	39	331	79	697	0	0	51	315
Pottery/CBM	7	24	14	15	1	1	0	0	9	33	6	19	0	0	10	37
Total	475	7459	1081	34006	391	12121	27	515	444	8400	633	13634	3	262	406	6747

	Phase												
	VII		**VIII**		**IX**		**IX/X**		**X**		**u/s**		*Total*	*Total*
Fabric	No	Wt (g)	No	Wt (g)	No	Wt (g)	No	Wt (g)	No	Wt (g)	No	Wt (g)	no	wt (g)
Samian	37	243	22	132	20	66	0	0	20	170	23	222	445	3811
Red cc	11	54	4	64	4	36	0	0	2	25	1	19	68	754
Black cc	9	58	5	31	3	8	0	0	3	89	1	8	75	553
Lead-glazed	0	0	0	0	0	0	0	0	0	0	0	0	1	1
Orange mica-dusted	2	17	4	23	1	7	0	0	1	4	0	0	48	527
White eggshell	1	1	0	0	0	0	0	0	0	0	0	0	4	7
Black-on-brown	0	0	1	4	1	21	0	0	0	0	1	39	68	415
Grey or black-on-brown	0	0	0	0	0	0	0	0	0	0	0	0	6	46
Grey	15	200	21	202	9	70	0	0	13	229	6	127	370	4728
Orange	197	2811	162	2274	90	1077	3	17	98	1686	145	2765	2162	39423
Orange or grey	0	0	2	61	0	0	0	0	1	8	0	0	10	165
Orange or CBM	6	19	3	12	7	29	0	0	2	12	0	0	65	201
Red-slipped orange	1	26	1	47	0	0	0	0	2	40	1	31	9	235
BB1	34	420	22	284	14	170	0	0	13	178	10	78	485	5654
BB1 or grey	0	0	0	0	0	0	0	0	0	0	0	0	1	4
Shell-tempered	2	35	3	89	1	7	0	0	0	0	3	93	23	413
Calcite-gritted	0	0	0	0	0	0	0	0	0	0	1	23	3	52
White-slipped orange	27	331	17	209	12	136	0	0	14	308	6	107	307	4952
White	20	324	15	136	13	259	0	0	11	180	7	221	165	3725
White or amphora	0	0	0	0	0	0	0	0	0	0	0	0	3	18
Amphora	28	1308	31	1652	14	787	2	20	16	1526	26	2830	465	42185
Indet mortarium fabric	0	0	0	0	0	0	0	0	0	0	0	0	1	70
Total	390	5847	313	5220	189	2673	5	37	196	4455	231	6563	4784	107939

	Phase												
	VII		**VIII**		**IX**		**IX/X**		**X**		**u/s**		*Total*	*Total*
Form	No	Wt (g)	No	Wt (g)	No	Wt (g)	No	Wt (g)	No	Wt (g)	No	Wt (g)	no	wt (g)
Flagon	3	122	4	40	8	142	0	0	1	12	3	223	128	3716
Flagon/amphora	0	0	0	0	0	0	0	0	0	0	0	0	1	8
Flagon/bottle	0	0	0	0	1	12	0	0	0	0	0	0	1	12
Flagon/bowl	0	0	0	0	1	13	0	0	0	0	0	0	1	13
Flagon/jar/beaker	0	0	0	0	0	0	0	0	0	0	0	0	1	11
Flagon/jar	0	0	0	0	0	0	0	0	0	0	0	0	2	25
Flagon/jug	0	0	0	0	0	0	0	0	0	0	0	0	5	229
Beaker	13	114	5	58	3	9	0	0	6	36	3	22	124	1027
Beaker/jar	0	0	0	0	0	0	0	0	0	0	0	0	1	8
Inkwell	0	0	0	0	0	0	0	0	0	0	0	0	1	7
Jar	8	116	17	330	7	78	1	7	7	160	13	250	250	4269
Outsize jar	0	0	0	0	0	0	0	0	0	0	0	0	2	619
Jar/beaker	0	0	1	6	0	0	0	0	0	0	1	6	11	49
Jar/bowl	1	4	0	0	1	7	0	0	0	0	0	0	8	309
Jar/flagon	6	395	2	212	1	67	0	0	5	258	0	0	30	2262
Cooking pot	7	65	5	40	4	41	0	0	9	122	2	15	143	1712
Mini cooking pot/beaker	0	0	0	0	0	0	0	0	0	0	0	0	1	8
Bowl	36	574	18	418	11	160	0	0	21	625	23	392	426	9516
Bowl/mortarium	0	0	1	6	0	0	0	0	0	0	0	0	3	19
Bowl/jar	0	0	0	0	0	0	0	0	0	0	0	0	3	152
Cup	7	39	5	26	3	15	0	0	6	29	8	85	89	551
Cup/dish	1	7	0	0	0	0	0	0	0	0	0	0	1	7
Feeding cup	0	0	0	0	0	0	0	0	0	0	0	0	1	13
Mortarium	8	370	11	186	4	169	0	0	10	481	5	237	131	6577
Dish/bowl	13	273	17	247	3	39	0	0	4	57	14	299	143	2592
Dish/platter	0	0	0	0	0	0	0	0	0	0	0	0	1	17
Dish	7	118	9	156	8	122	0	0	5	72	3	71	96	1950
Plate	1	2	0	0	0	0	0	0	0	0	0	0	11	26
Plate/bowl	3	15	2	13	1	4	0	0	2	16	0	0	24	193
Plate/bowl or bowl	0	0	0	0	2	9	0	0	0	0	2	18	12	183
Plate or plate/bowl	0	0	0	0	0	0	0	0	0	0	0	0	3	11
Platter	0	0	1	2	0	0	0	0	0	0	0	0	1	2
Lid	1	6	1	4	2	95	0	0	1	4	0	0	24	497
Strainer	0	0	0	0	0	0	0	0	0	0	0	0	1	11
Tazza	1	53	0	0	0	0	0	0	0	0	0	0	5	115
Counter	0	0	0	0	0	0	0	0	0	0	0	0	1	7
Clibanus	0	0	0	0	0	0	0	0	0	0	0	0	1	644
Amphora	28	1308	31	1652	14	787	2	20	16	1526	26	2830	457	42152
Amphora lid	0	0	0	0	0	0	0	0	0	0	0	0	9	44
Indet closed	148	1544	102	1286	62	578	0	0	71	725	119	1904	1840	21770
Indet open	15	191	19	164	8	77	0	0	9	195	4	149	263	3395
Indet	77	512	59	362	38	220	2	10	21	125	5	62	463	3010
Pottery/CBM	6	19	3	12	7	29	0	0	2	12	0	0	65	201
Total	390	5847	313	5220	189	2673	5	37	196	4455	231	6563	4784	107939

Table 5.1.11 Roman pottery: total amount quantified by source, phase and no sherds

			Phase							
		I		**II**		**III–IX**				
Source	No	% I	No	% II	No	% II--IX	u/s	% u/s	Total no	Total %
Local wares										
Holt	204	42.9	488	45.1	1407	46.9	137	59.3	2236	46.7
Cheshire Plain	175	36.8	91	8.4	386	12.9	16	6.9	668	14
Wilderspool	4	0.8	22	2	32	1.1	1	0.4	59	1.2
Wilderspool or Holt	0	0	0	0	0	0	1	0.4	1	0
Wilderspool or Severn Valley	0	0	0	0	5	0.2	3	1.3	8	0.2
Holt or Severn Valley	0	0	0	0	1	0	0	0	1	0
Total local wares	383	80.6	601	55.6	1831	61.1	158	68.4	2973	62.1
British traded wares										
East Yorkshire	0	0	0	0	2	0.1	1	0.4	3	0.1
Lower Nene Valley	0	0	11	1	46	1.5	1	0.4	58	1.2
Mancetter-Hartshill	1	0.2	8	0.7	65	2.2	3	1.3	77	1.6
Oxfordshire	0	0	4	0.4	60	2	5	2.2	69	1.4
Poole	12	2.5	166	15.4	297	9.9	10	4.3	485	10.1
Severn Valley	3	0.6	3	0.3	7	0.2	0	0	13	0.3
Verulamium region	5	1.1	4	0.4	1	0	0	0	10	0.2
Indet British	1	0.2	43	4	58	1.9	4	1.7	106	2.2
Total British traded wares	22	4.6	239	22.1	536	17.9	24	10.4	821	17.2
Continental wares										
S Gaul (samian)	37	7.8	27	2.5	50	1.7	1	0.4	115	2.4
C Gaul (samian)	3	0.6	83	7.7	208	6.9	22	9.5	316	6.6
S Gaul or C Gaul (samian)	0	0	0	0	8	0.3	0	0	8	0.2
E Gaul (samian)	0	0	2	0.2	4	0.1	0	0	6	0.1
North Gaul	2	0.4	1	0.1	3	0.1	0	0	6	0.1
C Gaul (black cc)	0	0	3	0.3	8	0.3	0	0	11	0.2
?Lyons	0	0	1	0.1	0	0	0	0	1	0
Trier	0	0	0	0	5	0.2	0	0	5	0.1
S Spain (olive oil amphora)	14	2.9	89	8.2	138	4.6	14	6.1	255	5.3
S Spain (fish sauce amphora)	2	0.4	1	0.1	1	0	0	0	4	0.1
S Gaul (wine amphora)	3	0.6	20	1.9	82	2.7	7	3	112	2.3
Italy (wine amphora)	0	0	0	0	4	0.1	2	0.9	6	0.1
Indet amphora	3	0.6	5	0.5	68	2.3	3	1.3	79	1.7
Indet amphora lids	4	0.8	0	0	5	0.2	0	0	9	0.2
Total continental wares	68	14.3	232	21.5	584	19.5	49	21.2	933	19.5
Indet source										
Indeterminate	2	0.4	9	0.8	46	1.5	0	0	57	1.2
Total indet source	2	0.4	9	0.8	46	1.5	0	0	57	1.
Total	475	100	1081	100	2997	100	231	100	4784	100

Table 5.1.12 Roman pottery: measure of condition by phase. (Percentages are based on no of sherds and indicate a proportion of each phase total, except where stated)

Phase	% v abraded	% abraded	% slightly abraded	% abraded & battered	% battered	%burnt & battered	% burnt	% slightly burnt	% burnt & abraded	% worn	% slightly worn	% sooted	No sherds examined	No sherds in phase
I	0	2.5	2	0	1.7	0.4	6.3	0.4	0.2	0.8	0.4	6	100	475
II	0.4	2.5	0.8	0.1	1.7	0.4	8.4	1.8	0.4	0.6	0.3	4.5	235	1081
III	0.3	1.8	0.5	1.8	2.5	3.6	11	2.3	0.3	0.3	0	5.6	116	391
III/IV	0	3.7	0	0	3.7	0	18.5	0	0	0	0	0	7	27
IV	0	1.3	2.2	0.9	3.6	1.6	8	3.6	0	0.2	0	3.8	113	444
V	0.6	2.5	3	1.6	2.8	0.9	12	5.6	3.8	1.2	0.3	2.4	228	633
V/VI	0	0	0	0	0	0	0	0	0	0	0	0	0	3
VI	0.7	3.2	2.2	0.9	6	0.7	10	4.2	1.5	0.3	0	3	131	406
VII	1.5	3.6	2.6	0.2	4.4	1.5	9	5	1.5	0.8	0	2.6	127	390
VIII	0.3	2.2	2.5	1.2	4.5	1	12	5.8	0.3	0	0	2.2	101	313
IX	1.6	8.5	2	1	6.3	0.5	7	3	1	1	0	2.6	66	189
IX/X	0	0	0	0	20	0	0	20	0	0	0	0	2	5
X	0.5	4.7	2.6	1.6	7	0.5	6	5	1	0.5	0	3.7	63	196
u/s	0	0.4	0	0.4	2.6	0.4	11	0.4	0	0.4	0.4	1.7	42	231
No sherds	129	158	177	87	48	37	8	21	23	154	47	442	1331	4784
% of site total	2.7	3.3	3.7	1.8	1	0.8	0.2	0.4	0.5	3.2	1	9.2	27.8	100

Post-Roman Pottery: Introduction
Julie E C Edwards

The excavations produced a large assemblage of post-Roman pottery of *c* 20, 270 fragments weighing 644,489 g, which was recorded from 956 different contexts.

As might be expected from such a large assemblage retrieved from a wide number and range of deposits, the condition varied considerably. In general, layer deposits produced poorly preserved material, whilst better preserved groups tended to be found in fills. A clear distinction could, however, be made between the Saxon/medieval and post-medieval assemblages. The former is fragmentary, residuality is high and its condition suggests that does not represent primary deposition. By contrast there are a number of well stratified groups that date from the late fifteenth century through to the early/mid-eighteenth century which contain well preserved assemblages, as well as three large groups from the nineteenth century. Their condition suggests a relatively low level of disturbance since deposition and that in general they were a result of single acts of disposal.

The evaluation excavations carried out on the site did not indicate any potential for a pottery assemblage of this size. The quantity of material therefore exceeded both in quantity and quality the estimated assemblage size that had been used to set a post-excavation budget prior to excavation. The tight timescale for assessment and publication and insufficient funds meant that a challenging programme and method of working had to be developed to meet the requirements of the brief and the developer.

In order to meet the minimum standards of a basic record by sherd count and weight, stipulated in the brief, and to attempt to keep to timetable, it was decided to identify pottery by ware and form when the material from each context was examined during the excavation, to provide 'spot' dates for the site director. The author sorted and labelled the pottery by common ware name, form if appropriate and any additional information of note. A list by context briefly described the pottery from each context and gave a date range for the context based on the pottery present. This list was then copied to the site director to enable each context to be phased.

Volunteers used the information written on the labels to compile the pottery record sheets and perform a basic quantification by sherd count and weight. This information was then entered into an Access database developed for the project. A minimum record was thereby completed for all the pottery from the site.

Key groups were selected for analysis, including additional quantification by Estimated Vessel Equivalent (EVEs), by the author, who was also working concurrently on the ceramic building materials. The selection of key groups was determined by size, condition, range, date, associated finds and the time/cost implications.

When compared to groups excavated elsewhere in the city, the assemblage has good potential to add to the overall knowledge of pottery supply and use in Chester.

A limiting factor was that it was difficult to make detailed comparisons with other excavated groups because of a lack of publication and because the quantified records were not in an easily accessible format. Ideally it would have been useful to physically examine groups from the city and elsewhere in the region in order to draw some general conclusions, but this was not possible within the timescale and budget. The author had therefore to rely on previously acquired knowledge of pottery from Chester and published sources in the region.

An urban assemblage of this size and stratification associated with documentary information relating to property boundaries, site function and the status of individuals offers the potential for comparisons between properties and a discussion on socio-economic themes. This was not possible within the bounds of the project, nor was a functional comparison of different materials, eg the ceramics and glass. It was decided to present as many of the groups as possible and to define and describe the wares and vessels in each in order to form a basis for future ceramic research in the city. With more time further division of the phases may have been possible based on the individual wares present, eg introduction of black wares; such ceramic phasing could then be transferred to other sites in the city.

Recording was carried out as far as possible in line with the Medieval Pottery Research Group's minimum standards (MPRG 2001). The terms used to identify the wares are largely those employed in the Chester fabric reference collection, modified for the post-medieval period by the common ware names recommended by the Potteries Museum during an English Heritage sponsored training course in 1999. Brief fabric descriptions are given for the principal wares found on the site; these used terminology employed in the DUA Pottery Archive Users Handbook 1984. The fabric numbers are those used in the Chester fabric reference collection. Fabric descriptions are not given for the continental wares; these can be found in Hurst *et al* (1986). Forms have been described as far as possible using the terminology employed in the *Guide to the classification of medieval ceramic forms* (MPRG 1998).

Saxon Pottery

Medieval Pottery

The Saxon pottery assemblage is very small and composed of relatively small sherds (19 sherds/239 g). It forms 0.07 % of the entire post-Roman pottery assemblage by sherd count. Thirteen fragments of late Saxon Chester ware were identified (*see* Rutter 1985 for a description of this ware), together with six other possible fragments. Only four of these sherds were stratified in pre-1066 deposits, namely Phase II and III contexts (1131) and (1132). As is common in the city, the majority of the sherds were residual to the phases in which they were found and were scattered throughout the phases and plots without any obvious distributional bias. Potentially the presence of Chester ware in Phase II is of great significance, but Phases I–III produced a total of fifty-nine fragments of medieval and post-medieval pottery, of which thirty were in Phase II. It would therefore be unwise to place much emphasis on the presence of Chester ware in these phases.

Phases II and III also produced some sherds which remain unidentified either because they are too small and abraded or because they are in fabrics not represented in the Chester Fabric Reference collection. Well stratified early post-Roman pottery is extremely rare in Chester, but the small size and condition of these sherds, the lack of any other finds of contemporary date and the presence of residual and intrusive pottery, glass and building material in these phases means that little significance can be placed on them. In the light of this insecure dating evidence and the budget no groups were selected for study and no work other than a basic identification was carried out on the pottery.

Table 5.3.1 Saxon pottery quantified by phase, plot, ware, no of sherds and weight

Phase	Plot	Ware	No	Wt (g)
II	3	Chester ware	3	16
III	3	Chester ware	1	6
IV	2	Chester ware?	2	8
V	3	Chester ware	3	93
	3	Chester ware?	1	16
	4	Chester ware	1	16
	6	Chester ware?	1	8
VI	3	Chester ware	3	36
	3	Chester ware?	2	9
VIII	6	Chester ware	1	24
IX	6	Chester ware	1	7

Introduction

A total of 3999 sherds/81614 g of medieval pottery were recorded from the site. Approximately half the assemblage came from stratified medieval contexts. The assemblage as a whole is fragmentary and there are few complete or partially complete vessels. When these do occur they are very late medieval/transitional types which were found in early post-medieval groups and are included in the post-medieval pottery report. Sherd size is not large and abrasion varies between contexts and often within context groups.

In general the range of wares appears to be typical of that found in Chester from the mid-thirteenth to fifteenth centuries. It consists largely of red/grey-firing wares made with local clays from at least *c* 1250 and pink/white wares made from Coal Measure clays and comparable to products of a suggested production site in the Ewloe/Buckley area of Flintshire in the fourteenth and fifteenth centuries. The transitional medieval/post-medieval period is represented by Ewloe-type wares of possible fifteenth–sixteenth century date, possible early Midland Purple-type wares and later red/grey wares. Imports to the region consist of Saintonge wares (mottled glaze, smooth green glaze, polychrome, *sgraffito* and unglazed fragments), Rouen ware plus other unidentified wares of possible French origin and a small number of sherds from elsewhere in Britain, eg Scarborough, Ham Green and developed Stamford wares. A fragment of a Dublin coarseware jug is a relatively unusual find in the city. Tudor Green-type wares are also present and there are a number of wares in white-firing fabrics which are not immediately recognisable but have features which may make them possible to identify in the future.

Whilst the wares present are generally typical, the range of forms, decoration and particular details of form is larger than can normally be expected, probably because of the large size of the assemblage. For example there are two pink/white ware decorated lids from Phase VI (671) and Phase V (760) (nos 1 and 2), various red/grey ware pipkin handles, a red/grey dripping dish and slip-decorated or incised decorated pink/white wares.

Given the large quantity of material and the time restraints on the project it was necessary to be selective in the groups for further study. The fragmentary nature of the medieval assemblage and relatively high number of residual wares within contexts and assemblages lowered the potential for further study. Consequently no groups from Phases III or IV were selected and only one from Phase V.

Table 5.4.1 Medieval pottery quantified by phase, no of sherds and weight

Phase	No	Wt (g)
I	1	2
II	28	489
III	16	269
IV	161	2936
V	1287	22234
VI	777	21425
VII	653	14333
VIII	507	10650
IX	298	5298
X	266	3833
Unphased	5	145

Table 5.4.2 Medieval pottery quantified by plot, no of sherds and weight

Plot	No	Wt (g)
1	255	4864
2	646	14971
3	911	15128
4	668	20186
5	165	3346
6	1226	20780
No plot given	128	2336

Catalogue (Ill 5.4.1)
1 Pink/white ware lid. (671): Phase VI, Plot 2; SF 10194.
2 Pink/white ware lid. (760): Phase V, Plot 2; SF 10195.

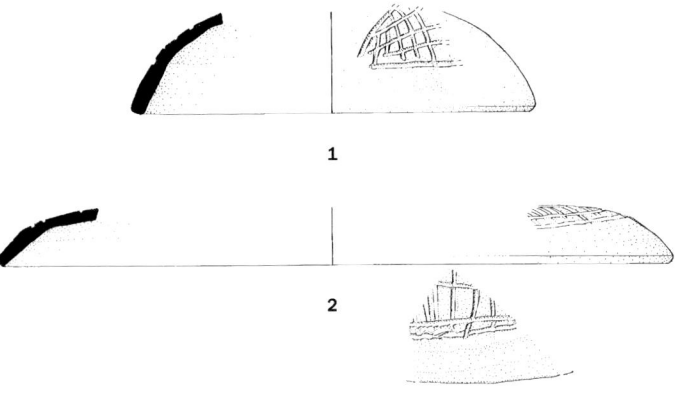

Ill 5.4.1 Medieval pottery. (Scale 1.4)

Phase V

Plot 6

Cultivation soil (836) and associated contexts

These contexts produced over 100 fragmentary sherds and contained a high proportion of apparently residual thirteenth- and fourteenth-century wares (60 sherds/1336 g fragments of medieval pottery) with a smaller group of post-medieval wares, (32 fragments/393 g). The post-medieval component consists of a fragment of black-glazed ware and a piece of tin-glazed ware, both of which are intrusive to this phase, and approximately twelve drinking vessels, all of which are either Cistercian-type wares or lower-fired glazed redwares paralleling Cistercian-type forms. Although only fragments of the vessels are present they are relatively unabraded and in good condition. All of these pieces exhibit some features of the new forms that were being introduced in the late medieval period. These fragments appear to be the earliest occurrence of such wares on the site. It was decided to apply the term 'Cistercian-type' to all the wares that display similar char-

acteristics of form to Cistercian wares: in this instance they are predominantly cups. It may be possible in the future to ascribe a provenance to those wares that differ from the more generally accepted Cistercian-type ware definition.

The fragments fall into four fabric groups, which are similar to the range found in Phase VI, particularly in the cess pit (487).

1 Fine, compact reddish-brown fabric with a glossy brown glaze, equivalent to Fabric 23 in the Chester Fabric Reference Collection.
2 Fine red-orange fabric with a glossy brown glaze; the vessels in this fabric tend to be thicker-walled and, whilst the glaze is thick and glossy, it could be sparsely applied in areas and some of the surface might be unglazed; Chester Fabric no 787.
3 Hard, fine purple fabric with lustrous purple/black glaze, equivalent to Fabric 24 in the Chester Fabric Reference Collection.
4 Red fabric similar to 2 but harder and darker in fabric colour, with occasional rounded white inclusions which appeared to be white clay; streaks of white clay might also occur. Glaze colour varies from a reduced greenish brown to black-brown; equivalent to Fabric 21 in the Chester Fabric Reference Collection.

The precise forms could not be determined because the fragments were not large enough, but the features that did survive, with two possible exceptions, suggested relatively small drinking vessels which could be divided into three cup forms:

1 Flared cups with splayed bases, which occurred in Fabrics 787 (nos 4 and 7 below); 24 (no 9; SF 10308) and 21 (not illustrated).
2 A necked cup in Fabric 24 (not illustrated).
3 A rounded cup with a slightly rounded foot which was the only example of Fabric 23 (no 3 below).

Handle fragments consist of small oval rod handles in Fabric 24; the remains of a handle on a Fabric 787 flared cup was similar (no 4). The rounded cup in Fabric 23 is finer thrown and has a thicker glaze, giving the vessel an overall well finished appearance, although the unglazed foot does not exhibit such a finish. The edges of some of the bases are blackened by soot.

In addition there are a cup or mug (no 5) with a rim radius of 38 mm and a relatively wide handle, and a splayed base fragment (no 6) too large to be from a cup. The form of no 5 is difficult to determine but it may have had flaring sides. The rim is well finished and glazed but is relatively thick compared to other Cistercian-type ware cups.

A slightly distorted rim and upper body fragment of a mug-like vessel, no 8 from (700), the parallel context to (836), was made in Fabric 24 and appears similar in form to a vessel from Norton priory (Greene & Noake 1977, 59, fig 20) (*see* also no 63 from pit (1541).

The pieces in Fabrics 24 and 21 fall into the same range as the cups in the cess pit (487) and other Phase VI examples of Cistercian-type wares. If the stratigraphic position of this layer is secure, then these fragments represent the first use of such wares on the site, if not in the city, in the fifteenth century. However, the fragments of intrusive material in (836) and the equivalent contexts (117) and (700) cast some doubt on the reliability of the context and the significance of these fragments, but it was thought useful to include illustrations and a brief description of these wares for future reference.

Catalogue (Ill 5.4.2)

3 Foot of rounded cup; Fabric 23. (836); SF 10307.
4 Flared cup with splayed base; Fabric 787. (836); SF 10341.
5 Cup or mug; Fabric 787. (836); SF 10342.
6 Splayed base; Fabric 787. (836); SF 10309.
7 Flared cup with splayed base; Fabric 787. (836); SF 10310.
8 Mug? Fabric 24. (700); SF 10332.
9 Cup; Fabric 24. (836); SF 10308.

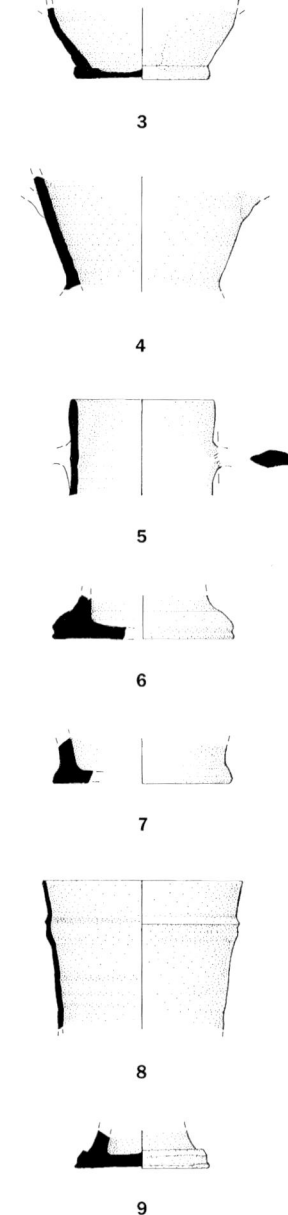

Ill 5.4.2 Phase V Plot 6: medieval pottery. (Scale 1/4)

Post-Medieval Pottery

Introduction

A total of 16278 post-medieval sherds weighing 562969 g were recorded from the site. Whilst the range of wares is typical of that found in excavations in Chester, the assemblage is remarkable for the large, well preserved groups that were retrieved in a stratigraphic sequence. These contain good examples of ware types and a large range of vessel forms. Early drinking vessels are particularly well represented in the late medieval and early post-medieval periods. There are good examples of imported continental wares and Chinese porcelains, but in terms of the total assemblage they are small in number and do not appear to exceed the proportion found in previous excavations; however, some pieces are uncommon finds in the city, eg two fragments of north Italian marbled slipwares found residually in Phases VIII and X (not illustrated). In Phase VII there are relatively large assemblages of tin-glazed wares, which is unusual; however, whether these are unique to the site or merely a reflection of a lack of opportunity to excavate other deposits of similar date in the city centre is debatable. While the best preserved material survived in fills, some of the linear deposits in Phases VII, IX and X produced good groups of material earlier than the phase date, eg (663), garden soil (301) and layer (1349), suggesting some disturbance and redeposition of earlier deposits.

Table 5.5.1 Post-medieval pottery: total amount quantified by phase, no of sherds and weight

Phase	No	Wt (g)
I	7	161
II	2	18
III	5	169
IV	22	614
V	92	2428
VI	864	33629
VII	4389	146973
VIII	2638	72408
IX	4562	217714
X	3267	77643
Unphased	430	11396

Condition

The assemblage is mixed in condition, ranging from contexts containing less than 10 small sherds to those consisting of over 300 pieces of semi-complete, complete or complete but smashed vessels. The proportion of material which is in good or very good condition is very high compared to other sites excavated in Chester; it is probably one of the largest stratified assemblages of early post-medieval pottery from an urban site in north-west England.

Range

A variety of wares is present but functionally the pottery is predominantly domestic. Of particular note is the fill of pit (1696) in Phase VII Plot 4, which contained a very large group which, with an accompanying glass assemblage, may represent an early eighteenth-century house clearance.

From the sixteenth century there is a good group of Cistercian-type wares, and spanning the sixteenth and seventeenth centuries Midland Purple-type ware storage vessels. Black-glazed wares dominate the seventeenth–early eighteenth-century assemblages and a good number of the fragments join to provide complete profiles, giving a better indication of the range available at any one time. Yellow-glazed wares are typical of seventeenth-century assemblages found in Chester, but, while they are present on this site, they form a relatively smaller proportion of the overall assemblage. This may reflect the poor representation of mid-to late seventeenth-century groups on the site. Slipwares and mottled wares complete the range of most common wares on the site for the seventeenth and early eighteenth centuries. There is also a small but good group of early English stoneware mugs comparable to types produced in Staffordshire, whose forms echo some of the mottled wares. Eighteenth-century finewares, eg early creamwares, are present but in relatively small quantities, and there are no good assemblages for the mid- to late eighteenth century.

In addition to these commonly found wares which were produced in the north-west, midlands and north Wales, there is a small but significant collection of pottery imported from further afield in Britain and also from Europe. Some of these wares are types not uncommon on excavations in Chester, eg North Devon gravel-tempered wares and post-medieval Saintonge wares, but some appear less frequently. In the latter group are a number of fragments of Rhenish stonewares and Italian wares. The quantified data from the site shows that continental imports make up a relatively small proportion of the total ceramic assemblage but a significant proportion of some individual assemblages. A lack of data makes it difficult to estimate the overall proportions of imports in assemblages from Chester, but perhaps the figures from this site can be used as starting point for future comparisons. Some of the individual imports have features that are themselves relatively uncommon. An almost complete Cologne stoneware mug is decorated with a pattern of trailing leaves and possible hop fruit rather than the more common roses or acorns (examples of which were also found). A Cologne/Frechen *schnelle* has elaborate relief moulding which does not appear to be paralleled in the principal published collections from Britain.

Other wares from the continent include Spanish olive jars, Valencian lustrewares, south Netherlands tin-glazed ware, Italian tin-glazed wares, North Italian Marbled Slipware, French chafing dish fragments, Beauvais ware and later post-medieval Italian oil jars. Amongst the imports from elsewhere in Britain are Surrey–Hampshire Border ware and a good collection of tin-glazed wares produced in London or Bristol and also, possibly in the eighteenth century assemblages, Liverpool.

A large group from Phase IX pit (1096) was apparently the result of clearance of a nineteenth-century chemist's shop and associated dwelling; it was notable for a large number of storage vessels. Other than this partly trade assemblage the other principal non-domestic feature of the site assemblage is a group of sugar cone moulds from Phase VII, used in the refining of sugar.

The assemblages selected for study and an associated group of ceramic building material are described below by phase and plot.

Phase VI

This phase includes a number of pit groups that contained pottery suggesting that they date to various times between the late fifteenth and the early to mid-seventeenth century. The evidence provided by the presence or absence of clay tobacco pipes and vessel glass supports the dating of the ceramic assemblages. The question one may be expected to ask is: could some of these groups be allocated a closer date range or perhaps be the basis for a relative dating framework, eg ceramic phases? In order to formulate an answer, further analysis of the finds assemblages in comparison with each other and with the stratigraphic evidence would be required. It has not been possible within the timing and budget of the project to ascertain the potential of the material for such analysis.

The groups chosen for publication here are those which contain either a large proportion of semi-complete vessels, a variety of imported pottery, or are accompanied by good vessel glass assemblages, or a combination of all three.

A range of continental wares is present which complement but also extend the range of wares previously found in the city. Some of these appear to be unusual as excavated finds, but it was not possible to carry out an extensive search for parallels to support this assertion, which is based on a limited examination of published sources and personal communications from various ceramicists around the country.

Plot 2

Cess pit (487)

A total of 187 sherds weighing 6486 g came from the fills of this pit (contexts (806), (798), (797), (791), (789), (787), (785), (786)). Of these, 145 (5768 g) are post-medieval and 42 (718 g) medieval.

Table 5.5.2 Phase VI Plot 2 cess pit (487): post-medieval pottery quantified by context, ware, no of sherds and weight

Context	Ware	No	Wt (g)
785	Blackware?	3	122
785	Cistercian-type	4	19
785	Midland Purple-type	2	130
789	Midland Purple-type	5	124
789	Merida-type	5	176
789	Saintonge?	4	16
791	Cistercian-type	12	162
791	Midland Purple-type	4	95
791	Merida-type	1	41
791	Saintonge?	5	72
797	Brown-glazed ware	2	31
797	Cistercian-type	14	345
797	Midland Purple-type	39	2431
797	Spanish micaceous ware	3	70
797	TGW - intrusive	2	15
798	Cistercian-type	3	226
798	Midland Purple-type	8	479
798	Midland Purple-type?	1	71
798	Cologne	5	311
798	Unidentified import	2	26
806	Cistercian-type	17	680
806	Midland Purple-type	1	29
806	Saintonge?	1	29
806	Spanish TGW	2	68
Total		145	5768

Table 5.5.3 Phase VI Plot 2 cess pit (487): post-medieval pottery quantified by ware, EVEs, no of sherds and weight

Ware	EVEs rim	EVEs base	No	Wt (g)
Blackware?	0	27	3	122
Cistercian-type	156	524	50	1432
Midland Purple-type	191	134	59	3288
Midland Purple-type?	0	8	1	71
Brown-glazed ware	0	10	2	31
Spanish TGW	0	12	2	68
Spanish olive jar	0	0	3	70
Merida-type	54	76	6	217
TGW	3	0	2	15
Cologne	100	50	5	311
Saintonge?	0	12	10	117
Unidentified import	0	0	2	26
Total	504	853	145	5768

Table 5.5.4 Phase VI Plot 2 cess pit (487): post-medieval pottery quantified by form, EVEs, no of sherds and weight

Form	EVEs rim	EVEs base	No	Wt (g)
Unidentified	0	27	18	429
Albarello	0	12	2	68
Cistern	100	100	38	2471
Cup/Mug	256	574	49	1682
Cup?	0	0	5	56
Dish	3	0	1	3
Dish?	0	10	1	30
Jar	91	42	14	698
Jug	0	12	9	88
Lid	54	76	6	217
Salt?	0	0	2	26
Total	504	853	145	5768

The lowermost fills of the pit, (806), (798) and (797), contained smashed and semi-complete vessels consisting of Cistercian-type ware cups, Midland Purple-type jars, including a virtually complete but smashed cistern, and continental imports. Residual pottery was restricted to Roman wares in (806) and (798) (7 sherds and 14 g). Whilst the Cistercian- and Midland Purple-types are broadly datable to the late fifteenth and sixteenth centuries it is difficult to be precise about the date of deposition. The Cistercian-type wares are similar to types at Norton priory but the published dating for these is quite broad and only places them within the sixteenth century. The imported wares may give a better idea of when the pit was first filled but there is the possibility of curation. The lowest fill, (806), contained fragments of a blue Spanish tin-glazed ware jar; such wares were being imported into Britain by the 1530s, when similar vessels appeared at Acton Court, near Bristol (Vince & Bell 1992, 107). In the New World it is suggested that they occurred from the late fifteenth century throughout the sixteenth (*see* below). The overlying context, (798), produced an almost complete Cologne stoneware mug with a relief pattern of trailing leaves and fruit. John Hurst (Hurst *et al* 1986, 209) commented that such mugs are generally dated 1520–40 but are found in pre-1520 contexts in England; vessels from Southampton are dated 1490–1510 (Brown 2002, 85). Context (798) also contained a fragment of a polychrome-glazed whiteware. Although much of the glaze is missing, the fragment is perhaps from a pedestal-shaped salt. The piece may be from Beauvais, in which case a date in the first half of the sixteenth century is again appropriate. Three sherds of a micaceous ware were found in (797). The fabric is coarser than that of Merida-type ware but the micaceous appearance suggests an Iberian origin. Initially the pieces were thought to be from an olive jar but they are perhaps too fine-walled; the lack of any features of form hinders precise identification

and dating other than that they are of Iberian origin and appear to be from some sort of plain storage vessel. Further comparative work would be required to identify them fully. Two fragments of tin-glazed wares were also found in (797): one is a seventeenth-century type and intrusive; the other is burnt but its fabric perhaps suggests an Italian or Spanish origin. Thus the imported pottery from the lowermost fills is broadly contemporary with the English wares, with a date range spanning the late fifteenth to mid-sixteenth century.

The incomplete nature of some of the imported wares suggests that these fragments were not from a primary deposit. However, the pit was not fully excavated and some sherds may remain on the site.

The uppermost two fills included a fragment of an early to mid-seventeenth-century glass beaker, and the topmost fill of the pit contained three fragments from the base of a blackware jar in a red fabric with a relatively fine lustrous glaze; its fabric equates to Fabric 121 (*see* below). However, there were no clay tobacco pipes; considering the size of the pit this suggested that the greater part of the pit was backfilled before the early seventeenth century.

There are a number of sherd joins between contexts in the fill, which increase towards the upper layers, while the topmost fills contained fragments of possibly intrusive seventeenth-century wares. A similar pattern of joins can be seen in the floor tile assemblage from the pit. The principal wares from the assemblage are discussed below.

Table 5.5.5 Phase VI Plot 2 cess pit (487): sherd joins between contexts

Context	SF no	Ware	Form	Joins context/s
785	9928	Midland Purple-type		778, 779, 776, 503
791	9927	Merida-type	Lid	789
791	9926	Saintonge?	Jug	789
797	9924	Midland Purple-type	Cistern	798
798	9921	Midland Purple-type	Jar	789
798	9924	Midland Purple-type	Cistern	797

Wares
Cistercian-type wares
The fills of pit (487) produced one of the largest groups of Cistercian-type ware in this phase: 50 pieces weighing 1432 g were found, providing 34% and 25% of the pit assemblage respectively, although if base EVEs are used this rises to 63% (rim 36%). The pit produced roughly a third of all the Cistercian-type wares from Phase VI (31% by sherd count, 36% by weight and 52 % by rim EVEs and 38 % base EVES where these were recorded).

Context (806), the bottommost fill of the pit, contained the greatest number of Cistercian-type ware sherds of any context in the pit, contributing 65% (rim EVEs) and 67% (base EVEs); the number of residual sherds was low (0 medieval and 6 fragments/12 g of Roman pottery). If considered with the overlying contexts, (798) and (797), the three contexts provided 68 % by sherd count, 87% by weight, 78 % of rim EVEs and 96% base EVEs of the Cistercian-type ware assemblage in the pit. All but one of the semi-complete and illustrated vessels came from these contexts.

The most distinctive feature of this group – all cups – is the variety in form and to a lesser extent fabric. Only two cups have a similar form. Three of the forms appear to be unusual locally, whilst two conform to a flared or funnel shape which seems to be relatively well represented in Chester and the north-west. This variety perhaps suggests a range of sources for these cups or alternatively a chronological difference. It is difficult to comment on whether they are all contemporary, but the number of semi-complete vessels and the distribution within the pit suggests close deposition and perhaps contemporary usage.

A similar range of Cistercian-type wares was found in the pit as in the Phase VI assemblage from cultivation soil (836), but Fabrics 24 and 21 predominate.

Fabrics
The vessels are described in their fabric group as follows.

Fabric 21: This is represented by the remains of two flared cups, nos 15 and 16, from which the rim, upper body and handles are missing. The two differ slightly with regard to size and possibly the number of handles. Both have walls which flare up and outwards from a constriction above a flared base with a bevelled or chamfered foot. At the broken edge the walls appear to stop flaring and begin to turn upwards. A fragment from no 16 has a raised cordon which appears to run below the rim.

Handles are only represented on each by the lower handle–body joins. No 15 has the remains of three handles spaced evenly around the cup; one of the broken edges is covered in glaze, suggesting that the handle was either badly cracked or broke away before or during firing. The base of the third handle is missing and is only represented by a scar in the glaze. No 16 has two opposing handles, the bases of which had been luted onto the vessel wall and finished with a final wipe to the left.

The bases differ slightly, with no 15 slightly kicked and that of no 16 being flat. Neither is well finished and displayed irregularities, some of which may have been caused by being picked up while the clay was still soft. Small fragments of clay also adhere to the surface of no 16, and fine parallel scratch marks on the underside show that a wire has been pulled straight across to detach the cup from the wheel-head. Similar marks appear on a base sherd from (791) but not on no 15. As on some of the base fragments in the assemblage from Phase V (836) there is soot around the edge of the base of no 15. The soot is particularly heavy around one side but it does not appear to relate to the position of the handles, unlike on later single-handled mugs and cups (eg *see* the assemblage from (1696).

The exteriors of both vessels are well glazed but the thickness varies between a glossy brown at its thickest and a lustrous sheen where thin. Smudged fingerprints are visible in the thinner glaze, especially around the handle joins. The glaze irregularly covers the foot of each but is sparse inside the base of no 15, unlike no 16 where the interior is well glazed.

The inside of no 15 is covered in a grey/white deposit which is particularly thick in the base; the deposit extends over the broken edges of the cup, suggesting that it relates to a secondary use of the broken vessel. No similar deposit was noted on other vessels in the assemblage. The deposit would need to be analysed in order to determine whether the sooting on the base was related to this secondary use or to use as a drinking vessel.

It is difficult to suggest a provenance for these wares. They are unlike forms found in Yorkshire (*see* Brears 1967; 1971; 1983; and Moorhouse & Slowikowski 1992) but they are similar to cup numbers 12–16 at Norton priory (Green & Noake 1977, 59), which are suggested to have been produced somewhere in the north-west. The flared form has also been found in Staffordshire (Ford 1995 59, fig 21, 177), where a wasted example was found at Bradwell Farm, although no kilns producing Cistercian wares have been excavated. Similar flared forms have also been found previously in Chester, although most of these are in darker fabrics with lustrous black/brown glazes, eg from 11 Watergate Street (Rutter 1984, fig 4.18 and .19); Nicholas Street Mews (CHE/NSM 88 unpublished); St Michael's Street, Browns extension (Newstead 1928, pl 21) and St John Street (Newstead 1939). None of these assemblages provide close dating evidence, nor do the Norton priory examples, which are broadly dated to the sixteenth century (Green & Noake 1977, 59). Speke Hall, Merseyside does have a deposit dated to the mid-sixteenth century, but while bases from that deposit may be from similarly shaped cups they are not conclusive enough to use for dating purposes. Two other Merseyside sites, Eccleston Hall near St Helen's (Edwards 1997) and Bewsey Old Hall near Warrington (Jenkins & Bearpark 1980), also produced similarly shaped cups.

Fabric 787: No 17, the only example of this fabric, is possibly a flared cup, although it is larger and does not have the splayed foot of nos 15 and 16 and the lower walls are relatively thick. A glossy clear glaze covers the exterior but becomes patchy on the lower part of the vessel, which is either unglazed or with a thin lustrous cover; finger prints can be seen in the latter. The interior is unglazed apart from the inside of the base and thin lines along the throwing rings. Two applied spots of white slip are present at what appears to be the girth of the vessel; they appear yellow against the golden brown background.

Fabric 24: The remains of three cups and several rims fragments in this fabric have a purple/brown fabric and dark glazes which tend to be lustrous. Two vessels are unusual forms.

No 12 has a short rounded body which opens into a wide funnel shape leading to the rim. Two opposing narrow strap handles are slightly off centre. The lower ends of the handles were applied just above the base whilst the upper is mid-way between the rim and the carination. The foot is slight and rounded and the base slightly kicked. Like many of the Cistercian-type wares from the site the foot and base are not well finished and are marked by small fragments of clay and also scuffing caused when the vessel was removed from the wheel. A glossy glaze covers both surfaces but in places, particularly above the base, it becomes thin and lustrous; the base is spotted with glaze.

A rim fragment from a similarly shaped cup in (806) has a slightly larger radius of 63 mm. A much larger but similar vessel, no 19, was found in Phase VI (251), where it was the only vessel apart from a fragment of Ewloe-type ware in pit (250). The form corresponds to Brears' type 14: short two-handled cups which have a height less than their rim diameter (Brears 1971, 22), although the rim is more exaggerated than Brears' illustrated example.

The form has been found at Potovens and also at Silcoats (Brears 1967, 21) where they fall into the late fifteenth- to sixteenth-century range. A similar but again not identical type also occurs in Staffordshire, classified by Barker as type 1b (Barker 1986a, 57 fig 1.1b), a wide-mouthed and low-waisted vessel.

No 11 is a cup with a rounded slightly pear-shaped body and no discernible waist: instead a sharply defined cordon marks the point where the wall curves out towards the rim, which is missing. The foot has been chamfered but it is slightly uneven and not cleanly finished. The underside of the base is covered in prominent parallel grooves, suggesting that a stranded wire had been used to remove the vessel from the wheel. Marks and smudges around the perimeter suggest that it was not removed cleanly from the wheel or had afterwards become attached to another surface. The base has been pushed upwards, giving a slightly concave surface.

Parallels for this form are not readily apparent. There is a similar vessel with what appears to be a sharply defined cordon from Wrenthorpe (Moorhouse & Slowikowski 1992, fig 53, no 53, 114) but again this is incomplete.

The body of no 13 is in the shape of an inverted baluster with quite a pronounced bulbous shoulder. An abrupt change of angle marks the beginnings of the rim, which is missing. Three narrow strap handles are rather weakly finished: each has been applied with the lower end to the left of the upper so that the handle slants to one side. One handle is set slightly higher than the others and one has been trimmed at the lower end with two blunt indentations. An attempt has been made to create a more finely shaped pedestal-type foot than on the other cups, but again it is not well finished. The lustrous black glaze is streaked with brown, particularly on the interior where brown tends to be the dominant colour. The cup is very highly fired and as a result there appears to be some distortion of the finer features. The remains of a yellowish deposit are encrusted on the inside of the base. The overall shape has some similarity to the flared cups from Chester and Norton priory (Greene & Noake 1977, nos 12 and 13), but it is shorter and has a squatter appearance.

No 14 is one of five rim fragments that are either similar to those from flared cups (eg types 12–14 at Norton priory (*art cit*, 59) and nos 15 and 16 in Fabric 4) or to those with funnel-shaped necks and small upright cordoned rims, eg no 62 from Phase VI (1540). All, however, have the purple fabrics and lustrous glazes of Fabric 24. The rim radii vary from 48 mm to 55 mm. It was not possible to relate these fragments to any of the more complete pieces.

Fabric 23: No 10 is the base of a round bodied vessel, possibly a cup or jug. The remains of one handle–body join can just be seen on the broken edge. The foot flares slightly and the edge is bevelled. In common with other examples the foot is poorly finished and the clay around the edge is scuffed and marked with stray fragments of clay. The flat base has parallel scratch lines across its surface. A very fine trace of glaze covers the base; within this is an unglazed rectangular kiln scar. The interior is well covered with a glossy but uneven glaze. The exterior glaze is also uneven and in places only present as a thin lustre; smudged finger prints are clearly visible in the latter.

It is difficult to suggest parallels for this form, which is more rounded than the other examples of this ware from the site. Some body sherds in the same fabric appear in context (791) but they seem to be from a more elongated type of vessel.

Decoration
Decoration is fairly limited on the majority of examples from 25 Bridge Street and the applied decoration that is well known on Yorkshire and Ticknall wares is only present on one example (*see* no 49 from (1697)). However, one fragment displays a style of decoration using applied prunts which appears to be associated with flared cups. No 18 is a fragment from the shoulder of a cup which, on comparison with a vessel from Norton priory, would have been a flared type (Green & Noake 1977, 59, fig 12). Conical-shaped prunts have been applied in line with the top of the handle. A similar feature is also present on a flared cup excavated during the 1920s extension to Brown's department store (Newstead 1928, 141 and pl 21.2)

General comment on Cistercian-type wares
Excavations in Chester have produced a variety of Cistercian-type ware cups; the examples from 25 Bridge Street reflect a similar variety. Independently dated assemblages of this size are rare so it is difficult to determine whether the variety here reflects chronological or geographical differences.

The assemblage from cess pit (487) does appear to be a sixteenth- or just possibly very late fifteenth-century deposit both on the range of pottery present and the absence of clay tobacco pipes, but placing the deposit within any particular part of the sixteenth century is currently difficult. However, one distinctive cup form of potentially late sixteenth-century date, a wide-necked waisted form exemplified by nos 59 and 60, is absent from the groups, which suggests that the deposit and wares date to before the later part of the sixteenth century.

Midland Purple-type wares
The term Midland Purple-type ware is used in this report to describe hard grey to brownish purple wares which may have almost vitrified fabrics and, when present, a relatively thin lustrous glaze. They are broadly similar to wares from the midlands made in the late medieval to early post-medieval period but they vary in fabric and form and there is no conclusive evidence as to their provenance. As Midland Purple ware is a generally understood term it was felt that it should be retained with the addition of '-type' until a more precise term linked to production site/s can be decided in the future. The wares from cess pit (487) and the immediately overlying contexts fall into three fabric groups.

Fabrics
Fabric 779: This is represented by a cistern, no 21, and is a comparatively fine, smooth-looking fabric, ranging in colour from red, brown to purple across the thickness of the sherd. It is a very hard fabric with a rough feel and a fine texture. The moderate inclusions consist of opaque white and colourless sub-angular quartz, fine pellets and streaks of dark red clay, fine streaks and sub-angular fragments of white clay and angular red-black iron-rich

fragments. The range of inclusions is similar to Fabric 780 but in general the fabric has a finer appearance. The glaze is thin and lustrous varying in colour from brown to purple/black.

The cistern or bunghole jar, no 21, has two strap handles (one missing) and a teardrop-shaped bunghole. The rim is simple and upright with a flattened top; a kiln scar is present around one side of the outer edge. The strap-handle tapers along its length and is concave on the exterior; it is splayed at the lower end to join the body. The bunghole opening was formed by piercing a hole from the outside. Clay was then applied around about three-quarters of the circumference to form a shelf below. The base is slightly concave; unlike similar storage vessels from the site the perimeter shows little wear. A curving kiln scar made of red clay and glaze encloses an unglazed area. The curve is approximately 75 mm in diameter and may have been from the rim of a cup. There is also an oblong scar possibly from a kiln spacer.

The area between the handles on the front of the vessel is decorated with two incised zigzag lines and three circular gridiron stamps. The glaze is generally sparse on both surfaces but there are thicker and unglazed patches. Wipe marks are present on the surfaces surrounding the bunghole and the handle joins.

The rim and upper body twist away from the main body as though the vessel had been moved by the handles when the clay was soft. The handles are not symmetrical around the bunghole, although they are more or less opposite each other. Unlike the base, which is an almost perfect, circle the rim is an oval.

Fragments of a similarly decorated vessel were found in pit (691) in this phase and others have been noted locally but none are from closely dated contexts.

Fabric 78: represented by jars 20 and 22, is a purplish-brown colour and where the walls are thick there is sometimes a black core. It is very hard with a rough feel and irregular texture. Inclusions consist of moderate colourless and opaque white sub-angular quartz grains which in general are well sorted but sparse coarse grains are present; also sparse angular red iron-rich fragments, sub-angular white fragments (possibly clay) and occasional streaks of white and red clay. The glaze varies from thick and glossy to a sparse patchy thin lustre particularly on the interior; the glaze colour appears brown.

Jar no 20 is a roughly barrel-shaped vessel which had been overfired; large blisters had formed inside the walls, distorting the outline of the vessel. The thickened rim had been squared but again was distorted and it is difficult to determine whether the top should have been flat or sloping. The walls have prominent throwing rings on the interior and exterior. Very little survives of the base but there had been trimming of the base angle, leaving pronounced blade-cut facets, and the edge of the base was worn. A thin patchy and lustrous purple/black glaze is present on both surfaces although it is sparser on the interior; unglazed surfaces are a dark red/purple to brown colour.

No 22 is again a barrel-shaped jar with pronounced throwing rings on the interior and exterior. The rim is everted, slightly flattened and thinned towards the outer edge, although this varies around the perimeter. The overall shape of the rim is an irregular oval. Little survives of

the base but it appears to be slightly concave with knife trimming around the base angle. The perimeter of the base is worn. An uneven purplish/brown glaze covers the interior and exterior. The glaze appears as though it had been splattered over the surfaces and varies from being thick and glossy to a thin lustre.

The vessel has some similarity to an example from Speke Hall, Merseyside (Higgins 1988–9, 63, fig 7:32) from a mid-sixteenth-century deposit, but the form is a very simple common type and without a direct comparison it cannot be said to be a good parallel. Another Chester example was also found with Cistercian-type ware cups during the Browns' extension excavation at St Michael's Street (Newstead 1928, pl 21). Sherds from this vessel were scattered throughout the topmost fill of the pit (785), the overlying oven deposits (778) and (779) and the deposits above the oven (776).

Fabric 95: (no vessels illustrated) This is purple, very hard and with a rough feel and an irregular texture. Unglazed surfaces can appear pimply. Inclusions consist of abundant colourless and opaque white sub-angular quartz grains, sparse rounded dark red iron-rich fragments and sparse irregular voids. Some examples are glazed, although often this may only be a thin lustre. When present the glaze varies from black to purple. Fragments were concentrated in the upper fills of (487) and included the base and lower wall of a jar (from 776) and fragments in (503), (776) and (797) (part glazed).

Spanish tin-glazed ware
No 23 consists of two fragments from a Spanish concave-sided jar or *albarello* in a tin-glazed ware with a pinkish buff fabric. The exterior is a rich blue but the surface of the glaze has a similar iridescent and opaque weathering to that found on glass. The interior has a thin white tin glaze containing numerous specks of blue. There are two kiln scars on the body: a curving scar in the glaze just above the foot, and an extra piece of clay adhering to the glazed surface. Monochrome tin-glazed ware jars are not common in Britain: similar vessels have been found at Acton Court, near Bristol (Vince & Bell 1992, 107 and fig 4, 112; Vince 2004, 324, fig 9.11), where they were identified as Spanish tin-glazed ware and were thought to have arrived on the site in the 1530s. In the New World similar vessels are identified as Caparra blue, which was produced in Seville (*azul lisa* in Spain: *see* Pleguezuelo & Lafuente 1995): they are suggested to occur from the late fifteenth century and throughout the sixteenth (http://www.flmnh.ufl.edu/histarch/gallery_types/type_index_display.asp?type_name=CAPARRA%20BLUE example sherd no 2921). The identification of Caparra blue wares in north-west Europe is problematic (Hurst *et al* 1986, 53; Hurst 1995, 51). No comparative work has been carried out on those fragments that have been found in Britain and it has not been determined whether they are all from the same source nor whether that source is Seville and therefore the same as the New World Caparra blue wares. In the absence of any readily available comparative material these fragments have been assigned the more general term used by Vince (2004, 309) of Spanish tin-glazed ware with the similar proviso as at Acton Court that this vessel may be a Caparra blue type.

Merida-type ware

No 24 is a Merida-type ware lid. A similar lid has been found in a late fifteenth–early sixteenth-century context in Exeter, but another also occurred in a late sixteenth–early seventeenth-century context in that city (Allan 1995, 311). Two similar shaped lids (Vince 2004, 324, fig 9.11, 301 and 303) were found in area 2 at Acton Court and may have been deposited between the mid-1530s and the mid-1550s (*op cit*, 299–301).

Cologne stoneware

An almost complete Cologne stoneware rounded mug, no 25, was found in context (798). It has a pale grey fabric with an overall salt glaze and an exterior that varies in colour from grey to pale and dark brown; the interior is pale grey. A groove is present just below the rim and a bevelled cordon marks the join between neck and body. Two finer cordons mark the constriction above the rounded foot. The underside of the base has concentric wire marks.

The body of the jug is decorated with applied curled tendrils from which single sprig-moulded serrate leaves spring at intervals. The tendrils terminate in a pair of fruits and a single leaf. The fruits were initially identified as perhaps strawberries or raspberries but hops have also been suggested (Ian Smith *pers comm*). Given the function of the vessel hops seem more appropriate and the leaves are closer to the smaller of the two types of hop leaf than those of the other fruits. The neck is decorated with four square-shaped motifs consisting of stylised foliage with a single fruit at the centre.

Whilst the sprigged motifs are finely moulded the overall scheme of decoration is imperfect and could be deemed substandard. Parts of some leaves and fruits had become detached during or before firing as the remaining scars are covered in salt glaze. One leaf appears to have been smoothed after application and had lost some of its surface detail. The applied tendril is also misshapen in some areas.

The form and general style of decoration is typical of Cologne drinking jugs or mugs (Hurst *et al* 1986, 208–9). Evidence at the kiln sites suggest that they were made in the first half of the sixteenth century (*ibid*), but there is evidence from excavations to suggest that they were reaching England in the late fifteenth century (Gaimster 1997, 191).

This particular vessel is unusual because the majority of known vessels have designs depicting oak leaves and acorns or roses and leaves. Five fragments of mugs with these designs have been found as residual fragments in Phases VII, VIII, IX and X.

In keeping with other Rhenish stonewares of the sixteenth and early seventeenth centuries, Cologne stonewares do not make up a large percentage of assemblages excavated in Chester. A total of 18 fragments (761 g) of Cologne or Cologne/Frechen stonewares were retrieved from the site as a whole (0.09%, 0.12%). Out of this total 55% by sherd count and 82% by weight were found in Phase VI deposits where they formed 2.1% of the assemblage by sherd count and 1.9% by weight.

Beauvais ware?

Context (798) also produced a fragment of a small poly-sided shallow dish which may have come from Beauvais in northern France (no 26). The piece is in poor condition. The upper surface has the remains of a lead glaze which appears pale yellow in the bowl although small areas of green, blue and brown glaze are present on the rim. The underside is unglazed and may not have been intended to be seen, suggesting that the dish perhaps fitted into a pedestal base such as were found on salts. Its provenance and function are unclear. The fabric and glaze colours are similar to Beauvais ware and this would agree with the overall date of the assemblage. An alternative is perhaps a Rhenish earthenware.

Saintonge ware?

Joining fragments from the base of a partially glazed whiteware vessel from contexts (791) and (789) are comparable in fabric and form to an almost complete vessel identified as a 'Saintonge flagon' in a group from 1–11 Crook Street 1973/4. This group contained artefacts ranging in date from the late sixteenth to the mid-seventeenth century but with a deposition date nearer the mid-seventeenth century (Rutter & Davey 1980, 56). (Not illustrated)

Catalogue (Ills 5.5.1–.2)

10 Cup or jug base; Cistercian-type ware; Fabric 23. (806); SF 9914.
11 Cup with pear-shaped body; Cistercian-type ware; Fabric 24. (797); SF 9923.
12 Cup; Cistercian-type ware; Fabric 24. (806); SF 9916.
13 Cup in form of inverted baluster; Cistercian-type ware; Fabric 24. (798); SF 9918.
14 Cup; Cistercian-type ware; Fabric 24. (798); SF 10328.
15 Flared cup; Cistercian-type ware; Fabric 21. (806); SF 9915.
16 Flared cup; Cistercian-type ware; Fabric 21. (797); SF 9922.
17 ?Flared cup; Cistercian-type ware with slipped dots; Fabric 787. (791); SF 9925.
18 Flared cup; Cistercian-type ware; Fabric 21. (949); SF 10343.
19 Cup; Cistercian-type ware; Fabric 24. (251); SF 10333.
20 Jar; Midland Purple-type ware; Fabric 780. (798), (789); SF 9921.
21 Cistern/bunghole jar; Midland Purple-type ware; Fabric 779. (797), (798); SF 9924.
22 Jar; Midland Purple-type ware; Fabric 780. (785), (776), (778), (779), (503); SF 9928.
23 Jar; Spanish tin-glazed ware. (806); SF 9917.
24 Lid; Merida-type ware. (789), (791); SF 9927.
25 Mug; Cologne stoneware. (798); SF 9919. (*see also* Ill 5.5.2*).
26 Dish; Beauvais ware? (798); SF 9920.

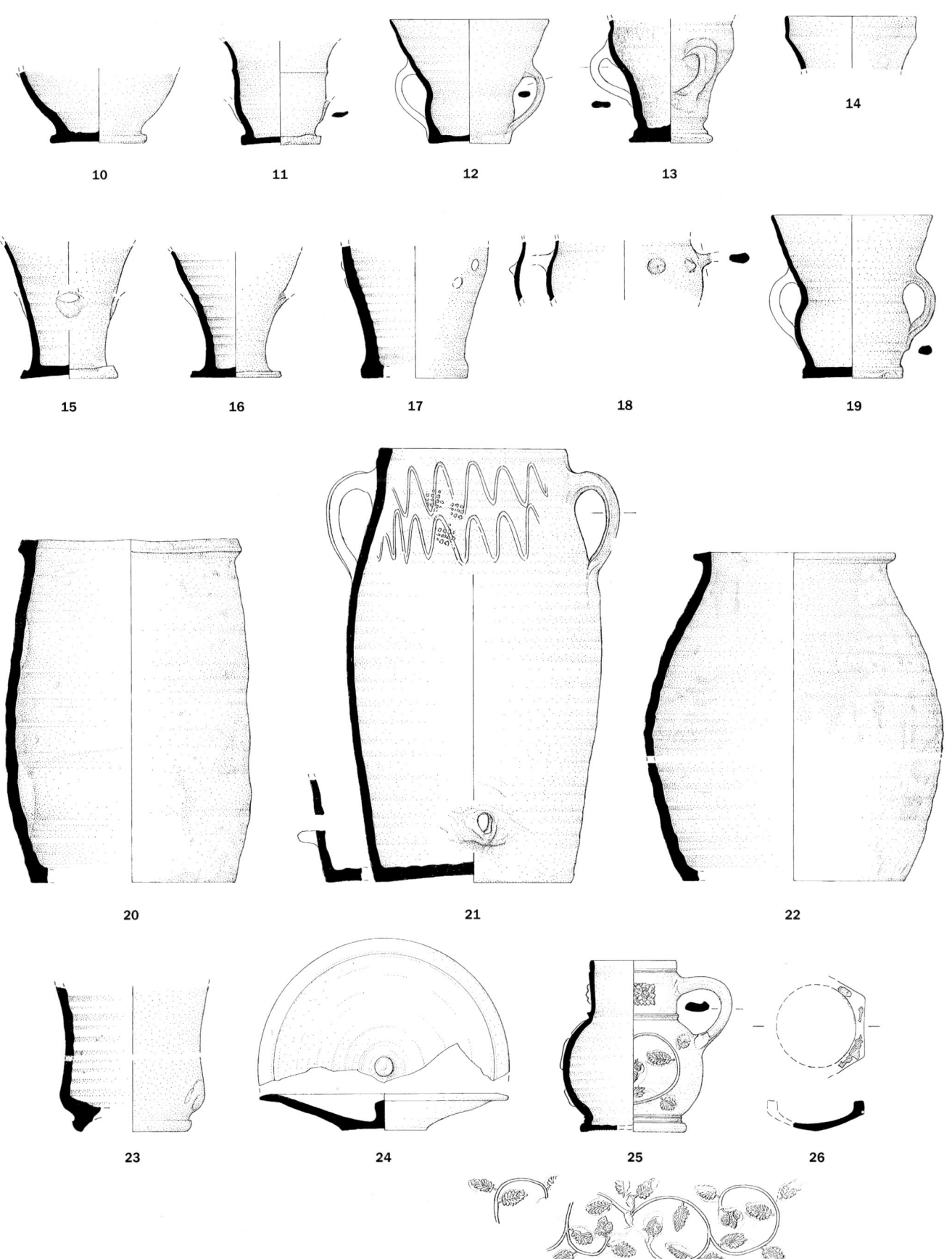

III 5.5.1 Phase VI Plot 2 cess pit (487): post-medieval pottery. (Scale 1/4)

Ill 5.5.2 Phase VI Plot 2 cess pit (487): Cologne stoneware mug (no 25).

Plot 3

Gully (1703)

Gully 1703 contained a small group of pottery consisting of semi-complete vessels of late sixteenth- and early seventeenth-century date. The presence of two fragments of eighteenth-century pottery and clay tobacco pipe suggests contamination during or after the eighteenth century. However the remains of an apparently curated Spanish lustreware dish make the assemblage noteworthy.

It is difficult to assign a date to the group: the only independently datable vessel is the late Valencian lustreware which is earlier than the generally accepted date of the introduction of the blackware, also in the group, *c* 1600. There is an absence of yellow wares and slipwares, both of which were present in an assemblage of Civil War date at Beeston castle. That assemblage did not contain Cistercian-type wares but Midland Purple-type wares were present and one (Noake 1993, 195, fig 133.63) had some similarity to no 27. The date of introduction of yellow wares is vague, but their absence suggests that this group may predate their introduction. However, the relatively small size of the group makes a consideration of the absence of wares difficult and the stratigraphy suggests some truncation. The vessel glass assemblage dates to the late sixteenth and the first half of the seventeenth century. The pottery seems to be of similar date, but perhaps nearer the beginning of the century than the middle. The absence of clay tobacco pipes other than the two potentially intrusive fragments also supports a date before the middle of the century.

Table 5.5.6 Phase VI Plot 3 gully (1703): post-medieval pottery quantified by ware, EVEs, no of sherds and weight

Ware	EVEs rim	EVEs base	No	Wt (g)
Blackware	10	0	1	41
Cistercian-type	0	200	8	367
Midland Purple-type	83	100	15	2633
Notts-type stoneware (intrusive)	0	0	1	10
Unglazed earthenware (intrusive)	0	0	1	18
Valencian late	15	0	3	154
Saintonge	0	0	4	93
Total	108	300	33	3316

Table 5.5.7 Phase VI Plot 3 gully (1703): post-medieval pottery quantified by form, EVEs, no of sherds and weight

Form	EVEs rim	EVEs base	No	Wt (g)
Cup	0	200	8	367
Dish	15	0	3	154
Jar	93	100	15	2642
Sugar mould? (intrusive)	0	0	1	18
Unidentified	0	0	6	135

Wares

Blackwares

These formed a minor part of the assemblage and there was only a single fragment from the everted rim of a jar (not illustrated). It had been slightly distorted during firing and has a red fabric (Fabric 121: *see* below).

Cistercian-type wares

Cistercian-type wares form the second largest ware group in the assemblage and are represented by the remains of four cups. One distinctively shaped vessel, no 27, is in the red Fabric 21 and the remainder Fabric 24.

No 27 is a cup with a short upright rim above a squat body that flares out and down before sharply turning into a narrow relatively high base. The base is very thin and slightly kicked. The centre of the base is broken and glaze covers part of the broken edge, suggesting that the base may have cracked during firing. The remains of the body join of one handle are present; the opposite side of the cup is missing but it would seem probable that there had been two handles. The glaze cover is patchy, varying from glossy to a thin lustre. Amongst the Cistercian-type wares from the site this cup is unusual. There are similarities, however, with Yorkshire forms (eg Moorhouse & Slowikowski 1992, 113, fig 52, nos 12 and 14; Le Patourel 1966, 265, fig 6.1).

The handles of cup no 28 are missing but the lower handle–body joins of two survive, one on each side of the cup but not symmetrically around the centre of the vessel. The foot splays out to one side but is rounded on the other, giving the vessel a lopsided appearance. Half of the base is sooted and the perimeter edge is quite heavily worn. The surface of the base has faint parallel scratch marks. A dark brown glaze covers both surfaces, but there are unglazed patches on the inside of the body. The vessel appears to fall into the same group as Brears type 14, the Staffordshire wide-mouthed forms (Barker 1986a) and nos 12 and 179.

Midland Purple-type wares

The remains of three jars were found. None of the fragments are glazed. Two are in high-fired purple wares (Fabric 95), whilst the third is an orange-purplish brown (Fabric 781; *cf* no 51 from (1697) below). Two of the vessels are relatively large with everted rims measuring 120 mm and 140 mm in radius. The third is the more complete but smaller of the three and is described below.

No 29 is incomplete but appears to be an unglazed medium rounded double-handled jar. The rim is upright with an internal bevel and a slight lid-seating. The opposing strap handles are set high on the shoulder. Each handle terminal has two pronounced thumb impressions at the join with the body. An applied thumbed strip is present just below the neck carination. The edge of the base had been thickened to create a slightly splayed foot; the base appears to be flat but large areas of the surface of the underside has broken away as though heat-shattered but there is no visible sooting. The perimeter of the base is worn.

As already noted there is some similarity between this vessel and an example at Beeston castle. These predominantly unglazed Midland Purple-types in Fabric 95 appear to have more in common with Staffordshire types than the other, better glazed, examples of Midland Purple-type wares from the site (*see* Ford 1995, 35–6 and fig 20.158; Kelly 1973, 2).

Late Valencian lustreware

No 30 is a flat-bottomed dish or basin. The centre of the base has the remains of a raised boss, which was either covered by incised decoration or had been incised to give a gadrooned appearance. The walls are missing but appear to have risen vertically from the basal angle. The upper surface is divided into two bands or zones. The inner zone is painted in overall lustre which has faded to a pale gold and is very faint in places. The decoration consists of six-petalled rosettes set amongst tendrils, stylised leaves, dots and possible small flower motifs. The outer zone consists of a band of lustre within which are reserved white discs divided into six segments by bisecting lines of lustre. The exterior is covered with concentric circles of reddish brown lustre bordered by wider bands at the perimeter and at the carination for the bossed centre. The surviving perimeter of the base is worn clean of glaze.

Two fragments from contexts (1448) (Phase VIII, Plot 3) and (1559) (Phase VII, Plot 4) appear to be from the same vessel. They have a similar concentric circle pattern on the reverse and pale gold overall lustre on the upper surface. The fragment from (1559) has a floral pattern on the upper surface. That from (1448), SF 10301, has a relief moulded or incised foliage design on the upper surface; shallow impressions on the reverse appear to be from fingers placed to support the vessel wall whilst the relief moulding was executed.

The dish has a complex form which appears to be unusual among excavation finds in Britain; complete vessels with comparable features of design and form are, however, present in museum and private collections. Dishes with gadrooned bosses are represented in the Wallace Collection (Norman 1976, C5, 45 and C6, 47) and suggested to be *c* 1500; each of these includes the motif made up of reserved discs in the lustre referred to as 'spoked wheels' by Norman. A dish with an incised bull set amongst incised floral and foliage designs is part of the Godman Bequest at the British Museum (Wilson 1995, 348, fig 28.8). This dish also features the reserved disc motif and is suggested to have been made in the Valencia region at the end of the fifteenth or first half of the sixteenth century. The incised decoration of this example also covers the bossed centre and it may be a closer parallel to no 29 than the gadrooned bosses.

Another, abraded, fragment of lustreware came from Phase VII, Plot 6, the fill of pit (925) (no 31). It has an overall pale gold lustre design on the upper surface and reddish brown lustre lines and dots on the reverse. It appears to be from a second dish with moulded or incised line decoration similar to the fragment from (1448).

Spanish lustrewares are not common finds in the city. Fragments from twenty-three vessels were noted in 1975

Ill 5.5.3 Phase VI Plot 3 gully (1703): Late Valencian lustreware dish (no 30).

(Davey & Rutter 1975), although they are arguably more numerous than elsewhere in the region. The majority that have been published to date appear to be late Valencian types (*see* Hurst *et al* 1986 for a definition and description), although it has not been possible to examine all the sherds from other sites in the city within the timescale of this project. Fragments of possible mature Valencian types were published in 1975 (*art cit*). Most fragments from the city are small and in relatively poor condition. Two pieces of late Valencian dishes with debased Arabic script are, however, well preserved. Both are poorly stratified: one was found in Hamilton Place in the centre of the walled city (Davey & Rutter 1977, 24–5, 18); the second piece was found recently in the back garden of a house in Handbridge, the southern suburb of the city (unpublished). One small fragment published from the Dominican friary and occurring in post-demolition deposits of the church (Rutter 1990b, fig 99.78) requires further examination because its illustration suggests that it was possibly also from a dish with relief or incised decoration similar to the piece from (1448).

By contrast nos 30 and 52 (*see* below) are the best preserved and the most substantial pieces of Spanish lustreware vessels found in the city. They are also relatively the best stratified, both appearing in pit groups, although the former is likely to be the remains of a curated or residual vessel. The fragments of no 30 suggest that it was an impressive object and if had survived to the present as a complete vessel would no doubt be highly prized.

Saintonge ware

The unglazed remains of a large rounded vessel were found in this ware. They are possibly from a *pegau* (*see* Hurst *et al* 1986, 76–8) (not illustrated).

Catalogue (Ills 5.5.3–.4)

27 Cup; Cistercian-type ware; Fabric 21. (1702); SF 10339.

28 Cup; Cistercian-type ware; Fabric 24. (1702); SF 10331.

29 Double-handled jar; Midland Purple-type ware; Fabric 95. (1702); SF 10336.

30 Dish; Late Valencian lustreware. (1702); SF 10302 + (1448); SF 10301.

31 Dish? Late Valencian lustreware. (824): Phase VII, Plot 6, fill of pit (925); SF 10303.

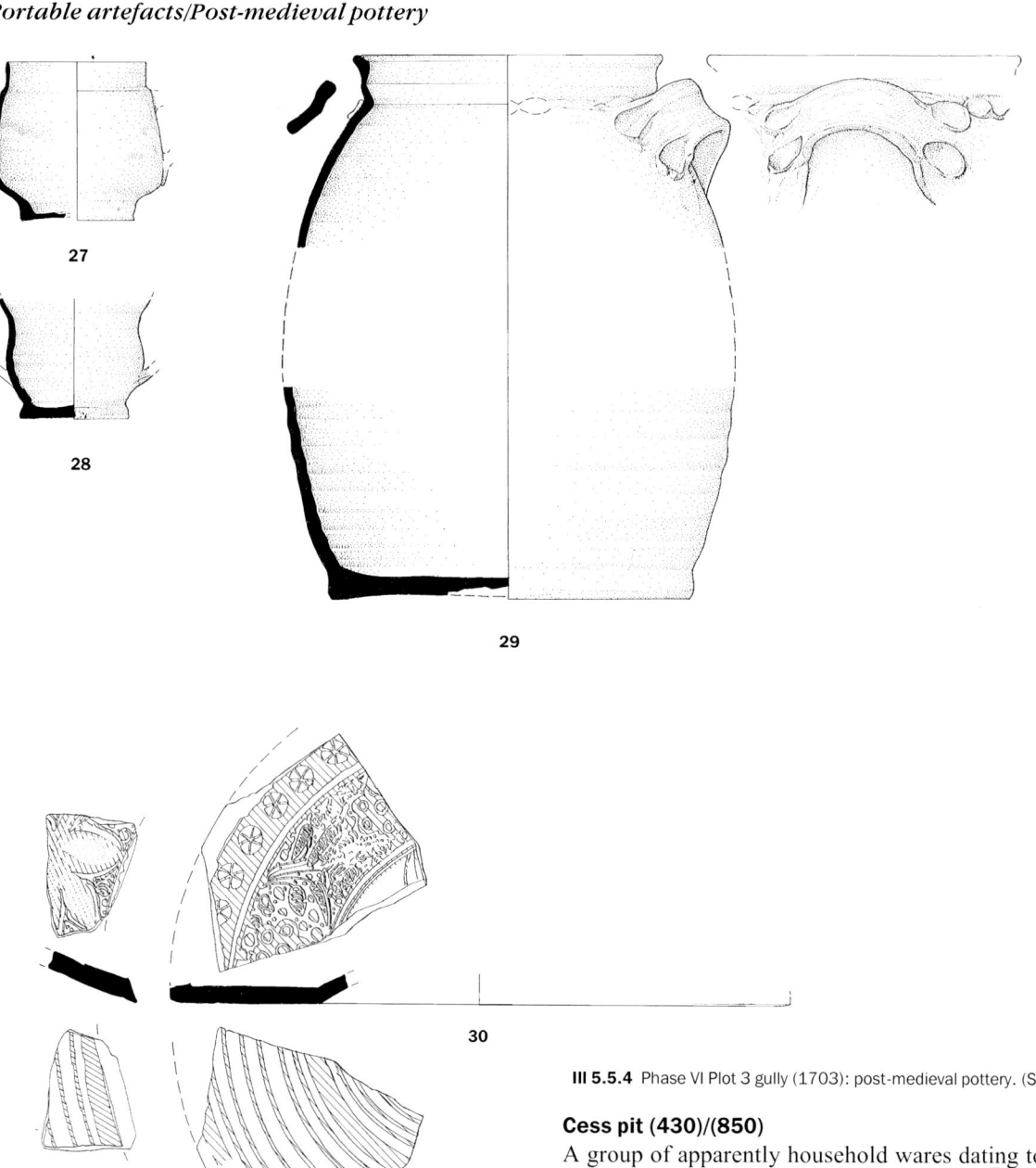

III 5.5.4 Phase VI Plot 3 gully (1703): post-medieval pottery. (Scale 1/4)

Cess pit (430)/(850)

A group of apparently household wares dating to some-time during the first half of the seventeenth century came from the fills of this pit ((429), (442), (800), (801), (802), (803), (804)). The group is mixed in condition, consisting of small unrelated fragments along with smashed but almost complete vessels and substantial pieces of vessels. The variable condition may be attributed to the pit being excavated in two phases and disturbed at some point in the twentieth century: the yellow ware jar no 39 had been partly encased in a fine grey extruded concrete or mortar. The group is included in this study because of the associated assemblage of vessel glass dating to the first half of the seventeenth century and pottery assemblages that can be associated with this period are relatively rare in the city. Whilst the pottery and vessel glass appear to be contemporary, the clay tobacco pipe assemblage is insignificant, mixed in date and includes much later fragments. These later pieces may reflect the later disturbance but the earliest date of *c* 1610 could possibly be used as a *terminus post quem* for the group.

In addition to the continued emphasis on drinking and storage vessels, a key feature of the group is the preponderance of blackwares and yellow wares, with lesser numbers of Cistercian-type wares and Midland Purple-type wares. Fragments of imported wares are present but they are too small to identify accurately as to form: Anglo-Dutch tin-glazed wares, a Rhenish stoneware (possibly Frechen) and a small sherd with a copper green coloured glaze, possibly a Surrey–Hampshire Border ware.

The group is relatively small so an absence of wares may not be related to date but it is potentially significant that the only use of slip in the group is a small stamped disc on a black ware mug fragment (not illustrated). The Civil War group at Beeston castle (Noake 1993) included trailed slipware dishes and hollow wares and is evidence that such wares were in use by the 1640s. It is thus possible that this pit group predates the Civil War; alternatively the predominance of drinking vessels and jars in the group may suggest a functional bias: dishes may have been provided by another material, eg pewter.

In comparison to some of the other assemblages continental imports in this group play a much reduced role, but it is perhaps worth noting that the glass, pottery and clay tobacco pipes all include imports or potential imports from the Low Countries. The pottery imports are less substantial than the glass but are indicative of contact either directly or indirectly with the Low Countries and south-east England.

Table 5.5.8 Phase VI Plot 3 cess pit (430)/(850): post-medieval pottery quantified by ware, EVEs no of sherds and weight

Ware	EVEs rim	EVEs base	No	Wt (g)
Blackware	218	200	66	1386
Cistercian-type	46	163	20	227
Midland Purple-type	19	72	8	403
Midland Purple-type?	0	0	1	69
Yellow	210	200	54	1801
Brown-glazed ware	17	0	1	23
Border ware	0	0	1	1
TGW	0	0	3	9
Frechen?	0	0	1	18
Total	510	635	155	3937

Table 5.5.9 Phase VI Plot 3 cess pit (430)/(850): post-medieval pottery quantified by form, EVEs, no of sherds and weight

Form	EVEs rim	EVEs base	No	Wt (g)
Unidentified	0	103	29	717
Cup	87	120	23	235
Cup?	17	0	1	23
Dish?	0	0	2	37
Jar	173	112	41	1912
Jar?	34	0	1	25
Mug	199	300	58	988

Wares

Blackwares

Blackwares are generally made from red/brown firing clay and have a dark glaze producing a black to dark brown finish. They formed a major component of the assemblage (43% sherd count, 35% weight, 43% rim eves, 32% base eves) and provided drinking vessels and storage jars and could be divided into three broad fabric groups.

Fabrics

Fabric 784: A fine reddish-brown to purple colour which often appears bright red. The fabric is hard with a smooth feel and fine texture. Inclusions consist of moderate to sparse colourless and opaque white sub-angular quartz grains which can vary from fine to medium size; sparse red to brown iron rich inclusions which may be rounded or sub-angular; sparse white inclusions (white clay?) that may be over 1 mm in size. A glossy black or dark brown glaze that can sometimes appear lustrous.

The forms that could be identified in this fabric consist of mugs, cups and what appears to be a small jar (no 33). Most of the drinking vessels are only represented by small fragments but two mugs whilst smashed are almost complete and are described below.

Nos 35 and 36 are flared mugs with single handles. These mugs are very similar to each other in form, method of decoration and manufacture, the major difference between them being height. The rims are simple and finely finished, that on no 35 flaring outwards slightly. Bands of narrow horizontal ridging appear at the top of the vessels just above the upper handle–body join, around the approximate centre and just above the base. Bases are splayed, more or less flat and the undersides are very smooth and cleanly finished. Both mugs are well glazed on the interior and exterior but the feet are unevenly covered.

Less survives of no 36 but it appears better made; no 35 is slightly off centre and leans away from the vertical as though the potter had started to lose control of the clay during throwing.

Although there were broad similarities with the assemblages dated to the Civil War period at Beeston castle, precise local parallels for the flared mugs were difficult to identify. The assemblage from a stone-lined cess pit excavated in St John Street in 1938 (Newstead 1939) contained similar mugs which were associated with a multi-handled vessel as below. That assemblage was dated to the first half of the seventeenth century.

Fragments from a large multi-handled mug, no 34, are decorated in a similar fashion to the above mugs. The mug has a wide flaring rim below which was a raised cordon above a band of horizontal ridging. A double loop handle survives and probably alternated with single loop handles.

Multi-handled mugs appear in Barker's blackware corpus (Barker 1986b) but these are from late seventeenth- to early eighteenth-century deposits. Earlier are similar vessels from the siege period at Sandal castle (Brears 1983, 220, fig 95, 77) and the Civil War period at Beeston (Noake 1993, 195, fig 133). Such vessels also occur in the earlier activity at Brookhill, Buckley (Amery & Davey 1979, 80), ie *c* 1640–60.

No 33 is the incomplete rim of a possible jar with a distinctive profile. The rim is upright with an internal bevel; a ridged neck flared out and down to a narrow sloping shoulder with a clearly defined carination above the body, which may have been cylindrical. The vessel is very finely thrown, has a highly fired purple-black body and a glossy black glaze. The shape is reminiscent of Italian tin-glazed ware *albarelli* (ie jars) and is unusual for blackwares in Chester, although copies of such vessels are known elsewhere in Britain, eg Surrey–Hampshire Border wares (Pearce 1992, 73, fig 44).

Fabric 121: Colour varies from red to a purple-brown colour, sometimes within the same vessel. The fabric is hard with a feel that can vary from smooth to rough and a fine texture. Inclusions consist of moderate but not very well sorted colourless and opaque grey/white quartz grains that are angular or sub-angular; sparse to moderate dark red/brown iron-rich inclusions angular or sub-angular in shape; sparse white clay inclusions appearing as lenses or pellets. The black to brown glaze is glossy but can appear lustrous.

This fabric is largely represented by featureless body sherds and the only identifiable vessels are jars; the only example with diagnostic features is described below.

No 32, a handled jar or chamber pot, has a flaring everted rim with an internal bevel. A strap handle is attached just below the rim edge and appears to be set quite high on the body. A band of ribbing marks the shoulder. The vessel is finely thrown and there is a glossy dark brown glaze on what survives of the exterior and the interior of the rim, but below the neck the glaze is a thin lustre. Similarly shaped single-handled jars in blackware and yellow wares appeared in the period 7 Civil War deposit at Beeston castle, (Noake 1993, fig 137, nos 116 and 118; fig 131, no 21). Such vessels made in Surrey–Hampshire Border wares in the early to mid-seventeenth century are identified as chamber pots (Pearce 1992, 68–9, figs 39–40) – a possible function for this vessel.

Fabric 785: Colour varies from orange to greyish purple, sometimes within the same vessel. Hard fabric with a rough feel and a fine texture. Inclusions consist of moderate, ill-sorted, sub-rounded quartz grains that are colourless or white; moderate flecks, particles and streaks of red clay; moderate streaks of white clay and sparse sub-angular fragments of white clay. The glaze varies in colour from dark brown to black and can be smooth and glossy or thin and lustrous.

Only nine body sherds in this fabric are in the group; several of them appear to belong to the same jar but none carry any diagnostic features and they have not been illustrated.

Cistercian-type wares

There was some difficulty in determining the precise quantity of Cistercian-type wares in the group. Some of the sherds assigned to this ware group are very small and featureless and it is possible that some are from high-fired blackware vessels; even so, Cistercian-type wares form a small percentage of the assemblage: (12% sherd count, 6% weight, 9% rim EVEs, 23% base EVEs). There are no complete vessels or any larger fragments that can be firmly identified. Thus it is difficult to ascribe precise forms or to draw parallels with possible production centres. However, the pieces that can be suggested to be Cistercian-type wares are from cups. All but one are in Fabric 24, the remaining sherd is in fabric 21. Some rims appear to be from short wide-mouthed forms such as nos 12 and 19 above, whilst others are perhaps from flared cups such as nos 15 and 16. A wider handle fragment (Fabric 21) has some similarity to no 59 below.

Enough survives of one vessel, no 37, to indicate that it is unlike any of the other Cistercian-type ware cups from the site. The squat rounded body is similar to no 12 but the foot is higher, more sharply defined and its upper edge marked by an incised line in similarity to no 59. Unlike that vessel the lower end of the handle joins the vessel just above the foot. It is perhaps nearer to Barker's type 2 pedestal form (Barker 1986a, 57 fig 1.2). The remains of the lower handle–body join suggest that the vessel had broader handles than is usual for Cistercian-type wares. The end of the handle had been splayed out quite broadly for such a small vessel and finished with a

sweep to the right. The underside of the base is marked by parallel scratches.

Midland Purple-type wares

Like the Cistercian type wares, Midland Purple-type wares are represented by a small fragmentary group (rim EVEs 4%, base EVEs 12%, sherd count 6%, weight 12%) and no complete vessels or substantial fragments remain. The only identifiable vessel forms are from jars. One base has the scar of a fine-rimmed vessel, possibly a cup in a red fabric, on the underside of the base. The three principal Midland Purple-type ware fabrics are present (ie Fabrics 95, 779, 780: *see* above).

Yellow wares

The yellow wares in this group form 80.3% (89% by weight) of all the yellow wares in Phase VI and are the earliest stratified group of yellow wares from the site. With the blackwares they form the bulk of the assemblage (35% sherd count, 46% weight, 41% rim EVEs, 31% base EVEs). Yellow wares have a relatively fine buff to pink fabric and a smooth glossy colourless glaze, producing a shiny yellow coloured ware. A white slip may sometimes underlie the glaze.

The majority of the identified yellow ware forms are drinking vessels and jars but two fragments may represent dishes. Rounded cordons or pronounced ribbing arranged singly or in bands of two or more are a feature of the jars and drinking vessels; any other decorative detail is uncommon on hollow wares. A large mug, no 39, is, however, distinctive both in its size and decoration. The jar fragments have everted rims and it is possible that some may be from tall chamber pots such as the black ware vessel in this assemblage, no 32.

There appears to be some difference in the quality of finish and production amongst the yellow wares. Two sherds from a cup, no 38, with a distinctive ribbed body and a narrow everted rim, are notably well thrown, thin walled and relatively finely finished, although the lower handle join is not set vertically below the upper veering off to the left. A speckled vessel is also distinctively sharply ribbed and finished. By contrast others, eg, the jar and mug, appear not to have received much attention to the finer details of finishing.

Fabrics

Three fabric groups are present, Fabrics 50 and 786, and a speckled yellow ware, Fabric 52.

Fabric 50: This is a pale pink to buff colour; it is hard with a rough feel and an irregular texture. Inclusions consist of abundant ill-sorted sub-angular quartz grains that are colourless, opaque white or pink stained in colour; flecks, rounded inclusions and sparse coarse sub-angular fragments of a red iron rich compound; sparse coarse rounded fragments of white clay. The glaze is clear and glossy.

No 39 in Fabric 50 is a narrow rounded jar with an internally bevelled everted rim and a slightly concave base. A band of four narrow cordons/ impressed lines mark the shoulder. It is glazed internally and externally but the lower quarter of the exterior is unglazed. There are occasional smudges of what appear to be a red slip under the glaze, making splatters of orange/brown colour. The

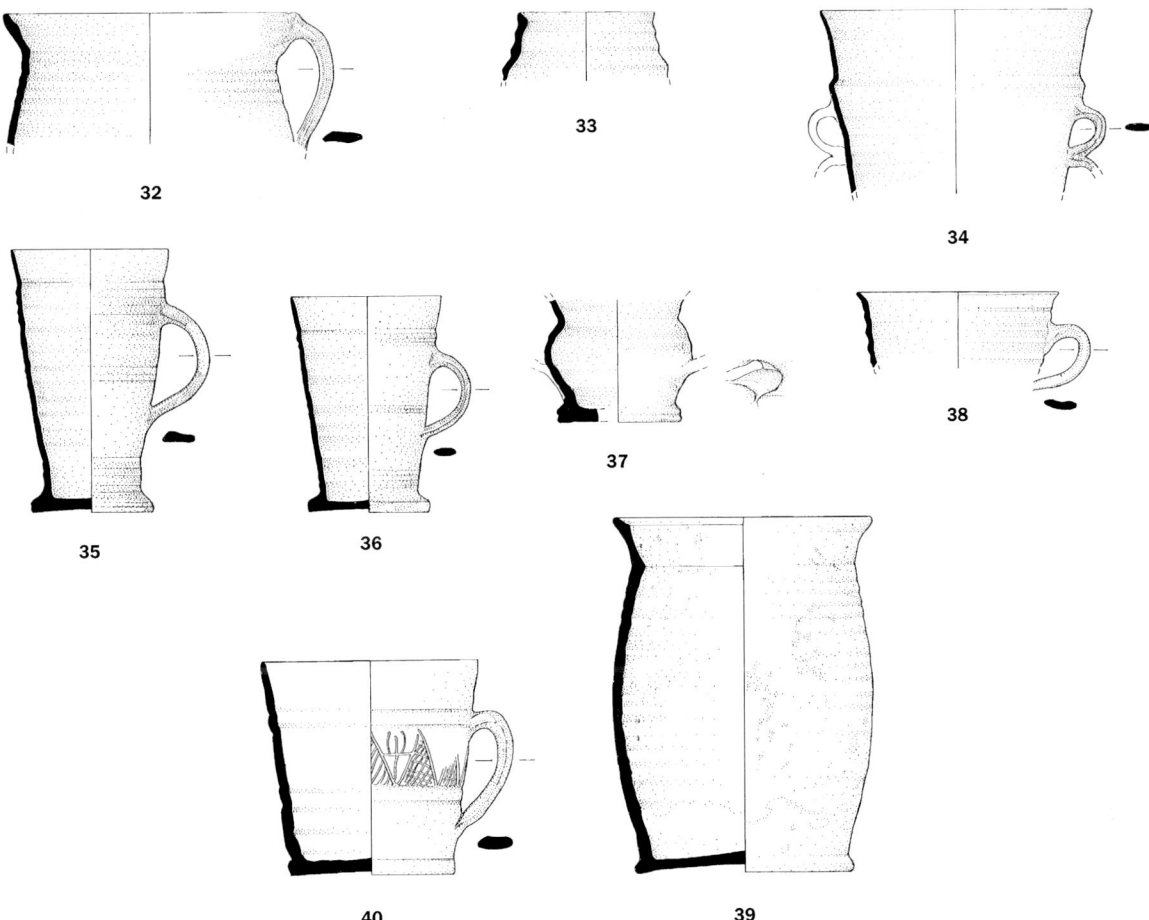

Ill 5.5.5 Phase VI Plot 3 cess pit (430)/(850): post-medieval pottery. (Scale 1/4)

vessel is smashed but complete. However, its surface condition is very poor, particularly in the base area which has a battered appearance as though repeated spalling has occurred over a period of time so that much of the original surface is missing. The base and rim edges are badly chipped. In addition there is sooting around the unglazed area of the lower body and under the base. The glaze is also crazed and has become detached from the surface in some places. A fine deposit or discoloration is present on the interior surface. This deposit and the condition of the base exterior suggest that the jar was placed near a heat source, perhaps to heat the contents.

Fabric 786: A buff hard fabric with a smooth feel and fine texture. Inclusions consist of: moderate ill-sorted opaque white and colourless sub-angular quartz grains; sparse fine flecks of red clay which can be present as coarse fragments. It has a smooth glossy glaze.

Mug no 40 is flared in form with a tapering vertical loop handle. A band of incised decoration bordered by two ribs marks the middle of the vessel. The band has been divided into alternating triangles, the majority of which are infilled with roughly vertical lines; most had been filled individually but on one or possibly two examples the lines had been continued over the border into the next triangle. Three triangles are cross-hatched rather than lined and one has a cross type symbol similar to an 'ankh'. The execution of the design appears not to have been done in a precise fashion.

The decoration is similar to that found painted on tin-glazed ware jars of the late sixteenth and early to mid-seventeenth century. Incised decoration is unusual on the yellow wares that have been found locally but it has been found at Ticknall, Derbyshire, on yellow wares suggested to have been produced there (Spavold & Brown 2005, fig 20, 89). Unlike jar no 39 the vessel is in good condition; it is smashed but a virtually complete vessel can be reconstructed.

No 38 is a rounded cup with a fine everted rim and pronounced ribbing on the body. The vertical handle is a tight loop, made from a tapered strap with a curved section. The upper and lower joins are not in line so the handle slants to the right. The vessel is quite finely thrown but the rim and handle were damaged before glazing. It was also glazed and fired with a waste fragment of clay sticking to the exterior of the rim. A fragment possibly from the same cup came from (802).

Fabric 52: Within the yellow ware category are three sherds which have a pinkish buff fabric and a brown speckle on the glazed surfaces. The fabric is similar to 786 but has more abundant red iron-rich inclusions and parallels Fabric 52 in the Chester Fabric Reference Collection. The three pieces consist of a featureless body fragment, the rim of a jar or chamber pot, and the remains of a pedestal bowl-type vessel perhaps a salt or chafing dish.

The jar (not illustrated) has a simple everted rim and pronounced ridging on the shoulder. Little remains of the vessel to identify its function but the rim form and high shoulder is similar to the potential chamber pot in this group, no 32.

Ill 5.5.6 Phase VI Plot 3 cess pit (430)/(850): Yellow ware mug (no 40).

Discussion of Yellow wares

The place of manufacture of these yellow wares is unclear. Rainford on Merseyside is one source (Davey 1986–7, 127); Staffordshire provides another and also potentially Ticknall in Derbyshire. Some forms found in Chester are similar to the Midlands Yellow-ware type-series described by Brears (1971, 31–7) and it is thus possible that they were derived from a variety of sources. More detailed comparative work is required. Speckled wares appear to be a variant of the ware and have been ascribed a possible provenance in south Lancashire (Rutter 1990b).

Yellow wares are generally ascribed a seventeenth-century date in the city and appeared sometime in the first half of the century (Rutter 1990b). This assemblage may confirm that dating. The large pit group (1696) from Phase VII Plot 4 (*see* below) suggests that they were not a major component of assemblages by the early eighteenth century and may have ceased production by then.

Catalogue (Ills 5.5.5–.6)

32   Handled jar or chamber pot; blackware; Fabric 121. (429); SF 10294.
33   Jar? Blackware; Fabric 784. (800); SF 10297.
34   Multi-handled mug; blackware; Fabric 784. (429); SF 10295.
35   Mug; blackware; Fabric 784. (429); SF 10292.
36   Mug; blackware; Fabric 784. (429), (800); SF 10293.
37   Cup; Cistercian type ware cup; Fabric 24. (800); SF 10299.
38   Cup; yellow ware; Fabric 786. (429); SF 10291.
39   Jar; yellow ware; Fabric 50. (429); SF 10296.
40   Mug; yellow ware; Fabric 786. (442); SF 10300.

Plot 1

Building debris (246)

This assemblage has been included to provide some context for the jack of plate found in the same layer. The pottery, whilst fragmentary, is in good condition. Curiously, while most vessels are represented by four sherds or less and cannot be reconstructed, one large blackware jar is virtually complete, although smashed into sixty-eight pieces. Two vessels were considered worthy of illustration and individual comment; otherwise the group has been summarised.

The wares present are blackwares (Fabrics 121 and 784), Cistercian-type wares (Fabrics 24 and 21), Midland Purple-type ware (Fabric 95) and yellow wares (Fabric 786), along with a small group of continental imports. The range of wares suggests an early to mid-seventeenth century date which is consistent with the clay pipe and glass evidence.

Jars and cups are the predominant forms where identification was possible, with the blackwares and Cistercian-type wares providing the drinking vessels. The Cistercian type-ware cups include a fragment decorated with two intersecting lines of slip on the exterior and a rim from a flared type. The Midland Purple-type and yellow wares present are jars.

Table 5.5.10 Phase VI Plot 1 layer (246): post-medieval pottery quantified by ware, EVEs, no of sherds and weight

Ware	EVEs rim	EVEs base	No	Wt (g)
Blackware	67	213	83	4451
Cistercian-type	2	33	6	107
Midland Purple-type	15	5	3	78
Yellow	0	60	4	129
Spanish coarseware	0	0	3	248
Saintonge	0	0	1	183
French import	0	0	1	9
Total	84	311	101	5205

Table 5.5.11 Phase VI Plot 1 layer (246): post-medieval pottery quantified by form, EVEs, no of sherds and weight

Form	EVEs rim	EVEs base	No	Wt (g)
Bowl - *lebrillo*	0	0	3	248
Chafing dish	0	0	1	9
Cup	2	46	7	120
Jar	82	265	84	4554
Pegau	0	0	1	183
Unidentified	0	0	5	91

Wares

Blackwares

Two smashed jars, one complete and the second represented by a base, make up the bulk of blackwares; both are in Fabric 121. The complete jar is described below.

No 41 is a tall, slightly rounded jar; the squared rim slopes inwards and has a bevelled and slightly concave exterior edge. Horizontal loop strap handles are placed on opposing sides and set so that the lower edge is wider than the upper. The jar has been well and finely thrown but leans slightly to one side. The convex walls are relatively fine for such a large vessel and become thinner around the shoulder.

A dark brown/black glaze covers the interior and exterior and becomes sparse and lustrous on the exterior of the lower body. It stops short of the rim on both surfaces, but patches of glaze are present on the rim and have spilled over to the exterior. Embedded in the glaze on the rim are two fragments of clay, presumably kiln spacers, suggesting that the glaze on the rim was derived from another vessel stacked above it in the kiln. The underside of the base is unglazed apart from a line around the perimeter which displays some signs of wear.

The inside of the jar is coated with a pale brown-buff deposit which when disturbed flakes away from the glazed surface; it covers the whole of the interior to just below the rim. It was not possible to analyse this deposit within the timescale of the project, but it is similar to that found inside chamber pots and is possibly a urine residue. The jar may therefore have been used to store urine, if not to collect it.

Continental imports

These consist of a fragment from a large unglazed Saintonge vessel, possibly a *pegau*, two fragments from a large green-glazed bowl or *lebrillo*, and a fragment from an elaborate chafing dish (no 42). Fragments of *pegau* were found elsewhere on the site and are occasional finds in the city. These large jug-like storage vessels have been found in late sixteenth and early seventeenth century deposits in England (Hurst *et al* 1986, 78). The large bowl or *lebrillo* is a type associated with coarse pottery production in the Seville area of Spain. Such bowls were produced from the medieval period but continued to be traded in the sixteenth and seventeenth centuries (*op cit*, 65–6). The bowls are thick walled heavy vessels with a thick coating of glaze on the interior and appear to fulfil a storage rather than table function.

No 42 consists of two joining fragments with green and yellow glazed moulded decoration in the style of architectural tracery. The second fragment came from Phase V (261). The two pieces form part of an openwork chafing dish and correspond to the tracery frill on the lower part of the bowl (Hurst 1974, 236, fig 4.1). This type of chafing dish was identified by John Hurst (1974, 237) and at that time only a small number of examples had been identified in London and Bristol. Examples of these vessels still appear to be rare, but fragments have since been found in Plymouth (Allan & Langman 2003, 55–6) and Hull (Armstrong 1977, 47, fig 17.160). This is the first example of the type to be recorded from Chester. The dating and precise provenance of the type is unclear but they appear to fit in with the more ornately decorated chafing dishes that appeared in the second half of the sixteenth and early seventeenth centuries (Hurst 1974, 234). The fragment is in a relatively poor condition in comparison with the rest of the assemblage, suggesting that it was perhaps not contemporary.

Catalogue (Ill 5.5.7)

41 Jar; blackware; Fabric 121. (246); SF 10289.
42 Chafing dish; French. (246), (261); SF 10290.

Plot 4

The fills of a sequence of pits at the western end of the plot (pit (1619): fill (1618); pit (1624): fills (1600), (1697), (1698); pit (1541): fills (1540), (1549)) contained assemblages which consist of a mix of transitional late medieval and early post-medieval wares. A number of vessels survive as large fragments or are almost complete but smashed. Sherd joins are present between the pit fills as well as with the assemblage in the overlying horn-core lined pit (1807) and with contexts assigned to Phase VIII in this plot. The deposits may have been disturbed as each successive pit was dug, as well as by the construction of the overlying horn-core lined pit. However, the confusion of cuts and fills may also be due to the difficult conditions under which the deposits were excavated. A further complicating factor is that an accident during finds processing led to a quantity of material being designated as unstratified. A number of fragments amongst this unstratified material either join pieces in the pit groups or appear to be from the same vessels. Whilst all these factors devalue the potential of the assemblages by compromising their stratigraphic integrity, the range,

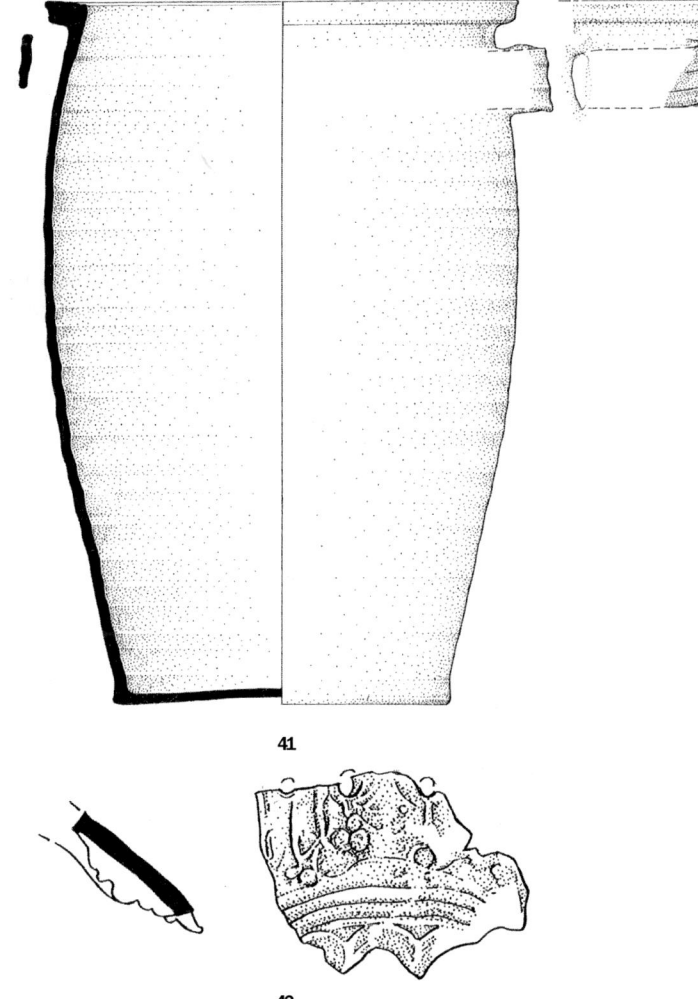

41

42

Ill 5.5.7 Phase VI Plot 1 building debris (246): post-medieval pottery. (Scale no 41: 1/4; no 42: 1/2)

quality and the potential date of the ceramics warrant their inclusion here.

The range of ceramics includes examples of late medieval pink/white wares and transitional Ewloe-type wares, alongside blackwares, Cistercian-type wares and Midland Purple-type wares. These are accompanied by a relatively wide range of continental imports: Italian tin-glazed wares, late Valencian lustreware, Rhenish stonewares, sixteenth-century tin-glazed ware, Saintonge and Beauvais wares. The substantial remains of a Cologne/Frechen mug (*schnelle*) is a rare occurrence in Chester. A group of three cups is unusual because, although stylistically related to Cistercian-type wares, their fabrics are unusual when compared to other Cistercian-types from the city. The fills of the lower pits in the sequence contained quite a large amount of medieval pottery which, apart from some well preserved fragments of Ewloe-type wares and pink/white wares, is in quite a fragmentary condition, suggesting that they were not primary deposits.

The small quantity of blackwares and yellow wares and an absence of slipwares suggest that the latest fills were deposited in the early seventeenth century, although one vessel, a blackware posset, no 57 SF 10054, is an anomaly. The low number of clay tobacco pipe fragments (five) in the combined assemblages also supports an early seventeenth-century date; an eighteenth-century fragment in (1618) appears to be intrusive. Vessel glass found in the sequence is also of a sixteenth-or early seventeenth-century date.

The fills of each pit have been described separately. Where sherds from the same vessel were divided between more than one pit fill they have been placed in the lowest deposit of the sequence. It is recognised that the mixing of the deposits may mean that this was not its original context of deposition.

Pit (1619)

This was the lowest pit in the sequence and contained thirty fragments (518 g) of medieval pottery which span the whole period and includes one small fragment of possible Rouen ware. Two later sherds are present: part of the base of a Cistercian-type ware jug or mug, no 43, which joins fragments from pits (1624) and (1541), and a small body sherd from a Midland Purple-type ware. If the first vessel was in its original place of deposition, an early to mid-sixteenth-century date could be suggested for its final filling.

Table 5.5.12 Phase VI Plot 4 pit (1619): post-medieval pottery quantified by ware, EVEs, no of sherds and weight

Ware	EVEs rim	EVEs base	No	Wt (g)
Cistercian-type	0	50	1	98
Midland Purple-type	0	0	1	34

Wares

Cistercian-type ware

No 43 is a small, pear-shaped jug or possibly a rounded mug made from the dark coloured Fabric 24. The rim is missing but the remains suggest that it was everted with a shallow raised cordon below. The tall narrow neck is slightly concave and widened out to sloping shoulders above a rounded body and a relatively wide base, giving a squat appearance. The base is thick relative to the walls. A single raised cordon defines the vertical foot. The base is slightly concave and there is a kiln scar or stacking mark in the form of a buff-brown disc edged in red and orange within the overall brown-purple colour. The lower handle–body join of a single oval-sectioned rod handle survives at the girth of the vessel. The exterior has a very dark reduced green-black patchy glaze which is sparse and lustrous in places. Glaze is present on the interior as spots and in small patches as a fine lustre.

The form of this vessel is unusual: it may have been an attempt to copy sixteenth-century Rhenish stoneware mugs. A similar but not identical vessel is known from Staffordshire (Barker 1986a, fig 1.8, 57).

Catalogue (III 5.5.8)
43 Jug or mug; Cistercian-type ware jug; Fabric 24.
    (1618), (1697), (1540); SF 9973.

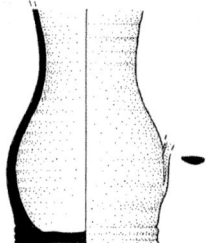

III 5.5.8 Phase VI Plot 4 pit (1619): Cistercian-type ware jug or mug (no 43). (Scale 1/4)

Pit (1624)

The lowest fill of this pit, (1697), contained the largest quantity of pottery, composed of large fragments, many of which join to form semi-complete vessels. Many of these fragments are coated to varying degrees with cess. Wares range from late medieval Ewloe-type and pink/white wares to sixteenth-century continental imports, Cistercian-type wares and Midland Purple-type wares. Only four relatively small fragments, of Cistercian-type ware, blackware and yellow ware, were found in (1600), the final fill, alongside twenty-six medieval pieces. However, clay tobacco pipes with a date range of 1610–40 were also present. No pottery, tobacco pipes or glass were found in the middle layer (1698). There are joins between the Cistercian-type ware vessels in this pit and the Phase VI pit (1541) and context (1796) in the Phase VII pit (1807); also between sherds of late Valencian lustreware in this pit and in pit (1696), which overlies the horn-core pit in Phase VII. Some of the later medieval or transitional wares in (1697) survive as large fragments, in one instance as an almost complete vessel. It is difficult to determine whether this is a result of pit fills being confused or whether these vessels were in use contemporaneously with the sixteenth- and possibly early seventeenth-century wares. It was decided not to rule out the latter, certainly in respect of the Ewloe-type ware cistern, and therefore the vessels have been described along side the later vessels rather than in the medieval section.

Table 5.5.13 Phase VI Plot 4 pit (1624): post-medieval pottery quantified by context, ware, EVEs, no of sherds and weight

Context	Ware	EVEs rim	EVEs base	No	Wt (g)
1600	Blackware	0	0	1	61
1600	Cistercian-type	0	0	1	13
1600	Yellow	0	0	2	14
1697	Cistercian-type	45	100	12	245
1697	Midland Purple-type	14	91	21	1208
1697	Valencian late	22	0	4	83
1697	Montelupo	9	0	1	10
1697	Beauvais?	9	0	1	38
1697	Saintonge	0	0	1	4
1697	Saintonge?	20	0	1	26
1697	Tudor Green	9	0	1	5
Total		128	191	46	1707

Table 5.5.14 Phase VI pit Plot 4 (1624): post-medieval pottery quantified by ware, EVEs, no of sherds and weight

Ware	EVEs rim	EVEs base	No	Wt (g)
Blackware	0	0	1	61
Cistercian-type	45	100	13	258
Midland Purple-type	14	91	21	1208
Yellow	0	0	2	14
Valencian late	22	0	4	83
Montelupo	9	0	1	10
Beauvais?	9	0	1	38
Saintonge	0	0	1	4
Saintonge?	20	0	1	26
Tudor Green	9	0	1	5
Total	128	191	46	1707

Table 5.5.15 Phase VI pit Plot 4 (1624): post-medieval pottery quantified by form, EVEs, no of sherds and weight

Form	EVEs rim	EVEs base	No	Wt (g)
Unidentified	0	0	12	361
Cistern	14	66	13	785
Cup	54	100	11	230
Cup?	0	0	1	5
Dish	60	25	8	311
Jug	0	0	1	15

Table 5.5.16 Phase VI Plot 4 pit (1624): medieval pottery quantified by ware, EVEs, no of sherds and weight

Ware	EVEs rim	EVEs base	No	Wt (g)
Ewloe-type	65	47	32	3861
Pink/white	0	70	19	1412
Other medieval wares			16	220
Total	65	117	67	5493

Wares

Pink/white and Ewloe-type wares

These wares are made from hard, coarse Coal Measure clays. The fabrics and forms are comparable to fragments found in a dump of kiln waste close to Ewloe near Buckley in Flintshire (Harrison & Davey 1977). It is possible that some of these wares may originate from other areas where Coal Measure clays outcrop, eg in Staffordshire, but detailed fabric analysis is required before this can be tested. The pink/white wares are found in forms which are characteristic of the fourteenth and fifteenth centuries; a hoard dating to *c* 1463 was found in 1901 in the remains of a pink/white ware jug (Rutter 1977).

No 44 is a cistern/bunghole jar with a rounded, everted rim with an internal lid-seating above a barrel-shaped body. An applied thumbed strip around the neck is the only form of decoration. The base has heavy knife-trimming and the whole vessel, whilst large and substantial, is not well finished. The handles and bunghole in particular appear insubstantial when compared to the bulk of the body and rim. The outside of the bunghole has been cut flat and wipe-marks are present around the join with the body. Two opposing vertical strap handles spring from the neck constriction. The handles veer to the left and their bases have been flattened and splayed at the join with the body. Throwing rings are prominent on the interior and exterior. A thin patchy glaze is present inside and out and varies in colour from a reduced greenish-brown to oxidised golden brown.

Ewloe-type ware bunghole jars are used as a marker of the late medieval period in Chester but there is no clear date of introduction nor any indication of when they went out of use. Their presence in this context with sixteenth-century wares suggests that they continued in use at that time. However, the mixed nature of this sequence of pit deposits makes it difficult to use this assemblage to refine the date of these wares.

No 45 is a Ewloe-type ware lid, highly fired to a purplish brown. It appears to have been almost flat.

No 46 is a baluster-shaped jug with a flaring base. The surface varies in colour from pink to dark brown and has spots of a reduced purple glaze. The form has some similarity to the Old Market Hall jugs (Rutter 1977), which are fourteenth- or fifteenth-century in date, but is much larger.

Cistercian-type wares

Cups nos 47–9 are in an unusual and coarser fabric than the other Cistercian-type wares, but their overall form is comparable, so they have been placed in this category until their provenance can be sourced. Two join with fragments in (1540) and the third with (1796) in Phase VII.

Fabrics

Fabric 788: This fabric has not been previously recorded in Chester. It is orange/red with a black core and

margins which fade in and out. The unglazed surfaces vary from a light to dark brown. The fabric is hard with a rough feel and a fine texture. Inclusions consist of numerous ill-sorted rounded or sub-angular quartz grains which are white or colourless; there are also occasional fine-grained rounded soft creamy white inclusions and sparse irregularly shaped iron-rich inclusions. The unglazed surfaces have smudges and wipe-marks. The glaze is brown. The surface of the pieces is marred by cess deposits but the glaze appears lustrous in patches and also crazed: how far this is its original state or the effect of deposition is unclear.

No 48 is the most complete of the vessels despite a missing rim and appears to be a necked cup with a rounded body and an everted neck. The cup originally had two opposing tapering squared rod handles, of which one survives. The upper end of the handle is splayed and joined to the cup just above the carination for the neck, whilst the lower is flattened into a triangular shape before joining at the girth. The base is flat with a small flared foot that has been roughly finished. The edge has been compressed in one place, perhaps when the pot was removed from the wheel. The underside of the base is smooth.

Only the upper part of the exterior is glazed; glaze is only present on the lower body where it had flowed down from above. These dribbles extend underneath the base. The border between the glazed and unglazed area is uneven, which with the excess overflows suggests that the glaze was applied in a less than careful manner. Most of the interior is glazed but patches inside the base and walls are not covered.

Two parallel horizontal lines were incised just above the girth and roughly mid-way between the girth and the carination below the rim. A disc of white clay had been applied mid-way between the handles so that it sits on the lower of these lines and covers the upper. The disc had been shaped into an eight-petalled rosette either by the use of a stamp or possibly by being shaped with a blade.

No 49 is similar to no 48 but less complete. It is again decorated with two parallel lines but there is no trace of any applied decoration. A large area of the underside of the base is covered in glaze which appears to have seeped down from the body. Neither of the cups display any kiln scars in the glazed area of the bases and it is difficult to determine how they were stacked in the kiln.

No 47 is a necked cup with a similar rounded profile but a shorter everted neck than no 48. The vessel appears to have been plain but there is a shallow indentation just below the rim. As with the other two cups the glaze stops just below the girth.

These cups are comparable in form and decoration to the Yorkshire Cistercian wares but are relatively low fired and their glazes have none of the lustrous purplish black colour usually associated with Cistercian-type wares. The lower firing and the fabric suggest that these may have been produced as local versions of Cistercian types but the location of that production is not apparent at present. No comparable cups have been published from Chester or observed by the author in the collections.

The Cistercian-type style suggests a date somewhere between the late fifteenth century and *c* 1600.

Midland Purple-type wares

Nos 50 and 51 were initially classified as a higher-fired, finer thrown variant of Ewloe-type ware. However, on closer inspection and after comparison with the other Midland Purple-type wares from the phase it was felt more appropriate to place them with these wares. Fabric 781 is similar to 780 in the range of inclusions but is rougher to the touch and without magnification its general appearance is similar to Fabric 95, differing only in colour, being a pale orange on the surfaces with purplish brown flashes and margins and a core that varies from yellow to grey. The remains of only three vessels from the site were noted. It is tempting to suggest that they were a development of the Ewloe-type wares into a local version of Midland Purple-type ware, but more well stratified examples and detailed fabric analysis would be required before any such conclusion could be drawn.

No 50 is a thin-walled finely thrown rounded jar form with prominent wheel-throwing rings. The rim is everted and very slightly thickened at the edge with an internal bevel. The remains of a single strap handle are present just below the rim, which had been neatly smoothed into the surface. The base is flat with trimming around the basal join so that it appears to have a chamfered foot. A prominent broad band of knife-trimming is present under the flat base around its perimeter. A circular hole had been cut through the vessel wall just above the base; the exterior surface of the surrounding area is missing, which suggests that the bunghole surround has fallen away, leaving just the pierced wall. The vessel is unglazed apart from the remains of a bib of purplish black glaze above the bunghole.

No 51 is a condiment dish made by joining two small dishes together and flattening the joining sides. A vertical handle with a curved terminal springs from one side of the join. The interior of the dishes is covered in a patchy reduced green glaze which had pooled in one corner of one of the dishes. The exterior and handle are unglazed apart from occasional spots. Smoothing and handling marks are visible on the exterior and the basal join below the handle had been knife-trimmed.

Late Valencian lustreware

No 52 is a bowl or dish with shallow vertical sides. Lobed panels are painted in a reddish brown lustre on the interior as though imitating gadrooning. The panels appear to alternate as sets of three: one is painted in solid lustre, the next in a scale-like pattern and the third with a 'flower on a leaved stem' motif. The walls have alternating square panels, one containing a flower head and the other painted in solid lustre. The exterior is painted with what appeared to be fern-like fronds and sweeping lines.

The panelling is almost exactly paralleled on a spirally gadrooned dish from the Godman Bequest (Wilson 1987, fig 19, 32) painted with the arms of Pope Leo X and dated to after 1513, but unlike the dish from the present excavation the British Museum example is painted in blue as well as lustre. Two other spirally gadrooned examples, one with overall lustre and the other in blue and lustre once in the Kassebaum collection, also have similarly decorated panelling (Sotheby 1992, 45, figs 119 and 120). The Bridge Street example only differs in that the scale-like pattern was painted in a more angular way.

A joining sherd was found in (1601) and another sherd possibly from the same vessel in (1552), both in Phase VII, Plot 4.

Montelupo tin-glazed ware

No 53 is a dish in a fine buff fabric with polychrome tin-glazed decoration on the upper surface and a plain tin-glaze on the reverse. Only part of the rim survives, decorated with a boldly painted orange-yellow lozenge decoration enclosing a yellow and red rosette. Finely painted circles surround the lozenge and the whole motif is bordered by finely painted blue lines. A blue and an orange-yellow band borders the edge of the dish.

The decoration is similar to that on a dish in the Van Beuningen de Vriese collection found in Dordrecht in the Netherlands and dated to the period 1500–50 (Hurst *et al* 1986, pl 1, fig 2.2, 15).

Montelupo is in Tuscany, north Italy and lies on the river Arno between Florence and Pisa. Tin-glazed ware manufacture was established in the town by the late fifteenth century and large quantities of the ware were produced in the sixteenth and seventeenth centuries (Hurst *et al* 1986, 12). The brightly coloured wares were exported around the Mediterranean, to the Americas and to northern Europe including Britain (*ibid*). The wares did find their way to Chester but, like other Italian wares, they are relatively rare finds in the city. Two other fragments of Montelupo tin-glazed ware were retrieved from the present site: both were residual finds in Phase VIII, a dish, no 54, from Plot 1, and a fragment from Plot 2, context (1439). The ware thus makes up 0.02% of the entire medieval and post-medieval pottery assemblage by sherd count and 0.01% by weight.

No 54 is a relatively small, incomplete dish. The walls are covered in bands of blue, green and orange-yellow, separated by lines of paler blue. Similar banding in the same colours appears on the wide rim flange, but a broad band of blue contains sgraffito decoration consisting of spirals alternating with a set of three diagonal lines. The motifs are smudged in places. The reverse is covered in a thin white tin glaze containing smudges of blue but the horizontal purple bands often found on the reverse of Montelupo dishes are missing.

The bold colours, sgraffito decoration and fine buff fabric are comparable with Montelupo wares but it is possible that no 54 is from elsewhere in northern Italy.

Beauvais ware

No 55 is a rim fragment from a dish or bowl with a pronounced beaded rim and combed wave decoration. A dark yellow glaze covers the upper surface and the exterior of the rim. The dish is unglazed on the reverse and there is a sooted/burnt area on the edge of the rim.

Beauvais is in northern France and earthenwares were produced there in the late fifteenth and sixteenth centuries (Hurst *et al* 1986, 106). A bowl decorated in a similar way but with a green glaze was found in a deposit of *c* 1490–1510 in Southampton (Brown 2002, fig 26. 244)

Saintonge? ware

No 56 is a dish or bowl with a narrow hammerhead flanged rim. The fabric is similar to Saintonge wares but the decoration is unusual. The glaze is a pale brown-buff colour as though it had been discoloured. Around the

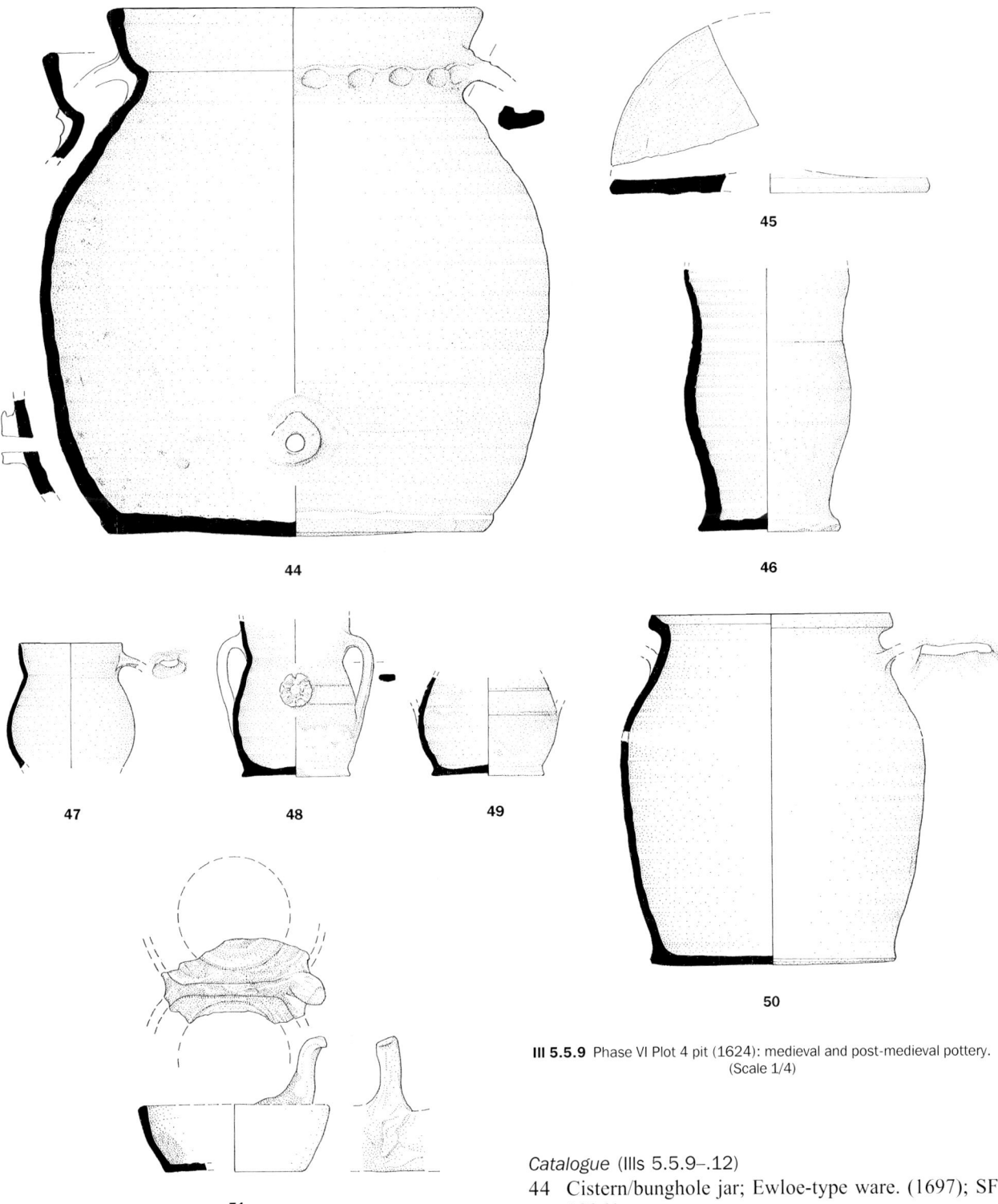

III 5.5.9 Phase VI Plot 4 pit (1624): medieval and post-medieval pottery.
(Scale 1/4)

Catalogue (Ills 5.5.9–.12)

44 Cistern/bunghole jar; Ewloe-type ware. (1697); SF 10061.
45 Lid; Ewloe-type ware. (1697); SF 9968.
46 Jug; Pink/white ware. (1697); SF 9967.
47 Cup; Cistercian-type ware; Fabric 788. (1697), (1796); SF 10344.
48 Cup; Cistercian-type ware cup; Fabric 788. (1697); SF 9980.
49 Cup; Cistercian-type ware cup; Fabric 788. (1697), (1540); SF 9978.
50 Cistern/bunghole jar; Midland Purple-type ware; Fabric 781. (1697); SF 9977.
51 Condiment dish; Midland Purple-type ware; Fabric 781. (1697); SF 9969.

broad rim flange is a painted green wavy line and under the glaze a combed wave decoration similar in style to that found on Beauvais dishes.

Saintonge green and brown dishes are found in sixteenth and early seventeenth century deposits in Chester; they are dated 1550–1650 (Hurst *et al* 1986, 83). This dish, however, does not really fit into that category and was possibly from another unknown French source.

Tudor Green ware

A small rim fragment possibly from a lobed cup, was also found in (1697) (not illustrated).

209

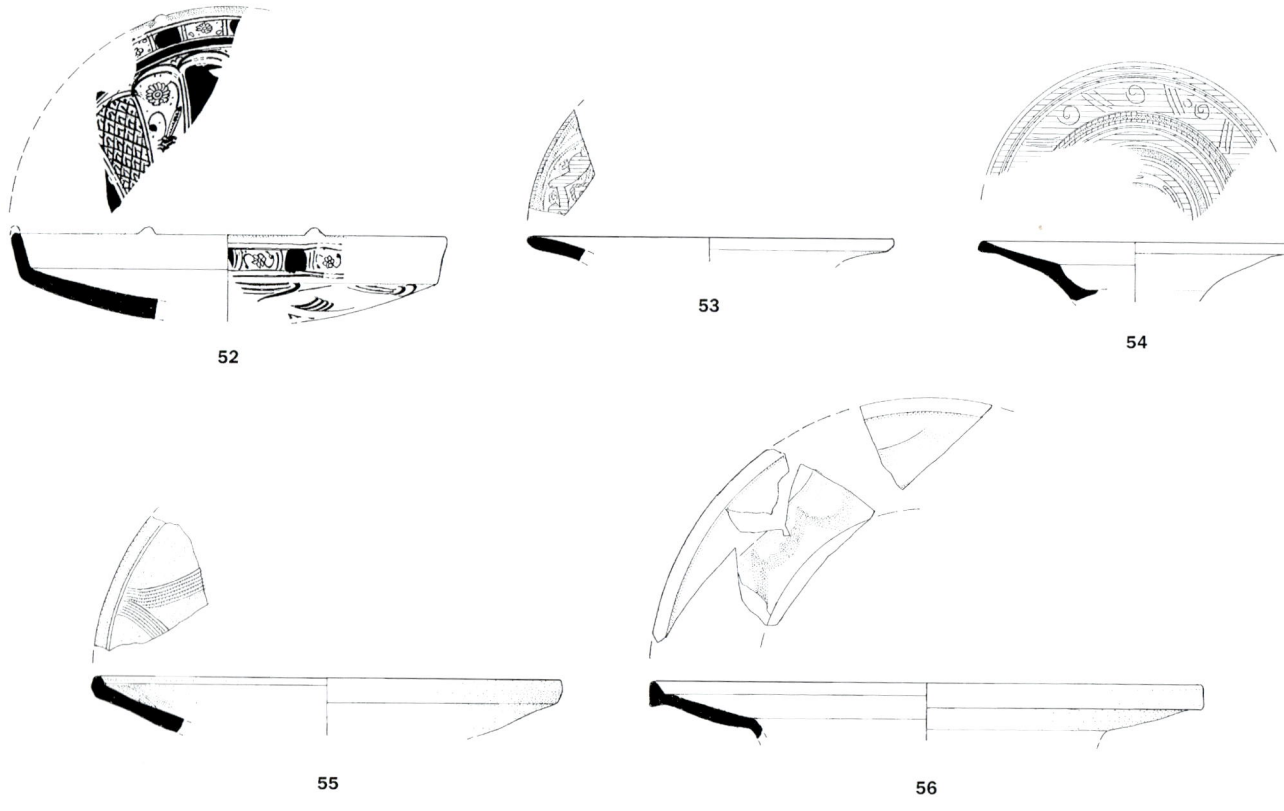

Ill 5.5.10 Phase VI Plot 4 pit (1624): imported pottery. (Scale 1/4)

52 Bowl or dish; Late Valencian lustreware. (1697); SF 9972.

53 Dish; Montelupo tin-glazed ware. (1697); SF 9971.

54 Dish; Montelupo? tin-glazed ware. Cut (1902): Phase VIII, Plot 1; SF 10108.

55 Dish or bowl; Beauvais. (1697); SF 10311.

56 Dish; Saintonge? (1697), (u/s); SF 10312.

Pit (1541)

Pit (1541) was the topmost pit in the sequence and underlay the horn-core pit (1807)/(1621). Its fills, (1540) and (1549), produced an assemblage that varied from complete but smashed vessels to relatively small single fragments. Unlike the lower pits only 12 sherds (738 g) of residual medieval pottery were found compared to the 58 (3341 g) of post-medieval. Only one fragment of clay tobacco pipe stem was found, with a date range of 1610–1710, and two fragments of vessel glass, one of the early seventeenth century and the other with a range from the mid-sixteenth to mid-seventeenth century. The types of pottery present largely date to the sixteenth and seventeenth centuries. Taking into account the tobacco pipe and glass dates, the suggested dates of some of the vessels present and the absence of slipwares, a date in the early seventeenth century is possible. However, two vessels, nos 57 and 64, are unusual for this period and it is not clear whether they were early examples of their type or there has been some confusion of the stratigraphy.

The upper of the two fills, (1540), produced the largest group of pottery but an almost complete Cistercian-type ware cup was found in the lower fill, (1549). Sherd joins were found between (1540) and contexts (1697) and

Ill 5.5.11 Phase VI Plot 4 pit (1624): Late Valencian lustreware bowl or dish (no 52).

Ill 5.5.12 Phase VIII Plot 1 cut (1902): Montelupo tin-glazed dish (no 54).

(1618) in the lower pits; the vessels concerned have been described with the material in those assemblages.

Table 5.5.17 Phase VI Plot 4 pit (1541): post-medieval pottery quantified by ware, EVEs, no of sherds and weight

Ware	EVEs rim	EVEs base	No	Wt (g)
Blackware	75	159	12	729
Cistercian-type	53	312	22	863
Cistercian-type?	0	0	2	31
Midland Purple-type	14	25	7	335
Midland Purple-type?	0	0	2	196
Buckley coarseware	33	45	5	838
Italian TGW	22	0	2	32
TGW	0	0	2	7
Cologne/Frechen	30	39	3	303
Saintonge unglazed	0	0	1	7
Total	227	580	58	3341

Table 5.5.18 Phase VI Plot 4 pit (1541): post-medieval pottery quantified by form, EVEs, no of sherds and weight

Form	EVEs rim	EVEs base	No	Wt (g)
Unidentified	0	25	11	333
Cup	112	375	25	1287
Cup?	0	0	1	6
Dish	22	0	2	32
Jar	47	45	6	883
Jug	0	37	7	325
Mug	46	98	6	475

Wares

Blackwares

Two identifiable vessels with a black glaze were found, as well as an undiagnostic sherd in Fabric 121. Whilst one, no 57, may have been local to the region the other, no 58, is suggested to be an import.

No 57, in Fabric 121 (*see* above), is a large fine-walled, bucket-shaped vessel. The rim is slightly everted and the walls narrow into the base. Single raised cordons are just below and just above the base. Two tapering vertical strap handles were placed equidistant either side of a very narrow spout. The spout consists of a very narrow tube which had been applied to the vessel wall, springing from a little above the base cordon and protruding above the rim; it had cracked where it passed over the upper cordon. The spout is so narrow in diameter that it more or less equates to a modern straw. The base is flat and unglazed apart from areas of the perimeter where glaze had run down from the walls and gathered in droplets, making the base uneven. The unglazed area is covered in fine parallel scratch marks from the use of a wire pulled straight across the base to detach the vessel from the wheel.

This type of vessel is known as a posset pot but these vessels are more common in the second half of the seventeenth century (eg Barker 1986b, 65). However, possets in other wares are known earlier in the seventeenth century. The earliest dated tin-glazed ware posset is 1631 (Lipski & Archer 1984, 200, no 886). An early seventeenth-century date for this vessel is not therefore impossible, particularly as in some ways the fine walls and the general finish of the vessel and the glaze are similar to Cistercian-type wares in Fabric 21. However, the stratigraphic problems with this sequence do pose some doubt over the date of this vessel and no 64. They could be intrusive or, given their size and virtual completeness, perhaps assigned to the wrong context.

No 58 is unusual locally in both form and fabric. The remains suggest a tall narrow mug. The lower part of the vessel has five raised cordons above a splayed rounded

foot, similar to the Rhenish mug no 66. The base is slightly concave. A thick black glaze covers the interior and exterior and extends to the perimeter of the base where it is heavily worn. The fabric is dark red and sandy and differs from the blackware types more commonly found in Chester. Both form and fabric are similar to those of the tall mugs found in the east and south-east of England (eg Nenk 1999, fig 27.1, no 7; 238 and 240 from Essex), where the type appears to be seventeenth century.

Cistercian-type wares

Cistercian-type wares make up the largest proportion of wares in the assemblage. An almost complete cup, no 61, was found in the lower fill accompanied by fragments from three others. The assemblage from the overlying layer, (1540), is larger and includes another almost complete cup, no 59, as well as fragments which join vessels in the lowest two pits in this sequence, (1619) and (1697).

The cup fragments, not all of which have been illustrated, include wide rims similar to no 59 as well as simple vertical and everted forms. A rim from a cylindrical vessel, no 63, appears similar to a mug-type form from Norton priory (Green & Noake 1977, 59, fig 20) and a fragment from Phase V (700), no 8. Also present in (1549) is the central part of a small multi-handled cup, no 62. Only the upper body and waist survive, suggesting a vessel with an hourglass profile which is not paralleled elsewhere on the site.

The two almost complete cups differ from each other in details of form but their general shape is a tall necked or waisted cup with handles spanning the central constriction.

No 61 in Fabric 21 is a mug with a flared neck above a tall pear-shaped body, a raised cordon marks the waist. The small flared foot has a bevelled/chamfered edge which was not trimmed after removal from the wheel, leaving a poorly defined edge. A narrow raised cordon marks the constriction between the foot and the body. The base is very slightly concave and, unlike other examples, has only faint straight parallel scratches across the surface. A narrow flattened rod handle spans the neck constriction and joins the body just above the girth. A fault is present at the upper handle–body join where glaze had seeped between the join and the rim has broken away at this point. The glaze varies in thickness over the surface of the vessel, being either glossy or thin and lustrous.

In overall shape this cup is similar to some of the type 4 cups from Wrenthorpe (Moorhouse & Slowikowski 1992, 114, fig 53), but in the absence of a rim a direct parallel cannot be drawn. The shape is also similar to a possibly curated cup from Phase VII (1507), no 60 (*see* below) which has a very different rim form to the Yorkshire examples and is more akin to that of no 59. The lower part of an apparently similar shaped vessel was found at Mickle Trafford near Chester in 1895 containing a hoard of thirty-eight Elizabethan silver coins ranging in date from 1561 to 1594 (Dolley & Webster 1952, 93). This vessel was unavailable at the time of writing so it was not possible to compare it directly with those from the excavation. However, previous writers have identified the hoard pot as a Cistercian-type ware (Rutter 1984, 62; Newstead 1939, 13) and the form as illustrated is similar to nos 60 and 61, suggesting that these types of vessel were possibly in use in the second half of the sixteenth century and certainly in the very late sixteenth and possibly the very early seventeenth.

No 59, also in Fabric 21, is a necked cup with a wide funnel-shaped neck which turns sharply upwards to form an almost vertical rim, the top of which is missing. The carination between the neck and rim is marked by a horizontal groove and cordon in a similar manner to no 60. A cordon also marks the constriction between the neck and the narrow, rounded body. The flared foot has straight-cut edges and is slightly distorted so that the base does not sit totally flat. The underside of the base is covered in parallel scratch marks and the perimeter is smudged and slightly scuffed. The handles are placed opposite each other spanning the carination between the body and neck. Unlike the rod handles commonly found on Cistercian-type wares from the site, the handles are a tapering strap shape with a curved section, resembling those found on blackware jars and mugs. One handle slants to the left more than the other and its base has a sweeping wipe mark to the left.

The glaze is a dark purple-black colour; on the exterior it varies from thick and glossy to sparse and lustrous. The interior of the neck is relatively well covered but the interior of the body is unglazed apart from spots.

This cup is similar to the waisted wide-mouthed vessels described above but the narrower body and tighter waist accentuates the funnel-shaped neck and vertical rim. Cups with this rim form have been recorded previously from Chester by Newstead (1928, pl 21.1; 1939, pls 3.14, 4.28). The group found in 1928 was assigned a seventeenth-century date, although the photograph shows flared Cistercian-type ware cups and Midland Purple-types which suggest a sixteenth- or possibly very early seventeenth-century date. The other groups were assigned a date in the first half of the seventeenth century and one contains blackware mugs as well as a flared Cistercian-type cup. Another example comes from a group of wares from Watergate Street (Rutter 1984, fig 4.20). This type of rim has been ascribed to the Mickle Trafford hoard pot (Dolley & Webster 1952; Newstead 1939, 13) but there is no evidence to suggest this on the published illustration.

Midland Purple-type wares
These are represented by a fragmentary assemblage, which consists predominantly of body sherds in Fabric 95. Some fragments are large and relatively well preserved and these include pieces from a jug or cistern which joined sherds in pit 1624 (1697).

Buckley? coarseware
Fabric 782: This is a red fabric which in areas has a dark grey core and margins. It is very hard with a rough feel and an irregular texture. The inclusions are numerous and ill-sorted and consist of moderate sub-angular colourless and opaque white quartz grains; moderate sub-angular white clay fragments up to 3 mm long; moderate rounded and sub-angular dark red iron-rich fragments up to 4 mm long; and fine streaks of red and white clay.

No 64 is a rounded slightly squat jar with two handles and the remains of tripod feet. The rim is everted and the neck marked by a raised cordon. One vertical loop handle survives and was applied over the neck cordon and terminates just above the girth. The handle is a tapered strap with a curved section and appears to be made from a finer clay fabric than the rest of the jar. The body curves into the concave base which is splayed and slightly rounded around the edge. Scars are present on the underside of the base close to the perimeter, suggesting that the jar had at least two or probably three applied feet. The vessel had been evenly thrown and has thick walls. The interior and exterior is covered in a slip that varies from dark red to purplish brown. A fine lustrous glaze is present on the inside of the base and as patches and spots on the interior of the body; the exterior is unglazed.

This jar appears to be the only one of its type and fabric from the excavation. The general form with tripod feet, handles in a finer fabric, thick slip over a coarse fabric and sparse glaze is similar to coarseware vessels in a buff fabric excavated at Buckley and dated to the period *c* 1640–60 (Amery & Davey 1979, 76, figs 133, 134) and also found in late seventeenth-century deposits at Beeston (Noake 1993, 210). Such vessels have also been found in seventeenth-century deposits in Chester but generally they are larger, have coarser, buff-coloured fabrics and a thick coating of soot on the exterior; this example was clean of soot and signs of burning.

Italian tin-glazed ware
No 65 is an unusual import which is probably from Venice. It comprises two fragments of a dish decorated in *berettino* fashion, ie dark blue painting on a pale blue tin glaze, but with the addition of polychrome decoration on the interior surface. The exterior has a simple overlapping petal or arch motif painted in blue. The glaze is in an extremely fragile condition and much has fallen away; that which remains shows a design of tendrils and foliage set amongst a sea of dots. The leaves and leaflets are painted yellow or turquoise green and the edge of a much larger motif appears outlined with a broad blue line and at least partly coloured yellow. Two additional fragments apparently from the same vessel were found in Phase IX, Plot 6 and in a group marked as unstratified. This style of decoration is unusual but is paralleled by a dish fragment found in Venice and a complete example in a private collection (Alvera' Bortolotto 1988, 77). These dishes, painted in similar colours, show a central deer or stag set amongst tendrils, foliage and dots as well as larger leaves and strangely shaped bell-shaped flowers similar to large thistle flowers. The remains of a motif on one of the Chester fragments compares quite well with the flowers on one of these dishes. Jars with a similar design of a mammal amongst tendrils, foliage and flowers are also known (Morley-Fletcher & McIlroy 1984, 88, figs 5 and 6).

In Britain *berettino* decoration is mainly associated with Ligurian wares, which are more commonly found on British sites than Venetian wares. Whilst there is some confusion in maiolica literature between Ligurian and Venetian sixteenth-century *berettino* the only parallels to this piece have been consistently described as Venetian and there appear to be no close parallels amongst material excavated in Liguria (Timothy Wilson *pers comm*). Thus this piece is likely to be from Venice with a suggested date in the middle or third quarter of the sixteenth century (Timothy Wilson *pers comm*); this would make it contemporary with the Rhenish stoneware in the same context.

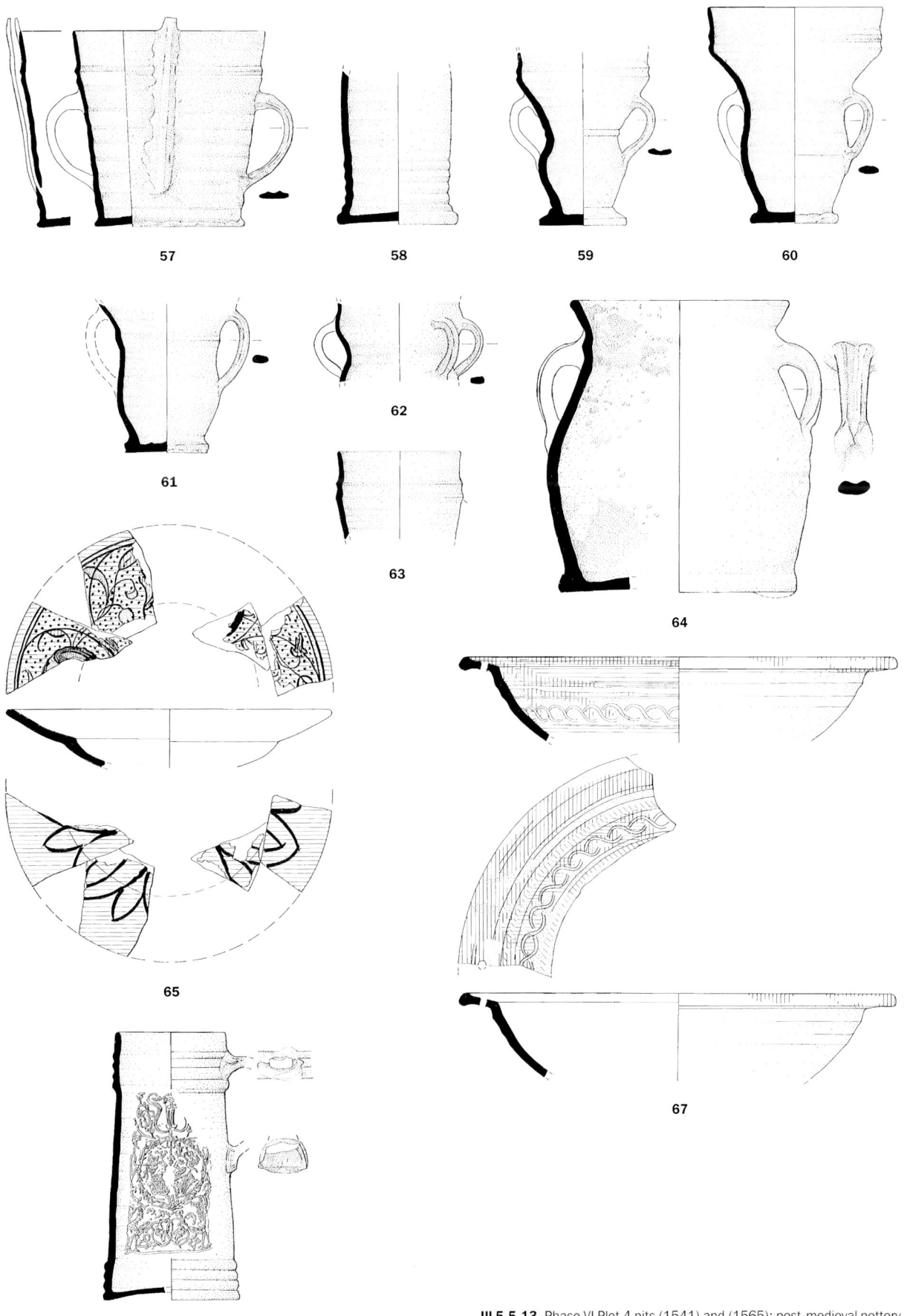

III 5.5.13 Phase VI Plot 4 pits (1541) and (1565): post-medieval pottery.
(Scale 1/4)

213

Low Countries and Anglo-Dutch tin-glazed wares

Two fragments were present in (1540): one is abraded but appears to be a late sixteenth- to early seventeenth-century Anglo-Dutch type; the other is a fragment from the cordoned neck of a small jug. The exterior has a mottled blue tin glaze and the interior a creamy white glaze smudged with blue. Commonly known as Malling jugs and once thought to have been an early English product, scientific analysis has now suggested that these tin-glazed ware vessels were produced in the Low Countries (Hughes 1995, 60).

Rhenish stoneware

There were two pieces of Cologne/Frechen stoneware: one is a small fragment from a jug with the remains of a bearded mask; the other is described below.

No 66 is a conical mug which tapered from base to rim, made from a dark grey stoneware with a mottled brown salt glaze. The density of the mottling varies and is more prominent in a vertical band between the rim and the base to the right of the handle. There are four raised cordons below the simple upright rim and three similar cordons are present above a rounded foot. The base is slightly concave and has 'cheese-wire' marks and a kiln scar in the form of part of an unglazed disc indicating how the vessel was stacked above another in the kiln. A strap handle has its upper end joined over the upper cordons and the lower set roughly in the middle of the vessel. A fragment probably from the same vessel has been labelled as unstratified.

The mug appears to have been decorated with three relief moulded panels, one of which survives. This consists of a central medallion bordered with a foliage wreath and containing two portrait busts of a man and woman shown in profile. The panel is surrounded by tendrils, foliage, grotesques and in each of the lower corners a long-legged bird holding what appears to be a small bough. A similar but not identical design appears on a smaller mug (*pinte*) found in Malmo, Sweden and attributed to Cologne *c* 1540–50 (Gaimster 1997, 68, fig 3.24).

Mugs such as this are known by the terms of *pinte* and *schnelle* in the Rhineland and elsewhere on the continent, and these terms are frequently used in Britain as well. This vessel could be termed a small *schnelle* as it was smaller than many of the illustrated *schnellen* but was larger than a *pinte*.

It is difficult to be certain as to the precise provenance of the vessel. It has cheese-wire marks on the underside of the base which Hurst identified as being characteristic of Frechen, but similarly shaped vessels carrying portrait busts appear to have been produced in Cologne as well in the period spanning the second and third quarters of the sixteenth century (*see* Hurst *et al* 1986, pl 40, 214 and pl 43, 219). During this period Cologne potters were leaving their city-centre workshops for the town of Frechen, 10 km away and production of vessels with similar forms and decoration was being carried on in both places, thus making it almost impossible to distinguish the provenance of individual vessels (Hurst *et al* 1986 208; Gaimster 1997, 193 and 209).

Catalogue (Ills 5.5.13–.15)
57 Posset; blackware; Fabric 121. (1540); SF 10054.
58 Mug; imported blackware. (1540); SF 10056.

59 Cup; Cistercian-type ware cup; Fabric 21. (1540); SF 9976.
60 Cup; Cistercian-type ware cup; Fabric 21. (1507): Phase VII; SF 10327.
61 Cup; Cistercian-type ware cup; Fabric 21. (1549); SF 9974.
62 Multi-handled cup; Cistercian-type ware; Fabric 24. (1549); SF 9975.
63 Mug; Cistercian-type ware; Fabric 24; (1540); SF 10330.
64 Jar; Buckley coarseware? (1540); SF 10053.
65 Dish; Italian tin-glazed ware, probably Venetian. (1540), (542), (u/s); SF 10057.
66 Mug; Cologne/Frechen. (1540); SF 10055.

Pit (1544)

This pit lay between (1624) and the overlying (1541) but unlike the others did not contain a well preserved assemblage. The only fill which produced pottery, (1543), largely contained fragments dating to the medieval period, including late medieval Ewloe-type wares. Only two small fragments of post-medieval pottery were present one a Cistercian-type ware. The assemblage has therefore not been included here.

Pit (1565)

Context (1566) in pit (1565) contained a fragmentary assemblage (20 sherds/735 g) which is in mixed condition and consists predominantly of blackwares, Cistercian-type wares, Midland Purple-type wares and residual medieval pottery. The wares possibly date to the first half of the seventeenth century and are accompanied by late sixteenth- to seventeenth-century glass. The assemblage is not of any significance other than that it includes part of a Beauvais double-sgraffito dish.

Catalogue (Ills 5.5.13 and .16)
67 Dish or bowl; Beauvais double-sgraffito. (1566); SF 10103.

The vessel has a slightly thickened, pierced, narrow flanged rim and boldly coloured decoration created by overlying a white slip over a red slip and cutting a pattern through the white to reveal the red below. The resulting yellow and red design was further coloured by green and blue mineral oxide colours in the glaze. Beauvais double-sgraffito wares were produced in the sixteenth century (Hurst *et al* 1986, 108). A small number of single- and double-sgraffito vessels have previously been found in Chester along with plain glazed Beauvais wares. This piece was the most substantial example from this site.

Plot 6

Pit (691)

This fill of this pit, (687), produced a small quantity of fragmentary material but this has been included because of the presence of the remains of a Midland Purple-type ware jar in a relatively uncommon fabric and an unusual Saintonge chafing dish. It was also thought that an attempt should be made to include an assemblage from each plot. The other wares include a fragment of yellow

Ill 5.5.14 Phase VI Plot 4 pit (1541): Italian tin-glazed dish (no 65).

Ill 5.5.15 Phase VI Plot 4 pit (1541): Cologne/Frechen mug (no 66).

Ill 5.5.16 Phase VI Plot 4 pit (1565): Beauvais double-sgraffito dish or bowl (no 67).

ware, four pieces of Cistercian-type ware cups, including one with dotted slip decoration, and two small fragments of blackware. Six fragments of residual medieval pottery were also retrieved. No clay tobacco pipes were recorded from this pit nor any vessel glass. A date sometime in the first half of the seventeenth century is suggested.

Table 5.5.19 Phase VI Plot 6 pit (691): post-medieval pottery quantified by ware, EVEs, no of sherds and weight

Ware	EVEs rim	EVEs base	No	Wt (g)
Black	0	0	2	24
Cistercian-type	0	0	4	29
Midland Purple-type	13	0	6	293
Yellow	0	0	1	10
Saintonge	21	0	1	77
Total	34	0	14	433

Table 5.5.20 Phase VI Plot 6 pit (691): post-medieval pottery quantified by form, EVEs, no of sherds and weight

Form	EVEs rim	EVEs base	Sherd no	Wt (g)
Unidentified	0	0	2	27
Chafing dish	21	0	1	77
Cup	0	0	5	36
Jar	13	0	6	293

Wares

Midland Purple-type ware

Fabric 783: This fabric has a purple colour with an occasional red margin or core. A hard fabric with a rough feel and a fine texture, the clay matrix does not appear vitrified as in other Midland-Purple type wares. Inclusions consist of abundant colourless and opaque white subangular quartz grains; sparse ill-sorted dark red iron-rich inclusions up to 3 mm; and sparse streaks and fragments of white clay. A brown glaze is present on the interior and exterior surfaces which generally have a smooth glossy finish but is sparse on part of the surviving exterior.

No 68 is a rounded jar or possibly bunghole jar/cistern with a collared rim. One handle survives and is a vertical tapered strap with an undulating section. The lower terminal is attached so that it is not quite in line with the upper, giving the handle a slight slant. The lower end of the handle has been splayed out and finished with finger or thumb impressions. The remains of a circular stamp and incised line decoration are present to the right of the handle. A fine glaze covers the interior and exterior surfaces. The interior is coated in a fine white deposit.

The jar is similar in shape to the cistern no 21 and is decorated in a similar manner using stamps and incised lines on the front. The method of joining the handle is also similar, but the more complex rim form, glossier finish to the glaze and different fabric set the present vessel apart; indeed, it perhaps verges towards a blackware. A similar vessel was found in Goss Street, Chester in 1973 (unpublished).

Saintonge or Central France chafing dish

No 69 is the remains of a chafing dish with a simple triangular shaped knob, the apex of which has been abraded and was darkened by burning or soot. A figure has been applied below the apex of the knob. The figure is not well modelled but is possibly that of a woman in a fulllength dress. The head is covered in some sort of closely fitting cap or headdress and the body is formed by an elongated triangle, the upper part of which shows modelling or moulding. The wall of the bowl has apparently randomly spaced piercings made with a roughly square-sectioned tool. A smaller single round piercing is present close to the body of the figure. The upper part of the dish is glazed green and yellow. The glaze extends as runs and splashes over the rim to the interior. The lower part of the bowl is unglazed on both surfaces and is partly blackened on the interior.

With the small triangular knob and bichrome glaze the vessel conforms to Hurst's type 1 vessel but the full-length figure and the pierced sides of the bowl are unusual. The piercings can be compared to the stabbed combing that is found between the faces on type 1 dishes (Hurst 1974, 240–1, figs 6 and 7), but pierced vessels were noted by Hurst from central France (*op cit*, 235) and a green-glazed chafing dish with pierced sides was found in Chester in 1935 (*op cit*, 239) although in a different form. The full-length figure is also unusual for a type 1 dish, although Hurst did note them as occurring elsewhere (Hurst *et al* 1986, 80). Hurst dated type 1 chafing dishes to the sixteenth century.

Catalogue (Ill 5.5.17)

68   Jar or cistern; Midland Purple-type jar; Fabric 783. (687); SF 10329.
69   Chafing dish; Saintonge or central France. (687); SF 10306.

Phase VI discussion

The site phasing was partly based on the range of pottery wares along with clay tobacco pipe and glass dates, so drawing conclusions on the range of wares in a particular phase carries some risk of setting up a circular argument. However, whilst it is possible that the precise dating of the phase may be open to debate, the groups placed in Phase VI do share a number of characteristics relating to the wares and forms present. With further analysis of groups, the wares and the stratigraphy it might be possible to further divide Phase VI, for example on the quantity or presence/absence of Cistercian wares, blackwares, yellow wares or Midland Purple types.

A total of 864 sherds of pottery (33629 g) was retrieved from the deposits assigned to Phase VI. Blackwares, Cistercian-type wares and Midland Purple-type wares predominate, comprising just over 73% of the assemblage by sherd count (79% by weight). Yellow wares comprise only 7.8% by sherd count (6%) of the assemblage. The remaining percentage is made up of continental imports, single sherds of Tudor Green ware, Surrey–Hampshire Border ware and North Devon gravel-free ware, as well as various brown-glazed wares, tin-glazed wares, unglazed ware fragments and two fragments of slipware. A group of later seventeenth- and early eighteenth-century wares was wrongly phased and make up some of the remaining wares. The lack of slipwares in any of the groups is notable and may be associated with the absence of any dishes that are not imports. Further definition of brown-glazed wares is required but not enough examples were present in the key groups to permit a discussion of their use and provenance.

Identifiable imported wares are dominated by continental imports: wares that can be definitely identified from elsewhere in Britain beyond the west midlands were very few. However, against this must be set the fact that the precise provenance of the majority of the wares com-

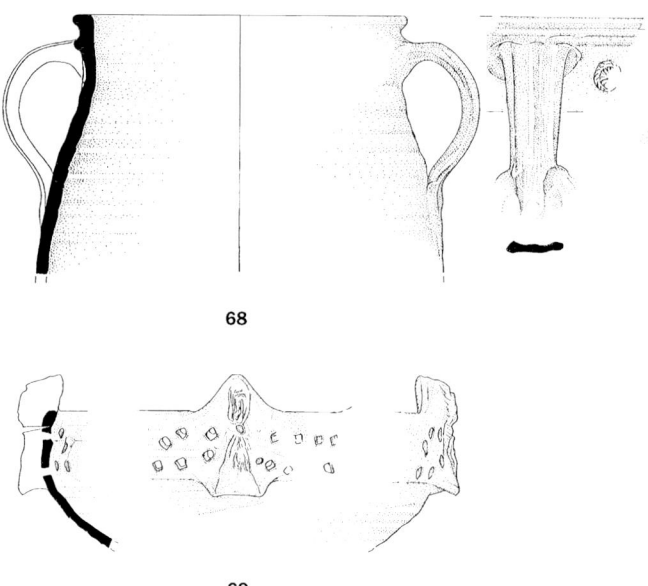

68

69

Ill 5.5.17 Phase VI Plot 6 pit (691): post-medieval pottery. (Scale 1/4)

monly in use in the city is unclear. No North Devon gravel-tempered wares are present yet these do occur in later phases on the site and are present on sites elsewhere in the city. The date of their introduction to the city is unclear but on the evidence from this site they were not common until after the mid-seventeenth century.

Two clear features of the chosen groups are the range and quantity of continental imports and the principal vessels forms represented and the changing wares in which they occur.

The 75 fragments of continental wares make up 8.7% by sherd count (7.8% by weight) of the entire Phase VI assemblage. Whilst this is a relatively small proportion, it is much larger than the 3.5% (2.5% by weight) present in Phase V or the 2% (0.9% by weight) in Phase VII. The proportion of continental imports from the entire medieval and post-medieval assemblage recovered from the site is 2% (1.6% by weight). Thus, the period of time represented by Phase VI clearly saw a greater use of continental pottery, and when the proportions of wares in the pit groups are examined the imported wares play a much larger role than is obvious from the overall totals.

Continental imports

The cess pit (487) provides the largest and earliest stratified assemblage in this phase. Whilst Cistercian-type wares and Midland Purple-type jars contribute the bulk of the assemblage, continental pottery contributes just over 20% by sherd count (14% by weight) but 31% by rim EVEs (base EVEs 17.6%). Unlike in some of the other assemblages in this phase (*see* below), these imports do not appear to have fulfilled a separate function from the 'local' wares. The Cologne stoneware mug, blue tin-glazed ware albarello, Merida-type lid and Iberian jars all served a drinking and storage function, as did the 'local' wares; the only potential serving vessels are the Saintonge jug and possible salt. Whilst the function of the imports may have been similar to that of local wares, it is likely that the contents would have been the initial differentiating factor. The jug and salt are both uncommon: jugs only form 2% of the phase assemblage (1.6% by weight) and the salt is the only one identified from the phase. There are no dishes or bowls and, if they were represented in other materials, they do not survive, although as the contents of the pit were not totally excavated this may not be a true representation.

The fill of cess pit (1624) may have been deposited in the early seventeenth century but contained pottery of predominantly sixteenth-century date. The proportion of imports is not dissimilar at 17.4% by sherd count (9.4% by weight) but leaps to 46.9% by rim EVEs; with the exception of a condiment dish in Midland Purple-type ware the dishes in the group are all provided by continental wares: Valencian lustreware, Montelupo, Saintonge and Beauvais. The remainder of the assemblage consists of cups and jars/bunghole jars in Cistercian-type ware, Midland Purple-type ware and Tudor Green ware.

The contents of cess pit (1541) were nearer the proportions for the whole phase, with continental imports providing 10% by sherd count (10% by weight) but again a much larger 22.9% by rim EVEs. The only dish in this group is an Italian tin-glazed ware. The remaining vessels are drinking or storage vessels, but two of these were provided by imports to the region: a blackware from eastern England and a Cologne/Frechen mug.

The much smaller pits (1703) and (691) had at least one quantifiable measure where continental imports were of similar proportions to the larger assemblages. In pit (1703) imports form 14% of the rim EVEs but 21% by sherd count, and in pit (691) 62% of the rim EVEs are imports; by sherd count the proportion falls to 7% but was 18% by weight.

How far these proportions are typical of early post-medieval assemblages in Chester is difficult to determine because quantified data is not readily available. However, one late fifteenth- to early sixteenth-century assemblage from the Hunter Street School site contains 21% imports (Davey 1983, 215). This was then considered unusually high, but it may suggest that the assemblage from cess pit (487) is not atypical. However, there is a clear reduction in continental ceramic imports in pit (430)/(850), where blackwares and yellow wares appear to have superseded the Cistercian-type and Midland Purple-type wares. The imports in this pit form only 2.5% by sherd count and less than 1% by weight and 0% by EVEs. In layer (246) the EVEs for imported wares were again 0% and the proportions for sherd count and weight 5% and 8.4% respectively. How far this was related to the function of these assemblages, to chronology or socioeconomic factors would require further comparative work on assemblages from the site and Chester as a whole. In both deposits drinking vessels and jars provide the overwhelming majority of vessel forms; dishes only represent 1% in (430)/(850) and an imported bowl and chafing dish in (246) form 4% by sherd count and 5% by weight. Whilst the function of particular assemblages and economics may have been factors in this reduction and dishes may have been supplied by another material, these groups from the first half of the seventeenth century are also indicative of the declining use of ceramics from the continent through the rest of the century that became manifest in Phase VII.

Taking into account all the assemblages studied in this phase the pattern of ceramic use appears to be that in the sixteenth and early seventeenth century the local or regional wares provided drinking and storage vessels and continental imports provided principally dishes and chafing dishes, which for whatever reason were not provided by British wares; it is noteworthy that the only chafing dishes recognised from the site are continental imports.

The question may be asked whether there was any significance in the range of imports in relation to trade or social status. French and Spanish wares contribute over 70% (by sherd count and weight) of the continental wares. The French, Italian and Spanish wares all contribute dishes, whilst storage wares are present in French and Spanish wares and drinking vessels in Rhenish stonewares. The Rhenish stonewares are largely Raeren, Cologne or Cologne/Frechen types. The Italian wares are all tin-glazed and consist of Montelupo, Ligurian *berettino* wares and the potentially Venetian dish. A slightly wider variety of sixteenth- and seventeenth-century wares appear as residual components in later phases, eg north Italian marbled slipware, Frechen jugs and Raeren biconical jugs. Whilst overall continental imports only make up a minor proportion of the pottery in use in Chester, they did in the sixteenth and early seventeenth century provide almost all the vessels with polychrome and applied decoration. How far this represented intentional choice on the part of consumers it is not possible to say. Considering that Cistercian or Midland Purple types consistently provided drinking and storage vessels whilst the dishes and 'minor' vessels varied in ware and provenance, it is possible that they were chance acquisitions. Alternatively, given that the Cistercian or Midland Purple types were perhaps also from a variety of sources (*see* below) despite their general similar appearance, it is possible that the dishes etc were deliberately acquired for their form, if not decorative novelty.

The bias towards France and Spain may be accounted for by the direct trade between those countries and the port of Chester (Wilson 1969). However trade between England and Spain and the Mediterranean was part of a complex network and simple connections between a merchant of one country and goods from the same cannot necessarily be made (*see* Childs 1995). It is difficult to find any reference to Italian contacts in the published literature, so it is harder to account for Italian pottery. However, the roles of Italians in Spanish trade (*ibid*) and Chester men travelling to and from Spain need to be considered, as do land routes to London (*see* Woodward 1970, 71–2) and the occasional visits of ships registered at southern ports such as Southampton (Wilson ed 1969, 46), which was an important port for Italian trade; personal contacts may also have had a role in the supply of imported ceramics.

In addition to land routes the coasting trade is particularly relevant to Rhenish stonewares found in Chester. Rhenish pottery was imported mainly through the south and east coast ports and was redistributed, with London playing a major role in this activity. Shipments of 'stone' pots are noted as arriving from London (Allan 1983, 40). However, the rarity of such recorded shipments to Irish Sea ports has led to the suggestion that overland routes were perhaps more favoured (Allan 1983, 39), although it may also account for the relatively low quantity of these wares in Chester, where they provided 13% (by sherd count) of the continental imports in Phase VI. Rhenish stonewares are well known for being exported in northern Europe as a commercial cargo, but the reasons for the presence of other continental wares are unclear. The French, Spanish and Italian pottery may perhaps be better understood if viewed in the context of the people who lived in Bridge Street and other imported goods in the city.

Whilst it has not been possible to link specific properties with documented individuals for this phase it was possible to identify the Row as the location of Mercer's Row in the sixteenth and early seventeenth century (Backhouse, *this volume*). Mercers were an important company in the local economy, and inventories for mercers elsewhere in the city show that their stock included a range of luxury goods: fustian, velvet, taffeta, damask, Spanish and Naples silk and exotic spices and dyestuffs (Backhouse *this volume*).

The people who sold such luxuries clearly had access to money to enable them to purchase stock and they had access to foreign merchants either directly or *via* middlemen. How far pottery was traded in its own right is unclear: alternatives are that it arrived at the port in the possession of foreign merchants either as gifts or for sale in its own right or for its contents. The presence of Spanish merchants and sailors in Chester is, of course, recorded but Chester men also carried out a large amount of the trade themselves, sailing to Spain on Chester-registered ships: indeed in the late sixteenth century a new councilman had to be elected as the previous incumbent was 'reputed to have died in Spain' (CCALS ZAB 1/217). The role and meaning of continental ceramics in this phase is therefore open to interpretation but clearly they played more than a minor role in several of the Phase VI assemblages.

It was not possible to carry out a comparison between the assemblages on each plot. However, it is clear that the pit deposits in Plots 2 and 4 in both Phases VI and VII contained large, varied groups. In Phase VI both plots contained significantly larger pit assemblages than the other plots and both properties had access to a range of continental imports and 'local' wares. While in Phase VII there is good documentary evidence for the occupants of Plot 4, the Phase VI occupants are unknown, but the assemblages have the potential to allow us to surmise the status of the occupants.

Forms and the introduction of new wares
As noted above, drinking vessels and storage vessels provided the majority of vessel types in each pit group or assemblage. Dishes were absent except as Spanish lustrewares, Italian tin-glazed wares or Beauvais wares. Chafing dishes were also only represented by Saintonge or other French wares, and bowls are only present as Iberian and French imports. Blackwares, Cistercian-type wares, Midland Purple-type wares and yellow wares provided the majority of the drinking vessels and jars. Whilst the jars and cups remained dominant in Phase VIa, a change can be detected in the wares that provided these vessels.

As might be expected, drinking vessels tend to be more numerous in comparison to jars when quantified by EVEs using rims and bases rather than by weight. When base

EVEs (the most consistently present measurement) are used, the proportion varies between 52% to 82% in all but two of the assemblages studied; the lowest reading is from pit (1624), where dishes form a much larger percentage than in the other groups (although if the Ewloe-type cistern is regarded as having been in contemporary use the EVEs figure for jars increases) and the largest is from pit (1541), where imported wares and blackwares are added to the Cistercian-type wares. In layer (246) drinking vessels represent only 15% and in (691) 0%, although if sherd count is used drinking vessels form 36% of the latter assemblage, which is within the range for sherd count in the other pit groups.

If the proportion of Cistercian-type wares is compared, again using base EVEs in pits (487), (1703), (1624) and (1541), the ware forms over 50% of each assemblage and in (487) and (1703) over 60%, but in pit (430)/(850) the proportion falls to 26% and in pit (691) to 29%, whilst in layer (246) it is only 11%, although the last figure also reflected the low number of drinking vessels in that group. However, pit (430)/(850) contained 66% drinking vessels by base EVEs and the fall in Cistercian-type wares was clearly compensated for by a rise in blackwares and yellow wares (a combined proportion of 63% by base EVEs) as providers of drinking vessels.

It is more difficult to compare the jars and Midland Purple-type wares from each assemblage because the survival of rims and bases was more variable than amongst the Cistercian-type wares. However, if rim EVEs are used the percentages of jars and of Midland Purple-type wares are similar in some groups: eg in (487) both were 38%, and in (1703) jars provide 86 % and Midland Purple-type wares 77%, but in pit (430)/(800) 41% are jars but Midland Purple-type wares have fallen to 9% by rim EVEs. As with the drinking vessels, the increased number of blackwares and yellow wares, 84% by rim EVEs, compensate for this fall. Layer (246) was difficult to interpret because of a single almost complete vessel being present amongst a number of fragments, but jars represented 98% by rim EVES, Midland Purple-type wares only 18%.

Each pit contained at least one large jar or bunghole jar/cistern. A question that could be posed is whether a time span can be placed on the popularity of bunghole jars/cisterns in comparison to jars and whether there was a change in the wares that supplied them. The later seventeenth-century groups on this site did not contain these vessels, although blackware bunghole jars are known elsewhere.

Clearly the appearance of blackwares and yellow wares is a key feature of Phase VI, but it is difficult to use comparative data from Phases V and VII to illustrate their arrival. Neither ware should have been present in Phase V but it contained a quantity of intrusive material ranging from the sixteenth to eighteenth century. Whilst there was an increase in the presence of blackwares in Phase VII from 34% to 39% by sherd count and 33% to 48% by weight, yellow wares remained relatively stable at 8% by sherd count and 6% to 5% by weight. However, as both phases overlapped the seventeenth century – the generally accepted timespan of yellow wares locally – it is difficult to track the rise and fall of the ware and any changes in the supply of blackwares. As pit (430)/(850) showed, it is the comparison of individual pit groups which indicates changing supply patterns rather than analysis of the phase groups as a whole. This pit group showed the highest use of each ware in the phase, with blackwares forming 43% by rim EVEs (43% and 35% by sherd count and weight) and yellow wares 41% by rim EVEs (34% and 45% by sherd count and weight). By contrast, in Phase VII pit (1696) yellow wares had fallen to 6% by rim EVEs (4% and 2% by sherd count and weight) whilst blackwares remained a relatively high but smaller component of the assemblage at 24% by rim EVEs (but 32% and 51% by sherd count and weight). Analysis is required of city assemblages dating to the mid- to late seventeenth century to further study the use and supply of these wares. However it seems from this site that yellow wares performed a significant function for a certain period after first appearing sometime during the first half of the seventeenth century. Whether their fall from use was due to a disruption in the source of supply or a deliberate preference for other wares, eg mottled wares, is as yet unknown.

Cistercian type wares and Midland Purple-type wares in Phase VI

Cistercian-type wares formed 17% (by sherd count) and 11% (by weight) of the total pottery assemblage from Phase VI but, as seen, the proportion within the key assemblages was much higher when quantified by EVEs. A more revealing statistic is that this phase produced 66% or 72% by weight of the total number of fragments of the ware from the site, thus placing the greater use of these wares firmly in this phase of activity. Midland-Purple type wares contributed 21% (by sherd count) and 34% by weight of the total Phase VI assemblage, while the phase contained 46% by sherd count and 59% by weight of the ware from the site. However, Midland Purple-type wares also formed 29% by sherd count and 21% by weight of the Phase VII assemblage, far higher than the Cistercian-type wares (0.5% by sherd count and 0.4% by weight): as indicated previously they probably carried on in use longer than Cistercian-type wares. However the two wares were contemporary in Phase VI and provided vessels serving different functions within the ceramic assemblages. The other major similarity between the two wares is that the fabrics and details of form show a diversity that could be said to indicate a variety of sources and also changes over time, although the latter is hard to quantify.

Whilst parallels outside of the region are harder to identify for Midland-Purple type wares, some can be suggested for the Cistercian-type wares. Links can be made between particular vessels from the present site and the form and size of some types excavated at Wrenthorpe (Moorhouse & Slowikowski 1992, 114, fig 53), but without direct comparison it is not possible to ascribe them a provenance in Yorkshire. There are also some clear differences, a key one being that many Cistercian-type wares from Chester are relatively large when compared to Yorkshire products; this was also noted for the examples from Norton priory (Greene & Noake 1977, 58). The Wrenthorpe vessels are described as being of high quality, being well thrown and fine walled (Moorhouse & Slowikowski 1992, 107). Whilst the Bridge Street vessels were well made they were not particularly fine-walled or well finished: bases in particular were left in an untidy fashion. The Wrenthorpe vessels were also noted as having concentric wire marks on their bases, showing the manner in which

they were removed from the wheel. However no concentric wire marks were noted on this site: where marks were present they were in the form of parallel lines suggestive of a wire pulled straight across the horizontal when the vessel was stationary. Some comparison has also been made with some of the published examples from Staffordshire, so it may be possible to suggest that some were imports from Staffordshire and Yorkshire or that they were made by potters strongly influenced by that production. Another possible source was Ticknall in Derbyshire. Documentary research has shown that this area was supplying some pottery to Cheshire in the late sixteenth and seventeenth century (Jean Spavold and Sue Brown *pers comm*). The wide variety in vessels forms seems to suggest a variety of sources, although some such as the wide-necked waisted vessels (nos 59 and 60) may also suggest a chronological difference between vessels and it is notable that none of these were present in cess pit (487). However, parallels for many of the vessels were only found in the Cheshire and Merseyside area, and some forms, eg funnel shaped cups, were so widespread in that area that, as others have already suggested, there was probably some as yet unknown production supplying at least the southern part of the north-west region (eg Green & Noake 1977, 58). Rainford has been suggested as a production source for one particular Cistercian-type ware, the facetted cup (Philpott 1982–3, 27) which, although recorded previously from Chester (Rutter 1990b, fig 99.76), was not identified on this site.

In short, a swift glance through the range of Cistercian-type wares found in Chester suggests that this site assemblage is not atypical for the city, and it could be suggested that this diverse range of forms represents a variety of suppliers. Whilst some parallels can be drawn with production outside the north-west region, distinctive features can be seen amongst some vessels to suggest a source of supply that may have been local to at least part of the region.

Whilst the evidence from this phase does not answer the many questions there are about Cistercian wares in Chester and the north-west it does provide one of the largest stratified assemblages from the city and provides a basis for comparison with other groups from the region.

The variety in form and fabric of the Midland Purple-type wares perhaps also reflects diversity of production. Some parallels can be drawn with other sites in Chester, Cheshire and Merseyside (particularly in the case of Fabric 95), and also in Staffordshire, but the precise sources are unclear and so far there is no evidence for production in the region. Whilst it is open to question whether the Ewloe-type ware bunghole jar in pit (1624) was in contemporary use, its function appears similar to the Midland Purple-type wares and prompts the question as to whether high-fired purple wares from that area supplied Chester and whether the coarser jars in the cess pit (487) could have been produced in North Wales.

Cistercian wares and Midland Purple-type wares were contemporary in this phase and formed a substantial role in the assemblages, providing the drinking vessels and storage jars until the appearance of blackwares and yellow wares. However assemblages elsewhere, eg at Beeston castle, suggest that Midland Purple types may have continued in use longer than the Cistercian-type wares, but an absence of groups clearly datable to the mid-seventeenth century at 25 Bridge Street means it was difficult to determine when they disappeared from use on the site. The assemblages in this phase provide relatively well dated, well preserved vessels which may provide a basis for future study.

Table 5.5.21 Cistercian-type and Midland Purple-type wares quantified by phase, EVEs, no of sherds and weight

Ware	Phase	EVEs rim	EVEs base	No	Wt (g)
Cistercian-type	V	34	106	32	440
	VI	300	1349	153	3908
	VII	0	0	24	634
	VIII	0	0	17	130
	IX	0	0	14	337
	X	0	0	7	135
Total		334	1455	247	5584
Midland-Purple	V	0	0	3	81
type	VI	349	435	178	11460
	VII	0	0	113	4166
	VIII	0	0	40	1796
	IX	0	0	31	1247
	X	0	0	24	716
Total		349	435	389	19466

NB EVEs only recorded for selective groups in Phase VI

Phase VII

The lack of any good ceramic groups of the mid- to late seventeenth century was disappointing. However, the late seventeenth- to early eighteenth-century period was well represented by the fills of a cess pit in Plot 2 and by a large assemblage of pottery and glass from pit (1696) in Plot 4.

Plot 2

Cess pit (465)
A large assemblage (671 sherds, 24136 g) predominantly of household wares but also including a group of sugar cone mould fragments came from the fills of this pit ((472), (463), (464)). The range of wares includes blackwares, yellow wares, brown-glazed wares, slipwares (including trailed, combed and feathered types), mottled wares and heavily sooted Buckley coarseware vessels. Imports to the region include Rhenish stonewares, fragments of Chinese porcelain, Surrey–Hampshire Border ware, North Devon gravel-tempered wares and a relatively large a large assemblage of plain undecorated tin-glazed wares with a smaller number of decorated wares. A Queen Anne ale-measure mark suggests a date of deposition of 1702 or later. The assemblage is comparable in its range of wares and date to that from pit (1696) in Plot 4. Given the more fragmentary nature of this assemblage and the time constraints on the project it was decided that (1696) should be examined in preference. However, an unusual find in this assemblage is a collection of seventy-two fragments (5304 g) of moulds which would have been made for use in the refining of sugar. Whilst not a large dump, the group appears to form the largest assemblage from the city to date. These are of significance in themselves and are discussed below.

Sugar cone moulds
A total of 153 fragments (8399 g) of sugar cone mould were found from the post-medieval phases on the site. Phase VII contributed 63% of the total found (by sherd

count, 70% by weight); the majority of these fragments came from pit (465).

Table 5.5.22 Phase VII Plot 2 pit (465): sugar cone moulds quantified by ware, no of sherds and weight

Context	Ware	Form/object	No	Wt (g)
463	Unglazed earthenware	Sugar mould	35	1410
464		Sugar mould	29	3711
472		Sugar mould	3	45
472		Sugar mould?	2	74
491		Sugar mould	3	64
Total			72	5304

The sugar-refining process has been described and summarised by Brooks (1983) and Allan (1984). Sugar was partly processed on the plantations in the Caribbean where the cane was crushed to extract the sweet juice which was then boiled. The liquid was left to crystallise and the partly refined sugar was shipped to Britain and other European destinations in wooden casks. At its destination the sugar was further refined using various processes, including boiling with water with the addition of egg white or bull's blood to clarify the syrup. Eventually the syrup was poured into earthenware cone-shaped moulds with open bases which were bunged at this stage. The syrup was left to crystallise in the cones which were placed over ceramic syrup-collecting jars. Once crystallisation had finished the bungs were removed from the cones and any excess syrup or molasses was allowed to drain away. Further processes were then carried out in order to obtain the required quality of sugar (*see* Allan 1984, 140 and Brooks 1983, 8–9). Finally, the loaves of sugar would be removed from the moulds and left to dry; meanwhile the moulds would be used again for the next batch of sugar that required refining. The whole process would take several weeks. The processing required access to water, a source of heat to boil the pans of syrup and a drying area to dry out the finished sugar loaves.

Fabrics
The fragments fall into three fabric groups. None of these have been described from Chester before and they have been added to the Chester Archaeological Service Fabric Reference Collection. Fabrics 777 and 778 are very similar but the latter is sandier and harder.

Fabric 777: A soft fabric with a slightly soapy smooth feel and a fine texture. The surfaces and broken edges are pale buff but a fresh break reveals a pink to pale orange core. At x20 magnification the fabric can be seen to be made up of a mix of white, pale buff, pink and orange clays that appear as fine threads and streaks. The inclusions consist of moderate fine mica, sparse grey or colourless sub-angular quartz grains which are ill-sorted; sparse pellets and lenses of orange-red clay.

Fabric 778: A slightly harder fabric than 777 with a rough feel and an irregular texture. The surface colour varies from buff to orange and the core is a pinkish orange with buff margins; as with 777 the broken edges appear paler than the fresh breaks. The inclusions consist of moderate quantities of grey, pink and colourless ill-sorted, sub-angular quartz grains; moderate pellets and irregular lenses of red iron-rich clay; sparse fine mica that appears more frequent on the surfaces; fine streaks and layers of white and red clay.

Fabric 779: A hard rough fabric with an irregular texture. The surfaces, core and margin are an orange to orange-red colour. On some examples the exterior surface can appear a darker red or orange. Inclusions consist of abundant fine to medium-sized, colourless, pink or opaque white quartz grains that are sub-angular in shape; sparse coarse quartz grains (as before); dark red iron-rich inclusions appear as pellets, and sub-angular fragments some of which are coarse or very coarse in size; moderate ill-sorted pellets and irregular-shaped fragments and streaks of white clay. The fabric has some visual similarity to some of the wares made from Coal Measure clays that outcrop in North Wales and Staffordshire.

It is difficult to suggest a provenance for these wares. It is possible that 779 was made at Buckley but there does not appear to be any evidence at the kiln sites for sugar cone moulds. Further fabric analysis is required before comment can be made on the paler fabrics; they do not resemble the wares described by Brooks (1983) or Allan (1984, 138–41), although the reference by the latter to white sugar moulds being used in France is intriguing. In the nearby region sugar cone moulds were made in the potteries at Prescot (McNeil 1982–3) and Liverpool. The fabrics from this group were different from the descriptions of those from Prescot (McNeil 1982–3, 63), although the latter types do occur in Chester, eg unpublished examples from the Chester amphitheatre 2004 excavation (CHE/AMP04) and a rim fragment stamped 'Prescot' found during excavations at 12 Hamilton Place in 1994 (CHE/12HP92 unpublished).

All the pieces are wheel thrown with throwing rings of varying pronouncement on the exterior. The insides of the cones had been shaved and smoothed with a blade of some sort, leaving very smooth surfaces that have occasional scratches and drag marks from where inclusions had been displaced. One fragment (in Fabric 779) has a narrow line of glaze along a broken edge.

Most of the fragments are body sherds but the remains of three pierced bases survive. Two of the holes are of similar diameter (4 mm and 5 mm), but one had been left with a plain rounded edge framed by an incised line, whilst the surround of the other, no 71, had been trimmed and flattened to form a sharply defined collar. The third fragment is incomplete but appears much wider (10 mm?) and is surrounded by a wide bevelled collar.

The rims of the cones in Fabrics 777 and 778 are clubbed. In addition no 70 had been trimmed to give a flat top. Only three rim fragments in Fabric 779 survive and each is slightly different. One fragment from (463) (not illustrated) is slightly thickened and had been trimmed to give a narrow external bevel and a flattened top. The other, no 72, appears to have been trimmed on the exterior of the rim so that it is no thicker than the walls. The top of the rim had also been flattened. Another fragment appears to have had an external bead.

The size of the cones is difficult to estimate. Radius measurements were taken where possible but some of the potentially larger cones are represented by relatively small pieces so that the radii are difficult to measure precisely. The pieces in Fabrics 777 and 778 have radii of approx-

imately 150 mm. The vessels in Fabric 779 have radii that are 95 mm and approximately 140 mm and 150 mm.

Sugar cone mould fragments are not unusual finds in Chester but they tend to appear as isolated sherds and only one group of fragments from the city has been published (Rutter 1990b, 194). There are no syrup-collecting jars in the assemblage and, whilst various sizes of moulds are represented, no complete ones could be reassembled. Collecting jars were an essential part of the refining process and their absence may suggest that the moulds were rubbish brought on to the site. It therefore seems unlikely that they represent sugar-refining on site but they do tie in with the arrival of sugar-refining in the city, which from documentary evidence appears to have begun in the second half of the seventeenth century (*see* below). The pottery assemblage from (465) contains material from the late seventeenth and early eighteenth century and thus the cones may be of similar date and from the early years of refining in the city.

Sugar refining in Chester
The Chester port books (Wilson ed 1969) document sugar coming in and going out of the port from at least the mid-1520s, eg June 1526 Anthony Peres arrived on the St Mary of Caminha with '3 coffers of sugar' (*op cit*, 138) and in July 1526 Gregory Fuce on the St Mary of 'Inda de Camyngo' with three hogshead; varying amounts of 'sugar' and 'white sugar' were carried to Dublin in 1566 (*op cit*, 76, 82). The term 'white sugar' suggests it was refined but that does not imply that termed 'sugar' was unrefined. Presumably refining was not taking place in the city at that time and refined sugar was being traded. Sugar was clearly valuable and sought after: in 1566 a man broke into a house and stole a loaf of sugar (CCALS ZQSF 24) and in an inventory of 1596 the Bishop of Chester was shown to keep in his chamber, along with his bedroom furniture and fine clothes, seven loaves of sugar, weighing eighty-five pounds (Bennett 1948, 86).

The date at which sugar refining began in Chester is unclear at the time of writing, The earliest reference to anyone involved in sugar refining appears to be to Giles Vanbrugh, who came to Chester in 1667 from London and carried on his business as sugar baker at the White Friars, formerly the Carmelite friary (Bennett 1935, 37). In 1679 Anthony Henthorne (*ibid*) acquired the lease of part of the White Friars and had probably previously been a tenant of the property. 'Anthony Henthorne, refiner of sugars' had already appeared in the Chester Assembly books on 22 November 1678 (CCALS ZAB 2/189), when he was in dispute with the City over collection of duty. A man of the same name was a witness to Vanbrugh's will of 1683. In 1683 and 1685 Anthony Henthorne was again in dispute with the leavelookers (collectors of duties) (CCALS ZAB 3/1v–4v: 8th December 1685) and in 1686 'Anthony Henthorne, sugar baker' had refused to pay the city duty on sugars he had bought and some of the sugar had been confiscated (CCALS ZAB 3/8v–9). 'Anthony Henthorne of White Fryers sugarbaker' also appeared in the consistory court papers for non-attendance at church (CCALS EDC 5); although the date of this is unclear it was perhaps before the renewal of toleration under the 1687 Declaration of Indulgence. Henthorne was a nonconformist and his house at White Friars was licensed as a meeting place for non-conformists after the 1672 Declaration of Indulgence (Bennet 1935, 37). Sugar-processing appears to have been a Henthorne family concern as Anthony was named as executor for his son Samuel Henthorne, sugar baker, in a will drawn up in 1694 (CCA-LS WS 1695); the will made no mention of the location of the sugar house but White Friars continued to be associated with men involved in the sugar business in the eighteenth century, so presumably the refining was carried on in a building on the site. In an indenture of 1686 Anthony Henthorne was shown as being in control of half of the 'messuages, houses, buildings, stables, yards, orchards, gardens, and lands, tenements and hereditaments called by the name of the Friars' and located between White Friars and Commonhall Street (Bennet 1935, 38). In 1707 Anthony's son John sold the lease to William Clayton of Liverpool (Bennett 1935, 39). William Clayton was referred to in 1714/15 in the Assembly files as having a sugar house in Chester (CCLAS ZAF 49g/25); his widow disposed of the lease in 1733 (Bennett 1935, 39). In 1722 the burial of Joseph Blease, a 'sugar-boyler' of St Martin's parish was recorded at Holy Trinity (Farrell 1914, 476).

It is not clear how long White Friars was associated with the sugar trade. Lavaux's map of 1745 shows a building named as 'The Sugar House' on Weaver's Lane between 'Common Hall Lane' and 'White Fryer's Lane' but a sugar house was being built in 1754 on the south side of Cuppins Lane (CCALS ZTCD/56). The available references to sugar making in Chester after this date appear to relate to this property, and after 1769 to another on Skinners Lane near the River Dee, although the White Friars building was still known as the Sugar House in 1781 (Bennett 1935, 39) and also in 1817 when it is shown on a map published by Ormerod (Ed 2, 1882).

There appears to have been a direct trade in sugar between Chester and the Caribbean in the late seventeenth century. A ship, the 'Friendship' of Chester, took a cargo including sugar from Jamaica to Chester in 1700 (Craig 1964, 49), and Craig suggests that commercial contacts with the West Indies had been fairly common before that date. Craig also describes a fall in direct links between Chester and the West Indies and, whilst Chester vessels still sailed to the Caribbean, they tended to do so *via* London or Liverpool (*ibid*).

Given the dates of the pottery in the assemblage from Bridge Street the White Friars sugar house appears to have been the likeliest source for the sugar-loaf moulds from the site. There was a tenuous link between the individuals at the two properties: as already described Anthony Henthorne was a non-conformist and his house was a licensed place of preaching, and Bennett describes connections with Matthew Henry (Bennett 1935, 37). In her will of 1696 Ann Fletcher, widow of Robert, requested that Matthew Henry preach her funeral sermon (*see* Backhouse, *this volume*). The occupiers of the two properties therefore appear to have been part of the same non-conformist congregation and would probably have been known to each other.

Catalogue (Ill 5.5.18)

70 Sugar cone mould; Fabric 778. (464); SF 10340.
71 Sugar cone mould; Fabric 779. (464); SF 10338.
72 Sugar cone mould; Fabric 779. (464); SF 10326.

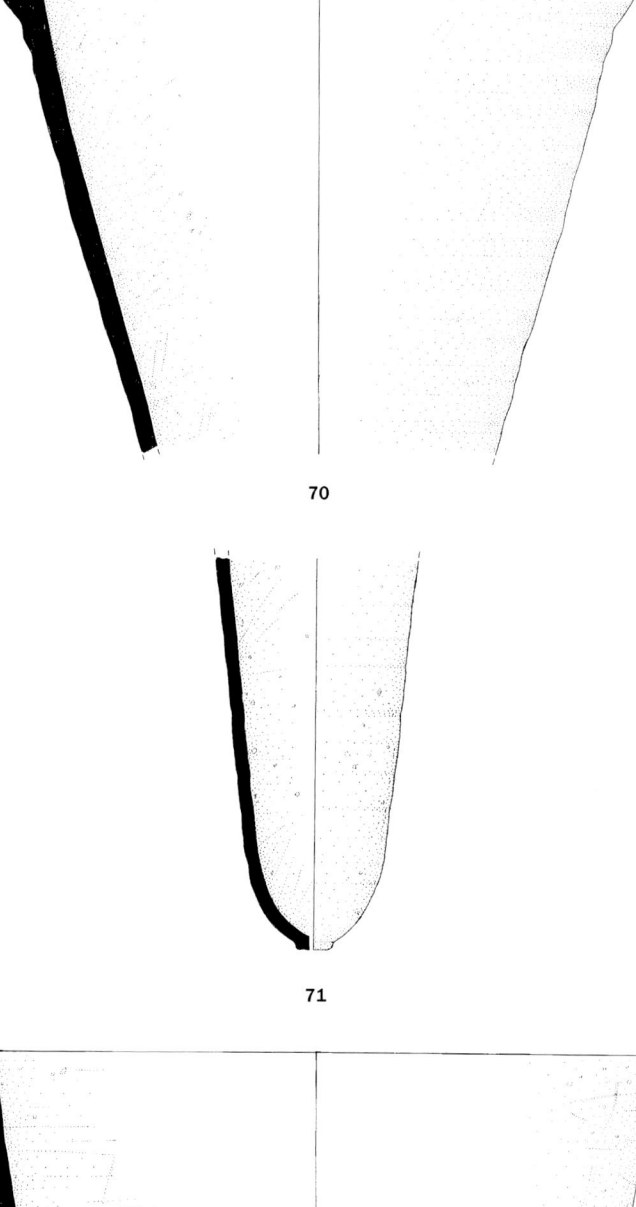

70

71

72

Ill 5.5.18 Phase VII Plot 2 pit (465): sugar cone moulds.
(Scale 1/4)

Pit (1696)/(1614)/(1625)

The assemblage from this pit is remarkable for its state of preservation and size, both in relation to the site and in comparison with other assemblages from Chester (895 sherds/33038 g). The ware and vessel types present date to the late seventeenth and early eighteenth century. Mugs from (1599) in the lower half of the pit have ale-measure marks with the initials, 'AR', of Queen Anne, thus placing the deposition no earlier that 1702. The total absence of any white salt-glazed stoneware suggest a *taq* of *c* 1720, from when the earliest dated wares of this type are known. The clay pipe and documentary evidence suggest a date *c* 1709/1710 (*see* Higgins and Backhouse, *this volume*). It is the largest post-medieval assemblage of this date and of such a close date to be excavated from Chester under PPG16 requirements. A large group of glass vessels found with the pottery further enhances the importance of the assemblage. Unfortunately, whilst other large post-medieval groups have been excavated in the city, there is no readily available quantified data which would permit any detailed comparisons to be made with this assemblage.

Of the six contexts filling the pit, pottery was retrieved from (1695), (1607), (1599), (1601), and (1604). Many fragments join to form complete or semi-complete vessels; these fragments were distributed throughout the five fills, suggesting that the pottery in the pit was deposited in one action or over a very narrow period of time rather than gradually accumulating as discrete deposits. Time did not allow for cross-context joins to be followed across the whole site, but joins observed during the spot-dating process were recorded. As a consequence a number of joins were noted between the pit and contexts higher in the stratigraphic sequence. A limited search was therefore carried out during the analysis stage amongst some of the more distinctive wares from the site, eg the tin-glazed wares. Joins were identified elsewhere in Phase VII and in Phases VIII and X (contexts (455), (1360), (1399), (1546), (1592), (1625), (1697)). All of these contexts were in Plot 4, except for (1399) which was in Plot 3. Clearly at some point activity within the plot had disturbed the pit fills but no obviously intrusive pottery was noted during recording. However, three small fragments of sugar mould are difficult to account for but are probably residual. One join was noted between (1601) and the late Valencian lustreware dish, no 52, in (1697), a fill of Phase VI cess pit (1624). This and other pits in the sequence underlying (1696) appear to have been disturbed by the later pit digging, although it would appear that no vessels from (1696) had intruded into the lower pits (but *see* no 57 and no 64 in pit (1541)).

It was quite difficult to estimate the total amount of residual pottery in the pit. Quantities of significantly earlier pottery were low: 28 medieval sherds (489 g) and 14 Roman sherds of pottery were found. Brick fragments and medieval roof tile fragments were also relatively small in number: a total of 29 fragments (3329 g) were kept and 8 fragments (807 g) discarded on site. The quantity of residual earlier post-medieval pottery was more problematic: fragments of sixteenth- and earlier seventeenth-century imports were easy to identify but other types more difficult unless they were in a significantly different condition to the bulk of the assemblage. However if condition is considered it would appear that residual post-medieval pottery is relatively low as well.

The relatively low residual component in the pit, the presence of a large, well preserved assemblage of glass vessels of similar date and the relative completeness of the ceramic vessels suggest that the assemblage was deposited as a single dump, perhaps the result of a house clearance. The documentary evidence for a well equipped substantial household on the plot in the late seventeenth to early eighteenth century, belonging to a prominent Chester family, suggests that this assemblage can be used to give an indication of the range of ceramic vessels in use in a relatively high-status urban household.

Table 5.5.23 Phase VII Plot 4 pit (1696): post-medieval pottery quantified by context, EVEs, no of sherds and weight

Context	EVEs rim	EVEs base	No	Wt (g)
1599	635	1023	176	7069
1601	2099	2351	529	20526
1604	263	575	101	3426
1607	423	393	74	1541
1695	10	0	15	476
Total	3430	4342	895	33038

The assemblage contained nineteen identifiable ware groups, although some of these are represented by single or very few fragments (Table 5.5.24). Many but not all of the less well represented wares are residual sixteenth- and early seventeenth-century types. The best preserved or largest ware groups in the assemblage consist of nine types: blackwares, yellow wares, brown glazed/coarse earthenwares, slipwares, mottled wares, English stonewares, Nottingham-type stoneware, tin-glazed wares and Chinese porcelain. These wares can be quantified by all of the four methods (Table 5.5.25). However, three of these – blackwares, yellow wares and brown-glazed earthenwares – were long lived types and thus the figures for them will include a residual element.

English wares dominate the assemblage but a change can be seen in the variety of wares represented and the use to which they were put. In comparison with Phase VI the pit shows an increase in the variety of wares and a corresponding drop in the proportion of long established wares in favour of new types.

Thus in the early seventeenth century blackwares formed 43% of the assemblage (pit (430)/(850)) by rim EVEs but in the present assemblage the proportion had fallen to 24%; the proportion by weight admittedly increased from 35% to 51% but this can be accounted for by the large number of blackware jars. Blackwares only provided 20% by rim EVEs of the drinking vessels – the largest vessel group in the pit; they did however retain a substantial role as a provider of jars, forming 50.9% by rim EVEs of that category, and provided 67.2% of chamberpots, which did not figure prominently in the earlier groups. This assemblage thus saw blackwares moving from a multi-functional role to one that had a predominantly storage rather than table function.

A ware which diminished even more was yellow ware, which only made up 6% of the assemblage (rim EVEs) in contrast to the 41% in the (430)/(850) assemblage where it almost equalled blackwares. Whilst this ware was reaching the end of its period of use, it did nevertheless make a notable contribution, providing 17.4% of the jars in the pit, two of the three candlesticks and the only money-box.

Pushing the blackwares and yellow wares to one side as a provider of tablewares were the mottled wares, English stonewares and tin-glazed wares. Apart from one example of a chamberpot, mottled wares appear to largely perform a table or serving function and provided 64.7% (rim EVEs) of the mugs, 15.3% of cups and 40.3% of the total number of drinking vessels. Along with the English stonewares, mottled wars provided 99% of mugs (rim EVEs, 96% base EVEs). The English stonewares were, however, quite restricted in their use, contributing only mugs and one jug. Tin-glazed wares however provided vessels in all the major categories: they seemed to be one of the most versatile wares providing tablewares as well as storage vessels, including chamber pots, 32% of which were in tin-glazed ware.

It is perhaps this ware, along with the vessel glass and the Chinese porcelain, that differentiates this assemblage and perhaps could be used to signify that it was from a household of some status. Tin-glazed wares in general form only a small component of excavated assemblages of late sixteenth- to early eighteenth-century pottery in the city. This is confirmed when the totals for Phase VI and Phase VII are examined. Tin-glazed wares formed only 1% by sherd count of the Phase VI assemblage but 7.5% of the Phase VII assemblage. The assemblage found in (1696) formed 49.5% of the Phase VII total and that from (465) 19%, although these two groups did contribute the major part of the total Phase VII assemblage. More work needs to be done on the supply of tin-glazed wares to the city, but archaeological deposits suggest that they were not widely available in the seventeenth and early eighteenth centuries. The specific mention of whitewares in the Anderton inventory (WS 1693) suggests that they were considered different to other pottery types and their linking with 'glasses' may also have some significance as to how they were regarded.

Some of the less well represented wares are known to be eighteenth-century types but were either not in common use at this particular time or may not have been common types. For example, one ware associated with eighteenth-century assemblages in Chester was black slip-coated ware (popularly also referred to as chocolate-dipped ware), but it is represented here by only one sherd, suggesting that its appearance in deposits in Chester did not become common until nearer the second quarter of the century or even perhaps the middle. Only 8 sherds (112 g) were recorded from the whole of Phase VII; in Phase VIII there are 21 fragments (174 g). There were few good pottery assemblages from Phase VIII but even in Phases IX and X only a total of 66 fragments (1263 g) were found as residual elements, suggesting that the ware perhaps never made up a large component of assemblages.

Similarly there was only one Staffordshire slip-coated ware vessel, the rim of a mug. 13 fragments (85 g) appear in Phase VII as a whole and only 21 fragments (304 g) in Phases VIII, IX and X, suggesting that the low numbers may have been due more to supply factors than to chronology.

As described above, the most obvious feature of the assemblage was the predominance of English wares. Whilst it is possible that some of the tin-glazed wares were Dutch, clearly identifiable overseas imports (excluding clearly residual material) were restricted to the small quantity of Chinese porcelain, represented by four or perhaps five vessels. The one contemporary continental import which might still have been expected to occur in an assemblage of this date, Westerwald stoneware, is conspicuous by its absence. Yet Westerwald stonewares were still popular in the early eighteenth century on both low and high-status sites (Gaimster 1997, 252–53). The low level of overseas imports was echoed in Phase VII as a whole; Westerwald wares only comprised 0.3% of the assemblage by sherd count (0.1% by weight) whilst Chinese porcelain was 0.7% by sherd count (0.1% by weight). However, the pit assemblage differed from the phase overall by having a higher proportion of Chinese porcelain. This formed 2% of the sherds in the pit (0.2% by weight; 2% and 4% of rim and base EVEs respectively) and contributed 68 % by sherd count of the Phase VII porcelain assemblage (60.7% by weight). The status of the household is perhaps reflected in this higher proportion.

The comparable assemblage in pit (465) did include 9 fragments of Westerwald stoneware (128 g) forming 0.78% of the assemblage by sherd count (0.3% by weight) although these only represent a single vessel. In contrast to pit (1696) the Chinese porcelain assemblage comprised 0.17% of the assemblage only consisting of 2 sherds. Whilst only a single vessel; the jug from (465) clearly indicates, as do assemblages elsewhere in Chester, that Westerwald stoneware was available. Its absence from such a large and discrete group as (1696) must therefore be considered. Three possible reasons are: because it was not accessible to the Andertons; they had no need of it for functional or decorative purposes; it reflected the long established sporadic supply of Rhenish stonewares to Chester. The presence of tin-glazed wares, Chinese porcelain and high quality glass clearly indicates that the first reason is unlikely. The range of vessel types in the ceramic assemblage suggests that the second reason perhaps in conjunction with the third is the most likely. Ceramic jugs are poorly represented in the assemblage (*see* below) and those present are mottled wares and Nottingham-type stonewares. Mugs and chamberpots are other common Westerwald forms. The former are well represented in the assemblage but are provided almost exclusively by mottled wares and English stonewares and the latter by tin-glazed wares and blackwares.

Thus it would seem that there was no need for Westerwald jugs, and other functions provided by this stoneware were amply provided by the mottled wares, English stonewares and tin-glazed wares. Elsewhere in the country Gaimster remarks (1997, 252) that Westerwald stonewares were not replaced by English stonewares at this time, but this assemblage suggests their function was not only carried out by English stonewares but other wares as well and indicates different conditions of supply and use in Chester. These may partly be due to geographical location, but the presence of the large group of tin-glazed wares – all probably imported to the city from areas where Westerwald stonewares were popular – suggests that is perhaps too simplistic a reason and more discussion is required than this project permits.

The documentary evidence suggests that the assemblage represents the range of wares available to a prosperous Chester household at the end of the seventeenth and early eighteenth century. Apart from availability the householders' personal choice would have also been a factor in the selection of wares and one which it is more difficult to understand. Clearly there was some acknowledgement of general fashion in choice of Chinese porcelain and tin-glazed wares decorated in a Chinese style but these were only present in relatively small quantities. Were these small cups used to drink tea or were they purely decorative? Does the presence of drinking glasses in the pit have any bearing on the choice of drinking vessels in the ceramic assemblage? And why were the majority of the tin-glazed wares undecorated? Was this choice related to function, cost or aesthetics?

Further comparative work of similarly dated assemblages elsewhere in the city and the region and also elsewhere in the country is required in order to begin to draw conclusions on whether this group could be said to be broadly typical.

Table 5.5.24 Phase VII Plot 4 pit (1696): post-medieval pottery quantified by ware, EVEs, no of sherds and weight

Ware	EVEs rim	EVEs base	Sherd no	Wt (g)
Blackware	857	1161	290	16926
Blackware?	13	10	2	111
Cistercian-type	0	0	1	8
Midland Purple-type	0	0	17	915
Yellow	211	386	40	984
Brown-glazed	74	121	46	2204
Black slip-coated	0	0	1	4
Border ware?	0	0	1	5
Unglazed earthenware	0	0	13	393
N Devon gravel tempered	0	0	10	155
Mottled ware	616	1217	192	4088
Mottled ware?	0	0	1	14
Slipware moulded	0	0	2	41
Slipware combed	103	0	15	330
Slipware feathered	0	0	2	46
Slipware trailed	83	45	24	1268
Staffs slip-coated	48	0	1	4
Slipware	0	0	4	39
Early English stoneware	160	330	34	1053
Notts-type stoneware	20	100	4	323
Valencian late	0	0	1	4
Ligurian	0	0	1	1
TGW	1163	779	164	3924
Frechen	0	0	2	5
Frechen?	0	0	1	3
Chinese porcelain	82	193	24	93
Unidentified	0	0	2	97

Table 5.5.25 Phase VII Plot 4 pit (1696): main post-medieval wares as a percentage of the pit assemblage, quantified by EVEs, no of sherds and weight

Ware	EVEs Rim %	EVEs Base %	Sherd no %	Wt (g) %
Blackware	24	26	32	51
Brown glazed	2	2	4	6
Yellow	6	8	4	2
Mottled ware	17	28	21	12
Slipware	5.4	1	5	5.1
Early English stoneware	4	7	3	3
Notts-type stoneware	0.5	2.3	0.4	0.9
Tin-glazed ware	33	17	18	11
Chinese porcelain	2	4	2	0.2

Function

A wide range of tablewares was present: dishes, bowls, cups, mugs and jugs, as well as chamberpots, candlesticks, small and large jars, a moneybox and a possible salt. This range of vessel types is in marked contrast to the Phase VI assemblages, where the range was relatively limited and concentrated on drinking vessels and storage jars. These vessels still played a strong role in (1696) but the balance had shifted.

Drinking vessels followed by storage jars made up the largest identifiable components of the assemblage. When the two categories are combined, the proportions by rim EVEs, base EVEs, sherd count and weight are 54.4%, 61.8%, 46.9% and 50.1% respectively. In the Phase VI pit (430)/(850), the largest group from the first half of the seventeenth century, drinking vessels and jars make up 100% of the assemblage by rim EVEs, 83.7% by base EVEs, 80% by sherd count and 81.7% by weight.

Predictably, storage jars formed the largest component by weight in (1696), but even by this measurement drinking vessels provided the second largest functional group. Bowls including the handled bowls or porringers provided the next most common vessels, followed by dishes and chamberpots.

Cups and cylindrical mugs were the principal drinking vessels, and of these mugs predominated using all methods of quantification. Mottled wares and stonewares provided the majority of vessels, with blackwares, tin-glazed wares, slipwares and Chinese porcelain present in smaller numbers. Small Chinese porcelain and tin-glazed ware cups provided a considerable contrast to the mugs in terms of size and delicate decoration. Clearly some of the vessels held different types of drink: a number of the mugs were blackened around the base, suggesting that they had been placed close to a fire or source of heat. When the drinking glasses are also considered the quantity and variety of drinking vessels is remarkable and gives rise to questions as to whether there were any differences in who used them, on what occasions and whether any were more for display than for use. This discussion is beyond the scope of this report.

Despite the preponderance of drinking vessels, storage containers for liquids were poorly represented amongst the ceramics. Jugs are the only identifiable vessels and appear as mottled ware, Nottingham-type stoneware and feathered slipware. These made up 4.9% by base EVEs but only 3% or less using other methods of quantification. The relatively large number of glass bottles in the pit may explain the small number of these ceramic vessels. Bunghole jars/cisterns are also noteworthy by their absence although blackware cisterns are known from later assemblages in the city. In earlier periods these vessels are generally thought to have been associated with small-scale brewing; their absence may be related to changes in this activity and is an area that needs further investigation.

Jars vary greatly in size and presumably served a wide range of storage functions. The majority are blackwares, but tin-glazed wares, and yellow wares provided the rest, particularly the very small jars often called ointment pots but probably used to hold materials which would only be required in small quantities.

Tin-glazed wares, mottled wares and blackwares provided various types of bowls; one particular type, the handled bowl or porringer, is only represented by tin-glazed wares. The different sizes of bowls appear to suggest that they were used both as tablewares and as utilitarian wares.

The dishes both decorated and plain were found principally in yellow wares, slipwares and tin-glazed wares. Whilst they were relatively numerous compared to the earlier seventeenth-century group, providing just over 10% of the recorded EVEs, they were still greatly outnumbered by drinking vessels, especially when the glass vessels are also considered. If this group represents a house clearance then clearly the inhabitants must have been eating from vessels other than ceramic. In comparison with plates, however, dishes were numerous: the only examples of plates were a small piece of a tin-glazed ware plate and a fragment of Chinese porcelain, although these did provide 6% of the assemblage by rim EVEs.

Chamberpots were only found in blackwares, mottled ware and tin-glazed wares. Whilst they fall into the minor of the form groups, chamberpots provided 7% of the assemblage by rim and base EVEs.

Candlesticks, whilst present, were again poorly represented in the group given the size of the household, and other materials must have also been used. Similarly ceramic cooking vessels (as the inventory indicates) were not present other than two fragments of pipkins, which were so small that they were probably residual.

Thus, if the documentary association is correct this assemblage gives a view of the range of ceramic vessels that might be expected to be found in the home of members of the upper ranks of town society in the late seventeenth to early eighteenth century. The vessels were biased towards the storage and table functions; the full range of vessels required for dining and to run a large kitchen was not present, although the latter were clearly present in the inventory in other materials, and a quantity of pewter was also listed although not defined.

In many ways the ceramics may seem quite mundane but the assemblage predated the introduction in the mid-eighteenth century of fine earthenwares and the family appeared not to be wealthy enough to acquire a large quantity of Chinese porcelain, or if they were it did not find its way into the pit. However, the porcelain that was present, as well as the English stonewares and decorated tin-glazed wares, shows that the Andertons were keeping up with new fashions and developments, and it is perhaps the quantity of material that signifies their wealth more than or as much as the range and quality of the pottery.

Table 5.5.26 Phase VII Plot 4 pit (1696): post-medieval pottery quantified by form, EVEs, no of sherds and weight

Form	EVEs rim	EVEs base	No	Wt (g)
Bowl	427	243	50	3165
Bowl - handled	327	250	39	819
Bowl - handled?	42	0	3	63
Bowl?	0	0	10	62
Candlestick	83	145	2	298
Candlestick?	0	17	1	15
Chamber pot	247	307	63	2692
Chamber pot?	0	15	1	17
Cup	434	719	79	1396
Cup?	11	0	6	32
Dish	283	149	76	3274
Dish - lobed	69	25	9	393
Dish?	0	29	2	190
Jar	599	477	152	11219
Jar?	0	151	5	414
Jar-miniature	368	340	7	286
Jug	58	212	25	835
Jug?	0	0	1	26
Lid?	0	0	1	7
Money box	0	43	3	75
Mug	441	1040	161	3214
Mug?	13	0	10	47
Pipkin	9	0	1	38
Pipkin?	0	9	1	16
Plate	6	16	2	43
Salt?	0	0	1	11
Saucer	0	0	1	1
Sugar mould	0	0	3	175
Unassigned	13	155	180	4215

Table 5.5.27 Phase VII Plot 4 pit (1696): post-medieval pottery forms as a percentage of the pit assemblage, quantified by EVEs, no of sherds and weight

Form	EVEs rim%	EVEs base %	No %	Wt (g) %
Bowl	12.4	5.6	6.7	9.8
Handled bowl	10.7	5.7	4.7	2.7
Candlestick	2.4	3.7	0.3	0.9
Chamber pot	7.2	7.4	7.2	8.2
Cup	13	16.5	9.5	4.3
Dish	10.26	4.7	9.7	11.7
Jar	17.5	14.5	17.5	35.2
Jar-miniature	10.7	7.8	0.8	0.9
Jug	1.7	4.9	3	2.6
Lid?	0	0	0.1	0.02
Money box	0	1	0.3	0.2
Mug	13.2	23	19.1	9.7
Pipkin	0.3	0.2	0.2	0.2
Plate	0.2	0.4	0.2	0.1
Salt?	0	0	0.1	0.03
Saucer	0	0	0.1	0.003
Sugar mould	0	0	0.3	0.5
Unassigned	0.4	3.6	20.2	12.8

Wares

Black wares (Ills 5.5.19–.20)

Table 5.5.28 Phase VII Plot 4 pit (1696): Blackwares quantified by form, EVEs, no of sherds and weight

Form	EVEs rim	EVEs base	No	Wt (g)
Bowl	27	0	7	1184
Chamber pot	166	294	50	2455
Cup	184	270	26	634
Cup?	0	0	3	18
Jar	480	392	112	10318
Jar?	0	151	5	414
Mug	0	0	3	50
Mug?	0	0	7	39
Unassigned	0	54	77	1814

Table 5.5.29 Phase VII Plot 4 pit (1696): Blackware forms as a percentage of the pit assemblage, quantified by form, EVEs, no of sherds and weight

Form	EVEs rim %	EVEs base %	No	Wt (g)
Bowl	0.8	0	0.2	0.03
Bowl - handled	2.2	1.2	1	2.3
Chamber pot	2.7	5.7	4.6	5.2
Cup	5.4	6.3	3	2
Jar	13	9.2	12.5	31
Mug	0		0.3	0.2

Blackwares comprised 32% by sherd count and 51 % of the assemblage by weight; the latter figure is biased by the preponderance of relatively large storage vessels. If EVEs are considered they made up *c* 25% and if rim EVEs are used alone blackwares actually take second place to tin-glazed wares. However, whichever criterion is chosen, it is clear that blackwares made up a substantial proportion of the assemblage. Within that proportion storage vessels of varying sizes dominated the ware.

Even a cursory examination of the blackwares demonstrates that the vessels in the group have fabrics of varying colours and coarseness. Fabric colour was influenced by firing conditions and also the position of a vessel within the kiln; thus some vessels, especially the larger storage jars, display a variety of colour within their clay bodies. The coarseness and fineness of fabric also varies according to the size and type of vessel.

A study of the blackwares from the site in comparison to groups from other sites in and beyond Chester was not possible within the bounds of this project. However, it was decided to attempt to isolate fabric groups in order to be able to begin to examine the blackwares within the chronological framework of the site. Broad fabric divisions were identified and these were then correlated with reference sherds already present in the Chester Fabric Reference collection. Some of the fabrics from the site clearly differed from those in the Reference Collection and these have been assigned new numbers. However, in some instances the fabric divisions for the site were broader than those in the Reference Collection, eg Group A equates to two fabrics in the Reference Collection. A review of the fabrics already recorded from Chester is required in the light of findings from this site.

Fabrics

Fabric Group A (Fabrics 24/33): Colour varies from a purplish brown to yellowish brown-pale orange/brown, this variation can be present within one vessel. A fine feel but a hackly fracture; the clay matrix is smooth-looking with round and lens-shaped voids. Inclusions consist of sub-angular and rounded white or colourless quartz; red iron-rich pellets and lenses; irregular yellow/white opaque vitrified fragments of white clay; occasional lenses and streaks of white and red clay. A fine layer of a reddish brown slip or wash is usually present between the glaze and the body on both surfaces but it is hard to see if this is present at the purple end of the colour scale. The slip can sometimes appear patchy. This fabric group is represented by vessels 73–8 and 88–9.

Fabric Group B (Fabric 775): Dark red/brown colour and a hard, dense-looking matrix with a fine feel and a hackly texture. Inclusions consist of well-sorted sub-angular and angular quartz grains which are colourless and opaque grey-white; occasional small irregular white clay inclusions and sparse large inclusions. Similar to the above but less variety in inclusions. No slip is apparent and is presumably unnecessary because of the colour of the fabric. This fabric is represented by vessel 79.

Fabric Group C (Fabric 121): A relatively finer looking fabric in comparison to A and B which varies in colour from red to a purple/brown, sometimes within the same vessel. Inclusions consist of moderate but not very well sorted colourless and opaque grey-white quartz grains that are angular or sub-angular; sparse to moderate dark red/brown iron-rich inclusions, angular or sub-angular in shape; sparse white clay inclusions appearing as lenses or pellets. Irregular texture. This fabric is represented by vessels 80–2.

When the blackwares from the earlier groups were examined it was found that Fabric 121 was a type which occurred in the first half of the seventeenth century. It was only represented in (1696) by fragments, and the jar rim forms were very different from the bulk of the vessels; it is therefore suggested these fragments were residual.

Fabric Group D (Fabric 776): Hard purple fabric with a fine texture. Inclusions consist of sparse sub-angular white and colourless fine quartz grains; sparse fine to coarse rounded and sub-angular dark red iron-rich inclusions; fine streaks and lenses of white clay. Well glazed on interior and exterior; glaze can be lustrous on the exterior. This fabric is represented by vessel no 87.

Fabric Group E (Fabric 24): High-fired purple fabrics similar to Fabric Group A with quartz inclusions and thin streaks of white clay. Possibly the same as Fabric Group A but from thicker parts of the vessel (Not illustrated).

Fabric Group F (Fabric 38): Similar to Fabric Group A but with large creamy white clay inclusions. A pale red to buff very hard fabric with an irregular texture. Inclusions consist of abundant fine to coarse sub-angular clear, colourless and opaque white quartz; moderate fine to coarse sub-angular and rounded red iron-rich material also present as fine streaks and lenses; moderate fine to very coarse rounded and sub-angular fragments and streaks of white clay. This fabric is represented by vessel no 83.

Fabric 789: A bright red fabric, varying to a dark purplish red on thinner areas of the vessel, hard with a rough feel. Inclusions consist of abundant fine to medium clear and opaque white sub-angular quartz; moderate fine to medium sub-angular red iron-rich fragments. A glossy slightly lustrous thick black glaze covers both surfaces. This fabric is represented by vessels nos 84 and 86.

Fabric 790: Purplish brown to orange very hard fabric with a rough feel and a fine texture. Abundant fine to coarse sub-angular and irregular red iron-rich fragments; moderate fine to coarse sub-angular clear, colourless, opaque white and red-stained quartz; sparse fine to coarse rounded and sub-angular pieces of white clay. A thick glossy black glaze covers both surfaces. This fabric is represented by vessel no 85.

Forms

Jars: The jars in Fabric 24/33, as with the other blackware vessels in the assemblage, are generally well constructed and finished. The storage jars, nos 73–5 and 79, share several features such as heavy thickened rims above walls which thin steadily from the base upwards, becoming very fine in comparison to the lower walls. Throwing rings are visible on the interior and exterior surfaces.

A characteristic of the rims is a vertical outer edge which is divided by a horizontal central indentation and an inner edge which overhangs the interior. The tops of the rims are flattened and an external bead is sometimes present. Glaze cover is good over the vessel walls but it can be sparse just below the rim on both surfaces. The tops of the rims are unglazed and the cover on the exterior vertical edge can be patchy. Finger prints and smudges in the glaze and slip can often be seen on the inside of the rim and occasionally on the exterior rim area. Bowl no 83 has a similar rim. The bases on these jars are finished to give a neat well defined basal angle and the undersides are slightly kicked and of even thickness. Kiln scars are often present on the interior and exterior of bases, the former indicating that some vessels were used to contain smaller vessels in the kiln.

Similar features can be seen on jars in the same fabric in pit (465), which appear to be contemporary with pit (1696). This rim form is also found elsewhere in Chester and in the region, eg Liverpool (Philpott 1980–1, fig 34).

Jar no 73 has flaring sides which curve to the vertical before joining the rim which, unlike no 74, has a concave top. The vessel is glazed over the interior and exterior but the glaze varies in thickness over the vessel and the surfaces appear rough where the glaze is thinnest. Finger prints and smudges of glaze are present on various parts of the vessel. The base is thin and uneven. On the interior of the base are three circular stilt marks and a fine crack around the perimeter had filled with glaze. On the exterior fingerprints made by glaze-covered fingers can be seen in the layer of slip covering the base and the perimeter edge is worn.

No 74 also has flaring sides which curve to the vertical before joining the rim. Fingerprints and smudges can also be seen on the interior and exterior of the rim area. The vessel is glazed from just under the rim to the base where the glaze has seeped underneath. The underside of the base is covered by a layer of red slip which contains smudge marks from handling. The kiln scar from the rim of another vessel is present under the base and the perimeter edge is worn.

One of two horizontal loop handles survives on jar no 75; it has a D-shaped loop and an undulating strap shape. The ends of the handle are splayed at the join with the body and terminate in three finger impressions. The handle is made from a darker clay than the body of the vessel.

The following two jars represent smaller vessels in this fabric group and are distinguishable by their finer walls, darker fabrics and slightly lustrous glazes. Each has finely formed rims. Two chamberpots are also present in the assemblage representing this finer production in Fabric 24/33.

No 77 is a barrel-shaped vessel with constrictions below the rim and above the base. The rim is everted and slightly hooked in profile. There is a lustrous black glaze on both surfaces but the coverage of the foot is uneven and on one side the glaze extends under the base, encasing fragments of buff coloured clay and causing the vessel to stand unevenly. The base perimeter, including the glaze area, has been worn smooth . The vessel form is similar to that of tin-glazed ware jars, which yellow wares also replicated, but it is not common amongst black wares in Chester.

No 78 is a rounded jar with a vertical loop handle. There appears to be a small pouring lip in the rim opposite the handle. The rim is thickened and flattened. The vessel has relatively thin, finely thrown walls and, as above, a good slightly lustrous glaze.

A much larger vessel than those already described was present in Fabric 775; its general characteristics were similar to the group of jars described in Fabric 24/3. No 79 is similar to no 75, with a squared, thickened rim that had a lightly concave top and overhung the interior. The walls gradually thin towards the rim. The base is slightly uneven and the underside is worn around its perimeter. A kiln spacer in the form of a rectangular piece of clay was attached to the edge of the underside and also displays wear marks. A kiln scar is also present inside the base. The vessel is well glazed on most of the interior and exterior but glaze is sparse on some areas of the exterior, especially on the lower wall above the base. It is also sparse around the rim, the top of which is unglazed. An even band of glaze has crept under the base. A red slip is present on the underside of the base and wipe marks and smudges can be seen in its surface.

The jars in Fabric 121 show more variety in rim form. The squared rims are similar to vessels in the same fabric

in the Phase VI groups and they were probably residual elements in this pit group.

No 80 is a rounded jar with an everted rim and external bevel. The horizontal strap handle has an undulating section and is made from a lighter, finer clay. The jar is well glazed on the interior and exterior and on top of the rim, unlike the more complete jars. A similar vessel is also present in (1601).

No 81 has a thickened, flat-topped rim with an angled, moulded external edge. The jar is well glazed on both surfaces but, as is common with types in Fabric 24/33, the top of the rim is unglazed. Dribbles of glaze running from the body towards the rim suggest that the vessel was fired upside down. The unglazed rim has patches of lighter red in the dark red-brown surface which are possibly kiln scars left behind by spacers.

No 82 is a jar with an everted rim thickened at the edge, giving a trumpet-shaped section. There is a good covering of glaze on the interior and over the rim but it is patchy on the interior.

Bowls: No 83 is a large bowl in Fabric 38. It has straight, flaring sides which become slightly concave just above the base. The rim is everted and squared but with a moulded outer edge; it appears to have been thickened. The walls had been evenly thrown so that thickness only varies slightly, although throwing rings are prominent on both surfaces. Only the interior is glazed but the glaze stops short of the rim. A fine red/brown slip is present on the interior and exterior.

Cups: The cup assemblage is fragmentary except for three more or less complete vessels. It is difficult to relate any of the fragments to the complete vessel forms. Some are obviously from cups in very different forms from those illustrated and it is possible that others are residual Cistercian-type ware fragments. Features of the fragments are bands of ribbing or raised cordons at either the handle–body joins, around the centre of vessels or just above the base. Handles appeared delicate, tapering and oval in section. Some of these are characteristics of earlier vessels. The majority of the cups are in a fine red fabric. No 85 is an exception: it has a fine orange-brown fabric which appears higher fired and denser in appearance than the other vessels.

All of these three complete cups can be paralleled with examples produced in Staffordshire in the late seventeenth or early eighteenth century (Barker 1986b).

No 84 is a three-handled flared or trumpet shaped cup with a thick glossy black glaze in Fabric 789.

No 85 in Fabric 790 has a wide pear-shaped body with a simple everted rim. There is a thick glossy black glaze which covers the lower part of the vessel and the foot unevenly.

No 86 in Fabric 789 is a rounded cup with flaring neck. The D-shaped loop handle tapers along its length and had been applied slightly off the vertical. The base is quite roughly finished and there is wear around the edge. The cup has a thick glaze which appears dull in comparison to the other examples. The glaze is uneven on the interior and the underside of the handle is unglazed. The rim has been squashed to an oval.

Chamberpots: Three chamberpots were reconstructed. All are fine-walled with prominent throwing rings. Two are rounded but the third unusually has straight sides.

No 87 in Fabric 776 is a round-bodied vessel with a high girth and a rim that is everted and flattened. A single handle was attached at the shoulder and girth. The body narrows to the base, which has a well shaped rounded foot bevelled on the upper edge. The pot is well glazed on the interior and exterior, but the glaze stops a few centimetres above the foot. The underside of the base is worn around its perimeter. The interior surface is heavily worn as though it has been scratched or scoured. A fragment of a similar shaped but smaller vessel was also found in (1604).

No 88 in Fabric 24/33 is similar in overall shape to no 87 but has a slightly more flaring rim. A kiln scar is present just below the rim on the inside. The handle is missing. Both the interior and exterior are glazed but sparsely on the underside of the rim flange. On the exterior the glaze stops just below the girth (three-quarters of the way down the vessel) but runs to the base and occasionally underneath were present. A fragment of buff-coloured clay is enclosed in the glaze under the base and has been worn smooth by the wear which extended around the perimeter of the base. The underside of the base has parallel scratches or drag marks across its surface, a feature which is also present on the base of another chamberpot base in the assemblage and on no 87.

No 89 in the same fabric is a vertical sided bowl with an everted and flattened rim and a D-shaped vertical loop handle applied to the lower part of the outer edge of the rim. The base of the handle is splayed and pressed into the body with a finger/thumb print that was smeared off to the right. The base is slightly kicked. The exterior is unglazed and the glaze on the interior is blistered and flaking. This is an unusual form for a chamberpot but its dimensions and overall appearance led to this identification.

Midland Purple-type wares

Seventeen pieces of Midland Purple-type wares (915 g) were present, representing only fragments of vessels. Many have a cess deposit on the surfaces and broken edges. The condition of the fragments of this assemblage is in contrast to that of the principal ware groups in the pit and it is possible that the pieces may have derived from pits underlying and cut by the horn core-lined pit (1807)/ (1621) and pit (1696). The fragments are mainly in Fabric 95 and are comparable to vessels in Phase VI. They were thus probably residual in this pit group.

Yellow wares

Table 5.5.30 Phase VII Plot 4 pit (1696): Yellow wares quantified by form, EVES, no of sherds and weight

Form	EVEs rim	EVEs base	No	Wt (g)
Unidentified	13	64	17	195
Candlestick	0	100	1	120
Candlestick?	0	17	1	15
Dish	11	22	10	427
Jar	10	0	1	4
Jar-miniature	168	140	5	105
Money box	0	43	3	75
Pipkin	9	0	1	38

The yellow ware assemblage was also fragmentary, and there were no large reconstructable vessels. The only complete vessel is a small jar, no 91. It is this, plus fragments of other jars, eg no 90, and a moneybox, which are in the best condition and comparable to vessels in the larger ware groups. It is arguable that these are relatively small vessels and thus more likely to survive intact if discarded in a good condition, but equally both are storage vessels and may have continued in use longer. The remaining fragments are generally in a relatively poor condition with abraded edges and flaking glazes. Those chosen for illustration are the better preserved fragments and include jars and a dish typical of the ware and, less common, the remains of a pipkin and money box. The fabrics are as those described above.

The generally accepted date span for yellow wares in Chester and elsewhere in the north-west is the seventeenth century. This assemblage suggests that, whilst a small number of yellow wares may have been still in use if not production in the early eighteenth century, the ware was not a major component of the principal types of pottery in use at this time. The assemblage thus confirms the largely seventeenth-century attribution.

No 92 is a small overfired or burnt fragment from the base of a pipkin, with soot present around the surviving foot. The money box, no 94, has a mammiform shape with a slot cut for coins just below the apex (missing). A thick white slip covers the vessel under the glaze.

Brown-glazed wares

There was a relatively large but fragmentary group of wares made from red to pale pink/buff fabrics with clear lead glazes which appear brown. There is some similarity with the fabrics of some of the blackwares and slipwares in the assemblage and most appear to have been made from Coal Measure clays. The group is in a poor condition relative to the other major ware types in the group and several sherds, including fragments from the same large dish, are coated in cess. The condition suggests that the wares were not contemporary with the bulk of the assemblage. An attempt was made to define fabric groups within this ware type but the task began to exceed the allotted time and as the majority of the fragments were likely to be residual to the pit assemblage it was decided not to proceed further. Their presence is noted here as a matter of completeness.

Table 5.5.31 Phase VII Plot 4 pit (1696): Brown-glazed wares quantified by form, EVEs, no of sherds and weight

Form	EVEs rim	EVEs base	No	Wt (g)
Unidentified	0	27	21	633
Bowl	0	0	1	61
Cup	0	0	1	8
Cup?	0	0	1	2
Dish	69	37	15	1162
Dish?	0	29	1	165
Jar	5	19	3	127
Pipkin?	0	9	1	16

Mottled wares

These wares, together with the stonewares, contributed the largest number of drinking vessels in the assemblage, the most common form being mugs. The assemblage consisted of smashed and semi-complete vessels in a relatively wide range of forms: straight-sided mugs, round-bodied cups, jugs including a fragment with a slip-trailed initial, and fragments of possible chamber pot and bowls.

Mottled wares are buff coloured with a glaze which appears speckled brown. The fabric is generally hard and fine in appearance but there is some variety amongst the wares, with some appearing slightly softer and sandier than others. A buff-coloured slip is sometimes present under the glaze.

Mottled wares were produced in a variety of places in the late seventeenth and eighteenth centuries: Staffordshire, Buckley and Prescot are all potential suppliers for Chester, although it is uncertain precisely when Prescot started to produce mottled wares (*see* Davey 1982–3). Most of the kiln evidence points to production *c* 1680 or later, eg Hanley in Staffordshire (Kelly & Greaves 1974, 3) and Brookhill at Buckley *c* 1690 (Amery & Davey 1979, 81). There is, however, a documentary reference that suggests that mottled ware may have been produced as early as the 1670s (Philpott 1985, 52) and a mottled ware jug was amongst a group of four hoard pots deposited at Congleton in the early 1670s (Edwards 2001). Further work is required to determine whether it is possible to relate the noted differences in fabric to the place of manufacture.

Table 5.5.32 Phase VII Plot 4 pit (1696): Mottled wares quantified by form, EVEs, no of sherds and weight

Form	EVEs rim	EVEs base	No	Wt (g)
Unidentified	0	0	5	78
Bowl	120	90	12	642
Chamber pot	1	0	1	17
Cup	57	226	18	559
Cup?	11	0	1	10
Dish	95	90	6	136
Jug	38	112	20	538
Lid?	0	0	1	7
Mug	281	699	126	2107
Mug?	13	0	3	8

Fabrics

Fabric 39: A buff hard, smooth-feeling fabric with a fine texture. Inclusions consist of moderate very fine colourless quartz, moderate fine to medium red iron-rich fragments and sparse fine red streaks, sparse fine streaks and medium to coarse rounded fragments of white clay.

Fabric 772: A pale whitish buff, hard, slightly rough feeling fabric with a slightly irregular texture. Inclusions consist of moderate fine colourless sub-angular quartz; moderate fine to coarse angular and hard opaque white fragments (possibly clay); moderate fine to coarse red (and sparse black) sub-angular and irregular iron-rich fragments.

Fabric 773: A yellowish buff, hard, slightly rough-feeling fabric with a fine texture. Inclusions consist of moderate fine to coarse sub-angular colourless, red-stained and opaque white quartz; moderate fine to medium red iron-rich fragments; sparse fine to very coarse irregularly shaped white clay inclusions.

Fabric 774: A dark grey very hard slightly rough feeling fabric with a fine texture. Inclusions consist of moderate fine to coarse colourless and opaque white sub-angular quartz; moderate fine to coarse (sparse very coarse) sub-angular fragments and flat lenses of white clay; moderate

red and black irregularly shaped fine to coarse iron-rich fragments; sparse flat voids *c* 1.25 mm in length that are ridged on one side and resemble ornamentation found on some shells. A slip which varies in colour from buff to a pale reduced grey covers both surfaces as well as a glossy smooth glaze which is a reduced yellowish green in colour.

Forms

The mugs are roughly cylindrical with distinctive bands of ribbing below the rim and above the base. The width and number of ridges varies; some have wide bands of ribbing below the rim, giving them a top-heavy appearance. In general they parallel the forms of the early English stoneware mugs.

No 95 in Fabric 39 has three bands of ribbing: above the foot, around the middle, and below the rim at the upper handle join with the body. An 'AR' ale-measure mark is stamped onto a small roughly circular pad of clay placed over the upper band of ribbing. The base is slightly kicked and soot blackened around the perimeter edge opposite the handle. The glaze is patchy over the lower band of ribbing and its thickness varies over the interior.

No 96 in Fabric 39 has a poorly defined band of eight ribs above the base. There is a wide band around the shoulder in which nineteen ribs are arranged in groups of three interspersed between four wider ribs. A 'WR' ale-measure mark was placed to the left of the handle join in the middle of the ribbed area. The handle is a flattened oval in section with a roughly kicked lower terminal; the upper terminal is joined to the vessel in the middle of the upper band of ribbing. The underside of the base is soot blackened around the edge opposing the handle. Chips around one edge of the base are covered by the soot. The glaze has a smooth appearance and is only lightly mottled. On the interior it unevenly covers the area just above the base. On the exterior it covers the foot unevenly and in places it has run down under the edge, necessitating part of the base to be chipped away, presumably to remove the mug from the kiln.

No 97 is a tapering cylinder in shape, narrowing towards the rim. Three bands of ribbing are present, one above the foot and two wider bands at the shoulder and below the rim. The lower band is squashed in places, apparently from finger impressions. A 'WR' ale-measure mark was stamped on a pad of clay placed on the middle band of ribbing close to and to the left of the handle. The handle is a flattened oval in section but the upper part is flatter with longitudinal moulding. The lower terminal is kicked. The upper terminal is attached between and slightly over the upper two bands of ribbing. Unlike other examples in this group the base is not soot blackened. The glaze cover is uneven, with thicker areas on the interior of the base and lower areas of the exterior. It stops short of the lower band of ribbing but runs of glaze extend down to the base.

No 98 in Fabric 772 has two bands of ribbing, which are more pronounced than on other examples. The wider, upper band consists of fourteen ribs; the lower, eight. The handle is missing but the lower terminal is kicked up and folded back against the base of the handle; the upper terminal is placed over the ribbed band. Finger impressions are visible over the lower ribbing. Concentric wiring-off marks are visible on the underside of the base as well as the shadow or ghost of three kiln spacer marks. The edge opposite to the handle is soot-blackened. The glaze cover is uneven over the lower band of ribbing, and glaze has pooled on top of the ribbing. In side the base a half-moon shaped area has been left unglazed.

No 99 in Fabric 772 has two bands of ribbing: the upper is at shoulder level and consists of thirteen ribs, whilst the second above a small rounded foot is composed of eight. None of the ribs are squashed as on some other examples. The handle is a flattened oval in section; the upper terminal was placed between the fourth and twelfth rib on the upper band and over the first two on the lower. The lower terminal is kicked up and placed slightly off-centre. The base is slightly kicked and the ghost of spacer marks is visible on the underside, which is also soot blackened opposite the handle. The glaze has gathered on the upper ribs of the ribbed bands and stops short of the base. On the interior it varies in density and has pooled to one side of the base.

No 100 in Fabric 39 has a cylindrical neck with a horizontal cordon below the rim. The body flares out and down into a rounded shape. The body is decorated with one or possibly more horizontal rows of indentations or dimples. The dimples were made when the clay was relatively hard because the inner surface has cracked under pressure, sometimes leaving a small hole in the centre of the dimple which has been sealed with glaze. The handle has a longitudinal central ridge and has been attached immediately below the neck cordon and terminates in one of the dimples.

No 101, again in Fabric 39, is straight sided but squat in appearance. A broad band of twelve ribs below the rim contributes to the squatness by giving the mug a top-heavy appearance. The handle is missing but a slightly kicked terminal remained. The band of ribbing above the foot is quite shallow and is almost hidden by glaze in places. The base is slightly kicked and sooting is present opposite the handle. The glaze extends to the very edge of the base and in one area has spilled over and stuck to whatever the vessel was placed on in the kiln.

No 102, also in Fabric 39, has three bands of ribbing, consisting of a band of six below the rim, a central band composed of a cordon with two ribs either side, and a band of four ribs above a rounded foot. The lower band has a finger impression, causing the ribs to be smudged. The handle is flattened oval with a central rib and a kicked terminal. The base is slightly kicked and the marks of three kiln spacers are visible. The surface of the base is discoloured but there is no soot blackening. The glaze has gathered in thicker, darker, denser patches, especially around the central cordon. It stops short of the lower cordon and on the interior the thickness varied, creating a thinner vertical strip.

No 103, in Fabric 772, is a shallow dish with a beaded rim and a rounded foot. A fine buff slip covers the interior and exterior and is clearly visible on the underside of the base. A kiln scar in the form of the remains of a drip of glaze under the base perimeter appears to have been partly chipped away, possibly when the vessel was removed from the kiln.

No 104, again Fabric 772, is a necked cup with a small loop handle which has an oval section. The base is slightly kicked. Glaze has seeped under the base and the scars of three spacers are present in the glaze. Fragments of red clay are embedded in the glaze and appear to be the remains of the spacers. A pinkish buff slip is present under the glaze on both surfaces.

No 105 is a large flared cup in Fabric 39 with a slightly everted rim and a rounded foot.

No 106 in Fabric 772 is a cup with almost vertical walls and a slightly everted rim. The walls curve down and round into a slightly kicked base. A kiln scar is present in the glaze which has crept under the base to edge the perimeter. The underside of the base is partly soot blackened but unusually the area below the handle is also blackened.

No 107 in Fabric 39 is a wide shallow cup. A band of seven ribs separate the slightly flaring rim from a short rounded body. The ring or loop handle is a flattened oval in section but with a central rib. There is a small foot. The base is flat and glaze has seeped underneath, enclosing the remains of two spacers, one of which is made of red clay. Some soot blackening is present under the base. The vessel had cracked either during or before firing; glaze has filled the crack, thus possibly making it unusable. Inside the base the glaze appears to have pooled on the side opposite to the handle.

No 108 in Fabric 773 is a fragment, probably from the shoulder of a jug or bottle with dark trailed slip lettering consisting of two dots placed one above the other followed by an 'R'. Another letter would probably have preceded the dots. Mottled ware jugs or bottles carrying sets of initials, whilst not common, are becoming apparent amongst late seventeenth-century assemblages in Chester, eg from Weaver Street 1994 (unpublished). There was another example amongst the group of four hoard pots discovered at Congleton thought to have been deposited before 1675 (Edwards 2001, 108–9). A similar practice was relatively common on plain tin-glazed ware bottles, where initials were often accompanied by a date; the word 'sack' also occurs, and it has been suggested (Lipski & Archer 1984, 307) that such bottles were given as gifts possibly containing wine.

No 109 is a jug in Fabric 772. It has a cylindrical but slightly outward flaring rim above an inverted baluster shaped body. A narrow raised cordon is present 15 mm below the simple rim. The rim is incomplete and the handle missing. The foot is bevelled and the base is slightly kicked; the scars of kiln spacers can be seen in its surface. The exterior is well glazed but it stops unevenly short of the foot although runs of glaze extend to the foot. Traces of a pinkish buff slip can be seen extending below the glaze above and on the foot, but the edge of this is also uneven. The interior is glazed apart from a band behind the shoulder. The interior is also slipped.

No 110 is a bowl in Fabric 772. It is straight sided with a flaring rim, a rounded foot with chamfered edge and slightly kicked base. Scars left by kiln spacers are present on the underside of the base. The vessel is glazed inside and out but the thickness of coverage is variable; the foot is unglazed.

No 111 in Fabric 39 is a fragment of a chamber pot. It has an everted rim that curves downwards. A rounded raised cordon is present at the shoulder. A thin buff slip is present on the interior and exterior. This is the only example of a mottled ware chamber pot from this pit assemblage but they do occur in other deposits on the site.

231

No 112 in Fabric 774 has been included with the mottled ware vessels because of its similarity to the mugs. Its fabric is unusual and it does not appear to have a mottled glaze. However it had clearly been highly fired and therefore it is difficult to decide whether it belongs to one of the common ware groups in the assemblage. It appears to be the only vessel of its type from the site. It has a hard reduced grey fabric which is an oxidised red under the base. A fine white slip covers the interior and exterior, stopping short of the base on the outside. The glaze appears to be colourless, so the vessel appears a greenish yellow on the slipped areas and a greenish brown on the unslipped. Patches in the slip give the vessel an unevenly coloured appearance.

Slipwares

While slipwares supplied 5% of the assemblage by rim EVEs they were quite fragmentary compared to the other major ware groups. Few of the vessels present had a complete profile and it was uncertain whether the pieces were contemporary with the bulk of the assemblage, although their date range was in keeping with that of the assemblage as a whole. The style of decoration did not appear to be of particularly high quality compared to the unpublished Weaver Street assemblage, where a number of pieces with particularly finely executed feather decoration were present. Buckley and Staffordshire were the potential sources for these wares but for most of the examples further comparative work would be required to identify the precise source.

Table 5.5.33 Phase VII Plot 4 pit (1696): Slipwares quantified by ware, form, EVEs, no of sherds and weight

Ware	Form	EVEs rim	EVEs base	No	Wt (g)
Slipware	unidentified	0	0	1	4
Slipware	Cup	0	0	1	16
Slipware - moulded	Dish	0	0	1	16
Slipware - moulded	Dish?	0	0	1	25
Slipware combed	Unidentified	0	0	1	9
Slipware combed	Dish	103	0	14	321
Slipware feathered	Cup	0	0	1	20
Slipware feathered	Jug?	0	0	1	26
Slipware trailed	Unidentified	0	0	1	12
Slipware trailed	Candlestick	83	45	1	178
Slipware trailed	Cup?	0	0	1	2
Slipware trailed	Dish	0	0	21	1076
Slipware?	Unidentified	0	0	2	19

Candlestick no 113 was made in a white-bodied fabric with a clear colourless glaze. It is decorated with red slip dots around the rim, red slip dashes along the handle and around the edge of the lower drip tray. It had possibly been made in two pieces, with an upper cylinder attached to a conical shaped lower pedestal, the underside of which had been heavily trimmed with a blade. A similar candlestick was found amongst a late seventeenth- to early eighteenth-century assemblage recovered during a watching brief at Weaver Street, Chester, in 1994 (unpublished).

No 114 is a press-moulded combed slipware dish. The scalloped rim has indented lines within the scallop marks, possibly from the ornamentation of a shell used to make the dents. The centre of the dish has a recessed well. The underside of the rim is soot blackened around approximately 50% of its area.

No 115 is another press-moulded combed slipware dish, with a raised cordon just below the rim and another in the

form of a circle framing the centre of the base. There is a slight trace of soot on the underside of the rim.

No 116 is a dish in a pale pink/buff fabric similar to a yellow ware fabric. A thin red slip covered the interior and a trailed wavy line of white slip decorated the rim flange. Vessels such as these appear to have been common in assemblages of the second half of the seventeenth century in Chester. The vessel is in poor condition relative to the rest of the assemblage. It is almost complete although smashed, but the pieces are more abraded than others in the collection and the broken edges and surface are coated in cess.

No 117 is a cup with a buff body covered on the exterior by a dark red slip over which had been trailed pairs of vertical lines alternating with vertical lines of dots. The style of decoration and form resemble cups produced in Staffordshire (*see* Mountford 1975, 16–17), which is more likely to have been the source than Buckley.

No 118 is the remains of a dish in a pink-bodied slipware. There is no slip coating over the interior, which appears a pale brown. A dark red and white slip floral design was trailed over the centre of the dish.

Early English stonewares

A group of buff bodied salt-glazed stonewares provided a number of the mugs in the assemblage. Stonewares were being produced in London, Staffordshire and the midlands from the late seventeenth century and it is difficult to distinguish wares from the different sources. Given the presence of potential London tin-glazed wares in the pit it is possible that the stonewares may also have originated there. It was not possible to examine any of the kiln material from the London stoneware potteries but material from Burslem was made available at the Potteries Museum at Stoke-on-Trent. Groups of early eighteenth-century stonewares from Swan Bank, Town Road and the Burslem Relief Road were compared to the mugs and cup from (1696). Most have a pale fabric and are finely thrown. Forms include mugs or tankards, jugs and 'capuchin' style cups as below. Vessels include those with a white slipped dipped lower body and brown upper body, as well as those with a smooth brown finish. A vessel similar in form to no 119 without a brown freckled wash on the upper body is also present. The stonewares from Burslem, especially those from the Relief Road, compared closely with the assemblage from (1696) and the town can be considered as a source for vessels found at Chester, although further comparative work with production assemblages from elsewhere is required to firmly identify a provenance.

Table 5.5.34 Phase VII Plot 4 pit (1696): Early English stonewares quantified by form, EVEs, no of sherds and weight

Form	EVEs rim	EVEs base	No	Wt (g)
Unidentified	0	0	4	15
Cup	0	30	1	24
Mug	160	300	29	1014

No 119 is a cylindrical vessel but, like no 120, the rim is slightly inverted. The vessel walls appear to be plain except for an incised line 3 mm below the rim. Unlike other vessels in the group this mug is pale coloured. A white slip is present on the lower part of the exterior and over the entire interior.

The slightly inverted rim of no 120 gives a barrel-shaped profile to the upper part of this mug. The upper part of the vessel has a band of moulding consisting of three narrow cordons or ribs either side of a wider raised cordon. Four cordons sit above a rounded foot. The base is slightly kicked and the edge is worn. Part of an 'AR' ale-measure mark remains on the upper band. The interior is a patchy pale brown, possibly caused by a wash. The exterior has a dark brown wash covering approximately three-quarters of the vessel; the lower quarter is a paler brown, similar to the interior. The fabric is similar to no 121 but more buff in colour.

Mug no 121 has a wide upper band of ribbing, in a similar style to the mottled wares, consisting of eighteen narrow horizontal ribs. The upper handle join is set over the first to twelfth ribs. Above the base there are six wider ribs. The handle is ribbed in profile and springs up high at the upper join before turning downwards. A brown wash is present under the glaze on the interior and over the upper half of the exterior and the upper three-quarters of the handle. A white slip is apparent on the lower half of the exterior. The fabric is a pale buff varying to a darker yellowish pink. Concentric wire marks are present under the base.

No 122 is the base of a large mug. A thick white slip covers the lower part of the vessel below the lower handle–body join but the remains of the upper body have a brown wash. A band of ribbing is present above the base. The remains of an 'AR' ale-measure mark survives on the body.

No 123 is the lower part of a wide-bodied vessel which has a squat rounded body below a wide flaring neck. The base of the neck is marked by a band of ribbing.

Nottingham-type stoneware

This type of stoneware has a fine buff fabric and appears lower fired than the stonewares above. It has a smooth glossy orange brown glaze; a distinctive white margin is present between the glaze and the clay fabric on both the interior and exterior. These wares were produced from the last decade of the seventeenth century in Nottingham and also in Derbyshire (Jennings 1981, 219).

Table 5.5.35 Phase VII Plot 4 pit (1696): Nottingham-type stoneware quantified by form, EVEs, no of sherds and weight

Form	EVEs rim	EVEs base	No	Wt (g)
Unidentified	0	0	2	63
Jug	20	100	2	260

No 124 is a jug with a simple upright rim that leans slightly inwards. A wide band of ribbing covers the upper part of the body and there is a narrower, similar band above the base. The handle is missing but the base survives, suggesting that it was at a right-angle to the pulled lip. This is the best preserved example of this ware surviving in the assemblage; the other examples are just fragments.

Tin-glazed wares

One hundred and sixty-four fragments (3924 g) of tin-glazed ware were found in the pit and provided 18% of the assemblage by sherd count (11% by weight) but 33% by rim EVEs. The majority of the wares are plain, ie they have an undecorated white tin glaze. Generally, where vessels are decorated they are generally painted in shades of blue or blue and purple with occasional black high-lighting/outlining.

Table 5.5.36 Phase VII Plot 4 pit (1696): Tin-glazed ware quantified by form, EVEs, no of sherds and weight

Form	EVEs rim	EVEs base	No	Wt (g)
Unidentified	0	0	8	40
Bowl	280	153	30	1278
Bowl - handled	327	250	39	819
Bowl - handled?	42	0	3	63
Bowl?	0	0	10	62
Chamber pot	80	13	12	220
Chamber pot?	0	15	1	17
Cup	63	0	6	35
Dish	5	0	8	132
Dish - lobed	69	25	9	393
Jar	91	66	31	602
Jar-mini	200	200	2	181
Mug	0	41	3	43
Plate	6	16	1	38
Saucer	0	0	1	1

Forms

Bowls, including the small handled bowls or porringers as they are better known, formed the largest component of the ware assemblage. Cylindrical storage jars of various sizes were the next most common, followed by dishes and chamber pots. Drinking vessels, whilst not a major component, were represented by the remains of a mug and a small decorated cup; the latter could be viewed functionally alongside the Chinese porcelain particularly as it was decorated in a Chinese style.

The chamber pots, porringers, some of the bowls, small jars and an impressive large lobed dish were undecorated and had a white tin-glaze on the interior and exterior surfaces. The larger vessels were particularly well glazed, whilst the small jars, or ointment pots as they are also known, tended to have thinner poorer-quality glazes.

It is remarkable that the Anderton inventory specifically mentions whitewares as being present in the 'dineing roome' and they were listed with glasses 'whiteware and glasses' (WS1693). Although it did not stipulate of what material these whitewares were made or the types of vessels, no other possible ceramic vessels appear to be listed. It is therefore possible, given the substantial number of plain white tin-glazed ware vessels, that the entry referred to these ceramics. A London inventory of 1664 for the house of Sir Kenelm Digby specifically listed 'white earthen ware' which was itemised as:

In: 12: white scollop fruite dyshes & basons, and 1: scollop bason & Ewer, 3: plaine creame dishes, 1 callender, 1: sillybub pott and another white pott with couers; 5: plates, 1: large plaine bason and with couers, 5: plates, 1: large plaine bason and Eure, 5: white chamber potts, 1: (harbinger) bason, 3: other plaine basons, 4: floure potts. (Stevenson & Davidson eds 1997)

The chamberpots, 'scollop' dish, plate, 'basons' could all be paralleled in the present assemblage. Whilst some plain wares were quite utilitarian vessels, others, such as the lobed or 'scollop' dish, were impressive objects and plain vessels appear to have been selected over decorated. A similar assemblage of plain vessels, including another lobed dish along with a posset pot and salt and other vessels, was found amongst a similarly dated assemblage during a watching brief in Weaver Street, Chester in 1994 (unpublished). Some of the vessels such as the lobed dish and porringers were similar to vessels produced in pewter or silver, and it is possible that the plain glaze served as an imitation of metal vessels.

The decorated wares are mainly painted in blue on a white background, but purple and black was used on some vessels. Chinese-inspired floral and abstract designs were popular, but abstract and pictorial scenes are also present. A small number have pale blue grounds as a base for designs executed in a darker blue, with black being used mainly for outlining. A particularly elaborate example of this is no 132, a relatively large vessel which appears to have a repeating pattern of a bunch of grapes interspersed with foliage and Chinese-inspired flourishes. A small tulip shaped cup, no 137, was painted in similar colours and includes similar Chinese-style abstract motifs.

Five decorated bowls are present. Two in particular stand out: one, no 130, is almost complete and has a ship or yacht in the centre painted in manganese purple and blue on a pale blue ground; an abstract foliage/floral border is present just below the rim. The other, no 128, has the central design missing but has a radiating pattern around the walls.

A small fragment of a porringer, no 134, is decorated in a manner that was rarely found in Chester. Instead of a blue on white decoration it is covered on both surfaces with a dark blue tin glaze onto which white spots had been painted. This style was known as 'bleu persan', a style dated in London to the late seventeenth and early eighteenth century (Orton 1988, 315). A fragment of a lobed dish decorated in the same style was found as a residual fragment in (1096).

As with the plain wares, the quality of decoration and glazing varies. Whilst some of the fragments have finely painted designs, a large cylindrical jar, no 145, has a pale blue cable and line decoration which appears to have been roughly painted without any regard to finish or neatness.

The majority of the vessels are types which by form and decoration can be dated to the second half of the seventeenth and early eighteenth century, but some earlier fragments are present, and their condition suggests that they were residual in the deposit. These ranged in date from the late sixteenth to the mid-seventeenth century and included a mottled manganese purple mug or jug, a waisted jar, a dish and a jug or mug with a trailing foliage design (none are illustrated).

It is difficult to be precise about where these wares were made. London was a major producer of tin-glazed wares in the seventeenth and eighteenth centuries. Production began in Bristol *c* 1650 and in Liverpool and Dublin in the early eighteenth century. London and Bristol are therefore the most likely sources for the vessels in this assemblage. Most attributions to Bristol are made on stylistic grounds, but it has been difficult to find any clear parallels for any of the more decorative designs. The forms, however, were all types that were being produced in London during this period and can be paralleled in waste dumps associated with potteries in Lambeth and Southwark on the south bank of the Thames, for example assemblages at Norfolk House (Bloice 1971) and Mark Brown Wharf (Orton 1988, 307–35).

Bowls: Bowl no 125 is a relatively thin-walled vessel with an everted and slightly downturned rim. The walls curve down to the base, which has a wide square footring that is heavily worn. Inside the base are two trivet marks. The glaze is plain with a slightly blue-grey tinge and covers the vessel well. The vessel was reconstructed from two contexts in the pit and sherds from Phase VIII; the pieces from pit context (1601) are discoloured.

No 126 is a bowl with curving walls and an everted rim which was turned down, giving a hook-shaped profile. The glaze is plain and there is no discoloration as on no 125. A peg mark is present on the reverse of the rim.

Bowl no 127 has an everted narrow rim pushed down to make a slightly hooked profile above a rounded body. The vessel is well glazed on both surfaces. The inside of the base is decorated, the only colour visible being blue. The design is unclear but the remains of a possible church spire are visible, and a powdered blue area which may have been part of a tree. A double line border frames the decorated area.

No 128 is a bowl with a flaring everted rim above rounded walls which thicken towards the base. The vessel is well glazed on both surfaces and is decorated in blue. The central circular zone is missing. The walls are decorated with a series of pyriforms constructed of vertical lines which radiate from the central zone. A seven-pointed star was placed between the points of each of the pyriforms. A wide band of blue decorates the rim bordered by a single line on the exterior and double lines on the interior.

No 129 is the remains of a bowl or shallow dish, decorated in blue.

No 130 is a bowl with an everted hook-shaped rim. The vessel is well glazed on both surfaces. A central design of a yacht or ship was painted in manganese purple and blue onto a pale blue ground. The upper part of the vessel has a border of foliage type patterns.

Bowl no 131 has a narrow everted rim pushed down into a wide hook. It has a blue-tinged glaze with a border of blue decoration just below the rim. The design consists of linked lozenges overpainted with simplified inverted pyriforms made of two horizontal brush strokes. Narrow lines border the motif band.

No 132 consists of twelve fragments that appear to be decorated with a repeating pattern of large bunches of grapes interspersed with stems, leaves and oriental style flourishes. The design was painted in shades of blue with black detailing on a pale blue ground. Two roughly painted lines encircle the base area. The form is incomplete and was initially identified as a rounded bowl with a relatively wide everted rim that curves outwards before turning up to meet the horizontal. A single kiln scar is present underneath the rim. The fragments probably formed part of the lid or cover from a punch bowl or large elaborate posset; the grape motif would have been in keeping with this function. However, no fragments were found that would have formed the lower part of such a vessel.

Handled bowls/Porringers: These were small bowls that may have had one or two handles, although at this period single handles were more common. The handles were flat and attached horizontally just below the rim. They were usually lobed around the edge and perforated, often with heart or circular shapes. The majority of the porringers in this assemblage have convex walls with narrow everted rims, a characteristic of the late seventeenth and early eighteenth centuries. Early vessels tend to have simple vertical rims. None of the vessels in this assemblage are decorated. They are thought to have been used for eating soft foods.

No 133 has convex walls with a simple narrow, everted rim. The single handle has five lobes and a heart-shaped perforation. The base has a narrow turned footring which is slightly worn. The glaze is plain and has a pink tinge in places. The underside of the footring is unglazed.

No 134 also has convex walls and a narrow everted simple rim. The vessel is covered on both surfaces with a dark blue glaze onto which white spots had been painted; this type of decoration is known as 'bleu persan' (*see* above). The glaze on the interior has been damaged, perhaps by burning.

No 135 is a relatively wide shallow form with convex walls an everted rim and a narrow turned footring. There appears to have been only one handle, which is missing. The base of the footring is worn. A plain white glaze which is thicker on the upper parts of the body covers the interior and exterior; the glaze is tinged pink on the thinner areas. Fragments of clay are stuck in the glaze around the footring.

No 136 has a convex body with an everted rim and a five-lobed handle with a central circular perforation. The handle is not symmetrical within itself. The plain white glaze has a pink tinge, especially where it is thinnest.

Drinking vessels: No 137 is a tulip-shaped cup. The vessel is decorated in an oriental style painted in black and dark blue on a pale blue ground. Cups of this shape have been described as capuchines and were probably used for drinking coffee or chocolate in the late seventeenth and early eighteenth century (Archer 1997, 349, H2).

No 138 is the base of a cylindrical mug with moulding/horizontal ribbing between the base of the handle and the base edge, similar in fashion to mottled mugs. The glaze is thin and glossy with a mottled blue band above the foot.

Chamberpots: Two styles of chamber pot were present: one type had everted rims and the other rolled. All are undecorated.

No 139 has a rolled rim, an indentation at the shoulder and a rounded body. The strap handle is attached to the lower side of the outer edge of the rim. At the join with the body the sides of the handle are pinched inwards before flaring outwards. The glaze has a pale blue tinge.

No 140 has an everted slightly flattened rim, a shoulder cordon and a pear-shaped body. The strap handle is joined to the underside of the rim and is kicked up at its base, which is formed into an unusual crescent shape. The glaze is in a poor condition on all the sherds.

Dishes: Dish no 141 has a smooth kicked base. The wall consists of two moulded rows of lobes: the inner are narrow and concave; the outer wider and convex, terminating in a scallop-edged rim. The plain glaze appears to be of good quality but it has slightly crawled away from the underside of some sections of the rim edge. A scar from a peg used to support the dish in the kiln is present underneath the rim. There is wear on the reverse of the lobes surrounding the base. The dish appears to be imitating the gadrooning found on silver and pewter ware dishes. A similar dish was found in a late seventeenth- to early eighteenth-century group from a watching brief at Weaver Street, Chester, in 1994 (unpublished).

Plate: No 142 is the only example of a plate. It has a flat base with convex walls which turn down into an interior central wall. The plain glaze covers the vessel thickly and evenly; it has a blue-grey tinge.

Jars: No 143 is a complete plain glazed small storage jar with straight sides. Its shape is typical of the form often known as a drug jar. The rim is slightly squashed to an oval shape. The base is kicked and has a comma-shaped mark from when it was removed from the wheel. No 144 is a more squat shaped example, also with a plain glaze.

No 145 is a drum-shaped or squat jar with blue decoration. The vessel has a simple everted rim, a foot trimmed to the vertical and a slightly kicked base. The white glaze is tinged with pink. A blue cable pattern decorates the middle of the vessel and is bordered by bands of blue. The painting was loosely executed and is untidy in places with frequent smudging of the blue.

In comparison to the other tin-glazed ware vessels in the assemblage this vessel is in a poor condition. The broken edges are quite abraded and the glaze has lost its surface gloss. The fabric is soft and the unglazed rim is quite worn, as is the edge of the base.

Chinese porcelain

Table 5.5.37 Phase VII Plot 4 pit (1696): Chinese porcelain quantified by form, EVEs, no of sherds and weight

Form	EVEs rim	EVEs base	No	Wt (g)
Cup	82	193	23	88
Plate	0	0	1	5

Twenty-four fragments of Chinese export porcelain were retrieved from the pit. They appeared to represent four different vessels: three drinking vessels and a plate. Two of the drinking vessels could be partially reconstructed, whereas there were only single fragments of the plate and a third drinking vessel, a tea bowl. The drinking vessels were comparable with the late seventeenth- or early eighteenth-century date of the pit; the plate may be earlier but the piece was too small to identify firmly.

No 146 is the base of a tall cup with a high footring. The surviving decoration was painted in underglaze blue on the exterior and consists of a low table with what appear to be decorated vessels. Under the base is a flower, also in underglaze blue. No 147 may be part of the same vessel.

No 147 consists of two rim fragments from a cup or tea bowl decorated in underglaze blue. A spray of flowers was painted on the exterior and on the interior a hatched band is present around the rim above a floral/foliage spray.

No 148 is a tall eight-sided cup with flaring sides and a footring. The decoration is divided into four panels outlined in red; each panel covered two sides of the cup. The panel is filled by a flowering shrub design painted in over-glaze enamel colours, red and two shades of green with black outlining. Some of the painted detail has worn

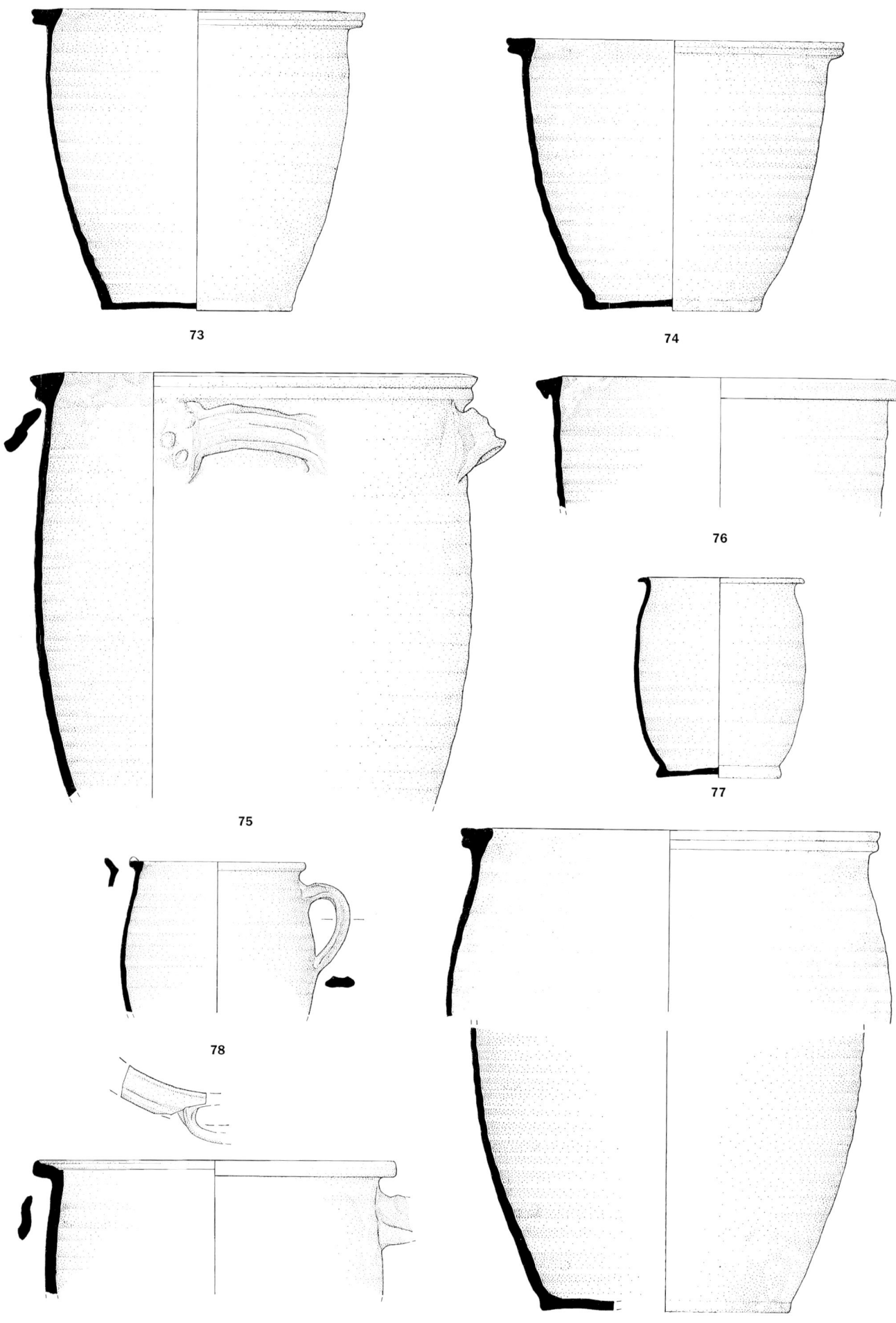

73

74

75

76

77

78

79

80

III 5.5.19 Phase VII Plot 4 pit (1696): Blackwares 73–80. (Scale 1/4)

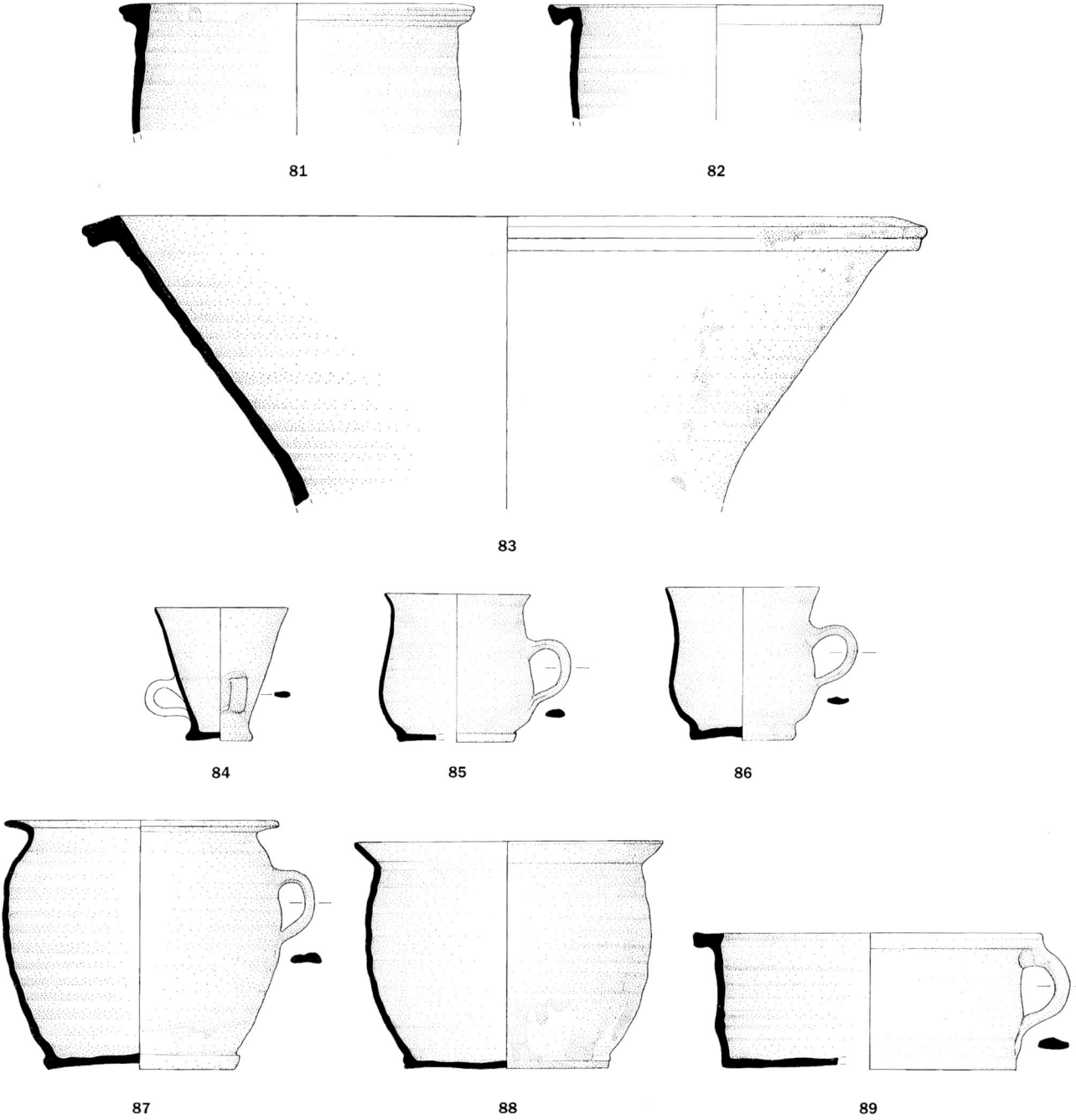

Ill 5.5.20 Phase VII Plot 4 pit (1696): Blackwares 81–9. (Scale 1/4)

away, leaving only a ghost of the design visible. Inside the base a single red flower surrounded by green leaves has been painted. Underneath the base a flower motif enclosed by a double circle was painted in underglaze blue.

Catalogue
Blackwares (Ills 5.5.19–.20)
73 Jar; Fabric 24/33. (1599), (1601), (1607), (455); SF 10163.
74 Jar; Fabric 24/33. (1599), (1601); SF 10164.
75 Jar; Fabric 24/33. (1601); SF 10176.
76 Jar; Fabric 24/33. (1601); SF 10287.
77 Jar; Fabric 24/33. (1599), (1601); SF 10160.
78 Jar; Fabric 24/33. (1601); SF 10177.
79 Jar; Fabric 775. (1599), (1601); SF 10175 & SF 10178.

80 Jar; Fabric 121. (1599); SF 10173.
81 Jar; Fabric 121. (1599), (1607); SF 10286.
82 Jar; Fabric 121. (1601); SF 10288.
83 Bowl; Fabric 38. (1599); (1601); SF 10174.
84 Cup; Fabric 789. (1601), (1604); SF 10052.
85 Cup; Fabric 790. (1599), (1601); SF 10159.
86 Cup; Fabric 789. (1601); SF 10157.
87 Chamberpot; Fabric 776. (1601), (1604), (1546); SF 10050.
88 Chamberpot; Fabric 24/33. (1601); SF 10161.
89 Chamberpot; Fabric 24/33. (1601); SF 10162.

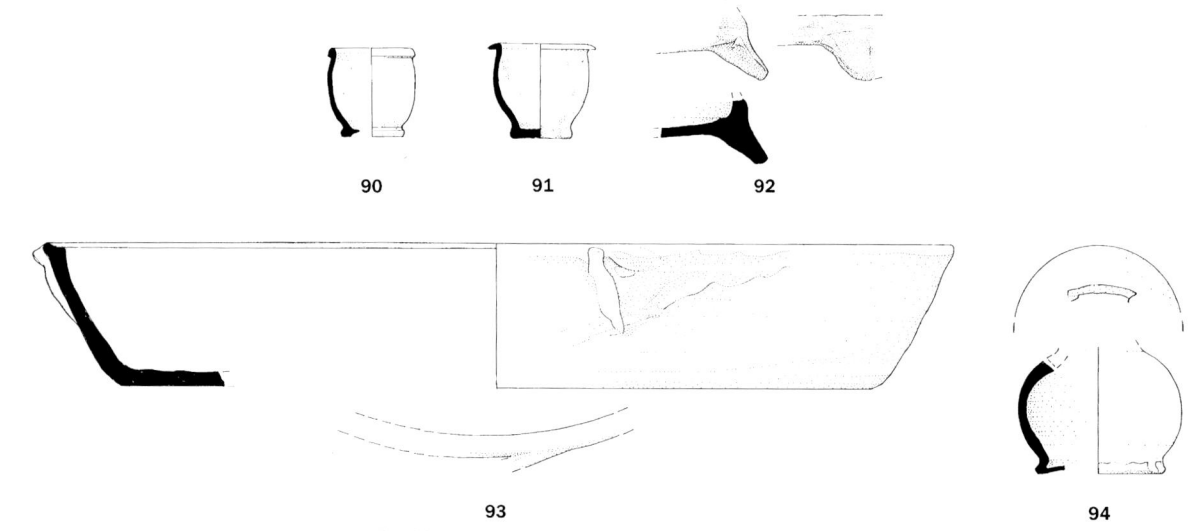

III 5.5.21 Phase VII Plot 4 pit (1696): Yellow wares. (Scale 1/4)

Yellow wares (Ill 5.5.21)
90 Jar; Fabric 786. (1601); SF 10185.
91 Jar; Fabric 786. (1601); SF 10183.
92 Pipkin foot; Fabric 786. (1607); SF 10186.
93 Oval dish; Fabric 50. (1601); SF 10184.
94 Money box; Fabric 50. (1604); SF 8698.

Mottled wares (Ill 5.5.22)
95 Mug; Fabric 39. (455), (1599), (1601); SF 9883.
96 Mug; Fabric 39. (1601); SF 9895.
97 Mug; Fabric 39. (1601); SF 9896.
98 Mug; Fabric 772. (1599), (1601), (1607); SF 10005.
99 Mug; Fabric 772. (1599), (1601), (1607); SF 10114.
100 Mug; Fabric 39. (1607), (1599); SF 10023 & SF 10027.
101 Mug; Fabric 39. (1607), (1695); SF 10026.
102 Mug; Fabric 39. (1599), (1601); SF 10030.
103 Dish; Fabric 772. (1599); SF 10022.
104 Cup; Fabric 772. (1599); SF 10024.
105 Cup; Fabric 39. (1599); SF 10025.
106 Cup; Fabric 772. (1607); SF 10028.
107 Cup; Fabric 39. (1599), (1601), (1604), (1360); SF 10031.
108 Jug; Fabric 773. (1601); SF 9894.
109 Jug; Fabric 772. (1601); SF 10032.
110 Bowl; Fabric 772. (1601); SF 9999.
111 Chamber pot; Fabric 39. (1601); SF 10116.
112 Mug; Fabric 774. (1604), (455), (1546); SF 10117.

Slipwares (Ill 5.5.23)
113 Candlestick. (1607); SF 9998.
114 Dish. (1599), (1601); SF 10123.
115 Dish. (1599), (1601), (1604), (1546); SF 10122.
116 Dish. (1599), (1601); SF 10197.
117 Dish. (1604), (1546); SF 10192.
118 Dish. (1601); SF 10305.

Early English stoneware (Ill 5.5.24)
119 Mug. (1601), (1546); SF 10118.
120 Mug. (1599), (1601), (455); SF 10120.
121 Mug. (1601), (1599); SF 10121.
122 Mug. (1599); SF 10179.
123 Cup. (1601); SF 10180.

Nottingham-type stoneware (Ill 5.5.24)
124 Jug. (1604), (1546); SF 10151.

Tin-glazed wares (Ill 5.5.25 and .27–8)
125 Bowl. (1599), (1601), (455); SF 10083.
126 Bowl. (1599), (1601); SF 10084.
127 Bowl. (1601); SF 10089.
128 Bowl. (1604), (455); SF 10094.
129 Bowl or dish. (1599), (1601), (1607); SF 10096.
130 Bowl. (1599), (1601); SF 10087.
131 Bowl. (1601), (1604); SF 10107.
132 Bowl or punch bowl lid. (1601), (1604), (455), (1360), (1399), (1592), (U/S); SF 10337.
133 Handled bowl/porringer. (1599), (1601); SF 10091.
134 Handled bowl/porringer. (1607); SF 10095.
135 Handled bowl/porringer. (1599), (455); SF 10101.
136 Handled bowl/porringer. (1601); SF 10085.
137 Cup. (1601); SF 10088.
138 Mug. (1601); SF 10090.
139 Chamberpot. (1599), (1601), (455), (1546); SF 10100.
140 Chamberpot. (1592), (455), *cf* (1607), (1601); SF 10102.
141 Dish. (1599), (1601), (1607); SF 10092.
142 Plate. (1607); SF 10099.
143 Jar. (1607); SF 10097.
144 Jar. (1607); SF 10098.
145 Jar. (1599), (1601), (1604); SF 10093.

Chinese porcelain (Ills 5.5.26 and .29)
146 Cup. (1601); SF 10190.
147 Cup. (1601); SF 10335.
148 Cup. (1599), (1601); SF 10191.

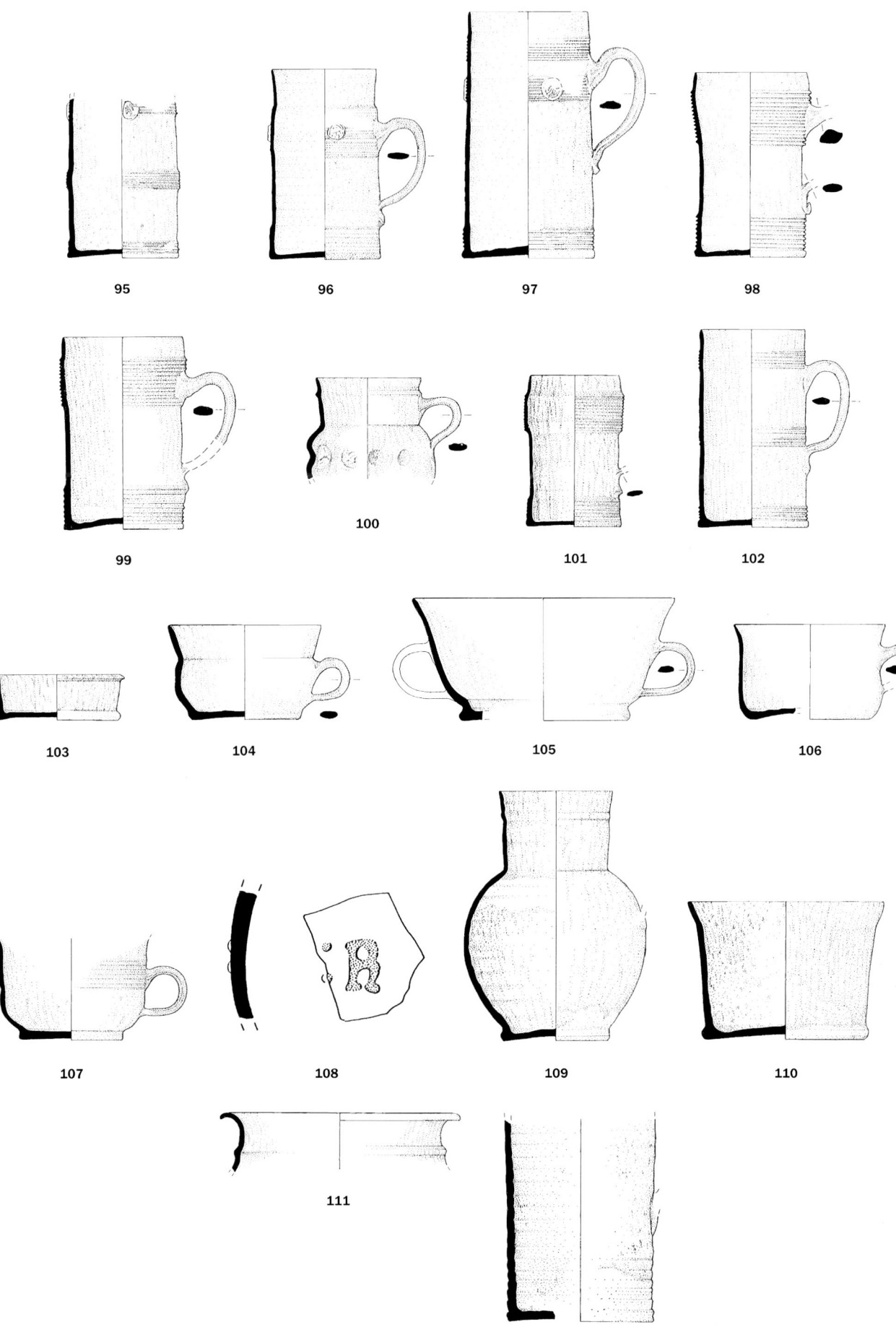

III 5.5.22 Phase VII Plot 4 pit (1696): Mottled wares. (Scale 1/4; no 108 1/2)

239

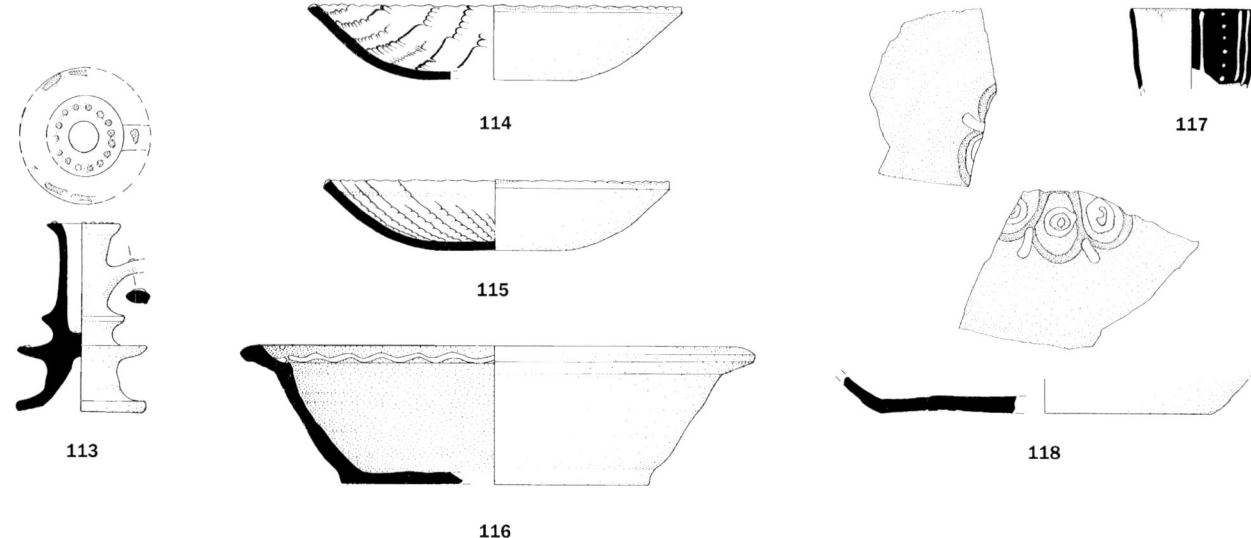

III 5.5.23 Phase VII Plot 4 pit (1696): Slipwares. (Scale 1/4)

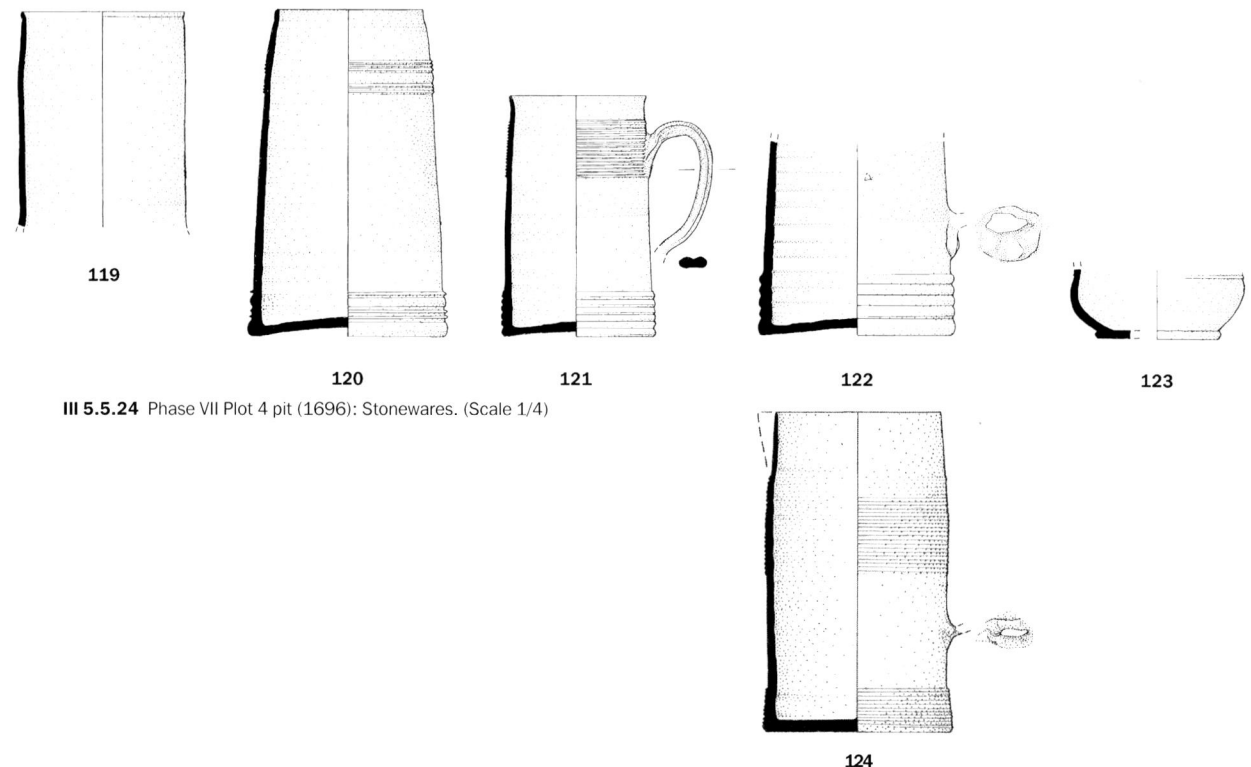

III 5.5.24 Phase VII Plot 4 pit (1696): Stonewares. (Scale 1/4)

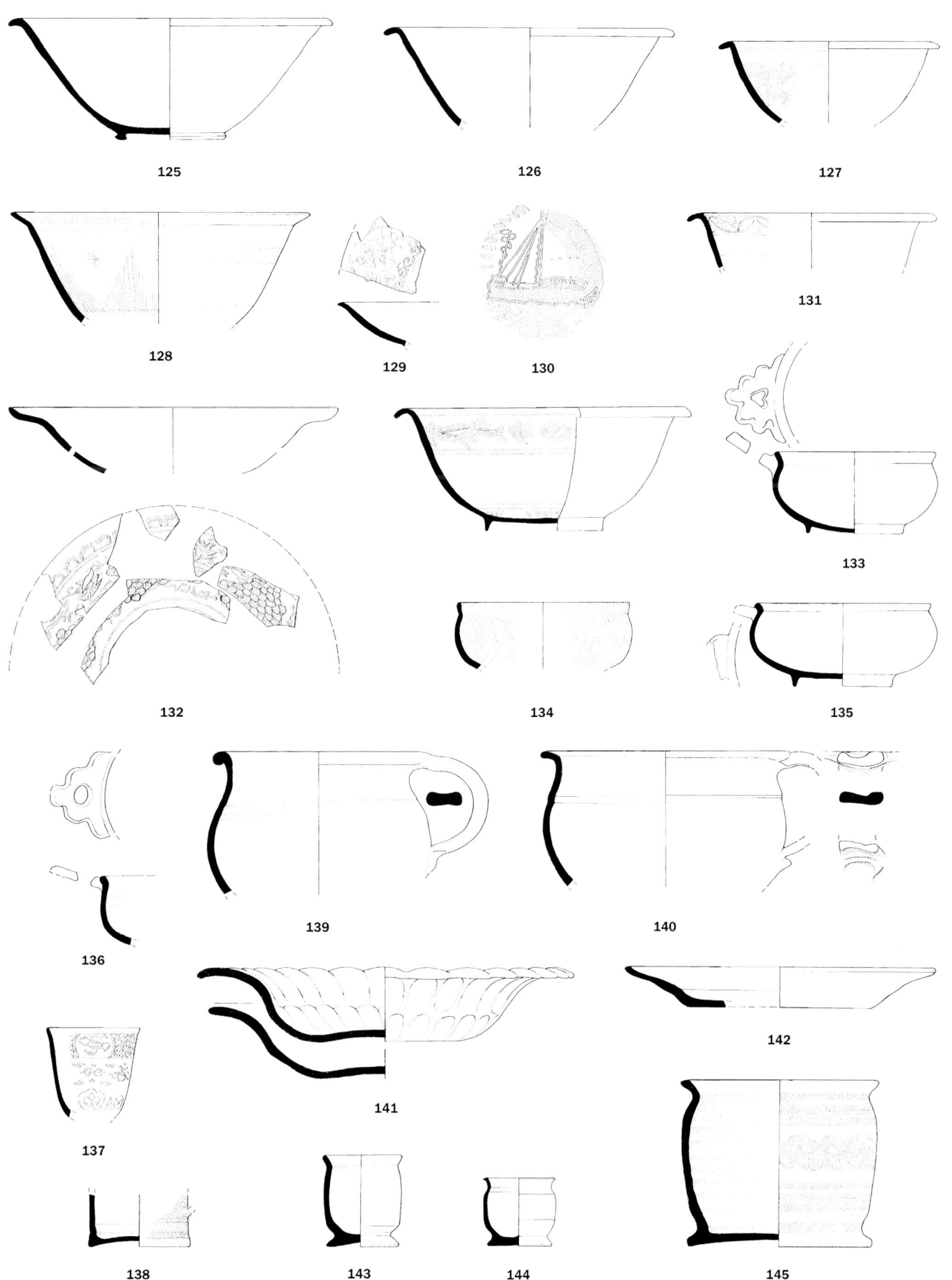

III 5.5.25 Phase VII Plot 4 pit (1696): Tin-glazed wares. (Scale 1/4)

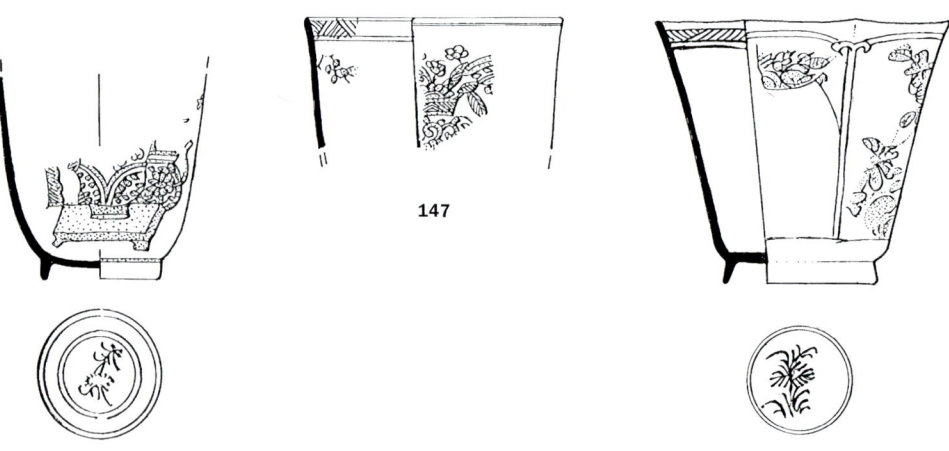

147

146 **III 5.5.26** Phase VII Plot 4 pit (1696): Chinese porcelain. (Scale 1/2) **148**

III 5.5.27 Phase VII Plot 4 pit (1696):
Tin-glazed ware bowl (no 130).

III 5.5.28 Phase VII Plot 4 pit (1696):
Tin-glazed ware cup (no 137).

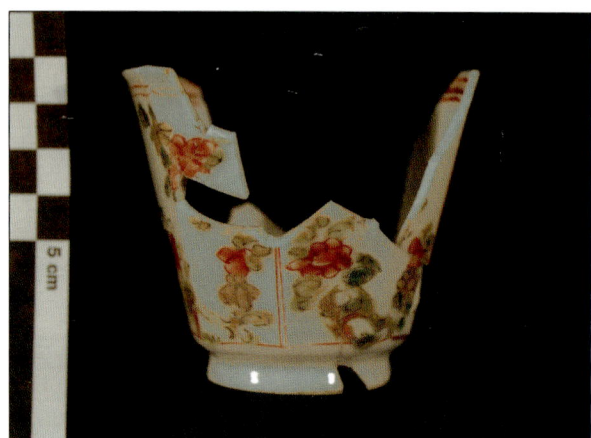

III 5.5.29 Phase VII Plot 4 pit (1696):
Chinese porcelain cup (no 148).

Acknowledgements

Many volunteers made an invaluable contribution to this project, both during the excavation and post-excavation stages. During the post-excavation stage in particular John and Liz Bailey assisted in the basic recording of the pottery and building materials, as well as dealing with the tasks of laying out and putting away material and typing and checking data; David Cartwright, Averil Downs, the late Geoff Rhodes and Rebecca Aspill undertook the laborious task of typing data into the database. Monica Webster assisted in checking the data. Susan Chambers, Liz Bailey and Simon Skelling worked hard in the early stages of the project assembling the discarded building material records into an easily useable order. I am extremely grateful to them all for giving up their time freely. I should also like to acknowledge the staff of Chester and Cheshire Record Office for their help whilst I was researching aspects of sugar refining in Chester.

I am also grateful for the help and advice on individual fragments and vessels from John Allan, Janet Axworthy, David Barker, the late Elizabeth Brotherton-Ratcliffe, Duncan Brown, Dave Evans, Mary Ginsburg, the late John Hurst, Clare McCutcheon, the late Bob Thomson, Alan Vince, Timothy Wilson; any errors in understanding that advice or identification are of course my own.

Clay Tobacco Pipes and Other Pipeclay Objects

David A Higgins

Introduction

The excavations produced a total of 5,570 pieces of pipe, comprising 987 bowl, 4,369 stem and 214 mouthpiece fragments. The pipes were recovered from 306 excavated contexts, in addition to which there is a group of 170 unstratified finds. About one third of the excavated groups, 205 contexts, produced between just one and ten fragments of pipe (Table 5.6.5). There were thirty-seven contexts which produced between eleven and twenty fragments, twenty contexts with between twenty-one and thirty fragments and thirty-five contexts with between thirty-one and one hundred fragments. There were eight contexts which produced large groups of between 101 and 200 fragments and one exceptionally large group ((1507): Phase VII, Plot 4) which produced 741 pieces of pipe. The larger the group of pipes, the more reliable the dating and interpretation of those fragments is likely to be. The site produced just over 100 context groups containing ten or more fragments of pipe, which provide a good basis for dating the post-medieval deposits on the site. Furthermore, the assemblage as a whole is exceptionally large, being by far the largest domestic assemblage that has been studied in detail from anywhere in the north-west and is one of the largest assemblages of its type from anywhere in the country.

In the report that follows, the pipes themselves are considered and presented first. This section examines the overall range of pipes present and provides a detailed discussion of various aspects of the assemblage, such as the bowl forms, makers' stamps and manufacturing techniques. The most significant context groups are described and illustrations provided of the significant bowl forms and marks. The report concludes with a short section considering the pipes as archaeological evidence and, finally, reports on the hair curlers and marbles from the excavations.

Methodology

All of the fragments were individually examined and details logged on an Excel worksheet based on a draft clay tobacco pipe recording system developed at the University of Liverpool (Higgins & Davey 1994). A summary, also prepared as a similar Excel worksheet, gives the overall numbers of fragments and date range for the pipes from each context; this is included below as Table 5.6.5. Digital copies of both the worksheet and the draft recording system have been provided for the site archive.

Several of the context groups contained more than one similar pipe bowl or marked stem which did not have a Small Find number. In order to identify the individual fragments, capital letters have been allocated to these pieces so that they can be cross-referred to the computerised record (A, B, C, … AA, AB, AC, etc). These letter codes have been pencilled onto the bowls following the context number. They appear under a reference column in the full catalogue as well as in the captions accompanying the figures. An assessment of the likely date of the stem fragments has also been provided in the catalogue. The stem dates should, however, be used with caution since they are much more general and less reliable than the dates that can be determined from bowl fragments.

A large number of stamped makers' marks or decorative borders were present within the excavated material. Some of these marks have been added to the national catalogue of clay tobacco pipe stamps which is being compiled by the author. Any die numbers quoted in this report refer to the unique die numbers which have been allocated within this catalogue.

A few pieces of pipe were cleaned of iron staining in a chemical solution of EDTA using the technique established for a group of pipes from Leicester (Higgins 1999). Cleaning was used for the fragments making up two complete pipes and for one or two decorated stems where encrustation and/or discoloration obscured the design. The cleaning process proved to be extremely effective, leaving blackening from smoking unaffected and site numbering intact, unless it had been applied over surface encrustation. Some site numbers were manually scrubbed off to allow the reconstructed pipes to be relabelled on one side, leaving the other clear for display purposes.

As a result of the cleaning one important observation was made. The fragments of the complete pipe from context (1503) were cleaned, leaving them looking fresh and white. In contrast, the remaining fragments from this group appeared off-white to pale buff in colour. The cleaning has shown that this coloration is due to an overall tint caused by general iron-staining from the ground and that it is not a true reflection of the original colour of the pipes themselves. This is significant in showing that colour descriptions of excavated fragments may well be unreliable, particularly for seventeenth- and eighteenth-century examples, which tend to have quite open and porous fabrics. These porous fabrics are likely to be very susceptible to iron-staining from burial, making fabric colour descriptions virtually meaningless unless the pipes have been freshly broken or chemically cleaned (any original coloration of the fabric from iron in the source material would be fixed in the fabric during firing and so should be unaltered by the subsequent chemical cleaning). Many previous publications of early pipes include colour descriptions and so these should now be used with caution, since they may merely reflect the burial conditions of the fragments rather than the actual clay types that were being exploited by the pipemakers.

Clay tobacco pipes

The pipe marks

The makers' marks and decorative stamps found on pipes provide one of the best means of dating them and tracing them to a particular source or manufacturer. Chester is fortunate in that a wide variety of different stamped marks are found in the city. During the 1970s a survey of the available evidence produced an extensive corpus of the various types then known from Chester (Rutter & Davey 1980). Comparison of the Bridge Street finds with this corpus has shown that many previously unrecorded marks

Table 5.6.1 Clay tobacco pipe bowl marks dating from c 1610 to 1660: summary showing their position (S = across the stem of the pipe; H = on the base of the heel; B = on the bowl facing the smoker), primary motif, the number of examples, the overall date range for the examples present, their likely place of origin and the figure numbers for any illustrated examples.

Position	Mark	No	Date	Origin	Ills
S	Snowflake	1	1610–1640	Uncertain, possibly Chester	2, 121
S	*Fleur de lis*	1	1610–1660	Probably Chester	3
H	Incuse 'star'	1	1620–1650	Uncertain	4, 110
H	Cross and dots	1	1610–1650	Uncertain	5, 111
H	Wheel with dots	6	1610–1660	Chester (? and/or London)	6, 109, 112
H	Crossed keys	1	1610–1650	Possibly Chester) (if not, Dutch	113
H	Running animal (? fox)	1	1640–1660	Chester	
B	GA	1	1640–1660	South Lancashire	7, 145
H	TB (probably)	1	1640–1660	Uncertain	8
H	NE	3	1610–1660	Chester	9–11, 124–6
H	EG	1	1640–1660	Chester	
H	IG	1	1610–1640	Uncertain	12, 127
H	RG	1	1640–1660	Probably Nantwich	13, 139
H	WK	1	1610–1640	Probably London	14, 108
S	AL	1	1640–1670	Chester	15
H	AL	8	1610–1660	Chester	
B	GL	1	1640–1660	Rainford	
H	HL	1	1640–1660	Probably Rainford	16, 138
H	IL	2	1610–1640	?West midlands	17, 114
H	PL	1	1630–1660	Probably Rainford	
H	M	2	1610–1640	West midlands	18, 115–16
H	AP	1	1630–1660	?London	19, 120
H	NT	1	1640–1660	Chester	
H	Illegible	3	1610–1660	Probably local (NW) types	

are represented, the majority of which are here illustrated at twice life size (Ills 5.6.1–.3, nos 1–57). In the following sections, the marked pipes from the site are considered by period and by type.

Late sixteenth and early seventeenth-century marks

This site is notable in that it produced a number of the earliest pipe forms, datable to *c* 1580–1610, which are very rare nationally, even as isolated examples. At least six bowl fragments and one stem dating from this period were identified, but only one of these pieces was marked. The marked piece is a bowl with part of the stem surviving, which has been decorated with a series of small lozenge-shaped marks containing a 'snowflake' design (Ills 5.6.1.1 and 5.6.6.92). Decoration of this type has most commonly been recorded from London and so it is usually presumed that these pipes were produced there. Almost identical decorative stem stamps, however, were also being used in Jamestown, Virginia, about 1608–10, where they can be attributed to Robert Cotton, a pipemaker who settled there in 1608. This not only provides a good date when this style of decoration was certainly in use, but also shows how easily London styles could be transmitted by pipemakers moving to set up in other centres. Although the Chester example is most likely to be a London import, the possibility of early pipemakers bringing this style to Chester cannot be entirely ruled out.

Early to mid-seventeenth-century marks

Excluding a large dump of spur bowls from (1507) which probably represent kiln waste, the excavations produced the remains of some 300 pipe bowls that are likely to have been produced between around 1610 and 1660. Amongst these were forty-two fragments with stamped marks on them, comprising thirty-seven heel stamps, of which thirty-four were identifiable, two bowl stamps and three pieces with stem stamps. This shows that, in broad terms, around 14% of the pipes in use at Chester during

this period were marked. The thirty-seven identifiable heel stamps can be further subdivided into two groups, the symbol marks (ten examples) and the initial marks (twenty-five examples), showing that initial marks were two and a half times as common as symbol ones during this period (Table 5.6.1).

Early symbol stamps

The most common type of symbol mark from the excavations was the wheel mark, of which there were six similar examples (eg Ills 5.6.1.6; 5.6.6.109 and .112). This mark is particularly difficult to source since it appears to have been used by a number of different makers up and down the country. It is quite common on early London pipes, which has often led to the suggestion that these pipes represent traded goods coming from the capital. While this may be true of some examples, the number found at Chester does seem to be particularly large. Furthermore, two pairs of these marks appear to match, that is, they were probably produced using the same die. This duplication of examples argues towards local production, either by someone moving from London or by a local maker copying London styles.

There are three other star or cross-like heel marks which, once again, are of types that were widely produced and/ or traded during the early seventeenth century (eg Ills 5.6.1.4–.5). The most interesting is a cross-like motif which was probably intended to represent a pair of crossed keys (Ill 5.6.6.113). An example of this type has previously been recorded from Chester (Pepper Street 1941; Rutter & Davey 1980, fig 32.12), when it was thought to be of southern English or Dutch origin. Since that time another example has been excavated from Chester (CHE/ 12HP92 context (1945)), bringing the total from the city to three. Comparison of the three mark impressions shows that, although they are all very similar, they were probably all made using different dies. The close similarity of detail in these three marks, however, suggests that the working dies were all produced from a common master, which in turn would indicate that all three examples were produced in the same workshop. Likewise, although the bowl forms are very similar, at least two different moulds appear to be represented. This range of mould and die types, together with the number of excavated examples, would all argue for local production in Chester itself. The situation is complicated, however, by the discovery of another example from Nuffield College, Oxford, now in the Woodstock Museum, Oxfordshire (Acc NUFF 5495; Higgins 1987a, fig 79.3). The Oxford example appears to have been marked using the same die as the Hamilton Place example from Chester. The occurrence of a fourth example reinforces the argument for an English origin for these pieces, since Dutch imports were always rare, with the most likely source being Chester. In any event, the Oxford and Chester examples demonstrate that both centres were sharing contact and a movement of goods across the country from a common source at this period.

The final symbol heel mark is very fragmentary but can be identified as part of a running animal stamp, possibly a fox, an example of which has previously been found in Chester (Rutter & Davey 1980, fig 32.15). This is a distinctive and unusual mark and one that was almost certainly made in the city. In addition to the heel marks, symbols were also used in a purely decorative way on the stems of pipes. There is one bowl of *c* 1610–40 with two lozenges made of smaller 'snowflake' type stamps on the stem (Ill 5.6.7.121). Enough survives to suggest that this is the complete decorative motif, that is, one lozenge of nine impressions adjoining another of four. The Dutch makers commonly used this style of decoration and so this finely burnished piece could be an import from overseas. On the other hand, the bowl is not milled, a characteristic of Chester pipes at this period, and there is other evidence that this style of stem decoration was being used in the city (*see* below). An interesting parallel for this particular stem comes from Eccleshall castle in Staffordshire, where an almost identical example has been found (E73 6/50). This piece has a lozenge of nine roughly applied lozenges with the same asymmetric motif as the Chester example. At Eccleshall, however, the outline of the die seems more rounded as if it is worn or the die is a second copy from the same master as the Chester example.

The final evidence for multi-stamped lozenge designs on the stem being used at Chester comes from the last symbol marked piece, a stem with the remains of a lozenge that would have been made up of nine individual *fleur de lis* impressions (Ill 5.6.1.3). The first point to note is that this stem is made of a very coarse gritty fabric with a granular fracture, like that produced by the local coal measure clays. This in itself suggests local production. As with the crossed key motif discussed above, there are also several local examples of this design, representing at least two different dies. There is a stem with a lozenge made up of nine individual *fleur de lis* impressions from the Cuppin Street 1986 site in Chester (CHE/CUS86 I (48) SF 13) which was made using the same die as an identical example from Beeston castle (Davey 1993, fig 58). In his report Davey says that there were two examples of this type from Beeston, but the author only has impressions of one with which to compare the Chester examples. Although the individual die used to create the

Cuppin Street and Beeston examples is slightly different to the Bridge Street one, they demonstrate a common motif and technique. In the Beeston report, Davey identifies that example as being Dutch, and dates it to *c* 1660–90, presumably based on similar Dutch examples using the *fleur de lis* motif. Single lozenge-shaped *fleur de lis* stamps can, however, be shown to have been used by the Chester makers. One was used as a heel mark on a local bowl form of *c* 1660–80 from Grey Friars Court in Chester (Rutter & Davey 1980, fig 32.18) and there is a stem decorated with both *fleur de lis* lozenges as well as an Alexander Lanckton stamp from another site in Chester, Sedan House 1989 (CHE/SH89 (1) SF 14). The Lanckton stem probably dates from *c* 1640 to 1660 and demonstrates that the Chester makers were certainly using this style of mark by the mid-seventeenth century. Given this fact, plus the evidence presented above, the author feels that these marks are almost certainly Chester products, foreshadowing the single large lozenge stamps containing many smaller *fleur de lis* which became characteristic of the late seventeenth century Chester pipes. If this is the case, then the Beeston examples may well derive from the Civil War deposits, rather than the later date which they have been assigned and, equally significantly, this reduces from three to one the number of Dutch imports found at that site.

Early initial stamps

The twenty-five initial marks are somewhat easier to attribute, since the lettering makes them more distinctive and they can often be matched with known distributions or documented makers. The majority of these marks were probably produced in Chester, where pipemaking was clearly well established by the second or third decade of the seventeenth century. There are three examples of NE marks, all from different dies (unidentified Chester maker; Ills 5.6.7.124–6), and eight examples of AL marks, from six different dies (seven heel stamps and one stem stamp, Ill 5.6.1.15). The AL marks can be attributed to Alexander Lanckton of Chester, who is recorded as a pipemaker in 1657 and was probably the same person who was buried there in 1670 (IGI). The products of both of these makers are well known from the city. It is interesting to note, however, that there are no examples of the SE marks, which are commonly found elsewhere in the city, but which are absent from this site.

In contrast to these more common marks, some of the less frequent marks are likely to have been imports from other parts of the country. The HL and PL marks, for example, are likely to have been produced in Rainford, south Lancashire (Ills 5.6.1.16 and 5.6.7.138), while the WK and AP marks may well be London types (Ills 5.6.1.14, .19; 5.6.6.108 and 5.6.7.120). The single letter M pipes (Ills 5.6.1.18, 5.6.6.115 and .116) can be paralleled by various examples from the west midlands, where these pipes seem almost certain to have been made, although the exact source has not yet been identified. Oswald illustrates an example from West Bromwich manor house (Oswald 1978–9, fig 4.15) and cites another from Shrewsbury, although his reference for this is incorrect in the literature. The single letter M has also been found at Eccleshall castle in Staffordshire, supporting the West Midlands distribution of this mark. Also from Eccleshall castle are six IL pipes, at least two of which were probably stamped using the same die as the Chester examples (Ills 5.6.1.17 and 5.6.6.114). The bowl forms for these pipes suggest that, like the single letter M marks, they are either local products or from the Broseley area industry in Shropshire. Similar IL marks have been found as far away as Worcester, suggesting a very wide distribution for this maker's products. Similarly, the RG mark (Ills 5.6.1.13 and 5.6.7.139) is almost certainly from Nantwich, where these initials occur in a wide range of different forms and in large numbers, suggesting a local maker. The two bowl stamps (GA and GL) are both crescent-shaped marks (eg Ills 5.6.1.7 and 5.6.8.145), which are characteristic of the south Lancashire industry, centred on Rainford.

These imported pipes clearly demonstrate the widespread trading connections of the city during the first half of the seventeenth century. Pipes from south Lancashire, Cheshire, the west midlands and London were all finding their way into Chester, where they circulated amongst the locally produced wares, in addition to which there was certainly some form of common link with Oxford. Although the 'imported' pipes form a significant proportion of the marked examples, around one third, this figure is unlikely to be representative of the unmarked examples, which form the bulk of the finds from the site. In some production centres, for example at Rainford, the majority of pipes of this date had stamps on them so any imports to Chester would be immediately apparent. In other cases, such as the west midlands area, local bowl forms were emerging which would help distinguish these pipes if they were present. This suggests that the low percentage of identified 'imports' to Chester is a true reflection of the situation and that the bulk of the finds, which are unmarked, are likely to have been produced in the city itself. Furthermore, the fact almost all the imports appear to be marked suggests that there is a correlation between marked pipes and those that were traded a significant distance from their place of manufacture, especially from places further afield such as the midlands and London. In this respect, the marks can be seen as an early form of branding that allowed the more established and large-scale manufacturers to identify their wares and this, in turn, made them more likely to be traded. The majority of the pipes found at this period, however, were unmarked and most of these are likely to have been produced in Chester itself.

Late seventeenth-century heel marks
After about 1660 there appears to have been a radical change in the use of stamps in Chester. The previous section has shown that just over 10% of the pipes made *c* 1610–60 found in Chester were marked. Excluding the large mid-seventeenth century kiln group in (1507), which would skew any results because of the large number of identical bowls from a single source, there were around 120 bowl fragments which are likely to have been produced within the period *c* 1660–1700. Of these, only one example had a stamp on it and that was an import to the city. The piece in question dates from *c* 1680 to 1710 and has the initials IP stamped on the heel beneath a distinctive scroll (Ills 5.6.1.20 and 5.6.8.149). Both the bowl form and mark are characteristic of pipes from Coventry, and the IP mark can be attributed to John Pottifer, who was recorded as a pipemaker there when his

son was apprenticed in 1710 (Muldoon 1979, 268–71; Gault 1979, 403). Even if the 137 bowl fragments from (1507) are included, none of these was marked, and so it is clear that the Chester makers effectively gave up using bowl stamps during the second half of the seventeenth century. This may be partly due to the preference for spur forms during the second half of the century, since this style of pipe was often unmarked, but it does go against the trend of the surrounding production centres. Pipes of this date from Nantwich, Broseley, Buckley and Rainford all continue to use stamped bowl marks and so it is clear that the Chester makers were setting their own styles. Where stamped bowls dating from after *c* 1660 are found in the city, they are almost invariably imports from elsewhere. What the IP example does show is that extent of the city's trading connections. Coventry lies in the heart of the midlands and so this pipe presumably represents overland trade from around one hundred miles away reaching the city.

Late seventeenth- and eighteenth-century stem marks
Although the Chester makers largely abandoned the use of bowl marks from the middle of the seventeenth century they did go on to produce some of the finest decorated stems ever produced. Although milled bands were occasionally used to decorate stems in many parts of the country from the early seventeenth century onwards, Chester was one of the centres to pioneer the use of decorative stem stamping. As noted above, the Chester makers were certainly using individual stamps to decorate stems by the middle of the seventeenth century, often employing them to make up decorative schemes. From around 1680 simple borders began to appear, sometimes used in association with decorative stamps or makers' marks placed across the stem. By around 1700 these had evolved into a range of elaborate decorative borders which were usually employed in conjunction with purely decorative stem stamps. Finely decorated stems became the hallmark of Chester pipes for nearly a century and their widespread distribution across Britain and beyond shows the extent of the city's trading influence during this period.

The excavations produced a total of eighty-four late seventeenth- or eighteenth-century stems with makers' marks or decorative stem stamps on them. These stems included seventy-eight with parts of one or more roll-stamped borders on them, forty-one with decorative stamps or marks placed across the stem and three with stem twists. These various marks range in date from around 1680 to 1790 and provide a representative selection of the styles produced in the city. Of the marks recovered, some ten borders and five stem stamps were too fragmentary to allow proper identification, leaving a total of 109 different marks which could be identified with reasonable certainty. Although well over 200 different Chester stem stamps of various types have already been documented (Rutter & Davey 1980), new types are regularly being discovered and around thirty of those from the Bridge Street excavation were of previously unrecorded types. This is more than a quarter of the stamps recovered and represents a 15% increase in the number of known types from the city as a whole. The large number of new types identified suggests that the known range of Chester stamps is far from complete and that many more types remain to be discovered.

The 1980 publication remains the standard work on Chester pipes and was used as a starting point in trying to identify the new finds from Bridge Street (Rutter & Davey 1980). In doing so a number of significant problems with the die drawings and accompanying catalogue were encountered which it is important to be aware of. For this reason, the defects which have become apparent in the 1980 catalogue will be described and discussed before moving on to an examination of the new finds.

The first problem encountered was in trying to establish exactly which pieces were used to define the various die types illustrated in the published catalogue. In the 1980 publication each different die type was illustrated with a catalogue entry listing all the known examples of that particular die. This catalogue entry, however, does not identify the exact context and small find number for each example, merely the site from which it was recovered. In some cases only one example of a particular die impression was known, making it relatively easy to identify the exact piece in the excavation archives. But in other instances multiple examples are listed, often from a number of different sites. This makes it very hard to even locate all the known examples, let alone to know which of them have been used to create the type drawing. This becomes crucial when doubt arises over the accuracy of the type drawing itself and comparison is required with the source material.

The type drawings themselves are very neatly drawn and presented, but the illustrations often appear to be slightly stylised. The drawings were prepared for publication at 1:1, which is not large enough to show the fine detail present on many of the dies. This fine detail can be very important, especially when trying to distinguish two very similar dies. Rutter and Davey, for example, illustrated a geometric border incorporating a panel containing alternate dots and cinquefoils (1980, fig 60.52). The die drawing was clearly created using a ruler, giving the horizontal lines a crisp and mechanical appearance. While this illustration superficially resembles a border from 25 Bridge Street, the new example seems to have a rope-like band above the dots and cinquefoils rather than a straight line (Ill 5.6.2.40). The rather stylised drawing gave rise to doubt as to whether the original drawing had simply omitted the finer detail or whether there were actually two different dies represented. The only way to tell if they were the same or not was to compare the type example that has originally been illustrated with the new find. However, Rutter and Davey list no less than fifteen examples of this die from at least six sites, making it impossible to know which piece(s) were used to prepare the original illustration. Spot-checking some of them, however, showed that a die does exist with straight lines above the dots and cinquefoils, and so the 25 Bridge Street example with its rope-like band does represent a new die type.

Although the 1980 drawing was accurate in this instance, this was not always found to be the case. A Chester oval from 25 Bridge Street (Ill 5.6.1.24), for example, appeared similar to an example illustrated by Rutter and Davey (1980, fig 56.49), except that it had only two dots flanking the shield and not a third above it, as shown in 1980. The 1980 drawing could have been any one of four examples listed in the catalogue, and so all of these impressions were compared with the drawing. This revealed that none of the quoted examples had a dot above the shield and that all four dies were, in fact, identical to the new Bridge Street example. Furthermore, none of the four original examples had the left-hand side of the mark properly impressed, so that the 'C' of 'CHESTER' was not present in any of them. The 1980 illustration, however, showed the lettering complete. From this it is clear that the 1980 illustrations are not always accurate and that, in some instances, detail has been added to complete a mark, even when there is no surviving impression to show that it is correct.

While checking the actual marks with the published catalogue further problems were found in that the examples of each die type listed in the 1980 paper were not always correct, ie similar but different dies had been identified as being the same and allocated to the same drawing number. This has a 'knock on' effect in that any of the associated marks listed in the catalogue do not necessarily date to the same period or belong to the same workshop.

Finally, there must also be a question over the accuracy of the dating of some of the stamp types, since some marks that were supposedly associated with one another sometimes have completely different date ranges given. For example, in 1980, one particular oval was identified as depicting the arms of the Grosvenor family and dated to *c* 1690–1715 (Rutter & Davey 1980, fig 54.9). Subsequent research has shown that these were, in fact, the arms of the Duke of Chandos (Brydges family), which were only granted in 1719 and that it may well have been as late as 1724 before these stamped pipes were actually commissioned (Cannon 2000). A dating of *c* 1720–30 would, therefore, seem more appropriate for this stamp, and this in turn has ramifications for the dating of all of the border types associated with it, including the type with alternate dots and cinquefoils, discussed above, which was previously also dated to *c* 1690–1715. This border, in turn, is associated with another six ovals, all of which were likewise dated to *c* 1690–1715. Given that the Chandos arms cannot date to before 1719, it seems likely that all of these interrelated marks need to be re-dated to the 1720s or later.

The attempt to use the 1980 paper to identify Chester die types has raised some important issues. On the one hand, there is no disputing either the importance or the continuing value of the 1980 paper. It was the first comprehensive study to bring together the existing documentary and artefactual evidence for the Chester pipe industry and to tackle what must be the most elaborate and complex series of decorative stamps from anywhere in the country. It established and classified the range stamped marks used in Chester and attempted to establish both a typology and chronology for them. While the present study does not question the broad overview established by the 1980 paper, it has shown that there are a number of problems with using the detailed die drawings and accompanying catalogue and that a reassessment of the die dating and associations is almost certainly required. Although this is beyond the bounds of the current study, it is clear that type examples for each different mark need to be identified so that there is a reference specimen against which new material can be compared. The existing illustrations also need to be redrawn in greater detail so that they show the distinguishing idiosyncrasies of each die and so that they can be published at 2:1. Finally, any duplicate examples need to be rigorously examined and identified so that correct associations can be determined and the dating of each class of mark reassessed.

What it has been possible to do within this study is to compare all of the new finds with the existing data and to establish which of them appear to represent new die types. These additional marks have been illustrated at 2:1 to provide new reference drawings to add to the corpus of known Chester dies. It has also been possible to correct and redraw some of the previously defined types where errors were discovered, for example, Ills 5.6.1.24, 5.6.2.45 and 5.6.3.51, or to prepare more complete drawings where better examples have now come to light, for example, Ills 5.6.1.31 and 5.6.3.51. Full details of all the decorative stamp types and associations can be found in the detailed catalogue in the site archive. The new and redrawn stem stamps dating from this period are shown in Ills 5.6.1.21–.32 and the new and redrawn borders in Ills 5.6.2–.3, nos 33–53.

The new stem stamps included an unusual *fleur de lis* shaped mark within a shield (Ills 5.6.1.21 and 5.6.9.161). Both the form and style of this mark are new to the Chester series. There was also part of a shield shaped mark containing the Chester arms (Ill 5.6.1.22). This example has been compared with the similar example marked RG illustrated by Rutter & Davey (fig 52.10) and it is from a different die, perhaps consisting of just the Chester arms, like that from Croydon (Higgins 1981, fig 28.14). Another partial shield of this type has been recorded from St Mary's Grove, Stafford, and so this style should be seen as an additional type to the more usual ovals with the place name 'CHESTER' beneath, for example, Ills 5.6.1.23–4.

As well as the Chester shields various other new arms and heraldic devices were discovered during the excavations. Perhaps the most distinctive was an arms with the motto 'FIDE.ET.CONS... ..' below (Ill 5.6.1.25). This finely executed die looks as though it represents an actual coat of arms which should be identifiable, although this has not been attempted within the confines of this study. It certainly appears that the Duke of Chandos commissioned pipes with his arms stamped on them in 1724, examples of which, produced in Chester, have been found at Tong castle in Shropshire (Cannon 2000; Wharton 1980). The duke was in negotiations to buy Tong castle during the 1720s, thus providing both a good context for their occurrence there and supporting evidence for the likely period when this type of heraldic stamp was being produced. Other new examples of heraldic ovals included a bird sitting on a bundle of arrows (Ill 5.6.1.28) and a coronet surmounted by a swan's neck (Ill 5.6.1.29). The swan's neck example is particularly interesting since it is flanked by the same border type (Ill 5.6.2.40) as that found with both the Chandos arms at Tong and with the Chester shield (Ill 5.6.1.22) from this site. In addition, there were half-a-dozen other known heraldic ovals from Chester associated with this border type. This not only suggests that all these marks date from around the 1720s but also that the same Chester workshop may have been specialising in producing specially commissioned heraldic pipes. It would be interesting to know if the Chandos (Brydges

family) papers, now in the Huntingdon Library in America, name the Chester pipemaker from whom Chandos ordered his pipes.

The excavations also produced a better example of a previously known crowned lion stamp (Ill 5.6.1.31), only a fragmentary example of which had been found before. As well as the heraldic stem stamps, the site also extended the range of other mark types, including two new lozenges produced by Elias Massey (Ills 5.6.1.26–7) and die variants for marks incorporating the initials TO (Ill 5.6.1.30) and RG (Ill 5.6.1.32). Both of these initialled marks are very similar to previously known examples, but they differ in detail. The previous TO mark has a serrated rather than a plain border while the previous RG mark has larger initials and additional small decorative elements around the Masonic emblems. The occurrence of at least two examples of almost identical and specially commissioned dies for each of these manufacturers is significant, since they must have been relatively expensive to produce. This would suggest that each of these manufacturers had sufficient journeymen working at any one time to warrant the additional expense of ordering these dies. Future excavations may well reveal other die variants, which in turn will refine our understanding of how these workshops operated and how many people they employed.

As well as the stem stamps the excavations produced seventy-eight examples of the roll-stamped borders which were often associated with them, sixty-eight of which were complete enough to allow reasonable identifications to be made. These borders included examples of nearly all the previously known range of Chester styles, including eighteen previously unrecorded dies. These included a number of stamps with 'lattice' decoration (Ill 5.6.2.34–6) which almost doubled the number of previously known examples (Rutter & Davey 1980, figs 58.27–.30). The author has seen various similar examples from other sites and so this style was perhaps more common than the 1980 publication would suggest. The excavations also produced a wide range of heart, star and *fleur de lis* borders, many of which were previously unrecorded (Ills 5.6.2.41–7). One of these types (Ill 5.6.2.45) had previously been recorded by Rutter and Davey (1980, fig 59.48) but their illustrator seems to have mistaken where the ends of the die were, so that the order of the *fleur de lis* and heart was reversed. Another error was found with a wide border that appears to contain a stylised crown motif (Ill 5.6.3.51). What appears to be a poor impression either of the same die, or a working copy made from the same master, was illustrated by Rutter and Davey (1980, fig 60.60). Their illustration, however, was drawn upside down and interpreted as perhaps Atlas holding up the world. Comparison of the actual marks, however, clearly showed that this was not the case and that, in fact, it should be paired with Rutter & Davey's fig 58.34, which shows a similar but different border employing the same stylised crown motif flanked by tendrils.

Late eighteenth- and nineteenth-century stamped marks
Only a relatively small number of late eighteenth and nineteenth century pipe fragments were recovered from the excavation and, of these, only nine had stamped marks. There were four examples of the long, single-line stamps with relief lettering which were placed on the top

of the stem. There were used from around 1770 to 1840, principally in Liverpool but with small numbers of manufacturers using this style as far east as Newcastle-under-Lyme and as far south as Worcester. All four of the 25 Bridge Street examples were made by the Fitzgerald family of Chester and at least three examples appear to be from the same, previously unrecorded die (Ill 5.6.3.54). This is characterised by a decorative motif at each end and two dots between the lettering.

There were also two examples of two-line stem stamps with relief lettering, which were used at much the same time as the single-line marks. Both were very poor examples reading 'AIRES / CHESTER' but, once again, they represent a previously unrecorded die type of *c* 1780–1830 (Ill 5.6.3.55). It is particularly fortunate that one of these marks joins to a bowl (Ill 5.6.10.176) since the Chester stem marks can only rarely be associated with their bowl forms and this is a period where the dating of bowl forms is particularly difficult anyway. There were various members of both the Fitzgerald and Aires families making pipes in Chester during the late eighteenth and early nineteenth century, making it impossible to attribute these marks to an individual maker. Rutter and Davey did not record any Aires marks in their study, but they did record a 'MAIRES & SON, CHESTER' stamp (1980, fig 68.3). There are no known Chester pipemakers with the surname Maires, although at least three makers named Aires are known. It seems likely that this stamp should, in fact, be read as M Aires, adding another member to this known family and removing an otherwise unknown name from the Chester pipemakers list.

The final stem mark is a fragmentary example comprising the unbordered, incuse lettering 'E.S... / BRO...'. This is part of an Edwin Southorn mark from Broseley in Shropshire. Edwin was an important and innovative maker at this production centre, where he used this style of mark from *c* 1858 to 1876 (Higgins 1987a, 490). Unfortunately, following Edwin's death in 1876, William Southorn & Co also occasionally used the mark until they closed in 1960. This makes it hard to date the mark exactly, but the unusual style of this particular stem (Ill 5.6.5.87) makes it more likely to be one of Edwin's products rather than a later piece. As such, it is most likely to date from around 1860–80.

As well as the stem stamps, there were also two later nineteenth-century bowl stamps. Both of these examples were recovered from (1096), the same context as the E Southorn mark of *c* 1860–80 discussed above. This context was a large rubbish deposit containing bottles and other debris associated with Davies and Shepheard's chemist's shop. This is a particularly useful association, since it allows the deposit to be securely dated to after 1857, which, in turn, fits with the E Southorn mark. The deposit date of *c* 1860–80 is important in establishing a good date for the two bowl marks, which are of types that are otherwise hard to date precisely. Both of the marks are incuse stamps on the bowl facing the smoker and both are slogans or pattern names which would have been used by a number of different manufacturers rather than specific makers' marks. One of these reads 'ISLAND BRIDGE' (Ill 5.6.3.57) and the other 'EVER-GREEN' below a shamrock leaf (Ill 5.6.3.56). This second mark is unusual in that it has inadvertently been placed upside-down on the bowl. Both of these marks are known from various sites in the north-west and so they were presumably produced within the region. By this date, however, pipes were being much more widely marketed and so they need not have been produced in Chester itself.

Late nineteenth- and early twentieth-century moulded marks

The final group of five marked pipes from the excavations all have incuse moulded marks on them. This style of marking emerged around the middle of the nineteenth century and became the most common technique employed in this area by the end of it. There is one fragment that would have had 'WHO . EMMA' on each side of the stem within a relief moulded and beaded border. This was a popular slogan or phrase, taken from the title of a popular song of the day, and is variously spelt 'Woa Emma!', 'Whoa Emma', 'Who Emma' or 'Wo'a Emma'. In fact, there appear to have been at least three completely different versions of this song, which circulated from around the 1850s onwards (Higgins 1988). The general theme of all three songs was that Emma was a hard-drinking and very popular girl, as was discovered to the horror of her upstanding and rather naive partner. This song was clearly popular since it was one of the more common titles appearing on the stems of pipes. Song titles appear to have been simply added to everyday pipe designs: for example, another song title, 'Not for Joe', has been found in the Liverpool area on a pipe the bowl of which is of typical Irish style, decorated with a harp and shamrock design (Higgins 1988, fig 1). A stem marked 'Wo'a Emma' has previously been recorded from Chester (Rutter & Davey 1980, fig 68.22), showing that least two different versions of this pipe were circulating in the city.

The other moulded marks were more mundane and included two identical stems marked 'BURNS CUTTY' (Ill 5.6.5.88), a popular pattern name for a spurless pipe style, and a stem marked '420'. This would have been a pattern number, used to identify a particular pipe style in the catalogue of a large pipemaking firm. This piece could have travelled quite a distance to get to Chester, since it is unlikely that any of the makers there used a numbering system running into the 400s. A good example of how far pipes could travel is provided by the final and very fragmentary moulded mark, which reads 'Mc... / ...W' (Ill 5.6.5.89). This was almost certainly part of a stem marked 'McDOUGALL / GLASGOW', one of the major Scottish manufacturers, who operated from 1846 to 1967 (Anon 1987, 354). McDougall's were major exporters of pipes and were listed in the Liverpool trade directories of the early 1890s, and they would almost certainly have had agents based there for even longer. Their pipes were common in the region and show how much more diverse the market for pipes was during the late nineteenth century.

Bowl forms

A wide range of bowl forms was represented, with the collection being particularly strong in material dating from the late sixteenth through to late eighteenth century. A large number of bowl forms from Chester has previously been published (Rutter & Davey 1980), but the new material not only added new variants for some of the known makers but also some new forms which had not been recorded from Chester before.

249

In the 1980 publication, an extensive type series was given for Chester pipes, running to some 107 different forms. Although this typology has been used to identify bowl types in the archive catalogue for this site, it was found too cumbersome to be of much general use in sorting the pipes. At one extreme, it often includes several very similar variants of a particular form so that it is impossible to determine which characteristics have been used to distinguish them. Some of the forms were so close that they seemed to be at the level of defining individual mould types rather than general classes into which groups could be divided. At the other extreme, some bowl forms which occurred with either heels or spurs were given the same number, making it impossible to distinguish them without adding some sort of suffix to the type number. Finally, the dating assigned to the various types was extremely poor. Instead of being individually dated, the bowl forms were lumped together into broad groups which gave only a general and often unreliable indication of date. There were no forms dated to before *c* 1630 but then there were sixty-three forms ranging from between 1630 and 1680, all but seven of which, on the basis of the typology, were in production during the 1640s. In contrast, no forms at all were allocated to the 1680–90 period. Some groups were given what appears to be an unrealistically precise date of only ten years, while others were given ninety-year ranges, even when some of the forms included were clearly much more closely datable than this. A new Chester typology is clearly required with a smaller but more useful range of bowl forms. These forms need to be carefully selected so as to produce an overlapping sequence of individually dated forms which will provide a more realistic and useable classification system for Chester pipes.

While it was not possible to prepare a new Chester typology as part of this project, it has been possible to illustrate both some key groups (discussed above; Ills 5.6.4.58–5.6.5.91) and a sequence of other bowl forms ranging from the late sixteenth century through to the end of the nineteenth century (Ills 5.6.6.92–5.6.10.178). These forms are not intended to provide a full sequence for the types found in Chester but rather to extend and supplement the corpus to be found in the 1980 paper.

Bowls of *c* 1580–1610 (Ill 5.6.6, nos 92–6)
The excavations produced five relatively complete examples of the earliest bowl forms to be found in this country. These are characterised by their small bowl size, a heel trimmed flush with the underside of the stem and their generally unmilled rims. The only milled example in this group had widely spaced milling (Ill 5.6.6.96), which differs from that generally adopted after *c* 1610 (eg Ills 5.6.6.97–.104). These early pipes often had relatively small stem bores of 4/64"–5/64" although the Chester examples ranged up to 7/64". All of them had burnished surfaces and some had a distinctive reduced, grey core to the fabric, which is typical of these early pipes. Pipes of this form are rare nationally since tobacco was still a scarce and expensive commodity, and no production sites have yet been located. These early pipes are usually presumed to come from London, although this does not necessarily have to be the case, with the distribution of Eglantine marks around Plymouth clearly suggesting that production had been established there

before *c* 1610. Likewise, Robert Cotton emigrated to Jamestown in 1608 where he appears to have set up a pipe workshop and so it is not out of the question that pipemaking could have started in Chester by the start of the seventeenth century.

Bowls of *c* 1610–60 (Ills 5.6.7–.8, nos 97–145)
After *c* 1610 smoking became much more common and a wide range of forms appeared, principally of heel types (Ills 5.6.6.97–5.6.7.140). Many of these are hard to source on form alone, since common styles were employed across the country, and it is mainly the distinctive makers' marks which reveal their origins (*see* above). There are, however, some manufacturing traits which are particularly characteristics of Chester, for example, the lack of milling on many of the locally produced bowls of *c* 1610–60 (Ills 5.6.7.121 and .123–.136). By the middle of the century local forms had become more distinctive. A good example is provided by the elongated bowl form and low set milling of Ill 5.6.7.139, which is characteristic of the pipes produced to the south of Chester; this piece probably comes from Nantwich.

A particularly unusual form is the miniature pipe shown in Ill 5.6.7.140. Although only the size of a late sixteenth-century pipe, the developed form and use of milling both mark this as a seventeenth-century piece. The pipe was made of a coarse clay, probably from the local coal measure deposits, suggesting that it was made in locally. If this is the case, then the quality of the form and finish would suggest that it was made in Chester itself, rather than in one of the neighbouring centres. The seams have some sharp lines scored along them, partially burnished over, which look like the trimming marks found on pipes from the Low Countries. This could be fortuitous or it could represent someone who had worked in the Low Countries bringing these techniques to Chester. A similar bowl form has been found at St Mary's City in Maryland, founded in 1634, and a small number of other examples are known, showing that these miniatures were occasionally produced by the mid-seventeenth-century makers.

Spur pipes also occurred in smaller numbers (Ills 5.6.8.141–6), the notable exception being the large kiln dump discussed below (context (1507); Ills 5.6.4.58–.62). This shows that spur pipes were being made in the city, even if they were not the dominant form. As with the heel pipes, local styles emerged so that particular shapes stand out as being imports, for example, Ill 5.6.8.145, which is from south Lancashire.

Bowls of *c* 1660–1790 (Ills 5.6.8–.10, nos 147–73)
Towards the end of the 1600s the standard 'barrel-shaped' bowl which had been dominant for nearly a century started to evolve rapidly. It became much larger and more elegant and the rim started to become more nearly parallel with the stem. In particular, the heel or spur area became much more dynamic, evolving into a wide range of different forms and sizes. There were changes, too, in finish, with the use of burnishing and milling dying out. These changes are poorly dated at Chester and a reassessment of the transitional forms is clearly needed to provide a better sequence and dating for this period. The two pit groups of *c* 1700 and *c* 1710, discussed below, help to define the changing styles at this time.

By the early eighteenth century a new range of spur and heel pipes had become established and it is basically these styles which dominated the eighteenth-century fashions. The heels were generally circular or oval and ranged from large to small (Ills 5.6.8.151–5.6.9.161) with distinctive tailed forms being particularly characteristic of the Chester makers (eg Ill 5.6.8.153). Sometimes the bases were cut at distinctive angle to the stem, for example, Ills 5.6.8.157–9. The larger types died out during the eighteenth century, the heels tended to become more cylindrical in form and trimmed parallel with the stem. Many of these types would have had decorated stems, as is shown by two surviving examples (Ills 5.6.9.161–2). The spur forms (Ills 5.6.9–.10, nos 163–73) developed in a similar manner and these forms would have had decorated stems too (eg Ill 5.6.9.165). Only one pipe of this period was found with possible moulded initials and even that is uncertain (Ill 5.6.10.173). Moulded initials were extremely common in other areas during this period, especially London, which might have been expected to set trends for the country as a whole. The distinctive bowl forms and finely decorated stems produced in Chester are distinctive to the city and show that London did not always dictate fashions.

Bowls after *c* 1790 (Ills 5.6.10, nos 174–8)
Later bowls are poorly represented from the excavations, making it hard to chart their evolution during this period. In general terms the bowls would have become more squat and upright during this period, with the frequent use of moulded decoration on the bowl sides and seams (Ills 5.6.10.174–5). One important discovery was that of an Aires stem stamp together with its associated bowl form (Ill 5.6.10.176). Not only was this a previously unrecorded mark but it is also extremely rare to recover the bowl forms that went with this style of stamp. There were only a few later nineteenth-century bowl forms from the excavations, at least some of which were imports to Chester (Ills 5.6.5.88–.91 and 5.6.10.177–8). By the late eighteenth century Chester had been eclipsed by Liverpool as a port and trading centre and its once vibrant pipe industry went into decline. The somewhat unreliable 1831 census figures recorded only eight pipemakers for Chester as opposed to thirty-nine for Liverpool and even the more thorough figures from 1841 and 1851 give only twenty-five and thirty-four for Chester as opposed to sixty-five and 130 respectively for Liverpool (Gault 1985; Cannon 2004).

Although pipemaking in Chester went into a terminal decline towards the end of the nineteenth century, the manufacturers there must have continued to respond to the changing demand for pipes. Pipemakers in the northwest as a whole were producing elaborate mould-decorated pipes from the late eighteenth century onwards, with distinctive regional styles developing during the early nineteenth century. Pipes of this period are rarely recovered from excavations, with the result that the Chester pipemaking industry from *c* 1780 onwards remains poorly understood. Production sites and good excavated assemblages of this period are a priority for further research.

Internal bowl marks
Internal bowl marks are occasionally found on pipes, most

usually comprising relief moulded crosses formed by the metal stopper that was used to create the bowl cavity. These marks seem to appear around 1700, when larger bowl forms were introduced, often with a flat internal base. These marks may have been used to help break the suction created with the wet clay during the moulding process, in the same way as the rough marks that were put onto nineteenth-century stoppers. Very rarely initials or other marks are found in this position and sometimes, especially in the nineteenth century, the internal bowl marks comprised ribs running up the internal surface of the bowl.

Internal bowl marks were never particularly common and there does appear to be some regional variation in the frequency with which they are found. These marks were not very common at Chester, as is shown by the fact that only five examples were noted from this assemblage. At least four of these dated from the eighteenth century. There was one example with rather irregular marks from Context (1406) (Ill 5.6.8.159) and three examples where a more organised upright cross had been cut as, for example, that from context (1700) (Ill 5.6.9.160). The final example was rather fragmentary, making it hard to date, and its context was slightly uncertain too. The fragment was stored in a bag labelled context (624), where it was later than all of the other finds, but the piece itself is labelled context (424). This piece had at least six short ribs or spikes extending up from the base of the bowl, on its internal sides, and is most likely to date from the late eighteenth or nineteenth century. These five examples all followed national trends in terms of their respective styles and dates, but their small number shows that internal bowl marks were infrequently used at Chester.

Modified stems and mouthpieces

Only a very small number of the fragments recovered showed any signs of additional treatment or reworking, either during manufacture or use. Out of the 987 bowl and 4,369 stem fragments only two bowls (from contexts (659) and (1111)) and two stems (contexts (201) and (463)) had any stem milling on them. These pieces were all of seventeenth- or early eighteenth-century date and both of the stems were probably milled to disguise repairs during manufacture. In contrast, the surviving milling attached to the bowls may have been purely decorative. One example had a criss-cross design (Ill 5.6.7.122) while the other had just two parallel bands surviving (Ill 5.6.8.145). The second piece also had a south Lancashire style GA mark on the bowl, showing that it was imported into Chester. These four fragments represented just 0.07% of the pipes recovered, showing that stem milling was very rarely found on the pipes used in Chester.

Towards the end of the eighteenth century some earthenware potters started extruding great lengths of stem to make elaborately coiled and painted pipes with glazed surfaces. The vogue for coiled pipes seems to have been taken up by the ordinary pipemakers who sometimes looped and twisted the stems of their long 'churchwarden' pipes. These coiled pipes generally seem to have been produced from the late eighteenth century through to the mid-nineteenth century, and the wide distribution of fragments suggests that they were fairly common across the country (Higgins 2005). One piece of curved stem from such a coiled pipe was recovered from these excavations (Ill 5.6.10.182). It probably dates from *c* 1780 to 1830 and was found in context (1802).

As with the stems, there was very little evidence for any particular treatment of the 214 mouthpieces recovered. From the end of the eighteenth century through until about 1910 glazed mouthpieces were sometimes produced. There were particularly common in the northeast of England, but less so in the north-west. Pipes of this period were not particularly well represented on this site, making it hard to assess how representative the seven stem examples with traces of glaze on them would have been. None of the actual mouthpieces survived, just sections of stem from close by with traces of glaze on them. There was one piece with a yellowish glaze and six with various shades of green. The yellow piece came from context (208) and the others from contexts (217), (563), (601), (1096), (1109) and (1802). In addition to the glazed fragments there were two fragments with traces of a red paint or wax coating surviving – a mouthpiece from context (1090) and a stem from near a mouthpiece in context (601). This type of finish does not survive well in the ground and may well be under-represented in the excavated sample.

The final type of modification found on the pipes occurred after they had been manufactured and sold and comprised modification or wear to the stems. A total of eighteen stems and one bowl showed evidence for reworking of the stems after firing. In most cases this was on seventeenth- or eighteenth-century pipes and simply comprised the smoothing or grinding into facets of the broken end of the stem. In some cases this may have been done to smooth a broken stem end so that a pipe could be reused. In other cases the broken stem may well have resulted from idle doodling or its use for drawing, like a stick of chalk. In most cases (thirteen examples) just one end was reworked, for example Ill 5.6.10.180. In two instances, however, both ends had been smoothed (eg Ill 5.6.10.181), in which case the stem may have been reused as a hair curler (*see* below). The only instance of a bowl with a ground end to the broken stem was on a much later pipe (Ill 5.6.10.177). At this date (*c* 1840–1920) some pipes were used with very short stems but it seems more likely that this example was ground for some other reason, perhaps even to remount it into some other sort of stem.

The last two pieces with modifications were rather different. There was one piece that had a worked facet on just one side of the stem at a shallow, sloping angle (context (201), SF 8136). This was very similar to the angle seen on a larger fragment which appears to have had at least two broad, shallow grooves cut into it, which just extended into the stem bore (Context (1098); Ill 5.6.9.179). There are documentary references to pipes being used as whistles or flutes and this careful modification may have been intended for this purpose. The illustrated piece had a relatively large bore (7/64") and is most likely to date from the seventeenth century, although, being cautious, it has been given a broad date range of *c* 1640–1740 in the catalogue. The other fragment must be from a different pipe since it had a much smaller bore (5/64"). It also had a decorative stem border (Die no 792; Rutter & Davey 1980, fig 61.79) and just the very edge of an oval on it. These two pieces came

from different plots (1 and 3) suggesting that, if they were modified as whistles, that this practice was not confined to a single household in this part of Chester.

Complete pipes

One of the objectives of this study was to see whether any complete pipes could be reassembled from the excavated material. Although documentary sources clearly show that different lengths of pipe were produced from the seventeenth century onwards, very little is known archaeologically about the complete form of seventeenth- and eighteenth-century clay pipes because they so rarely survive intact. This limits the way in which pipes can be interpreted because different stem lengths sold for different amounts (as a general rule, the longer the pipe, the more it cost). Some bowl forms appear to have been associated with pipes of a specific length, while others may have been produced in a range of lengths. There were also specific export styles of pipe being produced in Chester, some of which would also have had specific stem lengths.

Since no complete curated pipes of this date survive from Chester, information on stem length can only be recovered from archaeological material. Complete pipes can be reassembled from archaeological finds, but excavators rarely take the trouble to recover all fragments from key deposits, such as pit groups, and finds specialists do not often systematically search for joining fragments at the post-excavation stage. There are less than 100 complete seventeenth- or eighteenth-century pipes known from anywhere in the country, the majority of which have been reassembled by the author from various sites in London and the south-east. In the north-west complete pipes of this date have only been recovered from two sites: Church Field, Rainford (Higgins 1982) and the Royal Infirmary, Chester. There are no known pipes of later seventeenth- or eighteenth-century date.

The most promising group of pipes from the excavations, context (1507), was extensively sorted and searched for joins (*see* group summary below) but no complete pipes could be reassembled. Two other contexts did, however, produce complete or nearly complete pipes of early eighteenth-century date. The first was recovered from (1503), the fill of a cess pit containing pipes of *c* 1690–1720 but with *c* 1700–10 being the most likely deposition date (*see* group summary). This pipe was one of seven examples from the same mould recovered from (1503) and (1504) and had a stem length of 12 7/8" or 326 mm (Ill 5.6.4.67). This pipe appeared to be of middling quality: although the bowl had an average burnish on it, the stem was only poorly burnished and it had defects near the mouthpiece where insufficient clay was rolled to fill the mould.

In contrast, the second almost complete pipe, recovered from contexts (1699) and (1601), had a finely burnished bowl and stem. This pipe was also a spur form, in this instance dating to *c* 1710–20, and it was recovered from the pit (1696). This pipe was not quite complete since the very tip of the stem was broken (Ill 5.6.4.70). The stem survived to a length of 341 mm with an estimated original length in the region of 350 mm (13 ¾"). The overall quality and finish of this pipe was much finer than that from (1503) and this was perhaps reflected in its slightly longer stem, although this could equally be attributed to its different bowl form or slightly later date. Either way, the difference in stem length was not great, making it clear that pipes of a similar style and length were available in a variety of different qualities.

One point that was striking about both of these pipes was their very straight stems. English pipes were usually placed on frames or 'grates' to dry, most likely with wooden strips laid over the stems to try and prevent warping. Although the stems produced in this way were fairly straight, they were often not as good as those found on the Dutch pipes, which were placed on specially made wooden boards with grooves cut in them to take the stems. These boards ensured that the stems dried straight, thus enabling a better and more consistent result to be achieved. Although a sample of two is very small, the Chester pipes appear to have had notably straighter stems than examples of similar date from elsewhere in this country. If further examples show this to be a consistent pattern, then this would suggest that Chester employed a different drying method than elsewhere in Britain, perhaps using boards like the Dutch examples. In this connection it is worth noting that an early seventeenth-century pipe kiln muffle from the Royal Infirmary site at Chester is also unique in Britain, but very similar to Dutch examples. This may just be coincidence, but it would be worth considering links between pipe production in Chester and the Low Countries if further similarities come to light.

The straight stems from Chester and very fine finish of the pipe from (1599)/(1601) clearly demonstrate the quality of the early eighteenth-century pipes being produced there. From the late seventeenth century onwards Chester developed a reputation for fine quality pipes, with special orders being documented and examples of marked pipes having been recovered from many parts England as well as overseas. The two complete pipes had stem lengths of around 326–350 mm (12 7/8"–13 ¾"), which fall within the mid- to upper range of known examples of this date from elsewhere in the country (Higgins 1987a, 64). The total number of complete pipes recovered was, however, very small and may not be fully representative of the range originally produced. In 1710 the Bristol Company of Tobacco Pipe Makers passed an ordinance regulating the lengths that could be produced by the makers there: long pipes 16"; Dutch Pipes 14"; Jamaica Pipes 13"; Penned Heels and Gauntletts 11 ½" and Virginia Pipes 8 ½". Despite this, one maker was subsequently fined for making pipes of 24" (Jackson & Price 1974, 85). As a major pipemaking centre and trading port, it is highly probable that the Chester makers were producing a similar range of pipes to the Bristol makers at this date. This suggests that the Chester pipes recovered would have been firmly mid-range products and that both longer and shorter styles are to be expected. One of the priorities for pipe research in Chester is to recover more complete examples so that the range of pipes produced can be defined and comparisons made, both over time and with other production and export centres.

Production waste

There is no evidence that pipe production ever took place within the excavated area. There was, however, some production waste that appears to have been dumped on the site from workshops elsewhere in Chester. There was a large group of waste pipes dating to *c* 1640–70 from (1507), which are discussed below. Although no muffle or other kiln debris was passed on with the pipes for examination, the group from (1507) seems certain to represent production waste from a workshop that was operating during the mid-seventeenth century. This group of waste pipes appears to have been deposited on the excavation site about fifty years later.

The only other obvious production waste was a strip of pipe clay from (301) (Ill 5.6.10.185). This had been crudely hand-rolled and the surviving section included a join where two pieces of clay had been overlapped and then smoothed together. The surviving fragment was broken at both ends and ranged from about 8 to 11 mm in width. Two opposing faces had been slightly squashed and flattened, giving an average depth of about 7 mm. The roll was made of a very fine, white pipeclay and was typical of waste from pipe production sites, where rolls like this were used as bedding or sealing strips between larger elements of kiln furniture. Unfortunately (301) was a mixed context containing mainly seventeenth- and eighteenth-century pipes, but also some nineteenth-century or later fragments. This makes it impossible to accurately date the clay strip, which was presumably dumped on the site from elsewhere in Chester.

Significant context groups

As well as adding significantly to the number of known marks from Chester, the excavations also produced a number of good, homogenous-looking context groups that add to our knowledge of the range of bowl forms and finishes which were in use at particular moments in time. Twelve of the most significant context groups, from four discrete features or deposits, are described and discussed in chronological order below, with illustrations to show the range of forms present in each group.

Phase VII Plot 4 (1507): fill of pit (1506)

This context produced a total of 746 pieces of pipe, comprising 137 bowl, 564 stem and forty-five mouthpiece fragments, by far the largest group of pipes from the excavation. This deposit must have been laid down in the early eighteenth century since it contained a very distinct group of pipes (seven bowls, fifty-two stems and three mouthpieces), the bowl forms of which ranged from *c* 1690 to 1730. The associated stem fragments included a previously unrecorded heart, star and *fleur de lis border* (Ill 5.6.2.42), a style of border which Rutter and Davey dated to *c* 1700–20. If this dating is reliable, then the deposit seems most likely to date to the first two decades of the eighteenth century. In addition to this element, there were two or three early seventeenth-century bowl fragments, including one with an AL stamp on the heel, but these appear to comprise a small residual element of the main group.

All of the remaining fragments, 126 bowls, 512 stems and 42 mouthpieces, formed a very coherent group sharing the same slightly creamy-white fabric. All of the bowls were spur forms dating to *c* 1640–70, none of which were marked or decorated. Although the bowl forms were typical of Chester products, it was most unusual to find such a large number in one context and for them to dominate the mid-seventeenth-century pipes to the exclusion of all other forms. Furthermore, the majority of the bowls were unsmoked. Taken together, it seems almost certain that this group represents production waste from a kiln site, most likely dating to the 1650s. There was no other concentration of these spur forms elsewhere on the site, nor other evidence of production activity. This suggests that the kiln waste was imported to the site to fill this pit and that this redeposition occurred around fifty to sixty years after the waste was originally generated. Despite this, the deposit still provides an excellent opportunity to study a mid-seventeenth century kiln group from Chester.

Although the kiln group only included spur forms, there was quite a range in the precise size and profile of these pipes. The clean lines and extensive use of surface finishing on these pipes precluded the identification of individual mould flaws to determine the exact number of moulds represented, but it is certain that a number of different examples were present. Not only did the pipes range imperceptibly from one extreme of size to the other (Ills 5.6.3.58–.62) but they also varied in the lines of the bowl. Some examples had quite a marked waist and fairly globular bowl (eg Ill 5.6.3.61) while others had a more sleek appearance (eg Ill 5.6.3.59). This suggests that the workshop was producing just spur forms at this period, but that they offered a range of styles (probably differentiated primarily by varying stem lengths) and/or that they had sufficient journeymen employed to warrant running a number of different presses at any one time.

Analysis of the fragments from this group also shed some light on the workshop practices being employed. All of the surviving pipe rims had been bottered (finished with a tool to smooth and shape the rim) and ten of the 119 examples showed signs of internal trimming as well. All of the rims had also been finished with a band of milling. Of the 112 measurable examples, the majority were fully milled (eighty-nine examples; 79.5%). There were eighteen which were three-quarters milled (16%), three which were half-milled (2.7%) and just two which were one-quarter milled (1.8%). This clearly shows that all of the products from this workshop were expected to be milled and that usually this milling was applied with some care to ensure a full band. Similarly, the majority of the bowls had been given a burnished surface (ninety-five out of 122 measurable examples, or 78%). The quality of this burnishing can be further subdivided to show that twelve of the bowls had an average burnish (10% of the group as a whole) while eighty-three had a good burnish (68%). None of the bowls had a poor or a fine burnish, showing a mid-range consistency in the quality of output from this workshop.

In contrast to the bowls, only just over a half of the stem fragments were burnished (295 out of 512 fragments, or 58%) and an even smaller number of mouthpiece fragments (sixteen out or forty-two, or 38%). The mouthpiece figure is, however, less reliable since burnishing often faded out towards the tip of the pipe and some of these fragments were very small anyway, making it hard to see surviving traces of burnishing. Despite this, the overall picture is clear, with fewer stem fragments than bowls being burnished. In some instances it can be seen that only the bowl of the pipe was burnished and that the stem had been left unburnished, for example, Ill 5.6.3.61. In

other instances it can be seen that the burnishing finished part way along the stem. One particular characteristic of this assemblage was that there often appeared to have been a gap between the stem and bowl burnishing where the two burnished areas had not been joined up properly, for example, Ill 5.6.3.59. The evidence from this group suggests that four different grades of finish were being produced: completely burnished pipes; half-burnished pipes; pipes with just the bowl burnished and completely unburnished pipes. A burnished surface added value to the pipe and so these differences in burnishing may well have been reflected in the retail price.

The large sample size and discrete nature of this pit deposit offered the potential for complete pipes to have been recovered. The whole group was, therefore, sorted and laid out to try and reassemble the fragments, using a methodology previously described by the author (Higgins 1982, 197–9). Although a number of joins were found, the success rate in relation to the size of the assemblage as a whole was relatively low, despite a considerable amount of time having been spent searching for joins (only three of around twenty bowl/stem junctions fitted and stem joins were found with only four of the forty-two mouthpieces). No complete pipes could be reassembled but the stem tapers showed that these pipes would have originally have had stems of around twenty-eight cm in length. The stem length also affected the price of a pipe and so it is likely that this was an average and that different lengths would have been produced originally. Until more complete pipes are recovered, it is impossible to assess the range of lengths produced at Chester or how these lengths relate to the finishing techniques discussed above.

What this sample did allow, however, was a comparison of the burnishing and milling. In total there were 105 bowls where both of these variables could be recorded. These are shown in Table 5.6.2, where the columns represent burnishing and the rows the amount of rim milling. The percentages in brackets show the percentage that each figure represents within its own column.

What this table clearly shows is that it was the burnishing rather than the milling which was the principal variable. Between 73% and 88% of the pipes were fully milled, regardless of whether the pipes were burnished or not, which is close to the overall average of 79.5% for group as a whole. Given the small size of some of these samples, this figure seems remarkably consistent in all three columns. Similarly, the percentages for the three-quarters milled pipes are generally close to the group average of 16%. The only slight trend appears to be that the pipes with a good burnish always had at least a half-milled rim – none of this class had just one quarter milling, despite it being by far the largest sample. In contrast, the burnish on the pipes ranges from none to good quality. This shows that the rims were always finished with about the same degree of care while the surface could be treated in completely different ways.

Phase X Plot 5 (1503) and Phase VII Plot 4 pit (1522), fills (1504), (1505), (1513), (1558), (1559)

Context (1503) produced one of the freshest-looking and most significant groups of pipes from the site, comprising thirty-eight bowl, sixty-five stem and eleven mouthpiece fragments (total 114), with some of the bowls

Table 5.6.2 Clay tobacco pipe spur bowls from the kiln dump of c 1640–70 in context (1507) showing the relationship between burnish quality and the amount of rim milling

Rim milling	Unburnished		Average burnish		Good burnish		Total
One-quarter	1	(4%)	1	(9%)			2
Half					3	(4%)	3
Three-quarters	2	(8%)	2	(18%)	13	(19%)	17
Full	21	(88%)	8	(73%)	54	(77%)	83
Total	24		11		70		105

having up to 149 mm of surviving stem. It was possible to reconstruct a complete pipe from this deposit, the first of its date from anywhere in the north-west, and there were quite a number of joins between the generally large fragments. Apart from a few residual seventeenth-century pieces, the whole group comprised a narrow range of bowl forms, dating to *c* 1690–1720, plus contemporary-looking stems. The only problem with this group is that (1503) is recorded as the fill of a modern sewer pipe trench, which seems most unlikely for such a fresh-looking and coherent group of early eighteenth-century material.

A cross-join between pipe fragments in (1503) and (1513) was found, (1513) being one of the contexts within pit (1522). The other pipe-bearing deposits from the pit all produced pipe assemblages that would fit with (1503), and pipes from the same mould were present in (1503), (1504) and (1513), suggesting that all three deposits were closely contemporary. On the other hand, (1505) only produced one small chip of pipe from a sieved sample. This seems a very small quantity given the general occurrence of pipes within the pit as a whole. Likewise, there were no pottery or glass fragments recorded for (1505). It is suggested that the finds from (1505) were mislabelled (1503), thus explaining both the absence of finds from (1505) and the appearance of a first-rate assemblage of *c* 1690–1720 in a modern sewer trench. This would also explain the occurrence of late seventeenth- to early eighteenth-century assemblages of glass and pottery in (1503), including partially complete ceramic vessels. It would also explain the odd pieces of later material from (1503), which had already been identified as possibly intrusive in the pottery assessment, but which probably represent the actual finds that were in the sewer trench. For these reasons, (1503) will be considered as part of the pit sequence, where it was probably excavated as (1505). The pipe evidence suggests that the most likely date for the filling of this pit was around 1700–10.

The pipes from the pit as a whole included a small element of residual material, as might be expected. (1503), (1504), (1558) and (1559) all produced odd fragments ranging from *c* 1640 to 1680 but these pieces were generally smaller and more battered-looking than the bulk of the other pipes. The remaining material was extraordinarily consistent. One bowl form, a transitional spur type (Ills 5.6.3.63–7) dominated the assemblage, with thirty-one of the thirty-three substantially complete bowls being of this type. These were all so similar that, on first inspection, almost all might be taken as having been produced in the same mould. Detailed inspection, however, revealed that at least five different mould types were represented. Two of these types could be identified by their slightly different bowl forms (Ills 5.6.3.63 and .65) and three by mould flaws evident on the bowls or stems of the pipes (Ills 5.6.3.64, .66 and .67 – *see* figure captions for descriptions of the mould flaws). This still leaves sixteen examples, representing 52% of the spur bowls, which were

so smooth and well finished that mould types could not be identified. These could easily represent a further five mould types, suggesting that around five to ten different moulds of this specific type were represented in the pit.

In contrast to the spur bowls, only three heel bowls of this period were found (eg Ills 5.6.4.68–9). Two of these were almost identical, although it is not certain whether they were made in the same mould or not (Ill 5.6.4.69). Both had simple cut rims and neither was milled or burnished. None of the spur pipes were milled either, although half of them (fifteen out of thirty-one) had been given a good burnish to finish the bowls' surface. In addition, three of the spur bowls had bottered rims and a further four appeared to have been smoothed or wiped around the rim in some way. One of the heel bowls (Ill 5.6.8.68) also had a bottered rim.

The pipes from this pit group in Plot 4 suggests that the occupant of this property about 1700 favoured a particular form of spur pipe. The diversity of mould types may well indicate that this style was being produced by a number of different Chester makers at the time and that the pipes were being obtained from a variety of sources. Similarly, the total absence of any marked or decorated fragments from the pit suggests that this style of pipe was usually plain. The pipes being purchased at this date were not milled and only a few had bottered rims. This group provides a useful characterisation of the Chester pipes that were being consumed within a single household at this date.

Phase VII Plot 4 pit (1696) (fills (1599), (1601), (1604), (1607), (1625), (1695)

Pit (1696) contained six pipe-bearing deposits, which produced a total of 325 pieces of pipe, comprising eighty-one bowl, 231 stem and thirteen mouthpiece fragments. The pit fill also produced fragments of a tankard with a Queen Anne excise stamp on it and so must have been sealed after 1702. Despite the large size and fresh appearance of many of the pipe fragments, the pit produced a significant quantity of residual material, with at least twenty-nine of the pipe bowl fragments dating to before *c* 1680, including one very early bowl of *c* 1580–1610. Having said that, fifty of the bowl fragments formed a very consistent group, with the bowl forms ranging from *c* 1690 to 1730. All of these bowl forms would fit with a deposition date of around 1710–15, while the stamped stems are all of late seventeenth- to early eighteenth-century types. On balance, the later pipes would suggest a good group of *c* 1705–15, with a final deposition date of around 1710 seeming most likely. The pipe evidence suggests that the majority of the material represents a coherent group, probably discarded over a short period of time, but with the pit fill containing a significant quantity of residual material in its fill.

The latest material from this pit makes an interesting comparison with pit (1522) discussed above, in the same plot and probably sealed only about ten years earlier. Matthew Anderton Jr, who was Mayor of Chester in 1703/4, inherited this property following his father's death in 1693. Matthew Jr died in 1709 and his widow continued to occupy the property during the 1710s. Although parts of the building were rented out (*see* documentary section elsewhere in this volume), it is tempting to see pit (1522) as containing material discarded from the household during his occupancy and pit (1696) as a general clearance following his death in 1709. Either way, both pits relate to the same property and can be used to examine changes in pipe production and consumption over the first decade of the eighteenth century.

One of the principal changes from (1522) was the appearance of five marked or decorated stems in the (1696) assemblage. These five pieces still only represented a small percentage of the 150–200 stems of this date in the pit, suggesting that decorated stems were either still not particularly common or that they were not favoured in this household. The five pieces included parts of three lozenge marks and four different border types. One of the marks comprised the very tip of a lozenge divided into sections containing *fleur de lis* and two of the lozenges were marked Elias Massey, one of which proved to be a new die type for this maker (Ill 5.6.1.26). The Massey marks were associated with two different types of pinnacle and dot border (Rutter & Davey 1980, figs 58.10 and 59.19), one of which was duplicated as an isolated fragment without a surviving lozenge. The final border was a heart, star and *fleur de lis* border type (Rutter & Davey 1980, fig 59.40), which was important in that the bowl survived so that this stamp type could be associated with a specific bowl form (Ill 5.6.4.71). It is also interesting to note that this border appears to have been used by itself, without any accompanying stem stamp. The lozenge with *fleur de lis* appears to have been used in the same way, since it started 80 mm from a bowl junction without any border in between. The lozenge stem stamps and two different, fairly simply executed, styles of border all belong to the earliest styles of Chester stem decoration and support both the integrity of this group and its dating to the early eighteenth century. They also support the suggestion, alluded to above, that some of the more elaborate borders and ovals should be redated to the 1720s or later and that they do not belong to this early period.

Another difference between (1522) and (1696) can be seen in the range and form of the bowl types present. A number of very similar spur bowls dominated pit (1522), with just three heel pipes being present. In contrast, the forty substantially complete bowls from pit (1696) could be divided into almost equal proportions of spur pipes (twenty-one examples: Ills 5.6.4.70–7) and heel pipes (nineteen examples: Ills 5.6.5.78–.86). Some of the spur forms were very similar to those from (1522) (eg Ills 5.6.4.75–6), but none of the mould types could be cross-matched, suggesting that completely different supply sources and/or moulds were being used. Furthermore, the spur pipes tended to have slightly taller, more slender and elegant forms, often with a slight 'kick' in the profile just below the rim and facing the smoker. These subtle differences over no more than a decade show how bowl forms were continually changing and evolving, thus providing the potential for extremely accurate dating. The lack of common mould types also suggests that these had a relatively short life expectancy, either by virtue of wear or changing fashions. The evidence from these two pits would suggest a working life of less than a decade at this period.

The most marked change in style between the two pits, however, can be seen in the heel forms. About 1700 just one heel form was represented in pit (1522). By around 1710 nearly half of the forty pipes were heel forms, all of

which were characterised by quite marked flares to their heels. These heel forms could be further subdivided into those with round heels (thirteen examples or 33% of the group as a whole: Ills 5.6.5.78–.84) and those with tailed heels (six examples or 15%: Ills 5.6.5.85–6), both varieties of which came in a range of sizes. The round heels ranged from very large heels (Ill 5.6.5.84), like two of those from (1522), right through to examples with very small heels (Ills 5.6.5.78–9). The bowl forms associated with the round heel pipes were also extremely varied. Some of these forms were very forward-leaning, for example Ill 5.6.5.81, while others adopted a much larger and more upright bowl, resembling the contemporary London styles (Ill 5.6.5.82). Four of the six tailed heels were generally small, for example Ill 5.6.5.85, although two had rather larger heels to them (Ill 5.6.5.86). Pit (1696) produced a much greater range of bowl forms than (1522), but more detailed comparative studies would be needed to determine how far this reflected general changes in Chester's pipe production over this decade as opposed to specific changes in the consumption patterns in this particular household.

In terms of finishing techniques, there was a notable drop in the use of burnishing. Half of the spur forms in (1522) were burnished, whereas only four of the twenty-one spur forms in (1696) were burnished (19%) and only two of the nineteen heel forms were burnished (11%), giving an average of 15% for the pit group as a whole. This change almost certainly reflected a general trend in the Chester industry at this date, rather than a conscious move away from burnished pipes by the consumers at Plot 4. Most of the burnishing was of a typical standard for the local industry but one piece was finely burnished. This example (Ill 5.6.4.70) could be almost completely reconstructed, giving an estimated original stem length of 350 mm. This pipe is discussed in more detail above, but it is worth noting that it was not significantly longer than the complete pipe from (1503), despite having a very high quality finish. As with the group from (1507), suggested that the surface finish was one of the most important variables, as opposed to other characteristics, such as rim finish or stem length.

Out of the forty-three surviving rims in (1696), thirty-four were simply cut and nine were cut and wiped. Only one example had a milled rim and this was on an 'older' style of bowl (Ill 5.6.5.84). This confirms that the use of milled rims died out rapidly in the early eighteenth century and that, where it did occur, it was usually associated with 'old fashioned' bowls, where it was seen as part of the 'package' for that particular design.

Phase IX, Plot 2, layer (1096)

This layer produced an interesting assemblage of nineteenth-century pipes, which was important for a number of reasons. First, it was one of the few nineteenth-century assemblages recovered from the excavations. As such it helps complete the picture of changing pipe consumption on the site. Second, good nineteenth-century groups from controlled excavations are relatively rare nationally, and so this group helps establish the range and dating for the types present. Third, this pipe assemblage is associated with refuse dumped from a chemist's shop fronting onto Bridge Street, thus providing both a social context and independent dating evidence for this group.

The pipe assemblage totalled thirty-three pieces, comprising bowls bowl fragments, twenty-five stem fragments and one mouthpiece. The group itself was rather mixed, with about a half the material clearly being residual. The earlier pieces included both seventeenth- and eighteenth-century fragments, some of which could not have been much disturbed since their original deposition, since stem fragments of up to 166 mm in length were present. The latest material was, however, quite distinct and included five of the seven bowls, all of which had makers' names or slogans on them. There was also a marked stem, which provided the best dating evidence for the group.

The marked stem had part of an incuse stamp that would have read 'E. SOUTHORN / BROSELEY' on it (Ill 5.6.5.87). Edwin Southorn came from a prominent pipe-making family in Broseley, Shropshire, and established his own business there in about 1858 (Higgins 1987a, 490). He died in 1876 and the business eventually passed back into the family, who occasionally used Edwin's mark on their products until the business finally closed in 1960. Edwin was a particularly interesting and innovative maker, who experimented with different pipe designs and methods of decoration. This stem had been moulded with an unusual ridge or collar in its mid-section and was almost certainly from one of these designs. The combination of this unusual feature and the form of the other pipes from the layer clearly suggest that this pipe was made by Edwin rather than being a later product of the family. As such it can be dated to around 1860–80, providing a good date for the associated material from this layer.

One of the fundamental changes in pipe design during the nineteenth century was the introduction of short-stemmed pipes, which became known as 'cutties', about 1840. At least four out of the five later pipe bowls were of this type. These short-stemmed pipes were made in a wide variety of different styles, many of which had different pattern names. There were two examples of 'Burns Cutty' pipes, both of which were produced in the same mould and both of which had the pattern name moulded in neat, incuse lettering on both sides of the stem (Ill 5.6.5.88). This was one of the most popular nineteenth-century designs and was characterised by a plain, spurless bowl. There was a similarly shaped bowl but with raised ribs on the seams. This had just the very ends of an incuse moulded mark on the stem, which would almost certainly have read 'McDOUGALL / GLASGOW' originally (Ill 5.6.5.89). McDougall's were one of the principal Scottish manufacturers and operated from 1846 to 1967 (Anon 1987, 345). Their pipes were widely exported and circulated freely in the north-west during the second half of the nineteenth century. There was also a specifically shaped bowl that was a pattern known as a Gladstone pipe (Ill 5.6.5.90). This particular example had a shamrock and the slogan 'EVER-GREEN' stamped on the bowl. Irish slogans and motifs were very popular in the north-west but this example was unusual in that the mark had inadvertently been placed upside down.

The final bowl from this group was also designed to draw on the popularity of Irish designs and slogans. This bowl was of an Irish style, with thick walls and a band of hand applied milling around the rim. It also had a slogan stamped on the bowl, in this case reading 'ISLAND BRIDGE' (Ill 5.6.5.91). This pipe may have been a short stemmed cutty or it may have had a longer stem – some of these Irish style bowls had stems around 25 cm long. Apart from these bowls the only other diagnostic nineteenth-century fragment was a piece of stem with traces of a dark green glaze on it. This would have formed part of the mouthpiece coating and would probably have come from a long-stemmed or 'churchwarden' type of pipe.

This group was useful in that it provided a sample of the styles being used in Chester during the 1860s or 70s. The most marked contrast with earlier periods was in the range of styles and supply sources for the pipes. Prior to the mid-nineteenth century the majority of the pipes used in Chester would have fairly plain, long-stemmed varieties, the majority of which would have been produced locally. By this date, however, the majority of the pipes appear to have been short-stemmed cutties, made in a distinctive range of different patterns and by makers from as far afield as Shropshire and Glasgow. Irish styles and slogans were clearly popular but a larger sample is needed before the relative proportions of the different styles in use can be quantified.

The pipes as archaeological evidence

One of the most useful functions of pipe fragments is as a means of accurately dating and interpreting the archaeological deposits in which they occur. The detailed catalogue, deposited as part of the site archive, provides details of all the fragments recovered while a summary of this information is provided below (Table 5.6.5). The significant contexts have been described and discussed above. The following section briefly considers how this information fits into a broader interpretation of the site.

The first point to note is that the archaeological record only contains a partial and biased sample of what once existed. Despite being continually occupied during the post-medieval period, this site produced hardly any nineteenth-century pipes and, had the dump associated with the chemist's shop (context (1096), discussed above) not been within the excavated area, there would only have been scant remains of the nineteenth-century occupation. It would clearly be absurd to suggest that the site was unoccupied during the nineteenth century and so this dependency on survival must be kept in the fore when assessing the archaeological evidence. It is clear that the pipes only reflect events that have happened to survive in the archaeological record and their absence in other periods may simply reflect waste disposal taking place away from the main occupation site. The pipes that have been recovered, however, provide some useful evidence for the use of the site.

The second point to note is the uneven distribution of the pipes across the site as a whole. Table 5.6.3 shows the numbers of fragments excavated from each of the historic property plots (1–6). It is clear that much greater numbers of pipes were recovered from some plots than others, for example, Plots 1 and 4 both produced well over 1000 fragments each while Plot 5 produced only 176. This marked difference could well be the result of a combination of factors – such as the total area excavated within each plot or historic waste disposal patterns. If, however, this bias is peculiar to the pipes, then it may reflect differences in the smoking habits between the various households.

Table 5.6.3 Clay tobacco pipe fragments quantified by plot, pipe part and fragment count

Plot	Bowl	Stem	Mouthpiece	Total
Plot 1	171	884	23	1078
Plot 2	154	679	24	857
Plot 3	137	603	25	765
Plot 4	328	1263	98	1693
Plot 5	52	112	12	176
Plot 6	111	654	24	784
Unattributed	34	174	8	212
Total	987	4369	214	5570

One way to explore this theme is to look at the pipes from specific periods. The excavations produced six of the earliest bowl forms, dating from bowls around 1580 to 1610, plus one stem which appears to be of a similar date. These fragments, however, were not evenly distributed across the site with only one piece coming from each of Plots 1 and 4 but five of the fragments coming from Plot 6. This distribution does not in any way reflect the overall numbers of pipes recovered from each of the excavation areas and clearly suggests that there was a connection between early smoking and Plot 6.

In the late Tudor period tobacco was very expensive and the habit of smoking was only just being disseminated through the upper levels of society. This marked concentration of early fragments is interesting but, unfortunately, it may be more to do with patterns of waste disposal rather than identifying a particular owner who took up smoking at an early date. Plot 6 appears to have been an area comprising an open garden and then a yard or drying ground during the nineteenth century. This area may well have been open ground since the Tudor period and so the early pipes could have been discarded there as general rubbish or become spread on a garden with night soil as manure. The exact nature and degree of access to this plot in the late sixteenth century is uncertain and so it is not possible to link this concentration of early pipes with a particular owner or family.

Similar problems are encountered when trying to attribute pipes to particular events, such as the Civil War period in Chester. Although pipes dating from the mid-seventeenth century are certainly present in the excavated sample, there were no discrete features that stood out as being distinctive from this period, nor any marked change in the deposition of pipes to suggest a breakdown in waste disposal during at this time. This may be partly the result of collecting data from a crowded urban environment where there had been a lot of accumulated debris and reworking of deposits during the post-medieval period. As a result, the survival of key groups is perhaps more fortuitous and dependent on the individual history of the plot rather than a matter of course following national events.

While it may not be possible to follow these national events very closely, the excavated evidence proved particularly strong when it comes to individual events affecting the individual households. The excavation and filling of rubbish pits following a domestic agenda, for example, produced some of the best evidence from the site. Some of the larger groups may have accumulated over a period of time while others may have been triggered by a change of ownership or a death in the family, as has been tentatively suggested above. These groups not only provided an insight into the consumption patterns of individual households but, taken together, they provided a reflection of changing trends within Chester

as a whole. The pipes discussed above have not only provided important dating evidence for the post-medieval deposits from the excavations but also a broader window through which to view pipe manufacturing, trading and consumption patterns as well as the personal preferences of individual households.

Other pipeclay objects

In addition to the pipes, various other pipe clay objects were recovered from the site and these are discussed below.

Hair curlers

Although wigs had been used in England to hide baldness since at least the sixteenth century, they only became popular as fashion items following their introduction from the French court by Charles II in 1663 (Bullock *et al* 1996, 5) and they remained in common use until about 1800. The early curlers were comparatively crudely made and often show signs of being entirely hand-modelled, probably being made as a sideline by local pipemakers or potters. By the eighteenth century the demand was sufficient for specialist manufacturers to emerge and much more symmetrical and professionally made curlers were produced. There were three fragments of purpose-made curlers from the excavations, all of which were of a neat, symmetrical form, suggesting that they date from the eighteenth century.

Half of a medium-sized curler was recovered from (601), a context containing material of mixed date which was not sealed until at least the nineteenth century (Ill 5.6.10.183). This piece had a simple cut end 7 mm across; it was broken in half, where it was 12 mm in diameter, swelling to a maximum of 16 mm at the surviving end. A fragment from a curler of generally similar proportions was recovered from (344), but this was too fragmentary for any useful measurements to be made (both the ends and the middle were missing and the surviving piece is splintered diagonally across the maximum swelling). The pipes from (344) were of mixed seventeenth- and eighteenth-century dates, with final deposition most likely taking place around 1740–1800.

The final purpose-made piece was from a small curler and was interesting since it had the incuse stamped initials WB with a dot above and below on its surviving end (Ill 5.6.10.184). The end had been cut before the stamp was applied and was about 5 mm across. The maximum thickness of the surviving end was 13 mm. This piece came from context (208), which contained finds of mixed date but which was probably sealed during the first half of the nineteenth century. Maker's marks are relatively rare on curlers and, when they do occur, they tend to belong to a very restricted range and to be found on particularly well shaped and neatly finished products. This suggests that most of these marked curlers were made by a small number of specialist makers who marketed their products very widely. The WB mark is by far the most common to be found nationally and it is these initials that occur on about two-thirds of all marked curlers. The author has documented examples of this mark from all over England, ranging from as far afield as Carlisle to Cornwall, and these pieces must have been produced in a

Table 5.6.4 Marbles quantified by phase, plot, context and material

Phase	Plot	Context	Diam (mm)	Material	Date	Description
IV	1	265	15.2	Grey stone?	Medieval	Appears to be made of a fine-grained pale grey stone.
V	2	1311	13.5	Buff stone?	Late medieval	Pale white to buff-coloured object with a very weathered and eroded surface, possibly stone; rather irregular shape, surviving to 13.5 mm max diam.
IX	1	208	15.5	Grey stone	1800–1850	Appears to be made of a fine grained greyish stone.
		208	16.5	Marbled clay	1800–1850	Mainly white clay marbled with red veins.
		208	17.2	White clay	1800–1850	White clay marble.
IX	1	601	18	Pinkish clay?	1800–1910	Pale pinkish coloured marble - clay?
IX	2	1286	20	White stone	1810–1850	Slightly mottled white stone, probably marble. This example not as perfectly spherical as the others.
IX	6	375	13.9	Grey stone	1800–1900	Fine, darker grey stone.
		510	15.8	Buff stone	1790–1920	
X	3	1399	16.3	Marbled clay	19–20 cent	Mainly white clay marbled with red veins; slightly irregular form.
		1399	16.1	Buff stone	19–20 cent	Pale brownish buff coloured stone.
X	6	300	16.4	White clay	19–20 cent	Probably white clay (not certain).
		300	15.4	Buff clay	19–20 cent	Pale yellowish/buff coloured clay (probably).
		301	18.4	Grey stone	19–20 cent	Very fine pale grey stone with fine banding visible with lens.

large-scale workshop, most likely situated in London. One example has previously been recorded from Chester (Rutter & Davey 1980, fig 86.16).

As well as purpose-made hair curlers, it is known that other objects were sometimes used to curl hair, including pieces of pipe stem. At least sixteen of the pipe stems from the excavations had at least one of their broken ends ground smooth, for example, Ills 5.6.10.177, .180 and .181. Unfortunately, it is very hard to say whether this had occurred because a broken pipe has been adapted for reuse (as, perhaps, is the case with Ill 5.6.10.177), because a pipe fragment has been used to draw like a stick of chalk, because a fragment has been made into a hair curler or because it has simply been doodled with. In most examples just one smoothed end survived, making interpretation even more difficult, for example, Ill 5.6.10.180. In one instance, however, a stem fragment with both ends smoothed survived, raising the possibility that it had been adapted for use as a curler (Ill 5.6.10.181). The stem fragment had quite a large bore (7/64") and a rather oval section, which would suggest a date of around 1680–1730 for this piece. It was recovered from context (325).

Marbles

A total of fourteen marbles, or possible marbles, were recovered from the excavations (Table 5.6.4). Although these items are often recovered from excavations there appears to have been very little study of the materials from which they are made, the variations in size and finish that are evident or the dates at which they were produced. The finds from the 25 Bridge Street excavation are described below in the hope that they will contribute to a broader study of these objects at a future date.

Despite being sorted as clay objects the first point to note is that the majority of the marbles are, in fact, made of stone. There is one very weathered and irregular object from Context (1311) that is probably a natural stone nodule and so this will not be discussed further. Of the remaining thirteen marbles, at least eight and possibly as many as eleven appear to have been made of various types of very fine-grained stone. These ranged from 13.9 to 20.0 mm in diameter and the majority vary from a near white to a pale grey in colour. These examples are generally extremely well made, with a strongly spherical form, suggesting that they have been machine-turned. With

one exception, these were all recovered from Phase IX and X deposits, with the associated pipes suggesting a date of after 1800 for these examples. The one exception was from context 265 (Phase IV), a medieval context where it was presumably intrusive.

In contrast, only two of the marbles were certainly made of clay with two or three further examples that were possibly made of clay. The two certain examples were both made of marbled red and white clays and had diameters of 16.3 mm and 16.5 mm. These examples had a slightly less perfectly spherical form, although they were still of a good quality, and were presumably hand-rolled. The other three examples were pinkish, pale grey and buff in colour and it is not certain whether these are made of clay or stone – a proper geological examination is required to identify with certainty the materials from which all of these marbles were made. As with the stone examples, the clay marbles all came from Phase IX or X deposits and dated from after 1800.

In general terms, all of the marbles recovered appear to date from the nineteenth or twentieth centuries and range from 13.0 to 20.0 mm in size. This compares closely with the 15–18 mm range recorded for two nineteenth- or early twentieth-century clay marbles from excavations at Castletown on the Isle of Man (Higgins 1996, 96–7). The majority of the 25 Bridge Street marbles were found in Plots 1 and 6 (five examples each), with smaller numbers from Plots 2 and 3 (two examples each). Further work is clearly needed to establish the timespan over which marbles were commonly used and to see whether regional or temporal differences in size and material (glass, stone, clay, etc) can be discerned.

Summary

The pipes from this site not only provided a valuable means of dating and interpreting the deposits in which they occurred, but also an important reference point for future pipe studies. This is probably the largest domestic assemblage to have been recovered from Chester over the last twenty-five years and provided an opportunity to assess the sequences of bowl forms and makers' marks that were established for the city during the 1970s. While these still provide an invaluable framework, it has been found that the previously published corpus of marks needs to be redrawn at a larger scale and with greater precision. Similarly, the dating of the marks and their attribution to individual workshops needs to be reviewed and a new and more manageable typology established for the bowl forms. This study has also shown many more marks remain to be discovered, with this one assemblage contributing some thirty new marks to the known range – an increase of about 15%.

The excavations produced a good number of the earliest bowl forms, datable to *c* 1580–1610. These were concentrated in Plot 6 and reflected not only the affluence of the city at a time when tobacco would have been very expensive, but also the fact that it was 'moving with the times' by adopting new habits. The earliest pipes were probably imported from London, but by the early seventeenth century others may have been made locally, raising the question of exactly when production started in the city: a very early date seems likely. Around 14% of the early seventeenth-century pipes were stamped with makers' marks, initials being more than twice as common as symbol marks. These provided clues to the origins and trade in these pipes but it must not be forgotten that 86% of the pipes were still unmarked. The Chester makers went against the national trend by not using milling for much of the seventeenth century and this shows that many of the unmarked pipes were, as might be expected, produced in the city.

Both local and imported fabrics appear to have been in use and, during the seventeenth century, distinctive local styles of marking appeared. Stem stamps, and in particular individual *fleur de lis* marks, were used to make patterns, and these provided the inspiration for the more complex stem stamps and decorative borders that were to follow. A sudden decline in the use of maker's marks was noted after *c* 1660 and of burnishing towards the end of that century. In contrast, decorative stem borders appeared from the late seventeenth century and became much more complex and elaborate as they developed to become the hallmark of Chester pipes during the eighteenth century. The evidence from these excavations suggests that the early borders were generally simple and that some of the more elaborate and refined borders need to be redated to a slightly later period, most likely to the 1720s and later.

Tangible evidence for trade was provided by pipes with parallels from as far afield as the west midlands, Oxford and London, while individual groups provided information on manufacturing techniques and consumption patterns within Chester itself. The general quality of the pipes was good, with some exceptionally well finished pieces demonstrating how Chester achieved its reputation for producing outstanding pipes. One important discovery is the straightness of the stems that were produced, suggesting the use of special drying racks, such as were used in the Netherlands. The use of specially produced racks with stem grooves is unknown elsewhere in Britain and, if they were used here, they mark a distinct technological break with the rest of the country. Another discovery was the fact that iron-staining in the ground can significantly alter the overall appearance of buried pipes by giving them a colour cast. This overall tinting (as opposed to individual discoloured areas of staining) renders any description of the whiteness of the fabric meaningless unless the fabric has either been chemically cleaned or is freshly broken.

This site produced individual groups ranging from kiln waste to possible house clearance assemblages. Some of these groups can be traced back to individual families,

including those used by a former mayor of the city. Finds such as these provide insights into the day-to-day production of pipes and the choices made by domestic consumers. Similarly, the first complete eighteenth-century pipe from the city provides an initial step towards defining the range of stem lengths that were produced in Chester. Chester was an important production centre with a substantial export trade. The pipemakers would have produced a range of different patterns for their various markets, many of which would have also been produced in different qualities. Although many of the bowl forms and finishing techniques are well known, these cannot be fully understood without knowing the lengths of the pipes to which they belonged. The cost of a pipe was largely dependent on stem length and so assessing the social status of a group is also dependent on knowing the overall form of the pipes that it contains. The careful recovery of all fragments from discrete and undisturbed deposits is clearly a research priority if further complete pipes are to be reassembled. These are needed to not only provide fresh insights into the home markets but also into the styles that were produced for export to many other parts of the world.

Catalogue (Ills 5.6.1–.10)

Where there is more than one bowl fragment from the same context a letter (A, B, C, etc) has been allocated to each piece to identify it in the records. These letters have been pencilled onto the pipe fragments and are given in brackets following the context number. All die numbers refer to the numbers allocated in the National Clay Tobacco Pipe Stamp Catalogue, which is being compiled by the author. The illustrations are all at 1/1 with the exception of the stamp details, which are at 2/1, and the complete pipes, which are at 1/3.

Stamps

1   Die no 1983. Incuse stamped 'snowflake' mark across the stem of a heel pipe of *c* 1580–1610. This is an early bowl with bead rim and at least six 'snowflake' stamps forming a pattern on the stem. This particular design is known to have been in use *c* 1600–1610, suggesting that this mark may be more closely dated to the very early years of the seventeenth century. (1819): Phase VIII, Plot 1; SF 9275. Ill 5.6.6.92.

2   Die no 1986. Relief stamped 'snowflake' mark across the stem of a heel pipe of *c* 1610–40. The stem is decorated with two lozenges made up of a series of individual 'snowflake' type stamps (the first lozenge is made up of nine stamps and the second four). (429) A: Phase VI, Plot 3, fill of (850)/(430); SF 8648. Ill 5.6.7.121.

3   Die no 1985. Relief stamped *fleur de lis* mark across the stem of a pipe of *c* 1610–60 (and, most likely, 1610–50). This stamp occurs as part of a group of seven identical surviving impressions that would almost certainly have formed a lozenge of pattern made up of nine stamps originally. Very coarse gritty fabric, probably a Chester product. (223): Phase VIII; Plot 1, fill of (219).

4   Die no 1980. Incuse stamped star mark on the base of a heel pipe of *c* 1620–50. (1414): Phase X, Plot 3, fill of (1415); SF 9409. Ill 5.6.6.110.

5 Die no 1981. Relief stamped wheel mark on the base of a heel pipe of *c* 1610–50. Very shiny surface to the pipe but no obvious burnishing lines. (1371): Phase VIII, Plot 4, fill of (1545); SF 9236. Ill 5.6.6.111.

6 Die no 1979. Relief stamped wheel mark on the base of a heel pipe of *c* 1610–40 (1871): Phase VIII, Plot 1, fill of (1812); SF 9356. Ill 5.6.6.109.

7 Die no 1982. Relief stamped mark reading GA facing the smoker on the bowl of a spur pipe of *c* 1640–60. This is a south Lancashire style of mark with at least two bands of milling surviving on the stem. (659): Phase VII, Plot 2; SF 8653. Ill 5.6.8.145.

8 Die no 1987. Relief stamped mark reading TB on the base of a heel pipe of *c* 1640–60. Heel fragment only survives. Evaluation Trench F (17); SF 9872.

9 Die no 1990. Relief stamped mark reading NE (ligatured) on the base of a heel pipe of *c* 1620–60. Unidentified Chester maker. (301): Phase X, Plot 6; SF 9304. Ill 5.6.7.125.

10 Die no 1988. Relief stamped mark reading NE (ligatured) on the base of a heel pipe of *c* 1620–60. Unidentified Chester maker. (302): Phase X, Plot 6, fill of (303); SF 8327. Ill 5.6.7.126.

11 Die no 1989. Relief stamped mark reading NE on the base of a heel pipe of *c* 1610–40. Unidentified Chester maker. Evaluation Trench F (26); SF 9873. Ill 5.6.7.124.

12 Die no 1991. Relief stamped mark reading IG on the base of a heel pipe of *c* 1610–40. (1406) (B): Phase VIII, Plot 3, fill of (1413). Ill 5.6.7.127.

13 Die no 1992. Relief stamped mark reading RG on the base of a heel pipe of *c* 1640–60. Probably an unidentified maker from the Nantwich area of Cheshire. U/S; SF 9137. Ill 5.6.7.139.

14 Die no 1993. Relief stamped mark reading WK (ligatured) on the base of a heel pipe of *c* 1610–40. Probably a London mark. (1601) (AH): Phase VII, Plot 4, fill of (1696). Ill 5.6.6.108.

15 Die no 1999. Relief stamped hexagonal mark with a bird and the initials AL across the stem of a pipe of *c* 1640–70. This mark can be attributed to Alexander Lanckton of Chester (*fl* 1657, d 1670). (301): Phase X, Plot 6; SF 8131.

16 Die no 1994. Relief stamped mark reading HL on the base of a heel pipe of *c* 1640–60. Probably a Rainford (south Lancashire) maker. (1601): Phase VII, Plot 4, fill of (1696); SF 9565. Ill 5.6.7.138.

17 Die no 1988. Composite drawing of a relief stamped mark reading IL found on the base of two heel pipes of *c* 1610–40 (eg Ill 5.6.6.114). There is a similar IL mark from Eccleshall castle, Staffordshire. Drawing based on examples from contexts (1546): Phase VII, Plot 4; SF 9786 and (1556)/(1566): Phase VI, Plot 4; SF 9552.

18 Die no 1995. Composite drawing of a relief stamped mark reading M found on the base of two heel pipes of *c* 1610–40 (Ills 5.6.6.115 and .116). (663): Phase VII; SF 8667 and (1901), fill of (1902); SF 9423, both from Plot 1.

19 Die no 1996. Relief stamped mark reading AP on the base of a heel pipe of *c* 1630–60. Probably a London mark. (429) (B): Phase VI, Plot 3, fill of (850)/(430); SF 8555. Ill 5.6.7.120.

20 Die no 1997. Relief stamped mark reading IP on the base of a heel pipe of *c* 1680–1720. Coventry style bowl and stamp, attributable to John Pottifer, working at Coventry in 1710. U/S; SF 9793. Ill 5.6.8.149.

21 Die no 1984. Relief stamped *fleur de lis* mark across the stem of a pipe of *c* 1690–1715 made up of two joining fragments This pipe is very finely finished and has two shields, one above the other, each containing a single *fleur de lis*. Above and below these shields are two bands of milling, so neatly applied that it is impossible to see where each band starts or finishes. Made of a fine and probably imported fabric. This mark also occurs on the same pipe as a double milled border (Die no 826). Joining bowl from (463) (AE): Phase IX, fill of (465) and stem from (484): Phase IX, fill of (483); SF 8226; both Plot 2. Ill 5.6.9.161.

22 Die no 2000. Part of a new shield shaped Chester mark on a pipe of *c* 1690–1715. This is similar to the top of Die no 640, which includes the maker's initials RG (Rutter & Davey 1980, fig 52.10) but it is larger. This mark also occurs on the same pipe as a roll-stamped border, Die no 765 (Rutter & Davey 1980, fig 60, 52). (520): Phase VIII, Plot 6, fill of (519); SF 8381.

23 Die no 1768. Relief stamped Chester arms across the stem of a pipe of *c* 1700–30 This is on the same pipe as a heart and tendril border of previously unidentified form (Die no 1932; Ill 5.6.2.47). (301): Phase X, Plot 6; SF 8130.

24 Die no 703. Good impression of the Chester arms on a pipe of *c* 1730–60. This mark does not have a dot above the shield, unlike the 1980 drawing of the same die by Rutter & Davey (fig 56.49; their source material has been checked and none have a dot in this position). This mark also occurs on the same pipe as a decorative border (Die no 794; Rutter & Davey 1980, fig 61.81). (1867): Phase VIII, Plot 1, fill of (1866).

25 Die no 1770. Relief stamped arms with the motto 'FIDE.ET.CONS…' across the stem of a pipe of *c* 1700–20. The arms includes three crescents and the motto possibly ends with the letter 'A'. There is a very crisp tulip/heart/*fleur de lis* borders above and below arms (Die no 2008; Ill 5.6.2.46). (1406): Phase VIII, Plot 3, fill of (1413); SF 9350.

26 Die no 1967. Composite drawing of a relief stamped mark reading 'ELIAS MASSEY' across the stem of a pipe of *c* 1690–1710. This mark is associated with a stem border (Die no 733; Rutter & Davey 1980, fig 58.19). Examples from (1607): Phase VII, fill (1696); SF 9398 and (1546): Phase VII; SF 9355, both from Plot 4.

27 Die no 1968. Relief stamped mark reading 'ELIAS MASSEY' across the stem of a pipe of *c* 1690–1715. Shiny stem but no obvious burnishing lines. This mark is associated with a stem border (Die no 1975; Ill 5.6.2.39). (463): Phase VII, Plot 2, fill of (465); SF 8883.

28 Die no 1969. Heraldic mark comprising a bird sitting on a bundle of arrows stamped across the stem of a pipe of *c* 1690–1720. This has rather a thick burnished stem with a large bore. The mark is associ-

ated with a stem border (Die no 1971; Ill 5.6.2.37). (1892): Phase IX, Plot 1, cut; SF 9578.

29 Die no 1966. Heraldic mark comprising a swan's neck rising out of a coronet stamped across the stem of a pipe of *c* 1690–1720. The mark is associated with a stem border (Die no 1977; Ill 5.6.2.40). (1406): Phase VIII, Plot 3, fill of (1413); SF 9462.

30 Die no 1769. Relief stamped mark with a lion and the initials TO across the stem of a pipe of *c* 1700–20. This TO stem stamp is similar to a mark already known from Chester (Die no 676; Rutter & Davey 1980, fig 55.22) but with a plain border, as is the case with an example from Warrington Old Academy (Higgins 1987b, fig 11.6). These marks can be attributed to either Thomas or Timothy Ormes of Chester. The mark is associated with a stem border (Die no 1932; Ill 5.6.2.47). (559): Phase VIII, Plot 6, fill of (519); SF 8408.

31 Die no 681. Relief stamped rampant lion mark on a pipe of *c* 1700–1720. The mark is associated with a stem border (Die no 2004; Ill 5.6.2.44). (1404): Phase IX, Plot 3; SF 8948.

32 Die no 1771. Relief stamped Masonic mark with the initials RG across the stem of a pipe of *c* 1760–1790. The mark is associated with a stem border (Die no 816; Rutter & Davey 1980, fig 61.104). (601): Phase IX, Plot 1; SF 8440.

33 Die no 1970. Incuse stamped stem border on a pipe of *c* 1690–1720. This border is associated with a stem stamp (Die no 1168 which is a larger variant of Rutter & Davey 1980, fig 52.5). (1090): Phase IX, Plot 3; SF 8891.

34 Die no 1972. Relief stamped stem border from a pipe of *c* 1750–60. This border is associated with other stem stamps (Die nos 31 and 668; Rutter & Davey 1980, figs 63.1 and 54.14 respectively). (344): Phase IX, Plot 6; SF 8400.

35 Die no 1974. Relief stamped stem border from a pipe of *c* 1750–90. Appears to be a new border comprising a lattice pattern with dots. (1802): Phase X, Plot 1; SF 9511.

36 Die no 1973. Relief stamped stem border from a pipe of *c* 1690–1720. (1891): Phase VII, Plot 1; SF 9399.

37 Die no 1971. Relief stamped stem border from a pipe of *c* 1690–1720 that has rather a thick burnished stem with a large bore. This border is associated with a stem stamp (Die no 1969; Ill 5.6.1.28). (1892): Phase VII, Plot 1, cut; SF 9578.

38 Die no 1976. Relief stamped stem border from a pipe of *c* 1710–1800. The top edge of the stamp is missing but it would have mirrored the bottom. (300): Phase X, Plot 6.

39 Die no 1975. Relief stamped border across the stem of a pipe of *c* 1690–1715. Shiny stem but no obvious burnishing lines. This border occurs on the same pipe as the Elias Massey mark (Die no 1968; Ill 5.6.1.27). (463): Phase VII, Plot 2, fill of (465); SF 8883.

40 Die no 1977. Relief stamped stem border from a pipe of *c* 1690–1720. This border is associated with a stem stamp (Die no 1966; Ill 5.6.1.29). (1406): Phase VIII, Plot 3, fill of (1413); SF 9462.

41 Die no 2006. Relief stamped stem border from a pipe of *c* 1700–20. (558): Phase IX, Plot 6; SF 8407.

42 Die no 2005. Relief stamped stem border from a pipe of *c* 1700–20. Glossy fabric but not burnished. The border starts 50 mm from the bowl junction. (1507): Phase VII, Plot 4, fill of (1506); SF 9115.

43 Die no 2007. Relief stamped stem border from a pipe of *c* 1700–20. Very slag-encrusted stem. (1349): Phase X, Plot 4; SF 9119.

44 Die no 2004. Relief stamped stem border from a pipe of *c* 1700–20. This border is associated with a stem stamp (Die no 681; Ill 5.6.2.31). (1404): Phase X, Plot 3, fill of (1404); SF 8948.

45 Die no 761. Relief stamped stem border from a pipe of *c* 1700–20. This border is associated with a stem stamp (Die no 647; Rutter & Davey 1980, fig 53.7). (302): Phase X, Plot 6, fill of (303); SF 8137.

46 Die no 2008. Relief stamped stem border from across the stem of a pipe of *c* 1700–20. The border is associated with a stem stamp depicting a coat of arms with three crescents and the motto 'FIDE.ET.CONS...', the last word possibly ending with an A (Die no 1770; Ill 5.6.1. 25). (1406): Phase VIII, Plot 3, fill of (1413); SF 9350.

47 Die no 1932. Relief stamped stem border from a pipe of *c* 1700–20 with a TO stem stamp across the stem (Die no 1769; Ill 5.6.1.30) for Thomas or Timothy Ormes of Chester. (559): Phase VIII, Plot 6, fill of (519); SF 8408.

48 Die no 1934. Relief stamped stem border from a pipe of *c* 1700–30 This mark also occurs on the same pipe as Die nos 31 and 641 (Rutter & Davey 1980, figs 63.1 and 53.2 respectively). (1872): Phase VIII, Plot 1, fill of (1873); SF 9357.

49 Die no 1933. Composite drawing based on three examples of a relief stamped stem border of *c* 1700–30. In all three instances the border is associated with a Talbot stem stamp (Die no 642; Rutter & Davey 1980, fig 53.2) and in one case the complete decorative scheme of two Talbots and two of these borders can be seen (Ill 5.6.9.162). Drawing based on examples from (301): Phase X, Plot 6; SF 8323; (1399): Phase X, Plot 3; SF 9497; and (1406): Phase VIII, Plot 3, fill of (1413); SF 9349.

50 Die no 1243. Relief stamped stem border from a pipe of *c* 1720–60. This stem also has part of a Chester oval but it is too fragmentary to identify the individual die type. The tendril border has previously recorded at Beeston castle, but it is not in Rutter & Davey (1980). This composite drawing has been made from the 25 Bridge Street (1830): Phase IX, Plot 1; SF 9353 and Beeston castle examples.

51 Die no 773. Relief stamped stem border from a pipe of *c* 1720–60. (201): Phase IX, Plot 1; SF 8135.

52 Die no 2009. Relief stamped stem border from a pipe of *c* 1720–60. (1830): Phase IX, Plot 1; SF 9785.

53 Die no 2010. Relief stamped stem border from a pipe of *c* 1760–90. New type of tendril border with three lines of flanking geometric borders. Incomplete example, but the triple border is very distinctive. (438): Phase X, Plot 2; SF 8377.

54 Die no 1978. Composite drawing of a relief stamped mark reading 'FITZGERALD CHESTER' along the stem of a pipe of *c* 1770–1830. A number of pipemakers by the name Fitzgerald were working in Chester between *c* 1716 and *c* 1840. There are three

likely candidates for this particular mark, James I (*c* 1784–1835), James II (*c* 1773–1828) or Joseph II (*c* 1792–1840). Drawing based on three fragmentary examples, all from Plot 1: (601): Phase IX; SFs 8438 and 8439; and (653): Phase VIII. The fragment from (653) joins (601) SF 8439.

55 Die no 1767. Relief stamped mark reading AIRES CHESTER along the stem of a pipe of *c* 1780–1830. Another example of this mark with its associated bowl form is shown in Ill 5.6.10.176. (1802): Phase X, Plot 1; SF 9509.

56 Die no 1765. Incuse stamped mark reading 'EVER-GREEN' above a shamrock motif facing the smoker on the bowl of a spurless pipe of *c* 1860–1920. This particular bowl shape was generally known as a 'Gladstone'. The stamp has been applied upside-down on this pipe, the surface of which has been sanded, probably to take a "meerschaum wash" finish. (1096) (D): Phase IX, Plot 2. Ill 5.6.5.90.

57 Die no 1766. Incuse stamped mark reading 'ISLAND BRIDGE' facing the smoker on the bowl of a spurless pipe of *c* 1860–1900. Irish style bowl with hand impressed milling around the rim. (1096): Phase IX, Plot 2; SF 8845. Ill 6.5.5.91.

Bowls and stems

58 Spur bowl of *c* 1640–70. The rim is internally trimmed and bottered and three-quarters milled; the stem bore is 6/64". The surface has a good burnish. (1507) (BY): Phase VII, Plot 4, fill of (1506).

59 Spur bowl of *c* 1640–70. The rim is bottered and fully milled; the stem bore is 6/64". The surface has a good burnish. (1507) (CO): Phase VII, Plot 4, fill of (1506).

60 Spur bowl of *c* 1640–70. The rim is bottered and fully milled; the stem bore is 7/64". The surface has a good burnish. (1507) (BL): Phase VII, Plot 4, fill of (1506).

61 Spur bowl of *c* 1640–70. The rim is bottered and fully milled; the stem bore is 7/64". The surface has a good burnish. (1507) (DM): Phase VII, Plot 4, fill of (1506).

62 Spur bowl of *c* 1640–70. The rim is bottered and fully milled; the stem bore is 8/64". The surface is not burnished. (1507) (CU): Phase VII, Plot 4, fill of (1506).

63 Spur bowl of *c* 1690–1720. The rim is bottered but not milled; the stem bore is 7/64". The surface has a good burnish and the bowl has a slightly earlier looking, more cylindrical form to the other associated bowls from the same pit group. (1503) (AD): Phase X, Plot 5.

64 Joining spur bowl fragments of *c* 1690–1720 made in the same mould as bowls F, G H and I from this context. This mould is characterised by three very clear flaws just above the spur on the right-hand side of the bowl. The rim of this example is cut but not milled; the stem bore is 7/64". The surface is not burnished. (1503) (E): Phase X, Plot 5.

65 Spur bowl of *c* 1690–1720 with a surviving stem length of 149 mm. The rim is cut but not milled; the stem bore is 7/64". This bowl is distinguished from others in its group by having a particularly large,

wide-mouthed form and a chunky spur. The surface is not burnished. (1503) (J); Phase X, Plot 5.

66 Spur bowl of *c* 1690–1720 with a surviving stem length of 212 mm. The rim is cut but not milled; the stem bore is 6/64". The surface has a good burnish. A long, low ridge (mould flaw) running up from the spur on the left-hand side of the bowl distinguishes this mould type. Another example from the same mould was found in (1504) (E): Phase VII, Plot 4, fill of (1522). This example is from (1503) (Q): Phase X, Plot 5.

67 Spur bowl of *c* 1690–1720 and joining fragments making up a complete pipe. The rim is possibly wiped but not milled; the stem bore is 7/64". The surface has an average burnish. This mould type is characterised by a series of long, low lines (mould flaws) running back from the bowl on both sides of the stem. Six other examples from this mould were identified, five from (1503) (C, K, N, M and U): Phase X, Plot 5, and one from 1504 (D): Phase VII, Plot 4, fill of (1522). This example is from (1503) (A).

68 Spur bowl of *c* 1690–1720. The rim is bottered but not milled; the stem bore is 6/64". The surface is too abraded to tell whether or not it was burnished originally. (1503) (AE): Phase X, Plot 5.

69 Heel bowl of *c* 1690–1720 with a surviving stem length of 138 mm. The rim is cut but not milled; the stem bore is 7/64". The surface is not burnished. (1503) (R): Phase X, Plot 5.

70 Spur bowl and three two stem fragments from (1601) which join with two stems from (1599) to make up an almost complete pipe of *c* 1710–20. Stem bore variable from 5–6/64" along its length. The rim is cut and wiped but not milled. The surface has a fine burnish all over. (1601) (A) and (1599): both Phase VII, Plot 4, fill of (1696).

71 Spur bowl of *c* 1710–20. The rim is cut but not milled; the stem bore is 5/64". The surface is not burnished. (1604): Phase VII, Plot 4, fill of (1696); SF 9269.

72 Spur bowl of *c* 1710–20. The rim is cut but not milled; the stem bore is 6/64". The surface is not burnished. (1601) (L): Phase VII, Plot 4, fill of (1696).

73 Spur bowl of *c* 1710–20. The rim is cut but not milled; the stem bore is 5/64". The surface is not burnished. (1604) (N): Phase VII, Plot 4, fill of (1696).

74 Spur bowl of *c* 1710–20. The rim is cut but not milled; the stem bore is 6/64". The surface is not burnished. (1604) (O): Phase VII, Plot 4, fill of (1696).

75 Spur bowl of *c* 1710–30. The rim is cut but not milled; the stem bore is 6/64". The surface is not burnished. (1601) (S): Phase VII, Plot 4, fill of (1696).

76 Spur bowl of *c* 1710–30. The rim is cut but not milled; the stem bore is 5/64". The surface is not burnished. (1601) (T): Phase VII, Plot 4, fill of (1696).

77 Probably a heel bowl of *c* 1670–1720. The rim is cut but not milled; the stem bore is 5/64". The surface is not burnished. (1601) (W): Phase VII, Plot 4, fill of (1696).

78 Heel bowl of *c* 1710–20. No obvious burnishing lines but the surface is very glossy; stem end freshly broken but not joining fragment in this group. The rim is cut but not milled; the stem bore is 5/64". (1601) (P): Phase VII, Plot 4, fill of (1696).

79 Heel bowl of *c* 1 710–20. The base of the heel has not been trimmed. The rim is cut but not milled; the stem bore is 5/64". The surface is not burnished. (1604) (I): Phase VII, Plot 4, fill of (1696).

80 Heel bowl of *c* 1690–1715. The rim is cut but not milled; the stem bore is 6/64". The surface is not burnished. (1601) (V): Phase VII, Plot 4, fill of (1696).

81 Heel bowl of *c* 1710–20. The rim is cut but not milled; the stem bore is 7/64". The surface has a good burnish. (1601) (U): Phase VII, Plot 4, fill of (1696).

82 Heel bowl of *c* 1700–20. The rim is cut but not milled; the stem bore is 6/64". The surface is not burnished. (1601) (X): Phase VII, Plot 4, fill of (1696).

83 Heel bowl of *c* 1710–20. The rim is cut and possibly wiped but not milled; the stem bore is 7/64". The surface has a light but good burnish. (1599) (J): Phase VII, Plot 4, fill of (1696).

84 Heel bowl of *c* 1690–1720. The rim is cut and possibly wiped as well as being milled (probably three-quarters originally); the stem bore is 5/64". The surface has a good burnish. (1599) (N): Phase VII, Plot 4, fill of (1696).

85 Heel bowl of *c* 1710–20. The rim is cut but not milled; the stem bore is 5/64". The surface is not burnished. (1601) (F): Phase VII, Plot 4, fill of (1696).

86 Heel bowl of *c* 1710–20. The rim is cut but not milled; the stem bore is 6/64". The surface is not burnished. (1601) (E): Phase VII, Plot 4, fill of (1696).

87 Stem fragment of *c* 1860–80 with a stamped mark reading 'E S… / BRO….'. There is an unusual moulded 'collar' around the mid-section of the stem and part of an E. Southorn stem stamp from Broseley in Shropshire. This is similar to Die no 29 but incomplete so it cannot be identified to an exact match. This stem most likely dates to Edwin Southorn's period of production (1858–76) although the same mark was occasionally used later by William Southorn & Co. Stem bore is 5/64". The surface has a good burnish. (1096): Phase IX, Plot 2; SF 9162.

88 Spurless bowl of *c* 1860–1900 with a moulded mark reading 'BURNS CUTTY / BURNS CUTTY' in very neatly executed lettering. Appears to be from the same mould as SF 8847 from this context. The rim is cut but not milled; the stem bore is 4/64". The surface is not burnished. (1096): Phase IX, Plot 2; SF 8846.

89 Spurless bowl of *c* 1860–1967 with a moulded mark reading 'MC… / …W'. Almost certainly a product of McDougall's of Glasgow, who were working from 1846 until 1967. The rim is cut but not milled; the stem bore is 4/64". The surface is not burnished. (1096) (C): Phase IX, Plot 2.

90 Spurless bowl of *c* 1860–1920 stamped with a shamrock motif above which is the lettering 'EVERGREEN' (Die no 1765). This particular pipe bowl shape was known as a Gladstone. The stamped mark has been applied upside-down. The surface of the bowl has been sanded, probably to take a "meerschaum wash" finish. The rim is cut but not milled; the stem bore is 4/64". (1096) (D): Phase IX, Plot 2.

91 Spurless bowl of *c* 1860–1900 with a stamped mark reading 'ISLAND BRIDGE' (Die no 1766). Irish style bowl with hand impressed milling around the rim. The rim is cut and fully milled; the stem bore is 5/ 64". The surface is not burnished. (1096): Phase IX, Plot 2; SF 8845.

92 Heel bowl of *c* 1580–1610 with a stamped 'snowflake' mark (Die no 1983). This is a particularly early bowl with a bead rim and at least six 'snowflake' stamps forming a pattern on the stem, a design known to have been in use *c* 1600–1610. The rim is bottered but not milled; the stem bore is 5/64". The surface has a fine burnish. (1819): Phase VIII, Plot 1; SF 9275.

93 Heel bowl of *c* 1580–1610, very crudely finished and with a distinctive reduced core to the fabric. The rim is cut but not milled; the stem bore is 6/64". The surface has a good burnish. (316) (A): Phase IX, Plot 6, fill of (315).

94 Heel bowl of *c* 1580–1610 which appears to have been burnt. The rim is bottered but not milled; the stem bore is 7/64". The surface has an average burnish. (384): Phase IX, Plot 6, fill of (345).

95 Heel bowl of *c* 1580–1610. The rim is bottered but not milled; the stem bore is 7/64". The surface has an average burnish. (1604) (A): Phase VII, Plot 4, fill of (1696).

96 Stem fragment of *c* 1580–1610 with a very marked taper. The stem bore is 8/64". The surface has a good burnish right to the tip of the mouthpiece. (338): Phase IX, Plot 6, fill of (337).

97 Heel bowl of *c* 1610–40 made of a coarse local fabric. The rim is bottered and fully milled; the stem bore is 8/64". The surface has an average burnish. (454) (A): Phase X, Plot 4.

98 Heel bowl of *c* 1610–40 made of a coarse local fabric. The rim is bottered and fully milled; the stem bore is 8/64". The surface has a good burnish. (455) (D): Phase VIII, Plot 4.

99 Heel bowl of *c* 1610–40. The rim is bottered and fully milled; the stem bore is 7/64". The surface has a fine burnish. (1617): Phase X, Plot 4.

100 Heel bowl of *c* 1620–40. The rim is bottered but not milled; the stem bore is 6/64". The surface has a good burnish. (1514) (A): Phase VII, Plot 4, fill of (1506).

101 Heel bowl of *c* 1610–40. The rim is bottered and fully milled; the stem bore is 8/64". The surface has a good burnish. (656): Phase VIII, Plot 1, fill of (657).

102 Heel bowl of *c* 1630–50. The rim is bottered and milled; the stem bore is 7/64". The surface is not burnished. (301) (E): Phase X, Plot 6.

103 Heel bowl of *c* 1620–40. An average quality bowl with some folds visible in the surface of the clay. All of the surviving rim is milled and this pipe may well have been fully milled originally. The rim is bottered; the stem bore is 7/64". The surface is not burnished. (385): Phase X, Plot 6.

104 Heel bowl of *c* 1630–50 made of a coarse local fabric. The rim is bottered and fully milled; the stem bore is 8/64". The surface is not burnished. (420): Phase X, Plot 2.

105 Heel bowl of *c* 1610–40 made of a coarse local fabric. The rim is bottered and fully milled; the stem bore is unmeasureable. The surface has an average burnish. (455) (A): Phase VIII, Plot 4.

106 Heel bowl of *c* 1610–40 made of a coarse local fabric. The rim is bottered and fully milled; the stem bore is 8/64". The surface is not burnished. (455) (C): Phase VIII, Plot 4.

107 Heel bowl of *c* 1610–40 made of a coarse local fabric. The rim is bottered and fully milled; the stem bore is 8/64". The surface is not burnished. (455) (B): Phase VIII, Plot 4.

108 Heel bowl of *c* 1610–40 with a stamped mark with the ligatured initials WK (Die no 1993). The rim is bottered and fully milled; the stem bore is unmeasureable. The surface has a good burnish. (1601) (AH): Phase VII, Plot 4, fill of (1696).

109 Heel bowl of *c* 1610–10 with a stamped wheel mark (Die no 1979). The rim is bottered but not milled; the stem bore is 7/64". The surface has a good burnish. (1871): Phase VIII, Plot 1, fill of (1812); SF 9356.

110 Heel bowl of *c* 1620–50 with a stamped star mark (Die no 1980). The rim is bottered and fully milled; the stem bore is 8/64". The surface has a good burnish. (1414): Phase X, Plot 3, fill of (1415); SF 9409.

111 Heel bowl of *c* 1610–50 with a stamped wheel mark (Die no 1981). Very shiny surface but no obvious burnishing lines suggesting that it is not burnished. The rim is bottered and fully milled; the stem bore is 6/64". (1371): Phase VIII, Plot 4, fill of (1545; SF 9236.

112 Heel bowl of *c* 1610–40 with a stamped wheel mark (Die no 910). The rim is bottered and milled; the stem bore is 7/64". The surface has a good burnish. (663): Phase VII, Plot 1; SF 8225.

113 Heel bowl of *c* 1610–50 with a stamped crossed keys mark, which is very similar to Die no 532 but with very slight differences in detail – perhaps indicating two working dies created from the same master. The rim is bottered and fully milled; the stem bore is 8/64". The surface is not burnished. (456): Phase IX, Plot 4, fill of (1365); SF 9118.

114 Heel bowl of *c* 1610–40 with a stamped mark reading IL (Die no 1988). Similar example from Eccleshall castle, Staffordshire. Another example recovered from this site – (1546), SF 9786. The rim is bottered and fully milled; the stem bore is 7/64". The surface has a good burnish. Two labels in this finds bag; one for (1556) and one for (1566): both Phase VI, Plot 4; SF 9552.

115 Heel bowl of *c* 1610–40 with a stamped mark reading M (Die no 1995). Possibly the same die as that on a heel fragment from (663), SF 8667 (Ill 5.6.6.116). The rim is bottered and fully milled; the stem bore is 7/64". The surface is not burnished. (1901): Phase VIII, Plot 1, fill of (1902); SF 9423.

116 Heel bowl of *c* 1610–40 with a stamped mark reading M (Die no 1995). Possibly the same die as that on a heel bowl from (1901), SF 9423 (Ill 5.6.6.115). Stem bore 8/64". The surface is not burnished. (663): Phase VII, Plot 1; SF 8667.

117 Heel bowl of *c* 1610–40. The rim is bottered and fully milled; the stem bore is 7/64". The surface is not burnished. (386) (B): Phase X, Plot 6, fill of (385).

118 Heel bowl of *c* 1630–50. The rim is bottered and milled; the stem bore is 9/64". The surface has a good burnish. (1111) (D): Phase VII, Plot 3.

119 Heel bowl of *c* 1630–50 with no obvious burnishing lines, but a very glossy surface. The rim is bottered but not milled; the stem bore is 8/64". (429) C: Phase VI, Plot 3, fill of (850)/(430).

120 Heel bowl of *c* 1630–60 with a stamped mark reading AP (Die no 1996). The rim is bottered and fully milled; the stem bore is 8/64". The surface is not burnished. (429) (B): Phase VI, Plot 3, fill of (850)/(430); SF 8555.

121 Heel bowl of *c* 1610–40 with 13 stamped 'snowflake' marks (Die no 1986), which make up two lozenges on the stem – the first is made up of nine stamps, second is made up of four. The rim is bottered but not milled; the stem bore is 7/64". The surface has a fine burnish. Possibly a Dutch import. (429) (A): Phase VI, Plot 3, fill of (850)/(430); SF 8648.

122 Heel bowl of *c* 1630–50, the stem of which is decorated with milled bands. The rim is bottered and milled; the stem bore is 6/64". The surface is not burnished. (1111): Phase VII, Plot 3; SF 9794.

123 Heel bowl of *c* 1610–40 with the border of a circular heel mark. The rim is bottered but not milled; the stem bore is 6/64". The surface has a good burnish. (237) (A): Phase VII, Plot 1; SF 9258.

124 Heel bowl of *c* 1610–40 with a stamped mark reading NE (Die no 1989). The rim is bottered but not milled; the stem bore is 6/64". The surface has a good burnish. Evaluation Trench F (26); SF 9873.

125 Heel bowl of *c* 1620–60 with a ligatured NE stamp within a heart shaped border (Die no 1990). Stem bore 8/64". The surface is not burnished. (301) (L): Phase X, Plot 6; SF 9304.

126 Heel bowl of *c* 1620–60 with a ligatured NE stamp within a circular border (Die no 1988). Stem bore 7/64". The surface is not burnished. (302): Phase X, Plot 6, fill of (303); SF 8327.

127 Heel bowl of *c* 1610–40 with a stamped mark reading IG (Die no 1991). Stem bore is 7/64". The surface is not burnished. (1406) (B): Phase VIII, Plot 3, fill of (1413).

128 Heel bowl of *c* 1610–40. The rim is bottered but not milled; the stem bore is unmeasureable. The surface is not burnished. (663) (C): Phase VII, Plot 1.

129 Heel bowl of *c* 1610–40. The rim is bottered but not milled; the stem bore is 7/64". The surface is not burnished. (663) (B): Phase VII, Plot 1.

130 Heel bowl of *c* 1610–40. The rim is bottered but not milled; the stem bore is 6/64". The surface is not burnished. (663) (A): Phase VII, Plot 1.

131 Very neatly finished heel bowl of *c* 1620–40. The rim is bottered but not milled; the stem bore is 7/64". The surface is not burnished. (237) (B): Phase VII, Plot 1.

132 Heel bowl of *c* 1620–40. The rim is bottered but not milled; the stem bore is 8/64". The surface is not burnished. (237) (C): Phase VII, Plot 1.

133 Heel bowl of *c* 1620–40. The rim is bottered but not milled; the stem bore is 7/64". The surface is not burnished. (1906) (B): Phase X, Plot 1, fill of (1907).

134 Heel bowl of *c* 1630–50. The rim is bottered but not milled; the stem bore is 7/64". The surface is not burnished. (663) (F): Phase VII, Plot 1.

135 Heel bowl of *c* 1640–60. The rim is bottered but not milled; the stem bore is 7/64". The surface is not burnished. (301) (G): Phase X, Plot 6.

136 Heel bowl of *c* 1650–70. The rim is internally trimmed and bottered but not milled; the stem bore is 7/64".

The surface is not burnished. (237) (J): Phase VII, Plot 1.

137 Heel bowl of *c* 1640–60. The rim is bottered and milled; the stem bore is 6/64". The surface is not burnished. (406): Phase X, Plot 3.

138 Heel bowl of *c* 1640–60 with a stamped mark reading HL (Die no 1994). The rim is bottered and milled; the stem bore is 8/64". The surface is not burnished. (1601): Phase VII, Plot 4, fill of (1696); SF 9565.

139 Heel bowl of *c* 1640–60 with a stamped mark reading RG (Die no 1992). The rim is bottered and fully milled; the stem bore is 5/64". The surface has a good burnish. U/S; SF 9137.

140 Miniature heel bowl of *c* 1630–60. The rim is bottered and fully milled; the stem bore is 6/64". The surface has a fine burnish. This pipe is made of a coarse clay, probably from the local coal-measure deposits, suggesting that it was made in Chester itself. The seams have some sharp lines scored along them, partially burnished over, which look like the trimming marks found on pipes from the Low Countries. (1111) (A): Phase VII, Plot 3.

141 Spur bowl of *c* 1610–40. The rim is bottered and fully milled; the stem bore is 7/64". The surface has a good burnish. (1887) (A): Phase VII, Plot 1.

142 Spur bowl of *c* 1610–40. The rim is bottered and fully milled; the stem bore is 6/64". The surface has a good burnish. (1599) (A): Phase VII, Plot 4, fill of (1696).

143 Spur bowl of *c* 1620–40. The rim is bottered and fully milled; the stem bore is 8/64". The surface has a good burnish. (824): Phase VII, Plot 6, fill of (925).

144 Spur bowl of *c* 1630–50 with a stem bore of 5/64". The surface is not burnished. (300) (B): Phase X, Plot 6.

145 Spur bowl of *c* 1640–60 with a stamped Rainford style mark on the bowl facing the smoker reading GA (Die no 1982). There are at least two bands of milling visible on surviving stem. The rim is bottered and fully milled; the stem bore is 8/64". The surface has an average burnish. (659): Phase VII, Plot 2; SF 8653.

146 Joining spur bowl and stem of *c* 1640–80 in coarse gritty fabric. The bowl has a good burnish and part of the stem is burnished, but there is a band around the bowl/stem junction that has not been burnished. The rim is bottered and fully milled; the stem bore is 7/64". (459): Phase VII, Plot 2.

147 Spur bowl of *c* 1660–80 (two joining fragments). The rim is bottered but not milled; the stem bore is 6/64". The surface has a poor burnish. (229): Phase VIII, Plot 1, fill of (228).

148 Heel bowl of *c* 1660–1720. This is a strange heel form, which does not appear to be local. Stem bore 8/64". The surface has an average burnish. (441): Phase IX, Plot 1.

149 Heel bowl of *c* 1680–1720 with a stamped mark reading IP (Die no 1997). Coventry style bowl and stamp, attributable to John Pottifer, recorded working at Coventry in 1710. The rim is bottered and fully milled; the stem bore is 5/64". The surface is not burnished. U/S; SF 9793.

150 Heel bowl of *c* 1660–90 with a very large round heel. Although part of the rim is clearly broken in more recent times but it would appear that it had been broken and ground down prior to deposition, perhaps for reuse after it had become damaged. Traces of a ground edge can clearly be seen around the line of milling. The rim milled; the stem bore is 6/64". The surface has a good burnish. (488) (B): Phase VIII, Plot 2.

151 Heel bowl of *c* 1690–1720 with a stem bore of 5/64". The surface is not burnished. (316) (D): Phase IX, Plot 6, fill of (315).

152 Heel bowl of *c* 1680–1720. The rim is possibly cut but not milled; the stem bore is 6/64". The surface is not burnished. (301) (L): Phase X, Plot 6.

153 Heel bowl of *c* 1680–1720. The rim is wiped but not milled; the stem bore is 5/64". The surface is not burnished. (301) (M): Phase X, Plot 6.

154 Heel bowl of *c* 1690–1720. The rim is cut but not milled; the stem bore is 5/64". The surface is not burnished. (1891) (D): Phase VII, Plot 1.

155 Heel bowl of *c* 1690–1720. The rim is cut but not milled; the stem bore is 5/64". The surface is not burnished. (325): Phase IX, Plot 6, fill of (326).

156 Heel bowl of *c* 1710–20. The rim is cut but not milled; the stem bore is 6/64". The surface is not burnished. (1546) (O): Phase VII, Plot 4.

157 Heel bowl of *c* 1710–20. The rim is cut but not milled; the stem bore is 6/64". The surface is not burnished. (1546) (P): Phase VII, Plot 4.

158 Heel bowl of *c* 1720–50. The rim is cut but not milled; the stem bore is 5/64". The surface is not burnished. (559) (D): Phase VIII, Plot 6, fill of (519).

159 Heel bowl of *c* 1720–50 with an irregular internal bowl mark comprising a number of relief lines. The rim is cut but not milled; the stem bore is 5/64". The surface is not burnished. (1406) (C): Phase VIII, Plot 3, fill of (1701).

160 Heel fragment of *c* 1700–50 with an internal bowl cross and very edge of a stem border surviving, but not enough to identify the die. Stem bore 6/64". The surface is not burnished. (1700) (B): Phase VIII, Plot 3, fill of (1701).

161 Heel pipe of *c* 1690–1715 made up of two joining fragments from different contexts. This pipe is very finely finished and has two shield shaped marks, one above the other, each containing a single *fleur de lis*, on the stem (Die no 1984). Above and below these shields are two bands of milling, so neatly applied that it is impossible to see where each band starts or finishes (Die no 826). Made of a fine and probably imported fabric. Joining bowl from (463) (AE): Phase VII, fill of (465) and stem from (484): Phase IX, fill of (483); SF 8226, both Plot 2.

162 Heel bowl of *c* 1700–30, the stem of which is stamped with two talbot ovals and two borders (Die nos 642 and 1933 respectively). The rim is cut but not milled; the stem bore is 6/64". The surface is not burnished. (1406): Phase VIII, Plot 3, fill of (1413); SF 9349.

163 Heavily smoked spur bowl of *c* 1700–30. The rim is cut but not milled; the stem bore is 5/64". The surface is not burnished. (1406) (Q): Phase VIII, Plot 3, fill of (1413).

164 Heel bowl of *c* 1700–30. The rim is cut but not milled; the stem bore is 5/64". The surface is not burnished. (1406) (G): Phase VIII, Plot 3, fill of (1413).

165 Spur bowl of *c* 1690–1710 with a stem border (similar to Die no 717). The rim is cut but not milled; the stem bore is 6/64". The surface is not burnished. (1406): Phase VIII, Plot 3, fill of (1413); SF 9461.

166 Spur bowl of *c* 1700–30. The rim is cut but not milled; the stem bore is 5/64". The surface is not burnished. (1406) (E): Phase VIII, Plot 3, fill of (1413.

167 Spur bowl of *c* 1690–1740, possibly from same mould as bowl B from the same context. The rim is cut but not milled; the stem bore is 6/64". The surface is not burnished. (456) (A): Phase IX, Plot 4, fill of (1365).

168 Spur bowl of *c* 1690–1720. The rim is wiped but not milled; the stem bore is 8/64". The surface is not burnished. (463) (P): Phase VII, Plot 2, fill of (465).

169 Spur bowl of *c* 1690–1720. The rim is wiped but not milled; the stem bore is 7/64". The surface has a good burnish. (301) (K): Phase X, Plot 6.

170 Spur bowl of *c* 1740–1800 with a very thin spur; the surface of the bowl is burnt. The rim is cut but not milled; the stem bore is 5/64". The surface is too burnt to tell whether or not it was burnished originally. (206): Phase IX, Plot 1, fill of (205).

171 Spur bowl of *c* 1690–1720. Only a very small part of the rim survives so it is difficult to say how it is finished, but it appears to have been cut but not milled. Stem bore 6/64". The surface is not burnished. (440) (C): Phase VII, Plot 2.

172 Spur bowl of *c* 1740–1800. The rim is cut but not milled; the stem bore is 5/64". The surface is not burnished. (424): Phase X, Plot 2, fill of (423).

173 Spur bowl of *c* 1760–1800 with a moulded mark. Large, thin-walled, bowl that is unusual for Chester in that it has moulded maker's initials on the heel. The Christian name has been chipped away and the surname was damaged during production, but appears to comprise the letter C or O, placed upright on the heel (an unusual orientation). The rim is cut but not milled; the stem bore is 5/64". The surface is not burnished. (821) (D): Phase IX, Plot 6, fill of (820).

174 Spur bowl of *c* 1810–40. The rim is cut but not milled; the stem bore is 4/64". The surface is not burnished. (469) (A): Phase IX, Plot 2.

175 Heel bowl of *c* 1800–50. This is one of three bowls from the same context with leaf decorated seams, all of which appear to have been made from the same mould. The rim is cut but not milled; the stem bore is 4/64". The surface is not burnished. (208): Phase IX, Plot 1.

176 Spur bowl of *c* 1780–1830 with a stamped stem mark reading 'AIRES / CHESTER' (Die no 1767). The rim is cut but not milled; the stem bore is 5/64". The surface has a good burnish. (1802) (B): Phase X, Plot 1.

177 Heel bowl of *c* 1840–1920 with the broken end of stem facetted by rubbing – possibly used to write graffiti or smoothed for reuse as an extremely short pipe. Stem bore 6/64". The surface is not burnished. (300) (A): Phase X, Plot 6.

178 Spurless bowl of *c* 1870–1920, this particular style of bowl generally being known as a 'Woodstock'. The rim is cut but not milled; the stem bore is 4/64". The surface is not burnished. (386) (A): Phase X, Plot 6, fill of (385).

179 Stem fragment of *c* 1640–1740 which had been rubbed on one side to give an undulating profile that cuts through into the stem bore. This may have been done to make a simple whistle out of the pipe. Stem bore 7/64". The surface is not burnished. (1098): Phase VII, Plot 3, fill of (1189).

180 Stem fragment of *c* 1690–1730 which has been ground smooth at one end. Stem bore 7/64". The surface has a good burnish. (1503): Phase X, Plot 5.

181 Stem fragment of *c* 1680–1730, 47 mm in length with both ends ground smooth, possibly for reuse as a hair curler. Stem bore 7/64". The surface is very scratched and abraded but it is also very glossy between these marks, suggesting that it was given a good burnish originally. (325): Phase IX, Plot 6, fill of (326); <5020>.

182 Part of a coiled pipe, probably daring to *c* 1780–1830. The fragment has been very badly burnt. Stem bore 4/64". (1802): Phase X, Plot 1.

183 Half of a hair-curler dating to *c* 1700–1800. Quite a good form with striations around the body, probably from rolling against a shaped former. End cut and unmarked. (601): Phase IX, Plot 1.

184 Half of a hair–curler dating to *c* 1700–1800. Very neat, well made form with a cut end, which has been stamped with a neat incuse WB mark. (208): Phase IX, Plot 1.

185 Hand-rolled strip of pipe clay which has been slightly squashed between two opposing surfaces, resulting in one end being more flattened than the other. Strips such as this were commonly used when loading pipe kilns for firing and this fragment almost certainly represents waste from a pipe kiln. (301): Phase X, Plot 6.

Acknowledgements

I am grateful to Dr Susie White, who compiled almost all of the detailed pipe catalogue for this project. She also prepared the majority of the bowl form drawings, set and edited all the final digital images ready for publication and proof read the draft text. All of the detailed die drawings are by the author.

Ill 5.6.1 Clay tobacco pipe stamps 1–32. (Scale 2/1)

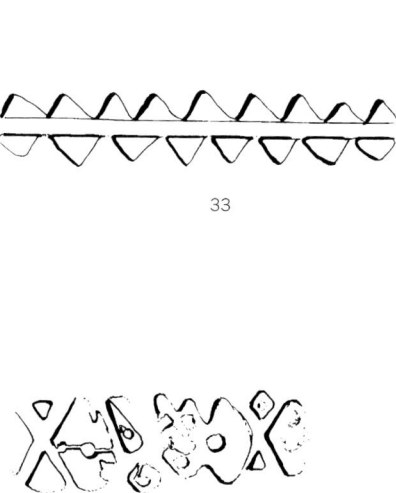

33

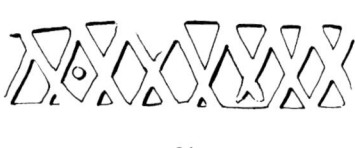

34

35

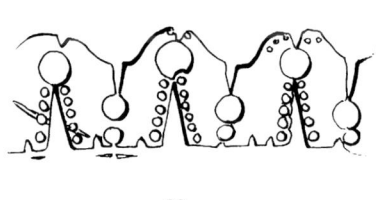

36

37

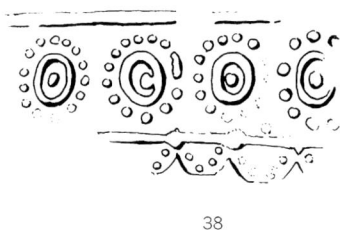

38

39

40

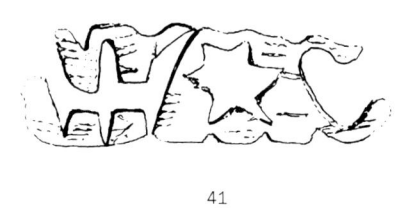

41

42

43

44

45

46

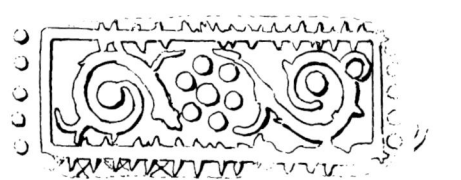

47

48

49

Ill 5.6.2 Clay tobacco pipe stamps 33–49. (Scale 2/1)

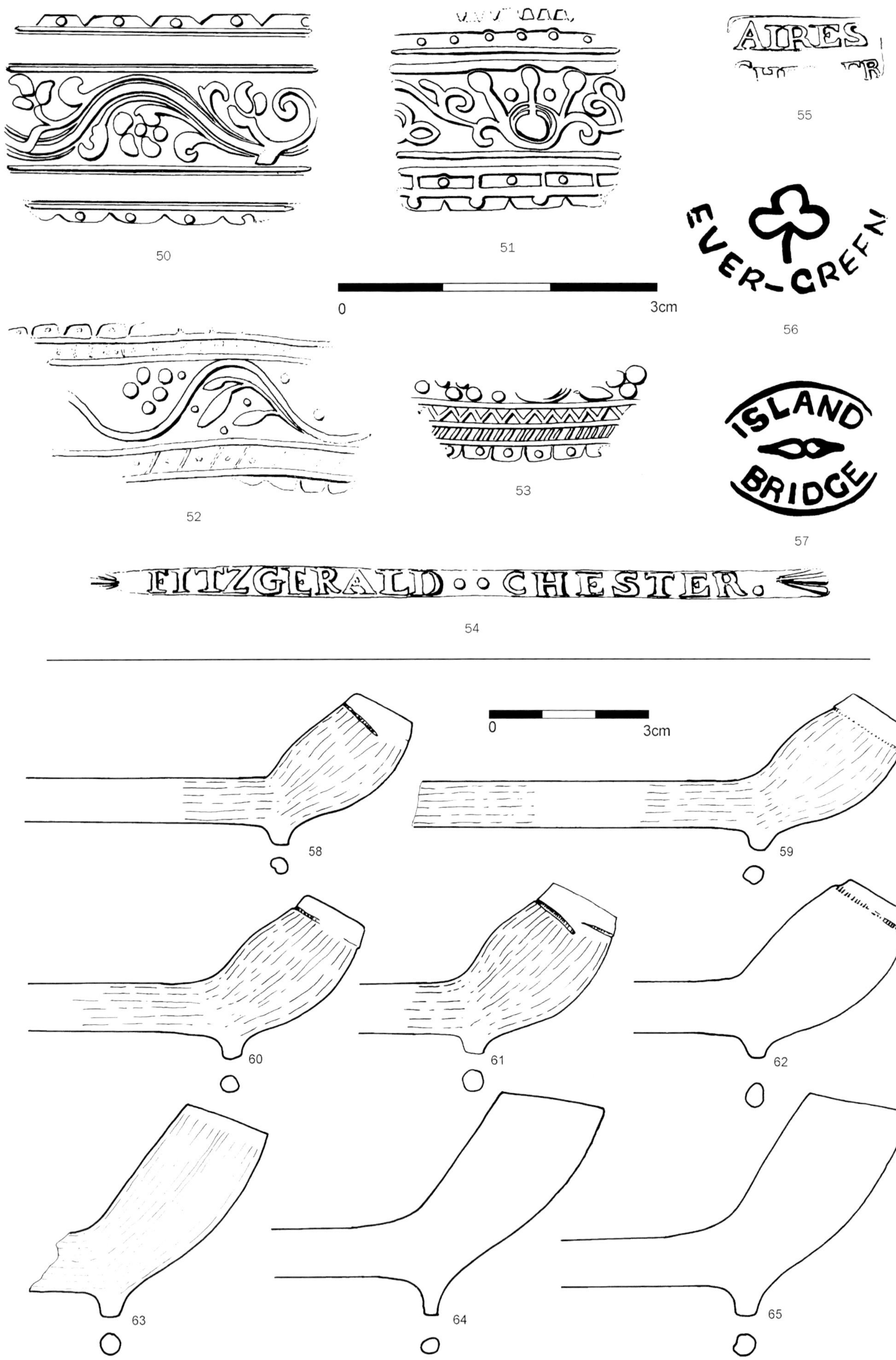

50
51
AIRES
55
EVER-GREEN
56
0
3cm
52
53
ISLAND
BRIDGE
57
FITZGERALD CHESTER.
54
0
3cm
58
59
60
61
62
63
64
65

Ill 5.6.3 Nos 50–7 clay tobacco pipe stamps (Scale 2/1): nos 58–62 kiln wasters of c 1640–70 from Phase VII Plot 4 context (1507) (Scale 1/1); nos 63–5 part of Phase VII Plot 4 pit group (1522) c 1700. (Scale 1/1)

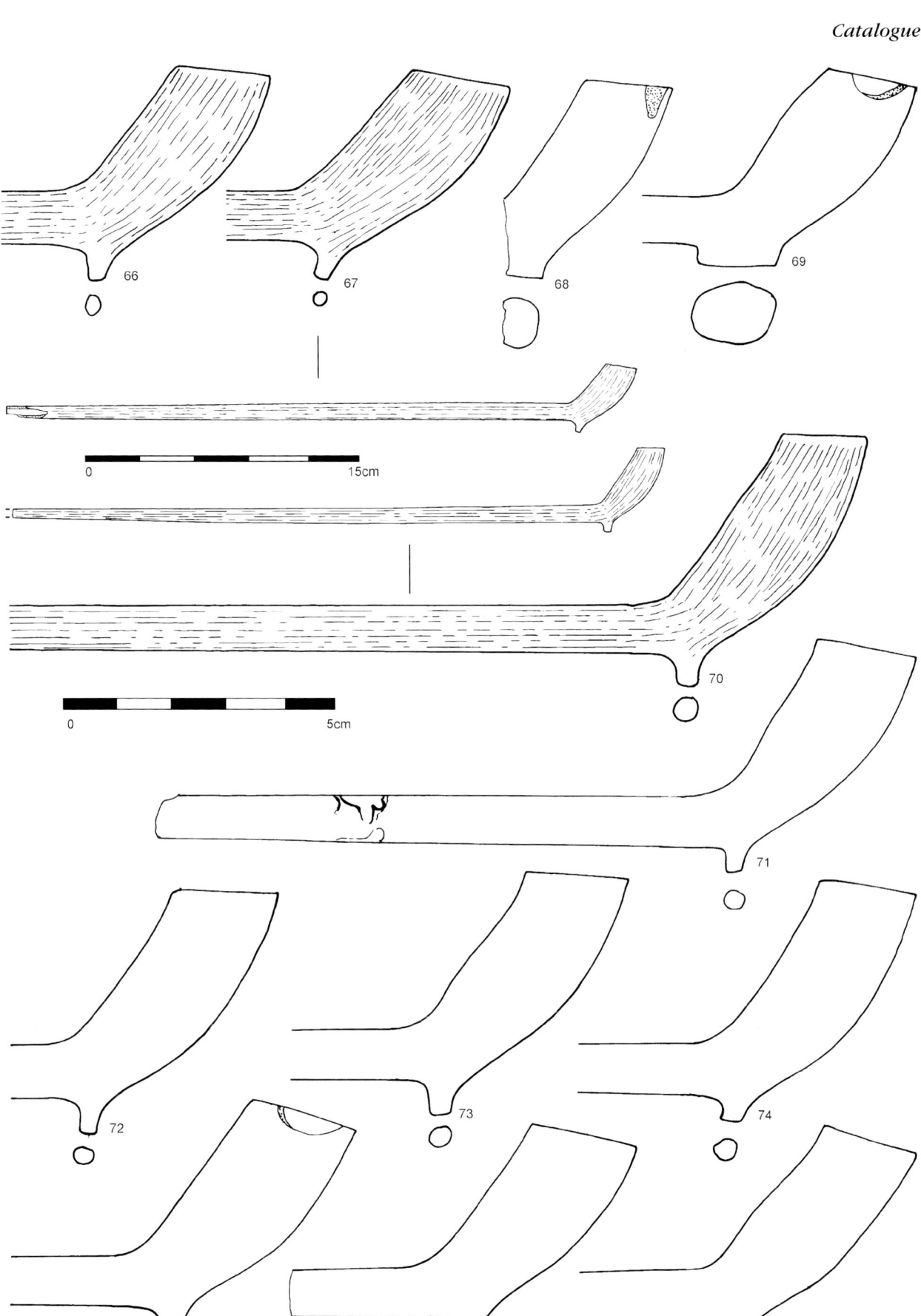

III 5.6.4 Phase VII Plot 4: clay tobacco pipes from pits (1522) c 1700 (nos 66–9) and (1696) c 1710 (nos 70–7). (Scale: bowls 1/1; complete pipes 1/3)

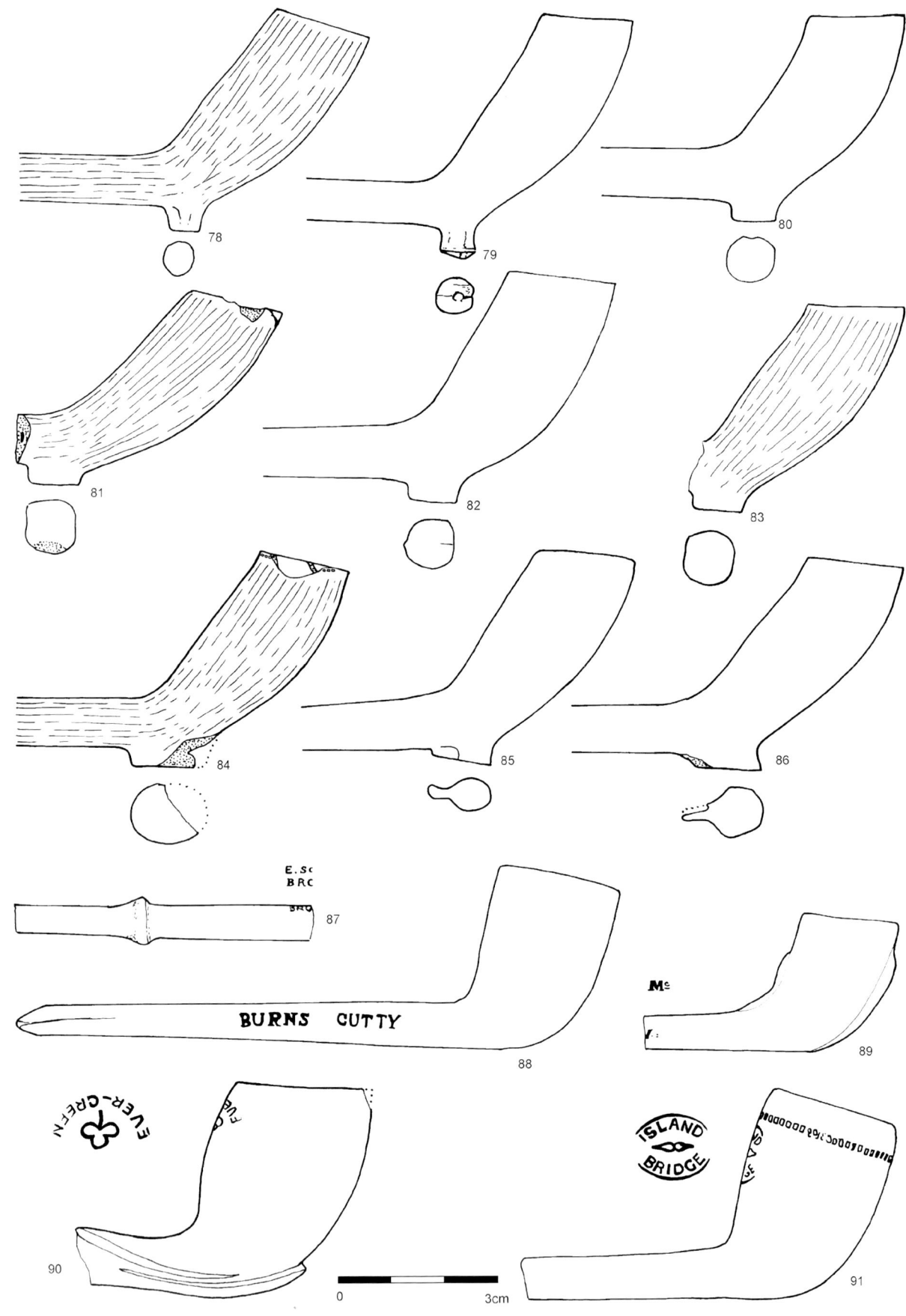

III 5.6.5 Clay tobacco pipes from Phase VII Plot 4 pit (1696) c 1710 (nos 78–86) and Phase IX Plot 2 layer (1096) c 1860–80 (nos 87–91). (Scale 1/1)

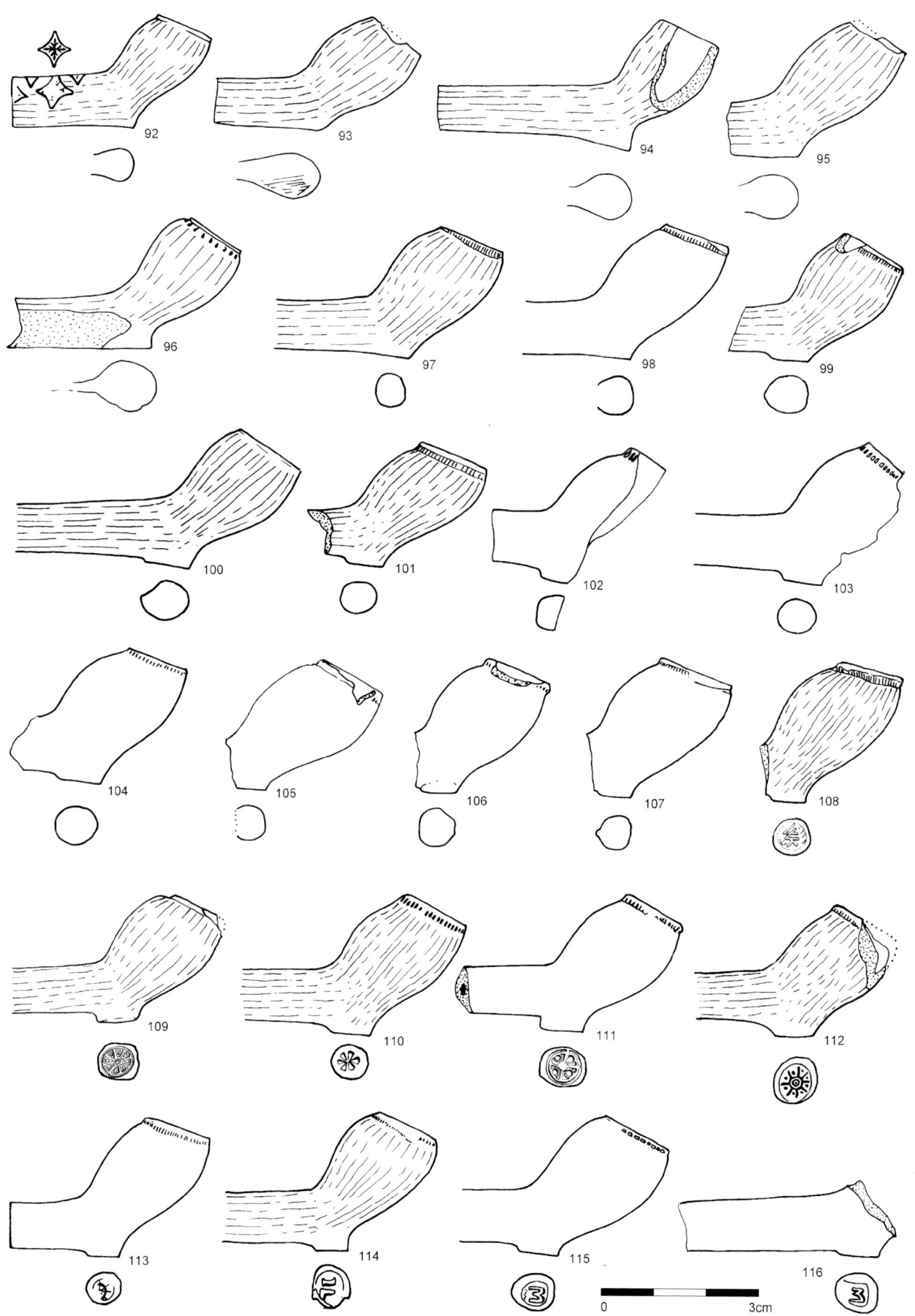

III 5.6.6 Clay tobacco pipe bowl forms ranging from c 1580 to 1640. (Scale 1/1)

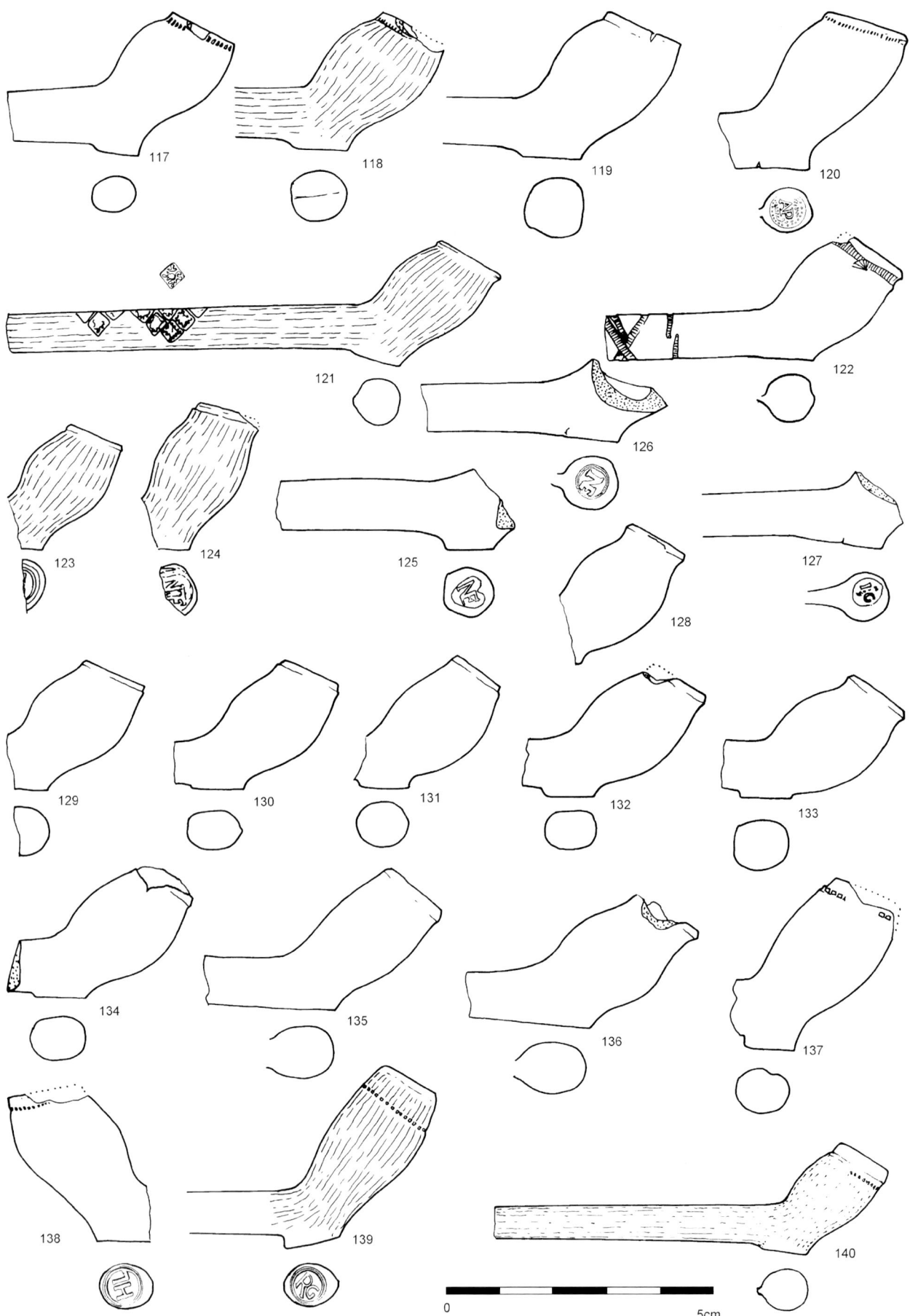

III 5.6.7 Clay tobacco pipe bowl forms ranging from c 1610 to 1660. (Scale 1/1)

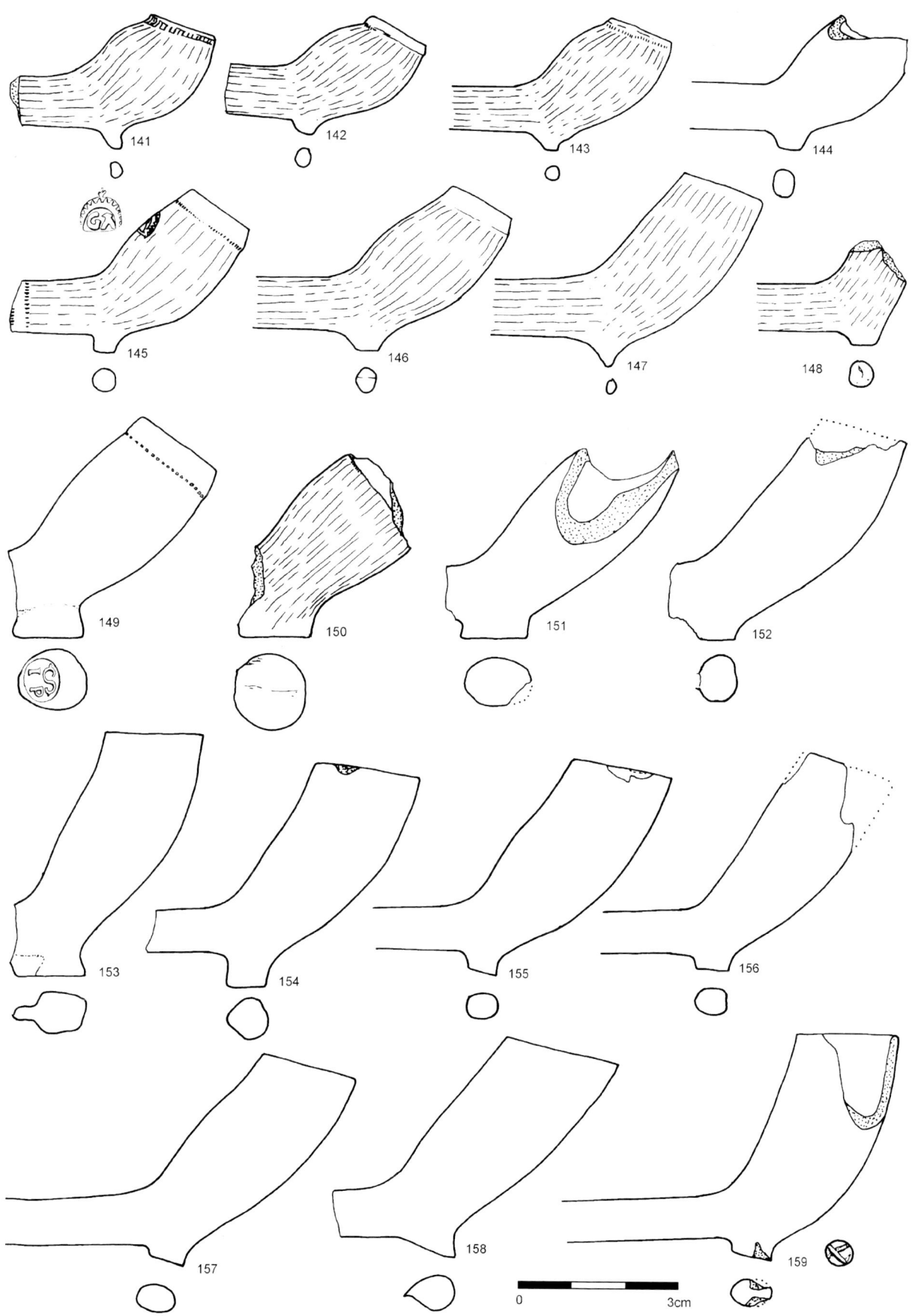

III 5.6.8 Clay tobacco pipe bowl forms ranging from c 1610 to 1720. (Scale 1/1)

275

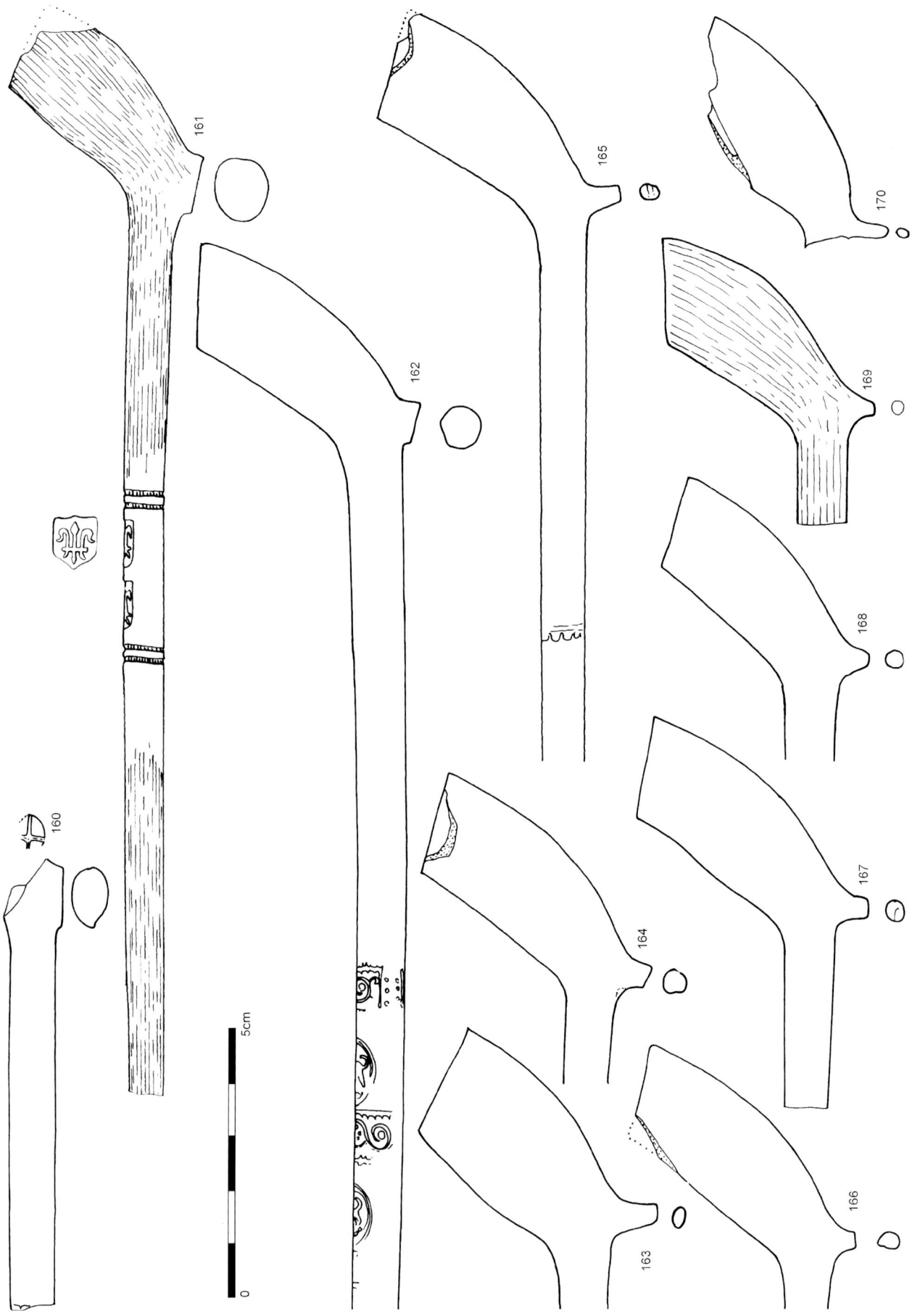

Ill 5.6.9 Clay tobacco pipe bowl forms ranging from c 1690 to 1800. (Scale 1/1)

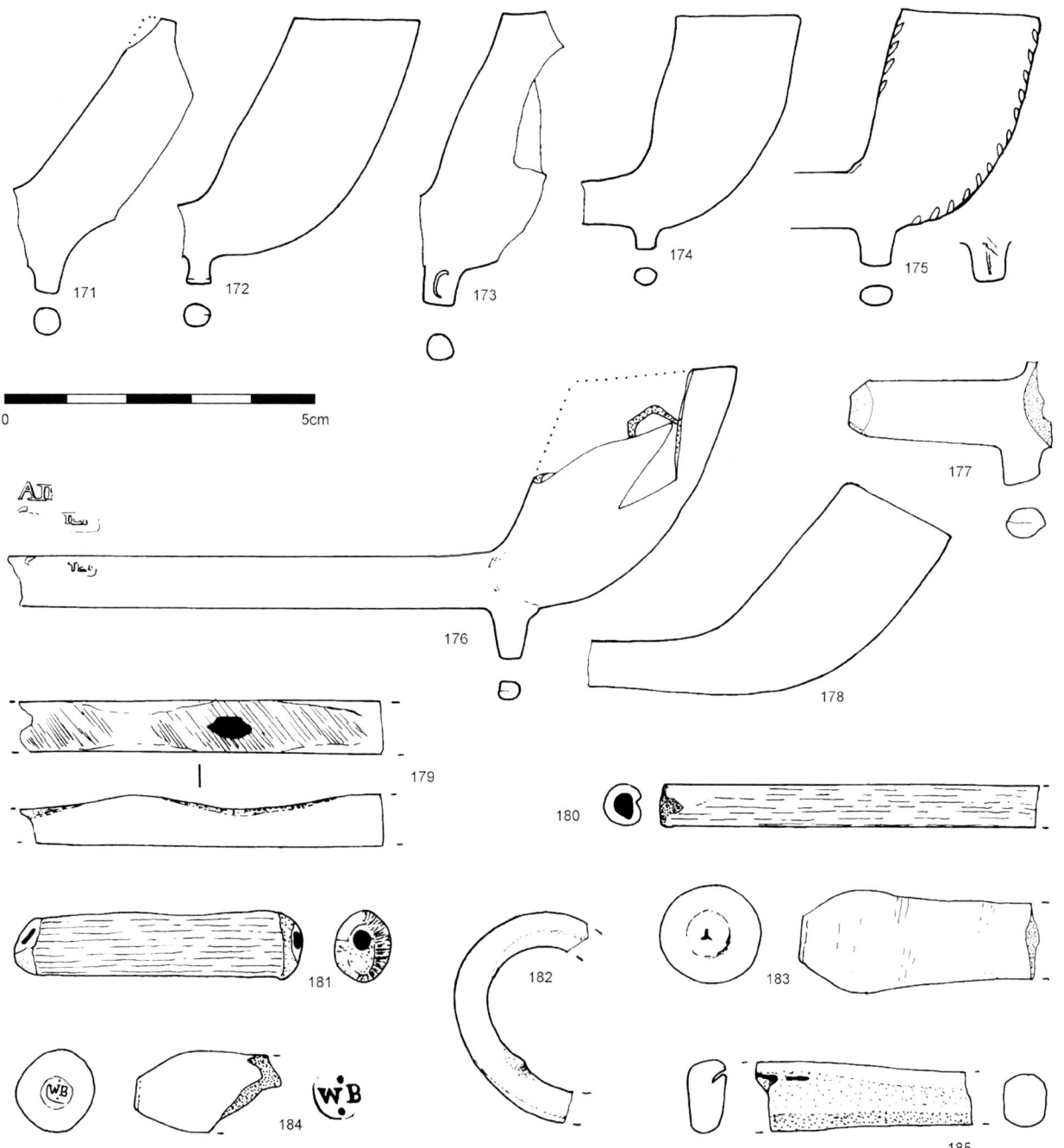

Ill 5.6.10 Clay tobacco pipe bowl forms ranging from c 1690 to 1920 (nos 171–8); modified or reworked stems (nos 179–82); hair curlers (nos 183–4); kiln debris (no 185). (Scale 1/1; detail of hair curler stamp 2/1)

Note on Table 5.6.5

This table provides a summary of the clay tobacco pipe evidence from the site. The phase and plot numbers are given first, followed by the context number and then the numbers of bowl (B), stem (S) or mouthpiece (M) fragments recovered from that context. These three columns are then added to show the total number of pipe fragments from the context as a whole. The overall date range of the pipes from each context is then given, followed by a suggested deposition date, based on the latest datable pipe fragments present (Deposit date). A summary of the makers' marks from each context (Marks) is then given,

followed by the total number of different stem stamps and stem borders present within that context. A brief note is then made of any notable or decorated pieces (Dec etc) and the illustration numbers for any illustrated examples. Bowl fragments, especially if they are marked, are much more closely datable than stem fragments. For this reason, the number and type of fragments present should be taken into account when assessing the reliance that can be placed on the suggested context dates given here.

Table 5.6.5 Clay tobacco pipes; total amount quantified by phase, plot, context and part (No B = no of bowl fragments; No S = no of stem fragments; No M = no of mouthpiece fragments; Stem stamps = no of different stem stamps; Stem borders = no of different stem borders)

Phase	Plot	Context	No B	No S	No M	Total	Date range	Deposit date	Marks	Stem stamps	Stem borders	Dec. etc	Ill nos	Comments
IV	6	1034		1		1	1710–1800	1710–1800						Plain 18-cent stem.
V	1	260		1		1	1710–1800	1710–1800						
		1893	2			2	1610–1660	1640–60						
	2	503		2		2	1610–1740	1610–1740						
		771		1		1	1710–1800	1710–1800						Shiny surface but no obvious burnishing lines visible.
		879		1		1	1610–1710	1610–1710						
	3	1334		1		1	1710–1800	1710–1800						
		870		2		2	1690–1780	1690–1780						
	6	1052		1		1	1710–1800	1710–1800						Plain 17-cent stem and mouthpiece.
VI	1	246		1	1	2	1610–1710	1610–1710						
		766		1		1	1610–1710	1610–1710						
	2	671	2	2		4	1610–40	1640–1700						All closely datable fragments are pre-1700.
		746	1			1	1700–70	1700–70						Spur fragment only; most likely to be 18-cent
	3	429	4	17	1	22	1610–1900	1800–1900	AP; Snowflake			Stem stamps	2, 19, 119–121	All bowls are c 1610–60. Most of stems are 17-cent but include some 18-cent fragments and one apparently 19-cent piece.
	4	800		13		13	1610–1710	1610–1710						
		1702		2		2	1710–1800	1710–1800						
		1540		1		1	1610–1710	1610–1710						
		1556/1566	1	1		2	1610–1750	1650–1750	IL				17, 114	Finds from bags with two labels, reading 1556 and 1566. Includes a bowl of c 1610–40 stamped IL. There is a similar example from Eccleshall castle, Staffordshire and another example recovered from context 1546 SF 9786.
		1561		1		1	1610–1710	1610–1710						
		1600	2		1	3	1610–1710	1640–1700						
		1618		1		1	1710–1800	1710–1800						
VII	1	26		2		2	1610–1910	1610–1910						
		237	15	44	1	60	1610–1910	1650–80	illegible			ground stem	123, 131–32, 136	Chips from sieving. All diagnostic forms are 1610–80 with latest types c 1650–80. Sieving chips gave broad date.
		243	1	1		2	1610–1710	1610–60	Wheel					Marked heel fragment of c 1610–60.
		663	16	48	2	66	1610–1710	1640–60	M; wheel				18, 112, 116, 128–130, 134	Good, consistent looking group with bowls all ranging from 1610–60 – most likely deposition c 1640–60.
		664		3		3	1610–1710	1610–1710						
		665	2	13		15	1610–1710	1620–60						Two small 17-cent heel fragments of c 1620–60; all other stems of 17-cent type.
		667	1	3		4	1610–1710	1630–50						Bowl frag of c 1630–50; stems all 17-cent types.
		670	9	47		56	1610–1910	1700–50						All more diagnostic fragments pre-1750 - but group includes 37 small chips from sieving that have been given a broad date range.
		1884	4	19		23	1610–1750	1690–1720	NT					Includes a NT mark attributable to Nathaniel Thorneley (1656–7).
		1887	5	15	1	21	1610–1750	1690–1750	AL				141	
		1891	10	58	2	70	1610–1760	1690–1720						
		1897	6	7		13	1610–1760	1730–60		1			36, 154	Mixed group with latest bowls of early 18-cent date.
		1898		3		3	1610–50	1610–50			1			

278

Phase	Plot	Context	No B	No S	No M	Total	Date range	Deposit date	Marks	Stem stamps	Stem borders	Dec, etc	Ill nos	Comments
VII	2	440	3	24		27	1610–1800	1710–1800					171	All 17-cent type fragments with bowl dating from c 1640–80.
		459	1	10		11	1610–1710	1640–80					146	
		463	45	140	7	192	1610–1750	1710–30	Pl; Lozenge; Elias Massey		2		27, 39, 161, 168	Bowls all range from 1650 to 1750 but with a high proportion of 1690–1730 forms and likely deposition date of c 1710–30. Good looking context. Bowl and decorated stem joins decorated stem in 484.
		464	32	125	3	160	1610–1840	1710–20	illegible					Large group with a range of bowl forms from c 1810 onwards. Latest forms appear to be c 1710–20 although one odd, damaged bowl could be later - perhaps intrusive.
		472	3	25		28	1610–1730	1660–1730						Mainly 17-cent material (up to c 1710), but one or two pieces appear to be 18-cent.
		482	3	6		9	1610–1800	1660–1800						
		491	6	21		27	1610–1750	1710–30		1			7, 145	Rainford style mark on the bowl facing the smoker; at least two bands of milling visible on surviving stem.
		659	1			1	1640–60	1640–60	GA					
		1304		1		1	1710–1800	1710–1800						
		1309	2	7		9	1690–1730	1710–20						Two joining fragments.
		1312			1	1	1610–1710	1610–1710						
		1343		1		1	1610–1710	1610–1710						Burnt.
		1454		4		4	1610–1710	1610–1710						
		1627		2		2	1610–60	1610–60						
		1628		2		2	1610–60	1610–60						
3		1098		7	1	8	1610–1800	1700–40				?whistle	179	Includes one modified stem with holes bored n it, possibly to create a whistle.
		1107		3		3	1610–1710	1610–1710						
		1111	18	70	3	91	1610–1800	1690–1720	EG	1		ground stem	118, 122, 140	All bowls range from 1630 to 1680 except for two fragments, which are c 1690–1730. Group includes one miniature bowl.
		1190		1		1	1610–1710	1610–1710						
		1191		6	1	7	1630–1710	1630–1710						
		1193	12	61	6	79	1640–60	1640–60	?A?L; GL					All bowls date from between 1640 and 1680 and all would fit with 1640–660 deposition. Just one 18-cent-looking stem - could be intrusive?
4		1495	1			1	1610–40	1610–40						Heel fragment only; no obvious burnishing lines but surface very shiny.
		1504	5	11	2	18	1610–1730	1690–1720						Very large group comprising two elements. The bulk of the material forms a tight group of c 1640–70 made up almost entirely of spur forms, which may represent a kiln dump. There is, however, also a small element of 1690–1720 material, which forms a second group within this context.
		1505		1		1	1610–1710	1610–1710						
		1507	137	564	45	746	1610–1720	1640–70 / 1690–1720					42, 58–62	
		1509	4	8		12	1640–1750	1690–1720						

Phase	Plot	Context	No B	No S	No M	Total	Date range	Deposit date	Marks	Stem stamps	Stem borders	Dec. etc	Ill nos	Comments
VII	4	1513	3	44	2	49	1610–1910	1690–1715						Includes general date from sieving chips.
		1514	2	5		7	1610–1710	1620–40					100	Two early bowls of c 1620–50 plus three 17-cent-type stems.
		1533	8	12		20	1610–1800	1710–1730						
		1546	23	53	1	77	1610–1800	1710–20	IL; ELIAS MASSEY	2	2		17, 26, 156–7	A little residual 17-cent material but almost all the remainder of early 18-cent date.
		1550		1		1	1610–1710	1610–1710						
		1551		3		3	1610–1710	1610–1710						
		1552		4	1	5	1610–1800	1700–1800						All 17-cent or early 18-cent plus one stem of general 18-cent type.
		1554	3	1		4	1660–1800	1680–1710						Bowl fragment of c 1640–60 plus a 17-cent-style mouthpiece.
		1558	1		1	2	1610–1710	1640–60						
		1559	1	10	2	13	1610–1800	1700–1800						
		1592	5	16	2	23	1610–1800	1700–1800						Bowls all range between 1630 and 1680 but group appears to contain a few 18-cent stems.
		1598		1		1	1610–1710	1610–1710						
		1599	15	48	1	64	1610–1910	1710–30	ELIAS MASSEY	1	1		83, 84, 142	Overall range distorted by chips from sieving. Some residual material, primarily of c 1630–80, but the majority a good early 18-cent group. Cross joins found with 1601, including an almost complete pipe.
		1601	37	83	6	126	1610–40	1710–30	Wheel; ?A?L; AL; HL; WK			ground stem	14, 16, 70, 72, 75–8, 80–2, 85–6, 108, 138	Some residual material, mainly of c 1610–1710, but principally a good group of c 1710–30. Cross joins with 1599 found, including an almost complete pipe.
		1604	18	42	2	62	1580–1800	1710–20		1	1		71, 73–4, 79, 95	Residual element ranging from c 1580 to 1650, but most forms a good group of c 1710–20.
		1607	9	49	4	62	1610–1910	1710–30	ELIAS MASSEY		1		26	A little residual early 17-cent material but almost all the remainder of late 17-cent to early 18-cent date. Sieving chips produced misleadingly wide date range, none of more diagnostic fragments had a range of later than c 1750.
		1608	1	1	2	4	1610–1910	1610–1910						Misleadingly wide overall date because of a chip from sieving.
		1625	2	1		1	1690–1710	1690–1710			1			
		1695		8		10	1610–1910	1660–1730						
		1699	1	10		11	1610–1910	1610–40						Bowl of 1610–40 plus two 17-cent stems and some widely dated chips from sieving.
		1881	1			1	1610–1910	1610–1910						Chip from sieving.
	6	389		2		2	1610–1710	1710–1800						
		686		1		1	1610–1710	1610–1710						
		824	1			1	1620–40	1620–40						
	1	207	6	36		42	1610–1850	1700–50?					143	Mainly small sieving chips, which are hard to date. Most of other material looks 18-cent and latest really diagnostic piece is c 1700–50.
VIII	1	218	3	13	1	17	1610–1800	1710–1800						
		220		1		1	1710–1800	1710–1800						Plain 18-cent stem.

Phase	Plot	Context	No B	No S	No M	Total	Date range	Deposit date	Marks	Stem stamps	Stem borders	Dec, etc	Ill nos	Comments
VIII	1	221	1	5		6	1610–1710	1610–60	illegible					Small heel fragment of 1610–60 with part of a stamp visible; other stems all 17-cent types.
		222		1		1	1610–1710	1610–1710						Plain 17-cent stem.
		223	5	4	1	10	1610–1910	1640–60	Fleur de lis			stem stamps	3	Late date derived from poorly attributable chips; all diagnostic pieces are early to mid-17 cent.
		225		7	1	8	1610–1800	1710–1800						Mixed 17- and 18-cent stems.
		227		3		3	1610–1800	1710–1800						Mixed 17- and 18-cent stems.
		229	1	5		6	1610–1710	1660–80					147	Bowl and joining stem of c 1660–80.
		233		1		1	1610–1710	1610–1710						Plain 17-cent stem.
		235		1		1	1710–1800	1710–1800						Plain 18-cent stem.
		604		1		1	1690–1750	1690–1750						
		643	1	3		4	1640–60	1640–60						Bowl of c 1640–60 and three 17-cent pieces of stem.
		653		12		12	1610–1710	1770–1830	FITZGERAL..				54	Latest piece part of a Fitzgerald stamp that cross joins with a piece in context 601.
		656	2	9		11	1610–1850	1750–1850			1		101	
		1812		3	1	4	1650–1820	1750–1820						
		1813		2		2	1750–1820	1760–1820			1			
		1819	6	20		26	1580–1720	1710–20	Fleur de lis			ground stem	1, 92	Mixed bowls of c 1580–1670, including a decorated example of c 1580–1610, plus one bowl of early 18-cent date.
		1821	6	28		34	1610–1820	1710–60						Mixed 17-cent and 18-cent material.
		1837		3		3	1690–1750	1690–1750						
		1867		2		2	1750–1850	1750–1850						
		1871	1	16		17	1610–40	1610–40	Wheel		1		24	Bowl stamped with wheel mark, c 1610–40, plus stems of c 1610–60 type.
		1872	1	5		6	1610–1800	1720–1800		1			6, 109	
		1879		1		1	1610–60	1610–60					48	
		1885	1	3		4	1610–1850	1750–1850						
		1901	1	4		5	1610–60	1620–40	M				18, 115	Bowl stamped 'M'; possibly the same die as a heel fragment from context 663.
2		488	2	4		6	1610–1710	1660–90						
		847	5	23		28	1630–50	1660–80?					150	Bowls all between 1630 and 1680 – all other fragments match except two apparently 18-cent stems. Could be intrusive?
		1305		1		1	1610–1710	1610–1710						
		1307	2	3		5	1610–1800	1710–20						
		1308		18	3	21	1610–1710	1610–1710						
		1417		1		1	1610–1710	1610–1710						
		1421	2	10		12	1640–80	1700–1800						Both bowls c 1640–80 but stems appear to include 18-cent types.
		1432	1	17		18	1610–1710	1660–80						
		1439	4	3		7	1610–1730	1690–1730						
		1645		3		3	1710–1800	1750–1800						
3		1405	3	11		14	1610–1840	1750–1840			1			
		1406	23	96	4	123	1610–1750	1700–30	IG	4	7		12, 25, 29, 40, 46, 49, 127, 159, 162–6	Odd residual pieces but almost all a good early 18-cent group, including borders and a new coat of arms with motto.
		1407		1		1	1640–1710	1640–1710						
		1408	1			1	1620–60	1620–60	Star					
		1435	1	3		4	1610–1710	1610–1640						Bowl of c 1610–40 plus three 17-cent stems.
		1437	2	3		5	1610–1910	1610–1910						
		1448		1		1	1610–1710	1610–1710						
		1449		2		2	1710–1800	1710–1800						
		1610			1	1	1610–1710	1610–1710						
		1637		3		3	1710–1800	1720–60		1				
		1684	4	21		25	1610–1750	1690–1750			1			
		1687		1		1	1610–60	1610–60						
		1700	2	25	1	28	1640–1800	1720–50		2	2		160	Chips from sieving.

Phase	Plot	Context	No B	No S	No M	Total	Date range	Deposit date	Marks	Stem stamps	Stem borders	Dec, etc	Ill nos	Comments
VIII	3	1701	11	23	1	35	1660–1750	1710–30						Almost all late 17-cent to early 18-cent material with a deposition date in early 18-cent likely.
	4	455	19	80	5	104	1610–1910	1690–1730					98, 105–7	Mixture of 17- and 18-cent stems. The bowls all range from 1610 to 1730, suggesting a deposit accumulating over this period with final sealing c 1690–1730. The deposit produced sieving chips with general date of 1610–1910 only. Pottery from this context cross joins with the 'big pit' complex and includes a post-1702 AR excise stamp.
		1357	2	1		3	1710–1800	1720–50						
		1371	3	1		4	1610–1710	1640–60	Wheel				5, 111	Three bowls all between 1630–60: one with a wheel stamp.
		1524		5		5	1710–1800	1800–1900						Four 18-cent type stems and one of 19-cent type.
		1535	1	13		14	1620–50	1620–50?						Bowl dates from c 1620 to 1650 and all other stems are of 17-cent type apart from one, which appears to be 18-cent.
		1539	2	20		22	1620–1760	1740–60			1			Both bowls date from c 1620 to 1650 and all stems except one could be contemporary. The exception is an 18-cent dec stem. If this were intrusive, could be a 1620–50 deposit.
	6	341	8	36		44	1610–1910	1710–1800						Includes poorly datable sieving chips.
		349		2		2	1610–1710	1610–1710						Plain 17-cent stems.
		515		2		2	1610–1910	1610–1910						Chips from sieving
		520	6	28	1	35	1610–1910	1710–1800		1	2		22	Latest well dated piece c 1710–20, so could be an early 18-cent deposit.
		534		1		1	1710–1800	1710–1800						
		559	6	48	1	55	1610–1800	1720–50		1	1		158	All bowls date to before c 1750.
		633	1	1		2	1610–40	1610–40						Bowl of c 1610–40 and a 17-cent stem.
		715		2		2	1640–1710	1640–1710						
		1573		2		2	1650–1750	1650–1750						
IX	1	11		4		4	1690–1750	1690–1750						
		201	1	74	1	76	1610–1840	1770–1840	RG; …D CHES…	3	3	ground end	51	Mainly 18-cent–early 19-cent finds; latest piece a Fitzgerald stem stamp of c 1770–1840.
		206	1	3	1	5	1610–1800	1740–1800					170	Very thin spur; surface of the bowl burnt.
		208	21	85	3	109	1610–1910	1800–50				8 fragts with leaf dec seams	175	Appears to be good contemporary group of c 1800–50 with several pipes from the same mould.
		211	1	3		4	1750–1850	1800–50				Leaf dec seams		
		212	1			1	1740–90	1740–90						Plain bowl fragment.
		217	7	21	3	31	1610–1910	1800–1900						Material of mixed date – latest is 19-cent.
		230		1		1	1610–1710	1610–1710				glazed stem		Plain 17-cent stem.
		441	1	20		21	1610–1800	1710–1800	ELIAS MASSEY	1			148	Mixed 17- and 18-cent pipes.
		577		1		1	1750–1850	1750–1850						
		581	3	24		27	1610–1800	1710–20						Latest bowl is c 1710–20, but other stems of general 18-cent type.
		601	8	54	1	63	1610–1910	1800–1910	…ERALD CHESTER; …D CH…	1	3	green glaze and red wax	32, 54	Mixed finds including two Fitzgerald stems and traces of coated mouthpieces. One of the Fitzgerald stamps joins with a piece in context 653.
		640		5		5	1610–1800	1710–1800						One a piece of 17-cent stem, ground at one end; possibly used as a piece of chalk.
		644		1		1	1610–1710	1610–1710						
		1809	1	1		1	1690–1750	1690–1750			1			Only a faint trace of a border survives – not enough to identify the die.

Phase	Plot	Context	No B	No S	No M	Total	Date range	Deposit date	Marks	Stem stamps	Stem borders	Dec, etc	Ill nos	Comments
IX	1	1815		1		1	1610–1710	1610–1710						
		1818		7	1	8	1720–1820	1720–1820						
		1828		2		2	1720–1800	1720–1800						
		1830	2	7		9	1610–1850	1720–1800		1	2		50, 52	Joining fragments.
		1839		4		4	1610–1660	1610–60						
		1869		8		8	1720–1820	1720–1820						
		1892		12	1	13	1660–1750	1690–1750						
		1912	1	3		4	1610–1720	1690–1720		1			28, 37	Heel fragment only.
		1913	1	4	1	6	1610–1710	1660–80						
	2	418	7	35	1	43	1610–1920	1860–1920	420		1			All bowls c 1660–80 apart from one of c 1690–1730. But stems are mixed 17- and 18-cent types and there is one late 19-cent stem with a moulded pattern number on it. 18-cent stems plus one chip from sieving.
		451	1	3		4	1610–1910	1710–1800						Plain 17-cent stem.
		452		1		1	1610–1710	1610–1710						Plain stem fragment.
		457		1		1	1610–1710	1610–1710						
		469	8	25	2	35	1610–1920	1850–1920	Ring & dot			5 with leaves etc		174 Some residual material but mainly 19 cent to early 20 cent in date.
		470		1		1	1610–50	1610–50						
		484		4		4	1610–1800	1710–1800		1	1		21, 161	Includes a very finely finished stem with two shields, one above the other, each containing a single *fleur de lis*. Above and below these shields are two bands of milling, so neatly applied that it is impossible to see where each band starts or finishes – joins bowl fragment in 463.
		1096	7	25	1	33	1610–1920	1860–1920+	2 x BURNS CUTTY/ BURNS CUTTY; SLAND BRIDGE; MC.../ ...W; EVERGREEN.	1		green glaze	56, 57, 87–91	Latest types in production into 20 cent and including a McDougall's fragment; working until 1967.
		1109		1		1	1800–1900	1800–1900				green glaze		Stem broken near mouthpiece end, pale green glaze visible. Iron stained.
		1114		4		4	1640–1800	1710–1800						
		1187		1		1	1710–1800	1710–1800						
		1201	6	24	2	32	1610–1800	1710–20						Looks like a good early 18-cent group of bowls.
		1286	1	16		17	1640–1920	1810–50				2 stems with leaf dec seams		Latest clearly diagnostic pieces are two stems of c 1810–50 with crude leaf decorated seams.
	3	1090	5	17	1	23	1610–1800	1690–1720	AL	2	1		33	Latest bowl of c 1690–1720: two stems of general 18-cent types and a mouthpiece of c 1790–1840 with red wax coating. Appears much later than the other elements of this group – possibly intrusive.
		1433		2		2	1610–1710	1610–1710						
	4	456	7	73	12	92	1610–1750	1720–40	Cross?				113, 167	Some residual 17-cent bowls but later examples all cluster c 1690–1740 with most likely date of deposition c 1720–40. Appears to be a good deposit.
		1279	1			1	1710–20	1710–20						
		1280		2		2	1710–1800	1710–1800						
		1491		1	1	2	1610–1800	1710–1800				ground stem		One 17-cent piece ground at one end.
		1527		2		2	1610–1710	1610–1710						
	5	1476	1	8		9	1650–1750	1690–1720						
		1486	10	33		43	1610–1910	1660–90		1				All bowls range from 1640–1700: sieving chips responsible for broad date of 1610–1910.

Phase	Plot	Context	No B	No S	No M	Total	Date range	Deposit date	Marks	Stem stamps	Stem borders	Dec. etc	Ill nos	Comments
IX	6	316	5	27	3	35	1580–1900	1780–1840+	…GERALD		2		93, 151	Includes a residual Tudor pipe; latest closely datable piece is a Fitzgerald stem stamp. Other stems could be 19 cent.
		325	4	10		14	1610–1910	1700–1800					155, 181	Includes chips from sieving and a stem fragment possibly modified as a hair curler.
		327	1	7	1	9	1610–1800	1710–1800						Plain 17- and 18-cent stems.
		329		2		2	1610–1800	1710–1800						
		338	2	18	2	22	1580–1800	1700–1800	Wheel				96	Unusual deposit in that it includes two very early fragments of c 1580–1610. Most of the finds, however, are 17 cent including a wheel stamp of c 1610–40 and three stems appear to be of 18-cent date.
		340	2	10		12	1610–1900	1800–1900						Mixed group: one stem appears to be 19-cent - but otherwise could end in 18 cent.
		344	3	45		48	1610–1800	1740–1800		1	2		34	Mixed 17- and 18-cent finds.
		346	1	4		5	1610–1750	1690–1750						Bowl fragment possibly very end of 17-cent or first half of 18-cent.
		351	1	2	1	4	1610–1710	1660–1710						
		352	6	11		17	1610–1910	1610–40?						Diagnostic bowls 1610–40 – all other datable fragments are 17-cent types plus some broadly dated sieving chips.
		353	2	6		8	1610–1910	1690–1750						Includes chips from sieving.
		358			1	1	1710–1800	1710–1800						
		359	1	5		6	1610–1800	1710–1800						Plain 18-cent stems
		367		4		4	1710–1800	1710–1800						Mixed 17- and 18-cent stems.
		368		3		3	1610–1800	1610–1800						
		374	3	6		9	1610–1800	1710–1800						
		375	1	2		3	1610–1910	1610–1710						Includes one chip from sieving; other two stems are 17-cent.
		381		4	1	5	1610–1710	1610–1710						Plain 17-cent stems and mouthpiece
		384	2	4		6	1580–1800	1710–1800					94	Includes a residual Tudor pipe together with 18-cent stems.
		395	1	3	1	5	1610–1800	1610–1800						
		401		7		7	1710–1800	1700–60						
		507	4	17		21	1610–1910	1710–1810			1			Includes poorly datable sieving fragments.
		510	1	4		5	1610–1920	1790–1920						Mixed material.
		512	4	5		9	1610–1910	1800–1910						Very neat early bowl with small heel; coarse gritty fabric
		513		2		2	1710–1800	1710–1800						
		524	1	2		3	1690–1800	1700–50						
		547		1		1	1610–1910	1610–1910						Chip from sieving.
		548		6		6	1610–1800	1610–1800						
		553	2	10		12	1610–1800	1700–20						Both bowls would fit early 18-cent deposit.
		554	3	10		13	1580–1800	1710–1800						Mixed finds, including a very early (1580–1620 style) stem, but most of stems are 18-cent in date.
		557		3		3	1610–1800	1700–1800						
		558		14	1	15	1610–1800	1710–1800		1	2		41	Mainly 18-cent style stems, including two early 18-cent stamped examples.
		568	2	1		3	1710–1850	1750–1850						
		571		1		1	1710–1800	1710–1800						
		607		7		7	1610–1710	1610–1710						
		620		1		1	1610–1710	1610–1710						
		629		2		2	1610–1710	1610–1710						
		630	1	1		2	1640–1800	1710–1800						
		821	5	13		18	1610–1800	1660–1800					173	Bowls mixed from c 1660–1800.
		827	1	2		3	1660–1700	1710–1800	illegible					Includes a small heel fragment of c 1660–1700 with traces of a heel stamp.

Phase	Plot	Context	No B	No S	No M	Total	Date range	Deposit date	Marks	Stem stamps	Stem borders	Dec. etc	Ill nos	Comments
IX	6	953	1	7		8	1640–60	1640–60				ground stem		Bowl of c 1640–60: all other stems of 17-cent type. One stem faceted at one end, most likely the result of being used like a piece of chalk.
X	1	200		1		1	1650–1750	1650–1750						Mainly appear 18 cent; just one piece looks 1800–1920.
		203		10		10	1610–1920	1800–1920						
		583	2	6		8	1610–1910	1710–1800						Mixed 17- and 18-cent material plus sieving chips.
		595	2	3		5	1610–40	1690–1715						Latest bowl c 1690–1715; other stems of general 18-cent type.
		597	1			1	1700–1800	1700–1800						Small spur fragment; quite neat spur.
		641		2		2	1610–1710	1610–1710						
		1802	6	47		53	1630–1830	1780–1830	AIRES CHESTER x 2		3	coiled pipe; green glaze	35, 55, 176, 182	Mixed finds but with latest pieces representing interesting material of c 1780–1830.
		1870		1		1	1640–1700	1640–1700						All finds would fit with c 1620–40 date except for one stem of c 1690–1730. Could be intrusive?
		1906	6	12		18	1610–1730	1620–40?					133	
	2	1919		2		2	1640–1710	1690–1710	ELIAS MASSEY		1			
		402		3		3	1720–1850	1750–1850			1			Mixed 17- and 18-cent stems.
		403		16		16	1610–1800	1710–1800						Bowls c 1640–70 and all rest 17-cent apart from three apparently 18-cent stems.
		409	2	8	2	12	1640–60	1700–1800						Coarse local fabric.
		410	1			1	1660–80	1660–80						
		420	1	6		7	1610–1820	1750–1820					104	
		424	1	1		2	1690–1800	1740–1800					172	
		435		2		2	1610–1710	1610–1710						
		438	1	23		24	1610–1800	1760–1800		1			53	Plain 17-cent stems.
		443		4	1	5	1610–1800	1710–1800						Mixed 17- and 18-cent pipes.
		497		1		1	1750–1850	1750–1850						
		405	1	3		4	1610–1800	1710–1800						Mixed 17- and 18-cent fragments.
		1206	2	11	1	14	1610–1850	1700–1800						
		1418	1	2		3	1610–1710	1660–1700						
		1426		3		3	1610–1710	1610–1710						Heel fragment only.
	3	406	1	2		3	1610–1900	1800–1900					137	Latest stem probably 19 cent.
		407	2	7	1	10	1610–1800	1710–1800			1			Bowls c 1640–70 and all rest 17 cent apart from one apparently 18-cent stem.
		415		2		2	1710–1800	1760–90						
		501		3		3	1610–1800	1690–1800			1			
		780	1	21	1	23	1610–1800	1710–1800						
		1082	6	9	1	16	1610–1900	1800–1900				ground stem		One stem with ground end. Latest bowls are 19 cent.
		1199	2	12		14	1610–1800	1700–1800						Small bowl fragment; thickness of walls suggests 17 cent.
		1398	5	4		9	1620–1920	1840–1920						
		1399	13	49	1	63	1610–1850	1720–50	AL	3	4		49	Bowls range from c 1620 to 1750 in date – mixed – but main deposition clearly in 18 cent. Five stems look as late as 1750–1850.
		1404	1	18		19	1610–1800	1720–50		1	2		31, 44	Latest diagnostic pieces are marked stems and bowl fragment of c 1720–50. Some residual 17-cent material.
		1412	2	29		31	1610–1850	1810–50		1	1	Leaf dec seams; 2 ground stems.		
		1414	15	43	1	59	1610–40	1700–50?	Star; ?Fox				4, 110	Mixed bowls: most range from 1610 to 1750. One or two pieces could be later, but uncertain.
		1683	2	10		12	1660–1800	1710–20						Bowl and joining stem (fresh break).

Phase	Plot	Context	No B	No S	No M	Total	Date range	Deposit date	Marks	Stem stamps	Stem borders	Dec. etc	Ill nos	Comments
X	4	454	5	24	3	32	1610–1800	1710–1800			1		97	Bowls all range from 1610 to 1720 but context appears to include 18-cent stems as well.
		1274		1		1	1800–1900	1800–1900						Bowls both 1640–80 but four stems appear to be 18-cent
		1276	2	12	1	15	1610–1800	1700–1800						
		1282		1		1	1700–1720	1700–20			1			
		1283		1		1	1750–1850	1750–1850						
		1349	5	40	4	49	1610–1800	1700–1800			1		43	
		1617	1	6		7	1610–1800	1700–1800					99	
5		1493	2	1		3	1610–1715	1690–1715						Large and very homogeneous group with almost all bowl forms dating from c 1690–1720. All stems look to be contemporary with bowls. One complete pipe reassembled and various other joins, so an apparently fresh group.
		1503	38	65	11	114	1660–1730	1690–1720				ground stem	63–9, 180	
6		1510	1	5	1	7	1610–1920+	1870–1920+	RAOB		1	ROAB		Latest piece an RAOB bowl.
		300	4	25	2	31	1610–1920	1840–1920			1	2 ground stems	38, 144, 177	Mixed group, mainly 18-cent but with odd pieces appearing to be 19-cent or later.
		301	21	167	8	196	1610–1920	1850–1920+	AL; ?NE; CHESTER	4	8	kiln debris	9, 15, 23, 49, 102, 125, 135, 152–3, 169	Large group, mainly of mixed 17- and 18-cent material. Almost all would fit with deposition at end of 18 cent but there are some possible 19-cent stems and one mouthpiece that is certainly c 1850–1920. Either late 18 cent deposit with odd intrusive material or earlier material redeposited c 1850–1920. Context also includes one fragment of pipe kiln debris.
		302	1	13	1	15	1610–1720	1700–20	NE	1	1		10, 45, 126	Includes ligatured NE within a circular border and an early 18-cent stamped stem.
		322		5		5	1610–1900	1800–1900						Plain 17- and 19-cent stems.
		323		4		4	1610–1900	1800–1900						Plain 17- and 19- cent stems.
		334		3		3	1610–1900	1800–1900						Mixed stems.
		361		2		2	1710–1800	1710–1800						Plain 18-cent stems.
		385	1	4		5	1610–1900	1760–1900					103	Latest pieces are two stems of late 18-cent or 19-cent date.
		386	2	1		3	1610–1920	1610–1920		1870–1920	WHO.EMMA		117, 178	Includes two late 19-cent–early 20-cent pieces.
		400		1		1	1610–1710	1610–1710						Plain 17-cent stem.
		563		13		13	1700–1900	1800–1900						Latest diagnostic piece is green glazed stem fragment.
		1356		4		4	1610–1800	1710–1800						
		B54		1		1	1610–1710	1610–1710						
		B85		1		1	1660–1730	1660–1730						
		C53		6		6	1640–1800	1730–1800						All c 1640–1710 except for one of c 1730–1800.
		C56		1		1	1730–1800	1730–1800						
		F16	1	5	1	7	1610–1850	1790–1850						
		F17	1	7		8	1640–1850	1750–1850	?TB				8	Includes heel fragment (only) of 1640–1700 with stamped mark.
		F19		8		8	1610–1710	1610–1710						
		F22		1		1	1750–1850	1750–1850						
		F26	1	5		6	1590–1660	1610–40	NE				11, 124	Includes very early stem fragment and could be early 17-cent deposit - bowl is c 1610–40.
		G4	1			1	1640–60	1640–60						
		G12		1		1	1750–1850	1750–1850						
		G30	1			1	1760–1820	1760–1820						
		U/S	29	134	7	170	1610–1750	NA	AL, RG, IP		1		13, 20, 139	Some of the bowls look very similar to finds 149 from 1507 and perhaps derive from this large deposit of possible kiln waste.
		Total	984	4356	214	5554								

Roman Glass

H E M Cool

Vessel glass

Introduction

In total forty-two fragments of Roman vessel glass were recovered from the excavations, approximately two-thirds of which were found in residual contexts. Approximately half of the recognised fragments came from robust blue-green bottles (nos 4–6, 15–19, 21, 29, 33–4), reflecting the fact that such fragments were more likely survive centuries of redeposition than many other forms. These bottles were in use during the later first to earlier third century (Price & Cottam 1998, 194–200) and are always very common on military sites of that date. Two fragments of cylindrical bottles were also present (nos 7–8); these were in use for a shorter period during the later first and early second century (Price & Cottam 1998, 191–4).

Of particular interest was a deep blue mould-blown fragment from a Phase 1 context (no 1). This clearly came from a late Neronian or early Flavian drinking cup. The fragment retains a vertical mould seam and parts of three horizontal ribs. The number of ribs rules out the possibility that it came from a cylindrical beaker with a scene of the circus or the arena, as the zones on these tend to be bounded by a single horizontal rib (*see*, eg, Cool & Price 1995, 43–8). Small ribbed cups (Price & Cottam 1998, 60) have multiple ribs but this fragment appears to come from a cylindrical-sided vessel rather than a hemispherical one. So, whilst it is possible to date the fragment with some certainty, the precise form of mould-blown beaker it came from is currently unknown.

Another first-century vessel is the globular jug represented by the handle fragment no 13. In general such jugs were in use from the middle of the first century to the early second century (Price & Cottam 1998, 150–2), but traces of opaque white marvering place this example in the first century as most vessels with this type of decoration had disappeared by the final decade of that century (Cool 1992, 64).

The colourless body fragment no 10 almost certainly came from one of the beaker forms most popular in early- to mid-second century (*see*, for example, the one from Watergate Street: Ward 1988, 22). This was the latest vessel that could be closely dated within the Roman period. The other forms that could be identified were either vessels in use during the later first to mid-second century (eg no 3) or functional forms such as jars (nos 2 and 14) which had wide first- to third-century *floruits*.

All vessels listed in the catalogue were blue-green unless otherwise stated.

Phase I

1 Body fragment, deep blue; mould-blown; fragment of cylindrical side retaining mould seam at junction of three horizontal ribs; dimensions 14 x 9 mm, wall th 1.5 mm. (1148); SF 9901; <5132>.

2 Jar rim fragment; tubular rim bent out and down, up, in and flattened; rim diam 130 mm. (1242).

3 Jug or jar, lower body and base fragment; side sloping into open pushed-in base ring, concave base; base diam 55 mm, present H 18 mm, wall th 5 mm.

4 Square bottle, six shoulder and side fragments; light green; broken at junction of neck and shoulder; horizontal shoulder curving over to side; outer diam of neck 30 mm, W of bottle 75 mm. (1148) with one of joining fragments from Phase II (1146).

5 Square bottle, body fragment; fragment retains complete width of bottle, broken at junction with base; present H 100 mm, W of bottle 75 mm. (1148).

6 Hexagonal bottle body fragment. (1242).

7 Cylindrical bottle base fragment; side curving into concave base; base diam 100 mm. (1242).

8 Cylindrical bottle body fragment; vertical scratch marks. (1239).

9 Two chips. (276); <5017>.

Phase II

10 Beaker body fragment, colourless; cylindrical side curving out to rim; horizontal wheel-cut line on upper body; dimensions 26 x 30 mm, wall th 1 mm. (1146); SF 9378.

11 Body fragment, colourless. (126).

12 Body fragment, colourless. (75).

13 Globular jug, light yellow-green; two joining handle and shoulder fragments; angular handle with six narrow prominent ribs; simple lower attachment retaining fragment of convex-curved side; traces of opaque white glass on outer and inner face of handle; present H 125 mm, handle section 27 x 6 mm. (1138).

14 Jar rim fragment; wide horizontal rim with rim edge rolled up and in; neck beginning to curve out; rim diam 75 mm; wall th 1 mm, present H 10 mm. (1219); SF 8814.

15 Square bottle, lower body and base fragment; corner of base retaining small part of circular moulding; heavy wear on base; also one other body fragment from a square bottle; present H 35 mm. (1225).

16 Square bottle, body fragment with vertical scratch marks; body W 70 mm. (1220).

17 Square bottle, body fragment. (1220).

18 Prismatic bottle; fragment from centre of base; base design: parts of two concentric circular mouldings; dimensions 34 x 18 mm. (1220).

19 Prismatic bottle, shoulder fragment. (1220).

Phase III

20 Jug, flask or bottle neck fragment. (106).

21 Hexagonal bottle body fragment. (281); <5019>.

22 Body fragment. (1022).

23 Chip. (973); <5094>.

24 Body fragment. (106).

Phase IV

25 Rim fragment; small fragment with rolled edge; dim 12.5 x 7 mm. (1015); <5096>.
26 Base fragment; concave base with central kick and edge of pontil scar; diam *c* 35 mm. (974).
27 Body fragment. (1030); <5114>.
28 Body fragments (2) plus two chips. (1015); <5096>.

Phase V

29 Hexagonal bottle body fragment. (487).
30 Body fragment. (992); <5097>.
31 Body fragment. (264); <5012>.
32 Body fragment. (1014).

Phase VII

33 Prismatic bottle body fragment. (1629).
34 Prismatic bottle body fragment. (31);<5101>.

Medieval and Post-Medieval Glass
Hugh Willmott

Introduction

The excavations produced a large assemblage of vessel glass from a wide variety of contexts. This is the largest group of post-Roman glass to have been excavated in Chester and, along with the wide range of forms present, is one of the most significant groups to have been excavated in England in recent years. Because of the size of the assemblage, not all the glass is discussed here, although a full catalogue has been submitted for the archive.

The vessels chosen for cataloguing and discussion are primarily those which came from group contexts, where a range of vessels can be seen to have been deposited. These groups were more informative for shedding light on glass use in the different plots during the different phases. In addition to these groups of glass, there were vessels which were of particular interest, but which were usually isolated finds.

Phase VI

Plot 2

Cess pit (487)

The earliest vessels on the site came from (806), the primary sediment in the cess pit constructed in Phase V, and are all late medieval in date. The first two, nos 1–2, are the pushed-in base and rim from potash glass globular flasks. Both are decorated with optic-blown wrythen ribbing and typical products of the fourteenth and fifteenth centuries (Tyson 2000, 122). The other vessel from this sediment, no 3, is the fragmentary remains of a very fine body, almost certainly from a urinal. Urinals are a relatively common form from the thirteenth until the sixteenth century, when inspection of the colour and consistency of urine was a popular form of health divination (Robbins 1970). The presence of these three vessels in this context is not surprising, as urinals and flasks, (which may have been used for the same purposes), are frequently found associated with garderobes and cess pits. A cylindrical beaker, no 4, decorated with optic-blown bosses, almost certainly manufactured in the Low Countries, came from a later fill of the pit.

Catalogue

1 Six fragments of pushed-in base from a globular flask, decorated with thick optic-blown wrythen ribbing; green glass with heavy weathering; base diam uncertain; 14–15 cent. (806); SF 10044. Ill 5.8.1.1.
2 Multiple fragments of everted rim from a flask, decorated with optic-blown wrythen ribbing; green glass, heavily devitrified; rim diam 75 mm; 14–15 cent. (806); SF 9599.
3 Ten small fragments of body, probably from a urinal; completely devitrified; late medieval. (806).

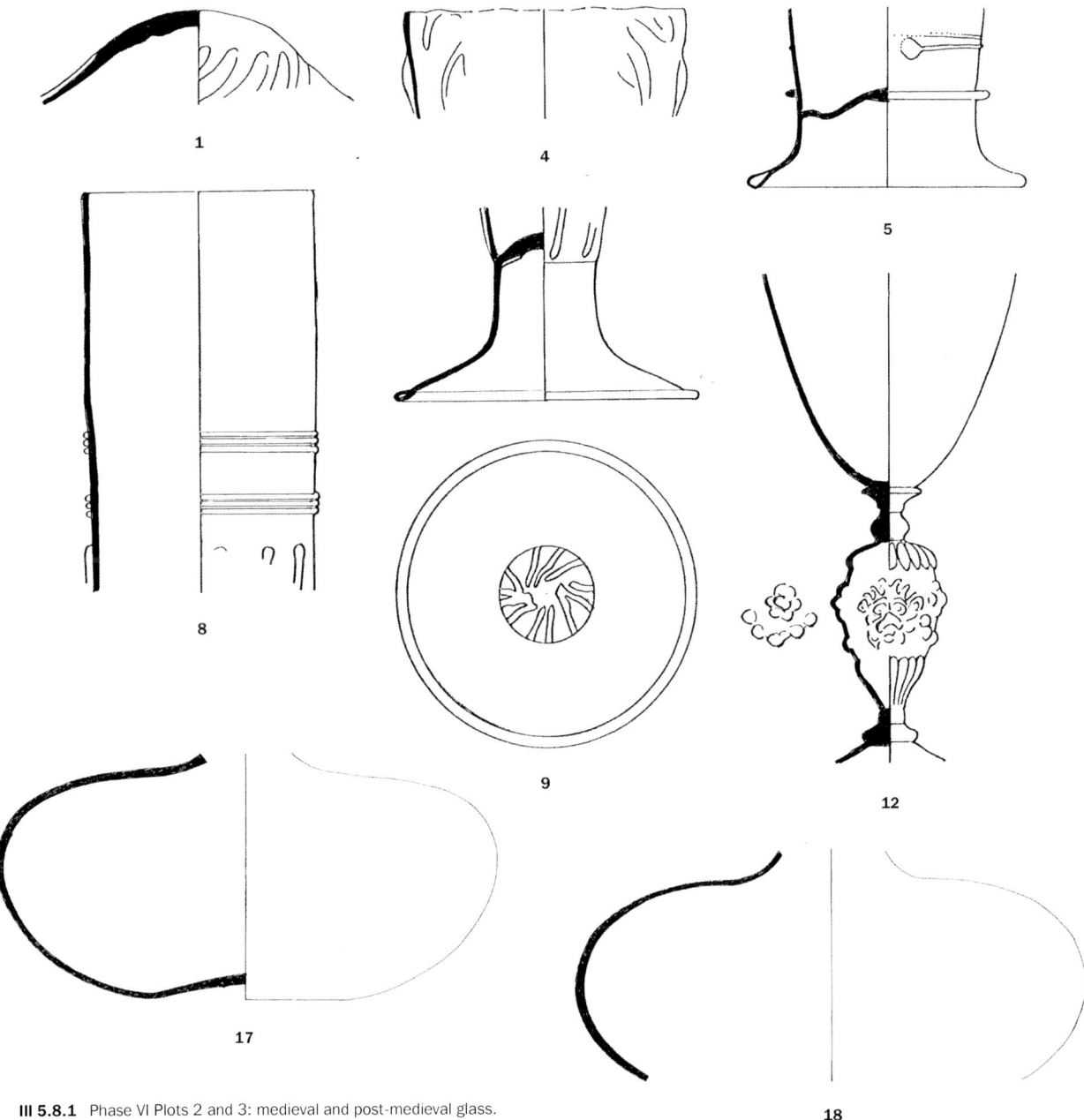

Ill 5.8.1 Phase VI Plots 2 and 3: medieval and post-medieval glass.
(Scale 1–12 1/2; 17–18 1/4)

4   One fragment of vertical rim from a plain cylindrical beaker, decorated with heavy optic-blown
bosses; clear glass with little weathering; rim diam
90 mm; early to mid-17 cent. Rim diam 90 mm. (789);
SF 8686. Ill 5.8.1.4.

Plot 3

Cess pit (430)/(850)

The earliest of these groups came from the fills of cess
pit (430), which contained vessels of sixteenth- and early seventeenth-century date. The earliest of these, from
the first decades of the sixteenth century, is the pedestal
base from a potash glass beaker, decorated with a prominent horizontal trail, no 5. Heavily weathered, this vessel
is very similar to a near complete example excavated at
Eynsham abbey in Oxfordshire. Fragments were found
in two different contexts from cylindrical beakers decorated with a thick spiral trailing, nos 6–7, cut by being

blown into a ribbed mould, although it is uncertain whether these come from the same vessel. These are relatively
common late sixteenth- or early seventeenth-century imports, traditionally thought to have been produced in
the Antwerp region (Tait 1967), but they are now real-
ised to have been made in northern Germany as well.

Fragments were also found in three different contexts
of a tall fluted beaker, nos 8–10, and it is probable that
these are from a single vessel. Unlike a pedestal beaker,
this type was formed from two separate paraisons of glass
and decorated with thick prominent opaque white vertical ribs on the body which go under the join of the two
pieces of glass. Further up the vessel the body is also
decorated with two horizontal bands of three opaque
white trails. Fluted beakers with this decoration are not
uncommon finds on sites from the first half of the seventeenth century, such as at Gracechurch Street, London
(Willmott 2000b), and this suggests an English provenance for them. Furthermore, fragments of such vessels

were found amongst the working waste at Old Broad Street associated with Sir Robert Mansell's nearby glass furnace at Austin Friars.

The remaining drinking vessels from this pit are all goblets. Two, nos 11–12, have embossed lion mask stems, formed by blowing a bubble of glass into a two-piece fixed mould. Consequently, it is often possible to match the different designs with other stems manufactured from the same mould (eg Willmott 2000a), although with these two stems no specific match was possible. In the case of no 11 this might be due to the fact the stem was quite heavily distorted when it was removed from the mould, and although no exact match for no 8 could be made it is very similar to two examples found at 1–11 Crook Street, Chester. Two further fragments, nos 13–14, are also the rim and base from goblets, although their form could not be reconstructed further. The only other tablewares from this feature are fragments from two different pedestal bowls, nos 15–16, both made in a green glass, but too fragmentary to identify more comprehensively.

The final fragments of glass from this feature are the most unusual. These are the remains from at least two different reniform, or kidney-shaped, bottles, nos 17–19. They have low bases, flattened bodies and rounded shoulders, although they are missing their necks. These bottles are virtually unique archaeologically in England. There are three nearly intact examples in the reserve collection of the Museum of London, but only one has a provenance, having been found in the attic of the 'Dick Whittington' tavern in Smithfield, London. However, they are unlikely to be English products, and more examples are known in the Netherlands. The most complete of these was found at Eiermarkt in Nijmegen dating to the first half of the seventeenth century (Henkes 1994, 244), whilst one also appears in a scene by Jan van der Velde II, engraved some time before his death in 1641. It is interesting to note that this reniform bottle predates the earliest occurrence of the classic wine bottle form around 1650, and it is no coincidence that no fragments of wine bottles were found in this feature.

Catalogue

5 Large cylindrical beaker; fifteen fragments of folded base and body, decorated with fine prominent horizontal trails; green glass with very heavy weathering; early 16 cent. (442); SF 8412. Ill 5.8.1.5.

6 Cylindrical beaker; five joining fragments of body, decorated with thick spiral chequered trails; clear tinted glass with medium weathering; late 16–early 17 cent. (429); SF 9849.

7 Cylindrical beaker; four fragments from body, decorated with thick spiral chequered trails; clear tinted glass with medium weathering; late 16–early 17 cent. (800); SF 8601.

8 Tall fluted beaker; four fragments of vertical rim and body, decorated with prominent opaque white vertical trails on its lower body and two horizontal bands further up; rim diam 70 mm; first half of 17 cent. (852); SF 8564. Ill 5.8.1.8.

9 Tall fluted beaker; complete base, decorated with prominent opaque white vertical trails; clear glass with no weathering; base diam 93 mm; first half of 17 cent. (429); SF 8413. Ill 5.8.1.9.

10 Tall fluted beaker; two body fragments, decorated with prominent vertical opaque white trails; clear glass with little weathering; first half of 17 cent. (800); SF 8561.

11 Goblet; one fragment of stem, in form of a mould-blown lion mask with side swags, distorted on removal from mould; clear glass with little weathering; first half of 17 cent. (429); SF 8516.

12 Goblet; four joining fragments of stem and lower U-shaped bowl; stem is a fine mould-blown lion mask with side swags; clear glass with little weathering; early 17 cent. (800); SF 8562. Ill 5.8.1.12.

13 Goblet; two fragments of rim from a very fine goblet bowl; clear glass with light weathering; late 16–early 17 cent. (429).

14 Goblet; two fragments of flaring base with under-folded edge; clear glass with no weathering; base diam 90 mm; first half of 17 cent. (429); SF 8506.

15 ?Pedestal bowl; one fragment of folded base; blue-green clear glass with light weathering; early 17 cent. (800); SF 8511.

16 ?Pedestal bowl; one fragment of folded base; green glass with quite heavy weathering; base diam 95 mm; early 17 cent. (429); SF 8393.

17 Reniform bottle; nineteen joining fragments of base and side; green thick glass with light weathering; base diam 75 x 115 mm; first half of 17 cent. (429); SF 10047. Ill 5.8.1.17.

18 Reniform bottle; twenty fragments of body and shoulder; green thick glass with heavy weathering; first half of 17 cent. (429); SF 10048. Ill 5.8.1.18.

19 Reniform bottle; eight fragments of side; green thick glass with light weathering; base diam uncertain; first half of 17 cent. (800).

Gully (1703)

The fill of (1703) contained a small but interesting assemblage of glass dating to the very late sixteenth and first half of the seventeenth centuries. This comprises parts of three different pedestal beakers with folded feet made in a green glass, nos 20–2. Although they vary in the degree to which they are weathered, they all appear to be plain and undecorated. The remaining vessel is represented by a small fragment of tapering neck in a deep blue glass, no 23. This is an unusual colour, but unfortunately due to the small size of the piece, could not be reconstructed further.

Catalogue

20 Three fragments of rim and very thick upper body from a pedestal beaker; green clear glass with light weathering; rim diam 88 mm; early 17 cent. (1702).

21 One fragment of upper folded base from a pedestal beaker; base diam uncertain; green glass with heavily devitrified; 16 cent. (1702).

22 One fragment of folded base from a pedestal beaker; green clear glass with light weathering; base diam 80 mm; late 16 cent. (1702).

23 One fragment of tapering neck possibly from a flask or bottle; blue glass with no weathering; 15–16 cent. (1702).

Plot 4

Pit (1541)

24 One fragment of base from a cylindrical beaker; decorated with optic-blown bosses and a rigaree base ring; clear glass with quite heavy weathering; base diam 78 mm; early 17 cent. (1540); SF 9343.

Phase VII

Plot 1

Unfortunately no known occupants of this plot could be identified during Phase VII, and glass of interest was only found in one context.

Context (663)

A small assemblage of glass was found in cultivation layer (663). In total five vessels could be identified, and with one exception all are tablewares. One, no 25, is part of the lower bowl from a goblet, although its precise form is uncertain. Two fragments, one rim, no 26, and one a base, no 27, are from green glass pedestal beakers, whilst fragments of a similar folded base ring, no 28, are from a bowl. The final fragment, no 29, is a rim and neck from a small case bottle. These are quite common forms and all date to the first half of the seventeenth century.

Catalogue

25 One fragment of lower bowl and merese from a goblet; clear glass with medium weathering; early to mid-17 cent. (663); SF 8465.

26 One fragment of slightly inturned rim from a plain pedestal beaker; green clear glass with light weathering; rim diam uncertain; early to mid-17 cent. (663).

27 One fragment of folded base from a pedestal beaker; green glass with medium weathering; base diam 70 mm; early to mid-17 cent. (663); SF 8296.

28 One fragment of folded base probably from a pedestal bowl; green glass with medium weathering; base diam 105 mm; early to mid-17 cent. (663); SF 8227.

29 One fragment of everted rim and short neck from a small case bottle; green glass with quite light weathering; rim diam 24 mm; early to mid-17 cent. (663).

Plot 2

Cess pit (465)

This pit overlay the Phase VI cess pit (487) and produced vessels which date to the later seventeenth and early eighteenth centuries. Although the documentary records are incomplete, it is possible that many of these vessels belonged to the family of Thomas Aspinwall, ironmonger and later his daughters Elizabeth, Hannah and Abigail in the second half of the seventeenth and early eighteenth century.

There is a single example of a large solid inverted baluster goblet, no 30, of a type identical to the more numerous examples found in Plot 4 pit (1696) (discussed *below*). Only two other fragments of drinking vessels were found in this feature, and both might have come from the same, or at least a similar, vessel. The first, no 31 is a small applied pad base in opaque white glass, whilst the second, no 32, is a portion of small looped handle. Al

though rare, opaque white cups with decorative handles are known in some late seventeenth-century contexts, and it is likely that they were imported from Italy (Willmott 2002, 52–3).

The remaining vessels are all storage wares. The first, no 33, is a small portion of rim from a seventeenth-century globular jar, whilst there are also fragments from at least five late seventeenth- to early eighteenth-century phials, nos 34–8. The remaining vessels are wine bottles of similar date, there being a single example of a shaft and globe bottle, no 39, from around 1650–80 and fragments from four different onion-shaped bottles, nos 40–3, of late seventeenth- or early eighteenth-century date.

Catalogue

30 One fragment of solid inverted baluster stem from a goblet; clear lead glass with medium weathering; early 18 cent. (463); SF 8233. Ill 5.8.2.30.

31 One fragment of small applied pad base from a cup; opaque white glass with quite heavy weathering; base diam 32 mm; late 17 cent. (463); SF 8527.

32 One fragment of small plain looped handle, possibly from a cup; opaque white glass with no weathering; late 17–early 18 cent. (463); SF 9345.

33 One fragment of widely everted rim from a globular jar; green glass with little weathering; rim diam 65 mm; early 17 cent. (472).

34 One fragment of widely everted rim from a phial; green clear glass with heavy weathering; rim diam 28 mm; late 17–early 18 cent. (464).

35 One fragment of basal push-in from a small flask or globular phial; green glass with light weathering; base diam uncertain; late 17 century. (463).

36 One fragment of base from a globular phial; green clear glass with light weathering; base diam 44 mm; late 17 cent. (491).

37 One fragment of base from a globular phial; green clear glass with light weathering; base diam uncertain; late 17 cent. (491).

38 One fragment of shoulder from a broad cylindrical phial; green clear glass with very little weathering; late 17–early 18 cent. (472).

39 One fragment of base from a shaft & globe wine bottle; green glass with medium weathering; base diam uncertain; date 1650 80. (491).

40 One fragment of base from an onion wine bottle; green glass with medium weathering; base diam 75 mm; late 17–early 18 cent. (463).

41 One fragment of base from an onion wine bottle; green glass with medium weathering; base diam 56 mm. Late 17–early 18 century. (463).

42 One fragment of rim and neck from an onion wine bottle; green glass with medium weathering; rim diam 28 mm; late 17–early 18 cent. (463).

43 Six fragments of body and base from an onion wine bottle; green glass with very heavy weathering; late 17–early 18 century. (472).

Soil layers (459) and (481)

Two fragments of interest were recovered from soil layers in this plot. The first, no 44, is the folded base from an early sixteenth-century bellied tankard. A typical *façon de Venise* product, these are sometimes further elaborately decorated with silver gilt mounts (eg Glanville 1971).

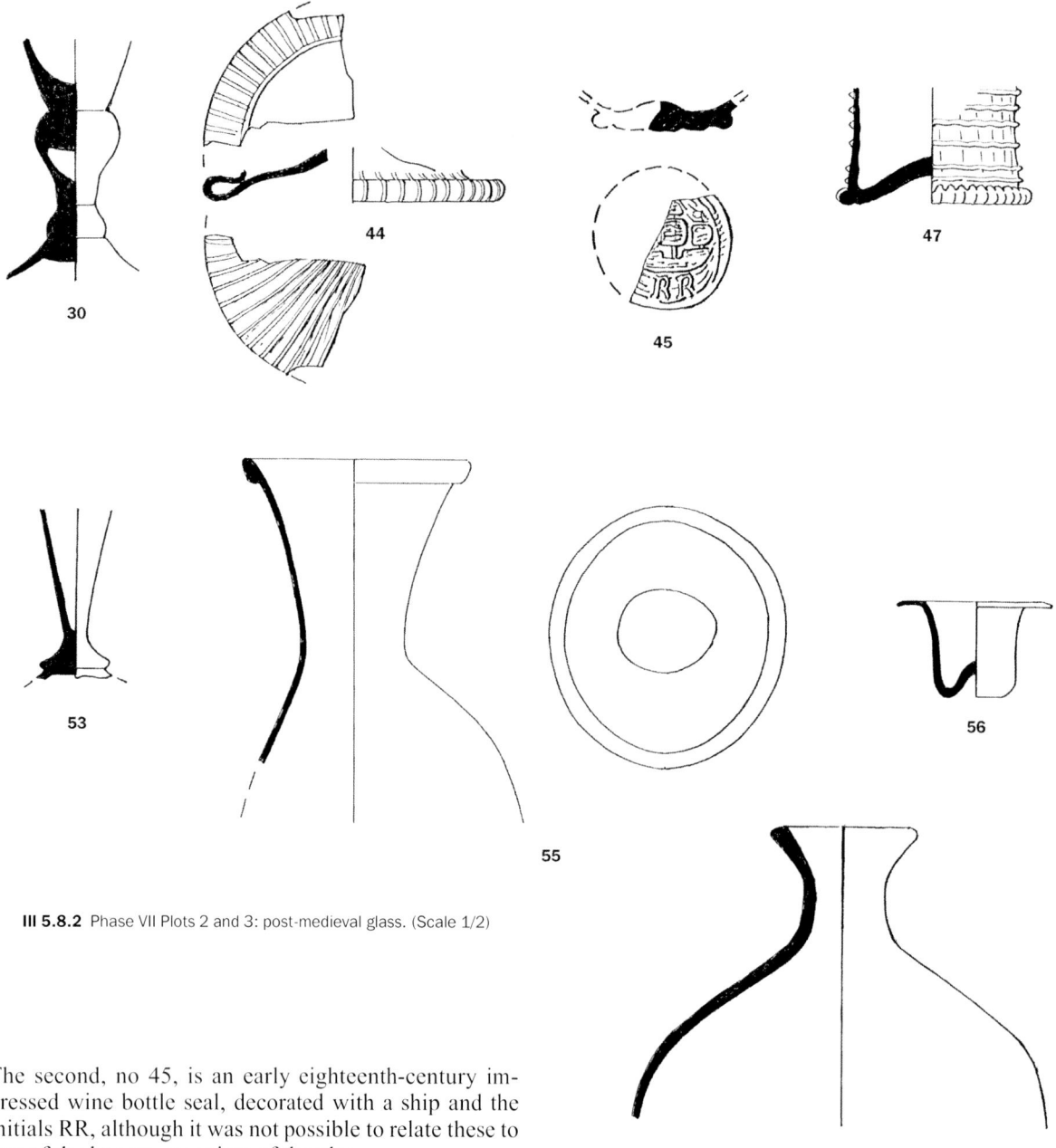

Ill 5.8.2 Phase VII Plots 2 and 3: post-medieval glass. (Scale 1/2)

The second, no 45, is an early eighteenth-century impressed wine bottle seal, decorated with a ship and the initials RR, although it was not possible to relate these to any of the known occupiers of the plot.

Catalogue
44 Five joining fragments of folded base, possibly from a bellied tankard or flask, decorated with broad bands of marvered opaque white vertical *vetro a fili*; clear glass with quite heavy weathering; base diam 100 mm; early to mid-16 cent. (481); SF 8298. Ill 5.8.2.44.
45 One fragment of stamped wine bottle seal, decorated with a masted ship and the initials RR below; green glass with no weathering; early 18 cent. (459); SF 8229. Ill 5.8.2.45.

Plot 3

Most of the glass from this phase in Plot 3 dates to the period when the property was owned by Randle Vause, a linen draper and various of his tenants during the later seventeenth century, and subsequently by his widow Sarah in the early eighteenth century.

Context (1111)
This layer contained a number of glass vessels, especially wine bottles, although only the most diagnostic of these are included here. They vary in date from the sixteenth to the early eighteenth century, but this is as might be expected given that this was a levelling-up layer. Three drinking vessels were found. The first, no 46, is a small fragment of base from a stemmed goblet, which is unusually decorated with vertical ribbing. The second, no 47, is a large fragment of base and lower side from a small green-tinted cylindrical beaker decorated with fine spiral trailing compressed in a vertical ribbed mould. The final drinking vessel, no 48, is less diagnostic, being a body fragment blown in a deep purple glass and probably from a footed cup. The remaining fragments are all from onion-shaped wine bottles, nos 49–52, dating to the late seventeenth or early eighteenth centuries.

46 One fragment of flaring base and base ring from a goblet, decorated with optic-blown vertical ribbing; clear glass with no weathering; base diam uncertain; late 16–early 17 cent. (1111).

47 One fragment of base and lower side from a cylindrical beaker, decorated with thin spiral chequer trails and a rigaree base ring; green clear glass with medium weathering; base diam 55 mm; late 16–early 17 cent. (1111); SF 8837. Ill 5.8.2.47.

48 One fragment of lower body, possibly from a small footed cup; purple glass with little weathering; mid- to late 17 cent. (1111).

49 One fragment of pushed-in base from an onion wine bottle; green glass with quite heavy weathering; base diam uncertain; late 17–early 18 cent. (1111).

50 One fragment of pushed-in base from an onion wine bottle; green glass with quite heavy weathering; base diam uncertain; late 17–early 18 cent. (1111).

51 One fragment of rim and neck from an onion wine bottle; green glass with quite heavy weathering; rim diam 28 mm; late 17–early 18 cent. (1111).

52 One fragment of rim and neck from an onion wine bottle; green glass with quite heavy weathering; rim diam 26 mm; late 17–early 18 cent. (1111).

Pit (1189)

This pit also contained a small collection of vessel glass dating to the seventeenth century. There is a fragment of lower stem from a cigar-shaped goblet, no 53, a typical English product of the first half of the seventeenth century, known to have been produced by Mansell at his Austin Friars furnace. There is also a fragment of base from a plain cylindrical beaker with a rigaree base ring, no 54, but this vessel has subsequently become badly heat distorted. The final tableware in this group, no 55, is more unusual, being a slightly out-turned rim with a folded-out edge from a possible decanter. The top of the shoulder also survives, showing that the body of the vessel was uneven in shape and apparently slightly flattened. Such out-turned rims are very rare indeed in early post-medieval glass, and no exact parallel for this form could be found in England. It might be that it was an import from rather further afield, such as Spain, but this remains speculative at present. Another unusual vessel, no 56, and again without exact parallel, is a small inkwell. In form, and in metal, its base resembles a cylindrical phial, but with a wide out-turned rim. Although it stood on its own, the design of the rim suggests that it was made to be inserted into an inkstand.

The remaining four vessels are all containers and date to the middle of the seventeenth century. One, no 57, is a small bottle-shaped phial, whilst two others, nos 58–9, are more common globular types. The final glass from this pit, no 60, is a complete neck and shoulder from a square-sectioned case bottle, a popular seventeenth-century form for the convenient storage and transport of liquids (Willmott 2002, 86–7), and known from other local sites such as Hunter Street, Chester.

53 One fragment of lower cigar-shaped stem from a goblet; upper portion of flaring base grozed away after

breakage; clear tinted glass with little weathering; first half 17 cent. (1096); SF 9372. Ill 5.8.2.53.

54 One fragment of base from a cylindrical beaker with solid rigaree base ring; heavily heat distorted; clear glass with medium weathering; base diam uncertain; early 17 cent. (1190); SF 9370.

55 Six joining fragments of out-folded rim and tapering neck from a possible flask or decanter; Clear tinted glass with little weathering, but many air bubbles and impurities; rim diam 70 mm; 17 cent? (1191); SF 9394. Ill 5.8.2.55.

56 One fragment of pushed-in base, short cylindrical body and widely everted rim, probably from an ink well; blue green glass with light weathering; base diam 23 mm, rim diam 40 mm, H 26 mm; late 17–18 cent. (1098); SF 9395. Ill 5.8.2.56.

57 Six fragments of neck and body from a small bottle-shaped phial; green clear glass with little weathering; mid-17 cent. (1191).

58 Two joining fragments of everted rim, short neck and shoulder from a globular phial; green clear glass with no weathering; rim diam 23 mm; 17 cent. (1098).

59 One fragment of everted rim and neck from a globular phial; green clear glass with little weathering; rim diam 30 mm; late 17 cent. (1098).

60 Fourteen joining fragments of everted rim, short neck and shoulder from a case bottle; green glass with heavy weathering; rim diam 38 mm; 17 cent (1191); SF 10046. Ill 5.8.2.60.

Plot 4

During this phase in Plot 4 there is particularly interesting biographical detail for the people living here during the late seventeenth and early eighteenth centuries. Between around 1660 and 1693 Matthew Anderton, an innkeeper, merchant, alderman, sheriff and significantly deputy controller of the port of Chester, occupied this plot, and this might explain the quantity and quality of the glass finds. After his death his son Matthew (who was mayor in 1703/4) occupied the site until he died in 1709. The vast majority of the glass from this period was found in the various fills of the pit (1696)/(1614)/(1625). Typologically it dates to the very late seventeenth or very early eighteenth centuries. Given the quantity of glass found in this feature, and its often relative completeness, it could be interpreted as a household clearance or dump. When this might date to is less certain, but obvious historical points might be the death of Anderton senior in 1683 or his son in 1709. If either is indeed the case, the date of the glass would probably support the latter. It was also possible that the glass recorded as coming (1503), Phase X, Plot 5 (*see* below), actually came from (1505), a fill of pit (1522) in Phase VII, Plot 4 and was mislabelled.

Horn core-lined pit (1807)/(1621)

61 One fragment of convex base with external pontil mark from a urinal; green clear glass with light weathering. 15–very early 16 cent. (1796). Ill 5.8.3.61.

62 One fragment of solid inverted baluster stem and lower bowl from a goblet; clear lead glass with little weathering; late 17 cent. (1609); SF 9134. Ill 5.8.3.62.

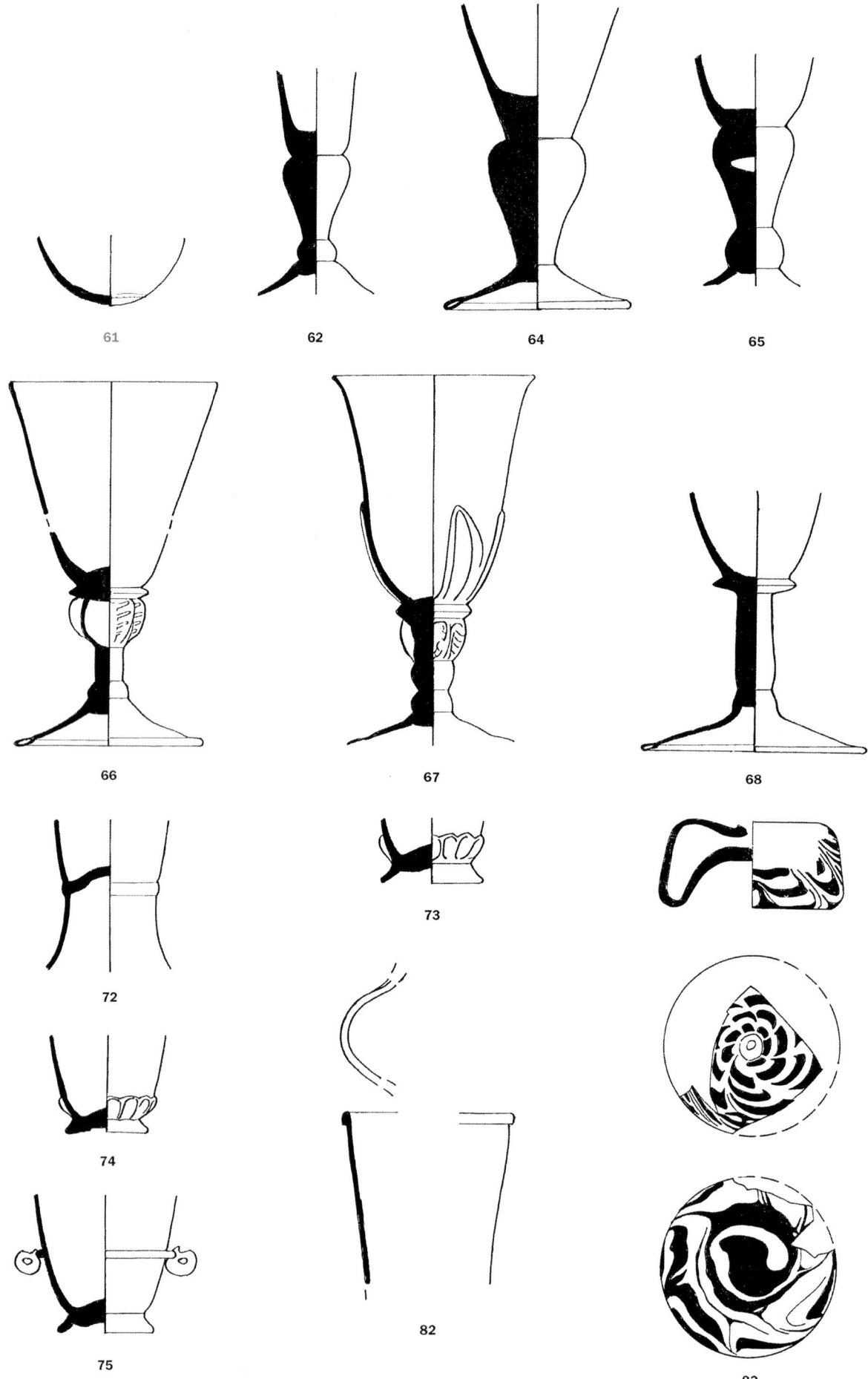

III 5.8.3 Phase VII Plot 4: post-medieval glass. (Scale 1/2).

Pit (1696)/(1614)/(1625)

The majority of the glass from Phase VII came from this feature. While fragments appear in a variety of contexts, there do not appear to be any chronological or typological differences, although there are no apparent cross-context joins either. With one exception, the glass was all contemporaneous with its depositional phase.

Amongst the rest of the assemblage tablewares dominate, of which a large number are high-status vessels such as goblets. Whilst there is a fragment of rim from an earlier seventeenth-century goblet, no 63, the rest date to the end of that century or the very beginning of the eighteenth century. Perhaps the most distinctive are two large goblets made in a lead glass with thick, heavy inverted baluster stems, nos 64–5. This form had its origins in the sixteenth century but was one of the types which made the transition between soda-based glass and the new lead crystal metal developed in the 1670–80s. Whilst these forms had earlier antecedents, the assemblage also contains examples of goblet forms which developed after the introduction of lead crystal. The most complete of these, no 66, has a deep U-shaped bowl and a 'propeller' stem formed by pinching the stem knop into a series if flattened vertical wings. There is a second glass with a similar stem, no 67, which has a slightly different bowl. This is covered on its lower portion with a prominent tooled decoration, formed from a manipulated double gather of glass. Another new form, again from the very end of the seventeenth century, has a much simpler stem, no 68. This is formed from a solid, thick, plain rod and has a prominent merese that joined it to the goblet bowl. The remaining fragments are also all from lead crystal goblets and consist of fragments from one further rim, no 69, and two different folded base rings, nos 70–1.

Only a single fragment of a beaker came from this feature, which was entirely consistent with its date. This, no 72, is the upper base and lower body from a tall fluted beaker made in a plain clear glass from two separate paraisons. Dating to around the middle of the seventeenth century, this vessel was probably quite old when deposited. The three remaining drinking vessels are all small footed cups. The first two, nos 73–4, are nearly identical bases with applied pad feet and decorated on their lower body with a heavy tooled gadrooning. These were again new products associated with early lead glass production, and fragments of similar vessels have been found at the Yorkshire glassmaking sites of Bolsterstone (Ashurst 1987, 197) and Silkstone (Willmott 2003, 2). The third cup, no 75, is a slightly different variation and not decorated with gadrooning, rather having the surviving remains of the lower portion of two decorative handle bases joined with a thick horizontal trail.

The other tablewares are all associated with the presentation and serving of foodstuffs. Amongst these are remains of five different bowls or dishes, although most are too fragmented for proper reconstruction of their form. At least one, no 76, is an everted rim and convex side from a bowl, made in a tinted opaque white glass. There are also fragments from at least five clear glass shallow bowls and dishes, nos 77–81, although their precise forms are hard to identify. Much more distinctive are the fragments of a rim and pouring lip from a jug made in a black glass, no 82. Vessels made in a black metal are generally very rare in England. However, the excavations at the

furnace at Haughton Green, near Manchester, which operated until 1653, did demonstrate that this metal was manufactured there (Hurst-Vose 1994, 33–5). It is possible that this jug was made at Haughton Green earlier in the seventeenth century, or may have been a product of another, as yet undiscovered, glasshouse elsewhere in the north-west.

The remaining vessels from the pit are all containers. The first, no 83, is a rare find and considerably older than the context in which it was found. It is a squat inkwell, with a relatively large basal kick and a narrow sheared rim. The vessel is made in a very dark brown-black glass and decorated with an opaque white spiral trail that is feathered or feathered and marvered flat into the body. Evison (2000, 82) has identified similar, but less complete, tops to inkwells of mid- to late Saxon date from Lurk Lane in Beverley, Brandon in Suffolk, and Southampton. However, the closest parallel in size and feathered opaque white decoration is a base from St Martin's Lane, Chichester, which she suggested was either from an Islamic bottle or an inkwell (*op cit*, 90). How this vessel came to be in this context is uncertain. It is possible that it was a residual find, but given its relative completeness it could have been found elsewhere and retained as a curio before finally being deposited in this feature.

The other containers are all rather ordinary types for the late seventeenth and very early eighteenth centuries. There are fragments from at least five different phials; two bottle-shaped nos 84–5, one cylindrical, no 86, and two globular, nos 87–8. Also present are fragments from at least three different case bottles, nos 89–91, and two onion-shaped wine bottles, nos 92–3, of the period *c* 1680–1720.

Catalogue

63 One fragment of rim from a very fine everted goblet bowl; clear glass with no weathering; rim diam 90 mm; early 17 cent. (1601); SF 9276.

64 Eighteen fragments of flaring base with under-folded edge, solid inverted baluster stem and bowl from a goblet; clear lead glass with little weathering; base diam 70 mm; late 17 cent. (1601); SF 9182. Ill 5.8.3.64.

65 One fragment of solid inverted baluster stem from a goblet; clear lead glass with medium weathering; early 18 cent. (1607); SF 9402. Ill 5.8.3.65.

66 Three fragments of base, stem, lower bowl and rim from a goblet; base is flaring with a folded-under edge, stem is a pinched 'propeller' type and the rim everted; rim diam 75 mm, base diam 70 mm; clear lead glass with medium weathering; late 17–early 18 cent. (1607); SF 9213. Ill 5.8.3.66.

67 Fourteen fragments of upper base, propeller stem, lower bowl with applied moulding and everted rim from a dwarf ale glass; clear lead glass with light weathering; rim diam 75 mm; late 17 cent. (1601); SF 9179. Ill 5.8.3.67.

68 Two joining fragments of flaring under-folded base, plain solid rod stem and lower U-shaped bowl; clear lead glass with slight weathering; base diam 84 mm; early 18 cent. (1601); SF 9264. Ill 5.8.3.68.

69 Five fragments of rim and everted bowl from a goblet; clear lead glass with medium weathering; rim diam 65 mm; late 17–early 18 cent. (1601).

70 Two fragments of folded-under base ring from a gob-let; clear lead glass with little weathering; base diam 70 mm; late 17–early 18 cent. (1601); SF 9268.

71 Two fragments of folded-under base ring from a gob-let; clear lead glass with little weathering; base diam 90 mm; late 17–early 18 cent. (1601); SF 9268.

72 One fragment of upper applied base and lower body from a tall plain fluted beaker; clear glass with little weathering; early to mid-17 cent. (1695); SF 9207. Ill 5.8.3.72.

73 One fragment of applied foot and lower body from a small cup, lower bowl decorated with thick gadroon-ing; clear lead glass with no weathering; base diam 36 mm; late 17–early 18 cent. (1601); SF 9366. Ill 5.8.3.73.

74 One fragment of solid pad base and lower side from a small, footed cup, lower side decorated with heavy applied gadrooning; clear lead glass with little weath-ering; base diam 31 mm; late 17–early 18 cent. (1599); SF 9363. Ill 5.8.3.74.

75 One fragment of solid applied foot and lower body from a small cup, decorated with a thick horizontal and with two handle termini still attached; clear lead glass with medium weathering; base diam 35 mm; late 17–early 18 cent. (1601); SF 9253. Ill 5.8.3.75.

76 Three fragments of folded-under everted rim, con-vex side and low pushed-in base from a shallow bowl or saucer; opaque white glass with heavy weather-ing; rim diam 140 mm; late 17 cent. (1601); SF 9365.

77 Four joining fragments of flat base from a shallow bowl or saucer; clear glass with medium weathering; base diam 85 mm; 17 cent. (1601); SF 9360.

78 One fragment of everted rim from a shallow bowl, clear glass with medium weathering; rim diam 120 mm. 17 cent. (1601); SF 9361.

79 Three fragments of lower base, vertical side and widely everted rim from a small bowl; clear glass with little weathering; base diam 90 mm, rim diam 140 mm; late 17 cent. (1601).

80 Two fragments of lower side from a shallow bowl; clear glass with light weathering; base diam uncer-tain; 17 cent. (1599);. SF 9362.

81 One fragment of a very fine widely everted rim from a small bowl; clear glass with little weathering; rim diam 105 mm; late 17 cent. (1604); SF 9367.

82 Three joining fragments of rim and spout with an out-folded edge from a jug; black glass with very little weathering; rim diam uncertain; late 17–early 18 cent. (1601), (1607); SFs 9274, 9855. Ill 5.8.3.82.

83 Four joining fragments of low pushed-in base, squat side, sharp shoulder and sheared rim from a small inkwell; decorated with an opaque white marvered and combed trail; dark brown-black glass with light weathering; base diam 56 mm; 8–11 century. (1599), (1601), (1604); SFs 9167, 9364, 9248. Ill 5.8.3.83.

84 One fragment of rim and tapering neck from a small bottle-shaped phial, green clear glass with little weathering; rim diam 19 mm; mid- to late 17 cent. (1601

85 Two fragments of rim, neck and low pushed-in from a small bottle-shaped phial; green clear glass with little weathering; rim diam 20 mm, base diam 76 mm; mid- to late 17 cent. (1607).

86 One fragment of base and lower side from a tall cy-lindrical phial; blue green glass with little weathering; base diam 16 mm; late 17–early 18 cent. (1601).

87 One fragment of basal push-in from a globular phial; green clear glass with light weathering; base diam uncertain; late 17–early 18 cent. (1599).

88 One fragment of base from a globular phial; green clear glass with little weathering; base diam 60 mm; late 17 cent. (1604).

89 One fragment of very small slightly everted rim, pos-sibly from a small case bottle; blue green glass with light weathering; rim diam 18 mm; 17 cent? (1601).

90 Sixteen fragments of base with low push-in, and ver-tical sides from a square case bottle; sides taper outwards slightly up the length of the vessel and base has a distinct pontil mark; green glass with heavy weathering; base diam 88 x 92 mm; 17 cent. (1601).

91 Two fragments of everted rim, probably from a case bottle; green glass with heavy weathering; rim diam 50 mm; 17 cent. (1601).

92 One fragment of base, body, neck and rim from a near complete onion-shaped wine bottle; green glass with heavy weathering; base diam 108 mm; late 17–early 18 cent. (1601). Ill 5.8.4.92.

93 One fragment of base from an onion wine bottle; green glass with medium weathering; base diam 93 mm; late 17–early 18 cent. (1599).

Pit (1508)/(1560)

This pit was the only other one from this phase in Plot 4 which contained a significant group of vessels. The most interesting of these, no 94, is a round knop from a goblet. On examination it is possible to see the faint remains of three attached lead strips, which are the remains of a con-temporary repair. At some point in its life the stem had snapped from the bowl and was reattached with a rela-tively crude cage of lead strips. Repairs to glass goblets are known from other sites but are rare (Willmott 2001). So far all have been found in London or the south-east of England and on glasses from the first half of the seven-teenth century. The Chester example is therefore interesting due to its more northerly location and the fact that it is on a late seventeenth-century glass. The only other repair with lead strips on a glass of similar date is on an early lead crystal baluster stem found on the Thames foreshore.

Other vessels are less unusual, but all appear to be ta-blewares. There is a fragment of a goblet bowl, no 95, decorated with thick vertical ribs, and a small fragment of cylindrical green glass body decorated with two trails, no 96, which probably comes from a Low Country or north German *roemer*. The final fragments are from the base and rim, nos 97–8, of two earlier seventeenth-centu-ry pedestal beakers as well as the terminal from the lower handle of a tankard of similar date, no 99.

Catalogue

94 One fragment of round knop stem and bowl merese from a goblet; faint remains of a contemporary repair using three strips of lead to reattach the now lost base to the stem; clear glass with little weathering; mid- to late 17 cent. (1509); SF 9113. Ill 5.8.4.94.

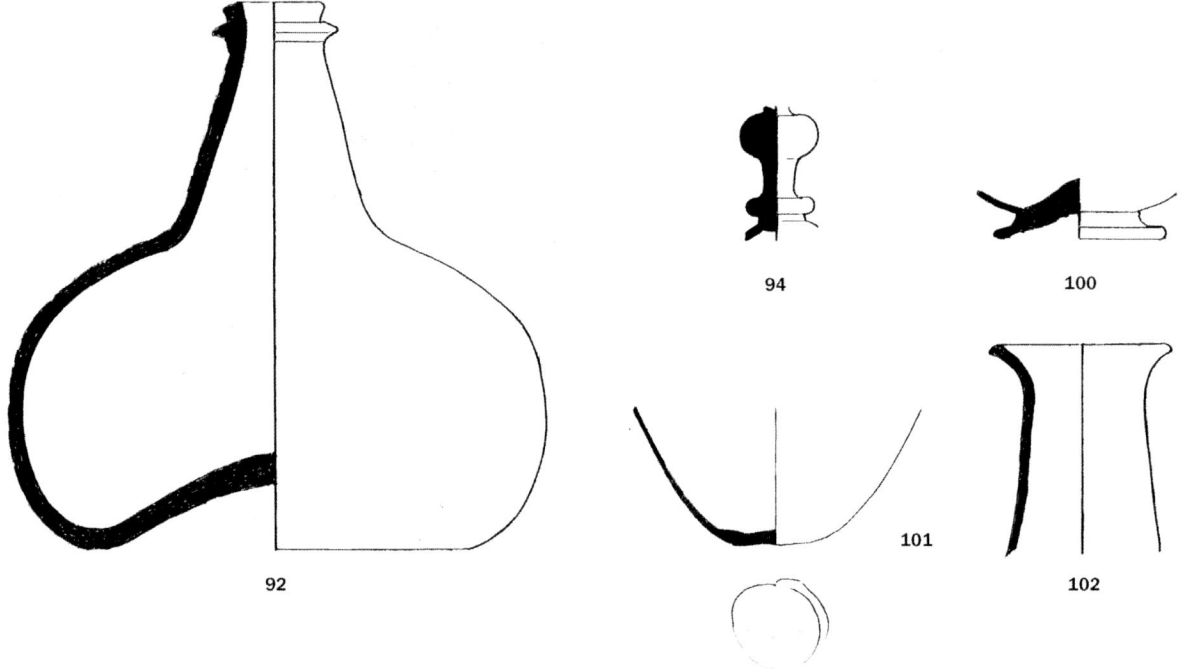

Ill 5.8.4 Phase VII Plots 4 and 6: post-medieval glass. (Scale 1/2)

95 One fragment of bowl, possibly from a goblet, decorated with one thick vertical rib; clear glass with cloudy weathering; mid- to late 17 cent? (1509); SF 9126.

96 One fragment of cylindrical body, possibly from a *roemer*, decorated with two prominent horizontal trails; green clear glass with little weathering; 17 cent. (1509); SF 9125.

97 One fragment of folded base from a plain pedestal beaker; green clear glass with quite light weathering; base diam uncertain; late 16–early 17 cent. (1509); SF 9123.

98 Four fragments of slightly everted rim from a pedestal beaker, decorated with optic-blown vertical ribbing; green clear glass with little weathering; rim diam 80 mm; early to mid-17 cent. (1516).

99 One fragment of lower terminus of an applied handle, probably from a cylindrical tankard; green clear glass with quite heavy weathering; early to mid-17 cent. (1509); SF 9142.

Context (1533)

This soil layer also produced a fragment which was in keeping with the glass from the pits, as did contexts in Phases VIII and X in the same plot (*see* below).

100 One fragment of applied pad base and lower spherical body from a jug or flask; opaque white glass with medium weathering; base diam 48 mm; late 17–early 18 cent. (1533). Ill 5.8.4.100.

Plot 6

Two fragments of note came from this plot, from the fills of pits (925) and (63) respectively.

101 One fragment of convex base with external pontil mark from a urinal; clear tinted glass with light weathering; late 15–early 16 cent. (824). Ill 5.8.4.101.

102 Four joining fragments of irregular everted rim and neck from a plain flask; green potash glass, heavily devitrified; rim diam *c* 50 mm; 13–15 cent. (62); SF 9548. Ill 5.8.4.102.

Phase VIII

Plot 2

Two vessels of interest were found in Plot 2. Both could have been imports or domestic products. No 103 came from the fill of pit (848); no 104 from levelling deposit (1439).

103 One fragment of pushed-in base from a plain cylindrical beaker, decorated with a rigaree base ring; clear tinted glass with medium weathering; base diam 54 mm; late 16–early 17 cent. (847); SF 8861. Ill 5.8.5.103.

104 Two fragments of folded base from a pedestal bowl; clear tinted glass with light weathering; base diam 115 mm; early to mid-17 cent. (1439); SF 9180. Ill 5.8.5.104.

Plot 3

Nothing appears to be known about the occupants of Plot 3 during the middle and late eighteenth century. A single pit, however, did contain a significant quantity of glass. Strangely the suggested date of this pit, mid-eighteenth century, was somewhat later than the glass found within it, suggesting that either the phasing was inaccurate or the glass was as much as fifty or more years old when discarded. Either way, the seventeenth- to eighteenth-century date of the glass suggests that it might have belonged to the Vause family or their tenants.

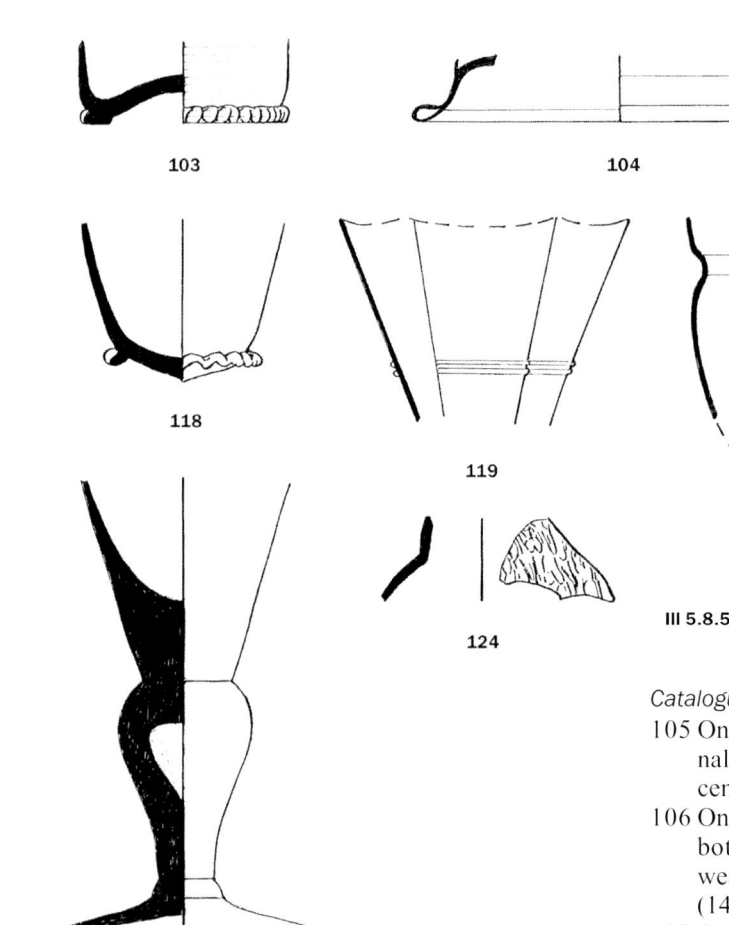
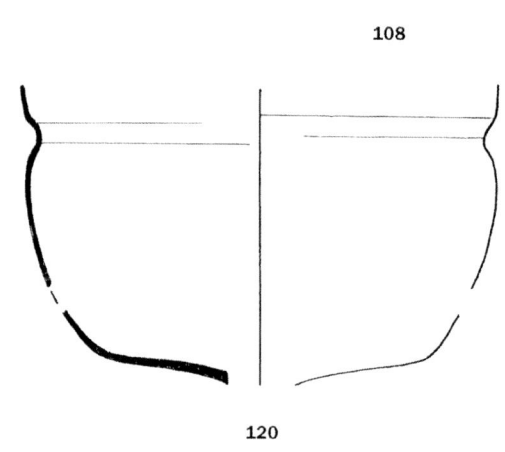

103   104   108

118

119

124

III **5.8.5** Phase VIII Plots 2, 3, 4 and 6: post-medieval glass. (Scale 1/2)

122

Pit (1413)

One find from this pit which must have been residual is a portion of rounded base, no 105, with an external pontil mark from a urinal. Although the quality of its metal is good, it cannot be later than very early sixteenth-century in date. The other finds are all more broadly seventeenth- or very early eighteenth-century in date. Interestingly, they are all from containers, there being no fragments from tablewares. This is slightly odd and this was the only group from any of the plots where this was the case. Most of these containers are phials, with all the ordinary late seventeenth-century varieties being present. Two, nos 106–7, are the rims and necks from bottle-shaped phials, whilst there is a very nearly complete example of a very small globular example, no 108. The remaining phials, nos 109–11, are all straight-sided and cylindrical in shape, and one, no 109, was heavily distorted towards the base when being made, yet was clearly still functional and used. A single fragment of ribbed neck, no 113, from this context is probably from a squat globular jar, whilst all the remaining vessels are wine bottles. Three of these, nos 114–16, are onion-shaped and date to the late seventeenth or early eighteenth centuries and one, no 117, is octagonal in cross-section, suggesting a mid-eighteenth-century date.

Catalogue

105 One fragment of convex base, probably from a urinal; clear tinted glass with light weathering; early 16 century? (1406).

106 One fragment of rim and tapering neck from a small bottle-shaped phial; green clear glass with little weathering; rim diam 20 mm; mid- to late 17 cent. (1406).

107 One fragment of rim and tapering neck from a small bottle-shaped phial; green clear glass with little weathering; rim diam 17 mm; mid-to late 17 cent. (1406).

108 One complete pushed-in base, globular body and everted rim from a small squat phial; green clear glass with very little weathering; base diam 30 mm, rim diam 25 mm, H 36 mm; first half 18 cent. (1406). SF 9440. Ill 5.8.5.108.

109 One complete profile of a small cylindrical phial; lower body is heavily distorted but vessel is still functional; green clear glass with no weathering; rim diam 21 mm, base diam 33 mm, H 88 mm; late 17 cent. (1406).

110 One fragment of base and lower body from a tall cylindrical phial; green clear glass with no weathering; base diam 18 mm; late 17–early 18 cent. (1406).

111 One fragment of base from a tall cylindrical phial; green clear glass with no weathering; base diam 20 mm; late 17–early 18 cent. (1406).

112 One fragment of base from a tall cylindrical phial; green clear glass with no weathering; base diam 22 mm; late 17–early 18 cent. (1406).

113 One fragment of neck from a globular jar, decorated with optic-blown wrythen ribbing; green clear with no weathering. 17 cent. (1406).

114 One fragment of rim and neck from an onion or bladder wine bottle; green glass with heavy weathering; rim diam 28 mm; late 17–early 18 cent. (1406).

115 One fragment of rim and neck from an onion or bladder wine bottle; green glass with heavy weathering; rim diam 30 mm; late 17–early 18 cent. (1406).

116 One fragment of rim and neck from an onion or bladder wine bottle; green glass with heavy weathering; rim diam 28 mm; late 17–early 18 cent. (1406).
117 Two joining fragments of base from an octagonal wine bottle; olive glass with very little weathering; base diam 90 x 48 mm; mid-18 cent. (1406).

Three further vessels of note were found in this plot. The first, no 118, is the lower portion of a fine bucket-shaped bowl from a goblet decorated with an applied wavy trail. Late seventeenth-century in date, this is a good example of the type of knopped goblet known to have been imported just prior the revival of the English glass industry. Nos 119–20 are the bowls from two seventeenth-century goblets of a rather unusual shape, although they are missing the rest of their form. The first, no 119, is a trumpet-shaped bowl which is hexagonal in cross-section and decorated with a pair of fine horizontal trails. The second, no 120, is more fragmentary but appears to be part of a larger more globular goblet bowl tooled into a series of vertical lobes. No 121 is a base ring, probably from a bowl.

Pit (1686)
118 One fragment of lower bucket-shaped bowl from a goblet, decorated with an applied pinched lower trail; clear slightly tinted glass with little weathering; late 17 cent. (1687); SF 9435. Ill 5.8.5.118.

Fill of undefined cess pit
119 One fragment of rim and upper hexagonal-shaped bowl from a goblet, decorated with at least one horizontal band of two prominent trails; clear glass with little weathering; rim diam uncertain; mid 17 cent? (1701); SF 9428. Ill 5.8.5.119.
120 Two fragments of nearly flat base and lower body, possibly from a lobed goblet bowl, body decorated manipulated horizontal flutes; clear tinted glass with no weathering; base diam 90 mm; 17 cent. (1701); SF 9495. Ill 5.8.5.120.
121 Two joining fragments of folded base ring, probably from a bowl; green clear glass with quite heavy weathering; base diam 100 mm; 17 cent. (1701); SF 9494.

Plot 4

No 122 from layer (455) is another very good example of an inverted baluster stem goblet, very similar to those from pits (1807) and (1696) in the previous phase.

122 One fragment of flaring base, large thick inverted baluster knop and lower everted bowl from a goblet; clear lead glass with little weathering; base diam 90 mm; late 17–early 18 cent. (455); SF 8978. Ill 5.8.5.122.

Plot 6

Two vessels of note came from garden soil (341).

123 One fragment of widely everted rim with up-folded edge from a urinal; green clear glass with quite heavy weathering; rim diam 85 mm. 15–early 16 cent. (341); SF 8147.

124 One fragment of lower neck from a small squat bottle or ?phial, decorated with opaque white splashing; brown glass with little weathering; late 17 cent. (341); SF 8259. Ill 5.8.5.124.

Phase IX

Two of the more interesting assemblages from the excavation were associated with Phase IX, Plots 2 and 4, in contexts (1096) and (1491). The former could be related to a series of chemists known to be trading at 27 (formerly 12) Bridge Street Row. The glass falls into two broad categories: vessels used for specific, usually temporary purposes, and containers for longer-term storage. Until recently, assemblages of nineteenth-century glass were rarely studied. Furthermore, the invention of press-moulding as a means for mass-producing vessels means that the numbers of containers found are potentially very large. Consequently, when dealing with late assemblages it is not possible to individually catalogue all the bottles, and only the most diagnostic fragments can be recorded (*see* Tables 5.8.1–.2).

Plot 2

Eight vessels were catalogued in detail from (1096). The first two of these are fragments from two different lead crystal wine glasses, nos 125–6, both typical mid-nineteenth century forms. There are also fragments from at least four vessels that are more unusual, nos 127–30. These are short, thick, mould-pressed vessels with hexagonal bases. Although they appear to be similar to vases, their rounded interiors suggest that they are, in fact, designed for mixing ingredients, and medicines in particular – not surprising given their association with a pharmacy. Other vessels are more unusual, and include a portion of shoulder, probably from a cupping glass, no 131, which would have been heated and applied to boils to draw out the pus.

Catalogue
125 Two joining fragments of flaring base with ground-out pontil mark, stem and lower bowl from a wine glass, stem and bowl decorated with simple vertical cutting; clear lead glass with very little weathering; base diam 62 mm; mid-19 cent. (1096).
126 One fragment of lower curved plain bowl, probably from a wine glass; clear lead glass with no weathering; mid-19 cent. (1096).
127 Four joining fragments of heavy hexagonal base, vertical side and rim from a mixing glass, decorated with cut flutes on the body and star-cut base; clear lead glass with some weathering; base diam 68 mm, rim 85 mm, H 124 mm; mid 19 cent? (1096).
128 One fragment of heavy hexagonal base and vertical side from a mixing glass, decorated with cut flutes on the body and star-cut base; clear lead glass with some weathering; base diam 68 mm; mid 19 cent? (1096).
129 One fragment of heavy hexagonal base and vertical side from a mixing glass, decorated with cut flutes on the body and star-cut base; clear lead glass with some weathering; base diam 68 mm; mid-19 cent? (1096).

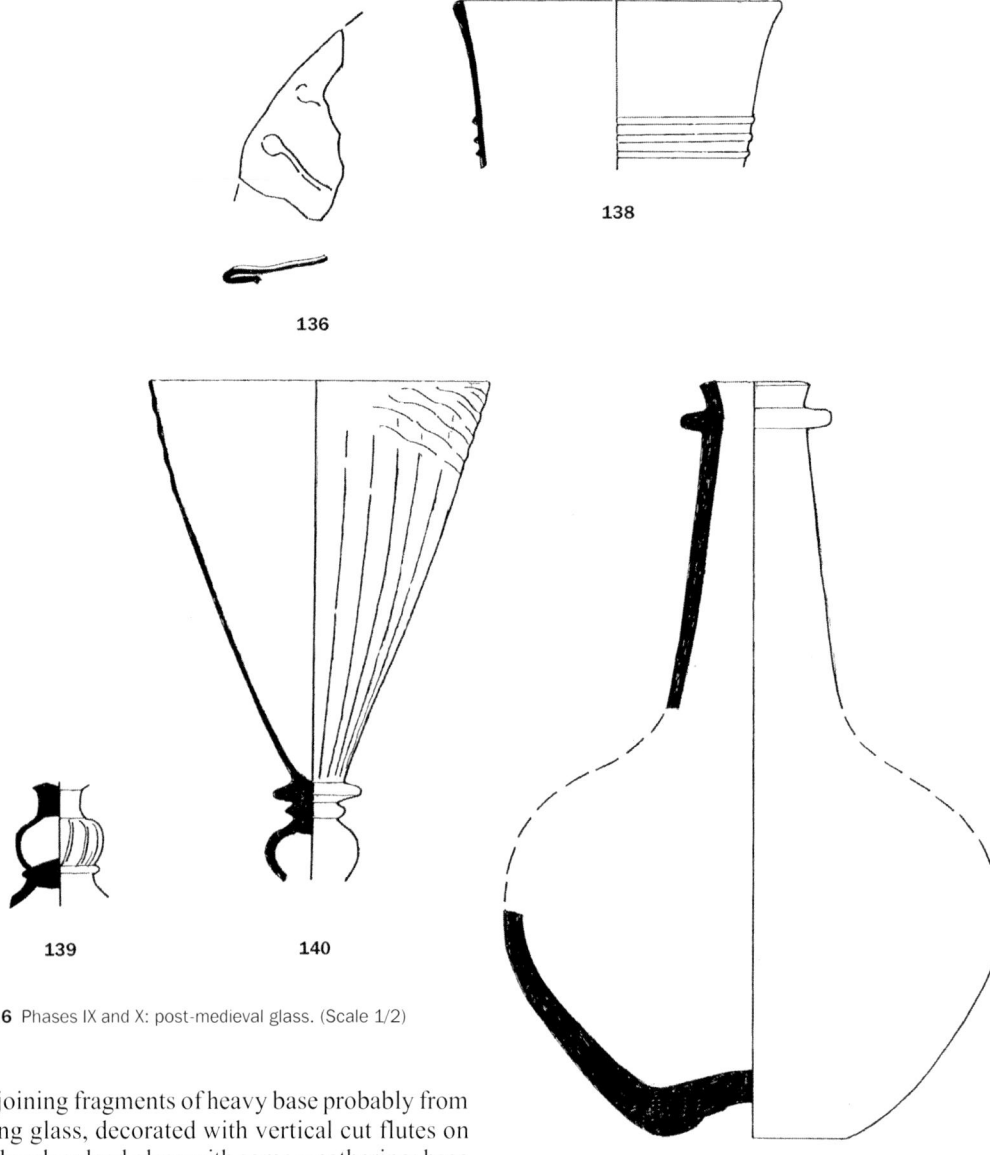

Ill 5.8.6 Phases IX and X: post-medieval glass. (Scale 1/2)

130 Three joining fragments of heavy base probably from a mixing glass, decorated with vertical cut flutes on the body; clear lead glass with some weathering; base diam 56 mm; mid-19 cent? (1096).

131 Four fragments of everted rim and tapering shoulder, possibly from a cupping glass; free-blown clear glass with no weathering; rim diam 45 mm; 19 cent. (1096).

132 One fragment of convex body, possibly from a large bowl or dish, decorated with one thick prominent rib; clear lead glass with little weathering; mid- to late 19 cent. (1096).

The majority of the vessels in this context are bottles. A minimum number of forty-two survive, although this will be an underestimate of the original total (summarised in Table 5.8.1). Amongst the earliest and best dated of these are fragments from fourteen Schweppes 'Hamilton' bottles, used to hold soda water. Interestingly two slight variations occur. The first are from when the company was based at 79 Margaret Street and can be dated to around the period 1823–31. The second are from after they moved to 51 Berners Street, and thus date from 1831 to the later nineteenth century. Other commercial firms identifiable through their bottles include Dinneford, manufacturers of milk of magnesia, and a wine bottle made by Powell & Co of Bristol. However, most interesting are bottles manufactured specifically for the chemist and embossed with his name. At least one cylindrical

phial and one octagonal bottle are embossed 'Davies Chester', whilst two have the names 'Davies & Shepheard, Chester'. The remaining bottles are plain but are likely to have held medicinal products. It is known that between 1828 and 1850 Samuel Davies ran his shop on the Row, but on his death in 1857 the business was taken over by Thomas Shepheard, who continued to trade under the dual name of Davies and Shepheard until 1923. It would seem that the deposit of (1096) was formed sometime shortly after Davies's death.

Plot 4

The assemblage from (1491) in Plot 4 was smaller, consisting of a minimum number of sixteen vessels, but still contained a number of bottles that can be related to the pharmacy (summarised in Table 5.8.2). Amongst these are a later nineteenth-century bottle of 'Mrs Winslow Soothing Syrup', an opiate-based product for teething children made by Curtis and Perkins. There is also a bottle manufactured for the unknown firm of Hewitts in

Chester. Interestingly there are also two Davies and Shepheard bottles and a number of plain examples. The fragments from two measuring cylinders, nos 133–4, also have clear pharmaceutical functions. The final fragment of non-bottle glass, no 135, is a single piece of opaque white oil lamp globe.

Catalogue

133 One fragment of rim and pouring lip from a large measuring cylinder with a single surviving abraded measuring mark; clear glass with no weathering; rim diam 84 mm. (1491).

134 One fragment of pad base and lower vertical side probably from a small measuring cylinder; clear glass with light weathering; base diam 42 mm. (1491).

135 One fragment of body from an oil lamp globe; opaque white glass with no weathering; late 19 cent. (1491).

Plot 6

Plot 6 produced a number of important residual fragments. The most important of these, no 136 from the fill of (315), are two fragments form wide flaring base with an underfolded edge from a tall-stemmed green glass goblet, decorated with mould-blown ribbing. Although very fragmentary, this is an example of a type of drinking vessel dating to the fourteenth century and usually associated with high status contexts, such as a near-complete example from Ludgershall castle, Wiltshire (Tyson 2000, 54–5). No 137 from the fill of (337) is a urinal, of which examples were found in earlier phases on the site, and no 138 from the fill of (544) is a slightly everted rim from a green tinted cylindrical beaker decorated with horizontal bands of trailing.

Catalogue

136 Two fragments of flaring base with a folded-over edge from a goblet, decorated with optic-blown ribbing; green clear glass with medium weathering; base diam 160 mm; 13–14 cent. (316); SF 8147 and 8198. Ill 5.8.6.136.

137 One fragment of convex base with external pontil mark from a urinal; green clear glass with quite heavy weathering; 15–early 16 cent. (338).

138 One fragment of rim from a cylindrical beaker, decorated with thin trails; green clear glass with medium weathering; rim diam 90 mm; late 16–early 17 cent. (545); SF 8306. Ill 5.8.6.138.

Phase X

Three residual fragments of interest came from this phase.

Plot 4

No 139 is a round ribbed knop from a goblet made in a soda-based metal. This can be related to the period when the Andertons were occupying the plot.

139 One fragment of round ribbed knop from a goblet; clear tinted glass with no weathering; late 17 cent. (1274); SF 9136. Ill 5.8.6.139.

Table 5.8.1 Phase IX Plot 2: chemists' bottles from (1096) quantified by form and metal

No	Bottle shape	Colour	Embossed	Date
4	Cylindrical phial	Clear		Mid-19 cent?
1	Cylindrical phial	Clear	Davies, Chester	c 1828–50
1	Cylindrical jar	Clear		Mid-19 cent
7	Hamilton bottle	Blue-green	J Schweppes & Co, Genuine Superior, Aerated Waters, 79 Margaret Street	c 1823–31
7	Hamilton bottle	Blue-green	J Schweppes & Co, 51 Berners Street, Oxford Street, Genuine Superior, Aerated Waters	c 1831–late 19 cent
1	Oval bottle	Blue-green	Dinneford's Solution of Magnesia	c 1840–80
3	Oval bottle	Blue-green		Mid-19 cent?
1	Oval bottle	Clear		Mid-19 cent?
1	Octagonal bottle	Green	Davies, Chemist, Chester	c 1828–50
2	Octagonal bottle	Blue	Davies & Shepheard, Chester	c 1857—1928
2	Octagonal bottle	Clear	Chester	Mid- to late 19 cent?
1	Octagonal bottle	Blue		Mid-19 cent
3	Octagonal bottle	Green		Mid- to late 19 cent
1	Octagonal bottle	Blue	6 oz (on base)	Mid-19 cent?
1	Rectangular bottle	Clear	Chester	Mid-19 cent?
1	Cylindrical bottle	Blue-green		Mid-19 cent
1	Cylindrical bottle	Amber		Mid- to late 19 cent
2	Wine bottle	Olive		Early to mid-19 cent
2	Wine bottle	Olive	Powell & Co, Bristol	Mid-19 cent

Table 5.8.2 Phase IX Plot 4: chemists' bottles from (1491) quantified by form and metal

No	Bottle shape	Colour	Embossed	Date
1	Cylindrical phial	Clear	Late 19 cent	
1	Jar	Clear	Late 19 cent	
1	Cylindrical bottle	Clear	Curtis & Perkins Proprietors Mrs Winslow's Soothing Syrup	Mid- to late 19 cent
1	Cylindrical bottle	Green		Mid- to late 19 cent
2	Square bottle	Clear	Davies & Shepheard, Chester	c 1857–1928
1	Oval bottle	Green	Hewitts Chester	Mid- to late 19 cent
2	Oval bottle	Green		Mid- to late 19 cent
1	Hexagonal bottle	Blue	2 oz (on base)	Mid- to late 19 cent
1	Hexagonal bottle	Green		Mid- to late 19 cent
2	Octagonal bottle	Green		Late 19 cent?
3	Wine bottle	Olive		Mid- to late 19 cent

Plot 5

No 140 is a very well preserved slightly tinted soda-based goblet, with a small round knop and trumpet-shaped bowl decorated with optic-blown decoration and dating to the later seventeenth century. Finally, there are also the fragments, making up the majority of the profile, from a typical shaft and globe wine bottle, no 141. This was the earliest form of the wine bottle produced in England and typically dated to between 1650 and 1680. It is possible that this glass actually came from (1505), a fill of pit (1522) in Phase VII, Plot 4 and was mislabelled.

Catalogue

140 Six joining fragments of everted rim, trumpet-shaped bowl and round knop from a goblet; bowl decorated with optic-blown vertical and twisted ribbing; clear glass with no weathering; rim diam 95 mm; late 17 cent. (1503). Ill 5.8.6.140.

141 One fragment of rim, neck, lower body and base from a shaft and globe wine bottle; green glass with quite heavy weathering; rim diam 30 mm, base diam 52 mm; c 1650–80. (1503). Ill 5.8.6.141.

Glass and Frit Beads and Ornaments

H E M Cool

Introduction

Forty-three glass and frit beads were recovered from the excavations, a number undoubtedly inflated by the extensive sieving programme. As can be seen from the catalogue they were found in all phases but this does not reflect the periods when they would have been used, as there were no examples of the types typical during the Saxon period, and glass beads do not appear to have been much in use during the medieval period (*see*, for example, Egan & Pritchard 2002, 316). Roman contexts produced two frit melon beads (nos 1–2), a very common mid-first to mid-second-century form, and a small spherical bead from a necklace that had been thread using copper alloy wire. Such necklaces were commonest in the late Roman period (*see*, for example, that from Gadebridge Park (Neal 1974, 133, no 75)).

Of the ten beads stratified in contexts belonging to the late Roman to late medieval periods (Phases IIa–V), one is another melon bead (no 4) and three (nos 6–8) are short blue biconical beads of a type commonest in the late Roman period (Guido 1978, 97) but occasionally found in contexts as early as the late second to early third centuries (Brewer 1986, 149, nos 62–5). The faceted cubic bead (no 13) has a date range similar to the short biconical beads (Brewer 1986, 149, nos 67–70; Guido 1978, 99). The small annular and spherical beads (nos 5, 10 and 11) are also typical of many late Roman deposits. Only the short cylindrical beads in translucent light yellow-brown glass (nos 9 and 12) would, in my experience, have been unusual in a late Roman context.

Of the beads from Phase VI, the spherical bead no 15 could again have been a residual Roman piece, whilst the pair of beads from context (1702) (no. 16), although coming from the primary fill of a cess pit, have all the appearance of being relatively modern machine-made pieces.

An interesting feature of Phase VII was the appearance of very small annular beads (nos 19–22). These also appeared in Phase VIII (no 26) and Phase IX (nos 33–43). Given the amount of sieving carried out, the appearance of the type in Phase VII appears to be a real one as it is likely that at least one or two would have been found if they had been in use earlier. The tiny size of the beads make it unlikely that they were from necklaces, and it is more likely that they were used in beaded embroidery which was a part of seventeenth- and eighteenth-century costume. If this is correct, then they may be another strand of the evidence that points to mercers being present on the site somewhat earlier than the documentary evidence shows.

Also of some interest amongst the beads from the later contexts were two large spherical beads made of very dark glass appearing black (no 17 from a Phase VII context and no 27 from one of Phase 9). Although they might have been from items of contemporary jewellery, another

possibility would be that they were residual medieval finds. Large beads such as this were a component of rosaries (Egan & Pritchard 2002, 305), and black materials seem to have been especially favoured for devotional items in the medieval period (Muller 1987, 27).

Phase I

1   Melon bead, turquoise frit; complete with shallow gadroons; L 9 mm, diam 11 mm, perforation diam 5.5 mm. (1148); SF 9899; <5132>.
2   Melon bead, turquoise frit; small fragment. (1148); SF 9900; <5132>.
3   Spherical bead, very dark blue glass appearing opaque and retaining fragment of copper alloy wire; L 3 mm, diam 3 mm, perforation diam 1 mm. (1243); <5133>.

Phase II

4   Melon bead, pale greenish frit retaining glaze; misshapen and gadroons very faint; L 8 mm, diam 12 mm, perforation diam 5 mm. (1220): Phase IIa; SF 8793.
5   Small annular bead, translucent light yellow-brown glass; L 2 mm, diam 5 mm, perforation diam 2 mm. (1040): Phase IIb; SF 9898; <5117>.

Phase III

6   Short biconical bead, translucent deep blue glass; L 2.5 mm, diam 4 mm, perforation diam 1 mm. (1022); SF 9744; < 5098>.

Phase IV

7   Short biconical bead, translucent deep blue glass; L 2.5 mm, diam 5 mm, perforation diam 2 mm. (1015): Plot 6; SF 9743; <5096>.
8   Short biconical bead, translucent deep blue glass; L 2.5 mm, diam 4 mm, perforation diam 1.5 mm. (1015): Plot 6; SF 9743; <5096>.
9   Short cylindrical bead, light yellow-brown translucent glass; L 3.5 mm, diam 3 mm, perforation diam 1.5 mm. (1015): Plot 6; SF 9743; <5096>.

Phase V

10 Spherical bead, translucent mid-green glass; L 3 mm, diam 2.5 mm, perforation diam 1 mm. (490): Plot 3; SF 9738; <5058>.
11 Spherical bead, translucent green-blue wound glass; L 3 mm, diam 3.5 mm, perforation diam 1.5 mm. (490): Plot 3; SF 9738; <5058>.
12 Short cylindrical bead, light yellow-brown translucent glass; L 5 mm, diam 4.5 mm, perforation diam 2.5 mm. (1162): Plot 1; SF 9863; <5122>.
13 Short cubic bead, deep opaque blue; triangular facets on corners on one side; L 3.5 mm, diam 2.5 mm, perforation diam 1 mm. (261): Plot 1; SF 9733; <5010>.
14 Sphere, translucent yellow-brown glass; diam 4 mm. (1162): Plot 1; SF 8904; <5122>.

Phase VI

15 Spherical bead, opaque mid-green glass; half extant; L 2.5 mm, diam 3.5 mm. (797): Plot 2; SF 9742; <5077>.

16 Square-sectioned cylindrical beads (2), translucent deep blue glass; lengths 6 mm, 5 mm; section 3 mm, perforation diameter 1 mm. (1702): Plot 3; SF 9861; <5169>.

Phase VII

17 Spherical bead, very dark glass appearing black; L 9 mm, diam 13 mm, perforation diam 4 mm. (1601): Plot 4; SF 9430.

18 Spherical bead, opaque brown glass; L 3 mm, diam 4 mm, perforation diam 2 mm. (245): Plot 1; SF 9732; <5008>.

19 Tiny annular bead, opaque white glass; L 1.5 mm, diam 2.5 mm, perforation diam 0.5 mm. (670): Plot 1; SF 9741; <5067>.

20 Tiny annular bead, opaque white glass; L 1.5 mm, diam 2.5 mm, perforation diam 0.5 mm. (1607): Plot 4; SF 9860; <5159>.

21 Tiny annular bead, translucent light yellow-brown; L 1 mm, diam 2 mm, perforation diam 0.5 mm. (489): Plot 4; SF 9897; <5060>.

22 Tiny annular bead, deep blue translucent glass; L 1 mm, diam 2.5 mm, perforation diam 1 mm. (1599): Plot 4; SF 9859; <5158>.

23 Roundel; translucent mid-blue glass wound; plano-convex, half extant; diam 19 mm, th 8 mm. (1111): Plot 3; SF 8844.

Phase VIII

24 Spherical bead; very dark glass appearing black; L 5.5 mm, diam 7 mm, perforation diam 2 mm. (520): Plot 6; SF 9740; <5037>.

25 Small spherical bead, cloudy mid-blue glass; L 2 mm, diam 3 mm, perforation diam 1.5 mm. (207): Plot 1; SF 9730; <5004>.

26 Tiny annular bead, cloudy mid-blue glass; L 2 mm, diam 3 mm, perforation diam 1 mm. (207): Plot 1; SF 9730; <5004>.

Phase IX

27 Spherical bead, very dark glass appearing black; L 8 mm, diam 11 mm, perforation diam 3 mm. (206): Plot 1; SF 8658.

28 Spherical bead, opaque turquoise glass with white decayed surfaces; half extant in two pieces; L 6 mm, diam 9 mm. (206): Plot 1; SF 8657.

29 Squashed spherical bead, translucent mid-blue glass; L 6 mm, perforation 8 mm, perforation diam 2.5 mm. (206): Plot 1; SF 9729; <5001>.

30 Hexagonal cylindrical bead, very dark glass appearing black; L 5 mm, section 4 mm, perforation diam 2 mm. (206): Plot 1; SF 9729; <5001>.

31 Hexagonal-sectioned cylindrical, translucent very dark blue glass; fragment only; present L 3 mm, section 2.5 mm, perforation diam 1 mm. (375): Plot 6; SF 9736; <5024>.

32 Faceted annular bead, translucent purple glass; surfaces covered by three rings of diamond facets; L 3 mm, diam 5 mm, perforation diam 1 mm. (469): Plot 2; SF 8464.

33 Tiny annular bead, opaque white glass; length 1.5 mm, diam 2.5 mm, perforation diam 0.5 mm. (507): Plot 6; SF 9739; <5028>.

34 Tiny annular bead; opaque white glass; L 1 mm, diam 2 mm, perforation diam 0.5 mm. (352): Plot 6; SF 9734; <5021>.

35 Tiny annular bead, translucent white; L 1.5 mm, diam 2 mm, perforation diam 1 mm. (206): Plot 1; SF 9729; <5001>.

36 Tiny annular bead; translucent white glass; L 1 mm, diam 2 mm, perforation diam 0.5 mm. (353): Plot 6; SF 9735; <5022>.

37 Tiny annular bead, cloudy mid-blue; L 1 mm, diam 1.5 mm, perforation diam 0.5 mm. (352): Plot 6; SF 9734; <5021>.

38 Tiny annular bead, cloudy mid-blue; L 1.5 mm, diam 3 mm, perforation diam 1 mm. (352): Plot 6; SF 9734; <5021>.

39 Tiny annular bead, cloudy mid-blue; L 1 mm, diam 2 mm, perforation diam 0.5 mm. (352): Plot 6; SF 9734; <5021>.

40 Tiny annular bead, cloudy mid-blue; L 1 mm, diam 2 mm, perforation diam 0.5 mm. (352): Plot 6; SF 9734; <5021>.

41 Tiny annular bead, translucent mid-green; L 1 mm, diam 1.5 mm. (507): Plot 6; SF 9739; <5028>.

42 Tiny annular bead, translucent mid-green glass; L 1 mm, diam 2 mm, perforation diam 1 mm. (217): Plot 1; SF 9731; <5003>.

43 Tiny short cylindrical bead, translucent white; L 2 mm, diam 3 mm, perforation diam 1.5 mm. (206): Plot 1; SF 9729; <5001>.

44 Button, black glass; moulded star pattern with raised dot border; broken scar from attachment of shank' diam 22 mm, th 4.5 mm. (418): Plot 2; SF 8313.

Coins and Tokens   Peter Guest

Fifty-two coins and tokens were recovered from the excavations, comprising thirty-one Roman coins, nineteen medieval and modern issues, and two objects might not in fact be coins (*see* the catalogue on Table 5.9.1).

The twenty-four Roman coins which could be accurately identified have been arranged according to their dates of production in Table 5.9.2. The earliest were a *sestertius* and an *as/dupondius* struck for Domitian (SFs 9195 and 8624 respectively), followed by a few coins of various denominations from the second and early third centuries. These included four *denarii* (two for the deified Faustina I and one each for Caracalla and Julia Domna), a *sestertius* for Hadrian (SF 9194), a *dupondius* of Trajan (SF 8775) and an *as* of Lucilla (SF 9196).

However, the majority of the Roman coins from the excavations were struck between the end of the third century to some time around 350 (Issue Periods 13 to 17). This is a characteristic feature of most Romano-British excavated assemblages and reflects the greater quantities of coins in circulation (and therefore available to be lost), as well as their smaller size (and lower value). It is interesting that the Bridge Street site produced more coins of the period 330–41 than later third-century radiates (including imitations), and that the period after 350 was represented by only a single Valentinianic issue. Table 5.9.3 also shows the general pattern of coin loss for Chester (an amalgamation of material from previous excavations), from which it is apparent that the composition of the 25 Bridge Street assemblage was determined to a large extent by the site's setting within the wider settlement (Shotter 1998–9).

The medieval and modern coins and tokens recovered from the site are an interesting and diverse group of objects. They included a cut Short Cross halfpenny of the twelfth–thirteenth centuries (SF 8797), four Long Cross pennies of the late thirteenth to late fifteenth centuries (SFs 5051, 8197, 9019 and 9231), a sixpence of Elizabeth I (SF 8159), seven Nuremberg jettons from the sixteenth and seventeenth centuries, and four bronze fractions of the seventeenth and eighteenth centuries (including a half-spade guinea of 1800 made by Simcox and Timmins of Birmingham). It is thought that the copper alloy jettons would have been used as counters or tokens to record the details of commercial transactions rather than as the medium of exchange, although one of these objects from 25 Bridge Street had been clipped to a reduced size, perhaps to allow it to be used as a licensed farthing (SF 9050). Excavations on the site of the Dominican friary at Grey Friars Court produced fifteen coins and tokens of the eleventh to sixteenth centuries, including four jettons (Lloyd-Morgan 1990).

Table 5.9.2 arranges the coins and tokens by phase and context, from which it is obvious that the overwhelming majority of Roman coins, like the other Roman finds, were deposited in deposits which date to the medieval and modern periods.

Table 5.9.1 Coin and token catalogue

SF no	Context	Denomination	Date
5051	1516	Penny	1279–1489
8004	261	AE3	318–24
8006	269	Denarius	201–2
8015	246	AE3	Late 3–4 cent
8056	340	Farthing	1613–25
8112	344	AE3	313–18
8159	520	Sixpence	1592
8160	546	Jetton	1586–1635
8161	546	Jetton	1586–1635
8162	208	½ spade-guinea	1800
8164a	217	AE3	340–1
8164b	217	AE3	340–1
8197	518	Penny	1351–61
8209	389	AE3	Late 3–4 cent
8353	386	AE4 minim	Late 3–4 cent
8357	367	Jetton	1515–59
8518	692	Jetton	16–17 cent
8571	793	Barbarous radiate	270–90
8606	799	AE3	Late 3–4 cent
8624	1022	AE2	91–6
8645	1022	*Denarius*	196–211
8663	318	AE2 (coin?)	Modern?
8684	873	AE3	337–40
8719	352	Barbarous radiate	270–90
8739	1177	Radiate	268–70
8740	1111	AE3 (coin?)	Modern?
8741	1161	*Denarius*	141–61
8744	1161	AE3	335–40
8763	1136	AE3	330–5
8769	1132	*Denarius*	141–61
8775	1225	*Dupondius*	98–117
8779	882	AE3	Late 3–4 cent
8789	883	Radiate	260–90
8790	1119	AE3	364–78
8795	785	Silver	Medieval/modern?
8797	600	Halfpenny	1180–1247
8800	1293	AE3	330–40
8834	464	Farthing/token	16–17 cent
8960	1417	Halfpenny	1727–60
8975	1399	Farthing	1625–44
9018	1509	AE3	Late 3–4 cent
9019	1217	Penny	1279–1489
9050	1406	Jetton	Early 17 cent
9057	1566	Jetton	1586–1635
9194	1668	*Sestertius*	117–38
9195	1668	*Sestertius*	87
9196	1668	*As*	161–9
9231	1654	Penny	1279–1377
9272	1744	AE3	330–5
9293	1819	AE3	330–5
9295	1689	AE3	Late 3–4 cent
9877	1033	Jetton	16–17 cent

Obverse	Reverse	Mint mark	Mint	Reference/Remarks
Illegible	Illegible (Long Cross)	-	-
Constantine I				
(l. facing bust)	VICTORIAE LAETAE			
	PRINC PERP	[.....]	-	-
CARACALLA	PART MAX PONT TRP	[..]	Rome	-
Illegible	Illegible	-	-
JAMES I	Lennox farthing	-	-
Constantine I	SOLI INVICTO COMITI	[.....]	-	-
ELIZABETH I	Standard reverse	-	-
Hanns Krauwinckel	GOTES.SEGEN.MACHT.			
	REICH (*Reichsapfel*)		Nuremberg	Stalzer 1989, 161, nos 433 ff
Hanns Krauwinckel	GOTES.SEGEN.MACHT.REICH		Nuremberg	-
	(*Reichsapfel*)			
GEORGE III	of Simcox & Timmins		B'ham	-
House of Constantine	VICTORIAE DD AUGG QNN	branch//[.....]	-	-
Constantius II	VICTORIAE DD AUGG QNN	leaf//TRP	Trier	LRBC **1**: 139
Illegible (Edward III)	Illegible (Long Cross)	-	Pre-Treaty coinage
Illegible	Illegible	-	-
Illegible	Illegible	-	-
IORG:SCHVLDE:S:IORG	OIVSGBANDETOIVSG:		Nuremberg	Stalzer 1989, 9, nos 47 ff
(Lion of St Mark)	(*Reichsapfel*)			
Illegible	Illegible (*Reichsapfel*)		Nuremberg	-
Illegible	as *Spes Aug*	-	-
Illegible	Illegible	-	-
DOMITIAN	Illegible	Rome	-
JULIA AUGUSTA	PIETAS AUGG	Rome	RIC **4** (1): 572
Illegible	Illegible	-	21 mm; worn flat
Theodora	PIETAS ROMANA	[.....]	-	-
Illegible	Illegible	-	-
VICTORINUS	*Salus?*	-	-
Illegible	Illegible	-	17 mm; worn flat
DIVA FAUSTINA	AETERNITAS - Juno	Rome	RIC 3: 344
House of Constantine	GLORIA EXERCITUS (1 std)	chi-rho//[.....]	-	-
URBS ROMA	Wolf & twins	[•]PLG	Lyons	LRBC **1**: 190
DIVA FAUSTINA	AUGUSTA - *Pietas*	Rome	RIC **3**: 373
TRAJAN	Figure seated l.	Rome	-
Illegible	Figure striding l.	[.....]	-	-
Illegible	Illegible	-	-
House of Valentinian	SECURITAS REIPUBLICAE	[.....]	-	-
Illegible	Illegible	-	9 mm, pierced
Illegible	Illegible (Short Cross)	-	cut half
House of Constantine	GLORIA EXERCITUS (? stds)	[.....]	-	-
Illegible	Illegible	-	-
GEORGE II	Britannia	-	-
CHARLES I	Richmond farthing	-	-
Illegible	Illegible	-	-
Illegible	Illegible (Long Cross)	-	-
Hanns Krauwinckel	*Apfelpfennig*		Nuremberg	Clipped (to pass as a licensed farthing?)
Hanns Krauwinckel	GOTES.REICH.BLIBT.EWICK		Nuremberg	Stalzer 1989,159, nos 418 ff
	(*Reichsapfel*)			
HADRIAN	Figure standing		Rome	-
	holding ?sceptre			
DOMITIAN	Illegible		Rome	-
LUCILLA	PUDICITIA SC		Rome	RIC **3**: 1759
Illegible (but HYB)	Illegible (Long Cross)	-	-
House of Constantine	GLORIA EXERCITUS (2 stds)	[.....]	-	-
URBS ROMA	Wolf & twins	• & cres [PLG]	Lyons	LRBC **1**: 200
Illegible	Illegible	-	-
Illegible	*Apfelpfennig*		Nuremberg	-

Table 5.9.2 Coins and tokens sorted by phase and context

Phase	SF	Context	Plot	Denomination	Coin issue/Type	Coin date
II	8006	269	N/A	*Denarius*	Caracalla	201–2
	8763	1136		AE3	Urbs Roma	330–5
	8741	1161		*Denarius*	Diva Faustina I	141–61
	8744	1161		AE3	*Gloria Exercitus* (1 standard)	335–40
	8739	1177		Radiate	Victorinus	268–70
	8775	1225		*Dupondius*	Trajan	98–117
III	8624	1022	N/A	AE2	Domitian	91–6
	8645	1022		*Denarius*	Julia Domna	196–211
	8769	1132		*Denarius*	Diva Faustina I	141–61
IV	8797	600	2	Halfpenny	Short Cross	1180–1247
	8606	799	3	AE3	-	Late 3–4 cent
	8684	873	3	AE3	Theodora	337–40
	8779	882	2	AE3	-	Late 3–4 cent
	8789	883	2	Radiate	-	260–90
	9877	1033	6	Jetton	*Apfelpfennig*	16–17 cent
	8790	1119	3	AE3	*Securitas Reipublicae*	364–78
V	8004	261	1	AE3	*Victoriae Laetae Princ Perp*	318–24
	9019	1217	3	Penny	Long Cross	1279–1489
	8800	1293	3	AE3	*Gloria Exercitus* (?2 standards)	330–40
	9231	1654	3	Penny	Long Cross	1279–1377
	9194	1668	5	*Sestertius*	Hadrian	117–38
	9195	1668	5	*Sestertius*	Domitian	87
	9196	1668	5	As	Lucilla	161–9
	9272	1744	2	AE3	*Gloria Exercitus* (2 standards)	330–5
VI	8015	246	1	AE3	-	Late 3–4 cent
	8518	692	6	Jetton	*Reichsapfel*	16–17 cent
	8795	785	2	Silver	-	Medieval/modern?
	9057	1566	4	Jetton	Hanns Krauwinckel	1586-1635
VII	8209	389	6	AE3	-	Late 3–4 cent
	8834	464	2	Farthing/token	-	16–17 cent
	8740	1111	3	AE3 (coin?)	-	Modern?
	9018	1509	4	AE3	-	Late 3–4 cent
	5051	1516	4	Penny	Long Cross	1279–1489
VIII	8159	520	6	Sixpence	Elizabeth I	1592
	9050	1406	3	Jetton	Hanns Krauwinckel	Early 17 cent
	8960	1417	2	Halfpenny	George II	1727–60
	9295	1689	3	AE3	-	Late 3–4 cent
	9293	1819	1	AE3	Urbs Roma	330–5
IX	8162	208	1	Half spade-guinea	George III	1800
	8164a	217	1	AE3	*Victoriae DD Augg QNN*	340–1
	8164b	217	1	AE3	*Victoriae DD Augg QNN*	340–1
	8056	340	6	Farthing	James I	1613–25
	8112	344	6	AE3	*Soli Invicto Comiti*	313–18
	8719	352	6	Barbarous radiate	-	270–90
	8357	367	6	Jetton	Iorg Schuldes	1515–59
	8197	518	6	Penny	Edward III	1351–61
	8160	546	6	Jetton	Hanns Krauwinckel	1586–1635
	8161	546	6	Jetton	Hanns Krauwinckel	1586–1635
	8571	793	3	Barbarous radiate	as *Spes*	270–90
X	8663	318	6	AE2 (coin?)	-	Modern?
	8353	386	6	AE4 minim	-	Late 3–4 cent
	8975	1399	3	Farthing	Charles I	1625–44

Table 5.9.3 Roman coins from 25 Bridge Street compared with the wider excavated assemblage from Chester

	25 Bridge Street 2001		Chester	
Issue Period	No coins	‰ coins	No coins	‰ coins
1	-	0	17	14.2
2	-	0	1	0.8
3	-	0	16	13.4
4	2	83.3	179	149.8
5	1	41.7	65	54.4
6	1	41.7	41	34.3
7	2	83.3	47	39.3
8	1	41.7	15	12.6
9	-	0	9	7.5
10	2	83.3	55	46
11	-	0	13	10.9
12	-	0	7	5.9
13	4	166.7	348	291.2
14	-	0	33	27.6
15	1	41.7	49	41
16	1	41.7	8	6.7
17	8	333.3	208	174.1
18	-	0	42	35.1
19	1	41.7	42	35.1
20	-	0	-	0
21	-	0	-	0
Total	24	1000	1195	1000
(late Roman)	7			

Note Issue Period XIII includes official radiates as well as their barbarous imitations

Metal

Copper alloy H E M Cool

Introduction

The excavations produced nearly 1000 items of copper alloy. In general it was in very poor condition. Many items were only identified following x-radiography and investigative conservation, carried out by Yannick Min-vielle-Debat of Bradford Conservation and Research. Her observations have been incorporated into the catalogue entries where appropriate, and I would like to place on record here my appreciation of her work which has made my job considerably easier.

Table 5.10.1 Copper alloy objects: distribution by phase and function

					Phase						
Function	I	II	III	IV	V	VI	VII	VIII	IX	X	*Total*
Personal	-	7	5	4	9	45	43	25	31	9	178
Toilet	-	-	1	-	-	-	-	-	-	-	1
Textile	-	-	-	2	-	1	-	1	-	-	4
House	1	-	1	-	1	1	1	-	2	1	8
Tools	-	-	-	-	-	-	1	-	1	-	2
Fasteners	6	12	7	10	3	4	9	13	9	15	88
Military	2	6	2	-	3	-	-	1	4	-	18
Pins	-	-	-	-	1	48	102	114	96	2	363
Miscellaneous	4	49	24	26	30	30	40	25	37	37	302
Total	13	74	40	42	47	129	196	179	180	64	964

The copper alloy artefacts are summarised by function and phase in Table 5.10.1. The extensive programme of sieving resulted in an inflated quantity of small fragments for which it is impossible to offer any interpretation. This accounts for the high quantity of items assigned to the Miscellaneous category, which also includes the less diagnostic items such as rings, lengths of wire etc This category will not be considered further here, but details of it are available in the archive database. In what follows the artefacts have been considered by phase. Where material was clearly residual in the context in which it was found, it has been catalogued and discussed in the phase during which it would have been in use. For some categories, such as fasteners, this was difficult to do because they tend not to be chronologically sensitive. A noticeable feature of the assemblage is the large number of medieval to post-medieval dress fittings such as lace tags and 'sewing' pins. A discussion of these will be found at the end of the phase-by-phase discussion as considering them as a whole provides a useful insight into the use of the area.

The copper alloy artefacts range in date from the first to the twentieth centuries but there are distinct gaps in the sequence. Roman material, mainly of second- to fourth-century date, was common, with the military component centring on the second and third centuries. There was nothing that needed to belong to the sub-Roman period, and little of late Saxon date. It was not until the fourteenth century that there started to be an appreciable number of independently dated items. Thereafter the sequence was good until the twentieth century.

Phase I

The Roman personal ornaments consist of a single hairpin and various bracelet fragments. The hairpin (no 1) is an example of a common second-century form (Cool 1990, type 3A). One of the bracelet fragments (no 2) might have been contemporary as they were in use from at least the late first century, but were commonest in the late Roman period (Cool 1983, 120, group I). The other fragments came from fourth-century light bangles. There is a single example decorated with a zigzag pattern (no 3: Cool 1983, group xxii) and an unknown number decorated with transverse grooves (nos 3–12: Cool 1983, group xix). Six of the light bangle fragments (nos 3–5, 10–12) came from Phase II contexts and so might have been contemporary with their context; all of the other items were residual.

Other second-century hairpins made of bone were also found on the site. The presence of these pins in the centre of the legionary fortress reminds us that it was not just soldiers who lived within them, but also the families of the officers. Contemporary hairpins are also known from inside the fortress at York (Cool *et al* 1995, 1543), and many were recovered from the bath house drain deposits of the later second to mid-third centuries at Caerleon (Greep 1986, 199). The proximity of the bath house to the present site may perhaps provide an explanation for the hairpins found here, as hairpins were a common loss during visits to the baths; but the rest of the very distinctive bath house rubbish suite seems to be missing from this site, so the pins probably reflect women going about their ordinary lives and perhaps living in the vicinity during the second century.

The only item in the household category is the bowl of a first- to second-century spoon (Crummy 1983, 69, type 1).

As noted in the introduction, most studs, tacks etc could only be dated by their context. Most Roman assemblages from urban and military sites have numerous items in this category, and it is to be suspected that many of the studs, split pins etc from Phases II and III, and some from later contexts, were residual Roman items. Normally these were catalogued according to the phases they were found in, but an exception was made for nos 19 and 20 as they are studs of composite composition which was typical of the sort of fittings found on Roman boxes: see for example those on a box found in a fourth-century grave at Colchester (Crummy 1983, 85).

The site also produced two copper alloy finials with iron shanks that are clearly decorative items, probably from furniture. No 14, although from a Phase II context, has the baluster shape seen in many Roman items and which was popular for this form of finial (*see*, for example, Allason-Jones & Miket 1984, 216, nos 3.733–6). No 15, by contrast, is quite extraordinary. It depicts a bulbous-eyed beast with curving lips or beak. Its context is given as (1260), which was the cut for the terrace of the road foundation. One would not normally expect to recover finds from cuts, as the correct attribution should be to the fill. The integrity of the attribution has to be considered as this currently appears to be a unique item; certainly I have not found any close comparanda for it. When originally found, this piece was an unrecognisable mass of copper alloy corrosion incorporating a large stone. It is possible, therefore, that it was found embedded into the surface of the cut and so the attribution is understandable. This context would date the piece to the first century. The beast, with its bulging eyes and scroll-like beak, has a 'celtic' rather than classical feel; and the possibility that this was the product of a craftsman working in a late pre-Roman Iron Age tradition seems very strong.

The military equipment present consists of two different types of armour, belt plates and horse fittings. Three groups of scales were found in contexts belonging to Phases II, V and IX (nos 25–7). These come from scale armour (*lorica squamata*), and all three groups are still wired together. All are narrow and have four pairs of perforations to allow them to be wired at top, bottom and sides. This style was a development of the Antonine period (Bishop & Coulston 1993, 117). Given the scarcity of metallic armour after the third century (*op cit*, 167), these pieces are most likely to have been in use during the later second to third centuries. The only possible fragment of a mail scale from a Phase I context (no 24) is larger than the undoubted examples, but the identification does seem likely. The folding would be consistent with the damage seen on no 25. Given the evidence of the mail rings made of iron (Mould, *this volume*), the damage on these fragments may be consistent with the interpretation that there was a *fabrica* in the area.

As well as the mail made of scales, there is also evidence for *lorica hamata* made of rings in both iron (Mould, *this volume*) and copper alloy. No 28 clearly shows the method of manufacture whereby rows of solid rings were linked together by riveted rings (*see* also Bishop & Coulston 1993, fig 137). The ring no 32 shows a similar expansion and so, although it came from a Phase VIII context, was included as a mail ring. The rings 29–31 are of a similar size to the undoubted mail rings and, given their contexts, seem most likely to be residual Roman pieces of first- to third- century date.

Two different types of belt plates are present. There are two examples (nos 33–4) of the very common Antonine form with openwork decoration (Bishop & Coulston 1993, 119, fig 80, no 2). No 35 is the side bar of an openwork enamelled belt plate. These were worn in chained bands, and were a third-century military fashion. They are found widely spread throughout the empire (Bishop & Coulston 1993, 153, fig 108, nos 1 and 4; and Allason-Jones & Miket 1984, nos 3.10–.11, pl vi). Another item of belt equipment is the strap end no 36. This is very similar to an example found during early excavations at Corbridge (Haverfield 1909, 409 fig 27). Unfortunately the context of that example is not recorded but in general a second- to third-century date would be most appropriate.

No 37 is a roundel from a set of horse harness. When complete there would have been a rivet with a decorative head through the central hole. A very similar piece was part of a hoard of fittings found in a mid-first-century context at Canterbury (Lawson 1995, 988, no 155). Mid-first-century equipment is frequently decorated by white metal coatings: the Canterbury roundel, for example, was tinned. No such coatings were observed during the conservation of this piece, and a later date might be possible. Strap fittings with circular frames and rectangular loops like no 38 this are known from Roman military sites such as South Shields (Allason-Jones & Miket 1984, 202, no 3.665), and this piece, too, is likely to have come from a piece of Roman horse harness.

Catalogue

Personal ornaments and dress accessories

1 Hair pin; oval baluster moulding head with two cordons above and one below; circular-sectioned shank tapering to (missing) point; present L 90 mm, shank section 2 mm. (1022): Phase III; SF 8627. Ill 5.10.1.1.

2 Bracelet; fragment of two-strand cable twist, right-hand twist; L 32 mm. (374): Phase IX; SF 8620.

3 Bracelet; rectangular-section, widest to wrist; simple zigzag formed by triangular nicks on alternate sides; L 31 mm, section 2 x 1 mm. (1219): Phase II; SF 8818.

4 Bracelet; D-sectioned, upper face decorated with diagonal grooves; both ends broken; present L 38 mm, section 2 x 1 mm. (1177): Phase II; SF 8761.

5 Bracelet; two fragments, D-sectioned, transverse grooves; total L *c* 100 mm, section 2 x 1.5 mm. (1135): Phase II; SF 8807.

6 Bracelet? D-sectioned, transversely ribbed; both ends broken; L 59 mm, section 2 x 1.5 mm. (1022): Phase III; SF 8627.

7 Bracelet? D-sectioned, transversely ribbed; both ends broken; L 25 mm, section 2 x 1 mm. (1030): Phase IV; SF 5114.

8 Bracelet? D-sectioned, transverse ribbing; both ends broken; L 24 mm, section 2 x 1 mm. (1015): Phase IV; SF 8640.

9 Bracelet? D-sectioned, transverse grooves producing beaded effect; L 11 mm, section 2 x 1 mm. (1030): Phase IV; SFs 9907, 5114.

10 Bracelet? D-sectioned, possibly with transverse ribs; both ends broken, much corroded; L 21 mm, section 2 x 1 mm. (99): Phase II; SF 9531.

11 Bracelet? D-sectioned, with transverse ribs; both ends broken; L 52 mm, section 2 x 1 mm. (76): Phase II; SF 9530.

12 Bracelet? D-sectioned, upper face transversely ribbed; both ends broken; L 40 mm, section 2 x 1 mm. (1132): Phase II; SF 8770.

Household items

13 Spoon; round bowl, stump of circular handle, joining bowl with triangular junction; diam of bowl 27 mm, section of handle 3.5 mm. (1148): Phase I; SF 8776. Ill 5.10.1.13.

Fittings

14 Terminal knob; baluster shape with knob and disc terminal, two fine grooves around body of the baluster; stump of square iron shank; total L 31 mm, L of

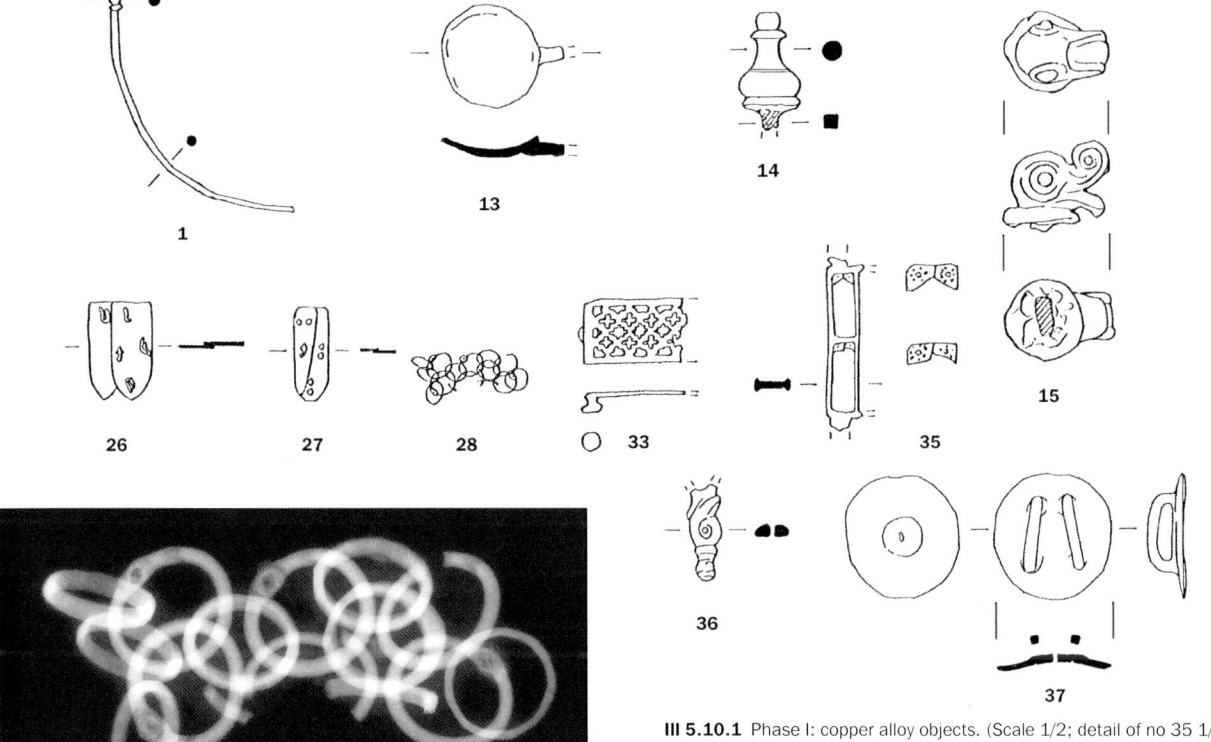

III **5.10.1a** Phase I: Roman copper alloy mail links no 28. (University of Bradford x-radiograph 464). (Scale c 2/1)

III **5.10.1** Phase I: copper alloy objects. (Scale 1/2; detail of no 35 1/1)

terminal 25 mm, max section 17 mm. (1142): Phase II; SF 8820. Ill 5.10.1.14.

15 Zoomorphic terminal; spherical head with bulbous eyes and curled lips, disc base; stump of rectangular tang; diam of base 21 mm, L 20 mm. (1260): Phase I; SF 8821. Ill 5.10.1.15.

16 Stud; flat disc head, shank broken; diam 10 mm. (1148): Phase I; SF 8822.

17 Stud; slightly domed disc head with rectangular sectioned shank bent at right angles; diam of head 11 mm, L of shank *c* 12 mm. (1242): Phase I; SF 8791.

18 Stud; flat disc head, tapering shank; L 15 mm, head diam 6 mm. (1148): Phase I; <5132>.

19 Stud; fragments of domed copper alloy sheet head covering lead alloy infill with void for missing shank; diam *c* 15 mm. (121): Phase II; SF 9634.

20 Stud; lead alloy hemispherical head with copper alloy and iron shank; L 23 mm, head diam *c* 20 mm. (879): Phase V; SF 8830.

21 Stud; shallow domed sheet head, possibly with some composite infill behind; short square-sectioned shank; diam 15 mm, L 9 mm. (1177): Phase II; SF 8761.

22 Tack; flat disc, short pointed shank; head diam 4.5 mm, L 7 mm. (276): Phase I.

23 Tack, slightly expanded head; L 9 mm. (1227): Phase I; SF 8803.

Military equipment

24 Mail scale? Folded sheet with small perforation centrally on one side and a possible pair of perforations centrally in upper side; present folded dimensions 22 x 19 mm. (144): Phase I; SF 9534.

25 Mail scales; parts of two still articulated and detached fragment of a third; narrow rectangular scales with rounded lower edge; four pairs of holes on each face; two scales wired together on long edge, lower edge retains wire from articulation; articulated scales folded in two. W of scales 8 mm. (1177): Phase II; SF 8765.

26 Mail scales; one complete and one broken at lower edge, these wired together on long edge; parts of four others wired to these. Complete ones are narrow rectangles with one rounded short edge; four pairs of holes on each face. Dimensions of complete scale 27 x 11 mm. (830): Phase V; SF 8622. Ill 5.10.1.26.

27 Mail scales; parts of three. Complete one is narrow rectangle with one rounded short edge; four pairs of holes on each face; fragment of second wired to it on one side, and small fragment of third at back. Dimensions of complete scale 24 x 8 mm. (620): Phase IX; SF 8435. Ill 5.10.1.27.

28 Mail rings; seven rows of articulated rings, sixteen complete and fragmentary rings extant; rows alternate with slightly smaller solid rings articulated by rows of rings where soldered join can be seen; diam of solid ring 7 mm, diam of soldered ring 8 mm. (1132): Phase II; SF 8783. Ills 5.10.1.28 and 5.10.1a.

29 Mail rings; two separate rings; diam (least corroded) 8 mm, section 1.5 mm. (1161): Phase II; SF 8758.

30 Mail ring? Two fragments of small rings; diam 8 mm. (1147): Phase II; SF 8970.

31 Mail ring? Fragment; diam 7 mm. (1175): Phase III; <5124>.

32 Mail ring; wire bent open and one terminal slightly expanded; diam 7 mm. (455): Phase VIII; <5142>.

33 Belt plate, missing one end; straight frame with openwork pattern internally of angular diamond-shaped pattern produced by outer triangular perforations, a central row of 8-rayed star perforations with a row of cross-shaped perforations on either side; a rivet with

integral washer at one end; present L 27 mm, W 18 mm. (1018): Phase III; SF 8641. Ill 5.10.1.33.

34 Belt plate, fragment; part of straight frame with open-work pattern internally of cross-shaped perforations giving angular diamond-shaped pattern; dimensions 16 x 10.5 mm, th 1 mm. (1014): Phase V; SF 8679.

35 Belt plate; hollow-backed side bar only; rectangular bar with two long cells retaining remnants of *mille-fiori* canes in ends of each; canes with opaque blue ground and opaque yellow flower pattern of central dot surrounded by ring of smaller dots; stumps of the bars which formed the peltiform end and the cross bar present at each end; present L 46 mm, section 9 x 4 mm. (1667): Phase V; SF 9297. Ill 5.10.1.35.

36 Strap end; terminal of flat-backed strap end with parts of curvilinear openwork decoration and knobbed terminal; L 26 mm, section 7 x 3 mm. (1119): Phase IV; SF 8792. Ill 5.10.1.36.

37 Strap union roundel; circular disc with central perfo-ration; front face slightly dished and has raised rib around perforation; two converging rectangular lugs behind; diam 33 mm, perforation diam 1.5 mm, L of lugs 21 mm. (1030): Phase IV; SF 8781. Ill 5.10.1.37.

38 Strap distributor; part of slightly hollow-backed cir-cular frame with rectangular loop on outer edge; present l mm, external diam of frame 60 mm. (1143): Phase II; SF 8969.

Phase II

Of the material found stratified in Phase II contexts, none was independently datable to the period. As noted, the items in the fastener category could easily have been residual from the Phase I contexts, whilst the buckle frag-ment could even have been intrusive from later phases.

Catalogue

Personal ornament and dress accessories

39 Buckle; fragment of square or rectangular frame; orig-inal W probably *c* 26 mm, frame section 2 x 2 mm. (1161): Phase II; SF 8750.

Fasteners

40 Stud; large gently domed head; now totally obscured by corrosion; diam *c* 24 mm. (119): Phase II; SF 9537.

41 Stud; fragment of hollow domed head; diam 10 mm. (1161): Phase II; SF 8758.

42 Stud, flat-headed, fragment. (1143): Phase II; SF 8786.

43 Split pin; ring loop with parallel legs slightly out-splayed at base; L 31 mm, diam of ring 16 mm. (1225): Phase II; SF 8756.

44 Split pin; rectangular-sectioned strip, tapering to pointed ends; oval loop, arms bent to one side; L 36 mm, diam of loop 14 x 10 mm, max section of bar 4.5 x 1.5 mm. (1132): Phase II; SF 8770.

45 Angle binding? Rectangular-sectioned; both ends broken, one expanding. (1143): Phase II; SF 8802.

46 Ferrule or collar; sheet bent into cylinder; large cir-cular perforation at one end; L 32 mm, present section 14 x 9 mm. (1135): Phase II; SF 8812.

47 Hollow copper alloy cylinder with central iron cor-rosion; L 45 mm, diam 9 mm. (1161): Phase II; SF 8759.

48 Cylinder; cast; L 30 mm, diam 8.5 mm, perforation diam 2.5 mm. (1161): Phase II; SF 8759.

49 Fitting; T-shaped with expanded terminal; L 18 mm, bar diam 4 x 2.5 mm. (1135): Phase II; SF 8806.

Phase III

It was not until Phase III that copper alloy artefacts again started to appear that might plausibly be contemporary with their contexts. Copper alloy beads such as no 50, for example, are rare in Roman contexts, but not uncommon in Norse contexts, and have been found in a ninth- to tenth-century context at Coppergate in York (Mainman & Rogers 2000, 2597, no 10527). The pair of tweezers no 53 would also fit more happily into a post-Roman mi-lieu, as collars or slides seem to be a much more common feature of the later examples than of Roman ones (Biddle 1990, 690). The bowl no 54 could not be independently dated, but seems most likely to be contemporary with its context, as white metal coatings are not a particularly common feature of Roman metal vessels.

Catalogue

Personal ornaments and dress accessories

50 Bead, squashed globular; diam 12 mm, perforation diam *c* 5 mm, L 7.5 mm. (70): Phase II; SF 9540. Ill 5.10.2.50.

51 Belt plate; sheet bent in half with hinge part broken; two rivets in central line; x-radiograph suggests the rivets are of a different alloy; dimensions 20 x 17 mm. (1022): Phase III; SF 9618; <5098>.

52 Gold; wire ring fragment, probably from chain; diam 3 mm, section *c* 0.25 mm. (1179): Phase III; SF 9865; <5127>.

Toilet equipment

53 Tweezers; rectangular-sectioned bar with closed loop and inturned jaws; strip collar around upper part of arms; L 27 mm, section 3 x 2 mm. (1179): Phase III; SF 8816. Ill 5.10.2.53.

Household items

54 Bowl; two joining rim fragments, bent out of shape; slightly outbent rim, vertical side. Conservation re-vealed a white metal coating on exterior and black deposit on exterior below rim. Rim diam *c* 140–150 mm, present height 20 mm. (1018): Phase III; SF 8715. Ill 5.10.2.54.

Fasteners

55 Studs; two corroded together, also one fragment pos-sibly from same group; much obscured. (1022): Phase III; SF 8672.

56 Stud; flat disc head and broken shank; head diam 8.5 x 6.5 mm. (1133): Phase III; SF 8760.

57 Stud; flat oval head; shank tapering to point; L 11 mm, head dimensions 7 x 3 mm. (1022): Phase III; <5098>.

58 Split pin; small loop; parallel arms with end of one bent back against itself to form a loop; L 33 mm. (1175): Phase III; SF 8809.

59 Mount; D-sectioned, shell-shaped with shank below; L 18 mm. (1022): Phase III; SF 9618; <5098>. Ill 5.10.2.59.

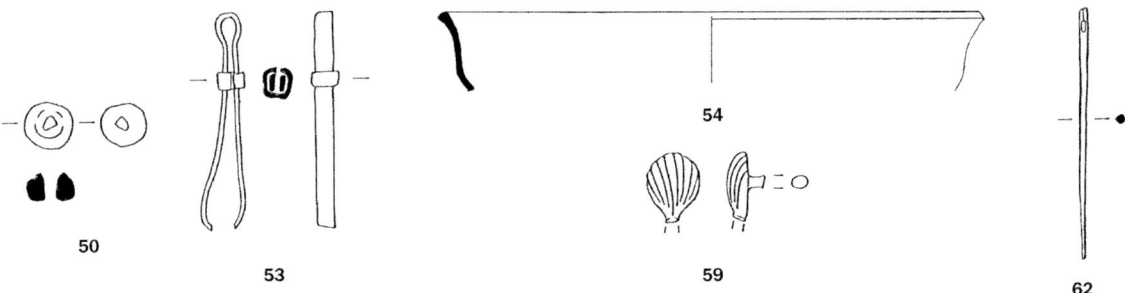

III 5.10.2 Phases III and IV: copper alloy objects. (Scale 1/2; no 53 1/1)

60 Mount; rectangular sheet strip with small perforation; L 35 mm, W 10 mm. (70): Phase III; SF 9539.

61 Mount; rectangular sheet with nail shank through centre; dimensions 31 x 19 mm. (70): Phase III; SF 9538.

Phase IV

Again, the assemblage did not include any items that could be independently dated to this period, and the items that were stratified in Phase IV contexts were not chronologically sensitive.

Catalogue

Textile equipment

62 Needle; oval-sectioned tapering to point; rectangular eye with groove above and below on both faces; straight head, now slightly curved; L 68 mm, section 2 x 1.5 mm. (69): Phase IV, Plot 6; SF 9526. Ill 5.10.2.62.

63 Needle; oval-sectioned shank tapering to sharp point; other end broken; L 39 mm, max diam 2 mm. (974): Phase IV, Plot 6; SF 9686.

Fasteners

64 Stud; shallow domed head, very short shank; head diam 7 x 5.5 mm, L 3 mm. (873): Phase IV, Plot 3; SF 8733.

65 Stud; hemispherical head; broken shank; head diam 17 mm, L 15 mm. (1125): Phase IV, Plot 2; SF 8831.

66 Stud; hemispherical head; broken shank; head diam 8 mm, present L 12 mm. (883): Phase IV, Plots 1 and 2; SF 8766.

67 Stud; shallowly domed head; bent rectangular-sectioned shank, tip missing; head diam 10 mm, L 20 mm. (266): Phase IV, Plot 1; SF 8002.

68 Head flat, square-sectioned pointed shank; head diam 3.5 mm, L 9 mm. Also one very corroded fragment. (1033): Phase IV, Plot 6; <5099>.

69 Square flat head; triangular-sectioned shank tapering to point; L 9 mm, head diam 4 mm. (1033): Phase IV, Plot 6; <5099>.

70 Disc, possibly a stud head; diam 12 mm. (1033): Phase IV, Plot 6; SF 8682.

71 Mount; rectangular sheet with curving line of five circular perforations down centre and centrally on a long edge; dimensions 28 x 16 mm. (1017): Phase IV, Plot 6; SF 9630.

72 Mount; rectangular with rectangular section and stumps of rivets at either end; L 13 mm, section 6 x 1.5 mm. (873): Phase IV, Plot 3; SF 8733.

73 Hook; circular bar tapering to point at one end and flat perforated plate for attachment at other; L 28 mm. (1015): Phase IV, Plot 6; SF 8639.

Phase V

The assemblage contained a wide range of personal equipment from this period, both stratified in contemporary contexts, and found residually. No 74 is the common buckle and plate form of the fourteenth century, possibly becoming commonest in the later part of that century and into the fifteenth century (Hinton in Biddle 1990, 507, nos 1158–9; Egan & Pritchard 2002, 80). Nos 75 and 76, composite strap ends with forked spacers, are another common fourteenth-century form (Egan & Pritchard 2002, 140—6); and so both were clearly residual in the contexts in which they were found. The buckle no 17 would have been in use contemporaneously with these strap ends (eg Hinton in Biddle 1990, 517, nos 1161, 1163, 1166, 1170–1), and again must have been residual. Buckle pins similar to no 78 have been found in contexts of the second half of the fourteenth century at London (Egan & Pritchard 2002, 115, nos 540–50, fig 75). In Winchester a very similar pin to this was found on a large double-sided buckle from an early to mid-fourteenth-century context (Hinton in Biddle 1990, 517, no 1152, fig 131); and on a D-shaped buckle from a fifteenth-century demolition context (*op cit* 521, no 1195, fig 132). Other types of strap fittings include a folding clasp (no 80) of a type in use from the late thirteenth to early fifteenth centuries (Egan & Pritchard 2002, 116); and a front plate (no 81) of a fourteenth- to early fifteenth-century two-piece strap end (*op cit*, 135). An example of the latter from London retains part of a silk tablet-woven girdle (*op cit* 49, fig 31). The use of paint to decorate the front of no 81 is noteworthy. As well as the strap ends and buckles, there is one example of the commonest type of decorative mount for leather or textile in the second half of the fourteenth-century and late into the fifteenth century (*op cit*, 186, *see* especially no 949). This piece, no 82, was very well made in comparison to many of these mounts and would have been a glittering addition to a strap as it was gilded.

Other finds relating to dress of this period are the tiny fragment of gold thread (no 83), and the pins and lace tags discussed below.

One item of household equipment was also recovered. No 84 is a patch with folded rivets of the type used to repair metal vessels. In London they have been found in late thirteenth- to fifteenth-century contexts (Egan 1998, 176–7), and so this piece is likely to have been contemporary with the context it was found in.

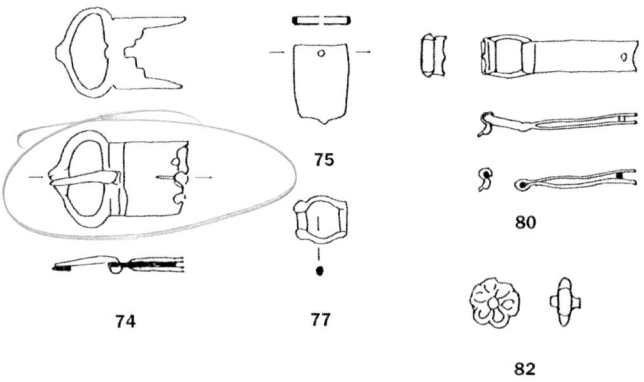

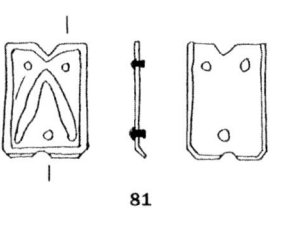

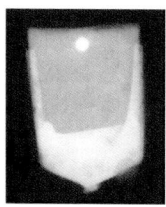

Ill 5.10.3a Phase V: Copper alloy strap end no 75. (University of Bradford x-radiograph 426). (Scale *c* 1/1)

Ill 5.10.3 Phase V: copper alloy objects. (Scale 1/2)

Catalogue

Personal ornaments and dress accessories

74 Buckle and plate; oval frame with lipped rest for pin; recessed hinge bar, stepped frame for plate; plain sheet coverings of plate extant, each with three perforations at outer end for rivetting strap in place; pin extant; L 37 mm, W of buckle 25 mm, W of plate 19 mm. (1641): Phase V, Plot 3; SF 9597. Ill 5.10.3.74.

75 Composite strap end with forked spacer; small terminal knob on frame; front and back plates present with straight upper edge; plates fastened by small rivet centrally on upper edge; L 22 mm, W 15 mm, (catalogued from x-radiograph). (1637): Phase VIII, Plot 3; SF 9517. Ill 5.10.3.75.

76 Composite strap end; lower part of forked cast spacer with knob and double-cordon terminal; detached fragment of sheet probably from cover; present L 18 mm, W 8 mm. (1304): Phase VII, Plot 2; SF 8981.

77 Buckle; single loop with recessed cross bar and triple ribbed outer edge; dimensions 13 x 14 mm. (663): Phase VII, Plot 1; SF 8472. Ill 5.10.3.77.

78 Buckle pin, cast, complete; open loop; transverse ridge on upper face at junction between loop and shaft; seating for frame at tip; L 51 mm. (1117): Phase V, Plot 2; SF 8737.

79 Buckle or brooch pin; part of shank with ring at one end; present L 20 mm. (1165): Phase V, Plot 2; SF 8736.

80 Folding strip clasp; folding plate has bevelled bar mount and scalloped end; frame has bowed sides; folded plate with central rivet at end; total L 41 mm, W of plate 13 mm. (1319): Phase V, Plot 3; SF 8966. Ill 5.10.3.80.

81 Strap end; front cover; rectangular with edges turned down on two long sides and one short; both short edges notched; front has slightly recessed field with edges diagonally punched giving a cable pattern; recessed area has decoration in black paint in V-shaped pattern delineated by narrow lines where copper alloy is visible; three iron rivets in situ. L 31 x 22 mm. (809): Phase V, Plot 3; SF 8507. Ill 5.10.3.81.

82 Sexfoil mount; sheet with recessed area in each lobe to accentuate petal pattern; separate ball-headed rivet centrally; surface of mount gilded; diam 14 mm, L of rivet 7.5 mm. (1656): Phase V, Plots 2 and 3; SF 9254. Ill 5.10.3.82.

83 Gold thread; fragment of thread with gold sheet spirally wrapped around; L 3 mm. (490): Phase V, Plot 3; SF 8905.

Household items

84 Repair patch; rectangular sheet with one broken end; upper parts of five folded sheet rivets visible on upper face; lower face retains plate of possibly different alloy held in place by rivets with outsplayed ends of rivets folded back against it; parts of other rivets broken; current dimensions 33 x 30 mm. (1293): Phase V, Plot 3; SF 8980.

Fasteners

85 Washer; square sheet with small central perforation; dimensions 12.5 x 11 mm, perforation diam 2.5 mm. (879): Phase V, Plot 2; SF 8836.

86 Mount; oval with one slightly waisted oval perforation and one small circular perforation in rounded end; L 25 mm, W 19 mm, th 1 mm. (261): Phase V, Plot 1; SF 8048.

Phase VI

In this phase strap fittings continued to be found, but in relatively small numbers. Instead, the personal equipment category is dominated by tie loops and lace tags. The latter are discussed below with the sewing pins, as there are grounds for thinking that, unlike the buckles and strap ends, these represented manufacturing or retail activity on the site rather than casual losses

There were two items of jewellery. The small ring, no 87, was designed for the upper joint of a small finger and belongs to a fifteenth-century tradition of small trinket rings (*cf* Egan & Pritchard 2002, 332). The figure-of-eight loop no 88 is probably from a necklace. Both of the buckles fit happily into a sixteenth-century milieu. D-shaped ones with notched lips such as no 89 were a long-lasting form (Whitehead 1996, 17), but a very similar buckle to this was found in a mid-sixteenth-century context at Winchester (Hinton 1990, 522, no 1212). Decorated spectacle buckles like no 90 were common between the mid-sixteenth and mid-seventeenth-centuries (Whitehead 1996, 60).

The dress fastenings consist of a hooked tag (no 91), a small wire hook (no 92) and six wire tie loops (nos 93–8). The hooked tag was clearly residual in the context in which it was found, as there were two periods when hooked tags similar to it were in use: the late Saxon and the late

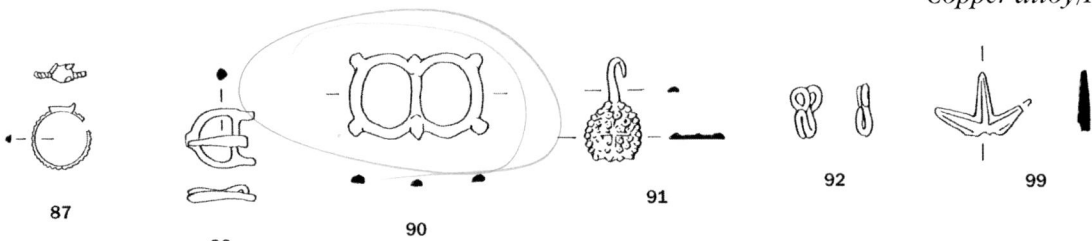

III 5.10.4 Phase VI: copper alloy objects. (Scale 1/2)

medieval (Mainman & Rogers 2000, 2576). Conservation clearly revealed the stumps of two projections opposite the hook, suggesting that this example originally had a rectangular projection with slot opposite the hook, as on one from Winchester (Hinton in Biddle 1990, 552, no 1428). This clearly places it in the late medieval category, when such hooks were a common dress accessory in the sixteenth century (Gaimster *et al* 2002). The small wire hook resembles the hook of a modern hook and eye and undoubtedly served the same purpose. It may have been residual in the context in which it was found as a similar example was found in a fourteenth-century context in Southampton (Goodall 1984, 339, no 121), but such a simple and functional fitting had a long life and it seems best to consider it contemporary with the context in which it was found.

Tie loops were in use elsewhere during the time covered by Period VI. They occurred, for example, in the post-Dissolution deposits at Denny abbey (Goodall 1980, 260, nos 48—9), and in a late sixteenth- to early seventeenth-century context at Bolingbroke castle (Goodall 1976, 33, no 78), but at other sites they were clearly in use earlier as well. At Exeter, for example, seventeen were found in contexts dating from the late thirteenth to late seventeenth centuries (Goodall 1984, 347) and there is an example at Leicester in a late fourteenth-century context (Clay 1981, 137, no 55). The sudden appearance of six in Phase VI contexts is noteworthy and is matched by greatly increased volume of lace tags and sewing pins. It seems likely that it was the result of new activities on the site and this will be further considered below.

The one other item of personal equipment from this phase is the rowel of a spur (no 99). Rowel spurs were in use in England from the thirteenth century onwards (Ellis 1991, 58). Simple rowels of modest dimensions such as this are not closely datable.

In addition to these personal items, there was a needle and a fragment from the rim of a bowl, as well as various small mounts and fittings.

Catalogue
Personal ornaments and dress accessories
87 Finger ring; D-sectioned hoop with beaded outer face; possibly penannular with square bezel with stumps of four claws originally holding a glass setting soldered over the join; traces of glass setting only remaining; diam 16 mm, section 2.5 x 1 mm. (862): Phase VI, Plot 2; SF 8602. III 5.10.4.87.
88 Figure-of-eight link; two fragments, one loop broken; original L *c* 15 mm. (798): Phase VI, Plot 2; SF 9614; <5079>.
89 Buckle; D-shaped loop with notched lip, cross bar with spurs; tongue present but detached; W 16 mm, L 20 mm. (947): Phase VI, Plot 6; SF 8604. III 5.10.4.89.

90 Spectacle buckle; double oval loop with mouldings at ends of cross bar and at outer edges of frame; L 38 mm, W 23 mm. (671): Phase VI, Plot 2; SF 9850; <5071>. III 5.10.4.90.
91 Hooked tag; circular with hook at one side and stumps of projecting bars at the other; face has scalloped edge with centre divided into four panels by raised cross-moulding; each face has four perforations, mostly obscured but visible in x-radiograph; present L 27 mm, disc diam 15 mm. (1638): Phase VIII, Plot 3; SF 9172. III 5.10.4.91.
92 Wire hook; wire bent in two with ends formed into loops and parallel end bent into hook; L 14 mm, W 9 mm. (798): Phase VI, Plot 2; SF 9852; <5079>. III 5.10.4.92.
93 Tie ring; wire, twisted, two examples; diam 12 mm, section 1 mm. (862): Phase VI, Plot 2; SF 8637.
94 Tie ring; wire, twisted; diam 12 mm, section 1.5 mm; also fragments of second example. (766): Phase VI, Plot 1; SF 8634.
95 Tie ring; wire, twisted ends; diam 13 mm, section 1.5 mm. (746): Phase VI, Plot 2; SF 8536.
96 Tie ring; wire, twisted ends; diam 12 mm, section 1.5 mm. (746): Phase VI, Plot 2; SF 8535.
97 Tie ring; wire, twisted ends; diam 9 mm, section 1.5 mm. (855): Phase VI, Plot 3; SF 8534.
98 Tie ring; wire, twisted ends; diam 11 mm, section 1 mm. (778): Phase VI, Plot 2; SF 8498.
99 Spur rowel; three points of six-point spur with faceted points; fragment retains small part of central perforation; original diam 45 mm, th 4 mm. (1618): Phase VI, Plot 4; SF 9299. III 5.10.4.99.

Textile equipment
100 Needle; oval-sectioned tapering to sharp point; rectangular eye with groove above and below on both faces; pointed head; L 76 mm, maxi section 3 x 2.5 mm. (37): Phase VI, Plot 1; SF 9525.

Household items
101 Bowl rim; horizontal out-turned rim fragment; diam 170 mm. (806): Phase VI, Plot 2; SF 9603; <5081>.

Fasteners and fittings
102 Hollow fitting; exterior much obscured by corrosion damage but resembles a beaked face; traces of lead infill; L 24 mm, max W 20 mm. (1320): Phase VI, Plot 3; SF 9032.
103 Mount; rectangular-sectioned, rectangular mount; one end broken across a circular perforation. L 25 mm, section 6 x 1.5 mm. (1215): Phase VI, Plot 3; SF 8799.
104 Mount? Circular disc with central raised circular cell; an arm on either side bent behind disc; diam 15 mm. (122): Phase VI, Plot 6; SF 9533.

105 Binding; U-shaped; three fragments; total L 135 mm,
    W 9 mm. (429): Phase VI, Plot 3; SF 8333.

Phase VII

The material associated with this phase included several
interesting pieces and continued to have a high level of
tie rings, lace tags and sewing pins. The strap buckles
(nos 107–8) are not particularly diagnostic but the features observed in the very corroded no 107 are consistent
with it being a buckle of later sixteenth- and seventeenth-
century date (Whitehead 1996, 77).

More noteworthy are the finger ring no 106 and the
fastener no 109. The ring has many similarities to posy
rings, popular in the fifteenth to eighteenth centuries.
These had short messages relating to love or religion on
their outer faces. Later ones developed more elaborately
decorated outer faces, and so the message moved to the
interior (Gere 1991, 40). This example is very heavily
corroded and it is possible that some details are hidden
below the worst corrosion crusts (Yannick Minvielle-
Debat *pers comm*). In as far as it is possible to be sure in
these circumstances, this ring does not have a message
internally and the mouldings on the exterior are not ex-
plicable as part of an inscription. Wirework fasteners such
as no 109 are found in sixteenth to eighteenth century
contexts (*see* Duncan 2002, 271 for references). It has
been thought they were used with chains, but it is rare to
find one still articulated to other elements as here, so this
example provides a valuable insight into how they were
used. This piece was found in a layer interpreted as a
garden soil accumulation, and the clay pipe evidence
suggests a date of 1640–60. This date would be consistent with the discovery of a fastener such as this from a
Civil War siege deposit (1644/5) at Pontefract castle (*op
cit*, 274, no 124). The chain fragment no 110 is likely to
have come from a similar artefact.

Another curious find is the bowl no 122. This vessel
had mortar-like deposits in the base and was recorded as
being found with a variety of artefact and ecofactual items
in an early eighteenth-century pit fill. Whether the association was deliberate, however, is open to question as
one of these, a clay pipe bowl, was corroded to the underside of the rim and was clearly not inside the bowl.

Catalogue
Personal ornaments and dress accessories
106 Finger ring; annular band; beaded border along each
    edge; central band bordered on each side by narrow
    horizontal rib with raised decoration between; ex-
    tant part shows unit of raised vertical bars with raised
    arrow-shaped motifs on either side. The pattern has
    only been revealed on approximately half of the cir-
    cumference as the ring is very heavily corroded and
    too fragile for further work; diam 21 mm, section 5.5
    x 1 mm. (824); Phase VII, Plot 6; SF 8644. Ill
    5.10.5.106.
107 Buckle; wide rectangular frame retaining central bar
    and parts of side arms; frame slightly curved; traces
    of herringbone moulding on either side of central
    bar; the whole much corroded. W *c* 33 mm. (463):
    Phase VII, Plot 2; SF 8216.
108 Buckle; one side of rectangular or square frame; W
    24 mm. (464): Phase VII, Plot 2; SF 8254.

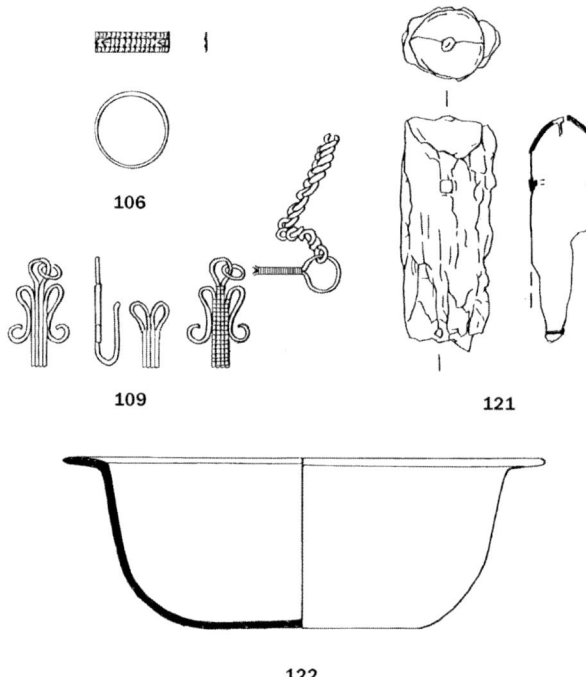

Ill 5.10.5 Phase VII: copper alloy objects. (Scale 1/2)

109 Wirework fastener and chain. Central area of fastener
    consists of parallel strands of wire bound together
    with finer-gauge wire, with parallel strands forming
    decorative side and end loop, and probably a hook
    at the other (currently obscured). Central loop artic-
    ulates with second fitting formed of one strand of
    wire bent to form circular loop at either end with
    ends forming central bar, also bound with finer gauge
    wire; larger loop of this fitting articulates with a four-
    strand plaited chain of square cross-section. L of
    fastener *c* 26 mm, W of central section 5 mm; L of
    articulating fitting 26 mm, chain section 2 mm,
    present L of chain *c* 50 mm. (663): Phase VII, Plot 1;
    SF 8213. Ill 5.10.5.109.
110 Chain; four plaited wires; all ends broken; present L
    19 mm, section 2.5 x 0.5 mm. (1898): Phase VII, Plot
    1; SF 9388.
111 Tie ring; wire, twisted; diam 12 mm., section 1.5 mm.
    (686): Phase VII, Plot 6; SF 8652.
112 Tie ring; wire, twisted ends; diam 11 mm, section 1
    mm. (663): Phase VII, Plot 1; SF 8471.
113 Tie ring; wire, twisted ends; diam 8 mm, section 1
    mm. (663): Phase VII, Plot 1; SF 8475.
114 Tie ring; wire, twisted ends; diam 13 mm, section 1.5
    mm. (237): Phase VII, Plot 1; SF 8010.
115 Tie ring; wire, twisted, oval; diam 9 mm, section 1
    mm. (1533): Phase VII, Plot 4; SF 9055.
116 Tie ring; wire, ends twisted together; diam 7 mm, L
    11 mm, section 1.5 mm. (1509): Phase VII, Plot 4; SF
    9031.
117 Tie ring; wire, twisted ends; diam 8 mm, section 1
    mm. (389): Phase VII, Plot 6; SF 8124.
118 Tie ring; wire, ends twisted together; diam 8 mm, L
    10 mm, section 1 mm. (341): Phase VIII, Plot 6; SF
    9608 ; <5026>.
119 Tie ring; wire twisted; diam 11 mm, section 2 mm.
    (630): Phase IX, Plot 9; SF 8291.
120 Tie ring; wire, twisted end, *c* one-quarter extant.
    (512): Phase IX; SF 8166.

Tools

121 Scale-tang knife handle, upper part; remnants of upper part of two wooden scales either side of iron tang; copper alloy terminal plate covering end; one iron rivet through scales and tang with copper alloy plating on head; diam 21 x 18 mm; present L 60 mm. (1516): Phase VII, Plot 4; SF 9507. Ill 5.10.5.121.

Household items

122 Bowl; now much fragmented but probably originally complete; much corroded; horizontal out-turned rim, slightly convex side with rounded junction to flat base; rim diam 130 mm, height 48 mm. (1601): Phase VII, Plot 4; SF 9160. Ill 5.10.5.122.

Fasteners and fittings

123 Stud; pointed oval head, slightly domed; broken square-sectioned shank; head dimensions 23 x 11 mm, L 9 mm. (463): Phase VII, Plot 2; SF 8217.

124 Stud; flat disc head; diam 17 mm. (1304): Phase VII, Plot 2; SF 8963.

125 Stud: hemispherical domed head with central perforation for missing shank; diam 13 mm. (663): Phase VII, Plot 1; SF 8477.

126 Chipped domed head; square-sectioned tapering shank; head diam 6.5 mm, L 7 mm. (463): Phase VII, Plot 2; <5045>.

127 Stud; broken flat head and shank. (663): Phase VII, Plot 1.

128 Stud; flat disc head with square-sectioned shank bent to one side; head diam 8 mm. (663): Phase VII, Plot 1.

129 Sheet mount; crescentic with central shank. (463): Phase VII, Plot 2; SF 9611.

130 Ferrule? Cylindrical with one rounded end, other broken, very corroded; L 18 mm, diam 11.5 mm. (463): Phase VII, Plot 2; SF 8237.

131 Collar; cylindrical tube; L 12 mm, section 5.5 x 4 mm. (1884): Phase VII, Plot 1; SF 9315.

Phase VIII

In this phase tie rings disappeared and lace tags declined markedly. It is noticeable that this was the earliest phase in which buttons occurred, as a single example (no 135) of a Winchester type C brazed button was found (Biddle & Cook 1990). In the light of the continuing presence of many pins, it may be noted that sewing was attested by a small thimble (no 136) which would have been appropriate for the little finger if worn by an adult.

Catalogue
Personal ornaments and dress accessories

132 Annular buckle; circular retaining pin (catalogued from x-radiograph); diam 17 mm, th of bar 3.5 mm. (847): Phase VIII, Plot 2; SF 9631.

133 Strap mount? Two rectangular sheets with two small rivets centrally on short edges and large central perforation; dimensions 27 x 17 mm. (1643): Phase VIII, Plot 3; SF 9174.

134 Pin; spherical head centrally perforated with circular-sectioned wire shank inserted, tip broken; L 45 mm, head diam 5 mm, shank section 1.5 mm. (341): Phase VIII, Plot 6; SF 8177.

135 Button; circular with broken back; diam 16 mm. (207): Phase VIII, Plot 1; SF 8614.

Textile equipment

136 Thimble; complete with mechanically milled diamond shaped pitting; L 13 mm, max diam 14 mm. (613): Phase VIII, Plot 6; SF 8396.

Fasteners and fittings

137 Stud; disc and diamond-shaped plate visible on x-radiograph; possibly stud with integral rove; disc diam 7 mm, diamond dimensions 22 x 14 mm. (847): Phase VIII, Plot 2; SF 8683.

138 Stud; broken round head, square shank; head diam 9 mm. (207): Phase VIII, Plot 1; SF 8614.

139 Stud; shallow domed head, tapering shank; L 13 mm, head diam 7 mm. (455): Phase VIII, Plot 4.

140 Stud; hemispherical hollow head, shank broken; head diam 9 mm. (1420): Phase VIII, Plot 2.

141 Tack; rectangular-sectioned shank with slightly expanded head; head diam 3.5 x 2 mm, L 9 mm. (559): Phase VIII, Plot 6.

142 Tack; small circular flat head, faceted tapering shank; head diam 3.5 mm, L 14 mm. (559): Phase VIII, Plot 6.

143 Mount; bar with expanded terminals each with rivet on underside; central hemispherical transversely ribbed dome; L 16 mm, max W 5.5 mm. (1439): Phase VIII, Plot 2; SF 9173.

144 Mount; hemispherical central boss; flat-backed with rivets at either end below projections; L 12 mm, section 9 x 3 mm. (612): Phase VIII, Plot 6; SF 8434.

145 Screw fragment from shank. (520): Phase VIII, Plot 6; SF 9626; <5035>.

146 Part of angular frame with fragment of sheet from possibly hinged attachment. W 14 mm. (341): Phase VIII, Plot 6; SF 8179.

Phase IX

One of the items catalogued here, the ring no 147, was clearly residual in the context it was found in. Finger rings with cabled hoops are very occasionally known in Roman (Johns 1997, 110, no 307) and medieval contexts (Hinton in Biddle 1990, 649, no 2064), but the extant fragments cannot be more closely dated. Apart from this the items were all likely to be of contemporary date. Buttons were relatively common and included brazed buttons of Winchester type C Biddle & Cook 1990) (nos 148–9), one of which (no 148) has the arms of the Royal Artillery on it, an interesting find given the cartridge casings (nos 164) also found. Other button included blazer buttons of Winchester type F (nos 146 and 150) and a metal suspender button of Winchester type E (no 153).

Catalogue
Personal ornaments and dress accessories

147 Finger ring; two fragments of three-strand cable-twisted hoop, left-hand twist, ends flattened for attachment of (missing) bezel; diam *c* 20 mm. (1476): Phase IX, Plot 5; SF 9159.

148 Brazed two-piece button with loose wire attachment loop at back; front has military insignia of the Royal Artillery; diam 23 mm, L 14 mm. (230): Phase IX, Plot 1; SF 8044.

149 Button; back plate with central cast loop; diam 28 mm. (640): Phase IX, Plot 1; SF 8437.

150 Button, slightly domed head with loop on back; much corroded; diam 17 mm, L 9 mm. (208): Phase IX, Plot 1; SF 8194.

151 Button; very heavily corroded; diam 15 mm. (601): Phase IX, Plot 1; SF 8416.

152 Button; slightly domed head with possible broken loop on back; much corroded; diam 17 mm. (418): Phase IX, Plot 2; SF 8195.

153 Button; circular with central dished perforated area; much corroded; diam 14 mm. (601): Phase IX, Plot 1; SF 8442.

154 Pop-stud head; domed with flange; diam 5.5 mm. (512): Phase IX, Plot 6; SF 8386.

Household items

155 Hinged box lid; possibly japanned and painted; dimensions 80 x 53 mm. (1279): Phase IX; SF 9148.

156 Key; trefoil handle; bar at right angles articulating with small cylinder in same plane as handle; L of handle 23 mm, L of bar 33 mm. (601): Phase IX, Plot 1; SF 8441.

Tools

157 Handle; lower part with central tapering tang and copper alloy sheet band around base; present L 40 mm. (1096): Phase IX, Plot 2; SF 8884.

Fasteners and fittings

158 Stud; shallow domed head; broken shank; head diam 9 mm. (469): Phase IX, Plot 2.

159 Stud; shallow domed head, possibly with broken flange; square-sectioned pointed shank; head diam 7 mm, L 13 mm. (352): Phase IX, Plot 6.

160 Tacks (2); slightly domed heads, one retains casting flanges at point and cannot have been used; lengths 17, 18.5 mm. (206): Phase IX, Plot 1; SF 8041.

161 Bolt. (640): Phase IX, Plot 1; SF 8436.

162 Collar; copper alloy sheet casing wooden rod. (1527): Phase IX, Plot 4; SF 9205.

163 Screw retaining washers; present L 26 mm. (1527): Phase IX, Plot 4; SF 9203.

Military items

164 Cartridge case; three copper alloy ends. (1527): Phase IX, Plot 4; SF 9202.

Lace tags and sewing pins

A notable feature of the assemblage is the numbers of lace tags and sewing pins which were recovered. As these showed interesting chronological patterns when considered as a whole, the discussion of them has been delayed until this point.

The lace tags were made of sheet with a vertical seam. It could occasionally be seen that they have small rivet holes at the top, but the majority were clearly made simply by clenching the sheet around the lace. One from a Phase VII context was possibly japanned, but the rest have no surface treatment. In length the complete tags range from 18 to 41 mm with a mean length of 28 mm. These tags or chapes were put on the ends of laces of leather or textile used for lacing clothes (Egan & Pritchard 2002, 281–6). As can be seen from Table 5.10.2, at the Bridge Street site lace tags only began to be common from the late fifteenth century, whereas in other urban centres they were much more visible in earlier centuries as well. As Egan and Pritchard have noted (2002, 284), the fashions from the fourteenth century onwards needed laces and their tags. There was a reasonably large assemblage of items from fourteenth and fifteenth century contexts and, given the amount of sieving that was carried on the site, it is to be expected that if the tags had been common they would have been recovered. The sudden rise in numbers from Phase VI thus appears to be a real one.

Table 5.10.2 Lace tags: comparison of chronological distribution at Chester, London and Winchester. (Sources: Egan & Pritchard 2002, 282–4; Biddle & Hinton 1990, table 79 (NB: - / indicates not applicable))

Chester Phase	Date	Complete	Incomplete	London	Winchester
IV	Late 11–13 cent	-	-	2	9
V	14–late 15 cent	2	-	33	18
VI	Late 15–mid-17 cent	10	12	/	43
VII	Mid 17– early 18 cent	14	10	/	56
VIII	Early 18–early 19 cent	3	9	/	5
IX	Early 19 cent–c 1900	9	7	/	28
X	20 cent and unphased	1	1	/	14
Total		39	39	35	173

A similar pattern could be seen when the distribution of 'sewing' pins was considered. Over 350 complete pins were recovered as well as many fragments. Virtually all of these are of the type with heads made of wire wrapped around the shank, although a few from Phase IX contexts have solid heads. No attempt was made to study the heads and the shank gauge in any detail, given the very poor condition of most of the copper alloy. They range in length from 16 to 55 mm with a mean of 28 mm. As can be seen in Table 5.10.3, they suddenly start to occur in quantity in Phase VI. These pins were multi-functional items, used to fasten veils and other items of clothing as well as for sewing, and were certainly being used in large numbers by the fourteenth century (Egan & Pritchard 2002, 297). Table 5.10.3 shows the chronological distribution of the pins on this site compared to those found at Winchester. The Winchester pattern can be taken as what is to be expected normally. Again Chester shows a sudden and dramatic increase only in Phase VI, and again the absence in Phase V seems to have been a real one.

Table 5.10.3 Sewing pins: comparison of chronological distribution at Chester and Winchester (Source: Biddle 1990, table 77)

Chester Phase	Date	Complete	Winchester
IV	Late 11–13 cent	-	14
V	14–late 15 cent	1	57
VI	Late 15–mid-17 cent	48	50
VII	Mid 17–early 18 cent	102	77
VIII	Early 18–early 19 cent	114	46
IX	Early 19 cent–c 1900	96	77
X	20 cent and unphased	2	49
Total		363	370

The sudden increase in the lace tags and pins in Phase VI was also matched by the patterns seen in the occurrence of tie rings, another class of small dress fitting which is certainly found elsewhere at an earlier date. Indeed, the inflated quantities of copper alloy artefacts seen from Phase VI onwards can be accounted for to a very great extent by the presence of these small fittings, as can be seen from Table 5.10.4. The documentary evidence shows that this part of Bridge Street was known as

'Mercers' Row' from at least the late fifteenth century, although it was not until the eighteenth century that there is firm documentary evidence of the presence of mercers and linen drapers. As these small items are precisely the sort of fittings which could be expected to form part of the stock of mercers, it is very tempting to suggest that they were reflecting their presence from the later fifteenth century onwards.

Table 5.10.4 Small dress fittings: occurrence by phase in comparison with other copper alloy artefacts

| | | | | | | Phase | | | | | |
Function	I	II	III	IV	V	VI	VII	VIII	IX	X	Total
Dress fittings	-	-	-	-	3	70	126	126	112	11	448
Other	13	74	40	42	44	59	70	53	68	53	516
Total	13	74	40	42	47	129	196	179	180	64	964

Iron   Quita Mould

Methodology

Twenty-one boxes of iron objects were recovered from the excavations. The material was scanned by Chester Archaeology and putative nails and other small fragments separated out; the other objects underwent x-radiography followed by selective investigative conservation, carried out by Yannick Minvielle-Debat at the University of Bradford. A jack of plate from Phase VI, Plot 1 is the subject of a separate report by David Starley and Thom Richardson (*below*). A basic record of all the remaining except nails was entered onto an Excel spreadsheet and is part of the site archive.

Introduction

The assemblage principally derived from the late medieval period onward and comprised domestic utensils, other household items and structural ironwork. A small number of objects of Roman, Saxon and Norman date were found, mostly occurring residually in later deposits. Certain functional categories of ironwork which include armour, tools, domestic utensils and household items were of particular relevance to the research agenda and are the focus of the following summary. Small amounts of bar iron, strap, strip and wire occurring across the site from Phase V onward suggested some small-scale ironworking but insufficient was recovered to suggest a focus of this activity, (*see* Tables 5.10.6–.7). The presence of small pieces of broken horseshoe may indicate that scrap iron was being collected but not all was recycled.

Phase I

No ironwork, other than nails, was recovered from deposits of Roman date (Phase I). A small number of iron objects of Roman date were recognised, however, occurring residually in later deposits. A slide key, SF 8297, was found in a spread of occupational debris and building refuse, (560), in Phase VII, Plot 6. Another, larger, example, SF 9259, was found unstratified. These slide keys are of a common Roman key type, (Manning 1985, 93, slide key type 2).

Two conical ferrules, SFs 8391 and 8461, of round section with open sockets are likely to be of Roman date. One, SF 8391, came from (542), the fill of a former bound-ary ditch (555), the other, SF 8461, from fill (620) of a rectangular cut for a telegraph pole stabilizer, (570), both attributed to Phase IX in Plot 6. Similarly, two curved strands of spirally twisted wire, SF 8326, apparently broken from a later Roman bracelet, were found in levelling deposit (418) in the same phase.

A possible medical instrument, SF 8118 (Ill 5.10.7.1), of Roman date was found in demolition rubble (301) in Phase X. The single-piece iron instrument is double-ended with a central handle which appears to have been ridged originally to aid grip. One end is straight, the other has a distinct and well made curve; both of the terminals are broken. The degree of curve differs from the known range of sharp and blunt hooks, however, and identification of the implement as medical is uncertain. While the majority of Roman medical instruments are made entirely or partly of copper alloy, single-piece surgical tools of iron have been found previously in Britain, most notably as part of the medical kit deposited in the mid-first-century burial of a healer at Stanway, Essex, (Jackson 1997). They also formed part of the extensive array of surgical equipment recovered from the Domus 'del chirurgo' at Rimini, Italy, destroyed by fire in the mid-third century (Jackson 2003). If not for medical use, such a tool might have been used for fine modelling in plaster.

Phase II

A small number of iron mail links were found in three deposits of late Roman/Dark Age date, two in Evaluation Trench F, the other at the eastern end of the site. Links were found in Phase IIb fills (126), (1040) of a shallow pit, (127), and a post hole, (1043), respectively. Others were found in a layer, (121), attributed to Phase IIc.

In all, approximately eighty iron chain mail links and link fragments were found during the excavations. The minimum number of individual links represented and their provenance are given in Table 5.10.5. All were retrieved from samples, suggesting that greater numbers were present but could not be detected by eye during excavation. The links occurred in small numbers in deposits dating from the late Roman/Dark Age to the early post-medieval period, (Phases II–VI). Residual Roman pottery was found in all of these contexts and all but one of the samples, (< 5039>). Mail links of copper alloy were found in Roman through to medieval contexts. It is likely, therefore, that the chain mail is of Roman date and derived from a single period of activity, although occurring residually in these later contexts.

Table 5.10.5 Iron chain mail links quantified by phase, plot and context

Phase	Plot	Context	SF no	Sample no	Min no
IIb	F	126	9647	5108	3
IIb		1040	9654	5117	3
IIc	F	121	9646	5107	2
III	Access pit	272	9640	5014	3
III	Access pit	281	9643	5019	1
III	Escalator Pit A	1022	9652	5098	4
IV	Access pit	266	9639	5013	13
IV	Plot 6	1015	9655	5096	9
IV	Plot 6	1030	9910	5114	4
IV	Plot 6	1033	9656	5099	4
IV	Plot 6	1034	9653	5116	2
V	Access pit	261	9638	5010	4
V	Plot 3 Ramp	490	9649	5058	2
VI	Plot 6	566	9700	5039	1
VI	Plot 2 Ramp	671	9651	5071	1

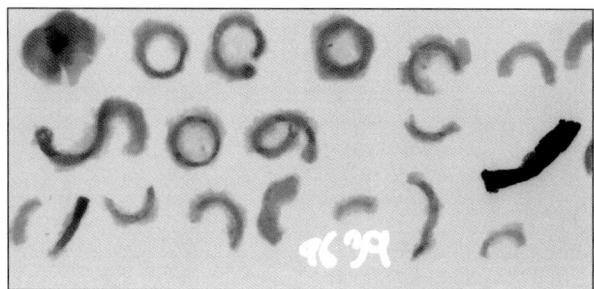

Ill 5.10.6 ?Roman iron mail links SF 9639, showing distortion. (University of Bradford x-radiograph 365). (Scale 1/1)

Plain, annular rings and rings with two ends joined together with a small rivet were present. The individual links of both types are of consistent size and measure 8–9 mm in diameter with a wire thickness of 1–2 mm. None of the links are articulated with others and three of the riveted links, SFs 9639 (Ill 5.10.6) and 9646, are distorted in a way which suggests that they had been reopened and that the mail was in the process of being taken apart. For these reasons one might suggest that the links are more likely to represent the manufacture or refurbishment of mail rather than being the result of the disintegration of a discarded item. However, I am advised by re-enactors that links easily become detached from mail during wear, so that it may be that recovery of individual links simply points to the wearing of mail rather than manufacture or refurbishment of such armour.

Phase III

A horseshoe heel, SF 8240, and a broken hinge strap, SF 8028, were found in late Saxon contexts in Evaluation Trench C. The broken horseshoe, SF 8240, found in pit fill (97) has a right-angle calkin, suggesting that it belonged to Clark's type 2, (1995, 86), and is likely to date to the end of Phase III, although a small number of tenth-century examples are known (Clark 1995, 95–6). Other fragments of horseshoes of Clark's type 2A, with round nail holes within rectangular, countersunk holes and 'wavy' outer edges, dating to the late Saxon and Norman periods (Phase IV *below*) were found occurring residually in later deposits. The plain heel of one example, SF 8547, was found in layer (683) in Phase VI, Plot 6. Another fragment of a Clark type 2A horseshoe, SF 8248, occurred residually in a spread of occupational debris and building refuse, (389), in Phase VII, Plot 6.

A spiked cramp, SF 8649, (Ill 5.10.7.2) a structural fitting used with stonework, was found in layer (1022) in Escalator Pit A. It is comparable to examples found *in situ* in the late fifteenth-century gatehouse at Berry Pomeroy castle, Devon (Mould 1996, fig 73, nos 1–2). A small hinge pivot, SF 9007, probably used on a window shutter or door, was recovered from a cultivation layer, (1131).

Phase IV

A small amount of domestic and structural ironwork was found in Phase IV. One object found in the area of the ramp in medieval cultivation soil, (883), dated to 1250+ was of interest (Ill 5.10.7.3). It comprises a long tapering point with a short socket at the other end; this is distorted and squashed out of shape, so that it is uncertain whether

it is complete or has been cleanly snapped off at this point. A number of possible identifications may be suggested, depending on whether one assumes the object was originally tanged or socketed. The long point may have been inserted as a tang into a wooden handle and the circular head at the other end used to make a hole. Tools of this type include a leatherworker's circular punch, (Manning 1985, 42 and pl 16 E34), and a blacksmith's cold drill. A cold drill, used to make a hole in cold iron, was amongst the Viking-age tools in a wooden chest found at Mästermyr, Gotland in Sweden, (Arwidsson & Berg 1983, 15 and pl 23.52). The examples of the tools cited had integral, solid handles, but there is no reason why wooden-handled examples would not have proved functional. A slight twist was observable above the socket. This may indicate that this end was fractured and that the item is a broken twist bit used to drill holes in wood. Alternatively, the object may have been a projectile with a short, open socket. Such needle-like projectiles were used as armour-piercing arrowheads. David Starley of the Royal Armouries, Leeds is of the opinion that the object is too large to be an arrowhead, although it should be noted that some examples of the larger military forms, (Jessop 1996, 198–9, types M7 and M8), are of a similar size.

A small amount of ironwork dating to the Norman period occurred residually in later deposits. In addition to the two fragments of horseshoe of Clark's type 2, (1995, 86), discussed above, a box binding, SF 8522 (Ill 5.10.7.4), of plano-convex section with a flat, circular terminal was found in a Phase VI layer, (835), in Plot 6. A fragment of another of flat section was found in another layer, (671), of the same phase in Plot 2. Each was plated with a white metal, likely to be of tin (not analysed). These bindings, used to decorate boxes or caskets, are commonly found at castles and manors and other sites of higher status. A possible textile-processing spike, SF 8274, potentially of pre-Conquest or Norman date, was found in a Phase VI layer, (776), in Plot 2. A whittle tang knife, SF 8462 (Ill 5.10.7.5), likely to date to the late Saxon or Norman period, was found residually in (620), the fill of a pit for a telegraph pole stabiliser in Plot 6, along with a conical ferrule, SF 8461, of Roman date. A small U-shaped bolt from a padlock, SF 8126, of a type in use during both the Roman and medieval periods, was found in (325), the fill of a tree bole pit, in Phase IX.

Phase V

Amongst the small group of structural and miscellaneous ironwork recovered from late medieval deposits were two household items. A ward plate, SF 9192, from a lock was found in fill (1217) of pit (1290) in Plot 3. A small, broken wall hook, SF 8841, tile pin or tenterhook was found in cultivation soil (830) in Plot 6. A second, complete, example, SF 8257 (Ill 5.10.7.6), was found in a Phase IX levelling deposit, (601). The use of these small hooks as tenterhooks, also to fix clay roof tiles and hang tapestries, was discussed by Goodall (in Biddle 1990, 235). Their occurrence still in place around a room in Nunney castle, near Frome, has shown that they were certainly used to hang textiles (Tony Harcourt *pers comm*). Two small, annular buckles, SFs 9637 and 9644, of a type commonly found on shoes of late fourteenth- and fifteenth-century date, were found in samples taken from deposits (217) and (352), dated to the late eighteenth to late nineteenth century (Phase IX).

Phase VI

Plot 1

A hinge pivot, SF 8650, was found in cultivation soil (766) in Plot 1 and the tooth from a rake, SF 8630, was found in a rubble deposit, (885), below (766) but possibly deriving from it. A jack of plate, SF 8001, came from context (246) and is reported on separately below.

Plot 2

A group of ironwork recovered from the fills of cess pit (487) in Plot 2 comprised domestic items, principally the remains of a plate stock lock, SFs 8508 and 8509, nailed bindings and a broken scale tang handle from a knife, SF 8573. A fragment of lock plate, SF 8508, was found in the bottom fill, (806), with organic remains preserved on one face, possibly textile with straw above. The scale tang handle, SF 8573, was bound with ten twists of cord/string (organic material not identified) at the junction of the blade and handle to aid grip or possibly as a repair. A sixteenth-century table knife, SF 8695 (Ill 5.10.7.7), with a plain end cap and a round-sectioned bolster was found in fill (779) of oven (778) above the cess pit. The knife has a wooden handle of two semicircular scales secured by three tubular rivets. A long, pointed shank, SF 8274, from layer (776), also above the oven, may have been a textile-processing spike, and if so, residual in this context.

Plot 3

A small hinge pivot, SF 9062, and a fragment of horseshoe, SF 9033, were found in pit- and ditch fills (1197/1106) and (1289) respectively, at the eastern end of Plot 3. A simple candleholder, SF 8449, (Ill 5.10.7.8) comprising a socketed spike bent at a right angle was found with other domestic waste in (467), the fill of a pit, (468).

Plot 4

Three iron items were found in the fills of cess pit (1624) in Plot 4. A 'leaf' from a wool-card or hand carder, SF 9408, was found in the bottom fill, (1697), believed to date to the mid-sixteenth century, while a pair of scissors, SF 9301 (Ill 5.10.7.9), and the remains of a tanged table knife or fork with a round-sectioned, ivory handle, SF 9305, were found in the top fill, (1600). Wool-cards were used in wool processing to align the wool fibres ready for spinning into yarn and indicate the processing of short staple wools into a soft woollen cloth (Walton Rogers 1997, 1721). The fragments comprise rows of fine wire hooks in a sheet of minerally preserved leather *c* 2 mm thick. Two edges of the leaf are preserved and indicate an original measurement in excess of 166 x 110 mm. This appears slightly larger than an example recovered from Meols, Wirral (Mould 2007, 239, pl 54 and 240, no 3278), and is possibly more comparable with one from a deposit dating to the end of the fourteenth to the fifteenth centu-

ry excavated at Saint-Denis (Seine Saint-Denis) in France (Montembault 1999, 4–6). The leather leaves from wool-cards are occasionally found in waterlogged deposits; more rarely the iron hooks and minerally preserved leather from the leaf are recovered, as occurred here. The Meols wool-card is of calfskin with hooks of bent wire, each 3 mm in length arranged in rows four per 10 mm. Such details are obscured by encrustation on the Bridge Street example. A small number of wool-cards of late fourteenth- and fifteenth-century date have been found in this country and abroad; similarly examples from early post-medieval deposits, contemporary with SF 9408, have also been found. These include fragments from Abbey Wharf, Reading, (late fourteenth to sixteenth century: Mould 1997, 118, fig 66, no 33); Newcastle upon Tyne, (sixteenth century: Vaughan 1981, fig 43, no 526); and Metz (Moselle) (end of the fifteenth to early sixteenth century: Montembault 1996, 153–64). A fragment of nailed binding, SF 9483, was found in (1543), the upper fill of a pit at the western end of Plot 4.

Plot 6

A small group of ironwork, including fragments from four horseshoes and household fittings, was found in Plot 6 in layers and pit fills. At least one of the horseshoe fragments, SF 8547, was residual in the layer, (683), in which it was found. A split-spiked loop, also known as a looped staple, SF 8206, was found in layer (625), associated with the formal knot garden.

Contemporary items were also found occurring residually in later deposits. A small annular shoe buckle, SF 9637, of a type used on shoes of late fourteenth- and fifteenth-century date, was found in sample <5003> from context (217) in Phase IX. A fragment of a table knife, SF 9004, with an oval-sectioned bolster dating to Phase VI was found in Phase X context (1399).

Phase VII

Plot 1

A tool, possibly for woodworking, and two blade fragments were found in cultivation soil, (237/663). The tool, SF 8096, has a tang for insertion into an organic handle, probably of wood, and a stop ridge to prevent the handle from being driven too far down the stem towards the blade. Details of the blade have been lost because of corrosion but the section suggests that of a gouge. A fragment of narrow blade from a table knife, SF 8549, and another from a larger blade, SF 8273, such as a boning knife, were found in the same deposit, (663).

Plot 2

A broken table knife with a wooden handle, SF 8247, and a fragment of strap or possibly a large blade, SF 8272, were found in fills (463) and (464) of cess pit (465). A leatherworker's awl, SF 8284, was recovered from layer (499), while the scale tang from a knife, SF 8481, and a small trowel, SF 8481, were found in a dump of domestic material, (481). A strap fragment which may have been the arm broken from an H-shaped pinned hinge was found in layer (1304) at the eastern end of the plot.

Plot 3

The hasp loop from a box fitting, SF 8983, and a broken horseshoe were found in layer (1111) at the eastern end of the plot. A large pair of scissors with long, pointed blades was found in fill (1193) of rubbish pit (1192) also at the eastern end of the plot.

Plot 4

A large hinge pivot from a door or gate, SF 9082, came from fill (1559) of a stone-lined cess pit, (1494), at the eastern end of the plot. Fragments of strap were present in (1516), the primary fill of pit (1560) in the same area. Three broken knives, SFs 9224, 9310 and 9405 (Ill 5.10.7.10), were found in fills (1601) and (1607) of rubbish pit (1696) at the western end of the plot. The best preserved example, SF 9405, has a scale tang handle with four tubular rivets, and a separate end cap and stop ridge. A heterogeneous dump of rubbish including heavily encrusted ironwork, pottery, a clay pipe bowl, wine bottle glass, roof tile, coal and cinder was found corroded together and said to be within a large, broken pot in an eighteenth-century pit fill, (1601). The iron appears to be fragments of sheet, a wide strap and two bars, one projecting at right angle to the other. No diagnostic features are preserved, but the suggestion of a V-shaped section visible in one area could suggest a fragmentary spadeshoe or more likely that the sheet was folded scrap. The encrustation was cindery and slag-like.

Plot 6

A Roman slide key, SF 829, and a fragment broken from a Norman horseshoe, SF 8248, were found occurring residually in a spread of occupational debris and building refuse, (389), (560).

Phase VIII

Plot 1

A broken lock plate, SF 9482, and a thin sheet fragment, SF 9375, were found in (1871), the fill of a brick fireplace, (1812). A second lock plate, SF 9335, was found in (1885), the fill of rubbish pit (1886). Part of a lock mechanism, SF 9311, also came from (1908), the fill of context (1909). A broken table knife, SF 8025, with a rectangular-sectioned bolster was found in (218), the upper fill of pit (219) and was likely to be residual.

Plot 2

A scale tang handle from a knife, SF 9222, came from (1305), the fill of post hole (1306) at the eastern end of the plot. Nailed bindings were found in (1636), the fill of pit (1642). A length of bar, SF 9052, and six pieces of strap, SF 9013, one with a nailed terminal, likely to be a broken hoop from a barrel, were found in a levelling or demolition deposit, (1421). A hinge pivot, SF 8986, and a small, square plate, SF 8985, were found in levelling (1417) for a paved floor.

Plot 3

The heel of a horseshoe, SF 9380, was found in layer (1637), and a bar, SF 9260, was found in (1437), a lower fill of pit (1438) at the western end of the plot. The head of a flat, circular button, SF 8972, with a central hole for a separate shank, was found in a sooty layer at the bottom of a fireplace, (1407). Preserved fibres present suggest that a garment had been burnt in the fireplace. A fragment broken from a slotted drain cover, SF 9490, was found in fill (1701) of pit (1703). A small hinge pivot, SF 8952, occurred in fill (1406) of rubbish pit (1413).

Plot 4

A fragment of nailed binding, SF 9026, and a knife with organic remains of the round-sectioned handle preserved were found in layer (455) at the western end of Plot 4.

Plot 6

The branch of a horseshoe with a feathered heel, SF 8373, a small cleat, SF 8182, strip fragments and bar, SF 8178, were found in layer (341). A nailed binding, SF 8515, came from a possible occupation layer, (698), and a piece of thick wire came from a planting hole, (696).

Phase IX

A range of domestic and structural ironwork was found in Phase IX contexts. The larger groups and items reflecting the day-to-day lives of the occupants are described briefly below. Items of earlier date occurring residually have been mentioned above.

Plot 1

A small group of ironwork was recovered from (208), the fill of fireplace (209). This includes a broken and burnt strap handle from a suspended vessel, probably a cauldron or bucket, SF 8022, and a fragment of strap, SF 8023, on which an area of stocking stitch knitted textile is preserved. Fragments of cast iron guttering, SFs 8399 and 8402, were found associated with the west wall of the existing department store, (582).

Plot 2

A fragment of sheet metal vessel with a rolled rim, probably a bucket, SF 8872, and the edge of a hobnailed shoe sole, SF 9014, were found in a layer of nineteenth-century rubbish from Davies and Shepheard's chemist's shop, (1096). A small group of ironwork was recovered from a levelling layer, (418), within structures (421) and (412), amongst which was a broken scale tang knife with a wooden handle, SF 8325. The toe of a boot iron, SF 8842, was found in (1093), the fill of a brick chute, (1086), at the eastern end of the plot. Fragments broken from a stove pipe, SF 8955, were found in layer (1201).

Plot 4

A group of domestic ironwork was found in (1491), the upper backfill of a brick-lined well, (1488). This includ-

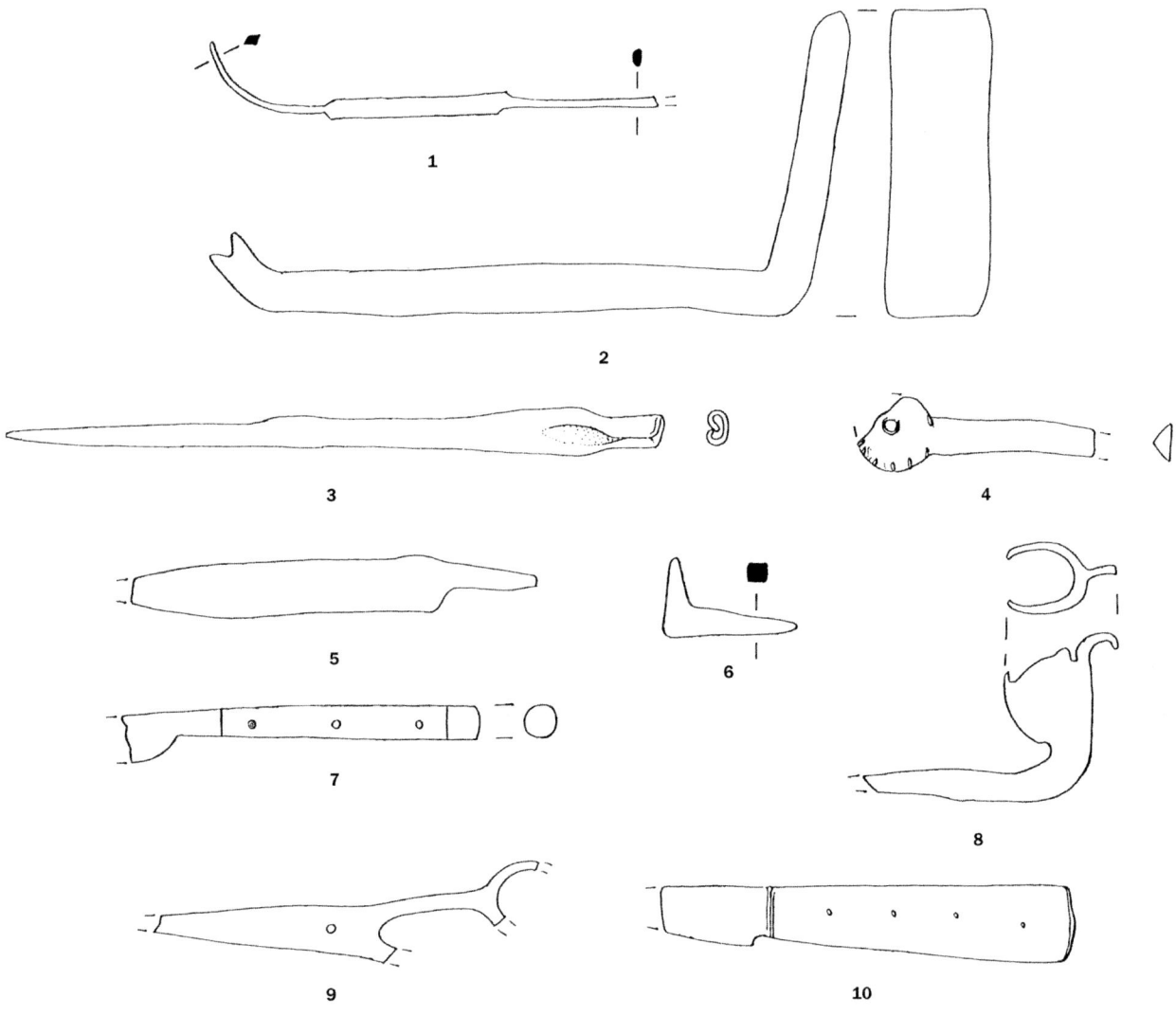

III 5.10.7 Iron objects. (Scale 1/2; drawn from x-radiograph)

ed a lock, the handle from a utensil such as skimmer or fire shovel, a socketed candleholder and the seam from a sheet metal vessel, possibly the join of side wall and base of a galvanised watering can, (SF 9156A–D respectively).

Plot 6

A bucket handle, SF 8115, was found in (340), the fill of a sewer/drainpipe, (355). A large drop hinge for a door, SF 8305, was found in (401), the backfill associated with a sandstone wall, (306), while a large H-shaped pin hinge for a cupboard door, SF 8566, was found in (395), the fill of the foundation cut for the western wall of the department store.

Phase X

A similar assemblage of ironwork was recovered from Phase X contexts, the largest group coming from demolition rubble (301) in Plot 6. The majority of the ironwork comprised structural fittings. Cast iron gutter fragments were found in Plot 6, (301), (302), and a gutter stop end, SF 9017, in context (1404) in Plot 3. Gutter hooks to hold them in place were found in Plot 3, SF 8690, context

(780); Plot 4, context (1274); and Plot 6, SF 8158, context, (334). A fragment of black-painted drainpipe, SF 8186, was found in context (322) in Plot 6, while a drain cover, SF 8191, was found in context (402) in Plot 2. Iron pipe with a 1/2 inch bore was found in Plot 6 and a strap with a porcelain electrical insulator, SF 8271, in context (403) in Plot 2. Wall anchors were found in Plot 1 (200), Plot 3 (1399), (1404), (1412), and Plot 4, (1283).

Household implements included a broken pair of scissors, SF 8093, from context (200) in Plot 1, the scale tang from a table fork, SF 9079A, from context (1414) in Plot 3, and a table knife, SF 8912, from layer (454) in Plot 4. A broken loop hinge, SF 9718, from a large box was found in context (80) in Plot 6.

Two tools were recovered. A straight-sided file, SF 9016A, with single cut teeth at an angle of 60 degrees, (*c* 12/1 cm, 28/1 in), was found in (1404), the fill of (1403), and a broken claw hammer or nail-puller, SF 8919, from (1410), both in Plot 3. A possible wire tooth, SF 9197A, from a long comb or rake-like implement was found in demolition rubble, (1802), in Plot 1.

A sexfoil mount, SF 8154, either a decorative feature on a box binding or a handle escutcheon, was found with nailed bindings, SFs 8153 and 8187 in (400), the fill of pit (399).

Table 5.10.6 Bar iron: occurrence by phase, plot and context

Phase	Plot	Context	SF no
V	1	1004	8917
V	4	1583	9404
V	3	1654	8205
VII	4	1601	-
VIII	6	341	8178, 8180
VIII	2	488	8277
VIII	2	1421	9052
VIII	3	1437	9260
IX	1	208	8036
IX	6	367	8352
IX	4	1491	9157A
X	3	1414	9077

Table 5.10.7 Iron wire: occurrence by phase, plot and context

Phase	Plot	Context	SF no
V	3	1319	8951
VI	6	532	8199
VI	6	565	8459
VII	1	670	8629
VIII	6	696	8666
IX	6	346	8189
IX	4	1491	9015
X	1	1802	9197B

Acknowledgements

I am most grateful to Ralph Jackson, (Department of Prehistory and Europe, British Museum), for his invaluable comments on the possible Roman medical instrument and information on comparanda and to Yannick Minvielle-Debat, (University of Bradford), for supplying photographs of the instrument.

Jack of plate
Thom Richardson and David Starley

Description

The remains of a type of body armour known as a jack of plates (SF 8001) came from Phase VI context (246) in Plot 1. The finds comprise forty concreted masses ranging from 350 mm in length down to about 40 mm. All are covered in a thick layer of ferrous corrosion but the overlapping structure of the plates was visible where some of the concretions had fractured. Detailed examination was carried out with heavy reliance on x-radiographs. To aid identification each fragment was assigned a code letter from A to Z and AA to AN

The jack of plate was a, or perhaps the, characteristic English body defence of the middle and later years of the sixteenth century. It was developed from the earlier quilted jack which had provided the mainstay of armour for the English infantry in the fifteenth century (Richardson 1998; Eaves 1989). Made in the form of a doublet, jacks of plate were composed of small square iron plates usually ranging between 20 and 40 mm square. These were secured through a hole in the centre of each plate by strong linen cord and were sandwiched between two layers of coarse canvas with an outer layer of fine linen. The finished armour characteristically showed the net or trellis pattern of cords on a 20–30 mm grid on the outside of the garment. They are amongst the least well researched forms of armour, due largely to the very small numbers which have survived compared to other forms. Their representation in collections is limited partly because of their construction, which relied heavily on easily degraded organic materials, but also because of their lowly status, which would have made them unattractive as display

items. In addition, it is likely that many excavated examples of jacks have simply not been identified as such. Archaeological finds such as the present one are therefore extremely important to our understanding of this once common, but now rare type of armour.

With relatively little understanding of the construction of jacks of plate, the Chester find led to a programme of re-examination of the largest surviving group, at the Royal Armouries, where

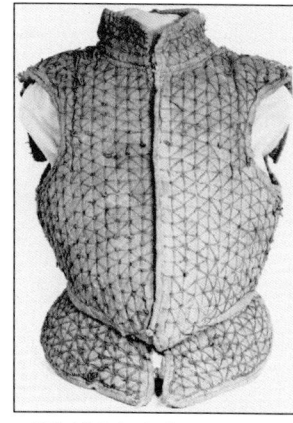

Ill 5.10.8 Jack of plate c 1580 in the Collection of the Royal Armouries.
© Board of Trustees of the Armouries

there are eight complete or near complete examples. The published details of a handful of archaeological finds from Camber (Biddle *et al* 2002), Beeston (Eaves 1989) and Pontefract castle (Roberts 2002) were also re-examined.

Construction

Initial examination of the fragments indicated that, although the jack had to some extent been broken up or fallen apart prior to deposition, some large sections of plates were still firmly held in their original positions until concreted by corrosion products after burial. The cord holding the plates in place and probably much of the textile was still in place at the time of disposal. Unfortunately, none of this organic material appeared to have been recognisably preserved by mineralisation. The materials used can only be suggested from other surviving examples, in which both cloth and cord (the use of crossbow strings is recorded) were of linen. Measurement of the dimensions of all fragments gave a maximum area of 0.36 m² about a third of what would be expected from a whole jack.

With only a few cleaned plates to work on, the size of the plates was calculated using reconstructions of the armour based on the x-radiograph images. This allowed figures from a sample of sixty-nine plates. The plates ranged in size from 34 to 56 mm with a mean of 46 mm and a standard deviation of 5 mm. This was significantly larger than any jack previously examined. It was also clear that the plates had been carefully cut and pierced in comparison with other jacks, at least suggesting a reasonably high standard of production for a garment which was often made with no attention to quality. As with the majority of jacks, but not all, the corners of the plates had been cropped. This is assumed to have helped to protect the cord ties from the sharp edges of the plates.

Examination of the x-radiographs showed a typical chequerboard pattern with brighter squares where the corners of four plates overlapped. Prior to the comparative study it had been widely believed that jack plates were sewn together in staggered rows in such a way that no more than three plates ever overlapped. However, the regular grid has now been shown to have been the norm for the main panels (ie back and front) of the jack. Where the garment needed to be 'tailored' this could be achieved

Table 5.10.8 Jack of plate: summary of fragments

Fragment (RA code)	Wt (g)	Dimensions (cm)	x -ray no	Joins	Notes
A	1983	26 x 15 & 2 x 15	346 (2) 345(2)	S	Two sections concreted together; possible tassets (skirt)
B	1123	23 x 22	338 (4)	C	Large section of 32 plates; front or back of body of armour. See x-radiographic interpretation
C	500	15 x 13	339 (3) 341(3)	B	Continuation of B, above. Further 15 plates
D	95	9.0 x 5.5	338 (3)	E, F	Multiple plates, regular grid, from body
E	308	15.5 x 9.0	338 (3)	D, F	Continuation of D
F	43	8.0 x 4.5	338 (3)	D, E	Continuation of D and E
G	1314	34.5 x 16.5	338 (1) 346 (1) 345 (1)		Large section of at least 31 plates; irregular grid suggests edge or tassets. See x-radiographic interpretation
H	8.1	4.5 x 4.1	344 (4)		Single plate, cleaned; th 1.5 mm
I	124	8.2 x 7.7	342 (4)		Multiple plates
J	237	14.1 x 8.2	339 (1) 341 (1)		Multiple plates; thickness suggests two layers
K	79	12.5 x 4.2	347		Multiple plates
L	385	13.1 x 9.8	342 (1) 344 (13)		Multiple plates
M	229	17.0 x 7.7	340 (2)		Multiple plates
N	96	9.8 x 5.1	342 (3)		Multiple plates
O	431	15.7 x 9.3	340 (1)		Multiple plates
P	114	8.3 x 5.1	339 (2) 341 (2)		Two plates with much concretion
Q	54	7.1 x 4.3	340 (3)		Two plates
R	58	5.6 x 5.4	340 (4)		Single plate
S	181	14.2 x 7.3	338 (3)	A	Multiple plates
T	28	6.3 x 4.4	343 (13)		One whole and parts of further plate
U	35	5.2 x 5.0	343 (9)		Single plate
V	40	6.5 x 4.6	343 (7)		Two plates
W	39	5.5 x 3.6	343 (2)		Not a jack plate
x	36	5.3 x 4.7	343 (12)		One whole and parts of further plate
Y	37	4.9 x 4.8	343 (11)		One whole and parts of further plate
Z	34	5.3 x 5.3	343 (6)		Single plate
AA	38	6.4 x 3.6	343 (3)		One whole and parts of further plate
AB	22	4.4 x 3.7	343 (4)		Single plate
AC	24	5.0 x 3.9	343 (10)		Not a jack plate
AD	63	6.7 x 5.3	343 (8)		Two overlapping plates
AE	56	7.0 x 4.8	343 (1)		Two overlapping plates
AF	21	4.7 x 3.9	343 (5)		Single plate
AG	23	4.6 x 4.3	344 (7)		Single plate
AH	17	4.2 x 4.2	344 (6)		Single plate
AI	17	5.6 x 3.0	344 (3)		Half of single plate
AJ	19	4.7 x 4.1	344 (8)		Most of single plate
AK	30	6.1 x 4.3	344 (2)		Two overlapping plates
AL	26	4.5 x 4.1	344 (5)		Single plate
AM	16	4.2 x 4.1	344 (9, 10, 11)		Single plate; now 3 fragments
AN	18	4.6 x 3.6	344 (1)		Single plate
Total	8001 g	3620 cm² 0.36 m²			Total 40 pieces including about 200 plates

either by a less regular pattern, increasing or decreasing the number of plates in adjacent rows, or by selective use of larger or smaller plates to distort the grid. Using this information it was possible to say that certain uniform pieces such as B, C, D, E and F were likely to have been central panels from the front or back of the body of the jack, whilst A and G with less regular grids were likely to be from parts of the jack which required more shaping, such as the area beneath the arms or the tassets (skirts) which hung from the main body of the jack. Most surviving jacks are sleeveless, but contemporary documents do refer to the wearing of (detachable) sleeves (Eaves 1989). A pair of surviving sleeves in the Royal Armouries show that their plates could be of very different form: thin, narrow but elongated. It therefore seems unlikely that the present find includes the remains of sleeves.

Where a few plates had been cleaned it was possible to see the direction in which each plate overlapped its neighbour and which row overlapped the next row. It was hoped this would help determine where in the jack the section was originally situated or whether an exposed surface was the interior or exterior to the armour. Unfortunately, reference to complete jacks showed that in most cases plates overlapped within rows away from the centre and the rows overlapped upwards (Royal Armouries III.44, .45, .46). In others, the plates overlapped in other ways such as III.1045, where the plates overlapped upwards within the column and the columns overlap away from

the centre. Thus there was no standard pattern of construction and it was not possible to be more precise in determining which parts of the Chester jack were present.

Many jack plates are known to have been made from recycled metal. A common source was old plates from earlier armours known as brigandines, as found in the Beeston jack (Eaves 1989) and also in Royal Armouries III.44, .45 and .1045. Evidence for this is usually evident as a distinctive pattern of rivet holes, although an occasional oblique angle on an otherwise square plate and/or tinning of the surface may also be recognised. Neither of the first two features were recognised on the present jack, though the advanced state of corrosion may have hidden some. A scattering of non-ferrous flecks was visible on the x-radiographs, but none were convincing as a surface coating.

The plates responded weakly to a magnet, indicating that little unmineralised metal remained. Metallographic examination to determine the nature and working of the ferrous alloy used was therefore not pursued. Only limited previous research on jack plates can be used to suggest the materials that might have been used. A single plate from one Royal Armouries jack was examined by metallography and microprobe analysis by Starley (1992, 247). This was found to be reasonably sound metal, with some carburisation of the outer surfaces and a modest increase in hardness (Hv 237, 241, 249) due to the presence of 0.1% phosphorus. Two plates from the Pontefract

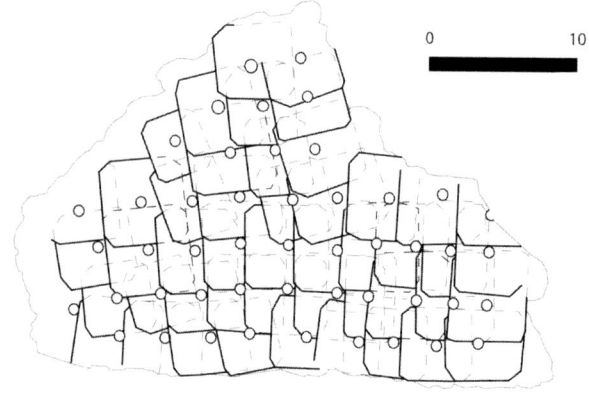

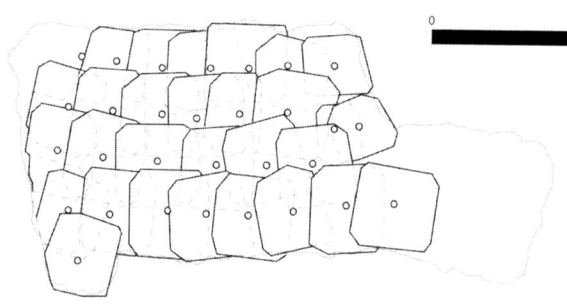

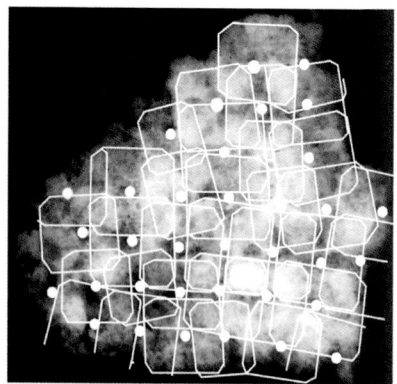

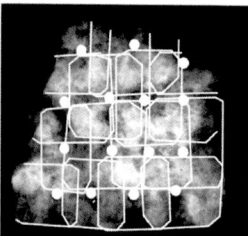

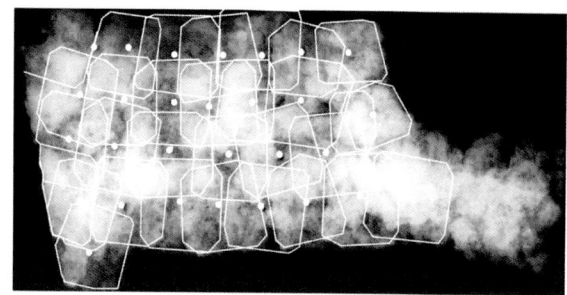

Ill 5.10.10 (*bottom to top*) Jack of plate fragment G: photograph; x-radiograph; reconstruction (irregular grid from shaped part, such as tassets). (Scale approx 1/5)

Ill 5.10.9 (*bottom to top*) Jack of plate fragments B and C: photograph; x-radiograph; reconstruction (regular grid from body of armour). (Scale approx 1/5)

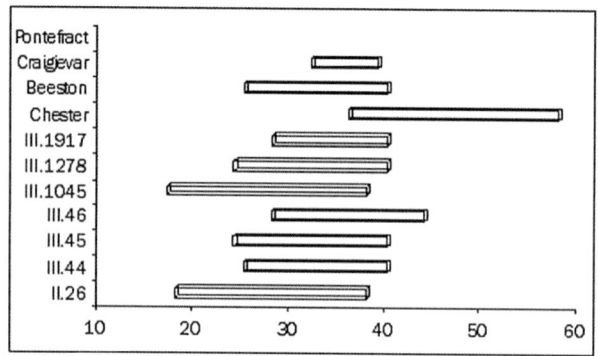

Ill 5.10.11 Plate sizes: comparison of the Chester and other jacks of plate.

find were also examined (Maclean & Starley 2002, 355–9). These were both heavily corroded and the results relied on interpretation of relict structures. The first plate was a low slag, ferritic iron and the second appeared to be a piled composite of ferritic and phosphoric iron. No evidence of steel was found. Taken together it would seem that jacks made use of a variety of iron, phosphoric iron or low grade steel: there was certainly no evidence of the high-quality steels found to have been used at this date for high-status armour (Williams 2003).

Dating

Although jacks of plate were made for a relatively short period of time – the second half of the sixteenth century – no manufacturing differences are known which would help narrow this window. Only when the whole garment survives in good condition can it be dated by the style of the tailoring, because the armour closely followed civilian fashion. During this period the cut of men's doublets changed considerably, from a deep-bellied form to a high-waisted form with a deep point or peascod at the centre. The question remains as to how long a jack of plates might ordinarily have survived in a usable condition. Is it likely that in 1617, when a jack is recorded in the inventory of Robert Fletcher (Backhouse, *this volume*), this armour was regarded as more than an outdated curiosity? Perhaps the most surprising fact about the archaeological finds of jacks is the late date of their archaeological contexts. Those from Pontefract castle came from a Civil War counter-mine shaft. The Beeston jack appears to have been disposed of well into the seventeenth century and the Camber plates were in a fill dated to the early seventeenth century. As described by Eaves (1989), jacks in use as late as the Civil War would have been old-fashioned to the point of inviting ridicule and probably in highly parlous condition. Although jacks were stored in the Tower of London during the seventeenth century, as is known from those which survived there until modern times, there is no evidence of their use at that time. By the seventeenth century it might be considered that with improvements in the efficiency, power and abundance of firearms, the small plates of these armours may have compounded any injuries rather than protecting the wearer.

Significance

In one respect the Bridge Street jack is very unusual. This is its civilian archaeological context and, if we can assume the inventory listing does indeed refer to this item, its documentary confirmation. The other English finds are from clear military contexts and it is believed that the Royal Armouries own examples are largely the residue of large government orders for such armours, which were within the Tower of London. Similarly, armour sent to the American settlements, where jacks have also been found, clearly included obsolete armour from the royal arsenals (Peterson 1956, 140). We may therefore have been examining one jack whose origin is different from the centralised (?London) products, and features such as the large plate size may reflect this. However, until more evidence from excavations becomes available, this must be speculative.

Nails and other objects   Peter Carrington

The excavation produced a large number of iron nails, small indeterminate lumps and fragments of sheet. Resources did not allow this material to be x-rayed to permit precise identification. The following table summarises the quantities and lists stratigraphic concentrations (five or more items per context).

Table 5.10.9 Iron nails and indeterminate objects quantified by phase and selected contexts

Selected context(-s)	Plot	Description	No items

Phase I
This phase produced a total of twenty-six items from seventeen contexts

Phase II
This phase produced a total of 131 items from twenty-nine contexts

(98)	N/A	Deposit over floor (99) of Building II(i)	7
(121)	N/A		12
(1138)	N/A	Fill of pit (1139)	19
(1161)	N/A	Cultivation soil	17
(1177)	N/A	Cultivation soil	14
(1220)	N/A	Secondary silting of N–S sewer	9
(1225)	N/A	Abandonment layer over Roman road surface (1226)	11

Phase III
This phase produced a total of fifty-six items from fourteen contexts

(1022)	N/A		26
(272)	N/A	Fill of pit (277)	5
(278)	N/A	Clayey silt layer	6

Phase IV
This phase produced a total of seventy-nine from twenty-five contexts

(266)	1	Cultivation soil	7
(1030)	6	Fill of pit (128)/(1029)	15
(1033)	6	Fill of pit (1031)	9

Phase V
This phase produced a total of 163 items from sixty-three contexts

(1012)	1	Wall of Building V(i)	8
(879)	2	Upcast from culvert (884)	9
(1117)	3	Fill of pit (1118)	8
(1293)	3	Cultivation soil	13
(1319)	3		5
(1579)/(1582)/(1583)	4	Fill of oven (1568)	7
(830)	6	Cultivation soil	6
(836)	6		12

Phase VI
This phase produced a total of 257 items from ninety-three contexts

(766)	1		12
(671)	2		6
(776)/(777)/(778)	2	Fills of oven (783) over cess pit (487)	7
(785)/(786)/791)/ (797)/(798)/(806)	2	Fill of cess pit (487)	47
(1635)	2	Fill of pit (1653)	6
(467)	3	Fill of pit (468)	30
(1215)	3	Fill of ditch (1289)	5
(1302)	3		8
(1697)	4	Fill of pit (1619)	5
(532)	6	Surface of timber building	6
(566)	6	Fill of pit (614)	14
(692)	6	Cultivation soil?	6

Phase VII
This phase produced a total of 201 items from sixty-seven contexts

(237)	1		6
(245)	1	Fill of pit (244)	6
(663)	1		25
(463)/(464)/ (472)	2	Fill of cess pit (465)	50
(481)	2		9
(1304)	2		9
(1629)/(1630)/(1631)/ (1634)	2	Fill of pit (1730)	13
(1509)/(1516)	4	Fill of pit (1560)	5
(1599)/(1601)/(1604)/ (1607)/(1695)	4	Fill of pit (1696)	12
(1796)	4	Lining of pit (1807)	2
(824)	6	Fill of pit (925)	5

Phase VIII
This phase produced a total of 175 items from fifty contexts

(1417)	2	Floor make-up for Building VIII(v)	12
(1421)	2	Floor make-up for Building VIII(v)	21
(1439)	2	Levelling deposit	7
(1636)	2	Fill of pit (1642)	12
(1405)	3	Building debris	5
(1406)	3	Fill of pit (1413)	5
(1448)/(1449)	3	Fill of pit (1450)	5
(341)	6	Cultivation soil	19
(520)/(559)	6	Fill of pit (519)	25
(698)	6		5

Phase IX
This phase produced a total of 277 items from seventy-five contexts

(201)	1	Layer over path (1186)	9
(208)	1	Fill of ash pit in Building VIII(i)	76
(217)	1	Soil in Building 8(i)	10
(601)	1	Make-up for floor (216) of Building VIII(i)	5
(418)	2	Building debris	11
(1093)	2	Fill of chute (1086) to cellar	7
(793)	3	Fill of pit (795)	8
(1491)	4	Construction trench of well (1488)	10
(1527)	4	Fill of cess pit (1359)/(1526)	5
(344)	5	Fill of soakaway (369)	5
(352)	6	Fill of root bole pit (336)	9
(353)	6	Fill of cat burial (3540)	9
(375)	6	Fill of dog burial (376)	16
(629)	6	Fill of pit (628)	7

Phase X
This phase produced a total of 127 items from forty-six contexts

Lead

Peter Carrington,
with a note on the cloth seals by Geoff Egan

Introduction

243 fragments of lead were recovered; of these eighty came from samples sieved on site. Most were small pieces of sheet, often offcuts in the form of strips. Finished objects included: lengths of drain lining; fragments of window came; shot?; cloth seals; a net-sinker?; a plumb bob?; weights; printer's equipment; wheels from a toy.

Phase I

1   Drain lining: U-shaped section: six fragments, total size 1000 mm x 180 mm x 70 mm x 2 mm; dished section: three fragments, *c* 590 x 340 x 2 mm. (1389): Phase Ic.
2   Plano-convex disc with hole in middle; diam 60 mm; H 17 mm; diam hole *c* 20 mm. (1243): Phase Ib; SF 9153.

Phase I also produced twenty-nine fragments of sheet, strip, lump and casting waste. A possible Roman weight was also found in a Phase X deposit (no 31).

Phase II

Phase II produced thirty-three fragments of sheet, strip, lump and casting waste.

Phase III

3   Sheet bent into flattened cylinder: net-sinker? 35 x 15 x 8 mm. (106); SF 9587.

Otherwise this phase produced only thirteen fragments of sheet, strip, lump and casting waste.

Phase IV

This phase produced twenty fragments of sheet, strip, lump and casting waste.

Phase V

4   Plano-convex disc with pattern of raised lines in the middle of the convex side; diam 65 mm, th 10 mm. (57): Plot 6; SF 9569.

The spoked wheel of a lead toy was recorded as being associated with (1069), the southern boundary wall of Plot 5. It was clearly intrusive in this phase and is described below with another example found in Phase VIII. Otherwise the phase produced only seventeen fragments of sheet, strip, lump and casting waste.

Phase VI

5   Circular section rod, curved and pointed at one end; L *c* 58 mm; diam 5 mm. (1288): Plot 3; SF 8815.
6   T-section strip, crudely cast; L 95 mm, max W arms 12 mm, depth flange *c* 20 mm. (956): Plot 6; SF 8692. *Cf* no 9 below.
7   Rectangular-section rod; two sections, with one end flattened and pierced by a hole; the other end tapers to a point; L 110 mm, diam 9 mm. Plumb bob? (692): Plot 6; SF 8521.
8   Circular-section rod; L 65 mm, diam 5 mm. (486): Plot 6; SF 8633.

Otherwise the phase produced twelve fragments of sheet, strip, lump and casting waste.

Phase VII

9   T-section strip, crudely cast; L 78 mm, max W arms 9 mm, max depth flange 20 mm, th arms *c* 3 mm. (237): Plot 1; SF 8018.
10 Ball; diam *c* 19 mm: gun shot? (237): Plot 1; SF 8013.
11 Window came; squashed; L 30 mm. (1601): Plot 4; SF 9316. Knight 1985, types A–D ('medieval').

Otherwise the phase produced eleven fragments of sheet, strip, lump and casting waste.

Phase VIII

12 Window came; two fragments, squashed; L 45 and 35 mm. (1687): Plot 3; SF 9491. Knight 1985, type E: late 16 century or later.
13 Spoked wheel from toy; seven spokes preserved; diam 76 mm. (1408): Plot 3; SF 9012. Three-dimensional cast toys did not become common until the 19 century (H Crowdy, Grosvenor Museum, *pers comm*). An identical wheel, but with only four spokes preserved, (SF 9011), was found associated with (1069), the southern boundary wall of Plot 5 in Phase V, where it was clearly intrusive or was wrongly recorded. A number of toy shops are recorded in Bridge Street Row in the nineteenth century (Backhouse, *this volume*).
14 Cast oval; *c* 65 x 50 mm, th 10 mm. (341): Plot 6; SF 8175.

The phase also produced fourteen fragments of sheet, strip, lump and casting waste.

Phase IX

15 Window came; eleven fragments, of which four are junctions, one with a fragment of clear glass; total L *c* 440 mm, H 9 mm. (208): Plot 1; SF 8016. Knight 1985, type G: 18–19 century.
16 Window came; flattened: L 55 mm, H 12 mm. (601): Plot 1; SF 8431. Knight 1985, type G: 18–19 century.
17 Ball; diam *c* 15 mm; gun shot? (217): Plot 1; <5003>.
18 Disc; diam 13 mm, th 2 mm, wt 2 g. (1816): Plot 1; SF 9393. Weight?
19 Pipe; oval section; L 30 mm; section 22 x 13 mm; wall th <3.5 mm. (469): Plot 2; SF 8278.
20 Cube with semicircular recess in back; broken transversely; 23 x 23 x 26 mm. (1286): Plot 2; SF 8988. ?Printer's type, presumably of lead alloy (*see* below no 36).
21 Pipe sweated onto lead sheet with stub of copper pipe projecting from sheet; L *c* 65 mm, OD *c* 35 mm, th 3 mm. (1527): Plot 4; SF 9083.
22 Pipe; squashed to triangular section; L 29 mm, section 40 x 28 mm, wall th 4 mm. (1527): Plot 4; SF 9059.
23 Ingot; oblong with sloping sides; L 95 mm, W 55 mm, H 23 mm. (1476): Plot 5; SF 9154. Printer's Monotype? ingot of lead/antimony? (Dr D Nuttall, Chester Archaeological Society *pers comm*). The *Chester Chronicle* printing office moved to Bridge Street Row in 1835 (Backhouse, *this volume*).
24 Window came; two sections; squashed; L 55 mm and 25 mm, H 8 mm. (353): Plot 6; SF 9746; <5023>.

Knight 1985, types E and G: late 16 century or later and 18–19 century.

25 Window came; squashed; L 25 mm, H 6 mm. (325): Plot 6; SF 9745; <5020>. Knight 1985, type E: late 16 century or later

26 Window came; junction piece; heavily encrusted, folded at one end; L *c* 50 mm, H *c* 10 mm. (375): Plot 6; <5024>. Knight 1985, type G: 18–19 century.

Cloth seals

The following two cloth seals were the first recognised from excavations in the city. Both appeared to be for imported textiles, presumably non-woollens or types of fabric not readily available from English looms, from the early post-medieval period. Both were residual in the contexts in which they were found.

27 Ornate letter A; corded border // Pinecone (represented by pellets) on round-based stand with pair of lateral projections; trefoil to each side; corded border; diam 20 mm // 18 mm. (553): Plot 6; SF 8322.

The letter stands for the city name Augsburg and the pine cone is its heraldic symbol. *Cf* Egan 1995, 106, fig 41, no 309 (where the trefoil was not noted) and VHA89 acc no 56 (Egan *forthcoming*) for similar issues, and Egan 2001, 70–1 figs 25–6, nos 143–54 for Augsburg seals which differ in minor details and were found in Salisbury. Neither of the closest parallels cited was from a dated context. The present find is most likely to date from the late sixteenth to the early seventeenth century.

The fustians from Augsburg in southern Germany (mixed linen and cotton textiles) were extremely popular in England and elsewhere in north-west Europe from at least the early sixteenth century to the 1630s, when the Thirty Years' War effectively put an end to the trade. Finds of seals representing these textiles have turned up right across England in greater numbers than those for any other branch of cloth imports (Egan 2002, 271; they occasionally match or outnumber the seals for locally woven woollens, as at Salisbury). The only other Augsburg seal noted so far from Cheshire was from Meols on the Wirral and was from a different stamp (Egan 2007, no 3134).

28 (Corroded in centre); crown between foliate motifs and over shield with: on a chief (?)three *fleurs de lis,* (main device illegible); tiny loop or scrolling to sides of shield // (weakly registered) ? rose; in border of ragged lozenges; diam 16 mm // 15 mm. (545): Plot 6; SF 9747.

The legible part of the arms suggested that this seal marked an imported French textile. Several towns and regions of France had arms with *fleurs de lis* in the upper part. From other French seals of the two-disc form recorded in England, Paris and Rouen are perhaps the most likely origins. The arms of Paris, however have a chief *semé de lis,* and so the most likely contender on this basis is Rouen, which had the paschal lamb (*agnus dei*) as the main device (*see* Harvey 1975, 269–70, fig 246, no 1907, assigned probably to the late sixteenth century, for a different seal with one of these stamps excavated in Southampton). Rouen was a major producer of traditional woollens at the end of the Middle Ages, but made cottons from the early sixteenth century and became the

most important centre for their manufacture in France by the late eighteenth century. This origin must be regarded as no more than a suggestion: there are several other potential identifications which so far lack parallels in England.

The phase also produced nine fragments of sheet and strip.

Phase X

29 Window came; ten fragments, including three junctions; H 8 mm; W 4 mm; longest fragment 65 mm. (1906): Plot 1; SF 9312. Knight 1985, type E: late 16 century or later.

30 Window came; L 40 mm, H 7 mm,, W 4 mm. (1817): Plot 1; SF (9425). Knight 1985, type E: late 16 century or later.

31 Disc engraved IIII; diam 40 mm, th 10 mm, wt 107 g. (1802): Plot 1; SF 9434. Probably Roman residual: in addition to the numerals, the weight is nearer to the Roman 4 *unciae* of 109 g than to the modern 4 ounces of 113.5 g.

32 Window came; L 59 mm, H 5 mm, W 5 mm. (420): Plot 2; SF 8453. Knight 1985, types C or D: early 15 century.

33 Printer's plate depicting car; front missing; L 90 mm, W 59 mm, th 2 mm. (435): Plot 2; SF 8378. Zincographic line plate (Dr D Nuttall *pers comm*).

34 Cube; 18 x 19 x 15 mm. (1399): Plot 3; SF 8984. ?Printer's type, presumably of lead alloy.

35 Window came; L 80 mm, H 10 mm, W 4 mm. (301): Plot 6; SF 8336. Knight 1985, type G: 18–19 century.

36 Printer's type with letter S; semi-cylindrical recess in back; presumably of lead alloy; 23 x 23 x 25 mm. (1274): Plot 4; SF 8987. Founder's display type *c* 1840 (Dr D Nuttall *pers comm*);

The phase also produced seventeen fragments of sheet and strip.

Unstratified

37 Printers' plate; L 155 mm; W 102 mm; th *c* 2 mm; advertisement for North West Securities. SF 8989. Zincographic line plate (Dr D Nuttall, Chester Archaeological Society, *pers comm*).

North West Securities was a Chester-based finance house established in 1948 as a subsidiary of a Colwyn Bay motor dealership to provide loans for buying cars. In 1958 it was bought by the Bank of Scotland. A small head office in Newgate Street was replaced by a large one, of eight storeys, in City Road in 1963. In 1997 it was renamed Capital Bank.

There were also three fragments of strip and casting waste.

Stone Objects
H E M Cool

Phase II

1   Hone; fine-grained, grey, micaceous; rectangular-sectioned, groove at each corner; both ends broken; present L 64 mm, section 24 x 17 mm. (98); SF 9777.
2   Hone; fine-grained, grey; rectangular-sectioned; both ends broken, groove parallel to corner; present L 50 mm, section 22.5 x 15 mm. (1132); SF 8911.

Phase III

3   Hone; fine-grained, grey, micaceous; rectangular-sectioned; one end broken, other has two vertical grooves; tapering to broken end; present L 75 mm, max section 25.5 x 20 mm. (1018); SF 8866.
4   Hone; fragment retaining one flat surface; present L 70 mm. (106); SF 9778.
5   Quernstone; lava; fragment without any worked surfaces. (70); SF 9776.
6   Quernstone; lava; fragment retaining small area with worked grooves. (70); SF 9776.

Phase IV

7   Bracelet; shale; lathe-turned, D-sectioned; c 18% of circumference extant; outer diam 80 mm, section 9 x 6 mm. (1017): Plot 6; SF 9635.
8   Hone; schist; rectangular-sectioned; both ends broken; one face has shallow rounded channel with rounded end, one face has two narrow grooves, one face smoothly worn; present L 79 mm, max section 27 x 19 mm. (1119): Plot 3; SF 8957.

Phase V

9   Touchstone ? Very fine-grained cream stone; rectangular-sectioned square block; one face has repeated vertical black streaks; 29 x 29 x 12 mm. (1660): Plot 4; SF 9568.

Phase VI

10 Counter; slate; circular with one side missing; diam 48 mm, th 4 mm. (532): Plot 6; SF 8529.
11 Burnisher or rubbing stone? Grey pebble with one face worn very smooth and very slightly concave; 71 x 59 x 15 mm. (831): Plot 6; SF 8730.

Phase VII

12 Counter; red sandstone; oval; 31 x 28 mm, th 4 mm. (663): Plot 1; SF 8530.
13 Counter; slate; circular; diam 24 x 23 mm, th 4 mm. (824): Plot 6; SF 8563.
14 Hone; fine-grained grey stone; rectangular, thinning to one end; face below the thin end worn very smooth;

vertical scratch marks on blunt end; L 113 mm, max section 50 x 32 mm. (481): Plot 2; SF 8285.
15 Hone; very dark grey fine-grained stone; end of rectangular hone; 24 x 14 x 11 mm. (49): Plot 1; SF 9767.

Phase VIII

16 Quern; coarse gritstone; three fragments, largest retaining dressed face; dimensions (largest) 78 x 80 mm, th 36 mm. (1879): Plot 1; SF 9764.

Phase IX

17 Mortar; white shelly limestone; vertical side curving into flat base; flat rim with part of spout and complete triangular lug; exterior with vertical and horizontal tooling forming a chequerboard pattern; interior worn smooth; approximately one-third extant; H 130 mm, rim diam c 220 mm, base diam 125 mm, wall th 30 mm. (1096): Plot 2; SF 9054.
18 Hone; pink sandstone; square-sectioned rectangular block with facetted corners; L 120 mm, section 39 x 38 mm. (524): Plot 6; SF 8348.
19 Hone; fine-grained grey micaceous stone; waisted rectangular bar with two conical sharpening pits on either face at one end; diagonal grooves on one flat face and both waisted faces show considerable wear; L 98 mm, max section 37 x 21 mm. (1476): Plot 5; SF 9415.
20 Disc; micaceous sandstone; approximately half extant; diam 80 mm, th 11 mm. (1491): Plot 4; SF 9150.
21 Slate pencil; circular-sectioned tapering to faceted point; other end broken; present L 39 mm, diam 5 mm. (353): Plot 6; SF 9779.

Organic Artefacts

Bone, antler and ivory   H E M Cool

Introduction

The artefacts made of skeletal material could be dated to the Roman, later medieval and the post-medieval to modern periods. The absence of finds typical of the Saxon and Viking periods was striking, given that skeletal material clearly survived in contexts of that date (*see* nos 2–9). The Anglo-Scandinavian period was one when bone and antler was exploited for a variety of very distinctive items (*see*, for example, MacGregor *et al* 1999), but none can be identified here.

Nearly all of the material found in Phases I to III could be identified as Roman. Two hairpins typical of the second century were present. No 2 was an example of a Crummy type 2 hairpin, which was the commonest type found during the second century (Crummy 1983, 21). The more elaborately carved no 1 is rare in bone, but the shape was frequently manufactured in copper alloy (Cool 1991, group 3A; *see* especially fig 2.6). Bone needles were in use during the Anglo-Scandinavian period, but no 3 from a Phase II context had been stained green, which was a typical technique of the earlier Roman period (Crummy 1983, 65). The other needle and the shank fragment from Phase II (nos 4 and 5) were not closely datable. Bone handles are a common artefact in Roman assemblages but no 6 with its rectangular-section and elaboration at the terminal was unusual and did not fall into any of the standard categories (*see*, for example, Crummy 1983, 107–10). It clearly did not belong to the normal type of one-piece handle with a rectangular-section as these had waisted ends for use with a spring clip to hold the blade securely (*op cit*, fig. 110, nos 2921–6). It was found in a layer associated with the final occupation of the fortress and thus would appear to be a very late Roman type.

The Phase III context (1022) produced three items associated with gaming. The two counters (nos 7 and 8) were examples of Greep type 2 and 3 counters (Greep 1986, 202), which first started to appear in large numbers in the second century. The fragment no 9 was poorly preserved but had ring-and-dot markings as if it had come from a die. It was clear that it was not a die of the normal cubic form nor from a parallelepiped die. MacGregor (1985, 131) has noted that Viking contexts not infrequently produce irregularly shaped dice, so it may be that this piece was much later than the counters and that the association was just fortuitous.

The only worked skeletal item from Phases IV or V was the tip of an antler tine (no 10) which was probably a by-product of the manufacture of some other item as, apart from the sawn face, it showed no other evidence of utilisation. A similar fragment was recovered from a Phase VII context (no 13).

The spherical bead no 11 from a Phase VI cess pit fill would have been contemporary with its context, as both the beads and the waste from their manufacture have been recovered from a number of late medieval to early post medieval sites (MacGregor 1985, 101–2).

The commonest form of die for gaming since the Roman period has been the cubic form with the spots on the opposite faces adding up to seven. On the Bridge Street site, however, this form did not occur until the post-medieval period. In addition to no 12 from Phase VI, two examples were recovered from Phase VIII (nos 14 and 15) and a fourth was found unstratified (not catalogued).

One interesting feature of the worked skeletal assemblage from the site was that it reflected the increasing refinement in eating habits seen from the eighteenth century onwards which can often be seen in pottery assemblages. Ivory and bone handles from cutlery started to appear in Phase VIII (nos 16–17) and were also present in Phase IX (nos 27–8).

Finally, the very interesting group of articles from the chemist's shop Davies and Shepheard on the site may be noted. This included fragments from a double-sided comb (no 20), toothbrushes (nos 21–5) and a probable hairbrush (no 26). The toothbrushes were particularly interesting. On one (no 21) the method of attaching the bristles could clearly be seen. The grooves on the back provided the seating for the wires which were looped up through each perforation to emerge on the other face. The bristles were threaded through the loops and when the wires were tightened, the bristles were firmly bedded in the head (MacGregor 1985, 183). Two of the other toothbrushes showed a different method of fastening the bristles. Here the backs were smooth but the tip of the brush had the openings of four fine perforations. Presumably the wires were threaded through these, each perforation corresponding to a row of bristles. The hair or clothes brush (no 26) seems to have had its bristles attached in the same way as the toothbrush no 21. The back of the bristle plate was covered by a second plate riveted on, but at one end the two had pulled apart and it was just possible to see the tips of the grooves for the wires. The brushes frequently showed green staining and it may be assumed that the wires used were made of copper alloy. Three of the toothbrushes had the maker's name 'Davies Chester' inscribed on them. Another maker's mark was present on no 22 but unfortunately this was too worn for it to be legible.

Phase I

1   Hairpin; complete in two joining fragments; bone; head details cut into top of circular-sectioned shank; pointed terminal with rib below; baluster-shaped unit with two grooves forming two ribs below; shank tapering to point; L 99 mm, shank section 4 mm. (1227); SF 8828.

Phase II

2   Hairpin; head and upper shank fragment; bone; head details cut into top of circular-sectioned shank conical faceted terminal, three grooves below; tapering shank slight green staining; present L 39 mm, shank section 4 mm. (1142); SF 8871.

3   Needle; bone; broken head; oval-sectioned shank tapering to point; base of rectangular-sectioned per-

foration with groove on either side below it green-stained; present L 50 mm, shank section 3.5 x 3 mm. (1132); SF 8817.

4   Needle; bone; roughly facetted oval tapering shank; upper end broken across groove below perforation; present L 98 mm, shank section 4 x 3 mm. (1161); SF 9165.

5   Shank fragment; bone; circular-sectioned tapering; both ends broken; present L 30 mm, shank section 3 mm. (1135); SF 8829.

6   Handle; bone; rectangular-sectioned one-piece retaining oval-sectioned iron tang; upper end perforated with scalloped shoulders; L 76 mm, section 14 x 7 mm. (1225); SF 8787.

Phase III

7   Counter; circular, approximately two-thirds extant; bone; obverse dished, dot on reverse, rounded edges; diam 16 mm, th 3 mm. (1022); SF 9130.

8   Counter; circular; bone; six concentric ribs with central dot on obverse; plain reverse with dished edge on one side; diam 22 mm, th 3.5 mm. (1022); SF 8625.

9   Die; bone; end of rectangular-sectioned strip; three ring-and-dots parallel to finished edge; one corner has ring-and-dot on each face; present L 7.5 mm, section 12 x 3.5 mm. (1022); SF 9129.

Phase V

10 Antler; sawn tine tip; present L 40 mm. (1654): Plot 3; SF 9501.

Phase VI

11 Spherical bead; bone; turned; L 5 mm, diam 6 mm, perforation diam 2 mm. (1702): Plot 3; <5169>.

12 Die; bone; cubic; one corner chipped; simple drilled spots with opposite faces adding to 7; L 6.6 mm. (785): Plot 2; SF 9851; <5073>.

Phase VII

13 Antler; sawn tine tip; present L 43 mm. (693): Plot 6; SF 8290.

Phase VIII

14 Die; bone; cubic; ring-and-dot spots with opposite faces adding to seven; L 7 mm. (1737): Plot 2; SF 9186.

15 Die; bone; cubic; one corner chipped; simple drilled spots with opposite faces adding to seven; L 9 mm. (207): Plot 1; SF 8003.

16 Cutlery handle, in two joining fragments lacking parts lower end; ivory; tapering circular-sectioned with slightly rounded bulbous end, central void for tang; present L 68 mm, max section 22 x 21 mm. (1435): Plot 3; SF 9228.

17 Cutlery handle, one complete plate; bone; D-sectioned with slightly bulbous end; three perforations with iron-staining; three small pits on end in triangle and fourth and fifth pits between perforations,

copper alloy staining around all pits. L 73 mm, max section 22 x 6.5 mm. (1684): Plot 3; SF 9426.

18 Strips; bone; five rectangular-sectioned fragments, two tapering to point; Max section 7 x 3.5 mm. (1437): Plot 3; SF 9853; <5151>.

Phase IX

19 Double-sided comb; bone; sawn teeth on either side, ten and twelve teeth to 10 mm; large parts of both sides missing; L 64 mm, W 46 mm, th 2.5 mm. (1830): Plot 1; SF 9500.

20 Double-sided comb, fragment; bone; sawn teeth on either side, thirteen teeth to 10 mm; present L 23 mm, original W *c* 45 mm, th 3 mm. (1096): Plot 2; SF 8867.

21 Toothbrush; ivory; rectangular-sectioned head with rounded end, broken oval-sectioned handle with waist between; head has three rows of fifteen perforations on one face and has three grooves; traces of bristles in perforations; both faces have copper alloy staining; present L 100 mm, head section 10 x 4 mm. (1096): Plot 2; SF 8867.

22 Toothbrush; ivory? Rectangular-sectioned head with rounded end, oval-sectioned handle with waist between; one face of head has row of close-set perforations around edge, and two rows of twenty-four centrally; four perforations around tip of head; handle has inscription 'Extrafine' and 'Warr Wald' arranged in pointed oval around central motif that starts with 4; L 165 mm, head section 12 x 4 mm. (1096): Plot 2; SF 8867.

23 Toothbrush; ivory? Rectangular-sectioned head with rounded end, oval-sectioned handle with waist between; one face of head has row of close-set perforations around edge, and two rows of twenty-three centrally; four perforations around tip of head; handle has inscription 'Davies Chester'; L 165 mm, head section 13 x 4.5 mm. (1096): Plot 2; SF 8867.

24 Toothbrush; ivory; broken across base of head retaining two perforations on one face and possible tip of groove on other side; oval-sectioned pointed handle with waist between it and head; handle has inscription 'Davies Chester'; present L 117 mm. (1096): Plot 2; SF 8867.

25 Toothbrush; ivory; broken across base of head retaining base of perforations on one face; broken oval-sectioned handle with waist between it and head; handle has inscription 'Davies Chester'; present L 95 mm. (1096): Plot 2.

26 Brush plate; bone; two rectangular plates with rounded ends; lower plate has six rows of circular perforations, outer rows of nineteen perforations, inner rows of twenty perforations, rows set in quincunx; face has traces of green staining; upper plate fastened to lower by four small copper alloy rivets; L 101 mm, W 25 mm, th 8.5 mm. (1096): Plot 2; SF 8867.

27 Cutlery handle; ivory? One piece with fragment missing at end; rounded asymmetrical end; grooved foliate design on each face infilled with black; each face has five small perforations, each infilled by small circular bone rivet; L 74 mm, max section 17 x 9 mm. (470): Plot 2; SF 8468.

28 Handle; bone; tapering cylinder with open ends, narrow end retaining iron tang; L 76 mm, max section 16 mm. (553): Plot 6; SF: 8349.

29 Cylindrical fitting, open at top and bottom; bone; convex-curved side; upper side with rib on outside and six very fine grooves on inner side; upper diam 28 mm, lower diam 20 mm, L 32 mm. (1491): Plot 4; SF 9060.

30 Button? Sliver from edge; diam 20 mm, th 1 mm.

Textiles

Penelope Walton Rogers
The Anglo-Saxon Laboratory

Phase VII

A single fragment of matted wool textile was recovered from context (924). It is a medium-weight fabric woven in tabby (plain weave), with 9/Z x 12/S threads per cm, and the matted effect is probably the result of fulling (beating the cloth in water). Although heavily stained, the textile has a pinkish tinge, suggesting dye. This is a typical wool clothing fabric of the post-medieval period. Several identical pieces were recorded at Newcastle upon Tyne, amongst tailors' offcuts dated to the third quarter of the seventeenth century (Walton 1983, 220), and related types were found in Civil War layers at Pontefract castle, West Yorkshire (Walton Rogers 2002, 309), and Dudley castle, West Midlands (Walton Rogers unpublished), seventeenth-century High Street/Blackfriargate, Hull (Walton 1987a, 231), and seventeenth- to eighteenth-century Black Friars, Newcastle upon Tyne (Walton 1987b, 127). The pink tinge will almost certainly have been due to madder dye, which was used extensively for reds and tans at this time. This example probably belonged at the poorer end of the social scale, since better-quality woollens at this date generally had a dense teaselled nap.

1 A folded fragment of wool textile, tabby, 9/Z x 12/S per cm; fulled; pink tone, probably indicating dye; 40 x 20 mm. (924): Plot 6; SF 9215.

Phase IX

Four different groups of textile fragments may be attributed to Phase IX, two from context (208) and two from (1491). The two from (208), both SF 9217, are fine, lightweight fabrics woven in tabby weave, but one is cotton and the other linen. They both have yarn spun in opposite directions in warp and weft and relatively high thread-counts, 28/Z x 30/S in the case of the cotton and 20/Z x 40/S in the linen. The cotton is off-white and the linen black and carbonised, perhaps through charring. By the nineteenth century fine linens had been in use for centuries, for underwear, bedding and lightweight summer clothing. Cotton textiles, on the other hand, although available since the late medieval period, were rare until the later eighteenth century, when new technology allowed the short cotton fibre to be spun more easily into useable yarn. In burial textiles, such as those from Christ Church, Spitalfields (Janaway 1993, 96–100), cotton was predominantly a feature of nineteenth-century graves.

SF 9214 consists of several large, tattered fragments of a thick wool textile in an unusual weave. It is difficult to plot the structure exactly because of wear and damage, but it is clearly some form of double-faced weave. It seems to have been constructed by alternating one row of 1/3/1/3/1/1 with another which is a combination of 2/1 and tabby, possibly 2/1/2/1/1/1/1/1. Z- and S-spun yarns have been used in both warp and weft and there are approximately 12 x 12 threads per cm in both. One fragment has a deep fold, possibly the remains of a front jacket opening, 30–40 mm deep. This heavy wool fabric with loose floating pattern threads on one face was probably the sort of textile used for women's coats and jackets in the nineteenth century.

SF 9210 appears to be the remains of a very worn and fragmentary hat brim. When the fragments were pieced together, they formed a curled brim approximately 100 mm wide, with stitch holes along the outer edge where a braid or tape was probably once attached. Felt hats were common enough in the nineteenth century, but this felt has an unusual construction. At the cut outer edges it resembles an ordinary felt, just under 2 mm thick, but the torn edges shows that it has in fact been made as a sandwich, with a layer of white powdery filler between two thin layers of wool. This feature has not been encountered before and was presumably a cheap way of making felt from very little wool.

2 Two fragments of cotton textile woven in tabby, 28/Z x 30/S per cm; natural off-white; 7 x 7 mm and 6 x 5 mm. (208): Plot 1; SF 9217.1.

3 One fragment of linen textile woven in tabby, 20/Z x 40/S per cm; black, carbonised; fibres 8–11 microns diam; 4 x 3 mm. (208): Plot 1; SF 9217.2.

4 Several fragments of a wool double-faced weave (*see* text), 12/Z+S x 12/Z+S per cm; largest fragment 270 x 120 mm. (1491): Plot 4; SF 9214.

5 Several fragments of a wool felt made in two layers with an off-white filler in between; total th 1.6–1.9 mm. The fragments have remains of original curving edges, some convex, some concave. The outward curving edge has a row of stitch-holes, five holes per 20 mm, set 9 mm in from the edge. Largest pieces are 105 x 37 mm and 90 x 55 mm. (208): Plot 1; SF 9210.

6

ENVIRONMENTAL REMAINS

Mammal, Bird and Amphibian Bones
Ian Smith

Introduction

TO date this is the most important late medieval and later bone assemblage to have been recovered from within the City Walls. Animal bones were recovered from all of the phases. Most of the bones from the late medieval and post-medieval periods could be grouped by plot and period and this allowed intra-site comparisons.

The majority of the animal bones undoubtedly originated from the disposal of butchery and food waste. A few contexts also yielded bones that related to leather production which, it is suggested, took place here from late medieval times. There was also tentative evidence for some involvement in fur trading. Between approximately the late fifteenth and the eighteenth centuries there was an increased diversity of bird remains amongst the food waste, suggesting increasingly prosperous plot owners. The rise in numbers of calf bones is also taken to be another sign of this prosperity and of the developing dairy industry. It is suggested that other medieval and post-medieval groups resulted from the burial and disposal of horses, dogs and cats. The assemblage has contributed to our understanding of the nature of bone deposition and aspects of meat provisioning and animal husbandry in the city-centre backlands and it raises research issues regarding the development of other parts of the city over the medieval and post-medieval periods.

Methodology

Collection

The bulk of the bone was hand-collected, but a proportion was also recovered from the heavy residues resulting from wet-sieved samples recovered over a 1 mm mesh (*see* Jaques *et al this volume* for details). Remains from hand collection and samples are presented in separate tables. The wet-sieved contexts and processed volumes from Phases I to IX that produced mammal, bird or amphibian bone are listed in Table 6.1.50. Table 6.1.50 includes material from the evaluation and lists the relevant plot numbers for Phases V to VIII.

Analysis

The aim was to address the research issues raised by the post-excavation assessment report (Garner 2002). However, some of the more detailed questions regarding the Roman and immediate post-Roman periods could not be fully addressed because of the small numbers of bones from these phases (I–III). The bones from these phases were therefore studied in less detail than those from later phases.

The contexts studied in greater detail were chosen on the basis of the assessment report and discussions with the excavation director and other specialists, with the

Table 6.1.1 Cattle: hand-collected fragments (NISP) quantified by element and phase

	I		II		III		IV		V		VI		VII		VIII		IX	
Element	No	%	No	%	No	%	No	%	No	%	No	%	No	%	No	%	No	%
Horncore		0.0	4	1.2	3	1.9	1	0.6	21	2.6	21	3.2	558	39.1	87	11.4	25	5.4
Skull	1	4.3	9	2.8	10	6.3	1	0.6	16	2.0	32	4.9	43	3.0	21	2.8	59	12.7
Hyoid													1	0.1	2	0.3	2	0.4
Maxilla		0.0	1	0.3	4	2.5		0.0	4	0.5	5	0.8	5	0.4	3	0.4	2	0.4
Maxilla loose teeth		0.0	16	4.9	19	12.0	11	6.3	38	4.8	27	4.2	31	2.2	39	5.1	27	5.8
Mandible fragments	1	4.3	38	11.7	7	4.4	13	7.4	47	5.9	23	3.6	40	2.8	27	3.5	21	4.5
Mandible loose teeth	2	8.7	30	9.2	9	5.7	13	7.4	53	6.7	21	3.2	44	3.1	40	5.3	22	4.7
Teeth		0.0		0.0		0.0		0.0	7	0.9	10	1.5	17	1.2	2	0.3	5	1.1
Atlas	1	4.3	4	1.2	1	0.6	1	0.6	6	0.8	4	0.6	5	0.4	4	0.5	2	0.4
Axis		0.0	3	0.9	1	0.6		0.0	3	0.4	3	0.5	4	0.3	3	0.4		0.0
Vertebrae		0.0	24	7.4	3	1.9		0.0	23	2.9	34	5.3	33	2.3	30	3.9	24	5.2
Ribs	2	8.7	6	1.8	1	0.6		0.0	2	0.3	8	1.2	26	1.8	27	3.5	7	1.5
Scapula	2	8.7	18	5.5	7	4.4	9	5.1	39	4.9	37	5.7	54	3.8	46	6.0	14	3.0
Humerus	1	4.3	10	3.1	6	3.8	10	5.7	58	7.3	50	7.7	55	3.9	43	5.7	17	3.7
Radius		0.0	17	5.2	12	7.6	10	5.7	45	5.7	22	3.4	48	3.4	37	4.9	32	6.9
Ulna		0.0	7	2.2	8	5.1	5	2.8	23	2.9	16	2.5	20	1.4	18	2.4	13	2.8
Radius/ulna		0.0				0.0	1	0.6	2	0.3	1	0.2		0.0	5	0.7	1	0.2
Metacarpal	4	17.4	27	8.3	6	3.8	12	6.8	21	2.6	19	2.9	32	2.2	19	2.5	13	2.8
Metapodial		0.0	5	1.5	2	1.3	6	3.4	13	1.6	8	1.2	21	1.5	13	1.7	7	1.5
Sesamoids													2	0.1	1	0.1	2	0.4
Sacrum		0.0	1	0.3		0.0		0.0	8	1.0	4	0.6	11	0.8	3	0.4	7	1.5
Pelvis	3	13.0	14	4.3	12	7.6	13	7.4	43	5.4	43	6.6	57	4.0	44	5.8	23	4.9
Femur	3	13.0	17	5.2	6	3.8	11	6.3	65	8.2	51	7.9	73	5.1	69	9.1	27	5.8
Patella		0.0		0.0	1	0.6	1	0.6	3	0.4	3	0.5	3	0.2	1	0.1	4	0.9
Tibia		0.0	15	4.6	9	5.7	8	4.5	71	9.0	66	10.2	80	5.6	49	6.4	32	6.9
Carpals+tarsals		0.0	3	0.9	1	0.6	2	1.1	26	3.3	20	3.1	25	1.8	20	2.6	11	2.4
Calcaneus		0.0	9	2.8	3	1.9	10	5.7	35	4.4	25	3.9	22	1.5	18	2.4	12	2.6
Astragalus		0.0	1	0.3	1	0.6	9	5.1	28	3.5	20	3.1	22	1.5	16	2.1	7	1.5
Metatarsal	1	4.3	17	5.2	11	7.0	10	5.7	31	3.9	30	4.6	19	1.3	27	3.5	10	2.2
Phalanx 1		0.0	15	4.6	7	4.4	11	6.3	36	4.5	21	3.2	38	2.7	14	1.8	15	3.2
Phalanx 2	1	4.3	7	2.2	6	3.8	5	2.8	15	1.9	12	1.9	21	1.5	15	2.0	12	2.6
Phalanx 3	1	4.3	7	2.2	2	1.3	3	1.7	11	1.4	11	1.7	16	1.1	18	2.4	10	2.2
Total	23	100.0	325	100.0	158	100.0	176	100.0	793	100.0	647	100.0	1426	100.0	761	100.0	465	100.0

Table 6.1.2 Pig: hand-collected fragments (NISP) quantified by element and phase

	I		II		III		IV		V		VI		VII		VIII		IX	
Element	No	%	No	%	No	%	No	%	No	%	No	%	No	%	No	%	No	%
Skull		0.0	15	6.4	2	2.2	1	1.6	7	3.6	10	6.9	27	10.7	10	6.3	14	10.4
Maxilla	1	2.5	2	0.9	7	7.9		0.0		0.0	5	3.4	4	1.6	4	2.5		0.0
Maxilla loose teeth	2	5.0	16	6.8	4	4.5	1	1.6	9	4.6	1	0.7	11	4.3	9	5.7	7	5.2
Mandible fragments	5	12.5	26	11.1	13	14.6	7	11.1	13	6.7	12	8.3	22	8.7	12	7.5	10	7.4
Mandible loose teeth	6	15.0	26	11.1	10	11.2	10	15.9	25	12.8	12	8.3	24	9.5	13	8.2	13	9.6
Teeth		0.0		0.0		0.0	1	1.6	4	2.1	2	1.4	2	0.8	1	0.6	4	3.0
Atlas		0.0	1	0.4	1	1.1	2	3.2	5	2.6	1	0.7	3	1.2	3	1.9		0.0
Axis		0.0		0.0		0.0		0.0		0.0		0.0	1	0.4		0.0		0.0
Vertebrae		0.0	5	2.1	1	1.1		0.0	6	3.1	3	2.1	14	5.5	7	4.4	1	0.7
Ribs	1	2.5	3	1.3		0.0		0.0	1	0.5	5	3.4	8	3.2	3	1.9	6	4.4
Scapula	1	2.5	5	2.1	5	5.6	2	3.2	7	3.6	3	2.1	7	2.8	3	1.9	2	1.5
Humerus	2	5.0	9	3.8	3	3.4	8	12.7	16	8.2	15	10.3	18	7.1	13	8.2	11	8.1
Radius		0.0	7	3.0	9	10.1	4	6.3	13	6.7	5	3.4	6	2.4	5	3.1	6	4.4
Ulna	1	2.5	8	3.4	5	5.6	4	6.3	13	6.7	6	4.1	9	3.6	10	6.3	10	7.4
Metacarpal	7	17.5	25	10.7	7	7.9	4	6.3	18	9.2	9	6.2	12	4.7	7	4.4	6	4.4
Metapodial	2	5.0	12	5.1	1	1.1		0.0	3	1.5	5	3.4	8	3.2	8	5.0	6	4.4
Sacrum		0.0		0.0		0.0		0.0	1	0.5		0.0	1	0.4	2	1.3		0.0
Pelvis		0.0	6	2.6	2	2.2	2	3.2	6	3.1	4	2.8	8	3.2	4	2.5	3	2.2
Femur	4	10.0	7	3.0	7	7.9	4	6.3	10	5.1	9	6.2	16	6.3	8	5.0	6	4.4
Patella		0.0		0.0		0.0		0.0		0.0	1	0.4		0.0		0.0		0.0
Tibia	3	7.5	11	4.7	3	3.4	5	7.9	15	7.7	17	11.7	24	9.5	9	5.7	10	7.4
Fibula	2	5.0	6	2.6	1	1.1		0.0	3	1.5	2	1.4	1	0.4	3	1.9	2	1.5
Carpals+tarsals		0.0		0.0		0.0		0.0		0.0		0.0	2	0.8		0.0	1	0.7
Calcaneus		0.0	5	2.1	2	2.2	3	4.8	6	3.1	5	3.4	3	1.2	2	1.3	1	0.7
Astragalus	1	2.5		0.0		0.0		0.0		0.0	1	0.7	1	0.4	2	1.3	2	1.5
Metatarsal	2	5.0	33	14.1	4	4.5	4	6.3	10	5.1	8	5.5	6	2.4	11	6.9	7	5.2
Phalanx 1		0.0	6	2.6	2	2.2	1	1.6	3	1.5	3	2.1	7	2.8	8	5.0	3	2.2
Phalanx 2		0.0		0.0		0.0		0.0	1	0.5	2	1.4	6	2.4	2	1.3	4	3.0
Phalanx 3		0.0		0.0		0.0		0.0		0.0		0.0	1	0.4		0.0		0.0
Total	40	100.0	234	100.0	89	100.0	63	100.0	195	100.0	145	100.0	253	100.0	159	100.0	135	100.0
Pig teeth %		35.0		29.9		38.2		30.2		26.2		22.1		24.9		24.5		25.2

aims of excluding any contexts with small groups or clear evidence for post-depositional disturbance and high residuality and focussing on those that had good potential for identification to species level. Contexts and features selected for detailed recording included:

1 Those that appeared to relate to specific structures or activities (such as the possible leatherworking and horn-core-lined pit).

2 Groups of pits or undisturbed dumps of material associated with a single phase of occupation.

Table 6.1.3 Sheep and sheep/goat: hand-collected fragments (NISP) quantified by element and phase

											Phase							
	I		**II**		**III**		**IV**		**V**		**VI**		**VII**		**VIII**		**IX**	
Element	No	%	No	%	No	%	No	%	No	%	No	%	No	%	No	%	No	%
Horncore		0.0	3	2.6		0.0	1	2.8	7	1.5	6	1.7	4	0.9	1	0.3	3	0.8
Skull		0.0	1	0.9	1	1.4		0.0		0.0	2	0.6	6	1.3	2	0.5	3	0.8
Maxilla		0.0		0.0		0.0	1	2.8		0.0	1	0.3	2	0.4	3	0.8	1	0.3
Maxilla loose teeth	1	6.7		0.0		0.0	2	5.6	8	1.7	5	1.4	10	2.2	8	2.1	10	2.7
Mandible fragments		0.0	3	2.6	4	5.6	1	2.8	4	0.9	4	1.1	7	1.5	8	2.1	19	5.2
Mandible loose teeth		0.0	3	2.6	1	1.4	2	5.6	5	1.1	8	2.2	10	2.2	12	3.1	10	2.7
Teeth		0.0		0.0		0.0		0.0		0.0		0.0		0.0		0.0	1	0.3
Atlas		0.0	2	1.8		0.0		0.0	4	0.9	6	1.7	14	3.0	4	1.0	5	1.4
Axis		0.0		0.0	1	1.4		0.0	5	1.1	6	1.7	5	1.1	4	1.0	1	0.3
Vertebrae	2	13.3	3	2.6	4	5.6		0.0	6	1.3	11	3.0	8	1.7	18	4.7	6	1.6
Ribs		0.0		0.0		0.0		0.0	8	1.7	31	8.6	8	1.7	5	1.3	5	1.4
Scapula		0.0	4	3.5	10	14.1	1	2.8	16	3.5	32	8.8	46	9.9	32	8.3	28	7.6
Humerus	1	6.7	18	15.8	7	9.9	5	13.9	30	6.5	30	8.3	47	10.1	44	11.4	44	12.0
Radius	1	6.7	8	7.0	8	11.3	7	19.4	30	6.5	48	13.3	47	10.1	46	11.9	42	11.4
Ulna	1	6.7	2	1.8	2	2.8	4	11.1	7	1.5	13	3.6	15	3.2	13	3.4	12	3.3
Radius/ulna		0.0		0.0		0.0		0.0		0.0	1	0.2		0.0	1	0.3		
Metacarpal	3	20.0	10	8.8	2	2.8	2	5.6	90	19.6	17	4.7	27	5.8	16	4.2	14	3.8
Metapodial	1	6.7	2	1.8	1	1.4	1	2.8	18	3.9	5	1.4	4	0.9	8	2.1	5	1.4
Sacrum		0.0		0.0		0.0		0.0	2	0.4	2	0.6	4	0.9	2	0.5		0.0
Pelvis		0.0	2	1.8	7	9.9		0.0	30	6.5	29	8.0	46	10.3	36	9.4	29	7.9
Femur	2	13.3	9	7.9	8	11.3	3	8.3	25	5.4	20	5.5	52	11.2	42	10.9	37	10.1
Patella		0.0		0.0		0.0		0.0		0.0		0.0		0.0		0.0		0.0
Tibia	1	6.7	41	36.0	12	16.9	2	5.6	36	7.8	38	10.5	54	11.6	44	11.4	47	12.8
Carpals+tarsals		0.0		0.0		0.0		0.0	2	0.4	5	1.4	1	0.2	3	0.8	1	0.3
Calcaneus		0.0	1	0.9		0.0	2	5.6	3	0.7	10	2.8	8	1.7	16	4.2	5	1.4
Astragalus		0.0		0.0		0.0		0.0	1	0.2	5	1.4	12	2.6	5	1.3	8	2.2
Metatarsal	2	13.3		0.0	1	1.4	2	5.6	70	15.3	22	6.1	18	3.9	12	3.1	15	4.1
Phalanx 1		0.0	2	1.8	1	1.4		0.0	47	10.2	6	1.7	5	1.1	1	0.3	14	3.8
Phalanx 2		0.0		0.0	1	1.4		0.0	1	0.2		0.0	1	0.2		0.0	2	0.5
Phalanx 3		0.0		0.0		0.0		0.0	4	0.9		0.0		0.0		0.0		0.0
Total	15	100.0	114	100.0	71	100.0	36	100.0	459	100.0	362	100.0	464	100.0	385	100.0	368	100.0

Table 6.1.4 Goat: hand-collected fragments (NISP) quantified by element and phase

				Phase					
Element : No	I	II	III	IV	V	VI	VII	VIII	IX
Horncore			1	1	9	2	2	2	1
Skull			1						
Mandible fragments					1				1
Mandible loose teeth						1			
Metacarpal				1	1			1	1
Phalanx 1					2	1			1
Phalanx 2							1	1	
Total	0	0	2	2	13	4	3	5	3

Table 6.1.5 Domestic mammal bone: weight (g) by phase

									Phase									
	I		**II**		**III**		**IV**		**V**		**VI**		**VII**		**VIII**		**IX**	
Species	Wt	%	Wt	%	Wt	%	Wt	%	Wt	%	Wt	%	Wt	%	Wt	%	Wt	%
Cattle	1307	47.0	11234	55.9	5618	48.4	5526	57.5	23138	59.9	20290	58.8	102920	86.1	23178	64.6	12943	52.4
Large mammal	904	32.5	4726	23.5	3472	29.9	2972	30.9	2844	7.4	8568	24.8	9042	7.6	6759	18.8	5873	23.8
Pig	374	13.5	2363	11.8	1407	12.1	601	6.3	1886	4.9	1555	4.5	2347	2.0	1594	4.4	1270	5.1
Sheep/goat	35	1.3	1139	5.7	735	6.3	361	3.8	9964	25.8	3086	8.9	4246	3.6	3556	9.9	3764	15.2
Medium mammal	160	5.8	626	3.1	370	3.2	151	1.6	770	2.0	1025	3.0	1049	0.9	794	2.2	839	3.4
Total	2780	100.0	20088	100.0	11602	100.0	9611	100.0	38602	100.0	34524	100.0	119604	100.0	35881	100.0	24689	100.0

3 Groups of related contexts within a burgage plot or other defined area.

4 Any sequence of context groups which contained closely dated material assessed to have good potential (*see* O'Connor 1989, 191).

5 Material that was exceptionally well preserved (*see* Huntley & Stallibrass 1995, 85).

6 Contexts with apparently little disturbance and containing particularly large samples of bones.

For the medieval and post-medieval periods it was possible to address many of the original and revised aims and research questions. The process of selecting bone groups for detailed study may have discriminated against some context types. However, in common with the artefact remains, counts and weights of all fragments were also recorded to allow comparisons between material types and to give a basic overview of all the recovered bones from each phase of the site.

The hand-collected animal bone was recorded through:

A Counts of all fragments from the site by species (or genus/order) and anatomical part

B Weight for each of the main domesticated mammals and birds

C An Access database of a sample of bones from selected contexts from Phases IV to IX consisting of the following fields: site code; context number; context type; phase; element; species; proximal fusion; distal fusion; side; zones; gnawing; burning; fine cutting; hacking; sawing; fracture types; sex; age; pathology; notes; tooth wear; measurements.

Table 6.1.6 Mammal bone zones (mainly zones recorded by Rackham)

Element	Zone	Description	Abbreviation
Horncore	1	base, (where there is >50%)	hc1
	2	tip	hc2
Skull	1	paraoccipital process	sk1
	2	occipital condyle	sk2
	4	external acoustic meatus	sk4
	5	frontal sinus	sk5
	6	ectorbitale	sk6
	0	infraorbital foramen	sk0
Mandible	3	lateral diastemal foramen	ma3
	4	coronoid process	ma4
	5	condylar process	ma5
	6	angle	ma6
	7	anterior dorsal ascending ramus	ma7
	8	mandibular foramen	ma8
	9	deciduous d4	ma9
	10	permanent M3	ma10
Vertebra	1	whole centrum or atlas	ve1
	2	partial centrum >50%	ve2
Rib	1	proximal articulation	ri1
Scapula	1	supraglenoid tubercle	sc1
	2	glenoid cavity	sc2
	3	origin of the distal spine	sc3
	4	tuber of the spine	sc4
	5	posterior of neck with foramen	sc5
	6	cranial angle of blade	sc6
Humerus	1	head	hu1
	2	greater tubercle	hu2
	5	deltoid tuberosity	hu5
	6	dorsal angle of olecranon fossa	hu6
	7	capitulum	hu7
	8	trochlea	hu8
	9	coronoid fossa	hu9
	0	teres tubercle	hu0
Radius	1	medial half of proximal epiphysis	ra1
	2	lateral half of proximal epiphysis	ra2
	3	posterior proximal ulna scar and foramen	ra3
	4	medial half of distal epiphysis	ra4
	5	lateral half of distal epiphysis	ra5
	6	distal shaft immediately above distal epiphysis	ra6
Ulna	1	olecranon tuberosity	ul1
	2	trochlear notch-semilunaris	ul2
	3	lateral coronoid process	ul3
	4	distal epiphysis	ul4
Metacarpus	1	medial facet of proximal articulation, MC3	mc1
	2	lateral facet of proximal articulation, MC4	mc2
	3	medial distal condyle, MC3	mc3
	4	lateral distal condyle, MC4	mc4
	5	anterior distal groove and foramen	mc5
	6	medial or lateral distal condyle	mc6
	7	mid-shaft MC3	mc7
	8	mid-shaft MC4	mc8
	9	mid-shaft MC3 or 4 (incl SD)	mc9
Innominate	1	tuber coxae	pe1
	2	tuber sacrale + scar	pe2
	3	body of ilium with dorso-medial foramen	pe3
	4	iliopubic eminence	pe4
	5	acetabular fossa	pe5
	6	symphyseal branch of pubis	pe6
	7	body of ilium	pe7
	8	ischial tuberosity	pe8
	9	depression for medial tendon of rectus femoris	pe9
Femur	1	head	fe1
	2	trochanter major	fe2
	3	trochanter minor	fe3
	4	supracondyloid fossa	fe4
	5	distal medial condyle	fe5
	6	distal lateral condyle	fe6
	7	distal trochlea	fe7
	8	trochanter tertius	fe8
Tibia	1	proximal medial condyle	ti1
	2	proximal lateral condyle	ti2
	3	intercondylar eminence	ti3
	4	proximal posterior nutrient foramen	ti4
	5	medial malleolus	ti5
	6	lateral aspect of distal articulation	ti6
	7	distal pre-epiphyseal portion of the diaphysis	ti7
Astragalus	1	>50%	as1
Calcaneum	1	calcaneum tuber	ca1
	2	sustentaculum tali	ca2
	3	processus anterior	ca3
Metatarsus	1	medial facet of proximal articulation, MT3	mt1
	2	lateral facet of proximal articulation, MT4	mt2
	3	medial distal condyle, MT3	mt3
	4	lateral distal condyle, MT3	mt4
	5	anterior distal groove and foramen	mt5
	6	medial or lateral distal condyle	mt6
	7	mid-shaft MT3	mt7
	8	mid-shaft MT4	mt8
	9	mid-shaft MT3 or 4	mt9
Metapodial	1–9	as in metatarsus	mp1-9
First phalanx	1	proximal epiphysis	1stph1
	2	distal articular facet	1stph2
Second phalanx	1	proximal epiphysis	2ndph1
	2	distal articular facet	2ndph2
Third phalanx	1	>50%	3rdph

Table 6.1.7 Bird bone zones

Key Numbers in right column are corresponding Cohen & Serjeantson 1996 zone numbers

Element	Zone	Description	Zone no
Skull	1	occipital condyle	
	2	premaxilla	
	3	dentary	
Coracoid	1	bicipital tuberosity	2
	2	glenoid	1
	3	sternal facet	7, 8
Scapula	1	proximal articular surface	
Humerus	1	proximal fossa	2
	2	deltoid crest	3
	3	branchial depression	
	4	distal articular surface	
Ulna	1	proximal articular surface	1
	2	impression for branchialis anticus	3
	3	distal articular surface	7, 8
Radius	1	proximal articular surface	1, 2
	2	distal articular surface	7, 8
Carpo-metacarpus	1	process of metacarpal 1	
	2	intermetacarpal tuberosity	
	3	distal articular surface	7, 8
Femur	1	greater trochanter	2
	2	femoral head	1
	3	distal articular surface	7, 8
Tibio-tarsus	1	proximal articular surface	2
	2	fibular crest	4
	3	supracondylar fossa	
	4	distal articular surface	
Tarso-metatarsus	1	proximal articular surface	
	2	calcaneal ridge(s)	
	3	1st metatarsal facet	5
	4	distal foramen	
Pelvis	1	>50% of acetabulum	3, 4
Sternum	1	anterior margin	
	2	apex of keel	4
	3	posterior metasternum	

The diagnostic zones to be counted were chosen after assessment. The system used for recording diagnostic mammal zones followed that devised by James Rackham. However, some changes were made to allow comparability with zones counted in Chester in the past. These included a reduced number of zones for the skull (five instead of ten), mandible, humerus and vertebrae, and extra zones for the mandibular deciduous d4 and the permanent M3 and for the medial and lateral mid shafts of ungulate metapodials. In the case of the ungulate metapodials it was concluded, after assessment, that immature animals would be under-represented unless mid-shaft zones were included. Amongst the pigs, the third and fourth metapodials only were zoned. A full list of the mammal zones counted can be found in Table 6.1.6. For the majority of the mammal zones, Rackham's original zone numbers and descriptions are replicated. The bird zones counted included some of the zones and descriptions of Cohen and Serjeantson (1996) and all are listed in Table 6.1.7. Amongst both mammals and birds, zones were consistently counted only where more than 50% of a zone was present.

As well as diagnostic zones the text also refers to NISP or number of individual bone specimens and to calculations made by Judith Cartledge of MNI or minimum numbers of individuals. NISP totals have been arrived at by consistently counting all fragments even where it was suspected that they might belong to a single bone. All fragments of hand-collected bone were counted. Each wet-sieved group was carefully scanned and all identifications and recognisable parts from the samples were counted. Generally (after the removal of any small mammal, bird and fish bone) no attempt was made to count the many tiny nondescript unidentified fragments of compact and spongy mammal bone recovered over the 1 mm mesh, but, as a trial, this process was completed for Phase V (*see* 343 and Table 6.1.17). References in the text to numbers of bone fragments have been given in parentheses and are preceded by n=, to distinguish them from context numbers. Suggested epiphysial fusion ages follow Silver (1969), but these should be regarded as approximate only since, as Silver recognised, the ages at which domesticates mature varies widely. Suggested ages according to tooth wear and eruption have been made with the aid of Silver 1969, Payne 1973 and 1987, Grant 1982 and Halstead 1985 and 1992.

Identifications

The wild mammals and some sheep/goat were checked against bones at York University, Liverpool Museum, Manchester Museum and the Natural History Museum stores in Kensington and Wandsworth. Identifications of the majority of the domesticated animals were made through comparisons with bones in the Chester Archaeology reference collection. Sheep and goats were differentiated with the aid of the criteria defined by Boessneck 1969, Kratochvil 1969, and Payne 1985. The text refers to sheep and goats and to caprovids (sheep and/or goats). Fallow and red deer were identified with comparative skeletons at Chester and with the aid of Lister 1996. Bird remains were identified with the aid of reference material at the Natural History Museum at Tring and at Liverpool Museum and York University and with the aid of Cohen & Serjeantson 1996. Identifications of amphibian bones were carried out through comparison with modern reference specimens and with the aid of Böhme 1977. Measurements of mammals and birds were taken following von den Driesch 1976. The butchery codes of Binford 1981 were used where possible and some are referred to in the text. Additional butchery codes were devised where this was necessary. Butchery codes, brief descriptions and presence by phase are listed in Tables 6.1.43–.49. Withers height calculations were made following Harcourt 1974 for dogs and Kiesewalter 1888 and May 1985 for horses. Comparisons have been made to various modern dog and horse breeds to give those unfamiliar with withers height estimates an idea of the approximate size of the animals described. It is not suggested that any of these specific breeds were represented amongst the bones.

Phase I

Sample size

The sample recovered from this period was small (n=263 hand-collected fragments and 179 from samples) (Tables 6.1.8–.9), and thus any conclusions must be tentative. Wet-sieved bone was recovered from eleven contexts (Table 6.1.50). When the phase was divided into sub-phases, many of the fragment totals for individual species were reduced to single figures. The largest proportion of hand-collected bone came from sub-phases Id (n=135) and Ie (n=78). From Ib (n=20) and Ic (n=30) there was considerably less bone and there were only fifteen identifications to species. Whilst some reference has been made to these sub-phases (*see* below), the totals were too small for the recognition of significant trends.

Table 6.1.8 Phase I: hand-collected fragments quantified by taxa

Vernacular	Taxon	No	%
Bird			
Goose	*Anser/Branta* sp	2	0.8
Chicken	*Gallus* f domestic	2	0.8
Mammal			
Hare	*Lepus* sp	1	0.4
Pig	*Sus* f domestic	40	15.2
Roe deer	*Capreolus capreolus*	1	0.4
Cattle	*Bos* f domestic	23	8.7
Sheep	*Ovis* f domestic	3	1.1
Sheep/goat	*Ovis/Capra*	12	4.6
Large mammal	Mammalia	74	28.1
Medium mammal	Mammalia	49	18.6
Unidentified		56	21.3
Total		263	100.0

Table 6.1.9 Phase I: fragments from samples quantified by taxa

Vernacular	Taxon	No	%
Bird			
Goose	*Anser/Branta*	6	3.4
Chicken	*Gallus* f domestic	7	3.9
Woodcock	*Scolopax rusticola* L	2	1.1
cf Blackbird	*Turdus* cf *merula* L	1	0.6
Small passerine	Fringillidae/Passeridae	2	1.1
Crow family	Corvidae	2	1.1
Mammal			
Rabbit	*Oryctolagus cuniculus* L	1	0.6
Hare	*Lepus* sp	2	1.1
Mouse	Muridae	10	5.6
Small rodent	Rodentia	8	4.5
Rat	*Rattus* sp	4	2.2
Dog	*Canis* f domestic	1	0.6
Cat	*Felis* f domestic	4	2.2
Pig	*Sus* f domestic	77	43.0
Pig (neonate or suckling)	*Sus* f domestic	18	10.1
Cattle	*Bos* f domestic	16	8.9
Cattle (calf)	*Bos* f domestic	4	2.2
Sheep/goat	*Ovis/Capra*	11	6.1
Sheep	*Ovis* f domestic	3	1.7
Total		179	100.0

Main domestic species
Cattle

Cattle bones made up 47% of the total weight from the phase (Table 6.1.5). Another 32.5% of the total weight was classed as 'large mammal': given that there were no identifications of horse, it is suggested that most or all of this bone may also have come from cattle. Thus one can speculate that cattle elements may have contributed nearly 80% of the weight of bone from this small group. Certainly cattle bones comprised a large proportion of the weight of recovered and identified fauna, and this suggests a large proportion of beef in the diet. A high proportion of cattle bones is to be expected from Roman military sites (King 1984, 189; 1999, 139) although other studies have shown that there can be major variations in species ratios within a particular settlement (Maltby 1994, 86).

When one looks at the hand-collected and sampled NISP totals (Tables 6.1.8–.9), cattle appear considerably less abundant. However, if we again assume that the large mammal fragments were from cattle and combine the two categories, it can be seen that they constituted 36.8% of the fragments. A note of caution is needed, however, since it is also quite probable that a higher proportion of the relatively robust cattle bones survived the range of taphonomic processes than the bones of smaller domesticated and wild fauna. Carnivore gnawing had affected some pig and sheep bones in contexts (1242) and (1138), for instance, and other bones from these animals may have been taken away or eaten. Thus, whilst cattle remains were relatively common, their relative abundance may in part have been a product of pre- and post-depositional processes. Cattle bones are generally larger and, in this period, were generally more extensively chopped than those of the other species and thus there were more fragments to count.

Carcass representation
Amongst the cattle fragments there were bones from various parts of the skeleton. The numbers were too small to investigate in a detailed manner. Whilst one cattle mandible fragment came from sub-phase Ib, all of the other cattle bones were from sub-phases Id (n=14) and Ie (n=9). However, what was clear from this small sample was that various parts of the skeletons of cattle were deposited on the site. The same applied to the pig bones, which came from head, limb bone and distal parts of the skeleton. Thus it is plausible that beef and pork were not being deposited or supplied as a restricted range of joints. Cartledge (1991, 5) drew the conclusion that skeletal elements were generally distributed non-selectively throughout the contexts on the Chester sites she examined and suggested that the majority of animals were brought to Chester on the hoof and slaughtered here. However, she did detect some skeletal patterning, including some 'pockets' with disproportionately high numbers of cattle scapulae (1991, 5, 13 and *see* below). Of course, some concentrations of particular elements are to be expected even where whole carcasses were brought onto a site, and Roman forts were complex sites where the animal bones may well reflect social and internal/external differences (Stokes 2000, 151; Stallibrass 1991, 62). A factor of importance on many Chester sites, as in Carlisle (Stallibrass 1991, 59) is the dumping of animal bone, amongst other materials, in derelict buildings and the disturbance of animal bone during subsequent building work. Where such processes operated they will certainly have obscured the original species and skeletal part distributions. Another important factor is that there appear to be higher proportions of cattle bones on sites close to, but outside, the fortress (Ingrem 2003; Baxter 2007).

Butchery
Many of the cattle long bones and ribs bore hack marks. This butchery would have exposed the marrow inside the long bones and reduced sides of beef into smaller joints.

Two cattle scapula fragments were recovered from these deposits: both were spinous process fragments that bore chop marks that would have separated the spinous process from the blade (Ill 6.1.9). This butchery pattern is common in assemblages of the Roman period in Chester (Cartledge 1991, 5) and elsewhere in the north of England and on the continent (Stallibrass 1991, 33–5). They may represent brined and cold-smoked joints and have been interpreted as being products of systematic processing (Dobney *et al* 1996, 27).

Pig
It is clear from a number of Roman bone assemblages in Chester that there was a good supply of pork in the fortress. It seems possible that pigs outnumbered cattle, although given the size difference between these animals beef was probably the most commonly consumed meat on the Chester sites examined so far. In the much larger sample (19,000 fragments) examined by Judith Cartledge (1991, 3) cattle dominated the fragment counts and were followed in abundance by pig and then sheep/goat.

In this assemblage, pig bone fragments were the most common in each of sub-phases Ib to Ie apart from Id, where twelve fragments were from pig and fourteen from cattle. The largest number of pig fragments came from sub-phase Ie (n=21). Overall, fragments of pig bone were more abundant than those of either cattle or sheep (Tables 6.1.2, .1 and .3 respectively) and the pig bones weighed nearly eleven times as much as the sheep bones (Table 6.1.5). Dividing the medium-sized mammal fragments in the proportions of the identified bones from these two species reveals that pig could potentially have contributed 17.9% of the total weight of hand-collected bone. Identifications of definite pig contributed 12.9% of the total bone weight. In addition, they dominated among fragments from the samples (Table 6.1.9).

A high proportion (93.4%) of pigs were estimated by Cartledge (1991, 8) to have been killed before reaching maturity in Chester. Whilst the proportion of young pigs is not unusual (Stallibrass 1991, 56) the proportion of pig bones (compared to the other main domesticates and especially as compared to sheep) in Chester does seem high as compared to some other military sites in the north, where sheep bones are more frequent than those of pig (Berg 1999, 259; Stallibrass 1991, 30; 2002, 395–7; Stallibrass & Nicholson 2000, 378). The bones of younger mammals have been shown to be discriminated against by taphonomic processes (Symmons 2005, 1691–8; Munson & Garniewicz 2002, 405–16). Thus it is seems reasonable, given that there was evidence for taphonomic processes such as carnivore gnawing, to suggest that younger pigs would have been discriminated against as compared to the adult pigs in most archaeological animal bone assemblages from Chester, as elsewhere. It is also probable that pigs, and sheep, would have been discriminated against as compared to cattle which have larger bones and, the ageing data suggests, were more likely to survive into adulthood than the pigs (Cartledge 1991, 6). In the present assemblage the proportion by weight of bones from pigs, as compared to the other main domesticates, was highest in Phase I (Table 6.1.5) and fell until Phase V, after which it stabilised at between 4 and 5%. The higher frequency of pig over sheep within the fortress at Chester also holds true whether one quantifies by fragment count, MNIs based on the appendicular skeleton, or MNIs based on the mandibles (Cartledge 1991, 3).

Horse

The post-excavation assessment report (Garner 2002) raised the possibility that any horse bones recovered might reflect the stabling of cavalry in this area of the fortress. In fact, no horse bones were recovered from Phase I. However, this proves little since the volume of deposits excavated in the phase was small and in any case horse carcasses may not have been disposed of near to the stables. Some horse fittings were, however, recovered (*see* Cool, *this volume*).

Other fauna

No exotic mammals or birds were recorded from the Roman contexts. The proportion of recovered wild fauna in Roman urban centres is generally small (Maltby 1994, 100; Dobney *et al* 1996, 68 fig 5) and so the relatively low proportion of wild mammals and birds here is not unusual. Woodcock was present amongst the sampled material here and on sites such as Goss Street 1973 and 1–11 Crook Street 1973/4 (Cartledge 1991, bird bone archive) and from the amphitheatre (Smith *in preparation*) and is an indication that some wild fowling took place. One rabbit mandible was recovered from context (1148), which also produced an intrusive post-medieval black cup sherd, so the presence of this rabbit bone in a Roman context should be treated with caution. Other fauna included hare, chicken and goose, which were represented by a few bones only, and roe deer which was represented by a single radius (Tables 6.1.8–.9).

Environmental factors and the military

One of the original research aims was to reveal how the composition of the faunal assemblage might relate to military activity. Certainly this assemblage shared some features of interest with other Roman legionary sites in the north-west provinces. Perhaps the most characteristic feature was the hacked cattle bones, which are typical of Romano-British military sites (Stallibrass 1991, 31; O'Connor 1988, 82). It is of interest that sheep comprised only 5.7% of the hand-collected total from the phase. Cartledge (1991) drew attention to the increase in cattle and pig percentages toward the later Roman period (and *cf* King 1978, 216). This is detectable at Chester when one compares the sheep/goat with cattle and omits the pig (Cartledge 1991, 12). However it is important to restate that this assemblage largely came from the later Roman period and that there were few bones of any species from the early Roman phases (Ib and Ic) and none from sub-phase Ia. This, together with the fact that there were only fifteen sheep bones in total, means that it is impossible to draw any meaningful conclusions about changes in the frequency of sheep bone deposition.

King (1978, 212) noted that assemblages with 30% or more of sheep bones are largely restricted to the lowland area and to dry light soils. The principal soils around Chester and across much of the western plain and Welsh borders are fine loamy over clayey argillic stagnogley soils and are typically characterised by surface wetness (Furness 1978, 116–23). The nature of these soils, combined with their generally flat or undulating aspect, restricts drainage. Thus one might reasonably presume that environmental conditions near Chester would have favoured the rearing of cattle and pigs over sheep in the Roman period. Certainly cattle were more numerous in Cheshire than sheep in the medieval period (Trow-Smith 1957, 142) and they still are today. Prior to the widespread drainage schemes of the post-medieval period, freshwater flukes might well have made conditions even more unsuitable for sheep across much of the county.

However, there is no simple environmental equation that dictates that sheep cannot be reared in wet areas (*see* Dobney *et al* 1996, 58–9, for instance). Also, of course, sheep could have been herded from suitable grazing areas outside Cheshire. A number of Chester sites do show a decrease in the proportions of sheep/goat bones through the Roman period (Cartledge 1991, 12). It is assumed that sheep would have been more numerous on civilian sites than within the fortress (Stallibrass 1991, 64). However, as elsewhere in Britain (King 1999, 139), the rearing of sheep in some of the areas that supplied Chester with animal products may have been important prior to the Roman conquest and declined thereafter. One can hypothesise that cultural rather than environmental factors may have been the key to declining sheep bone deposition within the fortress. Obviously this needs to be tested and the recovery of well dated assemblages from Chester and its rural hinterland is crucial.

Summary and further research

It is unfortunate that this group of bones was too small to divide into sub-phases. However, it was possible to recognise that the fauna and butchery practices were typical of the Roman period in Chester. Hacked cattle and pig bones dominated amongst what were mainly food remains. Issues regarding possible declining frequencies of sheep and increasing numbers of pigs through the Roman period in Chester deserve further investigation through the recovery of larger well dated assemblages from both inside and outside the fortress.

Phase II

Sample size

1712 fragments were hand-collected and there were 177 identifications from samples (Tables 6.1.10–.11). Wet-sieved bone was recovered from twelve contexts (Table 6.1.50).

Main domestic species

Cattle

Cattle fragments comprised 19% (NISP=325) of the total fragments recovered (Table 6.1.1). Cattle were represented by a range of elements from different parts of the carcass, cranial, axial, main limb and distal limb bones being present. Cattle bones also contributed 56% of the weight of bones from the main stock animals (cattle, sheep and pig) plus the large and medium mammal categories. If one combines the cattle bones with the large mammal bones this percentage rises to 79% of the main stock animals by weight. Potentially this could mean that beef constituted 79% of the meat that came from these stock mammals (Reitz & Wing 1999, 200). It is, however, likely that cattle bone survival exceeded that for the smaller species and it seems appropriate to assume that the latter

Table 6.1.10 Phase II: hand-collected fragments quantified by taxa

Vernacular	Taxon	No	%
Bird			
Swan	*Cygnus* sp	1	0.1
Goose	*Anser/Branta*	1	0.1
Duck	*Anas* sp	2	0.1
Chicken	*Gallus* f domestic	32	1.9
Golden plover	*Pluvialis apricaria* L.	1	0.1
Jackdaw	*Corvus monedula* L.	1	0.1
Bird unident	Aves	8	0.5
Mammal			
Hare	*Lepus* sp	3	0.2
Dog	*Canis* f domestic	47	2.7
Bear	*Ursus arctos* L.	1	0.1
Wild cat	*Felis sylvestris* Schreber	19	1.1
Horse	*Equus* f domestic	7	0.4
Pig	*Sus* f domestic	234	13.7
Red deer	*Cervus elaphus* L.	2	0.1
Red/fallow deer	*Cervus/Dama*	1	0.1
Roe deer	*Capreolus capreolus* L.	4	0.2
Cattle	*Bos* f domestic	325	19.0
Sheep	*Ovis* f domestic	31	1.8
Sheep/goat	*Ovis/Capra*	83	4.8
Large mammal	Mammalia	410	23.9
Medium mammal	Mammalia	189	11.0
Small mammal	Mammalia	14	0.8
Unidentified		296	17.3
Total		1712	100.0

Table 6.1.11 Phase II: fragments from samples quantified by taxa

Vernacular	Taxon	No	%
Amphibian			
Toad	cf *Bufo* sp	1	0.6
Frog	cf *Rana* sp	2	1.1
Frog/toad	*Rana/Bufo*	8	4.5
Bird			
Goose	*Anser/Branta*	3	1.7
Duck	*Anas* sp	1	0.6
Chicken	*Gallus* f domestic	7	4.0
?wader unidentified	Aves	1	0.6
Small wader	cf *Calidris* sp	1	0.6
Small passerine	Passeriformes	5	2.8
Thrush family	*Turdus* sp	1	0.6
Small passerine	cf Fringillidae/Passeridae	3	1.7
Small corvid	Corvidae	1	0.6
Mammal			
Common shrew	*Sorex araneus* L.	2	1.1
Pygmy shrew	*Sorex pygmaeus* L.	1	0.6
Shrew	Soricidae	3	1.7
Hare	*Lepus* sp	1	0.6
Hare/rabbit	Leporidae	1	0.6
Vole	cf *Microtus agrestis* L.	3	1.7
Vole	Microtidae	1	0.6
Mouse	Muridae	8	4.5
Small rodent	Rodentia	20	11.3
Rat-sized rodent	Rodentia	2	1.1
Dog	*Canis* f domestic	5	2.8
Cat	*Felis* f domestic	6	3.4
Pig	*Sus* f domestic	54	30.5
Pig (neonate or suckling)	*Sus* f domestic	4	2.3
Cattle	*Bos* f domestic	17	9.6
Cattle (calf)	*Bos* f domestic	0	0.0
Sheep/goat	*Ovis/Capra*	13	7.3
Goat	*Capra* f domestic	0	0.0
Sheep	*Ovis* f domestic	2	1.1
Total		177	100.0

are under-represented.

Metrical data

A few cattle horn core measurements from this phase indicated that cattle with quite small horns were present. One specimen which was classed as age class 3, and so probably approaching its maximum size (Armitage 1982, 41), had an outer length of only 90 mm and a basal circumference of 112 mm. This is the size of horn core one might expect of the cattle which were originally known

as *Bos longifrons* (Trow-Smith 1957, 22) but which are now recognised as being small domestic cattle and not of a discrete species (Clutton-Brock 1987, 65).

Butchery

It is of interest that six contexts produced cattle scapulae with chop marks at the base of the spinous process (Ill 6.1.9 *below*) similar to those referred to in Phase I and typical of the Roman period in Chester (Cartledge 1991, 5). Two of these contexts, (1142) and (1225) in Phase IIa, may relate to the final Roman activity. The presence of this distinctive butchery method in later contexts, (1132), (1135), (1138) and (1161), suggests that either organised processing and supply of such joints continued until late in Phase II or that these bones were residual.

Pig

Pigs continued to constitute a significant proportion (NISP=234 or 13.7%) of the assemblage. This might be explained most simply by a continuation in the consumption of relatively large quantities of pork. A number of the contexts that produced bone, (1142), (1219), (1220) and (1225) in Phase IIa, related to the final Roman activity on the site. However, some of the relatively large number of the pig bones are potentially residual (*see* below). Pigs made up a larger proportion of the fauna in Phase I–IV as compared to the later phases (Table 6.1.5).

Residuality

It is clear that there were high levels of Roman residual material in Phases II to IV, and it is possible that the pattern of bone redeposition mirrored that of the pottery and building material. Levels of residuality in bone are difficult to identify from the bone itself and there is no straightforward relationship between the levels of residuality in pottery and bone (*see*, for instance, Dobney *et al* 1996, 18, 19). However the radiocarbon dating results suggested that some (earlier Roman) residual bone was indeed present. The animal bone from the Phase IIb pit (1138) produced 2 sigma results of cal AD 60–240 (Beta – 170989) and cal 45 BC to cal AD 120 (Beta – 170988). Meanwhile, animal bone recovered from the upper fill of Phase IIa sewer (1219) produced a 2 sigma result of cal AD 115–339 (Beta – 170990).

Other fauna

Bear

There was one second phalanx of a bear from Phase IIc layer (1177) (Ill 6.1.1). The presence of this bone need not indicate the presence of a whole bear – possibly only the import of a skin with phalanges attached. Various sites of similar date have produced bones from the feet of bears, and some of these may well attest a long-distance trade in bear skins, including for use in burial ceremonies, or in live bears for baiting (Yalden (1999, 112, 115, 165). Wild bears may have been extinct in Britain from as early as Roman times or slightly later in Scotland.

Cat

Amongst the cat bones from pit fill (1138) there were metapodials with cut marks which suggested that a cat had been skinned (Ill 6.1.2). However, there was no evidence that there was any butchery in addition to the skinning. The bones came from a large animal, probably

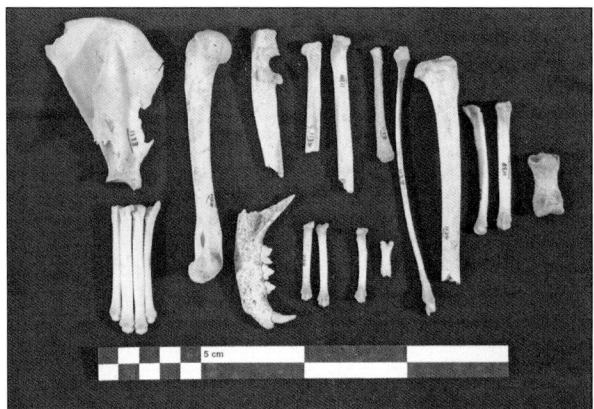

III 6.1.1 Phase II: cat skeleton and a single bear second phalanx
(far right).

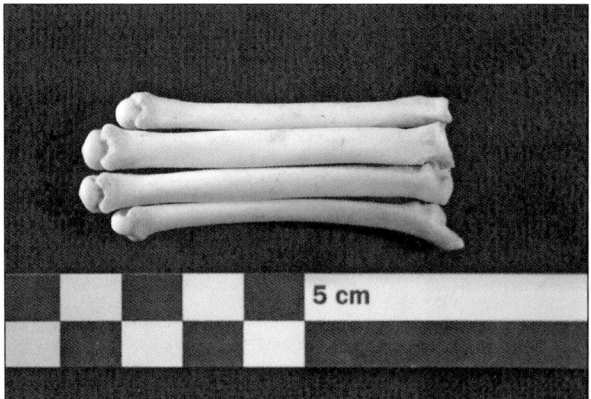

III 6.1.2 Phase II: cat metatarsals. Fine cut marks are just visible on the
second and third metatarsals.

a wild cat (*Felis sylvestris*). All of the main limb bones of
this specimen were compared to wild cat specimens at
York University (EAU 774, 776 and 783) and in each
case the specimens from context (1138) were larger. The
bones were very well preserved and the possibility that
they might relate to a later period was considered. There
were two sherds of intrusive pottery in this context, but
there was also a series of deposits and structures, including a sandstone oven, which overlay the area from which
the skeleton was recovered. After a consideration of the
stratigraphy (Dan Garner *pers comm*), it therefore seems
unlikely that a whole cat skeleton could be intrusive and
more probable that it was deposited prior to the backfilling of the pit.

Micro-fauna
A small number of frog and toad pelvic and other bones
were recovered from this phase (Table 6.1.11). Sample
<5125> from Phase IIb context (1179) produced some of
these. The context has been interpreted as being the fill
of a robber pit cut to extract stone from a sewer. These
amphibians may either have made their way into the sewer and after disturbance their remains might have been
incorporated into the fill of the robber pit, or they may
have fallen directly into the robber pit. The appearance
in this phase of amphibians and of pygmy shrew, common shrew and vole (Table 6.1.11) may at first sight
suggest a period when there was less intensive use of the
site. In fact shrews appear to have occurred regularly with
other urban synanthropic fauna, and the presence of frogs
and toads in such situations is not unusual (O'Connor

2003, 198). Another possibility is that amphibians were
part of the diet during the Roman period, since evidence
has been claimed for their consumption on a number of
European sites (*see* Luff 1982, 266). Vole were attested
by only three teeth, certainly identified as vole and almost certainly *Microtus agrestis*, which might have come
from a single animal. They suggest the possibility that
nearby there was some ground cover or cultivated land.

Summary and further research
Cattle and pigs continued to form a large proportion of
the fauna. This may reflect the continuation of practices
seen in Phase I. However, some of the radiocarbon dates
and finds force us to question the levels of residuality in
this material. If in future undisturbed groups of bone clearly dating to the late Roman and Dark Age periods are
recovered in Chester they will clearly be valuable. It
would be most instructive to compare Roman species
representation, butchery, age structures and so on with
assemblages from demonstrably Dark Age or Saxon contexts.

Phase III

Sample size
There were 887 hand-collected fragments and 50 identifications from samples (Tables 6.1.12–.13). Wet-sieved
bone was recovered from eight contexts (Table 6.1.50).

Main domestic species
Cattle dominated in numbers of fragments (NISP=158 or
17.8%) and weight, and the bones of pig (NISP=89 or
10%) were slightly more common than those of caprovids
(NISP=73 or 8.2%). Cattle, pigs and sheep were represented by all parts of the skeleton. Amongst the sheep,
meat-bearing parts predominated. Goat bones appeared
in this phase and in each of the succeeding phases, but
always as a small component of the assemblage and always represented by head and foot parts: there were no
identifications of the major meat-bearing bones of goats
(Table 6.1.4).

Pig and sheep
Bone weight and possible recording bias
The pig bones from this phase, and from each of Phases I
to IV, weighed considerably more than the sheep bones
(Table 6.1.5). It is possible that this was in part due to a
bias at the recording stage. Many fragmentary pig bones
are instantly recognisable as such, whereas some small
fragments of probable sheep bone can be difficult to distinguish conclusively from roe deer or other medium-sized
mammals. However, even if one assumed that all of the
medium-sized mammal bones from Phases I to IV were
from sheep, the pig bones would still have weighed more
than these combined with the identified sheep bone from
these phases.

Pig mandibles and possible taphonomic bias
Pig mandibular and maxillary fragment percentages as a
proportion of total pig fragments were highest in Phases
I to IV (Table 6.1.2) (mean percentage = 33 and 29.9% or
over in each of these phases) and lowest in Phases V to IX
(mean percentage = 24.5% and below 26.5% in each
phase). Any changes in the provisioning of carcasses (for

Table 6.1.12 Phase III: hand-collected fragments quantified by taxa

Vernacular	Taxon	No	%
Bird			
Goose	Anser/Branta	4	0.5
Duck	Anas sp	1	0.1
Chicken	Gallus f domestic	8	0.9
Bird unident	Aves	2	0.2
Mammal			
Dog	Canis f domestic	21	2.4
Cat	Felis f domestic	6	0.7
Horse	Equus f domestic	5	0.8
Pig	Sus f domestic	89	10.0
Red deer	Cervus elaphus L.	3	0.3
Red/fallow deer	Cervus/Dama	2	0.2
Roe deer	Capreolus capreolus L.	6	0.7
Cattle	Bos f domestic	158	17.8
Goat	Capra f domestic	2	0.2
Sheep	Ovis f domestic	6	0.7
Sheep/goat	Ovis/Capra	65	7.3
Large mammal	Mammalia	291	32.7
Medium mammal	Mammalia	121	13.6
Small mammal	Mammalia	3	0.3
Unidentified		94	10.6
Total		887	100.0

Table 6.1.13 Phase III: fragments from samples quantified by taxa

Vernacular	Taxon	No	%
Amphibian			
Toad	cf Bufo sp	1	2.0
Frog	cf Rana sp	4	8.0
Bird			
Swan	Cygnus sp	1	2.0
Small passerine	Passeriformes	1	2.0
Chicken	Gallus f domestic	6	12.0
Mammal			
Common shrew	Sorex araneus L.	1	2.0
Rabbit	Oryctolagus cuniculus L.	1	2.0
House mouse	Mus musculus L.	1	2.0
Mouse	Muridae	2	4.0
Small rodent	Rodentia	6	12.0
Rat	Rattus sp	1	2.0
Dog	Canis f domestic	1	2.0
Pig	Sus f domestic	14	28.0
Pig (neonate or suckling)	Sus f domestic	1	2.0
Cattle	Bos f domestic	6	12.0
Cattle (calf)	Bos f domestic	0	0.0
Sheep/goat	Ovis/Capra	3	6.0
Total		50	100.0

instance whether whole, without heads or as particular joints) must obviously have been important factors in this process. Possible industrial selectivity must also have been an important factor. In Phase V, for instance, there was a significant over-representation of distal bones among the sheep or goats which appeared to relate to leatherworking. It was clear that, in terms of weight, the whole assemblage could be divided into two. The weight ratios of pig to sheep switched at Phase V, with pig being dominant in the earlier phases and sheep in Phase V and later. The influence of the Roman army on the composition of the Phase I assemblage was clearly of great importance. Another possible influence is taphonomy. High values for pig in the earlier periods could plausibly relate to greater weight and chance of survival of their teeth over long periods as compared to post-cranial elements of pig (or sheep). This trend in pig bone and tooth survival deserves further investigation and comparison with other sites.

Other fauna

Dog

One of the larger groups of bone came from layer (1022). The finds from this context were exclusively Roman. Amongst these there were femora which suggested the presence of dogs of approximately 27 and 30 cm at the withers (Table 6.1.33). Dogs of this size and smaller appeared during the Roman period and it has been suggested that they included lap dogs which would not have survived without human shelter and protection (Harcourt 1974, 164). A markedly bowed ulna and two femora from context (1022) appeared to have morphologies and dimensions similar to the bow-legged dwarf dogs referred to and illustrated by Baxter (2006, 12–23). Meanwhile a tibia from the same context was notably straight and gracile and appeared to have more in common with the small, straight-limbed dogs identified by the same author (2006, 12–23). Thus it appears possible that both types of dwarf dogs defined by Baxter were represented. Evidence for dogs was also present in the form of carnivore (tentatively dog-) gnawed pig, sheep and cattle bones and by a possible dog coprolite identified in the bulk sample (*see* Jaques *et al* this volume).

Deer

Roe deer were represented by a small group of bones (NISP=6) which included two of the main meat-bearing bones (a humerus and a tibia), and the red deer (NISP=3) remains consisted of a femur, humerus and tibia.

Other animals from context (1022) and (1175)

Five of the cat bones from this phase (NISP=6) also came from (1022), as did a number of chicken, duck and goose bones. Horse (NISP=5) was represented by mandibular, axial and distal parts from this context. Rat, mouse, frog and toad bones also came from wet-sieved samples from context (1022).

Residuality and bone condition in context (1022)

When initial examination of all the bone from context (1022) was undertaken the surface preservation, colour and the angularity of broken edges suggested that this bone was unlikely to have been redeposited. The colour was relatively uniform, there was little evidence for the rounding of broken edges, and surface preservation was excellent except where dog gnawing had taken its toll. However, C14-dated animal bone, in a state characteristic of context (1022), produced a 2 sigma date of cal AD 215–400 (Beta – 170987). This and the fact that the datable finds such as the pottery were exclusively Roman suggest that there was a high degree of residuality among the bones. This possibility might be conclusively resolved by multiple radiocarbon dates from individual contexts, but such research was unfortunately outside the financial scope of the project.

Cess pit fill (1175)

Cattle, pig, sheep, chicken, house mouse, common shrew, frog and toad bones were identified in the sampled green silty lower fill (1175) of possible cess pit (1176). Whilst the pottery and building materials from this fill suggested some residuality, it may be the case that the micro-fauna included bones from individuals that fell into the pit.

Summary and further research
Residuality continues to be an issue worthy of further investigation as do continued high proportions of pig bones. As with the previous phase, the recovery of undisturbed groups of bone of this date would be of great value.

Phase IV

Sample size
There were 806 hand-collected fragments and 123 identifications from samples (Tables 6.1.14–.15). Wet-sieved bone was recovered from six contexts (Table 6.1.50).

Main domestic species
Cattle
Amongst the cattle (n=115; zones from seventy fragments with zones present) the most common zone was the sustentaculum tali of the calcaneus, followed by the glenoid cavity of the scapula and the astragalus. Metapodials, the distal trochlea of the humerus, the supracondyloid fossa of the femur and the angle of the mandible were also relatively common. Whole carcasses or a range of joints from different parts of the skeleton were apparently deposited.

No calf bones were recovered among the hand-recovered cattle bones. Instead, all (NISP=176) were either from sub-adult or adult animals. Likewise, amongst the sieved samples there were no calf bones. By contrast, each succeeding phase did produce calf bones. Cattle bones and unidentified large mammal fragments dominated the phase in terms of fragment numbers and weight (Tables 6.1.1 and 6.1.5).

Butchery
From Plot 2 (context (882)) there was a fragment of cattle maxilla with multiple cut marks (five main cuts and at least one much smaller) located under the facial tuberosity, some 10 mm over the maxillary P4 and over the empty and damaged socket of the P3. The cut marks ran approximately parallel to the alveolar border and possibly resulted from skinning. The presence of this fragment may suggest that the animal was skinned on site or perhaps that waste from that process was dumped here. Other butchery, such as the multiple cut marks on an astragalus that match Binford's butchery code TA-1 (1981, 120) and hacks through the calcaneus, related to dismemberment. The cattle metapodials included specimens hacked across the proximal shaft and mid-shaft and two were split longitudinally. Hack marks at the proximal end of radii were also recorded. Pelves were hacked through the ilium, pubis and across the acetabulum. Scapulae included examples that were hacked at the base of the spinous process, across the 'neck' and through the lateral tuberosity.

Some particular hack marks (such as those seen in the scapulae) had much in common with the butchery marks seen in Roman contexts. Whether this represented a continuation or similarity in butchery techniques in some parts of the city or was due to the redeposition of Roman period bones is not clear. The recovery of well sealed early medieval deposits containing butchered material is needed to help to elucidate this issue.

Table 6.1.14 Phase IV: hand-collected fragments quantified by taxa

Vernacular	Taxon	No	%
Bird			
Goose	Anser/Branta	3	0.4
Duck	Anas sp	1	0.1
Chicken	Gallus f domestic	6	0.7
Raven	Corvus corax L.	4	0.5
Bird unident	Aves	4	0.5
Mammal			
Rabbit	Oryctolagus cuniculus L.	1	0.1
Hare	Lepus sp	1	0.1
Dog	Canis f domestic	6	0.7
Cat	Felis f domestic	8	1.0
Horse	Equus f domestic	10	1.2
Pig	Sus f domestic	63	7.9
Red deer	Cervus elaphus L.	2	0.2
Red/fallow deer	Cervus/Dama	3	0.4
Red deer/cattle	Cervus/Bos	1	0.1
Cattle	Bos f domestic	176	21.8
Goat	Capra f domestic	2	0.2
Sheep	Ovis f domestic	5	0.6
Sheep/goat	Ovis/Capra	31	3.8
Large mammal	Mammalia	262	32.5
Large or medium mammal	Mammalia	2	0.2
Medium mammal	Mammalia	53	6.6
Small mammal	Mammalia	4	0.5
Unidentified		158	19.6
Total		806	100.0

Table 6.1.15 Phase IV: fragments from samples quantified by taxa

Vernacular	Taxon	No	%
Amphibian			
Toad	cf Bufo sp	1	0.8
Bird			
Chicken	Gallus f domestic	6	4.9
Small passerine	Passeriformes	2	1.6
Small passerine	cf Fringillidae/Passeridae	2	1.6
Mammals			
Common shrew	Sorex araneus L.	2	1.6
Pygmy shrew	Sorex pygmaeus L.	1	0.8
Rabbit	Oryctolagus cuniculus L.	1	0.8
Vole	Microtidae	2	1.6
Mouse	Muridae	2	1.6
Rodent	Rodentia	3	2.4
Small rodent	Rodentia	25	20.3
Rat-sized rodent	Rodentia	2	1.6
Dog	Canis f domestic	1	0.8
Cat	Felis f domestic	1	0.8
Pig	Sus f domestic	40	32.5
Red deer	Cervus elaphus L.	1	0.8
Cattle	Bos f domestic	15	12.2
Sheep/goat	Ovis/Capra	10	8.1
Sheep	Ovis f domestic	5	4.1
Human	Homo sapiens L.	1	0.8
Total		123	100.0

Documentary evidence
Documentary evidence is clearly of importance to an understanding of the management of cattle in all periods. During the early medieval period there was right of common pasture on nearby Saltney Marsh, and there were imports of Welsh cattle and meat into the city (Lewis & Thacker eds 2003, 41, 29). Thus some of the patterns of cattle trade and husbandry that existed in the post-medieval period can be traced back to early medieval times.

Pig and sheep
Both pigs and sheep were represented by parts of fore limb, hind limb and by distal elements such as metapodials (Tables 6.1.2–.3). One fragment each of goat and sheep horn core was recovered. The pig elements included small and delicate limb bones (humeri, radius, ulna and tibia n=5) from animals of neonatal size, suggesting that pigs were farrowing on the site. Salted meat was one of the

foodstuffs traded in Chester in considerable quantities (Lewis & Thacker eds 2003, 46) during this period and it is possible that some of the cuts of salted meat might have been 'boned out' and thus may be invisible at the site of consumption.

Butchery

The butchery mainly represented the dismemberment and filleting of carcasses to produce joints of mutton or lamb. No particular characteristics were identified to differentiate the butchery recorded here from that seen in later periods. Amongst the sheep bones there were fine cut marks at the proximal end of one metatarsal and fine cut marks indicative of filleting at the distal end of a humerus. Some hacking and possible hacking of sheep radii and of mid- and distal tibia shafts was recorded and one humerus had been hacked through medial and lateral distal condyles. One sheep skull had been split sagittally and the single goat horn core had been hacked at the base in a manner seen amongst the goat horn cores from the later phases. Documentary evidence suggests that sheep and sacks of wool, as well as pelts, horses and pigs, were amongst the goods traded at the Midsummer Fair at this time (Lewis & Thacker eds 2003, 45).

Other fauna
Deer

Red deer was represented by an unfused calcaneus (context (1030), <5114>) and by a scapula and tibia from layer (974). There were also three fragments of deer antler from Plots 1, 2 and 3. The antler might have originated from craftworking debris or be associated with the import of skins. Chester was known for its leatherworkers from the twelfth century and animal skins (especially the pelts of 'marten') were imported from Ireland at this time (Lewis & Thacker eds 2003, 29, 30). The presence of the meat-bearing bones almost certainly related to the consumption of venison.

The presence in layer (974) of leg and wing bones of raven might indicate that these birds were scavenging on the site, but it is also possible that they were eaten by humans.

Indeterminate fragments

The indeterminate fragments from the samples (pit fill contexts (1015), (1030), (1033)) appeared slightly variable in colour and variable also in angularity and state of preservation. Each of these groups of indeterminate bone also contained a proportion (between 5 and 20%) of white, black or blue burnt mammal bone and there were a few fragments of burnt bird bone. The variability in state of preservation might have been due to a proportion of residual finds which were present not only in the layers but also in these pit fills, which also contained *tesserae* and other finds of Roman date.

Summary and further research

Again, the artefactual evidence suggests that we should be wary of assuming that all of the animal bones necessarily originated from this phase. It is possible but also questionable whether some butchery methods characteristic of the Roman period were still practised at this late date. The recovery of demonstrably early medieval bone assemblages from Chester is clearly desirable.

Phase V

Sample size
3908 fragments were collected by hand and 1773 fragments were recovered from samples (Tables 6.1.16–.17). (*See* also Unidentified fragments, below). Wet-sieved bone was recovered from fourteen contexts (Table 6.1.50).

Distribution and frequency amongst context types
The majority of the hand-collected fragments (n=3908) recovered from this phase came from layers (62%), whereas fills produced 36% and structures nearly 2%. Many of the contexts had quite distinctive animal bone assemblages that were not shared with other contexts with close stratigraphic associations. As one method of revealing relative frequency (O'Connor 1985, 29), an assessment was made of the proportion of bone-bearing contexts in which a species occurred. Thus, cattle bones were recovered from 78% of the bone-bearing contexts, sheep from 56%, pig from 48%, and chicken from 23%. Cat bones were recovered from 20% and dog from only 13% of contexts.

The overall frequencies of individual species from this phase were not good predictors of the proportion of contexts from which they were recovered. There were, for instance, comparable numbers of hand-collected pig (NISP=196) and dog (NISP=190) fragments, and yet dogs were represented in a much smaller proportion of the contexts. The distribution was also biased by plot. For instance, dog bones made up between 0.3 and 25% of the fragment totals from individual plots (Table 6.1.16) and 83% of the dog bone fragments came from Plot 6. Pig bones appear to have been deposited more evenly and made up between 4% and 6% of the fragments from each plot. Horse and cat bones, like those of dog, were highly clustered in groups of contexts in particular plots. The clustered distribution seen amongst the bones of cats, dogs and horses clearly reflected the occasional disposal of whole or partial carcasses and thus there were discrete (sometimes large) groups of their bones in a small number of contexts. As one might expect, the bones of these cats and dogs were less fragmented than those of the common food species (Ill 6.1.24).

Unidentified fragments
Small fragments of bone made up a large proportion of the material from the samples. For Phase V, a fragment count demonstrated that the bulk of these were mammalian, although they could not confidently be identified to species (Table 6.1.17). Counts were not made for the other phases but all of the material was scanned and almost certainly fragments of mammal bone would have been the most frequent component in the samples from this and all other phases.

Main domestic species
Cattle
Carcass representation
Amongst the cattle bones various meat-bearing parts were most numerous. The glenoid cavity of the scapula and the supracondyloid fossa of the femur provided the most commonly recorded zones (n=85 fragments zoned and 115 zones recorded). The highest totals of fragment numbers were recorded for the tibia, femur and humerus (Table

Table 6.1.16 Phase V: hand-collected fragments quantified by plot and taxa

Vernacular	Taxon	1	2	3	Plot 4	5	6	Other	No	%
Bird										
Heron	*Ardea cinerea* L.						1		1	0.0
Goose	*Anser/Branta*	1		14	3	1		2	21	0.5
Duck	*Anas* sp						1		1	0.0
Chicken	*Gallus* f domestic	4	8	34	5	7	4	3	65	1.7
cf Curlew	cf *Numenius arquata* L.			1					1	0.0
Pigeon	Columbidae			1					1	0.0
Raven	*Corvus corax* L.		1	3					4	0.1
Bird unident	Aves	5	1	20	5	6	1		38	1.0
Mammal										
Rabbit	*Oryctolagus cuniculus* L.			1			1		2	0.1
Hare	*Lepus* sp			21	1				22	0.6
Rat	*Rattus* sp			2					2	0.1
Dog	*Canis* f domestic	21	1	9	1		158		190	4.9
Stoat	*Mustela erminea* L.	1							1	0.0
Cat	*Felis* f domestic	1	13	91	6		1	2	114	2.9
Horse	*Equus* f domestic	1		24			3	1	29	0.7
Pig	*Sus* f domestic	25	12	94	15	3	26	21	196	5.0
Red deer	*Cervus elaphus* L.				3				3	0.1
Fallow deer	*Dama dama* L.							1	1	0.0
Red/fallow deer	*Cervus/Dama*	1	1	6	3		4	1	16	0.4
Red deer/cattle	*Cervus/Bos*			1					1	0.0
Cattle	*Bos* f domestic	92	92	320	99	5	152	33	793	20.3
Goat	*Capra* f domestic			11	1	1	1		14	0.4
Sheep	*Ovis* f domestic			46	7		4	2	59	1.5
Sheep/goat	*Ovis/Capra*	27	13	277	32	1	26	24	400	10.2
Human	*Homo sapiens* L.				1				1	0.0
Large mammal	Mammalia	156	82	422	80	22	143	35	940	24.1
Large or medium mammal	Mammalia	2		2			1		5	0.1
Medium mammal	Mammalia	18	16	198	11	14	20	11	288	7.4
Small mammal	Mammalia	1	1	17					19	0.5
Unidentified		138	58	358	32	6	69	19	680	17.4
Total		494	299	1973	305	66	616	155	3908	100.0

Table 6.1.17 Phase V: fragments from samples quantified by plot and taxa

Vernacular	Taxon	1	2	3	Plot 4	5	6	No	%
Amphibian									
Toad	*Bufo bufo*	2						2	0.1
Frog	cf *Rana* sp	2						2	0.1
Bird									
Goose	*Anser/Branta*	1						1	0.1
Chicken	*Gallus* f domestic	2						2	0.1
Small passerine unident	Passeriformes	1	1				1	3	0.2
Bird									
Bird unident	Aves	12	9	2				23	1.3
Mammal									
Mole	*Talpa europaea* L.						1	1	0.1
Pygmy shrew	*Sorex pygmaeus* L.		1					1	0.1
Shrew	Soricidae			1				1	0.1
House mouse	*Mus musculus* L.	6	3	1				10	0.6
Rat	*Rattus* sp	2	1	1	6			10	0.6
Mouse-sized rodent	Rodentia		2	2	3		2	9	0.5
Rat-sized rodent	Rodentia				6		1	7	0.4
Rodent	Rodentia		3		6			9	0.5
Dog	*Canis* f domestic	15						15	0.8
Small carnivore	Mustelidae?	1						1	0.1
Cat	*Felis* f domestic	7			21			28	1.6
Pig	*Sus* f domestic	14	2	2	1		4	23	1.3
Cattle	*Bos* f domestic	4	1	4	4		1	14	0.8
Sheep/goat	*Ovis/Capra*	2	1	1	4		1	9	0.5
Mammal unident	Mammalia	829	205	180	165		89	1468	82.8
Large mammal	Mammalia	4	2		7			13	0.7
Unidentified		53	40		26		2	121	6.8
Total		957	271	194	249	0	102	1773	100.0

6.1.1). Since cattle bones were found widely amongst the contexts, this element representation is interpreted as reflecting the regular disposal of bones from joints of beef.

Age

Calf fragments constituted 9.4% of the zoned cattle fragments (Ill 6.1.3). Clearly calf carcasses or joints were arriving on site from this phase. A major source of these animals may have been the county of Cheshire itself. Large numbers of cattle were raised in Cheshire from the fourteenth century, although cattle were also driven to the city from Wales (Trow-Smith 1957, 108–9). Cestrians themselves had common rights of pasture on Hoole Heath and on the meadows by the Dee in Saltney, and there were private pastures to the north of the city (Lewis & Thacker eds 2003, 49). Certainly, numbers of calf bones increased as a proportion of the total number of cattle fragments zoned from this time through to Phase VII, and it is suggested that this reflected the rise of the Cheshire dairy industry. The considerable extent of ridge and furrow shows the that arable farming was at one time widespread in Cheshire, although many areas have been destroyed since 1945: it appears that the change from arable to dairying across much of the county had its origins in the 1350s and 1360s, although arable production was still very important at this time (Crosby 1996, 43, 45).

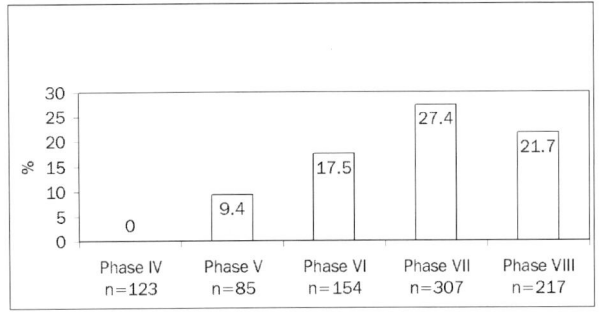

Ill 6.1.3 Phase V: calf fragments as a percentage of cattle fragments where zones could be counted (sample=886 fragments).

Fodder is another important factor to consider regarding the age structure amongst cattle, in that providing fodder for a large number of new cattle would have been difficult, especially so in severe winters. For farmers in the wetter parts of Cheshire, even in more recent periods prior to widespread drainage works, keeping breeding stock alive through the winter was difficult and securing enough fodder was a dominant concern (Dodd 1988, 50). This must surely have meant that control of stock levels was crucial, and that one of the main incentives regarding the slaughter of calves prior to the winter months was the availability of fodder.

Butchery

The recorded hack marks include some on vertebrae (n=7) that possibly related to the division of carcasses into left and right sides (Table 6.1.49). Six femora were hacked mid-shaft to divide the femur in two. Four scapulae had been chopped across the 'neck', apparently to divide the articular end from the blade.

Pig

The hand-collected pig bones came from all parts of the skeleton. Humeri, tibiae, radii and ulnae were well represented but the number of pelves was lower than might have been expected (Table 6.1.2). Dog-gnawing was recorded and certainly accounted for the reduction of some limb bone elements into cylinders. Butchery of pig bones included hacking through the distal shaft of a femur and through the mandibular coronoid process. One hand-collected humerus of new-born size was recovered from Plot 3 (context (807)). It is suggested that joints of pork were brought to the site and it is possible that some pigs were raised on site.

Sheep

There was a marked increase in the numbers of sheep or goat bones recovered between the early and late medieval periods (Table 6.1.3). A trend towards increased numbers of sheep bones can be seen at a number of cities around the country from the eleventh to seventeenth centuries (O'Connor 1989, 13–18) and can be linked to the development of the wool trade. However, there is sometimes considerable variation in sheep bone abundance between different sites within the same city (Gidney 2000, 172). It is possible that the increase in caprovid bones does reflect a regional drive to increase the numbers of sheep, but according to William Smith Cheshire was not 'heavily sheeped' from the sixteenth century (Trow-Smith, 1957, 210). Certainly Chester was not heavily involved in the wool trade in the medieval period but its merchants did obtain some wool for local supply and export, mainly from the monasteries in north Wales (Lewis & Thacker eds 2003, 47).

Carcass representation

Consideration of the recorded zones shows that there were two main groups of caprovid bones:
1   metapodials and phalanges of lamb or kid
2   meat-bearing parts of fully grown (sub-adult or adult) animals

Zones from metapodials were the most commonly recorded (Ill 6.1.4). The medial central shaft, lateral central shaft, anterior distal groove and foramen and the medial and lateral facets of the proximal articulation of the metapodials were all common, whereas the relatively small unfused distal condyles were under-represented. This may have been due to recovery bias since this material was collected by hand and tiny distal condyles of such small sheep were likely to be missed by anything other than fine sieving. However, it is also clear that all other bones were under-represented as compared to the metapodials. The metapodials were porous, unfused distally and generally between 65 and 90 mm long. The fusion data (Table 6.1.38) suggested the presence of many young animals, and indeed most of the metapodials were approximately the size of those illustrated by Amorosi, which are between birth and six weeks old (1989, 241, 305). Relatively large concentrations were found, with very few other parts of the skeleton. Some bore fine cut marks which ran around the proximal end of the shaft some 10 to 15 mm from the proximal articulation (code MTp5 in Table 6.1.39). The minority of zones relating to the major meat-bearing bones in this phase (Ill 6.1.4) came

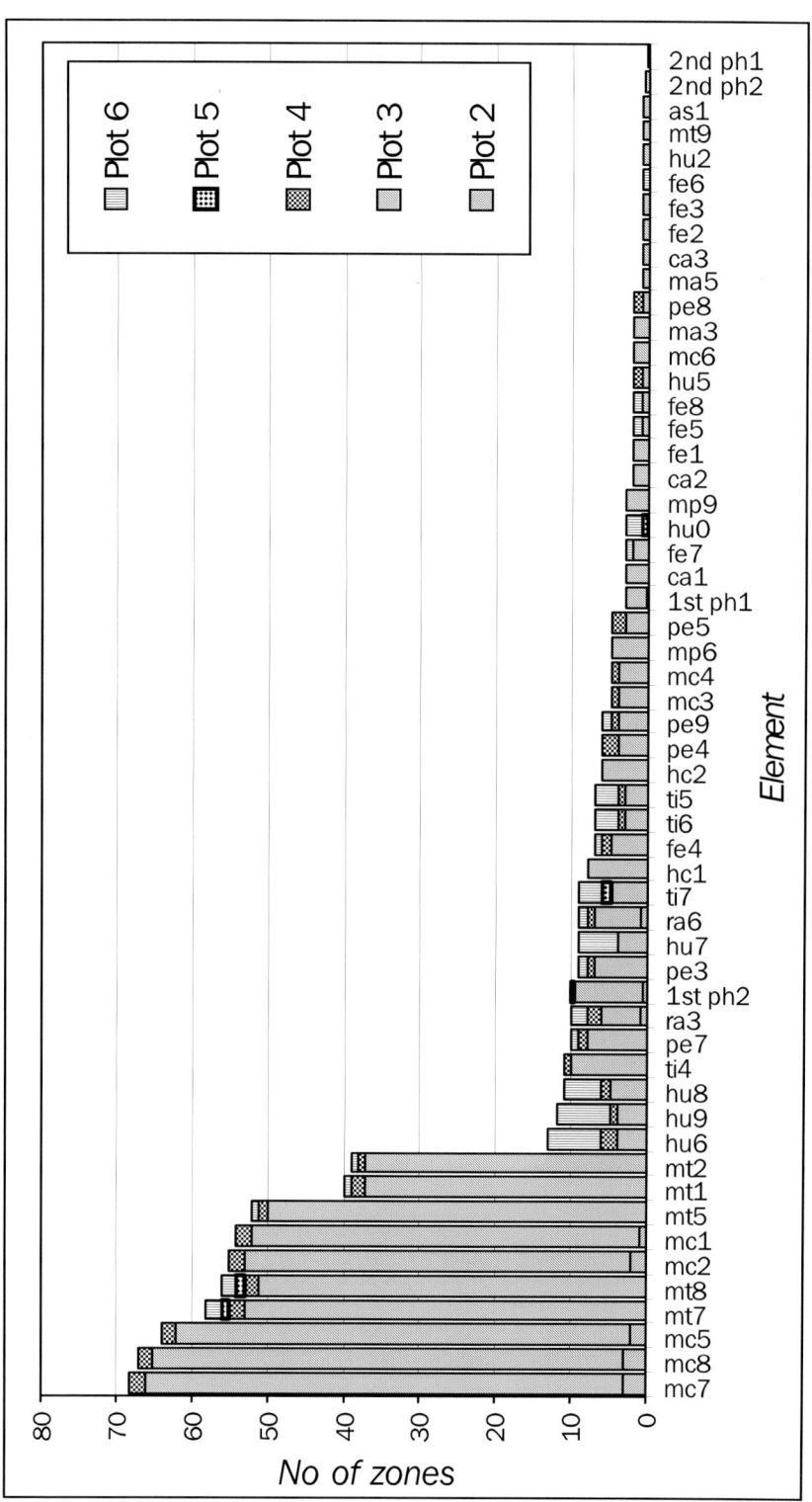

III 6.1.4 Phase V: frequency of sheep/goat elements quantified by zone.

mainly from adult or sub-adult animals and such bones largely originated from contexts that produced few metapodials.

The recovered metapodials showed an obviously biased spatial distribution (Ill 6.1.4). In Plot 3, 45% (n=359) of bone fragments were from metapodials (n=162) and a further 13.6% (n=49) were from phalanges. 117 fragments of metapodial came from fills, the remainder from layers. Amongst the fills there were some, such as pit fills (809) (*see* Ill 6.1.5) and (1217), that were dominated by small and unfused metapodials and phalanges. In contrast to the large numbers of metapodial fragments from Plot 3, only fourteen (or just over 14%) of the bone fragments from Plots 1, 2, 4, 5 and 6 combined were from metapodials. The concentration of distal elements in Plot 3 may represent specialised activity, most probably to do with the working of lamb- and possibly kid skins. Given the size and fusion state of these bones, it is plausible that they related to the processing of fine light skins of young animals such as might be used to produce gloves, purses or fine shoes.

Sheep or goat?

What was clear in the fusion data was that a large proportion of the animals represented here died in their first year of life. A small number (n=4) of third phalanges definitely indicated lambs as opposed to kids. The first phalanges (n=23 from context (809) and a total of thirty-one distal ends assessed and n=2 from context (809)) also appeared to resemble sheep rather than goat using the criteria of Boessneck (1969, 356–7). Admittedly it is not clear how applicable these criteria are to young sheep and goat phalanges, but comparisons with reference material appeared to confirm that the second phalanges were from sheep rather than goats. Amongst the metacarpals there was some variability in the mid-shaft dimensions. Most were quite gracile but a number (two from a sample of nineteen in context (809) for instance) were notably shorter and thicker at mid-shaft and one can speculate that these may have been either kids or male lambs.

Age

The age range of these animals could not be assessed by mandibular data (Table 6.1.41), since most mandibles were apparently not brought to the site. However, the unfused state of the metapodials (Table 6.1.38) did not correlate with what one might expect generally of the medieval period, in that the increased drive to produce wool from the fourteenth century onwards should have resulted in an increase in the number of older sheep brought to towns (Wilson 1994, 110). Therefore this assemblage raises questions regarding the supply and marketing of young lambs and kids in Chester.

Trade in sheep products

Doubtless Cheshire farmers kept some sheep during the late medieval period, but, as noted above, the county is not traditionally a sheep- or goat-rearing area. Clearly, however, there was an urban market for meat, wool and skins, which took a surplus of lamb products. One possibility that might explain large numbers of lamb bones would be that they came from milk flocks. However, William Smith in the sixteenth century said that the farmers here ran only enough for their own use for meat and wool

Ill 6.1.5 Phase V: some of the sheep/goat (including lamb) metapodials and phalanges from context (809).

(Trow-Smith 1957, 211). Prior to the Black Death, Cheshire seems to have been nearly empty of sheep apart from at Eaton and Frodsham (Trow-Smith 1957, 142). Sheep from Frodsham were sold in Chester (Lewis & Thacker eds 2003, 73) but it seems probable that many of the sheep products traded or worked on in Chester would have been imported from outside the county. Documentary evidence shows that wool was imported from the Wirral, Anglesey, Coventry and Derbyshire (Lewis & Thacker eds 2003, 74), so these are some of the possible sources of sheepskins and woolfells. By the late fifteenth century cargoes from Ireland included hides, skins and wool in the form of yarn, flocks and fells and it may also have been a source of light skins (Lewis & Thacker eds 2003, 46, 69).

Leatherworking

Chester supported a large number of tanners, glovers and other leatherworkers, and lambskins were a valuable resource. The present assemblage seems likely, in part, to reflect the importance of Chester as a producer of leather goods and the importance of the skins themselves. What is not so clear is the degree to which this kill-off pattern was also driven by a local demand for lamb. Certainly there was a crop of lamb (and possibly kid) meat which would have been consumed, but apparently not by the inhabitants of these plots since there were very few meat-bearing bones from these animals in Phase V.

There is documentary evidence for the presence of tawyers in Chester from the 1290s, and Thacker (Lewis & Thacker eds 2003, 46) argues that this indicates a trade in light fine skins. The documentary evidence further suggests that there was a concentration of leatherworkers (skinners, tanners, saddlers and glovers) on Bridge Street (Backhouse *this volume*; Laughton *lecture to Chester Archaeological Society 2005*). According to a will dated to 1696 small-scale skinning took place in the seventeenth century either on Plots 2 or 3, and several glovers lived in this area during this period (Backhouse *this volume*). This picture gains support from and is extended by the zooarchaeological evidence, which suggests that tawing (sometimes called mineral tanning), chamoising (sometimes called oil tanning) or possibly fellmongering (Albarella 2003, 72, 77) was taking place on Plot 3 in the late medieval period. It seems less likely that the production of tanned sheep skins or 'bazan' (Kowaleski 1990, 58) took place on site, since no tanning features were discovered. One might expect that if one plot had evidence for leatherworking adjoining ones would also have had it, since shops tended to group by trade (Lewis & Thacker eds 2003, 50). However, the evidence recovered here suggests that leatherworking waste was probably disposed of on only one of the excavated plots during this period.

Goat

Goat bones were recovered from each of Phases III to IX (NISP=33, thirty-two of which were hand-collected) but were most common in this phase (NISP=13). However, none of the main-meat bearing bones was identified: indeed, the fragments from goats in all phases were all from either horn cores, skulls, mandibles, metacarpals or phalanges (Table 6.1.4). The single kid mandible came from this phase. One should state that the majority of caprovid (or sheep/goat) bones were identified to the level sheep or goat and that those body parts that were identified as goat were amongst the easiest to distinguish from sheep. However, a lack of the full range of goat body parts is common on English medieval and post-medieval sites (Albarella 2003, 80) and may reflect the transport of skins of goats with the attached horns.

Amongst the goat bones in Plot 3, context (792), which was closely associated with the pit fills such as (809), there were small parts of the skull and horn cores from adult goats. The hacking marks apparently associated with the separation of horn core from most of the skull were delivered from a posterior direction and impacted at the base of the horn cores. A lamb horn core from (809) was hacked in a similar fashion. The goat remains may relate to goat skins brought here for processing, but use might also have been made of the horn.

Horse

Twenty-nine horse bones were recovered in this phase. Twenty-seven came from layers; one came from the fill (1520) of a linear feature, possibly a ditch; and one was associated with a wall (496): none came from pit fills. Some of the horse bones may therefore have been residual. However, it is also possible that horse carcasses were disposed of in a different way from the other animals. Certainly the features used to dispose of domestic waste (or where domestic waste ended up) in this phase were too small to be used for the disposal of a whole horse carcass.

There was evidence from context (854) (again in Plot 3 and in association with some of the goat elements mentioned above) that a horse was skinned on the site during this phase. The evidence came in the form of fine cut marks running transversely around the shaft of a first phalanx. This animal may have been lame since there was a considerable amount of spongy bone growth over the majority of the anterior aspect of the second phalanx (Ill 6.1.6). This was possibly caused by tethering. The proximal articular surface was unaffected and appeared healthy. The distal articular surface had suffered some recent damage and so could not be fully assessed. Aged or declining individuals are common amongst the horse remains from medieval and post-medieval sites (Hamilton-Dyer 2003, 7). The presence of this skeleton could suggest that horses were stabled or tethered in the backlands when not working or that a lame horse was led to Plot 3 to be dis-

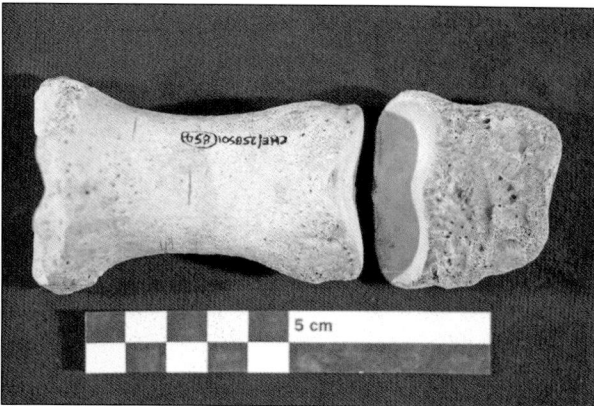

Ill 6.1.6 Phase V: horse phalanges (context (854)) showing cut marks indicative of skinning on the first, and extoses on the anterior aspect of the second.

patched, skinned and disposed of by the leatherworker or skinner who apparently worked here. According to at least one medieval reference, tawyers were certainly supposed to deal with horse hides (Cherry 1991, 299), but equally the hide could have been taken to one of the tanneries outside the City Walls, where most of the heavy hides, including horse, appear to have been dealt with. The fact that all parts of the body were represented perhaps indicates that the carcass was thought too heavy to remove. Although horses would probably not have been able to gain access to the backlands *via* Bridge Street it may have been possible for them to be brought in *via* Newgate Street.

According to a calculation based on the length of the femur (Kiesewalter 1888) this horse was about 130.9 cm or 13.75 hands at the withers. Recalculated using May (1985) this changes only slightly to 130.6 cm. This means that in height it was somewhere between the size of a Welsh pony and a Welsh cob. This is a typical size for the medieval period (Hamilton-Dyer 2003, 7).

Other fauna

Cat and hare

From one of the pit fills that produced a large amount of caprovid distal elements, (809), there was a number (NISP=74 or 62 zoned elements) of cat bones and also some hare bones. Although cat bones were relatively common, there was a minimum number of only two cats from this context based on the humeri and ulnae present. The proximal humeri, radii and tibiae were all unfused, but all were of approximately adult size. One cat appears to have been around eleven months old and one less than ten months. Those parts of the skull or mandible that might have shown evidence for skinning were not present and no cut marks were seen amongst the metapodials or other limb bones. However, related contexts from the same pit (845) produced more sheep metapodial (n=14) and phalanx fragments (n=4), and another context from the same area, (792), produced hare metacarpals (n=8), cat phalanges (n=2) and more sheep metapodial (n=10) and phalanx fragments (n=3). All of the (hand-collected) hare bones (NISP=10) were either metapodials or phalanges with the exception of a distal radius fragment. In total the cat, hare, distal sheep elements and a few goat horn cores made up 43% of the fragments from these contexts. The body part representation of cat and hare could either relate to the disposal of non-meaty extremities from

Ill 6.1.7 Phase V: pygmy shrew (*Sorex minutus*) mandible and shrew pelvis from wet-sieved samples.

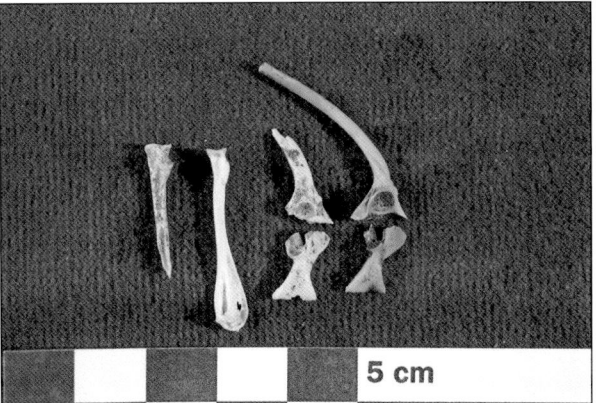

5 cm

Ill 6.1.8 Phase V: mole (*Talpa europaea*) scapula (*left*) with complete modern comparative specimen and two toad (*Bufo bufo*) pelvic bones (with modern *Bufo bufo* specimens to their right) from wet-sieved samples.

carcasses or of those same parts from a skin. However, the fact that these bones were present in context groups that were dominated by the distal parts of sheep or goat suggests that they may well reflect the activities of a skinner or leatherworker. Luff and Moreno Garcia (1995, 110) point out that an absence of cut marks may well indicate a highly skilled skinner.

Backlands environment
There is historical evidence that there were gardens and orchards and possibly a dovecote here during this phase (Hogenberg 1580, cited by Backhouse *this volume*). The zooarchaeological evidence can add some colour and scent to this scene. If horses were stabled or tethered here there would be implications in terms of other environmental remains. Fodder and manure would have been present. Certainly, manure or faeces from humans, pigs, cats, dogs and probably horses is likely to have been a feature of at least some of the backland plots. Rats, mice, shrews and toads were living in the area (Table 6.1.17) and moles may have been digging in Plot 6 (Ills 6.1.7–.8). An unfused pigeon (or squab) coracoid from Plot 3 (context (808)) could have come from the dovecote. One raven bone was recovered from Plot 2 and three from Plot 3 (Table 6.1.16), where we have evidence for leatherworking: one of these bones was found with a concentration of sheep metapodials in context (809). Bones and waste from leatherworking activities were undoubtedly present and this material may have attracted the ravens.

Summary and further research
It has been suggested that the age structure amongst the cattle bones from this phase reflected the developing importance of the dairy industry in Cheshire. It would be instructive to compare the cattle age structure from this site with those from contemporary sites of suspected lower status. The sheep and goat bones are taken to indicate that leatherworking took place on site from this period and that amongst the worked skins there were many from young animals such as might have been sought after by glovers.

Phase VI

Sample size
There were 4351 hand-collected fragments and 438 identifications from the sampled contexts (Tables 6.1.18–.19). Wet-sieved bone was recovered from twenty-five contexts (Table 6.1.50).

Main domestic species
Cattle
Carcass representation
The robust parts of the meat-bearing limb bones were common in this phase, suggesting the possibility that a proportion of the beef arrived on site as joints or carcasses without head or horns. Humeri, femora, pelves, tibiae and metatarsals contributed the most commonly recorded element zones from selected contexts (n=154 or 226 zones). Femora were highly fragmented and on average only one zone (from a possible eight) was recorded for each specimen. The supracondyloid fossa was the most commonly recorded, and amongst the pelves the ilium and the acetabular fossa were most frequent. The dorsal angle of the olecranon fossa was the most commonly recorded humerus zone (n=14) followed by the coronoid fossa and the capitulum. Amongst a NISP sample of 647 the tibiae, femora, humeri, pelves and scapulae were most common, followed by vertebrae, skull fragments and metatarsals.

Distribution and loss or residuality of cattle parts
Ubiquitous elements included humeri, which were recorded from thirty-three contexts. Horn cores were represented in only six contexts (twenty-one fragments). The majority of mandibular teeth (n=21) were isolated finds within a context and thus present an interesting problem since if they were *in situ* in whole mandibles at the time of deposition, one has to account for the post-depositional loss (including excavation loss) of nearly all the cattle teeth from the majority of contexts. Whilst post-depositional loss of all these teeth is possible, perhaps a more likely possibility is that many of these teeth (particularly the large robust adult cattle teeth) were residual.

Consideration of the taphonomic processes in operation is clearly relevant to this question and also to the proportions of calf and adult cattle. Condition varied from very poor preservation of teeth and other elements (context (467)) to excellent preservation of calf and adult teeth and other elements (context (797)). 5% (n=8) of the zoned cattle bones were gnawed by dogs (sample=154) and one femur had evidence for rodent damage. Of the eight bones gnawed by dogs, five were from calves. The gnawed sample was small, but it does appear probable

Table 6.1.18 Phase VI: hand-collected fragment quantified by plot and taxa

Vernacular	Taxon	Plot 1	2	3	4	5	6	No	%
Bird									
Heron	*Ardea cinerea* L.	1					1	2	0.0
Goose	*Anser/Branta*	13	34	16	11	1	4	79	1.8
Teal	*Anas crecca* L.	5		2				7	0.2
Duck	*Anas* sp	4		5	1		2	12	0.3
Grouse	cf *Lagopus lagopus* L.				1			1	0.0
Partridge	cf *Perdix perdix* L.	1					1		0.0
Chicken	*Gallus* f domestic	34	117	51	21	2	'	225	5.2
Oystercatcher	*Haematopus ostralegus* L.		1					1	0.0
Golden plover	*Pluvialis apricaria* L.		1					1	0.0
Lapwing	*Vanellus vanellus* L.			1				1	0.0
Jacksnipe	*Lymnocryptes minimus* Brunnich		1					1	0.0
Woodcock	*Scolopax rusticola* L.	10	11	5	1			27	0.6
Curlew	*Numenius arquata* L.		1					1	0.0
?Small wader*	Aves						60	60	1.4
Pigeon	*Columba* sp	1	1					2	0.0
cf Blackbird	*Turdus* cf *merula* L.	1						1	0.0
Thrush family	*Turdus* sp	1						1	0.0
Small passerine	Fringillidae/Passeridae	1						1	0.0
Small passerine	Passeriformes			1				1	0.0
Bird unident	Aves	38	34	29	18	1	102	222	5.1
Mammal									
Rabbit	*Oryctolagus cuniculus* L.	8	3	8	1		1	21	0.5
Hare	*Lepus* sp	3	17	1				21	0.5
House mouse	*Mus musculus* L.	1						1	0.0
Rat	*Rattus* sp	4		61			1	67	1.5
Dog	*Canis* f domestic	188	10	2	22		22	244	5.6
Cat	*Felis* f domestic	5	5	23	17			50	1.1
Elephant	*Loxodonta/Elephas*		1						0.0
Horse	*Equus* f domestic	1	1	1	1	2	2	8	0.2
Pig	*Sus* f domestic	13	29	48	13	1	41	145	3.3
Red deer	*Cervus elaphus* L.				1			1	0.0
Fallow deer	*Dama dama* L.	1	5	3	2	1		12	0.3
Red/fallow deer	*Cervus/Dama*	2	1	3		1	4	11	0.3
Cattle	*Bos* f domestic	84	150	153	83	17	160	647	14.9
Goat	*Capra* f domestic		1	1			2	4	0.1
Sheep	*Ovis* f domestic	27	21	21	2		5	76	1.7
Sheep/goat	*Ovis/Capra*	48	61	100	26	3	48	286	6.6
Large mammal	Mammalia	123	155	231	93	17	180	799	18.4
Large or medium mammal	Mammalia	3	5	7	1		1	17	0.4
Medium mammal	Mammalia	105	77	65	25	4	85	361	8.3
Small mammal	Mammalia	29	6	20	4	1	1	61	1.4
unidentified		233	84	248	78		229	872	20.0
Total		988	834	1106	422	51	951	4351	100.0

* cf sample <5039> which appears clearly to contain the same species/elements

Table 6.1.19 Phase VI: fragments from samples quantified by plot and taxa

Vernacular	Taxon	Plot 1	2	3	4	5	6	No	%
Bird									
Goose	*Anser/Branta*	1	1	1				3	0.7
Goose/duck	Anatidae		1					1	0.2
Chicken	*Gallus* f domestic	74	47	9				130	29.7
Snipe	*Gallinago gallinago* L.	1						1	0.2
?Small wader*	Aves						8	8	1.8
Woodcock	*Scolopax rusticola* L.		1	1				2	0.5
cf Blackbird	*Turdus* cf *merula* L.	1						1	0.2
Thrush species	*Turdus* sp			2				2	0.5
Mammal									
Rabbit	*Oryctolagus cuniculus* L.	1	5	4	1			11	2.5
Hare	*Lepus* sp			2				2	0.5
House mouse	*Mus musculus* L.	1						1	0.2
Mouse	Muridae	1	18	13	6			38	8.7
Small rodent	Rodentia		4	4				8	1.8
Rat	*Rattus* sp		5	1	10			16	3.7
Dog	*Canis* f domestic		3	1				4	0.9
Small carnivore	Carnivora		1					1	0.2
Cat	*Felis* f domestic	1	3	104	3			111	25.3
Pig	*Sus* f domestic	1	8	5	2			16	3.7
Pig (neonate or suckling)	*Sus* f domestic		25	12	4			41	9.4
Cattle	*Bos* f domestic	1	5	1	1		1	9	2.1
Cattle (calf)	*Bos* f domestic	2	5		1		1	9	2.1
Sheep/goat	*Ovis/Capra*		17	4	2			23	5.3
Total		85	149	164	30	0	10	438	100.0

* These eight specimens from <5039> (566) are comparable to hand-collected examples of the same species/elements

that the survival profile of cattle bones was age-mediated (Munson & Garniewicz 2003; Symmons 2005): that is, dog-gnawing, and possibly other taphonomic processes, discriminated against the survival of calf bones as compared to the bones of adult cattle and thus calf bones may originally have been more frequent at the pre-depositional stage than was apparent.

Age
From the early medieval period onward there was a steady increase in the numbers of calves as a proportion of the total cattle bones where zones could be counted. Calf fragment numbers reached 27% in Phase VII and then declined again in Phase VIII (Ill 6.1.3). There are a number of ways in which the increase in calf bone numbers might be interpreted. Firstly, we must consider the possibility that it reflected a taphonomic process whereby calf bones deteriorated more quickly than the bones of the adults and that the further back one goes (ie prior to Phase VII) the smaller the proportion of calf bones will be. Whilst this may be the case, it is worth noting that there were large numbers of unfused bones of young caprovids from Phase V which were apparently as well preserved as the bones of young animals from the later phases. The epiphysial fusion data show an increasing proportion of unfused early fusing cattle bones, which made up 26% of the total in this phase and which reached a peak in Phase VII. Thus the counts of definite calf fragments and the epiphysial fusion data show the same pattern of increasing numbers of calves and animals under eighteen months old.

Butchery
Amongst the calves, fine cut marks consistent with filleting were recorded on the proximal radius in the area of Binford's RCp-6 (1981, 133) and on the humerus at the proximal end at Hp-5 (1981, 133) and at approximately mid-shaft (Table 6.1.43). Hacking, probably with cleavers or heavy knives, was recorded in 53% (n=67) of the sub-adult or adult cattle bones. There was only one calf bone (a scapula hacked through the proximal end of the blade) on which hacking was recorded. Transverse hacking through adult scapulae to divide them into various proximal and distal proportions was recorded from this and later periods (Table 6.1.49). Such methods of dividing the blade were not noted in the earlier phases on this site and they are certainly rare in Roman deposits in Chester (Ill 6.1.9) where most scapulae appeared as near-complete bones (Cartledge 1991, 5).

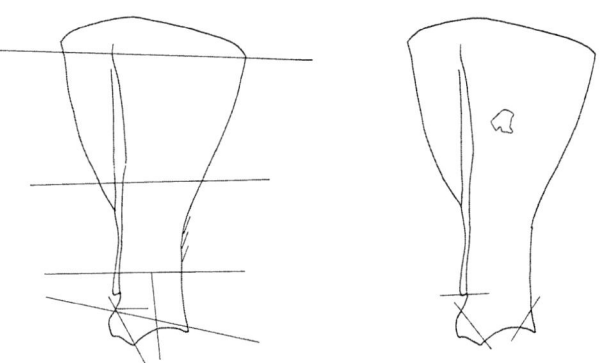

Ill 6.1.9 Hacking on adult cattle scapulae: (*left*) Phase VI and later; (*right*) typical butchery from Roman Chester.

Fragmentation
The average number of zones recorded per fragment for calf was 1.8, whereas for adult and sub-adult cattle it was 1.6. Whereas dog-gnawing may have been a major factor in the fragmentation or complete loss of calf bones, hacking appears to have been a major factor in the fragmentation of adult and sub-adult cattle bones.

Sawing
In Phase VI there was only a single sawn bone from the sample of bones studied in detail (n=606). In Phase VII there were five sawn bones (n=1122) and in Phase VIII there were four (n=637). Thus sawn bones made up less than 1% in each of these phases. The one sawn bone from Phase VI was a cattle femur fragment from context (791).

Management
The evidence relating to the sex of the cattle reaching the site was limited for all phases and in this phase it consisted of one definite and one probable female pelvis.

Status, veal and dairying
The increase in the numbers of calf bones may have reflected changes in status and diet. Briefly, the wealthy merchants who came to occupy the Bridge Street properties could afford to eat veal. The rise of cattle dairying and the slaughter of male calves from Cheshire farms made this meat available to the urban market.

According to the traditional view, dairying in Cheshire was undertaken with three main aims in mind: to obtain a supply of cheese; to obtain a supply of butter for domestic use; and for the breeding of calves, either to sell to urban butchers or to sell on to other farmers to fatten (Dodd 1989, 14). In fact the aims of cattle farmers varied across the county. In south Cheshire, for instance, many farmers concentrated on fattening cattle, some of which would have come from the dairy farms (Dodd 1988, 49). Cattle were also fattened by farmers in Christleton parish, near Chester (Lewis & Thacker eds 2003, 65). However, it is clear that dairying was the focus of the economy of many farms (Crosby 1996, 62–3) and that calves were sold off (Dodd 1988, 49). It may have been the calves from such dairy farms that were increasingly represented in the deposits on the present site.

Trade in calf skins and beef
From 1584 Chester was permitted under royal licence to export thousands of tanned calf skins to the continent. In fact, the trade to France and Spain had operated earlier than this, but illegally (Woodward 1970, 43, 62). Calf skins dominated exports from the city into the seventeenth century (Forster 2003, 104) and the port must have operated as a redistributive centre for these skins both for the county and for the surrounding region. It also received both tanned and raw hides from Ireland. Thacker (Lewis & Thacker eds 2003, 69) notes that Chester received 1,100 calfskins from Ireland in 1525/6. Other cattle that reached Chester probably included local oxen, which were only gradually being replaced by horses and might have been worked until they were nine or ten years old and then fattened for the autumn meat market (Dodd 1988, 48). Neighbouring parts of Wales also continued to be an important source of meat for Chester (Lewis & Thacker eds 2003, 65).

Pig

The pig bones from the samples included a relatively high proportion of suckling pigs. Some of these showed evidence of having been butchered, as in the group of from Plot 2 (context (785)). In this case two ribs had been sliced through and there were fine cut marks across the shaft of a femur which probably indicated that this bone was filleted. A small incomplete humerus from Plot 3 (context (429)) also bore a fine cut mark which suggested filleting. Four of the suckling pig bones from this phase were burnt; it is possible that these bones were tossed into a fire after the meat had been eaten.

Some other pig bones from the samples appeared small enough to be considered newly born. There was, for instance, a radius which was approximately half the size of the radius of a four-day-old piglet (Welsh x Large White EAU 708). According to Thacker (Lewis & Thacker eds 2003, 65) 'pigs roamed the streets in 1549' in Chester. Certainly, during the sixteenth century there were indictments relating to people keeping pigs to the annoyance of their neighbours (CCALS ZQSF 36, 44, 48). These concerned properties within the City Walls and 'near the High Cross', which is close to the present site. During the early seventeenth century the problem persisted within the walls and there are records of presentments and depositions regarding the erection of pig sties and the damage and smell caused by pigs (CCALS ZQSF 55, 56). It is suggested that pigs farrowed on these plots and that the smallest of the pig bones reflect infant mortality.

Sheep and goat

The majority of identifications were made to the level of sheep/goat (78%) but there were many more sheep (21%) than goats (1%) amongst the hand-collected caprovid NISP totals (Tables 6.1.3, .4 and .18). The body part representation for these animals differed markedly from that seen in Phase V, where the ten most common zones were all from metapodials. In Phase VI the four most common sheep zones were all from the proximal radius. The posterior proximal ulna scar and foramen and the medial half of the proximal epiphysis were most common. These zones were closely followed by the lateral half of the proximal epiphysis and the distal shaft immediately above the distal epiphysis. Metapodial zones were present but much reduced in number. After the radius, the scapula, tibia, humerus and pelvis provided the majority of the common zones and this, it is suggested, means that the bulk of the sheep and goat brought onto the site was in the form of meat-bearing joints.

Sheep butchery

Among the sheep bones there was evidence for filleting from pelves matching Binford's PS-3 (Table 6.1.45) and cuts on femora matching Fd-4, Fd-5 (1981, 132). Cuts on the humerus matching Binford's Hd-2 probably related to dismemberment (1981, 123). Amongst the zoned sheep vertebrae there were five split by medial hacking, which may have split the carcass into left and right halves and in two other cases there was hacking just into the centra, also in a longitudinal direction possibly to achieve much the same outcome. The hacked vertebrae came from six contexts, including four pit fills. Five other vertebrae from two pit fills and two layers were not hacked in this way. Thus it is possible that at least some sheep carcasses were being split lengthways into left and right halves. Another possibility is that vertebrae were hacked to expose marrow for the preparation of broths or stews.

Leatherworking and meat

The fragment totals for each element corresponded to the zones analysis. The radius (n=48) was the most frequent amongst the identified hand-collected fragments, followed by the tibia (n=38), scapula (n=32), humerus (n=30) and fragments of rib (n=31). Metapodials constituted 12% of the fragments compared to 39% in Phase V. It is therefore suggested that whereas in Phase V the bulk of the deposited sheep and goat bones related to leatherworking, in Phase VI there was a greater proportion that related to the consumption of lamb or mutton. Although it is impossible to discount the possibility that there had been a change in waste disposal practices or in the state in which skins were supplied (skins could have been supplied with no metapodials attached), the evidence appears to suggest that leatherworking activities were less intensive on these plots during Phase VI.

However, one cannot make generalisations about possible changes in the trade of sheep skins and wool in Chester on the basis of this change in recovered sheep parts. Documentary evidence demonstrates that the trade in sheep skins continued in the city. Alum for the tawyers continued to arrive from Gascony (Lewis & Thacker eds 2003, 71) and indictments from the sixteenth century give an insight into the value of sheep skins and wool (eg CCALS ZQSF 66, ZQSE 8/1). Documentary evidence relating to this part of the street also suggests that woollen felts were being traded here (Backhouse *this volume*).

Insubstantial evidence for a continuation in leatherworking activities was also provided by the four goat bones, which comprised two horn cores, a mandibular tooth and a first phalanx. Goat skins were amongst the commodities traded with Spain during the sixteenth century (Lewis & Thacker 2003, 71), and imports of kid skins are recorded from Ireland in the sixteenth and seventeenth centuries (Woodward 1970, 7). It is plausible that some goat bones arrived in Chester attached to skins and that they were disposed of in the backlands by the leatherworkers of the Bridge Street plots.

Other fauna

Dog

From Plot 2 (context (791), fill of cess pit (487)) there were two butchered dog femora. The two bones obviously came from different animals since one was fully fused distally and the other was unfused. The latter had multiple cut marks around the unfused proximal shaft under the 'neck' and at the base of the trochanter major (Table 6.1.48). The other had fine cut marks running approximately transverse to the distal shaft. These appeared unlikely to relate to dismemberment since they were located some 30 mm or more from the distal articulation and seemed most likely to relate to filleting.

Whilst it is possible that there was a time of hardship which caused people to resort to eating foods that they may not usually have eaten, there seems to be no other evidence for this in the deposit. The artefactual dating evidence suggested that this context fell somewhere in the sixteenth century and so was too early to be associated with the Civil War siege. Cheshire was, however, affected by periods of stress a number of times during the sixteenth century, including 1585–1610, when notably wet and cool conditions adversely affected agricultural production (Dodd 1988, 46). In fact, torrential rains and poor harvests were recorded across much of Britain and Europe in the mid-1590s, and this led to people eating cats, dogs and snakes (Woodward 1970, 52–3). If these bones do relate to a time of food shortage, this might plausibly have been the period.

If it was the case that waste from a number of different people or families went into backfilling this cess pit, then foods from rich and poor tables might have been mixed. One cautionary note is the possibility that people happily chose to eat the butchered dogs. Simoons (1994, 239) gives a slightly later (seventeenth-century) reference to the high regard in which the meat of young spaniels was viewed in England and France.

Pathology
Also amongst the dog bones there was a group from layer (766) that included many bones that appear to have come from a single unfortunate animal. This dog was approximately six to nine months old at the time of death since the bicipital tuberosity of the scapula was fused but the distal humerus was still unfused. It had suffered a broken atlas, which had fractured across one of its 'wings' in a line between approximately the alar notch and the foramina transversaria. There were further breaks to a right-hand side radius and ulna at approximately midshaft. Clearly the animal survived these injuries (at least temporarily), since there were signs of infection and there was substantial remodelling of the affected bones (Ill 6.1.10). However, despite considerable bone formation around the fore limb break, the proximal and distal parts of both bones remained separate. Whether these injuries did eventually lead to the dog's death is open to speculation but it seems plausible that this was a contributing factor.

Disposal
Another dog was deposited in contexts (1697) and (1698), the fills of cess pit (1619) in Plot 4. Although the breed of this dog is unknown it was approximately the height of a fox terrier (Table 6.1.33). Whether they were eaten or not it seems that these dogs were disposed of alongside domestic waste, cess and butchered animal remains. Another bone from a member of the Canidae was recovered from one of the late medieval lower backfill deposits, (791), of the cess pit (487) in Plot 2. This fifth metatarsal was particularly large (Table 6.1.33) and was a good match for Eurasian and Canadian wolf metatarsals in the Natural History Museum in London. This suggests that it belonged either to a domestic dog of considerable size; alternatively it could have been a wolf metatarsal which was brought here attached to a pelt.

Deer
Deer bones were recovered from each of the plots, with twenty-four identifications in total. Half of these were from bones identified as fallow deer (*Dama dama*) and included fragments of antler, ulna, radius, metacarpal, tibia and whole metatarsals (Ill 6.1.11). The single definite red deer (*Cervus elaphus*) bone was a radius. The bones identified as red/fallow deer included fragments

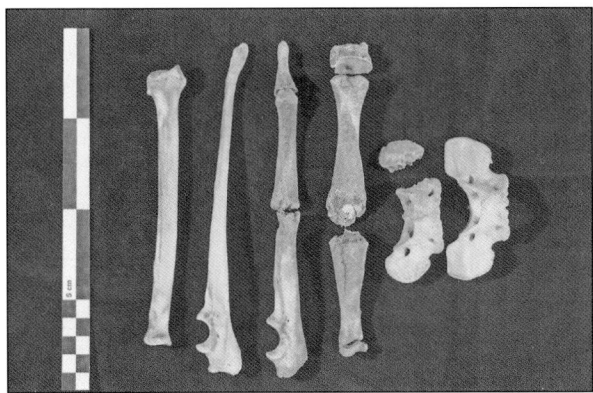

Ill 6.1.10 Phase VI: broken dog atlas, radius and ulna (*centre*) from (766) with modern comparatives.

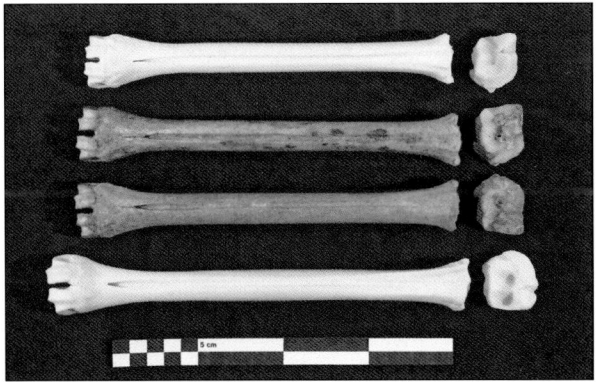

Ill 6.1.11 Phase VI: fallow deer metatarsals and navicular cuboids (*centre*) from the basal fill (806) of cess pit (407), with red deer (*bottom*) and fallow deer (*top*) modern comparatives.

of antler, maxillary tooth, scapula, humerus, metacarpals, pelvis, tibia, metatarsals and phalanges. Antler was recovered from Plots 4 and 5 and metapodials from Plots 1, 2, 3 and 4. Two of the antlers were from naturally shed fallow deer elements and thus were probably craftworking waste. The third was a sawn tine which was not identified to species. Two of these antlers had certainly been sawn and the third had probably been sawn but was poorly preserved. Whilst the fragments of antler reflected the working of this product and some of the metapodials might relate to the working of skins, other bones came from meat-bearing parts of the skeleton and certainly reflected the consumption of venison – another indicator of the relatively high status of some of the people who disposed of their food waste on these plots.

Rabbit
There was a fragment of rabbit mandible from Plot 1 context (766) which bore three fine transverse (at a right-angle to the diastema) cut marks just anterior to and in the region of the mental foramen. Given the location and orientation it seems certain that these represented skinning marks.

Wildfowl
In this phase the list of species recovered increased considerably (Tables 6.1.18–.19). Although not abundant, birds such as heron, teal, oystercatcher, snipe and lapwing appeared and the percentage of woodcock increased. The wider variety of birds recovered was seen in Plots 1, 2, 3, 4 and 6. There was low potential for recovery in Plot 5, since there were only six relevant contexts and three of

these were clay floors. Thus the lack of wild fauna in Plot 5 is not significant. The cess pit backfill contexts produced many of the bones of wild birds from Plot 2. The majority of the wild birds certainly appeared to have been eaten since they occurred in contexts that were also rich in the bones of butchered domestic animals. The presence of these birds could reasonably be interpreted as a reflection of the increasing wealth amongst those who disposed of their waste here.

How were these birds procured? It seems likely that wildfowlers had long operated along the floodplain of the River Dee and on the formerly large salt marshes to the west of Chester. It is also possible that from this time some of the birds traded in Chester came from duck decoys similar to that at Orford Hall or Hale, both on the Mersey. There is historical evidence for the existence of duck decoys from the time of King John, and they are mentioned in litigation in the thirteenth and fifteenth centuries (Payne-Gallwey 1886, 4). The decoy at Hale was in existence from at least as early as the first half of the eighteenth century and was in use until the mid-nineteenth century. It was said to take between 750 and 1,500 ducks per season. A large range of duck species was taken by this method and from Hale there are even records which document the changing proportions of mallard, wigeon and teal (Payne-Gallwey 1886, 98, 100).

Prior to the construction of such decoys, birds were driven between nets arranged in a large V which led to a net tunnel. In fact, there is evidence that this method continued to be practised into the seventeenth and eighteenth centuries. The driving of ducks was sometimes carried out at the time of the moult when many ducks would be unable to fly for a few days. As many as 3000 ducks might have been taken in a single drive (Payne-Gallwey 1886, 6). There would, of course, have been many other methods by which birds might have been caught. Interestingly, recent studies concerned with ringing and marking have shown that large numbers of the jack snipe (a species difficult to see and catch) can be caught with horizontally held nets carried by four people with two others flushing the birds into the net (Lepley *et al* 2005, 167–70).

Seasonality

The presence of a jack snipe (*Lymnocryptes minimus*) humerus in this phase, and also in Phase VII, might constitute tentative evidence that some of the wildfowling took place during the winter months. In modern times these birds are present between September and April (Sparks & Mason 2004, 57–60; Harradine 1986, 202–3) and migrate to the taiga for the summer. This species was formerly abundant in the marshes of the Dee and Mersey but declined during the latter part of the nineteenth century (Hedley Bell 1962, 117–18). The presence of woodcock, lapwing and teal might also indicate autumn or winter wildfowling (Gidney 1993, 11).

Chicken

Bones from tiny chicks made up 3.4% of the zoned chicken bones (n=341) from the whole site. 10.5% of chicken bones came from small or young chickens and most of these were from Phases VI and VII. In this phase a cluster of small unfused but well preserved chicken bones from a sample from Plot 2 (fill (806) of cess pit (487)) suggested

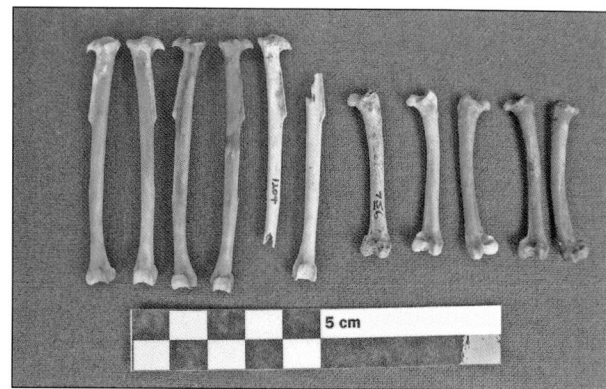

Ill 6.1.12 Bird tibiotarsi (*left*) and femora (*right*) identified as woodcock (*Scolopax rusticola*). The three archaeological specimens (*centre*) are from Phase VI and are surrounded by modern comparatives. Amongst wild birds, identifications of woodcock are one of the most common from archaeological deposits of Roman to recent date in Chester. (Photo: Ian Smith)

the presence of a whole unbutchered carcass since all of the elements were in a similar state of development and the wing and leg bones occurred in pairs. Other contexts within Plots 1, 2 and 4 also produced groups of chick bones and immature chicken bones which suggested the presence of whole carcasses. These groups of bone may relate to the death on site of young birds and this and the other groups of small and immature bones, may be an indication that chickens were reared on these plots (*see* Coy 1989, 32).

Elephant

The most surprising find from the fills of the cess pit (487) in Plot 2, and perhaps from the site as a whole, was an elephant (*Loxodonta/Elephas*) fore limb (ulna) bone (Ill 6.1.13). The surviving length was 460 mm but part of the distal end was missing; it is possible that the full length was about 850 mm. A smooth, straight, sharp-edged indent through the cortical bone (13 mm deep x 42 mm approximately medial to lateral) on the posterior side of the olecranon tuberosity was apparently a hack mark and suggested butchery. Comparisons were made between this elephant bone and others in the collections held at Liverpool University, Manchester Museum and at the Natural History Museum in London (collections at Wandsworth). Unfortunately attempts to identify the bone to species, although initially encouraging, became more inconclusive as the sample of consulted specimens grew, and thus it might have been either an African or Asian elephant. Although the bulk of the specimen has been conserved, samples remain which are untreated and could be subjected to isotopic analysis or an assessment to identify whether DNA survives. It has been radiocarbon (AMS) dated to 2 sigma cal AD 1290–1410 (Beta – 163943). No other bones from elephant were present in the pit. The origins of this bone are unknown, but the dating evidence suggested that it was a little too late to relate to the well known elephant presented to Henry III by Louis IX of France in 1254 and kept at the Tower Menagerie. One possibility is that this was a curio brought to Chester through the port. If so, the associated finds and stratigraphic dating evidence indicate that either it was only transported some considerable time after death or alternatively it may have been curated in Chester for over ninety years prior to disposal.

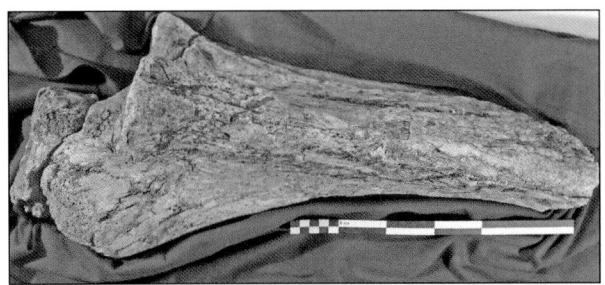

Ill 6.1.13 Phase VI: elephant (*Elephas/Loxodonta*) ulna from fill of cess pit (487).

Summary and further research
A factor that most obviously distinguished Phases V and VI was the range of wild birds recovered. The overall size of the assemblages from these two phases was similar in terms of numbers and weight of fragments. However, while there were relatively few wild birds from Phase V, they were relatively frequent in Phase VI. It would be instructive in future to compare these results with sieved medieval and early post-medieval assemblages from other parts of the city and from less prosperous situations.

The remains of suckling pigs, deer and a range of wild bird species were suggestive of increasing prosperity amongst the inhabitants. Increasing numbers of calf bones were also indicative of this trend and of the developing dairy industry.

Phase VII

Sample size
There were 5750 hand-collected fragments and 588 sampled identifications from this phase (Tables 6.1.20–.21). Wet-sieved bone was recovered from twenty-two contexts (Table 6.1.50).

Main domestic species
Cattle
Carcass representation
Cattle horn cores dominated this phase in terms of bulk and weight. Maxillary and mandibular parts were vastly under-represented relative to the number of horn cores (n=558 or 39%). After horn cores, the scapula (n=54), humerus (n=55), pelvis (n=57), femur (n=73) and tibia (n=80) had the highest fragment totals. Excluding the horn cores, the most commonly recorded zones were the femoral trochanter minor, the dorsal angle of the olecranon fossa in the humerus and the origin of the distal spine in the scapula. It is suggested that horn cores and joints of beef were the main cattle parts brought onto the site at this time.

Age
This phase produced a large proportion of calf bones (Ill 6.1.3 *above*), with a peak (twenty-eight or 68%) in the proportion of unfused early fusing bones (Table 6.1.36). These came from Plots 1, 2, 3, 4 and 6 (Plot 5 did not produce any contexts dating to this phase). The body part representation suggested that whole carcasses, or at least a range of bones from all parts of the skeleton, were disposed of on the site. Meat-bearing bones were well represented, implying that people were eating veal. It is possible that some calf skins were also processed on site;

if so, it is unlikely that many of them arrived on site with just the metapodials and phalanges attached, since no concentrations of these elements were recorded amongst the hand-collected or sampled contexts. The cattle bones from samples were nearly all from Plot 4 and were dominated by horn core fragments.

Gnawing
As in Phase VI, 5% (n=16) of zoned cattle parts had been gnawed by dogs (sample=307); of these, seven were from calves. Calf elements are more likely to have been completely destroyed than the adult cattle bones and are therefore are likely to be under-represented.

Butchery
Amongst the calf bones there were fine cut marks (Table 6.1.43) on the scapula matching Binford's S-3 (1981, 98) and consistent with filleting. Amongst the calf femora there were fine cut marks at approximately mid-shaft around the linea aspera and on the shaft between the level of the supra condyloid fossa and the trochanter minor. The latter probably also related to filleting, as did some cuts recorded on the proximal shaft of the tibia. Cuts to calf metatarsal condyles indicated dismemberment and others matching Binford's MTd-4 (1981, 132) may have resulted from filleting. In older cattle a fine transverse cut mark at the distal end of the humerus appeared to be associated with subsequent hacking through medial and lateral epicondyles, and cuts across the occipital condyles corresponding to Binford's S-1 (1981, 102) were consistent with cutting off the head.

The horn core structure
The group of horn cores in Plot 4 had been neatly stacked to line cess pit (1807)/(1621). This was the first such feature to be recorded in Chester. The walls were about 300 mm wide (the length of many of the longer horn cores) and lined a cut of 2.45 x 2.00 x 1.10 m. The cores had been laid with distal (pointed) ends pointing both into and out of the pit, although the latter were in the majority (*cf* Armitage 1989, 153). It seems clear that, latterly at least, the feature had been used as a cess pit. The primary fill of the pit, (1881), was a dark brown sandy clay which was covered by a black silty sand, (1699), containing burnt bone, wood charcoal and seventeenth-century pottery. The upper fill, (1608), was a black silt which contained clay tobacco pipes of seventeenth–eighteenth-century date.

The fact that there was a skinner, Robert Fletcher, who lived in this area makes it tempting to suggest that all of these horn cores may have come from the skinning of cattle here. However, by this time Fletcher was a wealthy man who owned four properties in this area, and although he may once have been a skinner, he almost certainly had no need to undertake such work any longer and was probably a merchant rather than a craftsman (Backhouse *pers comm*). Of course, he may have paid others to continue his trade but not necessarily in the centre of the city.

Concentrations of horn cores tend to be associated either with an area where primary butchery took place or where either tanning or hornworking was undertaken. It seems unlikely that a tanning operation (ie one which was dealing with the hides of cattle and horses) was based here for the following reasons:

Table 6.1.20 Phase VII: hand-collected fragments quantified by plot and taxa

Vernacular	Taxon	Plot 1	2	3	4	6	No	%
Bird								
Swan	*Cygnus* sp				1		1	0.0
Mute swan	*Cygnus olor* Gmelin				3		3	0.1
Goose	*Anser/Branta*	1	14	75	13	30	133	2.3
Wigeon	*Anas penelope* L.			1			1	0.0
Duck	*Anas* sp	1	2	9			12	0.2
Partridge	*cf Perdix perdix* L.	2	1				3	0.1
Chicken	*Gallus* f domestic	28	24	77	72	35	236	4.1
Turkey	*Meleagris gallopavo* L.					1	1	0.0
Cormorant	*Phalacrocorax carbo* L.			2			2	0.0
Heron	*Ardea cinerea* L.		1				1	0.0
Golden plover	*Pluvialis apricaria* L.		1				1	0.0
Lapwing	*Vanellus vanellus* L.	2					2	0.0
Woodcock	*Scolopax rusticola* L.	7	1	1	1	1	11	0.2
Common gull	*Larus cf canus* L.				1		1	0.0
Pigeon	*Columba* sp		1		1		2	0.0
cf Blackbird	*Turdus cf merula* L.	3					3	0.1
cf Song thrush	*Turdus cf philomelos* Brehm		1				1	0.0
Crow/rook	*Corvus corone/frugilegus*					1	1	0.0
Raven	*Corvus corax* L.	1					1	0.0
Jackdaw	*Corvus monedula* L.		2				2	0.0
Magpie	*Pica pica* L		1				1	0.0
Bird unident	*Aves*	35	38	50	10	13	146	2.5
Mammal								
Rabbit	*Oryctolagus cuniculus* L.	40	8	4	2	1	55	1.0
Hare	*Lepus* sp	5		1	2	4	12	0.2
Red squirrel	*Sciurus vulgaris* L.	3					3	0.1
Rat	*Rattus* sp	1		2	3	1	7	0.1
Dog	*Canis* f domestic	29	16	4	13	14	76	1.3
Red fox	*cf Vulpes vulpes* L.	1					1	0.0
Pine marten	*Martes martes* L.					2	2	0.0
Cat	*Felis* f domestic	8	254	14	88	6	370	6.4
Horse	*Equus* f domestic	1	3	1		1	6	0.1
Pig	*Sus* f domestic	66	48	15	51	73	253	4.4
Red deer	*Cervus elaphus* L.	1				2	3	0.1
Fallow deer	*Dama dama* L.	4	2			5	11	0.2
Red/fallow deer	*Cervus/Dama*	2	4	1	6		13	0.2
Red deer/cattle	*Cervus/Bos*	1	1				2	0.0
Cattle	*Bos* f domestic	274	148	78	712	214	1426	24.8
Goat	*Capra* f domestic	1			1	1	3	0.1
Sheep	*Ovis* f domestic	22	13	11	19	18	83	1.4
Sheep/goat	*Ovis/Capra*	161	52	40	65	63	381	6.6
Large mammal	*Mammalia*	299	143	59	156	261	918	16.0
Large or medium mammal	*Mammalia*	11	3	25	6	17	62	1.1
Medium mammal	*Mammalia*	248	80	62	49	134	573	10.0
Small mammal	*Mammalia*		8	1	4	1	14	0.2
Unidentified		503	139	25	91	153	911	15.8
Total		1761	1011	559	1368	1051	5750	100.0

1　The excavations uncovered no evidence of pits or other features associated with tanning.

2　The concentration of hand-collected horn core fragments was overwhelmingly from the lining of pit (1807) and some closely associated contexts. The results from the sampled contexts confirmed this limited distribution (Table 6.1.21). In a tannery one might expect a number of features to have produced such concentrations of horn cores.

3　There were no concentrations of hand-collected or sampled metapodials or phalanges. If the site had been a tannery one might expect the wet-sieved samples to have yielded some cattle phalanges and yet no concentrations of phalanges were recovered from samples in this phase.

4　Documentary, place-name and archaeological evidence show the known tanning sites of Chester to have been distributed outside the City Walls from the late medieval period onwards (Carrington ed 1994, 82).

One crucial reason why one might not choose to tan hides here is that the site is at a relatively high point in the city and thus would not have had a convenient supply of the copious water needed for tanning. Whilst there are examples in Chester of old water courses which are now hidden or non-existent, there appears to be no evidence for one here. Admittedly, one should not ignore the fact that other tanneries have been excavated hundreds of feet from rivers (Cherry 1991, 296), and at Chester it is clear from the documentary records that hides were transported some distance from the Bars site to the River Dee to be cleaned. (Laughton *pers comm c* 1999). Transportation of hides was routinely a source of conflict over rights of way and between landowners. The Bars site lies on the eastern side of the city, well away from the main settlement, yet even there it was recorded as a source of conflict. The present site is in the centre of the city, and the washing of hides from a tannery here would have necessitated transporting them through an area occupied by numerous prosperous and influential inhabitants. If it had taken place, one can speculate that the historical records would have documented the process, since the tanners would probably have been fined for causing a nuisance in the same way as those at the Bars had been in earlier periods.

Table 6.1.21 Phase VII: fragments from samples quantified by plot and taxa

Vernacular	Taxon	Plot 1	2	3	4	5	6	No	%
Amphibian									
cf Toad	cf *Bufo* sp				3			3	0.5
Frog	*Rana temporaria* L.				1			1	0.2
Frog/toad	*Rana/Bufo*	1						1	0.2
Bird									
Goose	*Anser/Branta*		2		1		3	6	1.0
Duck	*Anas* sp				1			1	0.2
Chicken	*Gallus* f domestic	2			11		2	15	2.6
Golden plover	*Pluvialis apricaria* L.				1			1	0.2
Snipe	*Gallinago gallinago* L.	1			1			2	0.3
Jacksnipe	*Lymnocryptes minimus* Brunnich	1						1	0.2
Woodcock	*Scolopax rusticola* L.				2			2	0.3
Pigeon	*Columba* sp				1			1	0.2
Small passerine	Passeriformes	1			3		5	9	1.5
cf Blackbird	*Turdus* cf *merula* L.	1						1	0.2
Thrush species	*Turdus* sp	1			1			2	0.3
Bird unident*	Aves				1			1	0.2
Mammal									
Common shrew	*Sorex araneus* L.	1			2			3	0.5
Rabbit	*Oryctolagus cuniculus* L.	1	2		2			5	0.9
Hare	*Lepus* sp		3					3	0.5
Mouse	Muridae	4			14			18	3.1
Rodent	Rodentia	3			2			5	0.9
Rat	*Rattus* sp	3	4		11			18	3.1
Dog	*Canis* f domestic		1		1		1	3	0.5
Cat	*Felis* f domestic	3	19		83			105	17.9
Pig	*Sus* f domestic	2			7		1	10	1.7
Pig (neonate or suckling)	*Sus* f domestic	1	1		38			40	6.8
Cattle	*Bos* f domestic	4			313			317	53.9
Sheep/goat	*Ovis/Capra*	1	4	2	2		2	11	1.9
Sheep	*Ovis* f domestic			1	2			3	0.5
Total		31	36	3	504	0	14	588	100.0

* From <5148> (1513)

Whilst we have uncovered no evidence of fines connected with the washing or transport of hides, there was a reference of 1718 to wet glover John Pendlebury being suffocated 'by smoke from fires for the drying of skins in the store house of William Jennings in Bridge Street' (CCALS ZQCI 19/16). Of course, these may not have been tanned skins: given that it was a wet glover who was suffocated it seems more likely that they were the light skins which a glover might typically process in a manner which did not involve tannins. The evidence for the drying of skins by fires is certainly of interest in itself. Perhaps the process that was being undertaken was that of loosening the hairs in wood smoke, which is recorded as being part of both the tawing and oil dressing processes (Clarkson 1960–1, 247).

Whilst there seems to be little to support the view that there was tanning on the site, it does not mean that some animals were not skinned here. Documentary evidence shows that people regularly got into trouble over the slaughter of animals on Eastgate Street and Bridge Street, inside or outside their shops (CCALS ZQSF 90–8), in which case they would surely have been skinned there as well. However the horn core group cannot easily be explained as relating to primary butchery waste since there were few of the other non-meaty extremities that typically stay at the primary butchery site.

It seems likely that the horn cores from the cess pit lining must have been approximately contemporary and that they probably largely related to a single building or depositional event. It is possible that they were carted to Plot 4 specifically to line the pit. They may for, instance, have been brought from the Bars, where, as seen above,

tanners dealing with cattle hides were based. Yet another possibility is that they came originally from Ireland and were brought *via* the port. Diane Backhouse (*this volume*) has suggested that Plot 4 probably belonged to one of two people (father and son) named Matthew Anderton who were contemporaries of the skinner Robert Fletcher. The Andertons both held office as alderman and sheriff and Matthew Anderton senior had been deputy controller of customs in the port of Chester. Of particular interest is the fact that both of them were involved in the import of cattle from Ireland. At this time Chester's leather industry was increasingly dependent on the tens of thousands of Irish skins and hides that were imported. Government legislation controlled this trade to some extent and there were complete bans, but smuggling was also important (Forster 2003, 139).

Worked horn cores

A proportion of the horn cores used to line the pit (6 or 1.6% of those where either the tip or 50% + of the base could be recorded) had been sawn, so it seems possible that these had received the attentions of a hornworker. The sawn edges were neat and regular and were noted both near the bases and pointed ends of the cores. Some cut marks were also noted (Table 6.1.35), 16% of which appeared to be associated with skinning. Another 4% were close to, or on, the base of the core, and amongst them there were some that extended some 40 mm up the core (Ill 6.1.14): the latter must surely indicate hornworking.

Amongst the horn cores from the lining of the pit there were some of juvenile age (Ill 6.1.15) which seemed too small to have been of great use to a hornworker (Armitage 1982, 41, 52). It is not clear what size of horn a worker might have rejected, but it seems plausible that in a big cartload of horns from a tannery there would have been some that a hornworker might not have selected.

Whilst there was some evidence of sawing and of cut marks on a proportion of the horn cores, the distribution of worked horn cores was limited to a relatively small number of contexts, as mentioned above. Whilst the presence of worked cores does not necessarily indicate hornworking on site, horn combs, amongst many other goods, were being sold by Thomas Minshull, who was one of Fletcher's tenants (Backhouse *this volume*). If horn was being worked on site, it seems that those involved were highly organised in their disposal of horn cores and perhaps that such activities took place over a limited period only.

Cattle types as indicated by metrical data

As to breed or type according to the lengths of the outer curve (Armitage 1982, 43) there was only one possible longhorn amongst the adult horn cores from the lining of pit (1807), with an outer length of over 360 mm. However, when one looks at the index of proportion, the latter core had a value of only 143, whereas in all longhorn cows and oxen the value for this index is greater than 180 (Armitage 1982, 43). Thus, this particular calculation suggested that even this large specimen was more likely to have been a medium-horn animal rather than a longhorn. All of the other horn cores between age classes 3 and 5 from the lining of the pit and associated contexts were shorter than those of longhorns (Ill 6.1.16), and the average index of proportion from a sample of thirty-four cores was 135.

Two other index of proportion values were of interest in that one was 180 and another 186, and yet both horn cores were only 320 mm long. In medium-horn cattle the index of proportion is always less than 180 and usually nearer to 100 (Armitage 1982, 43). It seemed unlikely that either core could have increased much more in length since the nuchal eminences were fused and the cores were made up almost entirely of compact bone: thus their lengths suggested that these were medium horns and yet the index of proportion measurement suggested that they are longhorns. It seems that these animals fall outside the types described by Armitage. He was fully aware that other types might be recognised and states that various districts, including Cheshire had their own longhorns (1982, 51). Trow-Smith (1957, 210) states that the cattle of Cheshire were certainly the ancestors of the longhorns.

Cattle breed and sex as indicated by morphological features

Regarding the cranial features that might determine cattle breed, there were some that appeared to characterise this group. Amongst these the intercornual ridge, seen from the front, nearly always formed a high double arch (Ill 6.1.14) and the frontal profile, seen from above, often had a slight boss. Such a combination of features has been recorded in Welsh and Irish (Kerry) cows (Grigson 1976, 126, 128). Historical accounts also suggest that Welsh and Cheshire stock were related (Trow-Smith 1957, 211). Where the horn cores were complete enough to determine orientation they were all oriented upwards and

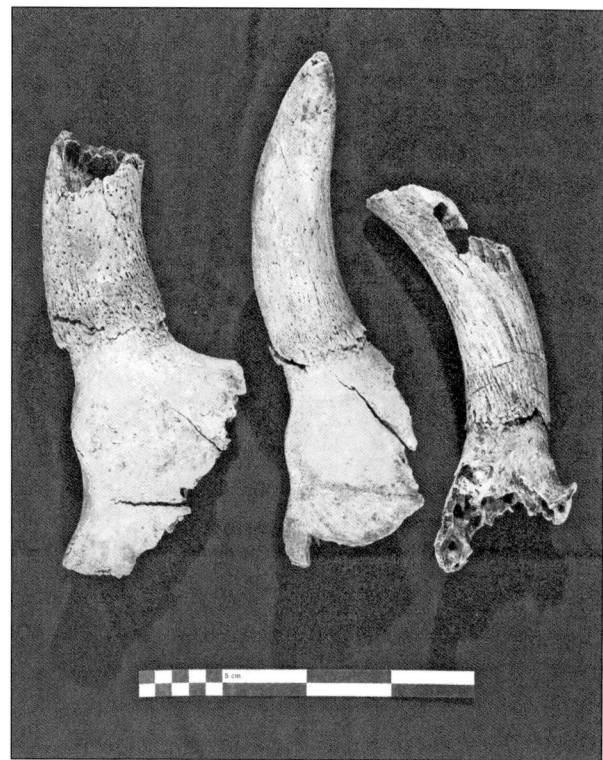

Ill 6.1.14 Phase VII: cattle horn cores showing the high double arch typical of the assemblage (*left two*) and cut marks (*right*).

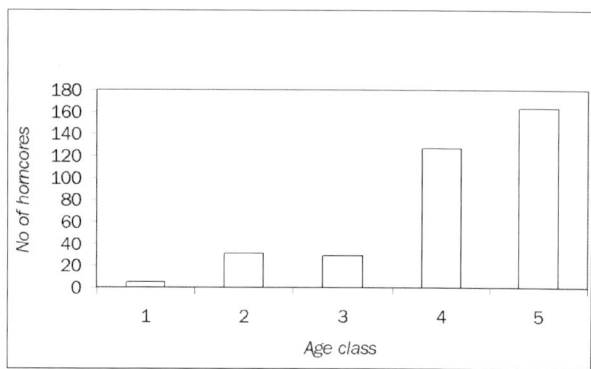

Ill 6.1.15 Phase VII: cattle horn core age stages (after Armitage 1982).

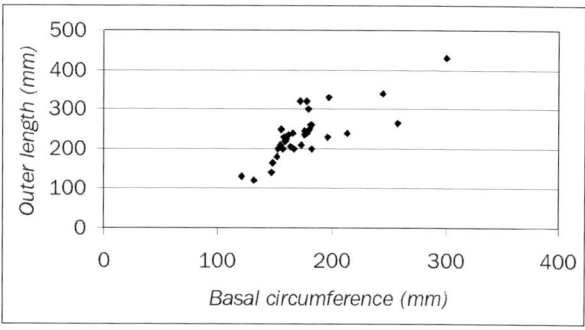

Ill 6.1.16 Phase VII: cattle horn core dimensions (Armitage 1982 age classes 3–5).

usually upwards and forwards (Table 6.1.35). In a smaller number of cases they were oriented upwards with tips pointing backward. One possible interpretation of this pattern of orientation amongst the medium horn cores is that it indicates a predominance of cows and oxen, since in bulls the cores generally curve downwards and inwards (Armitage 1982, 43). A note of caution is, however, appropriate here since recent work suggests that curvature

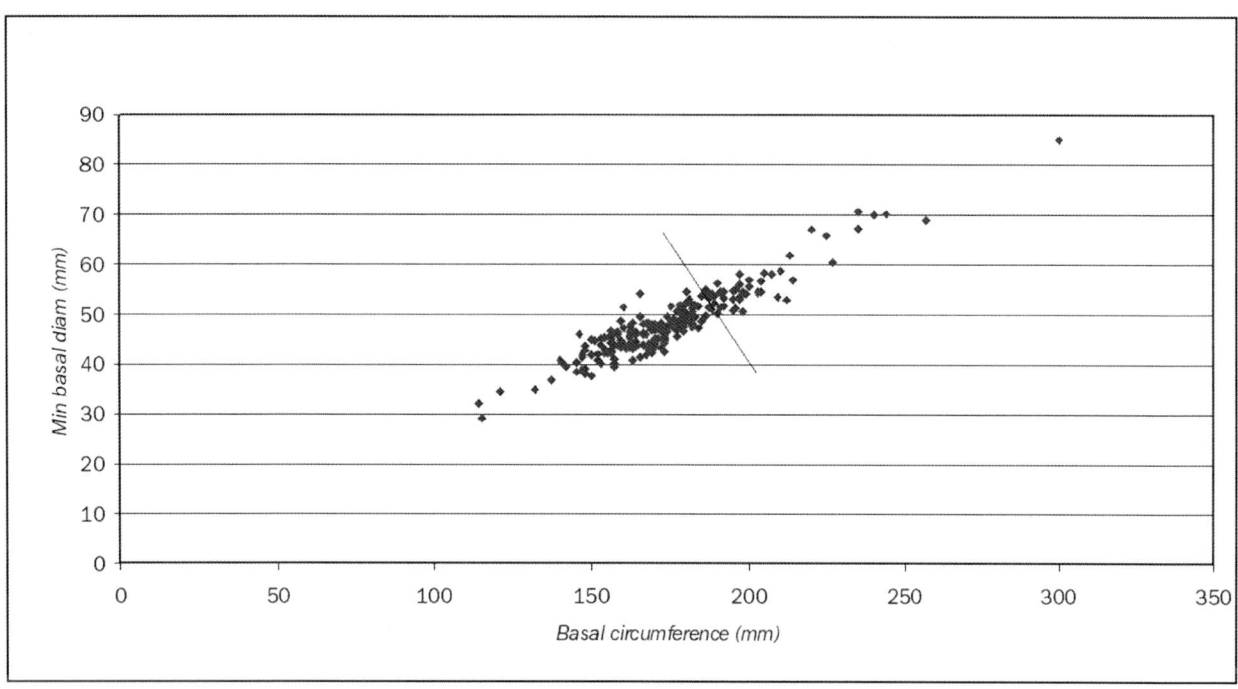

Ill 6.1.17 Phase VII: cattle horncore basal dimensions with female/male dividing line, based on the work of Sykes and Symmons.

and torsion cannot be linked unambiguously to sex (Sykes & Symmons *forthcoming*). There is also evidence that measurements of the minimum basal diameter and basal circumference (in animals over two years old) are better indicators of sex (*ibid*). These measurements are shown in Ill 6.1.17 with a male/female dividing line as predicted by work on cattle of known sex and age by Sykes and Symmons.

Trow-Smith (1957, 210) records that Cheshire long-horns had been crossed with Dutch cattle that Markham described as 'black, smooth coated, with exceedingly long white horns with black tips'. During the early part of the seventeenth century there certainly had also been importation of live cattle from both Ireland and Wales. Robert Brereton of Chester, for instance, leased lands, including some close to the centre of Chester at both Handbridge and on the Roodee, and had '28 Iryshe kyne among his stock' (Dodd 1989, 13). Meanwhile Henry Delves of Doddington introduced new blood into his herd with the addition of 'twenty Welch kyne' (Dodd 1989, 13). Clearly there would have been some potential for biometric and genetic variability. To allow one non-metric comparison with other assemblages it was calculated that 8% (sample=74) of these cattle skulls were characterised by occipital perforations (or non-traumatic holes in the skull).

Porosity and taphonomy

Potentially there were several processes of selection involved prior to the use of these horn cores in the pit lining and thus they might well constitute a biased sample. Certainly it seems highly likely that softer, more porous horn cores will have been discriminated against by post-depositional taphonomic processes. The problem of recovering the more porous horn cores was noted by the author during excavation. It is likely that damage to the bases and tips of many such horn cores will have led to a bias in favour of the recording of the zones of more compact specimens.

Age structure

The age pattern of the horn cores from this group relates to those animals whose horn cores were chosen to build the pit lining. Thus calves with tiny horns are less likely to be represented (Armitage 1982, 52). Despite this bias, the results of analysis using the ageing system proposed by Armitage (1982) suggest that cattle from a range of ages were represented (Ill 6.1.15). Whilst we cannot recreate a husbandry system from this sample, a proportion appeared to come from aged animals. Aged cattle are unlikely to have been reared primarily for beef, since it makes sense to kill such animals as soon as they reach maturity. Oxen were still an important part of the farm economy into the seventeenth century (Dodd 1988, 48). Therefore, as in Phase VI, it is possible that there were remains of cattle here that were used first for working the land or for dairying and that these cattle were only sent to the urban meat markets once they had past their working prime or become barren. It is important to temper these conclusions with the mention that amongst some researchers there is concern that, as presently applied, porosity and texture differences may be rather poor indicators of age. Some differences in porosity and texture might possibly relate directly to breed types (longhorn, medium horn) and so the age classes (Armitage 1982, 38–43) may not be similarly applicable to all horn cores in an assemblage with a mix of types (N Sykes *pers comm*). Reassessments of groups such as this will be desirable if new techniques for ageing cattle horn cores are developed.

Any possible age structure indicated by the horn cores from the site should not be taken as an indication of the ages of cattle consumed there. Doubtless the meat from these animals was consumed somewhere in the city (or elsewhere), but the main horn core producing contexts do not relate primarily to food waste.

Pig

Meat-bearing parts and skull and mandibular parts were

common among the hand-recovered fragments, but all parts of the pig skeleton were represented (Table 6.1.2). The most common zones were from the supracondyloid fossa in the femur and the proximal posterior nutrient foramen and distal pre-epiphysial portion of the diaphysis in the tibia. Fine cut marks that probably related to filleting were recorded (Table 6.1.44). Proximal and distal ends in the femur and the proximal end of the tibia had lower than expected values, apparently reflecting gnawing that had targeted late fusing epiphyses and reduced these relatively common bones to cylinders. Amongst the tiny pig bones from the samples (from a secure cess pit fill, context (1558)) there was a radius with a smallest diameter measurement (SD) of 8.11 mm and also various distal elements which would have been lost through a 5 mm sieve. The context has been interpreted as representing a period when this feature was open and slowly accumulating a silty fill. The bones suggest some pig-rearing took place on site and that some meat-bearing joints were brought in.

Sheep

The most common fragments from sheep all related to meat-bearing cuts (Table 6.1.3). The most common zones came from the scapula, humerus, radius, pelvis, femur and tibia. In the humerus the most common of these zones were the dorsal angle of the olecranon fossa, the trochlea and the coronoid fossa. In the femur the most common zone was the supracondyloid fossa. The femoral trochanter major was under-represented as were articular ends in general. It appears unlikely that many mandibles and skulls were brought onto site. As in other phases, the under-representation of mandible and skull parts meant that only a small sample of teeth could be aged (Table 6.1.41). The small sample size also meant that the mandibular wear and eruption results could not be trusted to reflect the age structure amongst the post-cranial sheep joints supplied to the site. The epiphysial fusion records (Table 6.1.38) gave a larger sample size and suggested that 95% of sheep were over ten months old when they were slaughtered and a considerable number reached their third year. Gnawing by cat and rodent was recorded (Table 6.1.42) and in total 10% of the sheep bones zoned were gnawed. Gnawing evidence characterised by the puncture marks typical of dog was most widespread: this may account for the reduction of many of these bones to cylinders. Gnawing probably biased the epiphysial fusion data in favour of the survival of fused older bones (Munson & Garniewicz 2003).

Comparisons with reference material in York suggests that joints of meat came from sheep smaller than a Shetland or Herdwick wether or ram and about the same size as a Shetland ewe (EAU 504).

Butchery

Fine cut marks (Table 6.1.45) consistent with dismemberment were recorded in the calcaneus and in the scapula matching Binford's code S-2, in the humerus matching Hd-2 and in the radius matching RCp-5 (1981, 122–5). Fine cut marks suggestive of filleting were recorded in the scapulae S-3 (1981, 98) and at various points around the shafts of the humerus, radius and femur including Fd-4 (Binford 1981, 132).

Other fauna

Dog

Butchery

A dog axis and femur from Plot 6 bore clear evidence of butchery. The axis was chopped through the anterior articular process to remove half of this part and the dens. There were a number of other hacking marks just behind this point and anterior to the intervertebral foramen (Ill 6.1.18). The decisive chop marks also removed the most anterior part of the spinous process. The femur bore a number of fine transverse cut marks along the trochanter major from its most proximal part to just above the level of the trochanter minor (Ill 6.1.19). These cut marks surely related to dismemberment and the most proximal of them corresponded closely to Binford's Fp-5 (1981, 117).

Disposal

From context (1601) in Plot 4 there were bones from a skeleton of what was certainly a small and apparently short-faced dog. The context from which these bones were recovered contained cess which coated part of the skull of the animal as a thin layer of yellow concretion. The humerus suggested a withers height of 26.5 cm, about the size of a Dandie Dinmont. It seems likely that this animal was either a small terrier or a lap dog. In contrast to some of the later burials this dog, like many of the cats, was unceremoniously dumped into a stinking pit.

Dog or pig damage to bone

In sample <5159> from context (1607) in Plot 4 there were many small fragments which may have been part digested. In many cases the cortical bone had largely disappeared, leaving the spongy bone underneath exposed. Where cortical bone survived it had a polished appearance. As well as small-sized fragments there were fairly large fragments of mammal cortical bone which a human would be unlikely to swallow. There was evidence on some of these bones that strong stomach acids had been at work. There were also yellow deposits on many fragments which may well have been the remains of cess. These bone fragments suggest that dog or pig faeces were one of the components of the deposit. The fact that very small pig bones were recovered from sampled contexts in Plots 2 and 4 raises the possibility that pigs were farrowing here. The possibility that pigs were active in this and other phases means that some types of bone may have been lost completely (Greenfield 1988, 476).

Cat

Disposal

A number of cats were deposited or buried on site at this time. On the basis of the context types that produced cat bones it is suggested that their deposition was less than reverential. The excavator of cess pit fills (463) and (464) in Plot 2 recorded the presence of a cat skeleton, although the contexts were not recorded as a burial. Certainly there was no whole cat skeleton from a single context, but by pairing similarly coloured and sized bones from these two contexts it was possible to pair up many of the bones that may have come from a single skeleton. However, also from these two contexts there were bones that certainly did belong to different cats of various ages from approximately new born to adult. The humeri of some of the smallest cats were 19.65 and 25.32 mm long with

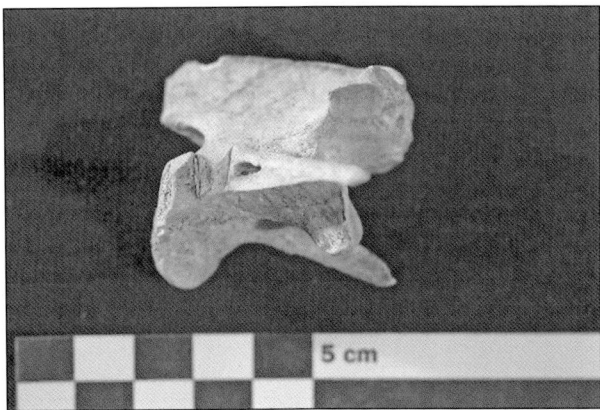

Ill 6.1.18 Phase VII: dog axis with hack marks.

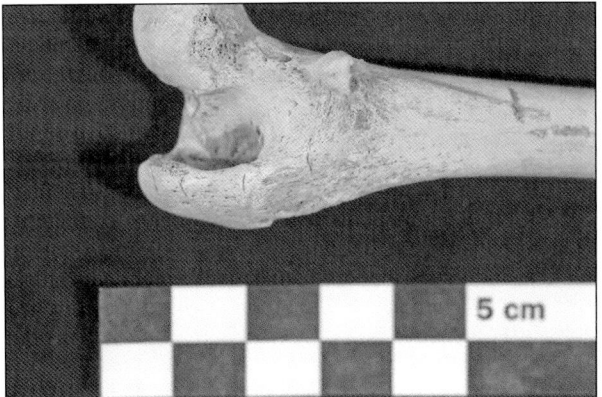

Ill 6.1.19 Phase VII: proximal end of a dog femur with cut marks.

smallest diameter measurements of 2.16 and 3.22 mm. The remains of the cats from Plot 2 were present in eight contexts, although most came from the cess pit fills.

Health
A number of the cats appear to have been in poor health for some time prior to deposition. Three of them had some dental problems. In two cases there was recession of the alveolar bone around the M1 and in the third case the M1 and most of the P4 has been lost and there was considerable remodelling of the sockets into a single cavity over 7 mm in length. In two other cases there was some bone recession and remodelling of the sockets of the P4. One pelvis (from context (440) in Plot 2) showed evidence of remodelling which suggested dislocation and the formation of a false acetabulum on the ilium.

Butchery
No skinning marks could be found above the orbits or at the anterior parts of the mandibles or maxillae or amongst the distal limb bones and no butchery marks were noted on axis, atlas or elsewhere. This does not prove that these cats were not skinned, since skilled skinners need not necessarily leave cut marks (Luff & Moreno Garcia 1995, 110). Metapodials and phalanges were recovered by hand from contexts (440), (463), (464), (472), (491) and (1451) and from wet-sieved samples of (464) and (489). The presence of these phalanges and of bones representing all of the other body parts was taken to suggest that whole carcasses were being disposed of. If these cats were skinned, the phalanges were apparently left attached to the carcass at the skinning stage. An inventory by the wife of

Robert Fletcher (the skinner) dated to 1696 lists cat, including wild cat, skins (Backhouse *this volume*). Of course it may be the case that some cat-skinning took place elsewhere and that cat skins arrived on site with no bones attached.

Cats breeding on site
The presence of very young cats from Phase VII contexts (464) and (489) in Plot 2 suggested that cats managed or were possibly encouraged to breed here, or alternatively perhaps that pregnant cats were skinned on site. The samples included neonatal bones from at least one cat from Plot 4 (context (1607)). On the basis of this evidence and the presence of some bones with small triangular puncture marks characteristic of cat, it is suggested that cats bred on site during this phase.

Rabbit
As well as young cats there were some small unfused metapodials from young rabbits in Plot 1, context (664). Small numbers of rabbit remains were also recovered from samples from Plots 1, 2 and 4 although the bulk of the rabbit remains were collected by hand (Table 6.1.18). One rabbit had definite cut marks on the pelvis that corresponded to Binford's PS-3 and PS-6 (1981, 130) and probably related to filleting.

Evidence for the fur trade
The fauna from this phase included small numbers of bones from various wild fur-bearing mammals. These were red squirrel, pine marten (Ill 6.1.20), a possible fox and hare. The bones identified as pine marten were a femur and tibia both from the left hand side and both fused proximally and distally. The presence of these bones (and of ferret/polecat and stoat in Phase VIII) suggested that the skins of such small animals may sometimes have been transported to the furrier with the main leg and sometimes skull bones still in place. Hare bones were not frequent but all those present were from distal parts of the skeleton. Red squirrel, pine marten and fox were much sought after by furriers and others, and from the sixteenth century a bounty could be claimed for their corpses (Yalden 1999, 176). Squirrel skins had apparently been one of the most important trade items of local skinners from the later medieval period but they also traded fox, rabbit and beaver (Lewis & Thacker eds 2003, 76). Given that pine marten survived in parts of Cheshire until 1800 (*see* Yalden 1999, 178, fig 6.5), the formerly extensive Delamere Forest would presumably have retained populations of these animals. However, each of these three fur-bearing species could also have been imports rather than local captures. Imports of hundreds of marten and fox skins are documented from Ireland from the sixteenth century (Lewis & Thacker eds 2003, 69).

Water birds
Each of the plots produced some wild birds, including some such as cormorant (Ill 6.1.21) and a possible common gull. The bones from Plot 4 were of particular interest. Amongst these there was a swan pelvis (context (1601) which had signs of butchery in the form of fine cut marks (Ill 6.1.23). This specimen was clearly a mute swan since there was no prominent ventral projection (Ill 6.1.22) at the anterior end of the synsacrum (*contra* the generally

excellent Cohen & Serjeantson 1996, 84). Associated bones from Plot 4 included another swan bone (the coracoid) and the usual range of domesticates as well as the pelves and femora of deer, and some bones from various wild birds including woodcock and snipe (Tables 6.1.20–.21). Such a range of food remains in urban post-medieval contexts is indicative of waste from high-status individuals, and it seems quite probable that at least some of it was waste from the table of the prosperous Anderton family who owned the plot.

Crow

The small number of corvid bones from this phase included raven, crow/rook, jackdaw and magpie specimens (Table 6.1.20). They were distributed in layers and fills from Plots 1, 2 and 6. Some of these bones may have been from human food remains but it is also possible that these birds were competing with the cats for scraps of food or butchery waste.

Summary and further research
The horn cores resulted from the large numbers of cattle and cattle hides that were either driven to Chester or arrived through the port at this time. It would be instructive in future to undertake stable isotope analyses to attempt to source these cores. As in Phase VI the diversity of wild birds, including swan, and the proportion of calves are taken to indicate some prosperous plot owners; the documentary evidence appears to be in agreement with this interpretation. Evidence was also recovered which suggests that waste from the preparation of furs was disposed of here. It is also suggested that cats, dogs, pigs and probably various members of the crow family were living and scavenging in the backlands.

Phase VIII

Sample size
There were 3559 fragments from hand collection and 224 identifications from samples (Tables 6.1.22–.23). Wet-sieved bone was recovered from nine contexts (Table 6.1.50).

Main domestic species
Cattle
Carcass representation
The small number of adult cattle teeth recovered (only two mandibular M3s from a total of five adult or sub-adult teeth) suggested that few adult cattle heads or mandibles arrived on site. Calf teeth were more numerous (n=11). Zones from the pelvis, femur, ulna, humerus, calcaneus, scapula and the mandibular deciduous d4s were the most frequent amongst the cattle bones. Although fragments of horn core were frequent (n=87), a large proportion (n=52) originated from context (455) in Plot 4, which overlay and had pottery joins to sherds from the horn core structure of Phase VII. Other fragments of horn core (n=6) were associated with sandstone wall (1531) that was also situated above the horn core structure. These horn core fragments may thus have been redeposited in Phase VIII and the horn core fragment count (Table 6.1.1) should therefore be viewed with suspicion.

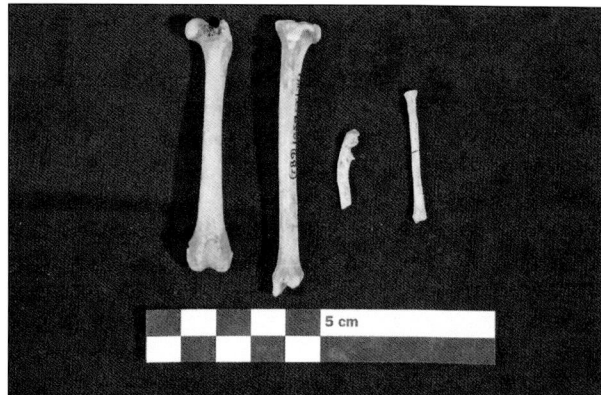

Ill 6.1.20 *(from left)* Phase VII: pine marten *(Martes martes)* femur and tibia, and red squirrel *(Sciurus vulgaris)* ulna and radius.

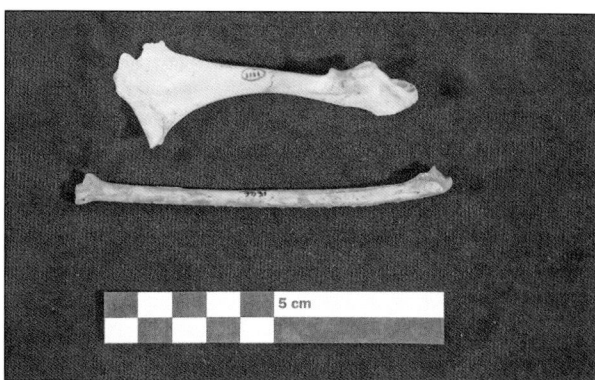

Ill 6.1.21 Phase VII: cormorant *(Phalacrocorax carbo)* coracoid and gull *(Larus cf canus)* ulna from Plots 3 and 4 respectively.

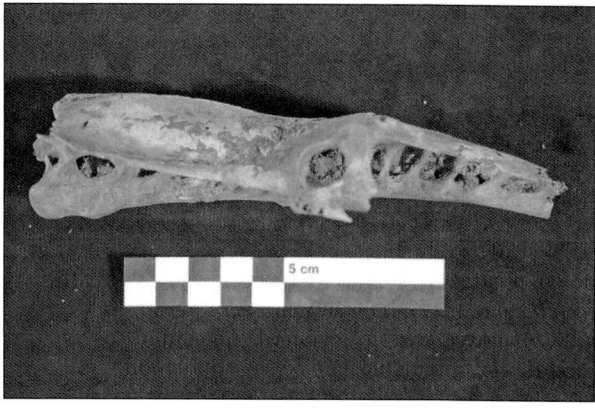

Ill 6.1.22 Phase VII Plot 4: mute swan *(Cygnus olor)* pelvis.

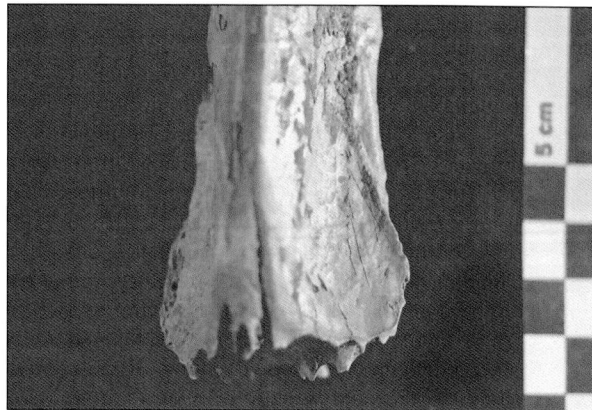

Ill 6.1.23 Phase VII: cut marks on swan *(Cygnus olor)* pelvis.

Table 6.1.22 Phase VIII: hand-collected fragments quantified by plot and taxa

Vernacular	Taxon			Plot			No	%
		1	**2**	**3**	**4**	**6**		
Bird								
Swan	*Cygnus* sp					1	1	0.0
Goose	*Anser/Branta*	11	10	10		15	46	1.3
Duck	*Anas* sp	1	1	2		2	6	0.2
Partridge	cf *Perdix perdix* L.					1	1	0.0
Chicken	*Gallus gallus* L.	7	18	11	6	33	75	2.1
Lapwing	*Vanellus vanellus* L.			1		2	3	0.1
Woodcock	*Scolopax rusticola* L.		1	2		1	4	0.1
Pigeon	Columbidae	1					1	0.0
Small passerine	Passeriformes					1	1	0.0
Bird unident	Aves	10	12	4	3	32	61	1.7
Mammal								
Rabbit	*Oryctolagus cuniculus* L.	18	11	5		1	35	1.0
Hare	*Lepus* sp	5	1	1		3	10	0.3
Dog	*Canis* f domestic	4				30	34	1.0
Red fox	cf *Vulpes vulpes* L.		1	1		1	3	0.1
Stoat	*Mustela erminea* L.		2				2	0.1
Polecat/ferret	*Mustela* sp		3				3	0.1
Cat	*Felis* f domestic	2	34	9	3	35	83	2.3
Horse	*Equus* f domestic			4		2	6	0.2
Pig	*Sus* f domestic	28	22	29	3	77	159	4.5
Fallow deer	*Dama dama* L.	3				6	9	0.3
Red/fallow deer	*Cervus/Dama*		2	2	1	1	6	0.2
Red deer/cattle	*Cervus/Bos*			1			1	0.0
Roe deer	*Capreolus capreolus* L.	1	2				3	0.1
Cattle	*Bos* f domestic	126	76	127	91	341	761	21.4
Goat	*Capra* f domestic				1	4	5	0.1
Sheep	*Ovis* f domestic	10	14	12	3	46	85	2.4
Sheep/goat	*Ovis/Capra*	52	31	67	13	137	300	8.4
Large mammal	Mammalia	121	77	86	47	271	602	16.9
Large or medium mammal	Mammalia	6		10		42	58	1.6
Medium mammal	Mammalia	113	50	64	8	145	380	10.7
Small mammal	Mammalia	11	2	4		6	23	0.6
Unidentified		207	22	115	38	410	792	22.3
Total		737	392	567	217	1645	3559	100.0

Table 6.1.23 Phase VIII: fragments from samples quantified by plot and taxa

Vernacular	Taxon			Plot				No	%
		1	**2**	**3**	**4**	**5**	**6**		
Amphibian									
Frog/toad	*Rana/Bufo*						1	1	0.4
Bird									
Goose	*Anser/Branta*						1	1	0.4
Duck	*Anas* sp	1						1	0.4
Chicken	*Gallus* f domestic			2	3		1	6	2.7
Snipe	*Gallinago gallinago* L.						1	1	0.4
Jacksnipe	*Lymnocryptes minimus* Brunnich						1	1	0.4
Woodcock	*Scolopax rusticola* L.						1	1	0.4
Small passerine	Passeriformes	1		1				2	0.9
cf Blackbird	*Turdus* cf *merula* L.	1						1	0.4
Mammal									
Shrew	Soricidae						1	1	0.4
Rabbit	*Oryctolagus cuniculus* L.	25		1	1		6	33	14.7
Hare	*Lepus* sp	1					1	2	0.9
Rabbit/hare	Leporidae				2			2	0.9
Mouse	Muridae	1		1	1		2	5	2.2
Rodent	Rodentia	4		1			1	6	2.7
Rat	*Rattus* sp	1		2	3		6	12	5.4
Dog	*Canis* f domestic			3			3	6	2.7
Cat	*Felis* f domestic			4	2		69	75	33.5
Pig	*Sus* f domestic	1					4	5	2.2
Pig (neonate or suckling)	*Sus* f domestic			5			7	12	5.4
Cattle	*Bos* f domestic	10			21		3	34	15.2
Cattle (calf)	*Bos* f domestic				2		5	7	3.1
Sheep/goat	*Ovis/Capra*			1			7	8	3.6
Sheep	*Ovis* f domestic				1			1	0.4
Total		46	0	21	36	0	121	224	100.0

Age

Dental evidence suggested an early peak in the kill-off pattern of the cattle arriving on site. Seven of the nine cattle mandibles and loose teeth recovered from this phase were from calves. One d4 was at wear stage d (Grant 1982, 92) and all of the others were at earlier wear stages (Table 6.1.39). Thus the teeth of these calves were just in wear, probably in the first few weeks of life. This evidence for a high proportion of calves was backed up by an assessment of the number of calf bones amongst the cattle. Just under 22% of the cattle fragments zoned were clearly from calves (Ill 6.1.3) (n=217). The two other cattle represented by teeth were an individual of around 30–36 months and another which was an adult when it died. The large proportion of calves is interpreted as being a product of the continuing importance of the dairying industry in the county and also of the continued prosperity of the people living in the adjoining properties. Dairying was the dominant farming concern over most of the county by 1800 and there were large surpluses of bull calves that were raised for veal (Crosby 1996, 89). However, the zooarchaeological evidence regarding the sex of the cattle from this phase was scant. Two cattle pelves were from females and one other was a probable female. No male cattle pelves were identified. It would be of great interest to compare the cattle age evidence from this site with contemporary properties of lower social status since one might predict that the numbers of calf bones in the latter should be lower.

Taphonomy

15 % (n=7) of the calf bones were recorded as having evidence for dog gnawing as compared to 2.3% of the adult or sub-adult ones. As elsewhere, dog gnawing probably discriminated against calf bones and some will have been completely destroyed. In addition, one calf and one adult cattle bone was gnawed by rodents. Although the proportion of calf among the surviving cattle bones was still high, we should start from the assumption that the mortality profile was biased toward the adult classes (Munson & Garniewicz 2003, 415).

Butchery

Fine cut marks consistent with dismemberment were recorded in the scapula corresponding to Binford's S-2 (1981, 122), in the ulna RCp-2 (1981, 125) and in a calf bone from the femur Fp-1 (1981, 117). Other fine cut marks were noted at the proximal superior surface of ribs (filleting) and at the cranial end of the ilium (Table 6.1.43). Among the most commonly recorded hack marks and impact scars there were a number which divided the main meat-bearing limbs in two. In the humerus the most common hack mark was a transverse one proximally of the nutrient foramen or at approximately mid-shaft. Another hack mark at the distal end of the humerus ran in a longitudinal direction and had the effect of separating the trochlea from the capitulum. In the femur the most common hack marks were located at mid-shaft and had the effect of dividing proximal and distal ends. In the tibia, hacking to divide the bone longitudinally was common as were oblique hack marks that divided the distal shaft.

Pig

Fragments of pig were less than half as common as frag-

ments from sheep or goat (Tables 6.1.22–.23). Most parts of the skeleton were represented (Table 6.1.2), with humeri being particularly common. Humeri were hacked through medial and lateral distal epicondyles and at approximately mid-shaft. Hacking apparently to divide the mandible into right and left sides was recorded, as were hacks through the diastema and longitudinal hacks through the vertebrae. The latter may well have originated from splitting the carcass into right and left sides. Fine cut marks to the astragalus and on the neck of the femur probably related to dismemberment (Table 6.1.44). Neonates or suckling pigs were recovered from the wet-sieved samples (Table 6.1.23) from Plots 3 and 6. It is suggested that some joints of pork were brought to site but it is possible that pigs were also reared here.

Sheep

The most commonly recorded zone was the coronoid fossa in the humerus. The humerus produced other common zones, as did the radius, scapula, tibia and pelvis. The fusion data (Table 6.1.38) indicated that most of the main meat-bearing bones were from adult or sub-adult animals. From a sample of 197 fragments there were only seven (3.5%) fragments of bone that came from either lamb or kid, six of which were from metapodials. Four of the latter, (from Plots 2 and 6) were metapodials with smallest diameters of between 6.6 and 9 mm and approximately the same length as those recovered from the late medieval phase. Whilst this raises the possibility that there was some continuation in leatherworking from the late medieval period the sample was far too small to be conclusive. In addition there was also a small femur (SD *c* 10 mm) and pelvis which clearly came from small immature animals, and so a few meat-bearing parts of lamb or kid meat appear to have been deposited alongside these metapodials during Phase VIII.

Butchery

Fine cut marks (Table 6.1.45) consistent with filleting were noted amongst scapulae (S-3), humeri (Hd-6) and femora (Fd-5). Cut marks associated with dismemberment were noted on scapulae corresponding to Binford's S-1 and S-2 (1981, 122) on humeri corresponding to Hd-2, in pelves corresponding to PS-7 (1981, 113) and in calcanea matching TC-3 (1981, 120). Fine cut marks possibly associated with splitting the carcass were also noted on the transverse process of a sheep vertebra.

Goat

As in earlier phases goat identifications were present but not common. They were represented by two horn cores, a metacarpal and a first and second phalanx. Bearing in mind that these were among the easier elements to distinguish from sheep, it is possible that these bones did represent some continuation of the leather-processing seen in earlier phases. Goats were widely prized for their skins and some parts of Britain had local traditions regarding the use of the goat and its products. Just across the border in North Wales goat haunches were apparently cured like ham (Whitehead 1972 in Noddle 1994, 122), and perhaps some of the skins from such goats were sent to the leatherworkers of Chester. However, there are various other possible sources for the origins of goat skins sent to Chester in this period. Tens of thousands of goat skins were exported from Scotland during the seventeenth century (Noddle 1994, 122) and there was a flourishing trade in goat skins over many parts of Europe from the medieval period onward (Albarella 2003, 81). From the mid-eighteenth to mid-nineteenth century the leather industry was the third largest industry in Britain (Noddle 1994, 123), although in Chester it had begun to decline from the early eighteenth century (Carrington ed 1994, 82). There is good evidence from the late medieval period onward that most of the tanneries in Chester were away from the centre, outside the City Walls (Carrington ed 1994, 82), but it is important to distinguish between the tanning of heavy hides and other leather-processing techniques. It is certainly possible that, in this period, some leatherworking activity (such as tawing) continued to take place inside the walls on sites such as this.

Other fauna
Fox and ferret
There were some signs that furriers may have been operating here. From Plot 6 there was a partial mandible from dog or fox. Comparisons with reference material suggest that it was most likely to be from a fox. This mandible had a number of fine cut marks spanning almost the whole fragment from just anterior to the mental foramina to the area supporting the carnassial. The location of these fine cut marks suggested that they resulted from skinning. Also, a skull and mandible from either a polecat or ferret had fine cut marks across the nasal area and across the most anterior part of the mandible that were taken to indicate skinning.

Dog
A dog femur from Plot 6, fill (637) was affected by a considerable amount of irregular remodelling which appears to have followed a break and infection of the proximal end of the shaft. The pit was excavated by trowel and the surviving part of the femur was reasonably well preserved, so it seems unlikely that most of the rest of the skeleton has been lost through taphonomic processes. However, this femur was the only part of the dog to be recovered, and so presumably this was part of a skeleton which had been disturbed and redeposited in this context.

Cat
Another mandible from Plot 6, but this time from a cat, bore fracture lines which isolated the canine and the mental foramina. Thus the foremost and lateral part of the mandible was broken from the main part of the ramus. The fracture was partially healed but the line of the fracture was still clearly defined and accompanied by slight lumps and rough areas on the lateral side and a smooth edged cleft which ran behind and below the symphyseal surface on the medial side. Clearly this cat managed to survive quite a serious injury.

Birds
Wild birds continued to feature on the menu of those depositing their food waste here (Tables 6.1.22–.23), although the proportion of chicken and goose fragments declined relative to Phase VII and the diversity of species was reduced.

Summary and further research
The proportions of calves to adult or sub-adult cattle may have continued to reflect the dairy industry and, together with the wild bird bones, suggest continued prosperity amongst inhabitants of the plots. It is possible, however, that this prosperity was on the decline, since both groups of remains occurred in reduced proportions compared with Phase VII. This is worthy of further investigation if other backlands sites are excavated, although of course, the prosperity of individual plot owners may very well have taken different courses. There is some evidence that furriers continued to practice in the area. As in the previous phase, groups of cat and dog bones probably indicated the demise or disposal of these animals on site.

Phase IX

Sample size
There were 3275 fragments from hand collection and 203 identifications from the samples (Tables 6.1.24–.25). Wet-sieved bone was recovered from fifteen contexts (Table 6.1.50).

Main domestic species
Cattle
Age
34% of all the identified cattle fragments came from calves (n=426) and calf remains occurred in thirty-nine contexts (59%). This proportion may reflect the surplus of calves sent to urban centres. Hanshall (1823, 58) recorded that there were in the region of 93,000 to 94,000 cows kept in Cheshire for dairying. He estimated that each cow produced an average of about 250 lbs of cheese and that annually the county produced 9791 tons or 23,500,000 lbs of cheese. It was claimed in 1837 that Cheshire was exporting up to 500 calves a week to the city of Liverpool during the summer months (Crosby 1996, 89).

Disposal
It is also worth considering the possibility (also raised by Higgins *this volume*) that people had largely ceased to dispose of their food waste in pits during this phase. If that were the case, one could argue that many of the bones from the food animals recovered from this phase were redeposited. Potentially then, many of the cattle bones and high levels of calf (and bones from other stock animals) could relate to earlier phases. We can identify some cattle and calf bones, from the fills of probable burials (*see* below), which do appear most likely to have been redeposited with the backfill of these features.

However, in at least one large context, (1491), a fill of the brick-lined well (1488) in Plot 4, there were indications that the mainly adult cattle bones clearly did represent primary deposition. The first indicator was the distinctively high level of sawing amongst the bones. Half (n=13 sawn) of the cattle bones and the majority (n=28 sawn) of the large mammal bones (many of which were probably from cattle) were sawn. The sawn bones included vertebrae that had been cut in a way which divided the carcass into left and right halves, and limb bones that had been divided into various joints. This sawing represented butchery rather than craft bone-working. However, this context was unusual in this phase since amongst the sixty-six contexts bearing cattle bones, there were

Table 6.1.24 Phase IX: hand-collected fragments quantified by plot and taxa

Vernacular	Taxon	Plot 1	2	3	4	5	6	No	%
Bird									
Goose	*Anser/Branta*	4	5	1	5		35	50	1.5
Teal	*Anas crecca* L.	1						1	0.0
Duck	*Anas* sp						4	4	0.1
Chicken	*Gallus* f domestic	4	9	6	6	10	42	77	2.4
Heron	*Ardea cinerea* L.						1	1	0.0
Lapwing	*Vanellus vanellus* L.					2	1	3	0.1
Snipe	*Gallinago gallinago* L.	2		3				5	0.2
Woodcock	*Scolopax rusticola* L.	1					7	8	0.2
Pigeon	*Columbidae*						6	6	0.2
Bird unident	*Aves*	5	3	8	5		42	63	1.9
Mammal									
Rabbit	*Oryctolagus cuniculus* L.	24	5	1	2		13	45	1.4
Hare	*Lepus* sp	5			1	1	3	10	0.3
House mouse	*Mus musculus* L.	2					1	3	0.1
Rat	*Rattus* sp						4	4	0.1
Dog	*Canis* f domestic	48		1			217	266	8.1
Cat	*Felis* f domestic	2	2	2	15	11	45	77	2.4
Horse	*Equus* f domestic						1	1	0.0
Pig	*Sus* f domestic	6	8	6	14	3	98	135	4.1
Red deer	*Cervus elaphus* L.						2	2	0.1
Fallow deer	*Dama dama* L.						5	5	0.2
Red/fallow deer	*Cervus/Dama*		1			1	3	5	0.2
Roe deer	*Capreolus capreolus* L.						1	1	0.0
Cattle	*Bos* f domestic	40	23	25	65	15	298	466	14.2
Goat	*Capra* f domestic				2		1	3	0.1
Sheep	*Ovis* f domestic	8	12	2	19	4	23	68	2.1
Sheep/goat	*Ovis/Capra*	32	31	20	65	6	146	300	9.2
Large mammal	*Mammalia*	52	35	28	71	8	331	525	16.0
Large or medium mammal	*Mammalia*		1	4	1		12	18	0.5
Medium mammal	*Mammalia*	48	50	7	37	6	264	412	12.6
Small mammal	*Mammalia*	47	8	2			16	73	2.2
Unidentified		95	32	40	55	10	406	638	19.5
Total		426	225	156	363	77	2029	3275	100.0

Table 6.1.25 Phase IX: fragments from samples quantified by plot and taxa

Vernacular	Taxon	Plot 1	2	3	4	5	6	No	%
Bird									
Chicken	*Gallus* f domestic	1					2	3	1.5
Lapwing	*Vanellus vanellus* L					1		1	0.5
Snipe	*Gallinago gallinago* L					1		1	0.5
Small passerine	*Passeriformes*					2		2	1.0
Thrush family	*Turdus* sp				1		1	2	1.0
Small corvid	*Corvidae*					1		1	0.5
Mammal									
Rabbit	*Oryctolagus cuniculus* L	5				1	1	7	3.4
Hare	*Lepus* sp	1						1	0.5
Rabbit/hare	*Leporidae*						6	6	3.0
Vole	*Microtidae*						1	1	0.5
Mouse	*Muridae*	3					2	5	2.5
House mouse	*Mus musculus* L						1	1	0.5
Rodent	*Rodentia*	1				5	8	14	6.9
Rat	*Rattus* sp	2				7	2	11	5.4
Dog	*Canis* f domestic						5	5	2.5
Cat	*Felis* f domestic					9	107	116	57.1
Pig	*Sus* f domestic	1				1	7	9	4.4
Pig (neonate or suckling)	*Sus* f domestic					5	2	7	3.4
Cattle	*Bos* f domestic						2	2	1.0
Cattle (calf)	*Bos* f domestic						1	1	0.5
Sheep/goat	*Ovis/Capra*				1	1	3	5	2.5
Goat	*Capra* f domestic					1		1	0.5
Sheep	*Ovis* f domestic					1		1	0.5
Total		14	0	0	2	35	152	203	100.0

only four which produced sawn bones. Could this possibly be an indication of the extent of residuality?

Further indications that the bones from context (1491) represented primary deposition were joins between the sawn edges; the radius and ulna fragments clearly belonging together; and the large size of the bones compared to those from the earlier periods. Unfortunately only a proximal radius produced a measurement to confirm the perceived large size (Table 6.1.26), but each of the other bones was notably large and it is suggested that this was a reflection of relatively recent breed 'improvements'.

Sheep

Sawn bones of sheep were also common in context (1491), and again there were adjoining sawn fragments and other signs that the bones belonged together and were thus unlikely to be redeposited. Each of the ten mandibles could be put into likely pairs according to tooth eruption stage and the degree of tooth wear. Three of these mandible pairs were from young sheep which had intact deciduous d4s. Measurements of the humerus, radius and tibia from context (1491) showed that these bones were large relative to any from the earlier phases (Table 6.1.28). As with the cattle bones, it is suggested that this was a biometric reflection of relatively recent breed improvements and that the bones represented primary deposition.

Horse

Only a single horse maxillary tooth was recovered from layer (827) which was cut by various recent service trenches. It is suggested that by this time disposal of horse carcasses on these backland plots was no longer practised.

Other fauna
Cat

By the late eighteenth to nineteenth century cats constituted a much larger proportion of the fragments. Dog fragment numbers were also high (Tables 6.1.24–.25). The cats and dogs differed from much of the rest of the fauna in that there were whole and partial skeletons and many of the bones were complete. There were a number of cat and dog skeletons from the area of the 'drying grounds' in Plot 6. The cut features associated with these skeletons corresponded closely to the size of the animals and it was clear during excavation that the fills were of a mixed, redeposited nature and that usually there was a single interred animal at the base of the cut. It is suggested that the digging of such features to inter individual animals indicates the burial of pets. Some other bones (butchered cattle bones, for instance) from these burials were probably residual in the backfill of the interments.

Double cat burial?

To complicate matters there was a group of cat remains which was interpreted on site as a double burial (context (353)). This was of interest since it seems unlikely that one would bury two pets at the same time, although such an event may have occurred after an outbreak of cat flu. No evidence for skinning was seen amongst these cat bones either at the most anterior part of maxilla and mandible on the metapodials or elsewhere. Of course, skinning can be undertaken in such a way that there is little or no

trace. However, in the absence of any evidence for skinning and given that pet-keeping was relatively common in the period, it has been assumed that these animals, too, were buried pets. Another possibility in the case of this double burial is that the line of a cut was missed during excavation since the contrasts between contexts in this area were difficult to define (D Garner *pers comm*). From the samples there were neonatal cat bones from Plot 5, context (1486), suggesting infant mortality and that cats bred here.

Dog

The dog remains included some from animals of quite small stature. From context (1818), for instance, probable pairs of humeri, femora and tibiae all indicated that one of the dogs was 29 or 30 cm in height at the withers. Other bones (some broken and some unfused) from the same context came from at least one other diminutive dog. The measurements suggest the dog was the size of a Jack Russell terrier or lap dog.

Most of the bones from another dog from Plot 6, context (375), were exceptionally well preserved. We can be confident that this dog was an adult male since the penis bone was recovered and all of the recovered bones had fused epiphyses. It stood between 55 and 57 cm at the withers (approximately the height of a labrador) according to factors based on the combined humerus/radius and femur/tibia (Harcourt 1974, 154). The other finds within the fill of the cut were randomly distributed and it is clear that the cut was made specifically for the burial of this dog. In this respect it differed from some of the dog skeletons from earlier phases. This appears to have been a careful burial and it is suggested that again this indicated a valued animal.

Summary and further research

There is a strong possibility that there was a large proportion of residual bones in this phase. There may have been some changes in waste disposal practices from the associated properties. However, in a small number of contexts there was clear zooarchaeological evidence for primary deposition. In these contexts there were distinctive metrical and butchery traits, as well as joins and possible matching pairs of elements which set these groups of bones apart from those in the rest of the phase. Many of the other contexts reflecting primary deposition seem to represent the burials of pet cats and dogs.

Acknowledgements

Many thanks to James Rackham for kindly providing details of the animal bone zones that he records. Many thanks also to Joanne Cooper, Terry O'Connor, Clem Fisher, Tony Parker, Richard Sabin and Henry McGhie for access to reference collections, and to Kim Norman for access to *Bufo calamita* specimens; to Sue Stallibrass for discussions on site; and to Sue Stallibrass, Stig Walsh, Naomi Sykes, Cluny Johnstone, Ian Baxter and Andy Hammon for sending me relevant papers. Particular thanks to Monica Webster who was involved in most of the recording work and who compiled the bulk of the fragment and weight data. Many thanks to Sarah Viner who helped to sort sieved bones and to input measurements, to Debbie Morton who ordered all bags and boxes by context after they came off site and to Heather Hidden who helped to organise the assessment data. Many thanks to Sonia O'Connor and Adrian Doyle who both offered invaluable bone conservation advice and to staff at York Archaeological Trust for work on bone conservation. Many thanks also to Geoff Couling who processed the samples on site and organised the sorting of sampled material, and to Peter Carrington for constructive comments on an earlier draft of this text.

Table 6.1.27 Pig measurements

Key Measurements as in von den Driesch 1976

Element	Phase	Plot	Context	GL	BP	Bd
Radius	VII	4	1516		25.1	
Tibia	IV	3	799	*unfused, c 36 mm		
Tibia	V	4	1579			28.84
MC3	VII	1	663	68.95		
MC3	V	3	1217	81.95	20.97	20.87
MT3	VII	1	663	96.8		
Phalanx 1	VIII	3	1405		17.09	

Table 6.1.26 Cattle measurements

Key Measurements as in von den Driesch 1976. (*45 greatest diameter of the horncore base, 46* least diameter of the horncore base), *c = circa*, + = minimum (damaged: original size may have been larger)

Element	Phase	Plot	Context	GL	BP	BFp	SD/SC	Bd	BT	SLC	GLP	45*	46*	GB
Horncore	V	4	1579									67.59	52.92	
	VIII	3	1437									57.31	45.82	
Scapula	IV	6	1030							45.72	58.19			
	VI	2	787							48.06	65.75			
	VI	4	1540								63.57			
	VII	4	1516							50.89	c 65.35			37.61
	IX	6	553								57.62			
Humerus	III	6	1022					53.00						
	VI	2	1635					91.27	77.76					
	VI	4	1566					c 75.70	c 68.88					
	VI	4	1566						66.19					
	VII	2	463					80.00	72.34					
	VIII	1	1837					69.59	67.71					
Radius	VIII	1	1871			c 68.71								
	VIII	1	1871		75.73	68.94								
	VIII	6	341		72.89	67.11								
	IX	2	1299		87.75	79.83								
	IX	4	1491		88.24	c 82.59								
Femur	IX	5	1486					102.65						
Tibia	III	6	1022					min 60						
	V	3	808					55.24						
	VI	4	1697					49.02						
	VI	1	766					55.57						
Calcaneus	III	6	1022	118.00										
	IV	2	1125	137.11										
	VII	4	1604	133+										
Metacarpal	III	6	1022	50.75										
	III	6	1022					54.47						
	VI	3	429	178.50				47.51						
	VII	1	245	198.00		c 60	37.85	61.58						
	VII	3	1193					54.35						
	VII	4	1607			53.47								
	VII	4	1604					59.84						
	VII	6	824	200.00										
	VIII	1	1903	c 175		50.63								
	VIII	1	1819					59.91						
	VIII	6	637					c 50.00						
	IX	1	1839					58.57						
	IX	6	340					c 56.27						
Metatarsal	III	6	1022					50.52						
	III	6	1022					50.97				67.59	52.92	
	IV	2	1125					58.50				57.31	45.82	
	VI	2	787	207.00	44.57			51.02						
	VI	2	798	210.00	24.25									
	VI	2	798	210.00	25.24									
	VI	3	857	227.00	51.42		30.17	60.16						
	VI	3	429	c 217										
	VI	4	1697					63.11						
	VI	4	1540					52.87						
	VII	1	663	211.00	45.52			50.55						
	VII	1	670	213.00										
	VIII	3	1406	270.00				46.97						
	IX	2	1299	215.00			25.02	47.82						
	X	2	1802					54.68						
	X	2	1802					50.63						
	X	2	1802					c 50.95						
	X	2	1802					53.11						
	X	3	1404					49.16						
Phalanx 1	III	6	1022	55.02	31.86			30.32						
	III	6	1022	51.97	22.39			22.41						41.83
	VII	3	1193	53.32	24.41			22.72						

Table 6.1.28 Sheep measurements (*continued on page* 370)

Key Measurements as in von den Driesch 1976. For c and c+d *see* Boessneck 1969, 353. In scapula SLC taken between glenoid and pecten

Element	Phase	Plot	Context	GL	BP	BFp	SD/SC	Bd	BT	SLC	GLP	c	c+d	GB
Scapula	III	6	1022								30.23			
	V	4	1579								31.11			
	V	4	1579								33.80			
	V	4	1582							20.83	c 31.50			
	VI	1	766								30.37			
	VI	3	1702								32.88			
	VI	3	1702								29.13			
	VI	3	800								31.48			
	VI	3	429							20.38	33.13			
	VII	1	1897								28.63			
	VII	2	463							21.17				
	VII	3	1193								30.52			
	VII	3	1193								34.79			
	VII	4	1592							19.95	35.22			
	VII	6	694							22.00				
	VII	6	694							22.31	32.76			
	VIII	1	656							20.09				
	VIII	1	1819								34.13			
	VIII	2	847								32.68			
	VIII	3	1437							19.12	30.46			
	VIII	6	341							19.23	32.22			
	IX	4	1491							20.65	33.69			
	IX	5	1486							18.92	29.85			
	IX	6	553							18.51	27.74			
	IX	6	524								32.06			
Humerus	III	6	1022					26.43	24.90					
	III	6	1022					28.28	23.93					
	VI	1	766					30.17						
	VI	2	791					30.07	29.29					
	VI	3	629					27.97	26.79					
	VI	3	429						25.12					
	VII	4	1516					c 29.56	27.55					
	VII	4	1516					28.03	27.30					
	VIII	6	633					29.91	c 29.20					
	IX	4	1491					33.07	29.34					
	IX	4	1491					c 31.46	30.57					
	IX	4	1491					35.65	33.34					
	IX	4	1491					35.96	33.94					
	IX	5	1486					29.09	27.53					
	IX	6	553					28.07	25.97					
	X	1	1802					31.42	28.86					
	X	1	1802					29.90						
Radius	III	6	1022				13.45							
	III	6	1022				12.54							
	IV	6	974		26.98	25.45								
	V	4	1582		31.22	27.97								
	VI	1	766	142.65	29.19	27.07	15.60	27.45						
	VI	1	766		30.60	28.15								
	VI	2	789	147.00	29.53	26.53		27.25						
	VI	6	692	c 150	30.05									
	VII	6	682		29.89									
	VIII	1	1819		28.34									
	VIII	6	633					28.10						
	VIII	6	633		32.23	30.71								
	IX	4	1491		33.75	30.76								
	IX	4	1491					34.57						
	IX	6	316		30.97	28.69								
	IX	6	542					28.60						
	IX	6	337		c 31									
	IX	6	629					27.02						
	X	3	413	138.65	28.77									

Table 6.1.29 Goat measurements

Key Measurements as in von den Driesch 1976

Element	Phase	Plot	Context	GL	BP	SD/SC	Bd
Metacarpal	IV	3	1119	108.17	23.08	15.60	26.70
	V	4	1579	107.35		16.19	26.72
	VIII	6	559		23.76	c 16.14	

Table 6.1.30 Equid measurements

Key Measurements as in von den Driesch 1976

Element	Phase	Plot	Context	GL	BP	BF	BFp	SD/SC	Bd	BT	SLC	GLP
Scapula	V	3	854								58.42	83.58
Humerus	V	3	854						74.58	c 68.00		
Radius	V	3	854		74.20		c 67.00					
Femur	V	3	854	373.0				37.42	86.26			
Phalanx 3	IV	6	974			48.19						

Table 6.1.28 Sheep measurements (*continued*)

Element	Phase	Plot	Context	GL	BP	BFp	SD/SC	Bd	BT	SLC	GLP	c	c+d	GB
Tibia	III	6	1022		38.46									
	III	6	1022					25.73						
	III	6	1022					24.10						
	III	6	1022					20.00						
	III	6	1022					22.42						
	IV	6	974					23.65						
	V	3	1317					28.68						
	VII	1	1897					24.83						
	VII	3	1111					25.76						
	VIII	2	847					26.89						
	VIII	3	1437					25.92						
	IX	2	1299					26.62						
	IX	2	1299					26.71						
	IX	4	1491					29.56						
	IX	4	1491					30.42						
	IX	4	1491					29.31						
	IX	4	1491					29.15						
	IX	4	1491					30.78						
	IX	4	1491					29.32						
	IX	6	542					c 27.21						
	IX	6	337					25.29						
	IX	6	821					22.95						
	IX	6	821					23.33						
	X	3	1404					21.80						
	X	3	1399					26.01						
	X	3	1399					26.32						
Calcaneus	VIII	6	559	c 56.62								13.43	c 22.38	12.20
	IX	3	1090	52.19										
	IX	6	542	54.83										13.34
Metacarpal	III	6	1022		19.84		12.26							
	IV	6	974	120.14	19.32		11.95	21.39						
	V	3	1317					25.57						
	VII	2	491					24.38						
	VII	2	491					25.21						
	VIII	6	559	c 110.66	20.94		12.50	c 23.66						
	VIII	6	559				12.98	25.08						
	IX	6	553					25.55						
Metatarsal	III	6	1022		17.54									
	VIII	6	559					22.35						
	VIII	6	637					c 25.28						

Table 6.1.31 Deer, rabbit and hare measurements

Key Measurements as in von den Driesch 1976

Species	Element	Phase	Plot	Context	GL	BP	Bd	BT
Rabbit	Humerus	VII	2	463			8.99	
Hare	Metatarsal 3	VI	3	857	55.30			
Fallow deer	Humerus	VII	6	693			36.79	31.40
Fallow deer	Tibia	VI	3	803			32.31	
Fallow deer	Metatarsal	VI	2	806	224.5	27.63	31.58	
Fallow deer	Metatarsal	VI	2	806	224.5	27.44	31.72	
Fallow deer	Metatarsal	VII	1	663			c 26.55	

Table 6.1.32 Cat measurements

Key Measurements as in von den Driesch 1976

Element	Phase	Plot	Context	GL	BP	Bd	1	1	5	7	9	10
Cranium	VII	4	1515				94.12					
Mandible	VII	2	463					56.53	18.28	7.15	9.97	9.10
	VII	4	1515					61.92	20.35	7.83	11.50	9.66
Humerus	IV	2	1125			17.15						
	V	4	1579	90.21		19.19						
	VII	4	1515	97.16								
	VII	4	1599	101.53								
	VIII	2	1636	89.30								
Ulna	VIII	2	1636	103.44								
Pelvis	VII	2	463	73.36								
	VII	2	463	78.37								
Femur	VI	4	1697	94.76								
	VI	4	1697	95.32								
	VII	2	463	95.75								
	VII	2	463	95.79								
	VII	2	463	102.07								
	VIII	2	1636	96.58								
	VIII	2	847	98.47								
Tibia	VI	4	1697	101.94	17.51	13.45						
	VII	2	463	100.31								
	VII	2	463	100.35								
	VIII	2	847	95.95								
MT2	IV	2	1125	42.08								
MT3	IV	2	1125	46.59								
MT4	IV	2	1125	47.53								

Table 6.1.33 Dog measurements

Key Measurements as in von den Driesch 1976. GL stands for GLC in case of femur

Element	Phase	Plot	Context	GL	BP	Bd	SD	Approx withers height (cm)
Scapula	IX	6	375	GLP 35.04			SLC 28.68	
	IX	6	375	GLP 33.97				
Humerus	III	6	1022	85.12		17.83		27
	VII	4	1601	85.80				27
	VIII	6	559	144.50		30.04		47
	VIII	6	559	147.50		30.68		48
	IX	1	1818	92.16		22.69		29
	IX	1	1818	91.61		22.41		29
	IX	6	375	166.00		33.02		54
	IX	6	375	165.00		32.88		54
Radius	IX	6	375	172.00	19.06	25.89	14.63	57
	IX	6	375	171.00	18.69	25.24	14.54	56
Ulna	IX	6	375	200.50				56
Femur	III	6	1022	89.79		19.80	8.64	27
	III	6	1022	102.99	25.05			31
	VII	2	472	125.54				38
	VII	6	693	157.00	35.28	28.07		48
	VIII	6	559	163.20	33.03	30.27		50
	IX	1	1818	97.30	24.27	21.44		29
	IX	1	1818	96.43	24.01	21.47		29
	IX	6	375	187.00	40.37	35.37	13.53	57
	IX	6	375	186.00	40.18	34.40	13.77	57
Tibia	III	6	1022	132.00	24.02	15.97		39
	VI	2	789	241.00	40.32	25.65		71
	VI	4	1698	132.27	23.91	15.77		40
	VI	4	1697	130.31	24.21	15.54		39
	VII	4	1601	100.11	22.32	14.47		30
	IX	1	1818	98.54	22.58	14.69		30
	IX	6	375	190.00	36.91	23.79	13.28	56
	IX	6	375	190.00	35.80	22.42	13.74	56
mc3	VI	2	787	66.58				
	VII	6	824	81.57				
mc4	VI	1	885	80.56				
mt5	VI	2	791	88.36				

Table 6.1.34 Chicken measurements

Key Measurements as in von den Driesch 1976. Sex I = indeterminate

Element	Phase	Plot	Context	Sex	GL	BP	BF	Bd	Lm	Notes
Coracoid	VI	3	1702	I	68.69		15.06			
Carpo-metacarpal	VI	1	766	I	44.57					
	VI	3	800	I	38.67					
	VII	3	1111	I	56.48					
	VII	4	1607	I	43.51					
Humerus	VI	2	797	I	67.02					
	VI	2	806	I	69.63					
	VI	2	797	I	79.14					
	VI	3	1702	I	78.05			16.13		
	VI	4	1697	I	c 74.00	19.27				
	VII	4	1507	I	79.63	20.54		16.52		
	VII	6	725	I	65.83					
Radius	VI	3	1702	I	70.43					
	VI	4	1697	I	66.51					
	VIII	2	847	I	70.19					
Ulna	VI	2	797	I	67.18					
	VI	3	1702	I	78.11					
Femur	VIII	6	341	I					71.87	
	VIII	6	341	I					81.89	
Tibiotarsus	VI	2	787	I				13.24		
	VI	2	787	I				13.33		
	VI	4	1697	I				12.35		
	VII	2	464	I	130.59					
	VII	4	1599	I	107.28					
	VII	4	1507	I	120.83			11.41		
	VII	4	1507	I				13.83		
	VII	6	694	I	124.33					
	VIII	2	847	I	122.43			12.98		
Tarso-metatarsus	V	5	1671	M	86.66			14.70		
	VI	2	798	F	73.15					
	VI	2	787	M				15.02		
	VI	2	787	I				c 15.66		
	VII	4	1507	M	81.29					Spur sawn
	VII	4	1607	M	81.66					
	VII	4	1607	M	81.90					
	VIII	2	847	F	72.23					
	VIII	2	847	F	72.83					
	VIII	2	847	Male or capon	90.07					Recent break to shaft but can measure

6 Environmental remains/Mammal, bird and amphibian bones

Table 6.1.35 Phase VII: horn core data

Key I = indeterminate; Side L = left; R = right; Hacking 1HC = hacking at base of horn core; 2HC = hacking into the skull at approximately the frontal/parietal suture; S-2 = skull split into right and left sides (same as Binford 1981, 136). FINE CUT MARKS: S-4 = cut marks on skull (same as Binford 1981, 102); S-9 = cut marks adjacent to the knobbly base (more distally than S-4). SAWING: S = sawn. AGE CLASS follows Armitage 1982. TWIST: T = twisted; N = not twisted. ORIENTATION: U = upwards; F = forwards; B = backwards. CURVATURE: C = curved. OCCIPITAL PERFORATION: N = not present; P = perforation present. INDEX OF PROPORTION: as in Armitage 1982, 43. BASAL INDEX: as in Armitage & Clutton-Brock 1976, 345.

Specimen no	Context	Side	Hacking	Fine cut marks	Sawing	Max basal	Min basal	Basal circumference	Outer length	Age class	Twist	Orientation	Curvature	Supra-occipital perforation	Index of proportion	Basal index
676	1796	L	-	-	-	47.07	40.26	143	-	1	N	U	C	-		117
741	1796	R	-	S-9	-	58.11	51.94	180	-	1	N	U	C	-		112
850	1796	L	2HC	-	-	45.60	40.84	139	-	1	T	F	C	-		112
858	1796	I	-	-	-	-	-	-	-	1	T	I	C	-		
957	1796	L	-	-	-	49.10	44.20	149	-	1	T	I	C	-		111
677	1796	R	-	-	-	59.69	49.90	175	-	2	I	I	I	-		120
678	1796	R	2HC	S-9	-	62.67	52.66	187	-	2	T	U/F	C	N		119
679	1796	R	2HC	-	-	48.23	39.83	145	-	2	T	U	C	N		121
700	1796	R	-	S-4	-	-	-	-	-	2	T	I	C	N		
701	1796	R	2HC	-	-	55.89	49.36	170	-	2	T	U/F	C	-		113
708	1796	R	2HC	S-4	-	-	-	-	265	2	T	U/B	C	-		
719	1796	I	1HC	-	-	54.60	-	-	-	2	T	I	C	-		
725	1796	R	-	-	-	76.33	68.51	231	-	2	T	U/B	C	-		111
727	1796	L	-	-	-	48.41	44.57	154	225	2	T	U	C	-	146	109
754	1796	R	-	-	-	66.90	62.07	211	-	2	T	I	C	-		108
774	1796	R	-	-	-	65.72	52.28	181	-	2	T	U	C	-		126
778	1796	L	-	-	-	57.91	44.35	167	-	2	T	U/F	C	-		131
781	1796	R	-	S-4	-	65.04	53.18	190	-	2	T	I	C	-		122
791	1796	R	-	S-4	-	50.71	41.22	150	-	2	T	U/F	C	-		123
799	1796	R	2HC	S-4, S-9	-	63.97	-	-	-	2	T	I	C	-		
809	1796	L	2HC	S-4, S-9	-	58.24	54.37	184	230	2	T	U/F	C	-	125	107
825	1796	I	-	-	S	-	-	-	-	2	N	I	C	-		
836	1796	R	-	-	-	-	43.90	-	-	2	N	I	C	-		
848	1796	L	-	-	-	51.18	-	-	-	2	T	U/F	C	-		
857	1796	L	-	S-9	-	50.48	41.99	147	-	2	T	U/F	C	-		120
860	1796	R	-	S-4	-	66.55	60.82	205	-	2	T	U/F	C	-		109
865	1796	I	-	-	-	-	-	-	-	2	T	I	C	-		
873	1796	L	-	-	-	-	-	-	-	2	T	I	C	-		
885	1796	I	-	S-4	-	-	-	-	-	2	T	I	C	-		
947	1796	L	-	-	-	-	-	-	-	2	N	I	C	-		
953	1796	L	2HC	-	-	-	-	-	-	2	T	I	C	-		
972	1796	R	-	-	-	58.83	48.72	175	-	2	T	I	C	-		121
1001	1601	L	2HC	-	-	72.62	62.24	219	-	2	T	I	C	-		117
1002	1601	R	-	-	-	-	-	-	-	2	T	I	C	-		
1014	1604	L	1HC, 2HC	S-4	-	52.52	-	-	-	2	T	U	C	-		
1023	1607	L	2HC	-	-	-	-	-	-	2	T	U/F	C	-		
680	1796	L	-	-	-	-	-	-	-	3	T	U/B	C	N		
681	1796	L	-	-	-	58.90	54.48	180	-	3	T	U/F	C	-		108
682	1796	L	2HC	-	-	64.64	54.61	191	-	3	T	U	C	-		118
699	1796	R	-	S-4	-	56.70	44.12	163	-	3	T	I	C	-		129
707	1796	R	-	S-4	-	77.72	60.35	227	-	3	T	U/F	C	-		129
724	1796	L	-	S-4	-	79.63	69.90	240	-	3	T	U/F	C	-		114
734	1796	R	-	S-4	-	59.46	-	-	-	3	T	I	C	-		
738	1796	L	-	-	-	65.84	56.12	197	-	3	T	I	C	N		117
760	1796	R	-	-	-	51.78	40.77	152	-	3	T	I	C	N		127
780	1796	R	-	-	-	77.32	70.66	235	-	3	T	U/F	C	-		109
783	1796	R	2HC	-	-	59.39	48.56	175	-	3	T	I	C	N		122
793	1796	R	2HC	-	-	74.51	-	-	-	3	T	I	C	P		
798	1796	R	2HC	-	-	51.69	45.23	156	-	3	T	U/F	C	-		114
810	1796	R	2HC	-	-	64.88	54.62	192	-	3	T	I	C	-		119
845	1796	L	2HC	-	-	54.29	46.79	170	-	3	T	U/F	C	N		116
886	1796	L	-	-	-	-	-	-	-	3	T	U/F	C	-		
897	1796	R	-	-	-	68.44	56.92	200	-	3	T	I	C	-		120
899	1796	R	2HC	-	-	63.64	51.48	187	-	3	T	U/F	C	N		124
906	1796	R	-	-	-	-	-	-	-	3	T	I	C	-		
909	1796	R	-	-	-	59.83	45.45	173	-	3	T	I	C	-		132
946	1796	L	-	-	-	-	-	-	-	3	T	I	C	-		
979	1796	L	2HC	-	-	85.08	70.13	244	340	3	T	I	C	-	139	121
1005	1601	R	1HC, 2HC	-	-	68.05	61.91	213	240	3	T	U	C	-	113	110
1006	1601	L	2HC	-	-	68.80	56.71	204	-	3	T	U/F	C	-		121
1021	1607	L	1HC, 2HC	S-4	-	73.69	58.68	210	-	3	T	F	C	N		126
1022	1607	L	2HC	-	-	38.46	32.03	114	-	3	T	U	C	-		120
1024	1607	R	2HC	-	-	48.24	44.88	151	-	3	T	U/F	C	-		107
1036	1695	I	-	-	S	-	-	-	-	3	T	I	C	-		
1045	1796	L	-	S-2	-	101.12	85.00	300	430	3	T	U/F	C	-	143	119
683	1796	L	-	-	-	51.65	42.98	156	-	4	T	U/F	C	-		120
684	1796	R	-	-	-	59.21	50.65	177	-	4	T	I	C	-		117
685	1796	L	-	S-4	-	59.44	47.35	176	-	4	T	I	C	N		126
691	1796	L	2HC	-	-	-	-	-	-	4	T	U/F	C	-		
698	1796	L	-	-	-	69.46	53.20	197	-	4	T	U/B	C	-		131
703	1796	L	-	-	-	58.78	43.61	167	-	4	T	U/F	C	-		135
705	1796	I	2HC	-	-	54.28	47.67	168	-	4	T	I	C	-		114
706	1796	L	-	-	-	63.51	56.28	190	-	4	T	U/F	C	-		113
714	1796	R	-	-	-	59.07	46.20	173	-	4	T	U/F	C	-		128
716	1796	R	2HC	-	-	58.29	43.97	164	-	4	T	I	C	-		133

Specimen no	Context	Side	Hacking	Fine cut marks	Sawing	Max basal	Min basal	Basal circumference	Outer length	Age class	Twist	Orientation	Curvature	Supra-occipital perforation	Index of proportion	Basal index
717	1796	R	2HC	-	-	46.57	45.07	150	-	4	T	I	C	-		103
718	1796	L	-	S-4	-	52.06	41.87	150	-	4	T	U	C	-		124
726	1796	R	-	S-4, S-9	-	-	-	-	-	4	I	I	C	N		
728	1796	R	1HC, 2HC	-	-	55.32	40.94	157	-	4	T	U/B	C	-		135
729	1796	L	-	-	-	61.17	54.13	187	-	4	T	U	C	N		113
731	1796	L	2HC	S-4	-	56.08	48.39	167	-	4	T	U/F	C	N		116
732	1796	R	2HC	-	-	53.17	47.69	162	235	4	T	U/F	C	-	145	111
733	1796	L	-	-	-	64.97	47.51	182	200	4	T	U	C	-	110	137
735	1796	R	-	-	-	62.67	52.18	182	-	4	T	I	C	-		120
736	1796	L	2HC	S-4	-	-	50.20	-	-	4	T	I	C	-		
737	1796	L	-	-	-	55.11	46.63	163	-	4	T	I	C	-		118
739	1796	L	-	-	-	59.61	47.49	172	-	4	T	I	C	-		126
744	1796	L	2HC	-	-	74.24	53.55	209	-	4	T	I	C	-		139
745	1796	L	1HC	S-9	-	59.40	42.98	169	-	4	T	U/F	C	-		138
750	1796	L	2HC	-	-	55.60	45.73	162	-	4	T	U	C	N		122
752	1796	L	-	-	-	53.49	44.16	160	-	4	T	U/F	C	N		121
755	1796	L	1HC	-	-	-	-	-	-	4	T	U/F	C	N		
756	1796	L	2HC	-	-	66.07	49.71	186	-	4	T	U/F	C	-		133
757	1796	R	2HC	-	-	77.44	-	-	-	4	T	I	C	-		
758	1796	L	-	S-4	-	64.46	47.29	184	-	4	T	U/B	C	-		136
759	1796	L	-	-	-	54.78	43.05	161	-	4	T	U/F	C	-		127
761	1796	L	-	-	-	66.16	52.29	189	-	4	T	U/F	C	N		127
762	1796	R	-	-	-	61.77	55.09	186	-	4	T	U/F	C	-		112
763	1796	R	-	S-4	-	56.12	46.95	169	-	4	T	U/F	C	-		120
767	1796	L	2HC	S-4	-	54.63	43.93	162	-	4	N	U/F	C	-		124
769	1796	R	-	-	-	60.02	47.57	172	-	4	T	U/F	C	-		126
770	1796	R	2HC	-	-	73.81	56.90	214	-	4	T	U/F	C	-		130
771	1796	L	1HC, 2HC	S-4	-	60.81	46.70	172	-	4	T	I	C	-		130
782	1796	R	-	-	-	55.25	43.80	162	-	4	T	I	C	-		126
785	1796	R	-	-	-	63.68	-	-	-	4	T	U/F	C	N		
787	1796	R	-	-	-	60.94	49.04	179	-	4	T	I	C	-		124
788	1796	R	2HC	-	-	61.47	49.68	179	-	4	T	I	C	-		124
794	1796	R	-	-	-	-	46.42		-	4	T	I	C	-		
795	1796	L	2HC	S-4	-	56.71	41.45	165	-	4	T	U/F	C	-		137
796	1796	L	-	-	-	-	-	-	-	4	T	U/F	C	N		
801	1796	L	2HC	-	-	-	-	-	-	4	T	I	C	-		
805	1796	R	-	S-4	-	54.30	42.57	156	-	4	T	U/F	C	N		128
806	1796	L	-	-	-	58.56	50.96	178	240	4	T	U/F	C	-	135	115
812	1796	R	-	S-4	-	58.29	50.50	-	-	4	T	U	C	-		115
817	1796	L	2HC	-	-	71.26	54.28	203	-	4	T	U/F	C	-		131
818	1796	R	2HC	-	-	68.10	50.81	195	-	4	T	U/F	C	-		134
821	1796	L	-	-	-	57.77	47.86	168	-	4	T	I	C	-		121
822	1796	L	-	-	-	54.37	46.01	167	-	4	T	U/F	C	N		118
823	1796	L	-	-	-	53.47	42.71	154	-	4	T	I	C	-		125
826	1796	R	-	-	-	55.72	37.76	150	-	4	T	U/F	C	-		148
829	1796	R	2HC	-	-	58.92	52.32	181	-	4	T	U/F	C	N		113
830	1796	R	-	S-4	-	54.47	45.97	158	-	4	T	I	C	-		118
831	1796	L	-	S-4	-	77.10	-	-	-	4	T	U	C	N		
832	1796	R	-	S-4	-	55.76	-	-	-	4	T	I	C	-		
834	1796	R	-	-	-	59.40	43.11	163	-	4	T	I	C	-		138
835	1796	L	2HC	S-4	-	59.38	54.27	165	-	4	T	I	C	N		109
839	1796	R	-	-	-	56.64	-	-	-	4	T	I	C	-		
840	1796	L	2HC	S-4	-	61.48	47.26	176	-	4	T	I	C	-		130
847	1796	L	-	S-4	-	63.44	47.30	-	-	4	T	U/F	C	-		134
852	1796	L	2HC	-	-	53.72	44.16	162	-	4	T	U	C	-		122
854	1796	R	-	-	-	-	-	-	-	4	T	I	C	-		
861	1796	L	1HC, 2HC	S-4	-	52.82	45.50	154	-	4	T	U	C	-		116
862	1796	R	2HC	-	-	49.74	41.88	147	-	4	T	U/F	C	-		119
868	1796	R	2HC	-	-	54.24	40.27	153	-	4	T	I	C	-		135
869	1796	L	2HC	-	-	62.39	49.79	179	-	4	T	U/F	C	-		125
874	1796	L	2HC	-	-	60.53	42.45	173	-	4	T	I	C	-		143
877	1796	L	-	-	-	62.49	51.05	182	-	4	T	U/F	C	N		122
880	1796	L	2HC	-	-	55.58	45.95	166	-	4	T	U/F	C	N		121
890	1796	R	-	S-4	-	58.93	42.98	168	-	4	T	I	C	-		137
902	1796	R	-	S-4	-	-	-	-	-	4	T	I	C	-		
912	1796	R	-	-	-	52.58	44.34	159	-	4	T	I	C	-		119
913	1796	L	-	-	-	66.39	51.01	188	-	4	T	U	C	N		130
914	1796	L	2HC	-	-	60.32	51.83	183	-	4	T	U	C	-		116
915	1796	L	2HC	-	-	49.51	41.48	147	-	4	T	U/F	C	-		119
921	1796	L	2HC	-	-	-	48.19	-	-	4	T	F	C	N		
922	1796	R	2HC	-	-	50.09	45.95	146	-	4	T	U	C	N		109
923	1796	R	-	S-4	-	57.70	43.34	161	-	4	T	I	C	N		133
925	1796	R	-	-	-	62.24	44.34	173	-	4	T	I	C	N		140
926	1796	I	1HC	-	-	39.26	29.25	115	-	4	N	I	C	-		134
927	1796	L	1HC, 2HC	-	-	47.47	40.18	141	-	4	T	U/F	C	N		118
930	1796	R	-	-	-	-	-	-	-	4	T	I	C	-		
934	1796	R	2HC	-	-	53.86	46.44	162	-	4	T	I	C	-		116
939	1796	L	2HC	-	-	54.21	47.25	160	-	4	T	U	C	N		115
944	1796	L	-	-	-	-	-	-	-	4	T	U/F	C	-		
948	1796	I	1HC	-	-	-	-	-	-	4	T	I	C	-		
950	1796	R	2HC	-	-	53.77	49.57	165	-	4	T	I	C	N		108

Specimen no	Context	Side	Hacking	Fine cut marks	Sawing	Max basal	Min basal	Basal circumference	Outer length	Age class	Twist	Orientation	Curvature	Supra-occipital perforation	Index of proportion	Basal index
951	1796	L	2HC	-	-	58.11	46.75	174	-	4	T	U	C	-		124
954	1796	L	-	-	-	59.61	53.05	181	-	4	T	U/F	C	-		112
955	1796	L	-	-	-	42.97	34.97	132	120	4	N	U	C	N	91	123
958	1796	R	-	-	-	59.73	46.54	174	-	4	T	U/F	C	-		128
961	1796	R	-	-	-	63.20	54.28	191	-	4	T	I	C	-		116
964	1796	R	-	-	-	91.59	-	-	-	4	T	I	C	-		
965	1796	L	2HC	S-4	-	-	63.00	-	-	4	T	I	C	-		
968	1796	L	2HC	-	-	67.01	54.98	196	-	4	T	U/F	C	-		122
969	1796	R	2HC	-	-	79.95	67.39	235	-	4	T	U/F	C	-		119
971	1796	R	2HC	-	-	-	-	-	-	4	T	I	C	-		
973	1796	I	-	-	-	85.09	69.00	257	265	4	T	I	C	-	103	123
980	1796	R	2HC	-	-	53.49	-	-	-	4	T	I	C	-		
981	1796	L	2HC	-	-	61.80	-	-	-	4	T	I	C	-		
982	1796	L	-	-	-	-	50.00	-	-	4	T	I	C	N		
985	1796	R 1HC, 2HC		-	-	46.44	40.84	140	-	4	T	I	C	-		114
991	1546	R	2HC	-	-	67.34	50.31	190	-	4	T	I	C	-		134
993	1546	L	-	-	-	54.15	48.29	168	-	4	T	I	C	-		112
994	1546	L	-	-	-	59.05	45.18	171	-	4	T	I	C	-		131
995	1599	R	-	S-4	-	68.73	53.21	195	-	4	T	U/F	C	N		129
997	1599	I	-	-	S	-	-	-	-	4	N	I	C	-		
998	1599	I	1HC	-	S	-	-	-	-	4	T	I	C	-		
1015	1604	L	-	-	-	-	-	-	-	4	T	U/F	C	-		
1017	1607	R	-	-	-	66.97	51.43	191	-	4	T	I	C	-		130
1019	1607	L	-	-	-	51.12	48.31	163	-	4	T	U/F	C	-		106
1020	1607	R	2HC	S-4	-	59.24	47.50	178	-	4	T	I	C	N		125
1026	1607	R	2HC	-	-	38.20	34.53	121	130	4	T	U/F	C	-	107	111
1027	1607	R	-	-	-	-	-	-	-	4	T	I	C	-		
1028	1607	L 1HC, 2HC		-	-	65.45	51.42	191	-	4	T	U/F	C	-		127
1029	1607	L	-	-	-	76.47	-	-	-	4	T	I	C	-		
1030	1695	R	2HC	-	-	48.73	36.97	137	-	4	T	U/F	C	-		132
1032	1695	L	-	-	-	-	-	-	-	4	T	I	C	-		
1033	1695	R	2HC	-	-	73.71	67.05	220	-	4	T	I	C	-		110
1034	1695	L	2HC	-	-	53.26	45.98	158	-	4	T	I	C	-		116
1035	1695	L	1HC	S-9	-	-	-	-	-	4	T	I	C	-		
1038	1695	L	1HC	-	-	53.18	42.24	154	-	4	T	U/F	C	N		126
686	1796	R 1HC, 2HC		-	-	-	48.91	-	-	5	T	I	C	-		
687	1796	L	2HC	-	-	54.99	44.45	169	-	5	T	U/F	C	-		124
695	1796	R	2HC	-	-	48.97	43.80	148	-	5	T	I	C	-		112
696	1796	I	-	-	-	-	48.78	-	-	5	T	I	C	-		
697	1796	R 1HC, 2HC		-	-	55.08	42.46	156	250	5	T	I	C	-	160	130
704	1796	R	2HC	S-9	-	58.70	50.86	179	300	5	T	U/F	C	-	168	115
709	1796	L	2HC	-	-	69.25	54.26	199	-	5	T	I	C	-		128
712	1796	R	2HC	S-9	-	60.29	45.29	170	-	5	T	U/B	C	N		133
720	1796	R	-	S-4	-	-	-	-	-	5	T	I	C	-		
721	1796	R	2HC	-	-	57.20	47.09	173	-	5	T	U/F	C	-		121
722	1796	L	-	S-4	-	55.44	46.40	164	-	5	T	U	C	-		119
730	1796	L	-	S-4	-	66.38	54.85	195	-	5	T	U/F	C	N		121
740	1796	R	2HC	-	-	61.42	43.45	170	-	5	T	U/F	C	-		141
742	1796	R	-	-	-	51.56	38.08	148	165	5	T	I	C	-	111	135
749	1796	R	2HC	-	-	58.64	47.68	176	235	5	T	I	C	-	134	123
751	1796	L	-	-	-	57.71	-	-	255	5	T	I	C	-		
753	1796	R	2HC	-	-	61.27	49.13	182	-	5	T	U	C	-		125
764	1796	R	2HC	-	-	57.90	41.89	167	-	5	T	I	C	-		138
765	1796	R	2HC	-	-	65.47	-	-	-	5	T	I	C	-		
766	1796	R	-	S-4	-	67.52	55.54	200	-	5	T	I	C	-		122
773	1796	I	1HC	-	-	-	-	-	-	5	T	I	C	-		
776	1796	R	-	-	-	57.74	48.92	176	245	5	T	I	C	-	139	118
777	1796	R	2HC	-	-	54.15	42.28	156	-	5	T	I	C	-		128
779	1796	R	2HC	-	-	59.93	42.24	169	-	5	T	U	C	-		142
784	1796	R	1HC	-	-	-	-	-	-	5	T	I	C	-		
786	1796	L	-	S-4	-	55.78	46.60	156	-	5	T	U	C	-		120
789	1796	R	-	-	-	55.71	44.48	164	205	5	T	U/F	C	-	125	125
790	1796	R	-	-	-	52.15	42.34	155	210	5	T	U	C	-	135	123
797	1796	R	2HC	-	-	63.12	48.18	182	-	5	T	U	C	-		131
800	1796	L	-	-	-	50.46	38.92	147	-	5	T	I	C	-		130
802	1796	R	-	-	-	66.19	58.33	205	-	5	T	U/F	C	N		113
803	1796	L	-	-	-	-	-	-	-	5	T	U/F	C	-		
804	1796	L	2HC	-	-	75.33	53.00	212	-	5	T	U/F	C	P		142
807	1796	L	2HC	-	-	60.43	50.29	180	-	5	T	U/F	C	N		120
808	1796	L	-	-	-	62.17	44.81	173	-	5	T	U/F	C	-		139
811	1796	L	2HC	S-9	-	64.76	58.13	197	-	5	T	U	C	-		111
813	1796	L	-	-	-	-	-	-	-	5	T	I	C	-		
814	1796	L	1HC	S-4	-	68.63	54.52	198	-	5	T	U/F	C	-		126
815	1796	R	-	-	-	64.58	49.54	183	-	5	T	U/F	C	N		130
819	1796	L	-	-	-	-	47.93	-	-	5	T	U	C	N		
820	1796	R	2HC	-	-	-	-	-	-	5	T	U	C	-		
824	1796	I	1HC	-	-	54.39	45.60	162	-	5	T	I	C	-		119
828	1796	L	-	-	-	60.30	49.63	174	-	5	T	I	C	N		121
833	1796	R	-	-	-	59.10	45.99	166	-	5	T	U/F	C	-		129
843	1796	L	-	S-4	-	66.12	53.82	189	-	5	T	I	C	-		123
844	1796	L	-	S-4	-	51.21	43.89	157	-	5	T	I	C	-		117

Specimen no	Context	Side	Hacking	Fine cut marks	Sawing	Max basal	Min basal	Basal circumference	Outer length	Age class	Twist	Orientation	Curvature	Supra-occipital perforation	Index of proportion	Basal index
846	1796	L	2HC	-	-	56.83	49.23	176	-	5	T	U/F	C	-		115
851	1796	L	-	-	-	61.96	51.18	182	-	5	T	I	C	-		121
853	1796	R	-	-	-	57.10	48.08	166	-	5	T	I	C	-		119
855	1796	L	-	-	-	56.41	46.53	-	-	5	T	U	C			121
856	1796	R	2HC	-	-	54.19	43.23	162	-	5	T	U/F	C	-		125
863	1796	R	-	-	-	55.27	43.56	164	-	5	T	U	C	-		127
864	1796	L	-	-	-	50.29	39.64	142	-	5	T	U	C	-		127
867	1796	L	-	-	-	-	49.34	-	265	5	T	U/F	C	-		
870	1796	R	-	S-4	-	60.52	49.05	179	-	5	T	U	C	-		123
871	1796	R	-	-	-	52.55	44.39	156	-	5	T	U	C	N		118
876	1796	R	1HC	S-4	-	66.65	56.12	197	-	5	T	I	C	-		119
878	1796	R	2HC	-	-	58.16	40.85	163	-	5	T	I	C	-		142
879	1796	L	2HC	-	-	62.90	47.90	177	-	5	T	U	C	P		131
881	1796	R	2HC	-	-	70.49	50.68	198	-	5	T	U/F	C	-		139
882	1796	R	1HC, 2HC	-	-	55.02	43.30	159	-	5	T	I	C	-		127
883	1796	R	-	S-4	-	59.58	49.09	176	-	5	T	U/F	C	N		121
887	1796	L	2HC	S-4	-	52.78	44.87	159	220	5	T	U/F	C	-	138	118
888	1796	L	-	S-4	-	58.34	50.99	182	-	5	T	U/F	C	-		114
889	1796	R	2HC	S-4	-	49.11	42.99	148	-	5	T	I	C	-		114
891	1796	L	1HC, 2HC	-	-	53.54		-	-	5	T	I	C	-		
893	1796	L	-	-	-	64.53	49.00	-	-	5	T	I	C	-		132
895	1796	R	2HC	-	-	54.67	-	-	190	5	T	I	C	-		
896	1796	R	2HC	-	-	53.15	42.38	155	-	5	T	I	C	-		125
898	1796	L	-	-	-	61.13	42.58	168	-	5	T	I	C	-		144
901	1796	R	-	-	-	54.07	39.51	157	200	5	T	U/F	C	N	127	137
903	1796	R	-	-	-	61.71	53.39	187	-	5	T	I	C	-		116
905	1796	R	-	-	-	63.53	45.66	177	-	5	T	I	C	-		139
907	1796	I	-	-	-	70.11	54.48	204	-	5	T	I	C	-		129
910	1796	L	-	-	-	58.60	48.34	177	-	5	T	I	C	N		121
911	1796	L	-	-	-	58.03	46.13	164	-	5	T	U/F	C	N		126
917	1796	I	-	-	-	70.22	54.56	203	-	5	T	I	C	-		129
919	1796	L	2HC	-	-	60.30	52.52	180	-	5	T	U/F	C	N		115
920	1796	L	2HC	-	-	59.25	48.21	169	-	5	T	U/F	C	N		123
924	1796	R	2HC	-	-	50.48	43.94	153	-	5	T	I	C	-		115
928	1796	I	-	-	-	-	-	-	-	5	T	I	C	-		
931	1796	R	-	-	-	60.29	46.93	177	-	5	T	U/F	C	-		128
933	1796	R	2HC	S-4	-	-	52.64	-	-	5	T	I	C	-		
935	1796	R	-	-	-	-	-	-	-	5	T	U/F	C	-		
936	1796	L	1HC	-	-	56.28	44.03	166	-	5	T	U/F	C	-		128
937	1796	L	-	-	-	59.12	51.59	175	-	5	T	U	C	P		115
938	1796	R	2HC	-	-	64.44	53.74	185	-	5	T	I	C	-		120
940	1796	L	2HC	-	-	-	-	-	-	5	T	U/F	C	N		
941	1796	R	2HC	-	-	51.95	48.83	159	-	5	T	I	C	-		106
942	1796	L	-	-	-	-	-	-	-	5	T	U	C	-		
943	1796	L	2HC	-	-	59.89	48.37	182	-	5	T	U/F	C	-		124
945	1796	R	-	-	-	-	-	-	-	5	T	I	C	-		
949	1796	R	-	-	-	52.72	45.33	162	-	5	T	I	C	-		116
952	1796	L	2HC	-	-	62.63	48.86	180	-	5	T	U/F	C	-		128
956	1796	R	1HC, 2HC	-	-	-	45.78	-	210	5	T	I	C	N		
959	1796	R	2HC	-	-	52.04	43.14	154	-	5	T	U/F	C	-		121
960	1796	R	2HC	-	-	66.35	51.74	192	-	5	T	I	C	-		128
962	1796	L	2HC	-	-	50.93	39.26	148	-	5	T	I	C	-		130
966	1796	L	-	-	-	59.18	47.14	174	-	5	T	U/F	C	-		126
967	1796	L	-	-	-	-	-	-	-	5	T	U/F	C	-		
970	1796	L	2HC	-	-	64.23	53.97	186	-	5	T	I	C	N		119
974	1796	R	-	-	-	49.06	38.60	145	-	5	T	I	C	-		127
975	1796	R	2HC	-	-	55.30	40.20	157	-	5	T	U/F	C	N		138
976	1796	L	-	-	-	62.46	49.66	182	260	5	T	U/F	C	N	143	126
977	1796	L	2HC	S-4	-	60.69	44.97	173	-	5	T	U/F	C	N		135
978	1796	R	-	-	-	56.77	46.29	166	240	5	T	U/F	C	N	145	123
984	1796	R	2HC	-	-	-	-	-	-	5	T	I	C	-		
990	1546	L	-	-	-	49.52	45.26	153	200	5	T	U	C	-	131	109
992	1546	L	-	-	-	63.47	45.19	171	-	5	T	I	C	-		140
996	1599	L	2HC	-	-	-	-	-	-	5	T	I	C	N		
999	1599	L	1HC, 2HC	-	-	-	49.88	-	-	5	T	I	C	-		
1000	1601	L	1HC	S-9	-	64.76	54.10	188	-	5	T	I	C	-		120
1003	1601	R	2HC	-	-	61.29	43.77	167	200	5	T	U/F	C	N	120	140
1004	1601	L	-	S-4	-	60.70	44.11	168	-	5	T	I	C	-		138

Table 6.1.36 Cattle epiphysial fusion states: quantified by no of fragments (from hand-collected and zoned sample) and phase

Key F = fused; UF = unfused; p = proximal; d = distal. Scapula supra refers to the supraglenoid tubercle

		Phase IV		V		VI		VII		VIII		IX	
	Age (months)	F	UF	F	UF	F	UF	F	UF	F	UF	F	UF
Early													
Scapula supra	7–10	2		5		2	2	3	7	1	3		
Pelvis, acetabulum	7–10	2		2		12	2	7	7	8	4		
Humerus d	12–18	4		1		10	4	6	6	6	6	1	1
Radius p	12–18	2	1	2	1	3	1	7	3	4	1	1	1
Phalanx 1–2 p	12–18	10		2		7		18	5	10	2	1	
Intermediate													
Metacarpal d	24–30	1		1				6	5	3	5		
Tibia d	24–30			3	2	3	2	10	4	3	1	2	
Metatarsal d	27–30	2	1	1				4	1	3	3		
Late													
Calcaneum	36–42	1	2	2		3	1	6	1	3	2		
Femur p	42	1		3	2	3	1	6	10	7	3	1	
Ulna p	42–8			1		1				5	1	1	1
Radius d	42–48	1											
Tibia p	42–48	1		2	1	6	3	6	8	3	3	1	
Femur d	42–48		2		3	1	6	2	11	3	6		1
Humerus p	42–48			2		1	4			2	6		1

Table 6.1.37 Pig epiphysial fusion states: quantified by no of fragments (from hand-collected and zoned sample) and phase

Key F = fused; UF = unfused; p = proximal; d = distal. Scapula supra refers to the supraglenoid tubercle

		Phase IV		V		VI		VII		VIII		IX	
Fusion state	Age (months)	F	UF	F	UF	F	UF	F	UF	F	UF	F	UF
Early													
Scapula supra	12							2		1			1
Pelvis, acetabulum	12	1		1		1		1		1			
Humerus d	12	1			1	1	1	2		1	2		
Radius p	12	1	1						2	1			2
Phalanx 2 p	12								1	1			
Intermediate													
Tibia d	24		4	1				5		5		4	
Metacarpal	24		3	1				4	2			3	
Phalanx 1 p	24							1	5	1	1		
Calcaneum	24–30				1			2		1		1	
Metatarsal	27		2			1	1	1	2		3		1
Late													
Ulna p	36–42		2						1	1			2
Femur p	42				2	3		2		1			
Radius d	42	1				1		2					
Tibia p	42	1				4		5					
Femur d	42			1	1	2		3		3			
Humerus p	42		2		1	4							

Table 6.1.38 Sheep epiphysial fusion states: quantified by no of fragments (from hand-collected and zoned sample) and phase

Key F = fused; UF = unfused; p = proximal; d = distal. Scapula supra refers to the supraglenoid tubercle

		Phase IV		V		VI		VII		VIII		IX	
Fusion state	Age (months)	F	UF	F	UF	F	UF	F	UF	F	UF	F	UF
Early													
Scapula supra	6—10			6		8	1	18				3	
Pelvis, acetabulum	6—10			10	1	3		11	2	7		3	
Humerus d	6—10			10	3	5		15	1	16		10	1
Radius p	6—10	1		8		14		15		14		5	1
Intermediate													
Metacarpal d	13—28	2		6	63			5	1	2	5	2	1
Tibia d	13—28	1	2	7	2	5	1	6	2			1	7
Metatarsal d	13—28			2	59			4	2	1	2	7	2
Phalanx 1—2 p	13—28			7	40	1	1	2	1		1		
Late													
Calcaneum	30—36		1	2	1	1	1	4		4	2	1	2
Femur p	30—36			2	1	1	2	3	1	3	4		2
Ulna p	30—36			1		4		2	4				
Final													
Radius d	36—42	1		3	2	4	1	4	5	6	1	2	5
Tibia p	36—42			2	4	5		3	4			2	2
Femur d	36—42			2	3	1	1	6	2	3	3		
Humerus p	36—42	2	1	2				4	2	6	1	1	

Table 6.1.39 Cattle: suggested age categories for hand-collected mandibles (Halstead 1985)

Age	Phase				
	IV	V	VI	VII	VIII
1–8 months		2	2	4	7
30–6 months					1
Adult	1	1		1	1
Senile				1	

Table 6.1.40 Pig: suggested age categories for hand-collected mandibles (Halstead 1992)

Age (months)	Phase				
	IV	V	VI	VII	IX
< 6		2	1		
6—12				1	
12—24	3	2		2	1
>24		1			

Table 6.1.41 Sheep: suggested age categories for hand-collected mandibles (age stages adapted from Payne 1973 and 1987)

Age	Phase				
	IV	VI	VII	VIII	IX
2–6 months					5
6–12 months					2
2 months–2 years			1		
1–2 years				1	
2–3 years	1			1	
3–4 years				4	
4–6 years		1		1	4
4–8 years				1	

Table 6.1.42 Gnawed fragments for the most common species quantified by no of fragments and phase

	Phase													
	IV	V		VI			VII			VIII			IX	
Gnawing by Gnawed bone from	Dog	Dog	Rodent	Dog	Rodent	Cat	Dog	Rodent	Cat	Dog	Rodent	Cat	Dog	Totals
Cattle	4	1	1	8	1	0	16	1	2	11	2	0	0	821.00
Pig	0	2	1	4	1	0	5	5	0	4	0	0	0	219.00
Sheep/goat	1	6	6	16	0	2	18	3	1	17	2	0	0	716.00
Chicken	0	0	3	0	2	1	6	1	0	1	1	1	342.00
Sampled totals*	146	526		654			1266			669			60	3321*
Total gnawed*	5	20		36			65			42			1	
% of all bones gnawed	3.4	3.8		5.5			5.1			6.3			1.6	

*Totals include species not listed here

Table 6.1.43 Cattle bones: fine cut marks

Element	Phase	Code	Description
Skull	VII	S-1	Binford - transverse cut on occipital condyles
Rib	VIII	RS-1	Binford - marks along superior surface just lateral to the rib head
Scapula	VII	Sc3	(Binford S-3) longitudinal marks up and down the lateral surface of the blade*
Scapula	VIII	Sc2	(Binford S-2) marks along the neck of the scapula
Humerus	VI	Hp-4 Hp-5	Binford - 'chevron' marks at insertion of teres minor and below the head*
Humerus	VII	Hd8	Fine marks across distal epicondyles associated with subsequent hacking
Radius	VI	Rcp-6	Binford 'chevron' marks below lateral and medial tuberosities*
Ulna	VI	Rcp-2	Binford - diagonal mark across lateral surface of olecranon
Ulna	VIII	Rcp8	Transverse marks across the olecranon parallel with the line of fusion
Metacarpal	VII	MCd-1	Binford - circular cut around distal shaft
Pelvis	VII	PS13	Transverse marks near and approximately parallel with the crest of the ilium
Pelvis	VIII	PS12	Transverse marks across pubis on dorsal side
Femur	VII	Fs1 Fs2	Transverse marks across mid-shaft on posterior and anterior sides
Femur	VIII	Fp-1	Binford - marks on the neck of the femur
Tibia	VII	Tps1	Transverse marks across the proximal shaft on medial side
Metatarsal	VII	MTd-2	Binford - circular mark around the distal shaft

*see Binford (1981, 136—42) for full description

Table 6.1.44 Pig bones: fine cut marks

Element	Phase	Code	Description
Femur	VI	Fs1 Fs2	Transverse marks across mid-shaft on posterior and anterior sides
Femur	VII	Fs1	Transverse marks across mid-shaft on posterior side
Tibia	VII	Tps1	Transverse marks across proximal shaft on medial side
Astragalus	VIII	TA3	Transverse marks on distal articular surface
Calcaneus	VII	TC-3	Binford - marks on dorsal side midway between tuber calcis and the articulator surface

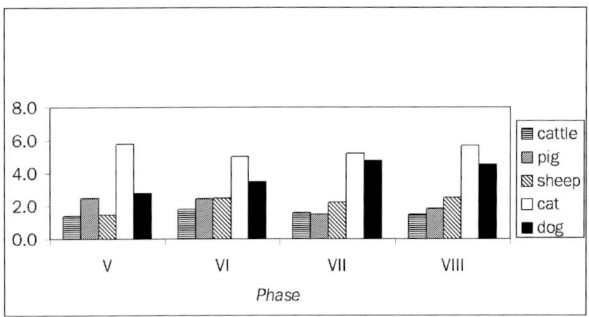

Ill 6.1.24 Fragmentation: average number of zones amongst humeri and femora (NISP=406).

Table 6.1.45 Sheep and goat bones: fine cut marks

Species	Bone	Phase(-s)	Code	Description
Goat	Horncore	VII	S-4 or S-9	(S-4 as in Binford 1981, 136) marks encircling base of horn cores, S-9 marks more distally (?and poss assoc with removal of horn)
Sheep/goat	Vertebra	VIII	Ve2	Marks across the transverse processes, parallel with the spinal column, on ventral side
Sheep	Scapula	VIII	Sc1	(Binford S-1) marks on lateral side near and parallel with lateral border of glenoid cavity*
Sheep	Scapula	VII, VIII	Sc2	(Binford S-2) marks along the neck of the scapula
Sheep	Scapula	VII, VIII	Sc3	(Binford S-3) longitudinal marks up and down the lateral surface of the blade*
Sheep	Scapula	VII, VIII	Sc5	Transverse marks across the 'neck' on the medial side
Sheep	Humerus	IV	Hp6	Transverse marks across the proximal end on the medial side
Sheep	Humerus	VII	Hs1	Transverse marks at approximately mid-shaft
Sheep	Humerus	VI, VII, VIII	Hd-2	Binford - transverse marks across medial surface
Sheep	Humerus	VIII	Hd-5	Binford - transverse mark across anterior face above articular end
Sheep	Humerus	VIII	Hd-6	Binford - oblique short 'chevron' marks clustered on neck of distal end on the anterior surface
Sheep/goat	Radius	VII	RCp-5	Binford - transverse marks on anterior margin of radial tuberosities
Sheep	Metacarpal	VIII	MCp5	Transverse cuts across the 'neck' of the proximal shaft
Sheep/goat	Pelvis	VI	PS-3	Binford - marks across the lateral face of the pubis
Sheep/goat	Pelvis	VIII	PS-7	Binford - marks above the acetabulum on arm of ilium
Sheep/goat	Pelvis	VIII	PS11	Transverse marks on medial side at proximal end of pubis
Sheep	Femur	VII, VIII	Fs1	Transverse marks across mid-shaft on posterior side
Sheep/goat	Femur	VII, VIII	Fs2	Transverse marks across mid-shaft on anterior side
Sheep	Femur	VI, VII	Fd-4	Binford - short 'chevron' marks obliquely grouped
Sheep	Femur	VI	Fd-5	Binford - short oblique marks on the anterior face above patellar surface
Sheep/goat	Tibia	IX	Tp-2	Binford - mark across the posterior face of the lateral and medial condyles
Sheep	Calcaneus	VIII	TC-3	Binford - marks on dorsal side midway between tuber calcis and the articulator surface
Sheep	Calcaneus	VII, VIII	TC-4	Transverse marks across the 'body' on the medial side
Sheep/goat	Metatarsal	V, V, VIII	MTp5	Transverse marks across and around the 'neck' of the proximal shaft
Sheep/goat	Metatarsal	VIII	MTs5	Transverse marks across mid-shaft
Sheep/goat	Metatarsal	VIII	MTd5	Clustered oblique marks on lateral and medial sides more proximally than Binford MTd-4

*see Binford (1981, 136—42) for full description

Table 6.1.46 Chicken bones: fine cut marks

Element	Phase(-s)	Code	Description
Coracoid	V	Cop1	Transverse marks on the caudal side, just distally of the glenoid
Femur	V, VI, VII,		
	VIII	Fe1	Transverse and oblique marks on the anterior side, between lesser trochanter and femoral head
Femur	VIII	Fe2	Oblique marks on the distal articular surface
Tibia	IV	Tbd1	Transverse marks across and/or just above the distal articular surface
Tarso-metatarsal	VIII	Tm1	Cuts affecting the proximal articular surface

Table 6.1.47 Goose bones: fine cut marks

Element	Phase	Code	Description
Scapula	VII	Sc1	Longitudinal marks on the external side near the humeral facet, parallel with the shaft
Humerus	VI	Hu2	Marks on the proximal articular extreme or 'head' of the humerus
Humerus	VII	Hu1	Transverse marks at the distal end of the humerus between the brachial depression and the articular end
Radius	VII	Ra1	Transverse marks at the proximal end of the radius on or just below the bicipital tuberosity
Ulna	VII	Ul1	Marks across the distal articular surface
Carpo-metacarpus	VII	Cmp1	Marks on the extreme proximal articular surface
Carpo-metacarpus	VII	Cmp2	Transverse marks across the process of metacarpal
Tibia	V	Tbd1	Transverse marks across and/or just above the distal articular surface
Tibia	VIII	Tbs1	Transverse marks across the distal shaft
Tibia	VIII	Tbs2	Transverse and oblique marks across the proximal shaft

Table 6.1.48 Other fauna: fine cut marks

Species	Element	Phase	Code	Description
Woodcock	Tibiotarsus	VII	Tbs1	Transverse marks across the distal shaft
Rabbit	Mandible	VI	MA1	Transverse marks on lateral side near the mental foramen
	Pelvis	VII	PS-3	Binford - marks near and parallel with the line of the pubic symphysis*
	Pelvis	VII	PS-6	Binford - longitudinal marks running caudally from obturator foramen*
Dog	Rib	VII	RS-1	Binford - marks along superior surface just lateral to the rib head
	Femur	VI VII	Fp-4	Binford - transverse marks on lesser trochanter
	Femur	VII	Fp-5	Binford - transverse marks on lateral surface of greater trochanter
	Femur	VI	Fp-7	Binford - short marks on the neck of greater trochanter, anterior face
	Femur	VI	Fs2	Transverse marks across mid-shaft on anterior side
Polecat/ferret	Skull	VIII	SK5	Transverse marks across the nasal bones
	Mandible	VIII	MA1	Transverse marks on lateral side near the mental foramen
Horse	Phalanx 1	V	PH1	Transverse marks encircling the first phalanx
Fallow deer	Radius	VIII	RCs1	Oblique and transverse marks at approximately mid-shaft

*see Binford (1981, 136—42) for full description

Table 6.1.49 Cattle bones: hacking quantified by location, no of fragments and phase

Element	Code	Phase IV	V	VI	VII	VIII	IX	Description
Skull	1SK		1		3			Hacking between the paraoccipital process and occipital condyle
	2SK		1			1		Skull split into left and right sides (same as S-2 of Binford 1981, 136)
	3SK		1	1	1			Hacking into, and sometimes just dorsally of, the occipital condyles
Mandible	1MA					1		Hacking through the coronoid process
	2MA		1			1		Hacking through approximate middle of premolar/molar tooth row
	3MA			2	1	1		Hacking through diastema
	5MA				1			Hacking through the condylar process
	7MA					1		Hacking through vertical part of the ramus
Vertebra	1VE	1?	7	5	9	5	2	Longitudinal hacking through vertebrae that divides them into left and right sides
	2VE			1				Longitudinal hacking along the centra, removes transverse process
	5VE		1					Transverse hacking at the cranial or caudal ends
Rib	1RI	1	2		3	2	1	Hacking through the 'neck' of the rib laterally of articular surfaces
	2RI			2				Transverse hacking through the flattened blade
Scapula	1SC	2	4	1		2		Oblique hacking through the 'neck' of the scapula from the medial side
	2SC	1	2					Hacking through the supraglenoid tubercle
	3SC				2	1		Transverse hacking from anterior side into the 'neck'
	4SC			1		1		Hacking through the blade to divide the most proximal third from the remainder
	5SC	2		3	3			Hacking into the base of the spinous process
	6SC				1			Transverse hacking into the 'neck' and distal blade from the medial side
	7SC			1	1	2		Transverse hacking through the blade from lateral to divide proximal from distal half
	8SC			2				Transverse hacking from lateral side to divide the most distal quarter from the rest
	9SC			1	1			Oblique hacking to remove much of the glenoid and the supraglenoid tubercle
	10SC			1		1		Hacking along the posterior border
	11SC				1			Longitudinal hacking into the glenoid, divides latter into cranial and caudal halves
Humerus	1H		1	1	6	1		Hacking through medial and lateral distal epicondyles
	2H	2	3	7	2	6		Transverse hacking through mid-shaft or just distally of this
	3H	2		5		2		Oblique hacking of distal trochlea
	4H			2	4	4		Longitudinal hacking that separates capitulum from trochlea
	5H		1		2			Transverse hacking across proximal shaft just distally of the head
	6H		1			1		Glancing longitudinal hacking at the proximal end into the 'head'
	8H	1						Oblique hacking that divides capitulum from trochlea
	9H	2						Longitudinal hacking, splitting the shaft
Radius	1RA	2		1		4		Transverse hacking through the proximal end of the shaft
	2RA				1	2		Oblique hacking that traverses the distal shaft and divides part of the articulation
	3RA	1	1	2	3	3	2	Longitudinal hacking dividing lateral and medial sides
	4RA			1		1		Hack through the middle of the proximal radius dividing part of dorsal from ventral
	5RA	1?	2	2	1	3		Transverse hacking through the mid-shaft
	6RA				1?			Transverse hacking across distal shaft
	7RA				2			Oblique hacking at proximal end, removing lateral epiphysis
	8RA				1			Oblique hacking at proximal end, removing medial epiphysis
	9RA		1					Oblique hacking across mid-shaft
Ulna	1UL					2		Hacking across the distal shaft
	2UL	1		3	1	2		Hacking across the proximal shaft distally of the articular surface
	3UL	1			3	1		Hacking across the proximal end between the processus anconaeus and the olecranon
	4UL				1	1		Hacking through the articulation
Metacarpal	1MP	1			1			Oblique hacking through the proximal shaft
	2MP				3			Oblique hacking through the distal shaft
	4MP	1			2	1		Transverse hacking through mid-shaft
	5MP	2		1				Longitudinal hacking through the middle of the bone, splitting medial from lateral
Pelvis	1PE	1		3	2	9		Transverse or oblique hack through the ilium
	2PE	1		4	1	2		Transverse hack through circa mid-acetabulum
	3PE	1		4	2	1		Transverse hack through the pubis close to or on the rim of acetabulum
	4PE		1?	4		3		Hack through the ischium close to or on the rim of the acetabulum
	5PE			1	2	1		Hack through the symphyseal branch of the pubis
	6PE				1			Hacking through the ischium
Femur	1FE					3		Hacking through the most proximal part of the head
	2FE				2			Hacking across proximal end, removing 'head' and greater trochanter
	3FE		3	1	1			Hacking at distal end, removing lateral or medial condyle
	4FE		6	3	10	9		Transverse hacking dividing the femur into proximal and distal halves
	5FE				4	3		Hack into the trochanter minor, sometimes slicing a triangle off the latter
	6FE		1	1		3		Longitudinal hack through the distal shaft
	7FE		1		1			Oblique hack at proximal end, removing greater trochanter
	9FE				1			Oblique hacking at proximal end just distally of the lesser trochanter
	10FE		1	1				Oblique hacking at distal end at level of supracondyloid fossa, removing distal end
	11FE		2					Longitudinal hacking at proximal end removes the 'head'
Tibia	1T		3	1	7	5	1	Oblique hack across the shaft which divides the most distal quarter from the rest
	2T	1	2	6	12	7		Longitudinal hacking through middle of the tibia to divide medial from lateral
	3T					1		Transverse hacking through the proximal shaft near the nutrient foramen
	4T	2	1	1	5	1		Hacking across the mid-shaft to divide proximal and distal halves
Astragalus	2AS		1	1				Longitudinal or oblique hack
Calcaneus	1CA		2	1		2	1	Transverse hack above sustentaculum tali which isolates the calcaneal tuber
	2CA	1	1			2	1	Hacking through the sustentaculum tali
	3CA	1		2	2			Hacking through the processus anterior
Metatarsal	1MP	1	1		1			Oblique hacking through the proximal shaft
	2MP				1			Oblique hacking through the distal shaft
	3MP				1			Oblique hacking at distal end, removing part of lateral or medial condyle
	4MP	3		2	3			Transverse hacking through mid-shaft

Table 6.1.50 Sampled contexts producing mammal, bird and amphibian bone (all wet-sieved over 1 mm heavy residue mesh; volumes in litres)

Phase

I Context	I Vol	II Context	II Vol	III Context	III Vol	IV Context	IV Vol	V Context	V Plot	V Vol	VI Context	VI Plot	VI Vol	VII Context	VII Plot	VII Vol	VIII Context	VIII Plot	VIII Vol	X Context	X Vol	Total vol
142	18	75	10	272	36	266	24	131	Eval	11	37	Eval	13	26	Eval	12	207	Eval	72	206	11	
143	10	98	10	278	12	1015	41	261	Eval	72	249	Eval	?	31	Eval	6	223	Eval	36	208	72	
157	8	121	10	279	12	1030	72	264	Eval	24	429	3	72	237	Eval	138	235	Eval	?	217	36	
161	10	126	10	280	12	1033	36	490	2	72	431	3	72	245	Eval	36	341	96	100	325	24	
276	12	129	36	281	12	1034	24	765	2	36	442	3	92	463	2	72	455	4	72	352	60	
1148	72	770	17	973	36	1041	12	768	2	36	467	3	?	464	2	72	515	6	36	353	6	
1242	72	1040	72	1022	72			888	1	24	493	6	6	489	1	24	520	6	72	375	72	
1243	36	1138	120	1175	60			992	6	36	566	2	6	663	1	?	559	3	36	384	36	
1250	48	1179	72					1021	2	60	671	1	72	670	6	36	1437		72	451	24	
1388	72	1219	72					1130	1	36	766	2	?	678	6	24				507	72	
1392	24	1220	72					1162	2	60	777	2	24	688	4	24				545	24	
		1221	24					1579	4	36	785	2	72	1505	4	72				546	5	
								1585	4	24	791	2	72	1513	4	36				547	6	
								1632	2	36	797	2	72	1515	4	30				1387	36	
											798	2	120	1558	4	?				1486	36	
											800	3	72	1590	?	?						
											804	3	36	1599	4	36						
											805	2	24	1607	4	36						
											806	2	72	1608	4	72						
											903	1	36	1695	4	36						
											984	1	24	1699	4	36						
											1556	4	36	1881	4	72						
											1635	2	36									
											1697	4	108									
											1702	3	72									
Total vol 382		463		252		209		563			1209			894			496			520		4988

Plant, Invertebrate and Fish Remains
Deborah Jaques, Allan Hall, Harry Kenward and John Carrott

Introduction

Deposits excavated on the site were generously sampled for the purposes of finds recovery and for the retrieval of biological remains. A series of 120 samples from 115 contexts, varying in size from five to 100 litres (seventy-one of which were of either thirty or sixty litres), was processed by 'bulk-sieving' (to 1 mm) on site; they yielded a heavy fraction ('residue') and lighter material ('washover' or 'flot'). A parallel series of unprocessed samples for many of these contexts was retained for subsequent examination of a 'GBA' subsample where deemed appropriate on the basis of the evidence from the BS samples (terminology follows Dobney *et al* 1992).

The extensive sampling programme produced a moderate-sized assemblage of fish remains. A smaller number of fragments was retrieved by hand during excavation, but these were mainly restricted to large vertebrae or single large elements. A couple of deposits also produced groups of bones representing articulated remains, mostly fins. Only a limited suite of species were present within the hand-collected material. Details regarding the fish assemblages are, therefore, mostly concentrated on information provided by the sieved assemblage.

Methods

Small numbers of plant remains, mainly charcoal, were sorted by excavation staff from the residues during on-site work and examined during the assessment, when 118 of the washovers, together with a small proportion of the residues, were inspected. Subsamples from a group of twelve samples for which unprocessed sediment had been retained and for which insects were considered to be worth investigating (on the basis of inspection of the washovers from bulk-sieving) were selected for laboratory processing. Their lithologies were recorded, using a standard pro forma, prior to processing, following the procedures of Kenward *et al* (1980; 1986), for recovery of plant and invertebrate macrofossils. In each case, only part of the washover could be inspected closely for insect remains; to examine all of the material would have required a prohibitive amount of time.

Following recommendations made during the assessment (Hall *et al* 2002a), the washovers from a group of twelve of the bulk-sieved samples were re-examined for plant remains during the main analysis phase. A selection of five of the samples processed for insect remains was likewise revisited (with paraffin flotation being applied to the washovers in an attempt to reduce the volume of material to be sorted).

Plant remains
Lists of plant remains and other components of the samples examined were recorded semi-quantitatively (using a simple, three-point scale from 1 – one or a few remains,

through 2 – moderately frequent remains, or a component representing between about 1 and 10% by volume of the original sample, to 3 – abundant remains or a component representing more than about 10% of the original sample volume), the data being entered, during inspection, on a computer database using Paradox software.

Insect remains
A record of the preservational condition of the insect remains was made using scales given by Kenward and Large (1998). This scheme provides scales for chemical erosion and fragmentation (0.5–5.5, the higher figure representing the greatest degree of damage), and colour change (0–4), in each case giving a range and a value for the position and strength of the mode (Kenward & Large 1998, tables 2, 3 and 5–7).

Insects were identified by comparison with modern reference material and using the standard works. Adult beetles and bugs, other than aphids and scale insects, were recorded fully quantitatively and a minimum number of individuals estimated on the basis of the fragments present. Other invertebrate macrofossils were recorded semi-quantitatively using the scale described by Kenward *et al* (1986) and Kenward (1992), again using estimates for extremely abundant taxa. Data pertaining to invertebrate remains were transferred from a paper record to computer databases (using Paradox software) for analysis and long-term storage.

The interpretative methods employed in this study were essentially the same as those used in work on a variety of sites by Hall, Kenward and co-workers (*see* Kenward 1978, with modifications outlined by, for example, Kenward 1988; Hall & Kenward 1990; and Kenward & Hall 1995). For the insect remains, interpretation rests primarily on a number of 'main statistics' of whole assemblages of adult beetles and bugs, and on the recognition of ecologically related groups of species.

Parasite eggs
Small subsamples from two sixteenth-century contexts from Phase VI, ((806) and (1697), the primary fills of cess pits (487) and (1624) in plots 2 and 4 respectively) were examined for the eggs of intestinal parasitic nematodes using the 'squash' technique of Dainton (1992). Six coprolites from deposits in Phases III, V, VI, VII and IX were also examined. Where possible egg measurements were taken using a calibrated eyepiece graticule at 600x magnification.

Shell
Nine boxes of hand-collected shell (representing material from 202 contexts) were submitted. All of the remains were identified as closely as possible during the assessment. The weight (in grammes) of shell from each context was noted and its preservational condition recorded using two, subjective, four-point scales for erosion and fragmentation. Scale points were: 0 – none apparent; 1 – slight; 2 – moderate; 3 – high.

For oyster (*Ostrea edulis*) shell, additional notes were made regarding: numbers of left and right valves; evidence of having being opened using a knife or similar implement; measurability of the valves; damage from other marine biota (polychaet worms and dog whelks); encrustation by barnacles.

The shell data were initially recorded on paper and later entered into a Paradox data table for subsequent interrogation.

Fish bone

The assessment of the fish remains recommended that all well dated fish assemblages from the samples should be recorded in detail, with the objective of providing basic information regarding species and body part representation; size range of species; and some interpretation concerning the exploitation of past fish stocks.

Where applicable, fragments were identified to species or species group, using the reference collections of Palaeoecology Research Services Ltd (PRS), County Durham, and of the Royal Museum for Central Africa, Tervuren, Belgium. Wim Van Neer and Wim Wouters (of the Royal Museum for Central Africa) also advised on some identifications. Selected elements were recorded (*see* Appendix for details). However, where other elements not in this list or fragments such as ribs, spines and pterygiophore could be identified to species or family group, these were noted and counted but not included in the tables of total fragment counts. These were recorded for their potential to provide additional information regarding skeletal element representation within certain context types.

Several methods of quantification were employed to calculate the significance of different species or groups within the assemblage. The simplest method used was to count the number of identifiable fragments for each species or group. Additionally, species were ranked on the basis of their frequency of occurrence, ie the number of contexts in which they were identified. It must be noted, however, that the relative abundance of different fish species in an archaeological assemblage is always difficult to ascertain. Differences in the number of identifiable elements for each species and differential preservation of certain bones are just two factors which can create an over- or under-representation of individual species.

Skeletal elements representing the olfactory, orbital, otic, oromandibular, hyoid and branchial regions of the fish skeleton were classified as being part of the fish head for interpretation purposes, whilst those from the appendicular region, vertebral column and caudal skeleton were classified as the body.

It was originally suggested that biometrical data be collected. However, measurable fragments were not numerous and many fragments were too incomplete or battered to provide biometrical data. Where size of fish is noted in the text, this was estimated by comparison of the remains with those of modern reference specimens of known size. Tail length (TL) rather than standard length (SL) was used.

Radiocarbon dates

Three samples of remains extracted from the sediment samples were submitted to Beta Analytic, Miami, Florida, for dating *via* Accelerator Mass Spectrometry (AMS). The results obtained are presented in the relevant sections following.

Results

Tables 6.2.1 and 6.2.2 present complete species lists of plant and insect (and some other invertebrate) remains, with, for the plant remains, an indication of the phases from which each taxon was recovered. Table 6.2.1 also includes records of other components of the washovers noted during examination of plant remains. Data concerning the insect assemblages are presented in Tables 6.2.3 and 6.2.4.

The assessment revealed that plant remains were often quite abundant and preservation was variously by charring, anoxic waterlogging, and (less often) mineral replacement. Sometimes all three modes of preservation were noted in the material from a single washover. Many of the deposits yielded only very small amounts of charcoal and perhaps a few other charred remains, such as cereal grains. In no case was there a very high organic content without the presence also of much other material, typically coal cinders. Naturally, some constraints on recording the 'waterlogged' plant remains were imposed by the examination of dried washovers but, given the broad chronological range of the deposits and the presence of large concentrations of cinders, it was thought important to concentrate on the bulk-sieved material to hand rather than to undertake extensive processing of further raw sediment.

Paraffin flotation of some of the samples failed to recover a significant proportion of the insects. This is not unknown for suites of very decayed remains: a case in point is presented by remains of *Trox scaber* in Anglo-Scandinavian and post-Conquest deposits at the Layerthorpe Bridge site, York (Hall *et al* 2000). A very large proportion of the fossils of *T scaber* from that site were recovered during botanical analysis from the residues from paraffin flotation, perhaps having failed to float because hydrophobic layers in the cuticle (to which paraffin normally attaches) had been modified or destroyed in the unusual environment of a tan pit: the *Trox* fossils were certainly in an unusual state of decay, and this was regarded as significant evidence regarding their pathway to the deposit. Further examples were offered by more conventionally decayed remains in samples from Cooper Farm, Long Riston, East Yorkshire (Jaques *et al* 2002) and peat from the Guardian Glass site, Goole (Hall *et al* 2003). In the present case, many of the remains in the washover from Sample <5161> were better preserved than those listed from the flot, perhaps contradicting the hypothesis that advanced decay was responsible for the failure of fossil remains to float. However, the same range of taxa was present in (subjectively) the same proportions. There was not time within project constraints to fully sort the washovers and identify the remains from them, but interpretation will not have suffered as a result. Notes on the insect remains from samples assessed but not examined further are given in Table 6.2.7 together with sediment descriptions for all twelve of the subsamples processed in the laboratory.

It seems likely that the organic remains in at least the more superficial deposits at this site have undergone recent decay *in situ*. Uniform decay of organics to red, orange or brown colours has been argued to be an indicator of gross decay of recently de-watered sediments, in contrast to the heterogeneous decay likely during deposit formation (Kenward & Hall 2000; 2004; 2006).

Measurements of the trichurid parasite eggs from contexts (806) and (1697) are presented in Table 6.2.6.

Small fragments of mostly marine shell were recovered from many of the samples which occasionally also gave a few fragments of eggshell (Contexts (37), (353), (671), (785) and (1513)). Only four of the contexts (*see* text following) gave more than the barest traces of highly fragmented shell and even these gave very few remains from large samples.

Hand-collected shell was recovered from 202 contexts (two of which remained unphased). Preservation was generally poor, with erosion and fragmentation scores for most contexts being recorded as either 2 or 3. Much of the shell was notably 'soft' and that the remains had continued to degrade after the excavation was evidenced by the many fragments and flakes of shell (mostly of oyster) present in almost all of the contexts. All of the material was examined and the taxa identified as closely as possible. Table 6.2.8 shows the total numbers of contexts assessed by phase. Table 6.2.9 gives a summary of the recorded shell by phase. The molluscs from almost all of the contexts included oyster shell, and summary information (again by phase) for this material is presented as Table (6.2.10.

The importance of the fish remains recovered was their potential for providing information from a sequence of deposits covering a broad chronological period. They were recovered from Phase I through to Phase X, although 43% of all identified fish fragments were from Phase VI, with a further 20% of the assemblage from contexts assigned to Phase VII. Material from samples representing 101 contexts was examined, resulting in the identification of 3638 fish bones to species or family group (Table 6.2.11 and Ill 6.2.1). Additionally, over 200 fragments were recovered by hand-collection from forty-six deposits, although Table 6.2.12 only shows those remains included in the recording protocol (*see* Appendix). Unless otherwise stated all comments, frequencies and total identified fragment counts refer to material recovered from the samples.

The contexts listed for each of the phase summaries presented below are those for which plant remains from the bulk-sieved washovers were examined in the assessment. Those underlined were re-examined for plant remains in the 'main phase', those examined in detail for insects *via* GBA subsamples being italicised. No further study of the parasite eggs remains or hand-collected shell was undertaken after the assessment. However, the assessment results have been revised for inclusion in this report by phase, with additional comments in the light of finalisation of the site phasing and further consideration.

Phase I

Plant remains
For the assessment, plant remains in washovers from samples from twelve contexts ((142), (143), (157), (161), (276), (1026), (1148), (1242), (1243), (1250), (1388) and (1392)) assigned to this phase were examined (although two of the separately numbered contexts are thought to represent the same deposit). All five of the sub-phases of Phase I and a variety of context types – fills of features and surface-formed layers – were represented. All twelve samples yielded at least a trace of charcoal, but otherwise the plant remains noted were restricted to uncharred seeds or seed fragments of elder (*Sambucus nigra*) in four sam-

ples, charred wheat (*Triticum*) grains in four samples, and charred hazel (*Corylus avellana*) nutshell in two. There was also a single tentatively identified charred plum (*Prunus domestica sensu lato*) fruitstone. The charcoal, where identified, was ash (*Fraxinus*) or oak (*Quercus*). These results are consistent with occupation in which accumulation of organic material was rare in the area excavated – not at all unusual for a Roman fortress.

Shell
No hand-collected shell was recovered from deposits of this phase.

Fish bone
Fish remains were recovered from samples from five deposits ((1148), (1242), (1243), (1250) and (1392)). A single fish bone was recovered by hand-collection. The largest collection of bones (fifty-six fragments) was produced by context (1148) (a primary silt in a substantial sandstone sewer, possibly of mid-third to fourth-century date); the remaining deposits all produced less than ten fragments. Most of the bones from (1148) were well preserved, but those from the other deposits were rather battered.

The identified bones totalled sixty-nine fragments and included the remains of eel, herring, flatfish (a few of which were more closely identified as flounder and plaice), salmon, sea bass and mullet. Additionally, several pre-caudal vertebrae from (242) were identified as being possibly the remains of Spanish mackerel. During the Roman period this Mediterranean species was commonly salted and transported in amphorae to all parts of the Roman empire (Van Neer & Lentacker 1994).

Although the remains of mullet appeared to be the most numerous, these fragments represented the part skeletons of just two separate fish (one being smaller than the other), with a range of elements suggesting that originally whole fish had been deposited (1148). Skeletal elements from the other fish identified were almost entirely restricted to vertebrae (both pre-caudal and caudal). Unidentified elements did, however, include fragments of spine, finray and pterygiophore.

The assemblage from this phase was small but somewhat different from that recovered from later phases. Fish are comparatively rare from deposits of Roman date in Britain, although mullet and ?Spanish mackerel are not unusual for this period.

Phase II

Plant remains
Plant material from a total of ten contexts ((75), (98), (121), (126), (1040), (1138), (1179), (1219), (1220) and (1221)) from this phase was investigated for the assessment (again, two contexts probably being the same layer, from the 'dark earth' deposits); seven of the remainder came from deposits interpreted as feature/cut fills. All three sub-phases were represented. Again, all ten samples yielded at least a little charcoal, and seven also some elder seed material. Charred cereal grains were occasionally present – barley (*Hordeum*), oats (*Avena*, including cultivated oats, *A. sativa*) and wheat (including bread/club wheat, *Triticum 'aestivo-compactum'*) – were all noted, and there were rare records of charred hazel nut-

shell. A pit fill (in cut (1139), Phase IIb), described by the excavator as having a 'midden-like' character, proved to contain traces of mineral-replaced material, including at least one apple (*Malus sylvestris*) seed, and did therefore perhaps contain some organic waste of faecal origin, mineral replacement usually being observed where there is other evidence for faeces.

Shell
Only three very poorly preserved oyster valves were recovered from a total of five contexts from this phase. For two of the deposits the remains amounted to no more than small fragments and flakes of shell.

Fish bone
Nine deposits ((98), (121), (126), (1040), (1138), (1179), (1219), (1220) and (1221)) produced the fish assemblage from this phase. A range of context types was represented, including pit- and post hole fills and occupation deposits. The overall total of identified fish remains was 186 fragments, of which 132 were recovered from just two of the deposits: (1138) (92 fragments), a pit fill and context (1220) (40 fragments), and a fill from the secondary silting of sewer (1182).

Flatfish remains (including flounder and plaice) were predominant, forming just over 50% of the assemblage. Herring bones were also numerous, whilst smelt and eel were present in small quantities. Very few gadid remains were identified, but fragments of both whiting and cod were recorded. Other bones present included the remains of shad, sea bass, salmon (and salmonid) and ray. Vertebrae recovered by hand-collection were identified as herring and ?trout.

Residual material from an earlier phase may be suggested by the presence of ?Spanish mackerel and mullet (possibly thin-lipped grey mullet) in (1138), the fill of pit (1139). Pit (1139) cut through the fill of another pit which had been dug to retrieve stone from the Phase I sewer (1182) and the presence of remains of these fish in (1138) may therefore suggest that this deposit contained reworked material originally deposited in the sewer.

Most of the deposits produced too few fragments for detailed analysis of their content. Where sufficient data were available from pit fills, eg (1138), it was evident that fragments representing the vertebral column and the appendicular skeleton of the fish were prevalent. Individual taxa such as herring and flatfish were represented by cranial elements, but for both vertebrae were the most commonly occurring bone. For herring from (1138), otic bullae from very small fish were also quite numerous, together with vertebrae and some cranial elements.

Fish remains from these deposits appeared to be waste from food preparation and consumption and possibly fish sauce or fish imported from the Mediterranean. When the fish were being prepared in the kitchen, the fish heads are likely to have been chopped off and disposed of, whilst the waste from the meal would mainly have consisted of vertebrae and would perhaps have been discarded elsewhere. However, the presence of both types of waste was noted here, which suggests that domestic refuse from the table and from the kitchen was all deposited together.

Phase III

Plant remains
All eight samples (from contexts (272), (278), (279), (280), (281), (973), (1022) and (1175)) yielded at least some charcoal at the assessment stage. Four of them (underlined above), from a series of fills of a single feature, were considered worthy of further examination. The feature from which they came has been interpreted as a hearth pit and, with the exception of some elder seeds and some cereal 'bran' and cereal caryopses, all the plant material recovered was charred or partly so. In a few cases, fossils were reduced to silica (*cf* Robinson & Straker 1991) through the same combustive processes. At the assessment stage, these deposits were thought to contain charred peat fragments and, indeed, the presence of charred sedge (*Carex*) nutlets in all four assemblages was thought to be consistent with this. However, closer examination revealed that most if not all of the fragments thought to be charred peat in fact contained fragments of seed coat (testa) of pea (*Pisum*), or in some cases bean (*Vicia faba*): both were certainly represented by the specimens of the diagnostic hila or seed attachment scars, together with some uncharred wheat/rye (*Triticum/Secale cereale*) and oat 'bran', and they should therefore be seen as charred food debris, presumably from the cooking of food consisting in large part of pulses and whole or milled grain. More conventional remains of food plants were the charred grains of oats (including cultivated oats), barley, rye and bread/club wheat, as well as charred seeds of blackberry, field bean and perhaps also pea.

It may be, in fact, that peat was being used as a fuel (hence the sedge nutlets), but was almost completely consumed, leaving only some fragments which consisted of pale yellowish material on one side and brownish material on the other, as seen in the washover from the sample from (278), the uppermost fill. Some of the charcoal identified as coming from hazel roundwood, may also represent fuel used in the cooking which evidently occurred at this hearth. The presence of grassy, non-woody material – perhaps tinder – may be indicated by some of the charred and silicified herbaceous material noted in at least two of these hearth samples, but very little other plant material was recognised, merely a few charred weed seeds.

The remaining samples from contexts assigned to this phase yielded only small amounts of charred plant material: a few cereal grains and hazel nutshell. There was one record of traces of uncharred seeds of fig (*Ficus carica*) found in a small assemblage with a few other probable plant food remains from a deposit, (1175), described as a 'cessy' fill of cut (1176). If truly pre-Norman Conquest, this represents a very rare record for fig, a species well known from Roman and from post-Conquest medieval (and later) deposits. In view of its abundance in later deposits at this site, the possibility of contamination in the ground, during sampling, or during processing should be considered.

Charred plant remains from two samples from this phase were subjected to radiocarbon dating. Cereal grains, mainly bread/club wheat and a little oats, with a trace of barley, from (272) and bread/club wheat and a little oats from (278) gave (2 sigma calibrated) AMS dates as follows:

Context (272): cal AD 785–1040 (lab no Beta -170531)
Context (278): cal AD 795–1000 (lab no Beta - 170532)

Shell

Hand-collected shell was recovered from one occupation deposit (1022) but amounted to only four grammes of small unidentified fragments and flakes.

Fish bone

Fish remains from this phase were recovered from six deposits, (272), (279), (280), (973), (1022) and (1175), mainly representing pit fills, cess and occupation deposits. In total, 148 fragments were identified, with the largest concentrations of remains being recovered from (272), a layer with a 'cess-like' appearance, (1175), the fill of a cess pit, and an occupation layer, (1022).

Preservation of the remains from this phase was mostly quite good. However, fragments from (272) and (1175) were of rather battered appearance, with a couple of vertebrae from (1175) showing characteristic damage associated with their possible consumption and subsequent passage through the digestive system (probably human). This deposit also included several burnt fragments.

The identified assemblage consisted primarily of flatfish remains, with herring, eel and small quantities of ray, smelt, gadid and ?trout. Although the predominance of flatfish was apparent in all of the larger assemblages, some variations were noted between the different context types.

Those deposits with a component that probably derived from cess, (272) and (1175), had lower frequencies of flatfish (43% in both cases) and quite high proportions of herring (37% and 29% respectively). In contrast, the occupation deposit, (1022), had a higher frequency of flatfish remains (68%), although similar frequencies of herring (26%). The larger quantities of the latter may be a result of the inclusion of cess within (272) and (1175); the herring bones (and probably the eel and smelt vertebrae from (272)), almost exclusively represented by vertebrae, probably derive from faecal matter. Flatfish remains, although represented chiefly by vertebrae, also included other elements from the oromandibular (eg dentary, premaxilla, quadrate and articular) and hyoid (eg hyomandibular and preopercular) regions of the head, together with fragments from the appendicular skeleton (eg cleithrum). These remains suggest the disposal of more general domestic refuse which could be either kitchen or table waste.

Coprolite

A coprolite recovered from an occupation deposit, (1022), was examined. It contained numerous small bone fragments and no parasite eggs were seen in the 'squash' subsample. It was thought most likely to be of dog.

Phase IV

Plant remains

The six contexts ((266), (1015), (1030), (1033), (1034) and (1041)) from this phase for which bulk-sieved samples were examined for plant remains were, with one exception, fills of pits or post holes. Again, all samples yielded at least some charcoal (including oak and ash) and usually also uncharred elder seeds, but ancient remains representing human activity were restricted to a few charred cereal grains, mostly wheat, with some barley, and perhaps also rye. Very few other remains were noted. They therefore offer comparatively little insight into this phase of occupation of the site and are at least consistent with the generally limited archaeological evidence from this site for the medieval period overall.

Charred plant material from (1034) was used for dating by AMS. It consisted of a few barley grains, one wheat and one ?rye; the 2 sigma calibrated date returned was:

Context (1034): cal AD 1055–1085 and AD 1150–1270
(lab no Beta - 170530)

Shell

No hand-collected shell was recovered from this phase.

Fish bone

None of the fish bone assemblages examined from Phase IV was particularly productive and few identified fragments were recovered. However, a total of fifty-six fragments was recorded from six deposits ((266), (1015), (1030), (1033), (1034) and (1041)), although only (1030) and (1033) produced more than ten identified fragments (thirteen and eighteen respectively). The deposits were mostly pit and post hole fills, together with a single cultivation soil.

Overall, preservation of the bone was described as good, although the small assemblage from (1034), a post hole fill, was of rather battered appearance. Burnt fragments were noted from (266), the cultivation soil. Most (64%) of the remains identified represented flatfish (including flounder), with 25% of the bones being herring. Additionally, remains of eel, ?trout, conger eel and gadid were recorded. Most of the fragments (80%) were vertebrae.

Phase V

Plant remains

The thirteen contexts ((131), (261), (264), (490), (768), (770), (888), (992), (1021), (1130), (1162), (1585) and (*1632*)) for which plant material was investigated included three associated with oven (767) and one with oven (1568), from Plots 2 and 4 respectively. Three others were pit fills and two came from the fills of culverts. Again, plant remains were rather restricted in their range and diversity, with charcoal (including oak and ash, but also willow/poplar/aspen, *Salix/Populus*) being recorded from all the samples. There were small numbers of charred cereal grains in several assemblages, but they were not noticeably more frequent in the deposits associated with the ovens; indeed, one deposit from oven (767) yielded traces of charred bean and pea seeds, whilst oven (1568) yielded only traces of wheat grains. The only sample revisited during the main analysis stage was (1632), the upper fill of pit (1455) in Plot 2, in which moderate numbers of fig and blackberry seeds were present, along with traces of mineral-replaced grape (*Vitis vinifera*) pips and some fragments of material (to 10 mm) which may well have been very decayed faecal concretions; there seems little doubt that this deposit, at least, contained food waste of faecal origin. It also, however, contained moderate amounts of cinders, indicating the first clear evidence for the use of coal as a fuel at the site.

Insect remains

The insect assemblage recovered from (1632) was also recorded in some detail. The flot was fairly small and contained generally very decayed insect remains, with rather numerous uncountable scraps of various taxa, especially *Cercyon* (E 3.5–5.5, mode 4.5 weak; F 2.5–5.5, mode 3.0 weak; trend to pale 2–4, mode 4 distinct). The washover was checked and found to contain very large numbers of remains, suggesting a serious failure of flotation, something occasionally noted in other samples with decayed remains (*see* above). In the present case, many of the remains in the washover were better preserved than those listed from the flot, although the same range of taxa was present in (subjectively) the same proportions. There were tens of *Cercyon depressus* and many histerines in the washover, including body sclerites of the latter, which were only represented by legs in the flot. There was not time within project constraints to fully sort the washover and identify these remains, but interpretation will not have suffered as a result. There were large numbers of remains (nineteen individuals at least in the flot) which appeared certainly to be *Cercyon depressus*, a surprising species in an occupation site pit fill since it is normally confined to stranded wrack and other salt-soaked litter. It may be that the pit fill included some salt waste (eg from brining), or that conditions in some other way mimicked those of wrack. *Aglenus brunneus* was also abundant, but may have been a post-depositional invader (Kenward 1975). Overall, most of the assemblage consisted of either 'house fauna' (eg six *Xylodromus concinnus* and four *Tipnus unicolor*) or species typically found together in fairly foul decaying matter (eg eight *Ptenidium* sp, four histerines, and two *Oxytelus sculptus*). The latter doubtless invaded the pit (though they gave little evidence of breeding in any numbers; fly puparia were rare, too), while the former may have strayed in or been dumped in rubbish from a house or other building. There were rare grain pests (*Oryzaephilus ?surinamensis* and *Sitophilus granarius)*, probably strays or brought in floor-sweepings, and certainly too few to suggest disposal of spoiled grain.

Shell

There was a small assemblage of hand-collected shell from this phase representing material from thirteen contexts. A total of 464 g of poorly preserved shell (average erosion: 2.75; average fragmentation: 2.38) was recovered, mostly oyster valves (thirteen), with a few remains of other edible shellfish (two valves each of mussel and cockle). Five of the oyster valves (38%) showed evidence of having been opened using a knife or similar implement. The small number of remains were thinly and fairly evenly distributed through the layers and fills of this phase.

Fish bone

Thirteen Phase V deposits produced a small assemblage of identified fish remains totalling 205 fragments. Only four contexts, (261), (490), (768) and (1162), produced more than ten identified bones, however. Several of the deposits were associated with, or backfilled, two different ovens ((768), (770) and (888), associated with oven (767) in Plot 2; (1579) and (1585) associated with oven (1568) in Plot 4), whilst a number of the contexts were pit fills ((1021), (1162) and (1632)). The largest concentra-

tion of fish remains (ninety-nine identified fragments) was recovered from (261), a cultivation soil in Plot 1, which appeared to have accumulated through the disposal of rubbish or midden-spreading. Preservation of the remains varied between contexts, but generally those fragments from the oven and flue fills were of reasonable preservation, whilst material from the pit fills and cultivation layers were less well preserved and rather fragmented and battered in appearance.

There was still a fairly restricted suite of species represented. Numerically, herring and flatfish were predominant; remains of eel, smelt, gadid, whiting, elasmobranch and salmonid were also identified. Taking the assemblage as a whole, the pattern (using frequency of total fragment counts) of the previous phases was reversed, with herring remains becoming dominant, forming 50% of the assemblage, and flatfish decreasing in significance to 35%. Frequency of occurrence, however, suggested that flatfish were still important, being found in 85% of the deposits examined from this phase, in comparison to 69% for herring. This technique increased the importance of gadid remains, the few fragments being recovered from seven of the thirteen deposits (ie 54%).

An examination of skeletal element representation for all fish from this phase showed that 81% of all the identified fragments represented the body of the fish, ie were either vertebrae (the majority) or skeletal elements representing the appendicular region of the skeleton. It can be seen from a closer examination of the two main groups (herring and flatfish) that whilst both were primarily represented by vertebrae (90% and 56% respectively), flatfish remains also included a wide range of elements from all parts of the head and appendicular skeleton.

Results from this phase were clearly influenced by the assemblage from (261), which produced almost 50% of the identified fragments. The prevalence of herring vertebrae can perhaps be attributed to the incorporation within this deposit of material deriving from night soil or cess, but the inclusion of other, more general refuse is indicated by the presence of the flatfish remains.

Comparison of the flatfish remains with modern reference specimens suggested that the individuals represented were quite small, ranging in overall length from 20 to 25 cm. Evidence from the whiting vertebrae from (261) indicated that the individuals represented were about 20 cm in overall length. Hand-collected material from this phase was restricted to just two fragments; one was a cod precaudal vertebra from a fish of approximately 1 metre in length (TL).

Coprolite

Context (992), the fill of culvert (994) between Plots 1 and 2, gave a single coprolite which the presence of numerous small bone fragments, and absence of parasite eggs within the 'squash' subsample, identified as most probably being of dog.

Phase VI

Plant remains

Almost all the twenty-one deposits investigated for plant remains ((37), (113), (429), (431), (442), (467), (493), (566), (608), (671), (765), (777), (785), (791), (797), (798), (806), (1556), (1635), (1697) and (1702)) came from pits, with five, (785), (791), (797), (798) and (806), being fills of cess pit (487) in Plot 2; (429) and (442) being fills of pit (430) in Plot 3; and (566) and (608) being fills of pit (614) in Plot 6. In addition to the material examined by AH, samples from (806) and (1697) (the primary fill of pit (1624) in Plot 4) were also studied by Fiona Johnson and David Shimwell, Palaeoecological Research Unit (PERU), School of Geography, University of Manchester. Comments on records additional to those made in the main study are included below.

Plant macrofossil assemblages from this phase were generally richer than in any previous deposits at the site, although cinders were frequent or abundant in a third of the washovers, indicating the regular use of coal as a fuel. Four samples were selected for re-examination after the assessment. The more frequent plant remains were seeds of fig (in two-thirds of the assemblages) and other probable food remains included blackberry, raspberry (*Rubus idaeus*) hazel nut, and grape. Strawberry (*Fragaria cf vesca*) was rather frequent in one of the assemblages rich in fig seeds (from (806)), but the range of foods represented was still quite limited: other edible taxa, usually only found in small amounts in one or two samples, included linseed (*Linum usitatissimum*), apple, sloe (*Prunus spinosa*); there was also a single record of charred field bean remains.

The other prominent component of the assemblages from the Phase VI deposits was a variety of remains of gorse (*Ulex*, perhaps all *U. europaeus*). The parts recorded were charred (and partly-charred) flower buds, charred, uncharred and mineral-replaced leaves (ie spines), and charred pods and twig fragments. Clearly dried flowering stems of gorse were being used at this time, most probably as fuel, the uncharred and mineral-replaced material representing that which had not been burnt prior to deposition in the pit concerned. Remains of gorse were most abundant in (785) from cesspit (487), and recorded from two of the other fills of this feature, but were also found in the fill of gully (1703) in Plot 3, (1702), and the fill of pit (39) in Plot 1, (37). Other plant remains in these deposits were a mixture of weeds of various kinds, perhaps largely arriving with cereal crops or straw, or growing in the vicinity of the deposits as they formed, but none was ever present in more than small numbers.

The samples from (806) and (1697) studied at PERU yielded much the same taxa represented by plant macrofossils as those investigated by AH, both assemblages consisting almost exclusively of remains of food plants. The group from (806) was very largely fig seeds with single apple, pear, ?cherry and medlar seeds or fruitstones. Neither pear (*Pyrus communis* L.) nor medlar (*Mespilus germanica* L.) was recorded by AH but neither is unexpected at this period.

Insect and parasite remains

Contexts (806) and (1697) were also examined (*via* 'squash' subsamples) for the eggs of intestinal parasitic nematodes during the assessment. For context (806), the 'squash' was mostly organic detritus with some inorganic material. Seven rather poorly preserved *Trichuris* eggs (all missing both polar plugs) were seen, as were many pollen grains and some ?fungal spores. Maximum lengths (though obviously not including polar plugs) and widths were recorded for five of the eggs. A maximum length

(including polar plugs) was calculated for these eggs by extrapolation from data from other archaeological records and their size range determined to be 52–64 microns long x 24–28 microns wide (Table 6.2.6). The 'squash' from context (1697) was also mostly organic detritus with some inorganic material. Twenty-one rather poorly preserved *Trichuris* eggs (again, all missing both polar plugs) were seen. Maximum lengths (not including polar plugs) and widths were recorded for eleven of the eggs. A maximum length including polar plugs was calculated as before and their size range determined to be 49–60 microns long x 24–30 microns wide (Table 6.2.6). A single ?*Ascaris* egg was also noted.

The insect remains from three of the deposits (italicised above) were recorded in detail. Context (806) (Sample <5081>) gave a moderate-sized flot composed of bright to pale orange plant tissue and insect fragments. There were many pale filmy remains which floated and migrated in the dish during sorting, and insects were consequently hard to see and to catch. Preservation was recorded as E 3.5–5.0, mode 5.0 strong; F 1.5–3.5, mode 2.5 weak; trend to orange (then pale) 3–4, mode 4 strong. Insect remains were fairly numerous (141 individuals of thirty taxa of adult beetles, though their concentration was quite low, this assemblage being from a subsample of 5 kg). Three species dominated: *Omalium ?allardi* (45 individuals), *Aglenus brunneus* (21) and *Tipnus unicolor* (17). The first of these is a likely invader of foul matter in the pit itself. On the other hand, *T. unicolor* is regarded as characteristic of long-lived somewhat damp buildings. (It is discussed further below). The species is regarded as a typical component of 'house fauna'. It may have been attracted to the odour of faeces, however, and many of the other beetles found in this deposit may also have been drawn to the smell, although their small numbers suggest that they did not establish breeding populations. Many are again components of 'house fauna' (notably *Mycetaea hirta*, *Xylodromus concinnus*, *Atomaria* species, *Anobium ?punctatum*, *Ptinus ?fur*, *Cryptophagus* species: Kenward & Hall 1995; Carrott & Kenward 2001), so they may alternatively have been introduced in floor sweepings, together with a flea (represented by a head which was too decayed to name, but quite probably *Pulex irritans* Linnaeus, the human flea). The blind, burrowing *Aglenus brunneus* may have been a post-depositional invader (Kenward 1975), together with *Trechus ?micros* and *Rhizophagus* sp (quite possibly *R. parallelocollis* Gyllenhal). This deposit yielded single specimens of the saw-toothed grain beetle *Oryzaephilus surinamensis* and the grain weevil *Sitophilus granarius*. Fly puparia, often very abundant in latrine deposits, were not particularly common. A characteristic *Ptinus* (spider beetle) pronotum could not be matched to any of the British species, having characteristics reminiscent of a cross between *P. fur* (Linnaeus) and *P. sexpunctatus* Panzer, but with very strongly developed lateral processes.

A smallish flot was obtained from (1635). It yielded quite large numbers of insect remains, including 196 adult individuals of 44 beetle taxa. Many remains were very decayed and typically pale orange, however, although in some cases with the wings of beetles still in place on the underside of the elytra: this sort of preservation suggests recent *in situ* decay of fossils which were formerly in excellent condition. Preservation was recorded as: E 3.5–5.5, mode 4.5 strong; F 1.5–3.5, mode 2.0 weak; trend to orange (then pale) 2–4, mode 4 strong. One taxon dominated the assemblage, an aleocharine staphylinid (111 individuals, although perhaps a compound taxon since Aleocharinae are very difficult even to divide into types when poorly preserved). This cannot be ecologically categorised, though many aleocharines are found in decaying matter of some kind. Of the remaining species, *Carpelimus bilineatus* (twelve) is rather typical of cess pit fills (although found in other kinds of deposits and, in nature, found in waterside litter: Kenward & Allison 1994; Kenward & Hall 1995). As in the case of the other deposits discussed here, *Aglenus brunneus* (nine) may have invaded post-depositionally, an hypothesis supported by records of *Trechus ?micros* and *Rhizophagus* sp. Most of the remaining fauna was composed of house fauna (eg *Xylodromus concinnus*, *Tipnus unicolor* and a *Cryptophagus* species, all with five individuals) and a few species found in fairly to very foul matter, although their numbers were small. There was a single grain weevil, *Sitophilus granarius*. A notable record was of the weevil *Apion ?genistae*, found in Britain on *Genista*, usually *G. anglica*, according to Morris (1990), but just possibly brought with the gorse recorded during the botanical analysis. The *Micrambe* recorded may be *M. villosus* Heer; Coombs & Woodroffe (1955) give no ecological data for this species, but the closely related *M. vini* Panzer is usually found on broom and gorse.

Context (1697) gave a quite large flot which contained moderate numbers of insect remains (although at a low concentration in the original sample material), many of which were strongly decayed and orange or pale (E 3.0–5.0, mode 4.0 weak; F 2.0–5.0, mode 2.5, weak; trend to pale/orange 2–4, mode 3 weak). The paraffin floatation process appears to have failed (*cf* Sample <5161>, context (1632)), as when part of the washover was checked it was found to contain appreciable numbers of fossils. It was, however, impractical to recover and record all of these remains, but the listed assemblage reflects the character of the whole well enough. Here, *Omalium ?allardi* (eleven individuals) appears to have colonised the pit fill, with a few other beetles which may have been attracted to foul matter and very large numbers of fly puparia of various kinds, doubtless breeding in rotting waste. The only other abundant species were house fauna components: *Tipnus unicolor* (17) and *Xylodromus concinnus* (11). How these entered the pit fill is not clear, though *T. unicolor* has occasionally been found in cesspits in abundance, perhaps living in the structure above the pits or attracted by faecal odours (*see* below). There was a single grain weevil, *Sitophilus granarius*, and one *Oryzaephilus surinamensis*. *Cercyon depressus*, typically found in stranded wrack and similar salt-soaked material, but also found in a sample from Phase V at this site, was represented by at least three individuals in this subsample.

Shell

Three Phase VI deposits gave traces of eggshell: contexts (37), (671) and (785).

A small assemblage (total weight 500 g) was recovered of hand-collected shell rather similar to that from Phase V; again it was thinly and evenly distributed through twenty-one contexts. The remains were rather poorly preserved (average erosion: 2.5; average fragmentation: 2.43) and mostly of oyster valves (twenty-two, seven of which, 32%, showed evidence for having been opened by humans), Small amounts of mussel (eleven valves) and cockle (six) were also recorded.

Fish bone

In total, nineteen deposits, mainly fills of rubbish or cess pits, produced 1551 identified fish bone fragments. The largest accumulations of fish bone were from a series of sixteenth-century fills from cess pit (487) (contexts (785), (791), (797), (798), (806)), and from context (1697), the primary fill cess pit (1624). The last produced the greatest quantity of identified remains from all phases from a single deposit. Two other contexts from this phase, (1635), the fill of pit (1653) in Plot 2, and (1702), the fill of gully (1703) in Plot 3, were also notable for their fish bone content.

Preservation of the fish remains was varied, and, in general terms, reflected the type of deposit from which they were recovered. Bones from cess pit fills tended to be quite fragmented and of rather battered appearance; this was particularly noticeable within the material from (1697). The assemblages from cess pit (487), however, were less fragmented and the remains from (798) were well preserved and included quantities of fish scales. Several herring and flatfish vertebrae recorded from (791), (798) and (1697) were crushed, characteristic damage associated with ingestion and passage through the human gut. These remains are likely to originate from faecal material

For this phase, numerically, eel provided a large component of the assemblage (39%), but both flatfish (including flounder, plaice, sole and turbot) and herring remains were numerous (30% and 21% respectively). On the basis of frequency of occurrence, flatfish become the most significant group, occurring in seventeen of the nineteen samples examined, whilst herring were present in thirteen and eel were recovered from ten. Other taxa present within the assemblages from this phase were gadid (mostly whiting), thornback ray, smooth hound, smelt, anchovy, conger eel, salmonid, cyprinid, stickleback and weever. Only the first three groups provided more than a few fragments.

Ill 6.2.2 shows that the relative frequencies of the various species or family groups differed between deposits, and some correlation with particular context types was observable. Eel remains were strongly represented in contexts (806) and (1697). These were both primary cesspit fills and the predominance of eel may be the result of the presence of a large component of faecal material within these deposits. The prevalence of flatfish remains representing all parts of the fish skeleton within contexts such as (791), (1635) and (1702) may suggest that these deposits were formed by the accumulation of more general domestic refuse, including kitchen and/or table waste. Context (1635) also included a larger number of gadid remains (mostly whiting) than was seen in other deposits, represented by elements other than just vertebrae, again suggesting domestic waste. In contrast to these deposits, the assemblage from (785) was dominated by herring. Vertebrae were abundant but not exclusive and a range of other skeletal elements was represented. A detailed examination of skeletal representation for herring suggested that there was an absence of cleithra and other fragments representing the appendicular skeleton. This may suggest that the herring had been gutted and that the remains represent cured rather than fresh fish. The profusion of herring vertebrae may indicate the presence of faecal matter within this deposit but, given that skeletal elements representing the head were also recorded, this may not necessarily be the case.

Most of the fish represented in these deposits were small, with flatfish ranging between 20 and 35 cm in overall length. Whiting and small gadid remains represented individuals between 10 and 25 cm in length, with a larger whiting, of approximately 55 cm, recorded from context (37). Larger fish, including ling and cod (with estimated overall lengths of around 1 metre) were also identified, mainly from the hand-collected material. The latter also included several flatfish bones from bigger individuals.

Coprolite

A single coprolite recovered from (442), the lower fill of cess pit (430) in Plot 3, contained substantial amounts of small bone fragments and was most probably of dog. No parasite eggs were recorded from the 'squash' subsample to support this theory. However, crushed fish bone was noted in this cess pit fill and the possibility that the coprolite was of human faecal material cannot be excluded.

Phase VII

Plant remains

A total of twenty contexts, (26), (31), (237), (245), (455), (463), (464), (<u>489</u>), (670), (1505), (1513), (<u>1515</u>), (<u>1516</u>), (1558), (1599), (1607), (<u>1608</u>), (1695), (<u>1699</u>) and (1881), was examined for plant remains by means of bulk-sieved samples, and five were selected for post-assessment re-examination. Almost all were fills of pits or other features, with three samples representing each of pits (465) in Plot 2 and (1522), (1696) and (1807) in Plot 4.

There was a moderate range of identifiable taxa in washovers otherwise largely dominated by cinders with coal and charcoal. Some assemblages rich in small fruit seeds, mainly fig, elder and blackberry, were noted, and there were several records of charred (and sometimes also uncharred) remains of gorse, as in the previous phase. Some of the deposits evidently contained an element deriving from faecal material, having some mineral-replaced plant macrofossils (but only one case with tentatively identified faecal concretions). Small numbers of charred cereals were also noted and there was a modest variety of weed seeds. A plant likely to have been cultivated or used as an ornamental locally was box (*Buxus sempervirens*) (leaf fragments from the primary fill of pit (1506) in Plot 4), other 'useful' plants including hops (*Humulus lupulus*) (moderately frequent in a fill in pit (1807), some of the material being mineral-replaced). The remains of hop seem unlikely to represent anything other than brewing, although they were found together with remains of fruits which otherwise suggest the deposition of food or faecal waste. There was also a tentatively identified specimen of a seed which appeared to be purslane (*Portulaca oleracea*), a non-British plant introduced from warm temperate or tropical areas and perhaps cultivated (presumably as the subspecies *sativa*) as early as 1200

(Preston *et al* 2002). Clement and Foster (1994) list it as an alien brought with bird-seed, wool, cotton, or tan-bark, when occurring in parts of the British Isles other than Scilly today. The fossil, if correctly named, probably represented an imported seed rather than a seed originating in a plant which grew in the city. Intriguingly, this plant has also been recorded, tentatively, from post-medieval (seventeenth– eighteenth-century) deposits in Dublin (Hall *et al* 2005) and would perhaps come to be a typical plant for the period were more deposits with good preservation to be examined.

Shell

Context (1513), a fill of stone-lined pit (1522) in Plot 2 gave traces of eggshell. The same deposit, as well as (237) and (1607), also gave small amounts of other (mainly marine) shell remains. The ?midden deposit, (1513), gave the greatest quantity of shell (340 g of heavily eroded and fragmented oyster) from a 60-litre sample. (1607), the fill of pit (1696) in Plot 3, yielded a single oyster valve (again heavily eroded and fragmented) from 30 litres. The ?cultivation deposit in Plot 1, ((237), Sample <5006>) gave remains of two rather poorly preserved oyster valves (one left and one ?right, the shell being heavily eroded and soft) and small shell fragments (including one fragment identifiable as cockle) from an 80-litre sample. In addition, a trace of unidentified land snail shell was recovered from (464).

Just over six kilogrammes of hand-collected shell were recovered from Phase VII deposits. Preservation was poor (average erosion: 2.86; average fragmentation: 2.59) and the remains were predominantly of oyster (171 valves, 30% of which showed evidence of having been opened by humans). Other edible marine taxa included periwinkle (six individuals) and cockle (five valves) and two flat periwinkles and a single top shell were also recorded. A little evidence of damage to the oyster valves by other marine taxa was noted in the form of polychaet worm burrows (on fourteen valves) and encrusted barnacles (on five valves). The remains were, in the main, rather thinly distributed between the forty-two shell-bearing deposits of this phase. Concentrations of remains were apparent in several pit fills, however. Contexts (463) and (464), fills of pit (465) in Plot 2; (1560), a pit in Plot 4; and (1601) and (1604), fills of rubbish pit (1807) in Plot 3, all gave larger numbers of edible shellfish valves, indicating disposal of food waste into these features.

Fish bone

Most of the nineteen deposits from which fish remains were recovered were from the fills of cess and rubbish pits, with some remains from two cultivation soils. Identified fish bone from this phase amounted to 719 fragments, the greatest quantities of remains coming from four groups of deposits: cultivation soils (237) and (663) in Plot 1; (463), (464) and (489), fills of cess pit (465) in Plot 2; (1505), (1513) and (1558), fills of the stone-lined cess pit (1522 in Plot 4; and the fills associated with horncore-lined pit (1807) and pit (1696) in Plot 4: contexts (1608), (1699) and (1881) and (1599), (1607) and (1695) respectively.

As with material from the previous phase, preservation was, to some extent, determined by context type. Material from the cultivation soils was recorded as being of fair preservation, although the bones were somewhat fragmented. Fish bones from the cess and rubbish pit fills were mostly very fragmented and battered in appearance. This was particularly true for the remains from (1513) and (1558), whilst material from (1607) was described as being of poor preservation. However, fish bones from the fills of cess pit (465) were well preserved, although the remains were not as numerous.

Distortion of some of the smaller vertebrae (including herring, smelt, small gadid, small conger and flatfish) was noted from several of the deposits ((31), (1513), (1588) and (1607)), including the cultivation soil (237). This damage is likely to be evidence of ingestion and passage through the digestive system and indicates the probable presence of faecal material within these deposits.

A quite diverse range of species was recovered from this phase, with many similarities to the assemblages recovered from Phase VI deposits. Overall, proportions of the main species (flatfish, eel and herring) were also similar to Phase VI, although the proportion of remains of eel decreased from 39% to 27%. Flatfish formed the largest component of the assemblage (30%), with herring providing 22%. Additionally, an increase in the remains of both gadidae and smelt was apparent. Gadidae remains largely comprised whiting, mostly small individuals.

Flatfish were identified from all nineteen of the samples examined; this corresponds with the numerical dominance of this group of taxa. Although eel remains were the next most numerous species represented, both herring and gadids occurred more frequently, in seventeen and fifteen of the deposits respectively. This perhaps gives a more accurate picture of the importance of the main species, given that eels are probably over represented since they have approximately twice the number of vertebrae of other fish.

Anchovy, first recorded in the previous phase, were slightly more numerous from these deposits, whilst salmonid remains (including trout and salmon), although not common, were also present. Other taxa identified included thornback ray, conger eel and Cyprinidae, together with a single fragment identified as weever. The hand-collected assemblage produced a further 147 fragments (including ribs, finrays, spines and pterigiophores) which included the remains of at least two cyprinids, of which some skeletal elements showed similarities with those of roach. Cod, ling, sea bass, salmon, turbot and carp were also present within this assemblage typically representing larger individuals than found in the sieved material.

When considered in more detail, some similarities were apparent between assemblages from the different context types (Ill 6.2.3). Generally, eel remains dominated the larger cess pit fill assemblages, eg (489), although different fills from the same feature varied and eels were not prevalent in all fills. Eel bones also provided 52% of the identified remains from (1607), one of the fills (described as being a 'green cessy' fill) within rubbish pit (1696). The high concentration of eel vertebrae (also herring and smelt in some of the deposits such as cess pit fill (1513)) is likely to indicate that these deposits contained a component originating from faecal matter. Crushed and distorted vertebrae, as seen in these deposits and in the cultivation deposits, are also suggestive of faecal materi-

al. In the case of the cultivation soils, this component may perhaps derive from night soil.

It is clear that cess was not the only source of the fish remains. Within the two cultivation soils (237) and (663) flatfish remains were the most frequently occurring fragments, and this was also the case for two of the fills ((1699) and (1695)) associated with the horncore pit and pit (1696), although these deposits only produced quite small assemblages. Flatfish remains were also recorded from the cess pit fills. These remains and those of thornback ray and larger flat fish (turbot) and gadids (as recorded from the hand-collected assemblages from (1601) and (1604) suggest the presence of more general rubbish from food preparation and table waste from consumption. Similarly, garden soil (455), rubbish pit fill (682) and cess pit fills (1193) and (1504) also produced hand-collected remains of larger specimens of fish such as turbot, ling, cod and salmon.

Skeletal element representation for the different species showed that, overall, vertebrae were the commonest element recorded. Regardless of context type, where herring, eel and smelt were identified, these taxa were almost exclusively represented by vertebrae, as were the small gadids, whiting and anchovy. However, for flatfish, cranial and appendicular elements were also relatively abundant and in some deposits (eg (237)), flatfish head bones were present in almost equivalent numbers to the vertebrae and, in one case, (1607), greater quantities.

Fish sizes varied but, generally, most of the fish represented in the deposits were small, including whiting and cod bones from individuals of an estimated tail length of between 15 and 20 cm. However, from (1513) there were several cod caudal vertebrae (probably from the same fish) which represented a far larger fish which must have been greater than a metre in overall length. Hand-collected remains included several cod and ling vertebrae which were from fish of a similar size ((682) and (1504)), together with a number of large gadid finrays and ribs from (1107). Flatfish ranged in size from around 20 cm to around 40 cm in length, with those fragments from the cultivation soil representing individuals between 18 and 25 cm. Hand-collected turbot remains from (455), (1601) and (1604), although rather fragmented, were clearly from somewhat larger fish, probably in the region of 100 cm in overall length.

Coprolite

A coprolite was recovered from the midden deposit, (1513). In common with the other coprolites recovered from the site, this was rich in small bone fragments and devoid of parasite eggs, and thought most likely to be of dog. *See* the *caveat* for the coprolite in Phase VI, however.

Phase VIII

Plant remains

Plant material from seven contexts ((207), (223), (341), (515), (520), (559), and (1437)) was investigated *via* bulk-sieved samples. Two were 'layers', the rest fills of features, with pit (519) being represented by two samples. None were thought worthy of further analysis subsequent to the assessment. Overall, the washovers had a rather similar composition to those from Phase VII, with cinders predominating, some coal and charcoal, and plant remains mainly comprising seeds of fig, elder and blackberry with small numbers of charred cereals.

Shell

This phase gave the largest hand-collected shell assemblage (total weight 6536 g), once again mostly of oyster valves (118) with traces of other edible taxa (including periwinkle, mussel, scallop and cockle; the last represented by twenty-five valves). Preservation was rather poor (average erosion: 2.6; average fragmentation: 2.28), but evidence of polychaet worm burrowing was visible on thirteen of the oyster valves and eroded barnacles visible on four. Evidence of the oysters having been opened using a knife (or similar) was recorded on twenty-three (19%) of the valves. A single *Helix* sp land snail was also recovered. Concentrations of remains were noted in two of the pit fills, (1406) and (1645), and in two layers, (1636) in Plot 1 and (1837) in Plot 2, but otherwise shell was rather sparsely distributed between thirty-five contexts.

Traces of unidentified land snail shell were recovered from context (341) in Plot 6.

Fish bone

Seven deposits produced a fish bone assemblage that amounted to 341 identified fragments. Of these remains, 40% were recovered from (1437), a fill of pit (1438) in Plot 3, whilst smaller assemblages came from (207), (223), (341), (515), (520) and (559); these included pit fills, occupation and cultivation deposits.

Preservation of the remains from this phase was, in general, good. Material from (207) and (1437) was somewhat fragmented and all the bone fragments from these deposits were small in size. Several vertebrae (of smelt, herring and eel), mainly from (1437), but including one from (559), had a crushed appearance, damage indicative of ingestion.

Taken as a whole, 43% of the identified fish assemblage was flatfish remains, with herring providing 24% and eel 18%. Other than the three main species, a number of other taxa were identified. These included gadid (mainly whiting), thornback ray, anchovy, cyprinid, conger and bass from (559), and perch from (314). A small number of scales that were probably perch were also recovered from this deposit. Additional species included ling from (341), cod from (1684) and salmon from (1871); all were identified from the hand-collected assemblage.

Individually, most of the smaller assemblages followed this general pattern, with flatfish remains occurring most frequently. However, a somewhat different pattern was observed from the material from (1437). Eel bones dominated this assemblage (34%), although flatfish were almost as numerous, forming 29% of the remains. Herring, at 17%, was rather less abundant than in this group of contexts taken as a whole (24% for the phase overall), whilst whiting and smelt contributed 11% and 6% respectively. Given the presence of high frequencies of eel vertebrae (and to a lesser extent, herring and smelt), and given that a number of these vertebrae showed evidence of having been eaten, it is likely that this deposit was composed largely of cess or faecal material.

Over 70% of the fragments from this phase were vertebrae. However, flatfish were typically represented by a range of skeletal elements, although generally vertebrae

were prevalent. The flatfish bones from (1437) were the exception, with 70% of fragments representing the head or appendicular skeleton rather than the vertebral column.

The fish represented in the deposits were again all fairly small with several herring vertebrae being from young individuals. Some of the whiting vertebrae, when compared with modern reference specimens, were from fish with a tail length of approximately 15 cm. Flatfish varied in size from 25 to 40 cm.

Phase IX

Plant remains

Although fifteen contexts ((*206*), (208), (217), (325), (352), (353), (375), (384), (451), (507), (545), (546), (547), (1387), and (1486)) were represented by samples for this phase, only one was thought appropriate for further analysis of plant remains following the assessment (but the washover from it could not, in the event, be relocated). All but three of the fifteen contexts were feature fills, with a slot, (544) in Plot 6, being represented by three of the samples. Washovers were rich in cinders and charcoal (both oak and ash being identified), and contained quite a diversity of identifiable plant remains, especially elder, fig and blackberry seeds, though usually in small numbers. There were also a few charred remains of hazel nutshell, barley, oat and wheat grains (including cultivated oat and bread/club wheat) and a single record of rather large numbers of tomato (*Lycopersicon esculentum*) seeds (from pit fill (451) in Plot 2). Other probable food plants present in very small numbers were strawberry, field bean, sloe and ?pea, with some part-charred rye rachis fragments perhaps originating in straw rather than grain. Fragments of heather shoot, some of them charred, from hearth (208) in Plot 1 might represent the use of this plant in various ways, perhaps most likely as fuel given the context; another possibility (given the later date and city-centre location) is that these fragments were debris from heather besoms (brooms). Also in this deposit were traces of tentatively identified box leaves, whilst (206), the fill of pit (205) in Plot 1, yielded traces of tentatively identified holly leaf. A single large solanaceous seed tentatively identified as thorn-apple, *Datura stramonium*, from (352) in Plot 6, is perhaps simply from a plant growing as a weed or garden plant.

Insect remains

The insect assemblage from (206) was fully recorded. The flot was of moderate size, but consisted primarily of yellow scraps of cuticle, brown 'felt' which consisted of fungal hyphae, and 'char'. The fossils were generally very poorly preserved, and tended to disintegrate when handled (E 3.5–5.0, mode 5.0 distinct; F 2.5–5.5, modes 3 and 5, distinct; trend to orange 3–4, mode 4 strong). The washover contained a few beetle remains, and abundant cuticular fragments which were probably mostly of cockroach (although no good diagnostic parts were seen, in contrast to the remains from the flot). Rather few adult beetles were found (twenty-two individuals of twelve taxa). There were also some insect larvae. Much the most numerous beetle was the golden spider beetle, *Niptus hololeucus* (probably a fairly recent introduction: *see* below, Discussion), and the only other species represented by more than one individual was a *Cryptophagus.* This limited fauna appears to point to a protected situation with direct access to a building. Such a conclusion is supported by the presence of remains of at least two individuals of the 'oriental' cockroach, *Blatta orientalis,* a warmth-demanding alien, again discussed below.

Shell

A trace of eggshell was recovered from (353), and the ash pit fill (208) in Plot 1 gave a small amount of cockle shell representing perhaps as many as five individuals and a single fragment of mussel shell from a sixty-litre sample. Additionally, traces of unidentified land snail shell were recovered from (353) and (375) gave a single *Vitrea* sp.

A total of 3763 g of hand-collected shell was recovered from the Phase IX deposits. The remains were almost entirely of poorly preserved (average erosion: 2.38; average fragmentation: 2.28) edible shellfish: oyster (126 valves), cockle (forty-four valves) and mussel (seventeen valves). A little damage from polychaet worm burrowing was noted on six of the oyster valves, with eroded barnacles noted on another. Evidence of the oysters having been opened by humans was recorded on one-third of the valves. Forty-eight deposits from this phase gave some hand-collected shell, mostly as a few oyster valves (and occasional other remains) per context. Slightly larger quantities of shell were recovered from three layers, (344), (1096) and (1187) and from (553), the fill of a boundary ditch in Plot 6.

Fish bone

Material from twelve deposits (mostly pit fills) was examined, and 320 fish bone fragments were identified. Most remains from this phase were well preserved, although material from (352), (1387) and (1486) was rather fragmented and of battered appearance. Approximately 10% of all the fish bone recovered from (352) was burnt. This phase included material from a number of deposits which possibly included reworked material. These included the fills of two features that had been dug for the specific purpose of burying animals (two cats and a dog). Most of the fish bones were recovered from (217), a layer in Plot 1; (352), (507) and (545), pit and gully fills in Plot 6; and (1486) a pit fill in Plot 5.

Total fragment counts for this phase showed that flatfish were the predominant species (44%), followed by herring (29%), eel (14%), smelt (9%) and gadid (4%). As seen from other phases, taxa such as eel, smelt and herring were typically well represented in cess pit fills and were often represented almost entirely by vertebrae. Material from (1486) showed these characteristics: eel and smelt remains contributed 78% of the assemblage from this deposit and were predominantly vertebrae. Very few fragments of other species were present, but a few flatfish and herring remains were identified, together with several vertebrae recorded as cyprinid, ?perch and ?whiting. Other deposits (eg (352), (507) and (545)) which produced assemblages of any size were mainly dominated by flatfish, including both plaice and flounder. One exception to this was the assemblage from (217) which consisted almost entirely of herring bones.

Overall, 69% of the skeletal elements identified were vertebrae. However, as seen throughout most of the medieval and post-medieval phases, flatfish were generally represented by a range of skeletal elements and this was also the case for this phase. In contrast to the herring remains where 75% were vertebrae, flatfish vertebrae amounted to 56% of the assemblage. Just over half of the flatfish remains from pit fill (545) were bones representing the oromandibular and hyoid region of the skeleton. There were fewer fragments from the appendicular skeleton and the branchial region, although two cleithra were recovered by hand collection.

Again, fish represented in these deposits were fairly small, with flatfish ranging in size from 25–40 cm, with one smaller individual of 15–20 cm.

Coprolite

A single coprolite was recovered from each of contexts (441), a ?tree bole pit fill, and (545), a pit fill. The presence of numerous small bone fragments and absence of parasite eggs within these, together with the context types of the deposits from which they were recovered, suggested that they were most probably of dog.

Phase X

Plant remains

Plant material from three contexts, (60), (424), and (583), dated to this phase was examined: a cess pit fill (from the evaluation stage of the field project), a drain fill, and the fill of a negative feature. Cinders were prominent in each of the washovers but identifiable plant remains were restricted to a few specimens of fig, grape, blackberry and raspberry, and with one record of tomato seeds.

Shell

A small assemblage of land snails was recovered from a drain fill, (424). Most of the shells were too poorly preserved to be identifiable but the better preserved remains were tentatively identified as *Oxychilus* sp. A few or single unidentified land snails were also recovered from (341), (353), and (464), while (375) gave a single *Vitrea* sp shell.

A little over five kilogrammes of hand-collected shell was recovered from deposits of this phase. The remains were poorly preserved (average erosion: 2.61; average fragmentation: 2.45) and mostly of oyster (178 valves) with a few other edible shellfish represented (mussel: six valves; cockle: thirteen valves). Damage to the oyster valves caused by opening using a knife (or similar) was noted on 21% of these remains. There were traces of damage from polychaet worm burrowing on four of the oyster valves and of eroded barnacles on a fifth. The remains were mostly evenly distributed between thirty-five contexts but two concentrations were apparent in (301) and (1503).

Fish bone

Fish bone of early modern date was recovered from five deposits ((60), (424), (443), (583) and (599)). Identified remains totalled 43 fragments, most of which were from (599). Preservation of these remains was mostly good. The three main species, flatfish, herring and eel, were identified, together with three fragments recorded as whiting. Herring and eel were predominantly represented by vertebrae, whilst a wide range of skeletal elements was recorded for flatfish. Similar flatfish remains were present within the hand-collected assemblage recovered from (443). Material from this deposit probably represents a single fish. The assemblage from this phase was too small to be of much interpretative value.

Discussion

The deposits at 25 Bridge Street exhibited a very variable content of plant and invertebrate remains, with some sediments very rich, others barren of recognisable material (other than, for example, wood charcoal). While most of the insect remains were preserved by anoxic waterlogging, plant material included specimens preserved by charring and mineral replacement as well. The earlier deposits (Roman to early medieval) tended to have only charred material surviving, whilst mineral replacement was, not surprisingly, prevalent in the deposits of the earlier post-medieval phases where most of the contexts examined gave evidence for food waste, probably largely faecal. Preservation in some of the more superficial deposits appears to have been excellent until recently, decay probably having been initiated in the past decades by a falling water-table consequent upon development.

The post-medieval groups of plant and invertebrate remains from this site are particularly valuable as rare examples of usefully large assemblages from a period all too infrequently sampled, yet in which major changes in resource utilisation and trade resulted in the appearance of many new species, often from tropical or subtropical regions (cockroaches, for example). The importance of the material makes the possibility that it is currently decaying *in situ* particularly disturbing.

Assemblages of plant remains where there was good waterlogged preservation – from the late medieval to later post-medieval periods – tended to be dominated by small fruit seeds, especially grape, fig, and apple, but the deposits in which they occurred often contained a variety of other remains which had clearly not been eaten, such as the frequent remains of gorse, and which probably represented domestic waste. Although not always charred, such remains from combustible raw material of this kind seem likely to have arrived, with the abundant coal and cinders, from hearths and fireplaces, if not ovens. The abundant hop remains in one sample are not unexpected in a context of this later period: there are a few examples from other post-medieval towns and, indeed, hop has been recorded from late deposits in other parts of Chester (Hall *et al* 2002b). There were a few hints of the kinds of plants which might have been grown in gardens, notably box, holly and columbine, the shortness of the list perhaps reflecting the density of occupation in this part of the city at this period, ie these were stray remains from gardens further afield. Another feature of the deposits that emerged from the long chronological sequence available was the changing use of raw material for fuel reflected in the charred plant remains (as well as the coal and cinders from the sediment matrix in the later contexts). Thus there is some evidence for the use of peat in the early medieval period, whilst later on, when coal was clearly important, gorse was nevertheless also being brought into the town in quantity.

Insect and parasite remains
The insect assemblages from Bridge Street were remarka-

ble for their low mathematical and ecological diversity. This may partly be a result of their generally poor preservation and the consequent difficulty of identification of species represented by only few remains, but undoubtedly it primarily reflects a restricted insect fauna, in turn indicating a very restricted range of local habitats for invertebrates in the phases examined. This is very much in accord with the limited evidence from other towns yielding post-medieval deposits (eg at sites in Coffee Yard and The Bedern, York: Robertson *et al* 1989 and Hall *et al* 1993a–c). The presence of species which are certainly or probably of exotic origin (the 'oriental' cockroach and the golden spider beetle respectively) reflects the increasing level of overseas trade and the ever more artificial and protected nature of the urban living environment.

The records of *Cercyon depressus*, normally confined to the sea shore, are surprising. A parallel is provided by *Ptenidium punctatum*, a small beetle primarily also associated with seaweed on the strandline, but found in large numbers in some Anglo-Scandinavian layers at 6–8 Pavement, York, by Hall *et al* 1983, 191–2; *see* also Kenward (2000), who discuss its significance at length, concluding that it probably exploited some specialised kind of decaying matter on the site. Rather remarkably, the species was not found at the nearby, and one would have imagined very similar, 16–22 Coppergate site (Kenward & Hall 1995, 747).

Niptus hololeucus is rare in the archaeological record and deserves discussion. There are records from Roman and other pre-modern deposits (Buckland 1976a; b), but these appear to relate to contexts where there was clear evidence, or at least a distinct possibility, of recent contamination. The record given by Roeder (1899) is perhaps suspect, too, in view of its antiquity and subsequent nomenclatural changes. The beetle's biology and possible geographical origins are discussed by Howe and Burgess (1952) and Buckland (1976b). It is common today and particularly likely to occur as a contaminant in archaeological samples which have been stored poorly sealed (eg in polythene bags), since it is often found in the sort of building typically used for sample storage; HK has noted several such contaminants. It may be that *N. hololeucus* was only brought to Britain in the past few hundred years. Alternatively, as appears to have been the case for the grain pest taxa, it may have been introduced on more than one occasion, starting in the Roman period, and only have become firmly established in modern, often permanently, heated buildings. Records of numerous individuals from securely dated and sealed Roman deposits would allow the early introduction to be accepted, though whether or not it later became extinct rather than just very rare would be hard to establish. There are several records of *N. hololeucus* from deposits of mid-seventeenth-century or later date at The Bedern, York, where it was found in company with the bedbug, *Cimex lectularius*, and an unidentified cockroach (Hall *et al* 1993a–c), so it appears to have become well established by this stage. From Germany there are records of the golden spider beetle from the fifteenth–sixteenth century (Cymorek & Koch 1969; Koch 1970; 1971), providing a source for its spread to Britain.

Although entomologists have regarded its introduction as rather recent (perhaps during the sixteenth century according to Ragge 1965), the oriental cockroach *Blatta orientalis* has been found in late Roman deposits at Lincoln, a discovery of considerable significance (Carrott *et al* 1995; Dobney *et al* 1998). It probably died out after this, however. A much later record from The Bedern, York (mid-seventeenth century or later: Hall *et al* 1993c, 32) appears to be the only other from an archaeological deposit in Britain. This specimen was unfortunately not identified closely when it was originally discovered, and it has proved impossible to locate the material in store. It was probably *B. orientalis*.

The spider beetle *Tipnus unicolor* is often present in insect death assemblages recovered from archaeological sites in Britain, occasionally forming a substantial proportion of the fauna. There are marked inter-period differences in its abundance, however, for *T. unicolor* is frequent in Roman and later medieval (post-Conquest) assemblages, but barely known from the intervening periods. This time distribution may have considerable importance in relation to changing urban conditions, and conversely the beetle may be a significant indicator species. The present records fit neatly into the established pattern of abundance. It is hard to believe that the beetle would have lived in a moist cesspit, as suggested by Osborne (1981); specimens in such situations are considered by the present author to be likely to be strays from the closet above in the case of latrines, or introduced in floor sweepings, a view shared by Girling and Robinson (in Hayfield & Greig 1989, 58–9). It may, of course, have been attracted to the odour of faeces, which in its natural habitats would not have been so hazardous as in a cesspit.

The *Trichuris* eggs seen in the 'squash' samples examined from contexts (806) and (1697) were all rather poorly preserved (all were lacking both polar plugs). Comparison of the calculated size ranges for these eggs with data for modern trichurids indicated that the eggs seen were almost certainly of either *Trichuris trichiura* or *T. suis*, the whipworms of humans and pigs respectively, or perhaps of both. It is particularly difficult to distinguish these two species purely by examination of their eggs as the normal size range for the eggs of *T. trichiura* is a wholly contained subset of that for *T. suis*.

Only a single ?ascarid egg was seen in the 'squash' from context (1697). A low ratio of ascarid to trichurid eggs has been interpreted as indicative of human rather than pig faeces (Taylor 1955), but this is not conclusive. Context (806) was interpreted as a cess pit fill and, as such, rather more likely to contain eggs of human parasites than those of pigs, though both it and the cess pit fill (1697) could perhaps contain faecal material of mixed origins.

The presence of the parasite eggs clearly indicates that faecal material formed a component of these deposits. However, their fairly poor state of preservation, together with the difficulties of identification outlined above, rendered a definitive determination of the source of the faecal content impossible, although the range of possible hosts indicated was limited to only humans and pigs.

No parasite eggs were found in the six coprolites examined *via* 'squash' subsamples. This, together with the presence of numerous bone fragments, suggested that the coprolites may be of dog faeces. However, in two cases the coprolites were recovered from a cess pit feature

(Phase VI (442)) and a midden (Phase VII (1513)) which also contained fish bone exhibiting damage characteristic of having passed through the human gut; for these the possibility that the coprolites may be of human origin cannot be excluded.

Most of the recovered shell was of edible shellfish from deposits of mid- to late seventeenth to twentieth-century date (Phases VII to X) but remains were recovered from most phases of the site. Oyster was by far the most commonly represented taxon with other edible marine taxa (eg cockle, mussel, and periwinkle) present in small numbers, again mostly concentrated in the later phases of the site. The other marine invertebrates represented were, with a few exceptions, other edible species commonly occurring off the coasts of Britain.

The bias of the recovered shell towards edible taxa (particularly oyster), together with the evidence of shells having been opened using tools, strongly suggests that these assemblages derived almost exclusively from human food waste, although this apparently never formed a significant component of the diet of the inhabitants of this site through the ages.

The most likely sources for the oysters from Phase VI and later were perhaps beds around the coast of Wales. Large quantities of both oyster and cockle were taken off Caernarvonshire in 1712; oysters were abundant on the east coast of Anglesey by the middle of the eighteenth century; there was a healthy trade oyster trade at Pwllheli (Cardigan Bay), and the oyster beds of Mumbles (Swansea Bay) were among the most prolific in Britain by the late seventeenth century (Starkey *et al* 2000, 88–9). Another relatively nearby supply of oysters would be Cornwall, though they had been traded widely from the Roman period so sources further afield (eg the Kent, Essex or Sussex coasts) are not necessarily ruled out. Most of the remains were from deposits of mid- to late seventeenth to twentieth-century date and certainly by the mid-nineteenth century oysters were being dredged in huge numbers all along the Sussex coast (to the point of exhausting the beds).

It seems likely that all of the remains of other edible marine taxa were also derived from human food waste, the extremely small number of non-edible species having been collected accidentally. All of these taxa are common off the coast of Britain today.

The land snail remains recovered were too few to be of any interpretative value.

Throughout, mostly marine or migratory fish were identified, with flatfish, herring and eel remains forming the bulk of the fish bones from most periods. Numerical dominance between these taxa fluctuated between phases, but, on fragment counts alone, they appeared to form the basis of the fish component of the diet of the inhabitants of this area of Chester from the Late Roman period through to the twentieth century. Gadids, although never present in any great quantities, became more prolific from Phase VI onwards, whilst rays consistently occurred throughout, albeit in quite small numbers. Rays are cartilaginous and are almost certainly under-represented (such tissue rarely surviving). Remaining taxa, with the exception of smelt, were represented by relatively few remains.

Generally, the fish remains from all phases represented waste from food. Some of the deposits produced refuse which was likely to be from the preparation of fish for cooking, whilst other deposits provided direct evidence for consumption. No material was recovered which was indicative of commercial waste from the processing of fish.

The fish remains are discussed further by period below.

Phases I and II: The fish assemblages from Phases I and II were rather small for detailed interpretative analysis and came from only a few deposits; they are not necessarily a representative sample from which to extrapolate the dietary preferences of the inhabitants of Chester during the Roman period. However, some of the remains were worthy of note.

The presence of the remains of Spanish mackerel was of some interest. During the Roman period, this Mediterranean fish was typically salted and transported in amphorae throughout the Roman empire (Van Neer & Lentacker 1994). Its presence, therefore, suggests the import into Chester of a Roman delicacy which would imply either a Mediterranean origin for some of the inhabitants or local residents adopting expensive Roman tastes. Confirmation of the import of such fish comes from an inscription on the side of an amphora recovered from Chester. This stated that the content was a sauce from Baetica (Southern Spain) made from mackerel tails (Alcock 2001). Although not common, this species has been identified from other sites in Britain. Some examples include six Spanish mackerel heads identified from a first-century amphora from excavations at Winchester Palace, Southwark (Locker 1994), whilst several pre-caudal vertebrae were identified from a late third-century well deposit at Great Holts Farm, Boreham, Essex (Murphy *et al* 2000).

Another species found only in Phases I and II was mullet, those fragments from Phase II possibly being more closely identified as thin-lipped grey mullet. This marine fish has also been recovered from Roman deposits at Colchester (Alcock 2001), Silchester (Boon 1974) and Dorchester (Hamilton-Dyer 1993), although the remains at the latter were identified as golden grey mullet. Whether these fish and those recovered from Chester arrived as fresh fish or had been salted/pickled cannot be established.

Phases III and IV: Deposits of late Saxon and early medieval date did not produce particularly large assemblages of fish. The range of species represented was small, with flatfish remains being predominant. The flatfish, eels and smelt could have been caught in estuarine waters, whilst the few gadid remains, mainly small whiting, could also have been caught in inshore waters. It is not impossible that herring were of local origin, although there is some evidence from other sites of Anglo-Saxon date of small-scale trade in herring, eg Fishergate, York (O'Connor 1991). However, in general, assemblages of this date appear to represent the exploitation of local fish resources in rivers and estuaries (eg Flixborough, North Lincolnshire: Dobney *et al* 2007; Melbourne Street, Southampton: Bourdillon & Coy 1980) with little evidence for extensive trade in fish during the eighth–eleventh centuries (Enghoff 2000). Trade in fish within Chester during the Anglo-Saxon and early medieval periods, therefore, was possibly not well established

or not particularly important for the economy of the settlement.

Phase V: Phase V showed many similarities with Phases III and IV, with a limited suite of species and very few gadid remains. In contrast to the previous periods, and indeed to the later ones, this period was dominated by the remains of herring. However, although herring was identified in nine of the thirteen deposits examined, over 60% of the bones were from a single deposit and its importance in this assemblage may therefore be somewhat exaggerated.

Phases VI and VII: Deposits of these phases produced the greatest accumulation of fish bones and, as in the earlier periods, herring, eel and flatfish were well represented. However, the contribution of both herring and eel to the late medieval–early post-medieval diet is likely to be biased since a large proportion of the fish bones were recovered from cess pit fills. Remains from this type of deposit can potentially represent material that has been subject to highly selective disposal processes. Within some of these deposits, herring and eel remains were represented almost exclusively by vertebrae, a small proportion of which showed characteristic damage associated with ingestion and passage through the gut. These remains most likely derived from faecal material. The presence of other species also appeared to be linked to the occurrence of cess. These tended to be small fish such as smelt, or in one or two cases, small gadids such as whiting, which were, perhaps, eaten whole. Anchovy was also identified, although not in any great quantities. Again these species were typically represented by vertebrae. The preponderance of this element is probably a taphonomic factor related to preservation, ie, only the most dense and robust elements are capable of surviving the rigours of mastication and digestion. Despite this concentration of small fish remains, some of the cesspit deposits clearly contained waste of a more general domestic nature from the preparation of fish for consumption and table refuse. This was represented by the remains of flatfish and small fragments of bones probably from larger gadids. The numerous spines, finrays, pterigiophores and other remains which mostly could not be identified more closely also represented waste from filleting and trimming and removing fins and tails.

A similar assemblage was recovered from the fill of a seventeenth-century cesspit in Antwerp, Belgium (Veeckman *et al* 2000). The range of species identified was somewhat more diverse than that recovered from the site at Bridge Street but included the remains of herring, eel, smelt, anchovy and flatfish. Characteristic of the assemblage was the presence of small individuals, although some cod bones from larger fish, probably from stockfish, were also present. Additionally, marine shell and remains of crustaceans, such as shrimp and prawn, a few bird and mammal bones (mainly small shaft fragments) were identified. The researchers concluded that these were remains from a variety of sources which included household refuse, faecal material and possibly from cleaning fishing nets (*op cit*). It was suggested that large organic remains (which take time to rot down) were not deposited in the cess pit so that the contents could be more easily reused as compost. Given that a number of the cultivation soils from Bridge Street contained remains which appeared to derive from faecal matter then the reuse of cess pit fills may also have occurred here.

Gadidae, both large (eg ling and large cod), and small (eg whiting and small cod) also provided components of the fish assemblage, with whiting generally providing the bulk of these remains. Their contribution in the earlier phases was small, but an increase in the frequency of gadids and other offshore marine species (eg thornback ray) can be seen from Phase VI, although their relative abundance appears small in comparison to the three main fish taxa.

Bones from larger gadids, such as cod and ling, were mainly restricted to the hand-collected material from this period and were not particularly numerous. Large cod and ling are found in more northerly deeper offshore waters and the remains identified as these species are likely to represent imported fish which had been dried and salted, pickled or smoked or a combination of these. Since all the ling bones and most of the larger cod bones identified from the site were vertebrae, this strongly suggests that these fish represented stockfish (ie they had been cured). The absence of cranial elements, as found here, is usually an indicator of stored rather than fresh fish: the heads of fish would have been removed at the processing site prior to salting or drying. Several of the vertebrae and neural spines had been chopped, and knife marks were also occasionally evident on these bones. The increased presence of gadid remains at this period probably reflects the growth of coastal fisheries and the expansion of trading networks.

Archaeological evidence from other sites, mainly on the east coast of Britain, suggests that the market for cod and related fish gradually increased from the eleventh century onwards (Enghoff 2000) and a large proportion of this was likely to be imported stock/store fish (Locker 2001a). The fish remains from Bridge Street suggest that the importation of cod and ling from deep sea fisheries occurred at a slightly later period (ie late fifteenth–mid-seventeenth centuries) than at sites on the east coast of England, such as King's Lynn (Wheeler 1977), Yarmouth (Wheeler and Jones 1976) and Newcastle (Nicholson 1989), where remains of large gadids were identified from deposits of the eleventh–thirteenth centuries (for the first two sites) and thirteenth-fourteenth centuries. Assemblages of twelfth–seventeenth-century date recovered from tenements in Bristol (Locker 2001b) are similar to those from Chester, with large gadids appearing in the late fourteenth-century deposits. However, it may be that large gadids were consumed (or traded) in Chester earlier, but that it was not until the early post-medieval period that they became more readily available and, perhaps, less expensive. The data from Chester correlate well with documentary evidence showing that, whilst other more prosperous centres were struggling in the late medieval period, Chester's trade and population were expanding and the quantity of fish imported during this period surpassed all other imports (Kermode 1996). Ships from Ireland provided much of this, with records showing trade in cod, ling, whiting, dogfish, eel, herring and salmon (Starkey *et al* 2000; Kermode 1996). More extensive evidence is available from port and custom records of the fourteenth and fifteenth centuries from Bristol, a similar, although somewhat larger, port which suggest the impor-

tation of a vast array of fish including a variety of dried and salted gadids (Carus Wilson 1967).

Herring remains from this period probably also represent imported fish, given that documentary evidence indicates that tons of herring from Irish Sea fisheries (Kermode 1996) were shipped into Chester from Cumbria, Wales and Ireland. Irish herring were particularly important at Chester, although it was Bristol which was the key port for Irish fish in the late medieval period (Starkey *et al* 2000). In the late sixteenth and seventeenth centuries, the Welsh fishing industry used Chester more and more as a market and source of salt for curing herring (*op cit*). From the archaeological remains, however, distinguishing the bones of processed herring which had been imported from those of herring eaten fresh is not easy, particularly since herring were typically processed whole. Sometimes they were gutted prior to processing but this depended on the manner of curing. Where an under-representation of skeletal elements representing the appendicular region (ie cleithrum, supracleithrum and coracoid) is detected, then this may point to remains of herring which had been gutted and probably represent salted rather than fresh fish. The taphonomic bias in favour of vertebrae seen from the cess pit deposits, and those other contexts which possibly contained a high proportion of faecal matter, mostly obscured any attempts at interpretation of the skeletal element representation. A single Phase VI deposit, however, produced an assemblage which suggested that the herring represented may have been gutted.

Another significant import from Ireland into Chester during the fifteenth and sixteenth centuries was salmon (Starkey *et al* 2000). Salmonid remains, including some more specifically identified as salmon, were recovered from several deposits but were few in number. Salmon bones do not preserve very well and this species may be under-represented. Alternatively, imported salmon may have been destined for other markets or distributed throughout the region and not consumed within this area of the city: it was a valuable commodity which attracted twice the custom that was charged for herring imports (Kermode 1996) and may have been too expensive for most of the people in this part of Chester.

When one considers evidence for status at this period, besides the few salmon and turbot remains, there was little to suggest high-status occupation. Large gadids were becoming increasingly available during this period and the importation of stock fish was more commonplace; however, they still represented a resource which was not necessarily available to all (Woolgar 1999). It is also evident from the increased diversity of the species represented in this period that at least some of the inhabitants of Bridge Street in the early post-medieval period were relatively affluent. The prevalence of flatfish (likely to be primarily flounder and plaice) in the assemblage, however, suggests that inshore fishing provided a greater contribution to the diet than imported fish. Local fisheries were probably supplying fresh flatfish, smelt, whiting and other species which commonly frequented estuarine and shallow inshore waters. Estuarine and river weirs were common and evidence of fish traps is widespread around the Welsh shores (Godbold & Turner 1994). These are likely to have represented a cheaper resource than imported fish. Evidence for the exploitation of freshwater resources was scarce but, in the medieval period, the supply of freshwater fish was carefully controlled and their consumption was restricted to the wealthy aristocracy (Dyer 1988). Although small numbers of cyprinid remains were identified from deposits of this period, these contributed less than 1% of the entire assemblage.

On balance, the evidence suggests that the inhabitants of Bridge Street at this time were sufficiently affluent to purchase imported large fish (sometimes in excess of a metre in overall length), such as ling and cod, but relied more on the cheaper products, such as herring, flatfish, eel and whiting.

Phases VIII, IX and X: The fish assemblages from the later period were smaller but showed a similar range of species to those seen in Phases VI and VII. Overall, despite a slight reduction in the frequency of eel remains, flatfish, herring and eel were the most commonly occurring species. Data from Phases VIII and IX generally show a continuation of trends noted for the previous phases, but the remains from Phase X were few and insufficient for detailed analysis.

Despite the decline in trade through Chester as a result of the emerging dominance of the port at Liverpool (Kermode 1996), fish were still being imported, especially from the Welsh fisheries. Historical evidence suggests that during the nineteenth century fishing activity around the northern coasts of Wales was considerable and, in one case, it is documented that at various times of year a fleet of boats from Flintshire sailed up the River Dee to Chester with cargoes of mackerel, turbot, whiting and sole (Matheson 1929).

Acknowledgements

The authors are grateful to Dan Garner, Geoff Couling, Anthony Martin and Tim Malim, of Gifford and Partners Ltd, for providing the material and the archaeological information, and for their hospitality and support during site visits and project meetings.

Deborah Jaques would like to express particular thanks to Wim Van Neer and Wim Wouters of the Royal Museum for Central Africa, Tervuren, Belgium, for the generous manner in which they gave up their time and their help with identifications. DJ is also grateful to Alison Locker for supplying a number of her unpublished reports.

Allan Hall and Harry Kenward thank English Heritage and the University of York for support during their work on the material from this site.

6 Environmental remains/Plant, invertebrate and fish remains

Table 6.2.1 Plant taxa (and other components) quantified by phase
Note: The table shows numbers of contexts in which each was recorded by phase. Taxa marked '*' were only recorded in one or both of the samples from Phase VI deposits examined at PERU *(see text)*. Numbers are underlined where at least one of the records for that phase yielded more than trace amounts of the taxon/material concerned. Material was uncharred unless otherwise indicated. Nomenclature and taxonomic order follow Tutin *et al* (1964–80).
Abbreviations: frags—fragments; '?' indicates cases where the taxon was recorded tentatively; 'f' indicates cases where only one or more fragments was recorded; 's' for some records of charred cereal grains indicates that material included specimens showing evidence of sprouting.

			Phase									
			I	II	III	IV	V	VI	VII	VIII	IX	X
No contexts examined per phase			12	10	8	6	13	21	20	7	15	3
Vernacular	Taxon	Parts recorded										
Conifer	Coniferae	Charcoal frags	-	-	-	-	-	-	1	-	-	-
Conifer	Coniferae	Wood frags	-	-	-	-	1	-	-	-	-	-
Yew	*Taxus baccata* L.	Leaves	-	-	-	-	-	-	1+?1	-	-	-
Willow	*Salix* sp(p)	Buds	-	-	-	-	-	-	1	-	2	-
Willow/poplar/aspen	*Salix/Populus* sp(p)	Charcoal frags	-	-	-	-	1	-	-	-	-	-
Alder	*Alnus glutinosa* (L.) Gaertner	Charcoal frags	-	-	-	-	-	-	-	1	-	-
Hazel	*Corylus avellana* L.	Charred nuts and/ or nutshell frags	2	1	2	-	2	6	3	1	3	-
		Charred roundwood frags	-	-	3	-	-	-	-	-	-	-
		Nuts and/or nutshell frags	-	-	-	-	-	-	-	-	1	-
Oak	*Quercus* sp(p)	Charcoal frags	1	1	4	1	5	3	3	2	7	-
		Charred roundwood frags	-	-	-	-	-	1	1	-	-	-
Fig	*Ficus carica* L.	Seeds	-	-	1	-	_3_	14	_18_	6	9	3
Hop	*Humulus lupulus* L.	Achenes	-	-	-	-	-	-	1	-	-	-
		Mineralised achenes	-	-	-	-	-	-	1	-	-	-
Hemp	*Cannabis sativa* L.	Achenes	-	-	-	-	-	-	2	-	-	-
Stinging nettle	*Urtica dioica* L.	Achenes	-	-	-	-	-	1	-	-	4	-
Knotgrass	*Polygonum aviculare* agg	Charred fruits	-	-	-	-	-	-	1	-	-	-
		Fruits	-	-	-	-	-	-	-	1	-	-
Persicaria/red shank	*P persicaria* L.	Charred fruits	-	-	1	-	-	-	1	-	1	-
Persicarias	*P persicaria/lapathifolium*	Charred fruits	-	-	1	-	-	-	-	-	-	-
Black bindweed	*Bilderdykia convolvulus* (L.) Dumort	Charred fruits	-	1	2	-	-	-	1	-	-	-
		Fruits	-	-	-	-	-	-	3	-	-	-
Sheep's sorrel	*Rumex acetosella* agg	Charred fruits	-	-	-	-	-	-	1	-	-	-
		Fruits	-	-	-	-	-	1	-	-	-	-
Docks	*Rumex* sp(p)	Charred fruits	-	-	-	-	-	1	1	-	-	-
Fat hen	*Chenopodium album* L.	Charred seeds	-	-	3	-	-	-	_1_	-	-	-
		Seeds	-	-	-	-	1	1	-	-	2	-
Oraches	*Atriplex* sp(p)	Charred seeds	-	-	2	-	-	-	1	-	-	-
		Seeds	-	-	-	-	-	1	2	1	1	-
?Purslane	cf *Portulaca oleracea* L.	Seed	-	-	-	-	-	-	1	-	-	-
Chickweed	*Stellaria media* (L.) Vill.	Seeds	-	-	-	-	-	-	-	-	1	-
Corn spurrey	*Spergula arvensis* L.	Charred seeds	-	-	-	-	-	-	1	-	-	-
		Seeds	-	-	-	-	-	1	-	-	-	-
Corncockle	*Agrostemma githago* L.	Charred seeds	-	-	3	-	-	-	-	-	-	-
		Mineralised casts/ moulds of seed frags	-	-	-	-	-	1	-	-	-	-
		Seed frags	-	-	-	-	-	-	1	-	-	-
Small-flowered catchfly	*Silene gallica* L.	Seeds	-	-	-	-	-	-	1	-	-	-
Meadow/creeping/ bulbous buttercup	*Ranunculus* Section *Ranunculus*	Achenes	-	-	-	-	-	1	-	1	2	-
		Charred achenes	-	-	-	-	-	-	1	-	-	-
Columbine	*Aquilegia* cf *vulgaris* L.	Seeds	-	-	-	-	-	-	-	-	1	-
Fumitories	*Fumaria* sp(p)	Seeds	-	-	-	-	-	1	_3_	-	-	-
'Turnip'	*Brassica rapa* L.	Charred seeds	-	-	-	-	-	-	1	-	-	-
		Seeds	-	-	-	-	-	1	1+?1	-	-	-
Brassica/charlock	*Brassica* sp/*Sinapis arvensis* L.	Charred cotyledons	-	-	-	-	-	-	1	-	-	-
Wild radish	*Raphanus raphanistrum* L.	Pod segments and/or frags	-	-	-	-	-	-	-	1	-	-
Raspberry	*Rubus idaeus* L.	Seeds	?1	-	-	-	-	6	_6_	2	5	1
Blackberry/bramble	*R fruticosus* agg	Charred seeds	-	-	2	-	-	-	-	-	-	-
		Seeds	-	1	2	-	1	9	_13_	4	9+?1	1
Blackberry etc/rose	*Rubus/Rosa* sp(p)	Charred prickles	-	-	-	-	-	-	1	-	-	-
(?Wild) strawberry	*Fragaria* cf *vesca* L.	Achenes	-	-	-	-	-	2	-	-	_1_	-
(Crab) apple	*Malus sylvestris* Miller	Endocarp	-	-	-	-	-	-	1	-	-	-
		Immature seeds	-	-	-	-	-	-	1	-	-	-
		Limpet-shaped structures at seed base	-	-	-	-	-	-	1	-	-	-
		Mineralised seeds/embryos	-	1	-	-	-	2	3	1	-	-
		Seeds	-	-	-	-	-	1	_3_	-	-	-
Medlar	*Mespilus germanica* L.	Seed	-	-	-	-	-	1	-	-	-	-
Hawthorns	*Crataegus* sp(p)	Thorns	-	-	-	-	-	1	-	-	-	-
Sloe	*Prunus spinosa* L.	Charred fruitstones	-	-	-	-	-	-	-	-	1	-
		Fruitstones	-	-	-	-	-	1	1	-	-	-
?Sloe	cf *P spinosa* L.	Charred thorns	-	-	2	1	-	-	-	-	-	-
Plums, etc	*Prunus domestica* ssp *insititia*	Fruitstones	-	-	-	-	-	1	-	-	-	-
?Gean, wild cherry	*Prunus* cf *avium*	Fruitstones	-	-	-	-	-	1	-	-	-	-
Sloe/plum/cherry, etc	*Prunus* sp(p)	Charred fruitstones	-	-	-	-	-	-	1	-	-	-
		Mineralised seeds	-	-	-	-	-	1	-	-	-	-
Pea family	Leguminosae	Charred cotyledons	-	-	-	-	-	-	1	-	-	-
		Charred seeds	-	-	2	-	-	-	1	1	-	-
Gorses	*Ulex* sp(p)	Charred flower buds	-	-	-	-	-	2	2	-	-	-
		Part-charred flower buds	-	-	-	-	-	1	-	-	-	-
		Charred leaf/leaves (spines)	-	-	-	-	-	9	9	-	1	-
		Charred pods and/or pod frags	-	-	-	-	-	1	-	-	-	-
		Charred twig frags	-	-	-	-	-	7+?1	5+?1	-	-	-
		Leaf/leaves (spines)	-	-	-	-	-	-	3	_3_	-	-
		Leafy shoot frags	-	-	-	-	-	-	-	1	-	-
		Mineralised spines	-	-	-	-	-	1	-	-	-	-

Table 6.2.1 Plant taxa (and other components) quantified by phase (*continued*)

Vernacular	Taxon	Parts recorded	I	II	III	IV	V	VI	VII	VIII	IX	X
		Phase	12	10	8	6	13	21	20	7	15	3
		No contexts examined per phase										
Gorses	Ulex sp(p)	Mineralised twig frags	-	-	-	-	-	1	-	-	-	-
		Pods and/or pod frags	-	-	-	-	-	-	1	-	-	-
		Twig epidermis frags	-	-	-	-	-	-	1	-	-	-
Field bean	Vicia faba L.	Charred cotyledons	-	-	-	-	-	1	-	-	1	-
		Charred hilum/a	-	-	1	-	-	-	-	-	-	-
		Charred seeds	-	-	1	-	2	-	-	-	-	-
		Charred testa frags	-	-	2	-	-	-	-	-	-	-
?Vetches, etc	cf Vicia sp(p) (non faba)	Charred seeds	-	-	1	-	-	-	-	-	-	-
Garden/field pea	Pisum sativum L.	Charred seeds	-	-	?1	-	1	1	-	-	?1	-
	cf P. sativum	Charred cotyledons	-	-	1	-	1	-	1	-	-	-
		Charred hilum/a	-	-	1	-	-	-	-	-	-	-
		Charred testa frags	-	-	4	-	-	-	-	-	-	-
Bur medick	Medicago minima (L.) Bartal	Pods and/or pod frags	-	-	-	-	-	-	1	-	-	-
?Clovers, etc	cf Trifolium sp(p)	Charred seeds	-	-	1	-	-	-	-	-	-	-
Cultivated flax	Linum usitatissimum L.	Seeds	-	-	-	-	-	1f	1	-	-	-
Sun spurge	Euphorbia helioscopia L.	Charred seeds	-	-	-	-	-	-	1	-	-	-
		Seeds	-	-	1	-	1	4	3	2	5	-
Holly	Ilex aquifolium L.	Charred leaf frags	-	-	-	-	-	1	-	-	?1	-
		Charred seeds	-	-	-	-	-	-	1	?1	-	-
Box	Buxus sempervirens L.	Leaf epidermis frags	-	-	-	-	-	-	1	-	-	-
Grape	Vitis vinifera L.	Mineralised seeds	-	-	-	-	1	4	5	1	1	-
		Seeds	-	-	-	-	-	4	3+1f	1	3	1
Violets/pansies, etc	Viola sp(p)	Seeds	-	-	-	-	-	3	4	3	4	-
White bryony	Bryonia cretica ssp dioica (Jacq) Tutin	Charred seeds	-	-	1	-	-	-	-	-	-	-
		Seeds	-	-	-	-	-	-	-	-	1	-
Coriander	Coriandrum sativum L.	Seeds (fr interiors)	-	-	-	-	-	-	1	-	-	-
Fool's parsley	Aethusa cynapium L.	Mericarps	-	-	-	-	-	1	5	2	6	-
Hemlock	Conium maculatum L.	Mericarps	-	-	-	-	-	1	1+1f	-	-	-
Heather, ling	Calluna vulgaris (L.) Hull	Charred shoot frags	-	-	-	-	-	-	-	-	1+?1	-
		Shoot frags	-	-	-	-	-	-	-	-	1	-
		Shoot tips	-	-	-	-	-	-	-	-	1	-
?Heather, ling	cf C vulgaris (L.) Hull	Charred root and/or basal twig frags	-	-	1	1	-	-	1	-	-	-
		Root and/or basal twig frags	-	-	-	-	-	-	-	-	1	-
Ash	Fraxinus excelsior L.	Charcoal frags	1	-	1	1	2	1	1	-	2	-
Borage family	Boraginaceae	Nutlets	-	-	-	-	-	-	1	-	-	-
Corn gromwell, 'Stone-hard'	Buglossoides arvensis (L.) I M Johnston	Nutlets	-	-	-	-	1	-	-	-	-	-
Annual dead-nettles	Lamium Section Lamiopsis	Nutlets	-	-	-	-	-	-	-	-	1	-
Woundworts	Stachys sp(p)	Nutlets	-	-	-	-	-	1	-	1	1	-
Selfheal	Prunella vulgaris L.	Nutlets	-	-	-	-	1	-	-	-	1	-
Deadly nightshade	Atropa bella-donna L.	Seeds	-	-	-	-	-	2	1	1	-	-
Henbane	Hyoscyamus niger L.	Seeds	-	-	-	-	-	2	1	-	-	1
Black nightshade	Solanum nigrum L.	Seeds	-	-	-	-	-	-	-	1	1	-
	Solanum sp(p)	Seeds	-	-	-	-	-	-	1	-	-	-
Tomato	Lycopersicon esculentum Miller	Seeds	-	-	-	-	-	-	-	-	1	1
?Hoary plantain	Plantago cf media L.	Charred seeds	-	-	-	-	-	-	1	-	-	-
Ribwort plantain	P lanceolata L.	Charred seeds	-	-	4	-	-	1	1	-	-	-
Elder	Sambucus nigra L.	Charred seeds	-	-	-	-	-	1	-	-	-	-
		Seeds	4	7	4	5	10+1f	12	19	5+1f	9	1
Stinking mayweed	Anthemis cotula L.	Charred achenes	-	-	-	-	-	-	1	-	-	-
Sea/scentless mayweed	Matricaria maritima L/M perforata Mérat	Charred achenes	-	-	-	-	-	-	1	-	-	-
Corn marigold	Chrysanthemum segetum L	Charred achenes	-	-	-	-	-	-	1	-	-	-
Thistles	Carduus/Cirsium sp(p)	Achenes	-	-	-	-	-	1	1	-	-	-
Dandelions	Taraxacum officinale sensu lato	Achenes	-	-	-	-	-	-	-	-	1	-
Nipplewort	Lapsana communis L.	charred achenes	-	-	-	-	-	-	1	-	-	-
Grasses	Gramineae	Charred caryopses	-	-	3	-	1	2	1	1	1	-
		Spikelets/spikelet frags	-	-	-	-	-	-	-	-	1	-
	cf Gramineae	Charred culm nodes	-	-	1	-	-	-	-	-	-	-
Grasses/cereals	Gramineae/Cerealia	Charred culm frags	-	-	1	-	-	-	-	-	-	-
Cereals	Cerealia indet	charred caryopses	-	2	-	-	-	1	1	1	1+?1	-
		Mineralised caryopses	-	-	-	-	-	-	-	-	1	-
Bromes, etc	Bromus sp(p)	Charred caryopses	-	-	-	1	-	-	-	-	-	-
Bread/club wheat	Triticum 'aestivo-compactum'	Charred caryopses	1+?1	1	5+?1	1	?1	3+?2	6	2	3	-
Wheats	Triticum sp(p)	Charred caryopses	2	1	6	4	5+?1	2	3	2	2	-
Wheat/rye	Triticum/Secale	Waterlogged caryopses	-	-	1	-	-	-	-	-	-	-
		Waterlogged periderm frags	-	-	3	-	-	-	-	-	-	-
Rye	Secale cereale L.	Charred caryopsis/es	-	-	2+?1	?3	1	-	1+?1	-	-	-
		Part-charred rachis frags	-	-	-	-	-	-	-	-	1	-
Barley	Hordeum sp(p)	Charred caryopsis/es	-	2	4	3	4	3+1s	8	2s+?1	4	1
Cultivated oat	Avena sativa L.	Charred spikelets/spikelet frags	-	1	2	-	-	?1	-	-	1	-
Oats	Avena sp(p)	Charred awn frags	-	-	-	-	-	-	1	-	-	-
		Charred caryopsis/es	-	2	6	-	3+1s	8+?2	11	2+1s	5	-
		Part-charred caryopsis/es	-	-	1	-	-	-	1	-	-	-
		Charred chaff	-	-	-	-	-	-	1+?1	-	-	-
		Waterlogged caryopsis/es	-	-	-	-	-	-	-	-	1	-
		Waterlogged periderm frags	-	-	1	-	-	-	-	-	-	-
Duckweeds	Lemna sp(p)	Fronds	-	-	-	-	1	2	-	-	-	-

Table 6.2.1 Plant taxa (and other components) quantified by phase (*continued*)

			Phase									
			I	**II**	**III**	**IV**	**V**	**VI**	**VII**	**VIII**	**IX**	**X**
No contexts examined per phase			12	10	8	6	13	21	20	7	15	3
Vernacular	*Taxon*	*Parts recorded*										
Common spike-rush	*Eleocharis palustris* sensu lato	Charred nutlets	-	-	1	-	-	-	-	-	-	-
		Nutlets	-	-	-	-	1	-	-	-	-	-
		Silicified nutlets	-	-	3	-	-	-	-	-	-	-
Sedges	*Carex* sp(p)	Charred nutlets	-	-	4	-	-	1	-	-	1	-
		Nutlets	-	-	-	1	4	7	4	3	2	-
		Silicified nutlets	-	-	2	-	-	-	-	-	-	-
	Sphagnum sp(p)	Leaf/leaves and shoot tips	-	-	-	-	-	-	1	-	-	-

Other components (recorded during examination of washovers and residues for macroscopic plant remains); excludes any material which was clearly modern
Abbreviations: ch—charred; frags—fragments; min—mineralised; sil—'silicified'

Artefactual materials

	I	II	III	IV	V	VI	VII	VIII	IX	X
Brick/tile	1	-	5	1	2	-	2	1	6	-
?Daub	-	-	-	-	-	-	-	1	-	-
?Glassy slag	-	-	-	-	-	-	-	-	1	-
Iron objects	-	-	-	-	-	1+?1	-	-	-	-
Leather frags	-	-	-	-	-	-	1	1	3	-
Mortar	1	-	-	1	2	-	2	2	3	-
Paper frags	-	-	-	-	-	-	1	1	-	-
Textile frags	-	-	-	-	-	-	1	-	-	-
Textile frags (ch)	-	-	-	-	-	-	-	-	1	-
Yarn frags	-	-	-	-	-	-	2	-	-	-
Yarn frags (ch)	-	-	-	-	-	1	-	-	-	-

Plant materials

	I	II	III	IV	V	VI	VII	VIII	IX	X
Bark frags	-	-	-	-	-	-	1	-	-	-
Bark frags (ch)	-	-	-	-	1	2	-	-	-	-
Catkin frags	-	-	-	-	-	-	-	-	1	-
Charcoal	12	10	8	6	13	19	19	7	12	1
Dicot leaf frags	-	-	-	-	-	-	-	1	-	-
Herbaceous detritus (ch)	-	1	4	2	1	6	4	1	2	-
Herbaceous detritus (sil)	-	-	2	-	-	-	-	-	-	-
Indet seed(s) (?sil)	-	-	-	-	-	-	1	-	-	-
Mineralised seeds/embryos	-	1	-	-	1	3	6	1	2	-
?Peat ash	-	-	1	-	-	-	-	-	-	-
?Peat frags (ch)	-	-	-	-	-	-	-	1	-	-
Root/rhizome frags (ch)	-	-	-	1	-	-	-	-	-	-
Twig frags	-	-	-	-	-	-	1	-	1	-
Twig frags (ch)	-	1	1	1	1	10	4	2	3	-
Wood frags	-	-	-	-	1	2	2	1	6	-
Wood frags (min)	-	-	-	-	-	3	2	-	-	1
Part-burnt wood	-	-	-	-	-	-	1	-	-	-
Woody root frags	-	1	-	-	-	-	-	-	-	-

Animal materials–invertebrate

	I	II	III	IV	V	VI	VII	VIII	IX	X
Beetles	-	-	1	-	1	6	6	2	4	1
Beetles (ch)	-	-	1	-	-	-	1	-	-	-
Bivalve periostracum	-	-	-	-	-	2	2	-	-	-
Earthworm egg caps	-	-	-	-	-	-	2	1	1	1
Earthworm egg caps (min)	-	1	-	-	-	-	-	-	1	-
Fly pupae (min)	-	-	-	-	-	1	1	-	-	-
Fly puparia	-	-	-	-	1	3	2	2	1	1
Fly puparia (ch)	-	-	3	-	-	-	-	-	-	-
Fly puparia (min)	-	1	1	-	-	2	6	1	1	-
Insect cuticle	-	-	-	-	-	-	1	-	1	-
Insects	-	-	-	-	-	-	1	-	-	-
Marine mollusc shell frags	-	-	-	-	-	-	1	-	-	-
Mussel shell 'fibres'	1	-	-	-	-	2	1	-	-	-
Mussel shell frags	-	-	-	-	-	-	-	-	1	-
Oyster shell frags	-	-	-	-	-	-	1	-	-	-
Snails	-	-	-	-	-	-	1	1	2	1
Woodlouse frags	-	-	-	-	-	4	1	-	-	-

Animal materials–vertebrate

	I	II	III	IV	V	VI	VII	VIII	IX	X
Amphibian bone	-	-	-	-	-	-	-	1	-	-
Animal hair (matted)	-	-	-	-	-	-	1	-	1	-
bird bone	1	2	-	-	-	2	3	-	1	-
Bird claw bone	-	-	-	-	-	-	1	-	-	-
Bird tracheal ring	-	-	-	-	-	1	-	-	-	-
Bone frags	4	4	4	2	4	16	18	6	10	2
Burnt bone frags	-	-	1	-	1	3	-	1	6	-
Burnt fish bone	-	-	-	-	-	2	-	-	-	-
Burnt small mammal bone	-	-	1	-	-	-	-	-	-	-
Cancellous bone frags	-	-	-	-	1	2	-	-	1	-
Eggshell frags	-	-	-	-	-	2	1	-	2	-
Eggshell membrane frags	-	-	-	-	-	1	1	-	1	-
Fish bone	1	3	3	1	3	8	9	4	5	-
Fish scale	-	2	1	-	-	7	7	4	6	1
Percid scale	-	-	-	-	-	-	1	-	1	-
Rodent droppings (min)	-	-	-	-	-	1	1	1	-	-
Small mammal bone	-	-	-	-	1	2	2	-	2	-
Small mammal tooth	-	-	-	-	-	-	-	-	1	-

Table 6.2.1 Plant taxa (and other components) quantified by phase (*continued*)

	I	II	III	IV	V	VI	VII	VIII	IX	X
						Phase				
No contexts examined per phase	12	10	8	6	13	21	20	7	15	3
Mineral component										
Chalk/lime	-	-	1	-	-	-	-	-	-	-
Cinders	1	3	2	2	8	18	20	7	14	3
Coal	1	1	3	2	4	11	15	6	9	1
Coal char'	-	-	-	-	-	1	1	-	-	'
?Lime	3	1	1	-	1	1	-	-	-	-
Part-burnt coal	-	-	-	-	-	-	1	1	1	-
Gravel	1	-	5	1	1	-	1	-	2	-
Quartzite	-	-	-	1	-	-	1	-	-	-
Sand	1	-	5	1	2	-	2	2	4	-
Sandstone	-	-	1	-	-	-	-	-	-	-
Triassic sandstone	1	-	3	1	2	-	2	2	3	-
Slate	-	-	-	-	1	-	2	2	3	-
Unwashed sediment	-	-	-	-	-	-	1	-	-	-
Other inclusions										
Ash concretions	-	-	-	-	-	1	-	-	1	-
Cenocccum (sclerotia)	-	-	-	-	-	-	-	1	2	-
Charred organic material	-	-	4	-	-	-	-	-	-	-
Concretions	-	-	-	-	-	-	1+?1	-	?1	-
Faecal concretions	-	-	-	-	?1	2+?1	?1	-	-	-
Fungal perithecia	-	-	-	-	-	1	-	-	-	-
Glassy ash	-	-	4	-	1	-	-	1	-	-
Glassy slag	-	-	1	1	-	-	-	-	-	-
Mineralised material	1	-	-	-	-	-	-	-	-	-
Plant ash silica	2	1	5	2	2	3	2	3	2	-
Pre-Quaternary megaspores	-	-	-	-	-	1	-	1	2	-

Table 6.2.2 Invertebrate remains from samples
Key Order and nomenclature follow Kloet * Hincks (1964–77) for insects. Where both secure and tentative identifications for a given taxon were recorded, only the former are listed here. Ecological codes used in calculating statistics (Table 6.2.3) are given (ec); they are explained in Table 6.2.5. * = not used in calculating assemblage statistics. The remains were of adults unless stated. 'Sp' indicates that record was probably an additional taxon, 'sp indet' that the material may have been of a taxon listed above it.

Taxon	ec	Taxon	ec	Taxon	ec
*?*Ascaris* sp (egg)	-	*Philonthus* spp	u	*Aglenus brunneus* (Gyllenhal)	rt-ss
**Trichuris* ?*trichiura* (Linnaeus) (egg)	-	*Quedius* sp	u	*Blaps* sp	rt-ss
* *Trichuris* ?*suis* (Schrank) (egg)	-	Staphylininae sp	u	*Anthicus* sp	rt
**Oligochaeta* sp (egg capsule)	u	*Tachyporus* sp	u	Halticinae *sp*	oa-p
**Blatta orientalis* Linnaeus	rt-ss	*Cypha* sp	rt	*Apion* (*Exapion*) ?*genistae* Kirby	oa-p
**Syrphidae* sp (larva)	u	*Falagria* sp	rt-sf	*Apion* spp	oa-p
**Diptera* sp (adult)	u	*Falagria* or *Cordalia* sp indet	rt-sf	*Sitophilus granarius* (Linnaeus)	g-ss
**Diptera* sp (puparium)	u	*Aleochara* sp	u	*Gymnetron* sp	oa-p
**Siphonaptera* sp	u	Aleocharinae spp	u	Curculionidae sp	oa
Trechus obtusus or *quadristriatus*	oa	Pselaphidae sp	u	Coleoptera sp	u
Trechus ?*micros* (Herbst)	u	*Trox scaber* (Linnaeus)	rt-sf	*Coleoptera sp indet (larva)	u
Carabidae sp	ob	*Aphodius* sp	ob-rf	*Hymenoptera Parasitica sp	u
Cercyon ?*analis* (Paykull)	rt-sf	Dermestidae sp	rt-sf	*Ponerinae sp	u
Cercyon depressus Stephens	rf	*Anobium punctatum* (Degeer)	l-sf	*Hymenoptera sp	u
Cercyon ?*terminatus* (Marsham)	rf-st	*Niptus hololeucus* (Falderman)	rd-ss	*Insecta sp (larva)	u
Cercyon sp *indet*	u	*Tipnus unicolor* (Piller & Mitterpacher)	rt-ss	*Pseudoscorpiones sp	u
Gnathoncus sp	rt-sf	*Ptinus* ?*fur* (Linnaeus)	rd-sf	*Acarina sp	u
Histerinae spp	rt	*Ptinus* sp	rd-sf	*Patella vulgata* Linnaeus	-
Ptenidium sp	rt	*Brachypterus* sp	oa-p	*Trochidae sp	-
Catops sp	u	*Meligethes* sp	oa-p	*Littorina littorea* (Linnaeus)	-
Lesteva ?*longoelytrata* (Goeze)	oa-d	*Rhizophagus* sp	u	*Littorina* ?*obtusata* (Linnaeus)	-
Phyllodrepa floralis (Paykull)	rt-sf	*Monotoma* ?*picipes* Herbst	rt-st	*?*Turritella communis* Risso	-
Dropephylla ioptera (Stephens)	u	*Monotoma spinicollis* Aube	rt-st	*Nucella lapillus* (Linnaeus)	-
Omalium ?*allardi* Fairmaire & Brisout	rt	*Oryzaephilus surinamensis* (Linnaeus)	g-ss	*Neptunea antiqua* (Linnaeus)	-
Omalium sp	rt	*Cryptophagus scutellatus* Newman	rd-st	*Mytilus edulis* Linnaeus	-
Xylodromus concinnus (Marsham)	rt-st	*Cryptophagus* spp	rd-sf	*Pectinidae sp	-
Carpelimus bilineatus Stephens	rt-sf	*Micrambe* sp	u	*Ostrea edulis* Linnaeus	-
Anotylus rugosus (Fabricius)	rt	*Atomaria* spp	rd	*Cerastoderma edule* (Linnaeus)	-
Anotylus tetracarinatus (Block)	rt	*Mycetaea hirta* (Marsham)	rd-ss	*?*Tellinidae* sp	-
Oxytelus sculptus Gravenhorst	rt-st	*Lathridius minutus* group	rd-st	*Vitrea* sp	-
Leptacinus sp	rt-st	*Enicmus* sp	rt-sf	*Oxychilus* sp	-
Gyrohypnus ?*angustatus* Stephens	rt-st	*Dienerella* sp	rd-sf	*Helix* sp	-
Gyrohypnus fracticornis (Müller)	rt-st	*Corticaria* sp	rt-sf		
Neobisnius sp	u	*Corticarina* sp	rt		

Table 6.2.3 Main statistics for assemblages of adult beetles and bugs (excluding aphids and scale insects) from samples. (For explanation of abbreviations, *see* Table 6.2.5).

Context	(206)	(806)	(1632)	(1635)	(1697)	Whole site
Sample no	<5001>	<5081>	<5161>	<5166>	<5172>	
Ext	/T	/T	/T	/T	/T	
S	12	30	41	44	24	89
N	22	141	116	196	72	547
ALPHA	11	12	23	18	13	30
SEALPHA	4	2	3	2	2	2
SOB	1	0	3	9	0	12
PSOB	8	0	7	20	0	13
NOB	1	0	3	11	0	15
PNOB	5	0	3	6	0	3
ALPHAOB	0	0	0	0	0	0
SEALPHAOB	0	0	0	0	0	0
SW	0	0	0	0	0	0
PSW	0	0	0	0	0	0
NW	0	0	0	0	0	0
PNW	0	0	0	0	0	0
ALPHAW	0	0	0	0	0	0
SEALPHAW	0	0	0	0	0	0
SD	0	0	1	0	0	1
PSD	0	0	2	0	0	1
ND	0	0	1	0	0	1
PND	0	0	1	0	0	0
ALPHAD	0	0	0	0	0	0
SEALPHAD	0	0	0	0	0	0
SP	0	0	1	6	0	7
PSP	0	0	2	14	0	8
NP	0	0	1	8	0	9
PNP	0	0	1	4	0	2
ALPHAP	0	0	0	0	0	0
SEALPHAP	0	0	0	0	0	0
SM	0	0	0	0	0	0
PSM	0	0	0	0	0	0
NM	0	0	0	0	0	0
PNM	0	0	0	0	0	0
ALPHAM	0	0	0	0	0	0
SEALPHAM	0	0	0	0	0	0
SL	0	1	1	1	1	2
PSL	0	3	2	2	4	2
NL	0	2	1	1	1	5
PNL	0	1	1	1	1	1
ALPHAL	0	0	0	0	0	0
SEALPHAL	0	0	0	0	0	0
SRT	7	19	28	23	15	91
PSRT	58	63	68	52	63	102
NRT	17	117	92	60	62	348
PNRT	77	83	79	31	86	64
ALPHART	0	7	14	14	6	40
SEALPHART	0	1	2	3	1	3
SRD	4	9	5	9	5	32
PSRD	33	30	12	20	21	36
NRD	14	22	7	15	9	67
PNRD	64	16	6	8	13	12
ALPHARD	0	6	0	0	0	24
SEALPHARD	0	2	0	0	0	5
SRF	0	0	2	2	1	5
PSRF	0	0	5	5	4	6
NRF	0	0	20	2	3	25
PNRF	0	0	17	1	4	5
ALPHARF	0	0	1	0	0	2
SEALPHARF	0	0	0	0	0	1
SSA	4	18	20	18	14	38
PSSA	33	60	49	41	58	43
NSA	14	66	50	54	49	233
PNSA	64	47	43	28	68	43
ALPHASA	0	8	13	10	7	13
SEALPHASA	0	2	3	2	2	1
SSF	3	9	9	8	5	20
PSSF	25	30	22	18	21	22
NSF	4	13	11	26	9	63
PNSF	18	9	9	13	13	12
ALPHASF	0	0	0	4	0	10
SEALPHASF	0	0	0	1	0	2
SST	0	3	7	6	3	10
PSST	0	10	17	14	13	11
NST	0	7	14	11	13	45
PNST	0	5	12	6	18	8
ALPHAST	0	0	0	0	0	4
SEALPHAST	0	0	0	0	0	1
SSS	1	6	4	4	6	8
PSSS	8	20	10	9	25	9
NSS	10	46	25	17	27	125
PNSS	45	33	22	9	38	23
ALPHASS	0	2	1	0	3	2
SEALPHASS	0	1	1	0	1	0
SG	0	2	1	1	2	3
PSG	0	7	2	2	8	3
NG	0	2	1	1	3	7
PNG	0	1	1	1	4	1
ALPHAG	0	0	0	0	0	0
SEALPHAG	0	0	0	0	0	0

Table 6.2.4 Species lists in rank order for invertebrate macrofossils from samples

For each sample assemblage the adult Coleoptera (beetles) are listed first, followed by the remaining invertebrates. Headers: ReM:D – recording method: detailed; weight is in kilogrammes; E - erosion; F - fragmentation (following Kenward & Large 1998); ec - ecological codes; n = minimum number of individuals; sq = semi-quantitative (e = estimate; - = fully quantitative, m = 'many', translated as 15 individuals; s = several, translated as 6). For translation of ecological codes, *see* Table 6.2.5.

Note it has not been practical to italicise specific epithets in this table.

Context (206) Sample <5001>/T ReM: D
Weight: 5.00 E: 5.00 F: 3.50

Notes: Entered HK 9/3/04. Four dish flot, yellow cuticle scraps, brown 'felt' (fungal mycelium) and char. Fossils tended to fall apart when handled. E 3.5-5.0, mode 5.0 distinct; F 2.5-5.5, modes 3 and 5, distinct; trend to orange 3—4, mode 4 strong. Washover contained a few beetle remains, and lots of scraps which were probably cockroach (no good diagnostic parts seen). Parts of at least one male and one female B orientalis in flot.

Taxon	n	sq	ec
Niptus hololeucus	10	-	rd-ss
Cryptophagus sp B	2	-	rd-sf
Carabidae sp	1	-	ob
Anotylus tetracarinatus	1	-	rt
Philonthus sp	1	-	u
Staphylininae sp	1	-	u
Cypha sp	1	-	rt
Aleocharinae sp	1	-	u
Cryptophagus sp A	1	-	rd-sf
Atomaria sp	1	-	rd
Corticaria sp	1	-	rt-sf
Coleoptera sp	1	-	u
*Coleoptera sp (larva)	15	m	u
*Blatta orientalis	2	-	rt-ss
*Insecta sp (larva)	1	-	u

Context: (806) Sample: <5081>/T ReM: D
Weight: 5.00 E: 5.00 F: 2.50

Notes: Entered HK 6/3/04 Four dish flot, bright to pale orange plant tissue and insect fragments Many pale filmy remains which floated and migrated in the dish: insects hard to see and to catch. E 3.5-5.0, mode 5.0 strong; F 1.5-3.5, mode 2.5 weak; trend to orange (then pale) 3-4, mode 4 strong. Peculiar Ptinus pronotum to own tube, sketch on sheet. Flea head too decayed to name.

Taxon	n	sq	ec
Omalium ?allardi	45	-	rt
Aglenus brunneus	21	-	rt-ss
Tipnus unicolor	17	-	rt-ss
Aleocharinae sp A	8	-	u
Philonthus sp	5	-	u
Atomaria sp B	5	-	rd
Mycetaea hirta	5	-	rd-ss
Xylodromus concinnus	4	-	rt-st
Atomaria sp A	3	-	rd
Histerinae sp	2	-	rt
Catops sp	2	-	u
Phyllodrepa ?floralis	2	-	rt-sf
Anobium ?punctatum	2	-	l-sf
Ptinus ?fur	2	-	rd-sf
Cryptophagus sp B	2	-	rd-sf
Lathridius minutus group	2	-	rd-st
Trechus ?micros	1	-	u
Tachyporus sp	1	-	u
Aleochara sp	1	-	u
Aleocharinae sp B	1	-	u
Trox scaber	1	-	rt-sf
Dermestidae sp	1	-	rt-sf
Ptinus sp	1	-	rd-sf
Rhizophagus sp	1	-	u
Oryzaephilus surinamensis	1	-	g-ss
Cryptophagus scutellatus	1	-	rd-st
Cryptophagus sp A	1	-	rd-sf
Enicmus sp	1	-	rt-sf
Blaps sp	1	-	rt-ss
Sitophilus granarius	1	-	g-ss
*Diptera sp (puparium)	15	m	u
*Insecta sp (larva)	15	m	u
*Diptera sp (adult)	6	s	u
*Oligochaeta sp (egg capsule)	1	-	u
*Siphonaptera sp	1	-	u
*Coleoptera sp (larva)	1	-	u

Context: 1635 Sample: 5166/T ReM: D
Weight: 5.00 E: 4.50 F: 2.00

Notes: Entered HK 6/3/04. Two dish flot. Recorded in flot and on filter paper. Many remains very pale orange, though in some cases with wings still in place on elytra: suggests recent in-situ decay. E 3.5-5.5, mode 4.5 strong; F 1.5-3.5, mode 2.0 weak; trend to orange (then pale) 2-4, mode 4 strong. Micrambe may be villosus

Taxon	n	sq	ec
Aleocharinae sp A	111	-	u
Carpelimus bilineatus	12	-	rt-sf

Context: 1635 Sample: 5166/T (continued)

Aglenus brunneus	9	-	rt-ss
Xylodromus concinnus	5	-	rt-st
Tipnus unicolor	5	-	rt-ss
Cryptophagus sp	5	-	rd-sf
Falagria or Cordalia sp	4	-	rt-sf
Micrambe sp	3	-	u
Anotylus rugosus	2	-	rt
Aleocharinae sp B	2	-	u
Mycetaea hirta	2	-	rd-ss
Lathridius minutus group	2	-	rd-st
Halticinae sp	2	-	oa-p
Apion sp B	2	-	oa-p
Trechus obtusus or quadristriatus	1	-	oa
Trechus ?micros	1	-	u
Cercyon ?terminatus	1	-	rf-st
Cercyon sp	1	-	u
Gnathoncus sp	1	-	rt-sf
Histerinae sp	1	-	rt
Dropephylla ioptera	1	-	u
Omalium sp	1	-	rt
Leptacinus sp	1	-	rt-st
Neobisnius sp	1	-	u
Aleocharinae sp C	1	-	u
Pselaphidae sp	1	-	u
Aphodius sp	1	-	ob-rf
Anobium ?punctatum	1	-	l-sf
Ptinus ?fur	1	-	rd-sf
Ptinus sp	1	-	rd-sf
Meligethes sp	1	-	oa-p
Rhizophagus sp	1	-	u
Monotoma ?picipes	1	-	rt-st
Cryptophagus scutellatus	1	-	rd-st
Atomaria sp A	1	-	rd
Atomaria sp B	1	-	rd
Dienerella sp	1	-	rd-sf
Corticarina sp	1	-	rt
Apion (Exapion) ?genistae	1	-	oa-p
Apion sp A	1	-	oa-p
Sitophilus granarius	1	-	g-ss
Gymnetron sp	1	-	oa-p
Curculionidae sp	1	-	oa
Coleoptera sp	1	-	u
*Acarina sp	15	m	u
*Diptera sp (puparium)	6	s	u
*Hymenoptera Parasitica sp	6	s	u
*Oligochaeta sp (egg capsule)	2	-	u
*Diptera sp (adult)	1	-	u
*Coleoptera sp (larva)	1	-	u
*Pseudoscorpiones sp	1	-	u

Context: 1697 Sample: 5172/T ReM: D
Weight: 5.00 E: 4.00 F: 2.50

Notes: Entered HK 6/3/04. Five dish flot recorded in flot and on filter paper. Many remains strongly decayed. E 3.0-5.0, mode 4.0 weak; F 2.0-5.0, mode 2.5 weak; trend to pale/orange 2-4 mode 3 weak. Washover checked and found to contain appreciable numbers of insects: impractical to recover and record them.

Taxon	n	sq	ec
Tipnus unicolor	17	-	rt-ss
Omalium ?allardi	11	-	rt
Xylodromus concinnus	11	-	rt-st
Phyllodrepa floralis	4	-	rt-sf
Cercyon depressus	3	-	rf
Mycetaea hirta	3	-	rd-ss
Aglenus brunneus	3	-	rt-ss
Cryptophagus sp B	2	-	rd-sf
Atomaria sp	2	-	rd
Sitophilus granarius	2	-	g-ss
Histerinae sp	1	-	rt
Gyrohypnus fracticornis	1	-	rt-st
Philonthus sp	1	-	u
Staphylininae sp	1	-	u
Aleocharinae sp A	1	-	u
Aleocharinae sp B	1	-	u
Aleocharinae sp C	1	-	u
Aleocharinae sp D	1	-	u
Trox scaber	1	-	rt-sf
Anobium punctatum	1	-	l-sf
Oryzaephilus surinamensis	1	-	g-ss
Cryptophagus sp A	1	-	rd-sf
Lathridius minutus group	1	-	rd-st
Blaps sp	1	-	rt-s
*Diptera sp (puparium)	100	e	u
*Insecta sp (larva)	15	m	u
*Coleoptera sp (larva)	6	s	u
*Ponerinae sp	4	-	u
*Oligochaeta sp (egg capsule)	3	-	u
*Pseudoscorpiones sp	3	-	u
*Acarina sp	2	-	u
*Diptera sp (adult)	1	-	u
*Syrphidae sp (larva)	1	-	u
*Hymenoptera sp	1	-	u

Table 6.2.5 Key to ecological codes (lower-case codes in parentheses) assigned to insect taxa and used in Tables 6.2.3 and 6.2.4. Indivs - individuals (based on MNI); No – number.

No taxa	S
Estimated number of indivs (MNI)	N
Index of diversity (ALPHA)	ALPHA
Standard error of ALPHA	SEALPHA
No 'certain' outdoor taxa (oa)	SOA
Percentage of 'certain' outdoor taxa	PSOA
No 'certain' outdoor indivs	NOA
Percentage of 'certain' outdoor indivs	PNOA
No OA and probable outdoor taxa (oa + ob)	SOB
Percentage of OB taxa	PSOB
No OB indivs	NOB
Percentage OB indivs	PNOB
Index of diversity of the OB component	ALPHAOB
Standard error	SEALPHAOB
No aquatic taxa (w)	SW
Percentage of aquatic taxa	PSW
No aquatic indivs	NW
Percentage of W indivs	PNW
Index of diversity of the W component	ALPHAW
Standard error	SEALPHAW
No damp ground/waterside taxa (d)	SD
Percentage D taxa	PSD
No damp D indivs	ND
Percentage of D indivs	PND
Index of diversity of the D component	ALPHAD
Standard error	SEALPHAD
No strongly plant-associated taxa (p)	SP
Percentage of P taxa	PSP
No strongly P indivs	NP
Percentage of P indivs	PNP
Index of diversity of the P component	ALPHAP
Standard error	SEALPHAP
No heathland/moorland taxa (m)	SM
Percentage of M taxa	PSM
No M indivs	NM
Percentage of M indivs	PNM
Index of diversity of the M component	ALPHAM
Standard error	SEALPHAM
No wood-associated taxa (l)	SL
Percentage of L taxa	PSL
No L indivs	NL
Percentage of L indivs	PNL
Index of diversity of the L component	ALPHAL
Standard error	SEALPHAL
No decomposer taxa (rt + rd + rf)	SRT
Percentage of RT taxa	PSRT
No RT indivs	NRT
Percentage of RT indivs	PNRT
Index of diversity of RT component	ALPHART
Standard error	SEALPHART
No 'dry' decomposer taxa (rd)	SRD
Percentage of RD taxa	PSRD
No RD indivs	NRD
Percentage of RD indivs	PNRD
Index of diversity of the RD component	ALPHARD
Standard error	SEALPHARD
No 'foul' decomposer taxa (rf)	SRF
Percentage of RF taxa	PSRF
No RF indivs	NRF
Percentage of RF indivs	PNRF
Index of diversity of the RF component	ALPHARF
Standard error	SEALPHARF
No synanthropic taxa (sf + st + ss)	SSA
Percentage of synanthropic taxa	PSSA
No synanthropic indivs	NSA
Percentage of SA indivs	PNSA
Index of diversity of SA component	ALPHASA
Standard error	SEALPHASA
No facultatively synanthropic taxa (sf)	SSF
Percentage of SF taxa	PSSF
No SF indivs	NSF
Percentage of SF indivs	PNSF
Index of diversity of SF component	ALPHASF
Standard error	SEALPHASF
No typical synanthropic taxa	SST
Percentage of ST taxa	PSST
No ST indivs	NST
Percentage of ST indivs	PNST
Index of diversity of ST component	ALPHAST
Standard error	SEALPHAST
No strongly synanthropic taxa	SSS
Percentage of SS taxa	PSSS
No SS indivs	NSS
Percentage of SS indivs	PNSS
Index of diversity of SS component	ALPHASS
Standard error	SEALPHASS
No uncoded taxa (u)	SU
Percentage of uncoded indivs	PNU
No indivs of grain pests (g)	NG
Percentage of indivs of grain pests	

Table 6.2.6 Measurements of trichurid eggs taken during assessment from Contexts (806) and (1697), with calculated total length measurements. All measurements in microns.

Context	Sample no	Measured length*	Calculated length**	Measured width
806	5081	50.2	52.9	24.4
		48.9	51.6	27.1
		51.6	54.3	25.8
		61.1	63.8	27.8
		49.5	52.3	26.5
1697	5171	55.6	58.4	29.9
		51.6	54.3	27.1
		46.1	48.9	29.9
		54.3	57	27.1
		54.3	57	27.1
		54.3	57	29.9
		51.6	54.3	24.4
		51.6	54.3	27.1
		51.6	54.3	29.9
		57	59.7	26.5
		51.6	54.3	25.1

* without polar plugs
** plug-to-plug

Table 6.2.8 Number of contexts containing hand-collected shell by phase

Phase	No contexts
I	0
II	5
III	1
IV	0
V	13
VI	21
VII	42
VIII	35
IX	48
X	35
Unphased	2
Total	202

Table 6.2.7 Summary notes on invertebrate remains for the GBA samples, including sediment descriptions.
Note Preservation notes follow Kenward & Large (1998). Processed subsamples were of 5 kg of sediment with the exception of Sample <5027>, which was 4.25 kg.

Context	Sample	Phase	Sediment description	Notes for macro-invertebrates
206	5001	IX	Dry, light to mid grey-brown, unconsolidated, ?ashy, silty sand. Stones (2 to 20 mm), cinder, rotted mortar/plaster, coal and a ?copper alloy pin were present.	See main text.
208	5002	IX	Dry, light to mid brownish-grey to mid grey-brown, unconsolidated, slightly silty sandy ash. Stones (2 to 6 mm), clay pipe fragments, pot, ?lead, wood (including ?worked chips) and cockle shell were present, coal was common, and cinder was abundant.	Some charred ?insect fragments. No identifiable invertebrates seen
245	5008	VII	Moist, mid to dark grey-brown, crumbly to unconsolidated, ashy sandy silt with occasional lumps of light to mid-brown clay (to 15 mm). Charcoal and ?burnt mortar and shale were present.	Traces of decayed cuticle.
424	5027	X	Moist, mid to dark grey-brown, unconsolidated, ?ashy, ?slightly clay sandy silt. Glass, mortar/plaster, brick/tile, pot, cinder, rotted wood, and cockle shell were present.	Small numbers of pale insect fragments including *Anobium punctatum* (Degeer) and several fly puparia; one landsnail.
429	5031	VI	Moist, mid grey-brown, unconsolidated (working more or less soft), slightly clay sandy silt. Stones (2 to 60 mm), coal, cinder, and bone (including ?bird bone) were present.	Earthworm egg capsule and fragments. No other invertebrates seen.
464	4046	VII	Moist, mid to dark grey-brown, crumbly (working soft), slightly sandy clay silt. Stones (6 to 60+ mm, including slate to 80 mm), mortar/plaster, brick/tile, cinder, rotted charcoal, and bone were present.	A few, very decayed, insect remains; *Omalium* sp, ?*Coprophilus striatulus* (Fabricius).
670	5056	VII	Moist, mid to dark brown to mid to dark grey-brown, stiff and sticky to crumbly (working soft), slightly gritty sandy clay silt.	Traces of cuticle including a dermestid beetle and some other beetle scraps, often unidentifiable. One *Coprophilus striatulus*, less pale and perhaps intrusive. Preservation: E4 F4 change to yellow 4
797	5077	VI	Moist, mid to dark grey-brown, stiff and sticky (working soft and somewhat plastic), silty clay sand with some rotted charcoal present.	Traces of cuticle, including some earthworm egg capsules.
806	5081	VI	Moist, mid brown to mid grey-brown (lighter in places), crumbly and slightly sticky (working soft), sandy clay silt. Stones (2 to 20 mm), charcoal and some ?humic patches were present.	See main text.
1632	5161	V	Moist, mid brown to mid grey (internally), crumbly to unconsolidated (working soft), sandy clay silt (more clay in places) with some coal present.	See main text.
1635	5166	VI	Moist, mid to dark grey-brown to mid brown, crumbly to unconsolidated (working soft), sandy clay silt. Stones (2 to 60 mm), mortar/plaster, coal, cinder and bone were present.	See main text.
1697	5172	VI	Moist, mid brown to mid grey-brown, crumbly (working soft), sandy clay silt. Cinder and charcoal were present.	See main text.

Table 6.2.9 Hand-collected shell counts by phase
Note Counts for bivalve taxa are minimum numbers of whole valves. Counts for other taxa are minimum numbers of individuals.

Vernacular	Taxon	I	II	III	IV	V	VI	VII	VIII	IX	X	Total
Limpet	*Patella vulgata* L.	-	-	-	-	-	-	-	1	1	-	2
Top shell	Trochidae sp indet	-	-	-	-	-	-	1	-	-	-	1
Periwinkle	*Littorina littorea* (L.)	-	-	-	-	-	-	6	1	-	-	7
Flat perinwinkle	*Littorina ?obtusata* (L.)	-	-	-	-	-	-	2	-	-	2	4
?Auger shell	*?Turritella communis* Risso	-	-	-	-	-	-	-	-	-	1	1
Dog welk	*Nucella lapillus* (L.)	-	-	-	-	-	-	-	4	-	-	4
Red welk	*Neptunea antiqua* (L.)	-	-	-	-	-	-	-	-	-	1	1
Mussel	*Mytilus edulis* L.	-	-	-	-	2	11	-	5	17	6	41
Scallop	Pectinidae sp indet	-	-	-	-	-	-	-	1	-	-	1
Oyster	*Ostrea edulis* L.	-	3	-	-	13	22	171	118	126	178	631
Cockle	*Cerastoderma edule* (L.)	-	-	-	-	2	6	5	25	44	13	95
?Tellin	?Tellinidae sp indet	-	-	-	-	-	-	-	4	2	-	6
Total (marine taxa)		-	3	-	-	17	39	189	157	188	201	795
Weight (g)		-	158	-	-	464	500	6083	6536	3763	5086	22589
Average erosion score for shell		-	3	-	-	2.75	2.5	2.86	2.6	2.38	2.61	-
Average fragmentation score for shell		-	3	-	-	2.38	2.43	2.59	2.28	2.28	2.45	-
Garden snail	*Helix sp*	-	-	-	-	-	-	-	1	-	-	1

Table 6.2.10 Additional notes on oyster valves, summarised by phase
Key 'Right valves' = number of right (or upper) valves; 'Left valves' = number of left (or lower) valves; 'Indet. valves' = number of valves of indeterminate side; 'Knife marks' = number of valves showing damage characteristic of the oyster having been opened using a knife or similar implement; 'Measurable?' = estimated number of valves intact enough to be measured; 'Worm burrows' = number of valves showing damage by polychaet worms; 'Barnacles' = number of valves with barnacles; 'Dog whelk' = number of valves showing damage from dog whelk boring.

Phase	Left valves	Right valves	Indet valves	Knife marks	Measurable?	Worm burrows	Barnacles	Dog whelk
I	-	-	-	-	-	-	-	-
II	1	3	-	-	-	-	-	-
III	-	-	-	-	-	-	-	-
IV	-	-	-	-	-	-	-	-
V	7	5	1	5	3	-	-	-
VI	6	14	2	7	3	1	-	-
VII	85	64	22	51	18	14	5	-
VIII	58	56	4	31	23	13	4	-
IX	52	62	12	42	26	6	1	-
X	74	80	24	38	11	4	1	-
Total	283	284	65	174	84	38	11	0

Table 6.2.11 Fish remains from selected sediment samples by phase

Vernacular	Species	I	II	III	IV	V	VI	VII	VIII	IX	X	Total
Smooth hound	*Mustelus sp*	-	-	-	-	-	1	-	-	-	-	1
Ray/shark/skate	Elasmobranch	-	1	-	-	1	2	3	-	-	-	7
Ray	Rajidae	-	1	4	-	2	26	2	2	1	-	38
Thornback ray	*Raja clavata* L.	-	-	-	-	-	12	2	1	3	-	18
Anchovy/herring	*Engraulis encrasicolus* (L.)/ *Clupea harengus* L.	-	-	-	-	-	1	-	-	-	-	1
Anchovy	*Engraulis encrasicolus* (L.)	-	-	-	-	-	1	13	1	1	-	16
Shad	*Alosa alosa* (L.)/*Alosa fallax* (Lacépède)	-	2	-	-	-	-	-	-	-	-	2
Herring	*Clupea harengus* L.	3	51	49	14	102	319	153	82	89	14	876
Salmon family	Salmonidae	-	3	-	-	2	2	4	-	2	-	13
Salmon	*Salmo salar* L.	2	3	-	-	-	1	2	-	-	-	8
Trout	*Salmo trutta* L.	-	-	-	-	-	-	1	-	-	-	1
?Trout	cf *Salmo trutta* L.	-	-	1	1	-	-	-	-	-	-	2
Smelt	*Osmerus eperlanus* (L.)	-	14	3	-	6	49	67	12	27	-	178
?Smelt	cf *Osmerus eperlanus* (L.)	-	-	-	-	1	-	1	-	-	-	2
Cyprinid	Cyprinidae	-	-	-	-	-	6	1	1	7	-	15
Eel	*Anguilla anguilla* (L.)	10	8	16	2	13	586	187	62	43	10	937
Conger	*Conger conger* (L.)	-	-	-	1	-	5	3	1	-	-	10
Cod family	Gadidae	-	-	-	2	2	9	10	3	1	-	27
Small gadid	Small gadidae	-	1	1	-	-	15	4	2	2	-	25
?Cod family	cf Gadidae	-	-	-	-	1	-	-	-	-	-	1
Whiting	*Merlangius merlangus* (L.)	-	1	2	-	5	39	41	24	5	3	120
?Whiting	cf *Merlangius merlangus* (L.)	-	-	-	-	-	7	7	1	3	-	18
Cod	*Gadus morhua* L.	-	1	-	-	-	2	7	-	-	-	10
?Cod	cf *Gadus morhua* L.	-	-	-	-	-	3	1	-	1	-	5
Ling	*Molva molva* (L.)	-	-	-	-	-	2	-	1	-	-	3
Bass	*Dicentrarchus labrax* (L.)	1	1	-	-	-	-	-	2	-	-	4
Perch	*Perca fluviatilis* L.	-	-	-	-	-	-	-	1	-	-	1
?Perch	cf *Perca fluviatilis* L.	-	-	-	-	-	-	-	-	1	-	1
Weever	*Trachinus sp*	-	-	-	-	-	1	1	-	-	-	2
?Spanish mackerel	cf *Scomber japonicus*	-	3	1	-	-	-	-	-	-	-	4
Mullet family	Mugilidae	34	2	-	-	-	-	-	-	-	-	36
?Thin lipped grey mullet	cf *Liza ramada* (Risso)	-	-	1	-	-	-	-	-	-	-	1
Stickleback	Gasterosteidae	-	-	-	-	-	1	-	-	-	-	1
Flatfish (turbot, brill, megrim etc	Bothidae	-	-	-	1	-	-	-	-	-	-	1
Turbot	*Scophthalmus maximus* (L.)	-	-	-	-	-	1	-	-	-	-	1
Flatfish (plaice, flounder, dab etc	Pleuronectidae	15	89	70	35	69	429	197	140	126	16	1186
Flounder	*Platichthys flesus* (L.)	1	2	1	1	1	17	5	-	6	-	34
?Flounder	cf *Platichthys flesus* (L.)	-	-	-	-	1	-	-	-	1	-	2
Plaice	*Pleuronectes platessa* (L.)	-	3	-	-	-	11	4	4	1	-	23
Sole	*Solea solea* (L.)	-	-	-	-	-	1	2	1	1	-	5
?Sole	cf *Solea solea* (L.)	-	-	-	-	-	1	1	-	-	-	2
Total		69	186	148	56	205	1551	719	341	320	43	3638
No contexts examined		5	9	6	6	13	19	19	7	12	5	101

405

Table 6.2.12 Hand-collected fish remains excluding spines, finrays, pterigiophore and ribs by phase

Vernacular	Species	II	V	VI	VII	VIII	IX	X	Total
Thornback ray	*Raja clavata* (L.)				1				1
Herring	*Clupea harengus* L.	1			2				3
Salmonid	Salmonidae	2							2
Salmon	*Salmo salar* L.				2	1			3
Cyprinid	Cyprinidae				1				1
Eel	*Anguilla anguilla* (L.)				1				1
Gadid	Gadidae			1	1	1			3
Cod	*Gadus morhua* L.		1	6	6	3		4	20
Haddock	*Melanogrammus aeglefinus* (L.)						1		1
Ling	*Molva molva* (L.)			2	2	1	1		6
?Ling	cf *Molva molva* (L.)				1				1
Bass	*Dicentrarchus labrax* (L.)				1				1
Turbot	*Scophthalmus maximus* (L.)				7				7
Flatfish	Pleuronectidae			12	11	2	7	8	40
Total		3	1	21	36	8	9	12	90

Appendix: List of selected fish skeletal elements identified to species or family group where possible (*see* Methods)

Anal pterygiophore
Articular
Casioccipital
Basipterygium
Branchial fragments
Caudal vertebra
Ceratohyal
Cleithrum
Coracoid
Dentary
Dermal denticle
Ectopterygoid
Epihyal
Frontal
Hyomandibular
Lower hypohyal
Maxilla
Opercular
Otic bulla
Otolith
Palatine
Parasphenoid
Pharyngeal
Pharyngobranchial
Post temporal
Precaudal vertebra
Premaxilla
Preopercular
Prevomer
Quadrate
Scapula
Scute
Subopercular
Supracleithrum
Symplectic
Upper hypohyal
Urohyal
Vertebra
Vomer

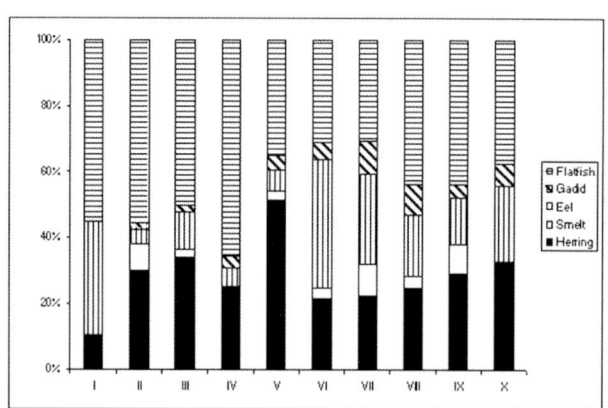

Ill 6.2.1 Frequency of the main fish species identified from samples sorted by phase.

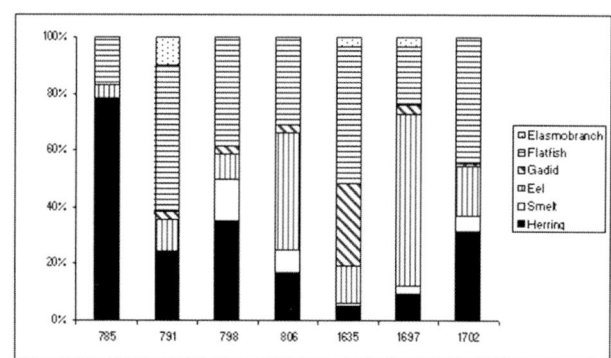

Ill 6.2.2 Frequency of the main fish species identified from selected Phase VI deposits.

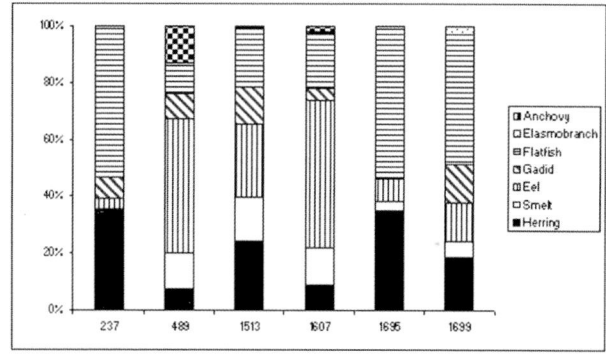

Ill 6.2.3 Frequency of the main fish species identified from selected Phase VII deposits.

Prehistoric Activity

IN the few areas (namely the ramp and access pit) where excavation was carried out to a level deep enough to encounter natural subsoil, it was clear that the early Roman construction levels had entirely removed any pre-Roman layers or surfaces. A few worked prehistoric lithics were found to be scattered throughout the Roman and later stratigraphy, but in all cases this material consisted of waste flakes or debitage which might simply have been derived from short-lived knapping episodes. None of this material could be ascribed to a particular prehistoric period; however, previous excavations within the Roman fortress and surrounding civilian settlement have yielded lithic tools which are ascribed to the Mesolithic, Neolithic and early Bronze Age periods. The material from the Bridge Street site can only be regarded as an indicator or 'background noise', which when added to the existing body of evidence lends further weight to the suggestion that Chester was an important site throughout prehistory.

Recent excavations at the Roman amphitheatre site in Chester during 2006 have revealed evidence for timber structures dating to the Middle Iron Age sealed by elements of a field system of Late Iron Age type (Garner 2007). Previously the only sound evidence for a pre-Roman Iron Age presence at Chester was a soil horizon containing a sherd of VCP buried beneath the fortress rampart at Abbey Green. The distance between these two sites was almost the entire length of the Roman fortress, and it would seem likely that the Iron Age occupation was thinly spread over a large area of the later Roman fortress and surrounding settlement. It is in this context that the 'celtic-style' copper alloy finial decorated in the form of a bulbous-eyed beast (cat no 15) must be considered. This object was recovered from the earliest Roman event encountered in the excavation, namely the cutting of a shallow terrace for the construction of road (1259), which was probably done during the initial laying out of the fortress *c* AD 75 (Mason 2001, 50).

Although the possibility remains that the celtic-style copper alloy finial arrived on the site with the Roman military, it is tempting to see it as an Iron Age object removed from its original context during the construction phase of the first Roman fortress. If so, it would constitute the first piece of decorative Iron Age metalwork to have been recovered from Chester and its environs. The decoration was reminiscent of an Iron Age copper alloy escutcheon found near Crewe, which has been argued to be derived from an iron tripod bucket of late Iron Age type (K Fitzpatrick-Matthews, *pers comm*). The material culture of Iron Age Cheshire (and indeed the North West of England in general) is somewhat elusive for reasons which have been recently summarised elsewhere (Hodgson & Brennand 2006, 51–8), and in this light the object from 25 Bridge Street is potentially of high importance in helping to elucidate the status of Chester during the Iron Age.

7

DISCUSSION

Phase I: Roman

The early fortress *insula*

The high level of residuality among the finds makes it extremely difficult to suggest firm dates for the Roman phases, or even to relate them to the established chronological framework for the fortress (which is itself less than secure). In particular, there is a considerable risk of dating phases too early.

As mentioned above, the earliest Roman event identified in the Bridge Street excavation was the cutting of a shallow terrace, (1260), in order to accommodate the construction of an east–west road running parallel to the southern boundary of the site (Phase Ia). This road would have been over 5 m wide and ran eastwards from the *via praetoria* along the northern edge of the baths to the *via sagularis* on the eastern side of the fortress; this is shown on Mason's conjectured primary fortress plan of *c* AD 75 (Mason 2001, 50). An evaluation trench excavated during 1996 had encountered this road further to the east, and pottery of late first-century date was recovered from its surface (Emery 1996), supporting an early date for the road's introduction. The position of the ramp excavation appeared to coincide precisely with a second road running north from the baths at right-angles to the first road. This was at least 3.5 m wide: its exact dimensions could not be established as the eastern edge had been removed during the construction of a later stone-founded building, whilst the western edge was not exposed within the excavation. A substantial portion of this road had been removed by the insertion of a stone-built sewer during the later third century.

These two roads survived for the rest of the life of the legionary fortress. They represent the first hard evidence that there was probably an additional *scamnum* between the baths and the tribunes' houses (*scamnum tribunorum*): previously it had only been conjectured (eg Carrington 1986); they also give us the first indications of how the *scamnum* was subdivided. The north–south road was in a slightly odd place as it was not a natural continuation of the road on the eastern side of the baths. The issue of layout will be returned to shortly when considering the later stone-founded building, but a natural inference would be that the block was subdivided into three *insulae* as the space between the *via praetoria* and the north–south road was approximately 60 m (200 *pedes*) and the entire block could not be more than 180 m (600 *pedes*) from east to west. On this basis the *insula* could conceivably have accommodated three pairs of *tabernae* of similar dimensions to those identified at the northern end of the Elliptical Building *insula* (Mason 2000, 100–2). No evidence was uncovered to indicate what might have occupied the area to the west of the north–south road during the first century. However, Evaluation Trenches B and C excavated in 1999 suggested that to the east of the road a series of deposits formed in the latter part of the first century which were consistent with a building

platform. Little artefactual evidence was retrieved from this early phase and none of it helped to suggest the function of this part of the fortress in its original plan.

Sometime towards the end of the first or in the early second century the east–west road was resurfaced (Phase Ib). At about the same time a shallow drainage channel was excavated along the northern edge of the road where it joined the north–south road. The reasons for doing this were clearly short-lived as once the drain became choked with silt it was not unblocked or replaced. The silt in this drain contained both charred wheat (*Triticum*) grains and both eel and possibly cod bones; a very small assemblage of some twenty mammal bones showing signs of butchery was also recovered. Generally this material was too meagre in quantity to draw any meaningful conclusions; however, it did indicate that a range of food waste was accumulating. This may indicate food preparation or consumption nearby, but it was unlikely to be derived from the baths to the south.

The second-century fortress *insula*

Pottery from the wall foundations and the make-up of the primary floor surface would suggest that a stone-founded building (Building I(i)) was erected during the early to mid-second century on the eastern side of the north–south road (Phase Ic). It is not clear whether this corresponded to the initial stone construction noted elsewhere in the fortress *c* 120 or that which may have taken place in the 160s (eg Ward & Strickland 1978, 16–23). This new building largely occupied an area to the east of the 2001 excavations, lying beneath a late nineteenth-century part of the Brown's department store. As the nineteenth-century building did not have a basement, it seems likely that much of this Roman building would have survived the 2001 development.

The south-western corner of the Building I(i) was located at the junction of the two roads and the foundation could clearly be seen to have been cut through the silts filling the earlier roadside drain. The western wall was traced north from the corner for a distance of approximately 10 m and was 0.8 m wide. The position of a short section of what was possibly the northern wall of the building was identified in Evaluation Trench B in 1999; this was of similar width to the western wall. To the north of the wall found in Trench B there was a series of sandstone surfaces that could have been external road or courtyard metalling, whilst on the southern side of the wall there was *in-situ* wall plaster adhering to the upstanding masonry and an internal mortar floor surface. This would give the building a north–south dimension of 18 m (61 *pedes*), which poses various problems of interpretation. The first problem is that the predicted *scamnum* measurement north–south is 30 m (100 *pedes*), meaning that the building would have occupied the southern three-fifths of the *insula*, leaving only a narrow building strip on its northern side. The second problem is that the thickness of the wall foundations would be in keeping with some of the fortress's smaller buildings, such as the barrack blocks (T Strickland *pers comm*). However, the dimensions of the building did not tally with those of the standard stone barrack blocks at Chester, which were 11.8 m (40 *pedes*) wide and 82.5 m (280 *pedes*) long (Mason 2001, 132). Furthermore, the position of the north–south road precluded the *scamnum* from being neatly divided into barrack blocks, which would seem to rule out this option for the building's function.

The north–south dimensions of the building, along with the thickness of the stone-founded walls, were broadly in keeping with a granary (*horreum*). However, there are again problems with this interpretation, as the interiors of such buildings tended to have raised floors supported on either sleeper walls or *pilae* in order to aid ventilation and prevent dampness. The interior of Building I(i) was only seen in two small evaluation trenches (B and C) excavated in 1999. In both instances it was possible to demonstrate that there were mortar floor surfaces inside the building at ground level. The use of solid ground-level floors in *horrea* is attested at several sites, such as Bar Hill (Gentry 1976, 58), and at Caersws a ground-level flagged floor followed the removal of a raised predecessor (*op cit*, 66). Certainly, ground-level flooring would have increased the loading capacity, and it seems reasonable to suggest that the preference for either solid or ventilated floors would have been dependent on what was being stored within (Wilmott 1997, 136). The case for the present building being a *horreum* ultimately flounders on the presence of an internal partition wall and other embellishments such as the mortar floors and plastered walls.

These embellishments were indicative of a slightly raised status in comparison with other buildings within the fortress. The mortar floors and plastered walls were comparable with the centurion's quarters at Crook Street and Northgate Brewery (Mason 2001, 133–5). An internal urinal was probably situated at the western end of the building, as indicated by the lead-lined drain emptying from the western wall into a larger drain or pit on the north–south road. This arrangement was again in keeping with the centurion's quarters at both Abbey Green and Northgate Brewery (Ward & Strickland 1978, 21–2). Only a small fraction of the total assemblage of Roman ceramic building material came from this phase and this comprised a limited range of forms – mainly roof tiles and a single box tile fragment. The latter would have come from a centrally heated building (eg a public building or high-status private accommodation), and this seems to be consistent with other indicators of raised status for the area. It is probably worth noting that the only evidence we have for the building on the western side of the north–south road was recorded in 1901 when a large pit (in the position of the brick cellared Building IX (iv) in Plot 2) exposed parts of two internal floor surfaces, the northern one being described as *opus signinum*, the southern as a mosaic (Newstead 1928, 104). It remains possible that these surfaces belonged to the tribunes' houses, in which case the latter would have been much larger and on a different spacing than has hitherto been conjectured.

As with the earlier phases the artefactual evidence comprised relatively small assemblages covering most material categories, both securely stratified material and residual objects dating to the second century and recovered from later phases of the site. The results revealed some interesting, if possibly conflicting, trends that may help shed some light on the function of the buildings in this *insula*. It is perhaps unsurprising that much of the metalwork had a distinctly military flavour, including two copper alloy military belt plates of Antonine form. A

single piece of scale armour (*lorica squamata*), also likely to be of Antonine date, was recovered from a deposit which had formed above the mortar floor in Building I(i); the object was damaged and may indicate that there was a *fabrica* in the area. Possibly of greater interest was the identification of two copper alloy fittings belonging to one or more horse harnesses, perhaps implying the presence of cavalry nearby. It is worth noting that the function of a second-century cavalry stables has already been ascribed to a stone building of similar dimensions to a barrack block, excavated in 1973 at Goss Street in the *latera praetorii* of the fortress (Strickland 1977, 26–7).

A meagre assemblage of butchered animal bone, charred wheat grains (*Triticum*) and fishbone (predominantly flatfish) was recovered, implying that food preparation/consumption was happening nearby. This activity was possibly confirmed by a substantial fragment from a portable oven (*clibanus*) which was recovered from the backfilling of the sewer connected to the lead-lined drain; *clibani* were generally used to bake bread/cakes, to roast meat and keep food hot (Jones 2006, 24). Two bone gaming counters of probable second-century type were recovered from deposits to the north of the building. Finally, a number of second-century copper alloy and bone hair pins were recovered from deposits associated with the north–south road, and it has been suggested that these artefacts perhaps indicate that women were living in the vicinity or visiting the baths to the south (Cool, *this volume*).

Despite some advances being made in characterising the types of building occupying this *insula* during the second century, their function remains a matter of conjecture. At present it is not even possible to be certain how many buildings occupied the *scamnum* or what their overall dimensions were. What can be established is that the interiors of these buildings were furnished to a level above that of the common barrack blocks. The building to the east seems to have been in keeping with centurions' quarters elsewhere in the fortress, implying that it was used as accommodation for personnel of this rank or higher. The mosaic floor noted in the building to the west in 1901 was undated. However, it is tempting to see this building as the residence for a more senior-ranking officer and possibly accommodating the women hinted at in the artefact assemblage.

Third-century developments

Probably in the first half of the third century the floor surfaces in Building I(i) were resurfaced with *opus signinum* which contained recycled fragments of painted wall plaster which may have decorated the second-century building (Phase Id). The nature and timing of this refurbishment work may be echoed at the centurion's quarters excavated at Northgate Brewery (Ward & Strickland 1978, 23–4), along with more extensive rebuilding elsewhere in the fortress (Mason 2001, 161–80). A small amount of evidence dating to the third century was recorded from the northern part of the *scamnum* prior to the 2001 excavations: this comprised a number of parallel stone-founded walls (Mason 2001, 177). In this light the *opus signinum* and mosaic floors noted to the west of the north–south branch road may also have belonged to this phase.

The east–west and north–south roads originally laid out during the first century were both resurfaced at about this time. Subsequently, the north–south road became covered in a thick layer containing domestic debris and ironworking waste, which implied that it had temporarily gone out of use. This state of affairs clearly did not last long, as after the middle of the middle of the third century the road had again been resurfaced and furnished with a substantial stone-lined sewer (Phase Ie).

Reviewing the artefactual evidence for the third-century occupation, it is first clear that there was a marked decline in the amount of contemporary pottery (much of the material being residual late first–second-century material). Amongst the metalwork assemblage there was an enamelled belt plate typical of third-century military fashion and a second- or third-century military strap end. As with earlier phases, evidence of food waste was present but in quite small quantities, which prevented meaningful analysis. One interesting identification from the third-century material was the presence in the fish bone assemblage of Spanish mackerel, which might suggest the use of the fish sauce known as *garum*. Even though this evidence was slight it might again suggest the preparation or consumption of food in the vicinity of the excavation – perhaps within the buildings flanking either side of the north–south road.

Phases II and III: Late Roman–Late Saxon

Phase II

It was suggested in the stratigraphic narrative that Phase IIa represented the final period of Roman occupation in this part of the Roman fortress. The first event in this sequence is likely to have been the laying of the new road surface (1226), the intermittent patching of which suggested prolonged use and maintenance. During the life of this road surface an overhaul of the Phase Ie sewer network appears to have included the addition of a tributary, (1147), which was a less substantial construction than the earlier sewer, (1182), but was apparently fit for purpose. This appeared to run towards the corner of Building I(i), where an earlier drain, (1390), had been placed in Phase Ic, suggesting that the building was still in use and that provision was still being made for the sewerage.

The evidence from Escalator Pit B suggested that Building I(i) fell in to disuse during this sub-phase and that it may even have been deliberately demolished, as was the case with other buildings in the fortress during the fourth century (Mason 2000, 148–9). This event may have given rise to the occurrence of relatively large amounts of Roman ceramic building material, mainly roof tile, during this sub-phase. The final event of Phase IIa was the formation of layer (1237/1225/1142), which contained fragments of *opus signinum*, quantities of loose *tesserae* and herringbone floor tiles (*opus spicatum*)

which could have been derived from the floors of the bath house to the south or other neighbouring buildings. It has been argued that the bath house remained in use into the late fourth century and beyond (Mason *et al* 2005), which may therefore give a rough indication of the date for the end of Phase IIa. On the other hand, these fragments could have been discarded during refurbishment of that building.

The silting of the main sewer (1182) and the tributary (1147) would presumably have happened after the abandonment/demolition of Building I(i) and the formation of layer (1237/1225/1142). Large numbers of *tesserae* were again found in the sewer silts.

Phase IIb seems to have been initiated by the excavation of a trench, (1229), through Phase IIa layer (1237/ 1225/1142), which in effect managed to uncover the capping stones of the main Phase Ie sewer (1182). This may have been done to bring the sewer (1182) back in to use (which might suggest that the silting discussed above in Phase IIa took place after this event), although the trench could have functioned as a drain in its own right. The fact that the trench followed the line of the sewer exactly suggests that the excavators were aware of its presence and wished to re-establish a drain running towards the main east–west road to the north of the bath house.

A byproduct of the excavation to re-establish the main north–south drain was the creation of a low earthen bank (1181) parallel and to the east of trench (1229) comprising the upcast material. This bank was subsequently cut into during the excavation of a series of substantial post holes which have been interpreted as the western side of Building II(i). The plan of this new building can only be guessed at; however, it might be significant that the post holes followed the line of the wall of Building I(i), suggesting that the general Roman site layout was still being respected. The date for the construction of Building II(i) was problematic: one of the post holes, (1137), produced a coin dated AD 330–5, while the beaten earth floor, (99), in Evaluation Trench C contained a fragment of fourth-century copper alloy bracelet, both of which provided a *tpq*, but the high level of residual material encountered in Phase II, together with the date of the finds in Phase IIa, raised the possibility that construction took place long after this date. The same post hole also produced a fragment of box tile which was probably derived from the bath house to the south and could not have migrated to the 25 Bridge Street site until the bath house had fallen into disrepair.

A single post hole, (1222), sat out of alignment with the western wall of Building II(i); this may represent a repair to the building, implying a period of prolonged use and maintenance. Evidence for the nature of the occupation of Building II(i) was hinted at. A layer of silt above floor surface (99) was interpreted as an occupation deposit; if so, the nature of the occupation would seem to have involved the working of copper alloy, (implied by the presence of crucible fragments and copper alloy working waste) and ironsmithing. This is potentially interesting, as the fragments of copper alloy and iron mail links from second–third century Roman armour first appeared in Phase II, and it has been suggested that the items may have derived from a single event involving the manufacture or refurbishment of mail armour (*see* Mould *this volume*).

During the construction and occupation of Building II(i) a number of pits were excavated along the line of the Phase Ie sewer, apparently in order to remove sections of the structure as part of a stone-robbing exercise. Amphibian bones were present in two of these pits, and this might suggest that once the stone-robbing had taken place the pits remained open; certainly pit (1139) seems to have found a secondary use as a cess pit, producing faecal material. All of these pits were subsequently backfilled, and the high level of residual Roman material in the fill would suggest that much of this was derived from their original excavation. Several elements from a large cat (possibly a wild cat) were recovered from pit (1139) and this may indicate that it was the result of primary deposition. The bone had marks suggesting the animal had been skinned, and this may suggest another manufacturing activity associated with the Phase IIb occupation.

Phase IIc comprised several cultivation soils or dark earth deposits, indicating that the entire area had been subject to a change of use. All of the elements of the Roman site plan had now become obsolete and the character of the site appears to have changed from urban to agricultural. Unfortunately, no reliable dating evidence was recovered to indicate when this change of use might have taken place.

Phase II was characterised by an extremely high level of residuality, almost to the point that there were no contemporary artefacts recovered from secure contexts. The phase produced the largest quantity of Roman ceramic building material of any phase on the site, and 30% of the Roman pottery assemblage recovered from the excavation came from Phase II contexts. This level of residuality was borne out by the radiocarbon dates from a selection of animal bone samples (Smith, *this volume*). This leaves us with a very loose chronological framework on which to base any useful discussion. What can be said with a degree of confidence is that some point within Phase II marked the end of the Roman occupation and the phase must therefore hold the evidence for any subsequent activity prior to the establishment of the early tenth-century Saxon *burh*.

Sub-phase IIb was notable for the first appearance of fourth-century pottery, including late shell-tempered wares with a date of *c* 360+; it also produced a coin dated AD 330–5. This could suggest that the start of Phase IIb could, in fact, be of mid-fourth-century date. However, the presence of large number of *tesserae*, if they were related to the demolition of part of the bath house, suggests a later date.

Phase III

The issues regarding the ephemeral nature of the archaeology of this period in Chester and the difficulties in identifying it have been adequately covered elsewhere (Ward *et al* 1994, 3–4). The quantity and nature of the remains encountered at the 25 Bridge Street site were typical of those found within the legionary fortress during this period. However, the artefact assemblage appeared on the whole to be rather meagre in comparison to previous interventions, with only one copper alloy bead of Norse type and a pair of tweezers likely to be contemporary *in-situ* artefacts. In fact, all of the Chester ware pottery was recovered as residual material from later phases of the site. In contrast to this, the environmental remains were relatively abundant, and two important assemblages were recovered from well sealed contexts scientifically dated to the late Saxon period. It is perhaps surprising to note that this was the first time scientifically dated environmental samples have been analysed from late Saxon levels at Chester, and consequently the information recovered is entirely new and potentially ground-breaking.

The first inference to be drawn from the environmental sampling was that the range of species represented in the fish bone assemblage suggests that trade in fish was not well established, or particularly important to the economy, during the Anglo-Saxon period in Chester. This conclusion is apparently at odds with the historical evidence which refers to the import of foodstuffs, including fish, from Ireland (Ward *et al* 1994, 124). The second important inference relates to agricultural production in Chester and its hinterland. The identification of pulses, including garden/field pea and field bean, alongside cereals including bread/club wheat, rye, barley and cultivated oat, suggests an agricultural regime which involved a crop rotation system. Similar evidence from late Saxon contexts from Wessex and Yorkshire has been interpreted in this way. Furthermore, sedge/peat and hazel appear to have been the dominant fuel types in the samples, and this may imply exploitation of targeted resources such as the peat deposits of the Gowy marshes. Some forms of wild fruits including sloe (?), and blackberry/bramble were also being harvested as part of the local diet. Imported fruit may be represented by a single fig seed, and again this has been noted at other late Saxon port sites such as Southampton. The general picture would suggest that the late Saxon economy of Chester's hinterland was similar to that of other parts of the country.

Phase IV: Early Medieval

Norman Chester has proved elusive in previous archaeological excavations within the city. However, it was almost certainly represented in Phase IV contexts, although the only recognisable contemporary artefacts were Norman-type horseshoes recovered residually from Phase VI context (683) and Phase VII context (389) and a possible textile-processing spike, potentially of pre-Conquest or Norman date, from Phase VI layer (776).

Post-conquest activity appeared to be confined to the accumulation of cultivation soils; at this time the entire site seems to have been open ground, with no initial evidence for property boundaries or land divisions. This may not be surprising as the excavation was located a long way from any of the main street frontages, where one would expect to find evidence for more formal arrangements. It has been argued that a number of parish boundaries were already established by this time, and the reference in Domesday Book to 500 burgages within the city in 1066 implies that some system of land division had been adopted within the Mercian *burh*.

The animal bone assemblage suggests that ravens were possibly scavenging on the site, which might be in keeping with midden deposits being spread on agricultural land. The textile-processing spike was probably introduced to the site as part of midden-spreading, but the object may also hint at textile-processing on the Bridge Street frontage.

The first evidence for land division was the creation of a north–south ditch, (1127), which was equidistant between the Bridge Street and Newgate Street frontages. This ditch may in fact be rather significant as it suggests that the block of land defined on all four sides by Bridge Street, Eastgate Street, Newgate Street and Pepper Street, was formally laid out as burgage plots. Scrutiny of the 25" 1st edition OS map of 1875 suggests that some burgage plots may have become fossilised in the townscape along the Bridge Street frontage. Taking the standard burgage plot width of 66 feet it is possible to extrapolate nine plots of equal width along Bridge Street between the corners of Eastgate Street and Pepper Street. Intriguingly, the central plot in this extrapolation appears to be perfectly preserved on the 1875 map, implying that much of the 25 Bridge Street excavation was located to the rear of the third plot south of Eastgate Street.

The later developments in Phase IV indicated that the large burgage plots were subsequently subdivided. This was clearly demonstrated by the stone boundary wall (600), which neatly defined the back of a property that was designated as Plot 2. This boundary wall followed the course of ditch (1127) and its construction trench had clearly been cut into the upper ditch fill; a coin dated 1180–1247 was recovered from the fabric of this wall. To the north of Plot 2 (the later Plot 3) a complex series of walls, clay surfaces and possible ovens/hearths were associated with pottery dated 1250+, while in Plot 6 a post hole dated cal AD 1150–1270 was covered by a clay surface associated with an oven base. The importance of Chester was raised after 1237 when it became the supply base for Henry III's and Edward I's campaigns in North Wales, heralding a period of economic growth and a rapidly increasing population. This suggests that the burgage plot subdivisions evidenced at 25 Bridge Street were a result of this economic growth in the city. Presumably the reduction in area for each property would have brought into use even the furthest reaches of each plot for activities earlier conducted nearer the street frontage. This suggests that ditch (1127) and the earlier cultivation soils did in fact date to the twelfth century.

Phase V: Late Medieval

The precise chronology of the later medieval developments on the site remains uncertain but at some point in the fourteenth–fifteenth century the area was formally divided by substantial stone property boundaries. As mentioned above, the main north–south boundary, marking the mid-point between Bridge Street and Newgate Street, was set out in Phase IV. In terms of site function, there was strong evidence for the construction of ovens at the backs of individual properties, some of which were quite elaborate in design. The precise use of these ovens remains obscure, but baking and brewing may have been some of the activities carried on. In one case the fabric of the oven contained a large quantity of reused medieval floor tile, which was of regional significance in its own right. The other activity ascribed to this period was the construction of pits for the disposal of cess and domestic waste. Within this category was a large stone-lined structure in Plot 2, context (487), which remained in use until the sixteenth century and is discussed in more detail in Phase VI. Enough of the pits were investigated to produce small assemblages of artefacts and ecofacts. Little could be inferred about activities on the site from the domestic debris with the exception of Plot 3, where a large number of sheep/goat metapodials appeared to indicate the presence of a leatherworker.

The plots that emerged in Phase IV could clearly be seen to develop during Phase V into six distinct properties which, once established, continued in existence until the later eighteenth century. Unfortunately some uncertainty remains over the ownership of these properties during the medieval period and this has limited the results of the documentary analysis undertaken for this report. However, a general rise in status could be inferred amongst the occupants, perhaps most graphically implied by a wide range of personal equipment including common fourteenth-century types of buckle and strap ends. The animal bone assemblage also indicated more sophisticated dietary tastes with calf carcasses or joints of calf/veal arriving on the site during Phase V; these have been interpreted as being early evidence for the dairy industry in Chester. Pigs may also have been farrowing in the area, dovecotes were possibly present, and dogs, cats and possibly ravens were scavenging in the open ground.

Phase VI: Late 15–mid-17 century

The date range for Phase VI has been established by a number of factors. A late fifteenth-century start was dictated by the appearance of Cistercian ware pottery and by the earliest documentary reference (dating to 1493) to Bridge Street Row East as 'Mercers' Row'. A mid-seventeenth-century close was again partly based on artefact assemblages.

In addressing the origins of Phase VI there are few tightly datable stratified objects belonging to this phase which were of fifteenth-century date, one exception being a small copper alloy finger ring (no 87) recovered from the stone surface (862) at the very back of Plot 2. This object tends to corroborate the argument for stone-lined cess pit (487) having its origins in Phase V. The lowest fills (806), (798) and (797) of the pit can be dated by imported pottery to the very late fifteenth or first half of the sixteenth centuries and it must have ceased to function as a cess pit by this time. Possibly another early artefact assemblage in the phase came from the primary fill (1697) of cess pit (1624) in Plot 4: here continental imports again suggest a date in the very late fifteenth or first half of the sixteenth century. Although it was not possible to identify individuals living at these properties during the early part of Phase VI the documentary evidence suggests that this part of Bridge Street Row comprised an enclave of mercers. This may be supported in the archaeological record by the heightened occurrence of copper alloy tie loops, lace tags and sewing pins from Phase VI onwards, and more specifically in Plot 4 by the leaf from a wool card (SF 9408) and a pair of scissors (SF 9301) that were recovered from cess pit fill (1697).

The Plots 2 and 4 cess pits (487) and (1624) provide valuable comparable assemblages as they are broadly contemporary and from closely neighbouring properties. It is clear that the assemblages are broadly similar with pottery groups being dominated by Cistercian ware cups and large jars/cisterns, whilst in each case there was a smattering of highly decorative (often polychrome) imported pottery (often in the form of a plate or dish). Iron table knives were also recovered in both assemblages, and it is notable that many of the glass vessels were identified as bottles and urinals. The most revealing information, however, comes from the palaeoenvironmental evidence recovered from the two pits. In the case of both pits fig seeds were found to be very common, along with blackberry, raspberry and grape; apple, pear, medlar and sloe were also present but only fill (806) had an abundance of strawberry seeds. This suggests that the occupants of the properties represented by Plots 2 and 4 had access to a wide variety of fresh fruits. Faunal remains from the fills of pit (487) included venison, suckling pig, calves (veal), and an increase in the range of wild bird species all indicative of high status. In both pits parasite eggs of whipworms were identified and were concluded to have been derived from human faecal matter deposited within the pits (whipworm can cause stomach pains and diarrhoea; it can make sufferers anaemic, and in extreme cases can cause rectal prolapse). Unfortunately other pits in this phase did not have the right conditions to preserve this sort of evidence so we cannot judge how common this sort of parasitic infection may have been in Chester's population at this time.

The documentary research suggested that by the later sixteenth to early seventeenth century it might be possible to begin to identify the names of some of the owners and occupiers of the properties fronting on to Bridge Street Row East. The status of these occupants can be illustrated by people such as William Wall, who was identified as an ironmonger in 1568/9 and who owed money to the City Assembly for extending a Row building out onto the public highway; again in 1573 he was listed as owing money to the City Assembly for rent on a piece of 'voide grond' on which he had built a substantial house; he served in the office of mayor in 1586/7 and was clearly a wealthy man on his death in 1599, as his will referred to several houses in Bridge Street. With reference to the current excavations it was possible to tentatively identi-

fy the owners or occupants of three plots in particular. The first and most tentative was a Robert Fletcher (feltmaker/hatmaker), who may have purchased the property identified as Plot 1 in 1612. Prior to this he had been elected alderman in 1608/9 and had held the office of treasurer in 1611; in the same year his son (also called Robert Fletcher) held the office of sheriff. Robert Fletcher's will of 1617 included an inventory which indicated a substantial house and shop. The most certain identification was for Plot 5 and established that the owner between 1605 and 1639 was a John Sparke, who was almost certainly related to or shared the residence with a William Sparke, a merchant and ironmonger who was mayor in 1632/3. This has led to us identifying the owner of Plot 4 in 1617 as William Edwards, ironmonger, who was originally William Sparke's apprentice; he became a common councillor in 1623, alderman in 1631 and mayor in 1636/7.

The 'Great Rebuilding'

During the latter part of the sixteenth and first half of the seventeenth century there was a great rebuilding of the town houses and shops of the merchant class in Chester, particularly those in the Rows. This has been attributed to a general rise in wealth in England during the period (Brown ed 1999, 77). In Chester the poor condition of many of the buildings in the city by the later sixteenth century is well documented. This has been attributed to limited repairs and reconstruction being undertaken in previous centuries, with the majority of building stock being of considerable age: the house of Thomas Ince, for example, was described as 'dating from before the memory of man'. The late sixteenth and early seventeenth century saw such a transformation in the buildings of the city centre that by the 1620s William Webb recorded that 'the streets, for the most part, are very fair and beautiful, the buildings on either side, especially towards the streets, of seemly proportion, and very neatly composed; whether of timber, whereof the most are builded; or of stone, or brick' (Smith & Webb 1696, 2, 19–20). Much of this rebuilding comprised timber frames built on top of the existing medieval stone undercrofts and cellars (Brown ed 1999, 77–9). It has been suggested that during this period in England people below the level of gentry became influential in demanding or building new forms of houses. These changes were reflected in a move away from large stone houses based on rural models to large timber properties built as homes for the builders or as speculation. This included the creation of a new building form towards the end of the sixteenth century which was a large house built of timber often referred to as a 'merchant's house'. At Shrewsbury this development has been seen as a deliberate move to create homogeneity and a sense of corporate, urban independence from previous forms of higher authority. This movement was driven by an urban oligarchy dominated by a few great men, in alliance with their like in the countryside (Schofield 1997, 141–2).

The documentary research undertaken for the excavation site has demonstrated that by the late sixteenth to early seventeenth century the properties fronting on to Bridge Street Row East were clearly changing ownership, with the new owners such as William Wall and

William Edwards developing their properties with extensions and new buildings. It has been noted elsewhere that in Elizabethan and Jacobean town houses, where the ground floor was a shop, domestic accommodation started on the first floor; and commonly the front room on the first floor would be the one most likely to be embellished with a plastered ceiling, the largest most ornate fireplace and decorative panelling (Schofield 1997, 140). It is perhaps significant in this context to note that the building belonging to Plot 4 which is attributed to William Edwards (15 Bridge Street and 17–19 Bridge Street Row), has a surviving room above the Row on the street front which retains a seventeenth-century panelled plaster ceiling, as does the room above it in the attic storey. This building is shown in its unaltered form in an engraving of 'St Peter's church and Bridge Street in 1700' and in a later engraving by Moses Griffith of 'Bridge Street and Mercer's Row' in 1777.

Some of the documentary evidence goes further in providing a picture of the grandeur of some of these new buildings. Robert Fletcher's will of 1617 listed his possessions room by room and indicated a substantial house and shop, possibly occupying the front of Plot 1. From this will it is possible to highlight various features of the building, even though no plans of it survive: at street level there was a cellar which was the site of 'The Moon Tavern' in 1612; at Row level there was a 'great chamber' a 'little chamber' and a 'parlour'; above this was a 'hall' and 'chamber'; and above this again was a 'gallery' and a 'chamber at the stair head'. These details indicate a four-storey building which would have been considered the height of fashion in the major towns of Tudor England. In particular both the 'great chamber' and the 'gallery' had noble overtones and there is reference to the sixteenth-century innovation of the staircase which occurred in houses which were large enough to have a hall and parlour block in a separate wing (Schofield 1997, 137). The will also mentions a 'parlour'; again this was a sixteenth-century development linked to a series of distinctions which operated in the emerging 'territorial unit', eg the front was public, as it was connected to the street, and the back was private and connected with the garden (Schofield 1997, 140). The parlour usually overlooked the garden to the rear of a property, and it is perhaps noteworthy that later in the seventeenth century the back of the Fletcher's property was described as having a 'long garden'. Further details to be gleaned from the 1617 will include references to service areas like the 'buttery', 'small buttery' and 'storehouse', as well as a servants quarters referred to as 'the nurses chamber'.

There appears to be some correlation between the archaeological record and this 'great rebuilding'. Many layers, deposits and pit fills in Phase VI were rich in waste building materials. Most notable of these was the complex sequence of fills in the Plot 2 cess pit (487), which contained many fragments of early hand-made brick and numerous glazed floor tiles. There were also several examples of large build-ups of grey roofing slate fragments (such as in the fills of Plot 6 pit (681)) which implied that buildings in several of the plots were receiving new slate roofs. Furthermore, there was evidence for a large build-up of stone masonry waste at the back of Plot 1 which could well have been associated with a new building on the Bridge Street frontage.

The documentary evidence, combined with surviving architectural details, supports an argument for the occupants of the properties on Bridge Street Row East being part of an affluent new urban elite who often went in to considerable debt rebuilding, altering and embellishing their new town houses. Many of these new owners were listed as 'ironmongers' (in this case probably middlemen dealing with the distribution of iron as a raw material to smiths and then organising the redistribution of the finished products to retailers), implying that allusions to the area as 'Mercer's Row' were no longer necessarily valid. These individuals would have been guildsmen and appear to have been upwardly mobile and heavily integrated into the social and political elite of Chester's society, with many reaching the offices of mayor, treasurer or sheriff. This shift may hint at a wider socio-economic change linked with the rise of the iron industry in the Welsh Marches during the seventeenth century, which ended the supremacy of the south-east in terms of the country's total iron production (Crossley 1990, 153–62).

It has been argued that in the case of towns such as Norwich the later sixteenth century saw an increase in the number of cess pits for each house, and that this was associated with a 'Tudor' trend towards the designation of spaces for waste and ablutions (Schofield 1997, 141). Furthermore, separate privies for male and female servants were reported in a large London merchant's house in 1543 (*op cit*, 140). It is perhaps in this context that we can find an explanation for many of the pits recorded in this and later phases of the Bridge Street site.

The Civil War siege

During the English Civil War between 1642 and 1646 Chester remained a staunchly Royalist city in a largely Parliamentary county and was thus in the 'front line' for most of the conflict (Ward 1987, 1). During the early part of the war Chester served mainly as a debarkation point and garrison for Royalist troops drawn from Ireland and North Wales. However, by September 1645 the city was under serious siege by Parliamentary forces. Supplies were virtually cut off by a close blockade, and this was accompanied by a sporadic bombardment from artillery pieces which included a mortar supplied by the Shropshire Parliamentary committee (Barratt 2003, 133). The effects of the siege are well documented by both the Royalist commander Lord Byron and notable citizens of the city like Randle Holme. Lord Byron stated that the mortar bombardment was '... very terrible to the people, causing great spoil in the part of the town where they fell' (thought to be along Watergate and Eastgate Streets). Byron also related an anecdote about a Parliamentary sympathiser living in the city who, along with his house, was blown up by a falling granadoe (Barratt 2003, 136). The most graphic account of the bombardment comes from Randle Holme describing the night of 10th December 1645:

> Eleven huge granadoes like so many tumbling demi-phaetons threaten to set the city, if not the world, on fire. This was a terrible night indeed, our houses like so many split vessels crash their supporters and burst themselves in sunder through the very violence of these descending firebrands. The Talbott, an house adjoining to the Eastgate flames

outright; our hands are bruised in quenching this whilst the law of nature bids us leave and seek our own security. Being thus distracted another thunder-crack invites our eyes to the most miserable spectacle that spite could possibly present us with – two houses in the Watergate slippes joint from joint and creates an earthquake, the main posts josell each other, whilst the frighted casements fly for feare, in a word the whole fabrick is a perfect chaos lively set forth in this metamorphosis. The grandmother, mother and three children are struck stark dead and buried in the ruins of this humble edifice, a sepulchre well worth the enemies remembrance ...

But for all this they are still not satisfied, women and children have not blood enough to quench their fury, and therefore about midnight they shoot seven more in hope of greater execution, one of these last light in an old man's bedchamber, and send him some fewe dayes sooner to his grave than perhaps was given him.

11 December six more break in amongst us, one of which persuade an old woman to bear the old man company to heaven, because the times were evill. Our ladyes all this while, like wise merchants, keep their sellars and will not venture forth in these tymes of danger lest they should miscarry, and indeed not without cause, for within the space of five nights following they shot twenty nine great granadoes which break down diverse houses in the Eastgate and Watergate Streets, but very few or none at all are hurt. (Barratt 2003, 144).

Along with the bombardment came the deprivation caused by the choking of supply lines to the city, with many references to some of the defenders (primarily the Welsh soldiery) starving to death. The commander of the Parliamentary besiegers, Sir William Brereton, stated that by the end of 1645: 'The better sort eat beef and bacon, but little cheese ... the poorer sort of the city that are not soldiers are ready to starve, they are compelled to eat horse flesh'.

Later in December two deserters from the Royalist garrison (one of whom was a John Fletcher) told their Parliamentary interrogators that: 'the poorer sort are in extreme want and of late some of the Welsh soldiers have perished for want of food' and that 'the soldiers, Irish and Welsh have 3d a day which they bestow in bread and beere to boil it in and that is their diet'. Lord Byron himself stated that: '...horse flesh grew in to such request that they who had any horses were forced to keep good guard upon them...' (Barratt 2003, 147).

It has, however, proved impossible to date any part of the archaeological record on this site with confidence to the period of the Civil War. The reason for this is largely due to the fact that artefactual dating evidence cannot be precise enough to isolate contexts dating to the 1640s. Furthermore, there were no obvious indicators in the structural record to suggest the sort of upheaval one might expect from the destruction wreaked by the Parliamentary bombardment of the city. That said, there were a few strands of evidence from the site which remain possible contenders for Civil War archaeology. Much of this evidence came from Plot 1 where a piece of armour known as a jack of plate was recovered from an early seventeenth-

century layer which was rich in building debris. Although this object is generally considered to be more in keeping with use during the sixteenth century, it is interesting to note that the inventory for the will of Robert Fletcher (who probably owned Plot 1) dated to 1617 listed a quantity of arms and armour including a 'Jacke'. These items have turned up in archaeological contexts associated with the Civil War at both Beeston (Eaves 1989) and Pontefract castles, which implies that although they were probably considered obsolete pieces of equipment by the 1640s they may have continued in use – particularly when arms and armour were in short supply. Associated with the jack in Plot 1 was a layer, (766), containing a young dog skeleton which had suffered extensive injuries leading to broken bones, subsequent infection and a premature death, and it is tempting to see this as a valued pet lost in the siege bombardment.

One of the dumps of material backfilling the cess pit (487) in Plot 2 produced the remains of two dogs, the butchery marks possibly indicating that the animals had been filleted. However, the dating evidence for this context spanned the late sixteenth and early seventeenth centuries and, as has been pointed out in the animal bone analysis, there were other periods of hardship during the late sixteenth century when people may have resorted to such extremes. The general indication from the Phase VI animal bone assemblage was one of increasing wealth, and this was supported in the documentary evidence. It is also worth noting that the documentary evidence for the siege implied that the wealthy still managed to maintain a reasonable level of diet, at a price: for example, Lord Cholmondeley had a turkey bought for him at a cost of seventeen shillings in December 1645 (Barratt 2003, 146). Thus it would seem that the residents of the Bridge Street site may have weathered the siege reasonably well. Some also managed to survive the political upheavals: the resident of Plot 4, William Sparke, was one of only seven aldermen in the city to retain his seat on the aldermanic bench after the end of the siege in 1646.

A treatise on the humble cess pit

The most common feature encountered during the excavations was the humble pit. Throughout the structural narrative the temptation to refer to anything as a 'rubbish pit' has been avoided, as it was unlikely that any pit on the site was dug specifically for the disposal of 'rubbish'; the fact that many of the pits contained 'rubbish' is considered to be secondary to their original function, ie an opportunistic use of a hole in the ground which needed to be filled in anyway to dispose of 'rubbish'. The debate over whether anything should be labelled as a 'cess pit' is also a complicated one, as even the presence of cess/faecal material in a pit need not be conclusive evidence for this attribution.

However, the interpretation of these pits is crucial to understanding site formation processes on the 25 Bridge Street site. A pit dug to dispose of, for example, noxious food waste, to prevent scavengers, flies etc from being attracted to living areas, would not have been left open for any length of time and could have been largely back-filled with the material generated by the digging of the pit. Rubbish burial would also mean that the area of the property where the pit was sited could go on to be used for other activities almost straight away. Amongst the pits encountered at 25 Bridge Street the smaller ones, which tended to only have a single fill, were generally not full of rubbish, but rather tended to have a mixture of fragments of building debris in their matrix.

A cess pit, on the other hand, needed to remain open for the duration of its use; ideally it would not have been full of water and generally it would have required some sort of covering. The presence of an open cess pit would have posed a hazard precluding any other activity nearby: people or livestock falling in; pathogens seeping into the ground water and causing outbreaks of cholera etc; and methane gas being generated by the decomposing sewage. The backfilling of the cess pit would also have been problematical: a large quantity of material would have been needed. Many of the pits in Phases V to IX had a basal fill of green silt – generally interpreted as cess – which would have been the first thing to be deposited in the pit after it was dug. Often this was covered by one or several dumps of material, which suggests deliberate and systematic backfilling; sometimes, but not always, these fills were rich in domestic rubbish. Some of the larger pits had a stone lining, and one example had a lining made entirely of cattle horn cores; these linings demonstrated that the pits needed to be kept open, making it easier to argue that they were indeed cess pits. However, many of the pits had no obvious lining, although timber or wicker linings would not have survived in the soil conditions prevalent on the site. It is thought probable that these pits were also primarily excavated for the disposal of cess.

The generic term 'cess pit' has been adopted in this report as a label for these pits, but it is vital to define what precisely is meant by that term if we are to understand the site formation processes correctly. It is first important to banish any comparisons with modern septic tank technology: there, sewage and grey water enter the tank; solids settle to the bottom and degrade to sludge; and excess water runs out of the tank *via* the outlet pipe to a buried drain-field or soakaway. The system works on the principle that the tank itself maintains the anaerobic conditions necessary for the sewage to be broken down into sludge, and as such requires a sealed environment with the constant presence of water. None of the pits recorded during the excavations could have functioned in this way.

The myriad varieties of 'cess pit' described in the structural narrative would have functioned in the same way as a 'compost toilet' or 'pit toilet', which is used solely for the disposal of sewage. This system usually works with a 'dry pit', ie a pit that is not deep enough to penetrate the water table and has porous sides and/or a porous base. If the soil conditions are right, liquids will leach out of promptly and some solids will decay and leach out of the pit over a period of time. However, some solids will accumulate, eventually blocking the escape of liquids and causing the pit to overflow. On the other hand, the system requires little maintenance as, when the pit becomes too full or prone to flooding, it can simply be backfilled and a new pit dug in a new area; any associated superstructure can also be moved or rebuilt over the new pit. In some cases the pit may have been large enough that the reduction in mass of the sewage or cess by decomposition would have allowed the pit to be more or less permanent (such as pit (487) in Plot 2). In this case it was more likely that the pit was emptied from time to time, a

task carried out from at least the medieval period by people known as 'gongfermors'. Pit toilets also fail to contain and sanitize human excreta since pathogens and nutrients seep into the groundwater. Deep pit latrines likewise fail to recycle, since the excreta are too deep for plants to make use of the nutrients. Earth, sand or sawdust could have been added after each use to cover the most recent deposit, helping to prevent smells and to discourage flies. However, the decomposition of human waste in these cess pits did create the dangerous byproduct of potentially explosive methane and other gases.

There are historical references to the flooding of cess pits in the Mayors' Books and Quarter Sessions files of the city, for example:

> A jaques or privy in the dwelling house of Jeffry Smith, draper, and near adjoining the stable of Ellis Johnes, ironmonger, in le Bridgestreete, for default of scouring and cleaning, is stopped up and filled with filth, earth, mud and sand; so that when it rains the said stable is flooded, and Ellis and his servants cannot go to and from the stable for their business. (CCALS ZMB/28a, 1599–1600).

> William Clough of Chester, cook, had made a privy in Watergate Street, adjoining the shop in which the said John Sconce of Chester sold victuals, and that the filth from the said privy ran in to the said shop. (CCALS ZQSF/44, 1594–5).

> Edward Button of Chester, innholder, on the last of September and many days and times after diverted a watercourse in and through a privy adjoining his dwelling house so that the excrement from the said privy was carried and flowed within the walls of the dwelling house of Richard Leegh in St John's Lane, and also flowed in and through the stable sellar of the same Richard, so that the 'parieties' stable and sellar have become foul and undermined and Richard Leigh scarcely dares to remain in his house on account of the fear of infection from the horrible stench. (CCALS ZQSF/53, 1604–5).

As already mentioned, cess pits are likely to have had some sort of covering – often a suspended wooden board floor, into which a hole or a number of holes could be cut. A provision for seating might also have been placed above a pit toilet, at sitting height. Alternatively, buckets inside the associated houses could have been carried outside and emptied into such covered pits as and when the buckets became full. It is also likely that the cess pits would have had some sort of superstructure over them (commonly referred to as an 'outhouse', 'privy', 'jaques' or 'earth closet'). This superstructure could have had a roof and walls to protect the user from the weather – it is likely that a roof would have been desirable anyway in order to prevent too much rainwater from entering the cess pit and causing it to flood. The superstructure would also have needed a door; illustrations of some relatively modern examples are sometimes seen decorated with a small crescent-shaped hole. The significance of the moon maybe associated with the advent of the finer inns beginning to offer separate outhouses for men and women. As most people were illiterate, symbols were used on outhouses to distinguish them, pictures of the sun commonly being used for men and the moon for women.

Ultimately, the longevity of these cess pits is a matter for speculation. It has been suggested that one person produces about 500 litres of urine and 50 litres of faeces per year. What does seem to be clear is that between Phases VI and VIII much of the areas investigated in Plots 1 to 6 appear to have been given over to the disposal of cess and rubbish. Very little evidence for any other form of land use at the back of these plots can be inferred from the structural record.

Phase VII: Mid- to Late 17–Early 18 century

Chester had been devastated by the effects of the Civil War and its citizens had suffered many hardships for their loyalty to the king (Carrington ed 1994, 91). This was compounded by an outbreak of plague during 1647/8 which is estimated to have killed 20% of the population: the city must have become fairly depopulated and grass was said to be growing in the streets around the High Cross in the centre of the town (Barratt 2003, 168). Nevertheless, the city's trade started to revive and its markets and fairs began to regain their regional importance so that by the end of the seventeenth century the city was the major wholesale and retailing market for Cheshire and North Wales (Carrington ed 1994, 91). The port recovered rapidly owing to an increase in trade caused by improved economic conditions in Ireland, and this far exceeded trade with the continent for the rest of the century.

Growing economic prosperity was reflected in the amount of new building which took place in Chester after the Restoration of the monarchy in 1660. This was partly due to the need to replace many of the buildings damaged or destroyed during the Civil War siege; however, there was a trend in many newer properties to move away from a mixed commercial-cum-domestic use to a purely domestic one. The new houses reflected a desire for more elaborate accommodation and were increasingly built entirely in brick in an effort to reduce the dangers of fire (Carrington ed 1994, 93). Many of these major new houses like Bridge House on Lower Bridge Street (built in the 1670s) resulted in the enclosure of parts of the Rows along all the major streets (Brown ed 1999, 95–101). Such rebuilding is indicated in the documentary evidence associated with Plots 1 and 3 owned by Robert Fletcher and Randle Vause respectively.

The Phase VII structural sequence was entirely dominated by cess pits which were filled with a variety of domestic and structural debris. The value of these features lies in the wealth of the artefactual assemblages recovered from them and how they might be related to the occupants recorded in the documentary evidence. There was one outstanding instance within the Bridge Street excavations where the documentary and archaeological evidence complemented one another very well. Plot 4 was occupied by two Matthew Andertons (elder and younger) between *c* 1662 and 1709. The documentary evidence attests that the Andertons were both members of the Innholders' Company and operated as merchants actively involved in trade with Dublin. They were clearly wealthy and successful men, one serving as sheriff in 1686 and the other being elected alderman in 1700, commissioner for the Dee in 1701 and mayor in 1703/4. It is clear from the documentary evidence that their property comprised a house of considerable size with a shop beneath, which was used to run a drapery business until *c* 1710, while the quantity of furniture, hangings, linen, crockery and glass listed in the inventory of the younger Anderton's will suggests a high-status dwelling.

Analysis of the animal bone demonstrated that the cattle horn cores recovered from Plot 4 in this phase were related to a single structure and are unlikely to indicate butchery, tanning or hornworking taking place on the site, although they do perhaps reflect the Andertons' links with the cattle trade from Ireland. Amongst the other bone recovered from Plot 4 were butchered deer and a range of wild bird bones, including those from a mute swan, which indicates a high-status household. High status is also indicated by the assemblage of fine drinking glasses recovered from the plot, dominated by lead crystal drinking goblets. The pottery recovered from Plot 4, by contrast, comprised vessels mainly produced in England, with only small quantities of imports – Chinese porcelain and Dutch tin-glazed earthenwares decorated in a Chinese style. These imports included a number of small tea cups and so may indicate that the household followed the contemporary fashion for tea-drinking. The reduction in continental imports might have been related more to changes in British pottery production than to the prosperity of the residents. English stonewares and significant numbers of white tin-glazed wares suggest that the occupiers kept up with new fashions and were able to exercise choice in their purchasing. The sheer quantity of pottery in pit fill (1696) is an indication of prosperity.

Phases VIII and IX: Early 18–End of 19 Century

Phase VIII

Chester grew steadily during the eighteenth century and then increased sharply during the first thirty years of the nineteenth century, when the population rose by more than one-third from 15,000 in 1801 to 21,000 in 1831 (Carrington ed 1994, 96). It became a centre for skills and craftsmanship, providing the luxury goods and quality services which polite society required. Chester city centre maintained its position as a sophisticated shopping centre, with a higher than average percentage of luxury shops run by wealthy shopkeepers. Perhaps the epitome of this new developing class was the erection of a new store by William Brown in Eastgate Street in 1831, which was the first purpose built store in the city stocking the latest fashions from London (Brown ed 1999, 110). Special market halls were also built to deal in specific commodities, such as the Linen Hall, built on Northgate Street in 1755 (*op cit*, 106). However, no new town houses were erected in the Rows during the second half of the eighteenth century of the size and quality of those erected during the previous fifty years. This was because better housing had moved to other parts of the city as attitudes about living in the commercial centre changed.

In this context it is interesting to note that during the latter part of the eighteenth century an increasing number of buildings appeared in the area of Plots 1, 2, 3 and 4, whilst Plot 6 continued to function as it did in earlier phases. Many of the buildings described in Phase VIII were clearly mapped on a plan accompanying a deed of 1879, and their description was largely unchanged from the time of their purchase by John Fletcher in 1813. Documentary research suggests that these buildings did not exist in 1770 and are most likely to have been built between 1803 and 1808. However, the archaeological evidence supports an earlier date, sometime shortly after 1760. It is clear that several of these buildings stayed in use during Phase IX as dwellings, and this has complicated our understanding of the stratigraphy. What seems likely is that the insertion of mortar floors and hearths in at least some of these buildings during the late eighteenth century indicates their use as dwellings. These buildings could possibly have accommodated some of the people occupying the property after its purchase in 1759 by Alderman Gabriel Smith.

During Phase VIII the structural evidence from the plots was again dominated by the creation and subsequent backfilling of numerous cess pits. This method of disposing of human waste appears to have become less and less common towards the end of the phase. This should not be seen as a deliberate move towards better sanitation but more as a response to declining areas of open ground and an increase in the number of dwellings towards the rear of the plots. The value of these cess pits again lay in the wealth of the artefactual assemblages recovered from them and how they might be related to the occupants recorded in the documentary evidence. Unfortunately, the artefactual analysis for Phase VIII failed to reveal any significant trends, with the possible exception of the animal bone, which might indicate a decline in the occurrence of high-status food waste reaching the site.

Phase IX

Chester was relatively unaffected by the dramatic effects of the industrialisation that transformed other towns and cities of the north-west and midlands: instead it remained a prosperous town reliant on its retailing centre and its increasing growth as a major tourist destination (Carrington ed 1994, 106). However, despite the evidence for prosperity, extreme poverty and appalling housing conditions were as rife in Chester as in other Victorian cities. Much of this was hidden from view in the courts of slum housing which grew up behind the main streets: by 1905 it was estimated that in Chester there were 122 courts, containing 747 houses and a population of 2,500 living in unsanitary conditions (*op cit*, 112).

The excavation site now accommodated a range of houses known as Fletcher's Buildings, which were apparently let as dwellings throughout the nineteenth century. The layout of these houses is clearly shown on the conveyance plan of 1879 and appears to take the form of a typical court development with communal wash house, drying ground and privies (marked as 'ash pit and closets') serving fourteen houses. The 1871 census return described the site as 'Fletcher's Court' with a population of sixty-eight. The census returns from 1841 onwards give details of the occupants of these houses. Although there were a large number of people living there it was not overcrowded by comparison with other courts, nor were the majority of the people migrants (none were of Irish origin, for instance), nor were they living in acute poverty. In fact, the population of Fletcher's Buildings should perhaps be seen more as the 'respectable poor', consisting of journeymen, professors of music and even a Chelsea pensioner. That said, the discovery of oriental cockroaches in one of the buildings in Plot 1 serves as a clear reminder of the generally poor sanitary conditions which people endured at this time.

The documentary research identified a particularly interesting connection with the archaeological evidence in Plot 2. It was established that a chemist's shop had existed on the Row on the northern side of Fletcher's Buildings since 1813: this was in the hands of Benjamin Whittell until 1826, then it was taken over by Samuel Davies who took on a partner called Thomas Shepheard in 1855, and this business remained in the trade directories until 1923. A series of deposits which formed in the area of the ash pit and closets at the back of Plot 2 contained numerous objects bearing the name of 'Davies & Shepheard' and it seems likely that this material related to intermittent clearances from the Row-level shop. The dump is thought to date to between 1860 and 1880 and contained several examples of bone tooth and nail brushes marked with a 'Davies' stamp.

By comparison, the building in Plot 4 appeared to be a warehouse rather than a dwelling, and was probably part of the dwelling house, shop and warehouse referred to in Robert Brittain's will of 1828. The will made clear that the younger Robert Brittain (a woollen draper) did in fact live in the property in 1828, whilst his father had retired to a property at Hoole Bank. The warehouse was almost certainly the Listed Building owned by the Ursula Keys Trust in 2001, which is described in the standing building section of this report. The Brittain family appear to have remained resident in the property until *c* 1860 and it is perhaps their occupancy to which much of the domestic refuse should be attributed which accumulated in the stone-lined cess pit and brick-lined well at the back of Plot 4.

The deed of sale of 1879 marked a crucial turning point in the development of the site. In 1882 the area marked as the 'drying ground' (Plot 6) was exchanged by Browns for a similarly sized plot further east owned by the Duke of Westminster. This was possibly done to facilitate the construction of an extension to Brown's store; the extension is clearly marked on the 2nd edition 1:2,500 OS map of 1899.

Chronological Trends

The stratigraphic sequence at 25 Bridge Street provided a sample through virtually every period of the known archaeological sequence at Chester. This should give an indication of the trends which should be anticipated in future excavations in the city centre. These relate mainly to the post-medieval phases of the site, as the earlier archaeology was not excavated in large enough areas for any trends to be valid.

Building materials

Brick and slate

Hand-made brick appears to have been far more abundant in pre-seventeenth-century contexts than had been previously thought. This either means brick buildings began to appear in Chester at an earlier date than is assumed or that the bricks are being manufactured for a specific function such as the construction of fireplaces and chimney breasts in an otherwise timber structure.

There was an increasing amount of grey roofing slate in the archaeological record from the late medieval period onwards. Many of the pits from Phase VI onwards contained dumps of slate fragments which were probably derived from shaping and trimming roofing materials. Presumably this reflected a growing desire to roof buildings in slate rather than straw for safety reasons.

Post-medieval pottery

Some significant trends emerged from the large pottery groups recovered from the numerous pits recorded in Phases VI and VII. It would appear that the sixteenth-century assemblages were dominated by local pottery, largely confined to drinking vessels in Cistercian wares and storage jars in Midland Purple wares, with most other pottery forms such as chafing dishes and plates being continental imports. Cistercian wares were replaced by blackwares and yellow wares by the early seventeenth century, possibly indicating an increased demand for ceramic tablewares. Yellow wares seem to have been a largely seventeenth-century phenomenon in Chester.

The large Phase VII pit group from Plot 4 had a suggested deposition date of *c* 1702–10, but the ceramics within the group spanned the late seventeenth to early eighteenth century. This group had some unusual indicators, most notable of which was the high proportion of undecorated white tin-glazed earthenware vessels as opposed to decorated examples. These items would have been imported to Chester, probably from the London or Bristol industries, and implied a conscious preference by Chester residents for undecorated vessels, perhaps in imitation of silver and/or pewter vessels.

The large Phase VII pit group also demonstrated a trend towards the blackwares being consigned to utilitarian forms and storage jars, with stonewares and mottled wares displacing the earlier blackware drinking vessels. The group also contained small quantities of black-slipped wares which became more prominent in later eighteenth-century contexts. The general trend seems to have been for an increasing range of pottery forms to be supplied from regional centres and for pottery to serve a wider range of functions: for example chamber pots appeared in relatively large numbers in the group.

Clay tobacco pipes

This site was notable in that it produced a number of the earliest pipe forms, datable to *c* 1580–1610, which are very rare nationally even as isolated examples. These were concentrated in Plot 6 and reflected not only the affluence of the city at a time when tobacco would have been very expensive, but also the fact that it was 'moving with the times' by adopting new habits This duplication of examples of early stamps argues towards local production, either by someone moving from London or by a local maker copying London styles. These imported pipes clearly demonstrated the widespread trading connections of the city during the first half of the seventeenth century. Pipes from south Lancashire, Cheshire, the west midlands and London were all finding their way into Chester. Chester makers effectively gave up using bowl stamps during the second half of the seventeenth century. This may have been partly due to the preference for spur forms during the second half of the century, since this style of pipe was often unmarked, but it did go against the trend of the surrounding production centres. By contrast, the Chester makers went on to produce some of the finest decorated stems ever produced.

Faunal remains

Mammal bone

The proportion of calf bones from Plots 1, 2, 3, 4 and 6 (no evidence from 5) has been interpreted as evidence for the rise of dairying in Chester's hinterland during the post-medieval period and the prosperity of the plot owners or occupants. Deer bones from each of the plots, and the increasing consumption of veal, and some suckling pig, have also been interpreted as being indications of increasing prosperity.

Bird and fish bone

There appears to be a trend towards the consumption of an increasingly diverse range of wild birds during the sixteenth and seventeenth centuries, tailing off during the later eighteenth century.

There was a transition from the exploitation of fresh water and estuarine fish stocks towards deep-sea fish in the later post-medieval period.

Plant remains

An exhaustive campaign of environmental sampling was undertaken. This produced low yields of plant macrofossils from unpromising soil conditions, the result of the well drained sandy soils and the lack of contexts with organic preservation. Despite this, environmental data was recovered from all phases of the site. The main trends observed were the occurrence of non-British plant species such as purslane in Phase VII and tomato from Phase IX, which may help to establish when these species were introduced to the area.

An abundance of hop seeds from a Phase VII context has been attributed to brewing activity; the dating of the context is likely to be mid- to late seventeenth century. Hop seeds have been recovered elsewhere in Chester, from a seventeenth-century context at the Deva Garage site on Grosvenor Park Road (Hall *et al* 2002b). It thus seems that the introduction of hops to the brewing process was well established in Chester by this time.

Wood charcoal appears to have been increasingly displaced by coal as the dominant fuel type from the sixteenth century onwards. This was clear from the bulk samples which become increasingly dominated by coal ash and hearth sweepings.

On the rare occasions that organic preservation was present on the excavation human parasite remains were recovered from the basal fills of two of the sixteenth-century cess pits. These remains were identified as the eggs from whipworm and maw-worm. Similar remains were recovered from a thirteenth-century cess pit excavated to the rear of a property on Watergate Street (Greig 1988, 62) and it seems increasingly likely that infestation was common among the inhabitants of central Chester during the medieval period.

Bibliography

Cheshire and Chester Archives and Local Studies Service (CCALS)

DBA	Barnston family of Churton, records, 12th century–20th century
DBC Acc 1720/4	Birch, Cullimore solicitors. Deeds *re* premises in Bridge Street 1681–1720
DBE 49	Bennett Collection. Notes on Chester Inns
DCH/DD/3, 5, 11, 12	Cholmondeley estate records. Deeds *re* Bridge Street *c* 1334–1598
DLE	Leche family of Carden, records, 14th century–20th century
DVE	Vernon and Warren family, records, 13th century–19th century
EDD 10/29	Survey of Chester estates of Dean & Chapter of Chester cathedral *c* 1790
P 63/7/1–9	St Peter's Chester rate books 1626–1808
EDC	Diocese of Chester records: Consistory Court Papers
WS	Diocese of Chester wills, inventories and administrations 1545–1858
ZAB	Chester Assembly minute books 1539–1835
ZAF	Chester Assembly files 1407–1835
ZCAS	Chester City assessments, subsidies, aids and taxes 1601–1813
ZCHB 3 and 6	Chester Corporation lease books 1356–1775
ZCHD 2/1–90	Deeds relating to Chester Corporation property in Bridge Street 1356–1805
ZCR 38	Brown family collection
ZCR 119/22	Frank Simpson. Alphabetical list of Chester inns
ZCR 119/24	Frank Simpson. Notes on Chester buildings
ZCR 465	Bavand family collection
ZCR 587/11	Chester Rows Research Project archive: Bridge Street East nos 1–35
ZCR 656/1–35	Papers of Matthew Anderton (Sr and Jr) *c* 1662–1716
ZD/JWW/1–42	Jolliffe, Wickham & Wood, solicitors. Deeds *re* premises in Bridge Street East 1698–1839
ZL/Ch	Unidentifiable references from index cards 1614–84
ZMB	Chester Mayors' books 1392–1874
ZQCI	Chester Quarter Sessions Coroners' inquisitions 1519–1839
ZQSE	Chester Quarter Sessions examinations and depositions 1522–1858
ZQSF	Chester Quarter Sessions files 1488–1971
ZSB	Chester Sheriff's books 1422–1624
ZTAP	Chester City rentals 1686–1835
ZTAR	Chester Treasurers' accounts *c* 1436–1672
ZTCD	City of Chester Town Clerk (pre-1835): draft Corporation conveyances
Microfilm 13/2	Hearth tax returns: St Michael's ward 1664. (NA E179/86/42)
Microfiche	1841 Census Returns: Bridge Street (NA HO107/130/10 ff 3v–9r)
Microfiche 34/93	1901 .. .. (NA RG13/3372 ff 10v–11v)
Microfilm 146/21	1881 .. .. (NA RG11/3559 ff 40r–42r)
Microfilm 2/35	1851 .. .. (NA HO107/2172 ff 248r–250v)
Microfilm 234/20	1861 .. .. (NA RG9/2630 ff 30r–34r)
Microfilm 24/35	1871 .. .. (NA RG10/3731 ff 41v–44r)
Microfilm 265/24	1891 .. .. (NA RG12/2864 ff 10v–11v)

Grosvenor Mss (Eaton Hall, Chester)

Box A 2, Bundle 4 and Box F 22	Documents relating to property in Bridge Street including the 'Rising Sun' public house purchased by Earl Grosvenor in 1815
Box E 2.4	Deed relating to exchange of 'Open Yard' forming passage into Fletcher's Buildings owned by William and Charles Brown, mercers, for 'Open Yard' to E of Fletcher's owned by the Duke of Westminster 1882

Bibliography

Other documents

Albarella, U 2003 — Tawyers, tanners, horn trade and the mystery of the missing goat. *In:* Murphy, P & Wiltshire, P E J eds. The environmental archaeology of industry. (Symp Assoc Environ Archaeol **20**). Oxford: Oxbow, 71–86

Alcock, J P 2001 — Food in Roman Britain. Stroud: Tempus

Allan, J P 1983 — Some post-medieval documentary evidence for the trade in ceramics. *In:* Davey & Hodges eds, 37–45

Allan, J P 1984 — Medieval and post-medieval finds from Exeter 1971–1980. Exeter City Council & University of Exeter. (Exeter Archaeol Rep **3**)

Allan, J P 1995 — Iberian pottery imported into south-west England c 1250–1600. *In:* Gerrard *et al* eds, 299–314

Allan, J & Langman, G 2003 — Appendix 1: The Dung Quay pottery. *In:* Stead, P. The excavation of the medieval and later waterfront at Dung Quay, Plymouth. *Proc Devon Archaeol Soc* **61**, 21–133

Allason-Jones, L & Miket, R 1984 — Catalogue of small finds from South Shields Roman fort. Newcastle upon Tyne: Society of Antiquaries of Newcastle upon Tyne. (Soc Antiq Newcastle upon Tyne Monogr Ser **2**)

Alldridge, N J 1981 — Aspects of the topography of early medieval Chester. *J Chester Archaeol Soc* new ser **64**, 5–31

Alvera' Bortolotto, A 1988 — Maiolica a Venezia nel Rinascimento. Venice: Edizioni Bolis

Amery, A & Davey, P J 1979 — Post-medieval pottery from Brookhill, Buckley, Clwyd. *Medieval and later pottery in Wales* **2**, 49–82

Amorosi, T 1989 — A postcranial guide to domestic neo-natal and juvenile mammals: the identification and aging of Old World species. Oxford: British Archaeological Reports. (BAR Int Ser **533**)

Anon 1914 — Chester pharmacies. *The Chemist & Druggist*, 153–7

Anon 1987 — Alphabetical list of pipemakers in Scotland. *In:* Davey, P ed. The archaeology of the clay tobacco pipe **10**: Scotland. Oxford: British Archaeological Reports (BAR Brit Ser **178**), 337–50

Archer, M 1997 — Delftware, the tin-glazed earthenware of the British Isles: a catalogue of the collection in the Victoria and Albert Museum. London: Stationery Office

Armitage, P L 1982 — A system for ageing and sexing the horn cores of cattle from British post-medieval sites (with special reference to unimproved British longhorn cattle). *In:* Wilson *et al* eds, 37–54

Armitage, P L 1989 — The use of animal bones as building material in post-medieval Britain. *In:* Serjeantson & Waldron eds, 147–60

Armitage, P L & Clutton-Brock, J 1976 — A system for classification and description of the horn cores of cattle from archaeological sites. *J Archaeol Sci* **3**, 329–48

Armstrong, P 1977 — Excavation in Sewer Lane, Hull 1974. *East Riding Archaeol* **3**. (Hull Old Town Rep Ser **1**)

Arwidsson, G & Berg, G 1983 — The Mästermyr find. A Viking-age tool chest from Gotland. Stockholm: Almqvist & Wiksell for Kungl Vitterhets Historie och Antikvitets Akademien

Ashurst, D 1987 — Excavations at the seventeenth–eighteenth-century glasshouse at Bolsterstone, Yorkshire. *Post Medieval Archaeol* **21**, 147–226

Aston charters — *Cheshire Sheaf* **3**, 28–9

Audsley, G A 1891 — The stranger's handbook to Chester, Eaton Hall and Hawarden castles and vicinity. Chester: Catherall

Barker, D 1986a — North Staffordshire post-medieval ceramics – a type series. Part 1: Cistercian ware. Stoke on Trent: Museum Archaeological Society. (Staffordshire Archaeol Stud new ser **3**), 52–7

Barker, D 1986b — North Staffordshire post-medieval ceramics – a type series. Part 2: Blackware. Stoke on Trent: Museum Archaeological Society. (Staffordshire Archaeol Stud new ser **3**), 58–75

Barker, E E ed 1953 — Talbot deeds 1200–1682. (Rec Soc Lancashire Cheshire **103**)

Barnston deeds — *Cheshire Sheaf* **3**, 42–3

Barratt, J 2003 — The great siege of Chester. Stroud: Tempus

Baxter, I L 2006 — A dwarf hound skeleton from a Romano-British grave at York Road, Leicester, England, UK, with a discussion of other Roman small dog types and speculation regarding their respective aetiologies. *In:* Snyder, L M & Moore, E A eds. Dogs and people in social, working, economic or symbolic interaction. Oxford: Oxbow. (Proceedings of the 9th Conference of the International Council of Archaeozoology, Durham, August 2002), 12–23

Baxter, I L 2007 — Delamere Street, Chester (CHE/DEL/06/BA1410): assessment of the animal bone for Birmingham Archaeology (site code CHE/DEL06). Unpublished document

Beamont, W 1866 — Arley charters: a calendar of ancient family charters preserved at Arley Hall, Cheshire. Newton: McCorquodale

Bennett, J H E 1921 — The Greyfriars of Chester. *J Chester Archaeol Soc* new ser **24** (1), 5–85

Bennett, J H E 1935 — The Whitefriars of Chester. *J Chester Archaeol Soc* new ser **31** (1), 5–54

Bennett, J H E 1948 — The Old Bishops's Palace, Chester. *J Chester Archaeol Soc* new ser **37** (1), 69–106

Bennett, J H E ed 1906–8 — The rolls of freemen of the City of Chester 1392–1805. (Rec Soc Lancashire Cheshire **51** and **55**)

Bennett, J H E & Dewhurst, J C 1940 — Quarter Sessions records.....for the County Palatine of Chester 1559–1760. (Rec Soc Lancashire Cheshire **94**)

Berg, D S 1999 — The mammal bones. *In:* Abramson, P, Berg, D S & Fossick, M R. Roman Castleford, excavations 1974–85 **2**: the structural and environmental evidence. Wakefield: West Yorkshire Archaeology Service, 223–80

Betts, I 2000 — The ceramic building material. Roman tile types. *In:* Bath Spa redevelopment project: results of the 1998/1999 excavations, 1–6. http://homepages.tesco.net/~cynbyn/cbmtype.htm. Accessed February/March 2006

Biddle, M 1990 — Object and economy in medieval Winchester: artefacts from medieval Winchester. Oxford: Clarendon Press. (Winchester Studies **7** (2))

Biddle, M & Cook, L 1990 — Buttons. *In:* Biddle, 571–81

Biddle, M *et al* 2001 — Henry VIII's coastal artillery fort at Camber castle, Rye, East Sussex: an archaeological, structural and historical investigation. Oxford: Oxford Archaeological Unit

Bidwell, P T 1979 — The legionary bath house and basilica and forum at Exeter. Exeter City Council and the University of Exeter. (Exeter Archaeol Rep **1**)

Binford, L R 1981 — Bones: ancient men and modern myths. New York: Academic Press

Bishop, M C & Coulston, J C N 1993 — Roman military equipment: from the Punic Wars to the fall of Rome. London: Batsford

Blockley, K 1989 — Prestatyn, 1984–5: an Iron Age farmstead and Romano-British industrial settlement in North Wales. Oxford: British Archaeological Reports. (BAR Brit Ser **210**)

Bloice, B J 1971 — Norfolk House, Lambeth: excavation at a delftware kiln site, 1968. *Post-Medieval Archaeol* **5**, 99–159

Boessneck, J 1969 — Osteological differences between sheep (*Ovis aries* Linné) and goat (*Capra hircus* Linné). *In:* Brothwell & Higgs eds, 331–58

Böhme, G 1977 — Zur Bestimmung quartärer Anuren Europas an Hand von Skelettelementen. Wissenschaftlich Zeitschrift der Humboldt Universität zu Berlin, Math-Nat R. **26** (3). Transl by Erika Strenski, Department of Archaeology and Prehistory, University of Sheffield

Boon, G C 1974 — Silchester: the Roman city of Calleva. Newton Abbot: David and Charles

Bourdillon, J & Coy, J 1980 — The animal remains. *In:* Holdsworth, P. Excavations at Melbourne Street, Southampton 1971–76. London: Council for British Archaeology. (CBA Res Rep **33**), 79–121

Braun, G & Hogenberg, F 1581 — *Cestria, vulgo Chester Angliae, civitas.* CCALS PM 14/1

Brears, P C D 1967 — Excavations at Potovens near Wakefield. *Post-Medieval Archaeol* **1**, 3–43

Brears, P C D 1971 — The English country pottery: its history and techniques. Newton Abbot: David & Charles

Brears, P C D 1983 — Post-Medieval Pottery. *In:* Mayes, P & Butler, L A S. Sandal castle excavations 1964–1973. Wakefield Historical Publications, 215–24

Brewer, R J 1986 — The beads and glass counters. *In:* Zienkiewicz **2**, 146–56

Brodribb, G 1987 — Roman brick and tile, Gloucester: Alan Sutton Publishing

Brooks, C M 1983 — Aspects of the sugar-refining industry from the sixteenth to the nineteenth century. *Post-Medieval Archaeol* **17**, 1–14

Broster, J 1781 — The Chester guide: or, an account of the antient and present state of that city.... to which is added, a directory ... [of] the city and market towns in the county. Chester: privately published

Broster, J 1821 — A walk round the walls and city of Chester. Chester: privately published

Brotherton-Ratcliffe, E & Axworthy, J A *in prep* — Medieval floor tile census for Cheshire

Brothwell, D & Higgs, E eds 1969 — Science in archaeology. Ed 2. London: Thames & Hudson

Brown, A ed 1999 — The Rows of Chester: the Chester Rows research project. London: English Heritage. (Archaeol Rep **16**)

Bibliography

Brown, D H 2002	Pottery in medieval Southampton c 1066–1510. York: Council for British Archaeology. (CBA Res Rep **133**; Southampton Archaeol Monogr **8**)
Brownbill, J ed 1913	Calendar of Moore family papers. (Rec Soc Lancashire Cheshire **67**)
Brownbill, J ed 1914	The ledger book of Vale Royal abbey. (Rec Soc Lancashire Cheshire **68**)
Brunskill, R W 1997	Brick building in Britain. London: Gollancz
Brushfield, T N 1885	The Roman remains of Chester with a particular description of those discovered in Bridge Street, in July 1863. J Chester Archaeol Soc old ser **3**, 1–106
Buckland, P C 1976a	The environmental evidence from the Church Street Roman sewer system. London: Council for British Archaeology. (Archaeol York **14** (1)), 1–44
Buckland, P C 1976b	*Niptus hololeucus* Fald. (Col., Ptinidae) from Roman deposits in York. *Entomologist's Monthly Mag* **111** (for 1975), 233–4
Bullock, T K, Tonkin, M B, Townsend, R R & Ford, T K 1996	The wigmaker in eighteenth-century Williamsburg. Colonial Williamsburg (VA)
Bulmer, M 1979	An introduction to Roman samian ware, with special reference to collections in Chester and the north-west. J Chester Archaeol Soc new ser **62**, 5–72
Cannon, P 2000	The clay tobacco pipe and the aristocracy: the example of the first Duke of Chandos, 1674–1744. *Soc Clay Pipe Res Newsl* **58**, 11–16
Cannon, P 2004	Pipemakers in the 1851 census. *Soc Clay Pipe Res Newsl* **61**, 3–35
Carrington, P 1977	Severn Valley ware and its place in the Roman pottery supply at Chester: a preliminary assessment. *In:* Dore, J & Greene, K T eds. Roman pottery studies in Britain and beyond. Oxford: British Archaeological Reports. (BAR Int Ser **30**), 147–62
Carrington, P 1986	The plan of the legionary fortress at Chester: further comparisons. *J Chester Archaeol Soc* new ser **68**, 7–17
Carrington, P ed 1994	Chester. London: Batsford
Carrott, J & Kenward, H K 2001	Species associations among insect remains from urban archaeological deposits and their significance in reconstructing the past human environment. *J Archaeol Sci* **28**, 887–905
Carrott, J, Issitt, M, Kenward, H K, Large, F, McKenna, B & Skidmore, P 1995	Insect and other invertebrate remains from excavations at four sites in Lincoln (site codes: WN87, WNW88, WF89 and WO089): technical report. (Reports from the Environmental Archaeology Unit, York **95/10**)
Cartledge, J 1991	Chester Roman sites: animal bone. Wakefield: West Yorkshire Archaeology Service. Unpubl report for Chester Archaeology
Carus Wilson, E M 1967	The overseas trade of Bristol in the later Middle Ages. London: Merlin Press
Catherall, T 1849	The stranger's companion to Chester. Chester: Catherall
Cherry, J 1991	Leather. *In:* Blair, J & Ramsey, N eds. English medieval industries: craftsmen, techniques, products. London; Rio Grande: Hambledon, 295–318
Childs, W R 1995	Anglo-Spanish trade in the later Middle Ages: twelfth to sixteenth centuries. *In:* Gerrard *et al* eds, 17–23
Clark, J ed 1995	The medieval horse and its equipment c 1150–c 1450. London: HMSO. (Medieval Finds Excav London **5**)
Clarkson, L P 1960–1	The organisation of the English leather industry in the late sixteenth and seventeenth centuries. *Econ Hist Rev* ser 2, **13**, 245–56
Clay, P 1981	The small finds: non-structural. *In:* Mellor, J E & Pearce, T. The Austin Friars, Leicester. London: Council for British Archaeology. (CBA Res Rep **35**), 130–45
Clement, E C & Foster, M C 1994	Alien plants of the British Isles. London: Botanical Society of the British Isles
Clutton-Brock, J 1987	A natural history of domesticated mammals. London: British Museum
Cohen, A & Serjeantson, D 1996	A manual for the identification of bird bones from archaeological sites. London: Archetype
Cool, H E M 1983	A study of the Roman personal ornaments made of metal, excluding brooches, from southern Britain. Unpubl PhD thesis, University of Wales
Cool, H E M 1990	Roman metal hair pins from southern Britain. *Archaeol J* **147**, 148–82
Cool, H E M 1992	The vessel glass. *In:* Caruana, I D. Carlisle: excavation of a section of the annexe ditch of the first Flavian fort, 1990. *Britannia* **23**, 63–8
Cool, H E M & Price, J 1995	Roman vessel glass from excavations in Colchester 1971–85. Colchester Archaeological Trust. (Colchester Archaeol Rep **8**)
Cool, H E M, Lloyd-Morgan, G & Hooley, A D 1995	Finds from the fortress. York: Council for British Archaeology. (Archaeology of York **17/10**)
Coombs, C W & Woodroffe, G E 1955	A revision of the British species of *Cryptophagus* (Herbst) (Coleoptera: Cryptophagidae). *Trans Roy Entomol Soc London* **106**, 237–82
Cowdroy, W 1789	The directory and guide for the city and county of Chester. Chester: privately published

Coy, J 1989	The provision of fowls and fish for towns. *In:* Serjeantson & Waldron eds, 25–40
Craig, R 1964	Shipping and shipbuilding in the Port of Chester in the eighteenth and early nineteenth centuries. *Trans Hist Soc Lancashire Cheshire* **116**, 39–68
Crosby, A 1996	A history of Cheshire. Chichester: Phillimore
Crossley, D W 1990	Post-medieval archaeology in Britain. Leicester U P. (The Archaeology of Medieval Britain)
Crummy, N 1983	The Roman small finds from excavations in Colchester 1971–9. Colchester Archaeological Trust. (Colchester Archaeol Rep **2**)
Cymorek, S & Koch, K 1969	Über funde von Körperteilen des Messingkäfers *Niptus holoeucus* Fald in Ablagerungen aus dem 15–16. Jahrhundert (Neuss, Niederrhein) und Folgerungen daraus für die Ausbreitungsgeschichte der Art in Europa. *Anzeiger für Schädlingskunde und Pflanzenschutz* **42**, 185–6
Dainton, M 1992	A quick, semi-quantitative method for recording nematode gut parasite eggs from archaeological deposits. *Circaea: Bulletin of the Association for Environmental Archaeology* **9** (2) (for 1991), 58–63
Darling, M J ed 1994	Guidelines for the archiving of Roman pottery. (Study Group for Roman Pottery Guidelines Advisory Document **1**)
Davey, P J 1982–3	Pottery production in Prescot. *In:* Archaeology in Prescot 1978–1986. *J Merseyside Archaeol Soc* **5**, 103–6.
Davey, P J 1983	Later medieval imported pottery in the Irish Sea Province. *In:* Davey & Hodges eds, 209–18
Davey, P J 1986–7	Post-Roman pottery. *In:* Tomlinson, P & Warhurst, M eds. The archaeology of Merseyside. *J Merseyside Archaeol Soc* **7**, 121–42
Davey, P J 1993	The clay pipes. *In:* Ellis ed, 172–80 plus fiche
Davey, P J ed 1977	Medieval pottery from excavations in the north west. University of Liverpool
Davey, P J ed 1979	The archaeology of the clay tobacco pipe **1**. Oxford: British Archaeological Reports. (BAR Brit Ser **63**)
Davey, P J ed 1980	The archaeology of the clay tobacco pipe **3**. Oxford: British Archaeological Reports. (BAR Brit Ser **78**)
Davey, P J & Hodges, R eds 1983	Ceramics and trade: the production and distribution of later medieval pottery in north-west Europe. Department of Prehistory and Archaeology, University of Sheffield
Davey, P J & Rutter, J A 1975	Medieval and early post-medieval finewares from France and Spain. *Cheshire Archaeol Bull* **3**, 14–21
Davey, P J & Rutter, J A 1977	A note on continental imports in the north west 800–1700 AD. *Medieval Ceramics* **1**, 17–30
Déchelette, J 1904	Les vases céramiques ornés de la Gaule romaine. 2 vols. Paris: Picard et Fils
Dobney, K M, Hall, A R, Kenward, H K & Milles, A 1992	A working classification of sample types for environmental archaeology. *Circaea: Bulletin of the Association for Environmental Archaeology* **9** (1) (for 1991), 24–6
Dobney, K M, Jaques, S D & Irving, B G 1996	Of butchers and breeds: report on the vertebrate remains from various sites in the city of Lincoln. City of Lincoln Archaeological Unit. (Lincoln Archaeol Stud **5**)
Dobney, K M, Jaques, D, Barratt, J & Johnstone, C 2007	Farmers, monks and aristocrats: the environmental archaeology of Anglo-Saxon Flixborough. Oxford: Oxbow. (Excav Flixborough **3**)
Dobney, K M, Kenward, H K, Ottaway, P & Donel, L 1998	Down, but not out: biological evidence for complex economic organisation in Lincoln in the late fourth century. *Antiquity* **72**, 417–24
Dodd, J P 1988	A view of Cheshire: livestock farming 1570–1603. *Cheshire Hist* **21**, 46–50
Dodd, J P 1989	A view of Cheshire: livestock farming 1604–1620. *Cheshire Hist* **23**, 12–16
Dodgson, J McN 1981	The place-names of Cheshire **5** (1(i)). Cambridge U P. (English Place-Name Soc **48**)
Dolley, R H & Webster, G 1952	An 1895 find of Elizabethan silver coins. *Brit Numis J* **27** ser 3, **7** (1), 93–4
Driesch, A von den 1976	A guide to the measurement of animal bones from archaeological sites. Cambridge (MA): Harvard University Peabody Museum of Archaeology and Ethnology. (Peabody Mus Bull **1**)
Duncan, H 2002	Domestic metalwork. *In:* Roberts, 249–80
Dyer, C 1988	The consumption of freshwater fish in medieval England. *In:* Aston, M ed. Medieval fish, fisheries and fishponds in England **1**. Oxford: British Archaeological Reports. (BAR Brit Ser **182** (1)), 27–38
Eames, E S 1980	Catalogue of medieval lead-glazed earthenware tiles in the Department of Medieval and Later Antiquities, British Museum. London: British Museum

Bibliography

Earwaker, J P 1898 — The history of the church and parish of St Mary-on-the-Hill Chester, together with an account of the new church of St Mary-without-the-Walls. Ed Morris, R H. London: Love & Wyman

Eaves, I 1989 — On the remains of a jack of plate excavated from Beeston castle in Cheshire. *J Arms Armour Soc* **13** (2), 81–154

Eaves, I 1993 — The jack of plate. *In:* Ellis ed, 161–4

Edwards, J E C 1997 — Eccleston Hall: unpublished Chester Archaeology assessment report on the pottery from excavations by Gifford & Partners

Edwards, J E C 2001 — Appendix 2: The Congleton hoard pots. *In:* Warhurst, M. Four seventeenth-century coin hoards from Congleton, Cheshire. *British Numis J* **71**, 106–10

Egan, G 1995 — Lead cloths seals and related items in the British Museum. London: British Museum. (Brit Mus Occas Pap **93**)

Egan, G 1998 — The medieval household: daily living c 1150–c 1450. London: HMSO. (Medieval Finds Excav London **6**)

Egan, G 2001 — Cloth seals. *In:* Saunders, P ed. Salisbury and South Wiltshire Museum medieval catalogue **3**. Salisbury and South Wiltshire Museum, 43–86

Egan, G 2002 — Seals of approval: archaeological evidence for an aspect of regulation in the textile trade in the late middle ages and the early modern era. *In:* Helmig, G, Scholkmann, B & Untermann, M eds. Medieval Europe Basel 2002. (Third International Conference of Medieval and Later Archaeology) pre-printed papers **1** (2): innovation, communication, interaction, 268–77

Egan, G 2007 — Lead cloth seals. *In:* Griffiths, D *et al*, 224–6

Egan, G *forthcoming* — The axis of the commonwealth: archaeological evidence for textile finishing from London sites, c 1200–1750

Egan, G & Pritchard, F 2002 — Dress accessories c 1150–c 1450. Rev ed. Woodbridge: Boydell Press. (Medieval Finds Excav London **3**)

Ellis, B M A 1991 — Spurs. *In:* Saunders P & Saunders, E eds. Salisbury Museum medieval catalogue **1**. Salisbury and South Wiltshire Museum, 54–78

Ellis, P ed 1993 — Beeston castle, Cheshire: excavations by Laurence Keen and Peter Hough. London: English Heritage. (Archaeol Rep **23**)

Emery, M M 1996 — Chester, 25–9 Bridge Street 1996: trial excavation. Chester City Council. (Archaeol Serv Eval Rep **46**)

Enghoff, I B 2000 — Fishing in the southern North Sea region from the first to the sixteenth century AD: evidence from fish bones. *Archaeofauna* **9**, 59–132

Evans, E 2000 — The Caerleon *canabae*. Excavations in the civil settlement 1984–90. London: Society for the Promotion of Roman Studies. (*Britannia* Monogr Ser **16**)

Evison, V 2000 — Glass vessels in England AD 400–1100. *In:* Price, J ed. Glass in Britain and Ireland AD 350–1100. London: British Museum. (Occas Pap **127**), 47–104

Farrell, L M 1914 — Parish register of the Holy and Undivided Trinity in the City of Chester 1532–1832. Chester

Ford, D A 1995 — Medieval pottery in Staffordshire, AD 800–1600: a review. Stoke on Trent: City Museum and Art Gallery. (Staffordshire Archaeol Stud **7**)

Forster, G C F 2003 — Early modern Chester, 1550–1762. *In:* Lewis & Thacker eds, 90–145

Frere, S S ed 1986 — Roman Britain in 1985. I: sites explored. *Britannia* **17**, 363–427

Furness, R R 1978 — Soils of Cheshire. Harpenden: Rothamsted Experimental Station. (Soil Survey of Great Britain Bulletin **6**)

Gaimster, D R M 1997 — German stoneware 1200–1900: archaeology and cultural history. London: British Museum

Gaimster, D R M, Hayward, M, Mitchell, D & Parker, K 2002 — Tudor silver-gilt dress hooks: a new class of treasure find. *Antiq J* **82**, 157–96

Garner, D J 2002 — Debenhams, Chester (CHE/25 BS 01): post-excavation assessment report. Chester: Gifford and Partners. (Rep **B2980E.01**)

Garner, D 2007 — Archaeology in the park: Grosvenor Park Chester 2007. Chester City Council

Gault, R 1985 — Abstracts from census returns. *Soc Clay Pipe Res Newsl* **5**, 24–30

Gault, W R 1979 — List of Warwickshire clay tobacco-pipe makers. *In:* Davey ed, 392–407

Gentry, A P 1976 — Roman military stone-built granaries in Britain. Oxford: British Archaeological Reports. (BAR Brit Ser **32**)

Gere, C 1991 — From the fifteenth century to the Victorians. *In:* Murdoch, T ed. Treasures and trinkets: jewellery in London from pre-Roman times to the 1930s. Museum of London, 38–49

Gerrard, C M, Gutiérrez, A & Vince, A G eds 1995 — Spanish medieval ceramics in Spain and the British Isles. Oxford: Tempus Reparatum. (BAR Int Ser **610**)

Gidney, L J 1993 — Leicester, The Shires 1988. Excavations: further identifications of small mammal and bird bones. London: English Heritage. (Ancient Monuments Lab Rep **92/93**)

Gidney, L J 2000 — Economic trends, craft specialisation and social status: bone assemblages from Leicester. *In:* Rowley-Conwy ed, 170–8

Gillam, J P 1968 — Types of Roman coarse pottery vessels in northern Britain. Newcastle upon Tyne: Oriel Press

Gillam, J P 1976 — Coarse fumed ware in north Britain and beyond. *Glasgow Archaeol J* **4**, 57–80

Glanville, P 1971 — The Parr pot. *Archaeol J* **127**, 147–55

Godbold, S & Turner, R C 1994 — Medieval fishtraps in the Severn Estuary. *Medieval Archaeol* **38**, 19–54

Goodall, A R 1984 — Objects of non-ferrous metal. *In:* Allan, 337–48

Goodall, I H 1976 — Metalwork. *In:* Drewett, P. The excavation of the Great Hall at Bolingbroke castle, Lincolnshire 1973. *Post-Medieval Archaeol* **10**, 26–9

Goodall, I H 1980 — Copper alloy objects. *In:* Christie, P M & Coad, J G. Excavations at Denny abbey. *Archaeol J* **137**, 255–60

Goodall, I A 1990 — Tenter-hooks. *In:* Biddle, 234–9

Grant, A 1982 — The use of tooth wear as a guide to the age of domestic ungulates. *In:* Wilson *et al* eds, 91–108

Greene, J P & Noake, B 1977 — Norton priory. *In:* Davey, P J ed, 1977, 58–9

Greep, S J 1986 — The objects of worked bone. *In:* Zienkiewicz **2**, 197–212

Greenfield, H J 1988 — Bone consumption by pigs in a contemporary Serbian village: implications for the interpretation of prehistoric faunal assemblages. *J Field Archaeol* **15**, 473–78

Greeves, T 2001 — Three hares – a medieval Mongol mystery. *Devon Today* April 2001, 58–63

Greig, J 1988 — Plant remains. *In:* Ward 1988, 59–69

Gresty & Burghall, nd — Gresty and Burghall's Chester guide. Revd Hicklin, J. Chester: J Gresty

Griffiths, D, Philpott, R A & Egan, G 2007 — Meols, the archaeology of the north Wirral coast: discoveries and observations in the 19th and 20th centuries, with a catalogue of collections. Oxford University Institute of Archaeology. (Oxford Univ School Archaeol Monogr **68**)

Grigson, C 1976 — Craniology and relationships of four species of *Bos*. *J Archaeol Sci* **3**, 115–36

Grimes, W F 1930 — Holt, Denbighshire: The works depot of the Twentieth Legion at Castle Lyons. *Y Cymmrodor* **41**

Groombridge, M J 1952 — The city guilds of Chester. *J Chester Archaeol Soc* new ser **39**, 93–108

Groombridge, M J 1956 — Calendar of Chester City Council minutes 1603–42. (Rec Soc Lancashire Cheshire **106**)

Guido, M 1978 — The glass beads of the prehistoric and Roman periods in Britain and Ireland. London: Society of Antiquaries. (Rep Res Comm Soc Antiq London **35**)

Haberly, L 1937 — Mediaeval English pavingtiles. Oxford: Blackwell

Hall, A R & Kenward, H K 1990 — Environmental evidence from the *colonia*: General Accident and Rougier Street. London: Council for British Archaeology. (The Archaeology of York **14/6**)

Hall, A R & Kenward, H K eds 1994 — Urban–rural connexions: perspectives from environmental archaeology. Oxford: Oxbow. (Symp Assoc Environ Archaeol **12**; Oxbow Monogr **47**)

Hall, A, Kenward, H K & Carrott, J 2003 — Evaluation of biological remains from a watching brief at the Guardian Glass site, Goole, East Riding of Yorkshire (site code: GGG2002). Shildon: Palaeoecology Research Services. (PRS Rep **2003/14**)

Hall, A R, Kenward, H K & Robertson, A 1993a — Investigation of medieval and post-medieval plant and invertebrate remains from Area X of the excavations in The Bedern (south-west), York (YAT/Yorkshire Museum site code: 1973–81.13 X): technical report. Portsmouth: English Heritage. (Ancient Monuments Lab Rep **56/93**)

Hall, A R, Kenward, H K & Robertson, A 1993b — Investigation of medieval and post-medieval plant and invertebrate remains from Area IV of the excavations in The Bedern (north-east), York (YAT/Yorkshire Museum site code: 1976–81.14 IV): technical report. Portsmouth: English Heritage. (Ancient Monuments Lab Rep **57/93**)

Hall, A R Kenward, H K & Robertson, A 1993c — Investigation of medieval and post-medieval plant and invertebrate remains from Area II of the excavations in The Bedern (north-east), York (YAT/Yorkshire Museum site code: 1976–81.14 II): technical report. Portsmouth: English Heritage. (Ancient Monuments Lab Rep **58/93**)

Hall, A R, Jaques, D, Carrott, J & Kenward, H K 2002a — Assessment of biological remains from excavations at Bridge Street, Chester (site code: CHE/25BS'01). Shildon: Palaeoecology Research Services. (PRS Rep **2002/16**)

Hall, A R, Jaques, D, Johnson, K, Carrott, J & Kenward, H K 2002b — Assessment of biological remains from excavations at the site of the former Deva Garage, 27 Grosvenor Park Road, Chester (site code: B3471A). Shildon: Palaeoecology Research Services. (PRS Rep **2002/30**)

Bibliography

Hall, A R, Kenward, H K, Jaques, D & Carrott, J 2000	Technical report: environment and industry at Layerthorpe Bridge, York (site code: YORYM 1996.345). (Reports from the Environmental Archaeology Unit, York **2000/64**)
Hall, A R, Kenward, H K, Williams, D & Greig, J R A 1983	Environment and living conditions at two Anglo-Scandinavian sites. London: Council for British Archaeology. (The Archaeology of York **14/4**), 157–240 plus pl 1 and fiche 1
Hall, A R, Whitehouse, N, Rogers, K, Carrott, J & Gardner, S 2005	Technical report: plant, insect and parasites (with brief notes on other biological remains) from excavations at 14–15 and 48–50 Newmarket Street, Dublin, Republic of Ireland (site code: 02W1692). Shildon: Palaeoecology Research Services. (PRS Rep **2005/06**)
Halstead, P 1985	A study of mandibular teeth from Romano-British contexts at Maxey. *In:* Pryor, F French, C, Crowther, D, Gurney, D, Simpson, G & Taylor, M. Archaeology and environment in the Lower Welland Valley **1**. *East Anglian Archaeol* **27**. (Fenland Project **1**), 219–24
Halstead, P 1992	Dimini and the 'DMP': faunal remains and animal exploitation in Late Neolithic Thessaly. *Annu Brit School Athens* **87**, 29–9
Hamilton-Dyer, S 1993	Fish remains. *In:* Woodward, P J, Davies, S M & Graham, A H. Excavations at the Old Methodist Chapel and Greyhound Yard, Dorchester, 1981–1984 . Dorchester: Dorset Natural History and Archaeological Society. (Dorset Nat Hist Archaeol Soc Monogr **12**), 345–6
Hamilton-Dyer, S 2003	Animal bones. *In:* Charter Quay, the spirit of change: the archaeology of Kingston's riverside. http://www.wessexarch.co.uk/projects/london/charter_quay/spirit/reports.html. Accessed 7 November 2007
Hanshall, J H 1817	The history of the county palatine of Chester. Chester: Fletcher
Harcourt, R A 1974	The dog in prehistoric and early historic Britain. *J Archaeol Sci* **1**, 151–75
Harradine, J 1986	Jack Snipe. *In:* Lack ed, 202–3
Harrison, H M & Davey, P J 1977	Ewloe. *In:* Davey P J ed, 92–9
Harrison, J 1850	On a tiled floor recently discovered in Chester. *J Chester Archaeol Soc* old ser **1**, 51–4.
Hartley, K F 1981	Painted fine wares made in the Raetian workshops near Wilderspool, Cheshire. *In:* Anderson, A C & Anderson, A S eds. Roman pottery research in Britain and north-west Europe: papers presented to Graham Webster. Oxford: British Archaeological Reports. (BAR Int Ser **123** (2)), 471–9
Hartley, K F & Webster, P V 1973	Romano-British pottery kilns near Wilderspool. *Archaeol J* **130**, 77–103
Harvey, Y 1975	The finds. *In:* Platt, C P S & Coleman-Smith, R. Excavations in medieval Southampton, 1953–1969 **2**: The small finds - catalogue. Leicester U P, 254–93
Haverfield, F 1909	Notes on the smaller objects. *In:* Knowles, W H & Forster, R H. Corstopitum: report on the 1908 excavations. *Archaeol Aeliana* ser 3, **5**, 305–423
Hayfield, C & Greig, J eds 1989	Excavation and salvage work on a moated site at Cowick, South Humberside, 1979. *Yorkshire Archaeol J* **61**, 41–70
Hedley Bell, T 1962	The birds of Cheshire. Altrincham: Sherratt
Hemingway, J 1831	History of the county palatine of Chester. Chester: Fletcher
Henkes, H 1994	Glas zonder glans: vijf eeuwen gebruiksglas uit de bodem van de Lage Landen, 1300–1800. Rotterdam: Coördinatie Commissie van Advies inzake Archeologisch Onderzoek binnen het Ressort Rotterdam. (Rotterdam Pap **9**)
Hewitt, H J 1929	Medieval Cheshire: an economic and social history of Cheshire in the reigns of the three Edwards. Manchester: Chetham Society
Hewitt, J 1887	Notes on the medieval architecture of Chester with special reference to the Rows and the crypts. *J Chester Archaeol Soc* new ser **1**, 30–52
Higgins, D A 1981	Surrey clay tobacco pipes *In:* Davey, P J ed. The archaeology of the clay tobacco pipe **6**. Oxford: British Archaeological Reports. (BAR Brit Ser **97**), 189–293
Higgins, D A 1982	Reconstruction and interpretation of the pipes. *In:* Davey, P J *et al*. Excavations on the site of a seventeenth-century clay pipe kiln in Rainford, Merseyside. *In:* Davey, P J ed. The archaeology of the clay tobacco pipe **7**. Oxford: British Archaeological Reports. (BAR Brit Ser **100**), 197–209
Higgins, D A 1987a	The interpretation and regional study of clay tobacco pipes: a case study of the Broseley district. Unpubl PhD thesis, University of Liverpool
Higgins, D A 1987b	Clay tobacco pipes from excavations near the Old Academy, Warrington, 1981. *In:* Higgins, D A. Some clay pipes from Cheshire and Merseyside. *North West Archaeol Trust Rep* **3** (Liverpool), 13–18
Higgins, D A 1988	Song pipes. *Soc Clay Pipe Res Newsl* **19**, 6–10
Higgins, D A 1988–9	Speke hall: excavations in the west range, 1981–2. *J Merseyside Archaeol Soc* **8**, 47–84

Higgins, D A 1996	Clay marbles (from excavations at Castle Rushen Stores). *In:* Davey, P J, Freke, D J & Higgins, D A. Excavations in Castletown, Isle of Man 1989–1992. Liverpool U P, 96–7
Higgins, D A 1999	The clay tobacco pipes. *In:* Connor, A & Buckley, R. Roman and medieval occupation in Causeway Lane, Leicester. University of Leicester Archaeological Services and Leicester City Museum Service. (Leicester Archaeol Monogr **5**), 215–34
Higgins, D A 2005	Coiled pipes. *Soc Clay Pipe Res Newsl* **67**, 31–9
Higgins, D A & Davey, P J 1994	Draft guidelines for using the clay tobacco pipe record sheets. Unpubl draft, University of Liverpool
Hinchliffe, J, Williams, J H & Williams, F 1992	Roman Warrington: excavations at Wilderspool 1966–9 and 1976. Manchester University. (*Brigantia* Monogr **2**)
Hodgson, J & Brennand, M 2006	Prehistoric periods resource assessment. *In:* Brennand, M ed. The archaeology of north-west England: an archaeological research framework for the north west region **1**. Resource assessment. *Archaeology North West* **8** (18), 23–58
Holbrook, N & Bidwell, P T 1991	Roman finds from Exeter. Exeter City Council and the University of Exeter. (Exeter Archaeol Rep **4**)
Hook, D R & Gaimster, D R M eds 1995	Trade and discovery: the scientific study of artefacts from post-medieval Europe and beyond. London: British Museum. (Occas Pap **109**)
Howe, M D, Perrin, J R & Mackreth, D F 1980	Roman pottery from the Nene Valley: a guide. Peterborough City Museum. (Occas Pap **2**)
Howe, R W & Burges, H D 1952	Studies on beetles of the family Ptinidae **7**: the biology of five ptinid species found in stored products. *Bull Entomol Res* **43**, 153–86
Hughes, H 1975	Chronicle of Chester: the two hundred years 1775–1975. London: Macdonald & Janes
Hughes, M J 1995	Neutron activation analysis of post-medieval European earthenware ceramics: a survey of current projects at the British Museum. *In:* Hook & Gaimster eds, 55–68
Hughes, T 1864	On the inns and taverns of Chester, past and present: part 1. *J Chester Archaeol Soc* old ser **2**, 91–110
Hunter, J 1789	Survey of the ancient and loyal city of Chester. CCALS PM 18/4
Hunter-Mann, K 2001	Ceramic building materials: minimum standards for recovery, curation, analysis and publication. Archaeological Ceramic Building Materials Group draft document
Huntley, J P & Stallibrass, S 1995	Plant and vertebrate remains from archaeological sites in northern England: data reviews and future directions. Durham: Architectural and Archaeological Society of Durham and Northumberland. (Res Rep **4**)
Hurst, J G 1974	Sixteenth and seventeenth-century imported pottery from the Saintonge. *In:* Evison, V I, Hodges, H & Hurst, J G eds. Medieval pottery from excavations: studies presented to Gerald Clough Dunning. London: John Baker, 221–55
Hurst, J G 1995	Post-medieval pottery from Seville imported into north-west Europe. *In:* Hook & Gaimster eds, 45–54
Hurst, J G, Neal, D S & Van Beuningen, H J E 1986	Pottery produced and traded in north-west Europe 1350–1650. Rotterdam: Museum Boymans-Van Beuningen. (Rotterdam Pap **6**)
Hurst-Vose, R 1994	Excavations at the seventeenth-century glasshouse at Haughton Green, Denton, near Manchester. *Post-Medieval Archaeol* **18**, 20–42
IGI	International genealogical index. Familysearch. http//:www.familysearch.org. Accessed 5 November 2004
Ingrem, C 2003	Assessment of the animal bone from the Bars, Chester: assessment carried out for Earthworks Archaeological Services on bones from 4 Boughton (site code CHE/4BOU01)
Jackson, R 1997	An ancient British medical kit from Stanway, Essex. *The Lancet* **350**, 1471–3
Jackson, R 2003	The domus 'del chirurgo' at Rimini: an interim account of the medical assemblage. *J Roman Archaeol* **16**, 312–21
Jackson, R G & Price, R H 1974	Bristol clay pipes. Bristol City Museum. (Res Monogr **1**)
Janaway, R C 1993	The textiles. *In:* Reeve, J & Adams, M. The Spitalfields project **1**: across the Styx. York: Council for British Archaeology. (CBA Res Rep **85**), 93–119
Jaques, D, Hall, A, Kenward, H K & Carrott, J 2002	Evaluation of bioarchaeological remains from excavations at Main Street, Long Riston, East Riding of Yorkshire (site code: MSR2001). Shildon: Palaeoecology Research Services. (PRS Rep **2002/07**)
Jenkins, J & Bearpark, P 1980	Bewsey Old Hall research report. Warrington New Development Corporation

Bibliography

Jessop, O 1996	A new artefact typology for the study of medieval arrowheads. *Medieval Archaeol* **40**, 192–205
Johns, C 1997	The Snettisham Roman jeweller's hoard. London: British Museum
Johnson, A M 1972	Politics in Chester during the Civil Wars and the Interregnum 1640–62. *In:* Clark, P & Slack, P eds. Crisis and order in English towns 1500–1700. London: Routledge & K P
Jones, A 2001	Roman ceramic building materials: a guide to on-site recording. Unpubl guidelines, Chester Archaeology
Jones, A 2003	Some unusual Roman antefixes from Chester. *J Chester Archaeol Soc* new ser **78**, 23–47
Jones, A 2006	Roman portable oven (*clibanus*) fragments. *In:* The Chester amphitheatre project: news from the finds room and laboratory. *English Heritage Res News* **4**, 23–4
Kelly, E R ed 1878	The Post Office directory of Chester. London: Kelly
Kelly, J H 1973	A rescue excavation on the site of Swan Bank Methodist church, Burslem, Stoke-on-Trent, Staffordshire, England SJ 870 499. Stoke on Trent: Museum Archaeological Society. (City Mus and Art Gallery Stoke on Trent Archaeol Soc Rep **5**)
Kelly, J H & Greaves, S J 1974	The excavation of a kiln base in Old Hall Street, Hanley, Stoke-on-Trent, Staffs SJ 885475. Stoke on Trent: Museum Archaeological Society. (City Mus and Art Gallery Stoke on Trent Archaeol Soc Rep **6**)
Kennett, A M 1984	The Rows in the city records. *J Chester Archaeol Soc* new ser **67**, 47–54
Kenward, H K 1975	The biological and archaeological implications of the beetle *Aglenus brunneus* (Gyllenhal) in ancient faunas. *J Archaeol Sci* **2**, 63–9
Kenward, H K 1978	The analysis of archaeological insect assemblages: a new approach. London: Council for British Archaeology. (The Archaeology of York **19/1**)
Kenward, H K 1988	Insect remains. *In:* Schia, E ed. Mindets tomt–Sondre felt. Øvre Ervik: Alvheim & Eide. (De arkeologiske utgravninger i Gamlebyen, Oslo **5**), 115–40
Kenward, H K 1992	Rapid recording of archaeological insect remains: a reconsideration. *Circaea: Bulletin of the Association for Environmental Archaeology* **9** (2) (for 1991), 81–8
Kenward, H K 2000	Data archive: insect assemblages from 6–8 Pavement (the Lloyds Bank site), York. (Reports from the Environmental Archaeology Unit, York **2000/39**)
Kenward, H K & Allison, E P 1994	Rural origins of the urban insect fauna. *In:* Hall & Kenward eds, 55–77
Kenward, H K & Hall, A R 1995	Biological evidence from Anglo-Scandinavian deposits at 16–22 Coppergate. York: Council for British Archaeology. (The Archaeology of York **14/7**)
Kenward, H K & Hall, A R 2000	Decay of delicate organic remains in shallow urban deposits: are we at a watershed? *Antiquity* **74**, 519–25
Kenward, H K & Hall, A R 2004	Actively decaying or just poorly preserved? Can we tell when plant and invertebrate remains in urban archaeological deposits decayed? *In:* Nixon, T ed. Preserving archaeological remains in situ? Proceedings of the 2nd [PARIS] conference. London: Museum of London Archaeology Service, 4–10
Kenward, H K & Hall, A R 2006	Easily decayed organic remains in urban archaeological deposits: value, threats, research directions and conservation. *In:* Brinkkemper, O, Deeben, J, Van Doesberg, J, Hallewas, D, Theunissen, E M & Verlinde, A D eds. Vakken in vlakken: archeologiche kennis in lagen. *Nederlandse Archeologische Rapporten* **32**, 181–96
Kenward, H K & Large, F 1998	Recording the preservational condition of archaeological insect fossils. *Environ Archaeol* **2**, 49–60
Kenward, H K, Hall, A R & Jones, A K G 1980	A tested set of techniques for the extraction of plant and animal macrofossils from waterlogged archaeological deposits. *Sci & Archaeol* **22**, 3–15
Kenward, H K, Engleman, C, Robertson, A & Large, F 1986	Rapid scanning of urban archaeological deposits for insect remains. *Circaea: Bulletin of the Association for Environmental Archaeology* **3** (3) (for 1985), 163–72
Kermode, J 1996	The trade of late medieval Chester. *In:* Britnell, R & Hatcher, J eds. Progress and problems in medieval England: essays in honour of Edward Miller. Cambridge U P, 286–307
Kiesewalter, L 1888	Skelettmessungen am Pferde als Beitrag zur theoretischen Grundlage der Beurteilungslehre des Pferdes. Phil Diss, University of Leipzig. (Conversion factors used but original text not seen)
King, A C 1978	A comparative survey of bone assemblages from Roman sites in Britain. *Bull Inst Archaeol London* **15**, 207–32

King, A C 1984	Animal bones and the dietary identity of military and civilian in Roman Britain, Germany and Gaul. *In:* Blagg, T F C & King, A C. Military and civilian in Roman Britain: cultural relationships in a frontier province. Oxford: British Archaeological Reports. (BAR Brit Ser **136**), 187–217
King, A C 1999	Animals and the Roman army: the evidence of animal bones. *In:* Goldsworthy, A & Haynes, I. The Roman army as a community. *J Roman Archaeol* Suppl Ser **34**, 139–49
Kloet, G S & Hincks, W D 1964–77	A check list of British insects. Ed 2. London: Royal Entomological Society
Knight, B 1985	Lead. *In:* Hore, J N *et al*. Battle abbey: the eastern range and the excavations of 1978–80. London: Historic Buildings and Monuments Commission for England. (HBMC(E) Archaeol Rep **2**), 154–6
Koch, K 1970	Subfossile Käferreste aus römerzeitlichen und mittelalterlichen Ausgrabungen im Rheinland. *Entomol Bl* **66**, 41–56
Koch, K 1971	Zur Untersuchung subfossiler Käferreste aus römerzeitlichen und mittelalterlichen Ausgrabungen im Rheinland. *Rheinische Ausgrabungen* **10**, 374–448
Kowaleski, M 1990	Town and country in late medieval England: the hide and leather trade. *In:* Corfield, P J & Keene, D eds. Work in towns 850–1850. Leicester U P, 57–73
Kratochvil, Z 1969	Species criteria on the distal section of the tibia in *Ovis ammon F aries* L and *Capra aegagrus F hircus* L. *Acta Veterinaria* (Brno) **38**, 483–90
Lack, P ed 1986	The atlas of wintering birds in Britain and Ireland. Calton (Staffs): Poyser
LRBC **1**	Carson, R A G, Hill, P V & Kent, J P C 1960. Late Roman bronze coinage, AD 324–498, part **1**: The bronze coinage of the House of Constantine, AD 324–346. London: Spink
Lavaux, A de 1745	Plan of the city and castle of Chester survey'd and drawn by Alexander De Lavaux engineer.
Lawson, A J 1995	A hoard of Roman harness equipment. *In:* Blockley, K, Detsicas, A P & Tatton-Brown, T W T. Excavations in the Marlowe car park and surrounding areas. Canterbury: Canterbury Archaeological Trust. (Archaeol Canterbury **5**), 984–1000
Lawson, P H 1928	Schedule of the Roman remains of Chester with maps and plans. *J Chester Archaeol Soc* new ser **27** (2), 163–89
Le Patourel, H E J 1966	The pottery. *In:* Mayes, P & Pirie, E J E. A Cistercian ware kiln of the early sixteenth century at Potterton, Yorkshire. *Antiq J* **46**. 252–9
Lepley, M, Defos du Rau P, Veille, M, Pineau, O & Monval, J 2005	Capturing Jack Snipe *Lymnocryptes minimus* with mobile horizontally held nets. *Ringing and Migration* **22**, 167–170.
Lewis, C & Thacker, A eds 2003	A history of Cheshire **5** (1). The city of Chester: general history and topography. Woodbridge: Boydell & Brewer for Institute of Historical Research. (Victoria History of the Counties of England)
Lewis, C & Thacker, A eds 2005	A history of Cheshire **5** (2). The city of Chester: culture, buildings, institutions. Woodbridge: Boydell & Brewer for Institute of Historical Research. (Victoria History of the Counties of England)
Lewis, J M 1999	The medieval tiles of Wales: census of medieval tiles in Britain. Cardiff: National Museums and Galleries of Wales
Lipski, L & Archer, M 1984	Dated English delftware. London: Sotheby
Lister, A M 1996	The morphological distinction between bones and teeth of Fallow deer (*Dama dama*) and Red deer (*Cervus elaphus*). *Int J Osteoarchaeol* **6**, 119–43
Lloyd-Morgan, G 1990	Coins and tokens. *In:* Ward, 165–6
Locker, A 1994	The fish bones from excavations at Winchester Palace, Southwark, 1983. Unpubl rep for Southwark and Lambeth Excavation Committee.
Locker, A 2001a	The role of stored fish in England 900–1750 AD: the evidence from historical and archaeological data. Sofia: Publishing Group
Locker, A 2001b	The fish bones recovered from excavations of medieval tenements at 76–96 Victoria Street, Bristol. Unpublished document
Lockwood, T M & Hewitt, J 1886	Notes on Bridge Street, Chester, 1886. Royal Archaeological Society Chester meeting. (Document in Chester Archaeological Society library)
Luff, R M 1982	A zooarchaeological study of the Roman north-western provinces. Oxford: British Archaeological Reports. (BAR Int Ser **137**)
Luff, R M & Moreno Garcia, M 1995	Killing cats in the medieval period: an unusual episode in the history of Cambridge, England. *Archaeofauna* **4**, 93–114
MacGregor, A 1985	Bone, antler, ivory and horn: the technology of skeletal materials since the Roman period. London: Croom Helm

Bibliography

MacGregor, A, Mainman, A J & Rogers, N S H 1999 — Bone, antler, ivory and horn from Anglo-Scandinavian and medieval York. York: Council for British Archaeology. (The Archaeology of York **17/12**)

Maclean, P & Starley, D 2002 — Analysis of metalworking debris, plate armour and domestic metalwork. *In* Roberts, 355–61

McNeil, R 1982–3 — Excavation of an eighteenth-century pottery in Eccleston Street, Prescot (site F). *J Merseyside Archaeol Soc* **5**, 49–94

McPeake, J C, Bulmer, M & Rutter, J A 1980 — Excavations in the garden of no 1 Abbey Green, Chester, 1975–1977: interim report. *J Chester Archaeol Soc* new ser **63**, 15–37

Mainman, A J & Rogers, N S H 2000 — Craft, industry and everyday life: finds from Anglo-Scandinavian York. York: Council for British Archaeology. (The Archaeology of York **17/14**)

Maltby, M 1994 — The meat supply in Roman Dorchester and Winchester. *In*: Hall & Kenward eds, 85–102

Manning, W H 1985 — Catalogue of the Romano-British iron tools, fittings and weapons in the British Museum. London: British Museum

Manning, W H ed 1993 — Report on the excavations at Usk 1965–1976. The Roman pottery. Cardiff: University of Wales

Mason, D J P 1990 — The use of earthenware tubes in Roman vault construction: an example from Chester. *Britannia* **21**, 215–22

Mason, D J P 2000 — Excavations at Chester, the Elliptical Building: an image of the Roman world? Excavations in 1939 and 1963–9. Chester City Council. (Chester Archaeol Excav Surv Rep **12**)

Mason, D J P 2001 — Roman Chester: city of the eagles. Stroud: Tempus

Mason, D J P 2002 — The construction and operation of a legionary fortress: logistical and engineering aspects. *In*: Carrington, P ed 2002. Deva Victrix: Roman Chester re-assessed. Papers from a weekend conference held at Chester College 3–5 September 1999. Chester Archaeological Society, 89–112

Mason, D J P forthcoming — Sedan House 1989: the western extramural baths. *In*: Ward, S W *et al*. Excavations at Chester, the western extramural settlement: a Roman community on the edge of the world. Chester City Council. (Archaeol Serv Excav Surv Rep **15**)

Mason, D J P *et al* 2005 — Excavations at Chester, the Roman fortress baths: excavation and recording 1732–1988. Chester City Council. (Archaeol Serv Excav Surv Rep **13**)

Matheson, C 1929 — Wales and the sea fisheries. Cardiff: National Museum of Wales

Matthews, K J 1995 — Excavations at Chester, the evolution of the heart of the city: investigations at 3–15 Eastgate Row 1990/1. Chester City Council. (Archaeol Serv Excav Surv Rep **8**)

May, E 1985 — Widerristhöhe und Langknochenmaße bei Pferd: ein immer noch actuelles Problem. *Zeitschr für Säugertierkunde* **50**, 368–82.

MPRG 1998 — A guide to the classification of medieval ceramic forms. Medieval Pottery Research Group. (Occas Pap **1**)

MPRG 2001 — Minimum standards for the processing, recording, analysis and publication of post-Roman ceramics. Medieval Pottery Research Group. (Occas Pap **2**)

Mees, A W 1995 — Modelsignierte Dekorationen auf südgallischer Terra Sigillata. Stuttgart: Theiss. (Forschungen und Berichte zur Vor- und Frühgeschichte in Baden-Württemberg **54**)

Montembault, V 1996 — Étude des cuirs. *In*: Catalogue de l'exposition Metz médiéval, mises au jour, Metz, 153–64

Montembault, V 1999 — Mystery object. *Archaeol Leather Group Newsl* **10**, 4–6

Morris, M G 1990 — Orthocerous weevils. London: Royal Entomological Society. (Handbooks for the Identification of British Insects **5** (16))

Morris, R H 1895 — Chester in the Plantagenet and Tudor reigns. Chester: privately published

Moorhouse, S & Slowikowski, A M 1992 — The pottery. *In*: Moorhouse, S & Roberts, I. Wrenthorpe potteries: excavations of 16th- and 17th-century potting tenements near Wakefield, 1983–86. Wakefield: West Yorkshire Archaeology Service. (Yorkshire Archaeol **2**), 89–149

Morley-Fletcher, H & McIlroy, R 1984 — Christie's pictorial history of European pottery. Oxford: Phaidon; Christie's

Mould, Q 1996 — The metalwork finds. *In*: Brown, S. Berry Pomeroy castle. *Devon Archaeol Soc Proc* **54**, 251–69

Mould, Q 1997 — Leather. *In*: Hawkes, J W & Fasham, P J. Excavations on Reading waterfront sites 1979–1988. Salisbury: Trust for Wessex Archaeology. (Wessex Archaeol Rep **5**), 108–41

Mould, Q 2007 — Leather objects. *In*: Griffiths *et al*, 233–40

Mountford, A R 1975 — The Sadler Teapot manufactory site Burslem, Stoke-on-Trent, Staffs. SJ 868499. Stoke on Trent: Museum Archaeological Society. (City Mus and Art Gallery Stoke on Trent Archaeol Soc Rep **7**)

Muldoon, S 1979 — Marked clay pipes from Coventry. *In*: Davey ed, 255–78

Muller, H 1987 — Jet. London: Butterworth. (Butterworths Gem Books)

Munson, P J & Garniewicz, R C 2003 — Age-mediated survivorship of ungulate mandibles and teeth in canid-ravaged faunal assemblages. *J Archaeol Sci* **30** (4), 405–16

Murphy, P, Albarella, U, Germany, M & Locker, A 2000 — Production, imports and status: biological remains from a late Roman farm at Great Holts Farm, Boreham, Essex, UK. *Environ Archaeol* **5**, 35–48

Neal, D S 1974 — The excavation of the Roman villa in Gadebridge Park, Hemel Hempstead. London: Society of Antiquaries. (Rep Res Comm Soc Antiq London **31**)

Neil, N R 1998 — Building to rear of 19 Bridge Street Row, Chester: standing building evaluation report. Nigel Neil Archaeological Services

Nenk, B S 1999 — Post-medieval redware pottery of London and Essex. *In:* Egan, G & Michael, R L eds. Old and New Worlds: Society for Post Medieval Archaeology; the Society for Historical Archaeology historical/post medieval archaeology papers from the societies' joint conferences at Williamsburg and London 1997 to mark thirty years of work and achievement. Society for Post Medieval Archaeology and the Society for Historical Archaeology. Oxford: Oxbow, 235–45

Newstead, R 1902 — A descriptive account of Roman and other objects recovered from various sites in Chester and District, 1898–1901. *J Chester Archaeol Soc* new ser **8**, 81–106

Newstead, R 1928 — Records of archaeological finds at Chester. *J Chester Archaeol Soc* new ser **27** (2), 59–191

Newstead, R 1939 — Excavations on the site of the new telephone exchange, St John Street, Chester. *J Chester Archaeol Soc* new ser **33**, 9–31

Nicholson, R 1989 — The fish remains. *In:* O'Brien, C C, Bown, L, Dixon, S, Donel, L, Gidney, L J, Huntley, J, Nicholson, R. & Walton, P eds. Excavations at Newcastle quayside: the crown court site. *Archaeol Aeliana* ser 5, **17**, 188–96

Noake, P 1993 — The post-medieval pottery. *In:* Ellis ed, 191–210

Noddle, B 1994 — The under-rated goat. *In:* Hall & Kenward eds, 117–28

Norman, A V B 1976 — Wallace Collection catalogue of ceramics **1**: pottery, maiolica, faience, stone ware. London: Trustees of the Wallace Collection

Nuttall, D 1967 — A history of printing in Chester. *J Chester Archaeol Soc* new ser **54**, 37–95

O'Connor, T P 1985 — On quantifying vertebrates – some sceptical observations. *Circaea: Bulletin of the Association for Environmental Archaeology* **3** (1) 27–30

O'Connor, T P 1988 — Bones from the General Accident site, Tanner Row, York. London: Council for British Archaeology. (The Archaeology of York **15/2**)

O'Connor, T P 1989 — Deciding priorities with urban bones: York as a case study. *In:* Serjeantson & Waldron eds, 189–200

O'Connor, T P 1991 — Bones from 46–54 Fishergate. London: Council for British Archaeology. (The Archaeology of York **15/4**), 209–98

O'Connor, T P 2003 — The analysis of urban animal bone assemblages: a handbook for archaeologists. York: Council for British Archaeology

OS 1875 — Chester town plan 1:500 ser. Southampton: Ordnance Survey

OS 1898 — 1:2500 ser. Ed 2. Southampton: Ordnance Survey

OS 1911 — 1:2500 ser. Ed 3. Southampton: Ordnance Survey

Ormerod, G 1882 — The history of the county palatine and city of Chester. Ed 2, rev Helsby, T. London: Routledge

Orton, C 1988 — Post-Roman Pottery. *In:* Hinton, P ed. Excavations in Southwark 1973–1976, Lambeth 1973–1979. Museum of London. (London Middlesex Archaeol Soc and Surrey Archaeol Soc Joint Publication **3**), 295–364

Osborne, P J 1981 — Coleopterous fauna from layer 1. *In:* Greig, J R A. The investigation of a medieval barrel latrine from Worcester. *J Archaeol Sci* **8**, 268–71

Oswald + no — Oswald, F 1936. Index of figure types on terra sigillata ('samian ware'). Suppl to *Annals Archaeol Anthropol Univ Liverpool*, 1936–7

Oswald, A 1978–9 — The clay pipes. *In:* Whiston, J W. Artefacts found in the moat of West Bromwich manor house, part 1. *South Staffordshire Archaeol Hist Soc Trans* **20**, 29–40

Payne, S 1973 — Kill-off patterns in sheep and goats: the mandibles from Asvan Kale. *Anatolian Stud* **23**, 281–303

Payne, S 1985 — Morphological distinctions between the mandibular teeth of young sheep, Ovis, and goats Capra. *J Archaeol Sci* **12**, 139–47

Payne, S 1987 — Reference codes for wear states in the mandibular cheek teeth of sheep and goats. *J Archaeol Sci* **14** (6), 609–14

Payne-Gallwey, R 1886 — The book of duck decoys: their construction, management and history. London: Van Voorst

Peacock, D P S & Williams, D F 1986 — Amphorae and the Roman economy: an introductory guide. New York: Longman

Bibliography

Pearce, J 1992	Post-medieval pottery in London, 1500–1700 **1**: Border wares. London: HMSO for Museum of London
Peterson, H 1956	Arms and armour in colonial America 1526–1783. Harrisburg (PA): Stackpole
Philpott, R A 1980–1	Black-glazed ware. *In:* Davey, P J & McNeil, R. Excavations in South Castle Street, Liverpool 1976 and 1977. *J Merseyside Archaeol Soc* **4**, 85–105
Philpott, R A 1982–3	The finds. *In:* A timber framed building at 21–23 Eccleston Street, Prescot (site 30). *J Merseyside Archaeol Soc* **5**, 23–33
Philpott, R A 1985	Mottled ware. *In:* Davey, P J & McNeil R. Excavations in South Castle Street, Liverpool 1976 and 1977. *J Merseyside Archaeol Soc* **4**, 1–158
Pigot, J 1818	The commercial directory for 1818-19-20. Manchester: Pigot & Dean
Pigot, J 1828	Pigot and Co's national commercial directory for 1828-9. London: Pigot
Pitts, L F & St Joseph, J K 1985	Inchtuthil: the Roman legionary fortress excavations 1952–65. London: Society for the Promotion of Roman Studies. (*Britannia* Monogr Ser **6**)
Pleguezuelo, A & Lafuente, P 1995	Ceramicas de Andalucia occidental (1200–1600). *In:* Gerrard *et al* eds, 217–44
Poole, J 1791	The Chester directory and guide. Chester: privately published
Preston, C D, Pearman, D A & Dines, T D eds 2002	New atlas of the British and Irish flora. Oxford U P
Preston, K 1986	Common Sandpiper. *In:* Lack ed, 224–5
Price, J & Cottam, S 1998	Romano-British glass vessels: a handbook. York: Council for British Archaeology. (CBA Practical Handbook in Archaeology **14**)
Ragge, D R 1965	Grasshoppers, crickets and cockroaches of the British Isles. London: Warne
Reitz, E J & Wing, E S 1999	Zooarchaeology. Cambridge U P
Richardson, T 1997	The Bridport muster roll of 1457. *Roy Armouries Yearb* **2**, 46–2
Robbins, R 1970	Medical manuscripts in Middle English. *Speculum* **45**, 393–415
Roberts, H 1851	The Chester guide. Chester
Roberts, I 2002	Pontefract castle: archaeological excavations 1982–6. Leeds: West Yorkshire Archaeology Service. (Yorkshire Archaeol **8**)
Robertson, A, Tomlinson, P & Kenward, H K 1989	Plant and insect remains from Coffee Yard, York. Unpublished report for York Archaeological Trust
Robinson, D J 2005	Reconstruction of the inscription RIB **1**, 463. *In:* Mason *et al*, 103–5
Robinson, M & Straker, V 1991	Silica skeletons of macroscopic plant remains from ash. *In:* Renfrew, J M ed. New light on early farming. Edinburgh U P, 3–13
Roeder, C 1899	Recent Roman discoveries in Deansgate and on Hunt's Bank, and Roman Manchester restudied (1897–1900). *Trans Lancashire Cheshire Antiq Soc* **17**, 147–89
Rogers + no	Rogers, G B 1974. Poteries sigillées de la Gaule centrale **1**: les motifs non figurés. *Gallia* Suppl **28**
RIB **2** (4)	Frere, S S & Tomlin, R S O eds 1992. The Roman inscriptions of Britain **2**: *instrumentum domesticum* fasc **4**. Stroud: Alan Sutton Publishing for Oxford University Haverfield Bequest
RIC **3**	Mattingly, H & Sydenham, E 1930. Roman imperial coinage **3**: Antoninus Pius to Commodus. London: Spink
RIC **4** (1)	Mattingly, H & Sydenham, E 1936. Roman imperial coinage **4** (1): Pertinax to Geta. London: Spink
Rowland, R nd	The Blue Posts: a story of bygone Chester…with original drawings. CCALS P/CHES
Rowley-Conwy, P ed 2000	Animal bones, human societies. Oxford: Oxbow
Rutland, S M & Whitwell, J B 1960	Browns's basement 1960. Grosvenor Museum Chester: unpubl archive
Rutter, J A 1977	Old Market Hall pit group. *In:* Davey ed, 18–20
Rutter, J A 1984	Lifestyle in the Rows, with particular reference to a collection of pottery from 11 Watergate St, Chester, found in 1894. *J Chester Archaeol Soc* **67**, 55–75
Rutter, J A 1985	The pottery. *In:* Mason, D J P. Excavations at Chester, 26–42 Lower Bridge Street 1974–6: the Dark Age and Saxon periods. Chester City Council. (Grosvenor Mus Archaeol Excav Surv Rep **3**), 40–60
Rutter, J A 1990a	Building materials from the Dominican friary: floor tiles. *In:* Ward 1990, 95–105 and 191
Rutter, J A 1990b	Other finds from the Domincan friary: pottery. *In:* Ward 1990, 138–63 and 192–6
Rutter, J A 1990c	Appendix 1: Floor tile catalogue. *In:* Ward 1990, 229–79
Rutter, J A & Davey, P J 1980	Clay pipes from Chester. *In:* Davey ed, 41–272
Schofield, J 1997	Urban housing in England 1400–1600. *In:* Gaimster, D & Stamper, P. The age of transition: the archaeology of English culture 1400–1600. Oxford: Oxbow. (Soc Medieval Archaeol Monogr **15**; Oxbow Monogr **98**), 127–44

Scott, S 1991	The animal bones. *In:* Armstrong, P, Tomlinson, D & Evans, D H. Excavations at Lurk Lane, Beverley, 1983–6. Sheffield University. (Sheffield Excav Rep **3**), 216–33
Serjeantson, D & Waldron, T eds 1989	Diet and crafts in towns: the evidence of animal remains from the Roman to the post-medieval periods. Oxford: British Archaeological Reports. (BAR Brit Ser **199**)
Shotter, D C A 1998–9	Chester: the evidence of Roman coin loss. *J Chester Archaeol Soc* new ser **75**, 33–50
Silver, I A 1969	The ageing of domestic animals. *In:* Brothwell & Higgs eds, 283–302
Simoons, F J 1994	Eat not this flesh: food avoidances from prehistory to the present. Ed 2. Madison (WI): Wisconsin U P
Simpson, F 1918	The City Gilds of Chester: the Bricklayers' Company. *J Chester Archaeol Soc* new ser **22**, 55–90
Smith, T P 1985	The medieval brickmaking industry in England 1400–1450. Oxford: British Archaeological Reports. (BAR Brit Ser **138**)
Smith, W & Webb, W 1696	The history of Cheshire: containing King's Vale-royal entire. Repr Chester: Poole 1778
Sotheby 1992	Early English and continental pottery from the John Philip Kassebaum Collection: sale catalogue. London: Sotheby
Sparks, T H & Mason, C F 2004	Can we detect change in the phenology of winter migrant birds in the UK? *Ibis* **146** (Suppl **1**), 57–60
Spavold, J & Brown, S 2005	Ticknall pots and potters from the late fifteenth century to 1888. Ashbourne: Landmark Publishing
Stallibrass, S 1991	Animal bones from excavations at Annetwell Street, Carlisle, 1982–4. Period 3: the earlier timber fort. London: English Heritage. (Ancient Monuments Lab Rep **132/91**)
Stallibrass, S 2002	An overview of the animal bones: what would we like to know, what do we know so far, and where do we go from here? *In:* Wilson, P R. Cataractonium, Roman Catterick and its hinterland: excavations and research 1958–1997 **2**. York: Council for British Archaeology. (CBA Res Rep **128**), 392–414
Stallibrass, S & Nicholson, R 2000	Animal and fish bone. *In:* Buxton, K & Howard-Davies, C. Bremetenacum: excavations at Roman Ribchester 1980, 1989–1990. Lancaster University Archaeological Unit. (Lancaster Imprints **9**), 375–86
Stalzer, F 1989	Kataloge der Staatlichen Münzsammlung München. Rechenpfennige Bd **1**: Nürnberg. Munich
S & S	Stanfield, J A & Simpson, G 1958. Central Gaulish potters. Oxford U P for Durham University
Starkey, D, Reid, C & Ashcroft, N eds 2000	England's sea fisheries: the commercial sea fisheries of England and Wales since 1300. London: Chatham Publishing
Starley, D 1992	Medieval iron and steel production: an assessment of the changing technology of European ferrous alloy production through the analysis of medieval and renaissance armour. Unpubl PhD thesis, University of Bradford
Starley, D & Richardson, T 2005a	Royal Armouries analysis record, Job 1880. Unpubl document
Starley, D & Richardson, T 2005b	Royal Armouries analysis record, Job 1881. Unpubl document
Starley, D & Richardson, T 2005c	Royal Armouries analysis record, Job 1882. Unpubl document
Starley, D & Richardson, T 2005d	Royal Armouries analysis record, Job 1883. Unpubl document
Starley, D & Richardson, T 2005e	Royal Armouries analysis record, Job 1885. Unpubl document
Starley, D & Richardson, T 2005f	Royal Armouries analysis record, Job 1886. Unpubl document
Starley, D & Richardson, T 2005g	Royal Armouries analysis record, Job 1887. Unpubl document
Starley, D & Richardson, T 2005h	The technological examination of jacks of plate in the Royal Armouries collection. Leeds: Royal Armouries. (Roy Armouries Tech Rep 2005/2). Unpublished document
Stevenson, J & Davidson, P eds 1997	The closet of the eminently learned Sir Kenelme Digbie Kt opened (1669). Blackawton (Devon): Prospect Books
Stewart-Brown, R 1934–8	Cheshire inquisitions post mortem: Stewart period 1603–1660. (Rec Soc Lancashire Cheshire **84**, **86**, **91**)
Stokes, P 2000	A cut above the rest? Officers and men at South Shields Roman fort. *In:* Rowley-Conwy ed, 145–51
Strickland, T J 1977	The fortress in the second and third centuries. *In:* Strickland, T J & Davey, P J eds. New evidence for Roman Chester. Liverpool University, 25–8
Swan, V G 1992	Legio VI and its men: African legionaries in Britain. *J Roman Pottery Stud* **3**, 1–17
Swan, V G 1999a	Legio XX Valeria Victrix and the Antonine Wall: new perspectives on the history of northern Britain'. *In:* Gudea, N ed. Roman frontier studies: proceedings of the XVIIth International Congress of Roman Frontier Studies. Zalau Museum, 539–45

Bibliography

Swan, V G 1999b — The Twentieth Legion and the history of the Antonine Wall reconsidered. *Proc Soc Antiq Scot* **129**, 399–480

Swan, V G 2004 — The historical significance of 'legionary wares' in Britain. *In:* Vermeulen, F, Sas, K & Dhaeze, W eds. Archaeology in confrontation. Aspects of Roman military presence in the Northwest: studies in honour of Prof Em Hugo Thoen. Ghent: Academia Press. (Archaeol Reps Univ Ghent **2**), 259–85

Sykes, N & Symmons, R *forthcoming* — Sexing cattle horn cores: problems and progress. *Int J Osteoarchaeol*

Symmons, R 2005 — New density data for unfused and fused sheep bones, and a preliminary discussion on the modelling of taphonomic bias in archaeofaunal age profiles. *J Archaeol Sci* **32**, 1691–8

Tait, H 1967 — Glass with chequered spiral-trail decoration: a group made in the southern Netherlands in the sixteenth and seventeenth centuries. *J Glass Stud* **9**, 94–112

Tait, J ed 1920–3 — The chartulary or register of the abbey of St Werburgh, Chester. Manchester: Chetham Society. (Remains, historical and literary, connected with the Palatine counties of Lancaster and Chester new ser **79**, **82**)

Taylor, E L 1955 — Parasitic helminths in medieval remains. *Vet Rec* **67**, 216

Thompson, F H 1967 — Notes on two building sites in Chester. *J Chester Archaeol Soc* new ser **54**, 21–2

Thompson, F H 1976 — The excavation of the Roman amphitheatre at Chester. *Archaeologia* **105**, 127–239

Tomber, R & Dore, J 1998 — The national Roman fabric reference collection a handbook. London: Museum of London Archaeology Service

Trow-Smith, R 1957 — A history of British livestock husbandry to 1700. London: Routledge & K P

Tutin, T G *et al* eds 1964–80 — *Flora Europaea* **1–5**. Cambridge U P

Tyers, P A 1996 — Roman pottery in Britain. London: Batsford

Tyson, R 2000 — Medieval glass vessels found in England c 1200–1500. York: Council for British Archaeology. (CBA Res Rep **121**)

Van Neer, W & Lentacker, A 1994 — New archaeozoological evidence for the consumption of locally produced fish sauce in the northern provinces of the Roman empire. *Archaeofauna* **3**, 53–62

Vaughan, J E 1981 — The leather. *In:* Harbottle, B & Ellison, M. An excavation in the castle ditch, Newcastle upon Tyne, 1974–6. *Archaeol Aeliana* ser 5, **9**, 184–90

Veeckman J, Van Hoof, W, Cooremans, B, Ervynck, A & Van Neer, W 2000 — De inhoud van de afvalput van de Groote Schalien Loove: speuren naar de 17de-eeuwse bewoners. *In:* Veeckman, J ed. Berichten en Rapporten over het Antwerps Bodemonderzoek en Monumentenzorg **4**. Stad Antwerpen, 115–90

Vernon Deeds — *Cheshire Sheaf* **3**, 56

Vince, A G 2004 — Medieval and later pottery (with Suzannah England). *In:* Rodwell, K & Bell, R. Acton Court: the evolution of an early Tudor courtier's house. London: English Heritage, 294–331

Vince, A G & Bell, R 1992 — Sixteenth-century pottery from Acton Court Avon. *In:* Gaimster, D M R & Redknap, M eds. Everyday and exotic pottery from Europe c 650–1900: studies in honour of John G Hurst. Oxford: Oxbow, 101–12

Walton, P 1983 — The textiles. *In:* Ellison, M & Harbottle, B. Excavation of a seventeenth-century bastion in Newcastle upon Tyne. *Archaeol Aeliana* ser 5, **11**, 217–40, 262–3

Walton, P 1987a — Medieval and seventeenth-century textiles from High Street/Blackfriargate. *In:* Armstrong, P & Ayers, B. Excavation in High Street and Blackfriargate. *East Riding Archaeol* **8**. (Hull Old Town Rep Ser **5**), 227–31

Walton, P 1987b — The textiles. *In:* Harbottle, B & Fraser, R. Blackfriars, Newcastle upon Tyne, after the dissolution of the monasteries. *Archaeol Aeliana* ser 5, **15**, 127–30

Walton Rogers, P 1997 — Textile production at 16–22 Coppergate. York: Council for British Archaeology. (The Archaeology of York **17/11**)

Walton Rogers, P 2002 — Textiles. *In:* Roberts, 308–14

Walton Rogers, P *unpubl* — Textiles from Dudley castle, West Midlands

Ward, S W 1981 — The Rows: the evidence from archaeology. *J Chester Archaeol Soc* new ser **67**, 37–46

Ward, S W 1987 — Excavations at Chester, the Civil War siegeworks 1642–6. Chester City Council. (Grosvenor Mus Archaeol Excav Surv Rep **4**)

Ward, S W 1988 — Excavations at Chester, 12 Watergate Street 1985. Chester City Council. (Grosvenor Mus Archaeol Excav Surv Rep **5**)

Ward, S W 1990 — Excavations at Chester, the lesser medieval religious houses, sites investigated 1964–1983. Chester City Council. (Grosvenor Mus Archaeol Excav Surv Rep **6**).

Ward, S W & Strickland, T J 1978 — Chester excavations, Northgate Brewery 1974/5: a Roman centurion's quarters and barrack. Chester City Council. (Grosvenor Mus Archaeol Excav Survey Rep **1**)

Ward, S W *et al* 1994 — Excavations at Chester, Saxon occupation within the Roman fortress: sites excavated 1971–1981. Chester City Council. (Archaeol Serv Excav Surv Rep **7**)

Warry, P 2006a — *Tegulae*. Manufacture, typology and use in Roman Britain. Oxford: Archaeopress (BAR Brit Ser **417**)

Warry, P 2006b — A dated typology form Roman roof tiles (*tegulae*). *J Roman Archaeol* **19** (1), 246–65

Warry, P 2007 — Roman tile, hardcore or hard data? *Current Archaeol* 209, **18** (5), 27–30

Webster, P V 1976 — Severn Valley ware: a preliminary study. *Trans Bristol Gloucestershire Archaeol Soc* **94**, 18–46

Webster, P V 1996 — Roman samian pottery in Britain. York: Council for British Archaeology. (CBA Practical Handbook in Archaeology **13**)

Wharton, A 1980 — Seventeenth- and eighteenth-century clay tobacco pipes excavated from Tong castle, Shropshire. *In:* Davey ed, 287–91

Wheeler, A 1977 — Fish bone. *In:* Clarke, H & Carter, A eds. Excavations in King's Lynn 1963–1970. (Soc Medieval Archaeol Monogr Ser **7**), 403–8.

Wheeler, A & Jones, A K G 1976 — Fish remains. *In:* Rogerson, A. Excavations on Fuller's Hill, Great Yarmouth. *East Anglian Archaeol* **2**, 208–24

White, G 1962 — The natural history of Selbourne. Ed 3. London: The Folio Society

Whitehead, R 1996 — Buckles 1250–1800. Chelmsford: Greenlight

Whitfield, S ed with Sims-Williams, U 2004 — The Silk Road: trade, travel, war and faith. London: British Library

Williams, A 2003 — The knight and the blast furnace: a history of the metallurgy of armour in the Middle Ages and the early modern period. Leiden: Brill

Williams, D F 2002 — Purbeck marble in Roman and medieval Britain. *In:* Hinton, D A ed. Purbeck papers. Oxford: Oxbow. (Univ Southampton Dept Archaeol Monogr **4**), 126–31

Williams, J 1846 — Williams's commercial directory of the city of Chester. Liverpool: Williams

Willmott, H 2000a — The classification and mould-grouping of lion mask stems from London. Annales du 14e Congrès de L'Association Internationale pour L'Histoire du Verre, Italia Venezia-Milano 1998, 389–95

Willmott, H 2000b — Recent research on the Gracechurch Street hoard. *Glass Circle News* **83**, 6–7

Willmott, H 2001 — A group of seventeenth-century glass goblets with restored stems: considering the archaeology of repair. *Post-Medieval Archaeol* **35**, 96–105

Willmott, H 2002 — Early post-medieval glass in England, c 1500–1670. York: Council for British Archaeology. (CBA Res Rep **132**)

Willmott, H 2003 — Some evidence for glassmaking from Silkstone, near Barnsley, South Yorkshire. Portsmouth: English Heritage. (Centre for Archaeology Rep **74/2003**)

Wilmott, A J 1997 — Birdoswald: excavations of a Roman fort on Hadrian's Wall and its successor settlements 1987–92. London: English Heritage. (Archaeol Rep **14**)

Wilson, B 1994 — Mortality patterns, animal husbandry and marketing in and around medieval and post-medieval Oxford. *In:* Hall & Kenward eds, 103–15

Wilson, B, Grigson, C & Payne, S eds 1982 — Ageing and sexing animal bones from archaeological sites. Oxford: British Archaeological Reports. (BAR Brit Ser **109**)

Wilson, K P ed 1969 — Chester custom accounts 1301–1566. (Record Soc Lancashire Cheshire **111**)

Wilson, T 1987 — Ceramic art of the Italian renaissance. London: British Museum

Wilson, T 1995 — Spanish pottery in the British Museum. *In:* Gerrard *et al* eds, 339–51

Wood, J 1833 — Plan of the City of Chester. CCALS PM 18/5

Woodward, D M 1967 — The Chester leather industry 1558–1625. *Trans Hist Soc Lancashire Cheshire* **119**, 65–111

Woodward, D M 1970 — The trade of Elizabethan Chester. Hull U P. (Occas Pap Econ Soc Hist **4**)

Woolgar, C M 1999 — The great household in late medieval England. New Haven (CT) and London: Yale U P

Yalden, D 1999 — The history of British mammals. London: Poyser

Young, C J 1977 — The Roman pottery industry of the Oxford region. Oxford: British Archaeological Reports. (BAR Brit Ser **43**)

Zienkiewicz, J D 1986 — The legionary fortress baths at Caerleon. 2 vols. Cardiff: National Museum of Wales and CADW: Welsh Historic Monuments

Zienkiewicz, J D 1993 — Excavations in the *scamnum tribunorum* at Caerleon: the Legionary Museum site 1983–5. *Britannia* **24**, 27–140